THE DAILY TELEGRAPH
SCHOOLS GUIDE
1998–99

The Daily Telegraph

SCHOOLS GUIDE

1998–99

THE DEFINITIVE GUIDE TO THE BEST INDEPENDENT AND STATE SCHOOLS

Edited by John Clare

ROBINSON
London

Robinson Publishing Ltd
7 Kensington Church Court
London W8 4SP

First published in the UK by Robinson Publishing Ltd 1998
Copyright © 1998 Telegraph Group Ltd

A copy of the British Library Cataloguing in Publication data is available from the British Library

ISBN 1-85487-975-8

Printed and bound in the EC

10 9 8 7 6 5 4 3 2 1

Contents

Introduction

CHOOSING the right school for your child can be an agonising business. State or independent? Day or boarding? Large or small? Single-sex or co-educational? Academic or sporting? Competitive or relaxed?

In each case, one alternative is likely to meet your child's needs better than the other. But how to tell which?

The Daily Telegraph Schools Guide is designed to lead you through the maze. Each of the 650 schools it describes – 75 prep schools, 575 senior schools, the latter divided equally between the state and independent sectors – has been meticulously judged against a variety of academic and other criteria.

They include most of the top 200 league table schools, all of which set stiff entry tests. Others are proudly non-selective. Some specialise in 'bringing on' less academically able children and those who suffer from specific learning difficulties such as dyslexia. All in their different ways are good schools – for the right child.

Unlike other guides, which invite schools to write their own entries, this one is as independent as it is authoritative. Every school has been visited by one of a team of experienced *Telegraph* inspectors. Their detailed reports form the basis of the entries that follow.

Each gives a frank account of the school's most significant features: its background, atmosphere and admissions policy; the character of the head; the nature of the teaching and curriculum; the latest exam results; the quality of the boarding accommodation, if any; and the strength of such extra-curricular activities as art, drama, music and sport.

All of it is vital information because league tables, valuable though they are, do not tell you everything you need to know. The schools at the top are not the best for every child; one nearer the bottom may very well be ideal.

Start, then, by making a realistic estimate of your child's abilities, aptitudes and interests. The company of other clever children is a stimulus, and the lack of it can lead to idleness. But always coming last can be demoralising, and always being top can lead to complacency. So aim high academically, but not too high.

An aptitude for a particular subject, whether it be music or science, languages or technology, deserves to be nourished. Take care, therefore, to ensure that the schools you are considering really are equipped to meet your child's needs.

Provided that the teaching is sound, less academically able children are more likely to flourish in a gentler, less competitive environment where they are offered a range of challenging activities outside the classroom.

Drama, outdoor pursuits, voluntary work, team and individual sports, a vocational slant to the curriculum: any of these can spell liberation to a child who struggles to keep up academically. So check that the schools you are considering make proper provision for them – and remember that boarding schools (state and independent) are often best placed to do so.

The schools in this guide are not, of course, the only good schools in Britain. They do, though, provide a template against which others may be judged.

Glossary of Terms

A-levels   Taken usually in at least three subjects two years after GCSE by pupils intending to go to university. The proportion of subjects graded A or B – the critical grades for entry to over-subscribed courses at good universities – determines a school's position in *The Daily Telegraph* league table.

Assisted places   A Government-funded bursary scheme introduced by the Conservatives to enable 40,000 bright children from less well-off homes to attend independent schools. The Labour Government is phasing it out over seven years, beginning in September 1998.

Boarding   Still in decline but fighting back with much improved facilities. For British and other European Community citizens, state boarding, with annual fees of less than £5,000, represents particularly good value. Further information from STABIS, the State Boarding Information Service, 01248 680542. Information about independent boarding schools is available from ISIS (qv) or the Boarding Education Alliance, which runs a helpline: 0171 388 8866.

City Technology Colleges   A group of 15 experimental state secondary schools specialising in maths, science and technology. Directly funded by the Government, with assistance from industry and commerce, they have spawned a network of technology and language colleges, which are required to meet high standards in return for extra funding. They are strongly represented in this guide.

Common Entrance   The entrance exam to independent senior schools taken by prep school pupils at 11, 12 or 13. The papers are set centrally but marked by the school to which the candidate is applying. Many schools now prefer to set their own tests in English, maths and verbal reasoning (a kind of IQ test).

Direct Grant   A status that used to be accorded to independent schools which, in return for a Government grant, admitted non-fee-paying pupils nominated by local education authorities. It was abolished by a previous Labour Government in 1976.

Dual award   The science qualification attempted by most 15-year-olds, which leads to the award of two GCSEs. Academic schools tend to regard it as an inadequate preparation for A-level sciences and prefer to prepare pupils for separate exams in physics, chemistry and biology.

Duke of Edinburgh award scheme   A judicious mixture of adventure training and community service, it sets young people challenging targets at three levels: bronze, silver and gold.

GCSE   The General Certificate of Secondary Education: usually taken in at least eight subjects after 11 years of full-time, compulsory education. The proportion of candidates who pass at least five at grades A–C is a common measure of the academic standing of comprehensive schools (most in this guide score at least 60%). Grammar and independent schools commonly score 95% to 100%.

Girls' Day School Trust   Founded in 1872 in the belief that girls do best in single-sex schools, it runs 25 of the best independent schools of their kind (most of which are included in this guide). Standards are uniformly high; fees are modest and bursaries generous.

GNVQs   General National Vocational Qualifications: a vocationally oriented alternative to GCSEs and A-levels in subjects such as business, art & design, leisure & tourism and health & social care. At advanced level, a GNVQ is equivalent to two A-levels and can lead to university entrance.

Grammar schools   Only 160 now remain, the rest having been swept away in the shift to comprehensive education. They select their pupils at 11 by academic ability.

Grant-maintained   The status accorded to state schools that opted out of council control to be directly funded by the Government. Under Labour, they are to be re-named 'foundation' schools and are likely to lose some of their freedom to run themselves. Most are exceptionally good schools and are strongly represented in this guide.

Highers   Scottish exams usually taken in five subjects one year after Standard Grade (qv) and leading to four-year Scottish degree courses. Although they are not equivalent to A-levels, most English universities accept them.

HMC Headmasters' and Headmistresses' Conference: an alliance of 240 leading boys' and co-educational independent schools which operates its own inspection system. Schools are usually happy to make a summary of their report available to parents (beware if they are not).

HMI Her Majesty's Inspectors: working under the umbrella of the Office for Standards in Education, they are the ultimate official arbiters of school quality.

IB The International Baccalaureate: a challenging, highly regarded alternative to A-levels that requires pupils to study both arts and sciences until they are 17. Few schools, alas, offer it.

ISIS The Independent Schools Information Service (0171 630 8794) provides factual information on the 1,300 independent schools (educating nearly 500,000 pupils) that it represents.

Ofsted The Office for Standards in Education is responsible for inspecting every primary and secondary school in England at least once every six years. Schools are required to make their inspection reports available to parents.

Oxbridge Shorthand for Oxford and Cambridge, the two best universities and the hardest to get into for most subjects. Academic schools keep a careful tally of how many of their pupils win places.

Performance tables Booklets listing the exam results of all the secondary schools – state and independent – in every English local education authority area are published annually by the Department for Education and Employment. They are available free by phoning 0800 242322.

Standard Grade The Scottish equivalent of GCSE.

Voluntary-aided A status largely confined to Church schools which – in return for meeting 15 per cent of their capital and maintenance costs – retain control over whom they admit.

Independent Schools' League Tables

1997 A-level league table: independent schools entering 45 or more candidates; percentage of subject entries graded A or B. Positions in 1996, 1995, 1994 and 1993 in brackets.

Note: – usually indicates years when fewer than 45 candidates were entered
* includes International Baccalaureate results

PREMIER LEAGUE

1 (22,19,35,19) Haberdashers' Aske's 90.46
2 (1,1,8,7) St Paul's Girls' 90.21
3 (24,8,16,9) Withington 89.5
4 (10,6,3,3) Winchester 88.18
5 (3,9,4,2) North London Collegiate 87.93
6 (9,13,15,21) Haberdashers' Aske's Girls' 86.73
7 (29,11,11,5) Manchester Grammar 86.68
8 (40,45,60,59) St Helen & St Katharine 86.36
9 (2,4,1,6) Westminster 86.28
10 (20,24,19,4) King Edward's, Birmingham 86.15

FIRST DIVISION

11 (5,15,10,22) Wycombe Abbey 86.13
12 (14,5,6,8) King Edward VI Girls' High 84.68
13 (16,7,13,16) KCS, Wimbledon 83.69
14 (36,27,36,36) James Allen's Girls' 83.64
15 (81,21,67,95) Oxford High 83.55
16 (45,40,18,17) South Hampstead 82.38
17 (4,41,29,–) St Swithun's 82.01
18 (6,3,5,1) St Paul's 81.25
19 (13,14,2,11) Eton 80.38
20 (23,36,39,75) Radley 79.95
21 (12,20,30,14) Godolphin & Latymer 79.87
22 (176,150,–,47) Ipswich High 78.83
23 (28,10,20,25) Lady Eleanor Holles 78.31
24 (26,116,111,115) Leeds Girls' High 77.78
24 (21,50,55,42) Loughborough High 77.78
26 (11,33,21,40) Cheltenham Ladies' 77.38
27 (19,59,22,43) University College School 77.23
28 (55,17,9,82) Downe House 77.1
29 (17,31,62,174) Bolton Boys' 76.83
30 (50,22,12,54) Malvern Girls' 76.45
31 (34,30,68,65) King's, Canterbury 75.73
32 (–,–,–,–) Fettes, Edinburgh 75.28
33 (201,23,23,55) Chetham's 75.0
34 (15,2,7,31) Royal Grammar, Guildford 74.94
35 (63,77,88,72) Rugby 74.82
36 (27,66,17,91) Notting Hill & Ealing High 74.76
37 (191,80,43,38) Sir William Perkins's 74.19
38 (143,150,69,137) Headington 74.07
39 (44,64,79,67) *Sevenoaks 74.06
40 (84,16,27,18) Perse Girls' 73.94
41 (69,42,40,37) Merchant Taylors', Northwood 73.89
42 (70,67,49,60) Nottingham High Girls' 73.6
43 (101,52,50,39) City of London Girls' 73.55
44 (38,93,26,83) Roedean 73.43
45 (31,–,–,–) St George's, Edinburgh 73.0
46 (52,12,14,12) Guildford High 72.9
47 (105,97,147,110) Stockport Grammar 72.78
48 (86,187,86,148) Redland High 72.35
49 (113,18,54,51) Benenden 71.89
50 (65,28,38,27) City of London 71.64
51 (48,63,74,70) Manchester High 71.16
52 (41,38,65,69) Shrewsbury 71.1
53 (98,35,108,190) Warwick 71.06
54 (–,–,–,123) St Catherine's, Guildford 70.97
55 (50,81,32,93) Putney High 70.64
56 (33,53,83,163) Sutton High 70.44
57 (32,99,63,118) Bradford Girls' 70.33
58 (61,43,46,81) Charterhouse 70.26
59 (72,160,112,88) Loughborough Grammar 70.24
60 (87,74,45,76) Bristol Grammar 70.07
61 (82,157,139,64) Haberdashers', Monmouth 69.79
62 (75,39,25,26) Wimbledon High 69.76
63 (103,60,66,33) Croydon High 69.75
64 (79,145,99,15) Leicester Grammar 69.55
65 (18,34,57,28) Tonbridge 69.51
66 (–,–,–,131)Talbot Heath 69.5

67 (56,46,116,125) King Edward VI, Southampton
69.45

68 (108,109,78,57) Maynard, Exeter 69.4

69 (64,91,106,61) Dulwich 69.29

70 (111,87,127,68) King's High, Warwick 69.12

71 (83,76,141,150) Bedford 69.08

72 (118,124,94,48) Bolton Girls' 68.93

73 (8,26,24,30) The Perse 68.86

74 (49,110,58,46) The Abbey, Reading 68.73

75 (7,–,–,–) St Mary's, Ascot 68.61

76 (59,37,64,49) Royal Grammar, Newcastle 68.6

77 (42,83,87,97) Whitgift 68.58

78 (161,92,132,109) Bromley High 68.37

79 (119,127,154,133) Marlborough 67.9

80 (93,100,44,111) Bancroft's 67.4

81 (73,71,34,34) Harrow 67.3

82 (46,25,71,13) Nottingham High Boys' 67.19

83 (–,–,–,–) *Atlantic College 67.0

84 (39,56,53,170) Abingdon 66.97

85 (58,61,122,24) Magdalen College School 66.82

86 (78,107,95,107) Central Newcastle High 66.67

86 (43,57,85,103) Sherborne Girls' 66.67

88 (88,70,101,95) Old Palace, Croydon 66.36

89 (129,105,73,50) Highgate 66.34

90 (62,89,211,92) King Henry VIII, Coventry 66.07

91 (130,208,182,231) Dame Alice Harpur 65.93

92 (102,148,142,113) Ipswich 65.84

92 (224,–,109,124) Queen Anne's, Caversham 65.84

94 (173,194,175,101) Newcastle-under-Lyme 65.8

95 (57,29,59,53) St Helen's, Northwood 65.67

96 (110,218,135,126) King Edward's, Bath 65.34

97 (71,49,47,78) Oundle 65.14

98 (117,171,110,146) Trinity, Croydon 65.03

99 (35,86,48,32) Queen's, Chester 65.0

100 (151,246,70,79) Hulme Grammar Girls' 64.84

101 (134,125,84,87) Norwich 64.55

102 (114,159,37,35) Woldingham 64.53

103 (157,68,150,142) Sheffield High 64.49

104 (152,32,123,105) Red Maids' 64.37

105 (68,90,41,52) Epsom 64.34

106 (116,166,120,218) Howell's, Llandaff 63.79

107 (200,–,240,215) Worth, Crawley 63.54

108 (30,155,92,121) Leeds Grammar 63.52

109 (76,114,137,77) Latymer Upper 63.47

110 (174,167,193,144) Bury Girls' 63.38

111 (140,85,140,180) Alleyn's 63.29

112 (67,–,–,–) Edinburgh Academy 63.27

113 (107,121,169,189) Ashford 63.23

114 (235,119,261,269) Westholme, Blackburn 63.19

115 (124,82,89,74) Eltham 63.0

116 (66,130,227,115) St Peter's, York 62.99

117 (182,143,98,182) Ampleforth 62.81

118 (114,44,50,20) St Albans Girls' High 62.57

119 (156,158,125,56) Grange, Northwich 62.5

120 (159,161,129,205) Uppingham 62.47

121 (205,182,138,263) Bromsgrove 62.46

122 (99,47,100,58) Merchant Taylors' Girls', Crosby
62.31

123 (97,87,75,71) King's, Chester 62.11

124 (210,147,159,210) Cheltenham 61.93

125 (184,229,195,162) Kingston Grammar 61.88

126 (91,78,33,61) Portsmouth Grammar 61.87

127 (96,96,56,43) Merchant Taylors', Crosby 61.86

128 (121,73,133,86) Wolverhampton Grammar
61.68

129 (89,83,175,154) Northampton High 61.54

130 (154,104,104,94) Sherborne 61.48

131 (25,106,90,160) Wakefield Girls' 61.44

132 (126,120,102,102) Chigwell 61.33

132 (171,206,214,176) Reigate Grammar 61.33

134 (177,216,144,117) Q E's Hospital, Bristol 61.14

135 (221,223,247,222) Dame Allan's 60.97

136 (165,179,128,138) Gresham's, Holt 60.86

137 (–,62,–,45) Francis Holland, Clarence Gate
60.42

138 (179,141,197,173) Canford 60.27

139 (141,245,186,128) Edgbaston High 60.23

140 (109,115,52,195) Norwich Girls' High 60.08

SECOND DIVISION

141 (209,130,118,106) Christ's Hospital 59.94

142 (122,111,75,168) Monmouth 59.93

143 (181,243,–,214) West Buckland 59.89

144 (145,55,28,122) Bablake 59.63

145 (53,69,115,120) Wellington College 59.53

146 (167,197,113,127) Arnold 59.4

147 (246,118,130,226) City of London Freemen's
59.3

148 (186,228,163,266) Kingswood, Bath 59.28

149 (77,58,31,10) Bradford Grammar 59.1

150 (204,190,191,98) Hampton 59.07

151 (153,210,146,107) Cheadle Hulme 58.81

152 (187,103,202,151) Hurtwood House 58.77

153 (146,138,80,73) Oakham 58.68

154 (158,156,119,140) Birkenhead 58.67

155 (207,217,126,237) John Lyon 58.64

156 (133,112,114,201) Birkenhead High 58.62

157 (94,140,93,99) Solihull 58.54

158 (264,165,177,198) Forest 58.53

159 (112,128,194,165) Hymers 58.43

160 (90,94,–,152) Clifton High 58.25

161 (131,205,184,134) Millfield 57.93

162 (100,137,145,208) Berkhamsted Collegiate
57.89

163 (232,72,207,145) Truro 57.82

164 (–,–,–,–) Northwood 57.75

165 (–,–,–,–) Shrewsbury High   57.66

166 (175,54,82,66) Caterham   57.4

167 (139,178,152,183) St Albans   57.38

168 (–,–,–,–) King's, Gloucester   57.33

169 (125,130,103,179) Walthamstow Hall   57.23

170 (85,154,161,155) Bryanston   56.65

171 (189,240,154,177) The Leys   56.62

172 (193,196,164,245) Wellington, Somerset   56.54

173 (163,146,171,260) Dauntsey's   56.52

174 (170,174,105,–) Farnborough Hill   56.05

175 (165,113,170,156) King's, Worcester   55.9

176 (80,176,166,143) Exeter   55.83

177 (188,139,96,100) Brighton College   55.25

178 (214,163,136,149) Wells Cathedral   55.14

179 (142,–,–,–) Godolphin, Salisbury   55.13

180 (168,149,151,114) Haileybury   54.91

181 (220,231,262,–) Belvedere   54.88

182 (263,250,157,185) St John's, Leatherhead   54.88

183 (–,–,–,–) Glenalmond, Perth   54.84

184 (241,168,180,129) Eastbourne College   54.78

185 (245,185,222,202) Leighton Park   54.76

186 (236,276,174,181) Queen's, Taunton   54.69

187 (138,122,107,–) Surbiton High   54.49

188 (180,181,189,199) Kimbolton   54.43

189 (147,193,167,139) Brentwood   54.3

190 (211,94,–,–) Concord, Shrewsbury   53.97

191 (291,244,233,246) Bloxham   53.69

192 (247,236,223,218) Stonyhurst   53.14

193 (128,75,216,136) Clifton   53.13

194 (255,123,117,234) St Mary's, Cambridge   52.99

195 (150,164,178,186) Bedford Modern   52.76

196 (–,177,212,240) New Hall, Chelmsford   52.74

197 (194,191,143,161) St Leonards, Mayfield   52.5

198 (127,189,160,158) *Malvern   52.36

199 (183,258,168,216) Cranleigh   52.26

200 (297,221,219,233) St Bede's, Manchester   52.14

201 (203,187,201,187) Stamford   52.13

202 (222,270,187,132) Lord Wandsworth   52.07

203 (164,241,204,–) Woodbridge   51.89

204 (239,213,190,172) Stamford Girls' High   51.61

205 (223,195,–,–) Birkdale   51.56

206 (271,275,199,229) Kent, Canterbury   51.1

207 (169,222,241,157) Taunton   51.0

208 (198,256,292,153) Elizabeth College, Guernsey   50.82

209 (253,234,188,216) King's, Macclesfield   50.63

210 (162,117,156,166) Felsted   50.62

211 (244,198,198,265) St Dunstan's, London   50.59

212 (240,102,158,90) Royal Grammar, Worcester   50.49

213 (190,200,149,141) Bedales   50.48

214 (149,175,192,167) St Edward's, Oxford   50.27

215 (275,226,165,214) Mill Hill   50.14

216 (196,51,91,112) Alice Ottley   50.0

216 (–,–,–,–) Derby High   50.0

216 (281,251,226,261) Durham   50.0

216 (–,–,–,–) Strathallan, Perth   50.0

THIRD DIVISION

220 (95,170,234,194) Repton   49.6

221 (212,214,204,80) Bury Grammar   49.58

222 (132,108,181,119) Wellingborough   49.5

223 (–,–,–,–) Guernsey Ladies'   49.28

224 (92,135,77,232) Bedford High   49.22

225 (54,173,148,89) Queen Elizabeth, Wakefield   49.19

226 (227,219,256,292) St George's, Weybridge   49.13

227 (172,220,266,130) Hulme Grammar   49.12

228 (252,206,253,264) Wisbech Grammar   49.06

229 (–,–,–,124) Casterton   49.04

230 (208,235,242,253) Churcher's   49.01

231 (285,249,244,159) Giggleswick   48.78

232 (233,201,153,243) Trent College   48.59

233 (192,277,284,193) Liverpool College   48.29

234 (–,–,–,104) St Margaret's, Exeter   48.03

235 (106,64,120,206) Dean Close   47.69

236 (160,184,179,184) Q E's, Blackburn   47.27

237 (136,142,248,220) Bishop's Stortford   47.26

238 (261,180,250,191) Wycliffe   47.2

239 (155,152,225,169) Bradfield   46.96

240 (262,212,258,212) King's, Bruton   46.95

241 (249,237,238,258) Christ College, Brecon   46.85

242 (272,254,213,–) Victoria College, Jersey   46.7

243 (294,–,–,–) Kingsley, Leamington Spa   46.25

244 (251,215,–,279) Culford   46.02

245 (237,202,185,251) Prior Park   45.95

246 (–,–,–,–) Sidcot   45.8

247 (226,204,244,171) Colfe's   44.83

248 (219,253,264,146) Ardingly   44.49

249 (217,233,288,195) St Edward's, Liverpool   44.39

250 (185,269,218,230) Barnard Castle   44.27

251 (225,266,172,178) Hereford Cathedral   43.92

251 (104,162,81,135) Lancing   43.92

253 (292,203,255,204) St Lawrence, Ramsgate   43.67

254 (295,287,249,278) St Mary's, Crosby   43.44

255 (238,186,209,262) Monkton Combe   43.29

256 (199,133,97,197) The Oratory, Reading   43.14

257 (195,153,196,236) Yarm   42.92

258 (230,263,246,254) William Hulme's   42.91

259 (258,172,232,244) Reading Blue Coat   42.86

260 (215,242,281,272) Blundell's   42.41

261 (213,238,260,209) King's, Taunton   42.36

262 (202,–,–,–)d'Overbroeck's, Oxford   42.27
263 (257,283,208,250) Batley Grammar   41.67
264 (274,–,215,290) King Edward VII, Lytham   41.62
265 (135,98,274,248) Bristol Cathedral   41.5
266 (302,272,268,282) Worksop   41.43
267 (248,134,162,211) St Benedict's, London   41.13
268 (–,–,–,277) Princethorpe, Rugby   40.97
269 (301,–,286,291) Wrekin   40.79
270 (260,–,–,–) Cambridge Sixth Form Centre   40.61
271 (–,–,–,–) St Columba's, St Albans   40.48
272 (197,261,183,241) Plymouth College   40.37
273 (178,211,200,275) Sedbergh   40.11

FOURTH DIVISION
274 (269,225,265,289) Emanuel   39.63
275 (259,230,217,200) Stowe   39.6
276 (286,232,210,188) Downside   39.47
276 (266,259,229,270) Rydal   39.47
278 (229,169,273,–) Ashville, Harrogate   38.95
279 (273,199,267,235) Framlingham   38.77
280 (288,136,294,–) Woodhouse Grove   38.1
281 (284,255,271,255) Sutton Valence   37.79
282 (279,247,203,–) St Bede's, Hailsham   37.71
283 (–,–,–,237) Sydenham High   37.32
284 (265,248,252,228) St Edmund's, Canterbury   37.28

285 (305,274,275,223) King's, Tynemouth   37.21
286 (283,264,293,225) Rossall   36.96
287 (254,209,221,273) Hurstpierpoint   36.82
288 (293,286,251,284) Pocklington   36.39
289 (234,273,231,249) Gordonstoun   36.11
290 (231,265,290,239) Kirkham Grammar   36.06
291 (243,259,279,–) Royal, Dungannon   35.59
292 (299,289,–,268) Colston's Collegiate   34.3
293 (218,281,228,238) St Ambrose   34.16
294 (256,182,276,224) St Joseph's, Ipswich   33.5
295 (308,–,–,–) Ursuline, Kent   32.24
296 (–,288,236,281) Denstone   31.62
297 (289,285,282,–) Royal Hospital, Ipswich   31.49
298 (296,284,235,276) Ryde   30.92
299 (304,291,291,–) Aldenham   30.29
300 (303,290,254,–) Ellesmere   30.18
301 (–,–,–,–) Farrington's, Chislehurst   29.38
302 (–,–,–,239) Royal Russell, Croydon   26.88
303 (280,282,272,288) Ratcliffe, Leicester   26.53
304 (298,257,259,213) King Edward's, Godalming   26.22
305 (–,238,242,280) Mount St Mary's, Sheffield   25.83
306 (268,252,173,256) King's, Rochester   24.26
307 (307,292,–,293) Shiplake   22.66
308 (306,293,287,–) Pangbourne   17.06

Independent schools entering between 25 and 44 candidates and having at least 50 per cent of subject entries graded A or B. Last year's position in brackets.

1 (1) Badminton, Bristol   88.33
2 (2) St Mary's, Calne   86.07
3 (8) Channing, London   74.75
4 (16) Burgess Hill   73.81
5 (3) Heathfield, Ascot   72.0
6 (–) St Leonards, Fife   71.43
7 (14) Mount, York   68.63
8 (–) *Marymount International   68.54
9 (–) Queen Margaret's, York   66.67
10 (–) Bath High   65.15
11 (–) Portsmouth High   64.84
12 (52) St Antony's-Leweston   63.01
13 (37) *Southbank International   62.75
14 (30) Truro High   62.7
15 (34) Hull Grammar   62.35
16 (49) Howell's, Denbigh   61.11
17 (13) Durham High   60.23
18 (6) Purcell Music   59.09
19 (–) Bootham, York   58.27

20 (–) Brighton & Hove High   58.02
21 (–) British, Brussels   57.94
22 (10) Harrogate Ladies'   57.55
23 (–) Duke of York's, Dover   57.32
24 (–) *American Community, Cobham   57.26
25 (–) Salesian, Farnborough   56.67
26 (26) Our Lady's, Abingdon   56.2
27 (25) St Mary's, Shaftesbury   55.56
28 (21) Tudor Hall, Banbury   54.81
29 (–) Our Lady of Sion, Worthing   54.44
30 (–) St Mary's, Worcester   54.29
31 (–) Westonbirt, Tetbury   54.08
32 (56) Moreton Hall, Oswestry   54.05
33 (4) Tormead, Guildford   53.57
34 (23) St George's, Ascot   52.59
35 (–) St Anne's, Windermere   51.96
36 (–) Thetford Grammar   51.81
37 (–) Streatham Hill & Clapham High   51.69
38 (–) Rendcomb, Cirencester   50.47

Preparatory Schools

ABBERLEY HALL ♂ *
Worcestershire WR6 6DD. Tel (01299) 896275

Synopsis
Boys (but going co-educational) ★ Boarding and day ★ Ages 8–13 (plus associated nursery and pre-prep) ★ 139 pupils (75% boarding) ★ Fees: £9,330 boarding; £7,230 day
Head: John Walker, 45, appointed 1996.
First-rate school; very good teaching; fine facilities; lots on offer.

Profile
Background Moved here from Blackheath 1916; rather austere Victorian mansion plus later additions on a magnificent hill-top site (clock tower can be seen from six counties) in 100 acres of gardens and woodland. Very good facilities, including new sports hall, library. Girls to be admitted at eight from September 1998 ('A new generation of parents accepts co-educational schools as the norm'). Nursery and pre-prep (ages two to eight) on same site.

Atmosphere Traditionally informal and unregimented: no uniform (but scruffiness frowned upon); staff addressed by first or nicknames. Boys friendly, well-mannered, articulate – and blissfully happy.

Admissions First come, first served (mostly by word of mouth – school has no prospectus); no entry exam; fairly wide range of abilities. Parents mostly landowners, farmers, business people; 80% live within an hour's drive. Rather functional dormitories (average eight bunks), some recently refurbished. Good food; staff eat with boys.

The head Recent appointment (predecessor, an old boy of the school, had been in post 22 years). Read psychology at Surrey; has spent all his career in boarding prep schools; previously head for four years of Bramcote. Keen sportsman; gets on well with pupils and parents. Married (wife much involved in school life); one son.

The teaching Enthusiastic, efficient; long-serving staff of 21 (a preponderance of bachelors). Common Entrance curriculum; Greek and German on offer; excellent facilities for art and design; plenty of computers. Pupils grouped by ability; lots of extra help for those with learning difficulties; average class size 11/12, never more than 15. Lots of music (nearly all learn an instrument); lively drama (all involved). Wide range of hobbies and activities, including pottery, calligraphy (a speciality), fishing, model-making, woodwork.

Results Very good: about 10% win senior school scholarships.

Destinations Principally Shrewsbury, followed by Eton and Winchester. Also: Malvern, Radley, King's Worcester, Marlborough.

Sport Good facilities for all main games. Particular success recently at cross-country, cricket. Golf, archery, fencing available.

Remarks Distinctive school; highly recommended.

---

* Key to symbols: ♂ = boys; ♀ = girls; ♂ ♀ = co-educational

ABERLOUR HOUSE ♂ ♀
Aberlour, Banffshire AB38 9LJ. Tel (01340) 871267

Synopsis
Co-educational ★ Boarding and day ★ Ages 8–13 ★ 110 pupils (60% boys, 85% boarding) ★ Fees: £8,985 boarding; £6,069 day
Head: John Caithness, 54, appointed 1992.
Small, happy school principally serving Gordonstoun (qv) whose ethos it shares; lots of outdoor activities.

Profile
Background Founded 1937; elegant Georgian country house plus extensive purpose-built additions in idyllic Spey Valley setting; 65 acres of wood and parkland. Co-educational since the early 1970s.

Atmosphere Homely, happy; emphasis on developing self-reliance; very good pastoral care. School is well-resourced; everything bright, tidy, clean.

Admission By interview; not unduly selective (entry to Gordonstoun not guaranteed); about 20% have learning difficulties. Parents mainly from professions and industry; most from within a radius of 100 miles. Pleasant, cosy dormitories but some rather crowded. Some financial assistance available through the Gordonstoun Foundation.

The head Educated at Merchiston Castle and St Andrews; taught in New Zealand for five years; formerly head of a prep school in Yorkshire. Gets on well with staff, parents and pupils. Married (wife much involved in pastoral side); two children (both educated at Gordonstoun).

The teaching Good; very committed staff. Standard Common Entrance curriculum; half take Latin (but Greek is no more); German on offer; good technology. Pupils grouped by ability as need dictates; lots of extra help for those who need it; average class size 16. Good music: 70% learn an instrument; small orchestra, choir. Lots of weekend expeditions. Pupils encouraged to develop interests, pursue projects; outdoor education is excellent.

Results Good Common Entrance record.

Destinations About 75%–80% to Gordonstoun.

Sport Chiefly rugby, hockey, cricket for the boys; netball, hockey, rounders for the girls; all do athletics, swimming; riding is popular. Extensive playing fields, sports hall, small heated pool, all-weather courts for basketball, netball, hockey, tennis.

Remarks Education not confined to the classroom: a school that develops free spirits and contributing citizens. HMI concluded (1996): 'The school has been successful in creating a very pleasant and stimulating atmosphere. Overall, the quality of teaching and learning was good.'

ARDVREK ♂ ♀
Gwydyr Road, Crieff, Perthshire PH7 4EX. Tel (01764) 653112

Synopsis
Co-educational ★ Boarding and day ★ Ages 3–13 ★ 160 pupils (66% boys, 65% boarding) ★ Fees: £8,700–£9,105 boarding; £900–£5,640 day
Head: Neil Gardner, 46, appointed 1995.
Pleasant, thriving school; good academic and sporting record.

Profile

Background Founded 1883 to teach boys 'patience, justice, obedience and unselfishness'. Moved to present purpose-built premises (Scottish baronial style) in extensive grounds 1885; later additions include fine music school, boarding houses, new classrooms. Co-educational since 1976; numbers up by 25% in past two years.

Atmosphere Busy, happy, well-ordered community; strong boarding ethos; hard-working staff (all of whom live in the grounds).

Admissions By assessment and interview ('children need to cope academically and socially'); fairly wide ability range. Parents mostly from professions, industry, multi-nationals, Services. Junior boarders in main building; separate houses for older boys and girls in the grounds; accommodation being up-graded.

The head Read law before switching to teaching; spent 10 years at Aberlour House (qv); previously head of the junior school at King's, Worcester. Married (to a teacher, much involved in school life); two children.

The teaching Mainly form teaching up to age eight; subject specialists thereafter. All do French from five, Latin from 10. Small classes; pupils grouped by ability in final year only; extra help both for the gifted and those with learning difficulties. Strong music: most learn an instrument; orchestra, choir. Frequent outings, visiting speakers. Extra-curricular activities include fly-tying, karate, cooking, rug-making. Sometimes the whole school spends a day in the hills, walking, climbing and fishing.

Results Common Entrance failures unheard of; average of six scholarships/exhibitions a year.

Destinations Mainly Strathallan, Glenalmond, Gordonstoun; significant minority south of the border to Eton, Radley, Downe House, Shrewsbury, Rugby etc.

Sport Chiefly rugby, cricket for the boys; hockey, netball, rounders for the girls; hockey, athletics, swimming for both; full inter-school fixture lists (and a good record). Riding, golf, skiing also on offer; very successful indoor .22 shooting. Facilities include five acres of playing fields and enclosed, all-weather surface.

Remarks Popular, successful school.

ARNOLD HOUSE ♂
3 Loudoun Road, St John's Wood, London NW8 0LH. Tel (0171) 286 1100

Synopsis
Boys ★ Day ★ Ages 5–13 ★ 231 pupils ★ Fees: £6,030
Head: Nicholas Allen, 45, appointed 1994.
Old-fashioned but enlightened school; good results.

Profile

Background Founded 1905; two amply-proportioned houses in quiet, tree-lined street; gardens back and front; two asphalt playgrounds. Facilities include well-designed science laboratory, fully-equipped computer room, art studio; space at a premium but school is uncramped by London standards.

Atmosphere Kindly; feels like a family; friendly relations between staff and pupils. ('The formation of character is regarded as of the greatest importance and the school aims to foster a spirit of self-reliance, cheerfulness and self-discipline,' says the prospectus. 'Particular emphasis is placed on good manners and neatness of person and work.') Uniform of cap, tie and blazer.

Admissions After interview with parents (early application advised). Fairly wide range of abilities but nearly all are capable of coping with Common Entrance.

The head   Able, experienced; keeps in touch with every boy's progress. Read history and archaeology at Exeter; previously head of Ipswich Prep. Married; three children (two are pupils here).

The teaching   Lively ('Teachers are selected for their ability to teach and relate to young children as well as for their personal qualities'). Both experience and enthusiasm are evident; parents can be confident their sons will receive a thorough grounding, and enjoy it too. Standard Common Entrance curriculum: all do French and Latin; Greek on offer; thriving art. Classroom arrangements vary from informal groups to front-facing rows; maximum size 17; extra help for dyslexics. (Reasonable conformity expected but great efforts made to accommodate individual needs.) Up to one hour's homework a night. Lots of music: 70% learn an instrument; two choirs, orchestra, jazz band. Extra-curricular activities include chess, current affairs, film studies, bridge.

Results   Good Common Entrance record; 17 scholarships since 1987. (Not a crammer but boys who merit scholarships tend to get them.)

Destinations   Many to Westminster; also Charterhouse, Eton, Haileybury, Harrow, Highgate, King's Canterbury, Winchester, Charterhouse, Rugby, University College School.

Sport   Two afternoons a week devoted to traditional games at school's own playing fields near Edgware; swimming at Finchley; cricket coaching at Lord's. Gymnastics taught to a high standard. Fully-equipped sports hall.

Remarks   Well-ordered, happy school with a deservedly good reputation.

ARNOLD LODGE ♂ ♀
Kenilworth Road, Leamington Spa, Warwickshire CV32 5TW. Tel (01926) 424737

Synopsis
Co-educational ★ Day and some weekly boarding ★ Ages 3–13 ★ 360 pupils (70% boys, 92% day) ★ Fees: £4,987 day; £6,822 weekly boarding
Head: Graham Hill, 53, appointed 1994.
Highly regarded school; good scholarship record; strong sport.

Profile
Background   Founded 1864 by a master from Rugby (and named after the great Dr Arnold). Attractive, solidly reassuring 1830s brick frontage plus later additions. Co-educational since 1979.

Atmosphere   A well-ordered, friendly, secure community in bright, cheerful surroundings. Big emphasis on social accomplishments (importance of good spoken English stressed – results apparent); civilised dining room; good food.

Admissions   At age three by interview with parents; at seven by tests in English, maths, verbal reasoning. Most pupils from business, professional families; 12% ethnic minority. Weekly boarding accommodation pleasantly furnished, homely.

The head   Able, experienced; previously head for 17 years of a large prep school in Surrey. Read English at Oxford (First). Married; two children.

The teaching   Styles range from formal (regarded as 'indispensable') to more modern approaches; all equally successful with highly responsive pupils. Experienced, well-qualified staff of 31 (equal numbers of women and men). Standard prep school curriculum; good technology; Spanish on offer. Pupils grouped by ability in maths, English; potential scholars streamed separately; maximum class size 18. Homework set daily, scrupulously corrected; effort and attainment reports to parents three times a term. Strong drama, music (flourishing orchestra, choir), art. Elegant dance studio; excellent library; lots of clubs and societies.

Results Good. About 10 scholarships a year to schools such as Oakham, Radley, Rugby, Shrewsbury.

Destinations Most girls move at 11 to King's High Warwick or Kingsley Leamington Spa. At 13, boys go on to about a dozen schools, particularly Warwick, Old Swinford.

Sport Strong in football, rugby, cricket, netball. Facilities include 12 acres of playing fields a mile away; leased swimming pool adjoining school.

Remarks Happy, high-achieving school. Good value for money.

ASHDELL ♀
266 Fulwood Road, Sheffield, South Yorkshire S10 3BL. Tel (0114) 266 3835

Synopsis
Girls ★ Day ★ Ages 4–11 ★ 125 pupils ★ Fees: £4,200–£4,500
Head: Mrs Jane Upton, 53, appointed 1984.
First-rate, traditional education for bright girls.

Profile
Background Founded in its present form in 1949 (previously a dame school). Delightful premises: two large, dignified, Victorian houses plus coach house surrounded by pleasant gardens in attractive residential area close to the city centre.

Atmosphere Busy, intimate community: happy, smiley faces (staff and children); bright, cheerful classrooms; neat, attractive uniforms. Everything maintained to a high order of good taste and style; big emphasis on good manners, consideration for others, self-discipline. School day ends at 4.30 pm.

Admissions At age four by interview; children need to show academic potential; head says of parents, 'I want to be sure they support what we are aiming for rather than just buying what we do'.

The head Warm, direct, humorous; totally absorbed in the school. Has very strong convictions; demands high standards from girls, parents and staff. Formerly taught French and German in large Sheffield comprehensives (her husband is deputy head of one).

The teaching Well-qualified, devoted staff; formal, structured methods; small classes. Great stress from the start on the basic skills of reading (parents required to play their part), writing (uniform style taught), spelling and arithmetic. Full curriculum ('a busy child is a happy child') includes science (handsome new lab), IT, French, Latin, woodwork. Extra help for those in difficulty (including dyslexia); enrichment groups for the very able. Regular homework, carefully marked. All required to do ballet, drama and learn a musical instrument.

Results Regular scholarships; virtually all win a place at their first-choice school.

Destinations About half to Sheffield High; most of the rest to boarding schools such as Cheltenham Ladies', Oakham, St Anne's Windermere.

Sport Netball, rounders on nearby sports field; swimming in university pool, half a mile away.

Remarks Excellent value for money; highly recommended.

ASHDOWN HOUSE ♂ ♀
Forest Row, East Sussex RH18 5JY. Tel (01342) 822574

Synopsis
Co-educational ★ Boarding and some day ★ Ages 8–13 ★ 214 pupils (75% boys, 95% boarding) ★ Fees: £8,280 day; £10,320 boarding
Head: Clive Williams, 52, appointed 1975.
Traditional prep school keeping up to date; good languages, music, art; château in France.

Profile
Background   Founded 1886. Fine Georgian mansion in 40 acres; classical Greek pillared entrance at the end of a long drive; extensive views across the games fields to Ashdown Forest. Some classrooms in rather ramshackle buildings. Co-educational since 1976.

Atmosphere   High expectations lead to a sense of purposefulness in games and lessons alike. Polite, friendly children (they stand aside for staff, open doors for visitors).

Admissions   No written admission tests but head interviews every child. Most from middle and upper-middle class backgrounds; half from London, a quarter expatriate. Pleasant boarding (new block opened 1994): pretty dormitories, wallpapered with matching curtains, carpets, duvets.

The head   Very long-serving; was a pupil here; returned to teach after Eton and Cambridge; still teaches part-time (scripture, scholarship Latin and Greek). Pleasant, relaxed manner (pupils find him very approachable). Wife, Rowena, teaches history and art, oversees the care side (with three qualified nurses).

The teaching   Styles range from the didactic to a lively, more dynamic approach. Staff of 20 (a third women); most live with their families on site. Standard prep school curriculum; good French (pupils spend periods at the school's château in Normandy, attend lessons with local children); all but a handful do Latin. Mixed-ability classes for first two years, streaming thereafter, including scholarship form; extra help for those with learning difficulties (but school claims no special expertise); average class size 15. Good music: two-thirds learn an instrument; three choirs, orchestra, various ensembles. Lots of extra-curricular activities.

Results   Good: 10 scholarships in past three years to Charterhouse, King's Canterbury, Wycombe Abbey, Downe House, Lancing.

Destinations   In the past three years, principally: Eton (21), King's Canterbury (18). Others to: Radley, St Paul's, Winchester, Benenden, Harrow, Roedean, Woldingham etc.

Sport   Chiefly soccer, rugby, cricket for the boys; netball, rounders for the girls; long list of fixtures against other schools. Hockey, tennis riding, golf also on offer; swimming in new indoor pool. Neighbouring farmer's barn converted into large sports hall for badminton, judo etc.

Remarks   Independent inspectors reported (1995): 'Ashdown House is an exceptionally pleasant, friendly and supportive environment where the children appear happy and confident. The school provides a sound all-round education with an emphasis on English, maths and languages. The children generally gain places at suitable senior independent schools when they leave.'

AYSGARTH ♂
Bedale, North Yorkshire DL8 1TF. Tel (01677) 450240

Synopsis
Boys ★ Boarding ★ Ages 8–13 (plus associated co-educational pre-prep) ★ 93
pupils ★ Fees: £9,108
Head: John Hodgkinson, 56, appointed 1988.
*Firmly traditional prep school; wide range of abilities; strong music, drama; lots
of sport.*

Profile
Background Founded 1877 at Aysgarth; moved to its present site in
Wensleydale 1890. Purpose-built red-brick premises, externally graceless but
redeemed by tranquil 50-acre woodland setting; later additions include well-
equipped science labs, music rooms, games/assembly hall; fine, late-Victorian
chapel (weekdays begin with a short morning service). Pre-prep (ages three to
eight, day only) in separate building under its own head.

Atmosphere Purposeful, cheerful – quintessential prep school ('The aim is to
give boys in their impressionable years secure foundations which will stand them
in good stead for the future'). Careful pastoral care system (friendly matrons,
domestic staff); fairly formal discipline with much emphasis on good manners
('We want to produce happy and well adjusted boys'). Lessons on Saturday mornings; television 'limited but available when the occasion demands'.

Admissions Entry by interview, predominantly at age eight; pupils of a wide
range of abilities (but expected to have reached 'levels of fluency in reading and
writing appropriate to their age and to know the basic rules of number work');
mainly from the North of England, some from the Midlands. Pleasant dormitories (some in need of up-dating); weekly boarding for first two years only. Some
financial help available for families in difficulty.

The head Relaxed, pragmatic style; formerly a housemaster at Uppingham.
His wife keeps a close eye on dormitories and domestic arrangements.

The teaching Claims to be unrepentantly traditionalist but keeps up to date.
National curriculum largely followed; good computing, electronics, design/tech-
nology; all do French, Latin. Specialist teaching throughout; expert remedial
provision for the less able; progress closely monitored (three-weekly grades);
average class size 10. Very strong music (orchestra, two choirs) and drama; the
art room, to quote the head, is 'a magic grotto'. Lots of extra-curricular
activities: something for everyone to do.

Results Good Common Entrance record; recent scholarships/exhibitions to
Loretto, Glenalmond, Harrow, Sedbergh.

Destinations Particularly Eton (37 places since 1989) and Harrow (27 places);
also Ampleforth, Radley, Stowe, Sedbergh, Uppingham, Winchester. Less academically able boys proceed to suitable schools.

Sport Main games: soccer, rugby, cricket (wicket would grace a county
ground). Other facilities include 17 acres of playing fields, indoor pool (due to
be replaced), rifle range, courts for squash, tennis, fives, six-hole golf course.

Remarks Well-run school (one of the last of its kind); prepares boys
thoroughly for Common Entrance. Highly recommended.

BEAUDESERT PARK ♂ ♀
Minchinhampton, Stroud, Gloucestershire GL6 9AF. Tel (01453) 832072

Synopsis
Co-educational ★ Day and boarding ★ Ages 4–13 ★ 294 pupils (80% day, 53% boys) ★ Fees: £3,510–£7,020 day; £9,534 boarding
Head: James Womersley, 40, appointed September 1997.
Happy, traditional school; good teaching and results; lots on offer.

Profile
Background   Founded 1908 as a boys' boarding school; moved 1918 to present 20-acre site (adjoining 500 acres of common); day boys admitted 1970s, girls 1981; pre-prep opened 1987. Elegant, timbered, Victorian mansion plus many later additions commanding fine Cotswold views; variable facilities.

Atmosphere   Bustling, friendly (like an extended family); warm relations between staff and pupils; academic expectations are high; 'good manners and consideration for others' a priority. Classrooms carpeted, curtained; pupils wear sensible sweaters, traditional shoes. Lessons on Saturday mornings.

Admissions   By interview and test; school is fairly selective. Boarders in tidy, characterful dormitories; weekly boarding popular.

The head   New appointment (the fourth in four years); previously a housemaster at the Dragon (qv). Keen to put a greater emphasis on drama, art, design/technology. Married (wife much involved in school life); three sons (all pupils here).

The teaching   Lively; traditional in style; mostly long-serving staff (equal numbers of women and men). Standard Common Entrance curriculum; French from age six, Latin from 10; well-equipped science labs. Pupils grouped by ability throughout; maximum class size 15, smaller for potential scholars. Very good music: choir; full orchestra performs regularly.

Results   Good Common Entrance record; up to 10 scholarships a year (academic, art, music, technology).

Destinations   Boys to Malvern, Cheltenham, Eton; girls to Cheltenham Ladies', Malvern Girls', St Mary's Calne.

Sport   Lots on offer. Facilities include 10 acres of playing fields half a mile away, indoor and outdoor pools, tennis courts, functional sports hall.

Remarks   Good school; childhood nurtured.

BELHAVEN HILL ♂ ♀
Dunbar, East Lothian EH42 1NN. Tel (01368) 862785

Synopsis
Co-educational ★ Boarding and day ★ Ages 7–13 ★ 90 pupils (78% boys, 85% boarding) ★ Fees: £9,120 boarding; £6,420 day
Head: Michael Osborne, 52, appointed 1987.
Most traditional of Scottish preps; good academic record.

Profile
Background   Founded 1923, since when its character has changed remarkably little (co-education, introduced in 1975, was abandoned in 1989 but reintroduced in 1994). Mid-18th century mansion (plus later additions) in 18-acre wooded estate on the outskirts of Dunbar, 30 miles east of Edinburgh; some

classrooms in battered huts.

Atmosphere   A happy, disciplined, civilised community; busy without being boisterous. Bright, socially polished children; staff–pupil relations friendly yet respectful. Day completely time-tabled from chanter practice before breakfast to end of prep at 7 pm.

Admissions   Entry by interview; selection by early registration rather than ability (word of mouth the only advertising). Mostly from land-owning classes, farming, professional backgrounds (90% Scottish). Boys' dormitories far from luxurious but being refurbished; girls in modern, purpose-built house.

The head   Former Belhaven pupil (1952–1958) and teacher (1973–1981); went to Radley and Cambridge. Well versed in, and keen to preserve, the traditions and character of the school. Wants to give greater prominence to music but otherwise sees little reason to tamper with a well-tried, successful formula. Leads a dedicated team and teaches a full timetable. Married with a young family.

The teaching   Mostly traditional chalk-and-talk; subject-based after first year. Full-time staff of 10 (three women), half graduates, half with teaching diplomas, all equally committed and versatile (most live on campus and are much involved out of the classroom). Standard prep school curriculum; French introduced from the start (French speaking at lunch twice a week), Latin a year later, Greek when required; design/technology not yet seen to justify investment of time and money – carpentry preferred. Junior classes of 17–18; older pupils grouped by ability in classes of eight to 12. Lots of music: all juniors learn the recorder; lessons also available in piano, violin, brass, woodwind and bagpipes. Rationed television favours the survival of archetypal boarding prep school hobbies: stamps, chess and other board games, model-making, gardening, table-tennis, model railway.

Results   Regular handful of scholarships to schools on both sides of the Border.

Destinations   Most boys registered for major English public schools (especially Eton, Harrow) but targets revised after careful assessment of a pupil's ability to face the competition. Approximately a third transfer to Scottish schools; Glenalmond the most popular.

Sport   Strong rugby, hockey and cricket; regular fixtures with other prep schools; girls' sports being developed. Heated, outdoor pool dates from 1930s; sports hall more recent.

Remarks   A school that adjusts slowly to change and continues to foster high academic standards. Unlikely to appeal to trendy parents but clearly fulfilling its aims.

BILTON GRANGE ♂ ♀
Dunchurch, Rugby, Warwickshire CV22 6QU. Tel (01788) 810217

Synopsis
Co-educational ★ Boarding and day ★ Ages 4–13 ★ 317 pupils (60% boys, 50% boarding, 8–13) ★ Fees: £9,333 boarding; £2,697–£7,464 day
Head: Quentin Edwards, 45, appointed 1992.
Fine school; good teaching and results; strong music and sport.

Profile
Background   Founded 1873; moved to present, immaculate, 156-acre parkland site 1887; regal Victorian mansion (interior designs by Pugin) joined to 18th-century farmhouse; delightful, scaled-down chapel. Spacious classrooms; later additions include science labs, technology block, theatre; facilities are first-rate. Co-educational since 1990. Independently run Montessori nursery in the grounds.

Atmosphere Secure, happy, well-ordered ('Any breach of common sense is a breach of the school rules'). Firm boarding ethos; day begins with an act of worship; lessons on Saturday mornings; two-thirds of staff live on site. Meals, taken in the original dining hall (lined with honours boards going back to 1875), are sociable occasions; good-quality food. Dens, treehouses in the grounds ('We offer them a childhood').

Admissions Entry is non-competitive: evidence sought of ability to cope with the work. Children drawn from fairly wide social spectrum; increasing proportion of parents are 'first-time buyers' of independent education ('There's no feeling now that prep schools are for snobs'). Boys' dormitories (up to 12 beds) recently refurbished (carpets, pastel shades, elegant lighting – 'Mums love it'); girls' boarding cosier, less formal; flexi-boarding on offer. Scholarships, bursaries available, including fee reductions for children of Service personnel, clergy, teachers.

The head Youthful, energetic, forthright; has made big changes (predecessor had been in post more than 20 years), including introducing co-education ('I find it very odd keeping boys and girls apart when they are growing up'). Read English at Oxford; taught at Bradfield for 17 years (10 as housemaster); determined supporter of boarding ('a magnificently rich supplement to family life'). Wife, Maggie, runs the pre-prep department (ages four to seven, day pupils only) and computing (enthusiastic about the benefits of laptops). They have two children.

The teaching First-rate: broadly traditional in style; meticulous attention to individual needs, including those of dyslexics. Staff of 27, a third appointed by present head. Broad curriculum: all do French from age five, Latin from nine, second modern language from 10; scholarship pupils add German/Greek; science taught as three separate subjects; IT across the curriculum (CD-Roms in Pugin library); outstanding design/technology (woodwork to robotics); very good art. Pupils grouped by ability from 10; further setting in maths, French for final two years; maximum class size 16. All do one hour's prep from age eight. Flourishing music: three-quarters learn an instrument; choir, orchestra, wind band, various ensembles. Lively drama; regular productions. Lots of extra-curricular activities.

Results Good: more than a quarter gain awards – academic, art, music, technology.

Destinations About 45% to Rugby; rest to Oundle, Uppingham, Oakham, Malvern, Bloxham etc.

Sport Strong. Major games: rugby, netball, hockey, cricket; all coached by qualified staff – as are tennis and squash. Fine facilities include extensive playing fields, all-weather surface sports hall, squash and tennis courts, large indoor pool.

Remarks Successful, go-ahead school; recommended.

BRAMBLETYE ♂
East Grinstead, Sussex RH19 3PD. Tel (01342) 321004

Synopsis
Boys ★ Boarding and day ★ Ages 8–13 ★ 215 pupils (70% boarding) ★ Fees: £9,600 boarding; £7,050 day
Head: Hugh Cocke, 42, appointed September 1997.
First-rate, traditional school; good teaching; lots of music; strong sport; wide range of extra-curricular activities.

Profile
Background Founded 1919; moved from Sidcup to present 130-acre site 1932.

Imposing Victorian country mansion approached by a long drive (cricket field and pavilion to the left, superb views of Weir Wood reservoir and Ashdown Forest to the right). Well-tended grounds and playing fields (six-hole golf course, small lake for fishing).

Atmosphere   Busy, friendly, very traditional (uniform includes distinctive pink blazer). Regular worship in chapel.

Admissions   No entry test: first come, first served – but detailed report requested from current school. Most come from a 50-mile radius, many from London. Cheerful, homely dormitories, recently upgraded.

The head   New appointment (predecessor had been in post 28 years). Read history at Culham College; previously head for six years of a prep school in Suffolk. Keen cricketer. Married; two daughters.

The teaching   Good; well-qualified staff of 23 (a third women). Standard prep school curriculum; all do Latin from third year; lots of computers. Pupils grouped by ability in maths, French after first year; class sizes range from 12 to 18; bright boys who reach the top of the school at 11 are prepared for scholarships in smaller groups; special help for dyslexics. Lots of music: opportunity to learn most instruments (including bagpipes, classical guitar); orchestra, swing band, two choirs; 270-seat arts centre has computerised stage lighting, good acoustics, orchestra pit, music practice rooms. Lots of art, craft, pottery. Choice of 24 extra-curricular activities: bridge, chess, fencing, cookery, stamp collecting, video-film making etc.

Results   Good: recent scholarships to Harrow, Charterhouse, Sherborne, Wellington, Millfield, King's Canterbury.

Destinations   In addition to the above: Harrow, Radley, Winchester, Eton, Cranleigh.

Sport   Excellent facilities, including gym, heated indoor pool, squash and tennis courts, assault course. Main games: soccer, rugby, cricket; regular fixtures against other prep schools. Also on offer: golf, athletics, shooting (.22 range), hockey, judo, fencing, fishing, rock-climbing, canoeing.

Remarks   Caring school; turns out confident, happy, well-rounded boys.

BRAMCOTE ♂ ♀
Filey Road, Scarborough, North Yorkshire YO11 2TT. Tel (01723) 373086

Synopsis
Co-educational ★ Boarding and day ★ Ages 8–13 ★ 100 pupils (90% boys, 88% boarders) ★ Fees: £8,640 boarding; £6,000 day
Head: Peter Kirk, 43, appointed 1996.
Well-run, happy, traditional school; good teaching; lots of extra-curricular activities; strong sport.

Profile
Background   Founded 1893; a row of red-brick Victorian houses (plus later additions) on an attractive five-acre site on the outskirts of the town, a short walk from the sea. Girls first admitted 1996.

Atmosphere   Happy, busy; high academic standards; clear Christian ethos. Staff give freely of their time; parents welcomed as partners.

Admissions   No entry test; fairly wide range of abilities; most pupils from upper-middle-class families (traditional prep school customers). Boarding accommodation functional, if not austere; communal rooms have a 'lived in' quality. Scholarships, bursaries offered.

The head Enthusiastic. Read maths at Heriot-Watt; joined the Royal Navy (instructor, Lieutenant Commander); previously a housemaster at Glenalmond (qv). Married (wife helps look after the younger ones); two daughters (both pupils here).

The teaching First-rate: mainly traditional in style; dedicated, long-serving staff of 12. Broad curriculum: all start French at eight, Latin at nine; Greek on offer; all but the youngest do one hour's prep a day. No grouping by ability until the final year, when a scholarship class is formed; average class size 14; extra help for those who need it (including mild dyslexia); progress closely monitored (three-weekly gradings, detailed termly reports). Strong music tradition; more than 80% learn at least one instrument; good choir. Exceptionally busy programme of extra-curricular activities.

Results Good scholarship record (average of four a year to leading schools over the past 10 years); virtually all go on to the school of their (guided) first choice.

Destinations Recently: Ampleforth, Bootham, Eton, Giggleswick, Gordonstoun, Loretto, Malvern, Oundle, Radley, Repton, Rugby, Sedbergh, Shrewsbury, Uppingham, Winchester, St Peter's York.

Sport Important; games played every day (winter timetable re-arranged to take advantage of the light). Main sports: soccer, rugby, cricket, athletics. Canoeing, cycling, squash, swimming, hockey, golf, tennis, archery, judo, basketball, badminton also on offer. First-class facilities, including immaculate playing fields, sports hall, indoor pool, floodlit tennis court.

Remarks Very good all round; recommended.

BUTTERSTONE ♀
Arthurstone, Meigle, Perthshire PH12 8QY. Tel (01828) 640528

Synopsis
Independent ★ Boarding and day ★ Girls ★ Ages 8–13 (plus co-educational pre-prep) ★ 57 pupils (82% boarding) ★ Fees: £9,375 boarding; £6,045 day
Head: Christopher Syers-Gibson, 64, appointed 1986 (retiring August 1998).
Traditional, well-run, 'family' school; good teaching; lots on offer.

Profile
Background Founded 1947 in Dunkeld; moved 1991 to elegant Georgian house plus Victorian extension on 25-acre estate (paid for by parents); entrance hall doubles as dance studio/theatre; gymnastics in girls' rococo common room; some classes in converted stable block. Co-educational nursery and pre-prep (50 pupils aged two to eight) on the premises. Everything well-maintained, spotlessly clean.

Atmosphere Warm, cheerful, friendly; genuine family feel; very good pastoral care; discipline exercised gently but firmly (a quiet word from the head is usually sufficient). Practical uniform of jumper and skirt. Many girls keep pets here; some bring their ponies.

Admissions By interview (no tests); fairly wide range of abilities; most are the daughters of Scottish landowners. Comfortable boarding accommodation in small, cheerful dormitories.

The head Gentle, avuncular, very experienced. Read English at Cambridge; has spent his career in the prep school world, including 18 years at Horris Hill (qv); previously head of The Downs, Colwall (qv). Married (wife teaches here and is much involved in school life); four children.

The teaching Good quality; varied styles; experienced, well-qualified, all-female staff (head teaches Latin and scripture). Standard Common Entrance curriculum; all learn to use computers. Pupils grouped by ability in English, maths, science; progress closely monitored (monthly reports to parents); no class larger than 12, some as small as five. Lots of music; choir, small orchestra. Wide choice of hobbies (knitting, fly-tying, silk painting, tap dancing).
Results Good Common Entrance record; two or three scholarships a year.
Destinations In Scotland: Gordonstoun, Kilgraston, St Leonard's, Glenalmond; about half go south of the border to Queen Margaret's York, St Anne's Windermere, North Foreland Lodge, Tudor Hall, Wycombe Abbey.
Sport Hockey, rounders, tennis, netball; skiing at Glenshee. Facilities include all-weather pitch, show-jumping/cross-country course.
Remarks Charming small school.

CALDICOTT ♂
Farnham Royal, Buckinghamshire SL2 3SL. Tel (01494) 646214.

Synopsis
Boys ★ Boarding and day ★ Ages 7–13 ★ 250 pupils (54% boarding) ★ Fees: £9,675 boarding; £7,245 day
Head: Mike Spens, 47, appointed 1993 (leaving August 1988).
Fine, well-run school; strong academic and sporting record.

Profile
Background Founded 1904; moved to present 20-acre site (attractive, well-maintained grounds) on the edge of Burnham Beeches 1938; another 18 acres recently acquired for further pitches and a lake. Large Victorian house plus purpose-built additions, including magnificent sports hall; facilities generally good.
Atmosphere Traditional values; strong Christian ethos (daily act of worship in chapel); high expectations. Committed staff (80% male); hard-working, well-mannered boys. Supportive parents raise substantial sums annually.
Admissions By interview and school's own exams in English, maths. Most boys live within a 20-mile radius; 20% of boarders from overseas. NB: all required to board for their final two years. Dormitories (five to eight beds) comfortable, carpeted, recently refurbished.
The head Able, experienced. Read geology at Cambridge; spent 19 years at Radley, including 10 as a housemaster; teaches older boys maths and science. Married (wife teaches dyslexics); three children. Moving to Fettes (qv).
The teaching High quality: mostly traditional in style; boys encouraged to participate. All do French from first year, Latin from second; German, Spanish on offer; very good provision for technology, computing; science much improved. Pupils grouped by ability from the start (including scholarship stream); extra help for those with mild dyslexia. Reports to parents three times a term. Good music: half learn an instrument; at least two concerts a year. Lots of art, drama. Wide range of extra-curricular activities: boys purposefully occupied at all times.
Results Excellent scholarship record, especially to Eton. Virtually all pass Common Entrance to (guided) first-choice school.
Destinations Mainly Eton, Harrow, Radley, Wellington, Marlborough.
Sport Notably strong, particularly in rugby (fine record in national sevens tournaments), cricket, hockey; athletics, tennis, shooting (.22 rifle gallery) also

offered; all boys play sport every day. Facilities include good playing fields, two squash courts, three tennis courts, outdoor pool.

Remarks   Ofsted inspectors concluded (1994): 'Caldicott is a very good school, with significant marks of excellence. It is highly successful in preparing its pupils for the next stage of their education.'

CARGILFIELD ♂ ♀
Barnton Avenue West, Edinburgh EH4 6HU. Tel (0131) 336 2207

Synopsis
Co-educational ★ Day and boarding ★ Ages 3–13 ★ 182 pupils (65% boys, 55% day) ★ Fees (upper school): £9,510 boarding; £6,810 day
Head: Andrew Morrison, 55, appointed September 1997.
Friendly, traditional school; good academic and sporting record.

Profile
Background   Scotland's oldest prep school; founded 1873 'to provide a liberal education and to teach the merits of work and honesty under conditions of happiness and well-being'; moved 1899 to present 20-acre, semi-rural site five miles from Edinburgh. Day boys admitted 1976; girls 1978; pre-prep department opened 1979; nursery 1982. Elegant, mock-Tudor, red-roofed buildings (with some less attractive modern additions). Charming chapel, which, with 180-degree turn of seating, becomes a theatre or dance hall.

Atmosphere   A happy, well-ordered (but not regimented) community; every effort made to maintain boarding atmosphere (working day ends at 6 pm, lessons on Saturday mornings). Strong family ethos; confident, well-mannered pupils.

Admissions   By interview; school is not particularly selective. Parents primarily from the professions and industry plus a significant number from the Services; 85% from Scotland. Boys' dormitories spacious but somewhat lacking in privacy; girls' dormitories smaller, cosier.

The head   New appointment. Educated at Eton (scholar) and Cambridge (classics); previously head of Mowden Hall (qv) and master of the under school at Charterhouse. Keen sailor and cricketer. Married (wife much involved in school life); three grown-up children.

The teaching   Healthy blend of experience and youthful vigour; relations with pupils friendly but not over-familiar. Nursery over-subscribed; bright, lively, well-staffed. Adjoining pre-prep department offers gentle but increasingly structured approach to learning; early emphasis on English and maths. Thereafter, full Common Entrance syllabus; Latin for the more able; Greek for the chosen few; Spanish and German on offer; computer studies and technology (show-piece studio) for all. Classrooms generally bright (class sizes average 12) but some prefabs and 'temporary' huts (one housing rabbits, guinea pigs, hamsters, gerbils etc). Music particularly strong; timetabled lessons plus private tuition; half learn an instrument; small orchestra, jazz band.

Results   Good Common Entrance record; 18 academic awards in past four years.

Destinations   Mostly Scottish independent schools: Fettes, Glenalmond, Loretto, Merchiston, St Leonards, Strathallan etc; south of the Border to Downe House, Eton, Harrow, Oundle, Rugby, Winchester.

Sport   Daily games for all: rugby, hockey, cricket for boys; hockey, rounders, netball for girls; busy fixture list. Good facilities, including new sports hall, well-

tended cricket square, three floodlit all-weather tennis courts. Archery, riding, squash, gymnastics, swimming etc on offer.
Remarks   Happy school; secure environment; sound education; wide variety of activities and sports.

CHEAM HAWTREYS   ♂ ♀
Headley, Newbury, Berkshire RG19 8LD. Tel (01635) 268242

Synopsis
Becoming co-educational ★ Boarding and day ★ Ages 7–13 ★ 130 pupils (70% boarding) ★ Fees: £10,176 boarding; £7,356 day
Head: Chris Evers, 58, appointed (to Cheam) 1985.
Traditional prep school: caring, family atmosphere in very pleasant surroundings.

Profile
Background   Result of a 1994 merger of two famous, long-established prep schools. Cheam was founded in 1645 by a Royalist clergyman for 'sons of gentlemen' (being out of London, they escaped plagues and dissension); became a nursery for the aristocracy; moved from newly-suburban Cheam, Surrey in 1934 (just after the Duke of Edinburgh left) to a lovely house on an 80-acre site four miles south of Newbury (where Prince Charles was sent in 1957). In 1994 the governors decided that, to preserve the essential character of Cheam as a good, smallish boarding school, it would be politic to make overtures to another such with a view to merger: they approached Hawtreys (founded 1869 by an Eton housemaster, housed in an elegant Palladian mansion in Savernake Forest), and the deal was done almost at once; most Hawtreys boys transferred to the Cheam site that September. ('It's like two regiments merging,' observed the head of Hawtreys. 'The regimental silver and the battle honours will not be lost.') Numbers, however, continued to decline and in March 1997 the school decided, 'in the light of market research into trends in the aspirations of potential parents', to admit girls from September; they will have their own, separate house. Pre-prep department to follow in 1998.
Atmosphere   Gracious, well-maintained Victorian mansion: spacious rooms, wide corridors, pleasant dining room. Small, homely dormitories and playrooms up a grand staircase; separate, delightfully domestic house for youngest boarders; photos of groups of grinning pupils all over the place. Boys play croquet or bowls on immaculate lawns; the outdoor swimming pool lies beyond the rose garden and the formal pond. Grounds include a barn for rough living, room for pitching tents and plenty of out-door opportunities. Day pupils (proportion is growing) follow the same routine as boarders, including Saturday school.
Admissions   Most start at age eight but a growing number of parents prefer to keep them at home a little longer. About 60% live within an hour's travelling; 10% from abroad. Exeats every three weeks; parents welcome to visit in between.
The head   Inspires immediate confidence; his Pooh-Bear-like solidity and obvious love of the school appeals to parents. Read PPE at Oxford (hockey Blue); has been a head for nearly 25 years (and comes from a family of heads). Runs the school more by instinct and seat-of-the-pants than theory or directives; 'Stick to what you believe, what you're good at,' he says, and he does. Beliefs include the unfashionable doctrine that boarding is wonderful for eight and nine-year-olds, who need and enjoy the constant diversion and entertainment that most parents cannot manage; fears schools are being pushed by parental expectations into

becoming 'sausage machines', concerned only with examination success. His wife, Penny, is in charge of the domestic side; they have two children.

The teaching   Staff – 13 men, five women, most appointed by the present head – give an impression of being tolerant, energetic uncles and aunts who like their little charges. Traditional prep school curriculum: most still learn Latin; French benefits from a rented château in Normandy; lots of computing; brand-new science block. Pupils grouped by ability; average class size 12–15. Plenty of music (choir, orchestra) and drama. Busy extra-curricular programme.

Results   Not many scholarships but good Common Entrance record.

Destinations   All major independent schools, particularly Eton, Harrow, Radley, Rugby, Marlborough.

Sport   Wide variety on offer: soccer, rugby, hockey, athletics, golf (nine-hole course), shooting, cricket, tennis. Not always a great deal of success in inter-school matches, perhaps because competition is not much encouraged. Boys make ample use of the grounds, being given time to themselves to do so.

Remarks   A happy place: not an exciting school, but a reassuring one, where boarding is home from home.

CLIFTON ♂ ♀
The Avenue, Bristol BS8 3HE. Tel (0117) 973 7264

Synopsis
Co-educational ★ Day and boarding ★ Ages 7–13 (plus associated pre-prep) ★ 360 pupils (70% boys, 83% day) ★ Fees: £6,630 day; £9,690 boarding
Head: Dr Bob Acheson, 48, appointed 1993.
First-rate, well-run school; very good teaching; strong sport.

Profile
Background   Founded 1873; shares governors and many facilities with the adjacent Clifton College (qv). Handsome set of adapted Victorian houses; later additions include new science block, IT centre, music school (£1 million spent over past three years). Pre-prep (180 pupils aged three to seven) on same site under its own head.

Atmosphere   Happy, well-ordered; strong pastoral care system (complaints boxes all round the school – head has the only key); good relations between staff and pupils; parents welcome at all times. Children may stay until 6 pm.

Admissions   By interview; school is not academically selective; range of abilities is wide. Boarding accommodation recently refurbished but rather over-crowded; boarders can stay for as few or as many nights as they want.

The head   Tough, dynamic, ambitious. Read history at Oxford, PhD from Kent; taught for 12 years at Duke of York's Royal Military (qv); previously head for eight years of a prep school in Berkshire; still teaches eight periods of history a week. Believes parents buy independent education because they 'want their children to grow up in an atmosphere of happiness, order, discipline and moral consistency: our independence affords us the chance to lift the eyes of children from the gutter of the 20th century; our future lies in keeping the torch of moral firmness burning brightly as the mists of a new dark age threaten to engulf us'. Married (wife teaches drama here); two children.

The teaching   Challenging, formal in style; well-qualified staff of 54 (equal numbers of women and men), half appointed by present head. National curriculum plus; languages on offer include Japanese, Mandarin. Pupils grouped by ability in

most subjects; plenty of extra help for those who need it, including dyslexics and high-flyers; maximum class size 16. First-rate art; lots of drama, music.
Results Good scholarship record: 60 awards in the past three years.
Destinations More than 90% go on to the senior school.
Sport Strong: wide range on offer; good coaching. Facilities shared with senior school include 93 acres of playing fields, two all-weather pitches, sports hall, indoor pool.
Remarks Very good all round; recommended.

COTHILL HOUSE ♂
Frilford Heath, Abingdon, Oxford OX13 6JL. Tel (01865) 390800

Synopsis
Boys ★ Boarding ★ Ages 8–13 ★ 260 pupils ★ Fees: £10,620
Head: Adrian Richardson, 53, appointed 1976.
Friendly, happy school; good teaching and results; château in France.

Profile
Background Founded 1870; beautiful old house with fine views in extensive, well-kept grounds; classrooms in modern, purpose-built block. School owns (and makes full use of) a 16–bedroom château in France.
Atmosphere Cheerful, good-humoured. Strong sense of community: no 'them-and-us' feeling between staff and friendly, high-spirited boys. Dormitories (mostly in main house) centrally-heated, carpeted, pleasantly furnished; partitions afford degree of privacy. Excellent food.
Admissions No entry test but boys are assessed during a visit to the school in the term prior to entry; head looks for an ability to shine in academic work, sport or social skills; most pupils of average intelligence but some significantly below and a few significantly above. Mainly from upper and upper-middle-class backgrounds in London and the South East.
The head Very long-serving. Gentle, but keeps firm discipline. Worked first for a shipping line (travelled extensively) and then in the City where he 'lost a lot of money and decided to become a schoolmaster'. Went to Oxford as a mature student; worked in a tough secondary modern. Teaches boys to be aware of their privileges while deriving maximum satisfaction from them. His wife, Rachel, shares responsibility for pupils' welfare: their front door always open; boys in and out all day.
The teaching Academically respectable – but this is not a hot-house. Standard Common Entrance curriculum; very good French (all 11 and 12-year-olds have a term's total immersion in French life and language). Pupils grouped by ability in third year; individual tuition for those with reading and writing problems; average class size 16.
Results Good Common Entrance record; most go on to their (guided) first-choice senior school.
Destinations Mainly Eton, Radley, Harrow and others of similar ilk.
Sport Daily games for all; good facilities (nine-hole golf course, shooting range). All boys can swim by the time they leave.
Remarks Well-run school; greatest strength is its concern for the boys' welfare and happiness.

COTTESMORE ♂ ♀
Buchan Hill, Pease Pottage, West Sussex RH11 9AU. Tel (01293) 520648

Synopsis
Co-educational ★ Boarding ★ Ages 7–13 ★ 145 pupils (70% boys) ★ Fees: £9,630
Head: Mark Rogerson, 54, appointed 1971.
Exceptionally friendly, happy school; strong family atmosphere; good academic record; first-rate music, drama, sport.

Profile
Background   Founded 1894 in Hove; moved 1947 (under present head's father) to stunning red-brick Victorian mansion (built by an ostrich-farming millionaire) in 30 acres of beautiful grounds adjoining a golf course. Most classrooms in adjoining, purpose-built block; very good facilities (£1.25 million spent over past 10 years); technology centre under construction. Co-educational since 1975.

Atmosphere   Exceptional: feels like an overgrown family, and a remarkably happy one at that. Daily 'coffee', when all adults congregate in the graciously proportioned original entrance hall, is typical: everyone on hand; children constantly in and out; very happy buzz. Staff (most of whom live within the grounds) vigilant and endlessly encouraging; high expectations of behaviour and effort; competition kept in its place, balanced by praise; children obviously happy and secure. Christian principles at the heart of it all: daily services in little chapel. Spacious, light dormitories (bunk beds, carpets, jolly duvets); girls one end, boys the other; very homely feel. One of the last all-boarding schools in England.

Admissions   By interview; numbers, remarkably, have held steady for 20 years. ('Through a period of great social change,' explains the head, 'the school has steered a steady course, and ridden the storms of fashion and recession.') Most from professional/middle-class families; a third from abroad (half are expatriates).

The head   Exceptionally long-serving, hugely experienced, very approachable; inherited the school from his father and runs it 'shoulder to shoulder' with his wife, Cathryn (known as Mr and Mrs Mark, they are very much surrogate parents). Educated at Eton and Cambridge (read history); met his wife while teaching at Windlesham House (qv); they have four grown-up children. Teaches five periods a week, knows every child well. Believes passionately in the value of boarding; no plans for weekly boarders, day pupils or further expansion.

The teaching   First-rate. Dedicated staff of 16, all but one appointed by present head; good spread of age and experience. First-years taught separately in cosy inter-linked classrooms; solid grounding in spelling, grammar, handwriting etc; Latin taught from second year; emphasis on learning through enjoyment (class of nine-year-olds singing French songs with total lack of inhibition and near-perfect pronunciation). Older children grouped by ability into two streams plus scholarship class in top year; very small classes; extra help for those with special needs; effort and achievement marks sent monthly to parents. Strong music tradition (sounds of someone playing in the background most of the time); impressive art; lively drama, involving everyone. Vast range of extra-curricular activities: 10-pin bowling, model railway, pottery, rifle shooting, chess, stamps. etc.

Results   Good Common Entrance record: all go on to their (guided) first-choice school; average of four scholarships a year.

Destinations   Wide range, but chiefly: Charterhouse, Eton, Lancing, Roedean, Benenden, St Mary's Calne, King's Canterbury, Sevenoaks.

Sport   Very strong. Main games: rugby, soccer, hockey, athletics, swimming, netball, cricket, rounders, tennis. Huge choice of minor sports includes judo, archery, riding, basketball. Good indoor pool (all learn to swim well); extensive, well-tended pitches.

Remarks   Pursuit of excellence combined with compassionate nurturing. Highly recommended.

CRAIGCLOWAN ♂ ♀
Edinburgh Road, Perth PH2 8PS. Tel (01738) 626310

Synopsis
Co-educational ★ Day ★ Ages 3–13 ★ 280 pupils (equal numbers of girls and boys) ★ Fees: £4,515
Head: Michael Beale, 49, appointed 1979.
Lively, successful school; small classes; wide range of activities.

Profile
Background   Founded 1952; nearly closed in late 1970s but has grown steadily under the present head. Large Victorian mansion plus modern additions (including technology centre, music suite, sports hall) set in 13 acres on the southern outskirts of Perth; splendid views of the surrounding countryside.

Atmosphere   Busy, purposeful; a secure environment with a strong sense of identity. Pupils confident, courteous, cheerful.

Admissions   By interview and previous school report; fairly wide ability range. Parental occupations mainly professional/business.

The head   Energetic (despite a long stint); expects equal commitment from staff and pupils; very much in charge (wife acts as bursar). Has a paternal, affectionate relationship with pupils; gets on well with parents. Keen sportsman: played cricket and hockey for Dorset.

The teaching   Unashamedly traditional (grammar analysed on the blackboard); Strong Scottish emphasis on the Three Rs; also much project work (crowded, lively wall displays). Subject-based specialist teaching for top three years; some Latin, lots of rigorously taught French, good technology. Long school day plus homework for all; termly exams. Pupils grouped by ability; plenty of individual attention; accelerated promotion for academically gifted; average class size 13. Lots of dance, drama, music (nearly two-thirds learn an instrument). Extra-curricular activities include debating, bird club, model-making etc.

Results   All do well enough in Common Entrance to proceed to the senior school of their (carefully guided) choice.

Destinations   Mostly to Scottish independent schools: Fettes, Glenalmond, Gordonstoun, Loretto, Merchiston, St Leonards, Strathallan; some to similar south of the Border, including Eton, Rugby, Downe House, St Mary's Ascot.

Sport   Rugby, hockey, cricket for the boys; hockey, rounders, netball for the girls. All do athletics, swimming. Facilities include eight acres of playing fields, three all-weather tennis courts. Saturday ski trips in season.

Remarks   Excellent preparation for senior school, whether boarding or day. Her Majesty's Inspectors reported (1993): 'The school was fully meeting its aims and providing a very good quality of education.'

THE DOWNS ♂ ♀
Colwall, Malvern, Worcestershire WR13 6EY. Tel (01684) 540277

Synopsis
Co-educational ★ Day and boarding ★ Ages 3–13 ★ 180 pupils (55% boys, 55% day) ★ Fees: £6,240 day; £8,670 boarding
Head: Mrs Jenni Griggs, 49, appointed 1994.
Distinctive, busy school; good teaching; strong music; wide range of extra-curricular activities.

Profile
Background   Founded by Quakers in 1900 as 'primarily a society, not an institution for instruction'. Pleasant, well-maintained red-brick buildings set in 55 acres of playing fields and gardens at the foot of the Malvern Hills. Co-educational since 1975. W H Auden used to teach here.

Atmosphere   Warm, welcoming; strong sense of community and purpose; friendly, open relations between staff and pupils (who thank their teacher at the end of each lesson). Senior school day lasts from 8.30 am to 7 pm Monday to Friday (siesta after lunch), 8.30 am to 4 pm Saturday ('We aim for at least 60 hours "contact time" between staff and pupils each week').

Admissions   By interview; fairly wide range of abilities ('enthusiasm and effort are attributes to be prized as highly as talent'). Home backgrounds mainly professional/managerial; some farming, Services (discounts offered), multinationals; nationwide catchment area. Homely boarding accommodation; 'flexi-boarding' on offer; boarders may bring 'small, warm-blooded, four-legged' pets.

The head   An internal promotion: came here to teach in 1987. Educated in former Rhodesia. Married; two sons (both were pupils here).

The teaching   Stimulating; styles range from Socratic questioning to practical project work ('hands-on experience being the natural way at this age'). Form teachers for younger pupils; subject specialisation thereafter. Standard prep school curriculum; Latin from 10; strong science. Some grouping by ability; scholarship class; extra help for dyslexics; small classes, average size 11. All encouraged to take part in full programme of extra-curricular activities ('hobbies liberate the imagination'): drama, art, craft, cookery, technology, sculpture, photography, computers, wildlife, needlework, textiles, pottery, skiing, horse-riding, squash, ballet, carpentry, etc; narrow-gauge railway (complete with steam engines). Music particularly strong; aim is to nurture the talented and encourage a love of music in all.

Results   Good Common Entrance record: all proceed to the school of their (guided) choice. Recent scholarships and music awards to King Edward's Birmingham, Marlborough, Millfield, Shrewsbury, Malvern.

Destinations   In addition to the above: Ampleforth, Bryanston, Dean Close, Downside, Eton, Harrow, Headington, King's Worcester, Malvern, Malvern Girls', Milton Abbey, Taunton etc.

Sport   Wide range; good facilities, including extensive playing fields, all-weather hockey pitch, tennis courts, heated outdoor pool. Cup awarded for bravery in rugby tackling.

Remarks   Good school with plenty to offer; recommended.

DRAGON ♂ ♀
Bardwell Road, Oxford OX2 6SS. Tel (01865) 315400

Synopsis
Co-educational ★ Day and boarding ★ Ages 3–13 ★ 800 pupils (including 200 in pre-prep, 70% boys, 65% day) ★ Fees: £6,837 day; £10,335 boarding
Head: Roger Trafford, 57, appointed 1993.
Marvellous school; challenging, spirited, informal.

Profile
Background Founded 1877 for the offspring of progressive Oxford dons. Conglomeration of buildings on a 15-acre site beside the Cherwell; classrooms grouped around a playground where generations of Dragons have played conkers and marbles (now they are more likely to be found rollerblading in the Rink, an ancient covered area for dodgem cars). Steep-roofed, octagonal brick folly topped by a dragon windvane is a boys' loo; more recent additions include superb new library; up-grading continues gradually. Pre-prep department (Lynams – named after the family that ran the school for 78 years) a mile away on the run-down site of a former prep school (transfer at age eight). Lessons on Saturday mornings.
Atmosphere Unique: 120 years of unconventional teachers and clever, questioning pupils have produced a school that is unconforming yet sensible, academic yet not selective, where things are run for, and often by, the pupils. What you say and mean counts, outward appearances are ignored (shirt tales sometimes out, school bags hanging open – but children deep in conversation). Visitors accepted and included without question; it is assumed they, too, will have something interesting to say (some, though, may miss the conventional prep-school courtesies). Behind the apparent spontaneity and freedom there are systems and lists: 600 young children in perpetual motion and debate are carefully monitored by a staff who amble about with casual alertness, never interfering unnecessarily but always on the spot. Boarding conditions vary in comfort, spruceness and modernity, but all areas well-staffed and cheerful; girls (first admitted as boarders in 1994) seem to fit in easily.
Admissions Over-subscribed; birth the safest time to register. No entrance test but children are individually assessed at age seven to help with placement; wide range of abilities. Pupils (including, still, a sizeable minority of dons' children) drawn from all over Oxfordshire (often at great parental sacrifice of time and money); few foreign nationals.
The head Able, experienced, totally unflappable; has a good understanding of the young and their needs. Left to himself, he would have the school tidy, but has adapted well to the Dragon style. Read history at Oxford; formerly head of Clifton prep (qv). Married (wife teaches history here and knows everyone's name); two grown-up sons.
The teaching First-rate: hard-working, relatively youthful staff; extra help for pupils at both ends of the ability range. Exceptionally broad curriculum: classics and modern languages particularly strong; nearly all do Latin; Greek, Spanish, German, Japanese (taught by teachers from Tokyo), even Mandarin on offer; geography includes serious overseas expeditions. Personal and social education taken seriously (taught by a partnership of the chaplain and an ex-policeman). Lots of music, drama, public speaking; more than 100 extra-curricular activities available (silversmithing to mah jong).
Results Good: ex-Dragons welcome at all top schools; about 20 a year win scholarships.
Destinations Currently, about 80 independent schools; Eton takes 25 a year.

Sport   Almost everything is available, and Dragons play to win. Particular strengths in girls' hockey, boys' rugby (14 teams fielded) and cricket; sculling on the river is popular, as is athletics. Facilities include large all-weather pitch; outdoor pool soon to be covered (by a new design/technology block).

Remarks   Should suit almost any child of active and enquiring disposition whose parents have the foresight to register and money to pay. Dragons leave with high expectations, a range of practical and academic skills and a cheerful readiness to cope with life as it comes.

DULWICH COLLEGE ♂
42 Alleyn Park, London SE2l 7AA. Tel (0181) 670 3217

Synopsis
Boys (plus girls in nursery) ★ Day (and some weekly boarding) ★ Ages 3–13 ★ 750 pupils (14 girls, 27 weekly boarders) ★ Fees: £6,447 day; £9,452 boarding
Head: George Marsh, 54, appointed 1991.
First-rate school; fine teaching and results; strong music and sport.

Profile
Background   Founded 1885; now the largest prep school in Britain; shares governing body with DCPS Cranbrook (qv). Imposing red-brick buildings on 20-acre site; recent additions include new three-storey classroom block, computer suite, science labs (money no object).

Atmosphere   Emphasis on the boys 'feeling safe'; discipline through encouragement – no negative criticism (occasional 'head's detention' regarded as serious); pupils breeze round in a purposeful way. To mitigate the effects of size, school is divided into four separate units: nursery (three to five), annexe (five to seven), lower school (seven to nine), main school (nine to 13); houses named after Red Indian tribes (very *Boys' Own*). Strong parental involvement (lots of matches and concerts to watch). Weekly boarders in rather spartan accommodation (very smelly lavatories).

Admissions   Selective; minimum IQ 120; elaborate entry procedures include one-to-one interviews at ages three, five, seven and eight. Strong family tradition: many boys are the sons of former pupils, some are grandsons. School broadly Christian but other religions accepted. Vast catchment area; parents organise minibuses. Some bursaries available but no free places ('An education for nothing is undervalued,' says head).

The head   Quietly spoken, unassuming (hovers around after assembly in case any pupil 'wants a word'), but determined. Read geography at Oxford; taught in comprehensives for 10 years; previously head of of Edgarley Hall (now Millfield Prep, qv). Teaches classical studies; keen on cricket and rugby. Married; two grown-up children.

The teaching   Styles vary from formal to informal: some teachers stand, some sit on desks, some use pupils' surnames (most don't). Full-time staff of 57: all female in the first three years; two-thirds male in main school. Specialist teaching from age nine, when pupils are grouped by ability; potential scholars identified at age 10; some help for dyslexics, slow learners; average class size 20. All do French; German, Latin, Greek also on offer. Very good art (several scholarships won); outstanding music (nearly two-thirds learn an instrument) and drama.

Results   Good: about 25 a year win scholarships.

Destinations A third to Dulwich; most of the rest to Westminster, Eton, Winchester, Harrow, King's Canterbury, Tonbridge.
Sport Huge range: rugby, soccer, cricket (a particular strength), athletics, squash, tennis, swimming, golf, squash, basketball. Facilities include spacious playing fields, indoor heated pool.
Remarks Highly recommended.

DULWICH PREP, CRANBROOK ♂ ♀
Coursehorn, Cranbrook, Kent TN17 3NP. Tel (01580) 712179

Synopsis
Co-educational ★ Day and boarding ★ Ages 3–13 ★ 532 pupils (equal numbers of girls and boys, 89% day) ★ Fees: £6,150 day; £9,420 boarding
Head: Michael Wagstaffe, 52, appointed 1990.
Very successful school; wide range of abilities; good teaching and results; plenty of sport and other activities.

Profile
Background Founded 1885; evacuated here from London 1939. Collection of rather squat buildings on a 40-acre site in quiet countryside; huts gradually being replaced as part of a five-year development plan; recent additions include £1.5 million classroom block, sports hall, swimming pool. School divided into three self-contained sections, including attractive, spacious nursery (parents encouraged into classrooms).
Atmosphere Emphasis is on breadth – everything on offer to discover each child's strengths; self-esteem (and equality between the sexes) paramount. Good work shown to the head; three bad slips for behaviour result in a 'chat' with him. Saturday morning lessons for pupils in their last two years. Supportive parents run fêtes and social events.
Admissions First come, first served (but siblings have priority); names put down at birth. Wide range of abilities, including substantial number of children with special needs (three full-time teachers). Catchment area has 15–mile radius.
The head Personable, friendly: a father-figure. Read history at Exeter; taught at Clifton, Dulwich, Bryanston (housemaster); teaches history and personal and social education. Keen sportsman (captained Dorset at cricket). Married (wife oversees the domestic side); three children (two were pupils here).
The teaching Variety of styles, formal and informal; some staff very long-serving. Specialist teaching in French from age six, Latin from 10. Pupils grouped by ability in maths from age nine (scholarship stream), French from 10; average class size 20 (but seven-year-olds in groups of five for spelling, reading); plenty of extra help for those who need it. Lots of music (three lessons a week). Vast range of extra-curricular activities: 80 on offer; head likes everyone to do two.
Results Good: up to 20 scholarships a year (academic, sport, music).
Destinations Principally Cranbrook (qv); also King's Canterbury, Tonbridge, Sevenoaks, Benenden, Eastbourne, Ardingly, Sutton Valence, Bedgebury.
Sport Lots on offer: football, rugby, cricket for boys; netball, lacrosse, rounders for girls; tennis (good), cross-country (strong), athletics, hockey for both; basketball on the up.
Remarks Hugely popular locally – and deservedly so.

GODSTOWE ♀
Shrubbery Road, High Wycombe, Buckinghamshire HP13 6PR. Tel (01494) 529273

Synopsis
Girls ★ Boarding and day ★ Ages 8–13 (plus associated co-educational nursery and pre-prep) ★ 275 pupils (50% boarding) ★ Fees: £9,630 boarding; £5,475 day
Head: Mrs Frances Henson, 44, appointed 1991.
First-rate, traditional prep school; good teaching and results.

Profile
Background   Founded 1900 (the first boarding prep school for girls) to give girls an academic education as good as their brothers'. Pleasant 10-acre site on a wooded cliff near the town centre; most recent additions include new music school, boarding house.

Atmosphere   Busy, orderly, unpretentious; clear Christian ethos; less attractive aspects of the consumer society carefully excluded (no pocket-money or expensive possessions, little television – 'Street cred is not cool here,' says the head). Lively, unassuming, well-mannered girls. Uniform (including navy cloak in winter, straw hats in summer) worn by all.

Admissions   No academic selection: first come, first served; 50% of places reserved for boarders (over-subscribed). Small, friendly dormitories in four houses (one for weekly boarders), 30–35 girls in each. Traditionally, many parents from diplomatic, Services background; sprinkling of foreign nationals, happily integrated.

The head   Calm, determined; good leader; fosters a strong academic tradition. Married; two children; lives in the grounds.

The teaching   Good: predominantly female staff; hard-working pupils. Broad curriculum ('a balance between the academic, physical, technical and creative'); strong languages; most do Latin; good art, design/technology. Maximum class size 16; extra help for those who need it. Lots of music: four choirs, orchestra, chamber groups.

Results   Good: average of 10 scholarships a year to respectable schools; high success rate at Common Entrance.

Destinations   Chiefly: Wycombe Abbey, Cheltenham Ladies', Downe House, Queen Anne's Caversham; others to co-educational schools and (at age 11) county grammars.

Sport   Lacrosse, netball, badminton, gymnastics in winter; tennis, rounders, athletics in summer; swimming year-round in covered pool. Riding, squash, golf available locally for older girls.

Remarks   Model school; discriminating clientele. Recommended.

THE HALL ♂
23 Crossfield Road, Hampstead, London NW3 4NU. Tel (0171) 722 1700

Synopsis
Boys ★ Day ★ Ages 5–13 ★ 375 pupils ★ Fees: £6,105–£6,255
Head: Paul Ramage, 57, appointed 1993.
Successful, traditional school; good teaching and results; stimulating environment.

Profile
Background   Founded 1889; a pleasant but confusing amalgam of buildings jammed into an expensive residential area of North London (break-times staggered

for lack of space); new middle school opens on adjoining site September 1998.
Atmosphere   Lively, stimulating; a traditional, rather formal school – not un-friendly but certainly not cosy. Staff and parents have high expectations, which the pupils generally meet; many are the sons of old boys.
Admissions   By interview and observation of social interaction and play. About four apply for each place but the school does not select on academic grounds alone.
The head   Likeable, easy-going; gets on well with staff, pupils and parents; has restored calm to the school after previous upheavals. Read history at Cambridge; his third headship. Married; three grown-up sons.
The teaching   Mostly formal in style: boys in rows facing the front. Experienced staff; equal numbers of women and men. Standard prep school curriculum; spelling, handwriting taught formally and firmly; all do Latin from age nine; science imaginatively taught. Pupils grouped by ability in English, French, Latin, maths from 10; some extra help for dyslexics, slow learners and the gifted; younger boys at the top of the school may repeat a year; average class size 18. Strong art, drama, music (many play an instrument, some to a very high standard). Lots of outings and trips abroad.
Results   Good Common Entrance record; average of four scholarships a year.
Destinations   Most to London day schools, including St Paul's, Westminister, City of London, Highgate, University College School; others to Eton, Bryanston etc.
Sport   Soccer, hockey, cricket played at Hampstead Cricket Club, 10 minutes' walk away. Fencing particularly strong.
Remarks   Good school for well-motivated boys.

HALL, WIMBLEDON   ♂ ♀
Stroud Crescent, Putney Vale, London SW15 3EQ. Tel (0181) 780 9612

Synopsis
Co-educational ★ Day ★ Ages 3–13 ★ 274 pupils (60% boys) ★ Fees: £1,590–£5,358
Head: Tim Hobbs, 38, founded the school 1990.
Dynamic, unusual school; broad-based education; happy children; good results.

Profile
Background   Started with nine pupils in a Wimbledon church hall; moved 1992 (by then 100 strong) to former premises of a state primary school. Well-designed 1950s building (spacious, light, airy) plus two temporary but solid classrooms (resembling miniature Swiss chalets) on a small site backing on to Wimbledon Common (discreetly concealed crematorium on one side, allotments on the other); bright, cosy nursery in separate house. New, good-quality equipment everywhere. Facilities include adventure playground, butterfly house, 'Beatrix Potter' garden, grazing for pet sheep and Gloucester pigs.
Atmosphere   Tangibly happy; a very lively buzz. Children friendly, open, keen to talk, self-confident, well-mannered. Lunch (after Latin grace said in unison) is a deliberately leisurely affair: children encouraged to converse. Relaxed relations between staff and pupils but strong underlying discipline: courtesy a priority; children taught to respect one another. Firm policy on bullying (definition includes 'belittling, undermining, humiliating or in any way spoiling a child's self esteem'). Practical, cheerful uniform: navy cords, (culottes, skirts or trousers for girls), emerald green sweatshirts (no ties), thick anoraks. Close partnership

between school and parents, who are encouraged into the classrooms (definitely not a 'dump-at-the-school-gate' place). Children notably complimentary about the school and enthusiastic about the head (who personally bakes a birthday cake for every child and invites family to join in lunch).

Admissions Non-selective; wide range of abilities. Parents (majority are 'first-time buyers' of independent education) phone for prospectus, visit and have lunch with the children. Numbers increasing rapidly; eventual maximum will be 340. Most from Wimbledon, Putney, Kingston, Barnes; a few from 'north of the river'; international element (15%) proclaimed by spread of national flags on poles round the all-weather pitch in front of the school.

The head Innovative, creative, energetic, idealistic, unmarried; the school is his life (works seven days a week, teaches two-thirds of the timetable). Read history at St Andrews; abandoned accountancy training; came to teaching by a chance introduction to Hill House (qv); left after six years to start his own school in its image. Believes passionately in developing children's sense of self-worth and ensuring that they are all happy and feel valued. Insists on high standards but rejects unrealistic expectations and demoralising pressures. Leads regular expeditions, including walking the 105–mile South Downs Way with 10 and 11-year-olds (Pennine Way next).

The teaching Mix of stimulating whole-class teaching and imaginative 'hands-on' learning (field trips and expeditions an integral part of the programme); well-qualified, mainly female staff. School divided into five units: children progress from octagonal tables in the nursery to individual desks for seniors; average class size 20 (but as small as seven in Common Entrance year). Hard work expected; regular testing; big emphasis on presentation and accuracy; extra help for those with special needs; one hour's homework from age eight. French taught throughout; Latin from 10; history, geography particularly strong; good art (bright displays everywhere); fledgeling music (lots of cheerful singing) and drama. Much teaching about the natural world (nesting box equipped with video camera linked to classroom television); all share responsibility for the animals.

Results Good Common Entrance record.

Destinations Wide range (mostly day schools). Boys to St Paul's, City of London, King's Wimbledon; also co-educational boarding at Bedales, Bryanston, Marlborough. Girls to Wimbledon, Putney and Guildford High schools, Francis Holland; boarding at Wycombe Abbey.

Sport Important, lively, enthusiastic; four specialist teachers (three male). Range includes rugby, football, cricket (pitches on Wimbledon Common) netball, lacrosse, short tennis, gym, ballet (but not swimming). Main sports are basketball (because it is accessible to boys and girls of all abilities) and tennis (good links with Wimbledon). Half-hour circuit training every morning at 8.30 from age 7.

Remarks Unusual, delightful, fast-developing school. Happy solution for parents wanting good day provision that is not single-sex, highly academic or pressured – but not for conventional parents wanting a traditional school.

HALSTEAD ♀
Woodham Rise, Woking, Surrey GU21 4EE. Tel (01483) 772682

Synopsis
Girls ★ Day ★ Ages 3–11 ★ 216 pupils ★ Fees: £4,380
Head: Mrs Annabelle Hancock, 56, appointed 1987.
First-rate, well-run school; good teaching; impressive results.

Profile

Background Founded 1927 in Kent; moved to Devizes during World War Two; re-opened on present, pleasant four-acre site 1947. Comfortable Edwardian villa (feels more like a house than a school) in a leafy part of Woking. Later additions include handsome new art block and spacious, purpose-built pre-prep department (designed by the staff).

Atmosphere Gentle, nurturing; every girl encouraged to explore her strengths and capabilities; discipline no problem ('One expects them to behave decently and therefore they do'). Competitiveness in class discouraged ('It is wrong to make children compete for anything other than to do their best if they have no hope of winning') but inter-house cups and shields keenly contested ('Every real effort is rewarded whenever possible'). Traditional uniform (turned up brims on winter hats, turned down on summer straws). Care facilities available until 6 pm.

Admissions At age three on first-come basis (no selection); at seven by assessment during a day at the school ('At this stage we reserve the right to take only children we feel will thrive'); registration at birth advised. Parents from City/professional backgrounds.

The head Able, determined. Aims to produce 'an embryo young lady, with charm and poise and courtesy, but with foundations and aspirations to climb any mountain and master any challenge'. Does no teaching but knows the children well and is about the school constantly. Staff (including two men – 'children are increasingly "under-fathered" ') say she has created an atmosphere in which individual talents can flourish.

The teaching High quality. Basic skills developed from the start (in bright, cheerful nursery); junior classes work more formally in small groups. Much cross-curricular teaching and project work; high standards of accuracy and presentation expected; computing integrated into the curriculum. Science taught to a high standard in custom-built lab; senior schools praise the quality of the girls' maths; English is strong, too; all do Latin, French. Excellent art and design includes pottery, textiles, drawing, painting (some work would do credit to GCSE pupils). No streaming or setting by ability; progress constantly monitored; extra help for those with dyslexia or similar learning difficulties (no such thing as failure); average class size 22 in junior years, 16 from age eight. Good music: instrumental lessons; 45-piece orchestra, four choirs. Timetabled dance (tap and jazz) and drama.

Results Excellent. Regular scholarships; all transfer to chosen school.

Destinations Mainly local day schools: Sir William Perkins's, Guildford High, St Catherine's Bramley, Tormead etc; boarders to Roedean, Wycombe Abbey.

Sport Enthusiastic; frequent matches against other schools; main games rounders, netball.

Remarks Happy, creative school; produces articulate, balanced children.

HILL HOUSE ♂ ♀

Hans Place, London SW1X 0EP. Tel (0171) 584 1331

Synopsis

Co-educational ★ Day ★ Ages 3–14 ★ 1,050 pupils (60% boys) ★ Fees: £4,056–£5,148

Head: Lt Col Stuart Townend, OBE, 88, founded the school 1951.

Thriving, unconventional school; strong ethos; good academic record; first-rate music and sport.

Profile

Background Founded in Switzerland (and still operates there). School is strongly international (half the pupils are 'non-English') and distinctive in style (not least the uniform: old-gold tops and rust-coloured knee-breeches). Six buildings scattered around Knightsbridge and Chelsea plus 100-strong nursery in Pimlico church hall. Principal premises in Hans Place (red-brick 'Pont Street Dutch') suggests a long-established institution; masses of school photos, cups galore. Accommodation throughout is well maintained, bright (lots of children's work, views of Switzerland everywhere) and practical (equipment designed for the size of the child). However, no shiny new science labs, well-equipped pottery studios or classy sports halls here (there are, though, excellent modern kitchens). Chalet in Glion, Switzerland has dormitories for 30: children aged nine and over go for three weeks at a time (gives them a taste of boarding).

Atmosphere Lively, business-like, disciplined; children well mannered, taught respect for others but apparently relaxed, despite packed timetable and lots of to-ing and fro-ing (mini-buses shunt them between various buildings). Colonel's ethos permeates the place: no nonsense, do your best, behave yourself; lots of praise (' "That's a damn good show", I tell 'em – you have to be careful with criticism'). Weekly assembly for 700 older children at local church taken by Colonel in hood and gown (begins with the national anthem). Easy relations between children and teachers (many of whom are young, from US, Canada, Australia, New Zealand, South Africa). Parents encouraged to drop in at any time. Former pupils include Prince of Wales, Sultan of Brunei (not all parents are rich and famous).

Admissions No selection (though dyslexics advised to go elsewhere): only requirement is that parents visit the school (any morning 8.30–9.30) to see for themselves, and that the Colonel likes the mother (not a foregone conclusion); no formal application form (no prospectus either); children can join any time. Catchment area: mainly Chelsea, Kensington, Fulham; half the parents come from all over the world (diplomats, foreign bankers, employees of multinationals); pupil roll fluid but numbers are constant.

The head A phenomenon: energetic, eccentric, forthright, élitist ('Aim for the top and be the best'); commands universal affection and loyalty; believes children should be proud of their parents, proud of their country, proud of their school. School is his, body and soul; runs it with army-style delegation (divided into five self-contained units); his finger firmly on the pulse. Read maths and science at Oxford; French, Italian, German in Switzerland; outstanding sportsman (athletics international); distinguished Army career. His priorities for the children are safety (nurse in each building), happiness, good manners and (lastly) preparation for the next school ('This is not a prep school: I do what I like and if people don't like it they don't have to come'). Spends Thursday to Monday in Switzerland (has done the journey 3,500 times). Heir apparent: son, Richard; organist, singer; runs thriving music department; similarly energetic and unconventional.

The teaching Not a forcing house: school motto, 'A child is a fire to be kindled not a vessel to be filled'; academic pressure deliberately delayed until the senior school (the change of pace can be daunting for some); only older children preparing for Common Entrance are grouped by ability. Traditional, whole-class teaching ('chalk-and-talk'); tables in rows or horse shoe facing white board; average class size 12–15 (some classrooms very cramped). Generally well-qualified staff of 127 (70% female), all picked by the Colonel; turnover is low. National curriculum plus; French from age six (excellent – taught by native speakers); Latin on offer; all do carpentry. Regular testing, strong emphasis on presentation, accuracy, spelling. Good art, outstanding music (most learn an instrument - two orchestras, various ensembles, first-rate choir).

Results Very good, especially given the range of abilities; all proceed to the school of their (guided) choice; some win scholarships (particularly for music).

Destinations Most boys to London day schools: Westminster, St Paul's, Dulwich, City of London; minority to a variety of boarding schools, including Bradfield, Charterhouse, Eton, Marlborough, Stowe. Girls mainly to Godolphin, More House, Francis Holland; some to St Paul's; minority to boarding schools.

Sport A particular strength: two sessions a day, and an astonishing range (27 in all). Aim is to teach basic principles of all games and to find something to suit each child. School has no facilities of its own, uses the 'best available in London': cricket at the Oval, shooting at Duke of York's barracks, swimming and tennis at Queen's. Rugby, soccer, athletics, rowing also on offer. No matches against other schools, but competitive instincts developed through inter-house fixtures. Colonel particularly keen on mountaineering in Switzerland: 'To reach the summit of a mountain requires discipline, determination and physical fitness; it gives something to a boy's and girl's character that no other sport does.'

Remarks Good all round but may not appeal to strictly traditionalist parents looking for standard prep school fare; extroverts probably thrive best.

HOLMEWOOD HOUSE, TUNBRIDGE WELLS ♂ ♀
Langton Green, Tunbridge Wells, Kent TN3 0EB. Tel (01892) 862088

Synopsis
Co-educational ★ Day and boarding ★ Ages 3–13 ★ 475 pupils (62% boys, 87% day) ★ Fees: £8,755 day (£2,100 nursery); £11,535 boarding
Head: David Ives, 60, appointed 1980 (retiring August 1998).
First-rate school; very good teaching and results; lots on offer.

Profile
Background Founded 1946. Pleasant, wooded, 30-acre site (the remnant of a gracious estate) near Tunbridge Wells; buildings range from brand-new red-brick to crumbling lean-to. Most of the teaching takes place in huts that must once have been called temporary (children thread their way through alleys of them in cheerful chatter); latest additions include music school, 400-seat theatre. Girls admitted 1989; school is expanding to a maximum of 580 pupils. Nursery and pre-prep department in adjacent, mostly new premises.

Atmosphere Bursting with action and enthusiasm. Boys board in the original country house (only the elaborate ceilings tell of its former glory); girls' boarding house in very good order. Lessons on Saturday mornings.

Admissions From age seven by tests; pre-prep pupils transfer automatically. Most from business/professional/middle-class homes within a 15-mile radius. Fees are among the highest in the country; lots of scholarships, bursaries.

The head Long-serving but still full of energy and idealism with plenty of schemes for the future; his study walls are covered with building plans, press-cuttings, team photos, oars, cups; a couple of large teddy bears stand waiting to comfort any child who feels like a cuddle (but they look as good as new – very few here are unhappy). Read English at Oxford; first headship at 31; still teaches French. Loves his job (long experience has made him a great picker of staff), and is helped by a committed wife, who oversees the domestic side.

The teaching Excellent: dedicated, confident teachers from varied backgrounds (two are ex-heads) who treat the children as interesting people. In the pre-prep department there is security, but also pressure to learn and be disciplined; in the main school, teaching is fairly traditional but very sound. Broad curriculum: Greek, Latin, German, Spanish, Mandarin ('the language of the future') on offer; very good art. Scholarship stream accelerated at an early stage; extra help for those with special needs, including non-English speakers.

Results Outstanding: up to 23 major scholarships a year, including music, art, sport.

Destinations Tonbridge takes the lion's share; Sevenoaks and King's Canterbury also popular.

Sport Very competitive; huge enthusiasm all round. Particular strengths in cricket, rugby, girls' gymnastics; hockey moving up for both sexes. Squash, tennis, netball, judo, fencing, athletics, archery, dancing also on offer. Impressive sports hall; shooting is in an outhouse; swimming in an outdoor pool.

Remarks Large, well-run school; vast range of opportunities; almost anyone would be happy here.

HOLMWOOD HOUSE, COLCHESTER ♂ ♀
Chitts Hill, Lexden, Colchester, Essex CO3 5ST. Tel (01206) 574305

Synopsis
Co-educational ★ Day and boarding ★ Ages 8–13 (plus associated pre-prep)
★ 225 pupils (70% boys, 80% day) ★ Fees: £7,455 day; £9,645 boarding.
Head: Stuart Thackrah, 47, appointed 1988.
First-rate, well-run school; good teaching; strong music, drama.

Profile
Background Founded 1922 to make boys 'self-reliant and adaptable and to help them face reality'; girls admitted 1985, otherwise aims remain unchanged. Well cared-for Victorian mansion plus later additions (including modern, purpose-built classrooms) in 20 acres; areas set aside 'for children just to sit and chat'. Staff room is by the front door enabling parents delivering their children to drop in for a chat. Pre-prep department in the grounds.

Atmosphere 'Happiness is the key to progress,' says the head: school bears witness. Big emphasis on self-discipline; children have friendly but respectful relations with teachers; strong tutor system (mixed-age groups of 12). Long day: older children stay until 7 pm. Bright, cheerful dormitories; boarders allowed home at lunch-time on Saturdays until Monday morning. Good food; wide choice.

Admissions School over-subscribed: first come, first served (names put down at birth); entry to the pre-prep at age four guarantees a place through to 13. All abilities (and dyslexia) catered for. Pupils come from up to 20 miles away (a sprinkling from abroad); parents mainly Colchester professionals, London commuters. Some scholarships, bursaries.

The head Kindly, sensitive; very much in tune with the needs of both pupils and parents (whom he expects to be fully involved in school life). First came here 1981; left to become deputy head of another prep school, then returned. Teaches maths, current affairs. Married (wife, Glenys, teaches reading, oversees the boarding); two children (both pupils here).

The teaching Formal, but plenty of opportunities for (relevant) fun. Staff of 39 (50% men), 75% appointed by present head. Children grouped by ability in most subjects; average class size 12; regular grades for effort and achievement; lots of extra help for those who need it (10 teachers dyslexia-trained). National curriculum followed but enriched: French from age four (French TV programmes by satellite, 80 seven-year-olds from Lyon come for a week every Easter); computing from age eight. Strong drama and music; two-thirds learn an instrument (19 ensembles, two choirs); splendid new premises for art.

Results Nearly all take Common Entrance and proceed to the school of their (guided) choice. Good scholarship record.

Destinations Wide range, including Felsted, Gresham's, Haileybury, Uppingham, Rugby.

Sport All main games played; particularly good squash, athletics.

Remarks Thriving school combining the best of the old and the new. Highly recommended.

HORRIS HILL ♂

Newtown, Newbury, Berkshire RG20 9DJ. Tel (01635) 40594

Synopsis
Boys ★ Boarding and day ★ Ages 8–13 (plus associated pre-prep) ★ 120 pupils (90% boarding) ★ Fees: £10,200 boarding; £6,900 day
Head: Nigel Chapman, 52, appointed 1996.
Strong, traditional school; good academic record; lots of sport.

Profile
Background Founded 1888 to prepare boys for Winchester. Large, red-brick Victorian house plus later additions in attractive 80-acre rural setting; purpose-built chapel accommodates the whole school. Numbers beginning to rise after a steady decline (affecting all such schools); day boys a recent innovation. On-site, co-educational nursery and pre-prep (ages three to seven) in converted stables.

Atmosphere Strongly traditional (previous head had been at the school for 37 years); hard-working, friendly, well-mannered (order without regimentation). Dormitories slowly being up-graded; bathrooms still to be modernised. Lots of space for hobbies (including model railway layout). Grey uniform but boys wear ties of their own (colourful) choice.

Admissions At age eight (occasionally seven) by informal interview and assessment; no academic selection. Most from professional, Home Counties background; one or two from abroad. Scholarships available.

The head Able, experienced (his second headship). Steeped in the prep school tradition (was senior housemaster at Summer Fields, qv) but introducing some overdue changes, including appointing younger staff ('We must learn to live with and adopt a more modern approach') and putting a greater emphasis on music and the arts. Married; three children.

The teaching Good quality. Formal in style but changing: school was very exam oriented; form orders posted every two weeks; top two years had little time for music or art. Prizes now for effort, progress, overall contribution, not just for coming top. Traditional curriculum: French from age eight, Latin from nine, Greek for scholars, German available; first-rate science, computing. Boys move up when they are ready; average class size 15; some help for dyslexics – but not a school for those with severe difficulties. Music being upgraded (and better housed), drama encouraged.

Results Very good scholarship record; most get into their first-choice school.

Destinations   Majority to Winchester or Eton (but passage no longer guaranteed); remainder to good boarding schools, including Radley, Sherborne.
Sport   First-rate facilities (including nine-hole golf course). Main games: soccer, cricket, hockey, athletics; squash, fives, tennis, swimming, badminton, basketball also on offer; weekly matches against neighbouring schools.
Remarks   Old-fashioned, well-regarded school now adapting to changing times.

KING'S COLLEGE JUNIOR SCHOOL ♂
Wimbledon Common, London SW19 4TT. Tel (0181) 255 5335

Synopsis
Boys ★ Day ★ Ages 7–13 ★ 460 pupils ★ Fees: £6,666–£7,050
Head: Colin Holloway, 60, appointed 1976 (retiring August 1998).
Well-run, successful school working closely with its senior partner, to where nearly all the boys proceed.

Profile
Background   Originally part of King's College School (qv); became separate in 1912 but still shares site and some buildings. First two years in pleasant, pink-brick, 19th-century house (own dining room and playground); older boys in re-built, modernised Gothic premises; facilities are first-rate.
Atmosphere   Carpet everywhere, space and light. No new-fangled ideas, and a feeling that the place is running on the right lines: an air of calm enjoyment prevails. Pupils – city boys in their quick self-confidence – seem more conventional and less showy than some, more likely to become solid citizens. Parents kept fully in the picture: the literature the school sends out is detailed and well-written.
Admissions   School heavily over-subscribed (more than three apply for each place); entry at any age between seven and 11 by interviews and tests – school is looking for 'academic appetite', someone who will use opportunities, 'pick the ball up and run with it'. Pupils drawn largely from professional families in a wide area of south-west London. Means-tested bursaries available.
The head   Approachable, affable, hides a firm grip under a calm, relaxed manner; spends vast amounts of time interviewing possible entrants and their parents to make sure he gets the best. His length of service and grasp of facts and figures makes him able to keep his end up against the big battalions in the senior school. 'We sing the same song', he says modestly, but actually composes his share of the tune. Cambridge classicist; married with a grown-up family. From September 1998: John Evans, 50, senior master at the senior school.
The teaching   Hard-working staff of 25 trying to cram a quart of subjects into a pint pot. Boys in the top years go up to the senior school for science (taught as three separate subjects); those who want German, Greek or Spanish miss part of morning assembly to fit them in. Technology, art and music have to take their turn in a balanced timetable, but extra is available at lunch-time. Touch-typing is taught and so is handwriting, with yearly tests of penmanship through the school. Boys grouped by ability from the start, but there is no undue competitiveness. Well-stocked library used to the full. Out-of-school activities and holiday trips are legion: staff work as hard outside the form room as in.
Results   Common Entrance holds no terrors for these hand-picked, well-taught boys; they win about half the available scholarships to the senior school.
Destinations   Almost all to the senior school.

Sport   All the senior school's facilities available; extra playing fields a short bus ride away.
Remarks   A first-rate start for able boys.

KING'S COLLEGE SCHOOL ♂ ♀
West Road, Cambridge CB3 9DN. Tel (01223) 365814

Synopsis
Co-educational ★ Day and (boys') boarding ★ Ages 7–13 (plus associated pre-prep) ★ 220 pupils (66% boys; 85% day) ★ Fees: £5,886 day; £9,120 boarding (£2,937 choristers)
Head: Andrew Corbett, 45, appointed 1993 (leaving August 1998).
Successful, happy school; very good teaching and results; exceptionally strong music (provides the choristers for King's College chapel).

Profile
Background   Founded 1453 by Henry VI as a choir school for 'poor and needy boys knowing competently how to read and sing'; non-choristers joined in the 17th century; moved to present five-acre site (next to the university library) 1878; girls admitted 1976. Large Victorian red-brick house plus later additions (all well loved and well used); King's College spending £1.2 million over the next five years on new classrooms and music school.
Atmosphere   Cheerful, busy (music floats out of the windows at every turn); friendly relations between staff and pupils. Distinctive purple blazers or sweatshirts.
Admissions   By interview and tests in maths, spelling, reading, verbal reasoning; audition day for would-be choristers (23 boys, all boarders). Most pupils of above-average IQ; about 30% are children of dons. Cheerful dormitories. Music scholarships and bursaries available.
The head   Read history of art at Edinburgh; previously head of history at The Hall, Hampstead (qv). Married (wife much involved in school life); two daughters (both pupils here).
The teaching   Fairly traditional in style; emphasis on pupil involvement. Enthusiastic, well-qualified staff; very low turnover. Standard Common Entrance curriculum; all start French in pre-prep at four; Latin from nine; German, Greek available; lots of computers. Older pupils divided into two scholarship forms and two Common Entrance forms; extra help for dyslexics; average class size 18. Credits for good work, behaviour; misdemeanour forms for those who stray. Music is at the heart of the school (though non-musicians are welcomed and happy): 80% learn at least one instrument (28 visiting staff); two large orchestras, three choirs; regular concert tours abroad. Lively art (regular scholarships). Busy programme of extra-curricular activities.
Results   Very good: numerous academic, music, art awards; virtually all go on to first-choice school.
Destinations   Wide range, including Eton, Oundle, Uppingham, Westminster, Downe House, Wycombe Abbey, King's Canterbury etc.
Sport   Chiefly: rugby, football, hockey, netball, squash, cricket, rounders, tennis, athletics, swimming, cross-country. Dance, fencing, gymnastics, canoeing also available. Facilities include three on-site pitches and two near by, tennis courts, outdoor pool.
Remarks   Attractive, vibrant school; recommended.

LAMBROOK & HAILEYBURY ♂ ♀
Winkfield Row, Bracknell, Berkshire RG42 6LU. Tel (01344) 882717

Synopsis
Co-educational ★ Day and boarding ★ Ages 8–13 (plus associated pre-prep)
★ 200 pupils (90% boys, 75% day) ★ Fees: £3,525–£6,660 day; £6,900–£9,300
boarding.
Head: John Hare, 57, appointed (to Haileybury Junior School) 1988.
Attractive, traditional school; good teaching; lots on offer.

Profile
Background   Result of a September 1997 merger between Lambrook, a small,
traditional boys' boarding school (with a co-educational pre-prep department),
and Haileybury, a boys' day school (with a declining number of boarders) in
Windsor. The Lambrook site is a beautiful 60-acre estate three miles from Ascot:
handsome 19th-century houses; first-rate games facilities and plenty of wilder play
areas. (Significant investment expected to follow the sale of the Windsor site.)
Atmosphere   Boarding-school ethos preserved: activities abound until bed-
time seven days a week (over-night stays encouraged). Big emphasis on kindness, consideration, building up self-confidence. Boarding accommodation
homely, intimate; seniors in their own house; no provision, as yet, for girls (who
first moved up to the prep school in September 1997).
Admissions   By interview and assessment; school is not aggressively academic. Parents a mixture of traditional prep school customers and 'first-time buyers'
('We have no flashy families').
The head   Able, experienced; a traditionalist but forward-looking (was a prime
mover in the merger). Read English at Oxford (soccer Blue). Married; two daughters.
The teaching   Good (by combined staff): traditional subjects taught with vigour
and thoroughness. Nearly all do Latin; Greek on offer; first-rate French; impressive
design/technology; good science. Pupils grouped by ability (scholarship form);
remedial help available; classes have been small (12–15) in both schools and the
intention is to keep them so. Lots of art, drama, music (chapel choir).
Results   Both schools had a good Common Entrance record and a steady trick-
le of respectable scholarships.
Destinations   Principally: Bradfield, Charterhouse, Cheltenham, Eton, Hampton,
Harrow, Marlborough, Oundle, Radley, Sherborne, Stoke, Wellington, Winchester.
Sport   Wide range; facilities include fine sports hall. Main games: soccer, hockey,
rugby, cricket. Also available: golf (on the school's own nine-hole course), indoor
swimming, fives, tennis, squash, croquet, athletics; dance and riding to be added.
Remarks   Good, safe school; off to a fresh start.

LLANDAFF CATHEDRAL SCHOOL ♂ ♀
Llandaff, Cardiff CF5 2YH. Tel (0122) 563179

Synopsis
Co-educational ★ Day and some boarding ★ Ages 3–13 ★ 300 pupils (80%
boys, 95% day) ★ Fees: £3,195–£4,830 day; £7,725–£7,875 boarding (reduced
fees for choristers)
Head: Lindsay Gray, 44, appointed 1994.
Traditional prep school; good teaching and results; strong music.

Profile

Background Re-founded 1880 (roots go back to the ninth century); housed in the former Bishop's Palace in attractive grounds close to the cathedral (monkey-puzzle trees in the garden). Roald Dahl was a pupil here in the 1920s.

Atmosphere Strong Anglican ethos (day starts in chapel); firm discipline. Choristers rehearse for two hours every morning.

Admissions By interview; school is not academically selective but boy choristers are required to 'satisfy the cathedral organist as to their musical ability'; girl choristers attend voice trials. Boy choristers pay one-third fees; £1,000-a-year awards available for girls choristers. Mock-Tudor boarding house: bunk beds, teddy bears; very good food.

The head Was a choral scholar at King's, Cambridge; became director of music at Cheltenham; previously head of a prep school in Gloucestershire. Conducts the girls' choir, which he started soon after arriving. Married; two daughters.

The teaching Bright, busy pre-prep department; extra help for dyslexics. Traditional teaching by specialists throughout the main school; national curriculum plus; Latin on offer; lots of computing; maximum class size 20. Homework carefully monitored. Music very strong: four choirs, two orchestras; frequent public performances.

Results Good Common Entrance record; more than 100 scholarships, awards and exhibitions over the past three years.

Destinations Chiefly: Malvern, Monmouth, King's Taunton, Clifton, Rugby, Harrow, Oundle, Stowe.

Sport Main games: rugby, cricket, tennis, hockey, netball. Football, cross-country, swimming also on offer. Facilities include 12-acre playing field, outdoor pool, fine sports hall.

Remarks Good all round.

LUDGROVE ♂

Wokingham, Berkshire RG40 3AB. Tel (0118) 978 9881

Synopsis

Boys ★ Boarding ★ Ages 8–13 ★ 195 pupils ★ Fees £9,600
Joint heads: Gerald Barber, 54; Nichol Marston, 56; appointed 1973.
Fine, traditional school; spacious, rural setting; civilised atmosphere; good teaching and results; strong sporting record.

Profile

Background Founded 1892 in Cockfosters; moved to present Victorian mock-Tudor premises (originally built as a school) 1937. Beautifully-tended grounds, huge stately trees, views over fields and woods; 130 acres in all (limitless space for small boys to make camps and dens). Prince William was a pupil here; Prince Harry still is. School has strong links with Eton.

Atmosphere Settled, family air and a certain timeless quality: Old Boys, returning as adults, might feel little had changed. School aims to create a happy environment, while insisting on good manners (all women addressed as Ma'am), consideration for others, respect for the environment (decent behaviour worked on constantly). Very high standard of pastoral care; boys relaxed, happy; parents encouraged to visit often.

Admissions Non-selective but severe learning difficulties cannot be catered for. Application at birth essential; lists full until 2005. Pupils overwhelmingly from upper-class homes. Boarding accommodation comfortable, if functional (though recently refurbished).

The heads Exceptionally long-serving. Both educated at Eton and Oxford and both born to the profession: Barber is the third generation of his family to run Ludgrove; Marston's father was head of Summer Fields (qv). Both love teaching and have heavy timetables: Barber takes Latin and scripture for 22 hours a week, Marston maths for a daunting 37 hours. Barber is married with teenage children (his wife oversees all domestic arrangements, and much else besides – her father was also a prep school head); Marston a bachelor. Barber puts great emphasis on traditional academic standards: 'Important to get the framework firmly established'.

The teaching Traditional: well-qualified, long-serving staff; desks (often ancient and ink-stained) in rows. Emphasis on grammar, spelling, 'discipline in thought' (Latin grammar from second year); particular strengths in maths, classics. Pupils grouped by ability from third year; potential scholars moved on to fast track; extra help for those with mild dyslexia; average class ('division') of 15. Fortnightly 'orders': boys given their place in division and grades for effort; reports to parents every three weeks. Excellent facilities for art, pottery, carpentry. Flourishing music: two-thirds learn an instrument; orchestra, good choir. Annual Shakespeare and pantomime in superb sports-hall-cum-theatre.

Results Most proceed to school of first choice; about two scholarships a year.

Destinations About 55% to Eton; Harrow, Radley also popular.

Sport First-class record, particularly in cricket; also soccer, rugby, hockey. Facilities include extensive playing fields, superb sports hall, tennis, fives and squash courts, nine-hole golf course, snooker tables. Indoor swimming pool is a period piece.

Remarks Very traditional school; turns out courteous, confident boys well prepared for public school life.

MAIDWELL HALL ♂
Maidwell, Northampton NN6 9JG. Tel (01604) 686234

Synopsis
Boys (plus some girls) ★ Boarding (boys only) and day ★ Ages 3–13 ★ 126 pupils (87% boys, 55% boarding) ★ Fees: £10,080 boarding; £6,720 day
Head: Peter Whitton, 44, appointed 1995.
Very traditional prep school; good teaching; everything on offer.

Profile
Background Founded 1933. Setting almost a cliché: a glimpse of turreted splendour among the trees, long drive flanked by rhododendrons, lawns running down to a lake (fly fishing, boating), sweep of gravel to the front door ('trunks will be unloaded by groundstaff – a quick goodbye normally works best'); 250 acres of grounds, 200 let out to neighbouring farmers. Late 16th-century mansion with Victorian interiors and additions; endless corridors of polished wood; classrooms in ancient drawing rooms with moulded ceilings. School now in (belated) transition: all-boarding, single-sex character abandoned in the face of the recession; pre-prep department opened 1993; day girls admitted 1994.

Atmosphere School's aim to give boys (and girls) 'a full education with a wide range of accomplishments' is achieved with dignity and style; emphasis on academic excellence and traditional values ('retaining and reinforcing the civilised manners the children are familiar with at home'); good pastoral care ('It can be helpful to let us know of any changes at home, such as a grandparent or pet dying, so that we are able to offer support to a boy at that time'). No uniform 'as such': boys wear tweed jackets, corduroy trousers; girls 'country coloured' kilts and sweaters. Lessons on Saturday mornings.

Admissions   By interview; most pupils from upper middle-class backgrounds. Pleasant boarding accommodation (lots of teddies and soft toys).

The head   Brisk, confident, decisive. Read English and American literature at Manchester; first came here in 1979; previously deputy head of Sandroyd (qv). Married (wife is assistant head); four children.

The teaching   A modernised traditional education: Latin (from age nine) at one end of the spectrum, computer studies at the other; bright boys may skip a form; remedial teachers come in twice a week (dyslexia catered for); weekly grades for effort and attainment; no class larger than 15. Lots of drama, music: orchestra, choir, more than half learn an instrument. Seniors spend four weeks at a château in Normandy.

Results   Good Common Entrance record; fair share of scholarships.

Destinations   Traditionally: a third to Eton; a third to Harrow; rest to Stowe, Rugby, Oundle, Milton Abbey, Sedbergh etc.

Sport   Organised games five days a week: just about everything on offer; regular matches against other prep schools. Facilities include three large playing fields, two tennis courts, squash court, heated pool. Evening options include snooker, chess, bridge, table tennis.

Remarks   Old-fashioned, socially-exclusive school keeping up its numbers.

MALSIS ♂
Cross Hills, North Yorkshire BD20 8DT. Tel (01535) 633027

Synopsis
Boys ★ Boarding and some day ★ Ages 7–13 (plus associated co-educational pre-prep) ★ 100 pupils (90% boarding) ★ Fees: £9,000 boarding; £6,600 day
Head: Norman Rowbotham, 45, appointed 1994 (leaving August 1998).
Attractive school; wide ability range; good teaching; first-rate facilities.

Profile
Background   Founded 1920 as a prep school for Giggleswick (qv). Grand 19th-century manor house (ceilings lovingly restored) set in 40 acres; later additions include splendid chapel; well-equipped technology department and art centre in converted stables.

Atmosphere   This really is a family: parents play an active part in the life of the school; staff include seven married couples (who all live near by); head and his wife always on hand. Tangible pride in everything achieved.

Admissions   By interview; intake genuinely comprehensive ('The school is particularly proud of the extra attention it gives to those who are academically weak'). Most live within a 100-mile radius, including the conurbations of South Yorkshire and Lancashire and the rural counties of the North. Warm, friendly dormitories (six to 12 beds), all refurbished; food ample and nourishing.

The head   Teaches French to the seniors and runs outdoor pursuits (keen on sailing, walking, camping and caving). Married; wife assists in the general care of the boys.

The teaching Formal without being dull; pupils acquire sound grounding in grammar and real love of reading. Youngest spend 40% of their time with one teacher to encourage feeling of security; specialised teaching thereafter. Standard prep school curriculum; technology achieves a nice balance between traditional skills and computer-aided design. Pupils grouped by ability; extra help for dyslexics; small classes. Very strong music: more than two-thirds learn an instrument; excellent concert band. Lots of extra-curricular activities.

Results Good Common Entrance record; seven or eight scholarships a year.

Destinations A total of 90 schools but chiefly Shrewsbury, Oundle, Sedbergh, Uppingham, Harrow, Giggleswick.

Sport Strong; particularly rugby, cricket, swimming, athletics. Golf (nine-hole course), fishing, canoeing, sailing also on offer. Facilities include ample playing fields, well-equipped sports hall, indoor pool, athletics track.

Remarks Good all round.

THE MANOR ♀
Faringdon Road, Abingdon, Oxford OX13 6LN. Tel (01235) 523789

Synopsis
Girls (plus boys aged 3–7) ★ Day ★ Ages 3–11 ★ 370 pupils (75% girls) ★ Fees: £2,010–£4,380
Head: Mrs Dot Robinson, 46, appointed April 1997.
Lively, cheerful school; very good teaching; strong family atmosphere.

Profile
Background Founded 1947; pleasant site six miles from Oxford. Accommodation includes three new classroom blocks, large multi-purpose hall, converted 14th-century barn for dancing (and playing in when it rains).

Atmosphere Warm, welcoming; strong sense of family (nearly three-quarters of the staff have, or have had, children here). Delightful classrooms, all with huge windows set low enough for even the smallest child (and tallest adult) to enjoy the splendid views. Walls covered in children's work and their photographs (marked with coloured spots showing how many books they have read during the term). Absolutely no peeling paint or any other sign of neglect. Hard to believe any child could be anything but happy here.

Admissions Not selective: school is prepared to cope with a wide range of abilities. Some registered at birth but two years prior to entry is best. Mostly from professional/middle-class homes.

The head Recent appointment. Read geography at Exeter; MBA from Nottingham; previously head for nine years of a prep school in Hertfordshire.

The teaching Challenging, stimulating ('They must understand, not learn like parrots'); lots of individual attention. All-woman staff: their cheerfulness and high morale pervade the school. Teaching styles change as pupils move up the school: in the nursery, project work, group activities, disciplined play; thereafter, increasingly front-of-class and subject-based; responsive children quick to volunteer answers and opinions. Specialist science teaching from age seven; French from seven plus two years of Spanish (emphasis on conversation); all girls take English Speaking Board exams. Detailed (nine-page) marking policy deems negative comments unacceptable: mistakes marked with a small dot to be turned into a tick as soon the correction has been made. Class sizes average 23 (each with teacher plus assistant);

smaller groups for older children; scholarship and remedial needs catered for.
Results All go on to their first-choice schools – though care is taken to ensure the choice is 'wise'.
Destinations Principally: Oxford High, Headington, St Helen & St Katharine, Downe House.
Sport All the normal games plus gym, football, ballet, country dancing, lacrosse. Swimming at Radley once a week.
Remarks Delightful, happy, well-run school.

MILBOURNE LODGE ♂
43 Arbrook Lane, Esher, Surrey KT10 9EG. Tel (01372) 462737

Synopsis
Boys (and some girls) ★ Day ★ Ages 7–13 ★ 200 pupils (20 girls) ★ Fees: £4,350
Head: Norman Hale, 77, appointed 1949.
Outstanding academic school; first-class teaching and results; keen sport.

Profile
Background Founded 1912; moved to present site 1948; attractive Victorian villa in seven acres plus access to limitless woodland. Some classrooms in cramped, converted bedrooms, others in wooden huts. ('Our overheads are low,' explains the head. 'We've no sports hall, no gym, no theatre, no school bus, no indoor pool, no governors, no bursar and we never advertise. We've got some decent chalk and a few blackboards.')
Atmosphere Vibrant, happy, highly academic. Hard work taken for granted; discipline not an issue. Eager, lively-eyed, well-mannered children (all leap to their feet when an adult enters the room). School exudes a family feel – with a strong competitive edge; three sides of the entrance hall are covered in gold-lettered honours boards listing the names of every pupil who has won a scholarship since 1950 (some 350 in all).
Admissions At age seven by 'a little test' in spelling, comprehension, basic arithmetic and reading aloud ('very important – at seven, they ought to have a reading age of nine if they've not been watching rubbish on television all the time'). Places offered to 30–35 (divided into two streams, one of which will be prepared for scholarships – 'I pride myself on picking winners; you get a feel for it'). No dyslexics ('because you can't teach them French and Latin'). Most from commuter-belt professional homes in Esher, Woking, Weybridge, Walton etc. Financial help available for above-average children (head regards this as more important than spending on 'facilities').
The head Longest-serving headmaster in Britain, and possibly the most successful. Larger-than-life; bursting with energy and enthusiasm ('One soldiers on'); believes passionately in the pursuit of excellence. Educated at Shrewsbury, where he gained his love of classics, and Oxford, where he read modern history. Teaches 17 periods a week: Latin to the youngest, Latin and Greek to the top set. No plans to retire in the foreseeable future: school is his life (and very much his and his wife's creation).
The teaching Lively, sometimes idiosyncratic, all of a high standard; desks in rows facing the teacher ('We rely on old-fashioned methods'). Big emphasis on traditional curriculum (no cross-curricular projects here) and solid grounding (work marked rigorously for grammar and spelling – corrections obligatory). Latin from the outset

(declensions learnt in less than two terms); more able half add Greek from 10; history taught without textbooks by inspired raconteur; imaginative science; lively maths; no design/technology until exams are safely out of the way. Nightly homework; progress closely monitored; grades sent to parents every three weeks. Average class size 20. Lots of music; all encouraged to learn an instrument; orchestra, choirs, string band. Thriving chess club; numerous trips to London theatres etc.

Results Outstanding: average of eight to 10 scholarships a year to top schools, including Winchester and Eton; no pupil has failed Common Entrance for 25 years.

Destinations Top six since 1981: Eton, Harrow, Charterhouse, Epsom, Winchester, Wellington; girls (a relatively recent innovation) to Benenden, Roedean, Wycombe Abbey, Marlborough.

Sport Chiefly football, rugby, cricket, tennis (one hard court in constant use), netball; athletics taken seriously (like everything else). Head believes keenly in sport and exercise: all play something for at least one hour a day. Good playing fields; heated outdoor pool.

Remarks Marvellous school, in the same premier league as Summer Fields, The Dragon, Pilgrims' and Horris Hill; warmly recommended.

MILLFIELD ♂ ♀
Glastonbury, Somerset BA6 8LD. Tel (01458) 832446

Synopsis
Co-educational ★ Day and boarding ★ Ages 8–13 (plus associated pre-prep)
★ 474 pupils (62% boys, 54% boarding) ★ Fees: £10,860 boarding; £7,335 day
Head: Simon Cummins, 35, appointed 1996.
First-rate, well-run school; very good teaching; lots of drama, music; exceptionally strong sport.

Profile
Background Founded 1946 (formerly known as Edgarley Hall); undistinguished, pre-fabricated concrete buildings on an attractive 90-acre rural estate on the slopes of Glastonbury Tor; some classrooms in 'temporary' huts; facilities for science, design/technology, music are first-rate. Same governors, principles, ethos as Millfield senior school (qv), three miles away.

Atmosphere Busy, happy, stimulating; very good pastoral care; 'a school where every child matters'.

Admissions By interview and previous school report; school is not academically selective; range of abilities is wide. Comfortable, spacious boarding accommodation in nine scattered houses; 20% of boarders come from 30 countries. Bursaries for those who are 'academically gifted or who are good academically and will offer a significant cultural or sporting contribution to the life of the school'.

The head Charming, energetic, extrovert; dynamic leader. Has qualifications in PE, history, educational management; first headship (of a small prep school in Kent) at 27. Married (to a teacher); three young children.

The teaching Good quality; enthusiastic, committed staff. Broad curriculum: sciences (a particular strength) taught separately; all do language 'taster' courses in French, German, Spanish, Latin (more able take two from age 10); all do course in 'thinking skills'; lots of computing. Pupils grouped by ability in most subjects to 'cater for all, both the academically gifted and those requiring remedial

tuition'; specialist help for dyslexics; maximum class size 16 ('to allow the individual pupil to be taught at his or her most appropriate pace'). Lots of drama and music; more than half learn an instrument (400 individual lessons a week); two choirs, two orchestras, various ensembles. Vast range of extra-curricular activities, including chess, ballet, riding, computing, modelling, animal care, canoeing.
Results   Good scholarship record.
Destinations   About 85% to Millfield; most of the rest to good, single-sex schools.
Sport   Exceptionally strong; regular county and national honours in athletics, tennis, skiing, badminton, hockey, rounders, gymnastics, fencing, swimming. Rugby, hockey, cricket, soccer, squash, netball also on offer. Facilities include 50 acres of playing fields, sports hall, indoor pool, nine-hole golf course.
Remarks   Fine school for children of a wide range of abilities and talents. Highly recommended.

MOOR PARK ♂ ♀
Ludlow, Shropshire SY8 4EA. Tel (01584) 876061

Synopsis
Roman Catholic (but most pupils are non-Catholics) ★ Co-educational ★ Boarding and day ★ Ages 7–13 (plus associated pre-prep) ★ 180 pupils (55% boys, 55% boarding) ★ Fees: £8,700 boarding; £6,285 day
Head: John Badham, 49, appointed 1988.
Attractive, happy school; first-rate teaching; strong sport.

Profile
Background   Founded 1964 as a Catholic boys' boarding school with a national catchment area; has become – in response to market forces – increasingly non-Catholic, co-educational and local. Magnificent 83-acre estate with woods, bogs, meadows, lakes and hidden dells – a wondrous fantasy land for any child's imaginings. Main building was originally Queen Anne but has been much messed about; modern classroom block; prefabs scheduled for demolition.
Atmosphere   Liberal, Christian ethos; carefree, unabashed children who respect authority and each other. All – whatever their faith – are treated as Catholics: no one opts out of Mass. Well-organised pastoral care system.
Admissions   Non-selective. Fairly wide social mix (not a snob school), mostly from within a radius of 30 miles; a third of parents are 'first-time buyers' of independent education; 25% of pupils are Catholics. Pleasant boarding accommodation: girls in beautifully decorated eight-bed dormitories (murals, fresh flowers); boys' boarding area recently refurbished; parents have free access. Day pupils stay until 6.30 pm.
The head   Charming, kindly, humorous. Catholic convert; keen to preserve the Catholicism that gives the school its identity; formerly head of a Catholic prep school in London. Married (wife responsible for domestic side).
The teaching   Good: youthful, enthusiastic staff of 25 (equal numbers of women and men); national curriculum followed. Relaxed atmosphere in pre-prep department: learning through fun. Pupils grouped by ability in maths, English, French from the start; specialist help for slow learners, including dyslexics. First-rate art and music; more than half learn an instrument; choir, orchestra. Vast range of extra-curricular activities and hobbies (rug making, Irish country

dancing, advanced computing, fencing, bridge etc). Lots of charitable work.
Results   Regular scholarships to Downside, Shrewsbury, Rugby, Eton, Moreton Hall, Ampleforth.
Destinations   As well as the above: Malvern, Monmouth, Cheltenham Ladies', Tudor Hall, Gordonstoun.
Sport   Taken seriously. Good record in netball, soccer, cricket, rugby, hockey, squash, tennis. Assault course and nine-hole golf course in the grounds; fishing and canoeing on the lakes; camping in the woods; large outdoor pool.
Remarks   Latin motto translates as 'To God who gives joy to my youth': a school that offers joy to any child.

MOUNT HOUSE ♂ ♀
Tavistock, Devon PL19 9JL. Tel (01822) 612244

Synopsis
Co-educational ★ Boarding and day ★ Ages 7–13 (plus associated pre-prep) ★ 165 pupils (85% boys, 51% boarders) ★ Fees: £8,835 boarding; £6,405 day Head: Charles Price, 55, appointed 1984.
Fine, well-run, traditional school; very good teaching; happy atmosphere; lots on offer.

Profile
Background   Founded 1881; moved 1941 to present, gracious, Georgian manor house in idyllic 50-acre estate on the southern slopes of Dartmoor by the banks of the Tavy (perfect setting for a happy, outdoor childhood); girls admitted 1996 ('a departure from a long-standing tradition' – to stave off falling numbers). Classrooms in attractively converted stables and out-buildings; later additions include design/technology centre, art school, sports hall. New (1996) purpose-built pre-prep in the grounds.
Atmosphere   Friendly, welcoming; very good relations between staff and well-mannered pupils; first-rate pastoral care. Smart, practical uniform. Day children stay until 7 pm or later; lessons on Saturday mornings, followed by sport. Religion taken seriously: daily prayers; strong parental attendance at traditional Sunday services.
Admissions   By simple tests in the Three Rs; applicants rarely turned away. Most children from professional and Service backgrounds; few from abroad (Hong Kong, Nigeria). Comfortable, cheerful boarding accommodation; dormitories of six to 12 beds. Boarding numbers have declined sharply (to the head's dismay). Food nourishing and plentiful (rice pudding always on offer).
The head   Able, affable, enthusiastic; very much in command. Married (wife closely involved in school life); two grown-up children (both working in prep schools).
The teaching   Very good across the board; dedicated, long-serving staff of 18 (four women). Standard prep school curriculum; all do French from the start, Latin from age 10. Pupils divided into Common Entrance and scholarship forms for last two years; regular form orders and grades for effort ('Academic work is competitive, high standards are expected and achieved'); average class size 15. Lots of art, drama, music; more than half learn an instrument; orchestras, robed choir. Wide range of hobbies, activities; ample opportunities for camping, caving, hill-walking, climbing.
Results   Good Common Entrance and scholarship record (nearly a third win awards).

Destinations Most to West Country schools: Sherborne, Blundell's, King's Taunton, King's Bruton; others to Eton, Marlborough, Radley, Shrewsbury, Wellington, Winchester etc.
Sport Chiefly: cricket, rugby, soccer, hockey; frequent matches against 'our sort of school'. Swimming, athletics, tennis, squash, golf, badminton, judo, sailing, shooting, gymnastics, cross-country, fly-fishing, sailing also on offer. First-rate facilities include well-kept playing fields, open-air pool, large (but unlovely) sports hall, two squash courts.
Remarks Very good all round; highly recommended.

MOWDEN HALL ♂ ♀
Newton, Stocksfield, Northumberland NE43 7TP. Tel (01661) 842529

Synopsis
Co-educational ★ Boarding and day ★ Ages 3–13 ★ 207 pupils (61% boys, 53% boarding) ★ Fees: £9,045 boarding; £6,480 day
Head: Andrew Lewis, 53, appointed 1991.
Attractive, friendly school; very good teaching and results; fine facilities; strong music, sport.

Profile
Background Founded 1935; moved 1945 to handsome, Georgian gentleman's country residence in 55 acres of woodlands and playing fields; girls admitted 1980; pre-prep opened 1993, nursery 1997. Later additions include attractive classrooms, spacious theatre, computer centre; first-class facilities (in what were the stables) for art, technology, science; £750,000 spent on improvements in past five years.
Atmosphere Happy, secure, civilised; like a busy family (much chatter and laughter). Discipline firm but kind; big emphasis on courtesy (doors held open; children stand when visitors enter). Smart uniform. Parents made to feel welcome.
Admissions School is non-selective: most children enter at ages four, five or eight, when entrance tests are felt to be inappropriate; fairly wide range of abilities; numbers are rising. Boarders from age eight; dormitories clean, bright, rather crowded. Good food.
The head Presides over the school with aplomb; hands-on manager; children find him sympathetic and approachable. Read maths and English at Cambridge; previously a housemaster at Repton, where he taught for 21 years; still teaches scripture and Common Entrance maths. Married (wife much involved in school life); four children.
The teaching First-rate: fairly formal in style; early emphasis on the basics of English and maths; specialist teaching begins at age eight. Standard Common Entrance curriculum: Latin, French from age nine. Pupils grouped by ability in some subjects; extra help for those who need it, including dyslexics (about 40 in all); scholarship class in final year for the most able; average class size 16–18. Lots of music: two-thirds learn an instrument; orchestra, three choirs. By arrangement with Cothill House (qv), 11-year-olds spend a term in France being taught all their lessons in French by French teachers.
Results Good: 32 scholarships in past six years.
Destinations A full spread: Oundle, Sedbergh, Repton, Uppingham, Eton, Fettes, Loretto, Merchiston Castle, Charterhouse, Ampleforth, Radley, Stowe, Dollar, Newcastle Royal Grammar, Austin Friars, Marlborough, Rugby, Millfield,

Shrewsbury, Wellington, Queen Margaret's, Wycombe Abbey.
Sport Strong; full fixture list. Main games: rugby, soccer, cricket, for boys; hockey, netball for girls; athletics, cross-country, tennis, swimming for both. Facilities include extensive playing fields, sports hall, indoor pool.
Remarks Very good all round; recommended.

NEWTON ♂ ♀
149 Battersea Park Road, London SW8 4BH. Tel (0171) 720 4091

Synopsis
Co-educational ★ Day ★ Ages 3–13 ★ 254 pupils (slightly more boys than girls) ★ Fees: £5,910
Head: Richard Dell, 51, appointed 1993.
Unusual school; some very able children; good facilities.

Profile
Background Opened 1991 in the spacious, renovated premises of a former primary school; named after Sir Isaac Newton and intended for gifted children. Large, bright classrooms; first-rate facilities (including three science labs, IT centre, gym, assembly hall); plenty of space to play.
Atmosphere Happy, multi-cultural, fairly traditional (but unorthodox behaviour tolerated); pupils of above-average ability, as in many London preps. Houses named after apple trees (but not Golden Delicious). Active parents' association (raises funds for scholarships). Mensa runs Saturday classes on the premises.
Admissions Entry at age three after one-to-one assessment by nursery teachers, at four by educational psychologist's report (paid for by parents). Most from South London (Battersea, Clapham, Stockwell); also Fulham, Chelsea, West London (popular with media folk). About 10% hold means-tested scholarships.
The head Caring, spiritual (says he 'came to heal' after the first head and most of the original staff departed); practises meditation; lectures on gifted children and mysticism. Left school at 16, went to Oxford at 27; his second headship. Married (wife is school matron); four children (one a pupil here).
The teaching Academic, formal but not stuffy; no hot-housing, head insists, but gifted pupils' needs met. Youthful staff of 34 (two-thirds female); children bright-eyed, attentive. School 'shadows' the national curriculum; science a strength; French starts at age seven. Pupils grouped by ability in maths, English from five; separate streams from eight; extra help for dyslexics; average class size 15. Homework (spelling, reading) introduced at seven. Good music (100 learn an instrument) and art. Extra-curricular activities include chess and 'Strategies', a popular game devised by the head.
Results Too soon to draw any conclusions.
Destinations Half to boarding schools such as Oundle, Winchester, Wycombe Abbey; half to day schools including St Paul's, James Allen's, the two Tiffins.
Sport Battersea Park for games and football; basketball popular; no swimming or rugby.
Remarks Interesting school for clever, quirky children who might not fit in at more orthodox establishments.

ORLEY FARM ♂ ♀
South Hill Avenue, Harrow, Middlesex HA13NU. Tel (0181) 422 1525

Synopsis
Independent ★ Day ★ Becoming co-educational ★ Ages 4–13 ★ 470 pupils
(85% boys) ★ Fees: £4,410–£5,640
Head: Ian Elliott, 53, appointed 1990.
Attractive, well-run school; good teaching; lots on offer.

Profile
Background   Founded 1850 as a boarding school to prepare boys for Harrow
(named after a novel by Trollope); moved 1901 to purpose-built, art nouveau
premises surrounded by 25 acres of playing fields and woodland at the bottom
of Harrow Hill; later additions include spacious pre-prep department. Girls
admitted 1994 (but traditions carefully preserved).
Atmosphere   Bustling, happy, well-ordered. First-rate staff; eager, well-
motivated pupils. Parents raise large sums.
Admissions   By a battery of tests taken at age three – of vocabulary, visual and
short-term memory, physical co-ordination, ability to get on with other children
and engage in simple conversation with adults. ('All very methodical,' says the
head. 'The parents get coffee and tranquilisers while the children are taken off
for an hour in groups of eight or 10.') About 180 apply; 60 are offered a place.
Catchment area extends from central London to Watford; 60% come from bilingual homes; nearly all have previously been to nursery school.
The head   Kindly, determined, quietly efficient. Manchester graduate; previously head for six years of Rossall Prep. Married; two grown-up children.
The teaching   Good quality; strong academic grounding; well-qualified, stable
staff. Standard prep school curriculum; science taught by specialists from age
seven (up-to-date labs); French from nine, Latin from 10. Pupils grouped by ability into three streams; extra help for those who need it, including dyslexics; weekly
grades for effort; largest class size 20. Good art; lots of music (orchestra, choirs).
Results   Good: scholarships to Merchant Taylors' Northwood, St Paul's, Eton.
Destinations   Wide range. 'Parents can have unreasonable expectations,' says
the head. 'I like to sit them down when their children are seven or eight and try
to agree a choice that won't waste everyone's time.' Most popular: Merchant
Taylors', Mill Hill, John Lyon, St Paul's, Dr Challoner's; a few to Harrow.
Sport   Lots on offer, including hockey, football, rugby, tennis, cricket, athletics,
basketball, golf, Eton-fives ('but it's OK not to be sporty'). Facilities include heated outdoor pool, all-weather tennis/hockey pitches.
Remarks   Good school for eager, able children.

ORWELL PARK ♂ ♀
Nacton, Ipswich, Suffolk IP10 0ER. Tel (01473) 659225

Synopsis
Co-educational ★ Boarding and day ★ Ages 3–13 ★ 200 pupils (75% board-
ing) ★ Fees: £10,080 boarding; £7,350 day
Head: Andrew Auster, 46, appointed 1994.
Good school; sound teaching; strong music; wide range of extra-curricular activities.

Profile

Background Founded by a clergyman in 1867; moved to present spectacular 90-acre site overlooking the Orwell estuary in 1937; fine 18th-century mansion with many later additions. Resources concentrated on essentials rather than frills; good science labs and technology workshops. Girls first admitted 1992, five-year-olds 1995 (numbers had been declining).

Atmosphere Wide range of games, hobbies and extra-curricular pursuits makes this an all-rounders' paradise. Strong commitment, too, to the traditional prep school values of discipline (shirt-tails tucked in, hands out of pockets), polite behaviour and academic excellence; all pupils help with the washing up and take part in a daily 'charring' routine. Parents invited to visit frequently (but no parents' association).

Admissions By informal interview with the child and extensive meeting with the parents; school is not selective (or full). Most live within a two-hour journey; 10% from abroad. Dormitories (maximum 10 beds) carpeted, tidy but most are rather crowded; new girls' wing is admirable. Some scholarships, bursaries available.

The head Tall, enthusiastic; has a passion for music (conducts school orchestra and choir), rugby and Aston Villa FC. Read music at Durham (plays bassoon, piano, trombone, tuba); formerly director of music at Shrewsbury and head of The Downs, Colwall (qv). Married (to a teacher); three children.

The teaching Designed to meet the needs of Common Entrance, scholarship exams and the national curriculum; particular stress on spelling, tables, reading skills; associated nursery department run on Montessori lines. French from age seven; all do three years' Latin; Greek on offer; lots of computing. Juniors grouped by ability; further setting in most subjects thereafter; plenty of extra help for slower learners (school is lavishly staffed); class sizes vary from eight to 16. Outstanding art studios; strong music (15 visiting teachers, more than 40 practice rooms). Observatory with 10-inch refractor telescope and radio station enables pupils to talk to astronauts and track their passage overhead. Big emphasis on hobbies and leisure pursuits.

Results All pass Common Entrance to their (guided) first-choice school; regular academic and music scholarships.

Destinations More than 60 senior schools in the past 10 years. Most popular, apart from East Anglian schools, are Eton, Harrow, Oundle, Uppingham, Rugby, Shrewsbury, Winchester.

Sport Strong tradition in team sports and individual pursuits. Facilities include extensive playing fields, splendid new sports hall with three squash courts, outdoor heated pool, five hard tennis courts, nine-hole golf course and Army-built assault course.

Remarks Hums with activity from before breakfast to past bed-time; it would be very hard to be bored here. HMI concluded (1996): 'The school is very successful in preparing its pupils for senior independent education. The teaching is generally sound and often good. The pupils are well motivated and make marked progress.'

PACKWOOD HAUGH ♂ ♀
Ruyton-XI-Towns, Shrewsbury, Shropshire SY4 1HX. Tel (01939) 260217

Synopsis
Co-educational ★ Boarding and day ★ Ages 4–13 ★ 232 pupils (66% boys, 57% boarding) ★ Fees: £8,976 boarding; £6,978 day
Head: Patrick Jordan, 57, appointed 1988.
Well-run, traditional prep school; very good teaching and results; lots of sport.

Profile
Background   Founded 1892; moved to present site 1941. Large Victorian country mansion plus sympathetic later additions beautifully situated in 65 acres of well-maintained grounds; farm buildings converted to classrooms.

Atmosphere   A cheerful, well-organised community; clear Anglican ethos; big emphasis on good manners, behaviour, neat appearance. School day ends at 6 pm; lessons on Saturday mornings. Half the staff live on campus.

Admissions   By interview and tests in maths, English; all abilities accepted; school is not full. Most from professional/business backgrounds and live within 50 miles; a few from abroad. Nearly all day pupils become boarders by final year; no weekly boarding. Pleasant boarding accommodation (in two houses); comfortable, carpeted dormitories (six/seven beds); soft toys abound. Two scholarships a year; fee reductions for clergy, armed forces.

The head   Able, hard-working, enthusiastic; strong leader. Read law and economics at Cambridge (choral scholar); previously head of a prep school in Dorset. Teaches Latin; keen musician and sportsman. Married (wife teaches here); two children.

The teaching   High quality: traditional in style; experienced, stable staff; aim is a 100% pass at Common Entrance. Standard prep school curriculum: all do Latin (six periods a week) and French; science labs small and inadequate; good provision for computing, design/technology. Pupils grouped by ability; specialist help for dyslexics; maximum class size 18. Good art, drama; flourishing music (orchestra, various ensembles). Lots of extra-curricular activities, including pets, model railway.

Results   Good Common Entrance record; average of 10 scholarships a year (Shrewsbury, Oundle, Cheltenham Ladies', Moreton Hall, Rugby, Malvern etc).

Destinations   Mainly Shrewsbury for boys, Moreton Hall for girls.

Sport   Strong: lots of teams (aim is to find everyone something he/she can do well); good facilities. Main sports: rugby, soccer, hockey, cricket for boys; hockey, netball, lacrosse, rounders for girls; cross-country, athletics, tennis, swimming for both. Extensive playing fields, all-weather pitch, nine-hole golf course.

Remarks   Good school: high standards in a secure, caring atmosphere.

PAPPLEWICK ♂
Windsor Road, Ascot, Berkshire SL5 7LH. Tel (01344) 21488

Synopsis
Boys ★ Boarding and day ★ Ages 7–13 ★ 200 pupils (75% boarding) ★ Fees: £9,810 boarding; £7,536 day
Head: Rhidian Llewellyn, 40, appointed 1992.
Good traditional prep school; lively teaching; friendly atmosphere; strong sport.

Profile

Background   Founded 1947; Edwardian mansion with later additions in 13 acres beside Ascot race course.

Atmosphere   Cheerful, kindly, busy; Christian values fostered (daily chapel service). Discipline based on thoughtfulness for others rather than on rigid rules; good manners, courtesy expected. Strong boarding ethos (all required to board for their last two years): most staff live on site; busy programme of weekend activities.

Admissions   Non-selective; £300 deposit secures a place (but apply early). Most from professional/business backgrounds in London and the Home Counties; 20% of parents live abroad. Boarding accommodation less than luxurious and rather crowded (iron bedsteads, 18 inches apart). 'We're not ritzy or grand,' says the head. 'We spend the money where it matters – on good staff and first-rate food.'

The head   Youthful, very able. Read history at London; wrote about cricket and racing (his passions) for *The Sporting Life*; previously a housemaster at the Dragon (qv). Married (wife teaches art here).

The teaching   Ranges from the traditional (rows of old-fashioned desks) to all kinds of innovative projects. Lively English (importance of grammar and spelling emphasised); compulsory Latin; lots of computing (excellent facilities); inspired teaching in art, design/technology. All pupils grouped by ability (to enable them to go at their own pace); scholarship boys 'accelerated' from age 10; extra help available for dyslexics, slow learners; regular grades for effort and achievement; average class size 12. Good music: nearly all learn an instrument; strong choral tradition. Wide range of hobbies and clubs; children make radio and television programmes in well-equipped media centre.

Results   Good: 42 scholarships since 1993.

Destinations   Wide range of boarding schools but especially Wellington, Charterhouse, Harrow, Eton.

Sport   Strong tradition: all play every day; good record against other schools, particularly in rugby and cricket ('The will to win is more important than winning itself'). Hockey, football, tennis, athletics also on offer; judo a strength. Facilities include all-weather pitch, three hard tennis courts, squash courts, small outdoor heated pool. Playing fields adequate but on the small side.

Remarks   Good all-round; recommended.

PILGRIMS' ♂
The Close, Winchester, Hampshire SO23 9LT. Tel (01962) 854189

Synopsis
Boys ★ Day and boarding ★ Ages 8–13 ★ 178 pupils ★ (55% day) ★ Fees: £6,480 day; £8,880 boarding
Head: Rev Dr Brian Rees, 48, appointed September 1997.
Delightful, traditional school; very good teaching and results; fine music; lots of sport.

Profile

Background   Founded 1931 as the choir school for Winchester Cathedral but open also to 'commoners'; Winchester College 'quiristers' added 1966. Medieval buildings plus high-quality later additions (main building said to be by Sir Christopher Wren) on a beautiful site between the cathedral and the college

Atmosphere   Busy, kindly, well-ordered; good pastoral care; big emphasis on praise and encouragement (boys take their work to 'show up' to the head after assembly). Long school day ends at 5 pm or 6 pm, depending on age.

Admissions By interview and tests in the Three Rs; school is not unduly selective but does not admit those with substantial learning difficulties; voice trials for a total of choristers and quiristers (who are all boarders and pay half fees). Pleasant boarding accommodation; weekly boarding available.

The head New appointment. Canadian; educated at McGill; PhD from St Andrews; ordained 1980; previously head of Bedford prep school. Married; three children (one a chorister here).

The teaching First-rate; experienced, well-qualified staff. Standard prep school curriculum; all start Latin at age 10; some add Greek; German on offer; good English, science, computing. Pupils grouped by ability from second year (and further divided in their last year according to whether they are taking the Winchester entrance paper, Common Entrance or scholarships); three-weekly grades for effort and achievement; average class size 18. First-rate music; nearly all learn at least one instrument; two orchestras, two school choirs. Hobbies include chess, drama, pottery, stamps.

Results Very good: since 1990, 48 boys have won music scholarships, 23 have won academic awards (including the top scholarship to Winchester).

Destinations Since 1990: Winchester 91, King Edward's, Southampton 23, Sherborne 19, Eton 8.

Sport Lots on offer; matches twice a week. Soccer, rugby, cricket, athletics, cross-country, hockey, fives, squash, rowing, swimming, tennis all on offer. School has its own playing fields (cricket nets in the dean's garden) and the use of Winchester's fine facilities.

Remarks Fine school for able, active boys. Highly recommended.

PORT REGIS ♂ ♀
Motcombe Park, Shaftesbury, Dorset SP7 9QA. Tel (01747) 852566

Synopsis
Co-educational ★ Boarding and day ★ Ages 3–13 ★ 393 pupils (55% boys, 62% boarding) ★ Fees: £11,520 boarding; £8,595 day
Head: Peter Dix, 47, appointed 1994.
Busy, well-run school; outstanding facilities; vast range of activities.

Profile
Background Founded 1891; moved 1947 to present, 152-acre estate (woods, lake, dens); late-Victorian, Tudor-style mansion (oak panelling, carved stairways, stone-mullioned windows) plus extensive modern additions, including fine design/technology centre, art & pottery studios, science labs, 450-seat theatre ('Tomorrow's school for tomorrow's child'). The Princess Royal sent her children here.

Atmosphere Fizzing; dedicated staff; friendly, articulate pupils; first-rate pastoral care; big emphasis on good manners, consideration for others; detailed policies on every aspect of school life (marketing is polished and highly effective). Lessons on Saturday mornings; weekend activities for boarders organised by 16 gap-year students who live and work at the school (70 hobbies on offer). Parents always welcome.

Admissions By interview; school is not academically selective; early application advised (up to two apply for each place). Most from the South West; many boarders have parents living abroad. Good, comfortable, 'home-from-home' boarding accommodation; high-quality furnishings; everything immaculately clean; juniors in dormitories of six to eight beds; seniors have sliding doors to create their own cubicles (complete with individual wash basins). Very good food. Scholarships: academic, art, music, gymnastics, sport, all-rounder.

The head Warm, enthusiastic, approachable; hands-on management style. Educated in South Africa and at Cambridge (classics); taught for 16 years at King's Canterbury (qv). Keen to raise academic standards. Married (wife much involved in the school); two daughters.

The teaching Good quality; generally formal in style; relatively youthful staff. Standard prep school curriculum; French from age seven; most do Latin, more able add Greek; sciences taught separately; very good design/technology. Specialist teaching from age nine; pupils grouped by ability in most subjects; extra help for those who need it; average class size 14. Lots of art, drama. First-rate music; more than half learn an instrument; three choirs, three orchestras.

Results Good Common Entrance record; regular scholarships (especially all-rounder).

Destinations Chiefly: Bryanston, Eton, Marlborough, Oundle, Canford, Charterhouse, Radley, Sherborne, Winchester.

Sport Strong; good coaching. Main sports: cricket, athletics, soccer, netball, rugby, hockey. Gymnastics (a particular strength), badminton, tennis, squash, trampolining, judo, archery, riding etc also on offer. Facilities include 30 acres of playing fields, all-weather pitch, sports hall, indoor pool, nine-hole golf course.

Remarks Attractive school; recommended.

RIDDLESWORTH HALL ♀
Diss, Norfolk IP22 2TA. Tel (01953) 681246,

Synopsis
Girls ★ Day and boarding ★ Ages 7–13 (plus co-educational nursery and pre-prep) ★ 78 pupils (35% boarding) ★ Fees: £9,765 boarding; £6,120 day
Head: David Dean, 46, appointed September 1997.
Small, grandly-housed school; good teaching and results; lots on offer.

Profile
Background Founded 1946; splendid Georgian mansion (substantially re-built after a disastrous fire) in 30 acres of attractive wooded parkland; cheerful class-rooms around two courtyards, one a converted 18th-century stable block; fine facilities for art, pottery, design/technology. Numbers have steadily declined. Pre-prep ('the Wigwam') in modern premises (19 pupils aged four to seven).

Atmosphere Very much a family school; emphasis on self-discipline, tolerance, kindness (but healthy competition encouraged); warm rapport between staff and children; good manners expected. Pets' corner houses lots of small, well-fed animals.

Admissions By interview and short, written test; fairly wide range of abilities. Most pupils from professional backgrounds in East Anglia; one or two from abroad. Boarding accommodation in bright, colourful dormitories. Scholarships, bursaries available.

The head Recent appointment; taught for 20 years at an international school in Switzerland. Admits that keeping the school viable is going to be a challenge. Married; two daughters.

The teaching Generally good; styles range from traditional to modern;

predominantly female staff. Standard prep school curriculum; French from age four, Latin from 10, German from 12. Average class size 14; extra help for dyslexics and those for whom English is a foreign language. Lots of music: three choirs, orchestra, jazz band. Extra-curricular activities include Brownies, puppetry, gardening, cookery.
Results Good scholarship record, most recently to Gordonstoun, Oundle, King's Ely, Malvern Girls'.
Destinations Chiefly boarding schools such as St Mary's Wantage, Heathfield, Downe House, Benenden, Queenswood, St Felix, Gresham's Holt.
Sport Strong emphasis on physical education. Facilities include fine indoor pool, two hockey pitches, four tennis/netball courts. Fly-fishing, clay pigeon shooting, riding available.
Remarks Small school, getting still smaller.

ST ANDREW'S ♂ ♀
Meads, Eastbourne, Sussex BN20 7RP. Tel (01323) 733203

Synopsis
Co-educational ★ Day and boarding ★ Ages 7–13 (plus associated nursery and pre-prep) ★ 301 pupils (62% boys, 79% day) ★ Fees: £6,930 day; £9,225 boarding
Head: Hugh Davies Jones, 53, appointed 1984.
First-rate, well-run school; high academic standards; good scholarship record; strong on arts and games.

Profile
Background Founded 1877 as a boarding school for boys (curriculum consisted of Latin and cricket); co-educational since 1977. Fine 19-acre site at the foot of the South Downs; original Victorian buildings modernised and extended. Nursery and pre-prep on the same site.
Atmosphere Still very much a boarding school, despite the preponderance of day pupils: lessons on Saturday mornings, supervised prep for all in the evenings; day children can stay until 7 pm (or over night) to take advantage of the vast array of extra-curricular activities. Pleasant environment ('Children notice their surroundings, even if only unconsciously,' says the head); lots of work displayed in classrooms and corridors. 'Competition,' says the prospectus, 'is seen as a useful stimulus to each child's effort.' Day begins with a chapel service led by the head or the school chaplain (Anglican but all faiths welcomed).
Admissions First come, first served; entry tests, for placing only, a term prior to admission. Most from business/professional families; day pupils drawn from 20-mile radius (school runs mini-buses); half the boarders are children of expatriates. Attractive, well-furnished boarding houses (one each for boys and girls); double-glazed, centrally-heated; single rooms for seniors. Cafeteria style meals; staff eat with children.
The head Enthusiastic, vigorous, very able; gets on well with staff, pupils and parents; previously head for 12 years of a Buckinghamshire prep school. Teaches scripture to the juniors; wife, Sarah, teaches maths, takes Brownies and Cubs, runs clothes shop, acts as registrar.
The teaching First-rate: well-qualified, hard-working staff of 33 (a third women); all subjects taught by specialists from age nine. Standard prep school curriculum: French from five, Latin from 10; German and Japanese on offer. Pupils grouped by ability from nine in English, maths, French; promotion by

stage rather than age; scholarship class for the brightest; extra help for those with learning difficulties; average class size 16. Children assessed weekly on effort, attitude, achievement, behaviour; outstanding work shown to the head and entered in honours book. Attractive, well-stocked library (plus bean bags). Excellent facilities for art, pottery, craft, technology. Good music centre (six practice rooms); several choirs; 60% learn an instrument. Lots of drama. Hobbies include bridge, computers, radio hams, cookery, tapestry etc. Outdoor education programme introduces seniors to life under canvas (winter and summer). Regular French exchanges (pupils stay with French families, attend local school).

Results   Good: about 15 a year win scholarships to senior schools such as Eastbourne, Lancing, Tonbridge, Moira House, Roedean, Sevenoaks.

Destinations   As well as the above: Ardingly, Benenden, Bryanston, Charterhouse, Eton, Harrow, Malvern, Marlborough, Oundle, St Bede's, Worth, Wycombe Abbey etc.

Sport   Huge range; good facilities; long fixture list. Main games: football, rugby, cricket (boys); netball, hockey, rounders (girls). Facilities include gym, heated indoor pool, two floodlit tennis courts. Full-time coaches for tennis, swimming.

Remarks   Independent inspectors concluded (1996): 'St Andrew's is a distinguished school. Above all, its success is the result of the firm but humane leadership of the headmaster supported by his wife and a loyal, hardworking and professionally committed staff.' Highly recommended.

ST AUBYN'S ♂ ♀
High Street, Rottingdean, East Sussex BN2 7JN. Tel (01273) 302170

Synopsis
Co-educational ★ Boarding and day ★ Ages 4–13 (plus associated pre-prep)
★ 130 pupils (90% boys, 50% boarding) ★ Fees: £9,630 boarding; £7,020 day
Head: Julian James, 59, appointed 1974 (retiring July 1998).
Small, traditional school; strong family atmosphere; good teaching and results; lots of sport.

Profile
Background   Founded 1895; fine Regency/Georgian buildings plus many recent additions in spacious grounds; lovely chapel. Co-educational since 1996.

Atmosphere   Homely, purposeful, exceptionally happy; head and his wife always on hand to sort out problems. Big emphasis on good manners, courtesy, consideration for others. Many pupils' fathers are old boys.

Admissions   Entry by assessment and tests in English, maths, IQ. Most pupils from London, Sussex; day pupils stay for supervised prep; lessons on alternate Saturday mornings. Pleasant dormitories (four to 10 beds); seniors in study-bedrooms ('The matron makes every effort to create a snug, homely atmosphere'). Academic and sporting scholarships available.

The head   Long-serving, totally committed. Was a pupil here (1947–52); went to Charterhouse, trained as a teacher and then came back in 1958; teaches French. From August 1988: Mr G A Gobat.

The teaching   Good: well-qualified, hard-working staff; emphasis on teaching the basics thoroughly. Standard prep school curriculum: French from age four; most do Latin, a few do Greek; good facilities for computing. Pupils grouped by ability; scholarship stream from age eight; extra help for those with special needs; average class size 14. Regular grades for work and effort; comprehensive termly reports. Good music (most learn an instrument) and art.

Results   Good Common Entrance record. Regular scholarships to Winchester, Cranleigh, Eastbourne, Lancing, Radley, St Bede's Hailsham, St Edward's Oxford, Stowe.

Destinations   In addition to the above: Eton, Harrow, Marlborough, Milton Abbey and many more.

Sport   Lots on offer; every child encouraged to play team and individual games. Main sports: soccer, rugby, lacrosse, hockey, netball, cricket, squash. Fencing a particular strength. Facilities include sports hall, heated outdoor pool, all-weather tennis and netball courts.

Remarks   Successful, old-fashioned school. Prospectus supplemented by delightful video featuring impressive endorsements by former heads of Harrow and Radley.

ST BEDE'S ♂ ♀
Duke's Drive, Eastbourne, East Sussex BN20 7XL. Tel (01323) 734222

Synopsis
Co-educational ★ Day and boarding ★ Ages 8–13 (plus associated nursery and pre-prep) ★ 320 pupils (68% boys, 73% day) ★ Fees: £6,375 day; £10,080 boarding Head: Peter Pyemont, 58, appointed 1964.
A forward-looking school with old-world values; very good teaching and results; wide range of extra-curricular activities, including strong music and sport.

Profile
Background   Founded 1895 as the prep school for Eastbourne College; moved to present spectacular site and purpose-built, five-storey, half-timbered villa on a cliff top near Beachy Head 1900; many later acquisitions and additions, including nursery and pre-prep. Co-educational since 1970.

Atmosphere   Lively ('Our aim is to ensure that each child shines') and well-ordered; firmly Christian ethos (but children of other faiths admitted). Values are traditional but the approach is up to date.

Admissions   By interview (no entry test); school is not rigidly selective but children must be able to benefit from the teaching. Most from professional/farming/business families; catchment area for day pupils extends in an arc from Brighton through Uckfield to Bexhill; 20% of boarders from overseas, including Hong Kong, Thailand. Two comfortable, unpretentious boarding houses; all eat in basement canteen (adventurous, well-balanced menu). Lessons on Saturday mornings from age nine. Scholarships, bursaries at head's discretion.

The head   Exceptionally long-serving. Enthusiastic, 'hands-on' style; door always open (children come in to play during break). Appointed at 25 (when there were just 39 boys on the roll); was a pupil here before going to Marlborough. Married (wife very much involved), grown-up children.

The teaching   Good. Formal in style; expectations geared to 100% success at Common Entrance; children's progress discussed in detail at weekly staff meetings. Broad curriculum; basic skills taught from an early age. Pupils grouped by ability in maths, French from age nine, in Latin ('a fine mind trainer') from 10; potential scholars spend last two years in separate sixth form (and add German or Greek); particular care for dyslexics and those for whom English is a foreign language; small classes (average size 16). Art well taught; exuberant pottery. Lots of drama (all encouraged to participate) and music; 70% learn an instrument (all pre-prep pupils learn the violin); 40–strong orchestra (including the head), three choirs. Huge range of extra-curricular activities, including carpentry, sailing, riding, computers, photography, chess, bridge etc. Much fund-raising for charity.

Results Regular scholarships to Eton, Benenden, Lancing, Roedean, Sevenoaks, Bedales etc (average of 18 a year).

Destinations In addition to the above: Harrow, Charterhouse, Wycombe Abbey, Sherborne, Tonbridge, Eastbourne, Moira House, St Bede's Hailsham.

Sport Taken seriously; particularly good netball, swimming, athletics, tennis, cricket. Rugby, soccer, hockey also on offer; other activities include judo, fencing, squash, shooting. Those who dislike games may do gardening instead. Facilities include thee pitches, fine sports hall, slightly steamy indoor pool.

Remarks Firm academic grounding; something for everyone to enjoy. Recommended.

ST JOHN'S BEAUMONT ♂
Old Windsor, Berkshire SL4 2JN. Tel (01784) 432428

Synopsis
Roman Catholic ★ Boys ★ Day and boarding ★ Ages 4–13 ★ 225 pupils (75% day) ★ Fees: from £3,762 day; £10,767 boarding
Head: Dermot St John Gogarty, 39, appointed 1987.
Small, well-run Jesuit school; high standards; good results.

Profile
Background Founded 1888 by Society of Jesus as prep school to Beaumont (now defunct). Fine 100-acre site on edge of Old Windsor; imposing, spacious, purpose-built premises designed by J F Bentley, architect of Westminster Cathedral (gives the school a gracious, civilised air); later additions include well-equipped science/art block.

Atmosphere Friendly, relaxed but with strong underlying discipline. Consideration for others a high priority; excellence in everything the aim; Roman Catholic faith and Jesuit ideals fundamental (fine Gothic chapel at the heart of the school). Confident, friendly, well-mannered boys, happy to explain what they are working at.

Admissions Selective entry (except at age four) by assessment day; most from Roman Catholic families, though boys of other denominations welcomed. Boarders housed in two light, high-ceilinged dormitories, divided into curtained cubicles (original 1888 design). Scholarships, bursaries available.

The head Young (appointed at 29), dynamic, determined; intolerant of anything 'sloppy' but with a lively sense of humour and jocular manner. Believes the 'common perception of a Catholic independent school is one of an austere, disciplined, almost 19th-century environment... This perception is far removed from the truth'. Runs school with a firm hand (and has transformed it); expects utter commitment from his staff. Constantly about the place, takes assembly morning and evening, sees every boy at least twice a week. Keen sportsman. Married; five children.

The teaching Traditional, but in a modern style. Rigorous standards of spelling, grammar, accuracy, presentation (specifics laid down in staff handbook); national curriculum taken very seriously. Staff of 17 (80% appointed by present head) kept up to the mark with regular in-service training. Standard prep school curriculum; French, Latin, science, computing introduced at age 10. Cheerful classrooms well equipped with overhead projectors, videos, computers. Pupils grouped by ability in top forms (additional help for dyslexics, special class for scholars); average class size 14. Regular testing (three-weekly orders); daily homework. Music encouraged: informal concerts every week so everyone has a chance to perform; two choirs. Regular drama productions (but facilities rather poor). Numerous hobbies and clubs run by staff.

Results   Impressive: regular scholarships; all pass Common Entrance to (guided) first-choice school.

Destinations   Catholic senior schools – Stonyhurst, Downside, Ampleforth, Oratory – also Eton, Harrow, Hampton, St George's Weybridge and state schools such as Windsor Boys'.

Sport   Strong tradition. All play games every day; regular matches with other schools. Main sports rugby and cricket (extensive pitches); minor ones include hockey, soccer, athletics, tennis. Indoor pool.

Remarks   Excellent grounding and a broad education in a structured, Christian environment. Recommended.

ST JOHN'S COLLEGE SCHOOL   ♂ ♀
73 Grange Road, Cambridge CB3 9AB. Tel (01223) 353532

Synopsis
Co-educational ★ Day and boarding ★ Ages 4–13 ★ 440 pupils (60% boys, 90% day) ★ Fees: £5,571 day; £8,975 boarding
Head: Kevin Jones, 40, appointed 1990.
First-rate school; very good teaching; strong music and sport.

Profile
Background   Founded 1660 as a choir school for St John's College, which still owns it (two-thirds of the governors are college Fellows). Moved 1955 to present handsome Edwardian premises (£2 million spent on recent additions, including new classroom block, music school); junior department (ages four to eight) 200 yards down the road – a colourful, child-centred habitat. Very good facilities for design/technology, computing.

Atmosphere   Happy, busy; strong sense of community. Friendly relations between staff and pupils; very good pastoral care system. Eye-catching scarlet blazers.

Admissions   By parental interview and informal assessment; voice trials for choristers (who pay one-third fees); fairly wide range of abilities. Boarding accommodation (for 50, including 20 choristers) being refurbished (mainly four-bed dormitories); lots of weekend activities.

The head   Youthful appointment; enthusiastic, deeply committed. Read English at Cambridge (First); previously deputy head of Yehudi Menuhin music school. Married; two sons (one a pupil here).

The teaching   Lively, effective: high-quality staff (nearly half appointed by present head); willing pupils. French taught from age eight, study skills from 10; Latin on offer from 10, Greek from 11; high-quality design/technology, computing (specialist staff). Pupils grouped by ability in some subjects from nine; extra help for those with specific learning difficulties or specific gifts; average class size 20. Supervised homework from seven. First-rate music: 80% play at least one instrument; four choirs (regular tours abroad), orchestras, various ensembles. Extra-curricular activities include dance, pottery, carpentry.

Results   Good: up to a third win scholarships (academic, music, art, IT).

Destinations   Wide range of schools, particularly boarding.

Sport   Important: all games timetabled; lots on offer. Main sports: soccer, rugby, cricket, netball (county champions), rounders, swimming, tennis, hockey. Squash, rowing, golf also available. Facilities include playing fields (shared with the college), all-weather pitch, covered pool.

Remarks   Very good all round; recommended.

ST PAUL'S (COLET COURT) ♂
Lonsdale Road, London SW13 9JT. Tel (0181) 748 3461

Synopsis
Boys ★ Day and boarding ★ Ages 7–13 ★ 440 pupils (95% day) ★ Fees: £6,910 day; £10,800 boarding
Head: Geoffrey Thompson, 51, appointed 1992.
A flying start for clever young Paulines: élite entry; excellent teaching.

Profile
Background   Founded 1881; functional, undistinguished 1960s buildings adjoining St Paul's (qv); amenities shared with the senior school include spacious dining hall, chapel, technology workshops, sports centre and playing fields.

Atmosphere   Relaxed, tolerant; little chattering figures playing with balls and bats almost redeem the dreary buildings, all grey pebble and utility slab. Inside, by contrast, seems almost cosy. Classrooms are a good size and bright with decoration; the large day room is set up for chess and bridge; in the hall two boys are practising their juggling routines for a Victorian music hall concert; a solitary bagpiper tunes up in the corner. The boarding house has friendly dormitories and a large games room; it also houses the computer room and the library, so there is a constant flow of day boys through the passages.

Admissions   Highly selective (these are Paulines in the making). Entry by interview and tests in English, maths, verbal reasoning; about 125 compete for 32 places at 7 and 180 for 40 places at 8. Waiting lists limited to 500 for each year (lists now closed until 2000). NB: a boy entered for Colet Court is automatically entered for St Paul's, and will only be accepted on the understanding that the senior school is his first choice. Some choir and music scholarships available.

The head   Formerly head of science here. Has a calm, easy authority. Married; lives next to the school.

The teaching   Intensive, structured, largely traditional in style. Some staff also teach in the senior school; most are graduates. Standard prep school curriculum; big emphasis on Latin, rather less on science and technology. Pupils grouped by ability in maths, French, Latin; scholarship class does ancient Greek; half-termly grades for effort and attainment (but no form orders). Dozens of out-of-classroom activities, nearly all generated by the enthusiasm of the staff; many take place at the weekend or in the holidays (cycling in Brittany, walking in Switzerland, rugby in Australia, chess at Pontins). Boys are treated as rational, likeable creatures; sports days, concerts and parents' evenings are amusing challenges rather than bores. Some staff believe the boys read less than they did, thanks to computer games and TV, but the library is well stocked and well used.

Lots of music: half learn an instrument; 50-strong orchestra, two choirs.

Results Boys are not specifically prepared for Common Entrance or for scholarships to senior schools other than St Paul's; nonetheless, some win scholarships to Eton and Winchester.

Destinations About 90% proceed to St Paul's.

Sport Rugby and cricket are both keenly played but there are many alternatives. Excellent facilities shared with the senior school.

Remarks Independent inspectors concluded (1995): 'Colet Court is is a distinguished preparatory school. The overall standard of teaching is very good. Expectations are very high and examination results are impressive.'

SALISBURY CATHEDRAL SCHOOL ♂ ♀
1 The Close, Salisbury, Wiltshire SP1 2EQ. Tel (01722) 322652

Synopsis
Co-educational ★ Day and boarding ★ Ages 8–13 (plus associated pre-prep)
★ 160 pupils (66% boys, 60% day) ★ Fees: £6,225 day; £8,625 boarding
Head: Christopher Helyer, 52, appointed 1991 (leaving April 1998).
Happy, well-run school; good teaching and results; lots of music.

Profile
Background Founded 1091 by St Osmund, first Bishop of Salisbury; became a prep school in the 1920s; moved to present 27-acre site in the cathedral close 1947; girl choristers admitted 1991. Main building is the former bishop's palace; space at a premium; most classrooms in 'temporary' huts (lack-lustre facilities compensated for by stunning surroundings). Pre-prep and nursery (ages three to seven) near by.

Atmosphere Happy, busy, well-mannered; very good pastoral care; warm relations between staff and pupils. Parents very supportive and encouraged to be involved. Firm anti-bullying policy states that all pupils have 'the right to enjoy their learning and leisure in an atmosphere free from fear and unpleasantness'.

Admissions By interview and assessment (automatic entry for pre-prep pupils); by interview and voice trials for the 25% who are choral scholars (competition severe). Boarding accommodation in the former palace (huge, double-glazed casement windows); eight-bed dormitories (boys on one floor, girls on another); everywhere clean and tidy.

The head Able, very experienced: previously head of the choir schools in Grimsby and Exeter. From April 1988: Robert Thackray, currently head of a church school in Suffolk.

The teaching Formal but friendly; dedicated staff of 11; pupils involved and interested. Emphasis on basic skills; form teachers for first two years, subject specialists thereafter; national curriculum followed. Pupils grouped by ability in maths, French, Latin; scholarship class formed in final year; lots of extra help for those who need it; progress closely monitored (three-weekly gradings to parents); average class size 15. Lessons on Saturday mornings. Music is at the heart of the school (pianos everywhere): nearly all learn at least one instrument; 250 lessons a week taught by 20 visiting staff; two choirs, one boys', one girls'. Drama (in the magnificent bishop's drawing room) valued too.

Results Good: 45 awards (academic, technology as well as music) worth £1.2 million won in the past two years.

Destinations Wide variety but particularly Marlborough, Bryanston,

Canford, Sherborne and other West Country schools.
Sports   Chiefly: rugby, football, hockey, cross-country, cricket, netball, rounders. Facilities basic (small gym), heated outdoor pool; extensive playing fields.
Remarks   Good school; beautiful, historic setting.

SANDROYD ♂

Rushmore, Tollard Royal, near Salisbury, Wiltshire SP5 5QD. Tel (01725) 516264

Synopsis
Boys ★ Boarding and day ★ Ages 8–13 ★ 117 pupils (90% boarders) ★ Fees: £9,750 boarding; £7,800 day
Head: Michael Hatch, 53, appointed 1994.
Delightful, old-fashioned school; good teaching and results; something for everyone.

Profile
Background   Founded in Surrey 1888; moved here 1939. Eighteenth-century mansion plus discreet additions on a 50-acre estate (complete with walled gardens, temple and ha-ha) surrounded by a 400-acre deer park in the heart of Cranborne Chase (beautiful views, as essentially English as the school). Classrooms spacious, functional; good facilities for art, science, computing, design & technology; simple chapel in converted Nissen hut. Two-thirds of staff live on site. Numbers (as in all such schools) have dwindled steadily.
Atmosphere   A welcoming, extended-family feel (blazing open fire, snooker in the panelled entrance hall, chintz curtains and flowers in the boys' drawing room). Pupils (muddied knees, undone laces, shirts awry) charming, smiling, unfailingly polite; prefects ('Deacons') take the lead against bullying. Casual uniform of corduroy trousers (any colour) and navy guernsey sweater. Lessons on Saturday mornings, tuck on Saturday evenings, letters home on Sundays. Aim is to prepare boys to 'make their way into the competitive world with confidence'.
Admissions   By an assessment morning; range of abilities is wide (specialist department for those with specific learning difficulties). Most parents from southern England (Kent to Devon); a third of pupils are the sons of Army officers. Dormitories for up to eight, slowly being up-graded; private showers; everywhere tidy and spotless. Formal meals, grace before and after; eat what is in front of you. Some scholarships, bursaries.
The head   Read maths at Oxford; previously a housemaster for 12 years at Sherborne. Married (wife much involved in school life – they both teach); two grown-up children.
The teaching   Generally formal in style but with plenty of pupil–teacher interaction; stable staff of 17 (nine women). Standard national curriculum augmented by the demands of Common Entrance; all take national curriculum tests at 11. Pupils grouped by ability in English, maths, science from 10; specialist teaching (and further setting) thereafter; scholarship form from 12 (at which age all spend a week in France – included in the fees); average class size 12, maximum of 16. Plenty of computing (touch-typing course on offer). Good music: two-thirds learn an instrument; three choirs, two orchestras. Lots of art, drama. Extra-curricular activities include vegetable gardening, badger-watching, looking after pets.
Results   Good Common Entrance record to all the major senior schools; one or two scholarships a year.
Destinations   Over the last eight years: 24% to Sherborne, 14% to Radley, 6%

to Eton. Others include: Bryanston, Harrow, Marlborough, Shrewsbury, Wellington, Charterhouse, Millfield.

Sport   An important part of life; main games rugby, hockey, cricket; good coaching. Golf, riding, swimming (indoor pool), basketball, sailing, fishing, archery also on offer.

Remarks   Safe, secure – if a little rarefied. Suits boys who like to be busy and independent (but the step to senior school could seem large).

STORMONT ♀
The Causeway, Potters Bar, Hertfordshire EN6 5HA. Tel (01707) 654037

Synopsis
Girls ★ Day ★ Ages 4–11 ★ 168 pupils ★ Fees: £4,140–£4,470
Head: Mrs Morag Johnston, 38, appointed 1993.
First-rate, traditional prep school; good teaching; excellent facilities.

Profile
Background   Founded 1940; established on present site 1944. Attractive Victorian house in delightful, one-and-a-half acre setting; stables converted into music rooms, art, pottery, design/technology centre; later additions include bright new classrooms; facilities are excellent. School has use of two-acre field behind.

Atmosphere   Delightfully cosy (perhaps a bit precious); uniformed domestic staff add to the impression of a bygone era. Very good pastoral care; friendly, committed teachers; polite, purposeful girls in pristine uniforms. Supportive parents.

Admissions   Strictly first come, first served; 24 places a year; 2000 filling up rapidly. Most live locally; predominantly from middle-class backgrounds; some are the daughters of former pupils.

The head   Friendly, approachable (children not in awe of her and keen to show their work); strong leader. BA from Durham; taught at the Dorset prep school founded by her parents; previously head of pre-prep at Thomas's, Battersea. Divorced; no children.

The teaching   Good: traditional in style; dependable, long-serving, all-female staff. National curriculum plus; French from age five; specialist teaching (and homework) begins at age eight; excellent science lab (would put many secondary schools to shame); lots of computers. Average class size 24 (but 12 for English, maths, science); specialist help for dyslexics; no scholarship class. Strong music: 60% learn an instrument; orchestra, choirs.

Results   Good; regular scholarships to Haberdashers' Aske's Girls'.

Destinations   Queenswood, St Albans High, North London Collegiate, City of London Girls' etc.

Sport   Lots on offer: netball, tennis, rounders, pop lacrosse, athletics; regular fixtures. On-site facilities include all-weather court for netball/tennis.

Remarks   Good all round; shrinking violets will flourish here.

SUMMER FIELDS ♂
Oxford OX2 7EN. Tel (01865) 554433

Synopsis
Boys ★ Boarding and day ★ Ages 8–13 ★ 255 pupils (95% boarding) ★ Fees: £10,620 boarding; £7,110 day
Head: Robin Badham-Thornhill, 43, appointed September 1997.
First-rate, lively school; very good teaching and results; exceptionally good facilities.

Profile
Background   Founded 1864. Elegant, golden brick buildings surrounded by 60 acres of gardens, playing fields and farmland; latest additions include art, design/technology centre.

Atmosphere   Whole school buzzes with activity and enthusiasm. Competition is the mainspring of life: boys divided into leagues, earn points for conduct, work and games. Classrooms mainly new, large, light, attractively furnished; dining hall (complete with high table and portraits) is imposingly panelled and echoes accordingly.

Admissions   Entry by tests in English and maths and observation during a half day at the school (to see whether the child will fit in); most of above average intelligence, some very clever indeed. Places cannot be guaranteed until 2001; names can, however, be placed on a waiting list. Pupils mainly from upper and upper middle-class families in London and the South East. Boarding houses carpeted, centrally-heated, comfortable; profusion of soft toys, garish posters, photographs.

The head   New appointment (predecessor had been in post 24 years). Read economics and politics at Exeter; previously housemaster at Cheltenham and headmaster for four years of Lambrook (now Lambrook & Haileybury, qv). Able, energetic. Married (wife much involved in school life); two young daughters.

The teaching   Varied in style but uniformly excellent. Able, enthusiastic staff have high expectations (suggested reading list for a nine-year-old runs to 44 titles) and offer constant encouragement; they make the boys want to learn. Maximum class size 16 but most much smaller; pupils grouped by ability in last three years; lots of prep. 'Tests', the boys complain engagingly, 'happen all the time'. Very strong music: 70% learn an instrument; 30 practice rooms; orchestras, choirs etc. Each form spends up to 10 days a year at a château in France to improve their French.

Results   Excellent: 24 scholarships to Eton since 1991; no Common Entrance disappointments since 1990.

Destinations   Mainly Eton and Radley; also Harrow, Marlborough, St Edward's Oxford, Stowe, Winchester.

Sport   Fine facilities, including new sports hall (with squash and fives courts), two swimming pools (indoor and outdoor), adventure playground, shooting range, nine-hole golf course. Respectable match record, but not a particularly sporty school; those who are not keen are allowed to opt out.

Remarks   Excellent, traditional school. Boys receive a solid grounding in the sciences and the arts in an atmosphere that encourages them to see learning as a pleasure.

SUNNINGDALE ♂
Sunningdale, Berkshire SL5 9PY. Tel (01344) 20159

Synopsis
Boys ★ Boarding ★ Ages 8–13 ★ 104 pupils ★ Fees: £7,950
Heads: Nick and Tim Dawson, 64, appointed 1967.
Small, traditional school; good all-round education for boys of a wide range of abilities; strong sporting tradition.

Profile
Background   Founded 1874; red-brick Victorian villa (feels more like a country house than a school) plus later additions (including a chapel) in 23 acres of lawns, playing fields and woodland close to Windsor Great Park; good facilities for art, design/technology, computing. School, which is privately owned, has an old-world style reminiscent of a more elegant and leisurely age: among the last of a dying breed.

Atmosphere   Very traditional: relaxed, cheerful but also orderly and well-mannered; boys (who automatically stand for visitors) on easy but respectful terms with teachers; firm Christian ethos (daily chapel, grace at meals). Good citizenship rewarded; anti-social behaviour leads to loss of privileges (eg missing the ice-cream van on Sunday).

Admissions   Non-selective (many register at birth – but school is not full); wide ability range. Most pupils from London (City, professional backgrounds); 10% from Scotland; some fathers are old boys; few are 'first-time buyers' of independent education. Pleasant boarding accommodation in light, freshly painted dormitories (six to 12 beds); seniors in individual small wooden cubicles (much adorned with posters); ancient communal bathing facilities (no showers); no weekly boarding. Wholesome, plentiful food.

The heads   Identical twins; courteous, engaging, completely dedicated; they carry on a remarkable double-act with evident *joie de vivre*. After Cothill and Eton (where they decided their ambition was to run a prep school) and a period in the Army, they went into teaching, bought the school in 1967, have run it jointly ever since and plan to go on doing so for at least another five years (when it will probably be taken over by Tim Dawson's eldest son, Tom). Both teach a full timetable, know all the boys very well and are involved in every aspect of the school. Nick Dawson a bachelor; Tim Dawson married (wife runs the domestic side); four children.

The teaching   Good: traditional in style and content; skilled staff (most stay about five years); emphasis on good grounding, grammar, spelling, punctuation. Particular strengths in maths, French (school owns a farmhouse in Normandy), classics (all do Latin, more able add Greek); good science (well-equipped new lab). Boys go at their own pace; extra help for those who need it; potential scholars may spend two years at the top; weekly grades for effort and achievement; fortnightly form orders; average class size 12. Lively drama, music; 75% learn an instrument.

Results   Good Common Entrance record; average of one academic scholarship a year.

Destinations   Most to Eton, Harrow, Stowe.

Sport   Strong tradition. Main activities: cricket, tennis, athletics, soccer, rugby, squash, fives, cross-country; good record against other schools. Facilities include small outdoor pool, sports hall, five-hole golf course.

Remarks   Old-fashioned, happy school. Recommended.

SWANBOURNE HOUSE ♂ ♀
Swanbourne, Milton Keynes, Buckinghamshire MK17 0HZ. Tel (01296) 720264

Synopsis
Co-educational ★ Day and boarding ★ Ages 3–13 ★ 334 pupils (80% day, 59% boys) ★ Fees: £1,830–£6,965 day; £8,895 boarding
Joint heads: Stephen, 41, and Julie, 39, Goodhart, appointed 1996.
Friendly, civilised school; good teaching; lots of extra-curricular activities.

Profile
Background   Founded 1920 as a small boarding prep school and expanded steadily; girls first admitted late 1970s; pre-prep department opened 1982, nursery 1993. Spacious Victorian mansion in attractive, extensive grounds on the edge of a sleepy village; later additions provide good teaching accommodation and facilities.

Atmosphere   Relaxed, friendly, cheerful; emphasis on care and consideration; not a competitive environment. High expectations of behaviour; very little need for sanctions; responsive, friendly, well-mannered pupils. Daily morning prayers in school chapel; strong Christian ethos but children of other faiths welcome. Boarding school timetable: pupils stay until 7 pm; lessons on Saturday mornings.

Admissions   Non-selective entry in early years; interview and assessment at age seven and after; most pupils from professional/middle-class backgrounds. Dormitories (four to eight beds) in high-ceilinged, pleasant rooms (lovely views); girls and boys on separate floors. Some scholarships, bursaries.

The heads   Warm, enthusiastic, experienced; he climbs mountains (seven times up Kilimanjaro), she sings folksongs; previously joint deputies and, later, acting heads, of Windlesham House (qv). Two children (one a pupil here).

The teaching   Thorough, from solid grounding in pre-prep (small classes in bright, cheerful rooms) to Common Entrance. Well-qualified, committed staff (a third live in the school grounds); mixture of formal and informal methods (multiplication exercises followed by enthusiastic 'hands-on' shopping). French introduced at seven, Latin from nine; good facilities for art, technology, computing, science (computer and art rooms never locked – children trusted to be sensible). Timetabled homework; high standards expected; spelling corrected. Pupils grouped by ability into two or three streams but can go ahead at their own speed; potential scholars may spend additional year at top of school; equally good support for those with learning difficulties (full-time remedial teacher); average class size 12. Music a strength: very good choral singing (young director with very high standards – no sloppy diction); good drama facilities in new hall. Wide range of extra-curricular activities.

Results   Good: no Common Entrance failure for four years.

Destinations   Wide range: Bedford, Oundle, Stowe, Sevenoaks, Tudor Hall, Queen Anne's, Eton, Rugby, Bloxham, Headington, Berkhamsted, Oxford High and some local state schools.

Sport   Quite a strong tradition: lots of matches against other schools; reasonably good record. Main games: rugby, soccer, hockey, cricket, cross-country for boys; netball, hockey, soccer, rounders for girls. Facilities include extensive playing fields, all-weather pitch, squash court, large gym, tiny swimming pool.

Remarks   Attractive school; recommended.

TOCKINGTON MANOR ♂ ♀
Tockington, near Bristol BS12 4NY. Tel (01454) 613229

Synopsis
Co-educational ★ Day and boarding ★ Ages 2–13 ★ 191 pupils (60% boys, 87% day) ★ Fees: £6,120 day; £9,090 boarding
Head: Richard Tovey, 48, appointed 1975.
Attractive, traditional school; good teaching; fine facilities.

Profile
Background Opened 1947 by present head's father; delightful Queen Anne manor farmhouse plus sympathetic additions in 28 acres of carefully tended gardens and woodland.

Atmosphere A family school: cosy chintz furniture; bowls of cut flowers on gleaming mahogany tables; huge boxes of muddy boots outside every door. Caring, friendly relations between staff and well-behaved children. Smart uniform (long, grey trousers at seven). Saturday morning 'enrichment workshops' at no extra charge.

Admissions First come, first served, plus informal interview. Most children from middle-class homes in Bristol, Bath and across the Severn Bridge (fleet of buses). First-rate boarding accommodation (cheerful dormitories, teddies galore, exceptionally good food); numbers are down but occasional boarding is increasingly popular. Some scholarships.

The head Able, enthusiastic, long-serving (the quintessential prep school head). Married (wife very much involved); four children (two are pupils here).

The teaching Good: formal in style; experienced, committed staff (equal numbers of women and men), nearly all appointed by present head. Broad curriculum: science taught as three separate subjects (in preparation for Common Entrance); French from age eight; Latin, Spanish, German on offer (languages are strong). Pupils grouped by ability in some subjects from eight; scholarship class in final year; extra help for dyslexics and the gifted; average class size 15. Lots of music: choirs, orchestra, various ensembles. Very good library, run by the children.

Results Regular scholarships, particularly to Clifton.

Destinations Wide range, including Malvern, Badminton, Dauntsey's, Marlborough, Cheltenham Ladies'.

Sport Facilities include two large games fields, five tennis courts, outdoor pool. Main sports: rugby, soccer, netball, hockey, cricket, cross-country (good record). Riding, judo, archery, gymnastics also on offer.

Remarks Happy, hard-working school; recommended.

TWYFORD ♂ ♀
Twyford, Winchester, Hampshire SO21 1NW. Tel (01962) 712269

Synopsis
Co-educational ★ Day and boarding ★ Ages 3–13 ★ 263 pupils (72% boys, 83% day) ★ Fees: £7,185 day; £9,780 boarding
Head: Philip Fawkes, 44, appointed Jan 1997.
Successful, traditional prep school; very good teaching and results; strong music, sport.

Profile

Background   Roots go back to 17th century (pupils are recorded as having cheered Charles II on his way to Winchester); moved 1809 to present Queen Anne house in 20 acres of attractive grounds; pleasant chapel; £2 million spent on facilities (including new classroom block and music school) in past 10 years. Thomas Hughes, author of Tom Brown's Schooldays, was a pupil here.

Atmosphere   Big emphasis on discipline, good manners; well-organised pastoral care; warm relations between staff and pupils. Day ends at 6 pm; lessons on Saturday mornings. Motto: 'It's dogged as does it'.

Admissions   School over-subscribed and becoming increasingly selective (IQs 115–130); entry to prep department at age eight by tests in English, maths. Parents mostly landowners, farmers, professionals. Boarders in dormitories of up to eight.

The head   Keen cricketer and ornithologist; previously head of a prep school in Scotland; has an MBA in educational management. Married (wife much involved in school life).

The teaching   First-rate; committed, well-qualified staff. Standard prep school curriculum: French from age seven, Latin from 10; strong science; very good art, design, technology. Pupils grouped by ability; scholarship class; maximum class size 18. Strong musical tradition: 150 learn an instrument; two choirs, two orchestras. Lots of clubs (chess, Scottish country dancing) and extra-curricular activities.

Results   Good Common Entrance record; regular scholarships.

Destinations   A third to Winchester; others to Bedales, Bradfield, Canford, Charterhouse, Eton, Harrow, King Edward VI Southampton, Millfield, Oundle, Radley, Shiplake, Wellington, Westminster.

Sports   An important feature of school life; all major sports offered; cricket a particular strength. Facilities include sports hall, indoor pool, tennis courts, netball court.

Remarks   Attractive school; good all round.

VINEHALL ♂ ♀
Robertsbridge, East Sussex TN32 5JL. Tel (01580) 880413

Synopsis
Co-educational ★ Day and boarding ★ Age 3–13 ★ 386 pupils (60% boys, 77% day) ★ Fees: £6,660 day; £8,970 boarding
Head: David Chaplin, 49, appointed 1977.
First-rate, well-run school; very good teaching; lots on offer.

Profile

Background   Founded 1938; former country house (imposing square tower) standing in 50 acres on a ridge over-looking the South Downs; pleasant modern additions include new classrooms, science labs, theatre, pre-prep department.

Atmosphere   Happy, busy, purposeful; strong Christian ethos (head is Anglican, his wife Catholic); big emphasis on rewarding good work and behaviour (the prize is is a tea party with the head and his wife). Camps built in the woods; fishing, cycling in the grounds. Parents much involved (and welcome to drop in any time).

Admissions   By interview; most children of above-average ability from professional/middle-class homes within a 20-mile radius; a third of boarders' parents live abroad. Pleasant dormitories in the main house; no weekly boarding. Means-tested bursaries available.

The head Long-serving; took over the headship from his father-in-law. Able, shrewd, boundlessly enthusiastic (school has flourished under his leadership). Read English at Durham; taught at Eastbourne and Tonbridge. Married (wife teaches here full time); three children (all were pupils here).

The teaching Generally formal in style; experienced staff, nearly all appointed by present head. Standard prep school curriculum; all do French, Latin from age nine; lots of computers. Pupils grouped by ability in maths, French for age eight; scholarship form from 10; extra help for dyslexics and others with special needs; progress closely monitored (monthly report cards); average class size 14. Strong music: nearly all learn an instrument; two choirs, two bands, various ensembles. Lots of extracurricular activities. Regular language exchange with a school in France.

Results Good: 45 scholarships over past five years to Benenden, Eastbourne, King's Canterbury, Lancing, Sevenoaks, Sherborne, Tonbridge, Westminster, Winchester.

Destinations As well as the above: Bradfield, Millfield, Cranbrook, Moira House, Stonyhurst etc.

Sport Plenty on offer: rugby, soccer, hockey, netball, tennis, cricket, swimming, golf, cross-country. Facilities include extensive playing fields, new sports hall, tennis courts, nine-hole golf course, indoor pool.

Remarks Very good school for able children; recommended.

WARWICK ♂ ♀
Bridge Field, Banbury Road, Warwick CV34 6PL. Tel (01926) 491545

Synopsis
Co-educational (girls 3–11, boys 3–7) ★ Day ★ 471 pupils (75% girls) ★ Fees: £1,545–£4,635
Head: Mrs Dianne Robinson, 39, appointed September 1997.
First-rate school; very good teaching; lots on offer.

Profile
Background Founded 1879 as part of King's High, Warwick (qv); separated 1944; moved 1971 to purpose-built premises on pleasant, secure four-and-a-half-acre site adjoining Warwick School (qv); later additions include nursery department, music block; some classrooms in 'temporary' huts. Numbers have risen steadily.

Atmosphere Happy, busy, well-ordered. Enthusiastically competitive house system; daily act of worship. Parents closely involved.

Admissions First come, first served. All from middle-class families; half the children have an IQ of more than 120.

The head New appointment (distinguished predecessor had been in post 16 years). Down-to-earth, experienced. Science graduate; previously head of the junior school at Wakefield Girls' High.

The teaching High quality: formal in style; experienced, first-rate staff; bright, confident children; computers in every classroom. Boys transfer to Warwick at age seven; girls stay on for specialist teaching of standard prep school curriculum; pupils grouped by ability in maths, English, science; extra help for dyslexics; average class size 22. Lots of art, drama, music; two-thirds learn an instrument.

Results   Good; frequent scholarships (including music).
Destinations   About half to King's High; remainder to other independent or grammar schools.
Sport   All take part in a balanced programme of games, gymnastics, dance. Main sports: netball, hockey, athletics, rounders, tennis. Sports hall shared with King's High.
Remarks   Very good all round; recommended.

WELLESLEY HOUSE ♂ ♀
Broadstairs, Kent CT1O 2DG. Tel (01843) 862991

Synopsis
Co-educational ★ Boarding and day ★ Ages 7–13 ★ 149 pupils (66% boys, 85% boarding) ★ Fees: £9,225 boarding; £6,852 day
Head: Richard Steel, 48, appointed 1990.
Successful, traditional school; good teaching; family atmosphere; lots on offer.

Profile
Background   Founded 1869; moved to present 16-acre site and solid, red-brick, purpose-built premises 1900; co-educational since 1974. Facilities are good.
Atmosphere   Traditional values; chapel central to school life; first-rate pastoral care (parents encouraged to phone whenever they want to); cheerful, chatty pupils; feels like an extended family. Beautiful gardens; croquet hoops on the front lawn; an oasis of calm and order. Practical, simple uniform. Small, caged animals welcome.
Admissions   By interview (with parents and child); tests in maths, English if head suspects a problem. Pupils drawn from all over the UK; many are the children of former pupils. Separate houses for juniors, girls; carpeted, curtained dormitories for up to 10 (lots of teddies, photos, posters). Good, home-cooked food. Scholarships, bursaries available.
The head   Read biology at London; previously head of a Hertfordshire prep school. Married (wife much involved in school life); three children (two are pupils here).
The teaching   Traditional in style ('Children are taught, not given a text book and told to get on with an exercise'); experienced, committed staff. Standard prep school curriculum; all do Latin; Greek on offer; all become computer-literate. Older pupils grouped by ability in maths; progress closely monitored (marks published fortnightly); extra help for those who need it; average class size 14. Very good art; lots of music; more than half learn an instrument; choir, orchestra. Wide range of extra-curricular activities, including Scottish and country dancing, ballet, needlework, astronomy, drama, modelling, carpentry; frequent trips to theatres, battlefields, castles, museums – and the beach.
Results   Good; regular scholarships to leading schools (Rugby, Charterhouse, Millfield, Fettes).
Destinations   Wide range, but principally Eton, Harrow, King's Canterbury.
Sport   Chiefly: soccer, rugby, hockey, tennis, athletics, rounders; cricket a particular strength; volleyball, badminton, golf (visiting professional) also on offer. Facilities include sports hall, indoor pool, tennis and squash courts, shooting range.
Remarks   Good all round.

WESTMINSTER CATHEDRAL CHOIR SCHOOL ♂
Ambrosden Avenue, London SW1P 1QH. Tel (0171) 798 9081

Synopsis
Boys ★ Roman Catholic ★ Day and boarding ★ Ages 8–13 ★ 90 pupils (30 boarders, all choristers) ★ Fees: £6,675 day; £3,300 choristers
Head: Charles Foulds, 41, appointed 1995.
Small, exceptional school; good teaching; outstanding musical training.

Profile
Background Founded 1901 by Cardinal Vaughan to provide 30 choristers for the new cathedral at Westminster; saved from closure in 1976 by Cardinal Hume, who reconstituted it with 60 places for fee-paying day boys. Rather cramped site in the shadow of the cathedral, overlooked by neighbouring blocks of flats; large asphalt playground put to maximum use.

Atmosphere Dedication to the life of the cathedral and devotion to the Roman Catholic faith are central. School pulsates with energy and purpose, yet has a noticeably kindly and nurturing feel. Pianos in odd corners, window ledges piled high with art work; the sound of someone practising a musical instrument always in the background. A high degree of self-discipline is implicit in the lives of the choristers, whose days are extraordinarily busy and demanding. No formal rules but decent behaviour and kindliness to others expected. All choristers board in one room: austere but homely.

Admissions Annual intake of six choristers (who must be Catholics) and 12 dayboys (who need not be); entry by tests and interview. Choristers selected after voice trials; head is looking not just for voice potential and musicality, but for the ability to fit into the community and a special indefinable quality that signals a potential chorister (stamina essential). Day boys mainly from professional and wealthy backgrounds.

The head Read German and French at Swansea; spent 16 years at Stonyhurst (qv) as housemaster, head of languages and deputy head. Married; four children (one a pupil here).

The teaching Imaginative and at times inspired; highly-qualified staff (half women); academic standards are high. Standard prep school curriculum; very good French; computers widely used. Pupils grouped by ability in all subjects. The music, not surprisingly, is superb; choristers all learn two instruments (they practise twice a day, once before breakfast, in addition to two choir rehearsals); most of the day boys learn at least one. Not much time for hobbies (or writing home).

Results Good: most go on to the school of their choice; choristers virtually certain of a music scholarship somewhere.

Destinations Chiefly Catholic public schools – Ampleforth, Stonyhurst, Oratory, Worth; also Westminster, St Paul's, Eton, Harrow.

Sport Apart from the playground (used extensively for roller skating), school has no facilities of its own; pupils have access to Westminster's playing fields for football and tennis; swimming and badminton in nearby sports centre; indoor cricket at the Oval.

Remarks HMI concluded (1994): 'The school is a civilised and supportive community with a friendly ethos. Pupils work hard and are eager to learn. Teaching is conscientious.'

WESTMINSTER UNDER SCHOOL ♂
27 Vincent Square, London SW1P 2NN. Tel (0171) 821 5788

Synopsis
Boys ★ Day ★ Ages 8–13 ★ 270 pupils ★ Fees: £6,870
Head: Gerry Ashton, 51, appointed 1992.
Happy, lively, academic school; first-rate teaching and results.

Profile
Background   Founded 1943 in the precincts of Westminster School (qv), with which it shares a governing body; moved 1981 to present exceedingly cramped premises (in some classrooms, boys are almost on each other's laps). Pleasant red-brick buildings overlooking Vincent Square; classrooms and corridors decorated in bright, cheerful colours.

Atmosphere   Busy, cheerful, well-mannered; free speech encouraged (indeed, required); boys great fun to teach. Intensely competitive house system; cups awarded termly for work, games and all-round achievement; good work earns a 'dig' (digniora), excellent work three 'digs' (dignissimum), bad work a 'scel' (scelera). Daily 20-minute silent reading period; chairman of governors hears every first-year read aloud at least once every three weeks. Pink and grey uniform for all.

Admissions   At age eight (120 try for 40 places) by written papers in maths, English plus an IQ test (no interview); at 10 (60 apply for 20 places) by exam and interview. School looks for (and finds) 'boys with ability to cope academically, who are sociable and responsive, and/or talented in other ways'. Pupils drawn from cosmopolitan backgrounds all over London, but particularly Kensington and Chelsea; 'feeder' pre-preps include Eaton House, Connaught House, Hampstead Hill, Garden House.

The head   (Master) Read modern languages at Cambridge; lectured at Birmingham and Strathclyde universities; joined the senior school in 1975 to teach Spanish and French. Married (to a professor of English at University College, London); three children.

The teaching   Enthusiastic, professional; mainly front-of-class (plenty of question and answer); Youthful, well-qualified staff of 22 (nine women). First-year pupils ('Petty B' – a corruption of petit) taught most subjects by a form teacher; specialist teaching from second year ('Petty A'). Very broad curriculum; all do Latin; Greek, German, Italian, Spanish on offer; computers in every classroom. Frequent tests from the start (spelling, tables); all work graded twice a term; marks for effort and attainment. Pupils grouped by ability in maths, French from third year; further division into scholarship and Common Entrance streams thereafter; average class size 17–20. Music particularly strong (nothing here is weak). Numerous extra-curricular clubs, societies; lots of trips, exchanges.

Results   Very good; all go on to first-choice school (after careful consultation between head, staff and parents); regular scholarships.

Destinations   Up to 80% to the senior school (but a place there is not guaranteed); remainder to Winchester, Eton, Radley, Bryanston, Dulwich, Highgate etc.

Sport   Good football but not great cricket ('No one is totally crestfallen if we don't win'). Facilities in Vincent Square include tennis courts, cricket nets and plenty of space for football; badminton, gymnastics, squash, swimming at Queen Mother Sports Centre; fencing, judo etc also on offer.

Remarks   Exciting school; delightful pupils. Recommended.

WINCHESTER HOUSE ♂ ♀
Brackley, Northamptonhsire NN13 7AZ. Tel (01280) 702483

Synopsis
Co-educational ★ Boarding and day ★ Ages 7–14 (plus associated pre-prep)
★ 186 pupils (75% boys, 54% boarders) ★ Fees: £9,615 boarding; £7,260 day
Head: Jeremy Griffith, 41, appointed September 1997.
Fine, traditional prep school; very good teaching and results; strong sport.

Profile
Background Founded as a boys' boarding school 1875; moved to present 18-acre site 1922; girls and day pupils admitted 1976. Victorian manor house (plus Elizabethan chapel) at the end of the town's main street; some classrooms in attractively converted stable block, others in 'temporary' huts. Lots of space to play. Pre-prep department (70 pupils aged three to seven) near by.

Atmosphere Charming: a real family feel; childhood protected here, 'sophistication' kept at bay. Very good relations between staff and well-behaved children (discipline impressive though unobtrusive); activities mostly structured and programmed (this is not a free-wheeling school). Day starts with scripture lesson and prayers.

Admissions By interview and informal tests; wide range of abilities. Few foreign pupils; a third of parents are 'first-time buyers' of independent education. Boys' boarding accommodation (in the manor house) is pleasant but slightly overcrowded; girls in new house.

The head Recent appointment (distinguished predecessor had been in post 21 years). Able, confident, experienced (has taught at Horris Hill, the Dragon, Windlesham House). Educated at Winchester and Bristol. Married (wife is in charge of the first-years); two small children.

The teaching First-rate: largely traditional in style but with plenty of pupil involvement; able, dedicated staff. Traditional prep school curriculum: all do Latin, French; Greek on offer; less emphasis on science, design/technology. Children grouped by ability in (unusually) all subjects from second year; extra help for dyslexics and slow learners; progress closely monitored (three-weekly 'bulletins' to parents); class sizes vary between 14 and 18. Lots of music (two-thirds learn an instrument) and drama.

Results Good Common Entrance and scholarship record; average of eight academic awards a year to leading schools.

Destinations Rugby, Oundle, St Edward's Oxford, etc.

Sport Strong: good coaching; impressive record. Main sports: cricket, hockey, rugby, netball, rounders, squash, shooting, athletics. Swimming, clay-pigeon shooting, golf, badminton, basketball, dance also on offer. Facilities include fine playing fields, outdoor pool, tennis and squash courts.

Remarks Attractive school; recommended.

WINDLESHAM HOUSE ♂ ♀
Washington, Pulborough, West Sussex RH20 4AY. Tel (01903) 873207

Synopsis
Co-educational ★ Boarding ★ Ages 8–13 ★ 241 pupils (62% boys) ★ Fees: £9,825
Head: Philip Lough, 44, appointed 1996.
Attractive, friendly school; good teaching and results; lots on offer.

Profile
Background   Founded 1837; run successfully for 157 years by five generations of the Malden family; numbers have since fallen quite sharply. Gracious Queen Anne house plus many later additions (including fine theatre-cum-sports hall) in idyllic 60-acre country estate on the edge of the South Downs; co-educational since 1967. Small pre-prep department (ages four to seven – day only) opened September 1997.

Atmosphere   Relaxed, cheerful; strong family feel; very good pastoral care; friendly relations between staff and pupils. Regular contact with home positively encouraged (phones in dormitories for bedtime chat); good food (emphasis on healthy eating); no uniform (but no logos on sweat shirts). Lessons on Saturday mornings; minimum of 100 on site every weekend.

Admissions   Non-selective; wide range of abilities. Most children from South London, Surrey, Sussex; 100 have parents based abroad (diplomatic, Services, multi-nationals). Comfortable boarding accommodation; carpeted, curtained dormitories of up to 12; own duvets; lots of soft toys.

The head   (Name pronounced 'Lock') Warm, energetic, approachable. Read modern languages at Oxford; previously a housemaster at Marlborough. Married (wife teaches here); three children.

The teaching   Good: informal but challenging; children encouraged to express and develop their ideas. Fairly youthful full-time staff of 28 (18 men). Standard Common Entrance curriculum; French from age 10; compulsory Latin from 11; IT used across the curriculum; very good design/technology. Pupils grouped by ability in English, maths from 10, French from 11; scholarship class in final year; extra help for dyslexics (but not for those severely afflicted); coaching for those who speak English as a foreign language; average class size 16–20. Three-weekly grades for effort but no form orders, to minimise comparisons and build confidence; nightly prep. Flourishing art, drama, music; two-thirds learn an instrument; two orchestras, two choirs. Lots of weekend activities (including building dens in the woods).

Results   Good: 48 scholarships in the past four years to senior schools including Marlborough, Sevenoaks, Bedales, Bryanston, St Leonard's Mayfield, Oundle.

Destinations   As well as the above: Eton, Harrow, Cheltenham Ladies', Woldingham, Rugby, Lancing, Roedean, Bedgebury, Ardingly.

Sport   Games twice a week: rugby, soccer, cricket for boys; netball, rounders for girls; hockey, tennis, cross-country, athletics for both. Facilities include sports hall, small indoor pool.

Remarks   Child-centred school which takes Common Entrance in its stride.

Secondary Schools

THE ABBEY ♀ *
17 Kendrick Road, Reading, Berkshire RG1 5DZ. Tel (0118) 987 2256

Synopsis
Independent ★ Girls ★ Day ★ Ages 11–18 (plus associated junior school) ★
755 pupils ★ 198 in sixth form ★ Fees: £4,620
Head: Miss Barbara Sheldon, 56, appointed 1991.
Strong, traditional, academic school; very good teaching and results.

Profile
Background Founded 1887; moved 1905 to present six-acre site in quiet, tree-lined road; red-brick buildings plus solid later additions, including good science labs, fine assembly hall, vast sixth-form centre reminiscent of an airport lounge (acres of curved, caramel-coloured sofas and little tables). Some classrooms rather crowded. Junior school (co-educational to age seven) near by.

Atmosphere Christian foundation (portraits of bishops line the stairs); reassuringly timeless ('Church of England teaching is given'). Warm heart of a proud, provincial grammar school still beats here: sensible green skirts and jerseys; rows of solid desks with lids (to whisper behind and bang down hard when cross); happy, chattering groups at the bus stop hung about with shapeless bundles and violin cases.

Admissions By competitive tests at 11 in English, maths, verbal reasoning (grammar-school standard required) plus interview. Virtually all junior school applicants (comprising half the intake) are admitted. Mostly from professional backgrounds; wide catchment area (parents arrange special buses). Scholarships, bursaries, music awards.

The head Read English at Birmingham; taught in state and independent schools before becoming deputy head of King Edward VI Handsworth. Strong believer in single-sex education; keen to reduce the proportion who leave after GCSE for co-educational sixth forms. Accessible, firm (but, say the girls, she listens).

The teaching Stable, happy staff; thorough, sensible teaching. Rigorous curriculum; big emphasis on sciences (taught as three separate subjects); computing starts at age four, compulsory to GCSE); all do French, Latin from first year and can add Spanish, Greek or German. Most take 11 GCSEs; more than half take science A-levels. Well-used art rooms; music, speech and drama available. Extra-curricular activities include Duke of Edinburgh award scheme.

Results (1997) GCSE: all gained at least five grades A–C. A-level: 69% of entries graded A or B.

Destinations About 75% stay on for A-levels; of these, nearly all proceed to university (up to 20 a year to Oxbridge).

Sport Lots available; hockey, netball, tennis all played to a high standard; rowing on the Thames. Facilities include all-weather tennis courts, fine indoor pool.

* Key to symbols: ♂ = boys; ♀ = girls; ♂ ♀ = co-educational

Remarks   Solid, well-run, purposeful school.

ABINGDON ♂
Park Road, Abingdon, Oxfordshire OX14 1DE. Tel (01235) 531755

Synopsis
Independent ★ Boys ★ Day and boarding ★ Ages 11–18 ★ 780 pupils (80% day) ★ 260 in sixth form ★ Fees: £5,946 day; £10,962 boarding
Head: Michael St John Parker, 56, appointed 1975.
Good academic school; first-rate teaching and results; strong music and sport.

Profile
Background   Known to exist in 1256 but re-endowed (after the dissolution of Abingdon Abbey) 1563 by John Roysse, mercer: Mercers' Company maintains a lively (and generous) interest. Moved to present attractive 35-acre site and purpose-built, red-brick premises 1870; later additions include £2.5 million teaching and sixth-form centre. Formerly Direct Grant, reverted to full independence 1976.

Atmosphere   Fizzing: intelligent, lively, unpretentious boys; able, hard-working teachers. Well-organised pastoral care.

Admissions   At 11 by school's own exams in English, maths, reasoning; at 13 by Common Entrance (60% mark required). Phasing out of assisted places, which about 100 hold, may force the school to lower its entry standards. Most from business, professional, Service families. Means-tested scholarships available. Pleasant, spacious boarding houses recently refurbished.

The head   Exceptionally long-serving; still enthusiastic. Read history at Cambridge; taught at King's, Canterbury and Winchester. Describes his management style as 'pragmatic' – 'high-handed' say some. Liked by the boys, who joke about his being a stickler for traditional standards (hates loud noise). Married, four children.

The teaching   Well-prepared, well-managed, interesting lessons; quieter boys drawn in by judicious questioning and gentle humour. All-graduate staff of 63 (six women), some of whom have been here even longer than the head. Broad curriculum: all who join at 11 take Latin for first two years plus German or Russian; French, Greek also on offer; science taught as three separate subjects; good computing; compulsory religious education. Pupils grouped by ability in maths, French, Latin; more able take GCSEs in these a year early. Wide choice of subjects at A-level, some in conjunction with girls at St Helen & St Katharine (qv); broad general studies programme. Lots of music: two-thirds learn an instrument. Extra-curricular activities include cadet force, Duke of Edinburgh award scheme, community service.

Results   (1997) GCSE: all gained at least five grades A–C. A-level: 67% of entries graded A or B.

Destinations   Nearly all go on to university (average 20 a year to Oxbridge).

Sport   All main games; everyone expected to participate at least twice a week; rowing a particular strength; fencing, sailing, golf also on offer. Facilities include extensive playing fields, modern sports hall, boathouse on the Thames, heated outdoor pool, eight tennis courts, shooting range.

Remarks   Good all round.

ADAMS' GRAMMAR ♂
Newport, Shropshire TF10 7BD. Tel (01952) 810698

Synopsis
Grammar (voluntary-aided, grant-maintained) ★ Boys (plus girls in sixth form) ★ Day and boarding ★ Ages 11–18 ★ 680 pupils (85% day) ★ 200 in sixth form (80% boys) ★ Fees (boarding only): £4,575
Head: James Richardson, 48, appointed 1994.
Well-run, traditional grammar school; boarding on offer; increasing emphasis on technology; good music.

Profile
Background Founded 1656 by William Adams, Haberdasher (links with the livery company retained); became voluntary-aided 1950; opted out of council control 1990; girls admitted to sixth form 1992; granted technology college status 1996. Hotch-potch of buildings of many styles and periods on original, now rather cramped, town-centre site; some classrooms bleak; recent additions include first-rate maths block, technology centre.

Atmosphere Pleasant, friendly, well-ordered; strong work ethic. Junior boarders live in style at Longford Hall, a Georgian mansion set in 100 acres a mile away; seniors in on-site, 18th-century town houses.

Admissions Over-subscribed: 250 apply for 100 places a year (up to 30 of which are reserved for suitably qualified boys living locally); entry by exam; top 25% of the ability range. Pupils mostly from middle-class/professional backgrounds in Telford, Wolverhampton, Stafford, Market Drayton, Shrewsbury; boarders from further afield, a few from abroad.

The head Enthusiastic, forceful; leads by example. Read economics at LSE; previously deputy head of Royal Grammar, Worcester (qv). Teaches business studies, politics, IT; believes technology is 'enriching the life-blood of the curriculum'. Married; two children (one was a pupil here).

The teaching Fairly formal but lively; particular strengths in maths, physics. Well-balanced curriculum; science taught as three separate subjects; good design/technology (links with local industry); homework closely monitored. Pupils grouped by ability in GCSE maths only; average class size 25, reducing to 15 at A-level. Good music (flourishing choir, orchestra, marching band). Wide range of extra-curricular activities, including well-supported cadet force, Duke of Edinburgh award scheme. Regular exchanges with schools in France, Germany.

Results (1997) GCSE: 97% gained at least five grades A–C. A-level: 46% of entries graded A or B

Destinations Nearly all go on to university (four or five a year to Oxbridge); head encourages pupils to take a 'gap' year first.

Sport Busy programme; good record; strengths in rugby, athletics, cricket. Facilities include five rugby, three hockey pitches, sports hall; also well-stocked fishing pool, shooting range.

Remarks Good all round.

ALDENHAM ♂
Elstree, Hertfordshire WD6 3AJ. Tel (01923) 858122

Synopsis
Independent ★ Boys (plus girls in sixth form) ★ Boarding and day ★ Ages 11–18 ★ 390 pupils (52% boarding) ★ 117 in sixth form (90% boys) ★ Fees: £8,685–£12,480-boarding, £5,463–£8,955 day
Head: Stephen Borthwick, 46, appointed 1994.
Small, supportive school; wide range of abilities; good sports facilities.

Profile
Background   Founded 1597; associated with the Brewers' Company, which still supports it. Victorian buildings plus later additions (including new junior house for 11 to 13-year-olds) on a 135-acre green belt site handy for the M25 and M1. Much refurbishment under way but some dingy corners remain. Numbers now the highest in the school's history.

Atmosphere   Caring community; wide range of abilities (including dyslexia); everyone treated with respect and tolerance. Boarding school ethos retained; compulsory chapel for all; day pupils stay until 9 pm. Parents predominately first-time buyers of independent education; 65% from abroad; 15% Jewish, 12% ethnic minorities. Staff accessible to parents and enjoy easy relations with pupils. Three boarding houses, one recently up-graded (attractive study-bedrooms); house loyalty taken seriously.

Admissions   Flexible: officially, 45%–50% mark required at Common Entrance but 10% score below that (and are thought to have something else to offer). Sixth-form entry for those with a 'reasonable expectation' of passing A-levels. Scholarships (including art, music, technology, sport) and bursaries on offer.

The head   Energetic, likeable; confesses to a 'love of children'; has a particular concern for those who fall outside the academic top 10% so assiduously courted by schools higher up the league tables. The school had been languishing and he has sharpened it up, winning praise from his HMC peers for the 'courage, intelligence, vision and determination' of his leadership. Grammar school educated; read physics at Bangor; taught at Rugby and Marlborough; his first headship. Married (his wife teaches English as a foreign language here); no children.

The teaching   Mainly traditional in style ('chalk-and-talk'). Staff of 44, a third appointed by the present head. Pupils grouped by ability in English and maths from the start, and in most other subjects subsequently. Up to a third (including 50 dyslexics) receive help from the learning support department. Standard national curriculum; Latin and Spanish on offer; first-rate provision for design/technology; enthusiastic music and drama. Most take nine GCSEs, including compulsory religious studies. Extensive programme of timetabled extra-curricular activities includes outdoor survival, camping, orienteering; well-supported Duke of Edinburgh award scheme.

Results   (1997) GCSE: 86% gained at least five grades A–C. A-level: modest 30% of entries graded A or B.

Destinations   Of 46 leavers, 26 proceed to university; most of the rest take vocational courses.

Sport   Extensive playing fields and magnificent hangar-like sports hall; facilities include Olympic-size indoor hockey pitch, cricket nets and bowling machine, fives courts, climbing wall. Main sports: soccer, basketball, cricket, hockey.

Remarks   Improving school; likely to instil confidence in boys who may not thrive in a more pressured environment.

ALICE OTTLEY ♀
Upper Tything, Worcester WR1 1HW. Tel (01905) 27061

Synopsis
Independent ★ Girls ★ Day ★ Ages 10–18 (plus associated junior school)
★ 561 pupils ★ 147 in sixth form ★ Fees: £5,406
Head: Miss Christine Sibbet, 56, appointed 1986.
Well-run, traditional school.

Profile
Background Founded 1883 as Worcester High School for Girls; renamed 1914 after its first head. Occupies a series of elegant Georgian houses on a cramped site fronting a busy main road close to the city centre; every nook and cranny in use; later additions include fine sports hall. Junior school in own grounds near by.

Atmosphere Happy, confident, well-ordered (everyone knows her place). Anglican by tradition but ecumenical in spirit. Sixth-formers have considerable freedom of dress.

Admissions Fairly selective: demand for places is strong; head admits any girl she feels will cope. Phasing out of assisted places (which 100 hold) will reduce the social mix. Pupils drawn from a 30-mile radius (coaches from most outlying towns); girls from junior school come up a year before the main entry at 11. Some scholarships, bursaries.

The head Only the fifth in 115 years. A traditional headmistress: quiet strength, patent authority, well respected. Read geography at Leicester (and teaches it to all 12-year-olds). Keen on gardening, walking, music, golf.

The teaching Formal in style (but girls are encouraged to speak their minds). Long-serving staff of 61 (four men), half appointed by present head. Pupils grouped by ability from the start; class sizes range from 20 to 24, smaller at A-level. Science (a strength) taught as three separate subjects; all do Latin from 11 and second modern language from 13. Good choice of subjects at A-level; nearly all take general studies. Strong drama, music (up to half learn an instrument). Lots of extra-curricular activities (school is a hive of activity at lunchtime), including Duke of Edinburgh award scheme.

Results (1997) GCSE: 94% gained at least five grades A–C. A-level: 50% of entries graded A or B.

Destinations Virtually all go on to university (six or seven a year to Oxbridge).

Sport Particular strengths in lacrosse (youth internationals), netball, trampolining. Tennis, athletics also popular. Playing fields a seven-minute walk away.

Remarks Good all round: not an academic hothouse but girls of middling ability do well.

ALLEYN'S ♂ ♀
Townley Road, London SE22 8SU. Tel (0181) 693 3422

Synopsis
Independent ★ Co-educational ★ Day ★ Ages 11–18 (plus associated junior school) ★ 920 pupils (equal numbers of boys and girls) ★ 261 in sixth form ★ Fees: £6,255
Head: Dr Colin Niven, 56, appointed 1992.
Attractive, well-run school; very good teaching and results; lots of art, drama, music, sport.

Profile
Background Founded 1620 by Edward Alleyn, Elizabethan actor-manager: the co-educational arm of the Dulwich triumvirate (with Dulwich College and James Allen's Girls). Established on present, 27-acre urban site 1882; formerly Direct Grant, opted for independence (and became co-educational) 1976. A jumble of buildings clustered round the original Victorian 'Big Hall': many are rather tired-looking 1970s additions but the most recent include a handsome sports hall (plus indoor pool), luxurious music school and custom-built junior school (ages 5 to 10, under their own headmistress); £1 million spent recently on refurbishment.

Atmosphere An exceptionally friendly, delightfully disorganised school that obviously works extremely well. Children expected to perform to their potential but no undue academic pressure; staff give freely of their time to help any who are struggling. First-rate pastoral care system; first and second years kept as discrete units (sixth-formers make themselves available for confidential chats). Neat uniform; sixth-formers in 'smart office dress'. Flourishing PTA runs after-school care scheme from 3.20 pm to 6 pm (and arranges parties to enable new parents to meet).

Admissions School is selective and over-subscribed: at 11, nearly 600 apply for 135 places. Entry by school's own tests in English, maths, verbal reasoning (minimum score of 110 required, average is 120); all applicants interviewed; 35% come from junior school, the rest split 60:40 between state primaries and prep schools. Labour's phasing out of assisted places, which 210 hold, will have a big impact: 'We'll become more socially exclusive, which I very much regret,' says head. Scholarships funded by the Saddlers' Company.

The head Able, enthusiastic, humane; insists on knowing what is going on in every corner of the school. Educated at Dulwich (head boy), Cambridge (modern languages) and has a doctorate from Lille. Was a housemaster at Fettes (taught Tony Blair French); previously head of Island School, Hong Kong and St George's, Rome. Bachelor; passions are opera, theatre and cats.

The teaching First-rate; formal in style (most classes in neat rows, teacher at the front) but informal in atmosphere. Well-qualified staff of 92 (slightly more men than women), a third appointed by present head. Broad curriculum: all must do two languages for GCSE (choice of French, German, Spanish, Latin); sciences taught as three separate subjects. Pupils grouped by ability in maths; extra help for dyslexics; average class size 26, reducing to 23 for GCSE, 10 at A-level. All do nine or 10 GCSEs and three A-levels (from a choice of 23, including art & design, music, theatre studies). Parents kept closely informed. First-rate provision for art (five studios) and music ('the jewel in the school's crown' – 400 individual lessons a week); strong drama (but no theatre). Extra-curricular activities include flourishing cadet force, Duke of Edinburgh award scheme; school has its own field centre in the Peak District. Regular language exchanges with schools

in France, Spain, Germany.
Results   (1997) GCSE: 98% gained at least five grades A–C. A-level: 63% of
entries graded A or B.
Destinations   Nearly 90% go on to university (about 10 a year to Oxbridge).
Sport   Everyone has a go, at a level and in a sphere appropriate to his/her abilities. Strongest areas are hockey, netball, soccer, cricket, swimming, athletics,
fives; opportunities also for basketball, gymnastics, dance, water polo, cross-
country, rounders, fencing, trampolining, badminton, volley ball. Good indoor
facilities; ample playing fields.
Remarks   HMC inspectors concluded (1995): 'Alleyn's is a very good school
where high standards are achieved across the curriculum and in a range of activities.' Warmly recommended.

ALL HALLOWS ♂ ♀
Crabtree Avenue, Penwortham, Preston PR1 0LN. Tel (01772) 746121

Synopsis
Comprehensive (voluntary-aided, Roman Catholic) ★ Co-educational ★ Ages
11–16 ★ 890 pupils (roughly equal numbers of boys and girls)
Head: Michael Flynn, 51, appointed 1984.
Sound, well-run school; good GCSE results; strong music, sport.

Profile
Background   Opened 1975 in response to local demand for a Catholic secondary school; achieved technology college status (with the help of British
Aerospace) 1994. Undistinguished, flat-roofed buildings on a 12-acre site in
an affluent suburb; well-equipped technology suite; over-crowded library;
lovely chapel.
Atmosphere   Very Catholic ('The aim of the school is to interpret human knowledge to its pupils in the light of the Gospel'); pastoral care of the highest order; few
disciplinary problems ('Pupils will walk quietly on the left, carrying their bags on
the right'). Uniform (episcopal purple) for all. Very supportive parents.
Admissions   Effectively confined to Catholic children; about 200 apply for 180
places; priority to those attending four 'feeder' primaries or living in five nominated parishes. Most from relatively well-off backgrounds; general level of ability is above average.
The head   Warm, shrewd; combines high ideals with a down-to-earth
approach (teaches regularly, does lunch duty); respected by staff, pupils and parents. Trained at Christ's College, Liverpool; came here as head of the upper
school. Married; two grown-up children.
The teaching   Mostly traditional in style; dedicated, long-serving staff (not all
are graduates), most appointed by present head. Standard national curriculum;
all take religious instruction; more able add German to French; good technology; lots of computing (80 networked PCs); vocational courses on offer. Pupils
grouped by ability from the start; maximum class size 30, reducing to 22 for
GCSE. Strong music (more than 200 learn an instrument); plenty of art, drama.
Participation in extra-curricular activities encouraged ('Those who wholeheartedly join in the wider life of the school rarely present problems and usually
progress academically as well').
Results   (1997) GCSE: 61% gained at least five grades A–C.

Destinations More than half go on to a Catholic sixth-form college.
Sport Strong netball, tennis; flourishing soccer, hockey, cricket, athletics, basketball, badminton. Facilities include playing fields, all-weather pitch, sports hall, gym.
Remarks Successful, if parochial, school.

ALSAGER ♂ ♀
Hassall Road, Alsager, Cheshire ST7 2HR. Tel (01270) 873221

Synopsis
Comprehensive ★ Co-educational ★ Ages 11–18 ★ 1,500 pupils (roughly equal numbers of girls and boys) ★ 270 in sixth form
Head: David Black, 46, appointed 1993.
First-rate, well-run school; good teaching and results; excellent sporting facilities.

Profile
Background Opened 1955 on the site of a 19th-century village school (still in use as an annexe); went comprehensive and expanded 1971. Spacious, functional buildings on a pleasant, well-maintained campus; fine theatre, recently refurbished.
Atmosphere Busy, hard-working; good relations between staff and pupils; clear code of conduct (bolstered by rewards and 'consequences'). High standard of pupil work displayed throughout. Parents predominantly middle-class, committed to and supportive of the school.
Admissions School over-subscribed but places guaranteed to all who live in the official catchment area; priority to others attending one of six 'feeder' primaries; 25% come from across the Staffordshire border. High proportion of pupils are of above-average ability.
The head Able, energetic, determined; insists on high standards (boys' GCSE results have improved markedly). Read physics at Portsmouth; has an MSc in education from Oxford; formerly deputy head of a comprehensive in Milton Keynes. Married (to a teacher); four sons (three are pupils here).
The teaching Good quality; traditional in style. Committed, relatively youthful staff of 87 (equal numbers of women and men), a quarter appointed by the present head (who measures their performance by pupils' exam results). Standard national curriculum; most take nine GCSEs; options include business studies, child development. Pupils grouped by ability in maths from first year and all other academic subjects from second: least able in smallest classes; extra provision for those with special needs. Unusually wide choice of 27 subjects at A-level (but no vocational alternatives – only 60% stay on). Strong drama, music (two choirs, orchestra, various ensembles). Lots of extra-curricular activities (up to 40 clubs meet at lunch-time and after school). Regular language exchanges with schools in France, Germany.
Results (1997) GCSE: 63% gained at least five grades A–C. A-level: 44% of entries graded A or B.
Destinations About 85% of those who stay on proceed to university (three or four a year to Oxbridge).
Sport First-rate facilities; leisure centre next door. Main sports: hockey, football, netball, rugby, cricket, rounders, tennis, squash, badminton, basketball, swimming, dancing, athletics, gymnastics. Canoeing, sailing, archery also on offer.
Remarks Very good all round; recommended.

ALTRINCHAM BOYS' GRAMMAR ♂
Marlborough Road, Altrincham, Cheshire WA14 2RS. Tel (0161) 928 0858

Synopsis
Grammar (grant-maintained) ★ Boys ★ Ages 11–18 ★ 950 pupils ★ 160 in sixth form
Head: David Wheeldon, 47, appointed September 1997.
First-rate, traditional grammar school; good teaching and results; high standards of work and behaviour.

Profile
Background Founded 1912; opted out of council control 1996. Solid red-brick building (bell tower, arched entrances, oak and wrought-iron staircases) on a 27-acre site in Cheshire stockbroker belt. Fine hall added 1938; less impressive flat-roofed science block dates from 1964; some classrooms in tatty huts; dining hall barely adequate. £1 million building and refurbishment programme underway; much more needs to be done.

Atmosphere Academic achievement highly prized; excellent relations between staff and hard-working, ambitious pupils within firm, well-ordered framework; strong sense of traditional virtues (honours boards, prefects in gowns etc). Blazer-and-tie uniform; sixth-formers in sober sports jacket or suit. Local community fiercely proud of the school and its history (which bodes well for its future under a Labour Government); teachers send their own children here.

Admissions School heavily over-subscribed; entry by verbal and non-verbal reasoning test; top 30% of the ability range from a wide range of social backgrounds in an extensive catchment area including Knutsford, Cheadle, Wythenshawe, Warrington (a third come from outside the borough). Numbers have been rising steadily.

The head New appointment. Enthusiastic, articulate, experienced. Read history at Birmingham, MSc in education management from Coventry; previously deputy head for seven years of King Edward VI Five Ways ('I believe strongly in academic selection'). Keen to increase numbers, particularly in the sixth form. Married (to a primary school head); two sons.

The teaching Formal, didactic; aims to stretch every pupil. Dedicated, hard-working staff of 51 (16 women); turnover virtually nil. Fairly broad curriculum: science on offer as three separate subjects; all do two languages (from French, German, Spanish, Latin). Demanding, carefully monitored homework policy. Pupils grouped by ability in maths, modern languages; maximum class size 30, reducing to 12–15 in sixth form. Good music and drama: more than 100 learn an instrument; two orchestras (with sister grammar school, qv), two choirs; annual plays (from Feydeau to Woody Allen). Stimulating extra-curricular programme, including famous Scout troop, strong chess.

Results (1997) GCSE: 94% gained at least five grades A–C. A-level: 41% of entries graded A or B.

Destinations About 80% stay on for A-levels; of these, 80% proceed to university (about six a year to Oxbridge).

Sport Main sports: soccer, rugby, cricket, tennis, athletics. Squash, sailing, golf also available. Extensive playing fields but no sports hall or swimming pool.

Remarks Ofsted inspectors concluded (1994): 'This is a very good school with considerable strengths in many areas. The school values learning and achievement and provides an effective education for its pupils.'

ALTRINCHAM GIRLS' GRAMMAR ♀
Cavendish Road, Bowdon, Altrincham, Trafford WA14 2NL. Tel (0161) 928 0827

Synopsis
Grammar ★ Girls ★ Ages 11–18 ★ 1,056 pupils ★ 213 in sixth form
Head: David Welsh, 53, appointed 1991.
Fine school; very good teaching and results; outstanding sport.

Profile
Background   Founded 1910; limited but pleasing grounds (mature trees, shrubberies, sweeping lawns) in leafy, Victorian-Edwardian stockbroker belt. Varied buildings (including 1960s extension in need of refurbishment) on two sides of a fairly quiet road; some classrooms in overcrowded 'temporary' huts; latest additions include new classroom block, three science labs. Sixth form on separate site five minutes' walk away. Parents have voted to opt out of council control.

Atmosphere   Lively, well ordered; strong bond between teachers and pupils (who are allowed a good deal of freedom); code of conduct agreed between girls, staff and parents. Tradition respected (silverware, honours board etc) but attitudes are modern.

Admissions   School heavily over-subscribed (more than 300 apply for 168 places) but not unduly selective. Entry by local authority 11-plus; top 35%–40% of the ability range. Pupils predominantly from professional/business backgrounds; 30% come from more than five miles away.

The head   Able; good leader; quiet, gentle manner (all welcome at his door). Read German at Durham; spent three years at a mission school in Zambia; came here as deputy head 1981. Believes in trusting children to behave well but sets firm limits. Methodist lay preacher; Francophile. Married; two grown-up daughters.

The teaching   First-rate; styles range from didactic chalk-and-talk to lively group work and dramatised French lessons. Hard-working, long-serving staff of 68 (60 women); most leave only for promotion or retirement. Standard grammar school curriculum; science on offer as three separate subjects; all do at least two languages (from French, German, Spanish). Choice of 17 subjects at GCSE and A-level; all sixth-formers do general studies. Homework carefully monitored. Pupils grouped by ability in maths, French from second year; class sizes average 25, reducing to 15 for A-level. First-rate music; modern dance taught to a very high standard. Lots of extra-curricular activities. Regular study trips abroad.

Results   (1997) GCSE: 97% gained at least five grades A–C. A-level: creditable 63% of entries graded A or B.

Destinations   About 75% stay on for A-levels; nearly 90% proceed to university (average of five a year to Oxbridge).

Sport   Strong – particularly hockey and netball but also tennis, rounders, athletics, trampolining. Excellent playing fields (all-weather hockey pitch reputed to be one of the best in England) but no sports hall or swimming pool.

Remarks   Identified by Ofsted (1996) as 'outstandingly successful'.

AMPLEFORTH ♂
York YO6 4ER. Tel (01439) 766000

Synopsis
Independent ★ Roman Catholic ★ Boys ★ Boarding and some day ★ Ages 13–19 (plus associated junior school) ★ 528 pupils (95% boarding) ★ 239 in sixth form ★ Fees: £13,305 boarding; £6,870 day
Head: Father Leo Chamberlain, 57, appointed 1992.
Fine Catholic school, remotely but beautifully situated; powerful ethos; very good teaching and results; lots of art, music, sport.

Profile
Background   Founded 1802 by Benedictine monks: run by the Abbot and Community of Ampleforth Abbey, now the largest Benedictine house in Europe; the abbey dominates the campus, the ethos of the Benedictine Order permeates the school. Splendid 1,000-acre site on the edge of the North Yorkshire moors; austere Victorian-Gothic buildings plus 1920s additions by Sir Giles Gilbert Scott; more recent additions include new music school, art/design/technology centre; fine library; some classrooms in 'temporary' huts, others too small. Junior school (115 boys aged eight to 13) across the valley.

Atmosphere   Strong Liberal-Catholic tradition ('Our mission is to encourage each boy towards a joyful, free and self-disciplined life of faith and virtue, ready to listen to the Holy Spirit'). Cheerful, courteous pupils; good pastoral care ('We ask much of the gifted and we support the weak'); discipline fairly strict. No uniform but boys 'should be tidily dressed'. Lessons on Saturday mornings.

Admissions   By Common Entrance; 60% mark required but consideration given to siblings, family connections (20% are sons of former pupils); junior school pupils guaranteed a place; range of abilities is fairly wide; 90% are baptised Catholics; 25% from abroad. Strong house system (eight of the 10 houses are run by monks); accommodation being refurbished (in some cases, not before time). Phasing out of assisted places, which more than 50 hold, will make recruitment more difficult. Scholarships (academic, music) available.

The head   Determined, congenial; devoted to the school. Was a pupil here (as were his father, grandfather and great-grandfather) and has taught here since 1968. Read history at Oxford; became a housemaster in 1972. 'There are no new values,' he says. 'There is only Christ, the same yesterday and today.'

The teaching   Good, in some cases outstanding. Full-time staff of 55 (14 monks, five women), more than half appointed by present head. Fairly broad curriculum; science on offer as three separate subjects; most do French; German available; all study Christian theology until they leave. Pupils grouped by ability in all main subjects; extra help for those who need it (including dyslexics and those for whom English is a foreign language); progress closely monitored; average class size 20, reducing to 15 at A-level. Good art, drama, music (70-strong orchestra, schola cantorum sings in the abbey and abroad). Extra-curricular activities include well-supported cadet force, Duke of Edinburgh award scheme.

Results   (1997) GCSE: 92% gained at least five grades A–C. A-level: creditable 63% of entries graded A or B.

Destinations   About 90% proceed to higher education (average of 15 a year to Oxbridge).

Sport   Very strong: good coaching; playing fields as far as the eye can see. Main activities: rugby, cricket, hockey, athletics, cross-country. Soccer, squash, badminton, golf, fencing, swimming, shooting, fly-fishing also available. Facilities include sports hall, indoor pool, rifle ranges.

Remarks   HMC inspectors concluded (1995): 'The school fully deserves its fine reputation. Most boys leave with an unmistakable hallmark on their character and personality, and are proud of their school for the rest of their lives.'

ANGLO-EUROPEAN, INGATESTONE   ♂ ♀
Willow Green, Ingatestone, Essex CM4 0DJ. Tel (01277) 354018

Synopsis
Comprehensive (grant-maintained) ★ Co-educational ★ Ages 11–18 ★ 1,150 pupils (equal numbers of girls and boys) ★ 222 in the sixth form
Head: Bob Reed, 48, appointed 1990.
Unusual, European-oriented school; good teaching and results; International Baccalaureate offered as an alternative to A-levels.

Profile
Background   Opened 1973 as a comprehensive with a strong European and international dimension; opted out of council control 1993, since when £250,000 has been spent on sorely needed refurbishment and £300,000 on first-rate 'lingua' block (school has language college status); much, however, still to be done.
Atmosphere   Everywhere buzzes with activity; European ethos pervasive. Big emphasis on tolerance (though Eurosceptics tend to get short shrift); confident children show maturity beyond their years (and are far too busy to waste time on petty squabbles); good pastoral care system (older pupils act as mentors to the younger ones). Strict uniform code below the sixth form.
Admissions   Over-subscribed (two apply for each place); no academic selection. Priority to those who have some connection with Europe; 20% non-UK nationals; 20% have dual nationality. Children bused in from up to 50 miles away (and 80 'feeder' schools). Parents tend to be university-educated and high achieving.
The head   An enthusiastic, energetic (and self-confessedly authoritarian) Welshman; expects high standards from pupils ('I want them to be well-rounded individuals who make a positive contribution'), staff and parents. Interest in Europe awakened at Bristol University; wide experience of state education.
The teaching   Teacher-dominated with active pupil participation; no room here for the lazy or uncommitted. Predominantly youthful staff of 84 (equal numbers of men and women); most speak a second language (22 in all). All take at least two languages from French, German, Spanish, Russian, Japanese; Arabic soon to be introduced; results are good. European studies compulsory at GCSE; lots of computing (and use of the Internet). Half take the International Baccalaureate as a broader, more challenging alternative to A-levels. Average class size 30, reducing to 26 for GCSE, 12 in the sixth form. Extensive programme of foreign visits: 700 pupils spend some time abroad each year (and 400–500 foreign children visit Ingatestone). Study visits for older pupils last up to two months; means-tested grants available (no child left behind for financial reasons).
Results   (1997) GCSE: 70% gained at least five grades A–C. A-level and IB: 40% of entries graded A, B or equivalent.
Destinations   Nearly all to university.
Sport   Wide range; high standards. Pupils have represented Great Britain in lacrosse, cycling, athletics, judo, kendo. Main games: football, rugby, netball.

Basketball, badminton, trampolining also on offer.
Remarks A centre of excellence (despite some shabby accommodation). Ofsted inspectors concluded (1994): 'This is a good school; the leadership is strong and positive; the teachers able and hard-working.'

ARCHBISHOP TENISON'S ♂ ♀
Selborne Road, Croydon CR0 5JQ. Tel (0181) 688 4014

Synopsis
Comprehensive (voluntary-aided, Church of England) ★ Co-educational ★ Ages 11–18 ★ 530 pupils (57% girls) ★ 200 in sixth form
Head: Richard Ford, 49, appointed 1988.
Happy, Christian school; good teaching and results.

Profile
Background Founded 1714 by Archbishop Tenison for 10 poor boys and 10 poor girls (one of the first co-educational schools); moved to present site in a quiet residential part of Croydon 1959. Functional building plus later additions, including well-equipped technology block: accommodation adequate if somewhat crowded (main foyer teems at break-time and doubles up as dining room at lunch-time); playground space is limited.
Atmosphere Strong Christian ethos; high standards of behaviour expected – but there is an unpressured, informal, reassuring feel. Friendly relations between staff and pupils; well-organised pastoral care system. Supportive parents (100% turnout at parents' evenings).
Admissions School heavily over-subscribed (and anxious to expand). Parents required to be committed members of the Church of England (attested to by parish priest) in the Archdeaconry of Croydon; 30% of places reserved for members of other Protestant churches. Most from middle-class backgrounds and of average or above-average ability.
The head Mild-mannered, tolerant, but has clearly made a big impact. Read English at Durham; taught at three comprehensives before coming here (strongly committed to the comprehensive ideal and regrets that local independent schools have creamed off many of the borough's most able children). Teaches English to second-years. Married; two children.
The teaching Sound. Long-serving staff; methods range from formal instruction to group work, depending on subject and individual teacher. Particular strengths in English, modern languages (all do French from first year, German from second), religious studies (taught throughout the school), art; plenty of computing. More than a third take GCSE sport; GNVQ in business studies available as an alternative to A-levels. Regular homework, rigorously monitored (parents sign weekly homework diary); house points awarded for achievement, good behaviour. Pupils grouped by ability in maths, science, languages from third year; average class size 30; less able in smaller groups; extra help for those with special needs (including Oxbridge candidates). Lots of music, drama.
Results (1997) GCSE: 65% gained at least five grades A–C grades. A-level: 31% of entries graded A or B.
Destinations More than half continue into the sixth form; of these, 65% proceed to higher education.
Sport Strong tradition but school is very pushed for space. Regular teams for

football, cricket, netball, athletics, tennis.

Remarks Popular, friendly school, offering good all-round education in a relaxed, supportive environment. Ofsted inspectors concluded (1995): 'The quality of education provided by the school is good. Pupils enjoy their work and have good attitudes to learning; they are co-operative and diligent and make good progress.'

ARDEN
Station Road, Knowle, Solihull, West Midlands B93 0PT. Tel (01564) 773348

Synopsis
Comprehensive ★ Co-educational ★ Ages 11–16 ★ 1,050 pupils (slightly more girls than boys)
Head: David Chamberlin, 51, appointed 1988.
Successful, well-run comprehensive; very good teaching and results.

Profile
Background Opened as a secondary modern 1959; went comprehensive 1973; language college status achieved 1996. Standard 1950s buildings plus later (and more attractive) additions on a pleasant site in a prosperous area; bright, spacious classrooms; everything cared for and well-maintained ('If we look good and feel good,' avers the head, 'then we are good'). School keen to open a sixth form.

Atmosphere Lively, friendly, well-ordered; easy relation between staff and pupils (who are generally a pleasure to teach). Emphasis on rewards rather than sanctions: book tokens, certificates, badges awarded for effort and achievement (some pupils have so many badges that they clank as they walk). Good pastoral care; highly competitive house system; green and gold uniform strictly enforced. Pupils raise large sums for charity.

Admissions School heavily over-subscribed; priority to those living in the catchment area. Most pupils of average or above-average ability, from professional, managerial backgrounds.

The head Very good leader; has fostered strong links with the community, local industry and commerce and the church. Read economics at Sheffield; wide experience in the state system. Married; three children.

The teaching Good quality: well-planned lessons; high expectations. Well-qualified, dedicated staff of 60, half appointed by the present head. Standard national curriculum; all start a second language in second year (choice of French, German, Spanish, Latin – Mandarin Chinese offered from third year); all do nine GCSEs (from a choice of 16); vocational alternatives available. Pupils grouped by ability in maths from first year, in science, languages, technology from second year; progress carefully monitored; average class size 28–30. Regular tests; strict homework policy. Exceptionally well-organised work experience and careers guidance.

Results (1997) GCSE: impressive 86% gained at least five grades A–C.

Destinations About 95% remain in full-time education after 16.

Sport Teams fielded in all major games; good record; staff give freely of their time. Facilities include sports hall, gym, dance hall, climbing wall and a full complement of courts, pitches and fields.

Remarks Identified by Ofsted (1996) as 'outstandingly successful'.

ARDINGLY ♂ ♀
Haywards Heath, West Sussex RH17 6SQ. Tel (01444) 892577

Synopsis
Independent ★ Co-educational ★ Boarding and day ★ Ages 13–18 (plus associated pre-prep and junior schools) ★ 460 pupils (57% boys, 68% boarding) ★ 198 in sixth form ★ Fees: £12,810 boarding; £8,850 day
Head: James Flecker, 57, appointed 1980 (retiring August 1998).
Sound, friendly school; good academic results; strong art, music, drama, sport.

Profile
Background Founded 1858 by Nathaniel Woodard, a Victorian clergyman who aimed to blanket the country with Anglo-Catholic boarding schools; moved to present beautiful 230-acre site and purpose-built, red-brick Victorian-Gothic premises (grouped round an imposing chapel) 1870. Original classrooms rather bleak and noisy, some others in 'temporary' huts; some science labs modern, others ancient and in need of refurbishment; recent additions include (unusually) a co-educational upper-sixth boarding house. Fully co-educational since 1982.

Atmosphere Relaxed (but not lax); exceptionally friendly; Christian ethos fundamental. First-rate pastoral care system; good working relations between staff and pupils; prefects help run the school.

Admissions By Common Entrance (minimum 50% mark required) or tests in English, maths, French and IQ. School is not unduly selective and admits a fairly wide range of abilities (including those who fail to win a place at their first-choice school). Lots of scholarships, bursaries (academic, art, music, drama, sport). Boarding accommodation of varying quality; juniors in dormitories (some large), seniors in study-bedrooms. Strong international element: 25% from abroad.

The head Engaging, approachable, bubbling with ideas and enthusiasm. Read classics at Oxford (and still teaches it); played hockey for England (and still coaches it); previously a housemaster at Marlborough (where he had been a pupil). Persuaded the governors to go fully co-educational; enthusiastic about Europe; has raised academic standards. Married (to a teacher); three grown-up daughters. From September 1998: John Franklin, 44.

The teaching Mixture of styles: some traditional chalk-and-talk but modern technology much in evidence as a teaching aid. Hard-working, well-qualified staff of 55 (80% appointed by present head). Broad curriculum: science on offer as three separate subjects; particular strengths in languages (French, German, Spanish, Japanese, Chinese – plus Italian, Russian in sixth form); first-rate art. A-level options include archaeology, theatre studies. Pupils grouped by ability; top sets take some GCSEs a year early. Thriving music for all abilities; orchestra, band, smaller ensembles; regular concerts. Flourishing drama: fully-equipped theatre and smaller studio; numerous productions. Extra-curricular programme includes large (voluntary) cadet force, Duke of Edinburgh award scheme. Plenty of educational and recreational trips; annual exchanges; everyone encouraged to spend time on the Continent each year.

Results (1997) GCSE: 97% gained at least five grades A–C. A-level: 44% of entries graded A or B.

Destinations About 80% stay on for A-levels; of these, 90% proceed to university (average of four a year to Oxbridge).

Sport Strong: good record against other schools. Wide range on offer, includ-

ing football, hockey, cross-country, netball, squash, lacrosse, cricket, athletics, rounders, tennis, swimming. First-rate facilities: extensive, well-tended pitches, all-weather surface, covered swimming pool, large reservoir for sailing, windsurfing, rowing.
Remarks Good all round: high-fliers well catered for, less able brought on.

ARNEWOOD ♂ ♀
Gore Road, New Milton, Hampshire BH25 6RS. Tel (01425) 610186

Synopsis
Comprehensive (grant-maintained) ★ Co-educational ★ Ages 11–18 ★ 1,500 pupils (51% boys) ★ 230 in sixth form
Head: Gordon Skirton, 53, appointed 1982.
Well-disciplined, firmly Christian school; good teaching and GCSE results; lots of sport.

Profile
Background Opened in the 1950s as a secondary modern; went comprehensive 1971; opted out of council control 1991; sixth form added 1995. Unattractive 1970s buildings plus many later additions (school doubled in size in 20 years) on a fairly cramped site on the outskirts of the New Forest (neighbouring premises recently acquired).
Atmosphere Strongly traditional: strict Christian ethos (daily act of worship, community service compulsory in the sixth form); hard work expected; competition fostered; rules clear (computerised attendance register taken for each lesson, making undetected truancy virtually impossible); uniform enforced; litter picked up by whoever is nearest. School has a good reputation locally.
Admissions Over-subscribed (290 apply for 240 places); priority to siblings and those who live in the catchment area and attend a recognised 'feeder' primary. Entry to sixth form requires five GCSEs at grade B or above for A-levels, at C or above for GNVQs (applicants required to 'recognise' the school's Christian ethos). About 80% live within three miles of the school, an area of mainly middle/lower-middle class housing.
The head Strong, charismatic leader; committed Christian, determined to promote a spirit of Christianity within his school. Read maths at London; has taught widely in the state sector. Relations with pupils are friendly but direct ('Pupils who do not behave themselves must expect to be punished,' says the prospectus).
The teaching Challenging; varied in style. Staff of 102 (55% women); good mix of age and experience. Broad curriculum: science taught as three separate subjects; more able take German as a second language (in addition to French); first-rate art (very good results); lots of computing. Pupils grouped by ability in all subjects from the start; some take GCSE maths, science, languages, art a year early; extra help for those with special needs; average class size 20–22. Choice of 22 subjects at A-level; GNVQs available in business, leisure & tourism, health & social care. Drama popular; music thrives.
Results (1997) GCSE: very creditable 70% gained at least five grades A–C. A-level: 33% of entries graded A or B.
Destinations Vast majority expected to go on to university.
Sport Wide range on offer, all taken seriously. Particularly good record in

athletics, football, hockey, netball. Sub-aqua diving, archery, fencing also available. Facilities include on-site recreation centre shared with the community; playing fields 500 yards up the road.
Remarks Unusually well-run school; recommended.

ARNOLD ♂ ♀
Lytham Road, Blackpool FY4 1JG. Tel (01253) 346391

> ### Synopsis
> Independent ★ Co-educational ★ Day ★ Ages 11–18 ★ 815 pupils (equal numbers of girls and boys) ★ 236 in sixth form ★ Fees: £4,140
> Head: William Gillen, 51, appointed 1993.
> *Well-run, academic school; good teaching and results; strong sport.*

Profile
Background Founded 1896; moved to present cramped, suburban site 1903; formerly Direct Grant, reverted to full independence 1976; co-educational since 1980. Stark, brick buildings plus later additions, including music school, sixth-form centre, fine design centre. Junior school (360 pupils aged three to 11) on same site.
Atmosphere Busy, warm – a family feel ('As many bricks build a house, so many hearts make a school'); dedicated staff; pupils proud to be here. Uniform for all. Modest fees.
Admissions By interview and tests in English, maths (no automatic promotion from junior school); school is fairly selective (top 25% of the ability range) but likely to become less so with the phasing out of assisted places, which about 200 hold. Scholarships, bursaries available.
The head Exuberant, charming; strong leader (a highly visible presence). Read English at Queen's, Belfast; previously deputy head of Guildford Royal Grammar (qv) and head of King's, Tynemouth. Bachelor; lives on site (a relic of the school's boarding past) .
The teaching Good quality; traditional in style; hard-working, well-qualified staff. Fairly broad curriculum: sciences taught separately (10 well-equipped labs); all do French plus German or Spanish; Latin available; lots of technology, computing; first-rate art; GCSE options include business studies, home economics; A-level options include theatre studies, geology; GNVQ in business studies on offer. Pupils grouped by ability in maths only (some take GCSE a year early); progress closely monitored; maximum class size 22. Plenty of drama, music. Extra-curricular activities include compulsory cadet force, well-supported Duke of Edinburgh award scheme. School owns an outdoor pursuits centre in the Lake District and has links with a village in Tanzania.
Results (1997) GCSE: 97% gained at least five grades A–C. A-level: 59% of entries graded A or B.
Destinations Nearly all go on to university (average of 12 a year to Oxbridge).
Sport Taken seriously; good coaching; crowded fixture lists. Particular strengths in hockey, rugby. Cricket, tennis, athletics, swimming, netball, basketball, badminton, squash, fencing, golf also on offer. Facilities include 13 acres of playing fields near by.
Remarks Attractive school; good all round.

ASHCOMBE ♂ ♀
Ashcombe Road, Dorking, Surrey RH4 1LY. Tel (01306) 886312

Synopsis
Comprehensive ★ Co-educational ★ Age 11–18 ★ 1,398 pupils (56% girls) ★ 222 in sixth form
Head: Arthur Webster, 57, appointed 1990.
A good comprehensive school dedicated to providing a sound education for all.

Profile
Background   Founded 1932 as a boys' grammar school; merged 1976 with a neighbouring girls' secondary modern. Range of buildings: some institutional and drab, others modern and attractive; £1.8 million spent recently on new class-rooms, labs, hall. Sixth-formers complain there is nowhere to park their cars.

Atmosphere   Open, egalitarian, well-disciplined; strong community spirit ('statement of values' prepared in consultation with pupils, staff, governors); anti-bullying policy prominently displayed. Lots of fund-raising for UK charities and overseas projects ('We want our pupils to understand that life in Dorking is not the norm'). On-site, self-financing nursery for staff.

Admissions   School full but not over-subscribed (numbers up by 200 in past four years); determinedly non-selective; catchment area extends to Reigate. Most pupils from middle-class backgrounds.

The head   Experienced, innovative; good manager; insists on close monitoring of performance to raise academic standards. Read history at London; his second headship. Married (to a teacher).

The teaching   Generally good. Fairly broad curriculum; choice of French, German, Spanish; Latin available; plenty of computing; vocational options include office technology, child development, GNVQ in business studies; 23 sub-jects offered at A-level; all do general studies. Pupils grouped by ability from sec-ond year and set individual targets; average class size 30. Strong drama, music (two orchestras, choir). Extra-curricular activities include well-supported Duke of Edinburgh award scheme. Links with European schools encouraged; regular trips abroad.

Results   (1997) GCSE: creditable 66% gained at least five grades A–C. A-level: 45% of entries graded A or B (as good as most grammar schools).

Destinations   About 75% proceed to higher education (including Oxbridge).

Sports   Lots on offer (early morning basketball and trampolining are popular).

Remarks   Ofsted inspectors concluded (1995): 'This is a very good school, where pupils are encouraged to achieve high standards and to value each other within a caring ethos.'

ASHFORD ♀
East Hill, Ashford, Kent TN24 8PB. Tel (01233) 625171

Synopsis
Independent ★ Girls ★ Day and boarding ★ Ages 3–18 ★ 530 pupils (380 in se-nior school, 76% day) ★ 115 in sixth form ★ Fees: £7,002 day; £12,168 boarding.
Head: Mrs Jane Burnett, 42, appointed September 1997.
Good school; high academic standards; happy atmosphere.

Profile
Background Founded 1898; moved 1910 to walled, 23-acre site in the middle of the town. Buildings a charming mixture of the old and new; everything well kept, brightly decorated; a feeling of space and calm.
Atmosphere Happy, friendly, studious; enthusiastic staff and pupils; good pastoral care. Smart uniform below the sixth form; seniors dress with flair. Boarding accommodation pleasant, spacious, well furnished; seniors have single study-bedrooms. Good quality food.
Admissions Entry at 11 by tests in English, maths, science; school is fairly selective. Admission to the sixth-form requires six GCSEs grades A–C, including A or B grades in intended A-level subjects. Scholarships (academic, music, art, sport) available.
The head New appointment. Read geography at Durham; previously deputy head of St Helen's, Northwood (qv); keen on swimming, tennis. Married; no children.
The teaching Good mix of the formal and informal; highly motivated girls constantly 'on task'. Experienced staff of 45 (67% female). Pupils grouped by ability in most subjects from the start; average class 15 (maximum of 10 in sixth form). All do French; most add German or Spanish from second year; Latin on offer; science taught as three separate subjects. Most take nine GCSEs and three A-levels (from a choice of 23); certificate in cookery also available. Lots of music: 60% learn an instrument; two orchestras, three choirs. Strong European links (international rail station near by); regular exchanges with schools in France, Germany, Spain. Flourishing Duke of Edinburgh award scheme.
Results (1997) GCSE: all gained at least five grades A–C. A level: 63% of entries graded A or B.
Destinations About 80% continue into the sixth form; nearly all proceed to university (half a dozen a year to Oxbridge).
Sport Enthusiastic participation; wide range on offer. Facilities include three hockey pitches, 11 hard courts, heated indoor pool; sports hall planned.
Remarks Good all round.

AUDENSHAW HIGH ♂
Hazel Street, Audenshaw, Manchester M34 5NB. Tel (0161) 336 2133

Synopsis
Comprehensive (grant-maintained) ★ Boys (plus girls in sixth form) ★ Ages 11–18 ★ 880 pupils (rising to 1,000 with recent addition of sixth form)
Head: Alan Crompton, 52, appointed 1994.
Popular, well-run, no-frills school; good teaching and results; high standards of behaviour.

Profile
Background Opened as a grammar school 1932; went comprehensive 1980; opted out of council control (among the first to do so) 1989; sixth form added September 1997. Solid, practical, well-maintained buildings fronted by extensive playing fields in an ageing industrial suburb; extensive recent additions include new classrooms, sixth-form block, extra science labs, art block, music suite and vast, well-equipped sports hall.
Atmosphere Strong sense of order. No-nonsense discipline tempered by

concern for each child's welfare and progress. Proper daily act of worship, beginning with school prayer. Strict uniform (including footwear) throughout. Highly supportive parents.

Admissions Heavily over-subscribed (and inundated with appeals). No selection: priority to siblings, those expressing a preference for a single-sex school, those living nearest (school serves predominantly working-class areas of Audenshaw, Droylsden and Denton). Full range of abilities.

The head Good manager: clear sighted; no time for educational gimmicks. Read languages (German and Swedish) at Newcastle; was deputy here. Magistrate, active church warden. Married; two children.

The teaching Varied styles but emphasis is on formal instruction and the imparting of knowledge. Stable staff of 50 (68% men). Pupils grouped by ability from second year; further setting thereafter; plenty of extra help for those who need it (including after-school 'twilight' classes for the most able). Class sizes 24–30, 8/9 in sixth form. Particularly good results in English, maths, science (dual award), French, history; Latin also on offer. Homework strictly monitored. Lots of music (including brass band) and drama. Wide range of out-of-school activities, including cadet force.

Results (1997) GCSE: creditable 61% gained at least five grades A–C.

Destinations Most expected to stay on in the new sixth form.

Sport Main game is rugby (in a soccer-mad area); athletics very strong. Volleyball, basketball, badminton, cricket (and soccer) also on offer.

Remarks Ofsted inspectors concluded (1995): 'This is a good school. It is popular, successful and provides education of a high quality for all pupils in an orderly, caring environment.' Hear, hear.

AUSTIN FRIARS ♂ ♀
St Ann's Hill, Carlisle, Cumbria CA3 9PB. Tel (01228) 28042

Synopsis
Independent (Roman Catholic) ★ Co-educational ★ Day and boys' boarding ★ Ages 11–18 ★ 305 pupils (60% boys, 92% day) ★ 78 in sixth form ★ Fees: £4,995 day; £8,748 boarding
Head: Rev David Middleton, 54, appointed 1996.
Successful, intimate school; strong religious ethos; good teaching and results.

Profile
Background Founded as a boys' boarding school in 1951 by the Hermit Friars of St Augustine in premises previously occupied by the Poor Sisters of Nazareth; girls admitted 1986; boarding numbers have steadily declined. Spacious, four-storey, pink sandstone buildings, including a magnificent chapel, on a 25-acre site overlooking the city; 1960s additions less distinguished; art in ramshackle hut; first-rate technology centre.

Atmosphere A joyous, hard-working, well-disciplined family ('We have fun but our standards are high'); ideals and dedication of the Augustinians permeate the school (although only a handful of friars remain). Day pupils stay until 5.30 pm.

Admissions By interview and tests or Common Entrance; school is fairly selective but admits less able children who show determination (and may have to become less discriminating with the phasing out of assisted places, which about a quarter hold); 60% non-Catholic ('Pupils from all denominations are welcome, giving all the opportunity to embrace the Christian traditions on which the school is founded'). Boarders from both sides of the Border and Hong Kong; accommodation was austere but is being refurbished. A few scholarships.

The head Friendly, relaxed; dedicated to the school. A former pupil; joined the order; taught here for many years before becoming head; gets on exceptionally well with staff and pupils. Teaches French with panache; keeps in close touch with parents.

The teaching Lively; mature, stable staff (a third female). National curriculum plus; all do Latin, German; sciences taught separately; good religious studies; choice of 17 subjects at A-level. Small classes: 16–18 for GCSE, reducing to a maximum of 10 for A-level; specialist help for dyslexics. Lots of art, music, drama. Big emphasis on outdoor pursuits, Duke of Edinburgh award scheme.

Results (1997) GCSE: 95% gained at least five grades A–C. A-level: 34% of entries graded A or B.

Destinations Nearly all who stay on for A-levels proceed to university.

Sport Strong rugby, cricket. Athletics, cross-country, tennis, hockey, netball, badminton also on offer.

Remarks Attractive, well-run school.

AYLESBURY GRAMMAR ♂
Walton Road, Aylesbury, Buckinghamshire HP2l 7RP. Tel (01296) 84545

Synopsis
Grammar (voluntary-controlled) ★ Boys ★ Ages 12–18 ★ 1,100 pupils ★ 380 in sixth form
Head: Ian Roe, 57, appointed 1992.
First-rate academic school; good teaching and results; strong music, sport.

Profile
Background Founded 1598; moved to present site and purpose-built premises 1907; formerly a co-educational independent school, joined the state sector 1952; became single-sex 1959 (girls moved next door to become Aylesbury High, qv); technology college status achieved 1997. Later additions include new science and technology blocks, first-rate computer centre.

Atmosphere Traditional, academic, hard-working; enthusiastic staff; lively, articulate boys; very good pastoral care; high expectations all round. 'We believe in encouraging pupils to develop an awareness of what constitutes acceptable and unacceptable behaviour in a community and to develop a sense of pride over appearance and conduct.' Blazer-and-tie uniform for all; prefects trained for their role. Highly supportive parents.

Admissions School heavily over-subscribed (about three apply for each place); entry by highly competitive Buckinghamshire 12-plus; top 25% of the ability range (minimum IQ about 120); up to 40 a year join the sixth form from other schools with a minimum of six GCSEs at grades A–C. Pupils drawn from more than 60 primaries and a fairly wide range of social backgrounds. Entry age to be lowered to 11 from September 1999.

The head Came here in 1961 to teach modern languages (read French at

Leicester) and has worked his way up through the ranks; previously deputy head. Married; grown-up children.

The teaching Good quality; committed, well-qualified staff of 55 (30% women). Broad curriculum; science taught as three separate subjects; languages include German, Spanish, Greek, Latin; all do at least 10 GCSEs (options include business studies, sport science, geology); choice of more than 20 subjects at A-level (including politics, sociology, computer science); many take four, some five. Pupils grouped by ability in maths, French for GCSE (some take it a year early); extra help for dyslexics; average class size 30, reducing to 26 at GCSE, maximum of 15 at A-level. Strong music, including jazz band, barber-shop group. Wide range of extra-curricular activities, including public speaking, Young Enterprise, Duke of Edinburgh award scheme. Lots of trips abroad for study, sport, recreation.

Results (1997) GCSE: 99% gained at least five grades A–C. A-level: 52% of entries graded A or B.

Destinations About 95% stay on for A-levels; of these, nearly all proceed to university (up to 20 a year to Oxbridge).

Sport Strong tradition, particularly in rugby, tennis; hockey, athletics, cross-country, swimming, shooting, squash, badminton also popular. Facilities include playing fields, indoor pool, squash courts, rifle range.

Remarks Identified by Ofsted (1995) as 'outstandingly successful'. Inspectors reported: 'This is a good school in which pupils learn effectively and achieve very high standards in a caring and sensitive environment. The school has a clear set of values and the ethos is excellent. Behaviour is very good and relationships are marked by mutual respect.'

AYLESBURY HIGH ♀
Walton Road, Aylesbury, Buckinghamshire HP21 7ST. Tel (01296) 415237

Synopsis
Grammar ★ Girls ★ Ages 12–18 ★ 1,100 pupils ★ 380 in sixth form
Head: Ms Jane Wainwright, 47, appointed 1992.
Successful, well-run school; good results; lots on offer.

Profile
Background Opened 1959 when Aylesbury Grammar (qv) was divided into two single-sex schools; close links maintained. Fifties glass-box buildings plus later additions, including £800,000 technology centre, on a narrow site between the boys' school and the police HQ. Eleven-year-olds admitted from September 1998.

Atmosphere Happy, relaxed, well organised; little need for rules ('any anti-social or thoughtless behaviour is discussed thoroughly with the offender'); good pastoral care system; older girls (regarded as 'mature young adults') given responsibility for the younger ones.

Admissions School heavily over-subscribed (nearly 400 apply for 180 places); entry by verbal reasoning tests administered by the county council; pupils drawn from more than 50 primary schools in Aylesbury Vale and beyond.

The head Alert, friendly; her style is understated but she knows her mind; has worked her way quickly up the administrative ladder. Grew up in Kenya; read geography at Oxford; taught in Ethiopia; still enjoys travel. Keen on technology; a champion of single-sex education; girls appreciate her approachability.

The teaching 'The entitlement of every girl to a broad curriculum' is the theme; all do French plus German or Spanish; nearly all take 10 GCSEs and three A-levels (from choice of 21, including technology, business studies, theatre studies) plus 'extension studies'; good results taken for granted. Pupils grouped by ability in GCSE maths only; average class size 30, reducing to 26 for GCSE, 12–18 at A-level. Strong art, lots of music (two orchestras, various choirs), new drama studio; joint concerts, plays, debates with boys' school. Choice of up to 50 extra-curricular activities, including Duke of Edinburgh award scheme; big emphasis on community involvement.

Results   (1997) GCSE: 88% gained at least five grades A–C. A-level: 52% of entries graded A or B.

Destinations   About 95% stay on for A-levels; of these, 90% proceed to university (about eight a year to Oxbridge).

Sport   Chiefly hockey, athletics, netball, tennis. Facilities include extensive playing fields, all-weather tennis and netball courts; pool shared with the grammar school.

Remarks   Good all round.

BABLAKE ♂ ♀
Coundon Road, Coventry CV1 4AU. Tel (01203) 228388

Synopsis
Independent ★ Co-educational ★ Day ★ Ages 11–18 (plus associated junior school) ★ 860 pupils (51% boys) ★ 220 in sixth form ★ Fees: £4,215
Head: Dr Stuart Nuttall, 50, appointed 1991.
Solid, academic school; good teaching and results; strong sport.

Profile
Background   Founded 1563; moved to present 11-acre site and purpose-built premises 1890; formerly Direct Grant, reverted to full independence 1975. Distinguished red-brick buildings plus later additions, including fine modern-languages block. Junior school (on adjoining site, under its own head) opened 1991. Shares a governing body with King Henry VIII (qv).

Atmosphere   Confident, relaxed, efficient; cheerful relations between staff and (neatly uniformed) pupils; good pastoral care (through house system). A 'comfortable' school, say parents.

Admissions   Selective: entry by exams in English, maths, verbal reasoning; two apply for each place at 11. Pupils drawn from a wide range of backgrounds in a catchment area with a 25-mile radius; 25% ethnic minority. Numbers may drop with the phasing out of assisted places (currently held by nearly 200); school hoping to raise extra funds. Up to 25 scholarships, bursaries a year.

The head   Able, experienced, unpretentious; gets on well with pupils. Has a First in chemistry from Salford and a PhD from Bristol; previously deputy head of Royal Grammar, Guildford (qv). Married; three children.

The teaching   Varied styles: plenty of exam-oriented written work as well as individual teaching; well-qualified staff of 70 (equal numbers of men and women), 24 appointed by present head. Pupils taught in mixed-ability classes up to GCSE (and encouraged to help each other); average class size 22. Broad curriculum: all start French, German, Latin; Italian, Spanish, Japanese also on offer; particular strengths in maths, science, geography; first-rate computing (across the curriculum); design/technology includes an engineering workshop. All A-level pupils take first-rate course in general studies (25 staff involved); strong business studies department. Good personal & social education programme; well-organised careers service; bright, stylish library (full-time librarian). Lots of art, drama, music.

Results (1997) GCSE: 99% gained at least five grades A–C. A-level: 60% of entries graded A or B.

Destinations Virtually all go on to university (including about eight a year to Oxbridge).

Sport Main activities: cricket, hockey, rugby, netball, athletics, cross-country, tennis; busy fixture list. Facilities include large sports hall, indoor pool, three squash courts; further 17 acres of playing fields (including all-weather pitch) near by.

Remarks Well-regarded locally; good value for money.

BACKWELL ♂ ♀
Station Road, Backwell, Bristol BS19 3PB. Tel (01275) 463371

Synopsis
Comprehensive ★ Co-educational ★ Ages 11–18 ★ 1,520 pupils (52% boys) ★ 310 in sixth form
Head: Richard Nosowski, 54, appointed 1988.
Large, well-run school; very good results.

Profile
Background Opened as a secondary modern 1954; went comprehensive 1969. Splendid Art Deco building plus later additions spread out over a large site in a semi-rural setting; clear signs of wear and tear; some areas crowded. Facilities include good library, theatre, new classroom block, lots of computers.

Atmosphere Bustling, purposeful, well-disciplined; effective pastoral care system; big emphasis on celebrating success; simple uniform. Parents contribute annually to school funds.

Admissions School over-subscribed (about two apply for each place); no academic selection; priority to those living in the extensive rural catchment area (parents move house) and to those living nearest. Most from middle-class backgrounds and of above-average ability.

The head Fiercely competitive; strong leader; very experienced. Read history at Oxford (soccer Blue); previously head for six years of a comprehensive in Warwickshire. Married (to a teacher); one grown-up daughter.

The teaching Good: generally formal in style; experienced, well-qualified staff (equal numbers of women and men). Standard national curriculum; most add German to French for two years; Latin on offer; good computing; GNVQ in business studies available as an alternative to A-level. Pupils grouped by ability from second year; extra help for those who need it; average class size 27, reducing to a maximum of 18 in the sixth form; homework closely monitored. Strong art; lively music (250 learn an instrument). Extra-curricular activities include Duke of Edinburgh award scheme. Regular trips abroad for study and sport.

Results (1997) GCSE: very creditable 74% gained at least five grades A–C. A-level: 42% of entries graded A or B (as good as many grammar schools).

Destinations About 70% go on to higher education.

Sport Competitive sport not a strong feature. Facilities include extensive playing fields, sports hall, tennis and squash courts.

Remarks   Ofsted inspectors concluded (1995): 'This is a very good school. Overall standards of achievement are high across the curriculum. Good quality teaching contributes to effective learning, and the school's high reputation in the community is fully justified.'

BACUP & RAWTENSTALL   ♂ ♀
Glen Road, Waterfoot, Rossendale, Lancashire BB4 7BJ. Tel (01706) 217115

Synopsis
Grammar (grant-maintained) ★ Co-educational ★ Ages 11–18 ★ 1,040 pupils (54% girls) ★ 308 in sixth form
Head: Martyn Morris, OBE, 52, appointed 1988.
Well-run, traditional school; good GCSE results; lots of sport.

Profile
Background   Founded 1701 as an endowed school for local children; moved to present Pennine valley site (lovely moorland views) 1913; opted out of council control (having successfully resisted being turned into a comprehensive) 1989; achieved technology college status 1994. Imposing Edwardian building with later additions, including excellent sixth-form centre, new art & design block; some classrooms in 'temporary' huts.

Atmosphere   Rather crowded (exacerbated by narrow corridors) but no hint of unruly behaviour ('discipline is essential for learning'); warm relations between staff and pupils. Honours boards, portraits of former heads and photographs reinforce sense of tradition. Compulsory uniform ('neglect and carelessness in school dress often indicate a deterioration in behaviour and work'); sixth-formers (a third of whom come from other schools) dress informally (but no denims, trainers or Doc Marten's). School enjoys strong parental and community support.

Admissions   School heavily over-subscribed (nearly 500 apply for 150 places) and growing steadily; entry by tests in English, maths, verbal reasoning; top 20%–25% of the ability range; predominantly from working-class homes.

The head   Quiet, modest, firm ('I believe in standards – students need good references and appropriate academic qualifications if they hope to proceed successfully'). Chemist with a research degree in education; active church-goer; OBE for services to education. Married; two children (both were pupils here).

The teaching   Generally good; high proportion of long-serving staff; methods range from chalk-and-talk to group discussions. National curriculum plus: all do French and German for at least two years; Spanish, Latin on offer ('We maintain a proud tradition of nurturing young classicists'); sciences taught by specialists; religious education taken seriously. Emphasis on neat presentation; strict homework policy. Mixed-ability teaching for first three years; some setting thereafter in English, maths, science; average class size 29, reducing to 24 for GCSE, 11 in sixth form. Lots of music: three choirs, string orchestra and highly popular jazz band. Extensive programme of extra-curricular activities: chess, drama, ice-skating, outdoor pursuits in the Lake District, Duke of Edinburgh award scheme. Regular trips to France, Germany, Spain.

Results   (1997) GCSE: 96% gained at least five grades A–C. A-level: 42% entries graded A or B.

Destinations   About 80% stay on for A-levels; of these, 75% proceed to higher education.

Sport   Wide range: football, rugby, hockey, cricket, basketball, netball, rounders, athletics; county and national representatives. Extensive playing fields half a mile away; other facilities are poor.

Remarks   A beacon of civilised values and hope to the community it serves. Her Majesty's Inspectors concluded (1994): 'Standards of work are generally high. The school provides a secure, well-ordered and pleasant environment for learning and teaching.'

BADMINTON ♀
Westbury-on-Trym, Bristol BS9 3BA. Tel (0117) 962 3141

Synopsis
Independent ★ Girls ★ Boarding and day ★ Ages 11–18 (plus associated junior school) ★ 280 pupils (62% boarding) ★ 90 in sixth form ★ Fees: £12,525 boarding; £6,975 day
Head: Mrs Jan Scarrow, 43, appointed September 1997.
Fine, academic school; very good teaching and results; first-rate facilities; strong music and sport.

Profile
Background   Founded 1858; moved to present 20-acre site 1900. Well-maintained Georgian house plus attractive later additions (library and music school by Sir Hugh Casson) set among mature trees and a fine terrace. Excellent facilities include stunning art block (better equipped than many colleges), good labs, theatre. Nothing here to offend the eye. Former pupils include Indira Ghandi, Claire Bloom, Dame Iris Murdoch.

Atmosphere   Exclusive, privileged, highly academic; no apologies for pursuing excellence (these are confident, responsible, high-flying girls who will go on to good universities – Miss Brodie would have been proud of them); big emphasis on doing things and doing them well (some have to be restrained from doing too much). Older girls given lots of freedom ('The style of Badminton is firm parameters and a welcome absence of pettiness').

Admissions   School always over-subscribed and can afford to be highly selective. Entry by interview and tests in English, maths, non-verbal reasoning or Common Entrance. Many girls live abroad (7% foreign). Very good boarding accommodation: juniors in light, airy, eight-bed dormitories; sixth-formers choose between double or single rooms. Day girls may stay for tea (food is excellent). Scholarships available.

The head   New appointment. Read history at Manchester; previously deputy head for nine years of Stonar (qv). Believes girls are disadvantaged in co-educational schools: 'It compels them to conform to stereotypical roles'. Married; no children.

The teaching   First-rate; highly professional, predominantly female staff. Broad curriculum: sciences taught separately; big emphasis on modern languages (French, German, Spanish); choice of 18 subjects at GCSE and A-level; maths and science particularly strong. Pupils grouped by ability in maths, French; regular grades for achievement and effort; average class size 16–18, reducing to 10 in the sixth form. Strong music: free term's tuition for every girl;

four choirs, three orchestras, numerous ensembles. Lots of drama (all required to be involved in the creative arts). Extra-curricular activities include well-supported Duke of Edinburgh award scheme.

Results   (1997) GCSE: all gained at least five grades A–C. A-level: impressive 88% of entries graded A or B.

Destinations   Nearly all proceed to university (including a few each year to Oxbridge).

Sport   Taken very seriously; games compulsory even in sixth form. Facilities include two hockey pitches, seven tennis courts, athletics track, gym, indoor pool.

Remarks   Very good school for able, hard-working girls ('dull puddings' need not apply); recommended.

BAINES   ♂ ♀
Highcross Road, Poulton-le-Fylde, Lancashire FY6 8BE. Tel (01253) 883019

Synopsis
Comprehensive (grant-maintained) ★ Co-educational ★ Day ★ Ages 11–18 ★
897 pupils (52% boys) ★ 149 in sixth form (56% girls)
Head: Mrs Muriel Ryding, 57, appointed 1987.
Successful, well-run school; good teaching and results.

Profile
Background   Founded 1717 (on the present site) as a boys' grammar school; went comprehensive and co-educational 1978; opted out of council control 1992; awarded technology college status 1994. Handsome original building plus a variety of later additions (some showing their age) in a pleasant residential area on the edge of the town.

Atmosphere   Cheerful, busy, well-ordered; good relations between staff and pupils.

Admissions   School over-subscribed; priority to siblings, those living nearest; fairly wide range of abilities and backgrounds.

The head   Able; strong leader. Came here 20 years ago and is largely responsible for the school's success.

The teaching   Very good; well-qualified, committed staff (equal numbers of women and men), most appointed by the present head. Standard national curriculum; good maths, science, technology; GCSE options include drama, media studies, sports studies; choice of 22 subjects at A-level. Lots of art, music. Extra-curricular activities include chess, debating, Duke of Edinburgh award scheme. Regular language exchanges with schools in France, Germany; good links with business, industry.

Results   (1997) GCSE: very creditable 70% gained at least five grades A–C. A-level: 33% of entries graded A or B.

Destinations   About 85% go on to university (three or four a year to Oxbridge).

Sport   Wide range; busy fixture list; strong basketball. Facilities include flood-lit, all-weather pitch.

Remarks   A sound education in a caring environment.

BALERNO HIGH ♂ ♀
5 Bridge Road, Balerno, Edinburgh EH14 7AQ. Tel (0131) 477 7788

Synopsis
Comprehensive ★ Co-educational ★ Ages 12–18 ★ 880 pupils (equal numbers of girls and boys) ★ 110 in (one-year) sixth form
Head: Rory Mackenzie, 49, appointed 1995.
Successful community school; good teaching and results.

Profile
Background   Established 1983; modern, functional buildings in a sylvan setting beside the Water of Leith; first-rate facilities.

Atmosphere   Not just a community school but a school in its community. Age range extends from toddlers to pensioners: some 4,500 attend leisure classes and clubs and join the fifth and sixth-year pupils for Highers. The heart of the school is a vast, covered social area with intimacy provided by partitions and informal seating; everything is immaculate, including an inviting cafeteria where pupils dine in harmony with adults and visitors (food is tasty and well presented). The discipline is that of a community rather than a school: there is an air of consideration, tolerance and industry.

Admissions   Virtually all drawn from the official catchment of Balerno, Kirknewton, Ratho and the surrounding area; furious competition for the remaining few places. The whole ability range is represented but with a large bulge at the upper end.

The head   Energetic, challenging; has stamped his mark on the school.

The teaching   First-rate: emphasis is on informality and individual learning; classrooms are effervescent; all abilities nurtured and strengthened. Broad curriculum; greatest strengths in maths, science, modern languages. All take seven subjects for Standard Grade (from choice of 20) in addition to a wide range of non-examined courses; fifth-years choose between Highers and vocational modules. Pupils grouped by ability from third year; average class size 25.

Results   (1997) Standard Grade: 48% gained at least five grades 1–2. Highers: 18% gained at least five grades A–C.

Destinations   About 85% stay on for Highers; of these, 80% remain for a sixth year; 50% of all leavers proceed to higher education.

Sport   Strong at team games: accent is on sampling and finding the ones that will endure beyond school. Good facilities, including sports hall, gymnasia, swimming pool, adjacent rugby and hockey pitches.

Remarks   Scottish schooling at its best: academic achievement combined with a broad liberal education. Recommended.

BANCROFT'S ♂ ♀
Woodford Green, Essex 1G8 0RF. Tel (0181) 505 4821

Synopsis
Independent ★ Co-educational ★ Day ★ Ages 11–19 (plus associated prep school) ★ 750 pupils ★ 220 in sixth form ★ Fees: £6,384
Head: Dr Peter Scott, 47, appointed 1996.
Traditional academic school; good teaching and results; equal emphasis on the practical and creative.

Profile
Background Founded 1737 under the will of Francis Bancroft who left his estate to the Drapers' Company; moved from Mile End to present site on the edge of Epping Forest 1884; formerly Direct Grant, reverted to full independence 1976. Handsome, Oxbridge-style, red-brick buildings (chapel, cloisters) plus sympathetic additions; Union Jack flies over the turreted gatehouse. Modern, purpose-built prep school (200 pupils aged seven to 11) in the grounds.

Atmosphere Busy, welcoming. Confident pupils concentrating on the task in hand; few disciplinary problems; well thought-out pastoral care system.

Admissions By tests in English, maths, IQ. Prep school pupils guaranteed a senior school place; another 50 admitted at 11; school heavily over-subscribed (extensive catchment area). Phasing out of assisted places, which nearly 100 hold, will not have a great impact; generous Drapers' scholarships (up to 13 a year) cover full fees; 25% of pupils Asian or black.

The head Thoughtful, charming, easy-going. Read chemistry at Oxford (DPhil); taught at Charterhouse for 17 years; previously deputy head of Guildford Royal Grammar (qv). Married; two daughters (both pupils here).

The teaching Good quality, diverse styles. Broad curriculum includes classics (all do Latin for at least two years, Greek on offer), electronics, technology, art. Pupils grouped by ability in maths, French (some take GCSEs a year early); average class size 24, smaller for GCSE, 10–15 in sixth form; all do general studies ('to guard against over-specialisation'). Lots of drama, music (orchestras, choirs). Extra-curricular activities include cadet force, Duke of Edinburgh award scheme.

Results (1997) GCSE: all gained at least five grades A–C. A-level: 67% of entries graded A or B.

Destinations About 90% stay on for A-levels and proceed to higher education (average of 12 a year to Oxbridge).

Sport Hockey, netball, tennis, athletics for girls; rugby, hockey, cricket for boys. Facilities include five acres of playing fields on site, 16 acres some distance away.

Remarks Good, safe school.

BARNARD CASTLE   ♂ ♀
Barnard Castle, Co. Durham DL12 8UN. Tel (01833) 690222

Synopsis
Independent ★ Co-educational ★ Day and boarding ★ Ages 11–18 (plus associated junior school) ★ 640 pupils (70% boys, 75% day) ★ 160 in sixth form ★ Fees: £5,610 day; £9,867 boarding.
Head: Michael Featherstone, 46, appointed September 1997.
Solid, traditional school; good teaching; respectable results; strong music and sport.

Profile
Background   Founded 1883; became Direct Grant but reverted to full independence 1976. Vast, late Victorian building plus far-flung later additions (including handsome chapel, new girls' boarding house) on 67-acre site (spectacular views of Teesdale). More than £1 million spent since 1992 on continuing programme of refurbishment but there is still much to do: shabby dormitories, bleak bathrooms, bare corridors, battered furniture; some classrooms in 'temporary' huts. Like many such schools, it has kept up numbers by going fully co-educational (in 1994, but some classes have only one girl) and admitting more day pupils. Immaculate junior school (ages four to 11) on adjoining site under its own head.

Atmosphere   Unpretentious, no-nonsense; few airs and graces. Accents local; parents intent on value for money. Emphasis is on achieving sound academic results, and learning 'how to get on with others, live happily and constructively, and respond positively to hard work and sensible discipline'. Pragmatic pupils take it for granted that staff are the legitimate source of authority; rules clear, well understood (breaches lead to lines, detention, fatigues, gating). Girls wear blazers, ties, join the cadet force – but few traces remain of school's 'macho' past: music now said to be stronger than rugby (Rob Andrew is an old boy). Good pastoral care system (professional counselling available); full-time chaplain. Girls' boarding accommodation high quality (pleasant double or single study-bedrooms); boys' bleak by comparison (facilities basic, institutional); houses command strong loyalties. Lessons on Saturday mornings; busy weekend programme. Parents tend to 'let the school get on with the job'.

Admissions   Entry by test and interview but school is not academically selective ('We don't turn many away and never refuse a sibling'); range of abilities similar to a good comprehensive's. Day pupils from Teesdale, Darlington, Bishop Auckland, Northallerton, Stockton (school buses run from most localities); boarders predominantly from the North; 10% from abroad, including Hong Kong. Some scholarships available; Labour's phasing out of 45 assisted places not a cause for concern.

The head   New appointment; his second headship; said to be 'a safe pair of hands, experienced and steady at the helm'. Read modern languages at Oxford; played hockey for England; formerly a housemaster at Radley. Married; three children (two are pupils here).

The teaching   Whole-class instruction plus small-group work 'where appropriate'; no undue formality but pupils line up quietly before lessons and are quickly settled. Well-qualified, relatively youthful staff of 53 (75% male). Broad curriculum: languages include German, Latin, Chinese; science on offer as three separate subjects (labs recently renovated); A-level options include politics, computing, ancient history (but no vocational alternatives). Pupils grouped by ability in most subjects from the start; progress carefully monitored (regular grades for effort, achievement); extra help for dyslexics, slow learners, those learning English as a foreign language; average class size 20, reducing to 12 at A-level (but larger in maths). Good music (three full-time teachers); orchestra, various ensembles; fine chapel organ. Well-supported cadet force, Duke of Edinburgh award scheme; busy programme of extra-curricular activities. Lots of study trips at home and abroad.

Results (1997) GCSE: 75% gained at least five grades A–C. A-level: 44% of entries graded A or B.

Destinations Nearly all go on to university (up to four a year to Oxbridge).

Sport First-class reputation, particularly in swimming, squash, cross-country, seven-a-side rugby; cricket, rugby, hockey, squash tours to Canada, Zimbabwe, Holland, Australia. Increasing emphasis on sport for all: athletics, netball, badminton, canoeing, fencing, football, golf, tennis also on offer. Facilities include extensive playing fields, well-equipped sports hall, small indoor pool, shooting range.

Remarks Sound school: what it lacks in polish or physical glitter is made up for in warmth, common sense, strength of character.

BEACONSFIELD HIGH ♀

Wattleton Road, Beaconsfield, Buckinghamshire HP9 1RR. Tel (01494) 673043

Synopsis

Grammar (grant-maintained) ★ Girls ★ Ages 11–18 ★ 800 pupils ★ 240 in sixth form
Head: Mrs Penny Castagnoli, 49, appointed 1996.
Lively school; good teaching and GCSE results; first-rate music.

Profile

Background Founded 1966; opted out of council control 1991; technology college status achieved 1996. Purpose-built, flat-top 1960s buildings on large, leafy site; recent additions include fine new technology block; some classrooms in 'temporary' huts.

Atmosphere Friendly, lively, buzzing with energy and purposeful endeavour. Confident, articulate, well-mannered girls, who are encouraged to take responsibility (well-organised school council); good pastoral care system. Traditional royal blue and grey uniform; sixth-formers required to look 'smart and professional' (trousers permitted, but no jeans).

Admissions By tests in verbal, non-verbal reasoning ('only girls reaching the required standard score of 123 be will eligible for a place'). Catchment area extends to neighbouring counties and London.

The head Came here as deputy 1993. Read comparative studies at Essex, MA from the Open University. Married, three children.

The teaching Good quality; styles vary from 'chalk-and-talk' (most classes traditionally arranged – desks facing the board) to project and group work; big emphasis on 'self-managed learning', using IT. Stable, well-qualified staff of 58 (seven men). Fairly broad curriculum: all choose two languages (from French, German, Spanish) for first three years; Latin on offer; good art; first-rate facilities for technology; lots of computers. Most take 10 GCSEs and three A-levels; options include industrial studies, psychology, government & politics. Girls grouped by ability in French, maths from the start, and in most other subjects for GCSE; progress closely monitored; average class size 25. Lively drama (regular productions); very good music (two orchestras, instrumental groups, numerous choirs). Lots of extra-curricular activities, including popular Duke of Edinburgh award scheme; well-established careers department. Regular language exchanges with schools in France, Spain, Germany.

Results   (1997) GCSE: 97% gained at least five grades A–C. A-level: 39% of entries graded A or B.

Destinations   Nearly 90% stay on for A-levels; of these, 95% proceed to university (up to 10 a year to Oxbridge).

Sport   Strong. Main sports: hockey, netball, tennis, athletics, cross-country; volleyball, basketball, badminton; rugby also on offer. Facilities include floodlit, all-weather pitch, 10 tennis courts.

Remarks   Good school; high standards expected and achieved in all fields.

BEAUCHAMP ♂ ♀
Ridge Way, Oadby, Leicester LE2 5TP. Tel (0116) 271 5809

Synopsis
Comprehensive ★ Co-educational ★ Ages 14–18 ★ 1,605 pupils (roughly equal numbers of girls and boys) ★ 680 in sixth form
Head: Mrs Maureen Cruickshank, 55, appointed 1981.
Well-organised, high-achieving comprehensive; liberal ethos; wide choice of subjects.

Profile
Background   Former grammar school with origins dating back to 1520; moved to present suburban site 1964, since when it has grown steadily; achieved technology college status 1996. Previous shanty-town of 'temporary' classrooms now largely replaced.

Atmosphere   Hectic, mature, purposeful ('Our aim is that our students should become competent, caring adults with the best possible qualifications, and that they should become life-long learners'). Pupils' motivation enhanced by the fact that, from day one, all are on examination courses; first-years take six-week introductory course in their rights and responsibilities as pupils ('If there are times when you break the spirit of community, when you make life hard and unhappy for others, you will find us consistent in upholding the values of decency and respect for others which we hold so highly'). High teacher morale (bolstered by well-furnished faculty offices); good relations with pupils, based on shared expectations of success ('No one is a failure at Beauchamp'). No uniform (head believes teachers 'should worry about learning, not articles of dress'). Income-generating nursery on site (open all year) for children of staff and local residents. Student counsellor available three mornings a week.

Admissions   Fully comprehensive intake (of 450 a year); two-thirds from two 'feeder' high schools (ages 10–14) in Oadby, a lower middle-class suburb; 20% ethnic minorities, mainly Asian. Numbers rising thanks largely to league-table success; school approaching full capacity but reluctant to turn applicants away.

The head   (Principal) Oxford-educated; calm, painstaking, resolute. Fastidious and prudent manager: she can reel off the cost of almost every item in her £3.25-million-plus budget; has appointed two-thirds of the 90 staff ('my most important job'). Strongly committed to maximising opportunities for girls and ethnic minority children. Widowed; three grown-up children.

The teaching Youngish staff (average age 37); well-qualified, open, enthusiastic. Impressive range of subjects: 23 at GCSE (including business studies, economics, Latin, Spanish), 33 at A-level (including social biology, PE, politics, photography and – highly popular – psychology); full range of GNVQs available as an alternative to A-levels. Pupils grouped by ability in most subjects from the start; lots of extra help for those who need it; average class size 23 for GCSE, about 12 for A-level. Large, automated library with satellite TV system for recording foreign language programmes. Strong music (100 pupils learn an instrument); thriving drama.

Results (1997) GCSE: 63% gained at least five grades A–C. A-level: 38% of entries graded A or B.

Destinations About 80% continue into the sixth form (joined by 70 pupils from other schools); of these, 75% proceed to higher education (four or five a year to Oxbridge).

Sport Good facilities; wide variety of games and activities, including lacrosse and orienteering. All sports except rugby and netball taught in mixed groups; GCSE and A-level PE courses increasingly popular.

Remarks Clear-sighted school; highly effective teaching; good preparation for university life. Ofsted inspectors concluded (1994): 'The school is strongly led and well managed. It has clear values which lead to excellent behaviour and a very orderly atmosphere.'

BEDALES ♂ ♀
Petersfield, Hampshire GU32 2DG. Tel (01730) 300100

Synopsis
Independent ★ Co-educational ★ Boarding and day ★ Ages 13–18 (plus associated pre-prep and prep schools) ★ 380 pupils (equal numbers of girls and boys, 75% boarders) ★ 153 in sixth form ★ Fees: £14,382 boarding; £10,851 day
Head: Mrs Alison Willcocks, 45, appointed 1995.
Informal, friendly, free-thinking school; good teaching and results; lots on offer.

Profile
Background Founded 1893 by J H Badley, a Fabian socialist committed to sexual equality and the outdoor life (cold baths, earth closets, manual labour); co-educational since 1898; no religious affiliations. Moved 1900 to beautiful, rural 120-acre site (includes a small farm); functional classrooms; fine library. Princess Margaret sent her children here.

Atmosphere Informal, anti-authoritarian; staff and pupils on first-name terms (and shake hands with each other to say good night); idiosyncrasy tolerated ('Children at Bedales have space to grow and develop at their own pace and in their own way'). Big emphasis on personal responsibility, managing relationships; no uniform (or dress code); no prefects; school run by 35 committees, some of which the pupils control. Lessons on Saturday mornings.

Admissions Half enter from the junior school; rest by interview, tests in English, maths, verbal reasoning and two-and-a-half-day residential assessment (including sport, art, drama, music and the ability to relate to others); up to 30% of those who apply are turned away. About 25% live abroad (mostly expatriates);

boarders in mixed-age, single-sex dormitories; upper sixth in co-educational boarding house with single-sex dormitories (visiting allowed during the day). Head says 'many parents are straight up and down'.

The head Forceful, popular (known as Alison throughout the school – 'Being on first-name terms means you have to earn their respect'). Read history at Cambridge, music at Birmingham; came here to teach history in 1980. Believes the most important lessons almost always take place outside the classroom. Divorced; two children (one was a pupil here, one still is).

The teaching Generally informal in style; pupils say some is inspirational, some quite orthodox and ordinary. Broad curriculum: all do art, design, music, drama (and must take at least one to GCSE); sciences taught separately; lots of computing; languages include Latin, German, Spanish; conventional choice of A-levels plus wide-ranging general studies. Strong music: choir, three orchestras, various ensembles; generous scholarships for the musically talented. Extra-curricular activities range from blacksmithing, baking and bell-ringing to fantasy role-play and meditation.

Results (1997) GCSE: all gained at least five grades A–C. A-level: 50% of entries graded A or B.

Destinations About 95% go on to higher education, including art, music and drama colleges.

Sport Lots on offer: football, hockey, netball, basketball, athletics, tennis, swimming etc; good facilities, including extensive playing fields, floodlit all-weather pitch, heated pool. Those not interested in games can work on the school estate.

Remarks 'Progressive' school holding true to its dissenting origins; unlikely to suit those who like or need a structured environment.

BEDFORD ♂
Burnaby Road, Bedford MK40 2TU. Tel (01234) 340444

Synopsis
Independent ★ Boys ★ Day and boarding ★ Ages 13–18 (plus associated prep school) ★ 730 pupils (65% day) ★ 300 in sixth form ★ Fees: £7,635 day; £12,120 boarding
Head: Dr Philip Evans, 49, appointed 1990.
Very well run, academic school; good teaching and results; wide range of extra-curricular activities.

Profile
Background Roots go back to 1128; granted Letters Patent 1552 by Edward VI for the 'education and instruction of boys and youths in grammatical learning and good manners'; endowed 1556 by Sir William Harpur, Bedford merchant who became Lord Mayor of London (one of four Harpur Trust schools – central London property rents provide a significant income). Moved to present 45-acre site and spacious, purpose-built premises 1891 (interior re-built after 1979 fire); £5 million spent on building and renovation since 1992; facilities are good (Great Hall seats the whole school).

Atmosphere Orderly, relaxed, very busy; strong spiritual dimension (all faiths catered for); respectful relations between staff and pupils; well-organised pastoral care system (anti-bullying policy a model of its kind). Compulsory uniform; traditional prefects; lessons on Saturday mornings (despite declining proportion of boarders). On-site prep school under its own head. Paddy Ashdown was a pupil here.

Admissions Unashamedly selective: average IQ 120. Entry at 13 by school's own tests or Common Entrance (55% mark required) and interview (on which great emphasis is placed). Pupils drawn from a wide range of social backgrounds (lots of scholarships, bursaries); school aims to compensate for the phasing out of assisted places, which nearly 100 hold. Boarding accommodation generally homely but standards of comfort vary considerably from house to house; juniors in dormitories of eight or nine, seniors in double or single study-bedrooms. Boarders include more than 100 foreign nationals (mainly from Asia, Western Europe).

The head Very able: clever, charming, enthusiastic; a complete professional. Read natural sciences at Cambridge (First); PhD from Imperial; previously head of chemistry at St Paul's (still teaches it); an influential Government adviser since 1990. Married (to a chemistry teacher); two grown-up sons.

The teaching Interesting, well-structured lessons; varied styles. Well-qualified staff of 87 (majority male), half appointed by present head. Broad curriculum: science taught as three separate subjects; modern languages include German, Spanish; Latin, Greek on offer; plenty of technology, computing. Pupils grouped by ability in all subjects; extra help for dyslexics, the gifted and those who speak English as a foreign language; maximum class size 24, reducing to 10–12 in the sixth form. Choice of 23 subjects at A-level (good results in sciences); wide range of non-examined options, including car maintenance, basic Japanese. Strong music: chapel choir, three orchestras, various ensembles; 45% learn an instrument. Lots of drama (in well-equipped theatre). Wide range of well-organised extra-curricular activities, including voluntary cadet force, well-supported Duke of Edinburgh award scheme. Good careers guidance. Regular language exchanges with schools in France, Germany, Spain. School owns a 140-acre estate eight miles away used for field studies.

Results (1997) GCSE: 98% gained at least five grades A–C. A-level: 69% of entries graded A or B (has risen steadily up the league table from 150th in 1993 to 69th in 1997).

Destinations At least 90% go on to university (about 10% to Oxbridge).

Sport Lots on offer; all encouraged to participate; regular tours abroad. Main sports: rugby, hockey, cricket, rowing. Archery, badminton, canoeing, fencing, golf, sailing, rock-climbing, water polo also on offer. Facilities include sports hall, all-weather pitch, indoor pool, rifle range, squash, tennis and fives courts.

Remarks HMC inspectors concluded (1996): 'Academic standards are high...the quality of teaching and learning is generally good.'

BEDFORD HIGH ♀

Bromham Road, Bedford MK4O 2BS. Tel (01234) 36O221

Synopsis

Independent ★ Girls ★ Day and some boarding ★ Ages 11–18 (plus associated junior school) ★ 745 pupils (92% day) ★ 228 in sixth form ★ Fees: £5,400 day; £10,170 boarding

Head: Mrs Barbara Stanley, 47, appointed 1995.

Successful, all-round school; good teaching and results; strong creative arts; lots of sport.

Profile

Background   Founded 1882, one of four Harpur Trust schools in the town; elegant Victorian-Gothic buildings (fine assembly hall, panelled library, sternly functional classrooms); sixth-form centre, music school in neighbouring houses. Purpose-built junior school (180 pupils aged seven to 11) on same site.

Atmosphere   Happy, homely, hard-working; good pastoral care. Smart, practical uniform below the sixth form (where navy check mini-skirts are worn).

Admissions   By interview and tests in English, maths, verbal reasoning; school is not unduly selective (top third of the ability range) and may become less so with the phasing out of assisted places, which about 150 hold. Catchment area has a 20-mile radius (including Luton, Milton Keynes); buses run jointly with other trust schools. Boarding houses recently refurbished; a third of boarders from Far East (foreign pupils limited to two per form). Generous bursary scheme.

The head   Approachable, unpretentious; good team player. Read geography at Queen's, Belfast; previously deputy head of Channing (qv). Married; two daughters (both pupils here).

The teaching   Good quality; traditional in style (rows of wooden desks); experienced, dedicated, predominantly female staff. Broad curriculum: a third take three sciences at GCSE; all start French, add Latin in second year, Spanish or German in third year; good technology; lots of computing; all do nine GCSEs; wide choice of 28 subjects at A-level, including politics, business studies, geology, history of art, home economics, textiles. Strong emphasis on creative arts; high standards in dance, drama; lively music (more than half learn an instrument). Careers guidance, work experience taken seriously. Well-supported Duke of Edinburgh award scheme.

Results   (1997) GCSE: 99% gained at least five grades A–C. A-level: 49% of entries graded A or B (not a good year).

Destinations   About 85% go on to university (average of six a year to Oxbridge).

Sport   Has a high profile; particular strengths in rowing, hockey, lacrosse, tennis, athletics, swimming. Facilities include 21 acres of playing fields, a few minutes' drive away.

Remarks   Very good all round.

BEDFORD MODERN ♂
Manton Lane, Bedford MK41 7NT. Tel (01234) 364331

Synopsis
Independent ★ Boys ★ Day and some boarding ★ Ages 11–18 (plus associated junior school) ★ 926 pupils (95% day) ★ 164 in sixth form ★ Fees: £5,263 day; £9,846 boarding
Head: Stephen Smith, 49, appointed 1996.
Sound, unpretentious school; good teaching and results; strong music, drama, sport.

Profile

Background   One of four Harpur Trust schools benefiting from a 16th-century endowment (including a large estate in central London); moved 1974 to present purpose-built premises on a wooded, hill-side site; formerly Direct Grant, became independent 1976. Good facilities; functional classrooms; later additions include attractive sixth-form centre. Junior school (200 pupils aged seven to 10) on same site.

Atmosphere   Unpretentious, grammar-school style; high standards of behaviour and appearance; good pastoral care; friendly relations between staff and pupils. Uniform worn throughout; complex system of ties to denote houses, sporting prowess, seniority etc. Parents kept closely informed.

Admissions   By interview and school's own tests; top 30% of the ability range from an extensive catchment area (buses organised by parents run in all directions). Phasing out of assisted places, which more than 150 hold, will reduce the broad social and cultural mix (though the fees are relatively modest and the trust aims to ensure that no able child is barred by reason of poverty). Modern, purpose-built boarding accommodation (four-bedded dormitories); most boarders from the Far East.

The head   Read history at Oxford; previously deputy head of Birkenhead (qv). Regular church-goer, local preacher; wants the school to be 'a loving place'; keen to build a 'spiritual centre' where boys of all faiths can worship together. Teaches religious education, drama, general studies; plays the piano and organ. Married; two grown-up children.

The teaching   Formal, traditional in style; stable staff of 87 (19 women). Fairly broad curriculum: most take science (a strength) as three separate subjects; all start Latin in second year; A-level options include computing, business studies, theatre studies; most take general studies. Pupils grouped by ability in maths (some take GCSE a year early), languages; extra help for dyslexics and those who speak English as a foreign language; average class size 23–25, reducing to 10 in the sixth form. Strong drama, music (more than 300 learn an instrument; large choir, orchestras, various ensembles). Regular language exchanges with schools in France, Germany. Extra-curricular activities include cadet force, Duke of Edinburgh award scheme.

Results   (1997) GCSE: 94% gained at least five grades A–C. A-level: 53% of entries graded A or B.

Destinations   Up to 95% proceed to university (average of 12 a year to Oxbridge).

Sport   Taken seriously. Main activities: rugby, soccer, hockey, cricket, athletics, rowing; regular, regional, county and national honours. Badminton, squash, judo, fencing, basketball, tennis also on offer. First-rate facilities include extensive playing fields, sports hall, indoor pool, boathouse on the Ouse.

Remarks   Good all round.

BEDGEBURY ♀
Bedgebury Park, Goudhurst, Cranbrook, Kent TN17 2SH. Tel (01580) 211221

Synopsis
Independent ★ Girls ★ Boarding and day ★ Ages 13–18 (plus associated junior school) ★ 213 pupils (72% boarding) ★ 97 in sixth form ★ Fees: £11,994 boarding; £7,449 day
Head: Mrs Lindsey Jane Griffin, 50, appointed 1995.
Small school offering an unusually wide range of academic and sporting choices; excellent facilities, including own riding school.

Profile
Background   Result of 1976 amalgamation of three schools. Very grand 17th-century mansion in 250 acres of well-kept parkland in attractive Kent country-

side; some classrooms in (recently upgraded) huts; junior school (ages three to 13) six miles away at Hawkhurst (there are plans to open a new one on the senior school site in September 1998). Immaculate and extensive riding school adds a tranquil and leisurely dimension.

Atmosphere Friendly, happy, relaxed: a close-knit, supportive environment; pastoral care evidently good; decent behaviour and personal responsibility expected. Spaciousness and the fine proportions of the house contribute to the unhurried calm of the place. Navy uniform with tartan skirts worn until the sixth form, then presentable mufti.

Admissions By Common Entrance; wide range of abilities; 25% from abroad (half expatriates). Boarding accommodation roomy and light; first three years in main house, divided by year and floor; initially in dormitories, many with spectacular views, later in study bedrooms. Purpose-built sixth-form block has very good facilities: well planned study-bedrooms, kitchens etc. Lots of scholarships (academic, art, technology, sport, music, drama).

The head Keen (not surprisingly) to raise the school's academic profile. Read English at Cardiff, medieval studies at York; previously head of a neighbouring girls' school that closed. Believes girls flourish best in girls' schools. Married.

The teaching Varied styles; well-qualified, predominantly female staff of 48. Fairly broad curriculum; languages include Latin, German, Spanish; maths a particular strength; good provision for science, computing, art, design/technology. Pupils grouped by ability in most subjects; extra help for dyslexics (two specialist teachers) and those for whom English is a second language; average class size 12. Most take nine GCSEs; vocational alternatives to A-level include GNVQ in leisure and tourism, diploma in fashion, British House Society assistant instructor qualification.

Results (1997) 83% gained at least five grades A–C. A-level: very modest 23% of entries graded A or B.

Destinations Most continue into the sixth form and proceed to university.

Sport Almost any taste catered for, but competitive sport not particularly strong. Fixture list includes lacrosse, tennis, netball, swimming, cross-country, rounders, athletics, squash, badminton, volleyball. Also on offer: fencing, judo, scuba diving, sailing, canoeing, wind-surfing (on school's own 22-acre lake). Riding centre has stabling for 60 horses (some girls bring their own), two covered schools, outdoor school, cross-country course. Superb facilities include lacrosse and hockey pitches, six tennis/netball courts, nine-hole golf course, heated outdoor pool, 15-stage assault course.

Remarks Unusual school; genuinely caters for individual requirements in a well-ordered, friendly environment.

BENENDEN ♀
Benenden, Cranbrook, Kent TN17 4AA. Tel (01580) 240592

Synopsis
Independent ★ Girls ★ Boarding ★ Ages 11–18 ★ 440 pupils ★ 140 in sixth form ★ Fees: £13,125
Head: Mrs Gillian duCharme, 59, appointed 1985.
Fine, well-run school; very good teaching and results; first-rate facilities; strong art, music; lots of sport.

Profile

Background Founded 1923 by three mistresses from Wycombe Abbey (qv) who wanted to break out of the traditional public school mould by creating 'a happy school where everyone would be given the chance to follow her own bent'. Grand, castellated, mock-Elizabethan mansion (re-built 1860s) set in 200 acres of farm and parkland; £14 million spent on development and refurbishment in past 10 years, including new sixth-form block, elegant design/technology centre, music school, labs – all furnished and decorated to a high standard. Princess Royal was a pupil here.

Atmosphere Cheerful, hard-working; deliberately not a hot-house; emphasis on sensible behaviour rather than petty rules; girls value the sense of space and the variety of things to do in their free time. Age groups mingle easily (older girls proud of their ability to sort out minor problems among the younger ones); relations generally calm, tolerant; firm anti-bullying policy covers sending someone to Coventry and 'making fun of her in an unpleasant way, especially if you are aiming to get other people to laugh at her too'. Smoking leads to suspension for a third offence; drugs absolutely forbidden.

Admissions Selective ('We don't take anyone who doesn't want to make something of herself'). Entry at 11 (25–30 places), 12 (10 places), 13 (35–40 places) by preliminary assessment weekend (short tests, group activities) followed by either school's own tests in English and maths or Common Entrance (60%–65% mark required); another 20 join for A-levels with at least GCSEs grade B plus further tests. Pupils are 60% Home Counties, 12% British expatriate, 10% foreign; parents in the City, media, fashion, industry, farming. Boarding in six houses of 40–50 (mostly two or three beds, functional furniture); seniors in separate modern blocks (well-equipped study-bedrooms). Good food; plenty of vegetarian and salad choice. Scholarships (academic, music, art) available.

The head Forthright, friendly, very able. Read modern languages at Cambridge (tennis Blue); previously head of a girls' day school in New York; still teaches French (and clearly enjoys it). Has modernised the school and successfully master-minded a huge development programme; not expected to retire before 2000. Divorced; no children.

The teaching Traditional, energetic and often high-powered. Committed staff of 72 (29% men), most appointed by present head; attentive pupils; first-rate facilities. Broad curriculum: science taught as three separate subjects (but dual-award GCSE); all do Latin for at least three years; Greek, German, Spanish on offer; particularly good results in English, science, design/technology, music, art; plenty of computing. Pupils grouped by ability in maths, languages from the start (more able take GCSE French, Latin a year early) and in science from third year; extra help for all who need it, including dyslexics and those speaking English as a foreign language; average class size 18, reducing to 10 for GCSE, smaller at A-level. A-level options include art history, economics, further maths; general studies compulsory. Strong music: more than 300 take instrumental or singing lessons; two choirs, two orchestras, numerous ensembles. Extra-curricular activities include Young Farmers' Club, bell-ringing, Duke of Edinburgh award scheme. Lots of trips abroad for study and recreation.

Results (1997) GCSE: 96% gained at least five grades A–C. A-level: creditable 72% of entries graded A or B.

Destinations Virtually all go on to university (up to 10 a year to Oxbridge).

Sport First-rate facilities; almost limitless in range. Main sports: lacrosse (eight pitches), netball, swimming (indoor pool), tennis (14 all-weather courts). Basketball, fencing, hockey, judo, rounders, riding, squash also popular. Ballet, sailing, clay-pigeon shooting available.

Remarks Good school for sensible, self-reliant girls with stamina and reasonable academic ability; not, though, for idlers or ravers.

BENNETT MEMORIAL ♂ ♀
Culverden Down, Tunbridge Wells, Kent TN4 9SH. Tel (01892) 521595

Synopsis
Comprehensive (grant-maintained, Church of England) ★ Co-educational ★ Ages 11–18 ★ 1,120 pupils (65% girls) ★ 240 in sixth form (85% girls)
Head: Rev John Caperon, 53, appointed 1992.
Successful school; clear Christian ethos; good teaching and GCSE results.

Profile
Background Opened as a girls' school 1953; went comprehensive 1976; boys admitted 1993; opted out of council control 1996. Early 20th-century mansion (the gift of Lady Elena Bennett) in 30 acres of parkland close to the town centre; later additions include large assembly hall and chapel.

Atmosphere Calm, well-ordered. Academic excellence encouraged (in competition with the town's grammar schools); strong pastoral care system; 'Christian values and standards provide the focus and inspiration for learning and for life'. Uniform below the sixth form.

Admissions Restricted to the children of practising members of the Church of England or other Christian churches (written reference required from parish priest); no academic selection.

The head Very able; strong leader; aims to produce 'youngsters who want to change the world for the better, serve their fellow human beings and make their Christian mark'. Read English at Bristol; MSc from Oxford; ordained 1983; formerly deputy head of a church comprehensive in North Yorkshire. Married (to a teacher), four daughters.

The teaching Good quality; mainly traditional in style. Staff of 80 (nearly two-thirds women), many long-serving. Broad curriculum: all do French from first year, add German from second and continue both to the end of the third year; science on offer as three separate subjects; religious studies compulsory to GCSE. Most do 10 GCSEs; options include child care, business studies. Choice of 21 subjects at A-level; vocational alternatives available. Pupils grouped by ability in most subjects from second year; extra help for those with special needs; progress closely monitored; average class size 26, much smaller in sixth form. Lots of music (orchestra, choirs, band). Extra-curricular activities include Duke of Edinburgh award scheme, active Christian Union, voluntary work for the handicapped and elderly.

Results (1997) GCSE: impressive 70% gained at least five grades A–C. A-level: 32% of entries graded A or B.

Destinations About 85% continue into the sixth form; the majority proceed to higher education.

Sport Usual games; reasonable facilities.

Remarks Popular school offering a solid Christian education.

BENTON PARK ♂ ♀
Harrogate Road, Rawdon, Leeds LS19 6LX. Tel (0113) 250 2330

Synopsis
Comprehensive ★ Co-educational ★ Ages 11–18 ★ 1,460 pupils (roughly equal numbers of girls and boys) ★ 230 in sixth form
Head: Mrs Anne Clarke, 46, appointed September 1997.
Successful school; good teaching; strong sport.

Profile
Background Opened 1959 as a secondary modern; became a grammar school 1970; went comprehensive 1975. Set in 15 pleasant acres overlooking outer Leeds suburbia to the south, open countryside to the north. Solid, four-storey building (wide corridors, staircases) plus later additions; some classrooms in 'temporary' huts, others cramped.

Atmosphere Orderly, purposeful, hard-working. Common-sense rules strictly enforced; uniform worn by all. Much attention paid to the rewarding of merit through colours, certificates, assemblies. Parents receive detailed, well-written reports.

Admissions Over-subscribed: priority to siblings, those living nearest; most come from Rawdon, Yeadon, Calverley, Horsforth.

The head New appointment (predecessor had been in post 21 years). Read modern languages at London; previously head of a girls' comprehensive in Kingston-upon-Thames.

The teaching Good quality, challenging: well-qualified staff of 88, nearly all appointed by present head. Pupils grouped by ability in all subjects from the start; extra help for those with special needs; average class size 23. Broad curriculum: science on offer as three separate subjects; all do Spanish or French; more able may add German, Latin; lots of computing. Wide choice of 23 subjects at A-level; general studies compulsory. Regular language exchanges with schools in France, Germany, Spain.

Results (1997): GCSE 53% gained at least five grades A–C. A-level: 35% of entries graded A or B

Destinations Most continue into the sixth form; about 75 a year proceed to university (including Oxbridge).

Sport Strong; busy fixture list. Main games: rugby, soccer, hockey, netball, athletics, cricket, tennis.

Remarks Ofsted inspectors concluded (1994): 'This is a good school with a positive ethos and sense of purpose; the behaviour of pupils is excellent.'

BERKHAMSTED COLLEGIATE ♂ ♀
High Street, Berkhamsted, Hertfordshire HP4 2DI. Tel (01442) 877522

Synopsis
Independent ★ Co-educational (but girls and boys taught separately from 11 to 16) ★ Day and boarding ★ Ages 11–18 (plus associated junior school) ★ 900 pupils (90% day, 60% boys) ★ 300 in sixth form ★ Fees: £7,479 day; £11,946 boarding
Head: Dr Priscilla Chadwick, 49, appointed 1996.
Sound, academic school; good teaching and results; strong sport.

Profile

Background   Result of 1996 merger ('pooling of resources') between Berkhamsted, founded 1541, and Berkhamsted Girls', founded 1888; boys' section in dignified, mainly Victorian premises (plus magnificent Tudor Hall modelled on a Venetian church) in the town centre; girls' section in attractive, 30-acre setting 10-minutes' walk away; co-educational sixth form on the site of the former. Junior school (400 pupils aged three to 11) near by.

Atmosphere   Traditional; emphasis on 'humane Christian values' (full-time chaplain); pupils expected to be 'considerate, courteous, honest and industrious'. Uniform for all. Governors believe there is a 'strong case for single-sex teaching, particularly during the period when pupils are studying for GCSE'.

Admissions   By tests; junior school pupils have priority (and provide 60% of the entrants); school is not unduly selective. Catchment area extends from North London to Milton Keynes. Pleasant boarding accommodation for up to 100 boys and girls in separate houses; 50% are weekly boarders.

The head   Able, business-like; good manager. Read theology at Cambridge, PhD in education; was head of a London comprehensive, then a senior manager at South Bank University. Not married.

The teaching   Good quality; stable, well-qualified staff. Broad curriculum: science (a strength) on offer as three separate subjects; good maths; languages include Latin, German, Spanish; wide choice of 27 A-levels. Pupils grouped by ability in maths, English from the start; average class size 20, reducing to a maximum of 15 in the sixth form. Lots of music, drama. Good careers advice. Extra-curricular activities include well-supported cadet force, Duke of Edinburgh award scheme.

Results   (1997) GCSE: all gained at least five grades A–C. A level: 58% of entries graded A or B.

Destinations   Nearly all go to university (four or five a year to Oxbridge).

Sport   Competitive games have a high priority. Lacrosse (a particular strength), netball, tennis, athletics, squash, gymnastic, dance for girls; rugby (very strong), soccer, cross-country, hockey, cricket, athletics for boys. Facilities include 40 acres of playing fields, all-weather pitch, indoor pool, courts for fives, squash, tennis

Remarks   Traditional school going through a period of organisational upheaval.

BIRKDALE ♂
Oakholme Road, Sheffield S10 3DH. Tel (0114) 266 8408

Synopsis
Independent ★ Boys (plus girls in sixth form) ★ Day ★ Ages 4–18 ★ 775 pupils ★ 151 in sixth form (70% boys) ★ Fees: £4,797
Head: Rev Michael Hepworth, 59, appointed 1983 (retiring August 1998).
Successful, well-run school; happy, well-rounded pupils.

Profile

Background   Founded as a prep school in the evangelical tradition 1904; moved to present rather cramped site in a quiet, residential area of the city 1915; senior school opened 1978, sixth form 1988. Mellow Victorian buildings plus many later additions; junior department (ages four to 11) half a mile away.

Atmosphere Lively, unpretentious, well-ordered. Enthusiastic staff; polite, self-assured pupils; clear Christian ethos. Uniform worn throughout.

Admissions Entry at seven and 11 by tests in English, maths, reasoning; at 13 by Common Entrance. Admission to the sixth form requires at least five GCSEs at grade C or above. Broad social mix; catchment area includes Worksop, Barnsley, Rotherham, Chesterfield.

The head A traditionalist with firm convictions who has moulded the school in his own image and will be hard to replace. Gets on well with staff (most of whom he has appointed) and pupils (whom he knows well). First came here as a pupil aged five (son of the local vicar); read theology at Cambridge. Married (wife is an integral part of the school – they live on site); two grown-up children. From September 1998: Robert Court, second master at Westminster (qv).

The teaching Lively; generally formal in style. Broad curriculum: all required to do French, German, Latin from 11–13; science on offer as three separate subjects; good computing. Pupils grouped by ability in maths, French (some take GCSEs in them a year early); extra help for dyslexics (trained staff); average class size 20. Progress closely monitored; firm policy on homework. Choice of 21 subjects at A-level, some in conjunction with girls at Sheffield High (qv). Very good art (inspirational teaching), music (orchestra, chamber quartet, blues band). Lots of extra-curricular activities; big emphasis on outdoor pursuits; all take part in Duke of Edinburgh award scheme.

Results (1997) GCSE: 96% gained at least five grades A–C. A-level: 52% of entries graded A or B.

Destinations Virtually all go on to university.

Sport Main games: rugby, soccer, cricket, athletics. Tennis, squash, hockey, basketball, netball also on offer. Sports hall on site; playing fields near by.

Remarks In the words of David Blunkett, Education Secretary and local MP: 'We want to offer the opportunities – the ethos – that exist in this school to every child in the city and in the country.'

BIRKENHEAD ♂
Beresford Road, Birkenhead, Merseyside L43 2JD. Tel (0151) 652 4014

Synopsis
Independent ★ Boys ★ Day ★ Ages 11–18 (plus associated prep school) ★ 1,065 pupils (685 in senior school) ★ 198 in sixth form ★ Fees: £4,155
Head: Stuart Haggett, 50, appointed 1988.
Strongly traditional, academic school; good teaching and results; lots of music and sport.

Profile
Background Founded 1860; formerly Direct Grant, became full independent 1976. Purpose-built Victorian premises plus many later additions (including new languages block, science labs) on an attractive campus; boys aged 11–13 housed separately ('a school within a school'). Prep school (plus kindergarten) on same site under its own head (provides half the entry to the senior school).

Atmosphere Hard-working, well-ordered, traditional; big emphasis on 'character building'. In the head's words, 'unashamedly committed to high standards of learning, integrity and self-discipline.' Chapel (plus full-time chaplain) plays a central role, offering 'spirituality without indoctrination and Christian witness without blunt evangelism'. Cheerful, polite, well-dressed pupils; prefects wear gowns; Saturday morning detention for those found guilty of 'offences against the community'.

Admissions Entry by exam and interview: school is fairly selective but likely to become less so with the phasing out of assisted places, which a third currently hold; numbers may fall, too. Most from the Wirral, Chester, North Wales (good train service, parents operate bus club).

The head Enthusiastic, shrewd, firmly in command; gets on well with staff and pupils. Read modern languages at Cambridge; teaches French, German, general studies. Married; two daughters.

The teaching Good quality: generally formal in style ('sometimes narrow, excessively didactic and teacher directed,' according to HMC inspectors); well-qualified staff of 50, half appointed by present head. Broad curriculum: science taught as three separate subjects; languages include Spanish, Greek, Latin; first-years do foundation course in computing; most take nine GCSEs and four A-levels, including general studies (all 'sensible' subject combinations accommodated). Pupils grouped by ability from age 13; average class size 24, reducing to 20 for GCSE, 10 in the sixth form. Academic progress carefully monitored (termly orders); homework systematically set and marked. Strong music: chapel choir; 200 learn an instrument (all first-years receive one term's free violin tuition); organ scholarships available; regular concerts. Extra-curricular activities include choice of cadet force or community service.

Results (1997) GCSE: 98% gained at least five grades A–C. A-level: 59% of entries graded A or B.

Destinations More than 90% proceed to university (including about 20 a year to Oxbridge).

Sport Strong team games (rugby, hockey, cricket, cross-country) balanced by a sport-for-all policy with an emphasis on general fitness and healthy living. Facilities include sports hall, all-weather pitch.

Remarks Despite some reservations about the teaching, HMC inspectors concluded (1996): 'The school's excellent reputation is well deserved and derives principally from four factors: its highly qualified, professional staff; its commitment to hard academic work; the good discipline of its pupils; and its great endeavour, often very competitive, over a broad range of activities from sport to music.'

BIRKENHEAD HIGH ♀
86 Devonshire Place, Birkenhead, Merseyside L43 1TY. Tel (0151) 652 5777

Synopsis
Independent ★ Girls ★ Day ★ Ages 11–18 (plus associated junior school) ★ 672 pupils ★ 191 in sixth form ★ Fees: £4,152
Head: Mrs Carole Evans, appointed September 1997.
Traditional, academic school; good teaching and results.

Profile
Background Founded 1901 by the Girls' Day School Trust; moved 1905 to present, peaceful, suburban site (intimate but not over-crowded) and purpose-built premises (major re-building under way); formerly Direct Grant, reverted to full independence 1976. Facilities are good. Junior school and nursery department

(300 pupils aged three to 11) on the same site.

Atmosphere Courteous, friendly, good-humoured; strong sense of community and family tradition (many pupils are the daughters of Old Girls); mutually respectful relations between staff and pupils. Black and white uniform below the sixth form.

Admissions By tests in English, maths, verbal reasoning; school is over-subscribed (about two apply for each place) and quite selective. Trust aims to replace assisted places, which about a third hold, with a scheme of its own. Catchment area includes Birkenhead, Wallasey, Wirral (parents organise buses). Scholarships available.

The head Recent appointment. Read economics at Bangor; previously head for five years of another trust school in Liverpool. Married; two daughters.

The teaching Good across the board; predominantly formal in style. Fairly broad curriculum: sciences taught separately; Latin, Greek, Russian, Spanish on offer; A-level options include business studies, theatre studies, geology. Pupils grouped by ability in maths, French; average class size 25, reducing to 16 for GCSE, maximum of 10 at A-level. Plenty of art, drama, music; well-supported Duke of Edinburgh award scheme. Regular language exchanges with pupils in France, Spain, Russia.

Results (1997) GCSE: all gained at least five grades A–C. A-level: 59% of entries graded A or B.

Destinations Nearly 90% go on to university (average of eight a year to Oxbridge).

Sport Participation encouraged, a balance being sought between team games – particularly lacrosse, hockey, netball – and individual sports, including athletics, squash, archery. Facilities include sports hall, indoor pool, tennis and netball courts.

Remarks Attractive, successful school.

BISHOP CHALLONER ♂ ♀
St Michael's Road, Basingstoke, Hampshire RG22 6SR. Tel (01256) 462661

Synopsis
Comprehensive (voluntary-aided, Roman Catholic) ★ Co-educational ★ Ages 11–16 ★ 600 pupils (equal numbers of girls and boys)
Head: Michael Whitty, 46, appointed 1995.
Good, academic school; strong Catholic ethos.

Profile
Background Opened 1975; conglomeration of functional, brick and concrete buildings surrounded by housing estates; parish church on campus. Much-needed £400,000 refurbishment in progress. Facilities just about adequate.

Atmosphere Friendly, hard working. Parents, teachers and children expected to respect the school's religious allegiance and to abide by the codes of behaviour and attitude that implies; each day begins and ends with classroom prayers. Mutually respectful relations between staff and pupils (friendly greetings as they pass one another). Younger children allotted an older pupil as confidant in case of anxieties, bullying etc. Uniform throughout.

Admissions Academically non-selective but Roman Catholic credentials required: regular attendance at local church or letter of recommendation from parish priest. Pupils admitted in parish order, beginning with the nearest; those belonging to other Christian denominations and other faiths (credentials required) accepted to a maximum of 15% (competition for these places is strong). Fairly wide social mix but few from socially disadvantaged or ethnic backgrounds.

The head Read English at Birmingham, MA from Nottingham; his second headship. Cheerful, optimistic Liverpudlian with an easy manner; strongly committed to the school's religious life. Says the 'magic ingredient' is parental interest and support (school is the first choice for virtually all its pupils). Teaches English to GCSE. Married, 3 children, all pupils here.

The teaching Businesslike. Quiet, well-ordered classrooms; homework consistently set and marked; last year's exam results on display. GCSE options include German, Spanish, Italian, Russian; science on offer as three separate subjects; good music (choirs and ensembles); religious knowledge compulsory. Class sizes up to 30; smaller for lower ability groups; extra provision for able children. Wide range of extra-curricular activities; drama a strength.

Results (1997) GCSE: creditable 64% gained at least five grades A–C.

Destinations Almost all go on to do A-levels at good, local sixth form colleges.

Sport Keen participation in football, rugby, cricket, hockey, netball, tennis. Facilities on site adequate; very good in leisure complex near by (ice-skating, swimming).

Remarks Identified by Ofsted (1996) as an 'outstanding' school. Will benefit from a facelift.

BISHOP OF HEREFORD'S BLUECOAT ♂ ♀

Hampton Dene Road, Tupsley, Hereford HR1 1UU. Tel (01432) 357481

Synopsis
Comprehensive (voluntary-aided) ★ Co-educational ★ Ages 11–16 ★ 1,150 pupils (equal numbers of girls and boys)
Head: Andrew Marson, 50, appointed 1986.
Traditional Christian school; good teaching and results; strong sport.

Profile

Background Result of 1973 merger between Bluecoat (founded 1710) and Bishop's (founded 1958); affiliated to the Anglo-Catholic Woodard Corporation. Functional, flat-roofed buildings on a compact site in a middle-class residential area on the outskirts of city. Bluecoat Foundation Trust helps pay for improvements; governors closely involved in school life (they sit in on lessons). Genuine concern for the disadvantaged: more than 40 pupils are disabled or have moderate learning difficulties. Technology college status achieved 1996.

Atmosphere Caring, ordered, friendly; an all-pervading Christian ethos ('We believe there is great value for all children in an education based on Christian principles given in a Christian atmosphere – but commitment is a matter which must ultimately be left to each individual'); regular worship, termly communion. Well-organised pastoral care; competitive house system; prefects 'contribute to the tone of the school'; blazer-and-tie uniform worn by all.

Admissions School becoming increasingly over-subscribed: priority to those with special needs, those living in named parishes and those whose parents are involved with the local church (parish priest's endorsement required – points system used to 'ascertain involvement'). Most from ambitious professional/middle-class homes (parents move house to secure a place here).

The head   Committed Christian; mild, approachable manner. Read geography at Hull; wide experience in the state sector; keen on 'child-centred' education.

The teaching   Progressive in style: emphasis on active learning, problem solving. Standard national curriculum; lively language teaching (French, German, Spanish); good science (seven well-equipped labs); all do an hour a week of RE. Pupils grouped by ability in English, maths after first term, in most other subjects thereafter; lots of extra help for those who need it; homework taken seriously. Active music: 120 learn an instrument; two orchestras, bands, smaller ensembles; lots of drama. Popular Duke of Edinburgh award scheme. Regular exchanges with schools in France, Germany, Spain.

Results   (1997) GCSE: creditable 72% gained at least five grades A–C.

Destinations   About 95% remain in full-time education after 16.

Sport   Good; enthusiastic staff. Main sports: rugby, netball, hockey, athletics. Facilities include sports hall, multi-gym, heated outdoor pool.

Remarks   Ofsted inspectors concluded (1995): 'The standards the school achieves are good. Pupils are well-motivated and willing learners and teachers have appropriately high expectations of them.'

BISHOP LUFFA ♂ ♀
Bishop Luffa Close, Chichester, West Sussex PO19 3LT. Tel (01243) 787741

Synopsis
Comprehensive (voluntary-aided, Church of England) ★ Co-educational ★ Ages 11–18 ★ 1,287 pupils (roughly equal numbers of girls and boys) ★ 243 in sixth form
Head: John Ashwin, 58, appointed 1981.
Popular, well-run school; good teaching and results.

Profile
Background   Opened as a secondary modern 1963; went comprehensive 1970; granted technology college status 1997. Functional, 1960s architecture plus later additions (including stylish new classroom block with vaulted, glass roof). Design/technology, art areas cramped; dining room crowded.

Atmosphere   Calm, cheerful, well-organised. Evident Christian ethos but school's aim is to 'help all our pupils make up their own minds about their own system of beliefs'. Staff clearly command respect; pupils polite, smartly turned-out (uniform below the sixth form), pleased to be here. Strong pastoral framework (including drop-in counselling service); good system of rewards (school colours for achievement) and sanctions (detention for poor work); possession of drugs leads to expulsion. Parents, mainly loyal Anglicans, much involved and raise significant sums.

Admissions   Over-subscribed (more than 300 apply for 210 places); academically non-selective. One hundred and eighty 'foundation' places allocated to: children of regularly communicant Church of England families or regularly participating families of other Christian bodies; children who, regardless of church membership have a special pastoral need; families who have an acknowledged connection with a local parish or with another Christian body within the area; children of practising Roman Catholics. Remaining 30 'community' places to children who, regardless of church connection, attend one of the Chichester 'family group' primary schools or live within three miles of the school. Pupils cover the whole ability range but most come from middle-class backgrounds; catchment area extends to Worthing, Littlehampton, Petworth, Emsworth, Hayling Island (foundation entrants qualify for help with transport costs).

The head   Able, experienced (his second headship); committed Anglican. Ofsted (1996) attributed much of the school's success to his 'high expectations and well-judged guidance'. Read English at Cambridge; teaches Latin to 14-year-olds. Married; three grown-up children (one was a pupil here).

The teaching   Good: varied styles; some whole-class, some group work; lively dialogue in modern languages; particular strengths in English, languages, geography, technology. Stable staff of 70 (55% male), nearly all appointed by present head. Broad curriculum: science on offer as three separate subjects; all do French and German (or Latin); Spanish on offer. GCSE options include business studies, textiles, drama; wide choice of A-levels, including philosophy, psychology, further maths; GNVQ in tourism available. Average class sizes 26, reducing to 15 for A-level; extra help for those with special needs (including 10 with 'statements'); homework taken seriously (monitored by staff and parents); good standard of presentation expected (and generally achieved). Lots of music: 220 learn an instrument; two choirs, two orchestras, various ensembles; good art, drama. Wide range of extra-curricular activities, including popular Duke of Edinburgh award scheme. Regular language exchanges with schools in France, Germany.

Results   (1997) GCSE: 80% gained at least five grades A–C. A-level: 40% of entries graded A or B.

Destinations   About 70% go on to university (including up to six a year to Oxbridge).

Sport   Adequate facilities; active fixture list. Main games: rugby, soccer, hockey, netball, tennis, cricket, basketball, athletics. Volleyball, cross-country, badminton, table tennis also on offer.

Remarks   Good all round; recommended.

BISHOP RAMSEY ♂ ♀
Hume Way, Ruislip, Middlesex HA4 8EE. Tel (01895) 639227

Synopsis
Comprehensive (voluntary-aided, Church of England) ★ Co-educational ★ Ages 11–18 ★ 1,111 pupils (equal numbers of girls and boys) ★ 205 in sixth form
Head: Mike Udall, 53, appointed 1992.
Strongly Christian comprehensive; good results; lots of music.

Profile
Background   Result of a 1977 merger between two schools half-a-mile apart (which is inefficient, inconvenient and expensive). Juniors (first three years) in solid, 1930s premises; seniors in mostly modern buildings on pleasant site bordering parkland. Parents encouraged to covenant annual donation of £120 a child (most do).

Atmosphere   Christianity is at the centre of school life: daily worship, regular Holy Communion, termly services, rooms set aside for quiet and prayer. Senior staff expected to be committed Christians; others to be in sympathy with Christian ethos; parents required to be regular worshippers. Big emphasis on community service, pastoral care, respect for others. Distinctive uniform of brown and old gold; sixth form smartly dressed (no denim).

Admissions School is heavily over-subscribed. Priority to: children of parents worshipping weekly over three-year period in an Anglican or other Christian church; siblings; children of parents worshipping at least monthly in a Christian church; and those of parents of other faiths. Full spectrum of abilities and social and ethnic backgrounds; about half drawn from suburban, middle-class Ruislip.

The head Read biology at London; taught in grammar and independent schools; came here as deputy head 1987. Careful to involve staff in all major decisions. Married; two sons (both pupils here).

The teaching Sound: wide range of styles, including much chalk-and-talk. Standard national curriculum; most do two languages (from French, German, Spanish) for two years and take nine GCSEs, including religious education. Wide choice of 26 subjects at A-level (in consortium with neighbouring schools); some pupils take three years rather than two; 25% take vocational alternatives. Pupils grouped by ability from second year; lots of extra help for those who need it. Music and creative arts (dance, drama, pottery, photography, poetry) particularly strong; annual arts festival; several orchestras, bands, ensembles, choirs. Popular Duke of Edinburgh award scheme; much charitable fund-raising; lots of trips abroad, including work experience in France, Germany, Spain.

Results (1997) GCSE: 63% gained at least five grades A–C: A-level: 45% of entries graded A or B.

Destinations About 75% continue into the sixth form; of these, 60% proceed to university.

Sport Wide range of activities, including soccer, rugby, cricket, netball, hockey, athletics, cross-country; swimming (in adjacent council pool) especially strong.

Remarks Good all round.

BISHOP WORDSWORTH'S ♂
The Close, Salisbury, Wiltshire SP1 2EB. Tel (01722) 333851

Synopsis
Grammar (grant-maintained) ★ Boys ★ Ages 11–18 ★ 761 pupils ★ 192 in sixth form
Head: Clive Barnett, 48, appointed 1992.
Traditional, poorly accommodated grammar school; good teaching and results; lots of music; strong sport.

Profile
Background Founded 1890 by John Wordsworth, Bishop of Salisbury; became a voluntary-controlled grammar school 1944; opted out of council control 1994 after decades of financial neglect, the effects of which are still evident. Assortment of buildings (the earliest is Tudor) in a glorious but cramped setting; most classrooms in 'temporary' huts; development appeal launched.

Atmosphere Robust, friendly, well-ordered; (big emphasis on self-discipline); clear Christian ethos (monthly services in the cathedral). Blazer-and-tie uniform (relaxed in the sixth form).

Admissions By tests in verbal, non-verbal reasoning; school is heavily over-subscribed (three apply for each place) but not severely selective (top 30% of the ability range); being a practising Christian helps. Catchment area has a 20-mile radius.

The head   Strong leader; an 'unashamed traditionalist'. Read history at Oxford; previously deputy head of Portsmouth Grammar. Keen sportsman; co-writer of a West End rock musical based on Nicholas Nickleby.

The teaching   Generally good: formal in style; long-serving, predominantly male staff. Fairly broad curriculum; sciences (a particular strength) taught separately; all take a second language from third year (choice of German, Spanish, Latin); very good art. Pupils grouped by ability in maths, French from third year, in science for GCSE; specialist help for dyslexics; maximum class size 30, reducing to 25 for GCSE, 10 at A-level. Lots of drama, music (more than 200 learn an instrument; strong choir).

Results   (1997) GCSE: 98% gained at least five grades A–C. A-level: 44% of entries graded A or B.

Destinations   About 95% go on to university.

Sport   Wide choice; rugby a particular strength, also hockey, cricket, athletics; regular fixtures against independent schools. Playing fields half a mile away.

Remarks   Ofsted inspectors concluded (1996): 'Despite inadequate accommodation, Bishop Wordsworth's provides a good quality of education for its pupils, who achieve high standards.'

BISHOP'S STORTFORD   ♂ ♀

Maze Green Road, Bishop's Stortford, Hertfordshire CM23 2QZ. Tel (01279) 838575

Synopsis
Independent ★ Co-educational ★ Day and boarding ★ Ages 13–18 (plus associated junior school) ★ 310 pupils (84% boys, 65% day) ★ 127 in sixth form ★ Fees: £8,670 day; £11,160 boarding
Head: John Trotman, 45, appointed September 1997.
Small school becoming co-educational; fairly wide range of abilities; strong sport.

Profile
Background   Founded 1868 to provide a 'liberal and religious education' for Non-conformist families. Purpose-built Victorian premises plus later additions on an attractively landscaped 100-acre site. Numbers have fallen but the proportion of girls is growing. Junior school (350 pupils aged four to 13) on same site.

Atmosphere   Friendly, unpretentious; good pastoral care; relaxed relations between staff and pupils (who are 'coaxed and encouraged to develop their individual talents'). Boarding school traditions retained: day ends at 5.45 pm; lessons on Saturday mornings (followed by compulsory sport).

Admissions   By Common Entrance; 55% mark required but the school is flexible – and not full; phasing out of assisted places, which about 50 hold, will not help. Most live locally; boarding accommodation of variable quality; dining hall somewhat functional. Some scholarships (academic, art, music, all-rounder) available.

The head   Recent appointment. Read English at Oxford; previously deputy head of The Leys (qv). Married; two sons (both pupils here); brother is head of St Peter's, York (qv),

The teaching   Generally traditional in style; predominantly male staff. Fairly broad curriculum; sciences taught separately; German, Latin on offer in addition to French; good design/technology; A-level options include business studies, media studies, history or art; all do general studies. Pupils grouped by ability; progress closely monitored (twice-termly grades for effort and attainment); extra help for those who speak English as a foreign language; maximum class size 24, reducing to 10 in the sixth form. Popular drama, music; 30% learn an instrument; orchestra, choir. Extra-curricular activities include Duke of Edinburgh award scheme.

Results   (1997) GCSE: 94% gained at least five grades A–C. A-level: 47% of entries graded A or B (not a good year).

Destinations   About 90% go on to higher education (including Oxbridge).

Sport   Strong; impressive fixture list. Boys concentrate on rugby, hockey, cricket, swimming; girls on hockey, netball, athletics, rounders, swimming. Facilities include extensive playing fields, all-weather pitch, large sports hall, ageing indoor pool.

Remarks   Sound school; main appeal is its size.

BISHOP'S STORTFORD HIGH ♂
London Road, Bishop's Stortford, Hertfordshire CM23 3LU. Tel (01279) 757515

Synopsis
Partially selective comprehensive (grant-maintained) ★ Boys (plus girls in sixth form) ★ Ages 11–18 ★ 1,077 pupils ★ 300 in sixth form (73% boys)
Head: Ian Shaw, 62, appointed 1980.
Robust, well-run school; good teaching and GCSE results; firmly traditional ethos; strong music, sport.

Profile
Background   Opened 1956 as a purpose-built secondary modern; went comprehensive late 1960s; opted out of council control 1993. Well-maintained buildings plus good-quality later additions (including technology centre) on a pleasant, landscaped site just south of the town.

Atmosphere   Busy, orderly; clear Christian ethos; emphasis on good discipline, manners, tidy appearance (all reinforced by merit marks); team spirit highly prized. Blazer-and-tie uniform strictly enforced. Good links with parents, Old Boys, local community.

Admissions   School over-subscribed (about 200 apply for 154 places); up to 23 places a year allocated to those with proven ability in music, drama, sport; A-level entry requires at least four GCSEs at grade C or above. Most from middle-class homes in a fairly extensive catchment area (both east Herts and Essex); ability level is above average.

The head   Enthusiastic, down-to-earth, fiercely individualistic; inspires great loyalty. Read history at Liverpool; wide experience in the state sector. Keen sportsman and Rotarian; teaches history to sixth-formers, coaches first-years at cricket; not interested in retiring (despite a long innings). Married; two grown-up children.

The teaching   Good quality; predominantly formal in style; relatively youthful staff (28% women). Standard national curriculum; good science, technology; Latin, German, Spanish on offer; GCSE options include business studies, economics; most take nine GCSEs; GNVQ in business studies offered as an alternative to a wide choice A-levels (some in conjunction with a consortium of other schools). Pupils grouped by ability from second year; extra help for those with special needs; progress closely monitored (termly reports to parents); average class size 30-plus. Lots of music (good facilities, choirs, orchestra, various ensembles) and drama. Regular study trips abroad (Germany, France, Japan). Wide range of extra-curricular activities, including chess, bridge (both strong), public speaking, Duke of Edinburgh award scheme.

Results   (1997) GCSE: creditable 70% gained at least five grades A–C. A-level: 31% of entries graded A or B.

Destinations   About 75% go on to university (average of five a year to Oxbridge).

Sport   Important; enthusiastic coaching; large fixture list (matches on Saturdays). Main sports: rugby, soccer, cricket, athletics; regular county honours. Hockey, badminton, basketball, tennis, netball also on offer. Facilities include on-site playing fields (others hired from local clubs), sports hall.

Remarks   Ofsted inspectors concluded (1994): 'This is an effective school, setting and achieving high standards in many subjects. It has a positive ethos characterised by a clear identity, a work ethic, high academic achievement, and maintenance of values which develop pride and worth for all pupils.' Recommended.

BISHOPSTON ♂ ♀
The Glebe, Bishopston, Swansea, West Glamorgan SA3 3JP. Tel (01792) 234121

Synopsis
Comprehensive ★ Co-educational ★ Ages 11–16 ★ 1,030 pupils (equal numbers of girls and boys)
Head: Mrs Jacqueline Williams, 50, appointed 1989.
Successful, well-run school; good teaching and GCSE results; flourishing music; strong sport.

Profile
Background   Opened 1976; grey brick, flat-roofed premises on a pleasant 20-acre site in a middle-class suburb; accommodation is barely sufficient; some classrooms in 'temporary' huts; high noise levels sometimes interrupt teaching and learning. Facilities include good library, drama studio, technology workshops; school desperate for a sixth form.

Atmosphere   Friendly, purposeful, well-ordered; emphasis on good behaviour, consideration for others; high standards expected and achieved in work and play. Uniform for all (unsuitably dressed pupils sent home); smoking results in automatic suspension. Staff and pupils eat together in a pleasant, relaxed atmosphere; good manners to the fore. Very supportive parents (they help re-decorate).

Admissions   School is full and aims to admit all who apply. Most from middle-class, English-speaking homes in a catchment area extending from the outskirts of the city to rural parts of the Gower (80% arrive by bus); average ability level is high.

The head   Friendly, able, clearly in control; liked and respected by staff and pupils. Read English at Cardiff; previously deputy head of a girls' comprehensive. Married (to a retired teacher); two grown-up sons.

The teaching   Lively; styles vary from formal to informal; committed, stable staff, half appointed by present head. Broad curriculum: science (a strength) available as three separate subjects; some take two languages (good results in French); Latin on offer; choice of 26 subjects at GCSE (most do nine). Pupils grouped by ability in English, maths; extra help for those who need it, including the gifted; homework closely monitored. Flourishing music (more than 100 learn an instrument). Good relations with local industry. Regular language exchanges with a school in Paris.

Results   (1997) GCSE: very creditable 72% gained at least five grades A–C.

Destinations   Nearly all remain in full-time education.

Sport   Lots on offer; high standards achieved despite limited facilities (no sports hall or all-weather pitch). Particular strengths in rugby, hockey, tennis. Athletics, cross-country, netball, soccer, cricket, volleyball, squash, badminton, basketball, archery also available.

Remarks   Ofsted inspectors concluded (1995): 'The school has a positive ethos which emphasises high academic standards.' Recommended.

BISHOP STOPFORD ♂ ♀
Headlands, Kettering, Northamptonshire NN15 6BJ. Tel (01536) 503503

Synopsis
Comprehensive (voluntary-aided) ★ Co-educational ★ Ages 11–18 ★ 1,358 pupils (slightly more girls than boys) ★ 344 in sixth form
Head: Dr Trevor Hopkins OBE, 64, appointed 1974 (retiring August 1998).
Successful, well-run school; very good GCSE results; lots of extra-curricular activities.

Profile
Background   Roots go back to 1535; opened 1965 on present 22-acre, suburban site as a purpose-built secondary modern; sixth form added 1975; went comprehensive 1976; technology college status achieved 1994. School is overcrowded ('bursting at the seams,' says the head) despite recent £3 million building programme; some classrooms in 'temporary' huts.

Atmosphere   Hard-working, well-disciplined; strong Christian ethos; friendly relations between staff and pupils (a family feel). Uniform strictly enforced. Supportive parents.

Admissions   School heavily over-subscribed (up to 400 apply for 180-plus places) but not academically selective. Priority to those demonstrating Christian church attendance and involvement over at least the preceding two years (helping to fill Sunday schools and church choirs). Pupils of a wide range of abilities and backgrounds from more than 50 'feeder' primaries in a catchment area covering 1,000 square miles of Northamptonshire, Leicestershire, Cambridgeshire.

The head   Long-serving; distinguished record; awarded OBE for services to education. Married; six children (one a teacher here).

The teaching   Widely varying styles; experienced, stable staff (equal numbers of women and men), nearly all appointed by present head. Fairly broad curriculum; all do German from first year, add French in second; lots of computing; choice of 20 subjects at A-level (economics, politics particularly popular); vocational alternatives include GNVQs in science, health & community care, business studies. Pupils grouped by ability from in English from the start, in maths, languages from second year, in science from third year; extra help for those who need it, including dyslexics; average class size 29 (and not much smaller for

A-level). Good art, music; 300 learn an instrument; five choirs, orchestra, various ensembles. Lots of extra-curricular activities, including popular Duke of Edinburgh award scheme. Close links with local industry and commerce. Regular exchanges with schools in France, Germany.

Results   (1997) GCSE: creditable 71% gained at least five grades A–C. A-level: 31% of entries graded A or B.

Destinations   About 80% proceed to higher education (average of three a year to Oxbridge).

Sport   Big emphasis on participation. Main games: hockey, netball, basketball, football, cricket. Facilities limited but lottery-funded sports hall due to open September 1998.

Remarks   Good all round; fully deserves its strong local reputation.

BLACKHEATH HIGH ♀
Vanbrugh Park, London SE3 7AG. Tel (0181) 853 2929

Synopsis
Independent ★ Girls ★ Day ★ Ages 11–18 (plus associated junior school) ★ 366 pupils ★ 66 in sixth form ★ Fees: £4,128–£5,180
Head: Miss Rosanne Musgrave, 45, appointed 1989.
Bustling, well-run, academic school; good teaching and results; lots of music.

Profile
Background   Founded 1880 by Girls' Public Day School Trust; moved to present three-acre site close to Greenwich Park 1994. Solid, Victorian building (Lady Baden-Powell's childhood home) plus later extensions and new additions, including huge dining hall/sports hall complex, science labs arranged around a large quadrangle laid to lawn. Juniors occupy the purpose-built Victorian premises on the other side of Blackheath formerly used by seniors.

Atmosphere   Girls hurry about, busy, involved, committed to the task in hand. A multi-racial school serving a multi-racial community, very much at ease with itself. Framed photographs of staff and governors displayed in entrance hall. Sixth-formers given lots of responsibility.

Admissions   Entry at age four by interview and group play; at 11 by interview and school's own exams in English, maths plus a test of 'nous' ('You can get a bright child who's dull as ditchwater'). No automatic entry to senior school for juniors. Some scholarships, bursaries; trust is replacing the assisted places scheme with one of its own.

The head   Very able. Shrewd, bursting with energy; a driving force. Read English at Oxford; previously head of English at Channing and head of sixth form at Haberdashers' Aske's Girls'. Appointed head here at 37. Strongly in favour of single-sex education for girls.

The teaching   Firmly academic; hard-working, experienced staff. National curriculum plus; science taught as three separate subjects; all do French from first year, add Latin and German in second and third years. All-roundedness encouraged (playing the tuba instead of taking a ninth GCSE not frowned upon). Music an important part of the life of the school: two-thirds learn an instrument; two orchestras, wind band, two choirs. Lots of community service, charity fundraising.

Results   (1997) GCSE: 91% gained at least five grades A–C. A-level: 47% of

entries graded A or B.

Destinations About 90% stay on for A-levels; of these, 90% proceed to university.

Sport Chiefly netball, hockey, rounders, volleyball; sixth-formers row. Five acres of playing fields a few minutes away.

Remarks Good school for bright girls; recommended.

BLUE COAT, COVENTRY ♂ ♀
Terry Road, Coventry CV1 2BA. Tel (01203) 223542

Synopsis
Comprehensive (voluntary-aided, Church of England) ★ Co-educational ★ Ages 11–18 ★ 964 students (roughly equal numbers of girls and boys) ★ 114 in sixth form

Head: Dennis Lewis, 58, appointed 1984.

Sound school; Christian ethos; good music and sport.

Profile
Background Roots go back to a charity school founded 1714: closed 1940; reopened as a comprehensive on the same site 1964. Functional, slightly shabby, 1960s buildings in spacious grounds backing on to parkland; new library urgently needed.

Atmosphere Courteous, well-ordered. Strong Christian ethos; well organised pastoral care system; firm anti-bullying policy.

Admissions Over-subscribed: about 250 apply for 174 places; 131 allocated to children of families committed to Church of England or other Christian worship (attested to by a minister); remainder to other faiths who can show that an Anglican school is the most appropriate. All parents interviewed; no academic selection; no catchment area (children drawn from up to 60 primary schools). Scholarships for musical tuition offered to 40 talented, promising instrumentalists (voice included).

The head Kindly, unassuming (teaches metalwork to first-years); practising Methodist. Married; three grown-up children.

The teaching Long-serving staff of 59 (equal numbers of men and women); particular strengths in English, maths, history, geography. Standard national curriculum; German but (unusually) no French; all do religious studies for GCSE. Pupils grouped by ability from the start; extra help for those who need it; average class size 30, smaller for GCSE. Lots of music: 200 learn an instrument. Extra-curricular activities include Duke of Edinburgh award scheme.

Results (1997) GCSE: 60% gained at least five grades A–C. A-level: 40% of entries graded A or B.

Destinations About 65% go on to university.

Sport Main games: netball, rugby, hockey, cross-country, basketball, athletics, rounders, tennis; fencing on offer. Facilities include playing fields, tennis courts (but no swimming pool).

Remarks Popular school; short of resources; highly praised by Ofsted (1996).

BLUE COAT, LIVERPOOL ♂
Church Road, Liverpool Ll5 9EE. Tel (0151) 733 1407

Synopsis
Grammar (voluntary-aided, grant-maintained) ★ Boys (plus girls in sixth form) ★ Ages 11–18 ★ 905 pupils ★ 267 in sixth form (80% boys)
Head: Michael Bell, 46, appointed September 1997.
First-rate, newly-selective school; very good teaching and results; exceptionally strong sport.

Profile
Background Chequered. Founded 1708 to help 'poor children to read, write and cast accounts'; moved 1906 from city centre to current site as an independent boarding school for disadvantaged boys and girls; became a voluntary-aided boys' grammar school 1949; went comprehensive 1967; nearly closed by Liverpool City Council 1986; opted out of council control February 1997; granted permission to select all new pupils on grounds of ability and aptitude September 1997. Edwardian buildings in imposing neo-classical style (Grade 2 listed) in dilapidated condition (peeling paint, falling plaster, broken lockers). Fine chapel (like a miniature St Paul's) seats 500. Some classrooms tiny and over-crowded.

Atmosphere Hard-working, well-disciplined; a sense of quiet pride in the school's considerable achievements. Prefects wear gowns on special occasions. Supportive parents raise £35,000 a year (mainly through covenants).

Admissions School always severely over-subscribed (more than 400 apply for 120 places). Entry (from September 1997) by tests in English, maths, non-verbal reasoning (previously by interview).

The head New appointment; previously head of a pioneering grant-maintained school in West Yorkshire.

The teaching Formal in style. Broad curriculum: science taught as three separate subjects; all add Spanish to French in second year; Latin on offer; choice of 18 subjects at A-level; nearly all do general studies. Pupils grouped by ability in maths only from second year; average class size 30, reducing to 20 for GCSE, five to 15 in sixth form. Lots of music (brass band, orchestra). Extra-curricular activities include chess (strong), debating, Duke of Edinburgh award scheme.

Results (1997) GCSE: impressive 98% gained at least five grades A–C. A-level: creditable 51% of entries graded A or B.

Destinations About 90% stay on for A-levels; of these, more than 90% proceed to university (10–15 a year to Oxbridge).

Sport Excellent record in football, cricket, athletics, hockey, basketball, swimming – despite inadequate facilities.

Remarks Identified by Ofsted (1996) as 'outstandingly successful'. Don't be put off by the state of the buildings.

BLUE COAT, OLDHAM ♂ ♀
Egerton Street, Oldham OL1 3SQ. Tel (0161) 624 1484

Synopsis
Comprehensive (voluntary-aided, Church of England) ★ Co-educational ★ Ages 11–18 ★ 1,261 pupils ★ 186 in sixth form
Head: Kenneth Pleasant, 52, appointed 1988.
Fine Christian school; good teaching and results.

Profile
Background   Founded 1834 as a charity school for boys; went comprehensive and co-educational 1966. Splendid stone building (Victorian battlements, imposing entrance) plus later additions – including some prefabs and a fine, purpose-built science block (10 labs) – on a rather restricted site overlooking the town.

Atmosphere   Cheerful, optimistic staff and spirited youngsters give the place a feeling of life and energy; large crucifix on main corridor symbolises Christian tradition and commitment ('We are a Christian community providing an education grounded in the teaching and principles of the Gospel'). Hard work, good behaviour, achievement all systematically rewarded; strong sense of people caring for one another. Strict blazer-and-tie uniform (lapels adorned with house names and team honours). The discovery of a drugs ring, involving nearly 50 pupils, was said by a judge in October 1997 to have brought disgrace on the school.

Admissions   School heavily over-subscribed (more than 400 apply for 211 places): priority to 'pupils who shall be, and whose families shall be, active members of the Church of England, supported by the recommendation of the Anglican clergy'. Wide range of abilities and social backgrounds; catchment area includes Rochdale, Tameside, Manchester, parts of Derbyshire.

The head   Committed Anglican; shrewd, warm-hearted, humorous. Read history at Lancaster. Married; two children.

The teaching   Variety of styles: didactic, group discussions, Socratic questioning; stimulating, well-prepared lessons; effective class control. Stable staff of 85, equal numbers of men and women. Standard national curriculum; all do French and German for at least three years; very good provision for computing; textiles taken seriously; homework carefully monitored. Choice of 19 subjects for GCSE, 22 at A-level; vocational alternatives available. Pupils grouped by ability in most subjects from second year; less able benefit from smaller classes and more attention (non-teaching staff and sixth-formers help – school works hard to avoid 'sink mentality'); average class size 25. Strong musical tradition: more than 300 learn an instrument; brass, wind and swing bands, large junior and senior choirs. Extra-curricular activities include Duke of Edinburgh award scheme, Christian Union, lots of charity work. Regular exchanges with schools in France, Germany.

Results   (1997) GCSE: 66% gained at least five grades A–C. A-level: 31% of entries graded A or B.

Destinations   About 45% stay on for A-levels; of these, 90% proceed to university.

Sport   Strong. Main games: soccer, netball, basketball, cross-country, trampolining; county and national honours. Facilities include two gyms but no sports hall.

Remarks   Oldham's flagship: gets the best from every child. Head says he is confident the drugs menace has been 'purged'.

BLUNDELL'S ♂ ♀
Tiverton, Devon EX16 4DN. Tel (01884) 252543

Synopsis
Independent ★ Co-educational ★ Boarding and day ★ Ages 11–18 ★ 460 pupils (70% boys, 50% boarding) ★ 164 in sixth form ★ Fees: £7,785 boarding; £4,500 day
Head: Jonathan Leigh, 45, appointed 1992.
Traditional mixed-ability school; attractive rural surroundings; strong music, sport.

Profile

Background   Founded 1604 under the will of Peter Blundell, a Tiverton merchant who simultaneously endowed Sidney Sussex College, Cambridge and Balliol College, Oxford; moved to present 100-acre site 1882; 13-year-old girls admitted 1993; junior department (11–13) opened 1996. Victorian-Gothic buildings of charm and character on both sides of a main road; latest additions include computer centre, sixth-form centre.

Atmosphere   Old-fashioned, happy, well-disciplined; good pastoral care; HMC inspectors found the spiritual atmosphere 'subdued'. Compulsory uniform throughout; lessons on Saturday mornings. Many staff live in the grounds.

Admissions   By Common Entrance or school's own tests; prospective pupils rarely turned away. Discount of 20% for those living within 10 miles; for an extra £150 a term, half the day pupils stay for one or two nights a week as 'day boarders'; 10% from abroad; boarding accommodation is of a good standard (though the boys' quarters are fairly untidy). Lots of scholarships (academic, music, art, design/technology, all-rounder, military) and bursaries available.

The head   Able, liberal, enthusiastic. Read history at Cambridge; taught it at Cranleigh (qv) for 16 years; became deputy head. Numbers were falling when he arrived: introduced co-education and lowered the entry age; keen to raise academic standards ('The move to league tables makes a statistical analysis *de rigueur*'). Married; two children (one a pupil here).

The teaching   Sound: formal in style but lively; enthusiastic, relatively youthful staff. Fairly broad curriculum; sciences taught separately; Latin, Greek, Spanish, German on offer; A-level options include design/technology, sports science, theatre studies. Pupils grouped by ability from the start; further setting in English, maths; extra help for slow learners and those who speak English as a foreign language; average class size 18–22, reducing to a maximum of 12 in the sixth form. Lots of music: two-thirds learn an instrument; choirs, orchestra. Extra-curricular activities include cadet force (compulsory for one year), lots of adventure training (on Exmoor and Dartmoor).

Results   (1997) GCSE: 91% gained at least five grades A–C. A-level: 42% of entries graded A or B.

Destinations   About 95% go on to university (average of four a year to Oxbridge).

Sport   Proud reputation. Strong rugby, cricket, hockey. Soccer, squash, netball, fencing, swimming, athletics also on offer. Facilities include extensive playing fields, sports hall, outdoor pool.

Remarks   HMC inspectors concluded (1995): 'Care must be taken to balance high sporting endeavours against the pursuit of academic and cultural aims.'

BOLTON ♂

Chorley New Road, Bolton BL1 4PA. Tel (01204) 840201

Synopsis

Independent ★ Boys ★ Day ★ Ages 8–18 ★ 1,000 pupils (850 in senior school)
★ 250 in sixth form ★ Fees: £3,429–£4,779
Head: Alan Wright, 54, appointed 1983.
Fine, hard-working school; very good teaching and results.

Profile

Background Founded 1524; re-endowed by Lord Leverhulme in 1913 as a single school with separate boys' and girls' divisions on the same 32-acre campus west of Bolton. Main building (imposing red sandstone) dates from 1897; linked to Bolton Girls' (qv) by battlemented tower. Recent additions include fine performing arts centre.

Atmosphere Exceptionally busy and friendly: a happy, hard-working, bustling school; excellent relations between staff and boys; behaviour in lessons is impeccable. Morning assembly in awe-inspiring hall with hammer beam roof; pupils sits on carved, high-backed chairs whilst one of their number plays the huge organ. All well turned-out in strict school uniform; sixth-formers may wear suits or jackets. Handbooks for parents are a model of clarity.

Admissions Highly competitive (400 apply for 125 places) but may become less so with the phasing out of assisted places, which a third hold. Entry at 11 by tests in English, maths, verbal reasoning (previous papers available for practice) and interview ('We're looking for teachability, a willingness to think for themselves, and a minimum IQ of 115'). Nearly all juniors admitted to senior school; others drawn from 90 primary schools within a 25-mile radius (school runs an elaborate coach service).

The head Very able and experienced; held in the highest regard by staff and boys. Educated at Manchester Grammar; read chemistry at Birmingham (First); taught at King Edward's, Birmingham and Royal Grammar, Newcastle-upon-Tyne. Committed Anglican, lay reader; married, three children (all were pupils here).

The teaching Outstanding. Formidably well-qualified staff of 76 (10 women); 10 PhDs, 20 with Oxbridge degrees; cheerful, dedicated and have the highest expectations of their pupils. Much of the teaching is properly didactic – chalk, talk and textbook – with plenty of pupil involvement; no streaming or setting (within a narrow ability band); heavy homework programme. Standard grammar school curriculum; all take two languages to GCSE (from Latin, Greek, French, German, Russian); sciences taught separately; first-rate technology. Average class size 28, reducing to 22 for GCSE, 12 in the sixth form. Vast range of extra-curricular activities; drama, debating, Christian Union etc shared with neighbouring girls' school. Regular foreign exchanges and visits, including annual four-week trek across Europe (staff and boys carry their food in tea chests – eccentric, obviously English). School owns an activities centre in the Lake District.

Results (1997) GCSE: 99% gained at least five grades A–C. A-level: impressive 77% of entries graded A or B.

Destinations About 95% continue into the sixth form; of these, 95% proceed to university (average of 15 a year to Oxbridge).

Sport All major games played, plus water polo; soccer the main sport but rugby is making rapid advances. Superb, modern sports hall and swimming

pool; very good playing fields and cricket pitch.
Remarks HMC inspectors concluded (1996): 'This is a very good school with a deservedly high reputation. Lessons are taught very effectively in a formal but friendly atmosphere.' Highly recommended.

BOLTON GIRLS' ♀
Chorley New Road, Bolton BL1 4PB. Tel (01204) 840201

Synopsis
Independent ★ Girls ★ Day ★ Ages 11–18 (plus associated junior school) ★
800 pupils ★ 215 in sixth form ★ Fees: £4,779
Head: Miss Jane Panton, 49, appointed 1994.
Well-run, academic school; very good teaching and results; strong music, sport.

Profile
Background Founded 1877; re-endowed 1913 by Lord Leverhulme (the soap king) as the separate but equal half of Bolton School, sharing a 32-acre campus with the boys' division (qv). Imposing red sandstone buildings (parquet flooring, oak fittings, magnificent hammer-beamed hall) linked to the boys' equivalent by a central archway topped by a crenellated clock tower. Spacious classrooms; first-rate facilities. Junior school (350 pupils aged four to 11) on same campus.

Atmosphere A sense of purpose and quality; fizzing with energy but no suggestion of disorder; importance of courtesy stressed; good pastoral care.

Admissions Entry by interview and competitive tests (shared with the boys' division) in English, maths, verbal reasoning; three apply for each place but the phasing out of assisted places, which more than 30% hold, will have a significant impact. Extensive catchment area; elaborate bus service.

The head Warm, enthusiastic; good leader. Read history at Oxford; previously head for six years of Merchant Taylors' Girls', Crosby.

The teaching Good quality; generally formal in style; highly-qualified, dedicated staff. Broad curriculum; science on offer as three separate subjects; all do Latin for at least one year; all take two languages for GCSE (choice includes German, Latin, Spanish); lots of computing; most take 10 GCSEs and four A-levels (from a choice of 26), including general studies. Pupils grouped by ability in maths, modern languages from second year; average class size 27, reducing to 10–12 at A-level. Strong musical tradition (joint orchestra with boys' school). Extra-curricular activities include well-supported Duke of Edinburgh award scheme. School has an outdoor activities centre in the Lake District.

Results (1997) GCSE: all gained at least five grades A–C. A-level: creditable 69% of entries graded A or B.

Destinations About 95% proceed to university (average of 10 a year to Oxbridge).

Sport Particularly strong at lacrosse, netball, tennis; regular county, regional and national honours. Facilities include extensive playing fields; sports hall and indoor pool shared with boys' division.

Remarks Very good all round.

BOOTHAM ♂ ♀
York YO3 7BU. Tel (01904) 623636

Synopsis
Independent ★ Co-educational ★ Day and boarding ★ Ages 11–18 ★ 361 pupils (72% day, 64% boys) ★ 93 in sixth form ★ Fees: £7,155 day; £10,995 boarding
Head: Ian Small, 53, appointed 1988.
Small, friendly school; good teaching and results; lots of music and sport.

Profile
Background Founded 1823 by Quakers (but pupils of all denominations and none now welcomed); fully co-educational since 1982. Variety of buildings, ranging from a Georgian terrace to an award-winning modern assembly hall, on a nine-acre site just outside the city walls. Numbers have held steady but proportion of boarders has fallen.

Atmosphere Warm, friendly; easy relations between staff and pupils; community spirit and Quaker traditions much in evidence; relaxed approach to discipline and uniform.

Admissions Entry at 11 by tests, at 13 by Common Entrance; school has been fairly selective but is likely to become less so with the phasing out of assisted places, which more than 50 hold (appeal launched to fund extra bursaries). About 10% of the pupils are children of Quakers; head recruits boarders in Saudi Arabia. Boarding accommodation plain but adequate.

The head Good leader; cheerful, approachable (insists boarding schools are 'bursting with happy, enthusiastic, well-adjusted youngsters'); dislikes rigidity and too much discipline (but discourages flamboyance). Read English and American studies at Sussex; previously housemaster at Stowe, head of English at Abbotsholme. His study has picture windows overlooking the playground, enabling him to keep closely in touch. Married (to a teacher); three daughters.

The teaching Good quality. Broad curriculum: science taught as three separate subjects; all do Latin or classical studies; choice of German or European studies from third year; 17 subjects on offer at A-level; all do general studies. Pupils grouped by ability in maths, French from the start and in other subjects thereafter. Lots of drama and music; all encouraged to learn an instrument. Wide range of extra-curricular activities, including astronomy (own observatory), debating, chess. Good links with local industry (especially Quaker companies).

Results (1997) GCSE: 90% gained at least five grades A–C. A-level: 58% of entries graded A or B.

Destinations Up to 80% stay on for A-levels; of these, 95% proceed to university (six or seven a year to Oxbridge).

Sport Strong fixture list in all major games. Facilities include cricket square, two soccer pitches, squash courts, heated indoor pool, ageing gym and – a short walk away – another 23 acres of playing fields, including netball and tennis courts, hockey pitches, athletics track.

Remarks HMC inspectors concluded (1995): 'Bootham is a good school. Its pupils reach high levels of attainment in relation to their abilities.' It should not, they added, be afraid to be 'bolder in propagating its Quaker ethos'.

BOTTISHAM   ♂ ♀
Bottisham, Cambridge CB5 9DL. Tel (01223) 811250

Synopsis
Comprehensive ★ Co-educational ★ Ages 11–16 ★ 920 pupils (equal numbers of girls and boys)
Head: Peter Hains, 44, appointed June 1997.
Sound school; good teaching and GCSE results; strong community involvement.

Profile
Background   Opened 1937 as the second of a pioneer chain of 'village colleges', intended to place education for all at the heart of rural life; became a secondary modern in the 1950s; went comprehensive 1974. Solid buildings of varied ages and styles (some needing refurbishment) in pleasant grounds (decorated with traditional and modern sculpture); £2 million building programme completed 1995; latest additions include new music suite. Varied community education and sports programme seven days a week.

Atmosphere   Calm, purposeful. Hard work and good discipline encouraged by merit-awards pyramid leading to 'warden's commendations' for outstanding achievement or behaviour; detention sometimes for poor work. Good relations between staff and pupils; close links with parents ('Learning is most effective when there is a strong partnership between families and the school'). Indistinct, blazer-less uniform.

Admissions   Over-subscribed; pupils drawn from a ring of 22 villages between Cambridge and Newmarket. Parents mainly from professional backgrounds.

The head   (Warden) Recent appointment. Read Law at Nottingham Trent; previously deputy head of Hinchingbrooke (qv). Married; one daughter, two foster children.

The teaching   Good. Well-qualified, stable staff of 58 (28 women). Standard national curriculum; half do German in addition to French; choice of 20 subjects at GCSE; very good results in science, technology; strong art. Pupils grouped by ability in maths, modern languages, science from second year; average class size 23, reducing to 20 for GCSE. Homework increases from 40 minutes a night to two hours as pupils move up the school. Good drama: high participation; superb, versatile, purpose-built studio. About one in six learns a musical instrument; school jazz band highly esteemed. Very successful Duke of Edinburgh award programme attracts 200 senior pupils a year, many returning to the school after 16 to complete silver or gold awards. Outward-bound opportunities for all, including compulsory summer camping week for all first-years. Regular language exchanges with schools in France, Germany.

Results   (1997) GCSE: 65% gained at least five grades A–C.

Destinations   About 90% remain in full-time education, 60% taking A-levels or equivalent.

Sport   Good facilities, including heated indoor pool, all-weather pitch, floodlit tennis courts, large sports hall. Coaching aims to introduce pupils to a variety of sports in eight-week spells; girls' soccer well-regarded; good record in cross-country.

Remarks   Ofsted inspectors concluded (1994): 'The school is successful in meeting its aims, which emphasise the all-round development of its pupils. It provides a positive learning culture through a broad and balanced curriculum taught by well-qualified and committed teachers.'

BOURNEMOUTH GIRLS' ♀
Castle Gate Close, Castle Lane West, Bournemouth BH8 9UJ. Tel (01202) 526289

Synopsis
Grammar (grant-maintained) ★ Girls ★ Ages 11–18 ★ 986 pupils ★ 277 in sixth form
Head: Mrs Margaret Matthews, 54, appointed 1984 (retiring August 1998).
Well-run, traditional school; good teaching; lots of extra-curricular activities.

Profile
Background Founded 1918; moved to purpose-built premises on present site (at the bottom of a hill dominated by the boys' grammar school, qv) 1961; opted out of council control 1992. Later additions include futuristic science block; new classrooms under construction; space is tight (and numbers increasing).

Atmosphere Lively, friendly; emphasis on pupil participation. Agreed code of conduct drawn up by girls (rules posted in every form room); detention for transgressors; strict uniform below the sixth form (where smart dress is required).

Admissions School is over-subscribed and highly selective (400 apply for 162 places a year); entry by English and IQ tests. About 40 a year join the sixth form from other schools (minimum of five GCSEs at grade C required). Most (but not all) from middle-class backgrounds.

The head Experienced, efficient manager; quiet, steadfast style. Read modern languages at Southampton; previously head of a grammar school in Kent.

The teaching Mostly formal in style; well-qualified staff of 68 (15 men), 75% appointed by present head. Broad curriculum: all do French and Latin in first year, add German in second; combined sciences taught by subject specialists; all take 10 GCSEs and at least three A-levels (from a choice of 24, some in conjunction with boys' school). Pupils grouped by ability in maths only; average class size 25. Lots of music: 150 individual lessons a week; two orchestras, numerous other ensembles. Wide range of extra-curricular activities, including Duke of Edinburgh award scheme. Regular language exchanges with schools in France, Germany. Good careers advice.

Results (1997) GCSE: 98% gained at least five grades A–C. A-level: 55% of entries graded A or B.

Destinations About 90% proceed to university (average of six a year to Oxbridge).

Sport Particular strengths in tennis, lacrosse, netball. Gymnastics, athletics, cross-country also on offer. Facilities include 32 acres of playing fields shared with boys' school.

Remarks Ofsted inspectors concluded (1994): 'This is a good school with many excellent features. Relationships are good, and mutual respect and trust are high.'

BOURNEMOUTH GRAMMAR ♂
East Way, Bournemouth, BH8 9PX. Tel (01202) 512609

Synopsis
Grammar (grant-maintained) ★ Boys ★ Ages 11–18 ★ 968 pupils ★ 300 in sixth form
Head: John Granger, 48, appointed 1996.
Successful academic school; good teaching and results; strong music.

Profile

Background Founded 1901; moved to present site and functional, purpose-built premises 1939; opted out of council control 1990. Drab classrooms; corridors lined with metal lockers; staff car park doubles as a playground; 'temporary' huts (erected in the 1940s) slowly being replaced.

Atmosphere Hard-working, well-disciplined; high standards expected. Pupils bright, courteous; taught to question and challenge. Efficient pastoral care system; bullying taken seriously and dealt with firmly. Grey-suited uniform; sixth-formers in dark business suits.

Admissions Over-subscribed (300-plus apply for 150 places); academically selective. Entry by tests in English, maths, verbal, non-verbal reasoning; top 15% of the ability range.

The head Read applied physics at Hull; spent 22 years at Torquay Grammar (qv), the last five as deputy head. Married; two daughters.

The teaching Generally traditional in style; long-serving staff of 59 (14 women). Broad curriculum: science (a strength) taught as three separate subjects; all do Latin for first three years and a second modern language from second year (from French, German, Spanish); lots of technology; all computer-literate by end of third year; very good art. Pupils grouped by ability in maths from first year, languages from second year; average class size 25–27; extra help for those who need it. Choice of 20 subjects at A-level (big emphasis on practising exam technique); GNVQ available in business & finance. Strong music: 130 learn an instrument; three choirs, orchestra, various ensembles. Extra-curricular activities include cadet force, well-supported Duke of Edinburgh award scheme. Regular language exchanges with schools in Germany, France, Spain.

Results (1997) GCSE: all gained at least five grades A–C. A-level: 53% of entries graded A or B.

Destinations About 90% go on to university (up to 10 a year to Oxbridge).

Sports Main games: rugby, hockey, cricket, tennis; regular fixtures. Volleyball, fencing, badminton and – unusually – netball also on offer. Gymnasium is past its sell-by date.

Remarks Good all round.

BRADFIELD ♂
Bradfield, Reading, Berkshire RG7 6AR. Tel (0118) 974 4203

Synopsis
Independent ★ Boys (plus girls in sixth form) ★ Boarding and some day ★
Ages 13–18 ★ 627 pupils (95% boarding) ★ 326 in sixth form (60% boys) ★
Fees: £13,425 boarding; £10,068 day
Head: Peter Smith, 53, appointed 1985.
Successful, well-run school; good results; first-rate facilities.

Profile

Background Founded 1850 for the 'careful education of boys as loving children of the Church of England' (sixth-form girls admitted 1977). Distinguished buildings of soft red brick and flintstone set around the village cross-roads in a 185-acre estate surrounded by beautiful countryside; sympathetic later additions (including fine library). Facilities are good.

Atmosphere Relaxed, friendly; a sense of space and timelessness (all wear academic gowns for morning school). Staff live on site and give freely of their time; day pupils encouraged to remain until 9 pm; parents welcome to visit any time. Compulsory chapel twice a week (all faiths welcomed).

Admissions School is over-subscribed (and expanding) but not unduly selective (minimum IQ 110 – head looks for 'doers and joiners'). Entry at 13 by Common Entrance (50% mark required) or school's own exams; at 16 (60 girls join each year) by interview and IQ test. Girls' boarding houses modern, well-equipped; boys' less so, but being upgraded; housemasters do their own recruiting. Most pupils from professional/middle-class backgrounds in the South East; 12% foreign (English taught as a foreign language), 8% expatriate. Lots of scholarships (academic, art, music, technology) and bursaries available.

The head Very able; school has flourished under his strong leadership (numbers up 25%); gets on well with staff and pupils. Read history at Oxford; previously a housemaster at Rugby. Married; two grown-up daughters.

The teaching Good (though HMC inspectors considered that 'many classes are passive, and there is seldom evidence that pupils are excited by the work they are doing'). Well-qualified, committed, relatively youthful staff of 69 (eight women), 70% appointed by present head. Broad curriculum: science on offer as three separate subjects; strong maths; modern languages include German, Spanish, Italian, Japanese, Russian; Latin, Greek available; good facilities for design/technology. All take at least nine GCSEs and three A-levels (from a choice of 23). Pupils grouped by ability in most subjects; extra help for those who need it. First-rate drama (including triennial performance of a Greek play in the original language) and music (choirs, orchestras). Wide range of extra-curricular activities, including cadet force, Duke of Edinburgh award scheme.

Results (1997) GCSE: 94% gained at least five grades A–C. A-level: 47% of entries graded A or B (not a good year).

Destinations About 85% stay on for A-levels; of these, 90% go on to university (average of seven a year to Oxbridge).

Sports Main games: football, hockey, cricket. Rugby, squash, fencing, athletics, lacrosse, gymnastics, netball, golf, basketball also available. Fine facilities include extensive playing fields, all-weather pitch, £3.5 million sports hall and indoor pool, plus 9-hole golf course, opens spring 1998.

Remarks HMC inspectors concluded (1997): 'Bradfield College is first and foremost a supportive and caring community. It espouses all that is best within the broad tradition of British liberal education.'

BRADFORD GIRLS' GRAMMAR ♀

Squire Lane, Bradford, West Yorkshire BD9 6RB. Tel (01274) 545395

Synopsis

Independent ★ Girls ★ Day ★ Ages 11–18 (plus associated junior school) ★ 681 pupils ★ 181 in sixth form ★ Fees: £4,461
Head: Mrs Lynda Warrington, 48, appointed 1987.
Successful academic school; very good teaching and results; strong music.

Profile

Background Founded 1875 (but roots go back to 1662); moved to present 17-acre site and purpose-built premises 1936; formerly Direct Grant, reverted to full independence 1976. Solid stone buildings plus many later additions, including new classrooms, sixth-form centre. Junior school (270 pupils aged three to 11) on same site.

Atmosphere   Busy, purposeful, warm (if somewhat formal). Strict, old-fashioned uniform; sixth-formers required to 'observe standards of dress appropriate to the school'.

Admissions   By interview and highly competitive tests; three apply for each place, more than half of which go to the junior school. Phasing out of assisted places, which about 75 hold, will reduce the social mix. Catchment area extends to Huddersfield, Halifax, Leeds.

The head   Strong leader; exudes confidence. Came here in 1979 having read physics at Leeds; promoted deputy head 1983. Married; no children.

The teaching   First-rate; generally formal in style; experienced, predominantly female staff. Broad curriculum; science on offer as three separate subjects; all do Latin for first three years; other languages include Greek, German, Spanish, Italian, Russian, Japanese; wide choice of 31 subjects at A-level. Lots of art, drama; very strong music (200 learn an instrument; two orchestras).

Results   (1997) GCSE: all gained at least five grades A–C. A-level: creditable 70% of entries graded A or B.

Destinations   About 80% stay on for A-levels; nearly all proceed to university (average of eight a year to Oxbridge).

Sport   Chiefly: hockey, netball, tennis, athletics, swimming. Facilities include sports hall, squash courts, indoor pool.

Remarks   Good, well-run school.

BRADFORD GRAMMAR ♂
Keighley Road, Bradford BD9 4JP. Tel (01274) 542492

Synopsis
Independent ★ Boys (plus girls in sixth form) ★ Day ★ Ages 11–18 (plus associated junior school) ★ 603 pupils ★ 298 in sixth form (90% boys) ★ Fees: £3,720–£4,695
Head: Stephen Davidson, 46, appointed 1996.
Strong, academic school; very good teaching and results; first-rate sport.

Profile
Background   Founded 16th century; granted Royal Charter by Charles II 1662; formerly Direct Grant, became independent 1976. Imposing 1930s building (assembly hall resembles a moderate-sized cathedral, complete with magnificent organ) plus later additions (including fine library, theatre) on a 20-acre site (shared with junior school) a mile from the city centre.

Atmosphere   Well-disciplined, down-to-earth, strongly academic; a beguiling combination of the traditional (head's corridor decorated with Oxbridge coats of arms) and the modern (electronic swipe cards carried by all); formal but friendly relations between staff and pupils.

Admissions   Entry to junior and senior school by tests in English, maths, reasoning; average IQ 120. Pupils come from a wide range of social and ethnic backgrounds in a far-flung catchment area; phasing out of assisted places, which one in four holds, will have a serious impact; co-education likely.

The head   Recent appointment (predecessor had been in post 22 years). Able, dynamic; strong leader; gets on well with staff, parents, pupils and old boys (who make up half the governing body). Read engineering at Manchester; previously head for eight years of the middle school at Manchester Grammar (qv). Married; one young son.

The teaching First-rate: formal in style but lively; very well-qualified staff (more than a dozen have PhDs). Broad curriculum: all take Latin from first year, German from second; Russian, Greek on offer; science taught as three separate subjects; good computing. Lots of drama, music; extra-curricular activities include debating, cadet force, Duke of Edinburgh award scheme.

Results (1997) GCSE: all gained at least five grades A–C. A-level: 59% of entries graded A or B (school has slipped steadily down the league table from 10th in 1993 to 146th in 1997).

Destinations Virtually all go on to university (up to 20 a year to Oxbridge).

Sport Strong, particularly rugby, athletics, cricket, rowing. Facilities include sports hall, indoor pool, running track.

Remarks Very good school for able boys.

BRENTWOOD ♂ ♀

Ingrave Road, Brentwood, Essex CM15 8AS. Tel (01277) 212271

> ## Synopsis
> Independent ★ Co-educational (but boys and girls taught separately to GCSE) ★ Day and some boarding ★ Ages 11–18 (plus associated pre-prep and prep schools) ★ 1,050 pupils (75% boys, 94% day) ★ 300 in sixth form ★ Fees: £6,471 day; £11,283 boarding
> Head: John Kelsall, 53, appointed 1993.
> *Sound school; good results; fine facilities.*

Profile

Background Founded 1558; reconstituted by Act of Parliament 1851; formerly Direct Grant, became fully independent 1976. Attractive, well-maintained buildings on delightful 70-acre site, including Old Big School (dating from 1568 and still in use), Victorian chapel, Edwardian classrooms plus many later additions (lavishly-furnished dining hall, applied science/technology centre). Girls first admitted 1988. Pre-prep and prep schools (ages three to 10) near by.

Atmosphere Air of academic calm: a sense of space, history, tradition (prefects wear gowns) and quality. Boys and girls taught separately up to GCSE; co-educational sixth form. Lessons on Saturday mornings; games on Saturday afternoons. Charcoal grey uniform designed by Hardy Amies (an old boy).

Admissions Entry at 11 by school's own exam, at 13 by Common Entrance; school is fairly selective but may become less so with the phasing out of assisted places, which more than 100 hold. Scholarships, bursaries on offer. Separate boarding houses for (55) boys and (25) girls.

The head Vigorous, forceful, radiates good cheer. Read economics at Cambridge; previously head of Bournemouth Boys' Grammar and Arnold. Married; two grown-up children.

The teaching Lively, stimulating; mostly traditional in style; fairly long-serving staff. Broad curriculum: all do Latin for at least one year; many take two modern languages (French plus choice of German, Spanish, Greek); science taught as three separate subjects; lots of computing. Most take 10 GCSEs (some take maths and French a year early) and three A-levels (from choice of 24).

Pupils grouped by ability in maths, languages; extra help for dyslexics; average class size 21, reducing to 19 for GCSE, 12 at A-level. Lots of drama and music; three orchestras, three large choirs, numerous ensembles. Extra-curricular activities include strong cadet force (450 boys and girls take part), Duke of Edinburgh award scheme, voluntary service. Regular language exchanges, educational visits, sporting tours.

Results   (1997) GCSE: 96% gained at least five grades A–C. A-level: 54% of entries graded A or B.

Destinations   About 85% stay on for A-levels; of these, 90% proceed to university (average of 12 a year to Oxbridge).

Sport   High reputation for boys' games, especially football and fencing; girls do well at hockey. Other strengths: cricket, athletics, netball, cross-country; many more activities on offer. Facilities include extensive playing fields, all-weather pitch, fine sports hall, gym, squash courts, fencing salle.

Remarks   HMI concluded (1995): 'Standards of achievement are generally well above average. The teaching is generally satisfactory or better. The school is well managed and runs smoothly.'

BRENTWOOD URSULINE ♀
Queen's Road, Brentwood, Essex CM14 4EX. Tel (01277) 227156

Synopsis
Comprehensive (grant-maintained, Roman Catholic) ★ Girls ★ Ages 11–18 ★ 750 pupils ★ 150 in sixth form
Head: Miss Helen Penny, 52, appointed 1996.
Successful, happy school; very good GCSE results; first-rate music; plenty of sport.

Profile
Background   Founded 1900 as a private boarding school by Ursuline nuns from Belgium; became a Direct Grant grammar school in the 1950s; went comprehensive 1979; opted out of council control 1994. Imposing brick buildings (old-fashioned, high-ceilinged classrooms) plus later additions, including flat-top 1950s block, in five acres of peaceful grounds.

Atmosphere   Lively, cheerful, friendly. Christian ethos and convent heritage very much in evidence (only two nuns still involved in the school); consideration for others and concern for those less fortunate are part of the fabric. Very good pastoral care system (seniors help juniors). Traditional uniform worn throughout.

Admissions   Wide range of abilities and social backgrounds from an extensive catchment area; 95% Roman Catholic (75% from four Catholic 'feeder' primaries).

The head   Energetic, friendly; came here as deputy head 1993. Read music; spent four years teaching in Nigeria.

The teaching   Mostly traditional in style; desks arranged in rows facing the blackboard. Very good grounding: emphasis on high standards of accuracy, presentation. Experienced, stable staff of 60. Broad curriculum: all do two languages (from French, German, Spanish) for at least three years; Latin also on offer; sixth-form options include Italian, Japanese; good results in English; sound science (on offer to the most able as three separate subjects from 1997); lots of computers but technology is embryonic. Pupils grouped by ability in maths from first year and in most other subjects thereafter; extra help for those with special needs both in the classroom and in a separate unit. Most take nine GCSEs (including compulsory religious studies); A-level options include law, theology, business studies. Imaginative art & design; thriving music (five choirs, orchestra, wind and string groups – regular concerts); drama less exciting. Well-established careers programme; extra tuition for Oxbridge entrance. Regular foreign exchanges, including links with other Ursuline schools in Europe.

Results   (1997) GCSE: very creditable 86% gained at least five grades A–C. A-level: 25% of entries graded A or B (head worries that her pupils' after-school jobs are interfering with their studies).

Destinations   About 65% stay on for A-levels; of these, 50% proceed to university (two or three a year to Oxbridge).

Sport   Lots on offer: hockey, netball, rounders, tennis, athletics taken seriously; swimming particularly strong; fencing, gymnastics, badminton, basketball also available. Facilities include 10 acres of playing fields near by, tennis courts, gym, indoor pool.

Remarks   Attractive school; caters well for all abilities.

BRIGHTON ♂ ♀
Eastern Road, Brighton, East Sussex BN2 2AL. Tel (01273) 704200

Synopsis
Independent ★ Co-educational ★ Day and boarding ★ Ages 13–18 (plus associated junior school) ★ 475 pupils (71% boys, 80% day) ★ 192 in sixth form ★ Fees: £8,760, day; £13,575 boarding
Head: Dr Anthony Seldon, 43, appointed September 1997.
Traditional, academic school; good teaching and results; strong sport.

Profile
Background   Founded 1845 to provide a 'thoroughly liberal and practical education in conformity with the principles of the Established Church'; girls admitted to the sixth form 1973, at 13 in 1988. Splendid quadrangle of Victorian-Gothic buildings (designed by Sir Gilbert Scott) plus sympathetic later additions; English Channel 500 yards from the front door. Co-educational junior school (360 pupils aged three to 13) near by.

Atmosphere   Formal, purposeful (pupils kept busy and have to work hard); good pastoral care; daily chapel service; strong house system (feels like a boarding school). Day pupils stay until 5.30 pm.

Admissions   By Common Entrance (50% mark required – school is not unduly selective) plus 'evidence of good character and conduct'; 60% join from junior school. Day pupils come from up to 30 miles way (school provides buses); pleasant boarding accommodation, recently refurbished (and unusually expensive); weekly boarding available.

The head   Very able; energetic, articulate; good manager (has an MBA). Read history at Oxford, PhD from LSE; previously deputy head of St Dunstan's. Prolific author and commentator; has written a biography of John Major; keen sportsman and dramatist. Married (to a teacher with a PhD); three children.

The teaching   Good quality: formal, demanding in style; hard-working staff (two-thirds male). Broad curriculum: science taught (and examined) as three separate subjects; more able do Latin and German; Greek on offer; choice of 25 subjects at A-level (sciences a strength). Pupils grouped by ability in most subjects; more able take GCSE maths a year early; good specialist help for dyslexics; maximum class size 24, reducing to 15 at A-level. Lots of art, drama, music; 20% learn an instrument; choir, orchestra. Extra-curricular activities include cadet force (compulsory for two years), Duke of Edinburgh award scheme.

Results   (1997) GCSE: 93% gained at least five grades A–C. A-level: 55% of entries graded A or B.

Destinations   About 95% proceed to higher education (up to 10 a year to Oxbridge).

Sports   Strong record; first-rate coaching; all required to take part. Main sports: rugby, hockey, cricket, squash, tennis, netball. Facilities include sports hall, indoor pool, tennis and squash courts; some playing fields one and a half miles away.

Remarks   Good all round.

BRIGHTON & HOVE HIGH ♀
The Temple, Montpelier Road, Brighton, East Sussex BN1 3AT. Tel (01273) 734112

Synopsis
Independent ★ Girls ★ Day ★ Ages 11–18 (plus associated junior school) ★ 512 pupils ★ 97 in sixth form ★ Fees: £4,152
Head: Miss Rosalind Woodbridge, 50, appointed 1989.
Successful, academic school; good teaching and results; liberal atmosphere.

Profile
Background   Founded 1876 by the Girls' Day School Trust to teach girls 'to govern themselves and their conduct in life by their reason and conscience'; moved 1880 to present site, a mansion built in 1819 as a 'Temple of Peace' to celebrate the end of the Napoleonic wars (pilasters of 44 spiked, inverted canons); formerly Direct Grant, reverted to full independence 1976. Later additions on a cramped site include ugly 1960s science block; much-needed refurbishment planned. Delightful junior school (250 pupils aged four to 11) near by.

Atmosphere   Bright, lively; a liberal-minded community; articulate, self-assured pupils. ('Don't complain when your daughter misbehaves at home,' the head tells parents. 'We're not turning out clones'.)

Admissions   By tests; 50% join from junior school (but have to qualify); school is over-subscribed and fairly selective; trust is replacing assisted places with a scheme of its own. Catchment area extends 20 miles.

The head   Able, shrewd, experienced; much liked by staff and pupils. Read history at York, MA from Birkbeck.

The teaching   Good quality; brisk pace; hard-working, well-qualified, predominantly female staff (70% appointed by present head). Fairly broad curriculum; science on offer as three separate subjects; Latin, Greek on offer; GCSE options include drama, computing, home economics, PE; choice of 18 subjects at A-level. Pupils grouped by ability in main academic subjects; average class size 28, reducing to 20 for GCSE, maximum of 10 at A-level. Very good art, music. Wide range of extra-curricular activities, including Duke of Edinburgh award scheme, Young Enterprise; school owns a field centre in mid-Wales.

Results   (1997) GCSE: 98% gained at least five grades A–C. A-level: 58% of entries graded A or B.

Destinations   About 65% stay on for A-levels; of these, virtually all proceed to

university (average of four a year to Oxbridge).
Sport Strong record in tennis, netball. Playing fields five minutes' drive away.
Remarks Attractive school.

BRISTOL CATHEDRAL SCHOOL ♂
College Square, Bristol BS1 5TS. Tel (0117) 929 1872

Synopsis
Independent ★ Boys (plus girls in sixth form) ★ Day ★ Ages 10–18 ★ 470
pupils ★ 112 in sixth form (83% boys) ★ Fees: £4,362
Head: Kevin Riley, 41, appointed 1993.
Sound school; good teaching and results; lots of art, music, drama, sport.

Profile
Background Roots go back to 1140; re-founded by Henry VIII 1542 ('When
bluff King Hal had leisure/From matrimonial joys/He took peculiar pleasure/In
educating boys' – school song); formerly Direct Grant, reverted to full independence 1976. Buildings in the cathedral precincts (surrounded by roads and
wasteland) span eight centuries (many are flag-stoned, lead-windowed and have
tiny, winding, stone staircases); space (inside and out) is very tight (but extra
land recently acquired near by); some classrooms in 'temporary' huts.
Atmosphere Friendly, informal, very male and noisy (lots of jostling and
charging in the claustrophobic corridors and staircases); discipline variable
(head says he has cracked down on bullying). Assembly in the cathedral three
times a week (all staff present). Lots of parental involvement.
Admissions Over-subscribed and fairly selective but phasing out of assisted
places, which more than 150 hold, is likely to have a significant impact. Entry at
11 (choristers start at 10) by tests in English, maths, verbal reasoning (shared
with Bristol Grammar, Queen Elizabeth's Hospital – qv). Large catchment area
(coaches from as far as Weston-Super-Mare, Bridgwater). Scholarships, bursaries available. Food not bad – but chaotic in the serving and eating.
The head Youthful, dynamic; good manager; open, consultative style. Came
here as deputy; promoted after his predecessor fell out with the Dean of Bristol,
chairman of the governors; has introduced many changes, making the school a
happier place. Degrees from Aberystwyth, Bristol; keen on rugby. Married; three
children (two are pupils here).
The teaching Good. Well-qualified staff of 41 (75% male), nearly half appointed by present head (a fairly brisk turnover). Standard national curriculum;
science (modern labs) taught as three separate subjects; Latin on offer; good
results in maths; first-rate art. Choice of 17 subjects at A-level; best results in
maths. Pupils grouped by ability in maths only from second year; extra help for
those with special needs. Lots of drama, music: half learn an instrument; strong
orchestra; cathedral choir. Extra-curricular activities include Duke of Edinburgh
award scheme, fund-raising for a school in Uganda.
Results (1997) GCSE: 95% gained at least five grades A–C. A-levels: 42% of
entries graded A or B.
Destinations About 80% stay on for A-levels; of these, 95% go on to university (four or five a year to Oxbridge).
Sport All traditional sports offered and encouraged (big emphasis on participation – competitive house system). Coaches to 18 acres of playing fields three

miles away.
Remarks   Robust school for children of a fairly wide range of abilities.

BRISTOL GRAMMAR   ♂ ♀
University Road, Bristol BS8 1SR. Tel (0117) 973 6006

Synopsis
Independent ★ Co-educational ★ Day ★ Ages 11–18 (plus associated junior school) ★ 1,043 pupils (60% boys) ★ 283 in sixth form ★ Fees: £4,293
Head: Charles Martin, 57, appointed 1986.
Well-run, academic school; very good teaching and results; lots of music and sport.

Profile
Background   Founded 1532; moved to leafy site behind the university 1879; imposing Victorian-Gothic buildings (stunning Great Hall) plus various additions, including underground design/technology centre. Junior school on same site.

Atmosphere   Serious, unpretentious, well-disciplined (policies on homework, bullying etc agreed between school, pupils and parents). Different age groups housed in separate buildings, which helps break down the size. Uniform worn by all.

Admissions   By exams in English, maths, reasoning (shared with Bristol Cathedral School and Queen Elizabeth's Hospital, qv). School is over-subscribed and has been fairly selective (more so than the two others) but phasing out of assisted places, which a third hold, will have a big impact – not least on the social mix. Scholarships available; more bursaries planned. Wide catchment area; parents run fleet of buses.

The head   Calm, thoughtful, in control: an exemplary head. Read English at Cambridge (still teaches it to the first-years); previously head of a grammar school in Birmingham. Strong opponent of bullying. Married; two children.

The teaching   Challenging; a mixture of traditional and modern methods. Very well-qualified staff of 85 (equal numbers of women and men), nearly half appointed by present head. Broad curriculum: science taught as three separate subjects; all do Latin for first two years; Greek, Russian, German on offer; first-rate design/technology. Pupils grouped by ability in English, maths, science, French; average class size 30, smaller in the sixth form. Lots of music: three choirs, three orchestras, various ensembles. Extra-curricular activities include very well supported Duke of Edinburgh award scheme.

Results   (1997) GCSE: all gained at least five grades A–C. A-level: creditable 70% of entries graded A or B.

Destinations   Nearly all go on to university (average of 15 a year to Oxbridge).

Sport   All required to participate below the sixth form. Very good facilities in on-site leisure centre for tennis, badminton, netball, basketball, squash, indoor cricket, football, climbing (but no swimming pool). Fifty acres of playing fields a short coach drive away; full fixture list in all main games.

Remarks   Very good all round.

BROMLEY HIGH ♀
Blackbrook Lane, Bickley, Bromley, Kent BR1 2TW. Tel (0181) 468 7981

Synopsis
Independent ★ Girls ★ Day ★ Ages 4–18 ★ 857 pupils (559 in senior school) ★ 132 in sixth form ★ Fees: £3,864–£4,968
Head: Mrs Joy Hancock, 49, appointed 1989.
Successful academic school; good facilities; wide range of activities.

Profile
Background   Founded 1883 by Girls' Day School Trust; moved 1981 to present, attractive 24-acre site; purpose-built red-brick premises (ranged around a central courtyard). Spacious facilities include good labs, technology block, smart dining room. Junior school has doubled in size since 1993.

Atmosphere   Quiet, friendly. Self-discipline is the aim; ethos based on co-operation and hard work; girls encouraged to think of themselves as all-round achievers ('Renaissance women'). Parents very involved.

Admissions   Entry at 11 by tests in English, maths; school over-subscribed (2–3 apply for each place) and fairly selective. From 1998, most places will go to girls moving up from the junior school. Wide social mix: 110 have assisted places, which the trust promises to maintain. Scholarships available. Catchment area includes Dartford, Sevenoaks, Orpington; school runs four coaches.

The head   Charming, humorous, astute; sees herself as an 'enabler'. Read history at Nottingham; taught in a secondary modern; previously deputy head of Brighton & Hove High (qv). Married; one daughter (a pupil here).

The teaching   Good quality; range of styles. Full-time staff of 46 (five men). Broad curriculum: science on offer as three separate subjects; lots of computing; head keen on one-year language 'taster' courses (Japanese, Russian, Italian etc); all take at least nine GCSEs and three A-levels. Pupils grouped by ability in maths only; average class size 26, reducing to 20 for GCSE, 10 at A-level. Good art, dance, music (two-thirds learn an instrument). Regular language exchanges with schools in France, Germany, Spain. Well supported Duke of Edinburgh award scheme; lots of community involvement.

Results   (1997) GCSE: all gained at least five grades A–C. A-level: creditable 68% of entries graded A or B.

Destinations   Virtually all go on to university (up to five a year to Oxbridge).

Sport   Lots on offer ('tasters' in cricket, rugby, soccer, lacrosse); netball outstanding. Facilities include all-weather hockey pitch, gym, heated indoor pool, new sports centre.

Remarks   Good all round.

BROMSGROVE ♂ ♀
Worcester Road, Bromsgrove, Worcestershire B61 7DU. Tel (01527) 579679

Synopsis
Independent ★ Co-educational ★ Day and boarding ★ Ages 13–18 (plus associated pre-prep and prep schools) ★ 690 pupils (66% boys, 60% day) ★ 260 in sixth form ★ Fees: £7,020 day; £11,025 boarding
Head: Tim Taylor, 52, appointed 1986.
Well-run, expanding school; good teaching and results; first-rate facilities; lots of extra-curricular activities.

Profile
Background   Medieval foundation re-established as a grammar school 1553; re-endowed 1693 and moved to present 100-acre tree-lined site on the edge of the town; co-educational since 1973. Harmonious collection of buildings spanning 150 years arranged around a spacious quadrangle; school is now nearing the end of an ambitious 10-year, £10 million building and refurbishment programme (including sixth-form centre, new boarding house, futuristic £2.5 million library). Facilities are first-rate. Very good on-site prep school (under its own head).

Atmosphere   Orderly, friendly; strong Christian ethos (full-time chaplain); warm relations between staff and confident, articulate pupils; big emphasis on pastoral care. Smart uniform; 'dress code' for sixth-formers.

Admissions   By interview and school's own tests or Common Entrance; fairly wide range of abilities (minimum IQ about 105), but becoming more selective. Boarding accommodation being upgraded: juniors in five-bed dormitories; seniors in double or single study-bedrooms (some with en suite showers); boarders include about 80 foreign nationals (chiefly Hong Kong, Taiwan). Scholarships (academic, music), bursaries (HM Forces, clergy, teachers) available.

The head   Able, energetic, kindly (knows all his pupils); strong leader; deeply committed to the school (numbers have nearly doubled since his arrival). Read biology at Oxford (athletics Blue); previously housemaster at Millfield, head of Millfield Prep (qv). Married; three children (one a pupil here).

The teaching   Good. Fairly youthful staff of 70 (two-thirds male). Broad curriculum: science available as three separate subjects; Latin on offer; modern languages include German, Spanish, Chinese; good computing. Most take nine GCSEs; sixth-form option include GNVQ in business studies; all do general studies. Pupils grouped by ability (some take GCSE maths a year early); progress carefully monitored (three-weekly grades for effort); extra help for those who speak English as a foreign language. Lots of drama, music (choir, orchestra, more than 400 individual lessons a week). Wide range of extra-curricular activities, including motor maintenance, cadet force, Duke of Edinburgh award scheme.

Results   (1997) GCSE: 94% gained at least five grades A–C. A-level: 62% of entries graded A or B (a good year).

Destinations   About 90% go on to university (up to 10 a year to Oxbridge).

Sport   Main games: rugby, hockey, cricket, netball, athletics, cross-country, tennis, swimming. Facilities include extensive playing fields, new sports hall, indoor pool, all-weather pitch, floodlit tennis and netball courts.

Remarks   Attractive, improving school; recommended.

BROOKE WESTON ♂ ♀
Coomb Road, Great Oakley, Corby, Northamptonshire NN18 8LA. Tel (01536) 460110

Synopsis

Comprehensive (City Technology College) ★ Co-educational ★ Ages 11–18 ★ 1,200 pupils (equal numbers of girls and boys) ★ 300 in sixth form
Head: Gareth Newman CBE, 57, appointed 1990.
First-rate, well-run school; very good teaching and results; excellent facilities.

Profile

Background   Opened 1991 as one of the Conservative Government's network of 15 experimental secondary schools, partly funded by business and industry, devoting 50% of the timetable to maths, science and technology (including a heavy emphasis on IT) and having a longer than usual school day and year. Modern, airy, purpose-built premises (carpeted throughout) on a 15-acre green-field site two miles from the town centre; school open until 6pm – and during the holidays. Ramps and lifts make it accessible to disabled pupils.

Atmosphere   Exceptionally purposeful: highly-motivated staff and pupils delighted to be working in such a high-tech setting; very good rapport between them. Smart, simple uniform; sixth-formers dress 'sensibly'. Parents invited to sit in on lessons (and receive five written reports a year).

Admissions   School is heavily over-subscribed (three apply for each place) but not academically selective; entry by interview to assess motivation, and non-verbal reasoning test to ensure a balanced intake from a catchment area with an eight-mile radius.

The head   Able and very experienced (his third headship); cheerful, bouncy, hard-working; highly visible around the school; has high expectations of everyone; described by Ofsted as an 'outstanding leader'; awarded CBE January 1998. Read physics at Aberystwyth. Married; one son (a pupil here).

The teaching   First-rate; varied styles (team teaching, group work, individualised learning); enthusiastic staff (equal numbers of women and men). National curriculum plus; big emphasis on maths, science (on offer as three separate subjects), technology; computers everywhere (one to every three pupils – first-years can access the school data-base from home); good facilities for media studies (recording and video studios). Unusually long 75-minute lessons (and 32-hour week); pupils group themselves by ability at one of four levels (basic, standard, extended, advanced); top 10% take GCSE maths, science a year early; maximum class size 25. Strong links with local business and industry.

Results   (1997) GCSE: impressive 83% gained at least five grades A–C. A-level: 30% of entries graded A or B.

Destinations   More than 90% continue into the sixth form; most are expected to proceed to higher education.

Sport   Wide range on offer; very good facilities, including sports hall, all-weather pitch.

Remarks   Ofsted inspectors concluded (1996): 'The college offers a high-quality education which combines a focus on technology with a very good ethos which permeates all its work. Students are mature, responsible learners who achieve high standards.' Highly recommended.

BRYANSTON ♂ ♀
Blandford Forum, Dorset DT11 0PX. Tel (01258) 452411

Synopsis
Independent ★ Co-educational ★ Day and boarding ★ Ages 13–18 ★ 624 pupils (57% boys,90% boarding) ★ 280 in sixth form ★ Fees: £14,025 boarding; £9,531 day
Head: Tom Wheare, 53, appointed 1983.
First-rate, well-run school; high academic standards; good art, music, drama; strong sport.

Profile
Background   Founded 1928 as a 'modern' public school to involve pupils 'as much as is possible in the process of their education'. Stunning red-brick and Portland stone mansion (by Norman Shaw) in 400-acre wooded estate by the River Stour; later additions include fine design/technology centre, striking art school, hideous science block.

Atmosphere   Friendly, informal, mature. Individuality recognised (no uniform 'but there are certain restrictions'); big emphasis on self-discipline, self-motivation; easy relations between staff and pupils (feels like a cross between a commune and a university). HMC inspectors found the pupils 'sometimes opinionated but notably more tolerant of one another and sympathetic to human weakness than many of their peers elsewhere'. Day pupils stay until 9 pm; lessons on Saturday mornings.

Admissions   By Common Entrance; school is fairly selective (but not full). First-rate boarding accommodation (including new house for boys); good food. Scholarships (academic, art, technology, music) available.

The head   Able, charismatic; manages by consensus ('The children are the plants, the teachers are the gardeners and I am the climate'). Read history at Cambridge (choral scholar); taught at Eton then became a housemaster at Shrewsbury; intends to stay until 2005. Directs plays, sings in the choir; door always open. Married; two children.

The teaching   Good. Hard-working staff of 70 (two-thirds male), fully committed to the school's distinctive approach. Traditional class teaching at first but pupils are encouraged to take progressively more responsibility for their work, the teachers playing a guiding and advisory role; progress closely monitored. National curriculum plus: science on offer as three separate subjects; Latin, Greek available; first-rate design/technology; big emphasis on creativity. Wide choice of 22 subjects at A-level; all spend at least a quarter of their time on wide-ranging general studies course. Very strong music: more than half learn an instrument; two orchestras, choir. Lots of drama. Extra-currricular activities (designed to 'encourage a sense of responsibility towards the community') include estate work, community service, Duke of Edinburgh award scheme.

Results   (1997) GCSE: 97% gained at least five grades A–C. A level: 57% of entries graded A or B.

Destinations   About 90% stay on for A-levels; of these, 85% proceed to university (up to 15 a year to Oxbridge).

Sport   Strong: all play at least three afternoons a week; facilities include extensive playing fields, all-weather hockey pitch, athletics track, 35 tennis courts, fine sports hall, gym, indoor pool. Sports include rugby, cricket, lacrosse, netball, rowing, fencing, archery, riding.

Remarks   Fine, liberal school for well-motivated children; highly recommended.

BRYMORE ♂
Cannington, Bridgwater, Somerset TA5 2NB. Tel (01278) 652369

Synopsis
Comprehensive (grant-maintained) ★ Boys ★ Boarding and day ★ Ages 13–17
★ 210 pupils (75% boarding) ★ Fees (boarding only): £3,720
Head: Tim Pierce, 47, appointed 1992.
Rare vocational school offering a blend of academic and practical subjects; emphasis on agriculture, horticulture, technology and sports

Profile
Background   Opened 1952 as a secondary technical school; opted out of council control 1994. Large country house plus later additions in 60 acres of parkland, which includes a working farm (dairy, beef, pigs, sheep, chickens) and a walled fruit and vegetable garden – all pupils fully involved in both (6.30 am milking). Stables converted into well-equipped technology centre (including foundry and forges); some classrooms in ageing huts; some areas in need of refurbishment, including shabby refectory.

Atmosphere   Aim is to give a 'sound general education to boys motivated by strong interests in agriculture, horticulture, crafts and the countryside – irrespective of their ultimate career'. Emphasis is on the 'Three Rs often lost in education: resilience, reliability, resourcefulness'; boys – many of whom have experienced limited educational success in their previous schools – offered 'genuine responsibilities – for animals and plants, for machinery and each other'. Firm discipline ('necessarily so, since work with animals and machinery requires strict adherence to rules of behaviour and safety procedures'); notably friendly relations between staff and hard-working boys (though bullying is not unknown). School uniform includes boiler suits, boots with steel toe caps.

Admissions   By assessment of aptitude for what the school has to offer ('We like to see what they're itching to get their hands on'); school has a waiting list. Nationwide catchment area but most live within 50 miles; boys drawn from all walks of life, but farming and engineering backgrounds predominate; 15% have 'statements' of special educational needs. Boarding accommodation in large dormitories (11–20 beds), carpeted but not curtained; everything clean and neat.

The head   An energetic visionary, committed to offering a 'relevant vocational education to as many pupils as possible'. Read physics at Southampton; wide experience in the state sector (interrupted by four years spent running his own garage). Very keen on sport. Married; two daughters.

The teaching   Varied styles (to cope with a fairly wide range of abilities); accent on 'learning by doing'. Well-qualified, hard-working, down-to-earth staff of 20 (five women – including the head of agriculture). Full national curriculum; excellent, practical technology (metals, wood, plastics); good computing (which is taken for granted). GCSE options include agriculture and horticulture. Some stay on after 16 to take a one-year vocational course. Pupils grouped by ability in English, maths, science; extra help for those who need it; average class size 24. Extra-curricular activities include badger-watching, photography, fishing; active Young Farmers' Club.

Results   (1997) GCSE: very modest 23% gained at least five grades A–C (not, in this case, a particularly useful measure).

Destinations   School says that for many years no boy has left 'without an assured job and/or place in further education'; highly regarded by employers.

Sport   Very important (the principal reason some boys are here); emphasis on team effort, participation, fitness. Main games: rugby, cross-country, hockey in winter; athletics, cricket in summer. Badminton, golf, swimming (in solar-heated outdoor pool) also on offer.

Remarks Highly recommended for boys with strong practical interests who would not, perhaps, fit into mainstream schools. (Why are there not more like it?) Ofsted inspectors concluded (1995): 'This is a strong school, in which a substantial majority of pupils succeed and achieve well. Pupils are confident and eager to learn, within the caring and secure environment provided by the school.'

BULLERS WOOD ♀
St Nicolas Lane, Logs Hill, Chislehurst, Kent BR7 5LJ. Tel (0181) 467 2280

Synopsis
Partially selective comprehensive (grant-maintained) ★ Girls (plus a few boys boys in sixth form) ★ 11–18 ★ 1,112 pupils ★ 160 in sixth form
Head: Miss Kathleen Clarke, 46, appointed September 1997.
Successful, well-run school; good teaching and results (especially in languages); strong sport.

Profile
Background Founded as a technical college; went comprehensive 1981; opted out of council control 1991; language college status achieved 1996. Gracious, wisteria-clad Victorian villa (decorated by William Morris) in 22 acres of attractive grounds and woodland. Extensive later additions include new science block, first-rate language centre, IT network, huge sports hall; sixth-form housed separately in congenial surroundings. School has a study centre in Normandy.

Atmosphere Lively, friendly, well-ordered: a very civilised community (much evidence of unprompted good manners). High standards of work and behaviour expected; amicable relations between staff and pupils; well-organised pastoral care; seniors help with junior classes and activities. Uniform (Black Watch tartan skirt, blouse and sweater) strictly enforced until sixth form, when 'respectable dress' demanded. Supportive parents help raise funds.

Admissions School heavily over-subscribed (three apply for each place); 15% of places allocated on general ability; priority for the rest to siblings, those living nearest. Fairly wide range of abilities and backgrounds but catchment area includes affluent, middle-class Petts Wood and Orpington.

The head New appointment (distinguished predecessor had been in post 20 years). Approachable, enthusiastic, committed. Read modern languages at Edinburgh; teaching experience all in Scottish state schools; previously a deputy head.

The teaching Good across the board: predominantly female staff; varied methods; big emphasis on traditional standards of presentation, accuracy, spelling; first-rate facilities. Broad curriculum: all study three languages for first three years (from French, German, Spanish, Italian); all do two languages for GCSE; all sixth-formers continue a language or take up a new one (Japanese on offer); sciences taught separately; good technology (wood, metal, textiles, graphics, electronics); vocational alternatives to A-level include GNVQs in business & finance, hotel & catering, leisure & tourism. Pupils grouped by ability in all subjects from the start; progress closely monitored; extra help for those with special needs. Good art; lively drama.

Results (1997) GCSE: very creditable 79% gained at least five grades A–C. A-

level: 38% of entries graded A or B.
Destinations   About 60% continue into the sixth form; of these, 80% proceed to university.
Sport   Strong tradition: high standards; good record against other schools, particularly in hockey, netball, tennis, athletics, cricket, swimming.
Remarks   Attractive school; caters well for girls with a wide range of interests and abilities. Ofsted inspectors concluded (1994): 'This is a good school.' Recommended.

BURGATE ♂ ♀
Salisbury Road, Fordingbridge, Hampshire SP6 1EZ. Tel (01425) 652039

Synopsis
Comprehensive (grant-maintained) ★ Co-educational ★ Ages 11–18 ★ 727 pupils (slightly more girls than boys) ★ 140 in sixth form
Head: Mrs Celia Nicholls, 44, appointed 1988.
Successful, well-run school; good teaching and GCSE results.

Profile
Background   Opened 1957 as a purpose-built secondary modern; went comprehensive 1981; opted out of council control 1991; sixth form added 1995. Attractive red-brick buildings plus later additions, including fine sixth-form centre, on 20-acre landscaped site.
Atmosphere   Happy, welcoming, well-ordered ('Discipline is firm, fair and friendly,' says the head); commendations for achievement; detention (even on Sunday mornings) for miscreants. Very good relations between staff and pupils; supportive parents.
Admissions   School over-subscribed (nearly 200 apply for 119 places); priority to those living in the catchment area, siblings; wide range of abilities.
The head   Friendly, enthusiastic, down-to-earth; good manager; much admired by staff. Read French and German at Nottingham; came here as deputy head 1982; has worked hard to raise academic standards. Married (to a college lecturer).
The teaching   Varied styles. Standard national curriculum; good science, drama, English; languages include German, Russian; choice of 22 A-levels. Pupils grouped by ability in most subjects; extra help for dyslexics; average class size 22, reducing to 20 for GCSE, 10 in the sixth form. Lots of music: 25% learn an instrument; orchestra. Regular language exchanges with pupils in France, Germany. Extra-curricular activities include public speaking, ballroom dancing, Duke of Edinburgh award scheme.
Results   (1997) GCSE: 72% gained at least five grades A–C. A-level: rather modest 27% of entries graded A or B.
Destinations   Most stay on for A-levels.
Sport   Usual range; particular strengths in hockey (boys), cross-country (girls and boys); rugby making a comeback. Good facilities, including sports hall.
Remarks   Good all round.

BURGESS HILL ♀
Keymer Road, Burgess Hill, West Sussex RH15 0EG. Tel (01444) 241050

Synopsis
Independent ★ Girls ★ Day and boarding ★ Ages 3–18 ★ 655 pupils (570 in senior school, 90% day) ★ 65 in sixth form ★ Fees: £2,790–£5,985 day; £10,125 boarding
Head: Mrs Rosemary Lewis, 55, appointed 1992.
Lively, civilised school; good teaching and results.

Profile
Background Founded 1906 on the then-radical principle that girls had as much right as boys to a good, rounded education. Pleasant Victorian buildings on secluded 12-acre site; £2 million spent since 1992 on new classrooms and facilities; sixth form in some unsightly 'temporary' huts.

Atmosphere Friendly; high spirits within a courteous environment (senior girls gently rebuke younger ones for failing to hold open doors or say 'thank you'). Highly developed system of pastoral care (several trained counsellors). Boarders in bright, converted villas.

Admissions Three and four-year-olds assessed during 'activity session'; admission from junior to senior school is automatic. Entry at seven, 11 and 13 by school's own exams. Broadly middle-class intake; 80% here by word of mouth; 30% of boarders from overseas (links with Malaysia). Music and academic scholarships available.

The head Experienced (15 years at Roedean, latterly as deputy head); a facilitator more than a leader. Read biology at Manchester; teaches it to A-level. Married; two grown-up sons.

The teaching Varied styles; classes orderly but not subdued. Current head has made several new appointments, lowering average age of staff to the late 30s (10% male). Strong science (on offer as three separate subjects); main languages French, German, Spanish; Latin available to A-level. Pupils grouped by ability in core subjects; some extra provision for dyslexics, slow learners; average class size 17. A-level options include psychology, social biology. Lots of art, drama, music (two orchestras). Duke of Edinburgh award scheme is popular.

Results (1997) GCSE: 96% gained at least five grades A–C. A-levels: creditable 74% of entries graded A or B.

Destinations About two-thirds continue into the sixth form (many of the rest switch to state sixth-form colleges); virtually all proceed to university.

Sport Enthusiastic staff. Main games netball, hockey, tennis, rounders. Reasonable facilities.

Remarks Safe, supportive school.

CAISTOR GRAMMAR ♂ ♀
Caistor, Lincoln LN7 6QJ. Tel (01472) 851250

Synopsis
Grammar (grant-maintained) ★ Co-educational ★ Ages 11–18 ★ 578 pupils
(54% girls) ★ 134 in sixth form
Head: Roger Hale, 36, appointed 1996.
Well-run, academic school; good teaching and results.

Profile
Background Founded 1630 (original ironstone hall still in use); opted out of
council control 1991; boarding phased out 1995. Variety of buildings – mainly
1930s and later – form two sides of a close around the parish church; good facilities for science, technology; some classrooms in shabby 'temporary' huts
(according to the prospectus, they 'enjoy a fine view'); limited play space.

Atmosphere Enthusiastic, purposeful, well-ordered; high expectations; competitive house system. Uniform below the sixth form (members of which are
required to dress like 'young professionals at work'). Supportive parents.

Admissions By two verbal reasoning tests ('to assess natural ability rather
than subject knowledge'); those living within a six-and-a-half-mile radius are
required to score a total of 220 marks (top 25% of the ability range) and take a
third of the 84 places; remainder are offered in order of merit to those living outside the catchment (about 125 are disappointed). Parents organise buses.

The head Youthful, energetic, shrewd. Read history at Cambridge; MA in
education from London; previously deputy head here for three years. Married;
two children.

The teaching Good quality ('Teachers respond well to the talents and abilities of the pupils, providing challenging and stimulating lessons,' was how
Ofsted put it). Fairly broad curriculum: sciences (a strength) taught separately;
all start either French or German and add a second language from second year;
Latin on offer; choice of 16 subjects at A-level. Pupils grouped by ability in
maths from third year, modern languages for GCSE; extra help for those who
need it (at both ends of the ability range). Lots of music (free instrumental
tuition); orchestra, two choirs. Extra-curricular activities include Duke of
Edinburgh award scheme.

Results (1997) GCSE: 98% gained at least five grades A–C. A-level: 45% of
entries graded A or B.

Destinations About 75% stay on for A-levels; of these, nearly all proceed to
university (average of two a year to Oxbridge).

Sport Good record in hockey (boys and girls), netball, tennis, athletics.
Playing fields eight minutes' walk away.

Remarks Identified by Ofsted (1996) as 'outstandingly successful'.

CALDAY GRANGE ♂
Grammar School Lane, West Kirby, Wirral L48 8GG. Tel (0151) 625 2727

Synopsis
Grammar (grant-maintained) ★ Boys (plus girls in sixth form) ★ Ages 11–18 ★ 1,310 pupils ★ 400 in sixth form (75 girls)
Head: Nigel Briers, 53, appointed 1987.
Good teaching; broad curriculum; strong sport; wide range of out-of-school activities.

Profile
Background   Founded 1636 as a small charity school; became a grammar school 1944; opted out of council control 1993; technology college status achieved 1996. Medley of buildings, including unappealing 1960s concrete slab, on a hillside with spectacular views of the Dee; recent additions include £1 million technology block; some classes in 'temporary' huts.

Atmosphere   Welcoming, tidy but somewhat cramped. Much thought given to pupils' social and emotional needs. Strict school uniform; sixth-formers soberly dressed.

Admissions   School heavily over-subscribed (450 apply for 180 places); entry by two verbal reasoning tests. Fairly wide range of abilities (top 25%) from a predominantly middle-class catchment area on the Wirral peninsula.

The head   Open, personable, good-humoured. Educated at Wirral Grammar and Manchester University (philosophy, politics and history); taught in Tanzania; previously head of a Cheshire comprehensive. Active in the community (chairman of Wirral Able Children Committee).

The teaching   First rate: highly-qualified staff; approaches range from chalk-and-talk to computers and language labs. Broad curriculum: science taught as three separate subjects; languages include German, Russian, Spanish, Latin (all do two); wide choice of 27 subjects at A-level (good results in law and business studies). Pupils grouped by ability in maths only; particular attention paid to the needs of the very able; class sizes 20–30, reducing to 12 in the sixth form. Good music (orchestra, school and house choirs, staff-student pop group) and strong drama (termly play). Wide programme of extra-curricular activities, including cadets, Christian Union, debating, war games, Duke of Edinburgh award scheme. Exchange visits to France, Germany, USA, Russia.

Results   (1997) GCSE: 98% gained at least five grades A–C. A-level: 39% of entries graded A or B.

Destinations   About 95% stay on for A-levels and nearly all go on to higher education.

Sport   Particularly strong. Main activities: cricket, hockey (teams regularly reach national finals), rugby, athletics, badminton, cross-country, golf. Table tennis, judo, fencing also on offer. Facilities include multi-gym, attractive swimming pool.

Remarks   Good school with a warm heart. Ofsted inspectors concluded (1996): 'The school achieves high levels of success in public examinations and is enabling pupils to develop into mature and responsible young people.'

CAMDEN GIRLS' ♀
Sandall Road, London NW5 2DB. Tel (0171) 485 3414

Synopsis
Comprehensive (voluntary-aided) ★ Girls (plus boys in sixth form) ★ Ages 11–19 ★ 830 pupils ★ 144 in sixth form (51% boys)
Head: Geoffrey Fallows, 56, appointed 1989.
Well-run school; good teaching and results; diverse intake welded into united, harmonious community.

Profile
Background Founded 1871 by Frances Mary Buss, pioneer of women's education, as sister school for North London Collegiate (qv), with which it retains slender links. Became a voluntary-aided grammar under 1944 Act; went comprehensive 1976. Buildings of varied periods and styles on a cramped inner-city site (war damage in the 1940s, cement failure in the 1970s); the result, surprisingly, is a sense of organic growth and continuity (though some areas need modernising and decorating); sixth form in 'temporary' huts. Parents invited to pay £10 a term to supplement funds (school has to pay 15% of the cost of any new buildings).

Atmosphere Old-fashioned comprehensive: mixed-ability teaching; competition played down; minimal supervision; no uniform. All talents encouraged by supportive staff; individualism flourishes in a context of mutual respect; big emphasis on girls achieving their full academic potential (Motto: 'Onwards and Upwards').

Admissions School heavily over-subscribed (about 200 apply for 107 places); priority to siblings, those who have medical or social needs which the school is particularly able to meet, and those living closest 'as the crow flies'; up to five places a year reserved for those demonstrating musical talent. Admission to sixth form by interview. Pupils drawn from a wide range of social, cultural, racial and linguistic backgrounds; 35% black or Asian.

The head Very able. Independent school (Shrewsbury) followed by classics at Oxford; taught in USA, boys' grammar school and large co-educational comprehensive before coming here as deputy head in 1975. His management style, despite the egalitarian ethos, is traditional and hierarchical, the emphasis being on consultation rather than consensus. Married; two grown-up daughters.

The teaching Good: teachers have high expectations; pupils are encouraged to take responsibility for their own learning and to judge themselves against their own potential, rather than in competition with others. National curriculum plus: classical studies for all (Latin an alternative); child development, dance, Greek also available. Wide range of A-levels plus technical and vocational qualifications offered in consortium with four neighbouring schools; all do non-examined general studies course. Pupils grouped by ability in some subjects; class sizes 26/27. Music and art are outstanding; large numbers opt for both at GCSE and A-level; ambitious programme of concerts for three choirs, two orchestras, various ensembles.

Results (1997) GCSE: 56% gained at least five grades A–C. A-level: 46% of entries graded A or B.

Destinations About 70% continue into sixth form; of these, 70% proceed to higher education, including art college.

Sport Emphasis is on individual activity rather than team games; limited competition with other schools.

Remarks   Ofsted inspectors concluded (1995): 'The pupils receive a good quality of education. The standards reached in all subjects are at least sound and standards in aesthetic subjects are exceptional.'

CAMPION, HORNCHURCH ♂
Wingletye Lane, Hornchurch, Essex RM11 3BX. Tel (01708) 452332

Synopsis
Comprehensive (voluntary-aided, Roman Catholic) ★ Boys ★ Ages 11–18 ★
810 pupils ★ 205 in sixth form
Head: John Johnson, 45, appointed 1993.
First-rate Catholic comprehensive; good GCSE results; strong music and rugby.

Profile
Background   Founded as a grammar school by the Society of Jesus in 1962; went comprehensive 1978; now run by laymen but strong Catholic ethos remains. Original buildings small and cramped; later additions include design/technology block, sixth-form centre. Pleasant site on the outskirts of Greater London.

Atmosphere   Well-ordered, caring; high standards expected. 'To lead young people to faith in Christ and to a mature understanding of the Christian faith' remains one of the school's aims; chapel, mass, Catholic assemblies central to its life. Very supportive parents (many of whom are former pupils).

Admissions   School heavily over-subscribed; entry restricted to practising Catholics from practising Catholic families recommended by their parish priest; most places reserved for those living in the deaneries of Havering and Brentwood.

The head   A former pupil here; read English at Cambridge. Wide experience in the state sector. Married; three children.

The teaching   Methods still largely traditional and didactic (every pupil has a textbook for every subject). Long-serving staff (60% men, some are former pupils) give freely of their time. Standard national curriculum; Russian, Latin on offer; most take 10 GCSEs; vocational alternatives to A-level available. Pupils grouped by ability in maths, science, modern languages. Very good music; strong choir. Extra-curricular activities include chess, public speaking, fund raising for charity.

Results   (1997) GCSE: very creditable 75% gained at least five grades A–C. A-level: rather modest 25% of entries graded A or B.

Destinations   About 85% continue into the sixth form; of these, 70% proceed to higher education.

Sport   Outstanding rugby (numerous overseas tours); soccer not neglected; full range of other activities on offer, including fencing, judo, sailing. Facilities include good playing fields, sports hall (paid for by parents), gym, swimming pool.

Remarks   Traditional values upheld in a caring environment.

CANFORD ♂ ♀
Wimborne, Dorset BH21 3AD. Tel (01202) 882411

Synopsis
Independent ★ Co-educational ★ Boarding and day ★ Ages 13–18 ★ 555 pupils (75% boys, 65% boarding) ★ 245 in sixth form ★ Fees: £13,425 boarding; £10,080 day.
Head: John Lever, 45, appointed 1992.
Successful, well-run school; good teaching and results; excellent facilities.

Profile
Background Founded 1923 as an Evangelical challenge to the Anglo-Catholic Woodard schools (and still conscious of its Christian roots). Nineteenth-century manor house plus many recent additions on a beautiful 300-acre country estate (Norman church in the grounds) bordered by the River Stour. Attached to a wall in the tuck shop was an Assyrian frieze thought to be a plaster cast but recently identified as the real thing and sold for £7 million – leading to further building (theatre, huge sports hall, girls' boarding house) and more scholarships. Facilities are good. Fully co-educational since 1995.

Atmosphere Civilised, cheerful, unpretentious, very well-ordered; strong boarding ethos and sense of community; good pastoral care (prefects help look after the juniors).

Admissions By Common Entrance: average 50% mark required; school is not unduly selective. No shortage of boarding applicants (popular with Service families); phasing out of assisted places, which about 70 hold, will not have a big impact. Comfortable boarding houses, some recently refurbished. Lots of scholarships (academic, music, art, Royal Naval) and bursaries (including some for children of Anglican clergy).

The head Able, energetic; committed Christian; keen to raise academic standards and make the school 'still more interesting, colourful and vigorous'. Read geography at Cambridge (rowing Blue); previously head of geography and a housemaster at Winchester (qv). Married; three young children.

The teaching High standard, varied styles; committed staff (predominantly male). Broad curriculum: science taught as three separate subjects; all do two languages (from French, German, Italian, Latin); very good art (enviable facilities); A-level options include business studies, design/technology, sports studies. Pupils grouped by ability in main academic subjects. Strong music: chapel choir, orchestra, string quartets. Wide range of hobbies and activities, including well-supported cadet force, community service programme.

Results (1997) GCSE: all gained at least five grades A–C. A-level: 60% of entries graded A or B.

Destinations About 95% go on to university (average of 12 a year to Oxbridge).

Sports Fine facilities include extensive playing fields, royal tennis court, nine-hole golf course, four squash courts, boathouse on the Stour (pupils may bring own sailing dinghies). Main sports: rugby, hockey, rowing, netball, cricket, tennis, athletics.

Remarks HMC inspectors concluded (1995): 'Canford is an impressive and well ordered school: not only for its appearance but, more importantly, for the quality of work achieved in the classroom, the standard of its games and the scope of its other activities.' Recommended.

CANON SLADE ♂ ♀
Bradshaw Brow, Bolton BL2 3BP. Tel (01204) 401555

Synopsis
Comprehensive (Church of England, grant-maintained) ★ Co-educational ★
Ages 11–18 ★ 1,500 pupils (55% girls) ★ 280 in sixth form
Head: Rev Peter Shepherd, 48, appointed 1989.
Well-run, firmly Christian comprehensive; broad curriculum; first-rate sport.

Profile
Background Founded 1855 by a committee chaired by Canon James Slade, vicar of Bolton. Became a Direct Grant grammar school 1946; opted for Church of England voluntary-aided status 1976; went comprehensive 1978; opted out of council control 1993. Moved to present 55-acre site two miles east of town centre 1956; mixture of flat-roofed 1960s buildings and more distinguished 1970s additions. School is over-crowded and parts are in need of redecoration; new 14-classroom teaching block will permit annual intake to rise from 240 to 270 from September 1998.

Atmosphere Permeated by Christian values: staff and pupils clearly share a strong sense of common purpose. ('Our mission is to prepare pupils for active Christian service in the community,' says the prospectus. 'The school motto, Ora et Labora – pray and work – identifies our priorities exactly.') Firm discipline; orderly movement between lessons; no litter; all pupils below the sixth form in strict school uniform. Good pastoral care system ensures no one gets lost; school council gives everyone a voice. Display cases crammed with evidence of sporting success; impressive artwork adorns the corridors.

Admissions School heavily over-subscribed; all pupils admitted without reference to ability or aptitude; admission based on points for frequence and length of attendance at Sunday worship at a Christian church by child and parent(s) as attested to by a member of the clergy (requisite number of points has risen from 13 to 31 in three years). Catchment area extends to Manchester and Bury; wide range of abilities and social backgrounds.

The head Lives his faith without advertising the fact; totally dedicated and very able. Grammar school boy from working-class background; read history at Reading. First teaching post was in a tough, inner-city secondary modern (he is 6'5"); given all the bottom streams and loved it. Later obtained divinity degree and MPhil from London (thesis on Christian-Hindu dialogue) and MA in education management; ordained but has not run a parish. First headship at 34; believes that the law requiring all state schools to hold a daily act of worship is 'entirely without educational, moral or theological justification'. Married; two daughters (both were pupils here).

The teaching Good. Lively, well-prepared lessons; teachers versatile in their methods. Broad curriculum (no premature specialisation); exceptionally wide choice of 35 subjects at GCSE (including German, Spanish, Latin, separate sciences) and 27 at A-level (including Greek, psychology, fashion, environmental science). Good technology; religious studies not a Cinderella subject; homework strictly monitored. Pupils grouped by ability from second year; special needs taken seriously; classes on the large side – 30 in the first year, gradually tapering to average of 12 in the sixth form. Strong drama and music; two choirs, brass band, orchestra, string ensemble etc. Huge range of clubs and societies (chess, Christian Union, computers, gardening, karate, model railways). Regular pupil exchanges with France, Germany, Spain, Japan. Generous support for charities.

Results (1997) GCSE: 65% gained at least five grades A–C. A-level: 31% of entries graded A or B.

Destinations About 50% proceed from GCSE to A-level; of these, 80% go on to higher education (about five a year to Oxbridge).

Sport Outstanding record, especially in basketball and soccer; other sports include hockey, netball, cricket, tennis, athletics, cross-country. Extensive playing fields; sports hall, swimming pool.

Remarks Impressive school; first-rate head. Ofsted inspectors concluded (1994): 'This is a high achieving and successful school. Pupils of all ages and abilities achieve well in a wide range of subjects. High standards of behaviour and discipline permeate the whole school and good learning flourishes.'

CARDIFF HIGH ♂ ♀
Llandennis Road, Cyncoed, Cardiff CF2 6EG. Tel (01222) 757741

Synopsis
Comprehensive ★ Co-educational ★ Ages 11–18 ★ 1,230 pupils (roughly equal numbers of girls and boys) ★ 275 in sixth form
Head: Mike Griffiths, 49, appointed September 1997.
First-rate comprehensive; strong academic record.

Profile
Background Result of a 1970 merger of two single-sex grammar schools; inadequate 1960s buildings (formerly a secondary modern) on prime 19-acre site in wealthy, residential Cardiff; £4 million building programme under way.

Atmosphere Purposeful, disciplined – a tight ship. Strict uniform (no jewellery); any petty thieving, racial harassment, rudeness taken seriously and dealt with swiftly.

Admissions Big pressure on places; automatic entry from two local 'feeder' primaries; rest from wide area who fit the criteria – medical reasons, siblings, ease of travelling etc. Most from professional/middle-class homes; 15% ethnic minority.

The head New appointment – but his third headship. Read economics at Cardiff. Married; two children.

The teaching Styles vary from traditional to workshop-based approach. Standard national curriculum; Welsh compulsory for first three years; strong science. Some classes up to 34. Particularly good special needs department (dyslexia a speciality). A-level options include sociology, law; GNVQ in business studies on offer. First-rate music (insulated recording studio). Regular exchanges with schools in France, Germany. Lots of charity work.

Results (1997) GCSE: creditable 76% gained at least five grades A–C. A-level: 51% of entries graded A or B.

Destinations About 80% continue into the sixth form; of these, 85% proceed to university (average of seven a year to Oxbridge).

Sport Wide choice: hockey, netball, cross-country, rugby, cricket, soccer, athletics. Facilities only adequate (unheated sports hall, no formal swimming lessons). Outdoor pursuits popular; rock climbing an option.

Remarks Successful school; parents move house to gain entry. Ofsted inspectors concluded (1995): 'The quality of learning is predominantly good. The majority of pupils show high levels of concentration, commitment and motivation. Overall, very good progress is made across the majority of subjects.'

CARDINAL VAUGHAN ♂
89 Addison Road, London W14 8BZ. Tel (0171) 603 8478

Synopsis
Comprehensive (grant-maintained, Roman Catholic) ★ Boys (plus girls in sixth form) ★ Ages 11–18 ★ 720 pupils ★ 180 in sixth form (68% boys)
Head: Michael Gormally, 42, appointed July 1997.
First-rate school; firm Catholic ethos; very good teaching and results; strong art, music.

Profile
Background Founded 1914 as a memorial to Cardinal Vaughan (who built Westminster Cathedral). Originally independent; became a voluntary-aided grammar school 1948, went comprehensive 1977; opted out of council control 1990. Splendid but slightly gloomy Victorian building plus functional 1960s block and later additions, including well-equipped technology centre, on a cramped, split site in leafy Holland Park.

Atmosphere Happy, hard-working, very well disciplined ('The school has never abandoned its traditional approach to teaching and learning'). Strong emphasis on high moral standards and aiming for excellence; Roman Catholicism and Christian values absolutely fundamental. Truancy rate negligible; no variation in uniform permitted. Enthusiastic, supportive parents; loyal Old Boys.

Admissions School always over-subscribed. Pupils of a wide range of abilities and social backgrounds from a catchment area that extends to Hillingdon and Richmond; membership of Roman Catholic Church the common factor; 10% of places reserved for those of high musical ability and aptitude.

The head New appointment – but not new to the school: came here 1980 as a post-graduate student; stayed and worked his way up. Read French at London; committed Catholic; accomplished linguist and musician. Unmarried ('I'm married to the school, a demanding spouse').

The teaching First-rate: formal, traditional, structured. Dedicated, well-qualified staff; much use made of target setting to raise attainment (progress closely monitored). Every lesson starts with the sign of the cross, every classroom contains a crucifix, to which reference is frequently made. Exceptionally broad curriculum: science on offer as three separate subjects (newly refurbished labs); strong language department (French, German, Spanish); more able take Latin from third year; Greek taught out of school hours; first-rate art; religious education compulsory throughout. Vocational alternatives available to A-level. Pupils grouped by ability in virtually all subjects; plenty of help for those with special needs; some classes over 30. Very good music: two orchestras, three choirs (one of which, the schola cantorum, regularly tours abroad). Lots of clubs: chess, computers, model railway (popular refuge at lunchtime, particularly for juniors). Regular language trips to France, Germany.

Results (1997) GCSE: very creditable 85% gained at least five grades A–C. A-level: 43% of entries graded A or B.

Destinations About 75% continue into the sixth form; most of these proceed to university (four or five a year to Oxbridge).

Sport Chiefly soccer, rugby, rowing; regular Saturday morning matches against other schools. Facilities include good gym for basketball, volleyball; playing fields at Twickenham.

Remarks   Ofsted inspectors concluded (1997): 'This is a very good, high achieving school with very high standards.' Strongly recommended.

CARRE'S ♂
Northgate, Sleaford, Lincolnshire NG34 7DD. Tel (01529) 302181

Synopsis
Grammar (grant-maintained) ★ Boys ★ Ages 11–18 ★ 570 pupils ★ 131 in sixth form
Head: Peter Freeman, 57, appointed 1983.
Traditional grammar school; good GCSE results; strong sport.

Profile
Background   Founded 1604; moved 1835 to present site on the edge of the town; became a voluntary-aided grammar school 1948; opted out of council control 1990. Mainly 1960s buildings (this is no architectural jewel); later additions include fine sports hall; technology block due for completion September 1998.
Atmosphere   Well-ordered, business-like; challenging without being intimidating. Good relations between staff and able, courteous boys. Uniform (black blazer edged with red braid) worn by all.
Admissions   Selective: top 25% of the ability range. Entry via 11–plus set by the Lincolnshire consortium of grammar schools: two verbal reasoning tests each containing 100 questions, which candidates have 50 minutes to complete. Pupils mainly from Sleaford and surrounding districts but some travel from Nottinghamshire and Leicestershire.
The head   Kindly, approachable but with a hint of steel (which the boys respect). Read English at Cambridge; teaches Latin, English, general studies, religious education for a quarter of the timetable. Married (to a teacher); two grown-up children (one was a pupil here).
The teaching   Long-serving staff of 45 (80% male). Standard national curriculum plus Latin; language options include German, Spanish; sciences taught separately; IT widely used. Pupils grouped by ability in maths from third year, French for GCSE; class sizes vary from 24 to 30. All take 10 GCSEs. Joint sixth form with neighbouring Kesteven & Sleaford High (qv) offers choice of 30 A-levels, including art, geology, computing, psychology, theatre studies; GNVQs available in business, health & social care. Lots of music (choirs, wind band, guitar group). Extra-curricular activities include drama, chess, fishing, Duke of Edinburgh award scheme.
Results   (1997) GCSE: 92% gained at least five grades A–C. A-level: 39% of entries graded A or B.
Destinations   Nearly all proceed to higher education (two or three a year to Oxbridge).
Sport   High standards in all the major games: soccer, rugby, cricket, basketball, hockey, badminton, tennis, swimming, athletics. Golf, weight training also popular.
Remarks   Good all round.

CASTERTON ♀
Kirkby Lonsdale, Carnforth, Lancashire LA6 2SG. Tel (015242) 79200

Synopsis
Independent ★ Girls ★ Boarding and day ★ Ages 8–18 (plus co-educational pre-prep) ★ 353 pupils (80% boarding) ★ 87 in sixth form ★ Fees: £7,881–£10,098 boarding; £5,499–£6,336 day
Head: Anthony Thomas, 53, appointed 1989.
Successful, well-run school; good teaching and results; fine facilities.

Profile
Background Founded 1823 to educate daughters of the clergy (one of the oldest girls' schools in England); moved to present site and purpose-built (now modernised) premises 1833; striking later additions include creative arts block, huge gym (swimming pool attached), £750,000 maths and science block. High standard of maintenance, decoration and equipment. Glorious views of the fells. The Brontës were pupils here.

Atmosphere Very much a family: intimate, friendly, informal. Every minute filled to good effect. Confident, articulate pupils, all of similar backgrounds, abilities and motivation; disciplinary problems virtually non-existent.

Admissions Most enter at eight or 11 by school's own tests designed to identify those capable of acquiring a good crop of GCSEs. Pupils mainly from the north of England, some from Scotland, a few from abroad; some are great granddaughters of former pupils. Juniors in warm, bright dormitories (up to six beds); seniors in five houses, each with own sitting room and kitchen; sixth-formers in cottages enjoy a good deal of freedom.

The head An enthusiast with a close knowledge of all his pupils. Read maths at Cambridge. Previously a housemaster at Sedbergh (qv), with which the school has strong links. Keen on music; coaches lacrosse.

The teaching Fairly formal in style; mature, highly-qualified staff who give unstintingly of their time and expertise. Traditional curriculum (home economics rather than food technology); main strengths in languages (French, German, Spanish, Latin) and sciences (taught as three separate subjects); all master word-processing (computing provision is generous and up to date). Choice of 20 subjects at A-level (creditable for such a small school). Very little setting by ability; small classes (maximum 15); some individual tuition in sixth form. Good library facilities; mini-theatre suitable for performances and ballet-training. Remarkably wide programme of extra-curricular activities.

Results (1997) GCSE: all gained at least five grades A–C. A-level: 49% of entries graded A or B.

Destinations Nearly all stay on for A-levels; 90% proceed to university (three or four a year to Oxbridge).

Sport Not a school that forces pupils to feats of outdoor endurance but active pursuits encouraged. Main activities: hockey, tennis, lacrosse, cricket, swimming, canoeing, hill walking. First-rate facilities, including stables (girls can bring their own horses).

Remarks A small jewel in an idyllic setting.

CATERHAM ♂ ♀
Harestone Valley Road, Caterham, Surrey CR3 6YA. Tel (01883) 343028

Synopsis
Independent ★ Co-educational ★ Day and boarding ★ Ages 11–18 (plus associated prep school) ★ 700 pupils (66% boys, 80% day) ★ 200 in sixth form ★ Fees: £6,396 day; £11,3799–£12,435 boarding
Head: Robert Davey, 50, appointed 1995.
Sound school; good teaching and results; beautiful setting.

Profile
Background Founded 1811 in Lewisham for the sons of Congregational ministers (strong links with United Reformed Church remain); moved to present rural, 80-acre site 1884; formerly Direct Grant, became fully independent 1976; merged with neighbouring Eothen Girls' School 1995. Gracious, three-storey, red-brick Victorian buildings plus many later additions, including new classroom block, music school. Pre-prep and prep schools in the grounds.

Atmosphere Calm, purposeful; friendly relations between staff and pupils. Smart uniform; sixth-form boys in suits, girls in elegant long skirts and blazers.

Admissions At 11 by interview and tests in English, maths, verbal reasoning (half join from the prep school); at 13 by Common Entrance; school is not unduly selective; 12% of pupils from abroad. About 25 a year join the sixth form with at least GCSEs grade B in intended A-level subjects. Comfortable boarding accommodation (two boys' houses, one girls'); seniors have single study-bedrooms. Scholarships (academic, music) and bursaries available.

The head Good manager. Read modern languages at Trinity College, Dublin; previously deputy head for eight years of Wells Cathedral School (qv). Married; three children (one a pupil here).

The teaching Good: lively, well-planned lessons; well-qualified staff of 65 (60% male); pleasant, co-operative pupils. Broad curriculum: all do French plus Spanish or German for first three years; Latin, Greek on offer; science taught as three separate subjects (but dual-award GCSE); lots of computing. Choice of 21 subjects at A-level; most take three plus general studies. Pupils grouped by ability from the start; further setting by subject thereafter; progress closely monitored (half-termly grades); average class size 22. Lively art, thriving music (two choirs, two orchestras, various ensembles). Extra-curricular activities include cadet force, popular Duke of Edinburgh award scheme.

Results (1997) GCSE: 93% gained at least five grades A–C. A-level: 57% of entries graded A or B.

Destinations Virtually all go on to university (average of five a year to Oxbridge).

Sport Good facilities, including extensive playing fields, all-weather pitch, sports hall, indoor pool. Main games: rugby, hockey, cricket for boys; hockey, lacrosse, netball, rounders for girls. Athletics, tennis, badminton, cross-country, basketball, volleyball, judo, squash also on offer.

Remarks Good all round and likely to get better.

THE CEDARS ♂ ♀
Mentmore Road, Leighton Buzzard, Bedfordshire LU7 7PA. Tel (01525) 375636

Synopsis
Comprehensive ★ Co-educational ★ Ages 13–18 ★ 1,305 pupils (roughly equal numbers of girls and boys) ★ 370 in sixth form.
Head: John Mitchell, 50, appointed 1994.
Sound school; good teaching and results; first-rate sports facilities.

Profile
Background   Founded 1921 as a grammar school; went comprehensive and moved to present semi-rural site on the outskirts of the town 1973. Well-maintained, purpose-built premises supplemented by 20 'temporary' huts (school is over-crowded); sixth-form centre under construction.

Atmosphere   More adult than most secondaries thanks to later starting age; self-discipline achieved without obvious supervision. Interior brightened by good displays of high-quality art. Sensible, simple uniform; sixth-formers required to be 'neat and tidy and suitably dressed for their work'. Many staff send their own children here (on-site nursery run jointly with an agency).

Admissions   School full but not over-subscribed; priority to those attending 'feeder' schools. Most from supportive middle-class homes.

The head   Read drama at East Anglia, MEd from London.

The teaching   Lively; varied styles (consumer research to identify what pupils find most helpful). Standard national curriculum; all take French plus German or Spanish; choice of 21 subjects at A-level; compulsory AS-level in general studies; GNVQs available in business, art & design, engineering, health & social care. Pupils grouped by ability in maths, modern languages from first year; parents asked to monitor homework. Strong music (three orchestras, bands, ensembles etc). Extra-curricular activities include well-supported Duke of Edinburgh award scheme. Regular language exchanges with schools in France, Germany, Spain, Italy.

Results   (1997) GCSE: 65% gained at least five grades A–C. A-level: 43% of entries graded A or B.

Destinations   More than 70% continue into the sixth form; of these, about 65% proceed to university (average of four a year to Oxbridge).

Sport   Excellent facilities include large sports hall for indoor tennis, cricket, volleyball, soccer, netball, basketball, hockey, gymnastics, badminton; impressive fixture list (Saturdays included). Extensive playing fields plus floodlit all-weather pitch; swimming pool and squash in adjacent leisure centre; canoeing on the Grand Union Canal.

Remarks   Committed staff; well-motivated pupils; good all round.

CENTRAL NEWCASTLE HIGH ♀
Eskdale Terrace, Newcastle-upon-Tyne NE2 4DS. Tel (0191) 281 1768

Synopsis
Independent ★ Girls ★ Day ★ Ages 11–18 (plus associated junior school) ★ 603 pupils ★ 190 in sixth form ★ Fees: £4,152
Head: Mrs Angela Chapman, 57, appointed 1985.
First-rate, well-run school; very good teaching and results; lots of art, drama, music.

Profile

Background Founded 1895 by the Girls' Public Day School Trust: a century's unbroken tradition of educating women for the professions. Purpose-built Victorian premises (solid redbrick and stucco) on a restricted site plus many later additions and acquisitions (including a former synagogue – head keeps a close eye on the property market). First-rate music school, fine art department; high standards of maintenance and furnishing throughout.

Atmosphere Notably friendly, welcoming; staff and pupils treat each other with affection and respect; 'the only rules are to do with health and safety – we have no crimes and no sanctions'. Girls are sensible, assured, co-operative. Good pastoral care (older pupils help look after the younger ones). Brown uniform below the sixth form, where elegant trouser suits are favoured. Parents enthusiastically supportive (though some would like to be more involved).

Admissions School is over-subscribed (three apply for each place) and highly selective; junior school pupils take two-thirds of the places; remainder by interview and school's own exam; average IQ 120. Most from middle-class/professional/business backgrounds in a wide catchment area (Northumberland, Durham, Tyne & Wear); 20% ethnic minority. Phasing out of assisted places, which 102 hold, is unlikely to affect numbers or entry standards but will reduce the (relatively classless) social mix. Some scholarships, bursaries available.

The head Able, experienced, very effective; direct, down-to-earth manner; popular with, and respected by, staff and pupils. Read modern languages at Bristol; diploma from the Sorbonne. Married (to a legal consultant); two grown-up sons.

The teaching First-rate: traditional in style but modern in spirit (much questioning and discussion); orderly, attentive classes. Well-qualified, conscientious staff of 60 (including 10 men), half appointed by present head; good mix of youth and experience. Broad curriculum: all do Latin; French, German, Spanish, Greek on offer (languages a speciality); science taught as three separate subjects (many go on to do medicine); sixth-form options include wide range of general interest courses. Pupils grouped by ability from second year in maths, French; average class size 25–28, reducing to 12–15 at A-level. Flourishing art (on display everywhere), drama, music; all learn to play the violin or viola for the first year; three choirs, two orchestras. Plenty of extra-curricular activities, including Duke of Edinburgh award scheme. Regular language exchanges.

Results (1997) GCSE: all gained at least five grades A–C. A-level: 67% of entries graded A or B.

Destinations Almost all who stay on for A-levels proceed to university (average of 10 a year to Oxbridge).

Sport Not dominant: games taught chiefly for fitness and enjoyment. Main sports: hockey, gymnastics, athletics, volleyball, badminton, swimming, netball. Good sports hall; playing fields, including all-weather pitch, a few minutes' walk away.

Remarks Very good school: a stimulating and civilising environment; hard-working but not an academic hot-house. Recommended.

CHANNING ♀
Highgate, London N6 5HF. Tel (0181) 340 2328

Synopsis
Independent ★ Girls ★ Day ★ Ages 4–18 ★ 496 pupils (340 in senior school) ★ 75 in sixth form ★ Fees: £5,715–£6,210
Head: Mrs Isabel Raphael, 59, appointed 1984 (retiring December 1998).
Small, successful school; very good teaching and results; plenty of extra-curricular activities.

Profile
Background Founded 1885 for the 'daughters of Unitarian ministers and others' (church links retained). Senior school in Georgian terrace plus later additions at the top of Highgate Hill; junior school (under its own head) near by; 12 acres in all. Facilities generally good.

Atmosphere Friendly, family school (lots of siblings and daughters of old girls); headmistress knows everyone. Good pastoral care; strong parental involvement.

Admissions At 11-plus by tests in English, maths (shared with North London Collegiate, City of London Girls etc) and interview; transfer from junior school not automatic; school heavily over-subscribed and can afford to be selective. Most from middle-class/professional backgrounds, one third Jewish; nearly all live within five miles. Scholarships, bursaries available.

The head Experienced, dedicated, very able (and can seem formidable). Read classics at Cambridge; first taught here in the 1950s then spent 20 years abroad. Teaches mythology to 10-year-olds, Latin to 12-year-olds, poetry to the sixth form. Has transformed the school (and will be hard to replace).

The teaching Well-qualified staff (nearly all appointed by present head), varied styles: younger girls in formal classrooms, old fashioned desks; sixth-form teaching more relaxed (but no less intense). National curriculum plus; lots of computing; pupils grouped by ability for maths, science (dual award), French. High-fliers well catered for but no provision for special needs; class sizes 24–28, reducing to a maximum of 20 for GCSE, 12 for A-level. Good art, drama, music (three orchestras). Wide range of extra-curricular activities; all required to do community service.

Results (1997) GCSE: all gained at least five grades A–C. A-level: very creditable 75% of entries graded A or B.

Destinations Nearly all go to university, including a handful each year to Oxbridge.

Sport Lots on offer: archery, badminton, dance, fencing, football, gymnastics, hockey, netball, rounders, squash, swimming, tennis, trampolining. Facilities include six netball pitches, seven tennis courts, sports hall.

Remarks Good school for able girls who might wilt in larger academic power-houses.

CHARTERHOUSE ♂

Godalming, Surrey GU7 2DJ. Tel (01483) 291600

Synopsis

Independent ★ Boys (plus girls in sixth form) ★ Boarding and some day ★
Ages 13–18 ★ 700 pupils (97% boarding) ★ 320 in sixth form (75% boys) ★
Fees: £13,941 boarding; £11,520 day
Head: Rev John Witheridge, 43, appointed 1996.
Distinguished school; good teaching and results; lots of opportunities for art, music, drama, sport.

Profile

Background Founded 1611 on the site of a Carthusian house in Smithfield by Thomas Sutton, wealthy Jacobean money-lender; moved 1872 to present fine, 200-acre site above Godalming. Gravely elegant Victorian buildings, turreted and Gothic, plus many later additions, including £3.7 million sports centre (opened by the Queen).

Atmosphere Happy: an uplifting mixture of old and new; some pupils always hurrying but there is time to notice the superb views (by Surrey standards). Civilised rules urge pupils to be 'clean, tidy and smartly dressed' and 'try to be cheerful and positive in all that you do' (and they do a lot); sixth-form girls fit in easily, after initial nervousness on both sides. Chapel compulsory and regular: a lofty building designed by Gilbert Scott, not ideal for audience participation but austerely beautiful.

Admissions 'At some time between the boy's 10th and 11th birthday, the opinion of his current headmaster will be sought concerning his suitability for Charterhouse,' observes the prospectus loftily. 'Parents can then be offered a guaranteed school place, subject to success in the Common Entrance examination.' School is quite selective. Boarding accommodation divided between modernised Victorian houses (high ceilings, honours boards and the hot pipes and radiators that comforted previous generations) and 1970s replacements (study-bedrooms radiating off a central stair; cosy sitting areas and all mod cons). Girls 'mainstream' during the day, each having a study in a boys' house, but at 10 pm are taken (by mini-bus) to their lodgings: in their first year a house of 12 other girls; in their second a family, usually a member of the teaching staff. Most pupils live within two hours' travelling; about 100 from abroad. Lots of scholarships, bursaries.

The head Recent appointment (after his predecessor left under an embarrassing cloud). Combines tough determination with friendly charm. Read English and theology at Kent and Cambridge; became chaplain to the Archbishop of Canterbury; previously senior chaplain for nine years at Eton. Married (wife much involved in school life); four children.

The teaching Some very good – enthusiastic, scholarly, dedicated – backed up by a system of 'calling over' two or three times a term, when the form master (an important figure) brings his charges in front of the head or deputy and goes through their placings and effort marks in detail. Lively staff of 80 (10 women) who obviously enjoy working here and have easy relationships with the pupils. School's reputation rests largely on its successes in the arts but times may demand changes: at present, combined rather than separate sciences are taken at GCSE; classics making a minor comeback but few boys enter with any Greek; main arts subjects still flourish but there is potential for modern languages to expand; impressive technology centre (open seven days a week). The timetable, as elsewhere, is becoming increasingly crammed; first-years given a busy time trying to fit in a bit of everything; pupils grouped by ability from the start. Choice of 70 extra-curricular pursuits: music has a notable reputation, both choir and orchestra; regular successes at Oxbridge; composer in residence. Fine Ben Travers theatre mounts 20 productions a year. Lots of outings: London theatres, Welsh mountains, activity centre in the Derbyshire Dales. Strong cadet force and Scout troop (Baden-Powell was a pupil here).

Results (1997) GCSE: 99% gained at least five grades A–C. A-level: creditable 70% of entries graded A or B.

Destinations Nearly all go to university (about 30 a year to Oxbridge).

Sport Vast array; particular strengths in soccer, cricket. Facilities include extensive playing fields, indoor pool, all-weather hockey pitch and athletics track, nine-hole golf course.

Remarks HMC inspectors concluded (1995): 'The standards of achievement are good. Exam results at GCSE and A-level reflect pupils who are performing in line with their high ability. Some lessons are inspirational, but others lack zest. There is a tendency for lessons to be too strongly teacher led and for the teaching to demand insufficient work of pupils.'

CHARTERS ♂ ♀
Charters Road, Sunningdale, Berkshire SL5 9QY. Tel (01344) 24826

Synopsis
Comprehensive ★ Co-educational ★ Ages 11–18 ★ 1,380 pupils (roughly equal numbers of girls and boys) ★ 230 in sixth form
Head: Mrs Marcia Twelftree, 47, appointed September 1997.
Good all-round school; happy atmosphere; creditable GCSE results.

Profile
Background Opened in the 1950s as a secondary modern; went comprehensive late 1960s; buildings (including some 'temporary' huts) added steadily since. Functional-looking, 30-acre campus in an up-market residential area; school has exclusive day-time use of an on-site leisure centre.

Atmosphere Happy, positive, purposeful: committed staff; eager, well-mannered pupils. Strong adherence to the slogan, 'Unity, Respect, Excellence'; older pupils have a duty of care to the younger ones; special provision for children with learning difficulties and physical disabilities. Strict uniform below the sixth form (sixth-formers have their own study and recreational centre). Art work displayed in all available spaces. High level of parental support and involvement. School owns a residential centre in Wales.

Admissions Heavily over-subscribed: more than 300 apply for 210 places. No academic selection; places allotted by Berkshire County Council according to geographical criteria (Sunninghill, Ascot etc); fairly wide social mix but few from disadvantaged or ethnic minority backgrounds.

The head New appointment; previously head for four years of a smaller comprehensive in Hungerford. Warm, outgoing personality; has a reputation for energy and innovation. Teaches A-level chemistry. Married; two grown-up children.

The teaching Calm, efficient; an atmosphere of quiet, well-ordered learning. Standard national curriculum; Spanish on offer as an alternative to French.

Impressive facilities for art (light, airy rooms); good metalwork, woodwork, graphic design. Class sizes 30, reducing to 20 for GCSE, 15 at A-level. Homework regularly set and monitored. Wide variety of extra-curricular activities; public speaking a speciality, drama a strength.
Results (1997) GCSE: 67% gained at leave five grades A–C. A-level: 46% of entries graded A or B.
Destinations Few leave after GCSE; most sixth-formers proceed to higher education.
Sport Wide choice; all participate. Traditional team games: football, rugby, cricket, netball, basketball; also tennis, athletics etc at leisure centre.
Remarks Ofsted inspectors concluded (September 1996): 'This is a very good school with some outstanding features'.

CHEADLE HULME ♂ ♀
Claremont Road, Cheadle Hulme, Cheshire SK8 6EF. Tel (0161) 488 3330

Synopsis
Independent ★ Co-educational ★ Day ★ Ages 11–18 (plus associated junior school) ★ 964 pupils (equal numbers of girls and boys) ★ 241 in sixth form ★ Fees: £4,530
Head: Donald Wilkinson, 42, appointed 1990.
Traditional academic school; good teaching and results; lots of extra-curricular activities.

Profile
Background Founded 1855 (as the Manchester Wharehousmen & Clerks' Orphan School); co-educational and non-denominational from the start; formerly Direct Grant, reverted to full independence 1976. Scattered collection of buildings ranging from Victorian (battered in parts) to post-modern (including superbly equipped languages block) on an 80-acre site 10 miles south of the city; boarding discontinued 1993.
Atmosphere Lots of smiling faces; warm, friendly relations between staff and pupils. HMC inspectors praised 'highly developed pastoral structure' which ensures every pupil has a number of adults ready to help and advise. Uniform worn throughout.
Admissions Heavily over-subscribed (600 apply for 150 places a year); entry by school's own tests. Phasing out of assisted places, which 150 hold, likely to have a significant impact on recruitment.
The head Friendly, courteous. Read history at Oxford (First); taught at Manchester Grammar (qv). Lives on campus; married (to a GP); two children.
The teaching Stimulating, imaginative; pupils participate enthusiastically. Well-qualified staff of 96 (62 women). Broad curriculum: all do French, German, Latin for first three years; science (a strength) offered as three separate subjects; all do nine GCSEs (from a wide choice); A-level options include business studies, theatre studies. Pupils grouped by ability in maths, French; average class size 28, much smaller at A-level. Good music: more than 200 learn an instrument; three orchestras, three choirs. Lots of art, drama. Wide range of extra-curricular activities, including pottery, chess, photography, bird-watching. Good careers advice.
Results (1997) GCSE: all gained at least five grades A–C. A-level: 59% of entries graded A or B.

Destinations About 85% stay on for A-levels; of these, virtually all proceed to university (average of 12 a year to Oxbridge).
Sport Lots on offer; everyone participates. Main games: rugby, hockey, cricket, netball. Soccer, fencing, badminton, volleyball, basketball, swimming (indoor pool) also on offer.
Remarks HMC inspectors concluded (1995): 'This is a happy and purposeful school well supported by staff, parents and pupils.' They said more should be done to 'enhance the teaching environment'.

CHELMSFORD COUNTY HIGH ♀
Broomfield Road, Chelmsford, Essex CM1 1RW. Tel (01245) 352592

Synopsis
Grammar (grant-maintained) ★ Girls ★ Ages 11–18 ★ 702 pupils ★ 210 in sixth form
Head: Mrs Monica Curtis, 51, appointed September 1997.

Profile
Background Founded 1906; opted out of council control 1992. Solid Edwardian buildings plus dilapidated 1950s extension on pleasant, 12-acre site near the town centre; later additions include £850,000 science block; further building (including new sixth-form centre) under way.
Atmosphere Dynamic; very good relations between staff and lively, confident pupils ('stretching very able girls is our speciality'); big emphasis on democratic discussion and decision-making. Traditional blazer-and-tie uniform below the sixth form (where there is a dress code). Supportive parents raise up to £20,000 a year.
Admissions School is severely over-subscribed (about 700 apply for 112 places) and highly selective. Entry at 11 by competitive tests in English, maths, verbal reasoning; to the sixth form (about 25 places a year) with at least five GCSEs at grade B or above. Extensive catchment area; numbers are rising.
The head New appointment. Able, experienced, very jolly ('an academic school doesn't have to be solemn'). Read English and history of art at Manchester; previously head of the lower school at Lancaster Girls' Grammar (qv), deputy head for seven years of Kesteven & Grantham Girls'. Married; two grown-up sons.
The teaching Outstanding: varied styles; hard-working, well-qualified, predominantly female staff. Solidly academic curriculum: all take science as three separate subjects; all do French and German from the start, add Latin from second year; all take at least 10 GCSEs and three A-levels (from a wide choice) plus general studies. Pupils grouped by ability in maths only from third year; average class size 28. Strong art, drama, music; choirs, two orchestras, jazz band. Wide range of extra-curricular activities, including public speaking, debating, Duke of Edinburgh award scheme.
Results (1997) GCSE: all gained at least five grades A–C. A-level: impressive 72% of entries graded A or B (best state school results in Britain).
Destinations Virtually all go on to university (average of 15 a year to Oxbridge).
Sport Lots on offer; particular strengths in hockey, athletics, netball. Swimming, tennis, fencing also on offer. Facilities include playing fields, indoor pool.

Remarks Identified by Ofsted (1995) as 'outstandingly successful'. Inspectors concluded: 'This is a very good school. The standards of achievement, the quality of teaching and learning are very high. Pupils are interested and take great pride in the quality and presentation of their work. Standards of behaviour, discipline and attendance are exemplary. Expectations by teachers of their pupils are high and the quality of relationships within the school is good.'

CHELTENHAM ♂
Bath Road, Cheltenham, Gloucestershire GL53 7LD. Tel (01242) 513540

Synopsis
Independent ★ Boys (plus girls in sixth form; going fully co-educational from September 1998) ★ Boarding and day ★ Ages 13–18 (plus associated junior school) ★ 565 pupils (85% boys, 68% boarding) ★ 290 in sixth form ★ Fees: £13,200 boarding; £9,975 day
Head: Paul Chamberlain, 49, appointed September 1997.
Sound, traditional school; good teaching and results; fairly wide range of abilities; strong sport.

Profile
Background Founded 1841 for the 'sons of gentlemen', the oldest of the Victorian public schools; imposing Gothic buildings on an extensive conservation site on the edge of the town; first-rate facilities. 'The spacious chapel,' reported HMC inspectors, 'induces a feeling of calm and reverence in all who are capable of awe.' Decision to admit girls at all ages taken, not without anguish, 'to make the school more responsive to the needs of parents and pupils in the 21st century'. Co-educational junior school (375 pupils aged three to 13) next door.
Atmosphere An easy, friendly air: hard-working staff; polite, orderly boys (main crimes are smoking and drinking, punished by fines or sending home); sixth-form girls well integrated. Compulsory daily chapel. Strong house system.
Admissions By Common Entrance (50% mark required); school is not unduly selective; the ability range is wide. Many boarders from the Cotswolds and Gloucestershire, some from West London; 14% live abroad (36 countries represented). Boys' boarding (five houses scattered within five or 10 minutes' walk) recently renovated; sixth-formers have single study-bedrooms; new girls' house to be built. Scholarships (academic, art, music, science, technology) available.
The head Recent appointment (his predecessor was forced to resign after the school plummeted down *The Daily Telegraph*'s league table). Crisp, decisive, strong leader; BSc from Durham; taught at Haileybury for 18 years, six as housemaster; previously head of St Bees (qv). Married; two children.
The teaching Good: well-qualified, committed staff of 58 (15% women). Fairly broad curriculum: science on offer as three separate subjects; languages include Greek, Latin, German, Spanish; good design/technology; lots of computing; all take at least nine GCSEs, some 11; choice of 24 subjects at A-level. Pupils grouped by ability in maths, science, English, French; extra help for those who need it (early evening clinics to treat 'grade disorders'); maximum class size 24, reducing to 14 in the sixth form. Lots of music; strong drama. Extra-curricular activities include cadet force (compulsory for one year, 'except in cases of religious or conscientious objection') and community service ('The aim is to adapt the 19th-century tradition of service to the Empire to that of service

to a modern industrial society').

Results (1997) GCSE: 93% gained at least five grades A–C. A-level: 62% of entries graded A or B (121st in the league table, its best position ever – ironic in view of the previous head's fate).

Destinations Nearly all go on to higher education (up to 20 year to Oxbridge).

Sport Taken seriously (boys support school matches from the touch-line, and a boy who is playing for his house is allowed to wear a house bow tie on the day of the match). Rugby (18 teams fielded), hockey, cricket and rowing are particularly strong; tennis, rackets, netball, golf, polo, athletics, cross-country, water polo, squash, badminton, sailing also on offer. Facilities include two large expanses of playing field (one is half a mile away), excellent pool and sports hall, two all-weather pitches, good tennis and squash courts.

Remarks HMC inspectors concluded (1994): 'The school fully deserves both its fine reputation and its popularity with the parents of its pupils.'

✓ CHELTENHAM LADIES' ♀

Bayshill Road, Cheltenham, Gloucestershire GL50 3EP. Tel (01242) 520691

Synopsis
Independent ★ Girls ★ Boarding and day ★ Ages 11–18 ★ 850 pupils (80% boarding) ★ 290 in sixth form ★ Fees: £13,345–£14,850 boarding; £8,595 day
Head: Mrs Vicky Tuck, 44, appointed 1996.
One of the few great boarding schools for girls; seriously committed to academic excellence.

Profile

Background Opened as a day school 1854; transformed by Dorothea Beale (founder of St Hilda's College, Oxford), who became head in 1858 and remained at the helm for 48 years; her aim, 'to raise the female sex in the world and with it, the world'. Slightly forbidding, pseudo-Gothic buildings set in a genteel residential area of the town; stained glass everywhere, featuring great scientists, poets, legends revered by the Victorians; statues abound – of ideal mothers, women patriots, great teachers (school has supplied heads for at least 40 schools world-wide). Excellent facilities: classrooms are spacious, corridors wide, libraries well stocked, science labs newly equipped; theatre seats 1,500.

Atmosphere A civilised community: polite, friendly girls; no feeling of rush or pressure. All wear distinctive sage-green uniform (plus 'sensible' shoes and brown stockings) and carry khaki canvas book sacks of ancient lineage. Boarding houses (resembling comfortable private hotels) spread round a network of quiet roads (girls walk in pairs, buses on dark evenings); juniors in dormitories of varying sizes; seniors have own study-bedrooms (plus cooking facilities and plenty of telephones). Lessons on Saturday mornings.

Admissions School is highly selective; entry by Common Entrance (approximately 60% mark required) or scholarship exam. Most girls from 100-mile radius; sprinkling of foreign nationals.

The head (Principal) Diffident, thoughtful, dignified; her natural warmth and sincerity have charmed her pupils. Accomplished linguist; firm believer in single-sex education; previously deputy head of City of London Girls' (qv). The first married head in the school's history; two young sons.

The teaching Traditional, purposeful: strong work ethic (but not unduly competitive); educational fads and jargon avoided (girls still told to date their work, watch their paragraphing). Well-qualified, stable, happy staff of 90 (two-thirds female). Broad curriculum; particularly good science (taught as three separate subjects), modern languages (including German, Russian, Spanish, Italian); lots of computing. A-level options include Latin, history of art, theatre studies, economics. Maximum class size 20, reducing to 12 at A-level. Very strong music: 800 individual lessons a week; orchestras, chamber groups, first-rate choir. All the usual trips and exchanges.

Results (1997) GCSE: 99% gained at least five grades A–C. A-level: very creditable 77% of entries graded A or B.

Destinations All go on to university (about 30 a year to Oxbridge).

Sport Very strong. Fine facilities include new sports complex, indoor pool, fitness centre (gleaming with metal and mirrors), all-weather pitch, battery of tennis courts. Main games: lacrosse, netball, hockey, tennis, squash. Golf, fencing, rowing, sailing, riding also on offer.

Remarks Excellent school: sets high standards and helps all to achieve them without undue competition or stress; not, though, for those who crave the bright lights.

CHERWELL ♂ ♀
Marston Ferry Road, Oxford OX2 7EE. Tel (01865) 558719

Synopsis
Comprehensive ★ Co-educational ★ Ages 13–18 ★ 990 pupils (roughly equal numbers of girls and boys) ★ 340 in sixth form
Head: Martin Roberts, 55, appointed 1981.
First-rate comprehensive; good teaching and results.

Profile
Background Founded 1963 as a secondary modern; went comprehensive and acquired a sixth form 1973, since when it has gone from strength to strength. Typical 1960s buildings plus later additions on a pleasant, well-maintained site; no classrooms in huts for the first time in 20 years thanks to £1 million building programme.

Atmosphere Unusually good relations between staff and pupils, based on respect and enjoyment on both sides; classrooms alive with the buzz of learning, reflecting teachers' high expectations of their pupils and their pupils' willing response. No prefects ('It wouldn't fit with the ethos of the school'); no uniform, nor do pupils seem to pay much attention to the request that they dress neatly; staff dress casually, too – but there is no sense that anyone is less purposeful in consequence. School does not meet the statutory requirement for a daily act of collective worship, though no one seems overly bothered about it.

Admissions Non-selective; places allocated by Oxfordshire County Council to pupils of a fairly wide range of abilities in North Oxford and Marston.

The head Very able, much respected; a man to whom things matter, and who believes they should matter to others too (has fire-and-brimstone views on educational politics). Read history at Oxford (and still teaches it 'for my sanity'); wide experience in the state sector. Married; two grown-up children (both were pupils here).

The teaching First-rate: well-prepared lessons; confident, enthusiastic staff

(60% women), clearly in control. Standard national curriculum; most take up to 10 GCSEs; remarkable choice of 40 subjects at A-level (in conjunction with other schools); vocational alternative on offer; some join the sixth form from independent schools. Pupils grouped by ability in most subjects; lots of support for those with learning and behavioural difficulties; average class size 21.

Results (1997) GCSE: creditable 66% gained at least five grades A–C. A-level: 49% of entries graded A or B.

Destinations About 75% continue into the sixth form; of these, 90% proceed to university (about 10 a year to Oxbridge).

Sport Lots on offer; particular strengths in basketball, football, cross-country. Modest facilities (two rugby pitches, three football pitches, four tennis courts) recently augmented by sports hall equipped for all indoor games.

Remarks Very good school, buzzing with enthusiasm; recommended.

CHETHAM'S ♂ ♀
Long Millgate, Manchester M3 1SB. Tel (0161) 834 9644

Synopsis
Independent ★ Co-educational ★ Boarding and day ★ Ages 8–18 ★ 285 pupils (55% girls, 80% boarding) ★ 120 in sixth form ★ Fees: £16,425 boarding; £12,714 day (all qualify for means-tested Department for Education grant); £4,125 for choristers (half paid by Manchester Cathedral)
Head: Canon Peter Hullah, 48, appointed 1992.
Musical powerhouse with an international reputation; first-rate all-round education; good exam results.

Profile
Background Founded as a charity school in 1653 by Sir Humphrey Chetham, local merchant; became independent in 1952 and a music school in 1969 (following publication of a report that pointed to the lack of national provision for musically-gifted children). Now the biggest of its kind in the country. City-centre site next to the cathedral (for which it is the choir school); varied buildings (some less than distinguished) dating from 15th century onwards.

Atmosphere Warm, busy; devotion to musical excellence almost religious in its intensity. Pupils all musically gifted and academically bright; all seem to accept that a gift means nothing unless nurtured and developed by professional guidance and systematic practice. Powerful sense of tradition (pupils wear Blue Coat dress on founder's day) and common purpose. Keen, conscientious, supportive parents.

Admissions Entry at any age; no academic requirements; sole criteria are musical ability and potential; 600 apply annually for 55 places. Some excellent boarding accommodation (two new, purpose-built houses), some rather basic.

The head Very able, enthusiastic. Read theology at King's College, London; taught in Uganda; returned to train for the priesthood; served as chaplain at Sevenoaks and King's, Canterbury. Not a musician; keen to stress that Chetham's offers a wide, not just a musical, education. 'Our pupils have music in their bloodstream,' he says. 'They want to be with others of a similar temperament. It's being all together that keeps them normal.' Married; two children.

The teaching Full academic curriculum – even though at least a third of the timetable is devoted to music. GCSE subjects include Latin, French, German, computer studies, drama, three separate sciences; 17 A-level courses, including business studies, further maths, theatre studies. Dedicated teaching staff of 40 (17 women) plus 90 part-time music tutors (many drawn from leading northern orchestras) who teach just about every musical instrument known to man on a one-to-one basis (97 practice rooms). School also offers courses in composition, conducting, singing, and Alexander Technique (for reducing tension and stage fright). Extra-curricular activities include regular trips to the countryside, youth hostelling, sailing etc.

Results   (1997) GCSE: 95% gained at least five grades A–C. A-level: creditable 75% of entries graded A or B.

Destinations   Nearly all do A-levels; two-thirds proceed to music colleges, rest to university.

Sport   No playing fields and no games against other schools but plenty of PE, recreation, indoor sports and swimming.

Remarks   A national centre of excellence getting the best out of highly gifted children.

CHIGWELL ♂

Chigwell, Essex IG7 6QF. Tel: (0181) 501 5700

Synopsis

Independent ★ Boys (plus girls in sixth form – going fully co-educational from September 1998) ★ Day and boarding ★ Ages 13–18 (plus associated junior school) ★ 382 pupils (93% day) ★ 157 in sixth form (82% boys) ★ Fees: £6,903 day; £10,494 boarding.
Head: David Gibbs, 50, appointed 1996.
Small, sound, academic school; good teaching and results; lots of sport.

Profile

Background   Founded 1629 'to supply a liberal and practical education, and to afford instruction in the Christian religion'; original schoolroom now houses the library. Mostly modern buildings in 70 acres of playing fields and woodland. Co-educational junior school (320 pupils aged seven to 13) on same site.

Atmosphere   Strong 'family' feel; good manners and self-discipline emphasised; easy relations between staff and pupils; good pastoral care. Uniform throughout. Parents kept closely informed. Lessons on Saturday mornings followed by compulsory sport.

Admissions   Main entry is to the junior school at 11 (300 compete for 65 places); school is fairly selective ('We offer an academic education, which doesn't suit everybody'). About a third of the pupils are Asian; substantial Jewish minority. Boarding accommodation cheerful but slightly shabby (like a seaside boarding house past its prime). Scholarships (academic, music, art) and bursaries available.

The head   Thoughtful, solid, quietly spoken. Read economics and economic history at Durham; previously head of economics & politics at Charterhouse, housemaster at Haileybury. Keen sportsman. Married (to a former probation officer); two children.

The teaching   Traditional in style; long-serving, predominantly male staff. Fairly broad curriculum: sciences taught separately; all do French; German, Greek, Latin on offer; plenty of computing. Pupils grouped by ability in maths, languages (more able take GCSEs a year early); average class size 20, reducing to 10 in sixth form. Strong drama; good art (weekly life classes); lots of music (a third learn an instrument, three orchestras, strong choir). Wide range of extra-curricular activities: astronomy, speech training, martial arts, cookery etc. Regular language exchanges to France, Germany.

Results   (1997) GCSE: 96% gained at least five grades A–C. A-level: 61% of entries graded A or B.

Destinations   About 90% stay on for A-levels; of these, 90% proceed to university (about six a year to Oxbridge).

Sport   Lots on offer; first-rate facilities. Main sports: soccer, cross-country, netball, hockey, rugby, cricket, athletics, swimming, tennis; full fixture list at all levels.

Remarks   Good all round.

CHISLEHURST & SIDCUP GRAMMAR ♂ ♀
Hurst Road, Sidcup, Kent DA15 9AG. Tel (0181) 302 6511

Synopsis
Grammar ★ Co-educational ★ Ages 11–18 ★ 1,280 pupils (roughly equal numbers of girls and boys) ★ 300 in sixth form
Head: Jim Rouncefield, 46, appointed 1994.
Well-run, traditional grammar school; good results; strong music, art, drama.

Profile
Background   Founded 1931; moved to present 'metroland' site 1954; became co-educational 1973. Dismal 1950s buildings (Festival Hall architecture on a bad day) set in pleasant, spacious grounds. 'Luckily,' says the head, 'buildings don't make a school.'

Atmosphere   Hard-working, very well-disciplined; pupils under pressure to do well ('but we're much more than an academic sweatshop'). Generally tidy purple and grey uniform; sixth-formers in 'office wear'. Supportive parents raised £20,000 in a year for new sixth-form block.

Admissions   School over-subscribed (nearly 400 apply for 192 places); entry by Bexley selection test. Prosperous suburban catchment area extends to Greenwich, Bromley, Orpington, Dartford; broad social and racial mix but predominance of white-collar backgrounds.

The head   Grammar-school educated; read geography at Goldsmith's College, London; early career in Inner London comprehensives; previously head of Chatham Boys' Grammar (appointed at 38). Says he believes strongly in a comprehensive system of education – including grammar schools. Keen on physical fitness, team games, mountaineering. Married; two children.

The teaching   Traditional in style and approach; high standards expected throughout; some very long-serving teachers. Broad, demanding curriculum; all do French and German from first year, Latin from second year; science taught as three separate subjects; maths particularly strong (good results at both GCSE and A-level). GCSE options include computer studies, home economics, graphical communication, physical education; sixth form offers wide choice of A-levels, including business studies. Pupils grouped by ability in some subjects. First-rate art, drama and music (full orchestra, chamber groups, large choral society). Extra-curricular activities include Air Training Corps, popular Duke of Edinburgh award scheme.

Results   (1997) GCSE: 97% gained at least five grades A–C grades. A-level: 48% of entries graded A or B.
Destinations   About 95% continue into the sixth form; of these, 65% proceed to higher education (about four a year to Oxbridge).
Sport   Main games: rugby, cricket for boys; hockey, netball, tennis for girls. Cross-country, athletics, golf, badminton, squash, swimming also on offer. Good playing fields, sports hall.
Remarks   Good all round.

CHRISTLETON HIGH   ♂ ♀
Village Road, Christleton, Chester CH3 7AD. Tel (01244) 335843

Synopsis
Comprehensive ★ Co-educational ★ Ages 11–18 ★ 1,256 pupils (roughly equal numbers of girls and boys) ★ 253 in sixth form
Head: Geoffrey Lawson, 53, appointed 1990.
Well-run, lively comprehensive; good teaching and results; lots of sport.

Profile
Background   Drab collection of 1960s steel and glass buildings in beautiful village location on the edge of the city; later additions include fine new music and drama facilities.
Atmosphere   Relaxed, friendly; great emphasis placed on the individual's responsibility 'to respect the world and its people'. School council has high profile in decision-making. Community dimension strong, too: parents invited to help in PE, library, science, languages etc.
Admissions   School regularly over-subscribed; 50% come from outside the catchment area. Fairly wide range of abilities and social backgrounds.
The head   A 'hands-on' leader: accessible, approachable (pupils constantly knocking on his door); supervises break daily; keen to improve the quality of school life. Trained at Culham, Oxford; took a maths degree through the Open University and a master's degree in education at Liverpool; previously head of another Cheshire comprehensive. Married; two sons (both were pupils here).
The teaching   Well-prepared lessons, delivered in a firm but friendly way; pupils constantly challenged and stimulated. Well-qualified staff of 81; good mix of experience and youth. Standard national curriculum; German on offer from third year; GCSE options include environmental & community studies, business studies, drama; choice of 22 subjects at A-level, including design, theatre studies, sociology; GNVQ in health & social care on offer. Pupils grouped by ability in English, maths, science, French from second year; specialist help for those who need it; most classes 25–28. Busy extra-curricular programme. Regular language exchanges with European schools.
Results   (1997) GCSE: creditable 72% gained at least five grades A–C. A-level: 42% of entries graded A or B.
Destinations   About 60% continue into the sixth form; of these, 85% proceed to higher education.
Sport   High participation rate: full fixture lists in netball, hockey, soccer, cricket, tennis; national champions at table tennis. First-rate facilities (shared by the community) include 11 acres of playing fields, sports hall, swimming pool.

Remarks   Ofsted inspectors concluded (1994): 'This is a very good school. Standards of achievement are very high.'

CHRIST'S HOSPITAL ♂ ♀
Horsham, West Sussex RH13 7YP. Tel (01403) 211293.

Synopsis
Independent ★ Co-educational ★ Boarding ★ Ages 11–18 ★ 793 pupils (60% boys) ★ 200 in sixth form ★ Fees: zero (see below) to £11,125
Head: Dr Peter Southern, 50, appointed September 1996.
Unusual school; wide social mix; means-tested fees; first-rate facilities.

Profile
Background   Founded 1552 by Edward VI to educate the children of London's poor; still gives priority to able children from needy families (fees subsidised by investments and property holdings worth more than £150 million). Awesome, purpose-built Victorian premises on a 1,200-acre estate; boys moved here from the City 1902, girls' section followed 1985. Impressive facilities for sport, music, drama. Barnes Wallis did his sums here, as did Coleridge.

Atmosphere   School nurses traditions as gothic as its architecture: pupils wear Tudor-style uniforms (ankle-length cassocks, clerical bands, saffron stockings) and march daily to lunch (in vast, panelled dining hall) behind a military-style band. Boarding houses include many that are open-plan and barrack-like: pupils should have 'a bit of spine, a bit of tenacity', says the head. However, some dormitories have recently been cubicled for privacy, a new boarding house to ease cramped conditions is likely, and there are plans to buff up bleak classrooms. New emphasis, too, on the views of the pupils (who are strongly supportive of the school – 18-year-old rugby giants have been known to weep on departure day).

Admissions   Residential entrance exam held each January (for admission the following September); candidates need to be of at least average ability. Priority to those with particular social, financial or academic needs; remaining places to those who performed best; 70% enter from primary schools. Fees are means-tested: parents earning less than £10,650 pay nothing (currently 38% of pupils); those earning £50,000 or more pay in full (currently 1% of pupils); those donating £12,000 or more have the right to nominate a 'child in need of boarding education'. Admission to sixth form dependent on 'academic performance and potential being considered to justify retention'.

The head   Has a tough streak but children and staff find him approachable. Read history at Oxford and Edinburgh; taught at Dulwich, Westminster (head of history); formerly head of Bancroft's (qv). Keen to modernise aspects of the school and to improve the exam results. Married; two grown-up sons.

The teaching   Varied styles but tone is essentially formal. Curriculum 'compatible with the national curriculum but not constrained by it'. Wide choice of 22 subjects at GCSE (including German, Russian, Greek, Latin), 26 at A-level. Average class size 22. Art and music exceptionally strong. Full programme of extra-curricular activities, including community service, Duke of Edinburgh award scheme.

Results   (1997) GCSE: 96% gained at least five grades A–C. A-levels: 60% of entries graded A-B.

Destinations   Nearly all continue into the sixth form; about 95% proceed to

university (including up to 10 a year to Oxbridge).
Sport Superb facilities: 200 acres of playing fields, £3 million sports hall, indoor pool. Rugby, football, cricket, swimming, tennis, hockey for boys; netball, hockey, swimming, tennis for girls.
Remarks Independent school married to a comprehensive ('a public school for the public'). Rather harsh image slowly being softened.

CHURSTON GRAMMAR ♂ ♀
Greenway Road, Brixham, Devon TQ5 0LN. Tel (01803) 842289

Synopsis
Grammar ★ Co-educational ★ Ages 11–18 ★ 849 pupils (56% girls) ★ 235 in sixth form
Head: Stephen Kings, 45, appointed September 1997.
Traditional grammar school; good GCSE results; lots of music, sport.

Profile
Background Opened 1957; dreary, purpose-built premises on 12-acre site plus more attractive later additions, including art & music block, sports hall; some classrooms in 'temporary' huts.
Atmosphere Purposeful; high standards set for work and behaviour.
Admissions School is heavily over-subscribed (about 300 apply for 120 places); entry by 11-plus; top 25% of the ability range. Catchment area includes Paignton, Kingswear, Dartmouth, Newton Abbot.
The head New appointment; previously deputy head of Torquay Boys' (qv).
The teaching Good quality; varied styles; experienced, stable staff. Standard national curriculum; good results in technology, religious education; choice of 18 subjects at A-level. Pupils grouped by ability in maths only; extra help for those who need it; average class size 30, reducing to 20–25 at GCSE, 12–15 in sixth form. Lots of music; about 100 learn an instrument; choirs, various ensembles. Extra-curricular activities include public speaking (a strength), Duke of Edinburgh award scheme. Regular language exchanges with schools in France, Germany.
Results (1997) GCSE: all gained at least five grades A–C. A-level: 39% of entries graded A or B (rather modest for a grammar school).
Destinations About 85% proceed to university.
Sport Usual range; good record; basketball a particular strength.
Remarks Sound school ready to move forward under a new head.

CITY OF LONDON BOYS' ♂
Queen Victoria Street, London EC4V 3AL. Tel (0171) 489 0291

Synopsis
Independent ★ Boys ★ Day ★ Ages 10–18 ★ 850 pupils ★ 250 in sixth form
★ Fees: £6,426
Head: Roger Dancey, 52, appointed 1995 (leaving August 1998).
Successful academic school; good teaching and results; strong music; fine facilities.

Profile

Background   A medieval foundation but present school dates from 1837; moved to superb, purpose-built premises 1986 – compact Thames-side site with spectacular views of St Paul's and the river, surprisingly insulated from its busy surroundings. Major funding by the Corporation of London (facilities are first-rate); all governors are members of the Common Council.

Atmosphere   Orderly, purposeful, no-nonsense; high energy levels contained by 'old-fashioned' discipline; decent behaviour insisted on. Boys on polite, easy terms with staff. Good pastoral care system.

Admissions   School over-subscribed by about four to one; entry (at 10, 11, 13) by 20-minute interview and competitive tests in English, maths, verbal reasoning ('We're looking for those who show quickness and flexibility of mind'). Pupils drawn from a wide range of social, racial and religious backgrounds in a catchment area that extends as far as Bromley and St Albans; phasing out of assisted places, which about 150 hold, is likely to reduce the social mix. Thirty scholarships offered a year.

The head   Able, enthusiastic, innovative; gets on well with staff and pupils. Read economics at Exeter; previously head for nine years of King Edward VI Camp Hill Boys' (qv). Interests include cricket and theatre (Christopher Hampton dedicated *Les Liaisons Dangereuses* to him – they were at Lancing together). Married; two grown-up children (both teachers). From September 1998: William Duggan, head of Batley Grammar.

The teaching   Lively, traditional: thorough grounding; regular testing; high standards of grammar, accuracy and presentation in written work. First-class staff of 83 (12 women); many here a long time. Fairly broad curriculum: all do Latin for at least two years; Greek, German on offer; very good science, taught as three separate subjects; lots of computing (200 screens); GCSE options include Japanese, electronics, technology; wide choice of A-levels. Pupils grouped by ability in maths, French (some take GCSE a year early); no specific help for dyslexics (in practice, school not suitable); average class size 21. Half-termly reports to parents giving grades for effort and achievement; full reports twice a year. Strong musical tradition; magnificent organ, two choirs, three orchestras, various ensembles; termly drama productions in well-designed, 200-seat theatre; good art studios. Plenty of extra-curricular activities; all boys join cadet force or do community service. Regular language trips to Paris, Hamburg.

Results   (1997) GCSE: all gained at least five grades A–C. A-level: creditable 72% of entries graded A or B.

Destinations   Virtually all stay on for A-levels and proceed to university (up to 25 a year to Oxbridge).

Sport   Wide range of options but not strongly competitive; playing fields eight miles away. Main games: football, hockey, cricket, tennis. Volleyball, basketball, badminton, fencing, swimming, water polo also on offer; cross-country run over Thames bridges. Facilities include fine sports hall, indoor pool.

Remarks   Good all round; highly recommended.

CITY OF LONDON GIRLS' ♀
Barbican, London EC2Y 8BB. Tel (0171) 628 0841

Synopsis
Independent ★ Girls ★ Day ★ Ages 11–18 (plus associated junior school) ★
546 pupils ★ 150 in sixth form ★ Fees: £5,886
Head: Dr Yvonne Burne, 50, appointed 1995.
Successful, academic school; good teaching and results; fine setting.

Profile
Background Founded 1894 after a coal merchant left a third of his fortune to the Corporation of London for the foundation of a girls' school 'corresponding as near as may be' to City of London Boys' (qv) 'making all proper allowances for the difference of the sexes'. Moved to present site in the Barbican 1969: vistas of soaring glass and concrete make it difficult to tell which buildings are part of the school. Facilities include impressive design/technology centre, eight science labs, two halls, indoor pool. Junior school on site.

Atmosphere Feels more like an office than a school: strong sense of the City on the doorstep. Girls busy, motivated, contented. Well-organised pastoral care system.

Admissions Entry at seven, 11 by tests in English, maths; a third of the places go to the junior school; no allowances made for siblings. Competition is severe; phasing out of assisted places, which more than 100 hold, will reduce the social mix but otherwise have little effect. About 70% come from North London but some travel from Essex. Substantial numbers of Asian, Jewish pupils (separate assemblies). Scholarships, bursaries available.

The head Quiet, competent. Read French and German at London (PhD); previously head for eight years of St Helen's, Northwood (qv). Married (to a diplomat); two children.

The teaching Fairly formal in style: most classes teacher-led and exam-oriented (ambitious girls, after their A grades). Experienced, predominantly female staff of 53. Broad curriculum: science on offer as three separate subjects; all do two languages in second year (from Latin, Greek, French, German, Spanish, Russian); good design/technology; outstanding art (90% A grades). Choice of 22 subjects at A-level (including home economics). Pupils grouped by ability in maths, science; average class size 26, reducing to 18 for GCSE, maximum of 15 in the sixth form. Very good drama (RSC workshops at the Barbican), music (choirs, orchestras). Well-supported Duke of Edinburgh award scheme.

Results (1997) GCSE: all gained at least five grades A–C. A-level: creditable 74% of entries graded A or B.

Destinations Virtually all go on to university (up to 15 a year to Oxbridge).

Sport Netball, swimming, gymnastics, tennis, fencing. Lots going on at lunchtime.

Remarks Good school for able, hard-working girls.

CLEEVE ♂ ♀

Two Hedges Road, Bishop's Cleeve, Cheltenham, Gloucestershire GL52 4AE. Tel (01242) 672546

Synopsis

Comprehensive ★ Co-educational ★ Ages 11–18 ★ 1,476 pupils (roughly equal numbers of girls and boys) ★ 283 in sixth form
Head: Brian Gardiner, 53, appointed 1987.
Big, busy school; good GCSE results; poorly accommodated and resourced.

Profile

Background Opened 1954 as a secondary modern for 400 pupils; went comprehensive and expanded in the 1960s. Tatty, flat-roofed, glass and concrete boxes on a restricted, over-crowded site on the edge of the village; some classrooms in ageing huts; much-needed but inadequate refurbishment in progress (coloured panels stuck on dismal façades). Governors and staff doing a heroic job but the whole sorry edifice should be razed to the ground and re-built. Technology college status granted 1997 (which will help a little).

Atmosphere Crowded, cheerful, laid back (some girls wear heavy make-up and several earrings; sixth-formers, who are allowed to wear jeans, say the staff treat them 'like partners'); pupils friendly, articulate. Lack of space means lunch has to be eaten in classrooms. Parents extremely supportive (nearly 100% attendance at parents' evenings).

Admissions No selection (except for sixth-form entry – minimum of five GCSEs at grade C). School over-subscribed; priority to those living in the catchment area; some come from 30 miles away.

The head Experienced (had been deputy here for six years). Good leader; inspires confidence, generates enthusiasm. Knows most pupils by name and all by reputation. Read geography at Hull (teaches it to GCSE); played county rugby, hockey, cricket. Married; two grown-up daughters (both were pupils here).

The teaching Well-planned lessons; high expectations; progress closely monitored. Full-time staff of 75 (55% female), 65% appointed by present head. Standard national curriculum. Pupils grouped by ability in all subjects from second year; extra help for those who need it; average class size 25 to GCSE, 13 at A-level. Nearly all take 10 GCSEs; some take four A-levels (from a choice of 23); Advanced GNVQs on offer. Well-supported Duke of Edinburgh award scheme.

Results (1997) GCSE: 62% gained at least five grades A–C. A-level: 30% of entries graded A or B.

Destinations Nearly 60% stay on in the sixth form; of those, 80% proceed to university.

Sports Soccer and basketball particularly strong; hockey, rugby, netball, tennis, badminton, athletics, dance, aerobics, squash, fitness training also on offer. Extensive playing fields near by; on-site sports hall but no swimming pool.

Remarks Well respected locally.

CLIFTON ♂ ♀
32 College Road, Clifton, Bristol BS8 3JH. Tel (0117) 973 9187

Synopsis
Independent ★ Co-educational ★ Boarding and day ★ Ages 13–18 (plus associated junior school) ★ 640 pupils (70% boys; 50% boarding) ★ 272 in sixth form ★ Fees: £13,245 boarding; £9,165 day
Head: Hugh Monro, 47, appointed 1990.
Sound, well-run school; fairly wide range of abilities; strong music, drama, sport.

Profile
Background Founded 1862; distinguished Victorian-Gothic buildings grouped round the Close (the inspiration for Sir Henry Newbolt's famous poem, 'There's a breathless hush in the Close tonight/Ten to make and the match to win/A bumping pitch and a blinding light/An hour to play and the last man in...'). Much-needed £6 million refurbishment in progress.

Atmosphere Confident, hard-working. Courteous, well-dressed pupils. Eleven boarding houses, most recently refurbished, include Polack's for Jewish boys (opened 1878 to be the 'intellectual nursery of liberal Jewish thought'); strong house system (standards of discipline vary).

Admissions By Common Entrance (also taken by the 75% who enter from the non-selective prep school); 50% mark required (but negotiable – pupil numbers have been falling); fairly wide range of abilities (including high-flyers). About 15% from abroad. Scholarships (academic, music, art), bursaries available.

The head Energetic, friendly; gets on well with staff and pupils; his influence felt throughout the school. Read history at Cambridge (rugby Blue); his second headship. Married; two children.

The teaching Good; fairly formal. Broad curriculum; particular strengths in English, maths, science (three Nobel Prize winners were pupils here); languages include German, Spanish, Greek; lots of computing. Pupils grouped by ability in most subjects; progress carefully monitored (formal exams twice a year); English taught as a second language to those who need it; extra help for dyslexics. First-rate music: choirs, orchestra, various ensembles; 'teaching is available on virtually all instruments and in all styles'. Good drama (in purpose-built Redgrave theatre). Well-supported cadet force, Duke of Edinburgh award scheme.

Results (1997) GCSE: 95% gained at least five grades A–C. A-level: 53% of entries graded A or B.

Destinations About 90% go on to university (average of 20 a year to Oxbridge).

Sport Compulsory; wide range; excellent facilities (sports centre, 100 acres of playing fields, two all-weather hockey pitches, 24 tennis courts). Good record, particularly in rugby, hockey, cricket; rowing (on the Avon), fencing, sailing also on offer.

Remarks Good all round.

CLIFTON HIGH ♀
College Road, Clifton, Bristol BS8 3JD. Tel (0117) 973 0201

Synopsis
Independent ★ Girls ★ Day ★ Ages 11–18 (plus associated co-educational junior school) ★ 390 pupils ★ 119 in sixth form ★ Fees: £4,710
Head (acting): Elizabeth Anderson, appointed April 1997; new head from September 1998.
Traditional academic school; good teaching and results; strong sport.

Profile
Background Founded 1877; original Victorian buildings plus many later additions (including fine creative arts complex) in an attractive area close to the Downs; ageing science labs being refurbished. Junior school in former boarding house (boarding finally phased out 1997).

Atmosphere Purposeful, traditional; lively, unpretentious girls; neat blue uniform worn by all.

Admissions Not unduly selective. Entry by interview and tests in English, maths, verbal reasoning. Most from middle-class, professional families; social mix will be further reduced by the phasing out of assisted places.

The acting head Was deputy head (and before that head of maths); stepped into the breach when the previous head was dismissed after 15 months in post having 'lost the confidence' of governors, staff and parents (her management style was regarded as heavy-handed).

The teaching Good; mostly formal in style. Broad curriculum: languages include Latin, Greek, French, German, Spanish; science (a strength) taught as three separate subjects; lots of computing; good results in maths, art. Pupils grouped by ability in most subjects; progress closely monitored. Good choice of 21 subjects at A-level. Regular language exchanges with schools in France, Spain, Germany. Well-supported Duke of Edinburgh award scheme.

Results (1997) GCSE: all gained at least five grades A–C. A-level: 58% of entries graded A or B.

Destinations About 60% continue into the sixth form; of these, 90% proceed to university.

Sport Good record, particularly in hockey, swimming, tennis (Jo Durie is an old girl). Netball, athletics, rounder, badminton, fencing, squash, volleyball also on offer. Facilities include gym, indoor pool; playing fields five minutes away by coach.

Remarks Sound school awaiting developments.

CLITHEROE ROYAL GRAMMAR ♂ ♀
York Street, Clitheroe, Lancashire BB7 2DJ. Tel (01200) 423118

Synopsis
Grammar (grant-maintained) ★ Co-educational ★ Ages 11–18 ★ 1,107 pupils (more girls than boys) ★ 488 in sixth form
Head: Stuart Holt, 54, appointed 1991.

Profile
Background Result of 1985 amalgamation of two single-sex grammar schools

(roots go back to 1554); opted out of council control 1991. Main school in premises of former girls' grammar (ageing 1950s concrete-and-glass plus later additions); sixth form two-thirds of a mile away (no frills here, either).

Atmosphere Relaxed, well-ordered ('conduct inconsistent with the work and behaviour of a civilised community is punished in a manner appropriate to the offence'); school has 200 pages of 'policies' on everything imaginable (including what to do when it snows). Uniform for all (frequently adapted as a fashion statement).

Admissions School is over-subscribed (400 apply for 120 places); entry by competitive tests in English, maths, verbal reasoning; places allocated (irrespective of sex) to the top 100 candidates from the Ribble Valley catchment area and the top 20 from outside. About 120 join the sixth form from other schools with at least five GCSEs at grades A–C. Most from middle-class backgrounds.

The head Self-confident, plain-speaking Northerner; good manager. Read zoology and biochemistry at Leeds (MPhil), MA in education from Lancaster; previously head of a Manchester comprehensive. Married; two children.

The teaching Good; generally traditional in style. Fairly broad curriculum: science on offer as three separate subjects; all do Latin; choice of French or German; lots of computing; all take 10 GCSEs; wide choice of 24 subjects at A-level (nearly all take four). Pupils grouped by ability in maths only; progress carefully monitored; average class size 25, reducing to a maximum of 20 in the sixth form. Strong music: four choirs, three orchestras, various ensembles. Lots of trips abroad; European work experience for sixth-formers.

Results (1997) GCSE: all gained at least five grades A–C. A-level: 43% of entries graded A or B.

Destinations Nearly all stay on for A-levels and proceed to university (average of six a year to Oxbridge).

Sport About 20 on offer. Chiefly: hockey, netball for girls; football for boys; others include athletics (strong), cricket, tennis, badminton, gymnastics, swimming, cross-country; regular district and county honours. Some playing fields a mile away.

Remarks Ofsted inspectors concluded (1997): 'This is a fine school with many outstanding features and very few weaknesses.'

COLCHESTER COUNTY HIGH ♀
Norman Way, Colchester, Essex CO3 3US. Tel (01206) 576973

Synopsis
Grammar (grant-maintained) ★ Girls ★ Ages 11–18 ★ 679 pupils ★ 182 in sixth form
Head: Dr Aline Black, 61, appointed 1987 (retiring August 1998).
Very strong academic school; first-rate teaching and results; lots of music, drama.

Profile
Background Founded 1909; became a grammar school 1944; moved to present, spacious site 1957; opted out of council control 1993. Purpose-built, utilitarian premise 'boasting much glass but little architectural merit'; some classrooms in 'temporary' huts; later additions include stylish new technology block. School bursting at the seams.

Atmosphere Warm, hard-working, well-ordered: academic ambition the norm; courteous, civilised behaviour expected and achieved; confident pupils on good terms with staff. Uniform worn (minor skirmishes over skirt length, nail varnish) below the sixth form (where jeans and trainers will do).

Admissions By highly competitive tests in English, maths and verbal reasoning set by consortium of eight Essex grammar schools; school is heavily over-subscribed (five apply for each place) and severely selective; top 10% (or less) of the ability range from largely middle-class homes within a 30-mile radius. 'We don't achieve simply because we have able pupils,' says the head. 'By bringing able pupils together, the quality of the interaction they enjoy with each other and with their teachers fosters levels of individual achievement far beyond what might have been expected.'

The head Able, experienced; softly spoken, very much in command. Read physics at Manchester, PhD in chemistry from Birkbeck; her third headship. Teaches A-level maths; helps run an 18-acre fruit farm (and drives a tractor). Married; no children.

The teaching First-rate; brisk pace; highly-qualified staff (half the science teachers have doctorates). Broad curriculum: 60% take science as three separate subjects; all do French and Latin for at least three years and German for two; most take 10 GCSEs; choice of 20 A-levels. Pupils grouped by ability in maths only; maximum class size 24. Strong art, drama, music; 170 learn an instrument; two orchestras, four choirs. Poet-in-residence adds spice to what one pupil described as the 'polite conservatism of a provincial girls' grammar school'. Extensive higher education and careers guidance. Regular language exchanges with pupils in France, Germany.

Results (1997) GCSE: all gained at least five grades A–C. A-level: creditable 61% of entries graded A or B (results are regularly among the best for state schools).

Destinations About 95% proceed to university (average of 12 a year to Oxbridge).

Sport Emphasis on keeping fit (activities include aerobics and 'dance for the seriously ungraceful'). Main sports: netball, hockey, tennis, athletics; teams do well (attributed by the head to 'intelligent tactical thinking'). Facilities include extensive playing fields, athletics track, netball and tennis courts, outdoor pool.

Remarks Ofsted inspectors concluded (1995): 'This is a very good school with many outstanding features. The quality of learning is consistently high and often outstanding. Pupils are highly-motivated, enthusiastic and intellectually lively.'

COLCHESTER ROYAL GRAMMAR ♂
Lexden Road, Colchester, Essex CO3 3ND. Tel (01206) 577971

Synopsis
Grammar (grant-maintained) ★ Boys (plus girls in the sixth form from September 1998) ★ Day and some boarding ★ Ages 11–18 ★ 668 pupils (95% day) ★ 187 in sixth form ★ Fees (boarding only): £2,925 weekly; £4,530 full boarding
Head: Stewart Francis, 59, appointed 1985.
First-rate academic school; very good teaching and results; strong sport.

Profile
Background Founded by Henry VIII 1539, re-founded by Elizabeth I 1584;

moved 1852 to attractive, eight-acre site (in leafy residential area a mile from the town centre) and purpose-built red-brick premises (assembly hall – pipe organ, founders' portraits – accommodates the whole school); opted out of council control 1993. Later additions include 1960s labs, classrooms; much recent refurbishment.

Atmosphere School is academically ambitious and proud of it (annual prize-giving recently revived); code of conduct emphasises that 'good behaviour and discipline are the key foundations of a good education'; mutually respectful relations between staff and boys. Distinctive uniform (purple blazer) below the sixth form (where jackets and ties are worn).

Admissions School is heavily over-subscribed (about five apply for each place) and highly selective; entry by tests (set by Essex consortium of grammar schools) in English, maths, verbal reasoning; top 10% of the ability range. Sixth-form entry requires at least three As and two Bs at GCSE. Pupils drawn from all over the county and beyond; boarders from Europe, Hong Kong (school eager to raise its international profile); accommodation in neighbouring converted houses; b & b available.

The head Able, energetic, determined; leads from the front (and teaches 12 periods a week of English and Latin). Read classics at Cambridge; previously head of a comprehensive in Oxfordshire. Keen sportsman (especially cricket); admits to being naturally competitive; seeks 'constant improvement' (and has no immediate plans to retire). Married (to a teacher); two grown-up children.

The teaching First-rate: lively, purposeful lessons, formal in style (tables in rows facing the teacher); hard-working, well-qualified, predominantly male staff. Broad curriculum: 70% take science as three separate subjects; very strong maths; nearly half do Latin; Greek on offer (sponsored by the Greek Government); plenty of computing; all take 10 GCSEs; choice of 18 subjects at A-level (40% take at least four, including general studies). Pupils grouped by ability in maths, French for GCSE; maximum class size 32, reducing to 27 for GCSE; much smaller at A-level. Good art; lots of music (100 learn an instrument); drama in conjunction with girls at Colchester County High (qv). Wide range of extra-curricular activities, including chess, public speaking, croquet. Regular language exchanges with schools in France, Germany.

Results (1997) GCSE: 99% gained at least five grades A–C. A-level: creditable 66% of entries graded A or B (results are consistently among the best in the state sector).

Destinations Almost all go on to university (average of 14 a year to Oxbridge).

Sport Has a high profile; good coaching; full fixture lists (against independent as well as state schools). Main games: rugby, hockey, cricket (a particular strength). Football, tennis, athletics, swimming, golf, basketball, badminton also on offer. Playing fields 10 minutes' walk away.

Remarks Fine school for able boys.

COLFE'S ♂
Horn Park Lane, London SE12 8AW. Tel (0181) 852 2283

Synopsis
Independent ★ Boys (plus girls in sixth form) ★ Day ★ Ages 11–18 (plus associated pre-prep and prep schools) ★ 731 pupils ★ 210 in sixth form (80% boys) ★ Fees: £3,690–£5,694
Head: Dr David Richardson, 51, appointed 1990.
Good, well-run school; first-rate teaching; strong music and sport.

Profile
Background   Origins go back to 1494; re-endowed by Abraham Colfe, vicar of Lewisham, 1652 'to provide education for pupils of good wit and capacity and apt to learn'; Worshipful Company of Leathersellers has supported the school ever since. Moved to present 18-acre site in a pleasant suburban area 1964; became independent 1974 to avoid being turned into a comprehensive. Facilities are good. Pre-prep and prep schools (ages three to 11) on same site.

Atmosphere   Business-like, well-ordered: a feeling of space and calm. Clear Christian ethos (full-time chaplain, daily assemblies, tradition of supporting charities); liberal and international in outlook. Good pastoral care; high standards of behaviour and dress.

Admissions   At 11 and 13 by exams in English, maths, verbal reasoning; school has been fairly selective (minimum IQ 110) but phasing out of assisted places, which more than 200 hold, will have a significant impact. Most pupils from Lewisham, Greenwich, Bexley, Bromley; those from the prep school make up half the intake.

The head   Able, experienced (his second headship); strong leader. Read economics at Nottingham (PhD); previously a housemaster at Rugby (qv) and head of Laxton for seven years. Married; four children.

The teaching   Good: experienced staff who give freely of their time and tend to leave only for promotion or retirement. Broad curriculum: science taught as three separate subjects; all take two languages (from Latin, German, French); Spanish on offer; particularly good results in maths, history. Most classes mixed-ability: pupils set in maths from third year; more able take 10 GCSEs (the rest do nine); average class size 20, reducing to 12 in the sixth form. Choice of 19 subjects at A-level, including computing, theatre studies, ancient history; all take three plus general studies. Homework closely monitored. Strong music: all encouraged to learn an instrument; two choirs, three orchestras, various ensembles. Extra-curricular activities include strong outdoor pursuits programme (in their first three years, pupils spend a week in the Lake District, North Wales and Scotland); popular Duke of Edinburgh award scheme. Frequent trips abroad for study and sport.

Results   (1997) GCSE: 96% gained at least five grades A–C. A-level: 45% of entries graded A or B.

Destinations   About 80% stay on for A-levels; of these, 85% proceed to university.

Sport   Strong; wide range on offer. Main games: rugby, football, cricket. Athletics, basketball, badminton, squash, tennis also popular. First-rate facilities include 30 acres of playing fields (half near by), large sports hall, indoor pool.

Remarks   HMC inspectors concluded (1994): 'This is a good school which deserves its strong local reputation. The pupils are taught and cared for by a well qualified, enthusiastic and highly committed staff.'

COLLINGWOOD ♂ ♀
Kingston Road, Camberley, Surrey GU15 4AE. Tel (01276) 64048

Synopsis
Comprehensive (grant-maintained) ★ Co-educational ★ Ages 11–18 ★ 2,100 pupils (equal numbers of girls and boys) ★ 380 in sixth form
Head: Jerry Oddie, 47, appointed 1996.
First-rate, purposeful comprehensive; wide range of abilities and backgrounds; good results.

Profile
Background Result of a 1971 amalgamation of two secondary moderns and a grammar school on adjoining sites on the edge of a (mostly privately-owned) housing estate; 1960s buildings, some showing signs of considerable wear and tear (money secured for refurbishment) recent additions include Halls-Dickerson technology centre, named after previous (long-serving) head. Technology college status awarded 1994.

Atmosphere Relaxed, happy, resourceful; a no-nonsense feel. Huge numbers of pupils move around the sprawling campus several times a day in an orderly fashion (but at a considerable cost in time). Good pastoral care system; children soon find their feet. Student council helps make decisions. Supportive parents raise more than £20,000 a year.

Admissions School is over-subscribed but non-selective; priority to siblings and those whose parents were pupils here or at one of the merged schools. Broad social mix; wide ability range.

The head (Principal) Strong leader; emphasises traditional values and firm discipline. Read French and Spanish at Birmingham; previous posts include 10 years in education administration; was head for six years of a grant-maintained comprehensive in Berkshire. Keen sportsman (football, cricket, tennis). Married; three children.

The teaching Sound; varied styles, some formal. Standard national curriculum; particularly good results in English, maths, history; good facilities for science and design/technology (but Ofsted inspectors noted that technology did not feature as strongly as it might, given the school's technology college status). GCSE options include business studies, sociology, food technology, computer studies; sixth-form options include GNVQs. Pupils grouped by ability from the start to enable them to go at their own speed; regular grades for attainment and effort (detention for bad work); average class size 26, reducing to 21 for GCSE. Homework rigidly enforced. Lively art, drama. Extra-curricular activities include very successful Duke of Edinburgh award scheme. Regular trips abroad.

Results (1997) GCSE: 62% gained at least five grades A–C. A-level: 48% of entries graded A or B.

Destinations About 60% continue into the sixth form; more than 80% of those who take A-levels proceed to university.

Sport Good range on offer, including hockey, soccer, rugby, athletics, tennis, squash, badminton, basketball.

Remarks Ofsted inspectors concluded (1996): 'Collingwood College provides a good education for its students, who are generally well motivated and keen to do well. The college is a moral community which teaches clearly the difference between right and wrong.'

COLOMA CONVENT ♀

Upper Shirley Road, Croydon CR9 5AS. Tel (0181) 654 6228

Synopsis

Comprehensive (Roman Catholic, grant-maintained) ★ Girls ★ 800 pupils ★ Ages 11–18 ★ 180 in sixth form
Head: Mrs Maureen Martin, 50, appointed 1995.
First-rate, traditional school; very good GCSE results; outstanding music.

Profile

Background Founded 1869 by the Daughters of Mary and Joseph (whose influence is still pervasive); moved to present, attractive 11-acre site 1965; became voluntary-aided 1978; opted out of council control 1994. Buildings well maintained but distinctly cramped; some classes in 'temporary' huts.

Atmosphere Busy, cheerful, well-disciplined; rules based on 'common sense and concern for others'; good relations between staff and confident, hard-working pupils. Big emphasis on spiritual and moral education; lessons begin with a prayer and end with expressions of mutual thanks; weekly voluntary mass to which parents are invited. Smart uniform (royal blue blazers) below the sixth form (where 'appropriate' dress is required). Strong support given to charities. Active parents' association raises money for the school.

Admissions No selection: school heavily over-subscribed; priority to Catholics irrespective of ability or aptitude; applicants interviewed to assess degree of commitment to church and Catholic education.

The head Humane, hard-working, widely respected; a deeply committed Christian providing strong spiritual leadership; role model for ambitious girls. Was a pupil here; has taught in East Africa, Mexico, Malaysia, India (husband works for the British Council); four children.

The teaching Lively, challenging. Committed, well-qualified staff of 55 (six men); low turnover. Pupils grouped by ability after first year; extra help for those who need it (including the very able); average class size 32, reducing to 20 for GCSE, 11 in the sixth form. Standard national curriculum; most take 10 GCSEs (including dual-award science); about a third add a second modern language; good computing; religious education is open and informative. Choice of 16 subjects at A-level; GNVQ in business studies on offer. Lively, imaginative art (good results). Music a real strength: half sing in choirs (which perform locally and nationally); 200 learn an instrument (two orchestras); profusion of concerts (Christmas production in Fairfield Hall); standards are high. Regular foreign exchanges; work experience in Germany.

Results (1997) GCSE: impressive 91% gained five or more grades A–C. A-level: 43% of entries graded A or B.

Destinations Two-thirds continue into the sixth form; nearly all proceed to university or college.

Sport Lacrosse a particular strength; netball, gymnastics, athletics, cricket, tennis also on offer. Facilities include large gym.

Remarks Ofsted inspectors concluded (1996): 'A very good school with outstanding features. The quality of teaching and the provision for spiritual, moral, social and cultural education are particularly good.' Recommended.

COLYTON GRAMMAR ♂ ♀
Colyford, Colyton, Devon EX13 6HN. Tel (01297) 552327

Synopsis
Grammar (grant-maintained) ★ Co-educational ★ Ages 11–18 ★ 682 pupils (54% girls) ★ 130 in sixth form
Head: Barry Sindall, 51, appointed 1991.
First-rate academic school; very good teaching and results; lots of offer.

Profile
Background   Founded 1546; moved to present, rural, nine-acre site and purpose-built, red-brick premises 1927; opted out of council control 1989 (one of the first to do so), since when £3 million has been spent on new facilities, including well-equipped technology block, good library, sixth-form centre.

Atmosphere   Friendly, purposeful, well-ordered; school hums with activity and enthusiasm; good relations between staff and attentive, ambitious pupils; strict blazer-and-tie uniform. Close links with local community; supportive parents raise large sums.

Admissions   School is over-subscribed (four apply for each place) and fairly selective; entry by 11-plus tests; top 25% of the ability range, with some priority to siblings and those living closest. Numbers have risen steadily; vast catchment area extends into Somerset, Dorset (the only grammar school for 50 miles).

The head   Enthusiastic, approachable; good manager; highly respected by staff and pupils. History graduate; taught here for eight years early in his career; previously deputy head of Torquay Boys' Grammar (qv). Loves his job; sets high standards ('Whatever we achieve this year is simply the baseline for next year's advance'). Married (to a teacher); two children.

The teaching   Good quality; formal in style (teachers teach); hard-working, well-qualified staff (equal numbers of women and men), nearly half appointed by present head. Broad curriculum: sciences taught separately; all take French and Spanish; German on offer; nearly all do nine or 10 GCSEs plus three A-levels (from a choice of 16, including business studies, theatre studies). Pupils grouped by ability in maths, modern languages; maximum class size 27, much smaller in the sixth form. Plenty of music; choir, orchestra. Extra-curricular activities include Duke of Edinburgh award scheme. Regular language exchanges with pupils in France, Spain.

Results   (1997) GCSE: all gained at least five grades A–C. A-level: creditable 58% of entries graded A or B.

Destinations   Virtually all proceed to university (eight or nine a year to Oxbridge).

Sport   Lots on offer, including rugby, soccer, hockey (girls' and boys'), athletics, tennis, netball, basketball, gymnastics, badminton. Facilities include limited playing fields (school hoping to buy part of a neighbouring farm), all-weather pitch, good sports hall.

Remarks   Attractive, well-run school. Identified by Ofsted (1995) as 'outstandingly successful'.

COMBERTON ♂ ♀
West Street, Comberton, Cambridgeshire CB3 7DU. Tel (01223) 262503

Synopsis
Comprehensive (grant-maintained) ★ Co-educational ★ Ages 11–16 ★ 920 pupils (slightly more boys than girls)
Head: Mrs Rosalie Clayton, 48, appointed 1987.
Lively, well-run school; strong arts programme; lots of sport.

Profile
Background   Founded 1961 as one of Henry Morris's 'village colleges' to provide for the community 'from the cradle to the grave' (now known as 'life-long learning'); opted out of council control 1993. Spacious, purpose-built premises plus later additions on a 26-acre site in a rural setting five miles west of the city; on-site youth club; adults attend evening classes. Some classrooms in 'temporary' huts; school is expanding but sixth-form proposal rejected.

Atmosphere   Lively, purposeful; older pupils involved in pastoral care system as 'sympathetic listeners'; aim is to 'send capable, caring and confident students out into the world'. Parents much involved.

Admissions   School is over-subscribed (245 apply for 180 places) but not academically selective; children drawn from Comberton and 15 surrounding villages (extensive coach service); parents range from farmers to dons; most pupils of above-average ability.

The head   Able, warm; good leader and manager; gets on well with staff, pupils and parents. Read English at University College, London; MBA from the Open University. Married; two grown-up sons.

The teaching   Fairly traditional in style; well-qualified staff of 51, two-thirds appointed by present head. Standard national curriculum; all do French and German for first three years; most take nine GCSEs. Pupils grouped by ability in maths, modern languages; progress closely monitored. Lots of music (free instrumental lessons); choir, orchestra, jazz and rock bands. Good art, drama. Extra-curricular activities include Duke of Edinburgh award scheme. Regular trips abroad for study and recreation.

Results   (1996) GCSE: 73% gained at least five grades A–C.

Destinations   About 90% remain in full-time education.

Sport   Facilities include sports hall, gym, outdoor pool, squash club, fitness centre, hard-court area for tennis and netball, extensive playing fields. PE staff run after-school sports club; regular district/county honours.

Remarks   A good, all-round education.

CONYERS
Green Lane, Yarm, Stockton-on-Tees TS15 9ET. Tel (01642) 783253

Synopsis
Comprehensive ★ Co-educational ★ Ages 11–18 ★ 1,200 pupils (roughly equal numbers of girls and boys) ★ 200 in sixth form
Head: John Morgan, 44, appointed 1995.
Successful school; good teaching and GCSE results.

Profile

Background Founded as Yarm Grammar School in 1590 by Thomas Conyers, gentleman; became a comprehensive 1975; moved to present site and undistinguished, purpose-built premises on the edge of town 1977; some classrooms in 'temporary' huts; no school hall.

Atmosphere Friendly, well-ordered; big emphasis on rewarding achievement ('There is no performance, however poor, that cannot be made worse by lack of praise,' says the head). High standards of dress and punctuality expected. Parents much involved.

Admissions Non-selective; about 70 out of 200 places available to children outside the (largely middle-class) catchment area; close liaison with 'feeder' primaries.

The head Enthusiastic, hard-working; gets on well with staff and pupils; keen sportsman. Read maths at Manchester; previously deputy head of comprehensives in Humberside and Greater Manchester. Married; two children.

The teaching Good; varied styles. Well-qualified staff of 75. Standard national curriculum but all do French and German in second and third years; particularly good results in maths and science; sixth-form options include vocational courses. Pupils grouped by ability in maths, languages from second year; extra help for those with special needs; average class size 25/26. Homework closely monitored. Extra-curricular activities include Christian Union, Duke of Edinburgh award scheme.

Results (1997) GCSE: 61% gained at least five grades A–C. A-level: 40% of entries graded A or B.

Destinations About half continue into the sixth form; of these, 90% go on to university.

Sport Good facilities for rugby, soccer, hockey, athletics, cricket (artificial wicket); nine tennis courts; sports hall (netball, basketball, volleyball, badminton).

Remarks Sound school.

COOPERS' COMPANY & COBURN ♂ ♀
St Mary's Lane, Upminster, Essex RM14 3HS. Tel (01708) 250500

Synopsis
Comprehensive (grant-maintained) ★ Co-educational ★ Ages 11–18 ★ 1,201 pupils (equal numbers of girls and boys) ★ 296 in sixth form
Head: Dr Davina Lloyd, 43, appointed 1995.
Lively, well-run school; strong traditional ethos; good academic results; excellent sporting record.

Profile

Background A 1971 amalgamation of two long-established East End grammar schools; opted out of council control 1993. Double-storey 1960s buildings with later additions, including first-rate science block and sixth-form centre, in 25 acres; three classrooms in 'temporary' huts; extensive playing fields.

Atmosphere Friendly, purposeful, lots going on. Strong underlying discipline; large numbers of children occupy small complex of buildings in orderly manner (no hurtling round corners) with a minimum of supervision. Courteous, well-mannered (hands up, wait your turn) relations between pupils and staff; plenty of support and praise. Very busy: lunch hours packed with extra-curricular activities; clubs after school; some sport every weekend. Traditional values: uniform (ties and blazers with crest); house system; school colours for games; cupboards full of trophies. Pupils articulate, open, take pride in school's achievements. Good pastoral care; juniors say it is easy to settle in. Lots of parental involvement and support (weekend matches, fund raising etc).

Admissions Heavily over-subscribed: 800 (from 80 'feeder' primaries) apply for 180 places, which go to those who do best in an interview (accounting for 70% of the marks) and tests (30%). Motivated children with wide interests/achievements likely to fare best; fairly wide range of abilities. Half live within three miles of the school; 80% from Havering; some from as far as Brentwood and Bow.

The head Highly qualified; read maths and science at Leeds; PhD in biological science; previously deputy head of Latymer (qv). Strong character; energetic; 'hands-on' management style; no qualms about discipline. Has high expectations of everyone and believes in incentives (house system being extended from sport to all aspects of school life to promote endeavour); children encouraged to come and show good work. Keen to expand languages, music and drama.

The teaching Good: lots of whole-class, traditional lessons plus group and individual work. High standards of presentation required; regular testing. Well-qualified staff, some very experienced; healthy turnover. Classes of 30–32 in lower school, 25 for GCSE, 10–20 in sixth form. Mixed ability throughout except for maths. Science very strong (separate sciences on offer as alternative to dual award); excellent facilities (eight labs); many opt for sciences and medicine at university. Languages another strength; unusually, all study two, from French, German, Spanish; Russian offered in sixth-form. GCSE choices include PE, design & technology, religious studies, home economics in addition to more academic subjects; A-levels include business studies, sociology, computer science (good facilities), government & political studies. Music expanding rapidly; enthusiastic young director has started up orchestras, choirs, ensembles of every kind; 600 learn an instrument but facilities limited. High standard of art and drama; A-level theatre studies expanding rapidly. Lots of extra-curricular activities; wide range of expeditions but Duke of Edinburgh award scheme in its infancy.

Results (1997) GCSE: very creditable 94% gained at least five grades A–C. A-level: 43% of entries graded A or B.

Destinations About 80% continue into the sixth form (others to college for vocational training; very few to employment). After A-level: 85% to wide variety of universities (handful each year to Oxbridge).

Sport Outstanding. Rugby a particular strength (currently coached by a member of the England squad); also hockey (indoor and outdoor), badminton, swimming, athletics and dance; pupils regularly reach national finals (not infrequently against such schools as Millfield). Facilities are good: large gym, excellent pool, several pitches (one all-weather). Sport every day at lunch time, after school and weekends; very dedicated staff.

Remarks First-rate school offering a good academic education and plenty of opportunities to pupils of very different abilities. Highly respected locally.

COPTHALL ♀
Pursley Road, Mill Hill, London NW7 2EP. Tel (0181) 959 1937

Synopsis
Comprehensive ★ Girls ★ Ages 11–18 ★ 1,127 pupils ★ 228 in sixth form
Head: Mrs Lynn Gadd, 44, appointed January 1997.
Successful, well-run school; good teaching and results.

Profile
Background   Opened as a grammar school 1936; merged with a secondary modern and went comprehensive 1973. School has recently benefited from an extensive programme of building (new science labs, design/technology workshops, sports hall) and refurbishment; facilities generally good.

Atmosphere   Friendly, supportive, well-behaved; strong sense of community; big emphasis on pursuit of excellence (high expectations underpinned by an elaborate system of merit awards). Distinctive uniform of Black Watch tartan kilts or trousers; sixth form in smart office dress.

Admissions   Heavily over-subscribed (nearly 500 apply for 180 places); no academic selection. Priority to: siblings, daughters of staff, former pupils; governors may reserve up to 15% of places for daughters of former pupils. Socially mixed intake (catchment includes large council estate); 30% ethnic minorities.

The head   Recent appointment. Strong leader; hands-on style. Has a BEd from Sussex, MA from Institute of Education; formerly deputy head of an inner London comprehensive. Married; one daughter.

The teaching   Good quality; varied styles ('whatever works'). Standard national curriculum; most do two languages (from French, German, Spanish); wide choice of A-levels; vocational alternatives on offer. Pupils grouped by ability in maths, French from second term and most other subjects subsequently; extra help for those who need it; average class size 30, smaller at A-level. Progress carefully monitored; homework diaries signed by parents. Strong drama, dance (regular public performances); lots of music (choir, orchestra). Wide range of extra-curricular activities, including Duke of Edinburgh award scheme.

Results   (1997) GCSE: creditable 68% gained at least five grades A–C. A-level: 41% of entries graded A or B.

Destinations   Two-thirds continue into the sixth form; of these, 85% proceed to university.

Sport   Main games: hockey, netball, tennis, rounders, athletics, cross-country. Aerobics, badminton, dance, football, gymnastics, volleyball also on offer.

Remarks   Identified by Ofsted (1995) as an 'outstanding' school.

CORFE HILLS ♂ ♀
Higher Blandford Road, Broadstone, Dorset BH18 9BG. Tel (01202) 697541

Synopsis
Comprehensive (grant-maintained) ★ Co-educational ★ Ages 13–18 ★ 1,600 pupils (equal numbers of girls and boys) ★ 465 in sixth form
Head: Andrew Williams, 47, appointed 1990.
Well-run, modern school; good teaching and GCSE results; first-rate facilities; lots of sport.

Profile

Background Opened 1976 as a purpose-built comprehensive – the summit of a pyramid of three middle schools and six primaries serving a mixed rural and suburban catchment area; opted out of council control (to avoid Poole's 12–18 selective system) April 1997. Spacious, sprawling, well-designed buildings (furniture colour-coded by department); pupils' work everywhere on display; good facilities for creative arts, science (14 labs), technology, computing.

Atmosphere Busy, stimulating, well-ordered; harmonious relations between staff and pupils; well-organised pastoral care (pupils encouraged to 'take ownership' of their problems and devise solutions); clearly-defined structure of rewards and sanctions ('public displays of affection' forbidden). Smart uniform below the sixth form (where there is a dress code). Strongly supportive parents.

Admissions School slightly over-subscribed; priority to those living in the catchment area (Corfe Mullen, Broadstone, Merley); full range of abilities. Sixth-form entry requires five GCSEs grades A–C.

The head Able, thoughtful, highly-regarded; very much in charge. Read history at Oxford; came here as deputy head 1986. Firmly committed to comprehensive education; teaches A-level history. Married; three children (two were pupils here, one still is).

The teaching Good quality; varied styles. National curriculum plus; all second-years add German or Spanish to French; 'self-study' Latin on offer; most take 10 GCSEs from a choice of 26, including sociology, business studies, child development; unusually wide range of 28 A-levels; GNVQs available in leisure & tourism, health & social care. Pupils grouped by ability in most subjects; plenty of extra help for those who need it; average class size 25, smaller in the sixth form. Some music (orchestra, choir); strong drama. Regular language exchanges.

Results (1997) GCSE: 62% gained at least five grades A–C. A-level: 34% of entries graded A or B.

Destinations Most continue into the sixth form; about 75% proceed to higher education (average of four a year to Oxbridge).

Sport Good record; everything on offer. Facilities include vast sports hall.

Remarks Comprehensive education at its best.

COTTENHAM ♂ ♀

High Street, Cottenham, Cambridge CB4 4UA. Tel (01954) 288944

Synopsis

Comprehensive ★ Co-educational ★ Ages 11–16 ★ 850 pupils (slightly more girls than boys)
Head: Tony Cooper, 44, appointed 1989.

Profile

Background Founded 1963, one of a ring of village colleges surrounding Cambridge, providing amenities and community education programme for 2,000 adults a week (open from 7 am to 11 pm all year round). Functional but pleasant buildings (some 'temporary'); school has an on-site unit for deaf children.

Atmosphere Positive, self-confident, well-ordered ('Good order does not just happen; it has to be worked for'); head takes a strong line on bullying. Traditional uniform. Extensive community use of the premises blurs the boundaries between school life and the adult world.

Admissions   School serves the surrounding, mostly middle-class villages; fairly wide range of abilities; pupil numbers planned to increase to 1,000.

The head (Warden)   Good leader; combines vision with a down-to-earth approach; firmly committed to comprehensive education. Read physics at Imperial; teaches maths and physics for six hours a week. Married; two children.

The teaching   Good across the board; experienced, committed staff (slightly more women than men). Fairly broad curriculum: science on offer as three separate subjects; some do two languages; more able take GCSE maths a year early. Pupils grouped by ability in most subjects. Lots of art, music, drama.

Results   (1997) GCSE: 56% gained at least five grades A–C (has been higher).

Destinations   More than 90% remain in full-time education.

Sport   Full range on offer; facilities include extensive playing fields, all-weather pitch, sports hall, outdoor pool.

Remarks   Ofsted inspectors concluded (1996): 'This is a well-run school. It caters fully for students of all abilities and backgrounds, promoting an ethos in which high standards are valued and achieved.'

COWBRIDGE   ♂ ♀
Aberthin Road, Cowbridge, South Glamorgan CF71 7EN. Tel (01446) 772311

Synopsis
Comprehensive ★ Co-educational ★ Ages 11–18 ★ 1,220 pupils (equal numbers of girls and boys) ★ 240 in sixth form
Head: Joan Dawson, 44, appointed 1995.
Highly successful (but poorly accommodated) comprehensive; very good academic record; excellent sport.

Profile
Background   Result of a 1974 merger of three secondary schools (the origins of one go back to 1608), inconveniently housed on three sites: lower school (first two years) in a rabbit warren of 19 'temporary' huts erected more than 40 years ago; middle school one mile away in functional, flat-roofed 1970s buildings (plus more huts); sixth-form centre a brisk walk away (underneath a by-pass) in the Victorian premises of a former girls' grammar school. One of the worst-sited schools in Wales, observed Her Majesty's Inspectors; a nightmare of organisation, magnificently managed. £1 million building and refurbishment programme under way.

Atmosphere   Happy, purposeful, caring; proud of its heritage (museum of memorabilia includes tasselled caps, ancient rugger shirts, honours boards dating back to 1870). Current successes recognised at twice-yearly merit ceremony and at prize day; trophies for sport and public speaking prominently displayed. Friendly, polite pupils (they stand when staff enter).

Admissions   School over-subscribed; priority to pupils from eight 'feeder' primaries. Most from middle-class backgrounds in an extensive rural catchment area.

The head   Friendly, approachable. Read engineering at Sheffield; previously deputy head of a comprehensive in Cardiff. Married; no children.

The teaching   Strong overall; staff have high expectations. Standard national curriculum; strong science (on offer as three separate subjects); good French; third years add German. Pupils grouped by ability in maths, languages from second year. Lots of music. Regular exchanges with schools in France, Germany, Japan.

Results (1997) GCSE: creditable 67% gained at least five grades A–C. A-level: 50% of entries graded A or B.

Destinations More than 60% continue into the sixth form; of these, 90% proceed to university (up to six a year to Oxbridge).

Sport Poor facilities, excellent results (characteristic of the school), particularly in rugby, hockey, athletics; numerous internationals and county players.

Remarks A triumph of spirit and determination. Ofsted inspectors concluded (1996): 'Standards of achievement are generally good. The quality of teaching is predominantly satisfactory or better. The school is not generously resourced; its accommodation is poor; the general appearance of all three buildings is uninspiring'.

CRANBROOK ♂ ♀
Cranbrook, Kent TN17 3JD. Tel (01580) 712163

Synopsis
Grammar (grant-maintained) ★ Co-educational ★ Day and boarding ★ Ages 13–18 ★ 720 pupils (52% boys, 58% day) ★ 280 in sixth form ★ Fees (boarding only): £5,100
Head: Peter Close, 54, appointed 1988.
Unusual co-educational grammar school with boarding; good results; strong sport.

Profile
Background Founded (on its present 70-acre site) 1518; Royal Charter (still proudly displayed) granted 1574; went through a bad patch in the 18th century (one head died in debtors' prison, another went mad, chairman of the governors absconded with the school funds); girls admitted 1974 (since when school has doubled in size); opted out of council control 1992. Main building dates from 1727; more recent additions include fine theatre, sixth-form centre, sports hall (plus dance studio), design/technology centre. All in reasonably good decorative order but looking well used.

Atmosphere Successfully combines the culture of a state and independent school (the best of both worlds). Common-sense discipline; big emphasis on house system (for day pupils as well as boarders). Pupils have a genuine say in how things are run; all do voluntary service once a week (and raise £12,000 a year for charity).

Admissions By Common Entrance or assessment over two years followed by written test. Day pupils required to live within six miles (which affects house prices); most boarders (who must be children of British or EU citizens) live within 50 miles; 20% from abroad. No scholarships or bursaries. Six comfortable boarding houses: juniors in dormitories (10–12 'funky bunks'); seniors have single or double study-bedrooms. Food is good, varied, healthy.

The head Tall, urbane. Read classics at Cambridge (cricket Blue); taught at both state and independent schools; previously head of a Dorset comprehensive. GCSE and A-level results have improved steadily under his leadership. Married; three daughters.

The teaching Generally formal in style: tables in tidy rows; attentive-looking pupils. Staff of 62 (60% male), nearly half appointed by present head. Standard national curriculum plus Latin; flourishing design/technology. Pupils grouped by ability from the start in maths, French, Latin; specialist help for dyslexics;

class sizes vary from 18 to 25, reducing to 10 at A-level. Choice of 23 subjects at A-level, including very popular home economics; best results in maths, further maths, physics. Good art, drama; lots of music. Well-organised careers advice. Popular cadet force. Regular language exchanges with schools in Germany, Spain; work experience in France.

Results (1997) GCSE: 97% gained at least five grades A–C. A-level: 50% of entries graded A or B.

Destinations About 75% go on to university (seven or eight a year to Oxbridge).

Sport A sporty school. Main games: rugby, hockey, cricket, cross-country, athletics, basketball, tennis for boys; hockey, lacrosse, netball, swimming, tennis for girls; many county and occasional national honours. Good facilities include all-weather pitch, squash courts, outdoor pool.

Remarks Good value for money; much sought after locally.

CRANLEIGH ♂
Cranleigh, Surrey GU6 8QH. Tel (01483) 273997

Synopsis
Independent ★ Boys (plus girls in sixth form) ★ Boarding and some day ★ Ages 13–18 (plus associated prep school on adjoining site) ★ 485 pupils (85% boarding) ★ 247 in sixth form (66% boys) ★ Fees: £13,710 boarding; £10,140 day
Head: Guy Waller, 46, appointed September 1997.
Sound, traditional school; fairly wide range of abilities; good drama; first-rate facilities for sport.

Profile
Background Founded 1865; imposing Victorian Gothic buildings plus Queen Anne-style extension in 240 elevated acres (fine views over Surrey farmland); later additions include new classrooms, theatre, indoor pool. Lovely chapel. Everything within easy reach: good community feel. Sister school to St Catherine's, Bramley (qv).

Atmosphere Gracious, adult: 'good manners, good sense and good humour' expected; strict policies on drugs, bullying. Pupils' progress carefully monitored (regular grades for attainment, effort); head gives personal commendations (and warnings) as appropriate; parents kept closely informed. Staff–pupil relations noticeably more relaxed and friendly in the sixth form. Smart uniform (blazers or badged sweaters) below the sixth form; girls wear 'office-style' dress. Eight boarding houses (boys and parents encouraged to choose); functional accommodation (some recently refurbished); juniors in dormitories, most seniors in single study-bedrooms, girls in separate premises. No weekly boarding; lessons on Saturday mornings.

Admissions By Common Entrance or interview; not unduly selective. Sixth-form entry requires six GCSEs grades A–C, including at least three at grade B or above. Most pupils from Surrey, Sussex, Hampshire, South London; 20% from abroad (half expatriate, half foreign). Scholarships (academic, art, drama, music) available.

The head New appointment. Read chemistry at Oxford (Blues for cricket, hockey); MSc in educational psychology. Taught at Radley for 19 years (housemaster); previously head of Lord Wandsworth (qv), where he revived classics and boosted the creative arts (plays the cello). Married; four daughters (all at St Catherine's, Bramley).

The teaching Most unusually, Mr Waller's predecessor (who retired early, having admitted he had 'run out of steam') refused to allow visitors into the classroom; exam results suggest particular strengths in English, maths, history, French. Full time staff of 53 (88% men); no teaching group exceeds 20 (10–12 in sixth form). Pupils grouped by ability from the start in science (on offer as three separate subjects), maths and French (in both of which the top sets take GCSE a year early); two-thirds add Spanish or German. Good choice of 22 subjects at A-level (all do at least three). Lively drama (up to 10 productions a year); good music (200 learn an instrument, three orchestras, regular scholarships to Oxbridge). Lots of out-of-school activities; popular cadet force. Regular exchanges with schools in France, Germany, Spain ('We are looking outwards to the new challenges of Europe').

Results (1997) GCSE: 96% gained at least five grades A–C. A-level: 52% of entries graded A or B.

Destinations About 95% go to university (up to 10% a year to Oxbridge).

Sport Wide range on offer: something for everyone ('Games are played seriously but not obsessively'). Rugby, hockey particularly strong; riding, fencing, sailing, shooting, badminton, karate also on offer. First-rate facilities include 100 acres of playing fields, two all-weather surfaces (one floodlit), nine-hole golf course, six squash courts etc.

Remarks Solid school ready to move forward under a new head.

CRICKHOWELL HIGH ♂ ♀
New Road, Crickhowell, Powys NP8 1AW. Tel (01873) 811033

Synopsis
Comprehensive ★ Co-educational ★ Ages 11–18 ★ 616 pupils (55% boys) ★ 130 in sixth form
Head: Andrew Timpson, 45, appointed 1993.
Well-run, orderly comprehensive; good teaching and results; strong sport.

Profile
Background Opened 1983 (after determined local pressure) to accommodate 550 pupils; pleasant buildings on attractive, 10-acre, split-level site now somewhat cramped (congested staircases, corridors); two 'temporary' huts; new buildings planned.

Atmosphere Lively, friendly, well-ordered (rules clearly set out, breaches incur detentions); warm relations between staff and pupils; daily act of broadly Christian worship (now something of a rarity).

Admissions Non-selective; places allocated by county council. Most pupils from middle-class backgrounds.

The head Energetic, decisive, very much in control (knows all his pupils by name). Read geography at Portsmouth; previously a deputy head in Dorset; teaches personal & social education, A-level general studies. Married; two sons (both pupils here).

The teaching Mix of formal lessons and group work (praised by Ofsted, 1995); experienced, stable staff of 41 (equal numbers of women and men), 20% appointed by present head. Standard national curriculum (Welsh a compulsory second language). Pupils grouped by ability in maths, science, languages; average class size 22–26; extra help for dyslexics, slow learners; gifted pupils encouraged to take more GCSEs (some do 11). Good choice of 22 subjects at A-level; particular strengths in maths, science; vocational options offered, including GNVQ in health & social care. Good art, drama (well-equipped studio but no stage), music (orchestra, choir). Extra-curricular activities include chess, computing, Duke of Edinburgh award scheme. Lots of trips abroad for study and recreation.

Results   (1997) GCSE: 62% gained at least five grades A–C. A-level: 35% of entries graded A or B.

Destinations   About 60% stay on for A-levels; of these, nearly all proceed to university.

Sport   A strength. All main games played; national and county representatives in football, netball, cross-country, badminton, athletics, tennis, cricket. Basketball, trampolining, volleyball also on offer.

Remarks   Good all round: everyone expected to give of his/her best.

CROSSLEY HEATH ♂ ♀
Savile Park, Halifax, West Yorkshire HX3 0HG. Tel (01422) 360272

Synopsis
Grammar (grant-maintained) ★ Co-educational ★ 793 pupils (roughly equal numbers of girls and boys) ★ 160 in sixth form
Head: John Bunch, 52, appointed 1991.
First-rate grammar school; good teaching and GCSE results.

Profile
Background   Result of a 1985 amalgamation of a 16th-century boys' grammar school and a 19th-century co-educational school for orphans founded by a local carpet manufacturer; opted out of council control 1991. Magnificent, rambling Victorian pile (reminiscent of St Pancras Station) set in own attractive grounds atop a hill with splendid views of the Pennines. Grant-maintained status has brought much-needed extra funding and state-of-the-art science labs.

Atmosphere   Calm, dignified (high ceilings, wide corridors, polished floors, founders' portraits, lots of sporting silver); a school that respects its history. Relaxed but professional relations between staff (who send their own children here) and bright, cheerful pupils. Proper Christian assemblies (and flourishing religious education); strong house system; uniform worn by all.

Admissions   By competitive tests in English, maths, verbal reasoning: top 20%–25% of the ability range. Most from business/professional homes in wide catchment area (some travel 15 miles); 10% ethnic minority.

The head   Scholarly, shrewd, courteous; very much in control. His connection with one of the merged school goes back to 1972. Read English at King's, London. Married; two grown-up children.

The teaching   Generally good: fairly wide range of styles but emphasis on didactic teaching; keen, hard working, stable staff of 51 (equal numbers of women and men). Standard national curriculum; dual-award science taught by specialists; all do nine or 10 GCSEs; choice of 22 subjects at A-level, including business studies, computer studies, design technology, geology. Pupils grouped by ability for GCSE maths only; maximum class size 30, reducing to 24 for GCSE, smaller in the sixth form. Strong music: 180 learn an instrument; choirs, wind band, orchestra. Wide-ranging programme of extra-curricular activities; regular overseas trips; language exchanges with schools in France, Germany.

Results (1997) GCSE: 97% gained at least five grades A–C. A-level: 43% of entries graded A or B.

Destinations About 90% stay on for A-levels; of these, 80% proceed to university.

Sport Main games: rugby (strong), basketball, fives, hockey, netball. Extensive playing fields, small swimming pool but no sports hall.

Remarks Thriving school. Her Majesty's Inspectors concluded (1996): 'The educational standards in the school are very good indeed and have been improving in the past two years.'

CROYDON HIGH ♀
Old Farleigh Road, Selsdon, Croydon CR2 8YB. Tel (0181) 651 5020

Synopsis
Independent ★ Girls ★ Ages 11–18 (plus associated junior school) ★ 700 pupils ★ 180 in sixth form ★ Fees: £4,968
Head: Mrs Pauline Davies, 47, appointed 1990 (leaving August 1998).
Fine, well-run, academic school; very good teaching and results; strong art, drama, music, sport.

Profile
Background Founded 1874 by the Girls' Day School Trust to provide a 'good and affordable' education (and still does); moved 1966 to purpose-built, starkly rectangular premises (masses of stairs and corridors) on attractive 20-acre campus. Junior school (300 pupils aged four to 11) on same site.

Atmosphere Lively, supportive, very well-ordered; simple rules clearly stated, consistently applied (no-smoking rule applies to staff, no-sherry rule to governors); very good pastoral care. Uniform below the sixth form (Muslim girls allowed to wear longer skirts).

Admissions By interview and competitive tests in English, maths, verbal reasoning; school is over-subscribed and quite selective; about half join from the junior department. Pupils drawn from a wide range of social and cultural backgrounds in an extensive catchment area; trust aims to replace assisted places, which more than 100 hold, with a scheme of its own. Music scholarship commemorates Jacqueline du Pre, who was a pupil here.

The head Very able, experienced. Read botany and zoology at Manchester; MEd in science education; previously deputy head of King Edward VI, Chelmsford (qv). Leaving to become head of Wycombe Abbey (qv).

The teaching Very good across the board: fairly formal in style; core of long-serving, dedicated staff. Broad curriculum: science taught as three separate subjects; all first-years do French and German; all second-years add Latin; Spanish on offer; excellent results in English; choice of 22 subjects at A-level, including economics, government & politics. Pupils grouped by ability in maths from second year, in French and science for GCSE; progress closely monitored; extra help for those who need it, including dyslexics; average class size 26–28, reducing to a maximum of 12 at A-level. Good art, drama, music; 250 learn an instrument; four choirs, three orchestras, various ensembles. Extra-curricular activities include well-supported Duke of Edinburgh award scheme.

Results GCSE: all gained at least five grades A–C. A-level: creditable 70% of entries graded A or B.

Destinations About 95% proceed to university (average of 15 a year to Oxbridge).

Sports Chiefly: netball, hockey, tennis, athletics, swimming, squash; regular county honours. Facilities include on-site playing fields, sports hall, indoor pool.

Remarks HMI concluded (1994): 'Croydon High is an excellent and highly successful school. The quality of education is first rate. Teaching is for the most part purposeful, thorough and challenging. Pupils are well prepared both for public examinations and for life in the wider community. The school is led with energy, flair and determination.'

DALLAM ♂ ♀
Haverflats Lane, Milnthorpe, Cumbria LA7 7DD. Tel (015395) 63224

Synopsis
Comprehensive (grant-maintained) ★ Co-educational ★ Day and boarding ★ Ages 11–18 ★ 682 pupils (54% girls, 92% day) ★ 170 in sixth form ★ Fees (boarding only): £4,695
Head: Derry Bancroft, 53, appointed 1991.
Successful, well-run school; good teaching and results; strong sport; boarding a plus.

Profile
Background Result of 1984 merger of a boys' grammar school (founded 1613) and a co-educational comprehensive in a neighbouring village; pupils aged 11–16 taught on the site of the former comprehensive in rather shabby, non-descript 1960s buildings (many classes in 'temporary' huts); sixth form and co-educational boarding accommodation in the rather more stately premises of the former grammar school (younger pupils spend a day a week here doing art, music, PE); campus has a college ambience. Language college status will lead to the opening of a new language centre (teaching four languages) in 1998.

Atmosphere Friendly, informal; discipline unobtrusive but effective (prefects apply in writing for the job); very good relations between staff and pupils (a family productively at work). Blazer-and-tie uniform (below the sixth form) worn with pride.

Admissions Non-selective; school is growing in popularity but not over-subscribed; wide range of abilities and backgrounds (all successfully integrated). Most pupils from surrounding villages; sixth-formers from further afield; boarders mainly from expatriate families, others from Hong Kong (after a marketing drive). Boarding accommodation is of a high standard, warm and well-furnished; juniors in dormitories of four to six beds, seniors in single study-bedrooms. Good, plentiful food.

The head Quiet, thoughtful, reassuring; firm leader; knows every pupil. Lives on the boarding campus with his family.

The teaching Lively; varied methods; stable staff. Standard national curriculum; all do two languages (from French, German, Spanish, Russian); choice of 19 subjects at A-level; vocational alternatives available. Pupils grouped by ability from third year; average class size 24, reducing to an average of 12 in the sixth form. Lots

of outdoor activities; well-supported Duke of Edinburgh award scheme.
Results   (1997) GCSE: 56% gained at least five grades A–C (has been higher).
A-level: 42% of entries graded A or B.
Destinations   Of those who continue into the sixth form, about 85% proceed
to higher education.
Sport   Strong – particularly rugby, hockey, soccer, basketball, athletics, crick-
et. First-rate facilities, including extensive playing fields, sports hall, tennis
courts, outdoor heated pool.
Remarks   Model comprehensive.

DAME ALICE HARPUR ♀
Cardington Road, Bedford MK42 0BX. Tel (01234) 340871

Synopsis
Independent ★ Girls ★ Day ★ Ages 11–18 (plus associated junior school) ★
734 pupils ★ 195 in sixth form ★ Fees: £4,992
Head: Mrs Rosanne Randle, 51, appointed 1990.
Sound, traditional school; generous bursaries.

Profile
Background   Founded 1882, one of four Harpur Trust schools in Bedford;
moved to present site in quiet residential area 1938; Direct Grant until 1976.
Main building 1930s red-brick plus sensible later additions. Everywhere spacious: wide corridors, airy classrooms; carpet creeping in slowly. Impressive
library. Junior school across the road.
Atmosphere   Calm, studious, disciplined (no one would think of shouting or
running). Happy, biddable girls, but not many thrusting high-flyers or open
rebels; in class they absorb rather than argue. The old-fashioned virtues of
respect and good manners still hold; uniform worn by all.
Admissions   Over-subscribed (two apply for every place); entry by school's
own tests; almost all juniors transfer to senior school. School claims to be 'not
unduly worried' by phasing out of assisted places, which 150 hold; trust provides
generous bursaries. Catchment area extends to Luton, Milton Keynes (well-
organised coach service).
The head   Quick-talking, straightforward, practical; knows her own mind and
is proud of the school. Read history and music at Southampton, educational
management at Hull; previously head of a state school. Married; two daughters.
The teaching   Sound; able, hard-working staff. Broad curriculum; science on
offer as three separate subjects; lots of computing; most take nine GCSEs and
three A-levels; choices range from classical civilisation to business studies;
general studies popular; supplementary activities include self-defence, car
maintenance, yoga. Lots of music (choirs, orchestras); lively drama in new
150–seat theatre.
Results   (1997) GCSE: all gained at least five grades A–C. A-level: creditable
66% of entries graded A or B.
Destinations   Most stay on for A-levels and proceed to higher education (up to
12 a year to Oxbridge).
Sport   Outstanding hockey. Facilities include indoor pool, large sports hall;
rowing on the Ouse.
Remarks   Independent inspectors concluded (1996): 'This is a school with a

strong sense of identity and purpose. Academic standards throughout the age range are very good.'

DAME ALICE OWEN'S ♂ ♀
Dugdale Hill Lane, Potters Bar, Hertfordshire EN6 2DU. Tel (01707) 643441

Synopsis
Partially selective comprehensive (grant-maintained) ★ Co-educational ★ Ages 11–18 ★ 1,300 pupils (equal numbers of girls and boys) ★ 300 in sixth form
Head: Mrs Aldon Williams, 53, appointed 1995.
Successful, well-run school; good teaching and results; strong music, sport.

Profile

Background Founded as a boys' school in Islington by Dame Alice Owen in 1613; girls' school added 1886; went comprehensive and moved to present fine 32-acre site 1973; opted out of council control 1993; achieved language college status 1997. Cheerful, well-maintained buildings, including grand technology centre, first-rate library, new language block; facilities generally good. School has links with the Worshipful Company of Brewers.

Atmosphere Busy, hard-working: an air of excitement and urgency. Polite, confident pupils at ease with staff and each other; few disciplinary problems. School assemblies accommodated in overflow room: head's address on closed-circuit television. Supportive parents raise considerable sums.

Admissions School is severely over-subscribed (1,200 apply for 200 places) and partially selective. Ninety places reserved for siblings; 90 allocated on the basis of an IQ test (minimum score 115) followed by tests in English and maths; 20 for those who excel in sport (county standard required) or music (at least grade four on an orchestral instrument). Wide catchment area (including Islington); parents arrange coach services.

The head Able, extrovert, dynamic; gets on well with staff, parents and pupils. Read maths at Aberdeen; taught it at South Hampstead (qv); came here as deputy head, left for a headship elsewhere and then returned. Raised £100,000 to secure language college status. Married; two grown-up children.

The teaching Varied styles – formal and informal – but all high calibre. Stable staff; equal numbers of women and men. Broad curriculum: science on offer as three separate subjects (fine labs); wide choice of languages, including Japanese, Russian, Italian, German. GNVQ in business studies available as an alternative to A-levels. Pupils grouped by ability from the start into two bands (upper and middle); further setting thereafter in maths, science, modern languages; extra help for dyslexics, slow learners and the gifted; class sizes 25–30. Resoundingly good music (but poorly accommodated). Lots of extra-curricular activities, including Duke of Edinburgh award scheme. Regular language exchanges with European schools.

Results (1997) GCSE: 86% gained at least five grades A–C. A-level: creditable 57% of entries graded A or B.

Destinations About two-thirds of those who continue into the sixth form proceed to university, including Oxbridge.

Sport Good; particular strengths in football, cricket; lots of inter-school fixtures. Facilities include extensive playing fields (next to the M25), floodlit all-weather pitch, sports hall, 12 tennis courts, four squash courts.

Remarks Good, highly regarded school.

DAME ALLAN'S ♂ ♀
Fowberry Crescent, Newcastle upon Tyne NE4 9YJ. Tel (0191) 275 0708

Synopsis
Independent ★ Co-educational (but girls and boys taught separately from 11 to 16) ★ Day ★ Ages 8–18 ★ 908 pupils (788 in senior school; equal numbers of girls and boys) ★ 210 in sixth form ★ Fees: £4,011
Head: David Welsh, 51, appointed 1996.
Happy, successful school; good teaching and results; aims to combine the best of single-sex and co-education.

Profile
Background Founded 1705 by Dame Eleanor Allan, widow of a wealthy tobacco merchant, to teach trades to 40 poor boys, and reading, writing, knitting and sewing to 20 poor girls; formerly Direct Grant. Moved to present site in the middle of a housing estate 1935: 13-acre campus dominated by red-brick building that looks like an ageing ocean liner moored beside the playing fields. Boys and girls occupy separate wings; behind are solid buildings in assorted styles with windswept walkways and tarred quadrangles; £2.6 million spent in the past four years to add an impressive sports hall, large science block and attractive music school. Scruffier parts gradually being brought up to standard (but refurbishment so far has done more for the girls than the boys).

Atmosphere A happy community. Children friendly, communicative, smartly turned-out; excellent relations between older and younger ones (sixth-formers help look after junior classes and run lunchtime clubs). Pupils attentive and responsive in class, quiet and sensible moving around the school. In-house catering is outstanding.

Admissions Entry (at eight, nine, ten and 11-plus) by exams in English, maths, verbal reasoning and interview; about 50 turned away each year (though school is not full); abilities range from average upwards (school is less selective than the Royal Grammar or Central Newcastle High, qv). Some 250 pupils have assisted places; as Labour phases out the scheme, the school is likely to reduce its intake to keep up standards. Catchment area has 40-mile radius; extensive school bus service.

The head (Principal) Recent appointment. Read French at St Andrews; his second headship. Cautious, thoughtful; has a clear sense of the school's direction and has tightened up on discipline; gets on well with staff, parents and pupils. Coaches rugby and cricket, produces plays. Married; one daughter.

The teaching High quality; whole-class instruction with plenty of opportunities for discussion (assisted by the absence of discipline problems, and the willing participation of pupils). Healthy balance of older and younger staff; predominantly male for the boys, female for the girls. Average class sizes 18–22, reducing to 12 in the sixth form. Pupils grouped by ability for GCSE maths and French only; extra help for those with dyslexia. Good modern languages (taught entirely in the target language from 11); English, drama, art show real creativity; design/technology not yet on offer (surprisingly), and computing is rudimentary. GCSE options include Latin (but only for boys) and dance (only for girls); science can be taken as three separate subjects. Music thrives: a third play an instrument; regular performances by orchestra, choirs, ensembles. Lots of extra-curricular activities (debating, cookery, chess, electronics, bridge); popular Duke of Edinburgh award scheme. Regular language exchanges with pupils in France, Germany.

Results   (1997) GCSE: 100% of boys and 98% of girls gained at least five grades A–C. A-level: 61% of entries graded A or B.

Destinations   Nearly all go to university (including four or five a year to Oxbridge).

Sport   Aim is to promote enjoyment and fitness. Main games (regular international tours): rugby, cricket for the boys; hockey, netball for the girls. Wide choice of minor sports: athletics, cross-country, swimming, badminton, lacrosse, basketball, table tennis, volleyball, dance, gymnastics, karate. Facilities include excellent new sports hall.

Remarks   Good school for boys and girls of a co-operative disposition and average and above-average ability.

DAUNTSEY'S ♂ ♀
West Lavington, near Devizes, Wiltshire SN10 4HE. Tel (01380) 818441

Synopsis
Independent ★ Co-educational ★ Day and boarding ★ Ages 11–18 ★ 667 pupils (55% boys, 55% day) ★ 206 in sixth form ★ Fees: £7,155 day; £11,622 boarding
Head: Stewart Roberts, 45, appointed September 1997.
Well-run school for children of a wide range of abilities; good teaching and results; lots of extra-curricular activities; strong sport.

Profile
Background   Founded 1542 by William Dauntsey, Master of the Mercers' Company (which still supports the school); moved to present 100-acre site and red-brick, purpose-built premises 1895; formerly Direct Grant, became fully independent 1975. Buildings and facilities regularly extended and refurbished.

Atmosphere   Robust, friendly, down-to-earth; strong family feel (45% of pupils have siblings who are or were pupils here). Christian foundation; full-time chaplain (but all faiths welcomed).

Admissions   By interview and tests or Common Entrance; school is not particularly selective (average IQ 112) and likely to become even less with the phasing out of assisted places, which about 150 hold. Most live locally (weekly boarding popular); junior boarders have their own country house (with golf course and trout stream).

The head   Recent appointment; came here as deputy head 1995. Read physics at Oxford; previously a housemaster for 15 years at Salisbury Cathedral School (qv). Very much in tune with the school's philosophy of finding every pupil something to be good at.

The teaching   Fairly relaxed in style (but discipline is good); energetic, hard-working staff. Fairly broad curriculum; most take two modern languages (choice includes Italian, Russian, Spanish, German); Latin on offer; good results in history. Pupils grouped by ability from second year in maths, modern languages; extra help for dyslexics (parents required to pay half the cost); maximum class size 20, reducing to 10 in sixth form. Lots of art, drama, music; more than half learn an instrument; choirs, orchestras, regular concerts. Extra-curricular activities range from bee-keeping to ballet.

Results   (1997) GCSE: 99% gained at least five grades A–C. A-level: creditable 57% of entries graded A or B.

Destinations   About 85% stay on for A-levels; of these, 95% proceed to higher education.
Sport   Strong – particularly rugby, girls' hockey, sailing. First-rate facilities include extensive playing fields, all-weather pitch, 12 tennis courts, indoor pool.
Remarks   Good school for active all-rounders; introverts might not thrive.

DAVENANT FOUNDATION ♂ ♀
Chester Road, Loughton, Essex IG10 2LD. Tel (0181) 508 0404

Synopsis
Comprehensive (grant-maintained) ★ Co-educational ★ Ages 11–18 ★ 975 pupils (roughly equal numbers of girls and boys) ★ 240 in sixth form
Head: Andrew Puttock, 35, appointed April 1997.
First-rate school; clear Christian ethos; good teaching and results; wide range of extra-curricular activities; strong sport.

Profile
Background   Founded 1680 by the Rev Ralph Davenant in the Whitechapel Road; became a grammar school and moved to purpose-built premises in Loughton 1965; went comprehensive 1981; opted out of council control 1991. Recent additions include technology block, new science labs; facilities generally good. Foundation provides £70,000 a year, supportive parents another £50,000 (mainly through covenants).
Atmosphere   Strong Christian commitment ('Davenant is a community which seeks to reflect the love of God in our relationships, our standards, our teaching and our way of life'); grammar school ethos carefully preserved. Discipline firm; behaviour good; uniform strictly enforced (sixth-formers wear suits or equivalent).
Admissions   Heavily over-subscribed (more than two apply for each place) but no academic selection; principal admission criterion is 'parental involvement in a place of mainstream Christian or Jewish worship'. Most pupils from relatively affluent homes in an extensive catchment area that includes Ongar, Harlow, Epping.
The head   Recent appointment. Ambitious for the school; promises to lead from the front. Read modern and medieval languages at Cambridge; previously deputy head of an Essex comprehensive; keen sportsman (plays hockey for Southend). Married (to a teacher); two young children.
The teaching   Rigorous, carefully planned, traditional in style. Standard national curriculum plus second modern language (from third year); most take 10 GCSEs (including compulsory religious studies); particularly good results in science, maths. Sixth-form options include GNVQ in business studies; all take general studies. Pupils divided into two broad ability bands from the start; further grouping in maths, French from second year; progress carefully monitored (grades for effort, achievement five times a year); class sizes range from 25 to 30. Homework diary signed weekly by parents. Strong drama, music (two orchestras, four choirs). Busy extra-curricular programmes includes well supported Duke of Edinburgh award scheme; regular trips abroad for study, sport, recreation.
Results   (1997) GCSE: impressive 75% gained at least five grades A–C. A-level: 38% of entries graded A or B.

Destinations   About 75% proceed to university (including one or two a year to Oxbridge).
Sport   Full fixture list; all expected to participate. Main games: rugby, soccer, cricket (boys), hockey, netball, rounders (girls), gymnastics, athletics, tennis, swimming (both).
Remarks   Ofsted inspectors concluded (1996): 'This is a good school in which the extremely responsive and highly motivated pupils achieve well in their formal studies, and most benefit greatly from the excellent range and quality of extra-curricular activities provided by the committed and able staff. Parents were notably fulsome in their praise of the school and the effectiveness of the school's Christian ethos.'

DEAN CLOSE ♂ ♀
Shelburne Road, Cheltenham, Gloucestershire GL51 6HE. Tel (01242) 522640

Synopsis
Independent ★ Co-educational ★ Boarding and day ★ Ages 13–18 (plus associated junior school) ★ 458 pupils (66% per cent boarding, 54% boys) ★ 196 in sixth form ★ Fees: £13,350 boarding; £9,300 day
Head: Christopher Bacon, 59, appointed 1979 (retiring August 1998).
Successful all-round school; good teaching and results; strong boarding ethos; first-rate facilities.

Profile
Background   Founded 1886 in memory of Francis Close, Rector of Cheltenham and later Dean of Carlisle, 'an uncompromising champion of the evangelical cause' (as the school still is); fully co-educational since 1972. Victorian red-brick buildings plus many later additions (including 550-seat theatre) on immaculate 80-acre site; new music school and library under construction.
Atmosphere   Genuinely friendly – tone set by the head, who greets everyone warmly (even at 80 yards distance). Strong religious tradition (aim is to 'combine the ideal of Christian service with sound learning'); compulsory chapel (full-time chaplain); emphasis on the relationship of personal faith to school life. Pupils cheerful, well-disciplined, smartly turned out. Standard boarding accommodation, some in gracious Regency houses near by. Busy programme of weekend activities (reassuring for expatriate parents).
Admissions   By Common Entrance: school can afford to be fairly selective. Most boarders' parents live abroad; prospective parents given names of current parents to consult. Numerous scholarships (science, arts, music) and bursaries.
The head   Long-serving: has transformed the school during his tenure. Warm, supportive but demands highest standards from staff and pupils. Read chemistry at Oxford (and still teaches it); farms on the Welsh borders in his spare time. Married; three daughters.
The teaching   Good quality; traditional in style. Well-qualified staff of 54, nearly all appointed by present head. Broad curriculum: all take science as three separate subjects ('we offer no mud-pie courses here'); language options include German, Spanish, Russian; all expected to be computer literate by end of second year (and own a laptop). Pupils grouped by ability in most subjects; extra help for dyslexics; average class size 23, reducing to 18 for GCSE, 10–12 at A-level. Strong music: four full-time teachers; more than half learn an instrument; two orchestras,

good choir. Lots of art, drama. More than 100 extra-curricular activities on offer, including well-supported cadet force, Duke of Edinburgh award scheme.
Results (1997) GCSE: 97% gained at least five grades A–C. A-level: 48% of entries graded A or B (not a good year).
Destinations Almost all go on to university (up to 10 a year to Oxbridge).
Sports Main games: rugby, cricket for boys; netball, tennis for girls; hockey, athletics for both; busy fixture list. Sailing, fencing, judo, shooting (indoor range) also on offer. Facilities include two all-weather pitches, sports hall, indoor pool.
Remarks Good school; recommended.

DEBENHAM HIGH ♂ ♀
Gracechurch Street, Debenham, Stowmarket, Suffolk IP14 6BL. Tel (01728) 860213

Synopsis
Comprehensive (voluntary-controlled, Church of England) ★ Co-educational
★ Ages 11–16 ★ 375 pupils
Head: Michael Crawshaw, 45, appointed 1989.
Fine, small school; high standards in a friendly community.

Profile
Background Opened 1964; pleasant buildings on green-field site on the edge of a picturesque village. Colourful wall displays; carpets almost everywhere; equipment more than adequate; books in good condition; impressive library.
Atmosphere Friendly, considerate; little need for discipline (pupils sit absolutely still in rows whilst the head addresses them in assembly, but laugh at the jokes). All are obviously trying hard in lessons: education is a serious business. Foundation commemorated annually in village church; school's values symbolised by the grace, formal communal meal and national anthem that mark the occasion. Supportive parents.
Admissions School takes almost all who apply from a large rural catchment area; numbers (and reputation) are rising.
The head An ample, slightly rumpled figure, who knows his pupils, cares about them, and is happy to be in a small school. He teases and is teased in a kindly way as he goes around, but underneath is pretty shrewd; keen to uphold traditions and standards, and not afraid to encourage competition (school has been amazingly successful at winning national competitions in art, music, literature). Married; two children.
The teaching Very good. First-rate, hard-working staff rise to the challenge of a small school with a full range of ability. Bright pupils entered for up to 11 GCSEs (firm, steady, exam-oriented teaching); others receive one-to-one help (school's size allows all to be discussed individually at morning staff meetings). Science very professionally taught by people who know and love their subjects; English is outstandingly good (many of the children can write poetry); art and home economics taught by enthusiasts; French and German have foreign assistants. About 60 learn musical instruments, which the head 'begs, borrows or steals'.
Results (1997) GCSE: 65% gained at least five grades A–C.
Destinations Nearly all remain in full-time education after 16.
Sport Lots on offer. Facilities include playing fields (with cows as spectators), gym and – right next door to the school – the local leisure centre.
Remarks Delightful school, united in sensible aims: children of widely

differing attainments and backgrounds all feel at home here. Ofsted inspectors concluded (1996): 'Debenham High offers a happy and caring learning environment in which pupils are encouraged to develop a sense of responsibility and concern for others and are challenged to achieve their full potential. The quality of teaching is high.'

DERBY HIGH ♀
Hillsway, Littleover, Derbyshire DE23 7DT. Tel (01332) 514267

Synopsis
Independent ★ Girls ★ Day ★ Ages 11–18 (plus associated junior school) ★ 313 pupils ★ 85 in sixth form ★ Fees: £4,680
Head: Dr George Goddard, 52, appointed 1983.
Attractive, well-run school; good teaching and results; lots of music, sport.

Profile
Background Founded 1892; moved to present 10-acre, suburban site 1957; good-quality buildings; school has steadily expanded. Co-educational nursery and junior school (250 pupils aged three to 11) on same site.

Atmosphere Happy, well-disciplined; first-rate pastoral care; strong Christian ethos. Much fund-raising for charity.

Admissions By interview and tests in English, maths, verbal reasoning; school is over-subscribed and fairly selective but may become less so with the phasing out of assisted places, which more than 40 hold ('It will certainly narrow the social environment and necessitate harder marketing'). Extensive catchment area (Burton, Belper, Ashbourne, Melbourne); 15% ethnic minority. Some scholarships available.

The head Cheerful, humane; good leader. Read chemistry at London; teaches science for up to a quarter of the timetable. Married; two children.

The teaching Traditional in style but with an emphasis on 'learning is fun'; experienced, hard-working, predominantly female staff (two-thirds appointed by present head). Standard national curriculum; sciences taught separately; all do French for at least three years, German for two; choice of 17 subjects at A-level. Pupils grouped by ability from the start in maths, French; extra help for dyslexics and those who speak English as a second language; progress closely monitored (half-termly grades for effort and achievement); average class size 24, reducing to a maximum of 10 at A-level. Strong music: up to half learn an instrument; several choirs, orchestras. Extra-curricular activities include popular Duke of Edinburgh award scheme. Regular language exchanges with pupils in France, Germany.

Results (1997) GCSE: 96% gained at least five grades A–C. A-level: 50% of entries graded A or B.

Destinations About 90% proceed to university (average of four a year to Oxbridge).

Sport Chiefly: netball, hockey (particularly strong), tennis, athletics; regular county honours. Squash, badminton, basketball, sailing also on offer. Facilities include extensive playing fields, sports hall.

Remarks Good all round; recommended.

DEVONPORT BOYS' ♂
Paradise Road, Stoke, Plymouth PL1 5QP. Tel (01752) 208787

Synopsis
Grammar (grant-maintained) ★ Boys ★ Ages 11–18 ★ 971 pupils ★ 191 in sixth form
Head: Dr Nic Pettit, 46, appointed 1993.
Successful school; good teaching and results.

Profile
Background   Founded 1896; moved to present imposing premises (originally a late 18th-century military hospital) 1945; opted out of council control 1996. Emphasis has always been on scientific excellence. Some pupils partially sighted or partially deaf.

Atmosphere   On first impression, as institutional and spartan as the traditional image of a public school – all tiled walls, cold corridors and asceticism – but swiftly redeemed by the warmth of the relations between staff and hard-working boys. Classrooms are large (ex-hospital wards) and bright; everything clean and tidy.

Admissions   Entry by tests in English and verbal and non-verbal reasoning; top 25% of the ability range. Catchment area extends into Cornwall in an arc from Tavistock through Callington to Liskeard.

The head   Quiet, unassuming; personal priorities are hard work, honesty and courtesy ('I give it and I expect it'). Educated at King's, Worcester; former research scientist (microbiology); previously deputy head of a grammar school in Buckinghamshire. Married; two children.

The teaching   Good quality; relaxed, informal style. Highly qualified staff of 58 (17 women); wide range of age and experience. Broad curriculum: all take French and Latin in first year, add German in second; strong science; first-rate art. Wide choice of subjects at GCSE (particularly good results in English, maths, sciences, French) and A-level (best results in maths, English literature, general studies). Pupils not grouped by ability (all are able); average class size 28. School owns a large house in Brittany converted into a study centre.

Results   (1997) GCSE: all gained at least five grades A–C. A-level: 37% of entries graded A or B.

Destinations   About 90% stay on for A-levels; of these, 90% proceed to university (about six a year to Oxbridge).

Sport   Important; wide choice of games.

Remarks   Good all round.

DEVONPORT GIRLS' HIGH ♀
Lyndhurst Road, Peverell, Plymouth PL2 3DL. Tel (01752) 705024

Synopsis
Grammar ★ Girls ★ Ages 11–18 ★ 670 pupils ★ 140 in sixth form
Head: Mrs Barbara Dunball, 56, appointed 1991.
Sound, academic school; good teaching and results; limited facilities.

Profile
Background   Founded 1911; moved 1947 to present barrack-like, red-brick

premises (Art Deco style) on cramped, city-centre site; later additions include attractive art school; some classrooms in ugly 'temporary' huts; money is tight.
Atmosphere Hard-working, well-behaved ('discipline is largely self-imposed'); cordial relations between staff and pupils. Uniform up to the sixth form (where there are few restrictions). School does not offer a daily act of collective worship.
Admissions By local authority 11-plus; top 25% of the ability range; about 230 apply for 100 places. Pupils drawn from a wide range of backgrounds in a fairly extensive catchment area (school runs buses).
The head Shrewd, cheerful, experienced ('We believe we triumph over our disadvantages'). Teaches English, general studies. Married; no children.
The teaching Good quality; well-planned lessons; fairly formal in style. Standard national curriculum; impressive languages (including Spanish, German, Italian, Latin); choice of 20 subjects at A-level. Pupils grouped by ability in maths, French; extra help for dyslexics; average class size 30–32, reducing to a maximum of 18 at A-level. Good art, music. Regular language exchanges with schools in France, Germany, Italy, Spain.
Results (1997) GCSE: 99% gained at least five grades A–C. A-level: 50% of entries graded A or B.
Destinations About 75% go on to university (average of three a year to Oxbridge).
Sport Good record despite limited facilities; regular county honours in hockey, netball, basketball.
Remarks Ofsted inspectors concluded (1995): 'The quality of teaching and learning is consistently sound. Pupils are generally well motivated. Overall, the school gives good value for money.'

DIXONS ♂ ♀
Ripley Street, Bradford BD5 7RR. Tel (01274) 776777

Synopsis
Comprehensive (City Technology College) ★ Co-educational ★ Ages 11–18 ★ 1,025 pupils (equal numbers of girls and boys) ★ 300 in sixth form
Head: John Lewis OBE, 50, appointed 1990.
Well-run, successful school; good teaching and results; emphasis on maths, science, technology.

Profile
Background Opened 1990, one of the first of a group of Government-inspired specialist schools, partly funded by commerce and industry. Purpose-built, high-tech, £7 million premises (lots of glass and tubular steel) on restricted, eight-acre inner-city site (no playing fields); everything immaculately maintained (no hint of litter, graffiti or vandalism). First-rate facilities for science, music, drama; IT provision is outstanding. Unusual five-term (eight weeks) year.
Atmosphere Energetic, creative; noisy and bustling at the end of lessons but classrooms are quiet, orderly places of learning. Hard-working pupils treated in an adult, trusting way, and respond accordingly; well organised pastoral care system. School open all hours; adult classes in the evening. Simple uniform with school insignia (no blazers).
Admissions Heavily over-subscribed: 450 apply for 150 places a year.

Catchment area restricted to Bradford; intake required to reflect full range of abilities as measured by non-verbal reasoning test (20% above average, 60% average, 20% below average) and socio-economic backgrounds. Pupils overwhelmingly inner-city working class; 35% ethnic minorities.

The head (Principal) Able, experienced; good manager with a clear vision of the school's future; gets on well with everyone; his second headship. Read history at Cambridge (soccer Blue); keen cricketer; created OBE in 1996 for services to education. Married (wife is deputy head of a comprehensive); three sons.

The teaching Wide range of styles using every available aid; plenty of formal teaching, too. Hard-working staff of 75 (60% female) plus 34 assistants (all appointed by present head). Full national curriculum with an emphasis on sciences (separate or dual award), maths, technology (first-rate computing – one machine between four), business education; all learn to touch-type from day one. Main languages German, Spanish; French on offer; some Japanese in sixth form. Pupils grouped by ability in most subjects from second year; lots of extra help for those who need it (at both ends of the academic spectrum); average class size 25 to GCSE, much smaller thereafter. Sixth-formers choose from 24 subjects, including GNVQs. Homework strictly monitored (and can be completed on the premises); good, heavily-used library (with CD-Roms). Lots of music (subsidised fees for instrumental tuition); wide range of clubs and societies; regular foreign trips and exchanges.

Results (1997) GCSE: creditable 77% gained at least five grades A–C. A-level: 35% of entries graded A or B.

Destinations About 70% continue into the sixth form; nearly all of them go on to university (and half are the first generation of their family to do so).

Sport All the usual games, including hockey, cricket, tennis, gymnastics, aerobics; playing fields hired for inter-school matches. Facilities include all-weather pitch, vast sports hall; use of playing fields one mile away.

Remarks A first-class, all-round education for children of all abilities. Ofsted inspectors concluded (1995): 'Pupils achieve high standards, and are well prepared for life in a modern, complex society.'

DOLLAR ACADEMY ♂ ♀
Dollar, Clackmannanshire FK14 7DU. Tel (01259) 742511

Synopsis
Independent ★ Co-educational ★ Day and boarding ★ Ages 12–18 (plus associated junior school) ★ 766 pupils (55% boys, 82% day) ★ 261 in sixth form ★ Fees: £4,599 day; £10,181 boarding
Head: John Robertson, 47, appointed 1994.
Sound academic school; fairly wide range of abilities; lots of extra-curricular activities.

Profile
Background Founded 1818 to educate the poor of the parish; dignified, purpose-built, classical style premises (re-built after a 1961 fire) plus many later additions (£4.5 million spent in past six years) on 40-acre campus 10 miles east of Stirling. Junior school (340 pupils aged five to 12) on same site.

Atmosphere Friendly, cheerful, hard-working; warm relations between staff and pupils. School has been co-educational from the start; boys and girls required to observe a 'six-inch rule' to prevent 'public shows of affection'. Uniform for all ('shirt-tails should be tucked in and top buttons fastened').

Admissions At age 10/11 by interview and competitive tests in English, maths, verbal reasoning; school is not unduly selective. Pleasant, spacious boarding accommodation. Scholarships (academic, art, music) available.

The head (Rector) Gentle, relaxed but very much in command (and knows everyone by name). Read English at Glasgow; spent 14 years at Stewart's Melville; came here as deputy head 1987. Teaches English to seniors, umpires 1st XI. Married; two children.

The teaching Efficient; experienced staff, a third appointed by present head. Standard Scottish curriculum; all do economics, computing, Latin, classical studies; German, Spanish on offer; all take seven Standard Grades (from a choice of 21); virtually all stay on for Highers (choice of 24). Pupils grouped by ability in English, maths; extra help for those who need it, including dyslexics; average class size 18. Strong drama, music; 20% learn an instrument; six choirs, two orchestras. Wide range of extra-curricular activities, including well-supported cadet force, Duke of Edinburgh award scheme; Scottish country and ballroom dancing popular, too. Regular language exchanges with schools in France, Germany.

Results (1997) Standard Grade: 81% gained at least five grades 1–2. Highers: 51% gained at least five grades A–C.

Destinations More than 90% remain for a sixth year; of these, about 90% proceed to university (mostly in Scotland, two or three a year to Oxbridge).

Sport Lots on offer; particular strengths in rugby, girls' hockey. Facilities include first-rate playing fields, sports hall, indoor pool, squash and tennis courts, rifle range.

Remarks Sound school; enjoys strong local support.

DOUAY MARTYRS ♂ ♀

Edinburgh Drive, Ickenham, Uxbridge, Middlesex UB10 8QY. Tel (01895) 635371

Synopsis
Comprehensive (Roman Catholic, grant-maintained) ★ Co-educational ★ Ages
11–19 ★ 1,300 pupils (equal numbers of girls and boys) ★ 200 in sixth form
Head: Lady Stubbs, 57, appointed 1986.
First-rate, well-run comprehensive.

Profile
Background Founded 1962 on a private housing estate in suburban Ickenham; opted out of council control 1993. Dreary 1960s architecture plus later additions enlivened by imaginative internal decoration (including a fine mural); two junior years housed a short walk away in workaday building and huts.

Atmosphere Vibrant, purposeful, bustling; an air of confidence and energy. Catholic ethos is fundamental: full-time chaplain, regular mass. Good manners strongly encouraged (children stand up for visitors); discipline, hard work, punctuality expected; uniform rigidly adhered to (head will not tolerate sloppiness – no shirts hanging out here); truancy virtually non-existent. Permanent reception desk manned by a succession of pupils (large 'Welcome to Douay' mat); big emphasis on doing everything with style. Parents receive 'entitlement' statements explaining in detail what to expect for their child; regular reporting, meetings, advice.

Admissions   School heavily over-subscribed (more than 400 apply for 240 places); membership of Catholic church essential ('entry is on the basis of faith rather than academic ability'). Wide range of ability and social background; most from Hillingdon and Harrow but also Brent and Buckinghamshire.

The head   Dynamic, bristling with ideas; constantly seeking to raise standards; will not countenance second best; trains everyone to be 'brisk' (her favourite word); commands loyalty and very hard work from her staff. Educated in Glasgow; wide and varied teaching experience in primary, secondary and special schools in Scotland, England and the USA. Married (to a prominent education-ist); three grown-up children.

The teaching   Formal, structured, challenging; strong emphasis on accuracy, presentation, grammar, spelling; some classes positively buzz. Enthusiastic, highly-qualified staff of 80, three-quarters appointed by present head (those who did not like her approach left). Broad curriculum: all first-years do classical civil-isation; second-years can choose between Latin and a second modern language; wide choice of options post-14 includes vocational GCSEs and GNVQs. A-level choice includes government & politics, media studies, psychology; vocational alternatives available. Daily homework, rigorously monitored; regular grades; full termly subject reports; achievement board on display to reward good work. Pupils grouped by ability in English, maths, science, modern languages; extra help for those with special needs; progress closely monitored (all set individual targets). All do two weeks' work experience, some in Europe and USA. More than 80 active clubs and societies; every pupil expected to participate in some-thing. Very good music: outstanding chamber choir performs annually at Montreux (head decreed she wanted 'patrician singing, no mid-Atlantic dron-ing'); two orchestras, numerous smaller ensembles. Annual Shakespeare play. Regular language trips to France and Spain.

Results   (1997) GCSE: 55% gained at least five grades A–C. A-level: 36% of entries graded A or B.

Destinations   Impressive 80% continue into the sixth form; of these, 80% pro-ceed to higher education (average of five a year to Oxbridge).

Sport   Not a particular strength, though good range on offer. Matches against other schools in football, cricket, rugby, hockey, netball, tennis, athletics. Badminton, basketball, swimming, dance also on offer. New £1.7 million sports hall; extensive playing fields on adjoining site.

Remarks   Ofsted inspectors concluded (1994): 'The school commands the respect and confidence of pupils and parents. It offers a good education. The standard of behaviour is very high.'

DOWNE HOUSE ♀
Cold Ash, Thatcham, Berkshire RG18 9JJ. Tel (01635) 200286

Synopsis
Independent ★ Girls ★ Boarding and day ★ Ages 11–18 ★ 629 pupils (95% boarding) ★ 161 in sixth form ★ Fees: £13,500 boarding; £9,786 day
Head: Mrs Emma McKendrick, 35, appointed September 1997.
Strong academic school; very good teaching and results; lots drama, music, sport.

Profile
Background   Founded in Kent 1907; moved 1921 to a 110-acre pine ridge

near Newbury, taking over the austere, Spanish-style buildings (red roofs, cloisters, white-washed walls) of the Order of Silence; school grew rapidly in reputation and size. Sudden departure of previous head and senior teachers (to North Foreland Lodge, qv) has caused dismay and upheaval; numbers now due to be reduced.

Atmosphere Gracious, friendly, well-ordered ('If a new girl doesn't realise that manners and respect for elders are important, it's pointed out to her'); relaxed, happy pupils with no fake sophistication or need to impress. Lessons on Saturday mornings; chapel ecumenical and compulsory; first-years spend a term at a château in the Dordogne.

Admissions By initial assessment day (to judge ability and enthusiasm) followed by Common Entrance; school is over-subscribed and quite selective (but reluctant to go into detail). Most pupils from London and the South East; sizeable contingent from Scotland. Boarding accommodation reassuringly domestic and feminine; five mixed-age houses vary in size and ethos; sixth-formers have study-bedrooms. Very good food (vegetarian chef).

The head New appointment; low-key, decisive (and unusually young for such a prestigious school). Read modern languages at Liverpool; previously head of Royal School, Bath, where she had taught since 1986.

The teaching First-rate: formal, demanding; much emphasis on independent learning. Broad curriculum: science (good labs) on offer as three separate subjects; lots of computing; all do Latin for first three years; Greek, Spanish, German, Russian, Italian available; all do cookery and needlework; wide choice of subjects at GCSE and A-level; all do general studies. Pupils grouped by ability; average class size 15. Strong drama (open-air theatre) and music (90% learn an instrument). Extra-curricular activities include well-supported Duke of Edinburgh award scheme; all required to develop a hobby ('If you have an interest, the teachers will support you').

Results (1997) GCSE: all gained at least five grades A–C. A-level: very creditable 77% of entries graded A or B.

Destinations About 90% stay on for A-levels; of these, virtually all proceed to university (average of 10 a year to Oxbridge).

Sport Good record; lacrosse a particular strength; squash popular; fencing, rowing available. Facilities include adequate playing fields, indoor pool, modest gym.

Remarks Good school looking forward to settling down under new management.

THE DOWNS ♂ ♀
Compton, Newbury, Berkshire RG16 0NU. Tel (01635) 578213

Synopsis
Comprehensive (grant-maintained) ★ Co-educational ★ Ages 11–16 ★ 650 pupils (roughly equal numbers of girls and boys)
Head: Graham Taylor, 53, appointed 1983.
Well-run, happy school; good teaching and results.

Profile
Background Opened as a secondary modern 1960; went comprehensive 1978; opted out of council control 1992; hopes to open a sixth form in 2000. Attractive, well-maintained buildings on a spacious, rural site (views over the west

Berkshire Downs); extensive re-building in progress (numbers rising due to league table success).

Atmosphere   Busy, warm, welcoming; everything well cared for (there is room to breathe here). Cheerful, well-disciplined pupils (no rushing about or excessive noise at break-time); all in uniform. Competitive house system (points for academic work, sport, drama).

Admissions   No selection: priority to siblings and those who live nearest. Fairly wide range of abilities and backgrounds from an extensive rural catchment area (33 'feeder' primaries).

The head   Able, confident; astute financial manager (effects visible in the wealth of books, computers, art equipment, musical instruments). Quiet, self-effacing manner; gets on well with staff and pupils (teaches physics to 12–year-olds). Married; four sons, the youngest a pupil here.

The teaching   Good: largely traditional in style; orderly lessons; enthusiastic, well-qualified staff; attentive pupils. Standard national curriculum; lots of emphasis on practical subjects. Average class size 22; pupils grouped by ability from the start in maths, science (dual award) and modern languages (French or German); extra help for those who need it – both the more able and those with learning difficulties. GCSE options include drama, business studies. High-quality music. Extensive work experience programme; good careers centre.

Results   (1997) GCSE: 69% gained at least five grades A–C.

Destinations   Nearly all remain in full-time education; parents anxious for a sixth form.

Sports   Keenly competitive soccer, rugby, cricket (girls and boys), netball, badminton, basketball, tennis. Facilities include playing fields, well-equipped sports hall, outdoor pool.

Remarks   Attractive, successful school.

DOWNSIDE ♂

Stratton-on-the-Fosse, Bath BA3 4RJ. Tel (01761) 235103

Synopsis

Independent ★ Roman Catholic ★ Boys ★ Boarding and some day ★ Ages 11–18 ★ 310 pupils (98% boarding) ★ 117 in sixth form ★ Fees: £12,180 boarding; £6,180 day
Head: Dom Anthony Sutch, 47, appointed 1995.
Firmly traditional Catholic boarding school; wide range of abilities; modest results.

Profile

Background   Founded 1606 in Douai, Flanders by the English Benedictine community of St Gregory to provide a Catholic education for English boys then denied one in England; driven out of France 1789; established at Downside 1814. Imposing but austere Victorian-Gothic buildings plus some ugly modern additions on a secluded 200-acre estate at the foot of the Mendips. Campus is dominated physically and spiritually by the pinnacles and flying buttresses of the magnificent abbey church; monastery library contains 150,000 volumes. Science labs and music school recently refurbished.

Atmosphere   Religious ethos powerful and all-pervasive: crucifix prominent in every classroom; compulsory prayers morning and evening; much emphasis on charitable activities. Courteous, good-natured, unpretentious boys (nearly a third are the sons of former pupils); traditional uniform of black jacket and pin-stripe trousers.

Admissions School is not academically selective: numbers have steadily declined and many teachers been made redundant; 25% of pupils come from abroad (particularly Spain and Malta); non-Catholics accepted only in exceptional circumstances. League table position has slipped too (from 188th in 1993 to 286th in 1996): head criticises those who think that more important than a fully Catholic education. Boarding accommodation recently refurbished but still spartan. Scholarships, bursaries available.

The head Very able; warm, portly, well-connected ('the Monk of Mayfair'); popular with monks, staff and pupils. Was a pupil here; read history at Exeter, theology at Oxford; became a chartered accountant; returned here 1975 and was a housemaster for 10 years.

The teaching Formal, structured. Broad curriculum: big emphasis on European languages (five offered – most take two for GCSE); Latin and Greek survive. Pupils grouped by ability in most subjects; small classes (many taught by monks, who forego a salary). Fine choral tradition (but standards of instrumental music are not high); lots of drama. Well-supported cadet force. Boys encouraged to take part in annual pilgrimage to Lourdes. Regular language exchanges with schools in France, Germany, Spain.

Results (1997) GCSE: 84% gained at least five grades A–C. A-level: 39% of entries graded A or B.

Destinations About 90% stay on for A-level and nearly all proceed to university.

Sports Strong tradition, particularly in rugby, hockey, cricket. Soccer, cross-country, tennis, athletics, swimming also available. Facilities include first-rate playing fields, sports hall, indoor pool.

Remarks HMC inspectors concluded (1995): 'The timeless values of the Benedictine tradition help to shape the school's strong sense of community. The standard of teaching in all subjects is sound. The pupils make progress commensurate with their abilities.'

DR CHALLONER'S GRAMMAR ♂
Chesham Road, Amersham, Buckinghamshire HP6 5HA. Tel (01494) 721685

Synopsis
Grammar (voluntary-controlled) ★ Boys ★ Ages 11–18 ★ 1,061 pupils ★ 400 in sixth form
Head: Graham Hill, 55, appointed 1993.
First-rate, traditional school; very good teaching and results; strong music, sport.

Profile
Background Founded 1624; moved to present site 1903. Formerly co-educational; girls moved to separate site 1962 (Dr Challoner's High, qv); strong links remain. Edwardian buildings plus various later additions, including shabby, 1950s, five-storey concrete block; state-of-the-art language lab paid for by parents and friends. School feels over-crowded; further building planned.

Atmosphere Courteous, well-ordered, hard-working; good rapport between staff and pupils.

Admissions School heavily over-subscribed (four apply for each place). Entry by county council 11-plus; top 30% of the ability range from an extensive, largely

middle-class catchment area; about 30% come from the independent sector.
The head Came here as deputy 1978. Scientist; teaches chemistry, writes textbooks. Married (wife much involved in school life).
The teaching First-rate ('The quality of teaching is a strength of the school,' said Ofsted inspectors); mix of formal and modern methods. Stable staff of 75 (66% women – a civilising element, says the head). Broad curriculum; all do French and German for first two years; science on offer as three separate subjects; strong maths. Pupils grouped by ability in maths, French (top 30% in each take GCSE a year early); average class size 20–25, reducing to a maximum of 16 at A-level. Good art, drama, music (three choirs, two orchestras). Extra-curricular activities include strong chess, debating, Duke of Edinburgh award scheme. Regular trips and foreign exchanges.
Results (1997) GCSE: 99% gained at least five grades A–C. A-level: 52% of entries graded A or B.
Destinations More than 90% stay on for A-levels; of these, 90% proceed to university (average of 20 a year to Oxbridge).
Sport All main games; soccer more popular than rugby; strong athletics, cross-country. Facilities are poor.
Remarks Identified by Ofsted (1995) as an 'outstandingly successful' school, 'highly regarded by parents and the wider community, with high academic standards, and attentive and well-motivated pupils'.

DR CHALLONER'S HIGH ♀
Cokes Lane, Little Chalfont, Amersham, Buckinghamshire HP7 9QB. Tel (01494) 763296

Synopsis
Grammar ★ Girls ★ Ages 12–18 (11–18 from September 1998) ★ 878 pupils ★ 282 in sixth form
Head: Mrs Sue Lawson, 51, appointed 1993.
Well-run, academic school; very good teaching and results; strong music.

Profile
Background Formerly part of Dr Challoner's (qv); became a separate school in purpose-built premises on a pleasant, wooded site 1962; much recent building but some classrooms still in huts.
Atmosphere Happy, vibrant: good rapport between dedicated staff and lively, well-motivated pupils. Big emphasis on moral values, mutual respect, tolerance (no prize-giving – head believes competing against oneself more important than competing against others). Highly supportive parents.
Admissions Selective – but not unduly so: top 30% of the ability range from a fairly small catchment area. Entry by verbal reasoning test (administered by the county council); 80% come from local primary schools.
The head Very able; strong leader. Read English at London; worked in industry; previously deputy head of a Surrey comprehensive. Holds a monthly 'clinic' for parents to discuss their daughter's progress.
The teaching Good quality, challenging; well-qualified, stable staff of 60 (five men), 20% appointed by present head. Broad curriculum: all introduced to French, German, Spanish, Latin and then choose two; science (new labs on the way) offered as three separate subjects; most take nine GCSEs. Girls grouped by

ability in GCSE maths only; average class size 25, reducing to 15 in sixth form. Strong music: 200 learn an instrument; three choirs, two orchestras, various ensembles. Busy programme of extra-curricular activities, including well-supported Duke of Edinburgh award scheme.

Results (1997) GCSE: 99% gained at least five grades A–C. A-level: 48% of entries graded A or B.

Destinations About 85% continue into the sixth form; of these, 90% proceed to university (up to 10 a year to Oxbridge).

Sport Main games: hockey, netball, cross-country, swimming, tennis, athletics; soccer, rugby also on offer.

Remarks Identified by Ofsted (1996) as an 'outstanding' school.

DUKE OF YORK'S ROYAL MILITARY ♂ ♀
Dover, Kent CT15 5EQ. Tel (01304) 245029

Synopsis
Independent ★ Co-educational ★ Ages 11–18 ★ 491 pupils (70% boys) ★ 100 in sixth form ★ Fees (subsidised): £849
Head: Colonel Gordon Wilson, 48, appointed 1992.
Sound, barely militaristic school for children of past or present Service personnel.

Profile
Background Founded 1803 in Chelsea by Frederick, Duke of York for soldiers' orphans seeking a military career; moved 1909 to present, 150-acre, cliff-top site and spacious, well-maintained premises; opened to all three Services 1991; girls admitted 1994. School is owned and funded by the Ministry of Defence (but 'executive agency' status gives it a degree of independence).

Atmosphere Firm discipline; impeccable courtesy; spotless uniform ('Everyone likes to have well-brushed shoes,' observed an earnest 12-year-old). Introduction of girls has softened the school's style (drama and music strongly ascendant, military attitudes subdued).

Admissions By tests in English, maths; top 25% of the ability range (about three apply for every place); one parent must have served in the armed forces as a Regular for at least four years; almost half are based overseas. Comfortable boarding accommodation (up to six share); very good food.

The head Charming, softly-spoken. Read history at Queen's, Belfast; previously a senior Army education officer in Germany. Married; two children (one a pupil here).

The teaching Formal in style; experienced staff (27% female). Standard national curriculum; all take six to 10 GCSEs; vocational alternatives to A-level include engineering, business studies. Free music lessons for first-years; strong drama. Extra-curricular activities include Duke of Edinburgh award scheme.

Results (1997) GCSE: 92% gained at least five grades A–C. A-level: creditable 57% of entries graded A or B.

Destinations Nearly all continue into the sixth form and proceed to higher education; about one in seven take up a Service career.

Sport Chiefly: cricket, hockey, rugby, netball, tennis; busy competitive calendar. First-rate facilities include all-weather hockey pitch.

Remarks Ofsted inspectors concluded (1995): 'The school is doing well and operating effectively with no major shortcomings.'

DULWICH ♂
College Road, Dulwich, London SE21 7LD. Tel (0181) 693 3601

Synopsis
Independent ★ Boys ★ Day and boarding ★ Ages 7–18 ★ 1,387 pupils (94% day) ★ 374 in sixth form ★ Fees: £6,270–£6,618 day; £13,263 boarding
Head: Graham Able, 50, appointed January 1997.
Strong academic school; good teaching and results; lots of music, sport.

Profile
Background   Founded 1619 by Edward Alleyn, Elizabethan actor-manager, as his 'College of God's Gift'; moved 1870 to present 60-acre site and fine (if institutional), purpose-built premises; many later additions, including attractive junior school. Whole school administered as a single unit with a common teaching staff.

Atmosphere   Academic, slightly lack-lustre (not a very strong pulse here – except in the junior forms, where there is a lively buzz); rudimentary pastoral care; formal, rather distant relations between staff and boys (little obvious evidence of warmth); competitive house system; traditional blazer-and-tie uniform.

Admissions   At seven by interview and practical assessment; at 10, 11 by tests in English, maths, verbal reasoning; at 13 by Common Entrance; school is fairly selective (top 20% of the ability range) but likely to become less so with the phasing out of assisted places, which 270 hold (at a cost to the Government of £1.2 million a year). Scholarships and many bursaries available (at a cost to the school of £1 million a year). Fairly broad social mix; most live within an hour's travelling time (fleet of buses); most boarders' parents live abroad. Adequate, if functional, boarding accommodation.

The head   Recent appointment (governors forced his predecessor to resign, after which there was an uncomfortable interregnum). Low-key, determined; sees his task as 'bringing the school up to speed without losing its past'. Read natural sciences at Cambridge; previously head for nine years of Hampton (qv). Keen sportsman. Married; two grown-up children.

The teaching   Generally good; mostly traditional in style; well-qualified staff. Broad curriculum: science on offer as three separate subjects; languages include Latin, Greek, Spanish, German; all take at least nine GCSEs and three A-levels; good general studies course. Pupils grouped by ability in most subjects; progress closely monitored (three-weekly grades for effort and attainment); extra help for dyslexics and those who speak English as a second language; class sizes vary between 18 and 25, reducing to 10 at A-level. Unexciting art; strong music tradition (choirs, orchestras); lots of drama. Wide range of extra-curricular activities (clubs and societies for all manner of things); popular cadet force; field study centre in Brecon Beacons.

Results   (1997) GCSE: all gained at least five grades A–C. A-level: creditable 69% of entries graded A or B.

Destinations   Nearly all go on to university (up to 30 a year to Oxbridge).

Sport   Traditionally strong; good coaching. Main games: rugby, hockey, cricket, swimming; wide range of others on offer. Facilities include extensive playing fields, all-weather pitch.

Remarks   Good school emerging from a bruising time, in need of (and grateful for) a new broom.

DUNBLANE HIGH ♂ ♀
Highfields, Dunblane, Perthshire FK15 9DR. Tel (01786) 823823

Synopsis
Comprehensive ★ Co-educational ★ Ages 12–18 ★ 770 pupils (equal numbers of girls and boys) ★ 122 in sixth year
Head: Jim Gardner, 56, appointed 1989.
Well-run, successful school; good teaching and results.

Profile
Background Opened 1976 in purpose-built premises (including imposing three-storey teaching block) on a pleasant site on the edge of the town (30 miles from Glasgow, 40 miles from Edinburgh). Classrooms generally spacious, light, well-equipped; some in 'temporary' huts; everything clean and tidy. Well-stocked library (full-time librarian) conducive to quiet study.
Atmosphere Disciplined, well-ordered (neither subdued nor boisterous); staff and pupils (who are given plenty of responsibility) working together towards common goals; well organised pastoral care system. Uniform encouraged but not obligatory (but no jeans or shell suits).
Admissions Places allocated by Stirling Council; most from professional/middle-class homes in a generally prosperous area.
The head (Rector) Able, professional; sets high standards. Read maths at Glasgow.
The teaching Good quality. Broad curriculum; choice of French or German; all do home economics, computing. Nearly all take eight Standard Grades; choice of 21 Highers plus vocational modules; most do a mixture of the two. Pupils grouped by ability in some subjects from third year; average class size 24/25. Sixth-formers draw up their own timetable, which may, or may not, involve daily attendance. Plenty of music: choirs, orchestra, smaller ensembles. Regular language exchanges with schools in France, Germany.
Results (1997) Standard Grade: 58% gained at least five grades 1–2. Highers: 17% gained at least five grades A–C.
Destinations Up to 90% stay on for Highers; of these, 90% return for a sixth year; 45% of leavers proceed to higher education.
Sport Main games: soccer, rugby, hockey, basketball, athletics, swimming; limited inter-school fixture list but individual talents nurtured. Facilities include sports hall, gym, two (ill-drained) rugby/soccer pitches, grass hockey pitch, all-weather surface.
Remarks Civilised, happy school.

DURHAM HIGH ♀
Farewell Hall, Durham DH1 3TB. Tel (0191) 384 3226

Synopsis
Independent ★ Girls ★ Day ★ Ages 3–18 ★ 400 pupils (250 in senior school) ★ 60 in sixth form ★ Fees: £3,120–£4,660
Head: Miss Margaret Walters, 51, appointed 1992 (retiring August 1998).
Traditional girls' school; fairly wide range of abilities; good teaching and results.

Profile

Background Founded 1884; moved to present purpose-built premises on self-contained 11-acre campus 1968. Pleasant, if undistinguished, buildings in economical 1960s style; later additions include sixth-form centre (drinks machine, comfortable sofas) and barn-like sports hall. Juniors in separate wing: bright, colourful classrooms; nursery extension opened September 1997.

Atmosphere A cosy haven ('Only when pupils are confident and comfortable will they achieve their full potential'); caring, Christian ethos; staff treated with respect and consideration; discipline not as strict as formerly but still fairly firm (rules on jewellery, make-up, uniform). Supportive parents. Best known (and perhaps typical) old girl is the actress Wendy Craig.

Admissions By interview for juniors; by entrance tests for 10 and 11-year-olds. Head says the school is 'mildly selective'; staff say a larger proportion of less able girls is being admitted. Anglican foundation but pupils of any religion welcome. Some scholarships, bursaries at 11 and 16.

The head Calm, efficient. Able administrator; seen as a moderniser; gets on well with staff and pupils (teaches first-years); 'at home' to parents on Thursday afternoons. Keen advocate of computer technology: has reformed the timetable to give it and science more weight. Read classics at Leicester; previously deputy head of Queen's, Chester (qv). Suffers from multiple sclerosis, and is much admired for being so open about it. Sings opera with the Durham Choral Society.

The teaching Good quality; traditional in style (much note-taking) but far from formal. Staff of 41 (including two young men appointed by present head); attentive, responsive pupils. Particular strengths in arts and humanities; maths, science (taught as three separate subjects) and computing not neglected; design/technology recently introduced. GCSE options include German, Spanish, Italian; Latin on offer to A-level. Pupils grouped by ability in most subjects; average class size 24, much smaller in the sixth form. Regular tests; homework carefully monitored. Lots of music: two-thirds learn an instrument; choir, orchestra, regular concerts. Sumptuous art rooms (after-school life drawing). Popular Duke of Edinburgh award scheme (more than 100 gold awards).

Results (1997) GCSE: 97% gained at least five grades A–C. A-level: creditable 60% of entries graded A or B.

Destinations Nearly all go to university (Durham, Edinburgh, London, Nottingham, Warwick and, occasionally, Oxbridge).

Sport Varied programme; suits all-rounders. Strong netball, tennis; soccer, rowing, karate also on offer.

Remarks Secure, happy school keeping up to date.

DURHAM JOHNSTON ♂ ♀
Crossgate Moor, Durham DH1 4SU. Tel (0191) 384 3887

Synopsis
Comprehensive ★ Co-educational ★ Ages 11–18 ★ 1,500 pupils ★ 290 in sixth form
Head: Dr John Dunford, OBE, 50, appointed 1982.
Comprehensive education at its best; first-rate teaching more than compensates for modest buildings and equipment.

Profile

Background Result of a 1979 amalgamation of a grammar school and two secondary moderns on two sites two-and-a-half miles apart; first two years in 1930s red-brick premises (light, airy classrooms and adequate facilities); seniors in rather stark 1950s buildings, constantly being up-graded.

Atmosphere Everything impeccable; staff and pupils radiate motivation and enthusiasm. Good pastoral care system; relationships are frank and open. Friendly, hard working, smartly uniformed pupils proud to be here. Overcrowded dining room has the air of a bubbling, courteous family.

Admissions School heavily over-subscribed; priority to pupils at seven main 'feeder' primaries and 20 smaller ones. Genuinely comprehensive intake; all seem to achieve their full potential. Up to 60 a year join the (open entry) sixth form from other schools, state and independent.

The head Calm, imaginative, very able. Read maths and economics at Nottingham; PhD at Durham. Two children; both pupils here.

The teaching Outstanding: wide range of styles, leaning towards the traditional; thorough grounding in the basics. First-rate staff: an ideal balance of age, maturity, experience. Mixed-ability teaching in first year, based on social groupings (mixing city and rural pupils); broad ability grouping from second year in English, maths, science, languages (French plus German or Latin); extra help in class for those with special needs; average class size 28 (smaller for the less able). Most do nine GCSEs and three A-levels; broad sixth-form programme includes general studies, preparation for higher education etc. Very good art, drama, music; excellent debating. Annual exchange with a high school in Japan.

Results (1997) GCSE: 63% gained at least five grades A–C. A-level: 50% of entries graded A or B.

Destinations About 50% continue into the sixth form; of these, 90% proceed to university (average of seven a year to Oxbridge).

Sport Particular strengths in football, cross-country, cricket, athletics, hockey; as much emphasis on participation as success. Good playing fields but no sports hall (school has access to university's facilities); many staff turn out on Saturday mornings.

Remarks Very good school offering pupils of all abilities a truly broad, balanced education. Highly recommended.

EASTBOURNE ♂ ♀
Old Wish Road, Eastbourne, East Sussex BN21 4JX. Tel (01323) 452320

Synopsis
Independent ★ Co-educational ★ Boarding and day ★ Ages 13–18 ★ 496 pupils (78% boys, 57% boarders) ★ 239 in sixth form ★ Fees: £12,690 boarding; £9,000 day
Head: Charles Bush, 45, appointed 1993.
Traditional school; firm values; good art, music; strong sport.

Profile

Background Founded 1867 (by the seventh Duke of Devonshire and others) in a residential area of the town, five minutes from the station and sea. Main building, in red-brick collegiate style facing a large cricket pitch, dates from 1920s; some areas rather bare and institutional. School expanded by admitting girls to the sixth form in 1969 (one of the first to do so) and at all ages from 1996 (but they are still heavily outnumbered); average of £1 million a year spent on developments since 1983; latest additions include art block, well-equipped design/technology centre. Library needs improving; some science labs in 'temporary' huts.

Atmosphere Purposeful; strong Christian ethos; school insists on high standards of work, honesty, respect, courtesy. Rules, rewards, sanctions (including Saturday night detention) clearly explained; firm line on drugs, alcohol, smoking (all of which can lead to expulsion); strict uniform. Friendly (but never casual) relations between staff and pupils; supportive house system. Boarding in late Victorian/Edwardian brick villas, some (but not all) recently refurbished and modernised. Ample food; plenty of choice. Twelve-hour school day (day pupils share the boarding experience); lessons on Saturday mornings.

Admissions By Common Entrance (minimum 50% mark required) or school's own tests; not unduly selective – range of abilities is fairly wide. Scholarships (academic, art, music, science, all-rounder) available. Pupils mainly from local prep schools (St Andrew's, St Bede's – qv); boarders from the London–Brighton–Tunbridge Wells triangle; few from abroad (English must be fluent).

The head Personable, determined; strong leader, 'hands-on' style; combines respect for traditional values with a clear (market-oriented) vision of an expanding future. Went to school in Australia; read history at Oxford; became a housemaster at Marlborough (qv). Teaches (non-examined) divinity to 16-year-olds. Married; three sons (two at Marlborough).

The teaching Good quality: challenging; formal in style. Enthusiastic staff of 50 (seven women); strong shared ethos. Broad curriculum: science on offer as three separate subjects; languages include German, Spanish, Latin, Greek; most take 10 GCSEs. Pupils grouped by ability in English, maths, science; regular grades for effort and achievement; individual help available for dyslexics; average class size 18–20, smaller for A-level. A-level options include economics and business studies, history of art, further maths; all take general studies. Good art (ceramics, plaster work, polystyrene sculpture as well as exuberant painting and carefully-observed watercolours); lots of music (chapel choir, more than 100 learn an instrument). Wide range of extra-curricular activities (debating, cookery, chess, bridge); compulsory cadet force; popular Duke of Edinburgh award scheme. Regular language exchanges with schools in France, Germany.

Results (1997) GCSE: 97% gained at least five grades A–C. A-level: 55% of entries graded A or B.

Destinations Most go on to university (including about 10 a year to Oxbridge).

Sport Strong, particularly in rugby and (boys') hockey; girls play netball, hockey, rounders and tennis; athletics, basketball, cross-country, fencing, fives, golf, judo, lacrosse, rowing, sailing, soccer, squash, swimming, trampolining, water polo, volleyball also on offer. Playing fields, including all-weather pitch, scattered within a mile's radius.

Remarks Robust school: suits able, physically-active children (but not trendy radicals or couch potatoes). HMC inspectors concluded (1996): 'This is a very good school with high standards of achievement.'

EATON ♂ ♀
Eaton Road, Norwich, Norfolk NR4 6PP. Tel (01603) 454015

Synopsis
Comprehensive ★ Co-educational ★ Ages 12–18 ★ 1,230 pupils (53% boys) ★ 360 in sixth form
Head: Dr Tom Elkins, 57, appointed 1978.
Well-regarded, rather formal comprehensive; high standards expected; respectable results; good music and art.

Profile
Background Founded 1910 as the City of Norwich School, the result of the local community's wish to have a grammar school to match those in other great cities. Magnificent purpose-built premises (including a fine hall) were opened by the then headmaster of Eton, and a tradition of academic excellence was rapidly established; went comprehensive 1970. Later additions rather less impressive; facilities, however, are generally adequate; those for music and art are good. School has a unit for the visually handicapped.

Atmosphere Demanding, purposeful. Traditional grammar-school ethos retained; academic expectations high; discipline firm. Distinct air of formality: not even the head is allowed to walk on the grass; silence expected at morning assembly the moment a member of staff appears on the platform. (Some pupils have difficulty accommodating themselves to the regime.) Strong parents' association; head produces weekly newsletter.

Admissions School is popular with parents and always full. Fairly wide cross-section of abilities and backgrounds.

The head Long-serving. Quietly dignified style; runs a tight ship. Read English at Queen's, Belfast; PhD in educational administration. Still teaches; keen on physical fitness. Married to a teacher; two grown-up children.

The teaching Very much in the academic tradition; hard-working, experienced, long-serving staff of 77 (nearly half have been here more than 10 years, some were here when it was a grammar school). Standard national curriculum; main languages French and German; maths and science results consistently good; first-rate art (many take it for GCSE). Large classes – 28 is typical – but smaller in the sixth form. Choice of more than 20 subjects at A-level, including Spanish, politics, music; many take a one-year vocational alternative; extra help for Oxbridge candidates. Good music: two orchestras, various bands, choir; active drama. Lots of charity fund-raising. Regular language exchanges with schools in France, Germany.

Results (1997) GCSE: 55% gained at least five grades A–C. A-level: 48% of entries graded A or B.

Destinations About 70% continue into the sixth form (no minimum entry qualifications); of these, 65% proceed to higher education.

Sport 'Unisex': boys and girls follow mixed PE programme. Strong tennis, hockey; basketball, cricket also popular. Facilities include extensive playing fields, sports hall, tennis courts.

Remarks Good school for average and above-average children. Ofsted inspectors concluded (1993): 'The quality of teaching and learning is generally satisfactory or good. However, there is scope to develop pupils' independent learning in more adventurous ways.'

ECCLESBOURNE ♂ ♀
Wirksworth Road, Duffield, Derby DE6 4GB. Tel (01332) 840645

Synopsis
Comprehensive (grant-maintained) ★ Co-educational ★ Ages 11–18 ★ 1,350 pupils (equal numbers of girls and boys) ★ 250 in sixth form
Head: Dr Robert Dupey, 57, appointed 1976.
First-rate, well-run comprehensive; good teaching and results.

Profile
Background Opened 1957 as a co-educational grammar school; went comprehensive 1976; opted out of council control 1990. Functional, single-storey buildings on large, leafy site; many classrooms in 'temporary' huts; recent building programme has improved facilities for technology, computing, business studies.

Atmosphere Friendly, purposeful, secure; high standards expected and achieved; traditional values retained. Articulate, polite pupils (they open doors for adults), confident without being cocky; disciplinary problems rare; neat uniform (designed by parents); sixth-formers wear suits. Most of the staff send their children here (a good sign); estate agents quote the catchment area (another good sign). Strongly supportive parents.

Admissions Over-subscribed: no academic selection; priority to those living in the rural and 'urban village' catchment area north of Derby.

The head Exceptionally long-serving. A tremendous enthusiast for comprehensive education; believes the school should fit round the child, not vice versa; liked and respected by staff and pupils. Read zoology at Leicester. Married, three children (two were pupils here, one still is); wife teaches children with special needs.

The teaching High quality; well-qualified staff of 90, nearly all appointed by present head. Standard national curriculum; all do French and two years of a second language (Spanish or German); strong religious education (many take it for GCSE and A-level). Choice of 24 subjects at A-level, including law, economics, computing; vocational alternatives include GNVQ in business and finance. Pupils set by ability in maths, languages from second year, science and English from third year; extra help for the gifted ('as resources allow') and those with special needs; progress carefully monitored. Burgeoning music; orchestra competes successfully at local festival. Regular language trips to France, Germany, Spain; arts visit to Paris; RE trips to Israel; lower-sixth pupils take part in month-long exchange with a school near Philadelphia.

Results (1997) GCSE: very creditable 80% gained at least five grades A–C. A-level: 41% of entries graded A or B.

Destinations About 65% continue into the sixth form; of these, 95% proceed to university (about five a year to Oxbridge).

Sport Regular county honours in hockey, football, rugby, cricket, athletics, tennis, netball, swimming.

Remarks Identified by Ofsted (1995) as an 'outstandingly successful' school.

EDGBASTON HIGH ♀
Westbourne Road, Birmingham B15 3TS. Tel (0121) 454 5831

Synopsis
Independent ★ Girls ★ Day ★ Ages 11–18 ★ 512 pupils (plus pre-prep and prep departments) ★ 120 in sixth form ★ Fees: £4,650.
Head: Miss Elizabeth Mullenger, 55, appointed January 1998.
Sound school; good teaching and results; lots of music and sport.

Profile
Background   Founded 1876 (the first girls' school in the city); moved 1962 to present, slightly cramped four-acre site (in a residential area next to the Botanical Gardens); pleasant, purpose-built premises plus later additions; playing fields some distance away.

Atmosphere   Bright, cheerful, well-ordered. Lively, enthusiastic girls; busy programme of lunch-time activities; much fund-raising for charity.

Admissions   By school's own tests in English, maths, non-verbal reasoning. Half the pupils come from the prep department, the rest from state primaries. Catchment area covers the West Midlands; 25% ethnic minorities. Scholarships (academic, music, sport) available.

The head   New appointment. Read English at Bangor; previously head of English at King Edward VI Camp Hill Girls' (qv) and then head for 12 years of St James's and The Abbey, Malvern.

The teaching   Good quality; varied styles. Full-time staff of 57 (five men), some long-serving. Fairly broad curriculum; science taught as three separate subjects; all do Latin plus two modern languages; plenty of computing. Pupils grouped by ability in maths, French. Average class size 22–26, reducing to 8–12 for A-levels. Strong music: choir, orchestra, various ensembles; lots of drama. Extra-curricular activities include public speaking, well-supported Duke of Edinburgh award scheme. Regular exchanges with schools in Denmark, Germany, France, Russia.

Results   (1997) GCSE: 97% gained at least five grades A–C. A-level: 60% of entries graded A or B.

Destinations   About 90% go on to university.

Sport   Wide choice; particular strengths in netball, tennis. Hockey, athletics, cricket, fencing, swimming also on offer.

Remarks   Attractive school; safe choice.

EDINBURGH ACADEMY ♂
42 Henderson Row, Edinburgh 6H3 5BL. Tel (0131) 556 4603

Synopsis
Independent ★ Boys (plus girls in sixth form) ★ Day and some boarding ★ Ages 10–18 (plus associated prep school) ★ 483 pupils (92% day) ★ 196 in sixth form (85% boys) ★ Fees: £2,673–£5,490 day; £10,065–£11,706 boarding
Head: John Light, 49, appointed 1995.
Traditional school, now in transition; sound teaching and results; strong music and sport.

Profile

Background Founded 1824 (Sir Walter Scott presiding); handsome, purpose-built neo-classical premises (including a magnificent hall) on the edge of the city's Georgian New Town; many later additions (some rather less grand). Prep school a mile away.

Atmosphere Courteous, purposeful; strong sense of community; good relations between staff and pupils; well-organised pastoral care system. Uniform of tweed jacket and school tie; kilts may be worn on formal occasions.

Admissions By tests in English, maths or Common Entrance (but most join from the prep school); fairly wide range of abilities (the school is not full). Most pupils from professional/middle-class backgrounds; phasing out of assisted places, which nearly 70 hold, will further reduce the social mix. Boarding accommodation homely (numbers small and declining). Scholarships available.

The head (Rector) Enthusiastic, very much in command. Read modern languages at Cambridge; worked in industry before switching to teaching; previously head of Oswestry. Keen on sport (runs marathons, plays squash) and music (sings in choir). Married; four children.

The teaching Sound; generally formal in style; well-qualified, predominantly male staff. Fairly broad curriculum: science taught as three separate subjects; all do Latin (but few continue it to GCSE); Russian, Greek on offer. Pupils grouped by ability in some subjects from 11, in all at 13; lots of extra help for those who need it; no class larger than 25. Most take five Highers in one or two years; more able do A-levels. Strong music: more than 300 learn an instrument; orchestras, choirs. Wide range of extra-curricular activities, including compulsory cadet force, well-supported Duke of Edinburgh award scheme; field centre in the Highlands. First-rate careers advice. Regular language exchanges with schools in France, Germany.

Results (1997) A-level: 63% of entries graded A or B.

Destinations About 80% proceed to university.

Sport Strong ('games are regarded as an integral part of the curriculum'); facilities include extensive playing fields (20 minutes' walk away), running track, all-weather tennis courts. Main games: rugby, hockey, soccer, cross-country, cricket, athletics, tennis, sailing. Fives, fencing, squash, swimming also on offer.

Remarks School has been through a bad patch recently (previous head left after only three years and numbers fell) but is now recovering.

EGGLESCLIFFE ♂ ♀

Urlay Nook Road, Egglescliffe, Stockton-on-Tees, Cleveland TS16 0LA.
Tel (01642) 783686

Synopsis

Comprehensive ★ Co-educational ★ Ages 11–18 ★ 1,320 pupils (roughly equal numbers of girls and boys) ★ 250 in sixth form
Head: Mrs Angella Darnell, 44, appointed 1994.
First-rate comprehensive; good results; very strong art, music, drama.

Profile

Background Founded 1962 as a secondary modern; went comprehensive 1969. Dreary buildings (leaking roofs, peeling paintwork) plus functional, graceless additions (some classrooms double as dining rooms) – but do not be deceived...

Atmosphere   Warm, welcoming, effervescent: a school that inspires superlatives. Staff and pupils give of their utmost within and beyond the curriculum; life busy from dawn to dusk. Exemplary pastoral care system. Very supportive parents (encouraged to be 'active participants' in their children's education).

Admissions   School heavily over-subscribed; priority to those in the local education authority's 'admission zone' and those living nearest 'as determined by the shortest convenient walking distance'. Wide range of abilities (at 11, 20% have a reading age of nine or less); middle-class, white-collar backgrounds predominate. Strict uniform below the sixth form (where platform shoes and leather jackets are not acceptable).

The head   Very able; strong leader; previously deputy head here for four years. Read history at Durham.

The teaching   First-rate: enthusiastic, knowledgeable teachers; good blend of youth and experience; particular strengths in science, maths, art, music. Standard national curriculum; choice of French or German (all have a taste of both); particular attention paid to cross-curricular themes such as equal opportunities, health, environment (school has its own nature trails and cares for parks and woodlands in the town). Good choice of 20 subjects at A-level; vocational alternatives include popular GNVQ in business studies. Pupils grouped by ability in maths from first year and later in languages; extra help for those who need it; average class size 25. Exceptional music: prize-winning orchestra and band; professional-standard recording studio. Flourishing Duke of Edinburgh award scheme (230 take part at any one time). Strong links with industry.

Results   (1997) GCSE: creditable 66% gained at least five grades A–C. A-levels: 34% of entries graded A or B.

Destinations   About 60% continue into the sixth form (to be joined by up to 60 others); of these, 80% proceed to higher education.

Sport   Good record in football, hockey, netball, athletics. Facilities include sports hall, gym, grass and all-weather pitches, athletics track, tennis courts.

Remarks   Ofsted inspectors concluded (1996): 'Egglescliffe provides a very good education for its pupils. In many areas of the curriculum, there is work of real excellence. Particularly impressive is the ability of pupils to debate issues and ideas, to think for themselves and to challenge received opinion. This independent way of thinking, which is not confined to the more able pupils, promotes high standards across the curriculum.' Model comprehensive; highly recommended.

ELTHAM ♂
Grove Park Road, London SE9 4QF. Tel (0181) 857 1455

Synopsis
Independent ★ Boys (plus girls in sixth form) ★ Day and some boarding ★ Ages ★ 11–18 (plus associated junior school) ★ 580 pupils (98% day) ★ 185 in sixth form (73% boys) ★ Fees: £6,000 day; £12,663 boarding
Head: Malcolm Green, 57, appointed 1990.
Well-run school; good teaching and results; fine facilities; strong music and sport.

Profile
Background   Founded 1842 as a school for the sons of missionaries; moved to present, attractive 25-acre site 1912; formerly Direct Grant, reverted to full

independence 1974. Gracious early 18th-century mansion plus rather more functional additions; facilities include fine performing arts centre, sports centre (named after Eric Liddell – former pupil, Olympic champion, China missionary). Governing body shared with Walthamstow Hall (qv). Junior school on same site under its own head.

Atmosphere   Friendly, well-ordered; 'an education based on Christian principles and practice'. Warm relations between staff and pupils; good pastoral care (bullying dealt with promptly and taken seriously). Smart uniform; sixth-form boys wear suits.

Admissions   At 11 by interview and exams (boys from junior school 'almost always' promoted); school has been fairly selective (and is socially and ethnically diverse) but phasing out of assisted places, which nearly 150 hold, will have a big impact. Some scholarships, bursaries. A handful of boarders, all of whom have single study-bedrooms.

The head   Able; strong leader; warm, courteous, unassuming; gets on well with staff, parents, pupils (teaches religious education to all first-years). Read English at Cambridge (and captained modern pentathlon team); his second headship. Married; three grown-up children.

The teaching   Challenging; varied styles. Hard-working, well-qualified staff of 58 (75% men), half appointed by present head. Fairly broad curriculum; science available as three separate subjects; German, Latin on offer; lots of computing; most take 10 GCSEs; choice of 22 subjects at A-level. Pupils grouped by ability in maths, modern languages; average class size 25, reducing to 17 for GCSE, 11 in the sixth form. Strong art, drama, music (more than 200 learn an instrument, two orchestras). Wide range of extra-curricular activities. Frequent study trips abroad.

Results   (1997) GCSE: all gained at least five grades at A–C. A-level: 63% of entries graded A or B.

Destinations   Virtually all go on to university (average of 12 a year to Oxbridge).

Sports   First-rate facilities include extensive playing fields, new sports complex. Main sports: rugby (strong), cricket, cross-country, athletics, gymnastics, swimming (indoor pool). Basketball, tennis, soccer, golf, lacrosse, netball, hockey also on offer.

Remarks   HMC inspectors concluded (1994): 'This is a very good school with a deservedly high reputation. The boys and girls achieve very high standards across an impressively wide range of subjects and activities.'

EMMANUEL ♂ ♀
Consett Road, Lobley Hill, Gateshead, Tyne and Wear NE11 0AN. Tel (0191) 460 2099

Synopsis
Comprehensive (City Technology College) ★ Co-educational ★ Ages 11–18 ★ 1,200 pupils ★ 250 in sixth form
Head: John Burn OBE, mid-50s, appointed 1993.
Fine modern school; strong Christian ethos; emphasis on maths, science, technology.

Profile
Background   Opened September 1990, one of 15 experimental secondary

schools set up by the Government and partly funded by business and industry. Solid, red-brick, purpose-built premises surrounded by playing fields; spacious, well-equipped classrooms (one computer between two), lecture theatres and labs; wide, carpeted corridors. School open from 8 am to 6 pm.

Atmosphere   Bustling, purposeful; a feeling of space and warmth (more like an industrial plant than a school). Ethos is strongly Christian ('Built and dedicated to the glory of God') and traditional (which might appear to sit uneasily with the emphasis on technology – but does not). Immaculately-uniformed pupils (fewer than five per cent of whom attend church regularly) clearly aware of the standards of behaviour and effort expected (discipline is unashamedly strict); staff dress like business executives. Sympathetic pastoral care system; exceptionally good parental support.

Admissions   School is more than four times over-subscribed. Entry by standardised tests and lengthy interviews with parents and children to establish requisite motivation; pupils selected with scientific care to represent the full range of ability and social and ethnic backgrounds (nearly half are entitled to free school meals, more than a third are from one-parent families); intake more comprehensive than in any normal comprehensive (some bright and middle-class children turned away). Catchment area covers most of Gateshead, inner-city areas of Newcastle and part of Derwentside.

The head   (Principal) Very able. Prominent Christian educationist ('To teach children that they are nothing more than developed mutations who evolved from something akin to a monkey and that death is the end of everything is hardly going to engender within them a sense of purpose, self-worth and self-respect'). Strongly committed to comprehensive education ('the Christian vision of opportunity for all') and has long experience of urban schools (taught chemistry); formerly head for 14 years of a community college in North Tyneside.

The teaching   Emphasis on ensuring a firm grasp of the basic skills; methods based on group and individual work as well as whole-class teaching. Highly-qualified staff (competition to work here is stiff), noticeably younger than average, collectively willing to go the extra mile. Half the timetable is devoted to maths, science, computing and technology (emphasis on electronics and automation); the rest to the normal range of national curriculum subjects. Pupils grouped by ability from first year in most subjects ('to give them the best opportunity to teach their highest potential'); average class size 28, reducing to 20 for maths, science, technology. Wide range of lunch-time and leisure activities.

Results   (1997) GCSE: very creditable 90% gained at least five grades A–C. A-level: 34% of entries graded A or B.

Destinations   All stay on into the sixth form.

Sport   Thriving rugby, soccer, hockey, netball, cross-country. Facilities include first-rate sports hall (but no swimming pool).

Remarks   A blend of firm Christian values with a curriculum that exploits the latest technology unhampered by academic tradition. A school that offers answers, not excuses. Identified by Ofsted (1996) as 'outstandingly successful'. Highly recommended.

EPSOM ♂ ♀
College Road, Epsom, Surrey KT17 4JQ. Tel (01372) 723621

Synopsis
Independent ★ Co-educational (since September 1996) ★ Boarding and Day
★ Ages 13–18 ★ 650 pupils (88% boys, 51% boarding) ★ 315 in sixth form ★
Fees: £12,825 boarding; £9,525 day
Head: Tony Beadles, 57, appointed 1993.
Successful, academic school; very good teaching and results (particularly in science); strong music, sport.

Profile
Background Founded 1855 for the sons of doctors (and still has strong links with the medical profession). Handsome Victorian buildings plus later additions on an attractive, 80-acre wooded site; girls admitted to sixth form 1976, at 13 in 1996 ('Society is changing – it seems a logical step'). Facilities are good (£6 million spent since 1990).

Atmosphere Fairly formal; firm work ethic. Strong house and prefect system; uniform for all. Pupils required to avoid 'overt displays of affection'; parents required to agree to random urine testing if drug use is suspected. Lessons on Saturday mornings.

Admissions By interview and Common Entrance (60% mark required) or school's own tests ('guaranteed place exam') in English, maths, IQ. Sixth-form entry requires five grade Bs or equivalent at GCSE. Most pupils from professional/business backgrounds ('company director' the most common occupation); 12% from abroad. Boarding accommodation varies according to age of house and state of refurbishment (better for girls than boys). Lots of scholarships: academic, music, art, sport, all-rounder plus up to three a year for children of doctors, one for children of solicitors.

The head Able; effective leader. Was a pupil here; read history at Oxford; housemaster at Harrow; previously head of King's, Bruton. Married; three grown-up children.

The teaching Good: formal in style; predominantly male staff (90% live on site). Broad curriculum: science (a strength) taught as three separate subjects; languages include Latin (popular), Greek, German, Spanish; good facilities for design/technology, computing; first-rate art (Graham Sutherland and John Piper were pupils here); all take at least 10 GCSEs. Pupils grouped by ability for GCSE; extra help for dyslexics; maximum class size 20. Flourishing music: 250 learn an instrument; strong choir, good orchestra. Wide range of extra-curricular activities, including cadet force (compulsory for two years), Duke of Edinburgh award scheme.

Results (1997) GCSE: all gained at least five grades A–C. A-level: 64% of entries graded A or B

Destinations Virtually all go on to university, many to study medicine (average of 10 a year to Oxbridge).

Sport First-rate facilities, including two sports halls, extensive playing fields, all-weather pitch, 10 squash courts, fencing salle, shooting range, indoor pool. All major games offered (including lacrosse for girls).

Remarks Good, well-run school; girls need a strong personality.

ERMYSTED'S ♂
Gargrave Road, Skipton, North Yorkshire BD23 1PL. Tel (01756) 792186

Synopsis
Grammar (voluntary-aided) ★ Boys ★ Ages 11–18 ★ 578 pupils ★ 148 in sixth form
Head: David Buckroyd, 59, appointed 1982 (retiring August 1998).
First-rate traditional grammar school; very good teaching and results; strong music, sport.

Profile
Background Founded 1492; imposing Victorian buildings (some in need of modernisation) on a pleasant, elevated site; later additions include fine sports hall.

Atmosphere Traditional, confident, hard-working; big emphasis on academic achievement. Warm relations between staff and pupils; uniform worn by all.

Admissions By North Yorkshire 11-plus; places for top 28% (about 50 boys) in the official catchment of Skipton and named surrounding villages; another 30 places for those in an extensive out-catchment area that extends into Lancashire and down the Craven valley towards Bradford and Keighley (priority to siblings, children of former pupils, those living nearest).

The head Able, long-serving; proud of the school and its achievements; demands the best of everyone. Read modern languages at Oxford; keen on rugby, music.

The teaching Good quality, varied styles (but predominantly formal). Experienced, long-serving staff of 37 (five women). National curriculum plus: all do Latin for at least one year; most take science as three separate subjects. Pupils grouped by ability in English, maths, French; average class size 25, smaller for GCSE, maximum of 16 at A-level. All do at least nine GCSEs and four A-levels, including general studies (very good results). Lots of drama, music (orchestra, bands, 60-strong choir). Regular language exchanges with schools in France, Germany.

Results (1997) GCSE: all gained at least five grades A–C. A-level: creditable 61% of entries graded A or B.

Destinations About 85% continue into the sixth form and proceed to university (average of four a year to Oxbridge).

Sport Has a high profile; particularly strong rugby, cricket, cross-country, athletics; fixtures on Saturday mornings. Playing fields eight minutes' walk away.

Remarks Ofsted inspectors opined (1995): 'The gaining of knowledge rightly enjoys a crucial place in a school which is noted for its academic success, but too few opportunities are provided for pupils to express their sensitivity and their growing understanding of humanity.'

ETON ♂
Windsor, Berkshire SL4 6DW. Tel (01753) 671000

Synopsis
Independent ★ Boys ★ Boarding ★ Ages 13–18 ★ 1,287 pupils ★ 516 in sixth form ★ Fees: £13,947
Head: John Lewis, 55, appointed 1994.
Distinguished academic school; fine teaching; stunning facilities.

Profile
Background Founded 1440 by Henry VI for the training of 70 'local boys of limited means' to the service of Church and State; buildings (scattered around the town) range from 15th-century (including fine chapel, original schoolroom) through functional Victorian to post-modern; facilities are outstanding (school's assets total £130 million). Old Etonians include 20 former Prime Ministers (also Fielding, Shelley, Swinburne, Orwell); Prince William is a pupil here.

Atmosphere Very hard-working, tightly disciplined (statutes lay down that 'there shall be no disputings, rivalries, factions, scurrilous talk or invidious comparisons in college'); superb pastoral care (regular and detailed reporting – hard for any boy to slip through the net); first-rate tutor system. Time-warp uniform of black tailcoats and waistcoats, pin-stripe trousers, winged collars, white bow ties – adopted in mourning for George III, who died in 1820. Drugs lead to instant expulsion (though in Charles II's reign smoking was compulsory, tobacco being thought a protection against the plague). Aim: to turn out 'men of the world who are not narrowly worldly'.

Admissions School 'properly aspires to a distinguished position' in the league tables but is not as academically selective as Winchester, for example. Entry procedures are complex: those registered with a house (as most are at birth) before 1990 take Common Entrance at 13 (minimum 60% mark required); rest (all from 2001) are interviewed and take a 'scholastic aptitude' test at 10-plus, on the basis of which they are either rejected or offered a place on condition they do sufficiently well at 13; 250 admitted a year, 750 turned away. Most come from a fairly narrow social stratum; 40% are sons of Old Etonians; current roll includes more than 30 princes, marquesses, viscounts, barons, lords, honourables. Very good boarding accommodation: Oppidans (non-scholars) in 24 houses (50 boys in each, all with individual study-bedrooms); 70 King's Scholars housed separately (an elite within an elite). In all, 220 receive some help with fees; up to eight scholarships a year reserved for pupils from state schools.

The head Scholarly, reserved, devoid of small talk. Brought up in New Zealand; read classics at Cambridge (double First); came here to teach classics 1971; Master in College (in charge of the scholars) 1975–80; left to become head of Geelong Grammar (Australia's Eton). A painstaking administrator admired for the quality of his paperwork ('Machinery, machinery, machinery should be the motto of every good school'). Hemmed in by powerful housemasters and heads of departments with the chairman of the governors – appointed by the Queen – living next door, he does what he describes as a lonely job. Will be in post until 2002. Married (wife is Danish); no children.

The teaching Outstanding: highly qualified, gifted, enthusiastic staff of 150 (just six women). Broad (if eccentric) curriculum: all take GCSEs in Latin, French and a science a year early, after which the 50% who study a second modern language (choice includes Spanish, German, Russian, Japanese) have to reach GCSE standard in one year rather than two; classics strong (a third take Greek for GCSE) but not as dominant as it was (English not introduced as a subject until 1960); sciences taught separately (a third take all three for GCSE); first-rate design/technology (in School of Mechanics – 'the interface between Eton and the real world'), silverwork a speciality. Pupils grouped rigorously by ability; average class size 20, reducing to a maximum of 12 in sixth form. Superb art school (recent £1 million refurbishment); marvellous music school (£2 million extension opens March 1998); half learn an instrument (900 lessons a week); first-rate drama. Vast range of extra-curricular activities.

Results (1997) GCSE: all gained at least five grades A–C (those who do not 'would normally be advised to leave the school'). A-level: impressive 80% of entries graded A or B (but 19th in the league table – its worst position since the table was introduced in 1991).

Destinations Virtually all go on to university (remarkable average of 60 a year to Oxbridge).

Sport Strong; more than 40 activities on offer (American Football to water polo), including cricket for the 'drybobs', rowing for the 'wetbobs'. Stunning facilities; 350 acres of famous playing fields.

Remarks An enclosed world in which many boys would feel (and have felt) uncomfortably alien. But those whom it suits receive an education – and a leg-up in life – without equal.

EXETER ♂ ♀
Exeter, Devon EX2 4NS. Tel (01392) 273679

Synopsis
Independent ★ Becoming fully co-educational ★ Day and boarding ★ Ages 11–18 (plus associated prep school) ★ 655 pupils (94% boys, 94% day) ★ 240 in sixth form ★ Fees: £4,695 day; £8,895 boarding
Head: Neil Gamble, 54, appointed 1992.
Successful school; good teaching and results; first-rate art; very good sport.

Profile
Background Founded 1633 as the town grammar; moved 1870s to present purpose-built premises; formerly Direct Grant, reverted to full independence 1976. Victorian red-brick buildings (including six-storey tower) plus well-designed modern additions on attractive 25-acre site (broad expanse of playing fields) a mile from the city centre. Facilities include music school, spacious art studios, technology centre, fine sports hall; £1 million spent recently on refurbishment but some classrooms rather gloomy. Girls admitted at seven (to the on-site prep school) and 11 from September 1997 – a development (designed to compensate for the phasing out of assisted places, which nearly 30% hold) that was tactlessly handled and has not been universally welcomed.

Atmosphere Generally cheerful and busy, but discipline in and out of class is on the casual side (off-hand responses to staff and chatter during lessons); some pupils look scruffy (especially in the sixth form) and litter is noticeable. Boarding accommodation rather bleak (fees are unusually modest); small dorms for younger boys, shared or single study-bedrooms for seniors (no boarding planned for girls). No Saturday morning lessons: weekend can seem long; many go home. Appetising food; good choice of dishes (in rather small dining hall).

Admissions Entry at 11 and 12 by school's own exam (about half who apply are turned away), at 13 by Common Entrance (few fail), at 16 with at least five GCSEs grades A or B. Fairly wide range of abilities: minimum IQ of 110 (but may be lower when assisted places disappear). Catchment area extends from Lyme Regis to Torquay; parents organise a network of private coaches. Some scholarships, bursaries.

The head Forceful, energetic, ambitious for the school; can seem rather abrasive. Read PPE at Oxford; taught at Repton for 13 years; previously head of King Edward's, Aston. Acknowledges that making co-education work is his biggest challenge. Married; three children (one a pupil here).

The teaching Formal in style; long-serving, hard-working staff of 67 (12 women). National curriculum followed; sciences taught separately; GCSE options include Latin; wide choice of 25 subjects at A-level. Pupils grouped by ability in some subjects; average class size 22 to GCSE, 10 in sixth form. Exceptionally good art; lots of music (250 learn an instrument, three orchestras, three choirs) and drama. Popular cadet force; wide variety of clubs and societies. Regular study trips abroad; annual language exchanges with schools in France, Germany.

Results (1997) GCSE: 99% gained at least five grades A–C. A–Levels: 56% of entries graded A or B.

Destinations Nearly all proceed to university (up to 15 a year to Oxbridge).

Sport High standards; all participate up to GCSE ; optional in sixth form. Good facilities indoors and out, including floodlit, all-weather pitch. Most successful recently in rugby, hockey, cricket. Squash, swimming (outdoor pool), tennis (two grass courts), basketball, athletics, cross-country, golf also on offer.

Remarks School in transition. Unusually, the head refused to disclose the contents of a recent HMC inspection report.

FAIRFIELD HIGH ♀
Fairfeld Avenue, Droylsden, Manchester M43 6AB. Tel (0161) 370 1488

Synopsis
Comprehensive (grant-maintained) ★ Girls ★ Ages 11–16 ★ 820 pupils
Head: Chris Penter, 48, appointed 1990.
Popular, well-run school; good teaching and GCSE results; strong drama, sport.

Profile
Background Founded 1796 by a Moravian community as part of their 'Christian duty to educate the young' (one of the first girls' schools); became a grammar school in the 1920s; went comprehensive 1974; opted out of council control 1993. Simple, red-brick buildings in in pleasant, wooded grounds; recent additions include well-equipped technology centre.

Atmosphere A calm, friendly place of learning; well-behaved pupils; code of conduct stresses respect for self, others, the environment.

Admissions School is over-subscribed but not academically selective; priority to those living nearest; numbers are rising.

The head Able, experienced; writes and directs plays; believes passionately in single-sex education for girls ('in the absence of sex-stereotyping, we can convince girls that there is nothing they can't achieve'). Married (to an opera singer).

The teaching Good; traditional in style; committed staff have high academic expectations ('this is not a vocational school'). Standard national curriculum.

Pupils grouped by ability in English, maths, science; average class size 30, reducing to 25 for GCSE. Flourishing drama. Regular language exchanges with pupils in France, Germany.
Results (1997) GCSE: creditable 67% gained at least five grades A–C.
Destinations About 95% remain in full-time education.
Sport Enthusiastic. Good record in netball, volleyball, football, athletics; regular county honours, despite limited facilities.
Remarks Very good all round.

FALLIBROOME HIGH ♂ ♀
Priory Lane, Macclesfield, Cheshire SK10 4AF. Tel (01625) 827898

> ### Synopsis
> Comprehensive (grant-maintained) ★ Co-educational ★ Ages 11–18 ★ 1,100 pupils (roughly equal numbers of girls and boys) ★ 168 in sixth form
> Head: Michael Batson, 55, appointed 1986.
> *Successful, well-run school; good teaching and results; strong IT.*

Profile
Background Opened 1979 as a purpose-built comprehensive; opted out of council control 1993; granted technology college status 1995. Attractive, airy, modern buildings (sloping pine roofs) in spacious grounds; many recent additions, including science labs, sixth-form centre, music and creative arts block; computing facilities are first rate; some classrooms in 'temporary' huts.
Atmosphere Feels intimate, despite the size. Big emphasis on self-discipline; lots of praise for good conduct ('We believe an ordered, disciplined atmosphere is the best environment for learning,' says prospectus). Competitive house system; uniform below the sixth form (where 'smart' dress is required – no jeans). Parental involvement encouraged.
Admissions School is popular, over-subscribed and growing. Priority to: siblings; pupils from five 'feeder' primaries to the west of Macclesfield; pupils from schools that have sent children here for at least three years. General ability level is above average.
The head Ebullient, energetic, humming with ideas: salesman, showman – aims for the heights. Read physics and chemistry at Leeds; came here as deputy head when the school opened. Teaches maths to first-years, general studies to the sixth form.
The teaching Good; fairly formal in style. Hard-working, relatively youthful staff of 65 (roughly equal numbers of women and men). Fairly broad curriculum: science on offer as three separate subjects; second language (German) introduced in second year; lots of computing. Pupils grouped by ability in maths from second year, in most other subjects from third year; extra help for those who need it (sixth-formers coach juniors); average class size 26 (but can be as large as 32 for GCSE), reducing to a maximum of 20 at A-level; progress closely monitored (twice-termly grades for effort, achievement). Choirs, orchestras (10% learn an instrument). Regular language exchanges with schools in France, Germany.
Results (1997) GCSE: 60% gained at least five grades A– C. A-level: 45% of entries graded A or B.
Destinations Just over half stay on for A-levels; of these, about 80% proceed

to university (two or three a year to Oxbridge).

Sport Good facilities; regular fixtures. Main sports: netball, hockey, badminton, soccer, basketball, rugby, athletics, cross-country, tennis.

Remarks Ofsted inspectors concluded (1994): 'This is a good school which serves its pupils well. It has high standards in all aspects of its work.'

FARNBOROUGH HILL ♀
Farnborough, Hampshire GU14 8AT. Tel (01252) 545197

Synopsis
Independent (Roman Catholic) ★ Day ★ Girls ★ Ages 11–18 ★ 527 pupils ★ 105 in sixth form ★ Fees: £5,163
Head: Miss Rita McGeoch, 45, appointed 1996.
Well-run, traditional school; good teaching and results; clear Christian ethos; strong creative arts.

Profile
Background Founded 1889 by the Religious of Christian Education on the 65-acre estate of the late Empress Eugenie of France; her former, mock-Gothic home (doors from the Tuileries Palace) is the centre of the school; additions include three wings and a chapel.

Atmosphere Quiet, civilised; emphasis on hard work, personal responsibility, consideration for others; warm relations between staff and pupils; well-organised pastoral care. Non-Catholics welcome provided they 'participate in the religious activity of the school and respect its Christian ideals'. Lots of fund-raising for charity.

Admissions By interview and tests in English, maths, verbal reasoning; school is over-subscribed (about 150 apply for 80 places) and fairly selective but is likely to become less so with the phasing out of assisted places, which more than 140 hold. About half join from state primaries; catchment area includes Woking, Basingstoke, Reading.

The head Warm, charming. Read English and drama at Glasgow (First), Bristol (MLitt); previously deputy head of St Leonards, Mayfield (qv).

The teaching Good quality; stable, predominantly female staff. Fairly broad curriculum; science on offer as three separate subjects; all do Latin for at least three years; other languages include Spanish, German, Greek; all do religious education for GCSE; strong drama (many do Guildhall exams) and art & design; A-level options include theatre studies. Pupils grouped by ability in maths, French from the start, in science for GCSE; maximum class size 30, reducing to 26 for GCSE, 12 at A-level. Lots of music; about 20% learn an instrument.

Results (1997) GCSE: 98% gained at least five grades A–C. A-level: 56% of entries graded A or B.

Destinations Nearly all go on to university.

Sport Strong competitive tradition in netball, gymnastics, hockey. Swimming, cross-country, athletics, tennis, rounders also on offer. Facilities include extensive playing fields, athletics track, indoor pool, golf course.

Remarks Attractive school; pupils made to feel valued.

FELSTED ♂ ♀
Dunmow, Essex CM6 3LL. Tel (01371) 820258

Synopsis
Independent ★ Co-educational ★ Boarding and day ★ Ages 13–18 (plus associated prep school) ★ 360 pupils (61% boys, 84% boarding) ★ 165 in sixth form ★ Fees: £13,620 boarding; £9,960 day
Head: Stephen Roberts, 41, appointed 1993.
Good, small school; fairly wide range of abilities; strong sport.

Profile
Background Founded 1564 (for 'goode lernyng of grammer and other vertues'); mid-Victorian buildings plus many later additions (including spectacular dining hall built in the style of a traditional Essex barn) set in 70 acres of quiet countryside. Fully co-educational since 1994; day numbers rising (as boarding declines).

Atmosphere Neat, tidy, well-ordered: head has added 'zip' to a previously rather plodding establishment (girls have helped, too). Sensible rules; good pastoral care system. Day pupils stay until 6.30 pm and can spend the night if they need to. Girls' boarding accommodation recently redecorated (very Laura Ashley), boys' could do with a lick of paint.

Admissions At 13, via Common Entrance: 50% required in each of maths, English, French and an average of 50% in other subjects. Pupils at the associated prep school guaranteed a place if they pass a test at 11 (as up to 90% do). Three-quarters live within an hour's drive; buses from Colchester and Maldon for day pupils; 15% from abroad (mostly expatriates). Scholarships (academic, music, art), bursaries available.

The head Very approachable; popular with staff, parents and pupils. Read physics at Oxford; became a merchant banker then switched to teaching; previously at housemaster at Oundle (qv). Teaches divinity; coaches hockey; demands high standards (not least in behaviour and uniform). Married (wife takes an active part in school life); two sons (one a pupil here).

The teaching Formal, enthusiastic (even the doziest pupils could not fail to be motivated). Predominantly youthful staff of 49 (25% women). National curriculum plus: science on offer as three separate subjects; classics available; choice of 18 subjects at A-level. Pupils grouped by ability from the start in maths, science, French, English; classes 16–18 up to GCSE, 10–12 for A-level. Lots of computing: 200 machines; pupils E-mail family and friends. Good art (sculptor in residence), drama, music; 40% learn an instrument; two orchestras, large chapel choir. Wide range of extra-curricular activities (40 societies flourish); well-supported cadet force and Duke of Edinburgh award scheme. Regular trips abroad.

Results (1997) GCSE: 94% gained at least five grades A–C. A-level: 51% of entries graded A or B.

Destinations Most proceed to university, a few every year to Oxbridge.

Sport Good record: all major sports on offer. Main games: rugby, hockey, cricket, netball; shooting (new £50,000 range) a particular strength. Facilities include floodlit, all-weather pitch, squash courts, indoor pool.

Remarks Good all round – and getting better.

FETTES ♂ ♀
Carrington Road, Edinburgh EH4 1QX. Tel (0131) 332 2281

Synopsis
Independent ★ Co-educational ★ Boarding and day ★ Ages 10–18 ★ 500
pupils (57% boys, 85% boarders) ★ 172 in sixth form ★ Fees: £9,225–£13,455
boarding; £5,790–£9,090 day
Head: Malcolm Thyne, 54, appointed 1988 (retiring August 1998).
Sound school; good teaching and results; first-rate music and drama.

Profile
Background Founded 1870; vast, neo-Gothic palace (a Disneyland cross
between a Scottish baronial castle and a château on the Loire) plus later additions on a commanding 100-acre site one-and-a-half miles from the city centre;
some classrooms in 'temporary' huts. Tony Blair was a pupil here (1966–71). Co-
educational since 1982.

Atmosphere Busy, friendly; big emphasis on politeness, courtesy. Clear
Christian ethos (compulsory daily chapel, evening prayers in houses); firm discipline ('There are no drugs at Fettes and that's that'); fairly formal relations
between staff and pupils ('If I go into a classroom I expect them to stand').

Admissions Entry at 10, 11, 12 by tests in English, maths; at 13 by Common
Entrance; school cannot afford to be very selective (minimum IQ 105). Fairly
comfortable boarding accommodation in recently-renovated, Victorian houses;
juniors on attractive, self-contained site. Most from professional/business backgrounds; 55% Scottish; 15% ceiling on foreigners (boarders from 40 countries).
Lessons on Saturday mornings. Lots of scholarships, bursaries available.

The head Has worked tirelessly to restore the school's somewhat faded glory.
Puts a big emphasis on academic achievement (and is well-armed with graphs to
demonstrate improving standards). His firmness and personal commitment
won the staff's respect. Believes in co-education but looks for a 60–40 split ('boys
need numerical superiority to counter more rapidly maturing girls'). Taught at
Edinburgh Academy and Oundle (housemaster); formerly head for eight years of
St Bees, Cumbria. Married, two sons. From September 1998: Michael Spens,
head of Caldicott Prep (qv).

The teaching Good: experienced, well-qualified staff of 66 (25 women). Broad
curriculum: science taught as three separate subjects; two-thirds do Latin; Greek
still available; all take 'taster' courses in German, Spanish. Pupils grouped by
ability in all subjects; some take GCSE maths, French, religious education a year
early; progress closely monitored (monthly grades for effort and achievement);
maximum class size 20 for GCSE, reducing to 12–14 for A-level. Top half take A-
levels; rest do Highers over two years; all take general studies and a course in IT.
Very good drama and music (nearly half learn an instrument; three orchestras,
four choirs). Extra-curricular activities include compulsory cadet force, well-
supported Duke of Edinburgh award scheme.

Results (1997) GCSE: 95% gained at least five grades A–C. A-level: creditable
75% of entries graded A or B.

Destinations More than 90% stay on for A-levels; of these, 95% proceed to
higher education (equal numbers to Scottish and English universities, seven or
eight Oxbridge).

Sport Games for all five afternoons a week: staple diet of rugby (strong), hockey, cricket for the boys; hockey, lacrosse (strong), for the girls; athletics for both;
much else on offer. Facilities include extensive playing fields, all-weather pitch,

indoor pool, shooting range, courts for fives, squash, tennis.

Remarks HMI concluded (1996): 'The school's strengths included well-behaved, courteous and hard working pupils; conscientious, hard working and caring staff; and high levels of pupils' attainment in almost all subjects.'

FINHAM PARK ♂ ♀
Green Lane, Coventry CV3 6EA. Tel (01203) 418135

Synopsis
Comprehensive ★ Co-educational ★ Ages 11–18 ★ 1,487 pupils (roughly equal numbers of girls and boys) ★ 318 in sixth form
Head: Chris Hunt, 50, appointed 1989.
First-rate, well-run school; good teaching and results.

Profile

Background Opened 1970 as purpose-built comprehensive serving a largely middle-class wedge of south-west Coventry. Typically dismal, flat-roofed buildings on otherwise pleasant suburban site. Reputation wobbled badly in late-1980s, but parents now clamour for places. School is over-crowded; new 'temporary' class-rooms being added, but substantial capital improvement required.

Atmosphere Welcoming, ambitious; high parental demands fuelled by 'chardonnay Socialist' academics at Warwick and Coventry Universities, relieved to be able to preserve their state-sector principles. An eight-form entry crammed into buildings designed for a six-form intake; stoical staff tolerate corridor and classroom congestion, which increases, not inhibits, school's comradely character (or, as Ofsted inspectors put it, 'The social and moral climate is excellent').

Admissions More than 300 apply for 240 places; local authority gives preference to siblings and to parents wanting co-education without a closer alternative. Prospectus (produced in-house and a model of its kind) includes a welcome in six languages.

The head Enthusiastic, forceful, persuasive; attracts near-universal admiration of staff and pupils. Has achieved big improvement in exam results with only minor changes in staffing; early teaching experience in working-class areas convinced him schools should have high expectations for all. Gained first headship at 34; still teaches GCSE history and examines it at A-level. Highly visible presence around the school; interviews all lower-sixth pupils and top and bottom 10 in each year. Married; four children.

The teaching Good: experienced, conscientious staff; lessons well structured to cope with needs of the less able. Standard national curriculum; particular strengths in maths, science, English; good computing; all do French and are introduced to German. Choice of 22 subjects at GCSE, 24 at A-level, including psychology, PE, law, geology; GNVQs well established in IT, media studies, business studies, art & design. Pupils grouped by ability in maths, science from third year, in modern languages and English for GCSE; class sizes average 28–30, reducing to 20–25 at GCSE, 14 at A-level. Thriving music: 25% learn an instrument. Expanding outdoor and residential education programme. Work experience opportunities in France for sixth-formers.

Results (1997) GCSE: creditable 65% gained at least five grades A–C. A-level: 35% of entries graded A or B.

Destinations About 60% continue into the sixth form; of these, 72% proceed to higher education.

Sport Outstanding gymnastics: school represents West Midlands in national acrobatic championships. Good tennis for both sexes (11 courts), and some team strength in rugby, soccer and netball. Spacious facilities; swimming taught off-site in first year. Wind-surfing available for enthusiasts.

Remarks Ofsted inspectors concluded (1995): 'This is a good school. On the whole, the pupils are sociable and hard working, and they are helped to thrive in an atmosphere of security and steady endeavour.'

FOLKESTONE GIRLS' ♀
Coolinge Lane, Folkestone, Kent CT20 3RB. Tel (01303) 251125

Synopsis
Grammar (grant-maintained) ★ Girls ★ Ages 11–18 ★ 694 pupils ★ 200 in sixth form
Head: Mrs Shan Mullett, 52, appointed 1989.
Successful, well-run school; good teaching and results.

Profile
Background Founded 1900; merged with adjacent girls' technical school 1983; opted out of council control 1993. Dismal collection of buildings (including many shabby 'temporary' huts) on a sprawling cliff-top site; much-needed refurbishment under way. Numbers have dropped recently but are planned to increase by 150 over the next three years.

Atmosphere Purposeful, orderly ('We insist upon courtesy and consideration for others at all times'); Christian ethos; discipline based on recognition of effort, achievement; poor work or behaviour may result in lunch-time detention.

Admissions From 'any local education authority that conducts selective tests'; top 30% of the ability range from varied social backgrounds.

The head Determined; strong leader. Read maths at Reading; qualified as a cost engineer; previously deputy head of a co-educational grammar school. Married; two children, two step-children.

The teaching Generally formal in style. Long-serving staff (some of whom were pupils here). Broad curriculum: choice of French or German (some do both); all first-years do Latin; science on offer as three separate subjects; choice of 22 subjects at A-level plus GNVQ in health & social care. Pupils grouped by ability in maths, science, modern languages for GCSE; extra help for those who need it; average class size 27, reducing to 17 in the sixth form. Strong art, drama, music (three choirs, two orchestras, various ensembles). Regular language exchanges with pupils in France, Germany. Extra-curricular activities include debating, Duke of Edinburgh award scheme.

Results (1997) GCSE: 96% gained at least five grades A–C. A-level: 44% of entries graded A or B.

Destinations About 90% continue into the sixth form; of these, nearly all go on to university (average of three a year to Oxbridge).

Sport Wide range on offer, including aerobics, dance, fencing, hockey, netball, rhythmic gymnastics; badminton, trampolining, skiing are particular strengths.

Remarks Good all round.

FOREST ♂ ♀
College Place, Snaresbrook, London E17 3PY. Tel (0181) 520 1744

Synopsis
Independent ★ Co-educational (but separate boys' and girls' sections to age 16) ★ Day (and some boarding) ★ Ages 11–18 (plus associated junior school) ★ 820 pupils (65% boys, 96% day) ★ 260 in sixth form ★ Fees: £6,038 day; £9,633 boarding
Head: Andrew Boggis, 43, appointed 1992.
Sound school; fairly wide range of abilities; strong music, drama, sport.

Profile
Background Founded 1834 by a group of City businessmen living in then-upmarket Walthamstow; fine Georgian building in beautiful grounds surrounded by Epping Forest; additions range from Victorian-Gothic to distinguished late 20th-century, including £1 million computer centre and fine theatre. Effectively three schools – junior, girls', boys' – on one campus (boys and girls mix in breaks and at lunch-times), coming together in a co-educational sixth form.

Atmosphere Happy, relaxed – but high standards demanded in work, behaviour and dress (uniform worn throughout). No air of élitism; pupils more socially mixed than in many independent schools; individual talents nurtured. Low-key Christian tradition (compulsory daily chapel, full-time chaplain); good pastoral care system. Much fund-raising by supportive parents.

Admissions By tests in English, maths and reasoning or Common Entrance; school is not unduly selective and likely to become less so with the phasing out of assisted places, which more than 100 hold. Fairly broad social and ethnic mix from a wide catchment area (400 bussed from 15-mile radius). Boarding house for 30 boys. Scholarships (some for music), bursaries; reduced fees for Service and clergy children.

The head (Warden) Quiet, authoritative style. Read modern languages at Oxford; formerly master-in-college at Eton for eight years, in charge of the scholars. Keen on cooking and opera. Married; three young children.

The teaching Good quality. Enthusiastic, committed staff of 106 (40 women); average age mid-30s. National curriculum plus; science on offer as three separate subjects (first-rate labs); all do Latin initially; German, Spanish available; all become computer-literate from an early age. Most take nine or 10 GCSEs and at least three A-levels (from a choice of 21) plus general studies. Pupils grouped by ability from the start; maximum class size 24. Excellent drama (including annual Shakespeare play since 1860) and music: more than a third learn an instrument; three orchestras plus many smaller ensembles; several choirs (strong tradition in singing). Flourishing debating society, cadet force, Duke of Edinburgh award scheme. Lots of ambitious foreign trips: Russia, China, India, Ecuador; regular exchanges with schools in France, Germany, USA, Russia.

Results (1997) GCSE: 95% of girls and 93% of boys gained at least five grades A–C. A-level: 59% of entries graded A or B.

Destinations About 90% stay for A-levels; of these, 90% proceed to university (average of 10 a year to Oxbridge).

Sport Chiefly soccer (strong), cricket, netball, hockey, tennis. Golf, riding, rowing also on offer. Regular county honours; busy fixture list. Facilities include 27 acres of playing fields, sports hall, squash courts, indoor pool.

Remarks Good all round; single-sex and co-education unusually combined.

FORTISMERE ♂ ♀
Tetherdown, Muswell Hill, London N10 1NE. Tel (0181) 444 5124

Synopsis
Comprehensive ★ Co-educational ★ Ages 11–18 ★ 1,450 pupils (roughly equal numbers of girls and boys) ★ 340 in sixth form
Head: Andrew Nixon, 53, appointed 1982.
Successful, urban comprehensive; good teaching and results.

Profile
Background Result of a 1983 merger of two schools on a 20-acre site at the top of leafy Muswell Hill; mainly 1950s buildings, some in need of up-grading and refurbishment. Technology College status achieved 1997.

Atmosphere No uniform, no prefects; big emphasis on self-discipline, mutual support, respecting the rights of others. Lots of admirable art work on display.

Admissions School is heavily over-subscribed (more than 400 apply for 240 places a year); priority to siblings and those living nearest. Diverse backgrounds, ranging from inner-city estates to middle-class suburbia; 30% ethnic minorities; wide spread of abilities but general level is above average. All successfully welded into a well-ordered, hard-working community.

The head Educated at a prep school, secondary modern and grammar school sixth form: strongly committed to the comprehensive ideal (as are many of the parents). Previously deputy head of a Camden comprehensive; appointed head of one of the merged schools 1980. Keen on 'open dialogue' with pupils, staff and parents. Married; three children.

The teaching Long-serving, committed staff; emphasis on 'experiential' learning and pupils developing at their own pace – but within a framework of rigour and high expectations. National curriculum plus: all take dance and drama and add a second language in third year. Mixed-ability teaching for first three years; some setting in maths; in-class support for those with special needs; largest classes 27. Most take nine GCSEs; choice of 21 subjects at A-level; vocational alternatives on offer. Lots of music: 130 learn an instrument; orchestra, instrumental groups, choirs. Much charity work and community involvement. Regular exchanges with schools in France, Germany, Spain.

Results (1997) GCSE: 62% gained at least five grades A–C. A-level: 41% of entries graded A or B.

Destinations About 60% go on to university.

Sport Choice of 20 activities; inter-school matches played regularly, including Saturdays. Facilities include ample playing fields, large all-weather pitch, 10 tennis courts, outdoor heated pool.

Remarks Effective school; good all round.

FRAMINGHAM EARL ♂ ♀
Norwich Road, Framingham Earl, Norwich NR14 7QP. Tel (01508) 492547

Synopsis
Comprehensive ★ Co-educational ★ Ages 11–16 ★ 544 pupils (roughly equal numbers of girls and boys)
Head: Mrs Wendy Down, 49, appointed 1990.
Well-run school; extra help for dyslexic children.

Profile
Background   Opened 1959 as a secondary modern; went comprehensive 1974. Well-designed and maintained buildings on the edge of a commuter village; reasonable facilities (though limited for sport). Parents pressing for a sixth form.

Atmosphere   School motto – 'Where happiness matters' – belies a serious academic drive. Strong emphasis on the special needs of dyslexic, gifted and disabled children. Strict code of behaviour ('You're sent out of class for the slightest infringement'); pupils sent home if uniform not up to standard. Very supportive parents.

Admissions   All who apply are admitted, but not for much longer: school's reputation is growing. Intake is of above-average ability.

The head   Calm, assured. Read theology at Oxford (teaches RE five hours a week). Formerly head of a small prep school but found it 'too comfortable'. Divorced; one grown-up child.

The teaching   Well-planned lessons, confidently delivered; particularly good history and modern languages. Experienced, stable staff of 32 (60% female); teachers always willing, children say, to give extra help at lunchtime and after school. Average class size 21; pupils grouped by ability in some subjects from the start. Thorough screening for reading and spelling difficulties; extra help for those more than a year behind; dyslexic children given three or four hours remedial work a week as well as good learning support. Lots of music and drama. Regular exchanges with pupils in Denmark, Germany, Russia.

Results   (1997) GCSE: 58% gained at least five grades A–C.

Destinations   About 80% stay on in full-time education; 35% proceed to university.

Sport   Good sports hall but other facilities limited. Main games: football, cricket, hockey (a particular strength), netball, basketball, tennis, cross-country, athletics.

Remarks   Attractive school: good teaching; articulate, confident pupils. Recommended.

FRANCIS HOLLAND ♀
Clarence Gate, London NW1 6XR. Tel (0171) 723 0176

Synopsis
Independent ★ Girls ★ Day ★ Ages 11–18 ★ 382 pupils ★ 98 in sixth form ★ Fees: £5,985
Head: Mrs Pamela Parsonson, 60, appointed 1988 (retiring August 1998).
Successful, academic school; very good teaching; first-rate art, drama, music.

Profile

Background Founded 1878 by Rev Canon Francis Holland; moved 1915 to rather gloomy, purpose-built premises in the heart of Marylebone; extreme pressure on space eased by addition of attractive new wing (including swimming pool with a rising floor that transforms it into a hall).

Atmosphere Lively, friendly, informal; girls self-assured, uninhibited; good pastoral care; warm relations between staff and pupils. Christian foundation (RE taught throughout) but most other faiths represented (15% Jewish). Traditional uniform (check blouses, sweaters or sweatshirts, grey skirts, black tights) until sixth form (typical teenage gear).

Admissions By interview and entrance exam (shared with other schools in the North London consortium); about 380 apply for 56 places; school looking for energy, interest, enthusiasm; ability range is fairly wide. Most pupils from North London professional backgrounds (lawyers, doctors, bankers, media). Some scholarships, bursaries.

The head Experienced, wise, unassuming; very popular with staff and girls (known to all as Mrs P). Read maths at Oxford; previously director of studies at North London Collegiate (qv). Married; four grown-up children. From September 1998: Mrs Gillian Low, deputy head of Godolphin & Latymer (qv).

The teaching High quality: thorough, stimulating, supportive; well-qualified, predominantly female staff, 75% appointed by present head. Fairly broad curriculum; sciences taught (but not examined) separately (five well-equipped labs); all do Latin for at least first two years; Greek on offer (classics are strong); modern languages include German, Spanish, Italian; A-level choices include economics, government & politics. Pupils grouped by ability in maths from second year, sciences from third year; average class size 28, reducing to 18 for GCSE, smaller in sixth form. High-quality art (techniques thoroughly taught, good pottery); lively music (two orchestras, chamber groups, two choirs) despite limited facilities; well-taught drama (major annual production). Good careers advice. Numerous extra-curricular activities, including Duke of Edinburgh award scheme.

Results (1997) GCSE: all gained at least five grades A–C. A-level: 60% of entries graded A or B.

Destinations About 80% stay on for A-levels; of these, nearly all proceed to university (three or four a year Oxbridge).

Sport Enthusiastic, but not a particular strength. Main games: hockey, netball, rounders, tennis; aerobics, badminton, volleyball, fencing also on offer. Outdoor games played in Regent's Park.

Remarks Small, happy school; recommended.

FRENSHAM HEIGHTS ♂ ♀

Rowledge, Farnham, Surrey GU10 4EA. Tel (01252) 792134

Synopsis

Independent ★ Co-educational ★ Day and boarding ★ Ages 11–18 (plus associated junior school) ★ 290 pupils (60% girls, 60% day) ★ 76 in sixth form ★ Fees: £8,700 day; £13,125 boarding
Head: Peter de Voil, 52, appointed 1993.
Unusual, liberal school; emphasis on creativity and the performing arts; results and facilities are good.

Profile

Background   Founded 1925 by three mildly eccentric Theosophists as an avowedly 'progressive' school, since when its history has been decidedly chequered; co-educational from the outset. Splendid Edwardian mansion plus ample outbuildings set high on a wooded hill (fine views over Surrey heathland). Lessons on Saturday mornings.

Atmosphere   Friendly, informal (pupils call staff – including the head – by their first names), easy-going (no one turns a hair if pupils hold hands or hug); big emphasis on the development of the individual ('a community where liberal values are expressed and put into practice'). No uniform (but detailed dress code advises that baseball caps 'may be worn only after tea on weekdays, and at weekends after lunch on Saturday'). Drug use may lead to random urine testing; tobacco 'strongly disapproved of' but sixth-formers who 'need' to smoke may do so 'in the designated smoking area at the times specified'. Parents include actors, musicians, film directors, media personalities.

Admissions   Entry by tests or Common Entrance; school is not unduly selective. Pleasant, comfortable boarding accommodation.

The head   Describes respectability as a 'ghastly' word but has introduced more 'structure' (noting that informality can easily become 'casual and sloppy'). Read classics and English at Cambridge; taught at Uppingham for 22 years (six as housemaster). Married; no children.

The teaching   Informal but business-like; many long-serving staff (equal numbers of men and women). Full academic curriculum; emphasis on creativity and the performing arts – dance, drama, design, music, ceramics; all take at least two for GCSE. Small classes (maximum size 19); plenty of individual attention; dyslexia catered for; competitiveness discouraged. Particularly good music: senior and junior choirs, two orchestras, various instrumental groups; frequent performances. Careful advice on higher education and careers.

Results   (1997) GCSE: 92% gained at least five grades A–C. A-level: 50% of entries graded A or B.

Destinations   More than 90% stay on for A-levels; most proceed to higher education, including colleges of art, drama, music.

Sport   Facilities include sports hall, tennis courts, playing fields, basketball court, outdoor pool; adventure centre in the woods.

Remarks   An alternative to mainstream schools; individual talents fostered.

FULNECK ♂ ♀
Fulneck, Pudsey, West Yorkshire LS28 8DS. Tel (0113) 257 0235

Synopsis
Independent ★ Co-educational (but girls and boys taught separately from 11 to 16) ★ Day and boarding ★ Ages 11–18 (plus associated junior school) ★ 320 pupils (56% boys, 84% day) ★ 76 in sixth form ★ Fees: £5,085 day; £7,575–£9,540 boarding
Head: Mrs Honorée Gordon, 44, appointed 1996.
Small, friendly school; distinctive ethos; fairly wide range of abilities.

Profile
Background   A 1994 merger of two single-sex schools founded by Moravians in 1753 to educate 'every child to be a complete human being'. Terrace of mid-

Georgian houses (snug, oddly-shaped rooms) plus later additions (including fine science block) in a pleasant, semi-rural setting between Leeds and Bradford. Junior school on site (ages three to 11).

Atmosphere   Emphasis on considerate, civilised behaviour, knowing right from wrong, practising what you preach. Warm relations between staff and pupils; pastoral care central to school's ethos. Daily religious assembly in Moravian community church within the grounds (parents of other faiths required to accept school's moral and spiritual values).

Admissions   At 11 by interview and school's own tests (but most come up from the junior school); fairly wide range of abilities. Boarding accommodation comfortable, homely (and recently upgraded). Some scholarships, bursaries available.

The head   Energetic Scot; full of ideas; gets on well with staff, parents, pupils. Read Russian and French at Bradford; previously taught in four state schools in Yorkshire (and was deputy head of one of them). Married; two children (one a pupil here).

The teaching   Traditional in style: long-serving staff; attentive pupils. Standard national curriculum (minus some technology); good science (offered as three separate subjects); all do French from nine, Latin from 11; sixth-form options include politics, sports studies, child care, Chinese. Extra help for those with special needs, including dyslexics and those who speak English as a foreign language; average class size 15–20, reducing to 10 or fewer at A-level. Lively drama, music (school pays for all to start learning an instrument); popular Duke of Edinburgh award scheme.

Results   (1997) GCSE: 85% gained at least five grades A–C. A-level: 31% of entries graded A or B.

Destinations   About 70% continue into the sixth form; most proceed to university.

Sport   Main games: rugby, hockey, netball, cricket, tennis; golf, sailing also available. Facilities include extensive playing fields, all-weather pitch, two gyms.

Remarks   Attractive school for children of a wide range of abilities.

GEORGE ABBOT ♂ ♀
Woodruff Avenue, Burpham, Guildford, Surrey GU1 1XX. Tel (01483) 888000

Synopsis
Comprehensive ★ Co-educational ★ Ages 11–18 ★ 1,919 pupils (51% boys) ★ 405 in sixth form
Head: Geoffrey Wilson, 58, appointed 1985.
Vast, efficient comprehensive; good teaching and results.

Profile
Background   Originally two single-sex schools; merged and went comprehensive 1976. Dowdy 1960s buildings (but light, airy classrooms) plus later additions (including attractive sixth-form centre) on a sprawling 30-acre campus (divided into age blocks) in a pleasant residential area. New £800,000 sports hall funded by the National Lottery. On-site unit for 20 visually impaired pupils.

Atmosphere   Calm, caring, orderly (despite the school's size); uniform strictly enforced; pupils' work attractively displayed. Staff run monthly 'clinics' to enable parents to discuss their children's work.

Admissions   Over-subscribed (370 apply for 300 places); priority to those living in the (largely middle-class) catchment area (which estate agents believe adds 10% to property prices); 10 buses bring children from outlying, rural areas.

The head   Able, meticulous, quietly spoken; strongly committed to comprehensive education. Read English at Manchester; previously deputy head of a comprehensive in Cheshire. Married; three grown-up children.

The teaching   High quality. Formal in style: emphasis on good classroom management. Hard-working staff of 126 (equal numbers of women and men). National curriculum plus: all do Latin in second year; German, Spanish on offer; more able take science as three separate subjects; particularly good results in maths, English; lots of computing. Pupils grouped by ability in maths from first year, other subjects from second; extra help for those who need it; average class size 30, reducing to 12–15 in sixth form. Lots of drama, enthusiastic music (a strong tradition). Careful attention paid to 'cross-curricular' issues such as gender, equal opportunities, the environment

Results   (1997) GCSE: 60% gained at least five grades A–C. A-level: 46% of entries graded A or B.

Destinations   About 80% continue into the sixth form; of these, about 75% proceed to university.

Sport   Main games: rugby, hockey, cricket (outstanding indoor facilities include six nets, bowling machine, video replay), football (girls' football a speciality). Basketball, canoeing, mountain-biking also encouraged.

Remarks   Popular school; a well-stocked (if a trifle bland) education supermarket.

GEORGE HERIOT'S ♂ ♀
Lauriston Place, Edinburgh EH3 9EQ. Tel (0131) 229 7263

> ## Synopsis
> Independent ★ Co-educational ★ Day ★ Ages 12–18 (plus associated junior school) ★ 950 pupils (58% boys) ★ 308 in sixth form ★ Fees: £4,131
> Head: Alistair Hector, 42, appointed January 1998.
> *A school proud of its historical setting in central Edinburgh; high standards; good all round.*

Profile

Background   Founded 1628 by George Heriot, jeweller, for the 'fatherless sons of Edinburgh burgesses' (72 fatherless children still offered free places); girls admitted 1979; school became fully independent 1985. Purpose-built premises ('a bijou of Scottish Renaissance architecture') plus many later additions on attractive eight-and-a-half-acre site near the city centre (fine view of Edinburgh Castle from the playground). Junior school (550 pupils aged three to 12) on same campus.

Atmosphere   Orderly; very good relations between staff and courteous, cheerful pupils. Uniform worn throughout. School 'deeply rooted in the Scottish tradition'.

Admissions   By tests; school is not unduly selective and may become even less with the phasing out of assisted places, which more than 250 hold; numbers likely to fall (no bad thing – school feels over-crowded). Scholarships available.

The head   New appointment. Read German at St Andrews; previously deputy head of Warwick (qv), where he has taught since 1985. Keen sportsman; plays the pipes. Married; three children

The teaching Enthusiastic, committed staff, many long-serving. Standard Scottish curriculum; sciences taught separately; big emphasis on literacy and linguistic competence (debating encouraged; generous prizes for creative writing; lots of foreign language exchanges); languages include German, Spanish, Latin; good maths. Pupils grouped by ability; many by-pass Standard Grade and go straight on to Highers; specialised help for dyslexics and those who speak English as a foreign language. Strong art, drama, music; 20% learn an instrument. Well-supported Duke of Edinburgh award scheme, cadet force.

Results (1997) Standard Grade: 78% gained at least five grades 1–2. Highers: 49% gained at least five grades A–C.

Destinations About 90% stay on for Highers; of these, 90% proceed to higher education (four or five a year to Oxbridge).

Sport Big emphasis on sport for all. Particular strengths in cross-country, hockey, rowing, rugby. Athletics, badminton, cricket, curling, fencing, golf, squash, tennis also popular. Playing fields one-and-a-half miles away.

Remarks Sound school.

GEORGE WATSON'S ♂ ♀
Colinton Road, Edinburgh EH10 5EG. Tel (0131) 447 7931

Synopsis
Independent ★ Co-educational ★ Day (and some boarding) ★ Ages 12–18 (plus associated nursery and junior schools) ★ 1,250 pupils (55% boys, 30% boarders) ★ 427 in sixth form ★ Fees: £4,512 day; £9,156 boarding
Head: Frank Gerstenberg, 56, appointed 1985.
Fine, well-run school; good teaching and results; lots on offer.

Profile
Background Founded 1741 by George Watson, merchant and financier; moved 1932 to present 40-acre, suburban campus and fine, purpose-built sandstone premises (endless corridors); later additions include state-of-the-art technology centre. Merged with girls' school 1974. Junior departments on same site.

Atmosphere Busy, well-ordered (but hectic at break-time); good pastoral care system helps counter the daunting size (parents encouraged to keep in touch – but mobile phones are banned: 'We've had our first go off in class, and I hope it will be the last'). Strict uniform ('The top shirt button must always be done up whenever a tie is worn').

Admissions By tests in English, maths, verbal reasoning; school is heavily over-subscribed (about four apply for each place) and fairly selective but may become less so with the phasing out of assisted places, which 240 hold. Most from solidly middle-class backgrounds: children of solicitors, chartered accountants doctors etc; 75% come from a 15-mile radius. Boarding accommodation is friendly and homely. Scholarships, bursaries available.

The head (Principal) Very able; genial, quietly spoken; strong leader (has revived the school). Read history at Cambridge; taught it at Millfield; his second headship. Married; three grown-up children.

The teaching Good quality: generally formal in style; experienced, well-qualified staff (more than half appointed by present head – 'It's the most important thing I do'). Broad curriculum: sciences (a strength) taught separately;

languages include German, Spanish, Russian, Latin; lots of computing; good technology; wide choice of Highers (most take five or six; brighter pupils tend to by-pass Standard Grade); most take Certificate of Sixth Year Studies. Pupils grouped by ability in maths, English, French; very good specialist help for dyslexics; maximum class class size 28. Lots of art, drama, music; four orchestras, four choirs; fine facilities; 'colours' for excellence in the performing arts. Vast range of extra-curricular activities, including well-supported Duke of Edinburgh award scheme. Regular exchanges with schools in France, Germany, Spain, Russia, USA.

Results (1997) Standard Grade: 65% gained at least five grades 1–2. Highers: 46% gained at least five grades A–C.

Destinations Virtually all do Highers and stay for a sixth year; 85% proceed to higher education (average of 14 a year to Oxbridge).

Sport Wide range on offer; particular strengths in rugby, hockey, rowing. Squash, fencing, athletics, swimming, tennis, badminton, golf, sailing, curling, cricket etc also on offer. Facilities include extensive playing fields, floodlit all-weather hockey pitch, indoor pool, tennis and squash courts.

Remarks Good all round; recommended.

GIGGLESWICK ♂ ♀
Settle, North Yorkshire BD24 0DE. Tel (01729) 823545

Synopsis
Independent ★ Co-educational ★ Boarding and day ★ Ages 13–18 (plus associated prep school) ★ 312 pupils (67% boys, 82% boarding) ★ 127 in sixth form ★ Fees: £12,750 boarding; £8,460 day
Head: Anthony Millard, 49, appointed 1993.
Happy, well-run school; good teaching and results; strong music, drama, sport; emphasis on outdoor education.

Profile
Background Founded 1499; moved 1869 to solid, purpose-built premises (now extensively modernised) on a commanding site on the edge of the village (copper-domed Gothic chapel dominates the surrounding countryside); became co-educational 1983. Prep school (Catteral Hall) on adjoining site.

Atmosphere Cheerful, purposeful; cordial relations between staff and pupils; full-time Anglican chaplain. Strict rules against drugs, bullying, sexual contact. Good food.

Admissions By interview and Common Entrance; school is not unduly selective. Boarding accommodation (four boys' houses, two girls') recently refurbished (at a cost of nearly £2 million); most boarders from North of England; 20% expatriates. Scholarships (academic, music, art, design/technology, drama, sport) available.

The head Straight-talking; strong leader; respected by staff and pupils. Read economics at LSE; previously deputy head of Wells Cathedral School and head for seven years of Wycliffe (qv). Married (wife much involved in school life); four children.

The teaching Lively, stimulating; enthusiastic staff of 44 (14 women). Fairly broad curriculum; science available as three separate subjects; lots of computing (all have palm-tops); Latin, Greek, German, Sapnish on offer; A-level options include business studies, theatre studies, sports studies; all do general studies.

All screened for dyslexia; extra help for those who need it; average class size 20, reducing to eight for A-levels. Good music (orchestra, chapel choir) and drama. Extra-curricular activities include cadet force (compulsory for two years) and well-supported Duke of Edinburgh award scheme; school has its own mountain rescue unit (big emphasis on outdoor education). Regular European exchanges.
Results   (1997) GCSE: 97% gained at least five grades A–C. A-level: 49% of entries graded A or B.
Destinations   About 90% proceed to university.
Sport   Taken seriously: strong coaching; good facilities. Main games: rugby, cricket for boys; hockey, tennis for girls; athletics, swimming for both; frequent tours abroad. Golf, fencing, canoeing, pot-holing, fell-walking, clay pigeon shooting also available.
Remarks   Good school: turns out well-rounded, confident, civilised young people.

GILLOTT'S ♂ ♀
Gillott's Lane, Henley-on-Thames, Oxfordshire RG9 1PS. Tel (01491) 574315

Synopsis
Comprehensive ★ Co-educational ★ Ages 11–16 ★ 885 pupils (52% boys)
Head: John Lockyer, 57, appointed 1987.
Successful comprehensive; good teaching and GCSE results; strong sport.

Profile
Background   Opened as a secondary modern 1945; went comprehensive in the 1960s; lost its sixth form in the 1970s. Buildings dating from 1960 and later grouped round a Victorian mansion on a 40-acre parkland site.
Atmosphere   Pleasant, hard-working. Uniform firmly enforced; prefects, sports colours.
Admissions   School is over-subscribed (about 200 apply for 180 places); county council gives priority to those at four 'feeder' primaries, siblings, those living nearest; up to a third come from across the county boundary with Buckinghamshire to avoid the selective system there. Most from relatively prosperous backgrounds
The head   Low-key, sympathetic. Read modern languages at Oxford; previously deputy head of Lord Williams's (qv). Married (to a head); two children.
The teaching   Sound; lively, hard-working staff. Standard national curriculum; top 60% add German to French; good results in science; GCSE options include photography, drama, art and design. Pupils grouped by ability in most subjects; class work geared to the level of the average; extra help before school for those who need it (28 have 'statements' of special educational needs). About 10% learn a musical instrument; choirs, orchestras, various ensembles. Regular language exchanges to France, Germany.
Results   (1997) GCSE: 67% gained at least five grades A–C .
Destinations   About 85% remain in full-time education after 16 (most take A-levels at Henley College).
Sport   Regular fixtures in hockey, netball, athletics, rugby, soccer, cricket, tennis; frequent district and county honours. Facilities include extensive playing fields, on-site sports centre shared with the community.
Remarks   Ofsted inspectors concluded (1996): 'This is a very good school. Pupils achieve high standards in many aspects of the curriculum.'

GLANTAF ♂ ♀
Bridge Road, Llandaff North, Cardiff CF4 2JL. Tel (01222) 562879

Synopsis
Comprehensive (Welsh-medium) ★ Co-educational ★ Ages 11–18 ★ 1,600 pupils (equal numbers of girls and boys) ★ 240 in sixth form
Head: Huw Thomas, 55, appointed 1995.
First-rate comprehensive; good teaching and GCSE results; strong sport.

Profile
Background Opened 1978, the only Welsh-medium school in Cardiff. Overcrowded, poorly constructed, flat-roofed 1950s buildings; lower school (450 pupils) inconveniently situated two miles away (but due to be re-located on the main site in September 1998). Special unit for those with physical disabilities.

Atmosphere Happy, homely: Welsh 'family' feeling underpinned with firmness; pride fostered in the culture and tradition of the Welsh nation (Welsh the official and social language of the school). Parents and governors have high expectations of academic success. Aim is that all should leave bi-lingual; criticisms of insularity and separatism wholeheartedly refuted.

Admissions Fairly wide range of abilities from an extensive catchment area. More than 80% come from English-speaking homes (the generation that missed out on learning Welsh); mix of social backgrounds – most white-collar, many professional.

The head Experienced; strong leader; wholly committed to Welsh-medium education (has edited a Latin/Welsh dictionary). Previously head for 15 years of a South Wales Valleys comprehensive; gets on well with staff, parents, pupils.

The teaching Highly effective; consistently good results (among the best in Wales). Standard national curriculum plus Welsh; vocational alternatives to A-level available. Pupils grouped by ability in most subjects; extra help for those with special needs. Strong drama and music; large choir, several orchestras. Regular language exchanges with schools in France, Germany.

Results (1997) GCSE: 65% gained at least five grades A–C. A-level: 47% of entries graded A or B.

Destinations About 65% continue into the sixth form; of these, about 50% proceed to university (average of five a year to Oxbridge).

Sport Outstanding: top-class rugby, very strong basketball (for boys and girls).

Remarks A happy, successful school, its commitment to the Welsh language epitomised by its motto: 'A country's crown is its mother tongue'.

GLASGOW ACADEMY ♂ ♀
Colebrooke Street, Glasgow G12 8HE. Tel (0141) 334 8558

Synopsis
Independent ★ Co-educational ★ Day ★ Ages 11–18 (plus associated prep school) ★ 594 pupils (69% boys) ★ 205 in sixth form ★ Fees: £4,665
Head: David Comins, 49, appointed 1994.
Traditional school now in transition; good art; lots of sport.

Profile
Background Founded 1845; moved to present purpose-built premises in a suburban Victorian terrace 1880s (latest additions include new music block);

went co-educational 1991 when it merged with a local girls' school. Pre-prep and prep school on the same site.

Atmosphere Becoming less sternly formal: more emphasis on pastoral care, valuing children as individuals. Meals still old-fashioned though – hardly a vegetable in sight.

Admissions At 11 by interview and tests in English, maths (but automatic entry from prep school); school is over-subscribed and fairly selective. Most pupils come from business/professional backgrounds; phasing out of assisted places, which 70 hold, will further reduce the social mix.

The head (Rector) Energetic, forward-looking; coaxing the school (in the face of some resistance) into the late 20th century. Read maths at Cambridge; taught at Glenalmond for 13 years; previously deputy head of Queen's, Taunton (qv). Keen on rugby and climbing mountains (Himalayas, Rockies, Alps). Married; three children.

The teaching Style is changing: less emphasis on formal instruction, more on a rounded education. Fairly long-serving staff of 60 (equal numbers of women and men), 11 appointed by present head. Broad curriculum: science (strong – many go on to do medicine) taught as three separate subjects; good maths. Pupils grouped by ability in English, French, maths from first year; progress closely monitored (effort grades every two months); maximum class size 24. Most take eight Standard Grades and then choose between one-year Highers and A-levels; vocational alternatives available. Very good art; music improving (choirs, two orchestras, pipe band). Extra-curricular activities include cadet force, Duke of Edinburgh award scheme.

Results (1997) Standard Grade: 90% gained at least five grades 1–2. Highers: 47% gained at least five grades A–C. A-level: 48% of entries graded A or B.

Destinations Nearly 90% go on to university, mostly in Scotland (average of five a year to Oxbridge).

Sport Wide range on offer, including athletics, basketball, cricket, cross-country, curling, golf, hockey, rugby, sailing, soccer, squash, shooting, swimming, skiing, tennis. Playing fields 2.25 miles away; all-weather pitch; large sports hall.

Remarks Sound school, improving slowly.

GLASGOW HIGH ♂ ♀
637 Crow Road, Glasgow G13 1PL. Tel (0141) 954 9628

Synopsis
Independent ★ Co-educational ★ Day ★ Ages 11–18 (plus associated junior school) ★ 638 pupils (roughly equal numbers of girls and boys) ★ 178 in sixth form ★ Fees: £1,656–£4,743
Head: Robin Easton, OBE, 53, appointed 1983.
Successful, well-run school; good teaching and results; lots of extra-curricular activities.

Profile
Background Roots go back to 12th century; closed by Glasgow Corporation 1976; re-born 1977 as an independent school in purpose-built premises on 27-acre site to the west of the city (junior school two miles away). Much new building, including £500,000 music suite; fund-raising not a problem.

Atmosphere Busy, friendly, well-ordered (transgressors dealt with firmly, sixth-formers required to sign good behaviour contract); uniform worn by all. Supportive parents.

Admissions Over-subscribed: at least two apply for each place. Entry at 11, 12 by school's own tests in English, maths, aptitude (top two candidates given scholarships worth 50% of fees). Most from professional/business backgrounds.

The head (Rector) Gentle, courteous Glaswegian; committed Christian (church elder); very much in control (without being overbearing). Read modern languages at Cambridge; previously a housemaster at Stewart's Melville, head of modern languages at George Watson's (qv). Married (to a teacher); two children (both pupils here).

The teaching Good; well-qualified, youthful, stable staff of 63 (rougly equal numbers of women and men) nearly all appointed by present head. Broad curriculum: Latin on offer from first year, German from second; science taught as three separate subjects. Choice of 17 subjects at Standard Grade (most take seven) and 19 Highers (nearly all take five in fifth year, followed by Certificate of Sixth Year Studies). Pupils grouped by ability in maths, science from second year and most other subjects thereafter; no class larger than 25. Lots of music (choirs, orchestras); wide range of clubs, societies (debating, satellite-tracking, chess, bridge etc).

Results (1997) Standard Grade: 96% gained at least five grades 1–2. Highers: 76% gained at least five grades A–C.

Destinations About 75% proceed to Scottish universities; average of six a year to Oxbridge.

Sport Main games: rugby, cricket, hockey, athletics, tennis. Football, cross-country, badminton, basketball, volleyball, netball, golf, gymnastics, squash, canoeing, sailing, skiing also on offer. Facilities include 23 acres of playing fields, new all-weather pitch, 12 tennis courts.

Remarks Attractive, well-balanced school; recommended.

GLENALMOND ♂ ♀
Perth PH1 3RY. Tel (01738) 880205

Synopsis
Independent ★ Co-educational ★ Boarding and day ★ Ages 12–18 ★ 330 pupils (76% boys, 88% boarding) ★ 125 in sixth form ★ Fees: £13,185 boarding; £6,600 day
Head: Ian Templeton, 53, appointed 1992.
Traditional boarding school in glorious rural setting; sound teaching; fairly wide ability range; strong sport.

Profile
Background Founded 1847 by W E Gladstone (four times Prime Minister) as a theological college and school for the Scottish Episcopal Church. Imposing Victorian neo-classical buildings (plus towers and turrets) in 230 acres in idyllic surroundings eight miles north-west of Perth 'away from the narrowing influences of town life'; later additions include music school by Sir Basil Spence and de luxe technology centre. Girls admitted to sixth form 1990, at all ages 1995; numbers have been rising steadily.

Atmosphere Pleasant, happy; good pastoral care. Splendid (500-seat) chapel, cloistered quadrangles, prefects in gowns – a Scottish public school on the English model. All staff live on site.

Admissions At 12 (from state primary schools) by tests in English, maths, verbal reasoning and a general paper; at 13 by Common Entrance; school is not unduly selective. Most pupils from Scottish professional/farming/business backgrounds. Boarding accommodation recently up-graded; new (1991) house for girls. Scholarships, bursaries available

The head (Warden) Has restored the school's flagging fortunes. Read maths at Edinburgh, philosophy at London (First); previously head of Oswestry. Keen golfer. Married (wife writes detective stories); two children.

The teaching Little evidence of any departure from well-tried and proven methods; long-serving staff of 43 (10 women). Broad curriculum: science taught as three separate subjects; most do Latin; Greek, Spanish, German on offer. Most take nine GCSEs; some do maths, French, Latin a year early. Sixth-formers choose between A-levels (taken by the more able two-thirds) and Highers. Pupils grouped by ability in maths, Latin; average class size 16. Lots of drama (350-seat theatre) and music: orchestras, pipe band, 90-strong chapel choir. Strong debating, active cadet force (the oldest in Scotland). Close links with schools in France, Germany, Italy.

Results (1997) GCSE: 89% gained at least five grades A–C. A-level: 55% of entries graded A or B.

Destinations About 95% continue into the sixth form; of these, nearly 90% proceed to higher education (about six a year to Oxbridge).

Sport Splendid pitches in parkland setting for rugby (long, proud tradition), hockey, lacrosse, cricket. First-rate facilities include sports hall, heated indoor pool, squash courts, nine all-weather courts for tennis and netball, well-manicured nine-hole golf course (designed by the architect of Gleneagles), artificial ski slope, private fishing on the River Almond.

Remarks HMI reported (1995): 'Most pupils were making good progress and attainment was mainly good or very good. Teaching was strong throughout the college.'

GLOUCESTER GIRLS' HIGH ♀
Denmark Road, Gloucester GL1 3JN. Tel (01452) 543335

Synopsis
Grammar ★ Girls ★ Ages 11–18 ★ 710 pupils ★ 175 in sixth form
Head: Mrs Margaret Bainbridge, 48, appointed 1992.
Well-run, traditional school; good teaching and GCSE results.

Profile

Background Founded 1883; moved 1909 to purpose-built, red-brick premises; some classrooms in 'temporary' huts. Numbers have been rising steadily.

Atmosphere Cheerful, orderly, hard-working; friendly relations between staff and pupils; traditional uniform below the sixth form. Supportive parents.

Admissions School heavily over-subscribed; entry by county council verbal reasoning tests; minimum score 110. Fairly extensive catchment area.

The head Able, good-humoured; leads from the front ('I must be in the middle of things'); teaches all first-years. Read French at Manchester; previously deputy head of a Lincolnshire grammar school.

The teaching Good quality; enthusiastic, predominantly female staff, nearly all appointed by present head. Standard national curriculum; most do two languages. Pupils grouped by ability in maths, French; average class size 30, reducing to 24 for GCSE, maximum of 15 at A-level. Lots of music; two choirs, four orchestras. Extra-curricular activities include Duke of Edinburgh award scheme.

Results (1997) GCSE: 97% gained at least five grades A–C. A-level: 37% of entries graded were A or B.

Destinations   Nearly all stay on for A-levels; about 90% proceed to university.
Sport   Main games: hockey, tennis (a particular strength), rounders. Netball, athletics, gymnastics also on offer. Playing fields near by.
Remarks   Good all round.

GLYN ADT ♂

The Kingsway, Ewell, Epsom, Surrey KT17 1NB. Tel (0181) 394 2955

Synopsis

Partially selective comprehensive (grant-maintained) ★ Boys ★ Day ★ Ages 11–18 ★ 1,231 pupils ★ 232 in sixth form
Head: Stuart Turner, 50, appointed 1988.
Successful school; good teaching and results; emphasis on technology; strong sport.

Profile

Background   Opened 1927 as a grammar school; went comprehensive 1972; opted out of council control 1992; technology college status achieved 1994 (ADT the principal commercial sponsors), since when substantial sums have been spent on facilities for science, technology, computing, sport; sixth-form centre opened September 1997.
Atmosphere   Businesslike; emphasis on standards, discipline. Competitive house system; strict blazer-and-tie uniform; prefects wear blue gowns; honours boards list Oxbridge successes; computers everywhere. 'A school of the future founded on the traditions of the past'.
Admissions   Thirty places (15%) allocated by entrance test; 170 to siblings and those living in the catchment area; school is over-subscribed. Most from middle-class backgrounds.
The head   Able, enthusiastic. Read history and maths at Cardiff; captained British Universities rugby; came here as deputy head 1980. Teaches for a quarter of the timetable. Married (to a teacher); two children.
The teaching   Good; generally traditional in style (but pupils encouraged to take responsibility for their own learning); relatively youthful staff (one third female). Emphasis on maths, science (taught as three separate subjects), technology, IT; languages include German, Spanish, Latin; all take at least 10 GCSEs; choice of 20 subjects at A-level; GNVQs available in science, business. Pupils grouped by ability in most subjects; extra help for those with special needs; average class size 26. Popular drama; lots of music. Wide range of extra-curricular activities, including engineering & technology club, chess, debating, Duke of Edinburgh award scheme.
Results   (1997) GCSE: 60% gained at least five grades A–C. A-level: 37% of entries graded A or B.
Destinations   About 70% continue into the sixth form; of these, nearly all go on to university (average of four a year to Oxbridge).
Sport   Good; emphasis on participation. Athletics, badminton, rugby, basketball, cricket, football, squash, tennis on offer; regular county and regional honours. Facilities include fine sports hall; five acres of playing fields a quarter of a mile away.
Remarks   Good all round.

GODOLPHIN ♀
Milford Hill, Salisbury, Wiltshire SP1 2RA. Tel (01722) 333059

Synopsis
Independent ★ Girls ★ Day and boarding ★ Ages 11–18 (plus associated prep school) ★ 400 pupils (55% day) ★ 112 in sixth form ★ Fees: £7,119 day; £11,886 boarding
Head: Miss Jill Horsburgh, 44, appointed 1996.
Successful academic school; good teaching and results; first-rate art, music, drama.

Profile
Background Founded 1726 under the will of Elizabeth Godolphin; moved 1840 to attractive, 16-acre, hill-top site (spacious, rural feel); late Victorian buildings plus many sympathetically designed additions. Exceptional facilities include new 350-seat performing arts centre, lavishly equipped blocks for art, technology, science. Everything high quality, well cared for.

Atmosphere Hard-working, well-ordered, conspicuously happy; warm relations between staff and pupils. Traditional uniform includes all-enveloping, royal blue pinafore worn by all below the sixth form (girls voted in 1996 to retain it). Pleasant, homely boarding accommodation; juniors in mixed-age dormitories for four or five; seniors in double or single study-bedrooms; day girls ('Sarums') well integrated into strong boarding ethos. Parental involvement encouraged.

Admissions Fairly stiff entrance test at 11-plus (also taken by children from the on-site prep school). Foundation scholarships worth 70% of the fees available to girls who have lost one or both parents through death, separation or divorce and have been brought up as members of the Church of England.

The head Shy, engaging manner; whole-heartedly committed to the school. Read history at Oxford; previously assistant head of Benenden (qv). Teaches history to the first-years; gets to know all pupils well.

The teaching Lively, challenging: able staff of 55 (75% female); well-behaved, hard-working pupils. Broad curriculum includes three separate sciences, two modern languages (French, German), Latin; all do at least nine GCSEs and three A-levels (from a choice of 21) plus general studies. Largest class size 15; all teaching areas well equipped. Very good quality art (artist in residence), music (orchestras, choirs) drama. Wide range of (compulsory) extra-curricular activities, including cookery, aerobics, Japanese, indoor cricket, lacemaking etc. Plenty of trips at home and abroad for study, recreation.

Results (1997) GCSE: all gained at at least five grades A–C. A-level: 55% of entries graded A or B.

Destinations Nearly all continue into the sixth form; of these, 85% proceed to university.

Sport More than 20 on offer: usual team games plus lacrosse; fencing, badminton, gymnastics on offer. All must participate; more than half are in school teams (lots of weekend matches). Facilities include on-site playing fields, heated outdoor pool; sports centre near by.

Remarks Purposeful, charming school; good choice for able, sociable girls.

GODOLPHIN AND LATYMER ♀
Iffley Road, Hammersmith, London W6 0PG. Tel (0181) 741 1936

Synopsis
Independent ★ Girls ★ Day ★ Ages 11–18 ★ 707 pupils ★ 191 in sixth form
★ Fees: £6,285
Head: Miss Margaret Rudland, 52, appointed 1986.
Well-run, highly academic school; first-rate teaching and results; lots of extra-curricular activities.

Profile

Background Founded 1861 as a boys' boarding school; turned into a girls' day school 1905; joined the state sector and became a voluntary-aided grammar school 1951; reverted to the independent sector 1977 'rather than become part of a split-site comprehensive'. Original Victorian yellow-brick buildings (wood block floors, high ceilings) and numerous later additions on surprisingly quiet, four-acre inner city site. Good facilities, despite pressure on space; some classes in 'temporary' huts.

Atmosphere Friendly, lively, purposeful; respectful relations between staff and pupils (junior girls stand behind their chairs before lessons until formal greetings have been exchanged); good manners expected; well-organised pastoral care; sixth-formers given lots of responsibilities (they help the juniors). Traditional uniform (check blouses, grey skirts, sweatshirts) until sixth form, then standard teenage wear.

Admissions By interview and highly competitive tests in English, maths; school over-subscribed by more than 4:1. Lacking endowments, it has launched a 'million for the millennium' appeal to compensate for the phasing out of assisted places, which 25% hold. Fairly broad social mix ('from cabinet minister to cabinet maker') but most from middle-class homes within a radius of five miles; 70% join from prep schools, 30% from primaries. Some music scholarships available.

The head Able, modest, courteous; very dedicated; much liked by staff and girls. Read maths and physics at London; was head of maths at St Paul's Girls' then deputy head of Norwich High. Teaches juniors four periods a week to get to know them.

The teaching Very good across the curriculum; generally traditional in style; experienced, well-qualified staff (85% female), more than half appointed by present head. Fairly broad curriculum; languages include Latin, German, Spanish, Russian (all do two in second year); particularly good results in English, French; sciences taught (but not examined) separately (well-equipped labs); lots of computing; wide choice of 25 subjects at A-level (including Greek, history of art, economics). Pupils grouped by ability in maths, French from second year, later for science; average class size 26, reducing to 12 in sixth form. High standard of art (good facilities); enthusiastic music (orchestra, three choirs); strong drama (girls encouraged to write and produce plays). Wide range of extra-curricular activities include thriving Duke of Edinburgh award scheme. Regular language exchanges with pupils in Russia, France, Germany, Spain.

Results (1997) GCSE: all gained at least five grades A–C. A-level: impressive 80% of entries graded A or B (21st in the league table).

Destinations Virtually all go on to university (average of 12 a year to Oxbridge).

Sport Hockey, tennis, rounders for juniors; wider range for seniors, including squash, volleyball, badminton, rowing (very popular), karate; numerous inter-school matches. Limited, but adequate on-site facilities; all-weather surface provides hockey pitch and nine tennis courts.

Remarks Successful, happy school; highly recommended for able girls.

GOFFS ♂ ♀
Goffs Lane, Cheshunt, Hertfordshire EN7 5QW. Tel (01992) 424200

Synopsis
Partially selective comprehensive (grant-maintained) ★ Co-educational ★ Ages 11–18 ★ 1,050 pupils (roughly equal numbers of girls and boys) ★ 220 in sixth form
Head: Dr John Versey, 49, appointed 1994.
Successful school; good GCSE results; strong music and sport.

Profile
Background Opened 1964 as a co-educational grammar school; went comprehensive 1976; opted out of council control 1993; achieved language college status 1996. Modern buildings on edge of suburban green belt.

Atmosphere Hard working, purposeful, well ordered; strong Christian ethos. Big emphasis on traditional values: house system, competition, team games, uniform, service to the community. Supportive parents raise £20,000 a year.

Admissions School is heavily over-subscribed; priority to those with an aptitude for music, sport, drama, languages. Most from suburban middle-class homes in Cheshunt, Goffs Oak, Cuffley.

The head Read zoology at Southampton; spent six years in medical research before switching careers; previously deputy head of a comprehensive in Essex. Married (to a teacher); two grown-up sons.

The teaching Traditional teacher-centred approach. Broad curriculum: all do French and German from the start (geography and general studies taught in French); science on offer as three separate subjects. Pupils grouped by ability from second year; progress closely monitored (elaborate system of rewards and incentives – half-termly grades, credit and merit marks, governors' commendations etc). Good music: 150 learn an instrument; two orchestras, four wind bands, two choirs, madrigal group; regular performances. House competitions in general knowledge, chess, public speaking, poetry reading. Regular language exchanges with European schools; annual cultural visit to Italy and to battlefields of Normandy or Flanders.

Results (1997) GCSE: creditable 70% gained at least five grades A–C. A-level: 30% of entries graded A or B.

Destinations About 75% continue into the sixth form; of these, 70% proceed to university (up to six a year to Oxbridge).

Sport Main games: rugby, soccer, cricket for boys; hockey, netball, tennis, rounders for girls; athletics, cross-country, swimming for both; inter-school fixtures on Saturday mornings. House competition also involves a wide range of lesser sports: basketball, volleyball, badminton, table tennis, gymnastics, squash, riding, golf, trampolining, dance, weight training. Facilities include on-site playing fields, six all-weather tennis/netball courts, sports hall, large outdoor heated pool.

Remarks Good school for children of all abilities.

GORDONSTOUN ♂ ♀
Duffus, Elgin, Moray IV30 2RF. Tel (01343) 830445

Synopsis
Independent ★ Co-educational ★ Boarding and some day ★ Ages 13–18 ★ 445 pupils (55% boys; 96% boarding) ★ 240 in sixth form ★ Fees: £12,918 boarding; £8,337 day
Head: Mark Pyper, 50, appointed 1990.
Distinctive school; lots of art, drama, music; big emphasis on outdoor activities.

Profile
Background Founded 1934 by Kurt Hahn, the influential educational reformer, after he had been forced to flee from Nazi Germany: his aim was to counteract the 'four social declines' of physical fitness, initiative, care and compassion. Regarding puberty as something of a deformity, he prescribed a rigorous regime of morning runs and cold showers (an image the school has had difficulty shaking off). Fine 17th-century buildings plus many later additions, including some rather basic wooden huts, on a pleasant 150-acre estate on the Moray Firth, six miles from Elgin. Prospectus quotes Plato: 'You should dwell in a land of health, amid fair sights and sounds, and receive the good in everything.' Princes Philip, Charles, Andrew and Edward were all pupils here, as was the Princess Royal's son – her daughter still is. Co-educational since 1972.

Atmosphere No longer the rugged, spartan place it was (a 'hell hole', according to Prince Charles) but much of Hahn's legacy survives: he was keen on self-reliance, outdoor education and community service; coastguarding, fire-fighting and mountain rescue are all important features of life here. Accent on internationalism (regular exchanges with schools in Australia, New Zealand, Canada, France, Germany, South Africa); 30% of the pupils come from abroad (both expatriates and other nationalities). Pastoral care is first-rate; some (older) members of staff complain that discipline is not what it was.

Admissions By interview and Common Entrance; school is barely selective. Phasing out of assisted places, which about 30 hold, will increase recruitment difficulties. Parents may apply for grants to supplement the standard fee (or pay more if they can). Boarding accommodation varies in age and quality; some of the eight houses are spartan and fairly crowded; others are new and of a high standard.

The head Modest, charming; has put his stamp on the school. Educated at Winchester and Oxford (read modern history); became head of a prep school in Sussex at 31; formerly deputy head of Sevenoaks, where he taught classics. His father, grandfather and great-grandfather were all heads. Advises his pupils: 'Be kind and be honest – it's what the world needs.' Married; three young children.

The teaching Sound; experienced, well-qualified staff. Fairly broad curriculum; science taught (but not examined) as three separate subjects; most do French plus at least one from German, Spanish, Latin. Pupils grouped by ability from the start; additional setting in maths, French; extra help for those with specific learning difficulties; progress closely monitored (regular reports to parents). Nearly all do nine GCSEs and three A-levels (from a choice of 21) plus wide-ranging general studies course. Lively interest in the arts: 40% learn a musical instrument; two orchestras and several smaller ensembles; 30-strong choir; lots of drama. Big emphasis on expeditions, seamanship (school owns 66-foot yacht) and Duke of Edinburgh award scheme (which Hahn invented).

Results (1997) GCSE: 90% gained at least five grades A–C. A-level: rather modest 36% of entries graded A or B.

Destinations   About 90% continue into the sixth form; of these, 90% proceed to higher education.

Sport   Not dominant (there is so much else going on) but facilities are first-rate: sports hall, indoor heated pool, squash and tennis courts, shooting range, athletics track, extensive playing fields, all-weather pitch.

Remarks   Plenty here to excite and inspire; the aim of stretching every pupil is very largely achieved (motto: *Plus est en vous* – There is more in you than you think). HMI (1996) praised the school's 'outstanding programme of outdoor education' but were less enthusiastic about some of the teaching.

THE GRANGE ♂ ♀
Bradburns Lane, Hartford, Northwich, Cheshire CW8 1LR. Tel (01606) 74007

Synopsis
Independent ★ Co-educational ★ Day ★ Ages 11–18 (plus associated junior school) ★ 600 pupils (roughly equal numbers of girls and boys) ★ 130 in sixth form ★ Fees: £4,020
Head: Mrs Jenny Stephen, 47, appointed September 1997.
Attractive school; good teaching and results.

Profile
Background   Founded 1933 as a prep school and kindergarten; senior school opened 1978, sixth form 1983. Attractive brick buildings plus later additions, including new classroom block, on 25-acre campus. New purpose-built junior school (ages four to 11) in own grounds near by.

Atmosphere   Crisp, business-like; strong pressure to achieve. Everywhere clean and well maintained; strict school uniform from age four. An attractive combination of the traditional (all staff in gowns) and modern (up-to-date facilities). 'The Christian religious influence is intentional,' says the prospectus, 'and underlies the corporate life and teaching of the whole school. Pupils of all denominations are accepted as long as they are prepared to take a full part in the life of the school.'

Admissions   At four by assessment; at seven by tests in reading, writing, vocabulary, punctuation; at 11 by tests in English, maths, verbal reasoning; school is fairly selective. Most pupils from middle-class homes (in an extensive catchment area midway between Chester and Manchester served by private coaches) but many parents make big sacrifices to afford the fees. Scholarships (academic, drama, music, sport) and bursaries available.

The head   New appointment (predecessor had been in post 20 years). Able, charming, strong leader; inspires loyalty and affection among staff and pupils. Read chemistry at Leeds; previously head of independent girls' schools in Bedford and Leeds. Married (to the High Master of Manchester Grammar, qv); three sons.

The teaching   High quality; lessons combine academic challenge with relaxed class control. Stable staff of 75 (34 women). Broad curriculum: science taught as three separate subjects; Latin compulsory for first two years; all do two modern languages (from French, German, Spanish). All take nine GCSEs and at least three A-levels (from a wide choice of 24) plus general studies. Pupils grouped by ability in maths, modern languages; progress carefully monitored (record card to parents every two or three weeks); maximum class size 24. Strict homework policy (beginning with spelling lists at age five). Strong music: 250 learn an instrument; orchestra. Extensive extrA–curricular programme, including Duke of Edinburgh award scheme, Christian Union, debating etc. Regular trips abroad; lots of visits to exhibitions, theatres, concerts.

Results   (1997) GCSE: 98% gained at least five grades A–C. A-level: 63% of entries graded A or B.

Destinations   About 80% stay on for A-levels; of these, 95% proceed to university (up to 10 a year to Oxbridge).

Sport   Main games: football, rugby, cricket, hockey, netball, rowing; many county representatives. Facilities include fine sports hall, 20 acres of playing fields (but no swimming pool).

Remarks   Model school; recommended.

GRAVENEY ♂ ♀
Welham Road, Tooting, London SW1 79BU. Tel (0181) 682 7000

Synopsis
Partially selective comprehensive (grant-maintained) ★ Co-educational ★ Ages 11–19 ★ 1,556 pupils (slightly more boys than girls) ★ 350 in sixth form
Head: Graham Stappleton, 51, appointed 1988.
Effective, well-run school; good teaching and results.

Profile
Background   Roots go back to 1669. Pleasant buildings on a large campus on either side of a residential road. School has technology college status.

Atmosphere   Calm, serious, well-ordered; good pastoral care; big emphasis on individual and collective responsibility; hard line on drugs and bullying. Parents regarded as 'co-educators'.

Admissions   School heavily over-subscribed: 50% admitted (since 1994) after tests in English, maths, non-verbal reasoning (900 apply for 125 places); nearly all the rest of the places go to siblings. Most from near by but catchment area is growing; 60% black or Asian; 18% entitled to free school meals.

The head   Dedicated, determined, pragmatic; strong manager; accepts no excuses for poor performance. Read history at Cambridge; has spent his entire teaching career here; gets on well with staff and pupils. Married; two children.

The teaching   Generally good: well-qualified staff; lively, well-prepared lessons (lots of pupil participation). Standard national curriculum; Latin on offer; A-level options include sports studies. Pupils grouped by ability into four bands and set individual targets; extra help for those who need it (including break-time and after-hours revision classes); maximum class size 20 (smaller than usual).

Results   (1997) GCSE: 53% gained at least five grades A–C. A-level: 38% of entries graded A or B.

Destinations   Most continue into the sixth form (some to re-take GCSEs).

Sport   Chiefly: football, cricket (good coaching), hockey, athletics, basketball. Facilities include new sports hall.

Remarks   Popular, improving school.

GRAYS CONVENT ♀
College Avenue, Grays, Essex RM17 5UX. Tel (01375) 376173

Synopsis
Comprehensive (voluntary-aided, Roman Catholic) ★ Girls ★ Ages 11–16 ★ 600 pupils
Head: Philip Kyndt, 46, appointed 1995.
Traditional, well-ordered school; good GCSE results.

Profile
Background   Founded 1906 by Roman Catholic Order of La Sainte Union des Sacrés Coeurs; went comprehensive 1969; lost its sixth form 1974. Solid 1930s building plus functional 1970s additions (some recently refurbished) on a small site in a quiet, tree-lined street; art and music in former convent house; some classrooms in 'temporary' huts.

Atmosphere   Orderly, disciplined; respectful relations between staff and well-mannered girls; decent behaviour and consideration for others expected. Christian ethos fundamental: crucifix in every room; regular (voluntary) Mass in small chapel. Strong pastoral care system. Traditional uniform rigorously enforced.

Admissions   Broad range of abilities; mostly working class backgrounds in Thurrock; 66% Catholic.

The head   School's first lay head; has taught here since 1976; previously deputy head. Read French at King's, London; MPhil from Birbeck. Married; three children.

The teaching   Formal, traditional, thorough; emphasis on high standards of accuracy, spelling, grammar, presentation; nightly homework. Dedicated, supportive staff (almost equal numbers of men and women, not all Catholics). Standard national curriculum; particular strengths in modern languages (French, Spanish) and English (extra help in the lunch-hour for those who need it); good science; computers used widely across the curriculum. Pupils divided by ability into two broad streams; further setting from the start in maths, English, French; progress carefully monitored. Lots of music: small orchestra, jazz band, two choirs.

Results   (1996) GCSE: 66% gained at least five grades A–C.

Destinations   About 90% remain in full-time education after 16.

Sport   Main strengths: netball, gymnastics, athletics. Limited on-site facilities.

Remarks   Disciplined but caring school; highly regarded locally.

GREENBANK HIGH ♀
Hastings Road, Southport, Merseyside PR8 2LT. Tel (01704) 567591

Synopsis
Comprehensive ★ Girls ★ Ages 11–16 ★ 894 pupils
Head: Mrs Pat McQuade, 45, appointed 1992.
Successful, well-run school; good teaching and GCSE results.

Profile
Background   Founded 1912 as Southport Girls' High; moved to present suburban site and purpose-built, functional premises 1958; went comprehensive 1978; achieved language college status 1996. Some areas in need of refurbishment; five classrooms in 'temporary' huts.

Atmosphere   Purposeful, friendly; discipline with a gentle touch. Green uniform worn by all (skirts short, medium, long, full or straight). Funds raised by supportive PTA.

Admissions   Places (200 a year) allocated by local council; pupils drawn from a wide range of backgrounds.

The head   Able, experienced, ambitious for the school; came here as deputy 1988. Gets on well with staff and pupils. Married; one son.

The teaching   Thorough; experienced, stable staff of 50 (10 men). Standard national curriculum with an accent on languages; sciences taught separately (good results in biology, chemistry); most take nine or 10 GCSEs (options include business studies, music, Latin). Pupils grouped by ability in maths, science, French; average class size 25. Well-supported Duke of Edinburgh award scheme. Regular language exchanges with pupils in France, Spain.

Results   (1997) GCSE: very creditable 69% gained at least five grades A–C.

Destinations   Most go on to sixth form college.

Sport   Chiefly: hockey, netball, gymnastics. Soccer, golf also available. Facilities include all-weather pitch; sports hall planned.

Remarks   Ofsted inspectors concluded (1994): 'This is a very good school with some outstanding features. Standards of achievement are well above national norms.'

GREENSWARD ♂ ♀
Greensward Lane, Hockley, Essex SS5 5HG. Tel (01702) 202571

Synopsis
Comprehensive (grant-maintained) ★ Co-educational ★ Ages 11–18 ★ 1,279 pupils (slightly more boys than girls) ★ 127 in sixth form
Head: David Triggs, 44, appointed 1994.
Well-run, forward-looking school; good teaching and GCSE results.

Profile
Background   Opened 1962 in functional, purpose-built premises on a spacious site; opted out of council control 1993; sixth form opened and technology college status achieved 1995; latest additions include new art and drama block.

Atmosphere   Busy, hard-working, well-disciplined; very good rapport between staff and confident, out-going pupils; well-organised pastoral care; school comes down on bullies 'like a ton of bricks'. Uniform 'very strictly' enforced.

Admissions   School over-subscribed (nearly 350 apply for 216 places); priority to pupils from four 'feeder' primaries; fairly wide range of abilities. Numbers have grown steadily since 1994 (school competes with two single-sex grammars).

The head   Dynamic, creative, autocratic; more like a businessman than a teacher; lists his priorities as D-U-L-L, Discipline, Uniform, Latin and Laughter. Has had a big impact on the school.

The teaching   Varied in style; lively, comparatively youthful staff (equal numbers of women and men). Fairly broad curriculum; big emphasis in the early years on the Three Rs; good technology. Pupils grouped by ability 'in all areas possible'; extra help for those who need it; average class size 23. Flourishing music. Regular language exchanges with schools in France, Germany.

Results   (1997) GCSE: very creditable 69% gained at least five grades A–C. A-level: very modest 17% of entries graded A or B (the new sixth form's first results).

Destinations   Up to 75% expected to continue into the sixth form.

Sport   Particular strengths in athletics and basketball. Rugby, swimming also popular. Facilities include extensive playing fields, gym, indoor pool.
Remarks   Good school, getting better.

GRESHAM'S, HOLT ♂ ♀
Holt, Norfolk NR25 6EA. Tel (01263) 713271

Synopsis
Independent ★ Co-educational ★ Boarding and day ★ Ages 13–18 (plus associated prep and pre-prep) ★ 523 pupils (60% boys, 60% boarders) ★ 210 in sixth form ★ Fees: £13,305 boarding; £9,480 day
Head: John Arkell, 58, appointed 1991.
Attractive school; good all round; first-rate music and sport.

Profile
Background   Founded 1555 by Sir John Gresham, local merchant and landowner; supported by the Fishmongers' Company. Moved 1900 to present, well-maintained, 50-acre site (plus 90 acres of woodland) three miles from the sea. Mostly 20th-century buildings (fine chapel); recent additions include design/technology centre, girls' boarding houses; £1.6 million theatre opens 1998. Lord Reith, Stephen Spender, W H Auden, Benjamin Britten were all pupils here.
Atmosphere   Friendly; warm relations between staff and pupils; tutor system ensures good pastoral care. Pleasant, spacious boarding accommodation in seven houses; juniors in small dormitories; seniors have single study-bedrooms. Most day pupils do homework in houses with boarders three evenings a week; lessons on Saturday mornings (full programme of games and activities in the afternoon).
Admissions   Entry to junior school by informal test, interview (more than 90% proceed to senior school); to senior school via Common Entrance or scholarship exams (wide range of awards, including five sponsored by the Fishmongers' Company). Most from professional backgrounds in East Anglia; about 60 from abroad, half expatriates.
The head   Warm, enthusiastic, experienced (his second headship). Read English at Cambridge; keen on sailing, old cars (drives to school in a 1931 Austin) and motor-bikes (recently took and passed his test). Grandfather of four.
The teaching   Generally formal in style; well-qualified staff of 51 (nearly 80% male), low annual turnover; particular strengths in maths, science (taught as three separate subjects) French, computing, technology. Pupils grouped by ability after first-year; extra help for those with dyslexia and other learning difficulties (two full-time special needs teachers); average class size 16. Wide choice of 24 subjects at GCSE (including Japanese) and A-level. Very strong music: first-rate choral tradition; orchestra, two jazz bands. Flourishing drama (open-air theatre in the woods). Exceptionally well-supported Duke of Edinburgh award scheme (40 currently going for gold); most join the combined cadet force.
Results   (1997) GCSE: 97% gained at least five grades A–C. A-level: 61% of entries graded A or B.
Destinations   About 95% proceed to university; Nottingham, Edinburgh, St Andrews the most popular (engineering, business studies the most popular courses); about seven a year to Oxbridge.
Sport   Very good reputation for team (rugby, cricket, hockey) and individual sports (particularly full and small-bore shooting). Wide range of recreational

activities on offer for non-athletes (including dinghy sailing). Facilities include sports centre, indoor pool, two floodlit, all-weather pitches.
Remarks Relatively small, rural school with lots to offer. Recommended.

GUILDFORD HIGH ♀
London Road, Guildford GU1 1SJ. Tel (01483) 561440

Synopsis
Independent ★ Girls ★ Day ★ Ages 11–18 (plus associated junior school) ★ 521 pupils ★ 131 in sixth form ★ Fees: £5,685
Head: Mrs Sue Singer, 55, appointed 1991.
Highly academic school; first-rate results; good music and sport.

Profile
Background Founded 1888; one of seven independent schools governed by the Church Schools Company (formed 1883 to create schools that would offer 'a good academic education based on Christian principles'). Red-brick, Victorian building plus later additions; school feels over-crowded.
Atmosphere Hard-working, formal, conformist. Strong Christian tradition. Decent behaviour and high standards expected; striving for excellence is fundamental to the school but overt competitiveness is discouraged. Big emphasis on concern for others, responsibility to the community (girls do lots of voluntary work). Parents supportive and involved.
Admissions Highly competitive; entry from age four by school's own tests and interview; over-subscribed at 11 by more than two to one. About 50% of parents are 'first-time buyers' of independent education.
The head Highly intelligent, strong personality, polished appearance. Came to the job by a slightly unorthodox route (finds this useful when talking to girls about careers): educated at St Mary's, Calne; abandoned her original plan to do medicine; married young and acquired a maths degree from the Open University while bringing up small children and running a playgroup; taught briefly in a comprehensive and then at St Paul's Girls', where she became head of maths. Teaches five periods a week, principally as a means of getting to know the girls. Much liked by her sixth-formers, who find her approachable and clued-up.
The teaching Thorough, mostly traditional in style. High academic standards across the curriculum; children well grounded, work well presented. Well-qualified, all-graduate, predominantly female staff of 42; some have been here a long time. Broad curriculum: science on offer as three separate subjects (extensive labs, excellent teaching); good languages (including German, Italian, Spanish, Russian). Wide choice of subjects at A-level; imaginative general studies course. Pupils grouped by ability in maths, French from second year; average class size 20. Strong musical tradition (both singing and instrumental); drama less developed. Excellent careers provision, including work experience. Regular French and German language exchanges.
Results (1997) GCSE: all gained at least five grades A–C. A-level: creditable 73% of entries graded A or B.
Destinations About 80% continue into the sixth form; of these, virtually all proceed to university (average of seven a year to Oxbridge).
Sport Strong sporting tradition. Lacrosse played to high standard, some girls reaching county level; also netball, swimming, tennis, rounders, athletics. Facilities include four acres of games fields, heated indoor pool, six tennis courts, good gym.

Remarks Very good school, run on traditional lines; highly recommended for able girls.

GUILDFORD ROYAL GRAMMAR ♂
High Street, Guildford, Surrey GU1 3BB. Tel (01483) 502424

Synopsis
Independent ★ Boys ★ Day ★ Ages 11–18 (plus associated junior school) ★ 850 pupils ★ 270 in sixth form ★ Fees: £6,255
Head: Tim Young, 45, appointed 1992.
Distinguished academic school; excellent teaching and results; strong sport.

Profile
Background Founded 1509; received Royal Charter from Edward VI 1552 for the 'education, institution and instruction of boys and youths in grammar at all future times for ever to endure'; left the state sector 1977. Fine, purpose-built Tudor premises in the High Street (chained library now the head's study); main school across the road in well-equipped 1960s building; space is tight; playing fields two miles away.

Atmosphere Orderly, traditional, strongly academic; day begins with assembly and short act of Christian worship; respectful relations between staff and able, confident boys. Good pastoral care system (seniors act as mentors to juniors); bullying rare and viewed seriously; strict uniform (sixth form in suits).

Admissions Highly selective: top 10% of the ability range. 'No boy will be offered a place at RGS unless it is felt he will flourish,' says prospectus. Entry at 11 (from primary schools) by school's own tests in English, maths, verbal reasoning; at 13 by Common Entrance (about 50% join from Lanesborough, the school's own prep). Pupils drawn mostly from professional/middle-class homes (20% of mothers are teachers) in a catchment area that extends to Reading, Redhill, Petersfield; phasing out of assisted places, which 100 hold, will further reduce the social mix.

The head Very able; strong leader (his influence felt throughout the school); teaches Latin and history to the younger boys (helps get to know them). Read history at Cambridge; taught in California, New Zealand; previously a housemaster at Eton. Married (to a consultant radiologist); two young children.

The teaching First-rate (classes buzz with purposeful activity). Well-qualified staff of 80 (75% male). Broad curriculum: all do Latin and, from third year, German; Greek on offer; science taught as three separate subjects. Pupils grouped by ability for GCSE maths, French; average class size 20–25, 10–12 at A-level. All do at least nine GCSEs and three A-levels from a choice of 21 ('more or less any combination is possible'); general studies in conjunction with girls at Guildford High and Tormead (qv). Very good music: 300 learn an instrument; choir, orchestra, various ensembles. Extra-curricular activities include Scouts, cadet force, Duke of Edinburgh award scheme.

Results (1997) GCSE: 99% gained at least five grades A–C. A-level: creditable 75% of entries graded A or B.

Destinations Virtually all go on to university (about 25% to Oxbridge).

Sport Strong. Main games: rugby, hockey, cricket. Tennis, swimming, cross-country, squash, basketball, badminton, shooting also available. Twenty acres of playing fields but no sports hall.

Remarks HMC inspectors (1996) commended the school for the 'outstanding academic achievements of its pupils, the commitment and expertise of the teaching staff, the impressive leadership of the head and the excellent quality of pastoral care'. Fine school school for able boys: highly recommended.

HABERDASHERS' ASKE'S BOYS' ♂
Butterfly Lane, Elstree, Borehamwood, Hertfordshire WD6 3AF. Tel (0181) 207 4323

Synopsis
Independent ★ Boys ★ Day ★ Ages 11–18 (plus associated prep school) ★ 1,120 pupils ★ 300 in sixth form ★ Fees: £6,378
Head: Jeremy Goulding, 47, appointed 1996.
Impressive, highly selective school; very good teaching and results; fine facilities.

Profile
Background Founded in Hoxton in 1690 from an estate left in trust to the Haberdashers' Company by Robert Aske; moved to Hampstead in 1898 and to its present 100-acre campus, shared with Haberdashers' Aske's Girls' (qv), in 1961. Purpose-built 1960s premises (showing their age) plus many later additions, including good sports centre, music block, new classroom complex.

Atmosphere Cheerful, competitive and extremely busy ('You need a certain robustness of character'); big emphasis on self-discipline, mutual tolerance. Pupils outgoing, resilient, alert, determined to make the most of their opportunities; rich North London ethnic and religious mix – faiths flourish in profusion (separate weekly assemblies for Christians, Hindus, Jews, Muslims, Sikhs and 'non-aligned'). Prefects in gowns; 'business-like' dress in the sixth form.

Admissions At seven, 11 and 13 by competitive exams, including written and oral tests of intelligence, literacy and numeracy. School heavily over-subscribed (450 apply for 100 places at 11) and likely to remain so even after the phasing out of assisted places, which 240 hold (bursaries will be increased to compensate). Coach service (£250 a term, 84 pick-up points) extends from Harpenden to St John's Wood.

The head Able, quietly spoken. Read classics, philosophy and theology at Oxford; housemaster at Shrewsbury; previously head for seven years (appointed at 38) of Prior Park, Bath. Keen musician (piano, cello) and fell-walker. Married (to a teacher); four children.

The teaching First-rate: hard-working, professional staff of 98 (21 women); wide range of expertise; low turn-over. Broad curriculum: science taught (and examined) as three separate subjects; all add a second language to French (from German, Spanish, Latin); art, computing (run by a woman of missionary zeal), design/technology all compulsory for at least three years (all take one GCSE in a creative or technical subject a year early). At A-level, boys are invited to select their own combination of subjects rather than being required to accept one of a set of compulsory groupings; science and arts attract the brightest in equal numbers; all do non-examined general studies. Pupils grouped by ability in maths, science, modern languages from third year; average class size 25, reducing to 20 for GCSE, 10–12 at A-level. First-rate drama, music (half learn an instrument, orchestras, 250–strong choir). Wide range of extra-curricular activities; cadet force and community service taken seriously.

Results (1997) GCSE: all gained at least five grades A–C. A-level: stunning 90% of entries graded A or B (top of the league table).

Destinations Almost all proceed to university (average of 40 a year to Oxbridge).

Sport Important to a lot of boys; keen inter-school rugby, hockey and cricket

in particular, plus many others, including water polo. Facilities include indoor cricket school, squash courts, indoor pool, athletics track, all-weather pitch etc.
Remarks Cosmopolitan school preparing the brightest boys in North London for successful careers – and doing it superbly well.

HABERDASHERS' ASKE'S GIRLS' ♀
Aldenham Road, Elstree, Hertfordshire WD6 3BT. Tel (0181) 953 4261

Synopsis
Independent ★ Girls ★ Day ★ Ages 11–18 (plus associated junior school) ★ 833 pupils ★ 240 in sixth form ★ Fees: £4,674
Head: Mrs Penelope Penney, 54, appointed 1991.
Well-run, highly academic school; very good teaching and results; lots of extra-curricular activities.

Profile
Background Founded in West London 1901, part of the ancient foundation of Robert Aske, haberdasher; moved 1974 to present 56-acre green-belt site. Linked (by the 'Passion Gates') to Haberdashers' Aske's Boys' (qv) next door (with which it shares a governing body). Accommodation strained by rising numbers; some areas looking drab and rather crowded; latest additions include technology complex, splendid new art/music centre.
Atmosphere Friendly, sensible, minimum of fuss or trouble – everyone is here from choice and knows the school's academic aims; girls observe the rules because they are keen to get things right (motto, Serve and Obey). Compulsory Christian assemblies (but careful of the sensibilities of the substantial minority of pupils who are Jewish).
Admissions Heavily over-subscribed and highly selective: hundreds apply at 11 for 60 places (another 60 are allocated to the junior school). Entry to junior school by play-group activity and interview, at 11 by tests in English, maths, verbal reasoning. Able girls obviously stand a better chance but head emphasises she is choosing a 'family' and wants a good mix, including a few eccentrics. Phasing out of assisted places, which more than 100 hold, will not have a great effect. Pupils drawn from an extensive, mainly North London, catchment area (elaborate coach service).
The head Able, energetic, decisive; admired by staff and pupils. Read English at Bristol; her third headship. Staunch supporter of single-sex education for girls ('university is the right time for co-education'). Married (to a clergyman); two grown-up children.
The teaching First-rate: generally formal in style, conducted at a brisk pace; well-qualified, predominantly female staff. Particularly good results in maths and science (on offer as three separate subjects); all do two modern languages plus three years' Latin. Individual work graded but no class rankings at any stage. Strong music (most learn an instrument), art, drama. Girls shine in inter-school debating and quizzes. (Last bus leaves school at 5.30 pm so everyone can join in the extra-curricular activities.) Regular language exchanges (in conjunction with boys' school) to France, Germany, Spain, Italy.
Results (1997) GCSE: all gained at least five grades A–C. A-level: impressive 87% of entries graded A or B (sixth in the league table).
Destinations All but a handful stay on in the sixth form; of these, 99% proceed to university (about 30 a year to Oxbridge).

Sport   All do something up to the sixth form. Lacrosse the great success (girls play for junior England team). Also: netball, gym, swimming (indoor pool), fencing, tennis (floodlit courts).
Remarks   Fine school for able girls; recommended.

HABERDASHERS' ASKE'S, HATCHAM   ♂ ♀
Pepys Road, New Cross, London SE14. Tel (0171) 652 9500

Synopsis
Comprehensive (City Technology College) ★ Co-educational (but girls and boys on separate sites from 11 to 16) ★ Ages 11–18 ★ 1,230 pupils (equal numbers of girls and boys) ★ 280 in sixth form
Head: Dr Elizabeth Sidwell, 47, appointed 1994.
Successful, heavily over-subscribed comprehensive; first-rate facilities; strong emphasis on maths, science, technology.

Profile
Background   One of the mixed (state and independent) family of Haberdashers' Aske's schools; founded 1875 as two single-sex schools; went comprehensive 1979; merged (with a huge injection of cash) as a City Technology College 1991. Attractive Victorian-Gothic buildings plus modern extensions on two sites an inconvenient half mile apart (bus shuttles between them).
Atmosphere   Orderly, traditional (formal speech days, strict uniform below the sixth form). Slightly embattled sense of security (buildings close to a busy main road); pupils have swipe cards. Busy programme of compulsory 'enrichment' activities, including sport, music, drama, computing (breakfast served from 7.45 am, school day ends at 4.30 pm).
Admissions   School severely over-subscribed (up to seven apply for each place); all applicants interviewed and take a non-verbal reasoning test to ensure that the intake is 'representative of the full range of ability'; parents asked to confirm support for the school's aims, 'in particular its promotion of full-time education to the age of 18'. Pupils drawn from more than 80 primaries across south-east London; high proportion are black or Asian.
The head   Brisk, calm, very competent. Read geography at LSE (PhD); previously deputy head of Forest (qv). Came here as head of the girls' school in 1991. Divorced; two grown-up children.
The teaching   Good: generally formal in style; fairly long-serving staff. Half the curriculum devoted to maths, science, technology (impressive facilities); all become computer literate ('The aim is to teach skills and life-time learning habits fit for the 21st century'); arts and humanities not neglected. Pupils grouped by ability in maths, science, technology, languages from age 13; average class size 23, reducing to 18 in (co-educational) sixth form. Lots of music; 60% learn an instrument. Close links with commerce and industry.
Results   (1997) GCSE: 59% gained at least five grades A–C. A-level: 25% of entries graded A or B.
Destinations   About 85% go on to higher education (average of two a year to Oxbridge).
Sport   Emphasis on rugby and cricket for the boys, tennis and netball for the girls. Small gyms on both sites; games field 10 minutes' walk from boys' site.
Remarks   Good all round.

HABERDASHERS', MONMOUTH ♀
Hereford Road, Monmouth, Gwent NP5 3XT. Tel (01600) 714214

Synopsis
Independent ★ Girls ★ Day and boarding ★ Ages 11–18 (plus associated junior school) ★ 543 pupils (81% day) ★ 153 in sixth form ★ Fees: £5,235 day; £9,192–£9,546 boarding
Head: Dr Brenda Despontin, 46, appointed September 1997.
Successful academic school; very good teaching and results; strong art, drama, music, sport.

Profile
Background Founded 1892 by the admirable Haberdashers' Company as a sister school to Monmouth (qv); moved to present 25-acre site and imposing purpose-built premises 1897; formerly Direct Grant, reverted to full independence 1976. New £2 million science block, on-site junior school; older buildings being refurbished.
Atmosphere Secure, purposeful, orderly; easy relations between staff and pupils; good pastoral care. Traditional uniform (candy-striped frocks, white socks).
Admissions By tests; school is quite selective; broad social mix from an extensive catchment area; Haberdashers' Company is replacing assisted places, which 79 hold, with a scheme of its own. 'Flexible' boarding: juniors in roomy dormitories; sixth-formers have double or single study-bedrooms. Scholarships (academic, music) and bursaries available.
The head New appointment. Read psychology at Cardiff (PhD); previously in charge of the girls' division at King's, Macclesfield. Married; one son.
The teaching Good quality; formal in style; well-qualified, experienced staff have high expectations. Broad curriculum: strong science (on offer as three separate subjects); all do German and French; Latin available; lots of computing; choice of 27 subjects at A-level (some in conjunction with boys' school); GNVQ in business studies popular. Average class size 25, reducing to maximum of 14 in sixth form. Strong art, drama, music; three orchestras, two choirs. Good careers guidance. Extra-curricular activities include Duke of Edinburgh award scheme.
Results (1997) GCSE: all gained at least five grades A–C. A-level: creditable 70% of entries graded A or B (results have steadily improved).
Destinations Nearly all go on to university (average of 10 a year to Oxbridge).
Sport Lots on offer. Good record in lacrosse, netball swimming, tennis, athletics, rowing. Facilities include ample playing fields, sports hall, indoor pool.
Remarks Very good all round; recommended.

HAILEYBURY ♂
Hertford, Hertfordshire SG13 7NU. Tel (01992) 462352

Synopsis
Independent ★ Boys (plus girls in sixth form, fully co-educational from September 1998) ★ Ages: 11–18 day; 13–18 boarding ★ 605 pupils (70% boarding) ★ 303 in sixth form (72% boys) ★ Fees: £13,980 boarding; £6,660–£10,140 day
Head: Stuart Westley, 50, appointed 1996.
Traditional boarding school; good teaching and results; first-rate facilities; lots of music, drama, sport.

Profile

Background Opened 1862 in the grand, neo-classical premises built 50 years earlier to house the East India Company's training college (quadrangle is the largest in Britain); spectacular Byzantine-domed chapel added 1877 (promptly burnt down and had to be re-built); merged 1942 with the Imperial Service College; sixth-form girls admitted 1973. First-rate facilities (more planned) on a 500-acre campus. School going co-educational in the belief that 'the uncertain years of adolescence are a time when girls and boys most need to be educated together to learn an understanding of each other as people'.

Atmosphere Cheerfully purposeful; organised but not regimented; courteous relations between staff and pupils; regular Anglican worship. Day pupils stay until 6.30 pm or later.

Admissions At 11 (from primary schools) by tests; at 13 (from prep schools) by Common Entrance; school is not unduly selective (top 35% of the ability range); girls entering the sixth form require at least six GCSEs at grades A to C, with at least a B in intended A-level subjects; admission of girls at 11 and 13 should compensate for the phasing out of assisted places, which about 40 hold; 10% non-British nationals. Boys' boarding accommodation refurbished (some consisting of vast dormitories divided by chest-high partitions); girls more luxuriously housed. Scholarships (academic, art, music, all-rounder) available.

The head (Master) Read law at Oxford; played professional cricket; previously deputy head of Bristol Cathedral School, head for 10 years of King William's, Isle of Man. Teaches maths to first-years, general studies to the sixth form. Married; one daughter.

The teaching Good quality; well-qualified staff of 69 (12 women). Standard national curriculum; sciences taught (but not examined) separately; all do French and may add German or Spanish; Latin, Greek on offer; choice of 22 subjects at A-level; all do general studies. Pupils grouped by ability in maths, science, languages; some take GCSEs a year early; three-weekly progress reports; average class size 22, reducing to 12 in the sixth form. Lots of drama (two theatres) and music; choirs, two large orchestras, various ensembles. Extra-curricular activities include cadet force, Duke of Edinburgh award scheme (both popular), community service (given a high priority). Regular language exchanges with pupils in France, Germany, Spain.

Results (1997) GCSE: 99% gained at least five grades A–C. A-level: 55% of entries graded A or B.

Destinations Nearly all go on to university (average of six a year to Oxbridge).

Sport Wide range on offer. Main sports: rugby, soccer, hockey (girls' and boys'), cricket, lacrosse, tennis. First-rate facilities include extensive playing fields, all-wether pitch, sports hall, indoor pool, two shooting ranges, courts for tennis, squash, fives, rackets.

Remarks Good school for all-rounders.

HAMPTON ♂

Hanworth Road, Hampton, Middlesex TW12 3HD. Tel (0181) 979 5526

Synopsis

Independent ★ Boys ★ Day ★ Ages 11–18 ★ 927 pupils ★ 277 in sixth form ★ Fees: £5,760

Head: Barry Martin, 47, appointed April 1997.

Well-run academic school; good teaching and results; lots on offer.

Profile

Background   Founded 1612; joined the state sector 1910; reverted to independence 1975. Plain 1930s buildings plus many later additions on a 27-acre site; good facilities.

Atmosphere   Academic but very relaxed; friendly relations between staff and pupils; 'a traditional academic education within a tolerant but ordered community'.

Admissions   At 11 by school's own tests in English, maths, verbal reasoning (280 try for 100 places); at 13 by Common Entrance (160 try for 50 places), 65% mark required; top 20% of the ability range but school is likely to become less selective with the phasing out of assisted places, which 175 hold. Extensive South and West London catchment area. Scholarships: academic, music.

The head   Able, experienced; friendly, outgoing personality. Read economics at Cambridge (hockey Blue); worked for the Bank of England; took an MBA at Loughborough in his spare time; previously head, for five successful years, of Liverpool (qv). Married; two children.

The teaching   Good quality; traditional in style; staff of 82 (25% female). Broad curriculum: science taught (and examined) as three separate subjects; all do Latin for first two years; modern languages include German, Russian, Spanish; more able take GCSE maths, French a year early; most take four A-levels (including general studies) and one AS (head cares more about breadth than league tables). Pupils grouped by ability in maths, science, French; extra help for dyslexics; progress closely monitored (half-termly grades for effort); average class size 25, reducing to 12 in sixth form. Lots of drama and music (some in conjunction with girls at neighbouring Lady Eleanor Holles, qv); 200 learn an instrument; choir, three orchestras. Extra-curricular activities include cadet force, Duke of Edinburgh award scheme. Regular language exchanges with pupils in Germany, France, Spain.

Results   (1997) GCSE: all gained at least five grades A–C. A-level: 59% of entries graded A or B.

Destinations   Nearly all go on to university (average of 10 a year to Oxbridge).

Sport   Lots on offer. Main sports rugby, tennis, cricket, athletics; soccer and rowing are particularly strong. Facilities include extensive playing fields, large sports hall.

Remarks   Attractive school; good all round.

HARROGATE GRAMMAR ♂ ♀

Arthur's Avenue, Harrogate, North Yorkshire HG2 0DZ. Tel (01423) 531127

Synopsis

Comprehensive ★ Co-educational ★ Ages 11–18 ★ 1,620 pupils (51% girls) ★ 400 in sixth form
Head: Kevin McAleese, 50, appointed 1992.
First-rate, well-run school; very good teaching and results.

Profile

Background   Founded as a grammar school 1903; moved to present, purpose-built, three-storey premises on the outskirts of the town 1933; went comprehensive 1973. Later additions include fine sixth-form centre; some classrooms in 'temporary' huts, others need modernising. Space at a premium; play areas far too small.

Atmosphere   Confident, hard-working, well-ordered (needs to be to accommodate so many on such a small site); pupils expect, and are expected, to succeed. Big emphasis on service to the community. Supportive parents raise £15,000 a year.

Admissions Heavily over-subscribed; local education authority gives priority to siblings, children from named local villages, those living nearest. Most are from middle-class backgrounds and of above-average ability. About 40 join the sixth form from other schools (with at least GCSEs grade B in their chosen A-level subjects).

The head Very able. Powerful, energetic leader; prefers 'wandering about the school' to sitting in his study; has a high regard for the traditional virtues. Left school at 16 to go to sea (and claims to be the only head qualified as an ocean-going navigator). Took degrees as a mature student at Keele and Kent; previously head of a comprehensive in Essex. Married (to a teacher); two grown-up children.

The teaching Good, largely traditional in style: long-serving, well-qualified staff of 112 (equal numbers of women and men); biddable children. Fairly broad curriculum: top 40% take science as three separate subjects; about 35% do French and German; more able take GCSE maths, French a year early. Pupils grouped by ability in most subjects; extra help for the least and most able; average class size 25, reducing to a maximum of 15 in sixth form. Most take four A-levels, including general studies; GNVQ in business studies increasingly popular. Good music (three choirs, three orchestras). Regular trips abroad for study and recreation.

Results (1997) GCSE: creditable 79% gained at least five grades A–C. A-level: 38% of entries graded A or B.

Destinations About 70% stay on for A-levels; nearly all proceed to university (up to 12 a year to Oxbridge).

Sport Lots on offer; large numbers participate. Main games: hockey (for girls and boys), rugby, netball, athletics, tennis, cricket, rounders. Golf, squash, orienteering also popular. Facilities include good sports hall, on-site playing fields.

Remarks Identified by Ofsted (1995) as an 'outstandingly successful' school.

HARROGATE LADIES' ♀
Clarence Drive, Harrogate, North Yorkshire HG1 2QG. Tel (01423) 504543

Synopsis
Independent ★ Girls ★ Boarding and day ★ Ages 10–18 ★ 350 pupils (58% boarding) ★ 100 in sixth form ★ Fees: £10,170 boarding; £6,570 day
Head: Dr Margaret Hustler, 47, appointed 1996.
Sound, academic school; good teaching and results; strong music, sport.

Profile
Background Founded 1893; purpose-built mock-Tudor premises in spacious grounds; later additions include music school, fine sixth-form centre.

Atmosphere Cheerful, cosy; friendly relations between staff and pupils; discipline unobtrusive. Lessons on Saturday mornings; compulsory chapel ('religious teaching is in accordance with the principles of the Church of England'). Sixth-formers play a big role in the running of the school and the houses. Neat uniform; upper sixth allowed smart casual wear.

Admissions By school's own tests; not unduly selective (numbers declined but are now picking up again). Boarders include daughters of Service, diplomatic, business families; some from Hong Kong, Russia. Pleasant, attractively furnished accommodation in spacious Victorian houses around the school's perimeter; gracious dining hall (and healthy menus). Academic, music scholarships available.

The head Professional; easy, informal manner. Read chemistry and bio-chemistry at London; worked for Unilever before entering teaching; her second headship. Gets on well with staff and girls. Married; eight children (three are pupils here).

The teaching Good quality, traditional in style; dedicated, enthusiastic staff of 40 (four men). Fairly broad curriculum; all do two languages (from French, Spanish, German); strong maths, science; lots of computing; choice of 20 subjects at A-level; GNVQ in business studies available. Pupils grouped by ability in maths and French; extra help for dyslexics and those for whom English is a second language; average class size 18–20, reducing to six or eight in the sixth form. Very good music; two-thirds learn at least one instrument; various ensembles, first-rate choir. Extra-curricular activities include Duke of Edinburgh award scheme; school has its own amateur radio station.

Results (1997) GCSE: 91% gained at least five grades A–C. A-level: 58% of entries graded A or B.

Destinations About 85% stay on for A-levels; of these, nearly all proceed to university.

Sport Strong lacrosse, athletics. Netball, riding, synchronised swimming also available. Facilities include vast sports hall, indoor pool, courts for squash and tennis.

Remarks Attractive school.

HARROW ♂
Harrow-on-the-Hill, Middlesex HA1 3HW. Tel (0181) 869 1200

Synopsis
Independent ★ Boys ★ Boarding ★ Ages 13–18 ★ 775 pupils ★ 318 in sixth form ★ Fees: £14,295
Head: Nick Bomford, 58, appointed 1991.
Socially exclusive, traditional school; good teaching and results; superb facilities; lots of art, drama, music; strong sport.

Profile
Background Founded 1572 by John Lyon, yeoman farmer. Listed Victorian buildings plus tasteful later additions surrounded by 300 acres of fields (including a farm); fine chapel; 800-seat Speech Room for concerts, Shakespeare, Harrow Songs. Modern de-luxe facilities include £3 million Ryan theatre, sumptuous design/technology centre. Old boys include Winston Churchill and six other prime ministers.

Atmosphere Exudes tradition (boys doff boaters to be-gowned 'beaks') and privilege but has a modern, friendly feel; good pastoral care (involving housemasters, tutors, matrons); strong house system.

Admissions By Common Entrance; 50% mark required (school is not unduly selective). About 25% are the sons of former pupils; 110 live abroad. Eleven boarding houses, all refurbished; boys have shared study-bedrooms for first two years, singles thereafter. Up to 20 scholarships a year (academic, music, art).

The head Able, experienced, low-key (a consolidator). Read history at Oxford; previously head of Monmouth (1976–82), Uppingham (1982–91). Married (wife much involved in school life); two daughters.

The teaching Good: mix of formal and informal methods; well-qualified, predominantly male staff (25% appointed by present head). Broad curriculum: sciences taught separately; all do Latin for at least one year; Greek, German,

Spanish on offer; lots of computing; choice of 25 subjects at A-level. Boys grouped by ability from the start; limited help for dyslexics (not included in the fees); average class size 20. Good art, drama, music (300 individual lessons a week); first-rate careers advice. Vast range of extra-curricular activities, including flourishing cadet force, Duke of Edinburgh award scheme.

Results (1997) GCSE: 99% gained at least five grades A–C. A-level: 67% of entries graded A or B (school has slipped steadily down the league table from 34th in 1993 to 79th).

Destinations Nearly all go on to university (up to 25 a year to Oxbridge); many join the Army.

Sport Everything on offer; particular strengths in cricket, rugby, rackets, fives, golf. Fine facilities include extensive playing fields, sports hall, indoor pool, nine-hole golf course, athletics track, cross-country course, indoor cricket school, courts for tennis, fives, squash, rackets.

Remarks Good all round.

HARRYTOWN RC HIGH ♂ ♀

Harrytown, Romiley, Stockport SK6 3BU. Tel (0161) 430 5277

Synopsis

Comprehensive (voluntary-aided, Roman Catholic) ★ Co-educational ★ Ages 11–16 ★ 700 pupils (equal numbers of girls and boys)
Head: Ged Roper, 50, appointed 1986.
An academically sound school in which the practice of the Roman Catholic faith is fundamental.

Profile

Background Founded as a girls' school by Catholic nuns 1913; went co-educational 1977 to provide both sexes with an education imbued with the values of Roman Catholicism. Buildings of various ages recently enhanced and refurbished at a cost of £1.6 million; pleasant, wooded grounds.

Atmosphere Entrance hall plastered with bright paintings, colourful pottery monsters and the names of those who have done especially good work, helped teachers or performed acts of charity ('They used to blush, now they like to gather around to see their names'). Commitment to Catholicism visible everywhere: crucifixes in every classroom, posters proclaiming the Christian message on every notice board; pupils expected to 'live the gospel' in their daily lives (and spend some time each year on retreat); half the staff are Catholic. Clear code of discipline; strong anti-bullying policy (any unkind action or comment – even if not intended to hurt – is regarded as bullying); uniform strictly enforced.

Admissions Non-selective; places allocated by Stockport council. Pupils' home backgrounds vary widely; 93% Catholic.

The head Deeply committed Catholic who believes Christian values should be apparent in the whole curriculum ('We are totally committed to academic achievement for all our pupils and constantly affirm that our Christianity requires us to use our gifts fully and creatively for our own fulfilment and to enable us to serve family and community'). Read classics at Manchester (teaches Latin up to GCSE outside the timetable); worked at two other Catholic schools. Married; three children.

The teaching Quality varies from the inspired to the competent; results suggest no particular strengths or weaknesses. Standard national curriculum; all take 10 GCSEs, including compulsory religious education; excellent satellite and computer facilities (underground optic-fibre network). Pupils grouped by ability from third year in English, maths, science, languages (French or German); extra help both for those with learning difficulties and the more able; average class size 26. Regular homework; parents sign weekly diaries. Music revived by new facilities; school band, choir. Good careers advice and work experience.

Results   (1997) GCSE: 58% gained at least five grades A–C.

Destinations   About 80% remain in full-time education after 16.

Sport   Main games catered for, including basketball, five-a-side football, indoor tennis, badminton, volleyball and cricket. Facilities include new sports hall (complete with sprung, maple floor).

Remarks   Ofsted inspectors concluded (1996): 'This is a good, successful and caring school which seeks to provide education of a high quality for all pupils.'

HARTFORD HIGH ♂ ♀
Chester Road, Northwich, Cheshire CW8 1LH. Tel (01606) 79233

Synopsis
Comprehensive ★ Co-educational ★ Ages 11–16 ★ 1,170 pupils (roughly equal numbers of girls and boys)
Head: Dr Peter Llewellyn, 54, appointed 1989.
First-rate, well-run comprehensive; good teaching and GCSE results.

Profile
Background   Result of a 1978 amalgamation of two single-sex secondary moderns built in the 1950s on same site 300 yards apart; first and second-years housed in former girls' school. Adequate, attractively decorated buildings but some classrooms rather cramped, others in 'temporary' huts; new science lab needed. School shares pleasant 123-acre site with other schools and a further education college.

Atmosphere   Orderly, civilised (code of behaviour 'negotiated' with pupils). Hardworking staff; co-operative, smartly-uniformed pupils; supportive parents. School takes a very strong line against bullying. Teachers send their own children here.

Admissions   School is full but not over-subscribed. Most from middle-class homes (30% from outside the official catchment area); ability range weighted towards the upper end.

The head   Open, welcoming; sets high standards and is very success-oriented. Left grammar school to work as a junior chemist, studied part time for chemistry diploma then full time at Salford; PhD in photo-chemistry. Trained as a teacher; became head of science; formerly head of a comprehensive in Chester. Plays the piano, builds computers. Married; three children.

The teaching   Styles cover the whole gamut of approaches; emphasis on fitting the system to the child rather than the reverse. Long-serving, committed staff of 60 (slightly more women than men) constantly striving to improve results (which are well above average). Broad, well-balanced curriculum; choice of 25 subjects at GCSE; science taught by specialists; plenty of computing; good art. Pupils grouped by ability in maths, science, modern languages (French, German, Spanish, Italian); more able take GCSE French a year early; lots of help for those with special needs (achievement in literacy and numeracy regarded as an absolute priority); average class size 24. Merit certificates for good behaviour, effort, achievement. Good music: 80 learn an instrument. Varied extra-curricular programme. Regular trips abroad.

Results   (1997) GCSE: 55% gained at least five grades A–C.
Destinations   About 70% proceed to some form of further education.
Sport   Good reputation. Main games: soccer, rugby, hockey, basketball. Dance, trampolining, table tennis, rounders also on offer. Facilities include extensive playing fields, running track, all-weather hockey pitch but no sports hall or swimming pool.
Remarks   Ofsted inspectors concluded (1996): 'Hartford High School is a good school with many outstanding features. The quality of teaching is frequently good and sometimes very good.'

HASMONEAN HIGH   ♂ ♀
(boys' section) Holders Hill Road, London NW4 1NA. Tel (0181) 203 1411
(girls' section) 2–4 Page Street, London NW7 2EU. Tel (0181) 203 4294

Synopsis
Comprehensive (grant-maintained) ★ Jewish ★ Co-educational (but girls and boys taught on separate sites) ★ Ages 11–18 ★ 952 pupils (slightly more boys than girls) ★ 200 in sixth form
Head: Dr Dena Coleman, 45, appointed 1993.
First-rate, traditional school for Orthodox Jewish children; very good teaching and results; strong religious and community ethos.

Profile
Background   Founded 1944 as two single-sex schools for refugee children from Nazi Germany; amalgamated 1984 on two sites one and a half miles apart; opted out of council control 1994. Boys' school in large Victorian villa plus various later additions on a small suburban site in Hendon (£4 million spent recently on re-building and refurbishment); girls in purpose-built, functional 1970s premises (some classrooms in shabby huts) on a four-acre site in leafy Mill Hill (refurbishment under way). Half the staff teach at both schools.
Atmosphere   Warm, friendly, supportive (an exceptionally close community); strong discipline; first-rate pastoral care; good rapport between staff and self-assured, articulate pupils. Orthodox Jewish faith absolutely fundamental: daily religious ceremonies; a quarter of the staff are Rabbis. Traditional uniform until the sixth form, then respectable dress; no jewellery, no 'cult' hairstyles; rules 'strictly enforced'. School raises £20,000 a year for charity. Parents asked to contribute to the cost of religious education.
Admissions   School heavily over-subscribed but no academic selection; priority to siblings; about four apply for each remaining place. Entry by interview (chiefly to check candidates' credentials as fully practising Orthodox Jews); most pupils from middle-class homes (where education is a priority) within a five-mile radius.
The head   Serene, elegant, highly intelligent; clearly loves her job and is much liked. Read botany and zoology at Manchester; PhD (in Victorian science education) from King's, London; was head of science at Queenswood (qv); came here as deputy head in charge of the girls' school. Married; grown-up children.
The teaching   Good across the board, mostly traditional in style; committed, long-serving staff (not all Jewish). Jewish studies (mostly taught by Rabbis) takes up 25% of the curriculum; science on offer as three separate subjects; good languages (French, German, Modern Hebrew); GNVQ in business studies available

as an alternative to A-levels. Pupils grouped by ability in maths, science, languages, RE; average class size 17. Lively music. Extra-curricular activities include flourishing Duke of Edinburgh award scheme.

Results (1997) GCSE: very creditable 78% gained at least five grades A–C. A-level: 50% of entries graded A or B.

Destinations Nearly all continue into the sixth form and proceed to university (usually after a gap year in Israel).

Sport Not a particular strength; limited on-site facilities at boys' site, better at girls'.

Remarks Ofsted inspectors concluded (1994): 'The school provides a demanding and rigorous education for its pupils.' Recommended.

HAYBRIDGE HIGH ♂ ♀

Brake Lane, Hagley, Stourbridge, West Midlands DY8 2XS. Tel (01562) 886213

Synopsis

Comprehensive ★ Co-educational ★ Ages 13–18 ★ 693 pupils (roughly equal numbers of girls and boys) ★ 237 in sixth form
Head: Dr Melvyn Kershaw, 50, appointed 1988.
Well-run school; good teaching and results.

Profile

Background Opened 1976; functional, crowded, single-storey buildings on a pleasant 20-acre campus on the edge of town; recent, much-needed additions include new science labs, technology suite, language block and £1.3 million sports complex.

Atmosphere Purposeful, secure, caring; strong pastoral care system; good relations between staff and pupils. High expectations (GCSE and A-level results prominently displayed, as are examples of pupils' work) but no feeling of pressure.

Admissions No selection; applications to local education authority; priority to siblings and those living nearest. Most pupils from middle-class/professional families.

The head Able, respected; knows and gets on well with everyone. Read chemistry at London; PhD from Manchester; previously deputy head at a local sixth-form college. Married; two grown-up daughters.

The teaching Good: wide variety of styles; enthusiastic, committed staff of 44, 70% appointed by present head. Pupils grouped by ability into two bands from the start; further setting in most subjects for GCSE; class sizes 20–30 (smaller for less able pupils). Standard national curriculum; A-level options include accountancy, sociology, Spanish; GNVQs also on offer. High standards of music (orchestral trips to Europe) and drama; annual arts festival. Good careers guidance and work experience (links with local industry and commerce). Language exchanges with pupils in France, Germany.

Results (1997) GCSE: creditable 80% gained at least five grades A–C. A-level: 44% of entries graded A or B.

Destinations About 85% continue into the sixth form; most proceed to university.

Sport All participate but optional for sixth form. Particular strengths: basketball, rugby, netball. New sports hall includes badminton and squash courts;

swimming at local leisure centre.
Remarks   Good school, inadequately accommodated.

HAYFIELD   ♂ ♀
Hurst Lane, Auckley, Doncaster DN9 3HG. Tel (01302) 770589

Synopsis
Comprehensive (grant-maintained) ★ Co-educational ★ Ages 11–18 ★ 1,160
pupils (equal numbers of girls and boys) ★ 200 in sixth form
Head: Tony Storey, OBE, 57, appointed 1971.
Successful, well-run school; good GCSE results; strong sport.

Profile
Background   Opened 1971 (under the present head) as a purpose-built comprehensive; opted out of council control 1995. Attractive, if isolated, green-field site; box-like architecture, flat roofs showing signs of age. Impressive technology facilities; good links with local employers.
Atmosphere   Friendly, relaxed, forward-looking; warm, open relationships between long-serving staff (25% have been in post since the school started) and pupils; few discipline problems. Strict uniform up to 16 ('We make no bones about this and it is not an issue for debate'). Remoteness of site contributes to high level of participation in lunch-time and after-school clubs (late buses provided). Racily-written, all-embracing prospectus. Parents supportive and involved.
Admissions   School is over-subscribed but non-selective: priority to those living in the catchment area and attending one of five 'feeder' primaries.
The head   Exceptionally long-serving. Affable, easy-going, idiosyncratic; has built the school from scratch and appointed all the staff ('You can't run a successful school by committee – it's not a biscuit factory'); awarded OBE for services to education in 1989. Strong communicator: keeps parents informed with frequent folksy newsletters. Divorced; two grown-up children.
The teaching   Sound; stable staff of 70 (rare for more than two to leave in same year). Standard national curriculum; good languages, creative arts; most take 10 GCSEs, including technology and a business-related course (local employers involved); GNVQ in business studies available as an alternative to A-levels. Pupils grouped by ability in maths, languages from second year, in science from third. Lots of music: 150 learn an instrument. Carefully-planned and monitored work-experience programmes for 15-year-olds; placements in France and Germany for some sixth-formers.
Results   (1997) GCSE: 60% gained at least five grades A–C. A-level: 26% of entries graded A or B.
Destinations   About 60% continue into sixth form; of these, about 65% proceed to higher education (average of three a year to Oxbridge).
Sport   Strong in rugby (large representation in South Yorkshire teams) and very strong in girls' basketball. Cricket benefits from head of PE's first-class playing experience, but suffers from lack of groundsman to tend pitches. Facilities include large gym, sports hall.
Remarks   Happy school; caters well for different abilities and aptitudes; highly regarded locally. Identified by Ofsted (1996) as 'outstandingly successful'.

HEADINGTON ♀
Headington, Oxford OX3 7TD. Tel (01865) 62711

Synopsis
Independent ★ Girls ★ Day and boarding ★ Ages 11–18 (plus associated junior school) ★ 517 pupils (65% day) ★ 160 in sixth form ★ Fees: £5,415 day; £10,438 boarding
Head: Mrs Hilary Fender, 56, appointed 1996.
Cosmopolitan school; good teaching and results.

Profile
Background   Founded 1915 as a school 'where girls could grow up in a Christian atmosphere' (faith remains firmly at its heart); moved 1920 to attractive, 22-acre site two miles from city centre. Main building dates from 1930; extensive additions blend in seamlessly. Junior school on same site.

Atmosphere   Lively (even boisterous); girls encouraged to formulate, express, argue for their opinions; good pastoral care; warm relations between staff and pupils.

Admissions   By Common Entrance and interview; school is fairly selective; phasing out of assisted places, which about 50 hold, will not have a great effect. Many pupils from abroad, particularly Malaysia, Hong Kong. Boarding accommodation (gradually being up-graded) ranges from small dormitories for juniors to single study-bedrooms for seniors.

The head   Friendly, accessible; gets on well with staff and pupils. Read history at Exeter and King's College London; formerly head for seven years of Godolphin (qv). Teaches history to 11-year-olds and some sixth-formers. Married; one son.

The teaching   Good. Interesting, well-prepared, orderly lessons; teachers have high expectations. Well-qualified staff of 65 (three men); some have been here more than 20 years. 'Careful attention' paid to national curriculum; three sciences taught separately (well-equipped labs); all do at least two years' Latin and one year's German or Spanish. GCSE options include home economics; GNVQ in business studies available as an alternative to A-levels; all do general studies. Pupils grouped by ability in maths, French; regular testing; lots of homework; class sizes vary widely from 30 to 10. Strong music; several orchestras, choirs. Popular Duke of Edinburgh award scheme.

Results   (1997) GCSE: all gained at least five grades A–C. A-level: creditable 74% of entries graded A or B (37th in the league table – its best performance ever).

Destinations   Two-thirds stay on for A-levels; of these, nearly all proceed to university.

Sport   Respectable match record but not a particularly sporty school. Main activities: hockey, netball, swimming, athletics, tennis, rowing, fencing. Facilities include new sports hall, indoor pool.

Remarks   Every girl challenged to make full use of her abilities.

HEATHFIELD ♀
London Road, Ascot, Berkshire SL5 8BQ. Tel (01344) 882955

Synopsis
Independent ★ Girls ★ Boarding ★ Ages 11–18 ★ 220 pupils ★ 57 in sixth form ★ Fees: £13,800
Head: Mrs Julia Benammar, 43, appointed 1992.
Small, graciously accommodated school; good teaching and results; first-rate facilities; lots of art, drama, music.

Profile
Background Founded 1880 by Eleanor Beatrice Wyatt, one of a formidable band of 19th-century pioneers of girls' education ('My girls come here not only to learn their lessons, but to learn how to live as well'). Moved to present site on the outskirts of Ascot 1899; gracious, white-painted Georgian house surrounded by well-tended lawns and lofty trees; later additions include first-rate science block, art studios, sixth-form centre, sports hall.

Atmosphere Cosy, friendly, extremely supportive ('The merit of one is the honour of all'); good manners de rigeur (badges awarded for 'bearing'); girls seem relaxed and happy. Strong Church of England tradition; regular worship in period-piece Victorian chapel. Very good pastoral care system (any difficulties picked up quickly). School has particular success with those who have not fitted into a less flexible mould. Independent inspectors detected (1994) 'a degree of insularity which isolates pupils in term time from the world outside the school's boundary walls' (which may be just what parents want).

Admissions Competitive (even though the school is all-boarding). Entry by Common Entrance and school's own assessment. Pleasant boarding accommodation ('the school is unashamedly comfortable'): juniors in cheerful, recently refurbished dormitories (up to eight beds); older girls have own bedrooms; sixth-formers live independently in custom-built bungalows. Some scholarships.

The head Strong, effective leader; well respected by staff and pupils. Grammar-school educated, has a First in modern languages from Leeds, MA from Lille; formerly a housemistress at Wellington.

The teaching Lively, traditional in style; emphasis on sound foundations – grammar, accuracy, presentation. Well-qualified, predominantly female staff. Broad curriculum: science taught as three separate subjects (well-equipped labs); all do Latin and French for at least three years, plus Spanish from second year; GCSE options include computer studies, law, almost any language (including Japanese); computing used across the curriculum. A-level choice includes economics, law, ceramics, business studies. Pupils grouped by ability in English, maths, science, French; regular grades for achievement and effort; remedial help where necessary; average class size 12–15. First-rate art (artist-in-residence) and drama; strong music tradition.

Results (1997) GCSE: 98% gained at least five grades A–C. A-level: very creditable 72% of entries graded A or B.

Destinations Most stay on for A-levels and proceed to university.

Sport Chiefly lacrosse, netball, rounders, tennis; other activities include badminton, basketball, volleyball, athletics, fencing, squash.

Remarks Happy, well-run school. Recommended.

HECKMONDWIKE ♂ ♀
High Street, Heckmondwike, West Yorkshire WF16 0AH. Tel (01924) 402202

Synopsis
Grammar (grant-maintained) ★ Co-educational ★ Ages 11–18 ★ 840 pupils (equal numbers of girls and boys) ★ 180 in sixth form
Head: Mark Tweedle, 42, appointed 1990.
First-rate, traditional grammar school; good teaching and GCSE results; lots of music; strong sport.

Profile
Background Founded 1898; a grammar school since 1944; opted out of council control 1989 (among the first to do so); achieved technology college status 1996. Splendidly confident Victorian building (fine central hall with hammer-beam roof and pipe organ) plus many later additions, including state-of-the-art technology suite and music rooms.

Atmosphere Hard-working, well-disciplined, civilised; everywhere gleaming, well-maintained; pupils' work widely and professionally displayed. Evident concern with timeless values (school's war dead formally remembered each year). Strong house system; strict blazer-and-tie uniform below the sixth form. Highly supportive parents.

Admissions School is heavily over-subscribed (500 apply for 150 places a year); entry by tests in maths, verbal, non-verbal reasoning (sample questions available); top 25% of the ability range. Pupils drawn from a wide range of social backgrounds; some come from as far as Leeds, Bradford, Huddersfield.

The head Very able. Courteous, quietly spoken; gets things done quickly and efficiently; has given the school a considerable fillip (numbers up 30% since he arrived). Read physics at Leeds; formerly deputy head of a grammar school in Kent. Chief examiner for A-level physics; conducts a brass band. Married; three children (all are, or have been, pupils here).

The teaching Good. Wide range of styles but predominantly formal; dedicated, well-qualified staff of 46 (equal numbers of men and women). Broad curriculum: science on offer as three separate subjects; languages include German, Spanish; good computing, technology; religious education taken seriously. Good presentation of work insisted on; rigorous homework policy. All take nine GCSEs and three A-levels plus general studies. Pupils grouped by ability in English, maths, French from second year, science from third year; maximum class size 30, smaller for GCSE, 15 or fewer at A-level. Lots of music: 200 learn an instrument (£60 a term); choirs, orchestras, ensembles. Extra-curricular activities range from canoeing to aerobics, chess to fell-walking; flourishing Duke of Edinburgh award scheme; much charity and community work. Regular field trips and foreign exchanges.

Results (1997) GCSE: 99% gained at least five grades A–C. A-level: 34% of entries graded A or B.

Destinations About 85% stay on for A-levels; of these, 80% proceed to university.

Sport Chiefly soccer, rugby league, cricket, hockey, netball, tennis, athletics. Facilities include extensive playing fields, all-weather pitch.

Remarks Identified by Ofsted (1995) as an 'outstandingly successful' school.

HELSBY HIGH ♂ ♀
Chester Road, Helsby, Warrington WA6 0HY. Tel (01928) 723551

Synopsis
Comprehensive ★ Co-educational ★ Ages 11–18 ★ 1,300 pupils (roughly equal numbers of girls and boys) ★ 210 in sixth form
Head: Mrs Elizabeth Lord, 53, appointed 1988.
Well-run, successful school; very good teaching and results; lots on offer.

Profile
Background   Result of a 1978 merger of two single-sex grammar schools (opened 1949) on a spacious, sloping site; solid, well-equipped buildings now becoming slightly cramped; some classes in 'temporary' huts.

Atmosphere   Busy, hard-working, well-ordered; aim is 'to encourage all pupils to develop lively, enquiring minds in preparation for adult life'. Strong sense of community; highly supportive parents.

Admissions   School over-subscribed by about 25%; no selection; priority to those living in the official catchment area (Helsby and surrounding villages), siblings, those attending a 'feeder' primary, and those living nearest; fairly wide range of abilities.

The head   Good leader; respected by staff, parents and pupils. Read French and Latin and at Nottingham and Strasbourg; previously a deputy head of another Warrington comprehensive. Married (to an Ofsted inspector); two grown-up daughters.

The teaching   Good quality; largely traditional in style; enthusiastic, well-qualified staff. Fairly broad curriculum; science on offer as three separate subjects; more able add German to French from third year; lots of computing. Pupils grouped by ability in most subjects from the start; average class size 25, reducing to 12 for A-levels. Good music (choirs, orchestra) and art. Extra-curricular activities include popular Duke of Edinburgh award scheme. Regular language exchange with pupils in France.

Results   (1997) GCSE: creditable 74% gained at least five grades A–C. A-level: 43% of entries graded A or B.

Destinations   About 55% stay on for A-levels; most proceed to university.

Sport   Wide range: basketball (a strength), netball, badminton, gymnastics, cross-country, hockey, rugby, football, athletics, cricket. Facilities include 35 acres of playing fields, large sports hall.

Remarks   Good, deservedly popular school; recommended.

HENRIETTA BARNETT ♀
Central Square, Hampstead Garden Suburb, London NW11 7BN. Tel (0181) 458 8999

Synopsis
Grammar (voluntary-aided) ★ Girls ★ Ages 11–18 ★ 660 pupils ★ 200 in sixth form
Head: Mrs Jane de Swiet, 56, appointed 1989.
Impressive, highly academic school; outstanding results.

Profile
Background   Founded 1911 by Dame Henrietta Barnett, tireless crusader for

social and educational betterment, particularly for women; she also helped found Hampstead Garden Suburb, in the middle of which the school is sited. Splendidly imposing Lutyens building (shared, uneasily, with adult education institute); 'temporary' huts behind.

Atmosphere Space and cash at a premium; premises over-used, ageing (much recent redecoration); desks in some classrooms packed closely together; head and staff make heroic efforts to cope. Ambitious, high-flying girls under strong parental and peer pressure to do well.

Admissions School heavily over-subscribed (850 apply for 93 places) and highly selective. Entry by interview and tests in English, maths. Some from money-eyed homes, others from disadvantaged backgrounds; large Jewish element, Asian numbers growing; 30% bilingual.

The head Very able. Nerve-centre of the school: good administrator; brisk, alert; holds decided views. Read classics at Cambridge; formerly at City of London Girls'. Keen to keep abreast of educational developments; great advocate of the ideals of state education.

The teaching First-rate: keen, loyal staff of 43 (11 men) doing their best to teach to a high level, cope with the ever-growing volume of paper-work and attend endless meetings. National curriculum plus; all do French and German; Latin, Greek offered up to A-level. Large classes, some over 30. Impressive science labs; adequate provision for art; poor facilities for music and drama. Well-used field studies centre near Shaftesbury – to introduce city girls to country life.

Results (1997) GCSE: all gained at least five grades A–C. A-level: impressive 70% of entries graded A or B (among the best state school results in England).

Destinations Virtually all proceed to higher education (average of 10 a year to Oxbridge).

Sport All take some sort of physical exercise; options include netball, tennis, hockey, rounders, basketball.

Remarks High-quality school; popular choice with parents who might otherwise consider going private. 'We don't have glamorous facilities', says the head. 'We don't have the polish, but what comes out is very good.' Identified by Ofsted (1995) as 'oustandingly successful'.

HENRY BEAUFORT ♂ ♀

East Woodhay Road, Harestock, Winchester, Hampshire SO22 6JJ. Tel (01962) 880073

Synopsis
Comprehensive ★ Co-educational ★ Ages 11–16 ★ 971 pupils (52% boys)
Head: David Dickinson, 48, appointed 1990.
Popular, well-run comprehensive; 'progressive' ethos; good teaching and GCSE results.

Profile
Background Opened 1972 as Winchester's first purpose-built comprehensive; grey, breeze-block buildings plus later additions (including circular, glass-roofed English department) on an attractive split-level site. Unit for hearing-impaired children.

Atmosphere Friendly, informal (sweat-shirts rather than blazers), well-ordered; 'non-macho' approach to discipline (praise in public, reprimand in private); pleasant children keen to succeed. Lessons end at 2.25 pm, leaving time for extra-curricular activities (last bus, 4 pm).

Admissions Slightly over-subscribed; priority to those living in the official catchment; pupils drawn equally from comfortable suburbia and surrounding villages. School is popular with parents.

The head Quietly spoken, determined, innovative; keen on equal opportunities (in particular, raising the attainment of boys to match that of girls). Read history and politics at Kent; worked as an equal opportunities adviser in Rochdale; previously head of a comprehensive in Gateshead. Divorced.

The teaching Good quality; emphasis on 'active learning' (staff study one another's teaching techniques). Standard national curriculum; second foreign language (French or German) offered from second year to those who show linguistic aptitude; particularly good results in English; inadequate access to computers. Pupils grouped by ability in some subjects; extra help for those who need it after school; average class size 30, reducing to 24 for GCSE. Music popular (orchestra, rock group, chamber ensembles). Lots of extra-curricular activities, including Duke of Edinburgh award scheme. Regular language exchanges with schools in France, Germany.

Results (1997) GCSE: 65% gained at least five grades A–C.

Destinations About 85% remain in full-time education.

Sport Strong rugby, hockey (county champions in both). Gymnastics, athletics, squash, tennis also popular. Facilities include extensive playing fields, sports hall, gym.

Remarks Ofsted inspectors concluded (1996): 'The quality of teaching is very high indeed. Behaviour and attitudes to work are excellent. It is an exceptionally civilised school.'

HEREFORD CATHEDRAL SCHOOL ♂ ♀
Old Deanery, Cathedral Close, Hereford HR1 2NG. Tel (01432) 363522

Synopsis
Independent ★ Co-educational ★ Day and some boarding ★ Ages 11–18 (plus associated junior school) ★ 627 pupils (52% boys; 96% day) ★ 170 in sixth form ★ Fees: £5,040 day; £9,015 boarding
Head: Dr Howard Tomlinson, 49, appointed 1987.
Traditional academic school; good music and drama.

Profile
Background Records go back to 1384 but foundation probably coincides with the cathedral's in the 7th century. Formerly Direct Grant, reverted to full independence 1976; co-educational since 1970; boarding numbers have continued to dwindle. Variety of charming Georgian and Victorian buildings plus later additions, including music school and art & technology centre, at the east end of the cathedral close; school feels over-crowded. Junior school admits cathedral choristers at age eight.

Atmosphere Happy, purposeful; strong Christian ethos (daily services in the cathedral).

Admissions At 11 by tests in English, maths, verbal reasoning; at 13 by Common Entrance; school likely to become even less selective with the phasing out of assisted places, which half hold. Remaining boarders live near by in characterful, immaculate accommodation.

The head   Quiet, scholarly; committed Christian. Read history at Cardiff; previously head of history at Wellington College. Married; four children.

The teaching   Generally traditional in style; enthusiastic staff, more than half appointed by present head. Fairly broad curriculum; science taught as three separate subjects; Latin on offer; all do religious studies; choice of 20 subjects at A-level plus wide-ranging general studies. Very good music; more than half learn an instrument; choirs, two orchestras, various ensembles. Lots of drama. Extra-curricular activities include cadet force, Duke of Edinburgh award scheme.

Results   (1997) GCSE: 98% gained at least five grades A–C grades. A-level: 44% of entries graded A or B.

Destinations   About 80% stay on for A-levels; of these, 90% go on to higher education (up to 10 a year to Oxbridge).

Sport   Choice includes rugby, squash, tennis, netball, rowing. Riverside playing fields near by.

Remarks   Attractive school facing considerable change with the scrapping of assisted places.

HERSCHEL GRAMMAR ♂ ♀
Northampton Avenue, Slough, Berkshire SL1 3BW. Tel (01753) 520950

Synopsis
Grammar (grant-maintained) ★ Co-educational ★ Ages 11–18 ★ 667 pupils (55% girls) ★ 205 in sixth form
Head: Julian King-Harris, 43, appointed 1996.
Sound, forward-looking school; emphasis on maths, science, technology.

Profile
Background   Opened 1957 as a technical school; opted out of council control 1992; achieved technology college status 1994. Large, featureless, four-storey block; a strip of playing-field behind and a car park in front (pupils wander round the bike sheds in break, and the grass edges merge into mud); sited in a commercial area of depressing aspect, not easy to reach by public transport. But do not be deceived...

Atmosphere   Inside, much is state-of-the-art – all computer screens and efficiency; classrooms carpeted, modern. Pupils are hard working, highly motivated, quietly conformist; parents anxious for them to succeed. School is small enough for everyone to feel known and secure.

Admissions   School over-subscribed; entry by tests in maths, verbal and non-verbal reasoning; top 30% of the ability range. Most from Slough; 70% Asian; large entry into the sixth form.

The head   Has a degree in educational management. Married; two children (both pupils here).

The teaching   Generally formal in style. Standard national curriculum; emphasis on maths, science (on offer as three separate subjects), technology; lots of computing; GNVQ in business studies very popular. Average class size 23. Extra-curricular activities include thriving Duke of Edinburgh award scheme.

Results   (1997) GCSE: 85% gained at least five grades A–C. A-level: very modest 21% of entries graded A or B.

Destinations About 80% continue into the sixth form; of these, 80% proceed to university.
Sport Facilities include good traditional gym, sports hall, four tennis courts, all-weather cricket pitch and pitches for rugby, soccer, hockey.
Remarks Ofsted inspectors concluded (1996): 'Herschel Grammar is an improving school with strong features and considerable potential for development. It provides an orderly, caring and secure environment where relationships are founded on mutual respect and co-operation.'

HIGHAM LANE ♂ ♀
Brookdale Road, Nuneaton, Warwickshire CV10 0BJ. Tel (01203) 388123

Synopsis
Comprehensive ★ Co-educational ★ Ages 11–16 ★ 1,200 pupils (equal numbers of girls and boys)
Head: Dr Ramsey Tetlow, 46, appointed 1990.
Attractive, well-run school; good GCSE results.

Profile
Background Founded 1939 on present 10-acre site as three separate schools (primary, secondary modern, sixth form); became a comprehensive 1974. Brick and concrete buildings designed by a naval architect to look like a Cunard liner; space at a premium; recent additions include new science labs, classrooms, sports hall. School has its own farm, including sheep and a Jersey cow presented by the Queen.
Atmosphere Industrious, orderly (corridors would be impassable if the pupils were not so well behaved), spotless (head takes a hard line on litter and graffiti). Neatly-uniformed pupils (bright red shirts). Strong anti-bullying policy.
Admissions School over-subscribed (more than 300 apply for 237 places); priority to pupils from 'feeder' primaries; most live within walking distance. Most of average or above-average ability from middle-class/professional homes.
The head Read biochemistry at Bristol, followed by a PhD at University College, London; previously deputy head of a comprehensive in Nottingham. Believes that 'the human condition can be improved by goodwill'; still teaches ('to be a role model in the classroom'). Married; three young children.
The teaching Good quality, mainly traditional in style; long-serving staff (60% men). Standard national curriculum; all start two modern languages (French plus German or Spanish) – but 20% do none for GCSE (in breach of the national curriculum); all become computer literate; good art. Pupils grouped by ability from first year in most subjects; extra help for the the less able; classes 28–30 (larger than usual). Wide range of extra-curricular activities: lots of music, strong debating, popular Duke of Edinburgh award scheme.
Results (1996) GCSE: 63% gained at least five grades A–C.
Destinations About 80% remain in full-time education after 16.
Sport Usual range of games; respectable match record.
Remarks Ofsted inspectors concluded (1996): 'This a very good school in which pupils attain high levels of achievement and personal development.'

HIGHCLIFFE ♂ ♀
Christchurch, Dorset BH23 4QD. Tel (01425) 273381

Synopsis
Comprehensive (grant-maintained) ★ Co-educational ★ Ages 11–16 ★ 918 pupils (53% boys)
Head: Fred Shepherd, 49, appointed 1987.
Popular, well-run school; good teaching and GCSE results; strong music, sport.

Profile
Background   Opened 1962 as a grammar school; went comprehensive (and lost its sixth form) 1974; opted out of council control 1992. Purpose-built, collegiate-style premises plus less attractive 1970s block on six-acre site in a quiet residential area; more recent additions include modern music school; some classrooms in 'temporary' huts; money is tight. Access for physically disabled children.

Atmosphere   Purposeful, well-ordered; good pastoral care system; academic expectations are high. Uniform for all.

Admissions   School is over-subscribed (about 250 apply for 180 places) but non-selective; priority to those from four 'feeder' primaries; ability level is above average.

The head   Able, experienced, approachable. Read modern languages at Cambridge; previously deputy head of a Northamptonshire comprehensive; teaches French and German for 20% of the timetable. Married; two children.

The teaching   Good quality; varied styles. Broad curriculum: science on offer as three separate subjects; good languages; Latin available; most take 10 GCSEs. Pupils grouped by ability in maths, French from the start and in most other subjects thereafter; first-rate extra help for those who need it; average class size 26/7. Strong music; a third learn an instrument; choirs, orchestras, various ensembles. Well-supported Duke of Edinburgh award scheme. Regular language exchanges with pupils in France, Germany.

Results   (1997) GCSE: creditable 69% gained at least five grades A–C.

Destinations   More than 85% remain in full-time education.

Sport   All main games played; cricket, tennis particularly strong; squash, fencing on offer. On-site pitches but facilities are modest.

Remarks   Attractive school.

HIGHGATE ♂
North Road, London N6 4AY. Tel (0181) 340 1524

Synopsis
Independent ★ Boys ★ Day ★ Ages 13–18 (plus associated junior school) ★ 600 pupils ★ 200 in sixth form ★ Fees: £7,875
Head: Richard Kennedy, 48, appointed 1989.
Traditional academic school; fairly wide range of abilities; good teaching and results; lots of extra-curricular activities.

Profile
Background   Founded 1565; Victorian-Gothic buildings plus later additions surrounded by swirling north London traffic. Well-equipped, carpeted, double-glazed

classrooms; 20 acres of playing fields and fine sports centre half a mile away. Co-educational pre-prep (ages three to seven) and junior school (seven to 13) near by.

Atmosphere   Well-disciplined; unusually powerful house system based on where boys live; strong community feeling (half the staff live in school accommodation).

Admissions   At ages seven and 11 by exam and interview, at 13 by Common Entrance; junior school provides half the senior school's intake. Range of ability is wider than at the top London schools (and may widen further with the phasing out of assisted places); head says 'bottom line' is the ability to cope with A-levels and university. Pupils mostly from Barnet, Hampstead, Islington.

The head   Warm, able, enthusiastic. Educated at Charterhouse and Oxford; taught at Shrewsbury and Westminster; formerly deputy head of Bishop's Stortford. Ran for Britain; now sings semi-professionally for the Academy of St Martin in the Fields. Married (to a civil engineer); two sons.

The teaching   Traditional subjects taught with traditional thoroughness but innovation encouraged. Well-qualified staff (a third are Oxbridge graduates), ranging from long-serving veterans to recent entrants. Broad curriculum: science taught (but not examined) as three separate subjects; most take Latin; choice of French, German, Russian, Spanish; all become computer-literate. Pupils grouped by ability in main subjects; class sizes vary between 15 and 25, reducing to an average of eight for A-levels. Big emphasis on extra-curricular activities: lots of drama, music (joint choir and orchestra with girls at Channing, qv); well-supported Duke of Edinburgh award scheme, cadet force. School owns a field centre in Snowdonia.

Results   (1997) GCSE: 98% gained at least five grades A–C. A-level: 66% of entries graded A or B.

Destinations   Virtually all stay on for A-levels; of these, 95% proceed to university (average of 12 a year to Oxbridge).

Sport   Strong soccer, cricket, fives, athletics, fencing, swimming, basketball. First-rate facilities (including Hampstead Heath for cross-country runs).

Remarks   Good all round.

HIGH STORRS ♂ ♀
High Storrs Road, Sheffield S11 7LH. Tel (0114) 267 0000

Synopsis
Comprehensive ★ Co-educational ★ 1,750 pupils (roughly equal numbers of girls and boys) ★ 400 in sixth form
Head: Dr Cherlye Berry, 48, appointed 1989.
First-rate, progressive comprehensive; excellent head; very good teaching and results; wide range of abilities and aptitudes equally well catered for.

Profile
Background   Founded 1880 as Sheffield Central Secondary School; became two single-sex grammar schools on adjacent suburban sites; merged and went comprehensive 1969. Remarkable Art Deco buildings (Grade 2 listed) woefully maintained (peeling paint, unkempt grounds) on 26-acre site ('Of course,' notes the prospectus, 'any school is much more than buildings and facilities'). Lift access for the disabled; special provision for the deaf. School enjoys a strong reputation locally.

Atmosphere Comprehensive in all senses of the word: school caters for the Oxbridge hopeful as well as the child with less demanding academic aspirations (earnest pupils thumbing Ovid alongside boys hauling out the innards of a Ford Escort in the motor maintenance pit). No uniform; heavy emphasis on anti-racism, anti-bullying and 'substance misuse' policies; much effort expended on home–school relations.

Admissions School is over-subscribed (about 300 apply for 240 places); city council gives priority to those living in the catchment area, siblings and pupils at 'feeder' primaries; about 12% ethnic minorities.

The head Dedicated, dynamic: a workaholic, always about, always involved; sets high standards for herself and others (school has won so many awards there is not space on her study walls for all the certificates). Read maths at Royal Holloway (First); PhD in business administration (sees herself as chief executive of a large business but still finds time to teach); previously head of a secondary modern in Lincolnshire. Married (husband is retired).

The teaching Informal and seemingly casual but standards are high. Enthusiastic staff of 115, 35% appointed by present head. Broad curriculum; classics still on offer; sciences taught separately; good computing; wide choice of subjects at GCSE (food technology, automotive engineering, leisure studies, office management) and A-level; GNVQs available in health & social care, leisure & tourism, hospitality & catering. Older pupils grouped by ability; extra help for slow learners as well as high-flyers; learning targets and programmes for all. Big emphasis on environmental studies, health education, citizenship, links with business. Lots of music: 350 learn an instrument.

Results (1997) GCSE: creditable 69% gained at least five grades A–C. A-level: 40% of entries graded A or B.

Destinations About 60% proceed to university.

Sport Not a strength (no one seems to have the time to organise it). Facilities include all-weather cricket pitch, nine tennis courts.

Remarks Fine school marked by integrity of purpose, compassion, real learning.

HIGHWORTH WARNEFORD ♂ ♀
Shrivenham Road, Highworth, Swindon, Wiltshire SN6 7BZ. Tel (01793) 762426

Synopsis
Comprehensive ★ Co-educational ★ Ages 11–16 ★ 861 pupils (52% boys)
Head: John Saunders, 43, appointed 1995.
Successful, well-disciplined school; good teaching and results; wide range of abilities.

Profile
Background Established 1975 in premises that previously housed a secondary modern; unprepossessing buildings, including eight dilapidated huts, enhanced by good-sized games pitches and uninterrupted views over Wiltshire country-side. Facilities vary enormously: many parts of the school are cramped (dining hall designed for 300) and rather scruffy (some classrooms very shabby) but the new library is spacious and well equipped and the computer provision excellent.

Atmosphere Calm, orderly (no hurtling down corridors): decent, disciplined behaviour expected; staff constantly vigilant; pupils find it a happy, friendly place. Truancy negligible; uniform worn throughout (distinguishing shields and badges).

Admissions   School serves a large, semi-rural community (coaches to outlying villages); wide range of abilities and backgrounds.

The head   Read geography at Bristol; previously deputy head for eight years of a Somerset comprehensive. Married; three children.

The teaching   Lively, varied, thorough; enthusiastic, stable staff of 47. Standard national curriculum; strong languages (choice of French or German for first two years; more able take both from third year); good art, science, technology; computing across the curriculum. Most take nine GCSEs. Pupils grouped by ability in most subjects from second year; lots of extra help in and out of class for those who need it; average class size 25; regular homework, rigidly enforced (notebook for parents to check and sign). Music developing (two small orchestras, choir). Very good careers education; all do work shadowing and have work experience; well-established links with local companies. Extra-curricular activities include Duke of Edinburgh award scheme. Regular language exchanges with schools in France, Germany.

Results   (1996) GCSE: creditable 69% gained at least five grades A–C.

Destinations   About 80% remain in full-time education after 16.

Sport   Emphasis on sport for all; everyone who turns up for practice gets a chance to represent the school at some stage. Main games: soccer, rugby, hockey (five pitches), tennis, netball (five courts), rounders, badminton, athletics, basketball (a particular strength).

Remarks   Successful school with a well-deserved reputation.

HIGH WYCOMBE ROYAL GRAMMAR   ♂

Amersham Road, High Wycombe, Buckinghamshire HP13 6QT. Tel (01494) 524955

Synopsis
Grammar (grant-maintained) ★ Boys ★ Day and some weekly boarding ★ Ages 12–18 ★ 1,167 pupils (54 boarders) ★ 395 in sixth form ★ Fees (boarding only): £4,284
Head: David Levin, 47, appointed 1993.
First-class academic school; very good teaching and results; strong sport.

Profile
Background   Founded 1562 (charter from Elizabeth I); moved 1914 to present 22-acre hill-top site and imposing, purpose-built premises; opted out of council control 1993; language college status achieved 1996. Most recent additions include new classrooms, the first for 33 years.

Atmosphere   Academic, competitive, well-ordered; strong emphasis on Christian moral values; fairly formal relations between staff and pupils. Strict blazer-and-tie uniform; sixth-formers wear dark grey suits. Supportive parents pay £150 a year to 'academic development' fund.

Admissions   School over-subscribed (about 300 apply for 192 places) and fairly selective (top 20% of the ability range). Entry by county council 12-plus (verbal reasoning test). Nearly all from middle-class/professional backgrounds within a 15-mile radius; 20% join from prep schools. Boarding accommodation spacious, if rather old fashioned (new house planned).

The head   Able, dynamic. Educated in South Africa (read economics); previously deputy head of Cheltenham. Married; no children.

The teaching Good; traditional in style; hard-working, long-serving staff have high expectations. Broad curriculum: science (a strength) taught and examined as three separate subjects (more than 150 take A-level physics); all do at least one year's Latin; modern languages include German, Spanish, Bahasa ('the language of Malaysia, Brunei and Indonesia, the fastest growing and most innovative economic region in the world'); most take 10 GCSEs; good choice of 24 subjects at A-level. Pupils grouped by ability in maths, languages for GCSE; lots of extra help for those who need it; average class size 32, reducing to a maximum of 16 at A-level. Plenty of drama; strong music (two choirs, two orchestras, jazz band). Wide range of extra-curricular activities, including debating, well-supported cadet force. Regular languages exchanges with pupils in France, Germany.

Results (1997) GCSE: all gained at least five grades A–C. A-level: creditable 60% of entries graded A or B.

Destinations All stay on for A-levels; about 95% proceed to university (impressive average of 26 a year to Oxbridge).

Sport Strong. Regular county and national honours in rugby, hockey, tennis, fencing, rowing. Other sports include cricket, athletics, squash, fives, swimming, shooting, sailing. Facilities include extensive playing fields, good sports hall.

Remarks Ofsted inspectors concluded (1995): 'This is a popular school with a deserved reputation for high academic performance. Pupils are proud of their school, motivated to work and have confidence in themselves.'

HINCHINGBROOKE ♂ ♀

Brampton Road, Huntingdon, Cambridgeshire PE18 6BN. Tel (01480) 451121

Synopsis
Comprehensive (voluntary-controlled) ★ Co-educational ★ Ages 11–18 ★ 1,811 pupils (equal numbers of girls and boys) ★ 348 in sixth form
Head: Dr Peter Sainsbury, 49, appointed January 1997.
First-rate, well-run comprehensive; superb facilities.

Profile
Background Founded 1565 as Huntingdon Grammar School (pupils included Oliver Cromwell and Samuel Pepys); went comprehensive and changed its name 1970. Since 1992 the whole school has been located in sparkling new premises in Hinchingbrooke Park; sixth form in renovated Hinchingbrooke House (mainly 17th century). Regular income from a local charitable foundation; £1.9 million building programme under way.

Atmosphere Vibrant, at times hectic, but the structure – lower, middle and senior schools occupy separate buildings for much of the day – helps keep pupils' educational orbit on a human scale. Many grammar school traditions retained (motto, Fear God and Honour the King); strong house system (thriving inter-house competition); modernised uniform of polo shirts and sweat shirts. Sixth-formers help the younger ones with clubs and activities. Very active parents' association.

Admissions Over-subscribed (about 350 apply for 278 places); geographical criteria rigorously applied (by the county council). Reasonable spread of abilities, though overall average is relatively high, reflecting predominantly middle-class backgrounds (many parents commute to London). Most from Huntingdon, Godmanchester, Brampton.

The head Recent appointment (predecessor had been in post 15 years). Read science at Manchester (PhD); widely experienced; previously head of a Leicestershire community college. Married; two children.

The teaching Generally good (but Ofsted inspectors found shortcomings and poor pupil behaviour in a tenth of lessons). Hard-working, relatively youthful staff of 102 (60% women). Standard national curriculum; all take a second modern language for at least one year. Wide choice of 21 subjects for GCSE, 23 at A-level; GNVQs available. Pupils grouped by ability ('We seek to combine optimism with realism') in maths, modern languages from second year and in most other subjects thereafter; class sizes average 30 in lower years, 26 for GCSE, 12–16 at A-level. Good drama (superb, 600-seat theatre) and music: tuition offered in virtually all instruments; huge range of musical events (including visits from professional groups who coach pupils during the day and play concerts in the evening). Extra-curricular activities include well-supported Duke of Edinburgh award scheme.

Results (1997) GCSE: 59% gained at least five grades A–C. A-level: 39% of entries graded A or B.

Destinations About 60% stay on for A-levels; of these, 90% proceed to university (about five a year to Oxbridge).

Sport Excellent facilities; wide variety of activities. Team strengths in rugby, girls' hockey, cricket. Wind-surfing and canoeing on the neighbouring lake, cross-country in the surrounding woods.

Remarks Ofsted inspectors concluded (1995): 'This is a good school with a number of outstanding features. The standards of achievement are very high.' Worth moving house for.

HOCKERILL ANGLO-EUROPEAN ♂ ♀

Dunmow Road, Bishop's Stortford, Hertfordshire CM23 5HX. Tel (01279) 658451

Synopsis

Comprehensive (grant-maintained) ★ Co-educational ★ Day and boarding ★ Ages 11–16 (11–18 from September 1998) ★ 400 pupils (50% boarders, roughly equal numbers of girls and boys) ★ Fees (boarding only): £4,180
Head: Dr Robert Guthrie, 48, appointed 1996.
Unusual boarding comprehensive; good GCSE results; strong European dimension.

Profile

Background Result of the 1980 amalgamation of two small boarding schools; opted out of council control 1994; hopes to open a sixth form September 1998. Grand Victorian buildings (formerly a teacher training college) in spacious, landscaped grounds; facilities include fine chapel, small farm (for rural studies).

Atmosphere Relaxed, friendly, well-disciplined. Clear Christian ethos; strong international flavour ('We strive to strengthen in our pupils a sense of European identity'). Uniform for all. Most staff live on site.

Admissions Forty places a year available for boarders, 67 for day pupils; all admitted 'without any reference to general ability or aptitude'; priority to those who have a boarding need or whose parents support the school's international aims. Wide range of abilities and backgrounds; 20% from abroad; 10% have parents in the Services. Four pleasant boarding houses; most pupils two to a room ('life as a boarder teaches the pupils independence, self-confidence, self-discipline, compassion, adaptability, tolerance, patience'); provision made for weekly and daily (7.30 am to 8.15 pm) boarders. Lessons on alternate Saturday mornings.

The head   Able, experienced. Read physics at Leeds (PhD in engineering ceramics), MBA from Durham; has taught in independent and state schools; previously head for five years of St George's, Rome (speaks Italian). Keen sportsman (schoolboy rugby international).

The teaching   Sound; big emphasis on individual and group work. National curriculum plus; all add German to French from third year; able linguists join *La Section Bilingue*, receive intensive tuition in French, take GCSE French a year early, learn some maths, history, geography in French and spend three weeks at a sister school near Lyon. Good technology; lots of computing; all do agricultural science. Pupils grouped by ability in English, maths, science, languages; lots of extra help for the least and most able (long-serving staff give freely of their time). School intends to offer the International Baccalaureate and vocational qualifications in planned new sixth form. Wide range of extra-curricular activities: music, drama, community service, Duke of Edinburgh award scheme, pets, horse riding, sailing etc. Regular exchanges with schools in Germany, France, Poland, Hungary; close links with others in Italy, Sweden, Hungary, Romania.

Results   (1997) GCSE: creditable 67% gained at least five grades A–C.

Destinations   Virtually all remain in full-time education after 16.

Sport   Intense coaching; regular practices. School competes on equal terms with many that are much larger; particular strengths in basketball, rugby, athletics, swimming, judo, football. Good facilities include floodlit, all-weather pitch.

Remarks   Interesting, innovative school; boarding is very good value for money; highly recommended.

HODGSON HIGH ♂ ♀
Moorland Road, Poulton-le-Fylde, Blackpool, Lancashire FY6 7EU. Tel (01253) 882815

Synopsis
Comprehensive ★ Co-educational ★ Ages 11–16 ★ 1,000 pupils (roughly equal numbers of girls and boys)
Head: Philip Wood, 39, appointed April 1997.
Successful school; good GCSE results; strong music, drama, sport.

Profile
Background   Founded as a secondary modern 1932; went comprehensive 1976; achieved technology college status 1996. Solid sandstone buildings (spartan – in urgent need of refurbishment) plus 1960s extension in wooded grounds on the outskirts of the town, a pleasant, middle-class enclave. Clean, bright classrooms and labs; good facilities for technology, computing, drama.

Atmosphere   Bustling, disciplined; relaxed, purposeful relations between staff and pupils, who take pride in the school and are clearly here to achieve. Smart, traditional uniform. Supportive, interested parents.

Admissions   School heavily over-subscribed (nearly 300 apply for 200 places); priority to siblings, those living nearest. Most from middle-class backgrounds; ability level slightly above average.

The head   Recent appointment but not new to the school; came here as deputy in 1993. Read history at Hull, MA from Nottingham; keen cricketer; plays the guitar. Married; two children.

The teaching Long-serving, well-qualified staff. Standard national curriculum; particularly good teaching in languages (choice of French or German), drama, technology, English; GCSE options include business studies, child development, tourism. Pupils grouped by ability in maths from first year and in most other subjects thereafter; average class size 25. Very good music and drama. Regular exchanges with schools in France, Germany, Ukraine.

Results (1997) GCSE: 53% gained at least five grades A–C.

Destinations About 75% remain in full-time education after 16, mostly to take A-levels.

Sport Team and individual games are strong. Facilities include good football and hockey pitches, grass and all-weather cricket wicket, athletics track, netball and tennis courts, sports hall, gym.

Remarks Ofsted inspectors concluded (1995): 'This is a very successful and caring school where pupils of all abilities realise their potential within a stimulating, cultural ethos. The education provided is of consistently good and sometimes outstanding quality.'

HOLMES CHAPEL ♂ ♀
Selkirk Drive, Holmes Chapel, Crewe, Cheshire CW4 7DX. Tel (01477) 534513

Synopsis
Comprehensive ★ Co-educational ★ Ages 11–18 ★ 865 pupils (roughly equal numbers of girls and boys) ★ 140 in sixth form
Head: Mrs Elizabeth Duffy, 47, appointed 1993.
Modern, middle-class comprehensive; good teaching and results.

Profile
Background Opened 1978 as a purpose-built comprehensive; attractive, modern buildings (which it has now outgrown) in spacious grounds on the outskirts of the village; numerous classrooms in 'temporary' huts.

Atmosphere Clear goals set within a supportive framework; good pastoral care; high standards of behaviour required (popular with parents). Sweatshirt uniform; sixth-formers in 'student' (rather than 'business') dress.

Admissions Places offered automatically to all pupils in two primary schools in Holmes Chapel and six in outlying villages; others come from further afield. Most from professional/middle-class homes and of above-average ability.

The head Energetic, forceful. Read English at Liverpool; taught in two grammar schools; previously deputy head of a London comprehensive.

The teaching Good. Hard-working staff of 58 (33% male). Standard national curriculum; all do French, about 60% add German. Pupils grouped by ability in most subjects; extra help for those with special needs; average class size 26, reducing to a maximum of 18 at A-level. Sixth-form options include GNVQs. Lots of music (130 have instrumental or singing lessons). Annual language exchanges with schools in France, Germany.

Results (1997) GCSE: 68% gained at least five grades A–C. A-level: 36% of entries graded A or B.

Destinations About half continue into the sixth form; most proceed to university.

Sport Chiefly: football (including a girls' team), rugby, hockey, tennis, basketball. Netball, gymnastics, trampolining, volleyball, badminton, cross-country, dance, tennis, athletics also on offer.

Remarks Ofsted inspectors concluded (1995): 'The school offers education of the highest quality. It has created a working atmosphere in which the learning of the pupils can flourish.'

THE HOLT ♀

Holt Lane, Wokingham, Berkshire RG41 1EE. Tel (01734) 780165

Synopsis

Comprehensive ★ Girls ★ Ages 11–18 ★ 1,185 pupils ★ 185 in sixth form
Head: Mrs Lorna Roberts, 54, appointed 1989.
Successful, well-run school; very good teaching and results.

Profile

Background Founded as a grammar school 1931; went comprehensive 1972. Red-brick premises (in need of refurbishment) on an attractive 13-acre site; sixth form cramped; many classes in 'temporary' huts.

Atmosphere Purposeful, hard-working; big emphasis on 'an orderly atmosphere and consideration for others'; easy relations between staff and courteous, articulate pupils (unusually, head girl and deputy attend governors' meetings). Sensible uniform strictly enforced (sixth form in appropriate casual dress); competitive house system. Very supportive parents.

Admissions School over-subscribed by about 50%; no academic selection; places allocated by county council; priority to those living in the catchment area. Most pupils from middle-class backgrounds; fairly wide range of abilities.

The head Good manager; very committed to single-sex education for girls. Read economics at Manchester. Married; two grown-up sons.

The teaching Good quality; stable, enthusiastic, staff (75% female). Standard national curriculum; German may be added to French from second year; good facilities for computing; wide choice of subjects at GCSE, including child development, business studies; A-level options include psychology, sociology, textiles (but no GNVQs). Pupils grouped by ability in all subjects; extra help for those with special needs; maximum class size 30, smaller for GCSE and A-level. Lots of music; choir, various ensembles. Extra-curricular activities include debating, community service. Regular language exchanges with pupils in France, Germany.

Results (1997) GCSE: creditable 83% gained at least five grades A–C. A-level: 41% of entries graded A or B.

Destinations About 50% continue into the sixth form; of these, 90% go on to higher education.

Sport Usual range; particular strengths in hockey, netball, cross-country. Facilities include adequate playing fields, sports hall.

Remarks Ofsted inspectors concluded (1995): 'The Holt is a very good school with many excellent features. It is a well-ordered community, which is purposeful and hard-working. There are high expectations of pupils and they respond well.'

HOWARD OF EFFINGHAM ♂ ♀
Lower Road, Effingham, Surrey KT24 5JR. Tel (01372) 453694

Synopsis
Comprehensive ★ Co-educational ★ Ages 11–18 ★ 1,515 pupils (roughly equal numbers of girls and boys) ★ 298 in sixth form
Head: Michael Marchant, 46, appointed 1989.
First-rate school; very good teaching and results; strong art, drama, music, sport.

Profile
Background Opened 1940 as a secondary modern (named after the admiral who defeated the Spanish Armada); went comprehensive in the early 1970s. Numbers have doubled since 1990: recent building includes £500,000 sixth-form centre, £1 million sports hall; classrooms, labs to follow (some areas currently over-crowded). Well-resourced, spacious library.

Atmosphere Lively, informal, good humoured; relaxed relations between staff and pupils. Good pastoral care system; strict rules on drugs, bullying. Smart uniform (black blazers, house ties) below the sixth form; seniors' dress expected to be 'clean and tidy, unobtrusive and appropriate'. Supportive parents raise £10,000 annually.

Admissions Over-subscribed but no selection: priority to siblings and those from defined catchment area (Effingham and surrounding villages); fairly wide range of abilities but most above average. Open access to sixth form.

The head Able, courteous; inspires trust. Read geography at Cambridge (First); worked in industry before switching to teaching. Committed Christian; keen sportsman, musician. Married; two children.

The teaching Good; particular strengths in English, maths, science, modern languages, art (vibrant department, exceptional results). All do French and German for first two years; Latin on offer from third year; science on offer as three separate subjects; most take nine GCSEs and three A-levels (from a wide choice of 28); GNVQs available. Pupils grouped by ability in most subjects after the first year; extra help both for slow learners and the very able; average class size 26, reducing to 24 for GCSE, 14 for A-level. Flourishing drama, music (two orchestras, two choirs). Full programme of study trips at home and abroad; annual exchanges with schools in France, Germany. Well-supported Duke of Edinburgh award scheme.

Results (1997) GCSE: 67% gained at least five grades A–C. A-level: creditable 45% of entries graded A or B.

Destinations About 75% continue into the sixth form; of these, 90% proceed to university (four or five a year to Oxbridge).

Sport Enthusiastic; lots on offer; district, county and national honours. Extensive playing fields, all-weather pitch; indoor facilities inadequate.

Remarks Ofsted inspectors concluded (1995) 'This is a good school; examination results are significantly above the national and county averages; the school benefits from the strong and effective leadership of the head.' State education at its best. Highly recommended.

HOWELL'S, LLANDAFF ♀
Cardiff Road, Cardiff CF5 2YD. Tel (01222) 562019

Synopsis
Independent ★ Girls ★ Day ★ Ages 11–18 (plus associated junior school) ★
570 pupils ★ 140 in sixth form ★ Fees: £4,152
Head: Mrs Jane Fitz, 50, appointed 1991.
Solid, well-run school; good teaching and results; lively music.

Profile
Background   Founded 1860 by the Drapers' Company as a boarding school for orphan maidens; formerly Direct Grant, became fully independent 1976; a member since 1980 of the estimable Girls' Public Day School Trust. Pleasant 18-acre site two miles from the city centre; attractive grey stone Victorian buildings with Gothic accessories, sympathetically modernised in the 1980s. Splendid octagonal concert room in music school (the boyhood home of Roald Dahl). Boarding accommodation recently phased out ('sad but inevitable'). Junior school (ages four to 11) on same site.

Atmosphere   Calm but purposeful. Good relations between staff and pupils (becoming less formal as girls progress through the school).

Admissions   By own exam (flexible pass mark); two apply for each place. Wide social mix but most parents are professionals commuting into Cardiff from a wide catchment area (pupils can stay until 6 pm). Trust aims to replace assisted places – which about 200 hold – with a scheme of its own.

The head   Courteous, accessible – but both staff and pupils 'know who's in charge'. Born and educated in Tasmania, BSc from London; formative 10 years as senior mistress at South Hampstead (qv); previously head of Notting Hill & Ealing High (qv). Keen on girls doing science; teaches chemistry. Married; one daughter (a pupil here).

The teaching   Sound; mainly traditional in style. Experienced staff of 44 (six men). Fairly broad curriculum; all take dual-award science (taught by specialists); consistently good maths results; strong modern languages (French, German); 40% take Welsh to GCSE; Latin recently re-introduced as a compulsory subject. Flourishing drama and music; more than 300 learn an instrument; three choirs, two orchestras, jazz groups, ensembles; electronically-equipped recording studio. Extra-curricular activities include Duke of Edinburgh award scheme. Work experience and exchange links with Germany, France.

Results   (1997) GCSE: 99% gained at least five grades A–C. A-level: 64% of entries graded A or B.

Destinations   About 85% stay on for A-levels (some leave for financial reasons); virtually all proceed to higher education (about five a year to Oxbridge).

Sport   Wide range on offer, including tennis, athletics, cross-country, fencing. New sports hall, fitness suite, dance studio.

Remarks   Highly regarded locally. A happy place; opportunities abound.

HUISH EPISCOPI
Wincanton Road, Langport, Somerset TA10 9SS. Tel (01458) 250501

Synopsis
Comprehensive ★ Co-educational ★ Ages 11–16 ★ 1,185 pupils (roughly equal numbers of girls and boys)
Head: Graham Roff, 43, appointed 1996.
First-rate, well-run school; good teaching; strengths in art, music, sport.

Profile
Background Opened 1939; closed during the Second World War and later re-opened as a secondary modern; went comprehensive 1974. Functional, single-storey buildings surrounded by green fields and Somerset wetlands; some classrooms in 'temporary' huts; equipment is less than lavish.

Atmosphere Calm, friendly, orderly (strong system of sanctions and rewards); lively displays of children's work in corridors and classrooms. Good pastoral care (older children counsel the younger ones); firm anti-bullying policy; uniform for all.

Admissions Anyone who wants to come is welcome: coachloads do, from all over the county – a genuine cross-section of a rural community.

The head Quiet, straightforward, unassuming; gets on well with staff, parents, pupils. Has an MEd from Keele; wide experience in the state sector; previously deputy head of a comprehensive in Stockport; still teaches geography, history. Married; two sons (one a pupil here – as are many teachers' children).

The teaching Varied styles (even the formal is pretty relaxed) but all moving at a good pace. Well-qualified staff of 66 (two-thirds women). Broad curriculum: all do French and German for first two years; Spanish on offer; science available as three separate subjects; very good art. Pupils grouped by ability in most subjects; lots of extra help for those who need it; average class size 24–30. Good music (choir, orchestra, various ensembles); strong careers advice ('For the last 15 years, no pupil has left the school without a college course or employer to go to').

Results (1997) GCSE: 58% gained at least five grades A–C.

Destinations About 80% remain in full-time education; half go on to university.

Sport Successful, lively; particularly strong football. Good indoor facilities (shared by the community).

Remarks Identified by Ofsted (1996) as an 'outstanding' school. 'The quality of teaching and learning is high, and the school fulfils its aim to provide a broad and balanced education for all its pupils,' the inspectors said. Deserves to be better resourced.

HULME GIRLS' GRAMMAR ♀
Chamber Road, Oldham OL8 4BX. Tel (0161) 624 2523

Synopsis
Independent ★ Girls ★ Ages 11–18 (plus associated junior school) ★ 529 pupils ★ 133 in sixth form ★ Fees: £3,912
Head: Miss Marlena Smolenski, 50, appointed 1992.
Traditional, academic school; good teaching and results; strong music, sport.

Profile

Background   Founded 1895 on the same site as Hulme Grammar (qv); moved into present, purpose-built premises 1925; formerly Direct Grant, reverted to full independence 1975. Junior school (120 pupils aged seven to 11) on same campus.

Atmosphere   Friendly, well-ordered; strong academic tradition; good pastoral support.

Admissions   By interview and tests in English, maths, verbal reasoning; school is over-subscribed and fairly selective but likely to become less so with the phasing out of assisted places, which 30% hold. Pupils drawn from a wide area north of Manchester, from Bury to Glossop.

The head   Read biochemistry at Manchester; taught in the state sector; previously deputy head of Leicester High.

The teaching   Good quality: mostly formal in style (desks in rows); experienced, predominantly female staff. Fairly broad curriculum; science on offer as three separate subjects; lots of computing; all do Latin in first year, can substitute German in second; all take nine GCSEs and at least three A-levels (from a choice of 18). Pupils grouped by ability in maths only; progress closely monitored (regular tests); maximum class size 30. Strong musical tradition: four choirs, two orchestras, various ensembles; joint drama and debating with boys' school. Extra-curricular activities include Duke of Edinburgh award scheme; much fund-raising for charity.

Results   (1997) GCSE: all gained at least five grades A–C. A-level: creditable 65% of entries graded A or B.

Destinations   Nearly all stay on for A-levels and proceed to university (three or four a year to Oxbridge).

Sport   Good record, particularly in athletics, hockey. Facilities include on-site playing fields, all-weather hockey pitch; sports hall and indoor pool shared with boys' school.

Remarks   Well-run school; good all round.

HULME GRAMMAR ♂

Chamber Road, Oldham OL8 4BX. Tel (0161) 624 4497

Synopsis

Independent ★ Boys ★ Day ★ Ages 11–18 (plus associated junior school) ★ 686 pupils ★ 166 in sixth form ★ Fees: £3,912
Head: Tim Turvey, 49, appointed 1995.
Traditional academic school; good teaching and results; lots of music, sport.

Profile

Background   Founded 1611; moved to present commanding site (shared with Hulme Girls', qv) and purpose-built premises 1895; formerly Direct Grant, reverted to full independence 1976. Later additions include new classrooms, science labs, sixth-form centre. Junior school (115 boys aged seven to 11) a few minutes' walk away.

Atmosphere   Masculine without being macho: a careful balance of self-expression and discipline; 'bullying and all forms of discrimination are taken very seriously and dealt with sensitively but firmly'; friendly relations between staff and boys. Uniform for all.

Admissions   By interview and tests in English, maths, verbal reasoning; school

is not unduly selective and likely to become even less with the phasing out of assisted places, which more than 200 hold; juniors promoted automatically. Pupils drawn from wide area north of Manchester; 17% ethnic minorities.
The head Promoted from deputy. Read botany and zoology at Cardiff; previously director of studies at Monkton Combe. Plays Dixieland jazz. Married; one son.
The teaching Formal, didactic in style (desks in rows); hard-working, well-qualified staff (applicants required to teach a sample lesson). Broad curriculum: all do science as three separate subjects; all start a second language in second year (choice of French, German, Latin, Spanish); limited computing; all take 10 GCSEs and three A-levels plus general studies. Pupils grouped by ability in maths, English; maximum class size 30. Good art; strong musical tradition (100 learn an instrument; choir, orchestra, various ensembles). Wide range of extra-curricular activities, including cadet force, well-supported Duke of Edinburgh award scheme.
Results (1997) GCSE: 96% gained at least five grades A to C. A-level: 49% of entries graded A or B.
Destinations About 80% continue into the sixth form; of these, 90% proceed to university (four or five a year to Oxbridge).
Sport Good record. Main games: football, cricket. Athletics, rugby, hockey, squash, swimming also on offer. Facilities include sports hall, modest playing fields.
Remarks HMC inspectors concluded (1995): 'This is a very good school, achieving high standards across a broad and balanced academic curriculum, and in a wide range of extra-curricular activities.'

HUMMERSKNOTT ♂ ♀
Edinburgh Drive, Darlington, Co Durham DL3 8AR. Tel (01325) 461191

Synopsis
Comprehensive ★ Co-educational ★ Ages 11–16 ★ 1,300 pupils
Head: David Henderson, 51, appointed 1984.
Well-run comprehensive, meeting the diverse needs of its pupils; good GCSE results; facilities need up-grading.

Profile
Background Opened 1968 on the site of a former girls' grammar school; graceless, flat-roofed 1950s buildings plus later additions on a grassy bank on the edge of the leafier suburbs of the town; school lost its sixth form in 1968 and is keen to replace it. Good library and computing facilities but provision for art and music is poor and some science labs are poorly equipped.
Atmosphere A mixture of workman-like application and high ideals: school has developed an enviable reputation (other teachers send their children here). Relaxed relations between staff and pupils; good pastoral care system.
Admissions School over-subscribed: more than 300 apply for 245 places a year. Pupils drawn from a mix of social backgrounds (one in six arrives by bus from a particularly deprived area of Darlington); general level of ability is above average.
The head Informal; prefers to be around the school than attending to paper-work (seems to know every child well); still enjoys teaching. Read maths at Durham; previously deputy head of a comprehensive in Sunderland. Keen

sportsman. Married (to the head of an infant school), two grown-up sons.

The teaching   High quality, informal in style: desks in groups rather than rows, but class teaching not neglected; long-serving, well-qualified staff. National curriculum plus; all sample Latin in third year; half do French and German for GCSE; some take up to 11 GCSEs; particular strengths in economics, business studies. Pupils grouped by ability from third year; those with special needs (including the gifted) well catered for; average class size 30. Wide ranging programme of extra-curricular activities at lunch-time and after school.

Results   (1997) GCSE: 61% gained at least five grades A–C.

Destinations   About 50% proceed to sixth form college; many go on to higher education.

Sport   Particular strengths in badminton, swimming. Facilities include first-rate sports hall, indoor pool.

Remarks   Successful school.

HUNTINGTON ♂ ♀
Huntington Road, York YO3 9PX. Tel (01904) 760167

Synopsis
Comprehensive ★ Co-educational ★ Ages 11–18 ★ 1,500 pupils (equal numbers of girls and boys) ★ 240 in sixth form
Head: Christopher Bridge, 49, appointed September 1997.
First-rate comprehensive; very good teaching and results; wide range of abilities.

Profile
Background   Opened 1966 as a secondary modern; went comprehensive 1973; sixth form added 1979; technology college status achieved 1996. Complex of inadequate, flat-roofed, 1960s buildings with numerous extensions (and 'temporary' huts) on a pleasant 22-acre site on the outskirts of the city; recent additions include new sixth-form centre; many areas in need of improvement.

Atmosphere   Bustling, friendly; school sets high standards in achievement and behaviour without being in the least stuffy or traditional. The accent is on common purpose rather than academic or social distinctions; pupils' general welfare a priority. School does not meet the legal requirement for a daily act of collective worship, arguing that worship can take place only in a 'gathering of believers' – and that does not apply to the normal school assembly.

Admissions   Non-selective: priority to siblings and those living nearest (more than half come from outside the official catchment area). Full range of social backgrounds and academic abilities.

The head   New appointment (his distinguished predecessor had been in post 15 years). Read English at Nottingham; previously head of a comprehensive in Leeds. Married; two grown-up children.

The teaching   The best of modern methods: emphasis on group and individual learning backed by a sound approach to basic skills; self-evidently effective with the whole range of pupils, including the less able; staff are first-rate. Standard national curriculum; greatest strengths in English, maths, science (taught as three separate subjects), technology; more able take a second foreign language. Pupils grouped by ability in most subjects from second year; average class size 28, reducing to 21 for GCSE. Sixth-formers choose between 19 A-level subjects; GNVQ alternatives available. Lots of music (two orchestras) and drama. Wide range of extra-curricular activities ('There's no hanging about at lunch-time').

Results (1997) GCSE: 66% gained at least five grades A–C. A-level: 46% of entries graded A or B.

Destinations Between 55% and 65% continue into the sixth form; of these, about 80% proceed to higher education.

Sport Choice of 20 activities; strong netball, rugby, soccer. Facilities include sports hall, gymnasia, extensive playing fields.

Remarks Ofsted inspectors concluded (1995): 'This is an exceptionally good school which provides an excellent education for its students. It provides a secure and happy environment. Academic standards are consistently among the highest in the country. Students across an unusually wide range of abilities achieve high standards and fulfil their potential to a remarkable degree.'

HUTCHESONS' ♂ ♀
21 Beaton Road, Glasgow G41 4NW. Tel (0141) 423 2933

Synopsis
Independent ★ Co-educational ★ Day ★ Ages 12–18 (plus associated junior school) ★ 1,231 pupils (roughly equal numbers of girls and boys) ★ 380 in sixth form ★ Fees: £4,221
Head: David Ward, 61, appointed 1987.
Distinguished academic school; very good teaching and results; wide range of extra-curricular activities.

Profile
Background Founded 1641 by the brothers George and Thomas Hutcheson; moved 1960 to present, rather uninspiring, purpose-built premises; later additions include splendid new science block, classrooms. Co-educational since 1976 (when the boys' and girls' schools merged). Juniors in elegant, neo-classical buildings one mile away.

Atmosphere Well-organised and well-ordered (necessarily so given the large numbers); above all, hardworking and purposeful; good relations between staff and pupils. Uniform worn by all.

Admissions Entry to junior school by assessment, to senior school by exam and interview. School is regularly over-subscribed and quite highly selective but may become less so with the phasing out of assisted places, which more than 150 hold. Most pupils drawn from a 15–mile radius; backgrounds primarily in the professions, industry, commerce. Scholarships available.

The head (Rector) Able, energetic; strong leader. Read history at Cambridge; previously head of Hulme Grammar. A man of authority, but by no means the authoritarian his imposing stature might suggest; although inevitably a remote figure for most pupils, he is a keen advocate of the corporate spirit.

The teaching Thorough; generally traditional in style. Broad curriculum: science taught as three separate subjects; all do Latin for at least two years; German, Spanish on offer; demanding homework programme. Most take seven Standard Grades and five Highers (from a choice of 19); A-levels available. Pupils grouped by ability in most subjects; extra help for those who need it; regular reports to parents; maximum class size 25. Lively music: a third learn an instrument; 70-strong orchestra; frequent concerts. Abundance of clubs and societies;

extra-curricular activities include Duke of Edinburgh award scheme. Good business contacts. Regular language exchanges with schools in France, Germany.

Results   (1997) Standard Grade: 89% gained at least five grades 1–2. Highers: 68% gained at least five grades A–C.

Destinations   All stay on for Highers; more than three-quarters stay on for a sixth year and proceed to higher education (up to 15 a year to Oxbridge).

Sport   Strong; wide participation. Chiefly rugby, athletics, cricket for the boys; hockey, athletics, tennis for the girls. Also on offer: swimming, soccer, netball, cross-country, badminton, squash, golf, curling, rowing. New sports hall; playing fields two miles away.

Remarks   HMI concluded (1995): 'Staff and pupils had a very strong sense of corporate identity with the school and its traditions and were happy at their work'.

HYMERS ♂ ♀

Hymers Avenue, Hull HU3 1LW. Tel (01482) 343555

Synopsis

Independent ★ Co-educational ★ Day ★ Ages 11–18 (plus associated junior school) ★ 750 pupils (60% boys) ★ 220 in sixth form ★ Fees: £4,032
Head: John Morris, 50, appointed 1990.
Good, traditional school; sound results; strong music, sport.

Profile

Background   Founded 1893 by Rev John Hymers 'for the training of intelligence in whatever social rank of life it may be found among the vast and varied population of the town and port of Hull' (catchment area has since widened). Splendid late-Victorian buildings (ornamental brick work, magnificent hall, fine clock tower) in attractive 30-acre grounds, formerly the city's botanical gardens; functional later additions; facilities generally good. Fully co-educational since 1989. Junior school on same site.

Atmosphere   Orderly, civilised; tradition respected (honours boards, portraits of former heads, cabinets full of sporting trophies) but no hint of stuffiness or coercion; warm relations between staff and pupils. Good pastoral care system.

Admissions   By tests in English, maths, verbal reasoning; school is not unduly selective – and likely to become less so with the phasing out of assisted places, which nearly a quarter hold. Catchment area extends from Bridlington to Grimsby, Goole to the coast.

The head   Quiet, courteous, approachable. Read history at Oxford; came here as head of history 1980; deputy head 1986. Member of Rotary; keen churchman. Married; three children.

The teaching   Styles vary from formal instruction to group work; enthusiastic, committed staff of 65 (20 women), who insist on high standards of work and behaviour. Good languages: all introduced to French, German, Spanish, Latin; science on offer as three separate subjects. All take 10/11 GCSEs and three A-levels; non-examined courses include computing (excellent facilities, evangelical teaching), photography, philosophy. Pupils grouped by ability in maths only; average class size 26/27, reducing to 22 for GCSE, 15 in sixth form. Strict homework policy. Strong music: 250 learn an instrument; choirs, three orchestras, wind bands etc; regular concerts. Busy extra-curricular programme includes

cadet force, Duke of Edinburgh award scheme, chess (good reputation), lots of charitable work, many outdoor activities. First-rate careers service. Regular overseas trips (Russia, North Africa, Iceland).
Results (1997) GCSE: all gained at least five grades A–C. A-level: 58% of entries graded A or B.
Destinations About 85% stay on for A-levels; of these, nearly all proceed to university (up to 10 a year to Oxbridge).
Sport Strong tradition. Main games: rugby, hockey, netball, cricket, rounders, athletics, tennis; minority sports include fencing, at which the school excels. First-rate facilities: gym, huge sports hall, extensive playing fields (but no swimming pool).
Remarks Successful school; all-round strengths.

ILFORD COUNTY HIGH ♂
Fremantle Road, Barkingside, Ilford, Essex IG6 2JB. Tel (0181) 551 6496

Synopsis
Grammar ★ Boys ★ Ages 11–18 ★ 700 pupils ★ 200 in sixth form
Head: Stuart Devereux, 47, appointed 1993.
First-rate grammar school; good music and sport.

Profile
Background Founded 1901; moved to present site and purpose-built premises in pleasant residential area 1934; survived Redbridge's switch to comprehensive education in 1972. Much of the original two-storey building has been modernised; later additions include computer rooms, electronics lab, technology suite.
Atmosphere Hard-working, cheerful, well ordered ('We expect boys to work hard and to allow others to do likewise'). Annual prize-giving recently re-instated; blazer-and-tie uniform worn with pride. Parents supportive of the school and their sons.
Admissions School is heavily over-subscribed (by about 10:1) and highly selective (top 10% of the ability range); entry by two nationally standardised tests of general ability. Wide spread of social and ethnic backgrounds (separate assemblies for Jews, Hindus, Muslims, Sikhs); catchment area shared with Woodford County High (qv).
The head Able, experienced; taught PE and geography before taking a degree in computer studies through the Open University; came here as deputy head 1990. Keen on consultation: involves all staff in major policy decisions.
The teaching Mix of traditional and more modern methods; first-rate staff, who tend to move only for promotion. Broad curriculum: all do two languages for at least two years (choice of French, German, Spanish, Latin) plus classical studies; science taught (and examined) as three separate subjects; maths exceptionally strong (100% have gained grades A–C at GCSE for the past three years and more than 70% do so at A-level). All take 10 GCSEs and at least three A-levels. Strict homework policy ('A pre-requisite for academic success is the establishment of good study habits'); average class size 30, reducing to 20 at GCSE. Good music: orchestra, brass band, jazz band, various ensembles. Wide range of extra-curricular activities during extended lunch hour and after school: active chess, bridge; lots of debating; well-organised Duke of Edinburgh award scheme. Regular field trips, expeditions, foreign visits.

Results (1997) 95% gained at least five grades A–C. A-level: 50% of entries graded A or B.

Destinations About 85% stay on for A-levels; of these, nearly 90% proceed to university (average of six a year to Oxbridge).

Sport Strong (staff give freely of their time). Good soccer, basketball, cricket, swimming. Hockey, badminton, rugby, trampolining, athletics, cross-country, water polo also on offer. Facilities include extensive, well-maintained playing fields, tennis courts, large gym, heated indoor pool.

Remarks Good school for able boys.

ILKLEY GRAMMAR ♂ ♀
Cowpasture Road, Ilkley, West Yorkshire LS29 8TR. Tel (01943) 608424

Synopsis
Comprehensive (voluntary-controlled) ★ Co-educational ★ Ages 13–18 ★ 1,070 pupils (equal numbers of girls and boys) ★ 300 in sixth form
Head: Peter Wood, 55, appointed 1979.
Well-run comprehensive; good teaching and results.

Profile
Background Founded 1607; moved to its present site between the moor and the town in 1893; merged with a secondary modern school to become a comprehensive in 1970. Solid, grey sandstone buildings plus 1970s additions; 12 classrooms in 'temporary' huts; overall impression is of a well-used rabbit warren. Facilities are generally good.

Atmosphere A conscious blend of the traditional and modern: the school is proud of its history but the teaching and the friendly relationships between staff and pupils are thoroughly contemporary.

Admissions Intake is genuinely comprehensive but predominantly middle-class; 20% come from outside the catchment area, including Bradford and Keighley.

The head Shows no signs of flagging despite an exceptionally long stint.

The teaching Methods range from the traditional to the most imaginative and up-to-date. National curriculum plus; science on offer as three separate subjects; all do either German or Spanish in addition to French; big emphasis on coursework and computing. Pupils grouped by ability in most subjects; extra help for those with special needs; average class size 24 (smaller for slow-learner groups). Sixth-formers choose between A-levels (options include economics, psychology, sociology) and vocational courses in business and health. Good careers advice. Lots of trips abroad.

Results (1997) GCSE: 64% gained at least five grades A–C. A-level: 43% of entries graded A or B.

Destinations About 60% continue into the sixth form; of these, 75% proceed to university.

Sport Chiefly soccer, cricket, tennis for the boys; hockey, volleyball, tennis for the girls. On-site facilities include sports hall, gymnasia, refurbished Victorian swimming pool; playing fields two miles away.

Remarks Attractive school; all abilities catered for. Ofsted inspectors concluded (1993): 'This is a very good school. Standards of achievement are good and at times outstanding. Across all subjects, the teaching is characterised by high expectation, challenge and rigour.'

IPSWICH ♂ ♀
Henley Road, Ipswich IP1 3SG. Tel (01473) 255313

Synopsis
Independent ★ Co-educational from September 1997 ★ Day and some boarding ★ Ages 11–18 (plus associated prep school) ★ 580 pupils (92% boys, 96% day) ★ 192 in sixth form (73% boys) ★ Fees: £5,097–£5,598 day; £8,295–£9,606 boarding
Head: Ian Galbraith, 48, appointed 1993.
Well-run, academic school; very good teaching and results; lots of art, drama, music; strong sport.

Profile
Background   Founded about 1390 by the Merchant Guild of Corpus Christi; moved to present site and fine, purpose-built premises 1852 (Prince Albert laid the foundation stone, which led to a riot); joined the independent sector 1945; girls admitted at 16 in 1972, at 11 from September 1997. Many recent additions, including fine sports hall (lit by a large stained-glass window). Expanding junior school (280 pupils aged three to 11) on same site.

Atmosphere   Friendly, well-ordered; good pastoral care; daily chapel service. Charcoal-suit uniform below the sixth form (where there is a dress code – 'If in doubt, err on the side of formality').

Admissions   At 11 by tests in English, maths, verbal reasoning (half join from the prep school); at 13 by Common Entrance; at 16 with at least six GCSEs grades A–C; school is not unduly selective (top third of the ability range, expected to be capable of coping with 10 GCSEs); admission of girls will help compensate for the phasing out of assisted places, which about 125 hold. Most from Sussex, Essex, Cambridgeshire; parents organise buses. Co-educational boarding house – a Victorian mansion in its own wooded grounds – being refurbished; weekly boarding available. Scholarships: academic, art, music, all-rounder.

The head   Genial, able, enthusiastic; good leader; takes an interest in everything, keeps everyone up to the mark. Read geography at Cambridge (starred First); previously head of the upper school at Dulwich (qv), where he had been a pupil. Teaches geography to the juniors. Married; two young children.

The teaching   Good quality; brisk, purposeful, challenging; well-qualified, predominantly male staff. Fairly broad curriculum; three-quarters take science as three separate subjects; GCSE options include German, Russian, Latin; choice of 18 subjects at A-level; all do general studies (and are encouraged to take an extra language). Pupils grouped by ability from age 13 in maths, French, Latin; maximum class size 24, reducing to 10 at A-level. Good art, drama, music; choirs, orchestras, various ensembles (concerts in Snape Maltings). Extra-curricular activities include cadet force, Duke of Edinburgh award scheme.

Results   (1997) GCSE: all gained at least five grades A–C. A-level: creditable 66% of entries graded A or B.

Destinations   Almost all go on to university (seven or eight at year to Oxbridge).

Sport   Strong, particularly rugby, also hockey, cricket; girls play hockey, rounders, tennis, netball. Archery, riding, golf, sailing also on offer. Facilities include fine cricket coaching gallery (shared with the community), small indoor pool, courts for squash, Eton fives; 30 acres of playing fields 10 minutes' walk away.

Remarks   Very good all round; recommended.

IPSWICH HIGH ♀
Woolverstone Hall, Woolverstone, Ipswich, Suffolk IP9 1AZ. Tel (01473) 780201

Synopsis
Independent ★ Girls ★ Day ★ Ages 11–18 ★ 450 pupils (plus associated junior school) ★ 100 in sixth form ★ Fees: £4,152
Head: Miss Valerie MacCuish, 51, appointed 1993.
Successful academic school; very good results; first-rate facilities in a magnificent, spacious setting.

Profile
Background Founded 1878 by the Girls' Day School Trust; formerly Direct Grant, became fully independent 1976; moved 1992 to Woolverstone Hall, splendid 18th-century mansion (formerly a boarding school) set in 80 acres of parkland five miles south of Ipswich (rustic mood enhanced by sheep grazing in the grounds under direction of a tenant shepherdess). Sympathetically-designed additions include large sports hall and 400-seat theatre. Junior school (ages three to 11) on same site.

Atmosphere Calm, intimate; warm relations between staff and girls; strong spirit of fellowship and co-operation; overt discipline almost unnecessary. Sixth-formers accommodated in space and comfort most universities would struggle to match. Daily morning assembly for all. Distinctive cherry-blazered uniform (older girls excused).

Admissions Entry by school's own tests in maths, English comprehension and essay; top 20%–25% of the ability range. Junior school takes half the 78 places in the senior school; up to 100 apply for the rest. One pupil in three receives help with fees; trust aims to replace the assisted places scheme with one of its own. Catchment area extends from Colchester to Woodbridge (buses arranged).

The head Approachable, informal, determined. Read French and Spanish at London; has wide experience in both state and independent girls' schools; previously head of Tunbridge Wells Girls' Grammar. Lives on site; teaches religious education to all first-years as a way of getting to know them.

The teaching Pacey, but not relentless; girls say teachers have time for them, and 'make everyone feel special, whatever their talents'. Stable staff of 46 (three men). Broad curriculum: science on offer as three separate subjects; all do Latin for first three years; exceptionally strong languages (half take both French and German for GCSE). Pupils set by ability in maths, French; average class size 26, reducing to a maximum of 20 for GCSE, 12 at A-level. First-rate music: 70% learn an instrument; three choirs, two orchestras, wind band, various smaller ensembles. Lots of extra-curricular activities, including Duke of Edinburgh award scheme. Regular, well-structured language exchanges.

Results (1997) GCSE: all gained at least five grades A–C. A-level: very creditable 79% of entries graded A or B (22nd in the league table – its best performance ever).

Destinations About 70% stay on for A-levels; of these, 95% proceed to university (about four a year to Oxbridge).

Sport Excellent facilities, including plentiful pitches. Strong hockey, tennis, netball (county honours in all three); national school champions in fencing. Other options include sailing, orienteering, swimming, athletics.

Remarks Very good all round; helps able girls maximise their talents.

JAMES ALLEN'S GIRLS' ♀
East Dulwich Grove, London SE22 8TE. Tel (0181) 693 1181

Synopsis
Independent ★ Girls ★ Day ★ Ages 11–18 (plus associated junior school) ★ 750 pupils ★ 207 in sixth form ★ Fees: £6,390
Head: Mrs Marion Gibbs, 46, appointed 1994.
Successful academic school; very good teaching and results; strong art, drama, music.

Profile
Background Founded 1741 (in two rooms of the Bricklayers' Arms) by James Allen, Master of Dulwich College, so that 'poor boys should be taught to read' and 'poor girls to read and sew'; became a girls-only school in 1857; moved to present 22-acre site 1886. Victorian building plus extensive later additions; large playing fields behind; famous botanical garden sadly neglected but slowly being restored. School is part of the Dulwich foundation, which includes Alleyn's and Dulwich (qv); close links with both maintained. Junior school on separate site.

Atmosphere Firmly academic: first-rate results expected and achieved without pupils appearing unduly pressurised; good pastoral care system. Girls drawn from a wide range of social and ethnic backgrounds: nearly 10% of families on income support; 49 different languages spoken at home; black and Asian minorities happily integrated. Muslim and Jewish pupils have option of their own assemblies three times a week. Pupils raise £10,000 a year for charity.

Admissions School is heavily over-subscribed and highly selective; entry (strictly on merit) by tests in English, maths, verbal reasoning (no exceptions made for siblings). School aims to replace assisted places, which about 250 hold, by significantly extending its scholarship scheme; 45% pay less than full fees. Dulwich Foundation bus service covers large parts of south-west and south-east London.

The head Able, energetic, experienced. Read classics at Bristol; MLitt in medieval Latin authors. Taught in grammar, comprehensive and independent schools, lectured for the Open University; became head of sixth form at Haberdashers' Aske's Girls' (qv) then joined Her Majesty's Inspectorate. Strong believer in single-sex education for academic girls but emphasises that JAGS is 'not a nunnery'; keen to strengthen the school's links with the local community by sharing sports facilities and running a literacy project with local primaries. Married (to a retired teacher); no children.

The teaching Great mixture of styles. Relatively youthful staff of 88 (18 men). Broad curriculum; languages a particular strength (all do two years' Latin and two modern languages); wide choice of 26 subjects at A-level. Pupils grouped by ability in maths, languages; lots of help for any in difficulty; class sizes up to 28 for first three years, reducing to a maximum of 25 for GCSE, 14 at A-level. Strong art (after-school life classes for A-level pupils); lots of drama (very good theatre, full-scale production every term); good music (early to electronic, 60% learn an instrument). Active Duke of Edinburgh award scheme; all first-years spend a week at an outdoor centre in Cumbria. Regular exchanges with schools in France, Germany, Italy, Spain, Russia.

Results (1997) GCSE: 99% gained at least five grades A–C. A-level: impressive 84% of entries graded A or B (14th in the league table – its best position ever).

Destinations Nearly all stay on for A-levels and proceed to university (20% to Oxbridge).

Sport   Strong hockey (four pitches), swimming, athletics; emphasis, too, on individual sports, especially fencing. Facilities include sports hall, four squash courts.

Remarks   Happy successful school; sewing has rather fallen by the wayside.

JEWS' FREE SCHOOL (JFS) ♂ ♀
175 Camden Road, London NW1 9HD. Tel (0171) 485 9416

Synopsis
Comprehensive (grant-maintained, Jewish) ★ Co-educational ★ Ages 11–18
★ 1,445 pupils (52% girls) ★ 308 in sixth form
Head: Miss Ruth Robins, 50, appointed 1993.
Fine Jewish school; powerful ethos; very good results.

Profile
Background   Founded 1732 as the Talmud Torah of the Great Synagogue; became the Jews' Free School 1817 (by the end of the 19th century it had 3,500 pupils and called itself 'the largest school in the world'); moved to its present cramped site on a busy North London main road after World War Two (during which its East End premises were bombed); opted out of council control 1993. Bleak concrete premises (dungeon-like corridors). Security is tight: parents organise a security rota to ensure that every visitor's credentials are checked; all staff and non-uniformed pupils wear identity cards; grounds surrounded by unclimbable wire fences.

Atmosphere   School aims to give every child, however unobservant his or her family, an identity as a Jew in the hope that he or she will 'opt in', become a practising Jew, and resist 'marrying out', thus contributing to the diminution of the Anglo-Jewish community (pupils emphasise, however, that they are not put under any pressure to become observant, and services in the synagogue are optional). Strongly Zionist, the school offers pupils the opportunity to spend five months in Israel in an orthodox community, studying Hebrew and Jewish history and culture. Relations between staff and pupils are warm, humorous and firmly traditional (pupils stand until the teacher tells them to be seated, and whenever an adult enters the room). Uniform includes kippa for boys; girls must observe 'the rules of modesty' (nothing sleeveless, no short skirts, no trousers). All pupils expected to eat school lunch in order to preserve the kashrut of the school: no outside food allowed in.

Admissions   School heavily over-subscribed. Entry by interview; pupils must be 'recognised as being Jewish by the Office of the Chief Rabbi'; full range of abilities (ensured by a quota system – 30% band one, 50% band two, 20% band three) from all over London and as far away as Luton; parents cover the social spectrum (170 pupils are entitled to free school meals) and 'every type of Jewishness imaginable' (those who send their children here are 'deemed to be stating a clear commitment to uphold the aims, standards and ethos of the school').

The head   Guarded, likeable, very committed (not only to the school but to Zionism and to Judaism in general); something of an enigma to her pupils (despite having taught here since 1968, apart from a two-year break lecturing in English at the university in Tel Aviv). Read English and modern languages at Cape Town.

The teaching   Good; very traditional in style (giving pupils, according to

Ofsted inspectors, 'too little scope for investigative and collaborative learning'). Exceptionally long-serving staff of 109 (61 women), 75 have been here more than 15 years; about a third are practising Jews. Up to a quarter of the curriculum is devoted to modern Hebrew and Jewish studies, rather restricting the time for other options. Choice of 20 subjects for GCSE, 15 at A-level; vocational alternatives available. Regular grades for effort, attainment, presentation (keenly monitored by highly competitive children); frequent and detailed reports to parents (with whom the school takes a firm line – 'We tell them where they're going wrong'). Pupils grouped by ability from the start; most able put into accelerated classes; further setting in maths, modern languages from second year and in most other subjects from third year; those with special needs catered for. Many extra-curricular activities are Jewish in nature but the Duke of Edinburgh award scheme and Young Enterprise flourish too. Regular trips to Poland to study the Holocaust.

Results   (1997) GCSE: creditable 70% gained at least five grades A–C. A-level: 54% of entries graded A or B (better than most grammar schools).

Destinations   Up to 95% go on to university (about eight a year to Oxbridge), some after doing national service in Israel.

Sport   Competition is not part of the school's ethos; matches (tennis, netball, football) tend to be friendlies. Facilities include large indoor pool, two gyms (girls and boys separated for religious reasons), all-weather courts – but no grass.

Remarks   Ofsted inspectors concluded (1996): 'This is a good school which provides a sound and effective education for its pupils.'

JOHN HAMPDEN GRAMMAR ♂

Marlow Hill, High Wycombe, Buckinghamshire HP11 1SZ. Tel (01494) 529589

Synopsis
Grammar ★ Boys ★ Ages 12–18 ★ 720 pupils ★ 290 in sixth form
Head: Andrew MacTavish, 58, appointed 1983.
Well-run, high achieving school; secure, friendly atmosphere.

Profile
Background   Founded 1893 for the study of art, science and technology; moved to present site 1960s; pleasant premises, including new sixth-form centre. Eleven-year-olds admitted from September 1998.

Atmosphere   Purposeful; much mutual respect between staff and friendly, well-mannered boys; good pastoral care system. Formal school assemblies; large body of responsible-looking prefects. All wear uniform, plus a selection of smart ties for positions of responsibility.

Admissions   School over-subscribed; entry by county council tests; pupils drawn from the whole of south Buckinghamshire and even beyond.

The head   Local boy, educated at Royal Grammar, High Wycombe and Cambridge. After spells in the Army and as an industrial manager, he taught in four boys' grammar schools, rising through head of English in Dorchester to deputy head at Devonport. Firm and traditional in his discipline, but his kindness and humanity show when someone is in trouble; he knows the boys individually, delighting in their achievements. Adamant that the school should remain at its present size, wishing to keep the relaxed relationships in the staff-room and the well-ordered framework. His 'hands-on' style with both boys and staff is very much the old grammar school way, but he abolished streaming by ability for the younger boys when he arrived, and stressed the importance of technology.

The teaching Staff are no-nonsense professionals, proud of the school and ready to give time to their pupils; new teachers are head-hunted by the management team, and there is no room for spent volcanoes or dead wood. Broad curriculum; all take 10 GCSEs, including three sciences; particularly good A-level results in maths, geography, physics, design, computing. Half-term grades and termly reports make slackers work harder than they otherwise might. School has cornered the market in offering GCSE re-takes to boys with potential from other schools ('adding value to lads of low performance'); two-thirds of these go on to A levels. Lots of music: more than 100 learn an instrument; choirs, bands.

Results (1997) GCSE: 99% gained at least five grades A–C. A-level: 44% of entries graded A or B.

Destinations Nearly all continue into the sixth form and proceed to university, some to Oxbridge.

Sport Main games: football, rugby, hockey, cricket, athletics. On-site playing fields; local sports centre just across the road.

Remarks Good school; gives boys the confidence and security to succeed.

JOHN LYON ♂

Middle Road, Harrow, Middlesex HA2 0HN. Tel (0181) 422 2046

Synopsis
Independent ★ Boys ★ Day ★ Ages 11–18 ★ 525 pupils ★ 140 in sixth form ★ Fees: £6,060
Head: Rev Tim Wright, 56, appointed 1986.
Well-run, relatively small school; good teaching and results; first-rate pastoral care; lots of sport.

Profile
Background Founded 1853 as a branch of Harrow (qv) to educate the sons of local townsmen; became independent 1868; moved to present spacious site 1876; strong links with Harrow remain. Buildings of various periods; most recent additions include 10 new science labs, library, sports hall.

Atmosphere Calm, friendly, relaxed (conducive to hard work, good behaviour). Very strong pastoral system: school divided into three blocks (lower, middle, sixth), ensuring everyone is known to all; close partnership between staff and parents (like an extended family). Smart uniform worn by all.

Admissions Not unduly selective. Entry by interview and exams in English, maths, verbal reasoning at 11-plus, and in English, maths, science, French at 13-plus. Most come from professional/business backgrounds in outer London suburbs. Phasing out of assisted places, which nearly 100 hold, will reduce the social mix. Academic and music scholarships available.

The head Strong leader; hands-on style (always around, knows the boys well). Read theology at London, spent six years as a parish priest; previously chaplain and housemaster at Malvern. Married; two grown-up children.

The teaching Good; varied styles; well-qualified, predominantly male staff. Fairly broad curriculum: all begin German and Latin as well as French; science taught as three separate subjects; choice of 17 subjects at GCSE and A-level; particularly good results in maths. Pupils grouped by ability from the start; progress carefully monitored; average class size 22. Homework increases from one-and-a-half hours a night for juniors to 15 a week in sixth form. Lots of extra-curricular activities; all expected to participate. Strong music (choirs, orchestras, various ensembles); well-supported Duke of Edinburgh award scheme.

Results (1997) GCSE: all gained at least five grades A–C. A-level: 59% of entries graded A or B.

Destinations About 90% continue into the sixth form; of these, 70% go on to university (including Oxbridge).

Sport First-rate facilities, some shared with Harrow; playing fields 10 minutes' walk away. Main games: football, cricket. Cross-country, athletics, tennis, swimming, badminton, archery, volleyball, basketball, golf, table tennis, squash, karate also available. Regular borough, county, national honours.

Remarks Good all round; particularly recommended for boys who might not thrive in a larger, more impersonal school.

JOSEPH ROWNTREE ♂ ♀
Haxby Road, New Earswick, York Y03 4BZ. Tel (01904) 768107

Synopsis
Comprehensive (voluntary-controlled) ★ Co-educational ★ Ages 11–18 ★ 1,200 pupils (slightly more boys than girls) ★ 145 in sixth form
Head: Hugh Porter, 46, appointed September 1997.
Successful school; good teaching and results; lots of music, sport.

Profile
Background Founded 1942 by the Joseph Rowntree Memorial Trust for the children of chocolate factory workers; became a comprehensive 1973. 'Flagship' 1940s buildings plus later additions on a 15-acre site.

Atmosphere Confident, open, caring; high expectations of work, behaviour, dress ('Strive and Succeed'). Strong links with parents.

Admissions School full but not over-subscribed; some places available to those outside the (largely middle-class) catchment area.

The head Recent appointment. Read history at Liverpool; his second headship. Married; two children.

The teaching Good quality; predominantly formal in style. Standard national curriculum; first-rate science; strong design/technology; choice of 20 subjects at A-level; vocational alternatives available. Pupils grouped by ability in most subjects; extra help for those who need it; maximum class size 25. Good careers department. Lots of music, drama. Extra-curricular activities include debating, Duke of Edinburgh award scheme; school owns a field centre on the North Yorkshire moors.

Results (1997) GCSE: 63% gained at least five grades A–C. A-level: 44% of entries graded A or B.

Destinations About 75% continue into the sixth form; of these, 65% proceed to university.

Sport Chiefly: rugby, football, netball, hockey, tennis, athletics; regular inter-house and inter-school competition. Facilities include extensive playing fields, tennis courts, large sports hall.

Remarks Good all round.

JUDD ♂
Brook Street, Tonbridge, Kent TN9 2PN. Tel (01732) 770880

Synopsis
Grammar (voluntary-aided) ★ Boys (plus girls in sixth form) ★ Ages 11–18 ★
800 pupils ★ 220 in sixth form (90% boys)
Head: Keith Starling, 53, appointed 1986.
First-rate, well-run school; very good teaching and results; strong music, sport.

Profile
Background Founded 1888 by the Skinners' Company from funds provided by the Sir Andrew Judd Foundation; moved to present site and purpose-built premises 1896; became a voluntary-aided grammar school 1944. Grimly Victorian buildings plus attractive modern additions, including £2 million classroom and technology block, music centre (paid for by voluntary donations); some classrooms in 'temporary' huts.

Atmosphere Lively, bustling, well-ordered; discipline based on 'high expectations of personal behaviour'. Blazer-and-tie uniform worn throughout. Parents generously supportive.

Admissions By Kent selection test (11-plus); school is over-subscribed and highly selective; 30 out of 120 places awarded to applicants from outside the official catchment area (nearly 200 apply). Entry to sixth form (for girls and boys) requires at least five GCSEs at grade A. Most from middle-class backgrounds.

The head Able, experienced; friendly, open manner; immensely proud of his school. Read geography at Cambridge; previously deputy head of Portsmouth Grammar (qv). Married; two sons (both were pupils here).

The teaching First-rate: essentially formal in style; well-qualified staff of 54 (16 women), half appointed by present head. Broad curriculum: sciences taught separately; all do French and German; Latin on offer; lots of computing; choice of 21 subjects at A-level. Pupils grouped by ability from the start in maths (some take GCSE a year early) and French; extra help for those who need it; average class size 28–30, reducing to 15 at A-level; homework closely monitored. Good art; strong music (three orchestras, two choirs). Wide range of extra-curricular activities, including well-supported Duke of Edinburgh award scheme, cadet force. Regular language exchanges with pupils in France, Germany.

Results (1997) GCSE: all gained at least five grades A–C. A-level: very creditable 63% of entries graded A or B.

Destinations Nearly all go on to university (about 12 a year to Oxbridge).

Sport Lots on offer; strong rugby, cross-country; regular county honours. Cricket, athletics, tennis, basketball, swimming (open-air pool), badminton also popular. Some playing fields one mile away.

Remarks Very good school for competitive, able boys.

KENDRICK ♀
London Road, Reading, Berkshire RG1 5BN. Tel (01734) 585959

Synopsis
Grammar (grant-maintained) ★ Girls ★ Ages 11–18 ★ 677 pupils ★ 200 in sixth form
Head: Mrs Marsha Elms, 50, appointed 1993.
First-rate school; very good teaching and results.

Profile
Background Founded 1877 after it was decided that an endowment made to the town in 1624 by John Kendrick (used to fund Reading, qv) should be extended to girls; moved to present site (facing the A4, near the centre of town) 1927; opted out of council control 1996. Vaguely classical buildings (red brick, formal entrance, pantile roof) supplemented by a sprawl of 'temporary' huts; classrooms barely adequate and still in the blackboard era (many with old, lidded desks); science labs not state-of-the-art. Much-used hall contains a portrait of John Kendrick behind a black-out curtain drawn back only on special days; large red Coke machine and a yellow telephone hood look almost too modern.

Atmosphere As soon as the bell rings, all these unprepossessing buildings and walkways come to life with bright-looking girls spilling out, talking hard. Staff pass them at the double, intent and earnest but ready to smile. School day is 'compressed', which means people eat on the hoof or dash into the canteen: head calls it 'being in work mode'. Strong pastoral support system. Uniform of 'Kendrick red' pullovers, grey skirts; sixth form allowed anything within reason.

Admissions School severely over-subscribed (nearly 600 apply for 93 places); entry by three verbal reasoning tests (best two taken into account); IQs range from 110 to 140; borderline interviews conducted by the school with much heart-searching. Extensive catchment area; 30% come from independent sector.

The head Dynamic, decisive, humane; says she is 'very into equal opps'; introduced a Speech Day, believing that effort should be seen to be rewarded. Read sociology in the late 1960s (partly at the London School of Economics); taught part-time for 10 years while bringing up a family (husband is a head); previously deputy head of a co-educational comprehensive (now a convinced convert to single-sex education).

The teaching Outstanding: experienced, stable staff of 50 (seven men) who teach because they love their subjects and want to pass them on. Standards are high but the teachers are protective of the girls, anxious not to be élitist or to over-emphasise academic competitiveness; pupils take their work seriously (and often stay behind at the end of a lesson to question further). Broad curriculum; all do at least one year's Latin and two modern languages; science on offer as three separate subjects; well-taught art (a third take it for GCSE). Large classes: average 32 (in small rooms). Music flourishes: 150 learn an instrument; two orchestras, two choirs. Lots of trips abroad for study and recreation.

Results (1997) GCSE: all gained at least five grades A–C. A-level: 57% of entries graded A or B.

Destinations About 90% stay on for A-levels; of these, 95% proceed to university (about three a year to Oxbridge).

Sport   Fairly low-key but there is hockey on the school field half-a-mile away and volleyball and badminton in the gym. Facilities include heated indoor pool (thanks to the parents) and four netball/tennis courts.

Remarks   Dedicated staff achieve good results with highly selected and motivated girls in buildings that sorely need attention. Identified by Ofsted (1995) as 'outstandingly successful'.

KESTEVEN & SLEAFORD HIGH ♀
Jermyn Street, Sleaford, Lincolnshire NG34 7RS. Tel (01529) 414044

Synopsis
Grammar ★ Girls ★ Ages 11–18 ★ 601 pupils ★ 124 in sixth form
Head: Mrs Alison Ross, 39, appointed 1996.
Sound, hard-working, traditional school; good teaching and results.

Profile
Background   Opened 1902; attractive listed buildings plus many later additions in a pleasant setting 100 yards from the town centre. Numbers rising steadily.

Atmosphere   Peaceful, academic, self-disciplined: strong sense of family and community; high standards of dress (compulsory uniform below the sixth form) and personal appearance. Supportive parents raise funds, organise social events.

Admissions   By county council administered verbal-reasoning tests; top 30% of the ability range, mostly from agriculture-related backgrounds in 100-square-mile catchment area.

The head   Read history at Lancaster, medieval studies at York; previously deputy head of Lancaster Girls' Grammar (qv). Married.

The teaching   Long-serving staff; styles range from traditional didactic to pupil-centred. Broad curriculum: science taught (but not examined) as three separate subjects; nearly half add German to French; Latin on offer from third year; most do 10 GCSEs and three A-levels; vocational alternatives available in conjunction with two other schools; good links with local industry. Pupils grouped by ability in maths, French from third year; progress closely monitored; extra help for those who need it. Very good art: A-level groups of up to 20; regular exhibitions. Lots of music (choirs, orchestra) and drama. Extra-curricular activities include popular Duke of Edinburgh award scheme, community aid programme. Regular foreign exchanges.

Results   (1997) GCSE: 86% gained at least five grades A–C. A-level: 41% of entries graded A or B.

Destinations   About 80% continue into the sixth form; of these, 80% proceed to university.

Sport   Main games: hockey (very strong), netball, basketball, tennis, athletics, cross-country. Badminton, swimming, football, lacrosse, cricket also on offer. Facilities include on-site playing fields, tennis courts.

Remarks   Good all round.

KESWICK ♂ ♀
Vicarage Hill, Keswick, Cumbria CA12 5QD. Tel (017687) 72605

Synopsis
Comprehensive (grant-maintained) ★ Co-educational ★ Day and boarding ★ Ages 11–18 ★ 950 pupils (roughly equal numbers of girls and boys, 90% day) ★ 210 in sixth form ★ Fees (boarding only): £3,900
Head: Michael Chapman, 44, appointed 1996.
First-rate comprehensive; good teaching and results; boarding option is a plus.

Profile
Background Roots go back to about 1400; re-founded as a grammar school 1898; amalgamated with a secondary modern and went comprehensive (on two sites half a mile apart) 1980; whole school now on the attractive site of the former secondary modern following £4.2 million building and refurbishment programme; opted out of council control 1995.

Atmosphere Friendly, disciplined: an attractive blend of the traditional and modern.

Admissions Of the 150 who enter each year, 80 are from local primary schools, 60 from outside the catchment area (more apply) and 10 are boarders – some from Europe and further afield. Children are above average in ability, mostly from middle-class backgrounds. One boarding house (second closed due to dwindling numbers): homely atmosphere, good facilities.

The head Recent appointment (predecessor had been in post 20 years). Good manager; has high expectations of all. Read natural sciences at Cambridge; previously deputy head of Sexey's (qv). Married; two children (one a pupil here).

The teaching Good (Ofsted inspectors complained it was too 'teacher-centred' – always a good sign); well-qualified, enthusiastic staff. Broad curriculum: all do science as three separate subjects; all take a second language from second year; good art, design/technology. Pupils grouped by ability in main subjects from second year. Vocational alternatives to A-level available; all take general studies. Extra-curricular activities include well-supported Duke of Edinburgh award scheme.

Results (1997) GCSE: 61% gained at least five grades A–C. A-level: 40% of entries graded A or B.

Destinations 80% continue into the sixth form; of these, 85% proceed to university.

Sport Strong in all the traditional team games. First-rate playing fields, new £1.2 million sports hall.

Remarks Ofsted inspectors concluded (1994): 'This is a good school, successfully promoting high expectations of staff and pupils.'

KIMBOLTON ♂ ♀
Kimbolton, Huntingdon, Cambridgeshire PE18 0EA. Tel (01480) 860505

Synopsis
Independent ★ Co-educational ★ Day and some boarding ★ Ages 11–18 (plus associated junior school) ★ 558 pupils (53% boys, 95% day) ★ 152 in sixth form ★ Fees: £5,858 day; £9,969 boarding
Head: Roger Peel, 51, appointed 1987.
Sound, well-run school; good teaching and results; lots of sport.

Profile

Background Founded 1600 as a grammar school; awarded Direct Grant status 1945; became fully independent 1978. Main building is Kimbolton Castle (once the home of Catherine of Aragon); later additions (including classrooms, labs, sports complex) dotted around a 160-acre campus; sixth-form common room in cellars; daily prayers in chapel. Pre-prep and prep departments (200 pupils aged four to 11) on same site.

Atmosphere Busy, hard-working; good relations between staff and pupils. Boarding ethos retained; lessons on Saturday mornings. Distinctive purple, black and white striped blazer; sixth-form boys can wear grey suits.

Admissions By interview and tests in English, maths, verbal reasoning or Common Entrance (50% mark required); school is not unduly selective, and likely to become less so with the phasing out of assisted places. Most pupils live locally (extensive bus service); two boarding houses in the High Street, a short walk away.

The head Energetic, enthusiastic; an imposing presence. Read chemistry at Nottingham; previously a housemaster at Trent College. Keen on sport and the outdoor life. Married (to a teacher); three children (all were pupils here).

The teaching Largely traditional in style; experienced staff, most appointed by present head. Fairly broad curriculum; science taught as three separate subjects (chemistry a particular strength); choice of 18 subjects at A-level (including Spanish, food technology, political studies); all do general studies. Pupils grouped by ability in most subjects; average class size 25, reducing to 22 for GCSE, smaller in sixth form. Lots of music; 200 learn an instrument; two orchestras. Extra-curricular activities include well-supported cadet force, Duke of Edinburgh award scheme.

Results (1997) GCSE: 96% gained at least five grades A–C. A-level: 54% of entries graded A or B.

Destinations About 85% stay on for A-levels; of these, 85% proceed to university (average of six a year to Oxbridge).

Sport Lots on offer. Main games football, hockey, cricket for boys; hockey, netball, tennis for girls. Fencing, aerobics, squash, badminton, sailing, canoeing also popular. Facilities include extensive playing fields, all-weather pitch, squash courts.

Remarks Good all round.

KING DAVID HIGH ♂ ♀
Childwall Road, Liverpool L15 6UZ. Tel (0151) 722 7496

Synopsis
Comprehensive (voluntary-aided, Jewish) ★ Co-educational ★ Ages 11–18 ★ 565 pupils (slightly more girls than boys) ★ 113 in sixth form
Head: John Smartt, 48, appointed 1994.
First-rate, well-run school; good teaching and results; excellent music.

Profile

Background Founded 1853; moved to present site (shared with a synagogue, Jewish primary school and community centre) 1957. The only Jewish secondary school in the city – but 60% of the pupils are non-Jewish and the head is a practising Catholic. Grey, drab, flat-roofed buildings; much-needed refurbishment under way.

Atmosphere   Strong community spirit; warm relations between staff and pupils (and among pupils); good discipline. School is faith-based but rules say 'no assembly should compromise the religious ideals held by any non-Jewish pupils or their families.' Sixth-formers attend week-long residential course on leadership and are given a lot of responsibility (including visiting 'feeder' primary schools and helping new pupils settle in); houses run by pupils (points for effort, achievement, care of the environment). Parents kept well-informed, made to feel welcome.

Admissions   School is over-subscribed (150 apply for 90 places) but not academically selective. Priority to: Jewish pupils from King David Primary School; all other Jewish pupils; non-Jewish pupils from the primary school; non-Jewish pupils who (along with their parents) can demonstrate an understanding of, and commitment to, the Jewish life and ethos of the school. Up to 15 places reserved for those with an aptitude for music. Catchment area includes the Wirral, Southport, Crosby; all applicants interviewed; most pupils are of above-average ability.

The head   Appears relaxed and easy-going but has his finger on every pulse; has spent his entire career here (previously deputy head) and is obviously devoted to the school. Gets on well with staff and pupils; active in the community and in adult education. Read biology at Leeds. Not married.

The teaching   Generally good, often formal in style ('heavily teacher-directed', according to Ofsted). Experienced, well-qualified, committed staff of 39; low turnover. Unusually broad curriculum: all do two languages (from French, German, Hebrew) for first three years; Jewish pupils take Jewish studies, including Hebrew and Latin (non-Jewish study world religions); science taught as three separate subjects in second and third years; computing not a strength. Pupils grouped by ability in maths, science; extra help for those with special needs; average class size 30, reducing to 24 for GCSE, 12 at A-level. Choice of 17 subjects at A-levels; GNVQ in business & finance available as an alternative. Progress carefully monitored; homework set regularly. First-rate music: choir, two orchestras, various other ensembles; 20 peripatetic teachers. Lots of other extra-curricular activities (debating, chess, drama): school buzzes at lunch-time.

Results   (1997) GCSE: creditable 74% gained at least five grades A–C. A-level: 45% of entries graded A or B.

Destinations   About 65% stay on into the sixth form; of these, about 80% proceed to university.

Sport   Wide range on offer; adequate facilities. (Girls' football a strength.)

Remarks   Popular, thriving school; highly recommended.

KING EDWARD'S, BATH   ♂ ♀
North Road, Bath BA2 6HU. Tel (01225) 464313

Synopsis
Independent ★ Co-educational from September 1997 ★ Day ★ Ages 11–18 (plus associated junior school) ★ 660 pupils (95% boys) ★ 222 in sixth form ★ Fees: £4,992
Head: Peter Winter 47, appointed 1993.
Good, well-run, academic school; very good teaching and results; strong sport.

Profile
Background Founded 1552; moved to fine, 14-acre, hill-top site 1961 (splendid views across the city); formerly Direct Grant, reverted to full independence 1976; girls admitted to sixth form 1986, at age 11 from 1997. Attractive, Georgian-style buildings recently refurbished; later additions include new music school, theatre, science labs. Co-educational junior school in modern, purpose-built premises.

Atmosphere A civilised community: courteous, well-disciplined pupils; committed, caring staff; diligent pastoral care.

Admissions School is over-subscribed, fairly selective and, with the admission of girls, likely to remain so – despite the phasing out of assisted places, which about 150 hold. Extensive catchment area.

The head Amiable, approachable; keen on 'open government'; has modernised the school. Read modern languages at Oxford; previously head of the international house at Sevenoaks (qv). Teaches first-years and lower-sixth general studies. Married; two children (one a pupil here).

The teaching Good quality: mostly formal in style; thoroughly professional staff (one third female). Broad curriculum: sciences taught separately; strong maths (but not computing); up to half add German or Spanish to French; choice of 17 subjects at GCSE, 20 at A-level. Lots of art, drama, music (choirs, orchestras, various ensembles). Extra-curricular activities include well-supported cadet force and a wide range of outdoor pursuits.

Results (1997) GCSE: all gained at least five grades A–C. A-level: creditable 65% of entries graded A or B.

Destinations About 95% proceed to university (10–15 a year to Oxbridge).

Sport Strong tradition. Main sports: rugby (a particular strength), hockey, cricket, netball, athletics. Tennis, swimming, fencing, badminton, squash etc also on offer. Facilities include 17 acres of playing fields about a mile away, all-weather pitch, sports hall.

Remarks Good all round – and getting better.

KING EDWARD'S, BIRMINGHAM ♂
Edgbaston Park Road, Birmingham B15 2UA. Tel (0121) 472 1672

Synopsis
Independent ★ Boys ★ Day ★ Ages 11–18 ★ 890 pupils ★ 260 in sixth form
★ Fees: £4,914
Head: Hugh Wright, 59, appointed 1991 (retires summer 1998).
Distinguished, highly selective school; excellent results.

Profile
Background Founded 1552 by Edward VI to foster godliness and good learning; one of seven schools (two independent, five grammar) in the generously-endowed King Edward's Foundation (owns a chunk of the city centre); climbed during the 19th century 'from insignificance to splendour'; formerly Direct Grant. Moved 1936 to present fine 40-acre site shared with sister school, King Edward VI High (qv). Purpose-built, slightly forbidding, Edwardian quadrangles; recent additions include music school, design/technology centre, sports hall.

Atmosphere Vibrant, well-ordered, highly academic ('We get people to be thorough, a terrific virtue,' says the head). Traditional, predominantly Christian ethos (in a multi-faith context). Able, ambitious pupils who waste no time on appearances. Library is full long before morning lessons begin; orderly mass movement between classes. Strong pastoral care system. Much parental support.

Admissions Four apply for every place at 11-plus; entry by school's own searching exams in English, maths, aptitude; applications in by mid-January. A third come from prep schools, the rest from state primaries in a catchment area with a 25-mile radius; 30% ethnic minorities. Nearly a third hold assisted places (including 50 boys who pay nothing and have free school lunches): foundation aims to replace the scheme with its own equivalent. Some scholarships (academic, music, art).

The head (Chief Master) Wise, amiable, experienced (his third headship – after Stockport Grammar and Gresham's); appointed to manage and lead (consultative style) not revolutionise. Read classics at Oxford; passionate about music. Married; three grown-up sons. From September 1998: Roger Dancey, head of City of London Boys' (qv).

The teaching Formal, traditional, gently humorous; tender plants may blossom but the boys expect no laggards ('no place for fop or idler', as the school song has it). All do 11 GCSEs (most take maths a year early) and four A-levels. First-rate technology (close links with industry); very strong languages, including Latin, Greek, Japanese, Russian. Staff of 80 (18 women); class sizes 20–26 to GCSE; 14–16 for A-levels. Some cross-timetabling with sister school (and much combining for drama and music). Regular exchanges with schools in France, Germany, Spain.

Results (1997) GCSE: all gained at least five grades A–C. A-level: impressive 86% of entries graded A or B (10th in the league table).

Destinations All go on to university (about 45 a year to Oxbridge).

Sport Extensive programme: in addition to cricket, hockey, rugby, athletics, swimming and tennis, there are facilities for badminton, basketball, Eton Fives, fencing, golf, sailing, squash and cross-country. ('Luck is good, the prize is pleasant, but the glory's in the game.')

Remarks Fine school for able boys who can keep up with the pace. Ofsted inspectors concluded (1994) that standards of achievement were excellent but there was not enough emphasis on aesthetic and creative subjects.

KING EDWARD VI, ASTON ♂

Frederick Road, Aston, Birmingham B6 6DJ. Tel (0121) 327 1130

Synopsis

Grammar (grant-maintained) ★ Boys ★ Ages 11–18 ★ 643 pupils ★ 174 in sixth form
Head: Peter Christopher, 53, appointed 1992.
Friendly, hard-working grammar school; good teaching and results; strong sport.

Profile

Background Founded 1883 as part of the King Edward VI Foundation (five grammar schools, two independents) in what was then a leafy suburb but is now an inner-city area showing signs of revival; opted out of council control 1993. Victorian-Gothic buildings (long, linoed corridors, high-ceilinged classrooms, vaulted library hung with portraits and rolls of honour) plus later additions, including a hall large enough to hold the whole school, design/technology suite, drama studio, sixth-form study area; sports hall added 1997.

Atmosphere Friendly, vigorous, hard-working ('You're very conspicuous if you're playing around'). Strong, common-sense discipline: no silly rules, and no doubt about the consequences of serious offences; excellent relationships across age groups and between staff and boys.

Admissions By tests administered by the foundation; about 750 compete for 96 places a year. Wide range of backgrounds from an extensive catchment area.

The head Enthusiastic, energetic, keenly ambitious for the school; clearly liked and respected by the boys. Read history and law at Cambridge; became a solicitor before switching to teaching; previously deputy head of a comprehensive in Staffordshire. Married.

The teaching Demanding, stimulating. Broad curriculum: strong science, taught as three separate subjects; all take two modern languages for first three years (40% continue both to GCSE); good facilities for design/technology, art, computing. All take three A-levels plus general studies. Extra-curricular activities include music (choir, many instrumental groups), public speaking, active Duke of Edinburgh award scheme. Strong links with local industry for careers and work experience.

Results (1997) GCSE: all gained at least five grades A–C. A-level: 41% of entries graded A or B.

Destinations Up to 90% stay on for A-levels; of these, up to 95% proceed to university (including Oxbridge).

Sport An important part of school life; lots of inter-house competitions. First-class rugby, athletics, cricket, swimming (despite lack of a pool). Orienteering, hockey, basketball also on offer. Playing fields 10 minutes' walk away.

Remarks Happy, well-balanced school; boys make the most of their abilities. Ofsted inspectors concluded (1994): 'The school expects and achieves high standards of work and behaviour from all of its pupils. Teaching and learning are conducted within a calm, purposeful and productive atmosphere and with excellent relationships between all those involved.'

KING EDWARD VI, CAMP HILL, BOYS' ♂
Vicarage Road, Kings Heath, Birmingham B14 7QJ. Tel (0121) 444 3188

Synopsis
Grammar (grant-maintained) ★ Boys ★ Ages 11–18 ★ 648 pupils ★ 185 in sixth form
Head: Mervyn Brooker, 43, appointed 1995.
First-rate academic school; very good teaching and results; strong sport.

Profile
Background Founded 1883, one of five grammar schools of the King Edward VI Foundation in Birmingham; moved 1956 to present spacious campus (shared with King Edward VI Camp Hill Girls', qv) and purpose-built (recently refurbished) premises; opted out of council control 1993. Many later additions, including new sixth-form centre shared with girls' school.

Atmosphere Lively, purposeful, well-ordered; good pastoral care ('Boys respond best to encouragement and praise rather than criticism and denigration'); older pupils help the younger ones. Traditional blazer-and-tie uniform for all.

Admissions By highly competitive tests administered by the foundation in maths, verbal and non-verbal reasoning (minimum IQ 115–120); school severely over-subscribed (nearly 800 apply for 93 places). Pupils drawn from a wide range of backgrounds (20% ethnic minority) in an extensive catchment area.

The head Able, experienced, enthusiastic. Read geography at Cambridge (cricket Blue); previously deputy head of Wolverhampton Grammar (qv); came here as deputy head 1992. Favours tradition: wears a gown to assemblies. Married; two children.

The teaching First-rate; generally formal in style; well-qualified staff of 42 (six women). Broad curriculum: science taught as three separate subjects; first-years take Latin for half the year, German for the other half; all take 10 GCSEs; some A-levels taught jointly with girls' school. Pupils grouped by ability in maths, French only for GCSE; extra help for the exceptionally able; average class size 31, reducing to 28 for GCSE. Plenty of drama, music (free instrumental tuition). Extra-curricular activities include chess, computing, photography. Very good careers guidance.

Results (1997) GCSE: all gained at least five grades A–C. A-level: very creditable 68% of entries graded A or B.

Destinations About 90% go on to university (average of six a year to Oxbridge).

Sport Good record, particularly in rugby, football, basketball, hockey, fencing, badminton. Athletics, cross-country, cricket, swimming also on offer. Facilities include extensive playing fields; indoor pool shared with girls' school.

Remarks Ofsted inspectors concluded (1994): 'This is a successful school with many good features. Standards are high. It is an orderly and happy community where relationships are good and pastoral care is well developed.'

KING EDWARD VI, CAMP HILL, GIRLS' ♀
Vicarage Road, Kings Heath, Birmingham B14 7QJ. Tel (0121) 444 2150

Synopsis
Grammar (grant-maintained) ★ Girls ★ Ages 11–18 ★ 700 pupils ★ 209 in sixth form
Head: Mrs Joan Fisher, 54, appointed 1992.
Strong academic school; very good teaching and results.

Profile
Background Founded 1883, one of five grammar schools of the King Edward VI Foundation in Birmingham; moved 1958 to present, spacious, parkland site shared (as are the music block and sixth-form centre) with King Edward VI Camp Hill Boys' (qv); opted out of council control 1993. Functional, purpose-built premises plus many later additions, including new science labs, classrooms, assembly hall. Numbers planned to rise to 820 by 2002 after the city council was found guilty of sex discrimination by providing fewer grammar school places for girls than boys.

Atmosphere Earnest, academic, well-ordered (perhaps a bit sombre); very good relations between staff and pupils. Tidy uniform below the sixth form (where most wear black skirts and jumpers).

Admissions By highly competitive tests in maths, verbal and non-verbal reasoning (administered by the foundation); top 10% of the ability range; no interview, no priority to siblings; school is severely over-subscribed (up to eight apply for each place). Girls come from a wide range of backgrounds in an extensive catchment area (nearly 100 primary schools).

The head   Able, experienced. Read modern languages at Leeds, MA from Birmingham; previously deputy head of a girls' grammar school in Essex. Married; four children (including triplets).

The teaching   First-rate; generally formal in style; well-qualified staff of 45 (a third male). Broad curriculum: sciences (a strength) taught separately; languages include German, Latin; good design/technology; business studies popular; some A-levels taught jointly with boys' school. Pupils grouped by ability in maths only for GCSE; average class size 30, reducing to 24 for GCSE, smaller at A-level. Music lessons are free; 20% learn an instrument. Extra-curricular activities include chess, debating, well-supported Duke of Edinburgh award scheme.

Results   (1997) GCSE: 98% gained at least five grades A–C. A-level: creditable 62% of entries graded A or B.

Destinations   About 95% go to university (average of six a year to Oxbridge).

Sport   Strong netball, hockey. Badminton, tennis, athletics, rounders, karate also on offer. Indoor pool shared with boys' school (but used at different times).

Remarks   Ofsted inspectors concluded (1994): 'Standards seen in the classroom nearly always reflected the high ability of the intake. Pupils are courteous and well behaved and, when given the opportunity to do so, exercise responsibility with good humour and maturity.'

KING EDWARD VI, CHELMSFORD
Broomfield Road, Chelmsford, Essex CM1 3SX. Tel (01245) 353510

Synopsis
Grammar (grant-maintained) ★ Boys (plus girls in sixth form) ★ Ages 11–18 ★
740 pupils ★ 240 in sixth form (85% boys)
Head: Tony Tuckwell, 54, appointed 1984.
Fine academic school; first-rate teaching and results; strong music, sport.

Profile
Background   Founded 1551; moved to present Victorian premises (cloisters, quadrangles) 1892; opted out of council control 1992. Space is tight; some classrooms in 'temporary' huts; sixth-form centre dilapidated. Recent additions include art, design & technology block.

Atmosphere   Hard-working, well-ordered, humming with activity; friendly relations between staff and pupils; supportive pastoral care system. Uniform worn throughout.

Admissions   School is heavily over-subscribed (550 apply for 108 places) and highly selective; entry by competitive tests (no interview); top 5% of the ability range from up to 40 'feeder' primaries in a catchment area with a 15-mile radius. Promotion to the sixth form requires at least seven Bs at GCSE; those joining from outside (40–50 a year) need five As and two Bs. Sixth-form girls not overwhelmed but need to be strong.

The head   Able, experienced; strong leader, good manager. Read history at Oxford; MBA in education management; has taught in state schools for 30 years (and still enjoys it). Married (to a teacher); no children.

The teaching   Very good; predominantly formal, traditional in style; experienced, well-qualified staff of 47 (75% male). Standard grammar school curriculum (three sciences, Latin); lots of computing; all do at least three A-levels (up to 40% do four) plus general studies. Pupils grouped by ability in maths only; termly grades; average class size 24, reducing to 13 at A-level. First-rate music; fine choir, two orchestras, various ensembles. Extra-curricular activities include cadet force (and corps of drums).

Results   (1997) GCSE: all gained at least five grades A–C. A-level: creditable 64% of entries graded A or B.

Destinations   Nearly all proceed to university (average of 12 a year to Oxbridge).

Sport   Strong. Main activities: rugby, soccer, hockey, cricket, athletics, cross-country, tennis; regular county honours. Playing fields three miles away.

Remarks   Ofsted inspectors concluded (1996): 'This is a very good school which gives good value for money. There is a powerful ethos related to a learning culture. Leadership by the headmaster is outstanding.' Recommended.

KING EDWARD VI, FIVE WAYS ♂ ♀
Scotland Lane, Bartley Green, Birmingham B32 4BT. Tel (0121) 475 3535

Synopsis
Grammar (grant-maintained) ★ Boys (plus girls in sixth form) ★ Ages 11–18 ★
704 pupils ★ 220 in sixth form (equal numbers of girls and boys)
Head: John Knowles, 48, appointed 1990.
Successful, expanding school; good teaching and results.

Profile
Background   Founded 1883 (part of the King Edward VI Foundation) on one of the city's biggest traffic islands; moved to present site and purpose-built premises surrounded by parkland and playing fields 1958; recent additions (more to come) include music centre, state-of-the-art science labs; some classrooms in 'temporary' huts. Opted out of council control 1992; going fully co-educational from September 1998; numbers expected to reach 1,050 in 2002.

Atmosphere   Warm, welcoming; pupils well-disciplined, courteous (they hold doors open for one another). Strict uniform below the sixth form (when smart dress is expected).

Admissions   Over-subscribed. Entry by tests (administered by the foundation) in maths, verbal and non-verbal reasoning; 96 boys admitted each year, rising to 150 boys and girls in September 1998. Girls admitted to sixth form on the basis of predicted GCSE grades and interview. A third of pupils are from ethnic minorities.

The head   Gentle; practising Christian; gets on well with staff and pupils. Read physics at Manchester Institute of Science and Technology; previously head of physics at Watford Grammar (qv). Married; three daughters.

The teaching   High quality, challenging; mainly formal in style; well-equipped classrooms (videos, computers). Pupils not grouped by ability; average class size 32, reducing to 25 for GCSE. National curriculum plus; science taught as three separate subjects; Latin on offer as an alternative to a second modern language (French or German); good computing (school was a pioneer). Lots of music (regular concerts), art, drama. Good links with local engineering and computing companies; all have two weeks' work experience.

Results   (1997) GCSE: 95% gained at least five grades A–C. A-level: 49% of

entries graded A or B.
Destinations   About 85% proceed to university (medicine, law are popular); a few each year to Oxbridge.
Sport   Chiefly: rugby, hockey, soccer, cricket, athletics, cross-country, swimming. Basketball, badminton, golf, squash, tennis, sailing also on offer. Lots of fixtures against other schools.
Remarks   Good all round.

KING EDWARD VI, HANDSWORTH ♀
Rose Hill Road, Handsworth, Birmingham B21 9AR. Tel (0121) 554 2342

Synopsis
Grammar (grant-maintained) ★ Girls ★ Ages 11–18 ★ 877 pupils ★ 237 in sixth form
Head: Miss Elspeth Insch, 47, appointed 1989.
Well-run, academic school; very good teaching and results.

Profile
Background   Founded 1883, one of seven schools (five state) belonging to the King Edward VI Foundation; moved 1911 to present purpose-built premises on pleasant nine-acre site in a run-down area; opted out of council control 1993. Elegant main building (wide corridors and staircases, high-ceilinged, well-lit classrooms) plus later additions, including striking new sixth-form centre.
Atmosphere   Competitive, enthusiastic, warm; friendly relations between staff and pupils; very good pastoral care. Uniform (navy skirts, blazers, light blue blouses) below the sixth form. Supportive parents help raise funds.
Admissions   Selective: entry by exams in maths, verbal and non-verbal reasoning; 900 apply, places offered to the 128 with the highest scores; head discourages coaching, preferring the girls to get in on 'their native wit'. Rich social and ethnic mix: catchment area extends from inner-city to leafy suburbia, including Wolverhampton, Sutton Coldfield, Dudley (girls travel by school buses and public transport); 30% Asian.
The head   High profile; very able; indefatigable (says she has resigned herself to being an autocrat). Read geography at London and Edinburgh.
The teaching   Stimulating. Aims are: 'learning for life, enjoyment of learning, independent thought'; classroom furniture moved around to accommodate different styles. Broad curriculum: science taught as three separate subjects; all do Latin for first three years; nearly all take 10 GCSEs. Pupils grouped by ability in maths only; classes of 20–25 for GCSE, 10–20 in sixth form; homework regularly set and marked (head has cautioned parents not to let their daughters spend too much time doing it). A-level sciences particularly strong (80% take at least one). Good music (choirs, orchestras, various ensembles), drama (in a converted cloakroom). Extra-curricular activities include well-supported Duke of Edinburgh award scheme (an enthusiasm of the head's).
Results   Good. (1997) GCSE: all gained at least five grades A–C. A-level: 68% of entries graded A or B.
Destinations   Almost all go to university (about eight a year to Oxbridge).
Sport   Main activities: hockey, tennis, netball, gymnastics, dance, swimming, golf; emphasis on skills and fitness for life rather than 'hammering the opposition'.
Remarks   Identified by Ofsted (1996) as an 'outstandingly successful' school.

KING EDWARD VI HIGH ♀
Edgbaston Park Road, Birmingham, B15 2UB. Tel (0121) 472 1834

Synopsis
Independent ★ Girls ★ Day ★ Ages 11–18 ★ 550 pupils ★ 165 in sixth form
★ Fees: £4,725.
Head: Miss Sarah Evans, 44, appointed 1996.
First-rate, highly academic school; excellent teaching and results.

Profile
Background   Founded 1883, part of the King Edward VI Foundation; moved to
its present 40-acre site (shared with King Edward's, qv) 1940; formerly Direct
Grant. Secure, elegant buildings, mostly modernised; teaching facilities excellent
(but no proper theatre/concert hall).

Atmosphere   Academic, friendly, impeccably well disciplined; hands-off management style. Sixth-formers in 'appropriate' dress (liberally interpreted).

Admissions   Severely selective; more than three apply for each place. Entry by
school's own exams in English, maths, verbal reasoning ('no special preparation
is advised'). Pupils come from a 25-mile radius (more from state primaries than
prep schools); substantial ethnic minority element, which the school prefers not
to identify or quantify; 'girls of all faiths or none are equally welcome'. Assisted
places, which more than 100 hold, will be replaced by the foundation's own
scheme; some scholarships.

The head   Recent appointment; still watching rather than reforming (not that
much needs changing); low key but makes her presence felt; wants girls to 'have
the world at their feet' when they leave. Read English at Sussex (BA), Leicester
(MA); previously head of a Quaker school in Essex. Married; one son.

The teaching   Brisk, expository, carefully planned. Well-qualified, predominantly female staff of 57; pupils not grouped by ability; average class size 26.
Broad curriculum: all do Latin for two years; German, Greek on offer; science
taught as three separate subjects; most take 11 GCSEs. Wide choice of subjects at
A-level (some in conjunction with King Edward's); all do general studies plus
courses in English, maths, languages, word processing. Lively music (in conjunction with boys). Numerous lunch-time activities.

Results   (1997) GCSE: all gained at least five grades A–C. A-level: impressive
85% of entries graded A or B (12th in the league table).

Destinations   Virtually all go on to university (about 15 a year to Oxbridge);
medicine, finance the two leading career choices.

Sport   Particularly strong netball, hockey, swimming. All do tennis, athletics,
dance, gymnastics, rounders for first two years; later options include badminton,
squash, lacrosse, archery, golf, fencing. Facilities include sports hall, indoor
pool, squash courts, all-weather pitches.

Remarks   A fast route to excellence for bright, well-motivated girls.

KING EDWARD VI, LICHFIELD ♂ ♀
Upper St John Street, Lichfield, Staffordshire WS14 9EE. Tel (01543) 255714

Synopsis
Comprehensive ★ Co-educational ★ Ages 11–18 ★ 1,350 pupils (slightly more girls than boys) ★ 290 in sixth form
Head: Duncan Meikle, 39, appointed April 1997.
Sound school; good teaching and results.

Profile
Background   Founded 1495 and became a solid provincial grammar school (Dr Johnson was pupil); moved to present site 1909; amalgamated with neighbouring secondary modern and went comprehensive 1973. Former grammar school building (covered in virginia creeper) has wide corridors, ample classrooms, a life-sized statue of Dr Johnson (head ruefully in hands), a computerised library and a cluster of scruffy huts round the back; former secondary modern premises on the hill behind are an eyesore – a clump of featureless, functional, poorly-maintained boxes; constant flow of pupils between the two (regularly resulting in late arrival to lessons). Music block a day's march away: across the cricket pitch, near the main road. Recent additions include a sports complex (shared with the community). School is not well funded (parents raise considerable sums).

Atmosphere   Orderly, hard working but somewhat staid; good pastoral care system. Parents are supportive and ambitious.

Admissions   School is over-subscribed; pupils predominantly from middle-class homes, about a quarter from outside the immediate catchment area.

The head   New appointment (predecessor had been in post 24 years). Read history at University College, London (First); MPhil from Manchester (wrote a 60,000-word thesis in his spare time); previously deputy head for six years of a comprehensive in Northumberland. Married; three daughters.

The teaching   Variable in quality but generally rigorous. Conscientious staff; good mix of age and experience. Standard national curriculum; all have at least a taste of both French and German; good science. Pupils grouped by ability from the start; further setting thereafter. Reasonable choice of subjects at A-level; vocational alternatives available. Some music and drama, but the facilities do not encourage them. Lots of educational trips, including foreign exchanges.

Results   (1997) GCSE: creditable 68% gained at least five grades A–C. A-level: 46% of entries graded A or B.

Destinations   About 70% continue into the sixth form; of these, 90% proceed to university.

Sport   Not a great strength. Hockey, tennis, athletics for both sexes; rugby; netball, basketball also on offer. Facilities include swimming pool, all-weather pitches.

Remarks   Solid school; over-due changes on the way. Ofsted inspectors concluded (1997): 'Overall standards are high but the most able pupils are rarely challenged to expand their knowledge and understanding beyond that necessary for external examinations.'

KING EDWARD VI, SOUTHAMPTON ♂ ♀
Kellett Road, Southampton SO15 7UQ. Tel (01703) 704561

Synopsis
Independent ★ Co-educational ★ Day ★ Ages 11–18 ★ 950 pupils (80% boys)
★ 259 in sixth form ★ Fees: £5,672
Head: Peter Hamilton, 41, appointed 1996.
Lively, successful school; very good teaching and results; lots of sport.

Profile
Background   Founded 1553; moved to present nine-acre site and purpose-built premises 1938; joined the independent sector 1979; girls admitted to sixth form 1983, at 11 in 1994 (aim is 50:50 balance). Facilities are good.

Atmosphere   Hard-working, well-ordered; very good pastoral care. 'Our aim is to provide a congenial atmosphere and a disciplined environment in which able pupils can develop as individuals'.

Admissions   By interview and tests in English, maths, verbal reasoning; school is heavily over-subscribed and quite selective (minimum IQ 112) but likely to become less so with the phasing out of assisted places, which more than 200 hold. Catchment area extends to Winchester, Salisbury, Bournemouth (parents arrange transport). Scholarships: academic, music.

The head   Able, enthusiastic. Was a pupil here; read modern languages at Oxford (First); taught at Radley, Westminster; still teaches (and thinks it a 'grave error' for heads not to). Married (to a teacher); one daughter.

The teaching   First-rate, mainly traditional in style; relatively youthful staff (two-thirds male). Broad curriculum: sciences (a strength) taught separately; languages include German, Spanish, Latin, Greek; most take 11 GCSEs; choice of 20 subjects at A-level plus extensive general studies programme. Pupils grouped by ability in maths from second year; extra help for dyslexics; average class size 22, reducing to a maximum of 12 at A-level. Lots of music; 150 learn an instrument; choir, two orchestras, various ensembles. Good careers advice. Extra-curricular activities include well-supported Duke of Edinburgh award scheme. Regular language exchanges with pupils in France, Germany, Spain.

Results   (1997) GCSE: all gained at least five grades A–C. A-level: very creditable 70% of entries graded A or B.

Destinations   Virtually all proceed to university (average of 10 a year to Oxbridge).

Sport   Regarded as an integral part of school life; no one excused except on medical grounds. Main sports: rugby, hockey, cricket for boys; netball, hockey, tennis, rounders for girls. Sailing, table tennis, acrobatics also on offer. Facilities include all-weather pitch, sports hall, squash courts; additional playing fields near Southampton airport.

Remarks   HMC inspectors concluded (1995): 'This is a successful and purposeful school. Standards achieved in public examinations are high. Pupils work effectively and behave well.'

KING EDWARD VI, STRATFORD-UPON-AVON ♂
Church Street, Stratford-upon-Avon, Warwickshire CV37 6HB. Tel (01789) 293351

Synopsis
Grammar (voluntary-aided) ★ Boys ★ Ages 11–18 ★ 432 pupils ★ 115 in sixth form
Head: Tim Moore-Bridger, 52, appointed April 1997.
Traditional academic school; sound teaching and results; strong sport.

Profile
Background   Roots go back to the 13th century (Guild of the Holy Cross endowment still produces an annual income of £250,000); re-founded 1553 by Edward VI. Half-timbered 15th and 16th-century buildings plus 20th-century additions (including new, £3 million, Tudor-style music/drama/sports hall) grouped around a spacious playground in the centre of the town. Guild chapel still used for morning worship; brass plate in schoolroom proclaims, 'Near this spot sat, according to old tradition passed on from scholar to scholar, William Shakespeare'.

Atmosphere   Traditional: no frills, no fuss; easy relations between staff and pupils (main sin is eating fish and chips in the street at lunch-time); strict blazer-and-tie uniform below the sixth form. Supportive parents.

Admissions   By county council 11–plus; about 250 apply for 60 places; top 15%–20% of the ability range. Boys come in equal proportions from the town, the Stratford area and as far afield as Coventry and Solihull.

The head   Recent appointment. Able, energetic, ambitious; keen to raise standards and modernise the school. Read modern languages at Cambridge; taught for 20 years at St Paul's; previously deputy head for eight years of Nottingham High. Married; three children.

The teaching   Formal in style; experienced, hard-working staff (25% female). Standard national curriculum; good English; Latin on offer; all do science as three separate subjects (well-equipped labs); limited computing; rather narrow choice of 14 subjects at A-level; most do three plus general studies (results are not outstanding). Pupils grouped by ability in maths from third year; average class size 30, reducing to 22 for GCSE, 16 in sixth form. Lots of music; drama offers the opportunity of walk-on parts at the RSC.

Results   (1997) GCSE: all gained at least five grades A–C. A-level: 43% of entries graded A or B (should be much higher, given the intake).

Destinations   About 80% proceed to university (including two or three a year to Oxbridge).

Sport   Rugby, fencing and rowing are strong. Facilities include indoor pool, extensive playing fields 15 minutes' walk away.

Remarks   Old-fashioned school in need of a shake-up.

KING HENRY VIII ♂ ♀
Warwick Road, Coventry CV3 6AQ. Tel (01203) 673442

Synopsis
Independent ★ Co-educational ★ Day ★ Ages 11–18 (plus associated junior school) ★ 820 pupils (roughly equal numbers of girls and boys) ★ 215 in sixth form ★ Fees: £4,215
Head: Terence Vardon, 49, appointed 1994.
Well-run, academic school; good teaching and results; lots of art, drama, music.

Profile
Background   Founded 1545; moved to present, rather confined, 11–acre site 1885; formerly Direct Grant, reverted to full independence (and became co-educational) 1976. Imposing Victorian building plus later additions, including science block, sixth-form centre. Newly-built (£1 million) junior school on adjoining site. Shares a governing body with Bablake (qv).

Atmosphere   Well-organised and disciplined (head believes rewards should have prominence over punishments); friendly relations between staff and pupils; strict uniform. Broadly Christian assemblies held twice weekly (main hall seats the whole school).

Admissions   Over-subscribed (230 apply for 120 places a year) and highly selective: top 10% of the ability range; those 'making little progress owing to persistent lack of effort or proved incapacity' liable to a term's notice. Entry by school's own tests in English, maths, verbal reasoning at 11 (taken also by those joining from the junior school), plus science, French at 13. 'Try before you buy' policy invites intending pupils to join for a day. Phasing out of assisted places, which 110 hold, will reduce the socio-economic mix; 25% ethnic minorities. Catchment area extends from Birmingham to Northampton. Scholarships, bursaries available.

The head   Vigorous, enthusiastic; efficient manager ('empower and delegate'); has modernised the school. Read history at Oxford; worked in state and independent schools; previously (and unusually) head of a comprehensive. Has a second career as an international musician (organ and harpsichord).

The teaching   Formal in style. Experienced staff of 75 (equal numbers of women and men). Broad curriculum: science (a particular strength) taught as three separate subjects; Latin, Greek on offer; lots of computing; choice of 22 subjects at A-level; all do general studies. Pupils grouped by ability in maths, French from third year; no provision for dyslexics. Maximum class size 24, reducing to 10–12 at A-level. Lively art, drama; good music (a third learn an instrument, lots of choirs, two orchestras, various ensembles). Regular trips to Europe for study and recreation; school owns a study centre in Normandy.

Results   (1997) GCSE: 98% gained at least five grades A–C. A-level: 66% of entries graded A or B.

Destinations   Virtually all go on to university (up to 12 a year to Oxbridge).

Sport   Main games: rugby (strong), hockey, cricket, netball. Extensive playing fields, including large all-weather pitch, two miles away; sports hall planned.

Remarks   Good school, and getting better.

KING'S, CANTERBURY ♂ ♀

Canterbury, Kent CT1 2ES. Tel (01227) 595501

Synopsis

Independent ★ Co-educational ★ Boarding and Day ★ Ages 13–18 (plus associated prep and pre-prep) ★ 738 pupils (57% boys, 81% boarding) ★ 317 in sixth form ★ Fees: £14,115 boarding; £9,750 day
Head: Canon Keith Wilkinson, 49, appointed 1996.
Lively, happy, traditional school in beautiful setting; first-rate teaching and results; accomplished music and drama; very good sport.

Profile

Background Founded in 6th century by St Augustine (school is as old as English Christianity); reconstituted 1541 by Henry VIII (who proposed to Anne Boleyn here). Steeped in history and tradition: setting is awe-inspiring; cathedral visible from practically every window; children walk through ancient cloisters and passages to classes. Girls first admitted to sixth form 1971; fully co-educational since 1992.

Atmosphere Vibrant, busy – but a quiet timelessness pervades. Tangibly happy and friendly; very good relations between teachers and well-mannered pupils. Exceptional standard of pastoral care (children clearly feel secure and valued); well-established tutor system (comprehensive reports every fortnight). Christianity central to the life of the school; regular services in the crypt and cathedral (but pupils say religion 'is not forced down our throats'). Co-education soundly established; girls' numbers set to rise still further. All wear 19th-century 'Canterbury dress': black jacket, striped trousers/skirt; King's scholars and monitors wear gowns. Six boarding houses for boys, five for girls, most in ancient and beautiful buildings; small dormitories, well-designed study bedrooms.

Admissions By Common Entrance; 60% mark required; school is quite severely selective. Sixth-form entry (60 apply for 30 places a year) requires at least six GCSEs at grade C or above, A or B in A-level choices, plus entry exam and interview. Most pupils from the South East; 30% 'first-time buyers' of independent education. Numerous scholarships, exhibitions.

The head Grammar-school educated; read English and theology at Hull, philosophy at Cambridge; became a curate and then chaplain at Eton (six years) and Malvern (five); previously head of Berkhamsted (qv). Quietly spoken, compassionate with a mental and spiritual toughness behind a mild exterior. Sees every pupil individually during the year; teaches English to first-years, religious studies and philosophy to the sixth form. Married (to a teacher); twin daughters (one at Oakham, the other here).

The teaching Very good across the curriculum and sometimes outstanding; mainly traditional in style. Well-qualified staff of 81 (high proportion from Oxbridge); 75% male. Sciences particularly strong (on offer as three separate subjects); languages include French, German, Italian, Japanese, Spanish; classics very well taught (all juniors do Latin or classical civilisation, Greek on offer). A-level choices include economics & politics, theatre studies, geology. Pupils grouped by ability from the start; some extra help for dyslexics; average class size 16–18, 10–12 in sixth form. High standard of art (in beautiful medieval building); lively drama (lots of productions, regular house plays); very good music (orchestras, chamber groups, choirs, regular concerts).

Results (1997) GCSE: all gained at least five grades A–C. A-level: creditable 76% of entries graded A or B (the top co-educational school).

Destinations   Virtually all go on to university (about 30 a year to Oxbridge).
Sport   Very strong: wide range of activities on offer, including rugby, hockey, rowing, cricket, tennis, netball, fencing, badminton, squash, swimming, netball, soccer, lacrosse. Facilities include extensive pitches, gleaming new sports hall, indoor pool.
Remarks   Successful, delightful school; highly recommended.

KING'S, CHESTER ♂
Chester, Cheshire CH4 7QL. Tel (01244) 680026

Synopsis
Independent ★ Boys ★ Day ★ Ages 11–18 (plus associated junior school) ★
460 pupils ★ 135 in sixth form ★ Fees: £4,494
Head: Roger Wickson, 57, appointed 1981.
Good academic school; first-rate teaching and results; lots of drama, music, sport.

Profile
Background   Founded 1541 by Henry VIII for the education of '24 poor and friendless boys'; moved to present 32-acre site (two miles south of the city) and attractive, purpose-built premises 1960; many later additions, including sixth-form centre, music school. Girls to be admitted to the sixth form in September 1988. On-site junior school under its own head.
Atmosphere   Happy, hard-working, well-disciplined; warm, courteous relations between staff and pupils. Uniform includes distinctive striped blazer. Supportive parents raise considerable sums.
Admissions   At 11 by tests in English, maths, reasoning; junior school pupils take 45 of the 75 places (but promotion is not automatic). School has been fairly selective but is likely to become less so with the phasing out of assisted places, which about 100 hold. Catchment area extends to North Wales, Shropshire, The Wirral.
The head   Long-serving; charming, scholarly, urbane; knows his pupils well (teaches all first-years). Read history at Cambridge; previously head of a grammar school in Dorset. Keen on medieval history, canals, Gilbert and Sullivan (directs and sings). Married; two children (one a pupil here).
The teaching   Good. Well-qualified, hard-working, relatively youthful staff of 35, nearly all appointed by present head. Broad curriculum: all do Latin for first two years; Spanish, German on offer (all do at least two languages for first three years); science taught as three separate subjects. Average class size 25. Lots of drama (first-rate facilities), music (two orchestras, church choir, 150 learn an instrument). Wide range of extra-curricular activities, including well-supported Duke of Edinburgh award scheme and cadet force. Regular trips abroad for study and recreation.
Results   (1997) GCSE: all gained at least five grades A–C. A-level: 62% of entries graded A or B.
Destinations   Virtually all go on to university (up to 15 a year to Oxbridge).
Sport   Good facilities, including 27 acres of playing fields, six all-weather tennis courts, grass athletics track, sports hall, indoor pool. Main sports: rowing (a particular strength), swimming, football, cricket; numerous fixtures throughout the year. Tennis, hockey, athletics, basketball, badminton, squash, golf also on offer.
Remarks   HMC inspectors (1997) praised the high standard of teaching and the school's demanding but supportive ethos.

KING'S COLLEGE SCHOOL, WIMBLEDON ♂
Southside, Wimbledon Common, London SW19 4TT. Tel (0181) 255 5300

Synopsis
Independent ★ Boys ★ Day ★ Ages 13–18 (plus associated junior school) ★
712 pupils ★ 288 in sixth form ★ Fees: £7,350
Head: Tony Evans, 52, appointed September 1997.
Distinguished academic school; excellent teaching and results; strong music, drama, sport.

Profile
Background Founded 1829 as the junior department of King's College, London 'to provide in the most effectual manner for the two great objects of education – the communication of general knowledge, and specific preparation for particular professions' (still does); moved to present 17-acre site on the edge of the common 1897; good quality buildings of varied periods and styles – feels like a university campus. (See separate entry for junior school.)

Atmosphere Courteous, well-ordered, highly academic; strong Anglican tradition (full-time chaplain); exceptionally good relations between staff and able, confident boys (no hint here of cynicism or arrogance).

Admissions By interview and Common Entrance (65% mark required): school is very selective; about 90 of 144 places a year go to the junior school. Most pupils live within five miles but some travel much further; parents mostly in professions, business. Scholarships, bursaries available.

The head New appointment (Robin Reeve, his distinguished predecessor, had been in post 17 years). Very able, experienced, determined; committed Catholic; strong Francophile; keen to broaden sixth-form studies. Read French and Spanish at Oxford; taught at Winchester, Dulwich; previously head for 14 years of Portsmouth Grammar (qv). Coined the phrase 'opulent neglect' – of children whose parents spend too much of their time amassing material wealth; believes that the 'twin pillars of religion and patriotism are tottering in our schools and the third pillar, the family unit, is dissolving'. Married (wife is French); two grown-up sons.

The teaching Excellent: styles vary from formal to informal; well-qualified staff of 73 (15 women), many long serving; pupils hard-working, responsive. Broad curriculum: science taught as three separate subjects; languages include Latin, Greek, German, Russian, Spanish (well-equipped language lab); very good art (especially ceramics); lots of computing. Pupils grouped by ability in most subjects; progress closely monitored. Strong drama, music; nearly 400 learn an instrument (three choirs, three orchestras, various ensembles). Well-organised careers advice and work experience. Lots of extra-curricular activities; fifth-formers choose between cadet force and Duke of Edinburgh award scheme.

Results (1997) GCSE: all gained at least five grades A–C. A-level: impressive 84% of entries graded A or B (13th in the league table).

Destinations Virtually all stay on for A-levels and proceed to university (average of 30 a year to Oxbridge).

Sport Very strong. Fine facilities include on-site playing fields plus 24 acres near by, two all-weather pitches, 18 tennis courts, sports hall, indoor pool, squash courts. Main sports: rugby, hockey, cricket, athletics, tennis, rowing. Fencing, basketball, badminton, golf, judo, archery, also on offer.

Remarks Fine school; highly recommended.

KING'S HIGH, WARWICK ♀
Smith Street, Warwick CV34 4HJ. Tel (01926) 494485

Synopsis
Independent ★ Girls ★ Day ★ 550 pupils ★ 120 in sixth form ★ Fees: £4,620
Head: Mrs Jackie Anderson, 55, appointed 1987.
High-achieving, friendly school; very good results; lots of music.

Profile
Background   Founded 1879; part of the Warwick Schools Foundation which
runs neighbouring Warwick (qv) and Warwick Prep (qv) schools; formerly
Direct Grant, became fully independent 1976 only 'with extreme reluctance'.
Unusual hotch-potch of buildings ranging over six centuries, including medieval
city wall tower, Queen Anne house, Victorian primary school and modern New
Brutalist block, all successfully blended on a compact urban site. Smallish,
homely, well-carpeted classrooms; some spectacularly aged laboratories (one
removed and placed intact in the Black Country Museum).

Atmosphere   Comfortable, dignified, an air of quiet industry; high standards
of behaviour expected and invariably obtained. Daily whole-school assembly in
rather worn Victorian main hall.

Admissions   By school's own exam and interview; top 25% of the ability range
from an extensive catchment area bounded roughly by Solihull, Alcester,
Banbury. Phasing out of assisted places, which more than 150 hold, could have a
considerable impact, not least on the social mix.

The head   Relaxed, unassuming, regarded by staff as good delegator. Educated
at a Kent girls' grammar and Keele; taught English in a mix of state and independent schools; previously vice-principal of Cheltenham Ladies' (qv). Teaches
first-years and upper sixth. Married (to Gloucestershire's director of education);
two grown-up children.

The teaching   Well-structured, intelligent: girls pushed hard; lessons flow
toward clear objectives, often leavened with wit and occasional Joyce Grenfell-like
admonitions ('No whistling, dear – ladies don't whistle'). Stable staff of 45 (five
men), average age 38. Standards very high across the curriculum, particularly in
maths and (combined) science; languages (French, German, Russian, Spanish,
Latin, Greek) also a notable feature, thanks partly to new specialist centre with
extensive video/audio equipment and libraries. Most take nine GCSEs; choice of
19 subjects at A-level, including business studies. Pupils grouped by ability from
second year in maths; GCSE years organised in upper and lower bands; class sizes
average 25–28, reducing to 18 for GCSE, nine at A-level. Abundant music: about
200 learn an instrument. Busy exchange programme includes a trans-Atlantic
link with a co-educational school in Albany, New York State.

Results   (1997) GCSE: all gained at least five grades A–C. A-level: creditable
69% of entries graded A or B.

Destinations   About 70% continue into the sixth form; of these, nearly all proceed to university (about six a year to Oxbridge).

Sport   Strengths in hockey, netball, tennis (11 grass courts, seven hard). Sixth-
form options include golf, canoeing, clay-pigeon shooting. Large gym; superbly-
equipped sports hall shared with prep school, five minutes' drive away.

Remarks   Intimate, cohesive school; knows its girls well and is good at getting
the best out of them.

KING'S, PETERBOROUGH ♂ ♀
Park Road, Peterborough PE1 2UE. Tel (01733) 751541

Synopsis
Partially selective comprehensive (grant-maintained) ★ Co-educational ★ Ages 11–18 ★ 853 pupils (55% boys) ★ 231 in sixth form
Head: Gary Longman, 43, appointed 1994.
Well-run, traditional school; very good GCSE results; first-rate music; strong sport.

Profile
Background   Founded 1541 by Henry VIII as the cathedral choir school; moved 1882 from cathedral precincts to four-and-a-half-acre site half a mile away; formerly a boys' grammar school, went comprehensive and admitted girls 1976; opted out of council control 1993. Small Victorian buildings plus extensive, unlovely, later additions; space is tight (technology block built on what was the cricket square).

Atmosphere   Friendly, traditional, well-ordered; competitive house system; prefects wear gowns; strict blazer-and-tie uniform for all (decorated with white braid for effort and achievement). Exceptionally supportive parents covenant about £40,000 a year.

Admissions   School is over-subscribed: 10% of places allocated on the basis of tests in English, maths, verbal reasoning (80 apply for nine places) or a test of musical ability (three places available); priority for remaining places to choristers (girls and boys), children of worshipping Church of England parents (50% quota), siblings, worshipping members of other faiths. Pupils drawn from mostly middle-class homes in a 30-mile radius; ability level is above average.

The head   Relaxed, friendly; good manager. Read botany at Nottingham; previously deputy head of a comprehensive in Lancashire. Married; two children.

The teaching   Good quality; dedicated staff. Standard national curriculum; Latin on offer; good results in maths, religious education; technology blossoming; most take nine GCSEs (options include child development, business studies, PE); choice of 18 subjects at A-level. Pupils grouped by ability in maths from first year, modern languages from second year, science for GCSE; extra help for those who need it; maximum class size 30, reducing to 20 for GCSE. First-rate music; two orchestras, two choirs. Good links with local industry. Extra-curricular activities include chess (strong), Duke of Edinburgh award scheme.

Results   (1997) GCSE: very creditable 86% gained at least five grades A–C. A level: 36% of entries graded A or B.

Destinations   About 75% stay on for A-levels; of these, nearly 80% proceed to university (average of five a year to Oxbridge).

Sport   Strong, despite the lack of on-site facilities (playing fields 15 minutes' walk away). Main games: rugby, football, netball, hockey.

Remarks   Ofsted inspectors (1994) praised the school for being 'both caring and rigorous'.

KING'S, TAUNTON ♂ ♀
South Road, Taunton, Somerset TA1 3DX. Tel (01823) 334236

Synopsis
Independent ★ Co-educational ★ Boarding and day ★ Ages 13–18 (plus associated pre-prep and prep school) ★ 453 pupils (66% boys; 75% boarders) ★ 200 in sixth-form ★ Fees: £12,600 boarding; £8,298 day
Head: Simon Funnell, 53, appointed 1988.
Attractive, traditional school for children of a wide range of abilities; good results; fine sporting facilities.

Profile
Background Founded 1880 by Rev Nathaniel Woodard as part of a country-wide network of Church of England boarding schools for parents of limited means; still controlled (like 30 others) by the Woodard Corporation. Imposing Victorian stone buildings (chapel is large enough to accommodate the whole school) plus less picturesque later additions on 100-acre site in walking distance of the town; premises generally well maintained, under- rather than over-crowded. Junior school (400 children under a separate head) three miles away.

Atmosphere Happy, purposeful; relationships based on appropriate mix of friendliness and respect. Strongly Christian ethos. Firm discipline: automatic expulsion for possession of illegal drugs or 'being found in bed together'; more minor infringements punished by chores (eg weeding at 7 am). Emphasis on full boarding (head says weekly boarding 'dilutes the ethos'): lessons on Saturday mornings; compulsory Sunday chapel; day-pupils barely go home except to sleep (and they can stay at school on b&b basis). Accommodation is comfortable, spacious, well furnished; no room with more than four beds; sixth-formers have own study-bedrooms in final year. Traditional uniform: tweed jacket, grey trousers for boys; blue blazer, skirt for girls; sixth-formers smartly dressed in sober styles and colours. Good food in impressive dining hall.

Admissions By Common Entrance; official pass mark is a modest 45% (school admits a fairly wide range of abilities); half enter from the prep school. Boarders mostly from Somerset, Devon; 25% from abroad (both expatriates and foreigners); unusually, boarding numbers are holding up – there is even some pressure on girls' places. Day pupils from Taunton and villages near by.

The head Highly regarded. Cheerful, efficient, charming; gets on well with staff and pupils; teaches first-years to get to know them. Read English at Cambridge; taught previously at Shrewsbury and Eastbourne. Married (his wife teaches music in the prep school); three children, one a pupil here.

The teaching Predominantly formal, whole-class. Hard-working, stable staff of 48, including eight women recruited since school went co-educational in 1992. Pupils grouped by ability from the start; average class size 15, smaller for A-level; full-time remedial teacher for dyslexic pupils. GCSE options include Latin, Greek, German, Spanish; choice of 17 subjects at A-level; non-examined Russian, art appreciation, war studies, accountancy etc also on offer. Spacious, well-equipped specialist areas for science, design/technology, art, music (orchestra, chapel choir, recording studio), drama (frequent plays, two theatres). Popular cadet force (nearly all volunteer) and Duke of Edinburgh award scheme. Regular trips abroad for study and sport.

Results (1997) GCSE: 95% gained at least five grades A–C. A-level: 42% of entries graded A or B.

Destinations Nearly 90% to university (seven or eight a year to Oxbridge).

Sport Very good for a small school; keen staff. Main games compulsory: rugby, cricket for boys; netball, tennis for girls; hockey for both. Squash, fencing, swimming, athletics, cross-country, soccer, badminton, basketball, archery, shooting, golf, sailing also on offer; sixth-formers must choose one. First-rate facilities include excellent playing fields, impressive sports hall (indoor cricket nets, heated pool), three good cricket squares, all-weather pitches, numerous tennis/netball courts.

Remarks Happy, well-run school; lots on offer.

THE KINGS OF WESSEX ♂ ♀
Station Road, Cheddar, Somerset BS27 3AQ. Tel (01934) 742608

Synopsis
Comprehensive (voluntary-controlled, Church of England) ★ Co-education-al ★ Ages 13–18 ★ 1,012 pupils (equal numbers of girls and boys) ★ 280 in sixth form
Head: Chris Richardson, 37, appointed 1995.
Successful school; good teaching and results.

Profile
Background Opened 1963 as a secondary modern (on the site of an Anglo-Saxon palace – hence the name); went comprehensive 1976. Clean, airy, well-maintained buildings plus a plethora of huts intended to be 'temporary' 20 years ago; later additions include well-built library and leisure centre. School has a unit for the hearing-impaired and is used as an adult education centre.

Atmosphere Well-ordered, close-knit community; firm Christian ethos (but collective worship does not satisfy the legal requirements). Friendly relations between staff and pupils; good pastoral care system.

Admissions Fairly wide range of abilities; most from middle-class/professional backgrounds within a one-mile radius of the Cheddar Valley.

The head Read Education at Warwick; previously deputy head of a Leicestershire comprehensive. Married; two children.

The teaching Styles vary: some lessons more formal than others. Stable staff of 67 (29 women). Standard national curriculum; choice of French or German (some do both); science taught (but not examined) as three separate subjects; lots of computing. GNVQs offered as an alternative to A-levels. Pupils grouped by ability in most subjects from second year; extra help for those who need it; no class larger than 30 (15 in sixth form). Extra-curricular activities include well-supported Duke of Edinburgh award scheme. Strong links with schools in Germany, Kenya.

Results (1997) GCSE: 63% gained at least five grades A–C. A-level: 45% of entries graded A or B.

Destinations About 50% continue into the sixth form; of these, 95% proceed to higher education.

Sport Chiefly: rugby, football, hockey, cricket, athletics, netball. Facilities include sports hall, squash courts, gymnasium, tennis courts.

Remarks Happy school, highly regarded locally. Identified by Ofsted (1996) as 'oustandingly successful'.

KING'S, WORCESTER ♂ ♀
Worcester WR1 2LH. Tel (01905) 23016

Synopsis
Independent ★ Co-educational ★ Day and boarding ★ Ages 11–18 (plus associated junior school) ★ 815 pupils (64% boys, 95% day) ★ 242 in sixth form ★ Fees: £9,600 boarding; £5,538 day
Head: Dr John Moore, 61, appointed 1983 (retiring August 1998).
Traditional school; sound teaching and results; good facilities.

Profile
Background   Roots go back to a 7th-century monastic school; re-founded 1541 by Henry VIII; formerly Direct Grant, reverted to full independence 1976; fully co-educational since 1991. Fine, 45-acre site in the cathedral precincts overlooking the River Severn; school hall is a 14th-century refectory; 17th- and 18th-century buildings plus first-rate later additions, including science labs, IT centre, language block. Extensive playing fields across the river; residential centre in Wales.

Atmosphere   Busy, friendly; strong Christian tradition.

Admissions   At 11, 13 by tests; school is not unduly selective and likely to become even less so with the phasing out of assisted places, which 170 hold. Day pupils from 25-mile-radius catchment area; boarding accommodation spacious, well-furnished, recently renovated (but numbers are declining).

The head   Long-serving. Educated at Rugby and Cambridge; PhD in classics. Delegates extensively to his senior management team (which would benefit from some new blood). From September 1998: Timothy Keyes, deputy head of Guildford Royal Grammar (qv).

The teaching   Styles range from traditional to informal; best results in English, maths, science (taught as three separate subjects), art. Well-qualified staff of 63, 75% appointed by present head. Pupils grouped by ability in maths, modern languages (French, German, Spanish); average class size 24 (but smaller for GCSE), 10 in sixth form. A-level options include Italian, Russian. Very good drama (fine theatre), music (lots of plays and concerts). Well-supported Duke of Edinburgh award scheme, cadet force. Regular trips abroad for study and sport.

Results   (1997) GCSE: 98% gained at least five grades A–C grades. A-level 56% of entries graded A or B.

Destinations   About 80% continue into the sixth form; of these, 95% proceed to university (about eight a year to Oxbridge).

Sports   Strong rugby, cricket, rowing, netball, fencing, sailing. Facilities include sports hall, Olympic-size pool, athletics track.

Remarks   Safe choice.

KINGSTON GRAMMAR ♂ ♀
70–72 London Road, Kingston upon Thames, Surrey KT2 6PY. Tel (0181) 546 5875

Synopsis
Independent ★ Co-educational ★ Day ★ Ages 10–19 ★ 600 pupils (60% boys) ★ 155 in sixth form ★ Fees: £5,880–£6,180
Head: Duncan Baxter, 44, appointed 1991.
Friendly, hard-working, academic school; good teaching and results; strong hockey and rowing.

Profile

Background Founded 1561 (but roots go back to the 14th century) as a 'free grammar school to endure for ever'; Elizabethan chapel of St Mary Magdalen still used as an arts centre. Formerly Direct Grant; became fully independent 1976, co-educational 1978. Buildings of many periods (some rather drab) on a confined site near the town centre; facilities generally good.

Atmosphere Orderly, open, friendly; hard-working but not fiercely competitive; good-humoured relations between sixth-formers and juniors.

Admissions School heavily over-subscribed (up to 400 apply for 60 places) but phasing out of assisted places, which 25% hold, will have a big impact. Entry at 10, 11 by tests, at 13 by Common Entrance; 50% of pupils from Kingston but many travel long distances. Head insists: 'Just because we are independent does not mean we have to be exclusive and our doors will remain firmly open despite the pressure to slam them in our faces.' Scholarships (maths, music, art, sport) and bursaries available.

The head Unassuming, scholarly, quietly determined. Read English at Oxford; taught at Gresham's, Holt and Wycliffe (qv). Married; two children (one a pupil here).

The teaching Generally traditional in style; committed staff of 60 (60% men), average age 38. Fairly broad curriculum: science taught as three separate subjects; some take GCSE maths a year early; A-level options include ancient history, sports studies. Pupils grouped by ability in most subjects. Flourishing music: choirs; a third learn an instrument. Extra-curricular activities include debating, cadet force, popular Duke of Edinburgh award scheme; regular language exchanges with France, Germany.

Results (1997) GCSE: all gained at least five grades A–C. A-level: 62% of entries graded A or B (122nd in the league table – its best position ever).

Destinations About 85% go on to university (average of six a year to Oxbridge).

Sport Taken seriously, particularly rowing and hockey (boys' and girls'); cricket, tennis, athletics, cross-country, squash, netball also on offer. Facilities include 22-acre sports ground across the Thames from Hampton Court, a 10-minute coach ride away.

Remarks Pleasant school; good all round. HMC inspectors (1995) considered that 'teaching strategies should be reviewed to encourage pupils to be more active in their learning'.

KINGSWINFORD ♂ ♀
Water Street, Kingswinford, West Midlands DY6 7AD. Tel (01384) 296596

Synopsis
Comprehensive (grant-maintained) ★ Co-educational ★ Ages 11–16 ★ 848 pupils (equal numbers of girls and boys)
Head: Geoff Harrison, 51, appointed 1986.
Well-run, cheerful comprehensive.

Profile
Background Founded 1939; went comprehensive 1975; opted out of council control 1993. Attractive red-brick premises in somewhat scruffy condition in a prosperous residential area on the western edge of Dudley.

Atmosphere Pleasant, well-ordered; strong sense of community; easy relations between staff and pupils; lots of pupils' work on display. Pastoral care system designed to promote self-reliance. Uniform strictly enforced.

Admissions School over-subscribed; priority to those with special needs, siblings and those living nearest 'as the crow flies'; about 30% come from further afield. Fairly wide range of abilities and social backgrounds.

The head Strong, effective leader; inspires confidence; has pulled the school round (since his arrival, GCSE results have improved 100%, pupil numbers have risen 30%). Trained at Sheffield College of Education; wide experience in the state sector. Married; three children (all have been pupils here).

The teaching Good: enthusiastic, cheerful staff of 51 (equal numbers of women and men), many long-serving. Standard national curriculum; all do French and German for first three years; computers used across the curriculum; good art and design. Most take eight or nine GCSEs (from a choice of 15). Regular homework; certificates of commendation for effort and achievement. Pupils grouped by ability from first year in maths, from second year in science and English, from third year in languages; progress carefully monitored (lots of movement between sets); extra help for both the more and less able; average class size 24. Good links with industry; thriving careers service.

Results (1997) GCSE: 52% gained at least five grades A–C.

Destinations Nearly 80% remain in full-time education after 16.

Sport Poor facilities: small playing field, three tennis/netball courts, one ancient gym. Nevertheless, school has a full fixture list and 'wins slightly more games than it loses'.

Remarks Good all round but poorly resourced.

KIRKHAM GRAMMAR ♂ ♀
Ribby Road, Kirkham, Preston, Lancashire PR4 2BH. Tel (01772) 671079

Synopsis
Independent ★ Co-educational ★ Day and boarding ★ Ages 11–18 (plus associated junior school) ★ 570 pupils (85% day; 53% boys) ★ 114 in sixth form ★ Fees: £4,095 day; £7,995 boarding
Head: Barrie Stacey, 56, appointed 1991.
Well-run, friendly school; good teaching and results; strong sport.

Profile
Background Founded 1549 as a charity school; became a voluntary-aided boy's grammar in 1944; reverted to independent status and became co-educational 1979; strong links with Drapers' Company. Moved to present 30-acre site and purpose-built premises 1910; main building in style of small Stuart mansion (ivy-clad walls, bell tower, oak-panelled interiors); block-like, flat-roofed addition erected by local council in 1965; later additions include sixth-form centre; some classrooms in 'temporary' huts. Junior school (ages four to 11) in modern premises across the road.

Atmosphere Calm, orderly, civilised; a happy blend of high seriousness and relaxed good humour. Real sense of Christian worship in morning assembly. Respect for tradition symbolised by honours boards, portraits of previous heads (mostly clergymen), display cabinets full of sporting trophies and ancestral silverware. Well-framed and striking pupil paintings adorn the corridors; everywhere clean and polished. Much laughter and leg-pulling in the staff room; pupils courteous to a fault.

Admissions By tests in English, maths, verbal reasoning; school has been consistently over-subscribed and fairly selective but phasing out of assisted places, which about 100 hold, will have an impact. Pupils predominantly from professional, middle-class homes in Kirkham, Preston, Wyre, Chorley, Blackpool (extensive coach service); boarders from Service, expatriate families and from Middle and Far East. Pleasant boarding accommodation recently upgraded. Scholarships, means-tested bursaries available.

The head Skilled manager; relaxed but clearly in control. Read history and education at Edinburgh, Oxford and Bradford. Athletics Blues from Edinburgh and Oxford; Amateur Athletics Association coach; still runs regularly. Has taught in both state and independent sectors; previously deputy head of Birkdale, Sheffield. Married; two grown-up children.

The teaching Immensely enthusiastic. Particular strengths in maths, science (taught as three separate subjects), technology. Choice of 20 subjects at GCSE (including Chinese), 18 at A-level (including sports science). Pupils grouped by ability in English, maths, French; class sizes 23–28, reducing to 20 for GCSE, 15 in sixth form. Lots of music: fine choir; 100 learn an instrument. Wide range of clubs and societies; cadet force of 200; sixth-formers undertake community work. Regular exchanges with schools in France, Germany, New Zealand.

Results (1997) GCSE: 98% gained at least five grades A–C. A-level: 36% of entries graded A or B (a bad year).

Destinations About 75% continue into the sixth form; of these, 90% proceed to university.

Sport Fine reputation: they regularly beat much bigger schools. Particular strengths in hockey and rugby (county honours). Netball, tennis, cricket, rounders, swimming (council pool next door) also on offer. Facilities include superb playing fields, floodlit all-weather pitch, lovely cricket square and pavilion.

Remarks Good all round: academically challenging; warm, family atmosphere.

LADY ELEANOR HOLLES ♀
Hanworth Road, Hampton, Middlesex TW12 3HF. Tel (0181) 979 1601

Synopsis
Independent ★ Girls ★ Day ★ Ages 11–18 (plus associated junior school) ★ 715 pupils ★ 192 in sixth form ★ Fees: £5,850
Head: Miss Elizabeth Candy, 54, appointed 1981.
Successful, well-run academic school; very good teaching and results; strong music, sport.

Profile
Background Founded 1711 under the will of Lady Eleanor Holles; moved 1936 to present 30-acre site and undistinguished, purpose-built premises (elegant Art Deco entrance hall is a later addition); facilities generally good. Junior school (200 pupils aged seven to 11) on same site.

Atmosphere Busy, self-confident, well-ordered; strong academic tradition; aim is to 'encourage every girl to develop her personality to the full so that she may become a woman of integrity and a responsible member of society'; independence encouraged.

Admissions By interview and competitive tests in English, maths, verbal and non-verbal reasoning, general knowledge; school is severely selective (top 10% of the ability range); up to 300 apply for 50–60 places; promotion from the junior school is not automatic. Phasing out of assisted places, which about 75 hold, will have little impact. Catchment area extends from London to Reading (coaches shared with boys from Hampton, qv). Scholarship, bursaries available.

The head Able, humorous, enthusiastic; strong leader ('l'état c'est moi'); dislikes 'policies' and being 'bogged down in paper'. Read chemistry at London ('a big mistake'); previously deputy head of Putney High (qv). Keen cyclist.

The teaching First-rate; fairly traditional in style; experienced, committed, well-qualified staff, 90% appointed by present head. Broad curriculum: science taught as three separate subjects; all do French and German for at least three years; Spanish, Russian, Greek on offer; religious education throughout; wide choice of 28 subjects at A-level; nearly all do general studies. Pupils grouped by ability in maths, French (some take GCSEs a year early); extra help for those who need it; average class size 24, reducing to 12 at A-level. Good art, music; more than 200 learn an instrument; three choirs, three orchestras. Extra-curricular activities include cadet force (in conjunction with Hampton boys) well-supported Duke of Edinburgh award scheme. Regular language exchanges with pupils in France, Germany.

Results (1997) GCSE: all gained at least five grades A–C. A-level: very creditable 78% of entries graded A or B.

Destinations Nearly all go on to university (up to 24 a year to Oxbridge).

Sport Strong, particularly netball, swimming, rowing, lacrosse. Facilities include extensive playing fields, indoor pool, courts for tennis, netball.

Remarks Her Majesty's Inspectors concluded (1995): 'The school provides an excellent education. Its pupils are highly successful in public examinations and they have outstandingly good achievements in a wide range of activities, including sport and music. The quality of teaching is very good.'

LADY MANNERS ♂ ♀
Bakewell, Derbyshire DE45 1JA. Tel (01629) 812671

Synopsis
Comprehensive (grant-maintained) ★ Co-educational ★ Day and some boarding ★ Ages 11–18 ★ 1,480 pupils (equal numbers of girls and boys, 97% day) ★ 330 in sixth form ★ Fees (boarding only): £4,422 weekly, £4,872 full-time
Head: Miss Mary Sellers, 45, appointed 1996.
Successful, well-run school; very good teaching and results; lots of music; strong sport.

Profile
Background Founded 1636 by Grace, Lady Manners for the 'better instructinge of the male children of Bakewell'; became a co-educational grammar school 1896; went comprehensive 1972; opted out of council control 1993. Moved to present site high above the town 1938; purpose-built premises now crowded and a little tired but well-maintained; most recent additions include six new science labs, fine library.

Atmosphere Strongly traditional: workman-like, calm, well-disciplined. Confident, respectful pupils mindful of school motto, *Pour y Parvenir* (Strive to

Achieve). Speech day retained; full uniform (blazers, ties, badges) worn by all.
Admissions Over-subscribed (about 280 apply for 220 places); no academic selection. Priority to those living nearest or having family connections with the school; most pupils come from small village primaries in an extensive Peak District catchment area. Boarders (limited to 45) comfortably housed at Castle Hill, a mansion on the other side of town.
The head Recent appointment (predecessor had been in post 18 years). Able, hard working; determined to maintain the school's values, traditions and academic record. Read modern languages at Oxford; previously head of a sixth-form college.
The teaching Good quality: varied styles but expectations uniformly high. Experienced, enthusiastic staff of 78 (slightly more men than women). Standard national curriculum but all do French and German for first three years. Pupils grouped by ability in most subjects from second year; extra help for those with special needs; average class size 27, smaller at A-level (good choice of subjects but no GNVQs). Lots of drama, music (choirs, orchestras, various ensembles). Wide range of extra-curricular activities. Regular language exchanges with schools in France, Germany.
Results (1997) GCSE: 66% gained at least five grades A–C. A-level: creditable 54% of entries graded A or B.
Destinations About half stay on for A-levels; of these, about three-quarters proceed to university (average of six a year to Oxbridge).
Sport Lots on offer; good record in rugby, hockey, netball, tennis. First-rate playing fields but no access to a swimming pool.
Remarks Ofsted inspectors concluded (1994): 'This is a good school. Academic achievement is matched by good relationships and a high level of care.'

LADY MARGARET ♀
Parsons Green, London SW6 4UN. Tel (0171) 736 7138

Synopsis
Comprehensive (voluntary-aided) ★ Girls ★ Ages 11–18 ★ 454 pupils ★ 104 in sixth form
Head: Mrs Joan Olivier, 56, appointed 1984.
First-rate, well-run school; clear Christian ethos; very good teaching and GCSE results.

Profile
Background Opened as a Dame's school 1917; became a grammar school 1944; went comprehensive 1977. Three large Georgian houses plus later additions facing the green – gardens in front, netball and tennis courts behind. School is expanding; money and space are tight.
Atmosphere Orderly, cheerful, crowded. Christian framework: assemblies four times a week; prospectus refers readers to Exodus 20, verses 1–16 (The Ten Commandments). Polite, obedient pupils, full of praise for smallness of school (friendships across age differences are common) and approachability of teachers. House system (cups and merit cards awarded termly); uniform of distinctive striped blazers (dress code for sixth formers). Supportive parents help raise funds.
Admissions School is heavily over-subscribed: nearly 500 apply for 90 places. Half are reserved for practising Anglicans (vicar's reference required); rest go to girls of good character whose parents undertake to support the school's aims and Christian ethos. School is not academically selective but all applicants take

tests in English, maths, non-verbal reasoning to assist in the allocation of places: 25 go to girls of above average ability, 50 to those of average ability, 15 to those below average. Most from Fulham, Hammersmith, Kensington, Chelsea, Putney, Wandsworth, Wimbledon; 25% ethnic minorities. School has benefited greatly from having its success identified in league tables. ('I'm competitive,' says the head. 'I want my girls to win.')

The head Dynamic leader. Scottish, energetic, talkative, roars with laughter. Read history at London (still teaches it to first-years and sixth-formers); came here as deputy 1973. Calls her pupils 'darling'; gives them five minutes' 'wriggle time' in the middle of double periods.

The teaching Good quality, varied styles; many long-serving staff. (If results are not up to the mark, head steps in: classes are monitored and new appointments made.) Standard national curriculum; pupils grouped by ability in English, maths from second year; extra help for those who need it (at both ends of the ability range). Lots of music: nearly a third learn an instrument; three choirs, orchestra.

Results (1997) GCSE: creditable 78% gained at least five grades A–C. A-level: 47% of entries graded A or B.

Destinations About 70% continue into the sixth form; most of these go on to university (one or two a year to Oxbridge).

Sport Netball strong (played on site); playing fields a coach ride away.

Remarks Ofsted inspectors concluded (1996): 'This is a very good school which has great strengths.'

LANCASTER GIRLS' GRAMMAR ♀
Regent Street, Lancaster LA1 1SF. Tel (01524) 32010

Synopsis
Grammar (grant-maintained) ★ Girls ★ Ages 11–18 ★ 760 pupils ★ 233 in sixth form
Head: Mrs Pam Barber, 50, appointed 1987.
Well-run, academic school; emphasis on technology.

Profile
Background Founded 1917; opted out of council control 1991; achieved technology college status 1996. Hodge-podge of ageing buildings on a crowded urban site sandwiched between the railway and the A6; recent additions include technology block, new classrooms, science labs, library; much recent renovation.

Atmosphere Happy, hard-working; formal but friendly relations between staff and pupils; compulsory uniform. Parents expected to 'support the school on issues of attitude and behaviour'.

Admissions Heavily over-subscribed (270 apply for 112 places). Entry by 11-plus; top 25% of the ability range, predominantly from middle-class backgrounds; priority to those living in Lancaster and the valley of the River Lune.

The head Strong leader ('You'll make it - go for it!'); forthright, energetic; likes to be in the vanguard of educational developments; keen to promote science, engineering, technology, computing. Previously deputy head of a comprehensive. Married.

The teaching Traditional in style. Well-qualified staff of 42 (two-thirds female). Broad curriculum: science taught as three separate subjects; languages include Latin, Greek, German, Spanish; all take nine GCSEs plus four A-levels (including general studies); options include psychology, fashion & fabric, domestic science. Pupils grouped by ability from third year in science, technology; average class size 29. Lots of music (in conjunction with boys of Royal Grammar, Lancaster, qv) and drama.

Results (1997) GCSE: 98% gained at least five grades A–C. A-level: 52% of entries graded A or B.

Destinations Nearly all go on to university.

Sport Particular strengths in hockey, tennis, athletics. Playing fields five minutes' walk away; girls have use of the sporting facilities at Lancaster University.

Remarks Good all round.

LANCASTER ROYAL GRAMMAR ♂
East Road, Lancaster LA1 3EF. Tel (01524) 32109

Synopsis
Grammar (grant-maintained) ★ Boys ★ Day and boarding ★ Ages 11–18 ★ 900 pupils (80% day) ★ 265 in sixth form ★ Fees (boarding only): £3,900
Head: Peter Mawby, 56, appointed 1983.
First-rate grammar school; very good teaching and results; strong sport; boarding available.

Profile
Background Founded in the 13th century; re-endowed 1472; opted out of council control 1990; granted technology college status 1995. Dignified 19th-century buildings plus attractive recent additions on a rambling, hill-top site overlooking the city. One of a small number of state schools to offer boarding.

Atmosphere Busy, hard-working, well-ordered; teachers in gowns, boys in uniform; good relations between staff, pupils, parents.

Admissions Heavily over-subscribed: about 300 apply for 100 places; entry by highly competitive tests; minimum IQ 120. Pupils drawn from a wide range of social backgrounds in a catchment area restricted to Lancaster and Luneside. Some boarders from near by, others from abroad (sons of British expatriates); pleasant; boarding accommodation recently renovated.

The head Very able: full of ideas; has revitalised the school and propelled it into the late 20th century. Read biology at Cambridge; previously head of biology at Cheltenham (qv). Visits all 80-plus 'feeder' primaries every year; has good links with local business, industry, community leaders. Married (wife is a magistrate); two children.

The teaching Very good. Formal but friendly in style; dedicated, well-qualified staff. Broad curriculum: science taught as three separate subjects (first-rate labs); all do Latin from second year; Spanish, German, Greek on offer; lots of technology, computing. Most take nine GCSEs and three A-levels. Good drama, music: choir, two orchestras, various ensembles. Strong European links (work experience, language exchanges). Extra-curricular activities include well-established cadet force.

Results (1997) GCSE: 98% gained at least five grades A–C. A-level: 54% of entries graded A or B.

Destinations About 90% go on to university (average of 12 a year to Oxbridge).

Sport Strong. Main sports: rugby, swimming, cross-country, cricket (fine ground), rowing (on the Lune), athletics. Golf, tennis, hockey, basketball also on offer.

Remarks   Ofsted inspectors concluded (1996): 'The school sets and achieves the highest standards. It provides an excellent academic education, enriched by an exceptional range of sporting, social and cultural opportunities.'

LANCING ♂
Lancing, West Sussex BN15 0RW. Tel (01273) 452213

Synopsis
Independent ★ Boys (plus girls in sixth form) ★ Boarding and day ★ Ages 13–18 ★ 497 pupils (85% boarding) ★ 236 in sixth form (70% boys) ★ Fees: £13,335 boarding; £10,020 day
Head: Chris Saunders, 57, appointed 1993 (retiring August 1998).
Traditional boarding school; good facilities; sound teaching; lots of music, sport.

Profile
Background   Founded 1848 by Rev Nathaniel Woodard as an Anglo-Catholic boarding school, the cornerstone of what he hoped would grow to be an empire. Stunning Victorian-Gothic chapel (England's largest rose window) plus imposing collection of flint and sandstone buildings arranged around two cloistered quadrangles on a 550-acre site (including a farm) high on the South Downs. Facilities are good. Evelyn Waugh was a pupil here.

Atmosphere   Busy, friendly; strong Anglican ethos (compulsory chapel, religious education); good relations between staff and pupils; individualism tolerated. Sixth-form girls feel well integrated (but need to be reasonably spirited).

Admissions   By Common Entrance; 55% mark preferred but numbers have fallen and school is not full; 10% from abroad. Ten houses, including two for sixth-form girls, play an important role; boys' accommodation fairly spartan; food unimpressive. Lots of scholarships: academic, music, art, clergy, Naval.

The head   Was a pupil here (and head boy) in the 1950s; read geography at Cambridge; previously head for 12 years of Eastbourne (qv). Has tightened up on discipline, dress code, lesson punctuality. From September 1988: Peter Tinniswood, head of Magdalen College School (qv).

The teaching   Sound; well-qualified, predominantly male staff. Broad curriculum: sciences taught separately (and well); all do French and Spanish; Latin, Greek, German, Russian on offer; most take nine GCSEs; wide choice of 25 subjects at A-level. Pupils grouped by ability from first year; some take GCSE maths, French a year early; maximum class size 22, reducing to 15 in sixth form. Good art, drama, music. Extra-curricular activities include cadet force, working on the college farm, Duke of Edinburgh Award scheme. Regular language exchanges with schools in France, Germany, Russia, Spain.

Results   (1997) GCSE: 97% gained at least five grades A–C. A-level: 44% of entries graded A or B (245th in the league table – worst position ever).

Destinations   Almost all stay for A-levels and proceed to university (up to 15 a year to Oxbridge).

Sport   Strong, particularly soccer, cricket, squash. Cross country, athletics, sailing, swimming (indoor pool), fives, rugby, hockey, tennis, netball, lacrosse also on offer. Facilities are good.

Remarks   Good all round.

LANGLEY PARK BOYS' ♂

South Eden Park Road, Beckenham, Kent BR3 3BP. Tel (0181) 650 9253

Synopsis

Partially selective comprehensive (grant-maintained) ★ Boys ★ Ages 11–18 ★
1,177 pupils ★ 239 in sixth form
Head: Roger Sheffield, 52, appointed 1990.
Well-run, firmly traditional school; good GCSE results; strong music, sport.

Profile

Background Founded as a grammar school 1901; went comprehensive 1976; opted out of council control 1991. Dreary, 1960s buildings on a spacious site; many classrooms in ageing 'temporary' huts; quite good facilities for computing, music, drama.

Atmosphere Strongly traditional, firmly disciplined (detention on Saturday mornings), big emphasis on 'old-fashioned' moral values: 'The school is seen first and foremost as a place of work; teachers are encouraged to adopt a firm, fair and friendly line with the pupils'; strict blazer-and-tie uniform; sixth-formers wear suits. Little contact with neighbouring girls' school (qv). Parents highly supportive.

Admissions School is over-subscribed: up to 15% admitted by general ability (tests in maths, verbal reasoning); up to 10% by aptitude for music or sport; priority for remaining places to those living nearest 'as measured in a straight line from the front door of the home to the front door of the school'. Most are drawn from eight primaries within a one-mile radius.

The head Traditional, autocratic, leads from the front; has brought about a steady improvement in results. Read psychology. Married; two grown-up children.

The teaching Formal in style; hard-working staff of 83 (65 men). Standard national curriculum; lots of computing; A-level options include sports studies, media studies, business studies; GNVQs available. Pupils grouped by ability in most subjects from the start; extra help for those with special needs; progress closely monitored. Lots of drama, music. Wide range of extra-curricular activities (most staff involved).

Results (1997) GCSE: 67% gained at least five grades A–C. A-level: rather modest 26% of entries graded A or B.

Destinations About 70% stay on for A-levels; of these, 75% proceed to higher education.

Sport Strong (and compulsory in the sixth form). Main sports: rugby, hockey, cricket, tennis (a particular strength), athletics, basketball; matches on Saturday mornings. Facilities include extensive playing fields.

Remarks Ofsted inspectors concluded (1997): 'This is a good school with several outstanding features. Pupils reach very good standards in public examinations. In sport, individual pupils and teams reach very high standards. Boys perform well in a wide range of musical activities.'

LANGLEY PARK GIRLS' ♀
Hawksbrook Lane, South Eden Park, Beckenham, Kent BR3 3BE. Tel (0181) 650 7207

Synopsis
Partially selective comprehensive (grant-maintained) ★ Girls ★ Ages 11–19 ★ 1,336 pupils ★ 233 in sixth form
Head: Mrs Jan Sage, 50, appointed 1993.
Thriving, well-run school; very good results; strong sport.

Profile
Background Founded as a grammar school 1919; moved to present site (adjoining Langley Park Boys', qv) and purpose-built premises 1959; went comprehensive 1976; technology college status achieved 1996. Most recent additions include new labs, classrooms, state-of-the-art technology block; facilities generally good; space is tight. Sixth-form centre shared with boys' school.

Atmosphere Busy, well-ordered; big emphasis on responsibility, integrity, self-discipline; very good relations between staff and pupils.

Admissions School heavily over-subscribed (up to 450 apply for 220 places); 15% (33 pupils) admitted by academic ability; priority for remaining places to those living nearest and siblings; 95% live in Bromley borough; 12% ethnic minority.

The head Charismatic leader; combines approachability with steely determination; demands the highest standards. Married; no children.

The teaching Generally good; varied styles; lively, relatively youthful staff of 69 (20 men). Standard national curriculum; first-rate technology; vocational alternatives to A-levels include GNVQs in leisure & tourism, health & social care, business & administration. Pupils grouped by ability in maths, science, modern languages; extra help for those with special needs (some have 'statements'); progress closely monitored; average class size 28, reducing to 24 for GCSE. Lots of music; orchestra, choir.

Results (1997) GCSE: impressive 79% gained at least five grades A–C. A-level: 39% of entries graded A or B.

Destinations About 70% go on to higher education.

Sport Good record, particularly in hockey, netball, swimming, tennis, athletics. Facilities include playing fields, all-weather pitch, sports hall.

Remarks Identified by Ofsted (1996) as 'outstandingly successful'.

LATYMER ♂ ♀
Haselbury Road, Edmonton, London N9 9TN. Tel (0181) 807 4037

Synopsis
Grammar (grant-maintained) ★ Co-educational ★ Ages 11–18 ★ 1,300 pupils (equal numbers of girls and boys) ★ 386 in sixth form
Head: Geoffrey Mills, 61, appointed 1983.
High-powered, selective school; very good teaching and results; outstanding music; strong sport.

Profile
Background Founded 1624; became co-educational and moved to present

sombre premises (behind high railings in a drab residential street) 1910; opted out of council control 1993; awarded technology college status 1994. Vast, arched assembly hall can seat the whole school; science labs recently refurbished.

Atmosphere Firmly traditional, extremely busy (can seem rather overwhelming at first – 'Reception is the 12th door on your left'); staff and pupils work, practise, rehearse on the premises from 7.30 am to 6.00 pm daily.

Admissions School heavily over-subscribed and highly selective; all applicants take a non-verbal reasoning test; top 650 proceed to tests of English and maths; places offered to the 180 judged likely to respond best to what the school has to offer. Wide social and ethnic mix from all over Enfield and beyond.

The head Effective and very experienced manager of a complex institution (don't be misled by his self-effacing manner). Read modern languages at Cambridge; previously head of a comprehensive in West Sussex. Married; four children (three have been pupils here).

The teaching Styles vary from formal whole-class teaching to less didactic group work. Enthusiastic, hard-working staff of 82 (average age late-30s); 85% appointed by present head. Strongly academic curriculum; good science (many go on to do medicine) technology improving; all take two languages for at least the first three years. Impressive choice of 25 subjects at A-level, including Russian, German (particularly strong), business studies (increasingly popular), theatre and media studies. First-rate library: nearly 20,000 volumes plus wide selection of periodicals. Outstanding music (despite lack of a purpose-built centre): 40% learn an instrument; three symphony orchestras plus a variety of smaller ensembles; four choirs (involving more than 300 pupils); 12 major musical events a year and regular foreign tours (all too much, complain some non-musicians). Much community service; charity fund-raising taken seriously. Residential centre in Snowdonia. Regular (and well-supported) exchanges with schools in France, Germany, Russia (and one with Sweden, established as a result of the school's entry in this guide).

Results (1997) GCSE: all gained at least five grades A–C. A-level: very impressive 65% of entries graded A or B.

Destinations More than 90% continue into the sixth form; of these, more than 90% proceed to university (about 20 a year to Oxbridge).

Sport First-rate; policy is to encourage widest participation in recreational sport, and competitiveness at the highest level. Soccer, rugby, basketball, hockey, netball, volleyball, tennis, athletics, cross-country, gymnastics all on offer; consistent success in borough, county, national competitions. Canoeing, sailing, swimming, golf, squash also available. Facilities include two gymnasia, full-size athletics track.

Remarks Exceptional school; highly recommended.

LATYMER UPPER ♂
King St, London W6. Tel (0181) 741 1851

Synopsis
Independent ★ Boys (plus girls in sixth form) ★ Day ★ Ages 11–18 (plus association prep school) ★ 925 pupils ★ 326 in sixth form (80% boys) ★ Fees: £6,540
Head: Colin Diggory, 43, appointed 1991.
Strong, academic school; good teaching and results; lots of music, drama, sport.

Profile

Background Founded 1624 to keep 'eight poore boyes from the town of Hammersmith' from vagrancy and idleness; moved to present site 1895; formerly a Direct Grant grammar, became independent 1976. A mass of functional, modern buildings behind an institutional red-brick façade on a narrow, restricted site stretching from King Street to the river, bisected by the Great West Road (subway link). Sixth-form girls admitted 1996. On-site prep school (ages seven to 11) under its own head.

Atmosphere Crowded, busy, happy. Big emphasis on tolerance; pupils, teachers, buildings all fairly scruffy (uniform casually interpreted). Unlikely to suit retiring girls.

Admissions School is heavily over-subscribed (about 350 apply for 120 places) and selective; entry by interview and competitive tests in English, maths, non-verbal reasoning (past papers available). Phasing out of assisted places, which more than 100 hold, will further reduce the social mix; governors' wish that 'no gifted boy should be denied a place through lack of parental means' likely to be further eroded – though a substantial number of scholarships are offered. Large West London catchment.

The head Able, vigorous. Read maths at Durham (First); taught at Manchester Grammar, St Paul's, Merchant Taylors'; came here as deputy head 1990. Principal task is to restructure the school to ensure its survival in the fee-paying market; still finds time to teach A-level maths. Married (to a teacher).

The teaching Didactic but lively; well-qualified staff of 87 (12 women). Broad curriculum: all do science as three separate subjects and can do three languages (from Latin, Greek, French, German, Spanish); more able take GCSE maths a year early; particularly good results in history. Pupils grouped by ability from second year; average class sizes 20–25, reducing to 12 in the sixth form. Lots of drama (Hugh Grant is an old boy) and music (several orchestras, choirs). Wide range of extra-curricular activities, some in conjunction with girls at Godolphin & Latymer (qv); well-supported Duke of Edinburgh award scheme.

Results (1997) GCSE: 99% gained at least five grades A–C. A-level: 63% of entries graded A or B.

Destinations Nearly all go on to university (average of 15 a year to Oxbridge).

Sport Emphasis on involvement, participation, choice. Main sports: rugby, soccer, rowing (own boathouse), cricket, athletics. Facilities include sports hall, squash courts, indoor pool; playing fields two miles away.

Remarks Good all round.

LAWRENCE SHERIFF ♂
Clifton Road, Rugby, Warwickshire CV21 3AG. Tel (01788) 542074

Synopsis
Grammar (voluntary-aided) ★ Boys ★ Ages 11–18 ★ 685 pupils ★ 235 in sixth form
Head: Dr Rex Pogson, 50, appointed 1985.
Well-run, traditional grammar school; strong sport.

Profile
Background Founded in the late 19th century as a town grammar with money diverted from Rugby (qv) which was originally endowed for the purpose by

Lawrence Sheriff in 1560 but grew into a national boarding school; granted voluntary-aided status 1944. Mock-Tudor buildings plus many later additions (including new classrooms, science labs, design/technology block) on a confined, traffic-encircled site

Atmosphere Busy, well-disciplined, unpretentious; grammar school traditions retained; emphasis on the pursuit of academic excellence (and, adds the head, compassion). Parents are highly supportive.

Admissions Heavily over-subscribed (350 apply for 90 places); entry by Warwickshire 11–plus; top 25% of the ability range from a 10-mile-radius catchment area.

The head Able, experienced; very strong leader ('I'm an interferer – open, visible and involved'). Read history at Cambridge (PhD); previously head of a grammar school in Kent. Has presided successfully over vigorous expansion. Married; three children.

The teaching Generally good; formal in style ('chalk-and-talk'). Experienced staff of 41 (65% male), 60% appointed by present head. Fairly broad curriculum: science on offer as three separate subjects; all do French and German for first three years. Pupils grouped by ability in maths only; average class size 31, reducing to 24 for GCSE, 14 in the sixth form. Choice of 23 subjects at A-level (many in conjunction with Rugby Girls' High, qv) ranging from ancient history to media studies and sociology. Lots of drama, music (choir, orchestra, various ensembles). Extra-curricular activities include much charitable work. Regular trips abroad for study, work experience, recreation.

Results (1997) GCSE: 95% gained at least five grades A–C. A-level: 31% of entries graded A or B.

Destinations About 90% go on to university (average of six a year to Oxbridge).

Sports Strong. Main games: rugby, hockey, cross-country, cricket, tennis, athletics. Playing fields about a mile way; sports hall on site.

Remarks Ofsted inspectors (1994) objected to the 'unduly limited variety of teaching styles' but concluded that standards of achievement were 'at least satisfactory'.

LEEDS GIRLS' HIGH ♀
Headingley Lane, Leeds LS6 1BN. Tel (0113) 274 4000

Synopsis
Independent ★ Girls ★ Day ★ Ages 11–18 (plus associated pre-prep and prep schools) ★ 603 pupils ★ 145 in sixth form ★ Fees: £4,837
Head: Mrs Susan Fishburn, 48, appointed September 1997.
Traditional, academic school; very good teaching and results.

Profile
Background Founded 1876; moved to present 10-acre-site two miles from the city centre 1906; formerly Direct Grant, became independent 1976. Elegant, three-storey, Edwardian red-brick buildings plus later additions; fine music and drama centre in converted chapel five minutes' walk away.

Atmosphere Lively, purposeful: a school confident in its well-established reputation; emphasis on hard work, academic achievement, community involvement. Attractive, practical uniform; smart dress code in the sixth form.

Parents keen, demanding, supportive in time and money and much involved in school life.

Admissions School is over-subscribed (three apply for each place) and highly selective – but likely to become less so with the phasing out of assisted places, which more than 100 hold. Entry at 11 by interview and tests in English, maths, verbal reasoning; half join from the prep school (promotion is not automatic). Catchment area encompasses Greater Leeds and extends to Huddersfield, Ilkley, Knaresborough, Tadcaster (fleet of private buses). Some scholarships, bursaries.

The head New appointment (predecessor had been in post 20 years). Read physiology and biochemistry at Birmingham (First); has taught widely in the state and independent sectors; previously deputy head of Stafford Grammar. Married; two children.

The teaching Traditional in style. Well-qualified staff of 53 (nine men). Fairly broad curriculum: science taught as three separate subjects; all do French, German, Latin; plenty of computing. Pupils grouped by ability in maths, French; average class size 24, reducing to 20 for GCSE, 15 or fewer at A-level. Most do nine GCSEs and four A-levels, including general studies. Lots of music (a third learn an instrument). Wide range of extra-curricular activities. Regular language exchanges with schools in France, Germany.

Results (1997) GCSE: all gained at least five grades A–C. A-level: very creditable 78% of entries graded A or B (24th in the league table – its best position ever).

Destinations Virtually all go on to university (average of 12 a year to Oxbridge).

Sport Main games: hockey, netball, tennis. Badminton, swimming also on offer. Facilities include sports hall, indoor pool, two hockey pitches.

Remarks Good school for able girls.

LEEDS GRAMMAR ♂
Alwoodley Gates, Harrogate Road, Leeds LS17 8GS. Tel (0113) 237 1997

Synopsis
Independent ★ Boys ★ Day ★ Ages 11–18 (plus associated junior school) ★ 1,010 pupils ★ 250 in sixth form ★ Fees: £4,845
Head: Bryan Collins, 59, appointed 1986.
Fine, academic school; very good teaching and results; brand-new campus.

Profile
Background Founded 1552 by Sir William Sheafield, who left £4 13s 4d for the education of 'all such schollars youths and children as shall come to be taught'. Moved September 1997 to splendid, £18.5 million, purpose-built premises on a 128-acre green-field site – complete with porte-clochère, campanile, piazza, rotunda and every state-of-the-art facility a school could possibly require.

Atmosphere As the relocation prospectus puts it, 'The Tradition Continues': history, achievements, culture all intact. Busy, lively; 'serious in purpose but light in spirit,' says head. Respectful but friendly relations between staff and pupils; good pastoral care (no gaps for boys to fall through); emphasis on recognising and rewarding achievement.

Admissions Highly selective but likely to become less so with the phasing out of assisted places which more than 200 hold (contributing significantly to the wide social and ethnic mix); head says he would encourage any boy of 'reasonably high ability' to apply. Half the intake comes from the junior school at 10, the rest from outside at 11 after interview and tests (the two streams merge at 12). Wide catchment area but the move to the city's middle-class, northern suburbs puts the school within a mile of 25% of its roll, and within three miles of 60%.

The head   Very able, experienced. Read biology at London and Bristol (MSc); previously head of a grammar school and a comprehensive; enthusiasm undimmed. Married; two children (one a pupil here).

The teaching   First-rate; largely traditional in style. Expert, dedicated staff of 93 (19 women). Broad curriculum: science taught as three separate subjects; all do Latin for at least one year; Greek, German, Spanish on offer; lots of computing and technology; most take 11 GCSEs and four A-levels (from a choice of 23) plus general studies. Pupils grouped by ability; some take GCSE maths, religious studies a year early; progress closely monitored (regular reports to parents). Lots of music (three orchestras, three choirs) and drama. Extra-curricular activities include cadet force, Duke of Edinburgh award scheme, more than 30 clubs, societies. Annual language exchanges with schools in France, Germany.

Results   (1997) GCSE: 99% gained at least five grades A–C. A-level: 64% of entries graded A or B.

Destinations   Almost all stay on into the sixth form and proceed to university (average of 20 a year to Oxbridge).

Sport   Main games: rugby, cricket (both played to a high standard). Cricket, athletics, swimming, tennis, basketball, badminton, squash, soccer also on offer. Facilities include extensive playing fields, sports hall, indoor pool.

Remarks   Highly recommended.

LEICESTER GRAMMAR
8 Peacock Lane, Leicester LE1 5PX. Tel (0116) 222 0400

Synopsis
Independent ★ Co-educational ★ Day ★ Ages 10–18 (plus associated junior school) ★ 610 pupils (equal numbers of girls and boys) ★ 130 in sixth form ★ Fees: £4,650
Head: John Sugden, 57, appointed 1989.
Strong academic school; very good teaching and results; lots of music.

Profile
Background   Founded 1981 (with 90 pupils) after the local education authority closed down one of the city's grammar schools (the city-centre premises of which it now occupies); two Victorian red-brick buildings adjacent to the cathedral (with which there are strong links); later additions include new classrooms, sixth-form centre, drama hall. Fully co-educational from the start.

Atmosphere   A young school with a powerful sense of tradition ('Atmosphere,' says the head, 'is what you have to work at most'); strong Christian ethos; emphasis on good discipline, hard work ('The pursuit of academic excellence lies unequivocally at the centre of school life'). Pupils smartly turned-out in sober grey uniform (prefects wear gowns); 20% ethnic minority ('because it's a school with principles').

Admissions   Entry at 11 by tests in English, maths and verbal reasoning; top 25% of the ability range. School is over-subscribed but likely to become rather less so with the phasing out of assisted places, which about 100 hold.

The head   Energetic, brisk, stimulating; insists education should be enjoyable. Read modern languages at Cambridge; taught at Portsmouth Grammar and King's, Canterbury, where he was a housemaster; formerly deputy head of Newcastle-under-Lyme.

The teaching   First-rate. Broad curriculum: science taught (and examined) as three separate subjects; half take two modern languages to GCSE; Latin, Greek, classical civilisation feature strongly; all do at least 10 GCSEs and three A-levels (from a choice of 18 – ranging from Greek to technology); particularly good results in maths, history. Pupils grouped by ability from third year in maths, French; average class size 26, reducing to 17 for GCSE. First-rate music; more than a third learn an instrument (including all first-years); orchestra, choir.

Results   (1997) GCSE: all gained at least five grades A–C. A-level: creditable 70% of entries graded A or B (one of the most successful fully co-educational schools).

Destinations   About 90% stay on for A-levels; virtually all proceed to university (up to 10 a year to Oxbridge).

Sport   Lack of on-site facilities has not prevented the school from producing performers of county standard in rugby, cricket, hockey, athletics, tennis, netball and swimming (splendid off-site facilities at local university and community centre). Planning permission has been obtained to develop 28-acre playing fields in the suburbs.

Remarks   Vigorous school offering a modern, grammar-school education. Founders' vision – which must have seemed idiosyncratic at the time – triumphantly vindicated. Highly recommended.

THE LEYS ♂ ♀
Trumpington Road, Cambridge CB2 2AD. Tel (01223) 508900

> **Synopsis**
> Independent ★ Boarding and day ★ Co-educational ★ Ages 13–18 (11–18 from September 1998) ★ 427 pupils (66% boys, 63% boarding) ★ 180 in sixth form ★ Fees: £12,780 boarding; £8,270 day
> Head: Rev Dr John Barrett, 54, appointed 1990.
> *Good all-round school; sound teaching and results; lots of extra-curricular activities; strong sport.*

Profile

Background   Founded 1875 by Methodists to provide a liberal Christian education (and still does); late Victorian buildings plus many later additions (including award-winning design/technology centre) on attractive 40-acre site half a mile from the city centre; fully co-educational since 1994.

Atmosphere   Big emphasis on individual care; strong spiritual and community ethos. Day pupils 'sleep at home but otherwise are able to enjoy all the opportunities of boarding school life'; lessons on Saturday mornings. Parents required to agree to random urine testing of pupils suspected of using drugs.

Admissions   By interview and Common Entrance (50% mark required) or tests; school is not unduly selective and may become less so with the phasing out of assisted places, which more than 50 hold. Good quality boarding accommodation; 22% of pupils from abroad. Scholarships: academic, art, music, sport.

The head   Solid, reassuring; good leader; strongly committed to the 'whole-person' approach to education; knows his pupils well. Read economics at

Newcastle, theology at Cambridge; ordained into the Methodist ministry but has spent all his career in schools; previously head of Kent College. Married; two grown-up children.

The teaching Sound; generally traditional in style; hard-working, enthusiastic staff, most appointed by present head. Fairly broad curriculum; sciences taught separately; languages include German, Spanish, Latin; good design/technology; all do religious studies; nearly all do nine GCSEs; choice of 21 subjects at A-level. Pupils grouped by ability in most subjects; extra help for dyslexics and those who speak English as a foreign language; average class size 18, reducing to 10 in the sixth form. Flourishing drama, music; very good art. Wide range of extra-curricular activities, including cadet force, Duke of Edinburgh award scheme.

Results (1997) GCSE: 90% gained at least five grades A–C. A-level: 57% of entries graded A or B.

Destinations About 90% stay on for A-levels; of these, 90% proceed to higher education (up to 10 a year to Oxbridge).

Sport Important feature of school life: wide variety on offer; good coaching; regular county and national honours. Impressive facilities include 40 acres of playing fields, all-weather pitch, state-of-the-art sports hall, indoor pool, three squash courts, boathouse on the Cam.

Remarks HMC inspectors concluded rather oddly (1995): 'The pupils are happy in their work and play. The quality of work and the standards of achievement measure up to the school's expectations.'

LIVERPOOL ♂ ♀
Queen's Drive, Mossley Hill, Liverpool L18 8BG. Tel (0151) 724 4000

Synopsis
Independent ★ Co-educational ★ Day ★ Ages 3–18 ★ 970 pupils (65% boys)
★ 150 in sixth form ★ Fees: £2,820–£4,515
Head: Jon Siviter, 40, appointed September 1997.
Successful school; good teaching and results; strong sport.

Profile
Background Founded 1840; moved to present fine, 26-acre site five miles south of city centre 1920. Varied collection of buildings (including three lovely mid-Victorian houses, graceful chapel, state-of-the-art technology centre) on both sides of a main road connected by a bridge. Co-educational since 1993, when the school inherited the pupils and staff of Huyton Girls', which closed.

Atmosphere Civilised, cultured but quite unstuffy; earnest, well-mannered children, keen to do well. School has a 'positive discipline' policy: reinforcement of good behaviour and achievement, firm sanctions for unacceptable conduct ('which is fortunately rare'). Strong house system. Corridors filled with confident art work.

Admissions At age three by interview, at five by tests in the Three Rs, at nine by tests in English, maths, general ability. School has been fairly selective but phasing out of assisted places, which 220 hold, will have a significant impact. Pupils from professional/business/middle-class backgrounds in an extensive catchment area (good transport links); more than a third are siblings. Scholarships, bursaries available.

The head (Principal) New appointment. Read physics at Oxford; worked for

Shell in Saudi Arabia; taught at St Paul's, Oundle, Uppingham; previously deputy head of Bancroft's (qv). Believes one of the most important things a school can do is 'teach its pupils how to learn'. Married (wife worked for Shell for 20 years); two daughters.

The teaching Broadly traditional. Well-qualified, hard-working staff of 82 (average length of service 15 years). Broad curriculum: science taught as three separate subjects; languages include Latin, Greek, German, Spanish; choice of 24 subjects at A-level, including business studies, theatre studies, geology; all do general studies. Pupils grouped by ability in English, maths from age nine and in most other subjects thereafter; maximum class size 20 for GCSE, 12 at A-level. Strict homework policy monitored by parents and teachers. Strong music: 220 learn an instrument (22 visiting tutors); choirs, orchestras, ensembles. Innumerable clubs and societies, and one of the biggest (compulsory) cadet forces in the country.

Results (1997) GCSE: 93% gained at least five grades A–C. A-level: 48% of entries graded A or B.

Destinations About 90% stay on for A-levels; of these, 90% proceed to university (average of five a year to Oxbridge).

Sport Lots on offer. Main sports: rugby, hockey, cricket for the boys; lacrosse, hockey, netball for the girls; athletics, tennis, swimming for both. Facilities include first-rate playing fields, sports hall, outdoor pool.

Remarks Good all round.

LONDON ORATORY ♂
Seagrave Road, London SW6 1RX. Tel (0171) 385 4576

Synopsis
Partially selective comprehensive (grant-maintained) ★ Roman Catholic ★ Boys (plus girls in sixth form) ★ Ages 7–18 ★ 1,300 pupils ★ 320 in sixth form (66% boys)
Head: John McIntosh, OBE, 52, appointed 1977.
First-rate, well-run school; very good teaching and results; strong art, drama, music.

Profile
Background Founded 1863 by the Fathers of the London Oratory; became a grammar school 1963; went comprehensive 1970 and moved to purpose-built premises on a two-acre site in a quiet backwater of Fulham; opted out of council control 1989. Later additions include impressive new arts block (fine theatre), lovely chapel, new junior house (for 80 boys aged seven to 11). Tony and Cherie Blair send their sons here.

Atmosphere Exceptionally orderly and purposeful ('a teaching establishment in which children are expected to learn and teachers to teach'); strong Catholic ethos (crucifix in every room, daily religious assemblies); first-rate pastoral care; civilised standards of behaviour expected and achieved; friendly relations between staff and secure, happy pupils; an almost tangible air of common endeavour. Traditional blazer-and-tie uniform for all, strictly enforced. Intelligently informative prospectus.

Admissions School heavily over-subscribed; 27 a year admitted at age seven on grounds of musical and general ability (plus voice test for Oratory Church choristers); entry at 11 by interview to determine Catholic credentials and parents' acceptance of school's rigorous aims; all expected to stay for A-levels; sixth-form entry (40–50 places) requires five GCSEs (B grades in intended A-level subjects). Pupils drawn from a wide range of socio-economic backgrounds and every London borough; 50% bilingual.

The head Very long-serving; outstandingly able; courteous, unassuming, totally dedicated (works a 12-hour day and most weekends); sets the highest possible standards and insists on parents' support (not least on the 'three Hs' – haircuts, holidays, homework). Read engineering at Sussex; has spent all his teaching career here. Music-lover; plays the organ.

The teaching Very good in all subjects: mostly traditional in style ('chalk-and-talk'); big emphasis on firm grounding, accuracy; highly-qualified staff, nearly all appointed by present head. Broad curriculum: science (a strength) on offer as three separate subjects; all do Latin for at least three years; modern languages include German, Spanish, Italian; Scottish Standard Grade offered in preference to some GCSEs; A-levels may be supplemented by Scottish Highers. Pupils grouped by ability from the start; further setting in most subjects (some take GCSEs a year early); lots of high-quality extra help for those who need it; progress closely monitored (regular testing); average class size 26, reducing to 16 in the sixth form. First-rate art, drama, music; several choirs, orchestras, chamber groups. Very good careers advice. Extra-curricular activities include cadet force; numerous clubs, expeditions, foreign exchanges.

Results (1997) GCSE: very creditable 86% gained at least five grades A–C. A-levels: 41% of entries graded A or B.

Destinations About 90% proceed to university (average of 10 a year to Oxbridge).

Sport Good, despite limited on-site facilities. Main sports: rugby, hockey, tennis, cricket, athletics (playing fields at Barnes). Basketball, volleyball, swimming, archery, badminton, fencing, rowing, squash also available.

Remarks Ofsted inspectors concluded (1996): 'This is a very good school that provides education of a high quality. It combines high standards of achievement with an emphasis upon the personal development of the pupil.' Highly recommended.

LORD WANDSWORTH ♂ ♀
Long Sutton, Hook, Hampshire RG29 1TB. Tel (01256) 862482

Synopsis
Independent ★ Boys (plus girls in sixth form – becoming fully co-educational from September 1997) ★ Boarding and day ★ Ages 11–18 ★ 470 pupils (70% boarding) ★ 150 in sixth form (70% boys) ★ Fees: £10,764 boarding; £8,376 day
Head: Ian Power, 36, appointed September 1997.
Solid, friendly, well-equipped school; good results; charitable support for a quarter of pupils.

Profile
Background Founded 1922, the result of a bequest by Lord Wandsworth to provide education for children who have lost one or both parents; foundation supports nearly a quarter of the pupils (who are not identified). Solid, well-proportioned buildings plus later additions, including sixth-form centre, in 1,200 acres of prime Hampshire farmland (which contributes to the trust's

financial stability); first-rate facilities. Girls first admitted to sixth form 1988, at 11 from September 1997.

Atmosphere   Low-key, friendly; pupils find the staff very approachable (almost all live on site). Christian ethos (Anglican chaplain) but children from other faiths welcomed. Traditional uniform worn throughout. Day pupils stay until at least 5 pm.

Admissions   At 11 by tests, at 13 by Common Entrance (50% mark required in English, maths); fairly wide range of abilities. Subsidised, means-tested places for foundationers (qualifying and deserving children of single-parent families – the result of death, divorce or separation) who come from up to 100 miles away; most non-foundationers live locally. Juniors in attractive boarding house (large, open dormitories) with own sports field and swimming pool; seniors in separate houses, some modern, others recently refurbished.

The head   New appointment. Read natural sciences at Cambridge; previously head of science and a housemaster at Millfield (qv). Married; two daughters.

The teaching   Wide range of style and approach, from 'chalk-and-talk' in traditional classrooms to stimulating, individualistic sixth-form teaching. Broad curriculum: science taught as three separate subjects; choice of Latin or classical studies; languages include Spanish, German; English a particular strength; good facilities for computing (used across the curriculum). Most do three A-levels; options include sports science, theatre studies. Homework (two hours nightly) throughout. Pupils grouped by ability from age 13; average class size 20. Flourishing drama (numerous productions) and music (choir, band, orchestra). Wide range of extra-curricular activities include cadet force, Duke of Edinburgh award scheme, community service, car maintenance etc.

Results   (1997) GCSE: 91% gained at least five grades A–C. A-level: 52% of entries graded A or B.

Destinations   About 80% continue into the sixth form; most go on to university.

Sport   Chiefly: rugby, cricket, hockey (extensive playing fields), tennis (hard and grass courts), squash, swimming (good indoor pool), badminton, golf (nine-hole course). Shooting, cross-country, lacrosse, athletics, basketball also on offer. Facilities include extensive games fields, two floodlit all-weather pitches.

Remarks   Good all round.

LORD WILLIAMS'S   ♂ ♀
Oxford Road, Thame, Oxfordshire OX9 2AQ. Tel (01844) 213681

Synopsis
Comprehensive (voluntary-controlled) ★ Co-educational ★ Ages 11–18 ★ 1,955 pupils (equal numbers of girls and boys) ★ 380 in the sixth form
Head: Mrs Pat O'Shea, 48, appointed April 1997.
Successful school; good teaching and GCSE results; lots of sport.

Profile
Background   Founded 1559 by John, Baron Williams of Thame; changed from boys' grammar to co-educational comprehensive 1971. School's lower (first three years) and upper sections on two sites two miles apart; teachers have to commute. Many classrooms in 'temporary' huts, despite recent £3 million building programme. School has a unit for autistic children.

Atmosphere   Strong sense of community, despite the huge size; pupils feel they and their opinions count; nearly every wall covered with displays of work, much of it excellent. Good pastoral care system (even the dinner ladies are trained to give help with emotional matters); regular newsletters keep supportive parents in touch.

Admissions Heavily over-subscribed; priority to those living nearest. Pupils represent a genuine cross-section: parents range from rural workers to senior business executives and Oxford dons; wide spread of abilities but the overall level is above average.

The head Recent appointment. Energetic, thoughtful, experienced. Read English at Oxford (First); taught in comprehensives then lectured in education before returning to teaching; previously head of Bottisham (qv). Married (to a professor); two young children.

The teaching Good. Well-qualified staff of 110 (60 women), four have PhDs. Most lessons last 70 minutes (to accommodate the split-site problems); teachers maintain friendly control, but noise levels can be high. Standard national curriculum; some take a second modern language; most do nine GCSEs (options include child development, dance, drama, business studies); GNVQs available as an alternative to A-levels. Pupils grouped by ability from third year; lots of extra help for those with special needs; maximum class size 30. Busy extra-curricular programme includes community service, public speaking, outdoor camp for all second years.

Results (1997) GCSE: 56% gained at least five grades A–C (results have steadily improved). A-level: 33% of entries graded A or B.

Destinations About 65% continue into the sixth form (most of the rest go to further education colleges); of these, 70% proceed to university (about three a year to Oxbridge).

Sport Extensive playing fields; high participation rate. Good match record at county and regional level in netball, football, rugby, hockey, cricket, athletics, tennis, squash. Indoor games (in two sports halls) include badminton, volleyball, basketball, trampolining. No swimming pool.

Remarks Ofsted inspectors concluded (1996): 'This is a good school. Its strengths lie in the support and guidance of pupils; very good GCSE performance; consistently good quality of teaching; well-established and effective links with parents, the community and local industry; and the provision for pupils with special educational needs.'

LORETTO ♂ ♀
Musselburgh, Midlothian EH21 7RE. Tel (0131) 653 4455

Synopsis
Independent ★ Co-educational ★ Boarding and day ★ Ages 13–18 (plus associated junior school) ★ 320 pupils (75% boys; 95% boarding) ★ 151 in sixth form ★ Fees: £12,870 boarding; £8,580 day
Head: Keith Budge, 40, appointed 1995.
Small, clearly Christian school; good teaching and results; strong family atmosphere; lots of sport.

Profile
Background Founded 1827; became renowned for its unorthodox emphasis on fresh air, exercise, open-necked shirts and communal singing. Pleasant 80-acre site (lawns, ornamental trees, flower beds everywhere) six miles from -

Edinburgh; earliest buildings date from late 14th century; latest additions include music school, design/technology centre. Fully co-educational since 1995. Junior school (ages eight to 13) on same site under its own head.

Atmosphere Small, close-knit community; firm Christian ethos; strong links between pupils, school and parents ('the wider Loretto family'); prefects have considerable authority. Very much a boarding school; lessons on Saturday mornings; day pupils 'go home to sleep'. Pupils in traditional uniform of red jackets and open-necked white shirts; all wear the kilt on Sundays.

Admissions By Common Entrance; not unduly selective; half come from the junior school. About two-thirds from Scotland, most of the rest from the north of England. Girls' boarding accommodation attractively furnished and decorated; boys' more austere (including, in Pinkie House, one of the largest dormitories in Britain – 'wonderful for cricket'). Good food (grace at the beginning and end of meals). Scholarships, bursaries available.

The head Hard-working, all-round schoolmaster. Read English at Oxford (rugby Blue); previously a housemaster at Marlborough. Married (wife plays an active role); three children.

The teaching Good: committed, relatively youthful staff of 38 (10 women), all of whom work at least a six-day week. Fairly broad curriculum (leading to GCSE and A-level): science taught as three separate subjects; Latin on offer; good design/technology. Pupils grouped by ability in most subjects; extra help for those with learning difficulties; average class size 17 (plenty of individual attention), even smaller in the sixth form. Lots of music: 60% learn an instrument (including pipe organ); chapel choir, orchestra, distinguished pipes and drums band. Extra-curricular activities include cadet force (compulsory for three years), well-supported Duke of Edinburgh award scheme. Regular language exchanges with France, Germany.

Results (1997) GCSE: 86% gained at least five grades A–C. A-level: 58% of entries graded A or B.

Destinations About 85% go on to university.

Sport 'It is a tradition in the school that every boy and girl should take regular exercise': games compulsory three days a week. Main sports: rugby, cricket, hockey, lacrosse, athletics, swimming, fives, tennis, squash, badminton, sailing. Games fields (including all-weather pitch) all within walking distance.

Remarks Sound school for children of a fairly wide range of abilities.

LOUGHBOROUGH GRAMMAR ♂

Burton Walks, Loughborough, Leicestershire LE11 2DU. Tel (01509) 233233

Synopsis

Independent ★ Boys ★ Day and some boarding ★ Ages 10–18 ★ 944 pupils (96% day) ★ 270 in sixth form ★ Fees: £4,815 day; £8,838 boarding
Head: Neville Ireland, 61, appointed 1984 (retiring August 1998).
Well-run, academic school; very good teaching and results; strong music, sport.

Profile

Background Founded 1495; moved 1852 to present 27-acre site (shared with Loughborough High, qv, and co-educational Fairfield Prep). Handsome, purpose-built Victorian-Gothic premises; formerly Direct Grant, reverted to full independence 1976. Modern additions include theatre, sixth-form centre, art and design centre.

Atmosphere Happy, hard-working; strong pastoral care; competitive house system. Grey-suited uniform for all. First-rate food. Very good links with parents.

Admissions At 11 by tests in English, maths, verbal reasoning (a third join from the junior school); at 13 by Common Entrance; school is highly selective and likely to remain so despite the phasing out of assisted places, which nearly 200 hold; extensive catchment area. Scholarships: academic, music.

The head Strong leader ('It's my vision which directs the school'); a little larger than life (boys' eyes light up when they see him); totally dedicated. Educated at Cambridge and King's College, London; previously head of the sixth form at University College School (qv). Married; three grown-up sons. From september 1998: P B Fisher, head of Mount St Mary's.

The teaching First-rate; fairly formal in style; experienced, predominantly male staff. Broad curriculum: sciences taught separately; all do Latin for first three years; Greek, German on offer; good facilities for art, ceramics; all take nine or 10 GCSEs and three A-levels plus general studies (to which a third of the timetable is devoted). Pupils grouped by ability in most subjects; progress closely monitored (half-termly grades); average class size 27. Good drama, music; two orchestras, bands, choir. Lots of extra-curricular activities, including Scouts, cadet force, Duke of Edinburgh award scheme.

Results (1997) GCSE: all gained at least five grades A–C. A-level: creditable 70% of entries graded A or B.

Destinations About 95% stay on for A-levels; of these, 98% proceed to university (average of 20 a year to Oxbridge).

Sport Main sports: rugby, cricket, athletics, hockey, tennis. Fencing, sailing, swimming, squash, badminton also on offer. Facilities include 57 acres of playing fields (some are 10 minutes' walk away), fine cricket square, indoor pool, large sports hall.

Remarks Very good all round.

LOUGHBOROUGH HIGH ♀
Burton Walks, Loughborough LE11 2DU. Tel (O1509) 212348

Synopsis
Independent ★ Girls ★ Day ★ Ages 11–18 ★ 540 pupils ★ 140 in sixth form ★ Fees: £4,347
Head: Miss Julien Harvatt, 54, appointed 1978.
First-rate, academic school; very good teaching and results.

Profile
Background Opened 1850 (the first girls' grammar school in England); shared foundation with Loughborough Grammar (qv). Moved to present, immaculate 39-acre site ('a dignified oasis of green') 1879; previously Direct Grant, became fully independent 1976. Stylish late Victorian buildings plus later additions of varying quality.

Atmosphere Happy, busy, highly academic ('a scholarly education in a disciplined atmosphere'). Prefects, competitive house system, uniform below the sixth form.

Admissions By tests in English, maths, verbal reasoning; school is quite selective (two apply for each place). Phasing out of assisted places, which 25% hold, is a blow; generous bursary fund will mitigate the effects. Predominantly middle-class pupils drawn from a 20-mile radius.

The head Long serving; able, energetic, humorous; leads by example. Read

German at London; previously senior mistress at Bolton Girls' (qv). Teaches European Studies to first years, German literature to the sixth form ('It's important for a head to teach – and anyway I enjoy it').

The teaching First-rate: committed, enthusiastic, well-qualified staff; attentive, hard-working pupils. Broad curriculum: sciences taught separately; all do Latin for at least one year; German, Greek on offer; all take nine GCSEs and three A-levels (from a relatively narrow choice of 19) plus general studies (run in conjunction with the boys' school). Pupils grouped by ability in English, French, maths, science. Lots of music.

Results (1997) GCSE: all gained at least five grades A–C. A-level: very creditable 78% of entries graded A or B (24th in the league table).

Destinations About 95% stay on for A-levels; of these, virtually all go on to university (about 12 a year to Oxbridge).

Sport Hockey, netball, tennis, athletics, swimming, squash, cross-country, fencing; regular county honours. Facilities include ample playing fields, gym, heated pool.

Remarks Good, well-run school; modest fees. Recommended.

MAGDALEN COLLEGE SCHOOL ♂
Oxford OX4 1DZ, Tel (01865) 242191

Synopsis
Independent ★ Boys ★ Day ★ Ages 9–18 ★ 513 pupils ★ 134 in sixth form ★ Fees: £5,394
Head: Peter Tinniswood, 49, appointed 1991 (leaving August 1998).
Successful academic school; very good teaching and results.

Profile
Background Founded 1478 by William of Waynflete as part of Magdalen College (and still educates the college choristers); formerly Direct Grant, became independent 1976. Unimpressive conglomeration of buildings on a fairly cramped site (leased from the college) plus 11 splendid acres of playing fields moated on two sides by the Cherwell and overlooking Christ Church Meadows. Cardinal Wolsey was Master here; William Tyndale was a pupil.

Atmosphere Informal but business-like; good relations between staff and pupils; effective pastoral care system. School professes to have only one rule – 'all boys must at all times behave sensibly and well' – but the rule's sub-sections run to three pages. Lessons on Saturday mornings (despite the phasing out of boarding).

Admissions At ages nine and 11 by tests in English, maths, verbal reasoning; at 13 by Common Entrance (minimum 60% mark required); school has been quite selective but phasing out of assisted places, which nearly half hold, is likely to have a considerable impact, and will certainly reduce the social mix. Aspirant choristers should apply to the Dean of Divinity at Magdalen College. Scholarships, bursaries available.

The head (Master) Able, enthusiastic, ambitious. Taught at Marlborough for 12 years and then did an MBA at Insead, Paris. Married; no children.

The teaching Highly professional; generally traditional in style; long-serving, all-graduate staff of 40. Broad curriculum: all take science as three separate subjects; all do two languages (third-years choose between a third and art – 65% take art). Nearly all take 11 GCSEs, some a year early, and three A-levels (from a wide choice) plus four non-examined subjects. Pupils grouped by ability in maths,

Latin, French; average class size 27, much smaller at A-level. Lots of music: choral society, two orchestras, various ensembles. Excellent library; strong careers guidance. All expected to participate in extra-curricular activities: 60% join the cadet force, 40% do community service; many other clubs and societies.

Results   (1997) GCSE: 99% gained at least five grades A–C. A-level: 67% of entries graded A or B.

Destinations   Nearly all continue into the sixth form; of these, 95% proceed to university (about 15 a year to Oxbridge).

Sport   Chiefly rugby, hockey, rowing, cricket, lawn tennis. Sailing, shooting, cross-country also on offer. Some playing fields three miles away.

Remarks   HMC inspectors concluded (1994): 'This is a very good school with a well-earned reputation for academic distinction which is achieved in a particularly happy and friendly environment.'

MAIDEN ERLEGH ♂ ♀

Silverdale Road, Earley, Reading, Berkshire RG6 7HS. Tel (01189) 262467

Synopsis

Comprehensive ★ Co-educational ★ Ages 11–18 ★ 1,535 pupils (equal numbers of girls and boys) ★ 295 in sixth form
Head: Wilton Wills, 57, appointed 1983.
Successful, well-run comprehensive; good teaching and results.

Profile

Background   Opened as a secondary modern 1962; went comprehensive 1974, since when it has tripled in size. Functional, flat-roof, open-plan buildings (some now partitioned); additions covered the playground so break-time was effectively abolished (day ends at 2.20 pm – though many pupils stay later). Good facilities for drama, music, design & technology; parents raise large sums.

Atmosphere   Busy, purposeful, well-ordered (staff refer to the school as 'the plant'); children attentive, tidy; no prefects.

Admissions   School is over-subscribed (350 apply for 250 places) but non-selective; places allocated by county council; priority to siblings and those living closest (on one of the largest private housing estates in western Europe). Most from middle-class homes (or, as Ofsted inspectors would have it, 'characterised by favourable socio-economic circumstances'); 15% ethnic minority.

The head   An engaging Welshman with a dry sense of humour ('We work hard to maintain standards in a changing world – a bit like Communist Albania'), committed to the comprehensive ideal. Read history at Swansea; came here as deputy head 1975, then left 1980 to become head of a small rural school; retiring in 2000. Teaches computing to the juniors ('It's important for them to know me'). Married; two grown-up children (both were pupils here).

The teaching   Generally good; committed staff. Standard national curriculum; more able add German to French; good results in maths, English; vocational alternatives to A-levels available. Pupils grouped by ability in maths, French; more able not sufficiently challenged in some subjects, Ofsted reported. Quite a lot of music: about 10% learn an instrument. Regular exchanges to France, Germany.

Results   (1997) GCSE: very creditable 73% gained at least five grades A–C. A-level: 38% of entries graded A or B.

Destinations   About 60% continue into the sixth form; of these, 60% proceed

to to university (one or two a year to Oxbridge).
Sport Lively programme of inter-house matches; facilities include sports hall, gym; playing fields one mile away.
Remarks Good school for children of a wide range of abilities.

MALVERN ♂ ♀
College Road, Malvern, Worcestershire WR14 3DF. Tel (01684) 892333

Synopsis
Independent ★ Co-educational ★ Boarding and day ★ Ages 13–18 (plus associated pre-prep and prep school) ★ 610 pupils (70% boys, 82% boarding) ★ 320 in sixth form ★ Fees: £13,350 boarding; £9,705 day
Head: Hugh Carson, 51, appointed January 1997.
Good, traditional school; fine setting and facilities; International Baccalaureate offered as an alternative to A-levels.

Profile
Background Founded 1865; impressive Victorian-Gothic buildings on a splendid 100-acre site on the eastern slopes of the Malvern Hills; later additions include science block, sports hall, attractive arts centre, superb (£2 million) technology centre. Prep department luxuriously housed in a former girls' school across the road.
Atmosphere A traditional country boarding school: lessons on Saturday mornings; very strong house system (pupils eat in their houses); firm discipline; day pupils stay to 9 pm; uniform worn until the upper sixth. High level of pastoral care. Boarding accommodation (especially the girls') is comfortable, clean, cheerful: dormitories for younger pupils, single study-bedrooms for seniors. Girls carry rape-alarms on the campus after dark as protection against possible intruders.
Admissions At 13-plus by Common Entrance (minimum 50% mark required); school is fairly selective. Twenty scholarships a year (academic, art, music, design/technology, sport); 60 hold assisted places. About 17% from abroad; mini buses provided for local pupils.
The head Recent appointment; his second headship. Gentle, courteous, quietly spoken; committed Christian; keen to be accessible to pupils (his door open two hours a day) and to increase the proportion of girls. Expected to introduce changes (leading to rather less formality) as soon as retirements allow him to appoint his own senior staff. Spent nine years in the Royal Tank Regiment before reading history at London (teaches first-years); became a housemaster at Epsom then head of Denstone. Married; wife (PhD in history) much involved in school life.
The teaching Mostly formal in style; fairly long-serving staff (average age 44), 75% men. Pupils grouped by ability in all subjects from the start; average class size 20 up to GCSE, 12 in sixth form; extra help from specialist teachers for those who need it; three-weekly reports on effort and attainment. Sixth-form choice is exceptionally wide: school is one of very few to offer the International Baccalaureate as a broader, more demanding alternative to A-levels. Good quality art, music (more than half learn an instrument) and drama (regular house and school plays). Frequent outings to galleries, museums and to theatres in Stratford, Birmingham, Bristol, Cardiff. Big emphasis on work experience in the lower sixth. Regular trips abroad for study and sport.
Results (1997) GCSE: 96% gained at least five grades A–C. A-level (including IB equivalent): 52% of entries graded A or B.

Destinations   90% to university (including up to 15 a year to Oxbridge).
Sport   Football, rugby, cricket (particularly strong) for the boys; hockey, net-ball, lacrosse for the girls; tennis, athletics, squash, swimming (Olympic-size indoor pool) for both. Also on offer: aerobics, badminton, judo, rowing, sailing, fly-fishing, riding, basketball, rackets, canoeing, mountaineering, shooting.
Remarks   Solid school; ready to move forward.

MALVERN GIRLS' ♀
15 Avenue Road, Malvern, Worcestershire WR14 3BA. Tel (01684) 892288

Synopsis
Independent ★ Girls ★ Boarding and day ★ Ages 11–18 ★ 460 pupils (87% boarding) ★ 170 in sixth form ★ Fees: £13,815 boarding; £9,480 day
Head: Mrs Philippa Leggate, 47, appointed September 1997.
Strong academic school; very good teaching and results; first-rate music, art, sport.

Profile
Background   Founded 1893 in a private house at a time when Malvern was becoming a popular spa town; gradually expanded by acquiring other Victorian houses; bought the old Imperial Hotel (luxurious centre for the water cure) 1919, marking the beginning of its climb to distinction as one of the premier girls' boarding schools. The building (imaginatively extended in the 1960s) is a sub-stantial red-brick and stone Gothic edifice six storeys high, surmounted by a commanding tower and with endless staircases and corridors; winged griffins maul the massive stone gateposts that still front the main entrance.
Atmosphere   A busy, purposeful, secure community; high expectations of work and behaviour; relaxed relations between staff and pupils, particularly in the sixth form. Lessons on Saturday mornings.
Admissions   By Common Entrance or school's own exams in English, maths, verbal reasoning; entry standard is fairly high (even though numbers have been falling); 20% from abroad (Malaysia, Hong Kong, Thailand, Africa, Europe, America). Comfortable boarding in disparate houses linked by grassy quads and gardens; smaller houses have a family feel; girls eat in their houses ('Living together in a community is an integral part of the education which we provide'). Scholarships (academic, art, music, PE) available.
The head   New appointment (the school's fourth head in three years). Read history at York, MEd from Bath; previously head of an independent school for expatriate pupils in Oman and of the Overseas School of Colombo, Sri Lanka. Married; one daughter.
The teaching   Solid, traditional; emphasis on academic success. Broad cur-riculum; big choice of languages, including French, German, Spanish, Italian, Greek, Chinese, Japanese; Latin compulsory for first three years; very good science (taught as three separate subjects) though facilities are old-fashioned. Pupils grouped by ability in maths, French. Stunning artwork displayed throughout the school (facilities, again, are poor). Strong music: 80% learn an instrument (particularly high standard of piano playing); choir, orchestra, wind bands etc. Extra-curricular activities include very successful Duke of Edinburgh award scheme. Big emphasis on community service.
Results   (1997) GCSE: 96% gained at least five grades A–C. A-level: creditable 77% of entries graded A or B.

Destinations   Nearly all stay on for A-levels and proceed to university (up to 15 a year to Oxbridge).

Sport   Usual team games; particular strengths in lacrosse, hockey. First-rate facilities include unusual sports dome (surrounded by a moat) for squash, volleyball, badminton, basketball, netball, indoor hockey, aerobics, dance; 18 tennis courts; indoor swimming pool; extensive playing fields. Outdoor pursuits include wind-surfing, canoeing, rock climbing, caving.

Remarks   Good school; facing up strongly to the challenge of a changing market.

MANCHESTER GRAMMAR
Old Hall Lane, Fallowfield, Manchester M13 0XT. Tel (0161) 224 7201

Synopsis
Independent ★ Boys ★ Day ★ Ages 11–18 ★ 1,415 pupils ★ 400 in sixth form
★ Fees: £4,560
Head: Dr Martin Stephen, 48, appointed 1994.

Profile
Background   Founded 1515 by Hugh Oldham, Bishop of Exeter, to foster 'god-linesse and good learning' and to ensure that 'grace, virtue and wisdom should grow, flower and take root in youths during their boyhood'; moved 1933 to present 28-acre site and purpose-built premises in south Manchester; Direct Grant until 1974. Imposing, if rather drab, red-brick buildings (green-tiled corridors the length of runways) plus later additions, including splendid, £1 million sports centre (named after Mike Atherton, an Old Mancunian); much recent refurbishment.

Atmosphere   Warm, civilised, mature; strong sense of common purpose; destructive aspects of competition eliminated, positive ones encouraged; rules kept to a minimum, based on common sense and mutual respect. Multi-ethnic boys confident without being arrogant; eccentricity is permitted, even encouraged, but sloppiness is not.

Admissions   By demanding, two-stage exams in English and arithmetic lasting more than four hours: only the brightest are advised to attempt them; 70% fail; all who succeed are clever, some are brilliant ('We educate like with like'). Pupils drawn in roughly equal measure from state and independent schools in an extensive catchment area stretching from Buxton to Blackpool and as far south as Stoke-on-Trent. No one who qualifies for entry is turned away on financial grounds ('Maintaining this tradition has become central to the culture of the school'); £10 million appeal launched to replace assisted places, which about a third hold.

The head   (High Master) Caring, articulate, exceptionally learned (author of 15 books on World War One social history and World War Two naval history). Read history and English at Leeds; PhD from Sheffield; worked in a remand home; taught at Uppingham (where he was a pupil), Haileybury (housemaster), Sedbergh (deputy head); previously head for six years of The Perse (qv). Loves teaching (first-years attend weekly English lessons in his study). Married (to the head of the Grange, qv); three sons.

The teaching   First-rate: brisk, challenging, primarily formal. Highly-qualified, exceptionally committed staff of 120 (27 women). Standard grammar school curriculum, including classics; science taught as three separate subjects; modern languages include German, Russian, Spanish; nearly all take GCSE maths and French a year early; A-levels restricted to three to leave plenty of time for wide-ranging, non-examined general studies courses (choice of 125 topics, philosophy compulsory). Pupils grouped by ability in maths only from second year; average class size 30, reducing to 25 for GCSE, 10–12 in sixth form. Good art; lots of music (two major concerts a year) and drama (at least six productions); masses of extra-curricular activities, including thriving community action programme and a strong tradition of trekking and camping.

Results (1997) GCSE: all gained at least five grades A–C. A-level: impressive 87% of entries graded A or B (seventh in the league table).

Destinations Nearly all stay on for A-levels and proceed to university (40–60 a year to Oxbridge).

Sport Impressive; regular national and regional honours in athletics, badminton, cricket, cross-country, hockey, soccer, squash, swimming, tennis, water polo. Facilities include extensive playing fields, indoor pool.

Remarks Marvellous school for able boys; highly recommended. HMC inspectors concluded (1996): 'The most significant feature of the school is the quality of its staff. Their academic ability, commitment and sense of vocation lead to a positive and alert response from the school's able pupils.'

MANCHESTER HIGH ♀
Grangethorpe Road, Manchester M14 6HS. Tel (0161) 224 0447

Synopsis
Independent ★ Girls ★ Day ★ Ages 11–18 (plus associated prep school) ★ 705 pupils ★ 175 in sixth form ★ Fees: £4,395
Head: Miss Elizabeth Diggory, 51, appointed 1994 (leaving August 1998).
First-rate academic school; very good teaching and results; strong drama and music.

Profile
Background Founded 1874 'to impart to girls the very best education which can be given to fit them for any future which may be before them' (Mrs Pankhurst sent her daughters here). Moved to present, pleasantly wooded site 1939, only to be bombed in 1940; girls returned 1949 to hastily constructed buildings which have been progressively improved or replaced; recent additions include sixth-form centre. Formerly Direct Grant, school reverted to full independence 1976.

Atmosphere Warm, harmonious, well-disciplined; humming with energy and enthusiasm. Big emphasis on respect, tolerance, co-operation; extra-curricular achievement regarded as important as academic success (first-rate art work on display). Smart, distinctive uniform.

Admissions Heavily over-subscribed (about 400 apply for 120 places) and very selective; entry at 11 by school's own exams and a one-and-a-half-hour assessment lesson. Phasing out of assisted places, which more than 200 hold, is likely to reduce the social mix (though the school hopes to offer more bursaries). Catchment area covers Greater Manchester and surrounding counties; large proportion of pupils from ethnic minority backgrounds.

The head Charming, forthright, very able. Read history at London; taught it for 15 years at King Edward VI High (qv); previously head for 11 years of St Albans High (qv). Committed Christian; strong supporter of single-sex education for girls; teaches general studies to the sixth form. Leaving to become head of St Paul's Girls' (qv).

The teaching Very good: generally formal in style; strongly academic, healthily competitive. Enthusiastic, well-qualified staff of 66 (five men). Broad curriculum: science taught as three separate subjects; all do Latin for first three years; other languages include German, Spanish, Russian, Greek; most take 10 GCSEs and three A-levels (from a choice of 23, including Latin, business studies, home economics). Pupils grouped by ability in maths, French; average class size 26–28. Strong music: all learn an instrument in the first year and most continue; choirs, orchestras, various ensembles. Enthusiastic drama. Good careers advice. Regular language exchanges with schools in France, Germany, Italy.

Results (1997) GCSE: all gained at least five grades A–C. A-level: very creditable 71% of entries graded A or B.

Destinations Nearly all stay on for A-levels and proceed to university (average of 10 a year to Oxbridge).

Sport Chiefly: gymnastics, swimming (indoor pool), netball, hockey, tennis, rounders; regular regional and national honours. Athletics, football, volleyball, basketball, badminton also available. Playing fields (including all-weather pitch) 10 minutes' walk away.

Remarks Very good school for able girls; highly recommended.

MARLBOROUGH ♂ ♀
Marlborough, Wiltshire SN8 1PA. Tel (01672) 892200

Synopsis
Independent ★ Co-educational ★ Boarding and some day ★ Ages 13–18 ★ 796 pupils (65% boys, 96% boarding) ★ 348 in sixth form ★ Fees: £14,100 boarding; £10,140 day
Head: Edward Gould, 54, appointed 1993.
Attractive, well-run school; very good teaching and results; strong art, drama, music, sport.

Profile
Background Founded 1843 for the sons of Anglican clergymen; pioneered the admission of girls into the sixth form 1968; fully co-educational since 1989. Elegant 18th-century and Victorian red-brick buildings ranged around a vast quadrangle on an 80-acre site; huge chapel; later additions include fine art school and three motel-like, mixed boarding houses. Facilities are first-rate. Sir John Betjeman was summoned by bells here.

Atmosphere Liberal tradition now tempered by tighter discipline: school is well-organised and purposeful. Strong religious ethos; good pastoral care; prefects take their responsibilities seriously; uniform for all. Parents required to agree to their child taking a urine test if drug-taking is suspected.

Admissions By interview and Common Entrance; 50%–55% mark required (not unduly selective); 20% receive some help with fees through scholarships (academic, art, music) and bursaries (including clergy). Victorian boarding houses (designed by the architect of Wormwood Scrubs) refurbished and up-graded; modern houses offer splendid accommodation; most sixth-formers have single study-bedrooms.

The head Very able: tough, determined, straight-talking; has restored the school's fortunes and raised its academic profile. Read geography at Oxford (rugby Blue, rowed for Britain); taught at Harrow for 16 years (including five as a housemaster); previously head for 10 years of Felsted. Gets to know the first-years by inviting them to dinner in small groups; takes time to visit houses. Married (wife much involved in school life); two daughters.

The teaching Lively, high quality; enthusiastic staff of 96 (30% female). Good languages; all do Latin for at least one year; Russian, Japanese, Mandarin, Arabic on offer; more able take GCSE dual-award science a year early; lots of computing, design/technology; choice of 19 subjects at GCSE, 25 at A-level. Pupils grouped by ability from second year; average class size 25, reducing to 15 at A-level. Very good art, drama, music: nearly half learn an instrument; three orchestras; strong choral tradition. Extra-curricular activities include cadet force, Duke of Edinburgh award scheme; weekend activities abound; school has its own beagle pack.
Results (1997) GCSE: 99% gained at least five grades A–C. A-level: creditable 68% of entries graded A or B (a good year).
Destinations About 95% go on to university (up to 20 a year to Oxbridge).
Sport Strong. Main sports: athletics, hockey, rugby, tennis, cricket, netball. Lacrosse, soccer, fencing, squash also available. Facilities include extensive playing fields, two all-weather pitches, athletics track, sports hall, indoor pool.
Remarks A fine all-round education. Recommended.

MARLWOOD ♂ ♀
Vattingstone Lane, Alveston, Bristol BS12 2LA. Tel (01454) 416844

Synopsis
Comprehensive ★ Co-educational ★ Ages 11–18 ★ 1,230 pupils (equal numbers of girls and boys) ★ 230 in sixth form
Head: Ken Williams, 52, appointed 1987.
Well-run comprehensive; good teaching and results; strong music, drama.

Profile
Background Opened 1972 (but has grammar school roots). Undistinguished flat-roofed buildings arranged around a quadrangle on 38-acre site with views of the River Severn and the Forest of Dean; some classrooms in 'temporary' huts; space at a premium. Supportive parents raise £15,000 a year.
Atmosphere Regime is firm, fairly traditional but unrepressive. Grammar school traditions preserved (gowns, speech day, founders' day service); staff, parents and pupils share the same values.
Admissions School 50% over-subscribed; priority to siblings and those living nearest. Most from middle-class backgrounds (definite 'flight from the city' syndrome).
The head Modest, open, welcoming; constantly about the school; sits in on lessons; knows pupils by name. Read history at Bristol; first headship at 37 (driven by a 'desire to be of obvious use'). Abhors bullying; thinks of the school as 'an oasis of moral standards'.
The teaching Good quality; varied styles (clear direction plus individual help). Staff of 77, half appointed by present head. Standard national curriculum; half take French, half German; good technology (120 computers); enthusiastic, first-rate history (visits to Russia, Berlin, concentration camps). Pupils grouped by ability from second year. Vibrant music (160 learn an instrument) and drama; ambitious productions; monthly theatre trips to Bristol. Lots of community involvement; regular charity fund-raising.
Results (1997) GCSE: 68% gained at least five grades A–C. A-level: 46% of entries graded A or B.
Destinations About 65% continue into the sixth form; of these, more than

80% proceed to higher education.
Sport   Rugby, soccer, cricket for the boys; hockey, netball for the girls. Facilities include on-site playing fields, large sports hall, athletics track (no swimming pool).
Remarks   Traditional values preserved.

MARPLE HALL ♂ ♀
Hill Top Drive, Marple, Stockport SK6 6LB. Tel (0161) 427 7966

Synopsis
Comprehensive ★ Co-educational ★ Ages 11–16 ★ 1,529 pupils (equal numbers of girls and boys)
Head: Miss Margaret Cuckson, 53, appointed 1989.
First-rate comprehensive; superb all-round education in delightful surroundings.

Profile
Background   Founded 1961 as a grammar school with 2,000 pupils; went comprehensive 1974; lost its sixth form 1989. Traditional 1960s premises (brick and panelling); vast classrooms; huge windows looking out on Cheshire countryside. A sense of (rather scruffy) spaciousness.
Atmosphere   Unusually relaxed and open: confident, cheerful pupils (full of praise for the school); frank, courteous teachers. No sign of disaffection or boredom anywhere; discipline so good as to be invisible to an outsider. Supportive parents, encouraged to come in whenever they like.
Admissions   Pupils drawn from a large catchment area south of Stockport; priority to those at nine 'feeder' primaries. Fairly broad social mix, but predominantly middle-class/professional families.
The head   Epitomises her school: ebullient, enthusiastic, exacting – and expects others to be the same. Read geography at Liverpool. Had taught here for 13 years before returning as head.
The teaching   Uniformly good: well-prepared, stimulating lessons; excellent facilities ('No need to make-do-and-mend here'); well-qualified staff of 89 (55% women). Standard national curriculum; science taught as three separate subjects; all do drama for first three years – 30% carry it on to GCSE. All take up to nine GCSEs from a choice of 20. Pupils grouped by ability in English, maths, modern languages; learning support for those who need it. Frequent testing; poor results lead to extra homework. Lots of extra-curricular activities; annual residential outing in the Lake District.
Results   (1996) GCSE: 65% gained at least five grades A–C.
Destinations   About 70% remain in full-time education after 16; rest go straight into jobs.
Sport   Impressive record in hockey, rugby, athletics, netball; other activities include football, tennis, golf, fencing, lacrosse. Good facilities but no sports hall or swimming pool.
Remarks   Good all round.

MAYNARD ♀
Denmark Road, Exeter EX1 1SJ. Tel (01392) 273417

Synopsis
Independent ★ Girls ★ Ages 11–18 (plus associated junior school) ★ 480 pupils
★ 112 in sixth form ★ Fees: £4,680
Head: Miss Felicity Murdin, 57, appointed 1980.
Attractive, lively school; very good teaching and results.

Profile
Background   Founded 1658 with an endowment by Sir John Maynard, local lawyer and MP who 'unlike most of his contemporaries held the enlightened belief that girls as well as boys should be educated'; moved to present attractive site and purpose-built premises (hammer-beamed hall) 1882; formerly Direct Grant, reverted to full independence 1975. Buildings are a pleasing blend of Victorian and modern, including fine new dining hall (very good food), sports hall, gym, sixth-form centre. Junior school (ages four to 10) on same site.

Atmosphere   Lively, friendly; 'committed to the inculcation of sound Christian principles' (girls practising other faiths welcome). Good relations between staff and confident, hard-working pupils ('social development and moral welfare closely monitored'). Motto: Manus justa nardus – The hand that deals justice is sweet-smelling.

Admissions   By exams in English, maths: school has been fairly selective ('We go at a cracking pace') but phasing out of assisted places, which more than 150 hold (and thanks to which 'the school has been able to sustain its former grammar school ethos, offering educational opportunities regardless of family background or parental income'), will have a big impact.

The head   Long-serving; very able; liked and respected by staff and pupils (not least for her sense of humour). Read French and Spanish at Oxford; taught at North London Collegiate (qv) for 17 years (senior mistress). Regards herself as first among equals; likes to 'get over rough ground lightly' – and faces a challenging last few years.

The teaching   High quality; varied styles. Enthusiastic, well-qualified staff of 52 (six men), nearly all appointed by present head; good spread of age and experience. Broad curriculum: science taught (and examined) as three separate subjects; all do Latin from second year for at least two years (half continue it to GCSE); Greek, Spanish, German, Russian on offer; English literature a particular strength; all do home economics (needlework or cookery). Wide choice of subjects at A-level, including sports studies. Pupils grouped by ability in maths, French, science; average class size 22–24, much smaller in sixth form. Good facilities for music, drama. Extra-curricular activities include Duke of Edinburgh award scheme; lots of community involvement; social and green issues taken seriously. Regular field trips and foreign exchanges.

Results   (1997) GCSE: all gained at least five grades A–C. A-level: 69% of entries graded A or B.

Destinations   About 80% continue into sixth form; of these, virtually all proceed to university.

Sport   Particular strengths in hockey, netball. Gymnastics, athletics, basketball, badminton, canoeing, cross-country, rounders, squash, swimming, tennis also on offer.

Remarks   Successful, well-run school; recommended.

MERCHANT TAYLORS', CROSBY ♂
Crosby, Liverpool L23 0QP. Tel (0151) 928 3308

Synopsis
Independent ★ Boys ★ Day ★ Ages 11–18 (plus associated prep school) ★
720 pupils ★ 173 in sixth form ★ Fees: £4,122
Head: Simon Dawkins, 52, appointed 1986.
Strongly traditional school; good teaching and results.

Profile
Background   Founded 1620 by John Harrison, merchant tailor; moved to present site and purpose-built premises on Liverpool–Southport road 1878 (leaving its original site to Merchant Taylors' Girls', qv). Main building a splendid pile: looks like a miniature Victorian town hall (soaring clock tower, chandeliers in the board room); many extensions and additions. Prep school (150 pupils aged seven to 11) near by.

Atmosphere   Disciplined, civilised; 'the building of character on firm, Christian foundations is among the school's first considerations'. No hint of disorder in classrooms or corridors; work ethic obviously respected. Honours boards and old photographs emphasise the school's history and traditions; prefects ('monitors') wear badges and undergraduate gowns.

Admissions   By tests in English, maths, verbal reasoning. School has been fairly selective ('grammar school standard') but phasing out of assisted places, which 280 hold, is likely to have a significant impact, not least on the social mix.

The head   Courteous, gentle. Read economics, philosophy and politics at Nottingham; formerly head of economics at Dulwich. Married; two children (one a pupil here).

The teaching   Purposeful, challenging. Hard-working staff of 58 (eight women). Broad curriculum: science taught as three separate subjects; all do Latin for at least three years; Greek, German, Spanish on offer. All take at least nine GCSEs and four A-levels, including general studies. Class sizes up to 29, reducing to 22 for GCSE, eight or nine in sixth form. Flourishing music – nearly a quarter learn an instrument – and drama, both shared with girls' school. Outstanding cadet force; lots of clubs and societies (everything from pottery to railways); regular trips and expeditions abroad.

Results   (1997) GCSE: 98% gained at least five grades A–C. A-level: 62% of entries graded A or B (school has slipped from 43rd in the league table in 1993 to 124th).

Destinations   About 95% stay on for A-levels; of these, 90% proceed to university (about 12 a year to Oxbridge).

Sport   Major games: rugby, hockey (particularly strong), cricket, athletics, tennis. (Blazers edged with yellow piping for boys who win sporting honours.) Fine playing fields, attractive pavilions, indoor swimming pool.

Remarks   An academically strong, no-nonsense school, successfully achieving its admirable aims.

MERCHANT TAYLORS' GIRLS', CROSBY ♀
Liverpool Road, Crosby, Liverpool L23 5SP. Tel (0151) 924 3140

Synopsis
Independent ★ Girls ★ Day ★ Ages 11–18 (plus associated junior school) ★
660 pupils ★ 180 in sixth form ★ Fees: £4,122
Head: Mrs Janet Mills, 50, appointed 1994.
Sound school; good teaching and results.

Profile
Background Founded 1888 on the site formerly occupied for more than 250
years by Merchant Taylors' Boys' (qv); original grey stone building plus many
later additions, some in need of refurbishment; space is tight. Formerly Direct
Grant, reverted to full independence 1976. Junior school in separate building
under its own head.

Atmosphere Friendly, happy, well-behaved; good relations between staff and
pupils; older girls help look after the younger ones. Uniform worn by all.

Admissions Entry by interview and tests in English, maths, verbal reasoning.
School is over-subscribed (about 200 apply for 100 places) and fairly selective
(weakest pupils are of average ability). But phasing out of assisted places, which
more than 200 hold (accounting for 25% of the school's £2 million income), will
have a significant impact – beginning with a 25% reduction in the intake; scholarship and bursary funds are limited. Wide catchment area includes Southport,
Ormskirk, Wigan, south Liverpool.

The head Experienced; good leader; gets on well with staff and pupils. Read
chemistry at York (and represented it at hockey, tennis, badminton); previously
deputy head of a girls' day school in Solihull. Keen golfer.

The teaching Formal in style (too formal for Her Majesty's Inspectors, who
said pupils were 'over-reliant' on their teachers and and needed to 'participate
more fully in their own learning'). Long-serving, predominantly female staff;
attentive, highly-motivated girls. Broad curriculum: science taught as three separate subjects; all do Latin in second year; Spanish, German, Russian on offer
from third year; particularly good results in history. Choice of 20 subjects at A-
level (largest entry for chemistry). Pupils grouped by ability in maths, French
from second year; average class size 23, reducing to 18 for GCSE, maximum of 16
in the sixth form. Lots of music: first-years offered free instrumental tuition; two
choirs, two orchestras. Extra-curricular activities include thriving cadet force,
popular Duke of Edinburgh award scheme.

Results (1997) GCSE: all gained at least five grades A–C. A-level: 62% of
entries graded A or B.

Destinations Virtually all stay on for A-levels; 90% proceed to university (four
or five a year to Oxbridge).

Sport More than 30 teams; extensive fixture list. Particular strengths in athletics, cross-country, tennis. On-site courts for netball, tennis; playing fields a short
distance away.

Remarks Despite their reservations about the teaching, HMI concluded (1996):
'The pupils achieve high standards. They learn well, making good progress in
most of their work and demonstrating high motivation and enjoyment.'

MERCHANT TAYLORS', NORTHWOOD ♂
Sandy Lodge, Northwood, Middlesex HA6 2HT. Tel (01923) 820644

Synopsis
Independent ★ Boys ★ Day and some boarding ★ Ages 11–18 ★ 750 pupils (95% day) ★ 120 in sixth form ★ Fees: £7,200 day; £12,045 boarding
Head: Jon Gabitass, 52, appointed 1991.
Well-run, traditional, academic school; very good teaching and results; first-rate sport.

Profile
Background Founded 1561 in central London by the Worshipful Company of Merchant Taylors (which still supports it); moved 1933 to grand, purpose-built premises on an idyllic 250-acre site in the heart of Betjeman's 'Metroland'; latest additions include computer centre, first-rate languages centre (no expense spared), excellent library; science labs need updating; some classrooms in prefabs. Clive of India was a pupil here; Cilla Black's son is.

Atmosphere A feeling of spaciousness, solidity, tradition (panelled walls, oak doors); some teachers wear academic gowns; common room has the air of a male club. Firm discipline; uniform worn throughout; well-organised pastoral care system (tutors keep in close touch with parents).

Admissions Heavily over-subscribed (at 11, 280 compete for 40 places), fairly selective (average IQ 120); entry at 11, 13 by school's own tests in English, maths, verbal reasoning. Intake largely middle-class, many from Jewish, Asian backgrounds; increasing number of parents are 'first-time buyers' of independent education; more than 200 pupils receive some financial help, including 80 on assisted places (funds set aside to compensate for phasing out the scheme). Boarding numbers small and dwindling (half from abroad); accommodation functional, facilities limited.

The head Formal, business-like, in command; believes in traditional values (including the character-building qualities of sport). Read English at Oxford (rugby Blue); previously deputy head of Abingdon. Married (to a teacher); two grown-up daughters.

The teaching Good: largely traditional in style (visitors not allowed into classrooms); long-serving, well-qualified staff (few women). Broad curriculum: all do Latin for at least one year (half take it to GCSE); Greek on offer to A-level; modern languages include Russian, German, Spanish, Japanese; science taught as three separate subjects; good facilities for design/technology. Pupils grouped by ability (more able take GCSE maths, French a year early); no special provision for dyslexics; average class size 20, reducing to 17 from third year, eight or nine at A-level. Limited art but lots of drama (some in conjunction with girls at St Helen's Northwood, (qv) and music (a third learn an instrument). Extra-curricular activities include well-equipped cadet force (assault course in the grounds) and Duke of Edinburgh award scheme – one of the two is compulsory from 14 for two years. Lots of trips abroad for study and sport.

Results (1997) GCSE: all gained at least five grades A–C. A-level: creditable 74% of entries graded A or B.

Destinations Virtually all go on to university (about 15 a year to Oxbridge).

Sport Outstanding facilities: playing fields as far as the eye can see; sports hall; indoor pool; courts for tennis, squash, fives, badminton; three lakes for sailing, wind-surfing, canoeing, fishing; rifle range; fencing salle. Main games: rugby, hockey, cricket; regular county, regional, national honours.

Remarks Good all round; particularly suitable for boys who are hard-working and sporty. HMC inspectors concluded (1996): 'The school is a friendly, disciplined, purposeful, happy and caring institution in which all have the opportunity to develop fully their own individuality.'

MERCHISTON CASTLE ♂
Colinton, Edinburgh, EH13 0PU. Tel (0131) 441 1567

Synopsis
Independent ★ Boys ★ Boarding and day ★ Ages 10–18 ★ 385 pupils (68% boarding) ★ 130 in sixth form ★ Fees: £9,150–£12,765 boarding; £5,970–£8,490 day
Head: David Spawforth, 59, appointed 1981 (retiring July 1998).
Successful, traditional school; good teaching and results; very strong sport.

Profile
Background   Founded 1833; moved 1930 to purpose-built, neo-classical premises on a romantic 96-acre estate (complete with ruined castle) four miles south-west of the city; fine chapel; modern facilities. The last boys' boarding school in Scotland.

Atmosphere   Down-to-earth, friendly, well-ordered (rules forbid 'dealing with betting shops'); warm relations between staff and pupils; strong family feel; traditional values upheld; boarding ethos retained (day boys stay for supper and prep). Aim is 'to give each boy in his way the capacity and confidence to live in an uncertain world and to make that life as rich as possible'. Smart uniform; kilts worn on Sundays and formal occasions. Lessons on Saturday mornings. Dances and discos in conjunction with St George's Girls' (qv).

Admissions   At 10 by interview and assessment, at 11/12 by tests, at 13 by Common Entrance; day places over-subscribed but school is not unduly selective. Boys drawn from a fairly broad social spectrum; 40% from northern England; 25% are the sons of expatriates or Servicemen. Five recently up-graded boarding houses in which, unusually, the boys live throughout their school careers with others of the same age – as juniors in small dormitories, as seniors in individual study-bedrooms; no weekly boarding but day boys may stay the night. Very good food. Scholarships: academic, music, technology, all-rounder.

The head   Charismatic, straight-talking, fiercely independent; coming to the end of a successful, 16-year reign. Married (wife has been much involved in school life).

The teaching   Good quality, generally formal in style; hard-working, relatively youthful staff of 49 (six women). Fairly broad (English) curriculum; science taught as three separate subjects; languages include Latin, German, Spanish; plenty of computing; most take nine GCSEs; sixth-formers choose between three A-levels and five Highers (more able tend to take the former); all do supplementary courses in computer studies, communications skills. Pupils grouped by ability in all subjects; progress closely monitored; first-rate extra help for those who need it; average class size 20, reducing to 10 or fewer in the sixth form. Lots of drama, music; 25% learn an instrument; two choirs, orchestra, pipe band. Extra-curricular activities include bridge, chess, debating, cadet force (compulsory for two years), Duke of Edinburgh award scheme.

Results   (1997) GCSE: 91% gained at least five grades A–C. A-levels (taken by 35%): 50% of entries graded A or B. Highers (taken by 65%): 54% of entries graded A or B.

Destinations   About 90% go on to university (average of three a year to Oxbridge).

Sport   Rugby is very strong; cricket, athletics, golf, swimming, football, squash,

shooting, tennis, sailing, fencing also flourish. Facilities include extensive playing fields, sports hall, indoor pool, courts for fives, squash, tennis.
Remarks Attractive school; good all round.

MILLAIS ♀
Depot Road, Horsham, West Sussex RH13 5HR. Tel (01403) 254932

Synopsis
Comprehensive ★ Girls ★ Ages 11–16 ★ 1,212 pupils
Head: Leon Nettley, 44, appointed January 1997.
Successful, well-run school; very good teaching and results; lots of music.

Profile
Background Opened 1957 as a secondary modern; went comprehensive 1978; achieved language college status 1996. Upper and lower schools in separate flat-roofed, functional buildings 100 yards apart on a spacious site; some classrooms in 'temporary' huts; school is poorly resourced (but language college status will help).

Atmosphere Brisk, purposeful, welcoming; girls attentive, absorbed in what they are doing, unabashedly aiming for success but without arrogance. Strong pressure to 'have a go', do well; rewards more important than sanctions (merit badges for achievement). Lively, broadly Christian assemblies; very good pastoral care. Firm uniform policy (no platform soles or sling-backs, no 'cult' hairstyles). Pupils' council meets regularly – and even has some of its ideas accepted. First-rate communication with parents, who contribute to many aspects of school life. Large sums raised for charity.

Admissions School slightly over-subscribed. Full range of abilities (one in five has a reading age below her chronological age) drawn largely from the fairly prosperous urban and rural community in and around Horsham; some from further afield.

The head Recent appointment but was previously deputy head here for seven years. Has a BEd from Exeter, MA from Sussex. Married; two daughters (both pupils here).

The teaching Good: mixture of formal instruction and group work; big emphasis on individual target setting. Keen, committed staff of 56 (11 men). Standard national curriculum; all take two foreign languages (from French, German, Spanish) for first three years; particularly good results in science, French; strong art. GCSE options include travel and tourism, drama, physical education, bilingual business studies (taught in Spanish), keyboarding. Pupils grouped by ability in most subjects from second year; extra help (in and out of class) for those who need it, including the gifted; progress closely monitored (half-termly grades for effort); average class size 26–28, smaller for GCSE. Music has an important place: 130 learn an instrument; two choirs, orchestra, wind band etc; frequent concerts. Lots of educational trips, expeditions; regular exchanges with schools in France, Germany, Spain.

Results (1997) GCSE: creditable 72% gained at least five grades A–C.

Destinations More than 90% remain in full-time education after 16.

Sport Enough variety to attract most girls; regular county honours. Main sports: gymnastics, dance, hockey, netball, rounders, tennis, athletics. Aerobics, badminton, basketball, football, trampolining, squash, swimming (off-site) also on offer. Ample playing fields (but sometimes water-logged); new sports hall.

Remarks Ofsted inspectors concluded (1996): 'Millais is a very good school with some outstanding features. The vast majority of pupils make better progress than expected given the comprehensive nature of the school's population.'

MILLFIELD ♂ ♀
Street, Somerset BA16 0YD. Tel (01458) 442291

Synopsis
Independent ★ Co-educational ★ Boarding and day ★ Ages 13–18 ★ 1,250 pupils (60% boys, 75% boarding) ★ 576 in sixth form ★ Fees: £14,385 boarding; £9,315 day
Head: Christopher Martin, 59, appointed 1990 (retiring August 1998).
Big, distinctive school; wide range of abilities; huge choice of subjects, activities; exceptionally strong sport.

Profile
Background Founded 1935 by Jack 'Boss' Meyer as a crammer for the sons of Indian princes; went co-educational in the 1960s and developed into a first-rate, most unusual school. Vast array of modern, rather ugly buildings on a 100-acre campus; excellent facilities include sculpture park, stabling for 47 horses. Boris Yeltsin and Deng Xiao-Ping sent their grandsons here.

Atmosphere Busy, purposeful, multi-national; 'existentialist,' says the head; 'people expect the school to be different tomorrow from today'.

Admissions By interview; enthusiasm is the main qualification ('enthusiasm for anything'); half come from the associated prep school. Many are the children of wealthy broken families (anorexia a growing problem); significant numbers are scholars (40% receive help with fees). Boarders in 30 houses, some in surrounding villages (pupils bussed in); accommodation adequate if slightly impersonal.

The head Experienced, brisk; taught modern languages at Westminster for 15 years; previously head of Bristol Cathedral School (qv). From September 1998: Peter Johnson, 49, head of Wrekin (qv).

The teaching Good quality; small classes (12 on average). Exceptionally broad curriculum: all do 13 subjects in their first year; sciences taught separately; languages include Russian, Spanish, Japanese; most take nine GCSEs from a choice of 37, including accounting, American studies, computer studies, environmental science, media studies; choice of 30 subjects at A-level; all take general studies; vocational alternatives available. Pupils grouped by ability in most subjects; extra help for the most able, those with learning difficulties and those who speak English as a foreign language. Lots of drama and music: more than 30 orchestras, choirs, instrumental groups; up to 15 music scholarships a year. Activities (60 on offer) range from archery to water-colour painting.

Results (1997) GCSE: 86% gained at least five grades A–C. A-level: 58% of entries graded A or B.

Destinations About 80% go on to university (20–25 a year to Oxbridge).

Sport Very strong; vast range; special coaching for 'outstanding performers' (former stars include Ian Botham, Duncan Goodhew, Mark Cox). Facilities include extensive playing fields, 23 tennis courts, all-weather pitch, Olympic-size pool, golf course.

Remarks All encouraged to find something at which they excel; very shy children may sink.

MILL HILL COUNTY HIGH ♂ ♀
Worcester Crescent, Mill Hill, London NW6 4LL. Tel (0181) 959 0017

Synopsis
Partially selective comprehensive (grant-maintained) ★ Co-educational ★
Ages 11–18 ★ 1,350 pupils (roughly equal numbers of girls and boys) ★ 260
in sixth form
Head: Dr Alan Davison, 40, appointed September 1997.
First-rate, go-ahead school; good teaching and results; big emphasis on technology.

Profile
Background Result of a 1984 merger between two small comprehensives; opted out of council control 1993; technology college status (leading to additional funding) awarded 1994. Fifties buildings plus later additions (including sixth-form centre) on a spacious, 21-acre site on the edge of the Green Belt; good facilities for science, computing, technology.

Atmosphere Business-like, well-disciplined (detention on Saturday and/or Sunday mornings); technology all-pervasive. Uniform below the sixth form (when pupils are required to be 'tidy, smart and clean in appearance' – and they are).

Admissions Heavily over-subscribed (four apply for each of the 240 places), partially selective: 30% admitted on the basis of their performance in three verbal and non-verbal reasoning tests; 10% of places for those demonstrating achievement and potential in music; 5% for achievement and potential in dance. Priority to siblings of current pupils, who make up nearly half the intake (drawn equally from middle-class homes, council housing estates).

The head New appointment. Able, vigorous, experienced (his second headship). PhD and MBA from Leicester in education management. Progressive in style but firmly committed to traditional values (uniform, discipline, high expectations). Married; two children.

The teaching Good quality; wide range of styles (school heavily involved in training new teachers). Standard national curriculum with an emphasis on technology, computing; wide choice of 25 subjects at A-level; vocational alternatives, including GNVQ in media studies (first-rate facilities), available. Pupils grouped by ability in all subjects at the end of the first term (top half take a second modern language or Latin) and, unusually, by sex in some subjects from third year (girls and boys taught separately for GCSE English and science); average class size 25, reducing to 10–14 in sixth form. Strong performing arts: three orchestras, three choirs; lots of drama. Extra-curricular activities include very well supported Duke of Edinburgh award scheme. Regular language exchanges to France, Germany.

Results (1997) GCSE: 60% gained at least five grades A–C. A-level: 40% of entries graded A or B.

Destinations About 60% continue into the sixth form; of these, 75% proceed to university.

Sport All main sports offered but the emphasis is on individual fitness and involvement with outside clubs rather than on team games and school matches. Sports hall but limited playing fields.

Remarks A school with lots to offer; recommended.

MILTON ABBEY ♂
Blandford Forum, Dorset DT11 0BZ. Tel (01258) 880484

Synopsis
Independent ★ Boys ★ Boarding and day ★ Ages 13–18 ★ 200 pupils ★ 72 in sixth form ★ Fees: £12,825 boarding; £8,565 day
Head: Jonathan Hughes-D'Aeth, 42, appointed 1996.
Small, friendly school; wide range of abilities.

Profile
Background   Opened 1954; fine Georgian mansion in beautiful grounds adjoining a medieval Benedictine abbey; tatty classrooms.

Atmosphere   Exceptionally friendly; high level of personal care; school capitalises on its intimate size; aim is to increase confidence, make boys believe in themselves (40% arrive with educational psychologists' reports, often indicating dyslexia); 'a supportive rather than a competitive environment'.

Admissions   Entry by interview and Common Entrance or tests; school is not academically selective. Most pupils from professional, farming, Service backgrounds from all parts of the country; a few from abroad. Boarding accommodation generally gloomy and spartan ('Our living quarters,' says the head, 'have begun to show signs of wear and tear – they are our Achilles heel').

The head   Enthusiastic, charming, able. Read geography at Liverpool; previously at Rugby (qv) for 16 years (housemaster). Married (wife much involved in school life); four young children.

The teaching   Sound; long-serving staff. Standard national curriculum; pupils grouped by ability in most subjects; extra help for dyslexics; average class size 15. Lots of music (three choirs), art, drama. Extra-curricular activities include cadet force, community service: lots for everyone to do.

Results   (1997) GCSE: creditable 76% gained at least five grades A–C. A-level: exceptionally modest 13% of entries graded A or B.

Destinations   Nearly all enter the sixth form; some go on to university.

Sport   All main games plus sailing, canoeing, golf (nine-hole course), fencing, squash. Heated indoor pool.

Remarks   Children who would be lost in a larger school may thrive here.

MINSTER ♂ ♀
Nottingham Road, Southwell, Nottinghamshire NG25 0HG. Tel (01636) 814000

Synopsis
Comprehensive (voluntary-aided, Church of England) ★ Co-educational ★ Ages 11–18 (but choristers and potentially able musicians admitted to junior department at eight) ★ 1,510 pupils (roughly equal numbers of girls and boys) ★ 330 in sixth form
Head: Philip Blinston, 42, appointed 1994.
Unusual, multi-faceted comprehensive; very good GCSE results; strong music.

Profile
Background   Roots go back to 956 when music and Latin were taught to choristers in Southwell Minster; re-founded 1313 and again in late 18th century; merged with a secondary modern and became a co-educational comprehensive 1976; one

of only two state choir schools (the other is King's, Peterborough, qv). School on two sites 15 minutes' walk apart. Junior department in self-contained unit.

Atmosphere Varies between sites: in the main school (first four years), rumbustious, hectic, slightly untidy; buildings are tatty, flat-roofed, drably decorated; some classrooms in 'temporary' huts (and one converted from a potting shed). In the upper school, in more attractive accommodation close to the Minster, the mood is calm, serious, reflective. Perceptible Christian ethos: almost all pupils have a daily assembly. Discipline fairly light for size of school. Uniform of navy blazer and tie; sixth-formers required to look 'tailored and professional'. Supportive parents raise/donate £10,000 a year.

Admissions Annual intake of 232: places guaranteed to children in the official catchment area and eight 'feeder' primaries; remainder (usually 30%) allocated to applicants from Nottingham, Newark, Mansfield on basis of Christian commitment or social grounds (up to 25% over-subscribed). Most pupils in middle-upper sections of ability range from professional/middle-class backgrounds.

The head Easy-going, cheerful, straightforward. Gained a BEd (and later MEd) at Nottingham, specialising in English and religious education. Came here as deputy head 1989. Practising Anglican; likes singing and Spain; owns a canal cruiser. Married (to a primary head); two children (both pupils here).

The teaching Clear, measured, well matched to individual needs; very stable staff of 86. Standard national curriculum; most take nine GCSEs; choice of 20 subjects at A-level, including graphics, performing arts; best results in maths, science, languages; all do (non-examined) general studies. Pupils grouped by ability from second year in maths, French; from third year in geography, history, English, religious education. Outstanding music: junior department admits about five choristers a year for the Minster, plus a number of talented instrumentalists; nearly 400 take part in weekly rehearsals for orchestras, choirs, bands, ensembles. Energetic drama department (good results). Exceptional Duke of Edinburgh award scheme involves more than 250 pupils and 40 staff.

Results (1997) GCSE: creditable 67% gained at least five grades A–C. A-level: 40% of entries graded A or B.

Destinations About 65% continue into the sixth form; of these, 90% proceed to university (about three a year to Oxbridge).

Sport Team strengths more in soccer than rugby; strong athletics, hockey, swimming. Ample pitches; use of sports hall, pool, squash courts at neighbouring leisure centre.

Remarks Rare cocktail of a school, combining characteristics of a neighbourhood comprehensive, choir school, church school and sixth-form college. Ofsted inspectors concluded (1995): 'This is a good school. Pupils show commitment to learning and behave well. The quality of teaching is good overall.'

MOIRA HOUSE ♀
Upper Carlisle Road, Eastbourne BN20 7TE. Tel (01323) 644144

Synopsis
Independent ★ Girls ★ Day and boarding ★ Ages 11–18 (plus associated nursery and junior schools) ★ 223 pupils (62% day) ★ 56 in sixth form ★ Fees: £3,300–£7,800 day; £9,270–£12,090 boarding
Head: Mrs Ann Harris, 50, appointed April 1997.
Lively, civilised school; wide range of abilities; good teaching and results; strong music.

Profile

Background   Founded 1875 by Charles Ingham, an enlightened Victorian engineer who believed young women should be able to follow challenging careers. Moved to present, compact site near Beachy Head 1887. Collection of Victorian/Edwardian red-brick buildings plus functional (but well-equipped) later additions; nursery and junior schools on same site.

Atmosphere   Friendly, courteous (unabashed emphasis on good manners – 'Other people matter'); individuals feel known and valued ('I was shy when I came,' says a 14-year-old, 'but I'm not shy any more'). Close, easy relations between head, staff and pupils; prefects known as The League, with titles of Squires, Standard Bearers, School Knights. Parents very supportive.

Admissions   School is not academically selective on principle; abilities range from average to potential Oxbridge. Entry chiefly by interview but applicants also take either Common Entrance or tests in English, maths at 11, plus French and science at 13; numbers have fallen but are rising again. Parents are self-employed business people, farmers, professionals; 5% expatriates, 9% foreign (Russia, Hong Kong, Lebanon, Thailand). Comfortable, spotless, non-institutional boarding accommodation. Scholarships, bursaries available.

The head   Recent appointment (predecessor had been in post 21 years and is now the bursar); previously head of the junior school, where she had been for 15 years. Pleasant, compassionate, popular with parents. Married; no children.

The teaching   Good: challenging, clearly presented lessons; pupils engaged, keen to participate. Experienced, stable staff of 46 (seven men). Broad curriculum: science on offer as three separate subject; languages include Latin, German, Spanish; good results in maths. Pupils grouped by ability in most subjects from the start; progress closely monitored (monthly grades for effort, attainment, attitude); extra help for those who need it (including dyslexia); average class size 15, maximum of 10 at A-level. Lots of music: 60% have singing or instrumental lessons; two orchestras, two choirs. Ambitious drama; well-supported Duke of Edinburgh award scheme. First-rate careers advice (full-time teacher). Regular language exchanges with pupils in France, Germany, Spain.

Results   (1997) GCSE: 85% gained at least five grades A–C. A-level: 49% of entries graded A or B.

Destinations   Most stay on for A-levels; more than 90% proceed to university (one or two a year to Oxbridge).

Sport   Chiefly: swimming (strong), hockey, netball (Sussex champions), rounders, tennis (five all-weather courts), athletics. Fencing, cricket, rugby, badminton, squash also on offer.

Remarks   Good school for well-motivated girls who might be swamped in a larger, more impersonal environment.

MONMOUTH ♂
Almshouse Street, Monmouth, Gwent NP5 3XP. Tel (01600) 713143

Synopsis
Independent ★ Boys ★ Day and boarding ★ Ages 11–18 (plus prep department) ★ 578 pupils (69% day) ★ 161 in sixth form ★ Fees: £5,202 day; £9,141 boarding
Head: Tim Haynes, 42, appointed 1995.
Successful traditional school; good teaching and results; strong sport.

Profile

Background Founded 1614 and substantially endowed by William Jones of the Haberdashers' Company, with which strong links remain. Mainly Victorian, grey stone buildings (plus some bleakly functional later additions) on a large, town-centre site beside the busy A40. Good facilities include extensive science labs, fine music school; 29 playing fields across the Wye.

Atmosphere Cheerful, hard working, well-ordered (shirts do not hang out here). Good pastoral care system (two chaplains, school counsellor). Some boarding houses still in urgent need of refurbishment.

Admissions Entry at 11 by school's own exam, at 13 by Common Entrance (55% mark required); fairly wide range of abilities. Local demand is strong; day pupils come from up to 25 miles away; boarding fees are modest. Assisted places, which 150 hold, will be replaced by the school's own scheme, at a cost of nearly £1 million a year. Sports scholarships available at 16.

The head Youthful, able, charming; well respected by staff and pupils. Read history at Reading; worked as a stockbroker before switching to teaching; previously surmaster (deputy head) of St Paul's (where he taught for 13 years). Married; two young children.

The teaching Good quality; generally traditional in style ('pedestrian', according to HMC inspectors). Stable staff of 55 (eight women). Broad curriculum: all do Latin for first two years; Spanish, Greek on offer; strong science. Wide choice of sixth-form subjects, some in conjunction with girls at Haberdashers', Monmouth (qv). Pupils grouped by ability in some subjects from 13; extra help available for dyslexics; average class size 20–24 to GCSE, 8–12 at A-level. Lots of music. Extra-curricular activities include voluntary cadet force, well-supported Duke of Edinburgh award scheme.

Results (1997) GCSE: all gained at least five grades A–C grades. A-level: 60% of entries graded A or B.

Destinations Nearly all go on to university (about 15 a year to Oxbridge).

Sport Main games: rugby (strong), rowing (boathouse on the Wye), cricket. Soccer, cross-country, athletics, badminton, squash, sailing, golf also popular.

Remarks Good value for money.

MORETON HALL ♀

Weston Rhyn, Oswestry, Shropshire SY11 3EW. Tel (01691) 773671

Synopsis
Independent ★ Girls ★ Boarding and day ★ Ages 11–18 ★ 260 pupils ★ (90% boarding) ★ 81 in sixth form ★ Fees: £12,600 boarding; £8,700 day.
Head: Jonathan Forster, 42, appointed 1992.
Attractive, go-ahead, small school with lots to offer girls of a fairly wide range of abilities.

Profile

Background Founded 1913 in Oswestry by Ellen Lloyd-Williams ('Aunt Lil') for daughters of the family; moved 1920 to present 100-acre parkland site. Compact cluster of buildings grouped around original Elizabethan hall; a sense of space and freedom. Facilities include large library, purpose-built art and design centre, music block, state-of-the-art recording studio.

Atmosphere Happy, purposeful, well-organised; clear code of conduct accepted by all; girls feel valued and secure. School has exceptionally strong business links: sixth-formers manage a travel agency (£360,000 turnover in 1996), a taxi service, the school farm, a licensed radio station and their local railway ticket office. Good quality boarding accommodation: juniors in small dorms (small pets allowed); seniors in university-style residence with study-bedrooms.

Admissions Entry by school's own exam and interview; fairly wide range of abilities; good provision for those with dyslexia. Girls come mostly from Shropshire, mid-Wales, Cheshire, the Midlands. Scholarships include one for tennis.

The head Affable, enthusiastic; his hands-on approach has given the school a clear direction. Read English at Leeds; previously head of English and a housemaster at Strathallan (qv). Married (to a teacher); two daughters (both pupils here).

The teaching Generally good. Youthful, well-qualified staff of 20 (equal numbers of women and men), half appointed by present head. Broad curriculum: German, Latin on offer from 13, Spanish from 14; science on offer as three separate subjects; choice of 20 subjects at GCSE and A-level (good results in business studies); GNVQ in leisure & tourism also available. Girls grouped by ability in most subjects; small classes of 10–15, reducing to six in sixth form; progress carefully monitored. Lots of art (good A-level results), drama (open-air amphitheatre), music (majority have singing lessons or learn to play an instrument).

Results (1997) GCSE: all gained at least five grades A–C. A-level: 54% of entries graded A or B.

Destinations About 85% continue into the sixth form; of these, 90% proceed to university.

Sport Strong tradition; very good facilities (well-equipped sports hall staffed from 7.30 am to 10 pm daily). Particular strengths in lacrosse, tennis (floodlit, all-weather courts). Volleyball, badminton, gymnastics, netball, hockey, athletics, swimming (heated outdoor pool), golf (nine-hole course) also on offer.

Remarks Ofsted inspectors concluded (1995): 'The school has particular strengths in its standards of achievement, quality of learning, excellence of boarding provision and development of personal qualities.'

MOUNT ♀
Dalton Terrace, York Y02 4DD. Tel (01904) 667500

Synopsis
Independent ★ Girls ★ Boarding and day ★ Ages 11–18 (plus associated junior school) ★ 255 pupils (55% boarding) ★ 65 in sixth form ★ Fees: £10,794 boarding; £6,645 day
Head: Miss Barbara Windle, 56, appointed 1986.
Small, successful school; friendly atmosphere; good teaching and results.

Profile
Background Founded 1831, the only girls' Quaker senior school in Britain. Mid-Victorian buildings plus many later additions on a lovely 20-acre site (an oasis of calm and restfulness) near the city centre. Junior school (ages three to 11) on same site.

Atmosphere Warm, friendly, purposeful; strong emphasis on the Quaker ethos of caring for the individual (school is small enough for every girl to be known well) and being involved in the community. 'Girls of all faiths and none are welcomed, although our intake is predominantly British and Christian.'

Admissions By interview and school's own tests in English, maths, verbal reasoning.

School is fairly selective but phasing out of assisted places, which more than 50 hold, is likely to lead to lower entry standards. A third of the intake comes from the junior school. Boarding in three houses divided by age; younger girls in small dormitories (four or five beds), seniors in single study-bedrooms; day girls can stay the night. Scholarships, bursaries available; means-tested fees for daughters of Quakers.

The head Personable, shrewd. Read English at Cambridge; previously head of sixth form at Bolton Girls' (qv).

The teaching Good quality; varied styles. Science taught as three separate subjects; all do French from first year, add Latin and German for second and third years and may drop Latin for GCSE; Italian, Russian, Spanish also on offer. Pupils grouped by ability in French, maths; extra help for dyslexics; average class size 15–20, reducing to a maximum of 12 in the sixth form. All do nine GCSEs and four A-levels, including general studies. Strong musical tradition: two-thirds learn an instrument; two orchestras, two choirs. Wide range of extra-curricular activities, including ceramics, woodwork, dressmaking, dancing, Duke of Edinburgh award scheme.

Results (1997) GCSE: 97% gained at least five grades A–C. A-level: creditable 69% of entries graded A or B.

Destinations About 80% stay on for A-levels; of these, nearly all proceed to university (four or five a year to Oxbridge).

Sport Strong record; good facilities (gym, indoor pool). Main sports: hockey, netball, rounders, tennis, swimming, athletics. Badminton, lacrosse, volleyball, squash, basketball, cricket, fencing also on offer.

Remarks Attractive school.

NEWCASTLE ROYAL GRAMMAR ♂

Eskdale Terrace, Newcastle-upon-Tyne NE2 4DX. Tel (0191) 281 5711

Synopsis

Independent ★ Boys ★ Day ★ Ages 11–18 (plus associated junior school) ★ 940 pupils ★ 280 in sixth form ★ Fees: £4,215
Head: James Miller, 47, appointed 1994.
High-powered, prestigious academic school; first-rate teaching and results.

Profile

Background Founded 1545; moved 1906 to present, dignified, red brick and stone buildings (oak-panelled walls, high-ceilinged classrooms) plus many later additions on 10-acre site close to the city centre; formerly Direct Grant, reverted to full independence 1976. First-rate facilities include new science & technology centre, music school, well-equipped sports hall; £6 million spent since 1995.

Atmosphere Busy, purposeful, civilised; emphasis on success, involvement; doing well taken almost for granted. Boys confident (no wilting violets), articulate (and not unquestioning). Friendly, respectful relations between staff and pupils; discipline good but low-key (breaches lead to detentions of varying inconvenience); good pastoral care system (new boys assigned a 'buddy' in the year above); strong line on bullying. Uniform evolves (a rite of passage) from blue blazers to black to a suit (in the sixth form). Notice boards bustle with club and society announcements. Parents well satisfied.

Admissions School heavily over-subscribed and seriously selective: entry at 11 by exam (sample papers published annually) and interview, at 13 by exam or Common Entrance; 50% of applicants turned away. Broad social mix (15%

ethnic minorities): 215 on assisted places; Labour's phasing out of the latter will have a significant impact, despite relatively modest fees. Catchment area covers the whole of Northumberland, Co. Durham, Tyne & Wear conurbation; good public transport (Metro station on the doorstep).

The head   Able, dynamic; very much in charge. Read PPE at Oxford; taught 17 years at Winchester (housemaster); his second headship. Keen on cricket, opera, car-rallying, crosswords. Married (wife specialises in teaching dyslexics); two sons (both were pupils here).

The teaching   Emphasis on traditional whole-class instruction (but more seminar-style in the sixth form). Highly qualified, relatively youthful staff of 75 (80% male), kept on their toes by lively, competitive boys. Particular strengths in maths, science (taught as three separate subjects) but also in English, history, art, economics, politics; religious studies imaginatively taught. Mainstream academic diet below the sixth form; options include Latin, Greek, German; many take GCSE maths a year early. Sixth-form curriculum broadened by extensive use of AS-levels (philosophy, computing, electronics, statistics); good general studies programme run in conjunction with girls at Central Newcastle High (qv). Pupils grouped by ability in maths from the second year, French from the third; typical class size 25, reducing to eight to 12 in the sixth form. Flourishing art, drama, music (orchestra, choir, choral and organ scholarships to Oxbridge). Busy programme of extra-curricular activities (debating, chess, cadets). Regular exchanges with schools in Germany, France, Russia.

Results   (1997) GCSE: 98% gained at least five grades A- C. A-level: creditable 69% of entries graded A or B.

Destinations   Nearly all go on to good universities (including Newcastle, Durham and up to 15 a year to Oxbridge); many do medicine.

Sport   Packed academic programme means time is limited; aim is to promote fitness, lasting enjoyment. Basic training in athletics, cricket, gymnastics, rugby; seniors can add badminton, basketball, cross-country, fencing, hockey, judo, karate, orienteering, rowing (boathouse on the Tyne), squash, table tennis, tennis, volleyball, water polo, weight training, soccer. Some playing fields five minutes' walk away.

Remarks   Very good school for able, highly motivated boys.

NEWCASTLE-UNDER-LYME ♂ ♀
Mount Pleasant, Newcastle-under-Lyme, Staffordshire ST5 1DB. Tel (01782) 633604

Synopsis
Independent ★ Co-educational (but boys and girls taught separately from 11 to 16) ★ Day ★ Ages 11–18 (plus associated junior school) ★ 1,100 pupils (equal numbers of girls and boys) ★ 305 in sixth form ★ Fees: £3,939
Head: Dr Ray Reynolds, 55, appointed 1990.
Sound, academic school; good teaching and results; lots of music, sport.

Profile
Background   Result of 1981 amalgamation of two Victorian, single-sex grammar schools on adjoining sites in a pleasant residential area a mile from the town centre; former girls' premises drab, utilitarian; boys more grandly accommodated. From 11 to 16, pupils are taught predominantly in single-sex classrooms ('within a co-educational environment'). On-site junior school (co-educational, ages eight to 11).

Atmosphere   Cheerful, purposeful, well-ordered; work-hard, play-hard ethos prevails. Competitive house system; smart uniform (colour-coded by achievement).
Admissions   By tests in English, maths, verbal reasoning (minimum IQ 105); promotion from the junior school not guaranteed; sixth-form entry requires six GCSEs, three at grade A or B. Phasing out of assisted places, which more than 350 hold, will have a big impact; to avoid lowering entry standards, numbers are likely to be reduced by a third. Catchment area extends to south Cheshire, east Shropshire.
The head   (Principal) Read physics at Queen's, Belfast (PhD); previously head of physics at Millfield (qv). Teaches general studies to sixth-formers. Married; one daughter.
The teaching   Good quality: fairly formal in style; well-qualified staff (slightly more men than women). Broad curriculum: sciences taught separately; all do French, German, Latin; Russian, Greek, Spanish on offer; choice of 22 subjects at A-level; general studies compulsory. Pupils grouped by ability in maths, English; average class size 28, reducing to 22 at GCSE, 12 in the sixth form. Strong drama, art, music; more than 300 learn an instrument; two orchestras, two choirs. Extra-curricular activities include public speaking, Scouts, cadet force. Frequent language exchanges to France, Germany; regular excursions to Flanders (history), Dublin (business studies), Spain (hockey), Colorado (skiing).
Results   (1997) GCSE: all gained at least five grades A–C. A-level: creditable 66% of entries graded A or B (a good year).
Destinations   About 95% go on to university (10–15 a year to Oxbridge).
Sport   Wide choice; fine facilities, including extensive playing fields, sports centre, indoor pool. Main sports: rugby, cricket, hockey, tennis, athletics, cross-country for the boys; hockey, athletics, netball, tennis, rounders for the girls. Golf, badminton, swimming, water polo etc also on offer.
Remarks   HMC inspectors concluded (1995): 'The school is a happy, open community with friendly, well-behaved pupils and a staff keen to do the best for them.'

NEW HALL ♀
Chelmsford, Essex CM3 3HT. Tel (01245) 467588

Synopsis
Independent ★ Girls ★ Day and boarding ★ Ages 11–18 (plus on-site pre-prep and prep) ★ 434 pupils (57% day) ★ 120 in sixth form ★ Fees: £7,275 day; £11,370 boarding
Head: Sister Anne Marie, 40, appointed 1996.
Attractive Christian school; good teaching and results.

Profile
Background   Founded 1642 in Liege, Belgium to provide a Catholic education for English girls then denied one in England; established on present 75-acre site 1799; magnificent Tudor house (once the home of Mary Tudor) plus unobtrusive later additions. Good facilities (including first-rate performing arts centre); bright, cheerful classrooms.
Atmosphere   Christian values all-pervasive: aim is to provide 'a broad-based Christian education for life' but girls of other faiths welcomed ('unity in diversity'). Big emphasis on 'community', enhanced by the presence of nuns of the Order of the Holy Sepulchre, who play an active part in school life; good pastoral care system (girls' welfare paramount). Boarding houses divided by age: girls

move house as they progress through the school; juniors in dormitories divided into cubicles; sixth-formers have own study-bedrooms.

Admissions 'Diagnostic' rather than selective: prospective pupils spend a day here; they take tests in maths, English, verbal reasoning, are asked to bring something of which they are particularly proud, and are interviewed by the head. School asks: 'Will the girl thrive at New Hall, and will New Hall continue to thrive because she is part of it?' Falling numbers countered by the introduction of weekly boarders and day girls and the development of a prep school (co-educational, ages four to 11). Fewer than 50% are Catholic; about 10% come from abroad. Scholarships (academic, performing arts) available.

The head Calm, totally committed. Was a pupil here; read history at Cambridge; trained in personnel management; returned in 1978 to teach history, Latin, religious education.

The teaching Mixture of traditional 'chalk-and-talk' and group work; mostly lay staff of 45 (11 men); particularly good maths, science (well-equipped labs); lots of computing. Pupils grouped by ability in some subjects; maximum class size 24, reducing to 14 in sixth form; extra help for those with special needs. Progress carefully monitored and reported to parents. Strong music: more than half learn an instrument; good choir. Extra-curricular activities include debating, photography, voluntary service, well-supported Duke of Edinburgh award scheme.

Results (1997) GCSE: 98% gained at least five grades A–C. A-level: 53% of entries graded A or B.

Destinations Majority go on to university.

Sport All the usual games plus basketball, aerobics, trampolining, weight-training. School planning to spend £1.5 million on enhanced facilities ('New Hall will not allow economic pressures to eclipse the priority we attach to the individual needs of pupils').

Remarks A welcome oasis of calm where girls are taught to think of others.

NEWLANDS ♀
Farm Road, Maidenhead, Berkshire SL6 5JB. Tel (01628) 25068

Synopsis
Comprehensive ★ Girls ★ Ages 11–18 ★ 1,068 pupils ★ 162 in sixth form
Head: Mrs Sue Benton, 53, appointed 1990.
Successful, well-run school; very good teaching and results; strong music.

Profile
Background Founded 1905 (as Maidenhead Girls' High); moved to present site on the outskirts of the town 1958; went comprehensive (and was renamed) 1973. Functional buildings of varying periods (school has steadily expanded); many classrooms in 'temporary' huts (some recently renewed); space is tight.

Atmosphere Friendly, well-ordered ('discipline is firm but not oppressive,' says head); good relations between staff and polite, confident pupils; bullying can lead to expulsion. Sensible uniform strictly enforced; sixth-formers in smart casual wear. Supportive parents (required to sign 'contract' with school).

Admissions Over-subscribed: nearly 300 apply for 186 places, which are allocated by Berkshire County Council; priority to those living in the catchment area. Pupils come from a wide range of backgrounds; 10% Muslims, Sikhs (attracted by single-sex education). Another 100 join at 16.

The head   Able, approachable, quietly-spoken. Read English at Leeds; has an MSc in educational management from Oxford; previously deputy head of a co-educational comprehensive in Oxfordshire. Married; two grown-up sons.

The teaching   Very good. Experienced, stable staff of 70 (90% women), 35% appointed by present head. Standard national curriculum; more able do French and German; Spanish, Italian (sponsored by the Italian Government) on offer; GCSE options include media studies, food technology, textiles. Choice of 16 subjects at A-level; GNVQs available (and popular). Pupils grouped by ability in maths, French; extra help for those who need it (including those who speak English as a foreign language); average class size 30, reducing to 25 for GCSE, smaller in the sixth form. Academic mentors set girls individual achievement targets. Very strong music: several choirs, orchestra, various instrumental groups; madrigal choir records for BBC. Extra-curricular activities include public speaking.

Results   (1997) GCSE: creditable 74% gained at least five grades A–C. A-level: 33% of entries graded A or B.

Destinations   About 60% continue into the sixth form; of these, about 70% proceed to university.

Sport   Wide range on offer: tennis, netball, hockey, gymnastics, swimming, athletics. Facilities include sports hall, indoor pool.

Remarks   Ofsted inspectors concluded (1994): 'This is a good school with some excellent features. It makes a very positive contribution to the development of its pupils.'

NEWPORT GIRLS' HIGH ♀
Wellington Road, Newport, Shropshire TF10 7HL. Tel (01952) 811040

Synopsis
Grammar ★ Girls ★ Ages 11–18 ★ 226 pupils ★ 69 in sixth form
Head: Mrs Kaye Harrison, 47, appointed 1992.
Small, well-run school; very good teaching and results.

Profile

Background   Opened 1925; traditional red-brick building on a compact site (no room for expansion) in quiet surroundings; later additions include new art and technology suite; eight classrooms and sixth-form centre in huts.

Atmosphere   Orderly, friendly, relaxed: everyone knows everyone else. Everything neat and tidy; pupils smartly dressed.

Admissions   Highly selective: top 15% of the ability range; about five apply for every place. Entry by tests in verbal, non-verbal reasoning and previous school reports. Priority to those living in and around Newport; catchment area includes Telford, Wellington, Shrewsbury, Stafford, Wolverhampton.

The head   Determined leader; commands strong loyalties. Read maths at York; previously deputy head of Queen Mary's Grammar, Walsall (qv). Married (to a teacher); no children.

The teaching   Good quality; predominantly traditional in style. Experienced staff of 21 (18 women), a quarter appointed by the present head. Broad curriculum: strong languages; all do French and German for first three years; science taught as three separate subjects. Pupils grouped by ability for GCSE only; average class size 32, reducing to 18 for GCSE, 15 or smaller at A-level. Lots of music (two choirs, orchestra); some extra-curricular activities (cadet force, debating) shared with boys at Adams' Grammar (qv).

Results (1997) GCSE: 97% gained at least five grades A–C. A-level: creditable 59% of entries graded A or B.

Destinations About 90% proceed to university.

Sport High participation; regular county honours. Main games: hockey, netball, tennis, rounders. Reasonable facilities but restrictively small gym.

Remarks High standards all round.

NEWSTEAD WOOD ♀
Avebury Road, Bromley, Kent BR6 9SA. Tel (01689) 853626

Synopsis
Grammar (grant-maintained) ★ Girls ★ Ages 11–18 ★ 829 pupils ★ 260 in sixth form
Head: Mrs Barbara Gibbs, 51, appointed 1994.
First-class, academic school; very good teaching and results; lots on offer.

Profile
Background Founded 1954; moved 1957 to purpose-built premises on a wooded site half-a-mile from the town; opted out of council control 1992. Most recent additions include new sixth-form centre. School is expanding.

Atmosphere Hums with activity. Lively, hard-working pupils; strong pastoral care system; few sanctions prescribed or needed. 'Girls aim confidently and successfully for demanding careers,' says the prospectus. 'No goal is considered unattainable.'

Admissions School heavily over-subscribed (more than 600 apply for 130 places) and highly selective (top 10% of the ability range); entry by tests in English, maths, verbal reasoning; most from middle-class homes in nine-mile-radius catchment area; 25% join from prep schools.

The head Alert, friendly, highly experienced. Chemistry graduate; MA in education; has taught widely in state schools; previously vice-principal of a sixth-form college. Married (to a teacher); two grown-up children.

The teaching First-rate; committed, stable, predominantly female staff; girls absorbed and intent, encouraged to take responsibility for their own learning. Broad curriculum: science taught (and examined) as three separate subjects; languages include German, Spanish, Latin; choice of 21 subjects at A-level; GNVQ available in IT. Pupils grouped by ability in maths only from third year; 'master classes' for the gifted; average class size 29, reducing to a maximum of 15 at A-level. Imaginative art, strong music; 60% learn an instrument; two choirs, two orchestras. Extra-curricular activities include well-supported Duke of Edinburgh award scheme. Regular language exchanges with pupils in Nantes, Barcelona, Bavaria.

Results (1997) GCSE: all gained at least five grades A–C. A-level: creditable 65% of entries graded A or B.

Destinations Nearly all go on to university (average of 10 a year to Oxbridge).

Sport Lots on offer: athletics, tennis, hockey, netball, dance, gymnastics, trampolining, swimming, archery, golf, fencing. Ample playing fields.

Remarks Ofsted inspectors concluded (1996): 'This is a first-class school. The pupils, all of high ability, respond very well to the high quality of teaching provided.'

NONSUCH HIGH ♀
Ewell Road, Cheam, Surrey SM3 8AB. Tel (0181) 394 1308

Synopsis
Grammar (grant-maintained) ★ Girls ★ Ages 11–19 ★ 917 pupils ★ 240 in sixth form
Head: Mrs Genefer Espejo, 48, appointed 1995.
Successful school; very good teaching and results; strong music.

Profile
Background   Founded 1938; opted out of council control 1991. Solid, well-proportioned 1930s brick building plus later additions, including technology block, in 22 acres of Nonsuch Park (once the site of a Tudor palace).

Atmosphere   Friendly, unpressured, no-nonsense (motto, Serve God and Be Cheerful). Everyone busily and constructively occupied; companionable relations between pupils and staff; strongly supportive parents.

Admissions   By competitive exam; school over-subscribed by nearly four to one. Predominantly middle-class catchment area.

The head   Read geography at Queen's, Belfast; previously head of a girls' comprehensive in Reading. Married; one son.

The teaching   Good: well-qualified staff; high standards across the board. Broad curriculum: nearly half do science as three separate subjects (good facilities – 10 labs); all take second language from third year (Spanish, German or Latin in addition to French); good computing; state-of-the-art technology. Wide choice of 27 subjects at A-level: most do four, including compulsory general studies. Pupils grouped by ability from second year in maths, science, French; average class size 25, smaller in sixth form. Homework obligatory throughout. Music a particular strength (three orchestras, several choirs); good art and textiles; regular drama productions. Extra-curricular activities include Duke of Edinburgh award scheme.

Results   (1997) GCSE: 97% gained at least five grades A–C. A-level: 40% of entries graded A or B.

Destinations   Most stay on for A-levels; almost all proceed to higher education.

Sport   Enthusiastic. Main games: hockey, netball, tennis, swimming, badminton, table tennis. Facilities include six hockey pitches, six tennis courts, outdoor pool.

Remarks   Ofsted inspectors concluded (1994): 'This is a very successful school. Of the lessons observed, 96% were deemed to be satisfactory or better, with 50% being good or very good. The school provides a caring and secure environment within which pupils learn. Standards of behaviour, discipline and attendance are excellent.'

NORTHAMPTON HIGH ♀
Newport Pagnell Road, Hardingstone, Northampton NN4 6UU. Tel (01604) 765765

Synopsis
Independent ★ Girls ★ Day ★ Ages 11–18 (plus associated junior school) ★ 600 pupils ★ 130 in sixth form ★ Fees: £4,410
Head: Mrs Linda Mayne, 52, appointed 1988.
Successful, well-run school; good teaching and results; excellent facilities.

Profile
Background   Founded by Anglicans 1878; formerly Direct Grant, became fully

independent 1976; moved 1992 to splendid, £17 million, purpose-built premises on a 27-acre site on the southern edge of the town (courtesy of the Cripps Foundation, established by a local businessman); first-rate facilities and equipment. On-site junior school under its own head.

Atmosphere Warm, purposeful, well-disciplined; emphasis on Christian values (but all faiths welcomed); mutually respectful relations between staff and pupils. Uniform below the sixth form, where 'appropriate dress' is required. Daily whole-school assembly in grand hall.

Admissions By tests in English, verbal, non-verbal reasoning; school has been fairly selective but is likely to become less so with the phasing out of assisted places, which 180 hold (head says: 'The choice is between going further down the ability range or making staff redundant'). Catchment extends to Wellingborough, Kettering.

The head Confident, forthright; good manager; gets on easily with staff. Read maths at Bristol (and still teaches it); previously deputy head of Shrewsbury High (qv). Strong proponent of single-sex education for girls ('boys get 70% of the teacher's time in a mixed class'). Married; one daughter (a pupil here).

The teaching Good; formal in style (teachers teach). Well-qualified staff of 41 (78% women), half appointed by present head. Broad curriculum: all do Latin for first three years; Greek, German, Spanish, French on offer; science taught as three separate subjects from third year; particularly good results in English, art; lots of computing. Choice of 21 subjects at A-level. Pupils grouped by ability in maths from first year, in science for GCSE; extra help for dyslexics; average class size 23, reducing to 20 for GCSE, maximum of 12 in the sixth form. Strong music: 200 learn singing or an instrument; choirs (including gospel), orchestra, various ensembles. Lots of trips abroad for study and work experience.

Results (1997) GCSE: 98% gained at least five grades A–C. A-level: creditable 62% of entries graded A or B.

Destinations Of those who stay on for A-levels, 80% proceed to university (up to six a year to Oxbridge).

Sport 'All must try,' says head. Main games tennis, hockey, netball; rhythmic gymnastics a speciality; golf, archery, fencing also on offer. Facilities include well-equipped sports hall, indoor pool, two squash courts, four hockey pitches, nine tennis courts.

Remarks Good school; recommended.

NORTH FORELAND LODGE ♀
Sherfield-on-Loddon, Hook, Hampshire RG27 0HT. Tel (01256) 882431

Synopsis
Independent ★ Girls ★ 11–18 ★ Boarding and day ★ 116 pupils (95% boarding) ★ 11 in sixth form ★ Fees: £11,580 boarding; £7,050 day
Head: Miss Susan Cameron, 56, appointed 1996.
Small, exclusive boarding school under new management.

Profile
Background Founded 1909; moved 1947 to Sherfield Manor, a substantial Victorian country house in 95 acres of parkland; later additions include new classrooms, science labs, music school, sports hall. Plans in hand to establish a branch in Switzerland, where pupils will spend half a term each year.

Atmosphere   Nurturing, intimate; socially exclusive; less than highly academic (but this could change). New head has tightened up on discipline (upper sixth are no longer allowed to smoke).

Admissions   By assessment; school is barely selective. Boarding has a family feel; juniors in dormitories (five or six beds); seniors in single study-bedrooms (encouraged to do their own catering). Scholarships available.

The head   Highly experienced, very able (and the principal reason for this entry). Read history at London; became head of Cobham Hall in 1985 and of Downe House in 1989; fell out with the governors of the latter over her plan to merge it with North Foreland Lodge. Having taken the school on herself, she aims to transform it; brought over several of her former staff to help. Girls will certainly have to work harder.

The teaching   Traditional in style. Fairly broad curriculum: science on offer as three separate subjects; languages include Latin, Greek, Spanish, German; professional cook's certificate available as an alternative to A-levels (choice of 18). Very small classes: average 12–15; even smaller in the sixth form.

Results   (1997) GCSE: 85% gained at least five grades A–C. A-level: modest 36% of entries graded A or B.

Destinations   All go on to some form of higher education.

Sport   Lots on offer, including tennis, lacrosse, netball, basketball, badminton, fencing, archery, aerobics.

Remarks   One to watch.

NORTHGATE ♂ ♀
Sidegate Lane West, Ipswich IP4 3DL. Tel (01473) 210123

Synopsis
Comprehensive ★ Co-educational ★ Ages 11–18 ★ 1,646 pupils (roughly equal numbers of girls and boys) ★ 599 in sixth form
Head: Neil Watts, 45, appointed 1992.
Well-run school; respectable results; some impressive facilities.

Profile
Background   A 1977 merger of two single-sex grammar schools; well-planned, mainly late 1980s buildings on rather bleak town-centre site (monitored by closed-circuit TV). First-rate facilities for drama, sport (shared with the local community).

Atmosphere   Orderly, calm (but less so in the sixth form). Good pastoral care system (pupils volunteer they feel safe here); first two years accommodated separately.

Admissions   No selection; school over-subscribed (about 260 apply for 210 places); priority to those living in the catchment area, a wedge extending from the town centre to the suburbs. Fairly wide range of abilities but mostly above average.

The head   Enthusiastic, experienced; had been deputy here before leaving to run another Suffolk comprehensive. Has appointed half the staff; GCSE results have improved materially. Read economics at Cambridge; teaches a cross-curricular module on careers, economics and citizenship. Married; two children.

The teaching   Strong emphasis on whole-class instruction (desks facing the teacher); lessons generally well planned and delivered, if occasionally lacking in imagination (pupils attentive but not often observed in eager discussion). Teaching

staff of 112: even balance of youth and experience. GCSE options include ancient history, Spanish, business studies; Latin, textiles, child development on offer at A-level. Pupils grouped by ability from the start; limited extra help for those who need it. Lots of drama; improving music (good choir). Chess club competes nationally.
Results (1997) GCSE: 50% gained at least five grades A–C. A-level: 32% of entries graded A or B.
Destinations About 60% proceed to university (including half a dozen to Oxbridge).
Sport Particular strengths in soccer, netball; cricket, rugby, hockey, badminton also on offer. Superb facilities include heated indoor pool, cricket square, athletics track.
Remarks Good school with the potential to do better.

NORTH HALIFAX GRAMMAR ♂ ♀
Illingworth, Halifax HX2 9SU. Tel (01422) 244625

Synopsis
Grammar (grant-maintained) ★ Co-educational ★ Ages 11–18 ★ 909 pupils (roughly equal numbers of girls and boys) ★ 207 in sixth form
Head: Graham Maslen, 42, appointed September 1996.
Successful, well-run school; good teaching and results.

Profile
Background A 1985 merger of two small grammar schools (one girls', one co-ed); opted out of council control 1991 (and has never looked back). Box-shaped, flat-roofed, Fifties buildings surrounded by a suburban housing estate (but good views of Yorkshire moors from upper floors); much recent repair and refurbishment (one 'temporary' hut remains). Large, sloping playing fields shared with two neighbouring comprehensives.
Atmosphere High expectations: academic rigour combined with concern for each child. Well-disciplined, courteous pupils, proud of their school. Smart uniform (dress code for sixth formers). Good links between home and school; active parents' association.
Admissions Heavily over-subscribed (three apply for each place). Entry by tests (shared with Crossley Heath, qv) in English, maths, verbal reasoning. Pupils from wide range of social backgrounds (but predominantly modest) in Calderdale, Keighley, Rochdale, Bradford, Huddersfield (good bus links).
The head Courteous, open; gets on well with everyone. Combines respect for academic tradition with a willingness to innovate. Read geography at London; formerly deputy head of a grant-maintained school in Essex. Married; two children.
The teaching High quality (the key to the school's success); lots of chalk, talk and textbook. Dedicated staff of 51 (55% male); low turnover but accent on youth. Standard national curriculum; science (a particular strength) on offer as three separate subjects; languages include German, Russian; Latin popular (and imaginatively taught); A-level options include art history, psychology. Homework an 'integral part of the curriculum'. Pupils grouped by ability in maths, English; average class size 27, reducing to 20 for GCSE, 12 in sixth form. Good music (orchestra, four choirs) and drama; wide range of out-of-school activities. Strong links with local industry and commerce.
Results (1997) GCSE: 93% gained at least five grades A–C. A-level: 40% of

entries graded A or B.

Destinations About 75% go to university (two or three a year to Oxbridge).

Sport Main games: soccer, hockey, netball, volleyball, tennis, athletics (but little cricket). Badminton, aerobics, gymnastics in leisure centre near by.

Remarks Identified by Ofsted (1995) as an 'outstandingly successful' school.

NORTH LONDON COLLEGIATE ♀
Canons, Edgware, Middlesex HA8 7RJ. Tel (0181) 952 0912

Synopsis
Independent ★ Girls ★ Day ★ Ages 11–18 (plus associated junior school) ★ 740 pupils ★ 225 in sixth form ★ Fees: £5,424
Head: Mrs Bernice McCabe, 44, appointed September 1997.
Distinguished academic school; excellent teaching and results; produces civilised career women.

Profile
Background Founded 1850 by Frances Mary Buss 'to provide an education for girls that would equal that of boys': they became the first girls to sit public examinations and the first women to graduate from Cambridge. Moved 1929 to Canons, elegant 18th-century mansion in 30 acres of parkland; has expanded and built steadily since – and remained in the forefront of women's education.

Atmosphere Lively, articulate girls everywhere: chattering under cedar trees, balancing on garden walls and pillars, hurrying down the broad staircase on to the Persian rugs in the polished hall. Oil paintings and sepia group photographs of strong-faced Victorian women gaze down, mutely exhorting the young ladies of today to noble endeavour. Adults are treated as amusing additions to a conversational group; relaxed informality is the tone. Music and art departments overlook pond and ducks; delightful rock garden tended one morning a week by a retired teacher.

Admissions Heavily over-subscribed; entry at 11 by highly competitive exams in English and maths (specimen questions available) and interview; 40% of the 104 admitted come from the junior school. Phasing out of assisted places, which 100 hold, will reduce the social mix; Asians, Jews, Greeks, Christians, Chinese all fit in amicably. Scholarships, bursaries available.

The head New appointment; previously head for seven years of Chelmsford County High (qv), one of the top state schools for girls. Read English at Bristol; MBA from South California. Able; skilled manager (masses of committees and working parties); strongly committed to academic excellence ('We want all our pupils to realise that it is attainable').

The teaching High quality, challenging; enthusiastic staff of 67 (10 men); relations with pupils are exceptionally warm. Broad curriculum: all do Latin for first three years; 70% take two modern languages for GCSE (French plus German or Spanish); science (taught – but not examined – as three separate subjects) and maths as important at A-level as arts subjects (increasing numbers take a mixture); all computer literate. Pupils not grouped by ability; competition between them discouraged. Music is a real strength; lots of instrumental teaching; two orchestras, two choirs. Lively drawing school staffed by practising artists teaches pottery, silkscreen printing, painting etc in four large studios. Career choices taken seriously; overseas work experience. Regular language exchanges with schools in France, Germany, Spain.

Results   (1997) GCSE: all gained at least five grades A–C. A-level: remarkable 88% of entries graded A or B (fifth in the league table).

Destinations   Nearly all stay on for A-levels and proceed to university (about 25% to Oxbridge).

Sport   Does not come very high on the list of things to shout about, but there are good tennis courts; lacrosse, netball (strong), athletics and cross-country are on offer, and there is a modern indoor pool. Treadmill in the gym for those who feel the tempo is not fast enough.

Remarks   First-rate school; hectic academic pace mitigated by a feeling of spacious style.

NORWICH ♂
70 The Close, Norwich NR1 4DD. Tel (01603) 623194

Synopsis
Independent ★ Boys (plus girls in sixth form) ★ Day ★ Ages 12–18 (plus associated junior school) ★ 600 pupils ★ 230 in sixth form (80% boys) ★ Fees: £5,088
Head: Christopher Brown, 52, appointed 1984.
Close-knit school in charming surroundings; good teaching and results; strong music and sport.

Profile
Background   Origins traced back to 15th century; re-founded by Edward VI 1547, when school moved to its present location in the cathedral close; reverted to full independence with the abolition of Direct Grant status in 1976; strong links with the Dyers' company. Girls admitted to sixth form 1994. Junior school in own purpose-built premises near by.

Atmosphere   Vital, intense (the academic pace is quick, and both sport and music have high profiles) but balanced by the generally beautiful architecture and tranquil mood of the close (some buildings, though, are rather quirky and cramped). Daily assembly in the cathedral (members of all religions welcomed) underpins the school's sense of history and identity; good pastoral care system based on houses; tight discipline (thanks largely to much-feared senior master, author of famously withering letters to miscreants' parents).

Admissions   By interview and school's own tests in English, maths, science, verbal reasoning; siblings of existing pupils have no advantage; those talented in music or sport do. Staggered entry system means that boys enter at eight, nine, 11 or 12 (roughly 25 places in each year); top 25% of the ability range. Phasing out of assisted places, which about 100 hold, will reduce the social mix; half-fee places for 20 choristers.

The head   Urbane, laconic, clear-sighted; has raised the academic tempo. Read English at Cambridge; previously head of English and director of studies at Radley (still teaches some English to younger boys). Married; two daughters.

The teaching   Intelligent, well-structured. Well-qualified, predominantly male staff of 57, including 20 Oxbridge graduates. Standard curriculum; choice of French or German; Latin available; technology optional. Choice of 19 subjects at A-level, supplemented by non-examined courses in computing, drama, film-making or philosophy (time allocated equivalent to half an A-level).

Pupils grouped by ability in maths, science, languages from age 13; average class size 25, reducing to 20 for GCSE, nine at A-level; half-termly grades for effort and achievement. Music plays a big part in school life: one-and-a-half days at the start of the year are given over to a festival in which all must participate; 40% learn an instrument; more than a dozen ensembles, from chamber group to jazz band. Extra-curricular activities include Sea Scouts, Duke of Edinburgh award scheme.

Results (1997) GCSE: all gained at least five grades A–C. A-level: 65% of entries graded A or B.

Destinations At least 90% stay on for the sixth form; virtually all proceed to university (about 10 a year to Oxbridge).

Sport Solidly traditional, seriously played. Compulsory games two afternoons a week: rugby in the autumn term, hockey in winter, cricket in summer; other options include fencing, rowing, sailing, shooting. Excellent playing fields: 10-acre site within cathedral close, 26-acres a short coach ride away; other facilities limited (ancient gymnasium, no sports hall or swimming pool).

Remarks Invigorating, high-octane education for able boys (and girls); very good value.

NORWICH HIGH ♀
95 Newmarket Road, Norwich, Norfolk NR2 2HU. Tel (01603) 453265

Synopsis
Independent ★ Girls ★ Day ★ Ages 11–18 (plus associated junior school) ★ 660 pupils ★ 165 in the sixth form ★ Fees: £4,212
Head: Mrs Valerie Bidwell, 49, appointed 1985.
Well-run, traditional grammar school; good teaching and results.

Profile
Background Founded 1875 by the Girls' Day School Trust; moved to present, attractively wooded, 12-acre site 1933; main buildings are Regency and Victorian, extended and modernised in 1996 at a cost of more than £1 million. Formerly Direct Grant, reverted to full independence 1976. Junior school (250 pupils ages four to 10) on same site.

Atmosphere Friendly, relaxed (within well-defined parameters); good pastoral care. Sixth-formers accommodated separately. School prides itself on providing a 'liberal education'. Drab green uniform being up-dated.

Admissions By tests in English, maths, verbal reasoning; school is fairly selective. Pupils drawn equally from the city and county (privately organised coach system). Trust aims to replace assisted places, which substantial numbers hold, with a scheme of its own.

The head Imposing, authoritative; lively sense of humour; gets on well with staff and pupils. Read modern languages at Newcastle and London. Married (to a former teacher).

The teaching Lively; traditional firm-but-friendly approach; well-qualified, stable staff of 66 (80% female). Broad curriculum: sciences taught separately; strong languages, including German, Spanish, Italian, Latin, Greek; lots of computing; choice of 21 subjects at GCSE and A-level. Pupils grouped by ability in maths only; specialist help for dyslexics; average class size 25, reducing to 12 in the sixth form. Very good music: a third learn an instrument; three choirs, three orchestras, various ensembles. Lots of extra-curricular activities, including well-supported Duke of Edinburgh award scheme (39 golds in two years). Annual language exchanges to Europe.

Results (1997) GCSE: all gained at least five grades A–C. A-level: 60% of entries graded A or B.

Destinations Nearly all go on to university (seven or eight a year to Oxbridge).

Sport Facilities include good indoor pool, gymnasium, tennis and netball courts – but otherwise tight for space outdoors. Lacrosse a strength; rowing popular.

Remarks Good all round.

NOTRE DAME ♂ ♀
Surrey Street, Norwich NR1 3PB. Tel (O1603) 611431

Synopsis
Comprehensive (voluntary-aided, Roman Catholic) ★ Co-educational ★ Ages 11–18 ★ 1,170 pupils (52% girls) ★ 305 in sixth form
Head: John Pinnington, 46, appointed January 1997.
Successful school; strong Christian ethos; limited facilities.

Profile
Background Founded as a convent school 1864; later became a Direct Grant girls' grammar; went comprehensive and co-educational 1979. Buildings of varying ages, styles and standards on a cramped, town-centre site; limited facilities but no one seems to mind (though Ofsted expressed concerns for health and safety).

Atmosphere Happy, well-disciplined (no jostling or shoving in the crowded corridors). Big emphasis on individual responsibility; sixth-formers play an important pastoral role; behaviour code states, 'Making someone unhappy is bullying.' Pupils with religious doubts encouraged to express them.

Admissions Non-selective; over-subscribed (nearly 300 apply for 205 places) but in practice all baptised Catholics are admitted. Large catchment area (school is the only Catholic comprehensive in Norfolk). Fairly wide range of abilities but most are above average.

The head Able, affable; staff say he gets the best out of everyone. Recent appointment but had been deputy here for 12 years; the school's first lay head (his faith is manifest). BSc in food science from Nottingham. Keen sportsman (rugby, soccer, marathon running). Married; three children (all were pupils here).

The teaching Well-structured lessons; classes fairly informal (but not chaotic). Long-serving staff of 70 (average age nearly 50). Standard national curriculum; GCSE options include Spanish, Russian; computing not a strength. Pupils grouped by ability in some subjects; average class size 23.

Results (1997) GCSE: 68% gained at least five grades A–C. A-level: 28% of entries graded A or B.

Destinations 90% continue into the sixth form; of those 65% proceed to university.

Sport Facilities include sports hall and tennis courts; boys' basketball and girls' netball are particularly strong. Football, rugby, cricket played at neighbouring school; no swimming.

Remarks Committed staff more than compensate for lack of facilities.

NOTTINGHAM GIRLS' HIGH ♀
Arboretum Street, Nottingham NG1 4JB. Tel (0115) 941 7663

Synopsis
Independent ★ Girls ★ Day ★ Ages 11–18 (plus associated junior school) ★
842 pupils ★ 255 in sixth form ★ Fees: £4,152
Head: Mrs Angela Rees, 52, appointed 1996.
First-rate academic school; very good teaching and results.

Profile
Background Founded 1875 by the Girls' Day School Trust; a line of inge-
niously-linked Victorian mansions plus later additions on a self-contained site
next to the arboretum. Junior school (275 girls aged four to 11) in modern buildings.

Atmosphere Enthusiastic, friendly; unashamedly academic.

Admissions By written tests (juniors move up automatically); school is heavily over-subscribed and severely selective; about 300 hold assisted places, which
the trust aims to replace with a scheme of its own. Extensive catchment area; half
travel on school buses.

The head Experienced, confident, down-to-earth. Read physics at Oxford; has
taught in a grammar school and a comprehensive; previously deputy head for
five years of Sheffield High (qv). Married (to a university lecturer); two grown-
up sons.

The teaching High quality; well-qualified, predominantly female staff of 85.
Fairly broad curriculum: sciences (first-rate) taught separately; English and
maths particularly strong; lively classics; modern languages include German,
Spanish; all become computer literate; choice of 23 subjects at A-level. Extra-curricular activities include public speaking (competitions won), well-supported
Duke of Edinburgh award scheme; lots of fund raising for charity. Regular language exchanges with pupils in France, Germany.

Results (1997) GCSE: all gained at least five grades A–C. A-level: very creditable 74% of entries graded A or B.

Destinations About 95% stay on for A-levels; of these, virtually all proceed to
university (average of 12 a year to Oxbridge).

Sport 'Not a big deal' but lots on offer; good record in hockey, tennis, netball,
cross-country. On-site facilities limited; 10 acres of playing fields a bus ride away.

Remarks Very good school for able, hard-working girls.

NOTTINGHAM HIGH ♂
Waverley Mount, Nottingham NG7 4ED. Tel (0115) 978 6056

Synopsis
Independent ★ Boys ★ Day ★ Ages 11–18 (plus associated prep school) ★
830 pupils ★ 234 in sixth form ★ Fees: £5,454
Head: Christopher Parker, 50, appointed 1995.
First-rate academic school; very good teaching and results; strong music, sport.

Profile
Background Founded 1513; moved to present urban site 1868; grand
Victorian-Gothic buildings plus many excellent later additions, including

science block, design/technology centre, music school. Prep school (185 boys aged seven to 10) on same site. D H Lawrence was a pupil here.

Atmosphere   Ambitious, hard-working, highly competitive; well-organised pastoral care. Traditional prefect system; blazer-and-tie uniform below the sixth form (where suits and pastel coloured shirts are worn).

Admissions   By interview and tests in English, maths, verbal reasoning; half the 120 places go to the prep school; about 160 apply for the rest; top 15% of the ability range; fairly wide social mix. Phasing out of assisted places, which 180 hold, will be off-set by increasing the already large number of scholarships (many funded by local employers, including Boots and Raleigh). Extensive catchment area; special bus services.

The head   Confident, voluble, experienced; strong leader. Read geography at Bristol; previously head for nine years of Batley Grammar. Married; two grown-up children.

The teaching   First-rate; largely traditional in style; experienced staff (88% male). Broad curriculum: science (a strength) taught as three separate subjects; all do Latin for at least two years, German (as a second modern language) for at least one; lots of computing (150 machines), design/technology; choice of 19 subjects at A-level (including economics, further maths, ancient history) plus a wide range of general studies courses. Very good music: two orchestras, two choirs. Extra-curricular activities include thriving cadet force, Duke of Edinburgh award scheme; chess and bridge both very popular.

Results   (1997) GCSE: all gained at least five grades A–C. A-level: creditable 67% of entries graded A or B.

Destinations   Virtually all stay on for A-levels (average of 15 a year to Oxbridge).

Sport   Strong reputation in rugby, cricket, swimming, cross-country, athletics; regular county and national honours. Facilities include sports hall, indoor pool; 20 acres of playing fields one and a half miles away.

Remarks   Fine school for able boys.

NOTTING HILL & EALING HIGH
2 Cleveland Road, London W13 8AX. Tel (0181) 997 5744

Synopsis
Independent ★ Girls ★ Day ★ Ages 11–18 ★ 560 pupils (plus associated junior school) ★ Fees: £4,968
Head: Mrs Susan Whitfield, 50, appointed 1991.
First-rate academic school; very good teaching and results; exceptionally happy atmosphere.

Profile
Background   Founded 1873 in Notting Hill by the Girls' Public Day School Trust; moved to present pleasant suburban site 1931; many later additions; some areas over-crowded and in need of refurbishment; extensive development under way. Delightful junior school (ages five to 11) on same site.

Atmosphere   Exceptionally happy and enthusiastic: all join in, feel they belong and enjoy what they are doing – bearing out the head's claim that 'if you get the pastoral care right, everything else will follow'. Pupils cosmopolitan, articulate, predominantly middle-class; smart navy blue and cherry red uniform below the sixth form. Much energy and ingenuity goes into fund-raising for charity.

Admissions To the junior school by interview and tests (jigsaws, drawing etc); to the senior school by highly competitive exams (set by a consortium of London schools) in maths, English ('We are an unashamedly academic school'). Virtually all juniors move on to the senior school, to be joined by roughly the same numbers from outside. Trust aims to replace assisted places with a scheme of its own. Some scholarships.

The head Very able, clearly in control. Read natural sciences and physical anthropology at Cambridge; taught biology at St Paul's Girls' for 12 years. Popular with pupils (makes an effort to know them all well); teaches health education to 14/15-year-olds ('It's good for them to see their headmistress demonstrating condoms and discussing diets'). Married; five children.

The teaching Ranges from good to inspired; staff of 65 (seven men), 40% appointed by the present head. Broad curriculum: sciences taught separately by specialists; at age 10, girls learn a term each of French, Spanish and German; at 11, all take Latin and one modern language, adding a second at 12. All do seven 'core' GCSEs plus two options from a choice of nine and at least three A-levels from a choice of 21. Pupils grouped by ability in maths only; regular tests, grades for effort and achievement; class sizes vary from 14 to 28. Very good music department. Busy extra-curricular programme.

Results (1997) GCSE: all gained at least five grades A–C. A-level: very creditable 75% of entries graded A or B.

Destinations Most stay on for A-levels and proceed to university (average of seven a year to Oxbridge).

Sport Facilities 'not good, to say the least' but a creditable match record in all the traditional sports, particularly hockey, netball and tennis. Main playing fields a 10-minute walk away.

Remarks School produces happy, confident girls with high aspirations and good qualifications: highly recommended.

OAKHAM ♂ ♀
Chapel Close, Oakham, Rutland LE15 6DT. Tel (01572) 722487

Synopsis
Independent ★ Co-educational ★ Boarding and day ★ Ages 10–18 ★ 1,030 pupils (50% boys, 50% boarding) ★ 325 in sixth form ★ Fees: £12,780 boarding; £7,440 day.
Head: Tony Little, 43, appointed 1996.
Attractive, well-equipped school; good teaching and results; strong music, sport.

Profile
Background Founded 1584 (simultaneously with Uppingham, qv); formerly a grammar school, reverted to full independence 1970; girls admitted 1971. Extensive collection of buildings, old and new, on an idyllic, 70-acre campus surrounding the town; £20 million spent on additions and improvements including, most recently, new classrooms and £2 million library. Facilities are first-rate.

Atmosphere Friendly, well-ordered: strong Anglican tradition; high quality pastoral care; happy, confident, well-adjusted pupils. Strict uniform (including kilt-like skirts for girls); dress code in the sixth form.

Admissions By interview and Common Entrance or tests in English, maths, verbal reasoning; school is not unduly selective (minimum IQ 110). Nearly half the pupils have, or have had, siblings here; day pupils from as far afield as Leicester, Northampton; a third of boarders from abroad. Boarding houses comfortable, well-equipped; juniors in dormitories; others have shared study-bedrooms; first-rate food. Scholarships (academic, music, art & design, chess, drama) available.

The head Able, experienced. Read English at Cambridge; previously head for seven years of Chigwell (qv). Married; one daughter (a pupil here).

The teaching Formal but friendly; well-qualified staff (a third are Oxbridge graduates). Broad curriculum: all start Latin; modern languages include German, Spanish, Russian; all take 10 GCSEs (from a choice of 17); 22 subjects available at A-level. Pupils grouped by ability in all subjects for GCSE; extra help for those who need it; maximum class size 22, reducing to 13 at A-level. Good drama (fine theatre); art & design centre offers pottery, sculpture, printing, textiles, computer-aided design etc; strong music (30% sing or play an instrument). Wide range of extra-curricular activities, including chess, cadet force, Duke of Edinburgh award scheme, numerous expeditions (Iceland, Sahara, Peru).

Results (1997) GCSE: 96% gained at least five grades A–C. A-level: 59% of entries graded A or B (school has slipped steadily down the league table from 73rd in 1993 to 150th).

Destinations About 90% go on to university (15–20 a year to Oxbridge).

Sport Lots on offer; regular fixtures; numerous county, regional and national honours. Facilities include extensive playing fields, sports hall, indoor pool. Main games: rugby, hockey, cricket for boys; hockey, netball, tennis for girls. Badminton, cross-country, Eton-fives, fencing, golf, lacrosse, riding, shooting, sailing, squash, sub-aqua also available.

Remarks HMC inspectors concluded (1995): 'This is a very good school with high standards of achievement and learning across the whole range of subjects.'

OATHALL ♂ ♀

Appledore Gardens, Haywards Heath, West Sussex RH16 2AQ. Tel (01444) 414001

Synopsis
Comprehensive ★ Co-educational ★ Ages 11–16 ★ 1,300 pupils (equal numbers of girls and boys)
Head: John Rimmer, 54, appointed 1981.
Well-run school; good teaching and results; on-site farm.

Profile

Background Opened 1938 as 'a school for the community and centre of excellence' – aims taken seriously by the current head, who oversees adult education on the same campus. Functionalist brick buildings, generally bleaker outside than in. Odd inclusion within the grounds of a five-acre farm (used as an educational tool) helps brighten things up: even the pigs win prizes here. Recent spending includes £1 million on new language and music centres.

Atmosphere Courteous, fairly relaxed though rules are firmly applied; big emphasis on academic achievement ('Children who work hard are happy at school'). Senior pupils gush with praise; younger ones confide, 'It's a bit strict' – a reasonable balance. Uniform worn properly by all ('a protection from the temptations of temporary extremes of fashion'); homework expected on time;

pupils spotted smoking on the way home given detention. Head has clearly been striving to drive up a once-moderate school.

Admissions Non-selective (but intake is largely middle-class). Priority to those living in the designated catchment area (Ardingly, Horsted Keynes, Lindfield, Scaynes Hill, most of Haywards Heath), then siblings, medical/social grounds, distance from the school.

The head Experienced, long-serving. Cornerstone philosophy: 'A passionate belief that people can exceed their own expectations of themselves'. Demands enthusiasm and dedication from his staff who, in turn, clearly respect him; pupils grin wryly at his repeated stress on the need to improve. Read civil engineering at Southampton. Married, four children.

The teaching Deliberately varied: head pops in and out to make sure styles change to avoid boredom. Staff of 84, 76 appointed by present head. Particular strengths in maths and (dual award) science; all do French and German for at least two years; vocational qualification for those who work on the farm. Pupils grouped by ability in most subjects from third year; extra help for those who need it, including the very able. Extra-curricular activities include Duke of Edinburgh award scheme, young farmers' club. Regular exchanges with pupils in France, Germany.

Results (1997) GCSE: creditable 70% gained at least five grades A–C.

Destinations About 90% continue in full-time education, many at the sixth-form college near by.

Sport Good facilities for rugby, basketball, hockey, swimming (heated outdoor pool), netball. The gym, though large, is barely adequate for 1,300 pupils: there are plans to build another.

Remarks Well-rounded, well-disciplined school. Pupils urged to raise their sights – and many do. Sheep, pigs and cattle add a pleasantly bizarre touch.

OLCHFA ♂ ♀
Gower Road, Sketty, Swansea SA2 7AB. Tel (01792) 201222

Synopsis
Comprehensive ★ Co-educational ★ Ages 11–19 ★ 1,897 pupils (roughly equal numbers of girls and boys) ★ 465 in sixth form
Head: Trevor Church, 44, appointed 1996.
Successful comprehensive; very good teaching and results; strong sport.

Profile
Background Opened 1960s; sprawling mass of red-brick, flat-roofed buildings on a pleasant 15-acre site surrounded by middle-class suburbs; intense pressure on space (some classrooms in 'temporary' huts); impressive sixth-form centre. Formidable local reputation: best results in the area.

Atmosphere Bustling, highly disciplined: emphasis on endeavour, commitment, achievement. Monthly certificates of merit handed out by head in assembly; pride in school and self the paramount goal; pupils required to sign code of conduct ('We speak politely to everyone, always trying to understand the other person's point of view...We wear the correct Olchfa school uniform with pride at all times'). Good pastoral care system helps break down the size: all pupils known to senior staff.

Admissions School over-subscribed: priority to those living in the catchment area or attending a 'feeder' primary; remaining places allocated with 'regard to the importance of ensuring that there is the appropriate balance of abilities and interests among pupils'. Most from professional/middle-class backgrounds.

The head Good manager; strong leader (regularly observes staff teaching). Read history at Exeter, psychology at Reading; formerly head of a comprehensive in Merthyr Tydfil.

The teaching Efficient, effective: academic tradition reflected in results across the board; styles vary from child-centred to traditional; highly motivated staff of 120 (slightly more women than men). Broad curriculum: science on offer as three separate subjects (good facilities – 12 labs); all do French and Welsh; German, Latin on offer. Impressive choice of 31 subjects at A-level including politics, psychology, sociology, theatre studies, physical education; GNVQs available in business, engineering. Pupils grouped by ability in maths from first year and most other subjects from second; extra help for those who need it. Enthusiastic music (120 learn an instrument); acclaimed orchestral, dramatic productions. Extra-curricular activities include popular Duke of Edinburgh award scheme (18 Golds in 1996), first-class debating, much fund-raising for charity. Regular expeditions (Greenland, Arctic, South Africa) and trips abroad: Russia, Spain, France, Germany.

Results (1997) GCSE: 67% gained at least five grades A–C. A-level: creditable 55% of entries graded A or B (better than many grammar schools).

Destinations About 60% continue into the sixth form; of these, nearly 90% proceed to university (a few each year to Oxbridge).

Sport Excellent facilities: sports hall, two gyms, indoor pool, on-site playing fields; six full-time specialist staff. All team games on offer (many county representatives); also golf, yachting, archery, orienteering.

Remarks Good school: high pressure and expectations have bred success. Recommended.

OLD PALACE ♀
Old Palace Road, Croydon CR0 1AX. Tel (0181) 688 2027

Synopsis
Independent ★ Girls ★ Day ★ Ages 11–18 (plus associated junior school) ★ 630 pupils ★ 150 in sixth form ★ Fees: £4,572
Head: Miss Kathleen Hilton, 60, appointed 1974.
Traditional, academic school; very good teaching and results; strong art, music.

Profile
Background Founded 1889 in a former residence of the Archbishop of Canterbury by the Sisters of the Church, an Anglican community; they withdrew in 1975 with the loss of Direct Grant status, and the school became independent; it was taken over by the Whitgift Foundation in 1993. Attractive, well-maintained premises (the new complementing the old) on a two-acre, town-centre site (little recreational space); further renovation and building planned. Preparatory department (210 pupils aged four to 11) on site.

Atmosphere Academic: highly-motivated girls encouraged (but not pressurised) to achieve; emphasis on Anglican teaching and worship ('a sound education based on Christian ideals'). Warm relations between staff and pupils; reasonable rules strictly enforced; uniform below the sixth form. Parents expected

to take a close interest in their daughters' education. School meals not provided.
Admissions At 11 by competitive exam for 55 places (another 35 go to girls from the prep department); school is highly selective. Pupils drawn from a wide range of backgrounds in an extensive catchment area (good public transport). About 250 hold assisted places, which the foundation aims to replace with a scheme of its own. Scholarships (academic, music) available.
The head Very long-serving and nearing retirement. Read history at Royal Holloway College, London (and still teaches it); previously head of history at Manchester High. A very visible presence; formal yet approachable; runs a tight ship.
The teaching First-rate; stable, predominantly female staff. Broad curriculum: sciences taught (and examined) separately (good results); strong maths; all do French for GCSE and Latin for at least two years; Greek, German, Italian, Spanish on offer; choice of 23 subjects at A-level. Pupils grouped by ability in maths, French; progress carefully monitored; average class size 30, reducing to 22 for GCSE. Outstanding art; flourishing music (three choirs, 40% learn an instrument). Well-supported Duke of Edinburgh award scheme. Regular language exchanges with pupils in France, Germany, Italy, Spain.
Results (1997) GCSE: all gained at least five grades at A–C. A level: creditable 66% of entries graded A or B.
Destinations About 90% stay on for A-levels; of these, 90% proceed to university (four or five a year to Oxbridge).
Sport Facilities limited (no sports hall or swimming pool) but school makes use of those at Whitgift and Trinity (qv). Activities include netball, hockey, tennis, rounders, athletics, cross-country, gymnastics, dance.
Remarks Good school for able girls.

OLD SWINFORD HOSPITAL ♂
Stourbridge, West Midlands DY8 1QX. Tel (01384) 370025

Synopsis
Partially selective comprehensive (grant-maintained) ★ Boys ★ Boarding and day ★ Ages 11–18 ★ 560 pupils (75% boarders) ★ 190 in sixth form ★ Fees (boarding only): £4,575
Head: Chris Potter, 57, appointed 1978.
First-rate state boarding school; good teaching and GCSE results; strong music and sport.

Profile
Background Founded and generously endowed by Thomas Foley in 1670 for 60 boys of 'poor but honest' parents (founder's descendants still administer the 600-acre estate); opted out of council control 1989 (one of the first to do so). Attractive buildings of varying periods (some 17th-century) on a six-acre site; latest additions include new classroom block, computer centre.
Atmosphere Happy, well-ordered, buzzing with activity; well-organised pastoral care system (firm line on bullying); school keeps in close touch with parents.
Admissions School is heavily over-subscribed. Boarders (200 apply for 70 places a year) are selected (at 11, 12, 13) by interview designed to ensure they would 'benefit from a boarding environment': head says he is looking for good, well-motivated all-rounders who show A-level potential and have keen,

supportive parents; day boys (180 apply for 16 places) selected by competitive exam (since September 1997); only British and EU citizens' children admitted. Modern, comfortable boarding accommodation: younger boys in dormitories of up to 12; all sixth-formers have single study-bedrooms. Scholarships and means-tested help with boarding fees available.

The head A genial figure; able, enthusiastic, long-serving. Read classics and archaeology at Cambridge; still teaches Greek to A-level and some Latin; runs the school's family history society (knows not only the boys but their backgrounds, too); both his father and grandfather were heads. Married; five children.

The teaching Good: traditional in style; well-qualified, long-serving staff of 40 (10 women), 35 of whom live on the campus; responsive, well-behaved pupils. Unusually broad curriculum: all do Latin for first two years, choice of Spanish, German in third year; sciences taught as three separate subjects. A-level options include Greek, media studies, electronics & computing. Pupils grouped by ability in maths, English, French, Latin; average class size 20, reducing to 12 at A-level; extra help for those who need it. Lots of music: choir, three orchestras, various ensembles; 170 learn an instrument. Busy extra-curricular programme. Annual language exchanges with schools in France, Germany.

Results (1997) GCSE: 98% gained at least five grades A–C. A-level: 41% of entries graded A or B.

Destinations About 90% go on to university (three or four a year to Oxbridge).

Sport All major games played: rugby a strength; soccer, hockey, basketball, sailing, cricket, athletics, table tennis, squash, tennis, fencing, archery, cross-country also on offer. Facilities include floodlit, all-weather pitch, tennis and squash courts, gym, indoor shooting range, huge climbing wall.

Remarks Well-run school; good value for money. Recommended.

THE ORATORY ♂
Woodcote, Reading, Berkshire RG8 0PJ. Tel (01491) 680207

Synopsis
Independent ★ Roman Catholic ★ Boys ★ Boarding and day ★ Ages 13–18 (plus associated junior and prep schools) ★ 380 pupils (65% boarding) ★ 134 in sixth form ★ Fees: £12,900 boarding; £9,030 day
Head: Simon Barrow, 55, appointed 1992.
Successful small school; fairly wide range of abilities; good teaching and results; strong art, sport.

Profile
Background Founded 1859 in Birmingham by Cardinal Newman 'to meet the educational needs of the Catholic laity'; moved to present, 180-acre hill-top site (glorious views) early 1940s. Gracious Queen Anne house plus sympathetic modern additions; first-rate facilities. On-site junior school (11–13); prep school two miles away.

Atmosphere Warm, cheerful, relaxed; friendly relations between staff and pupils; good pastoral care ('We exist to serve and support each boy separately'); many staff live on campus with their families and participate in full extra-curricular programme. Strong spiritual dimension (crucifixes on the walls); chapel seats the whole school (optional daily mass). Older dormitories showing their age (cubicles, wooden lockers); newer study-bedrooms bright and cheerful; everywhere carpeted, curtained ('more like a girls' school'). Day boys stay until 7.15 pm; lessons on Saturday mornings. Many parents are attracted by the Newman-inspired insistence on an all-lay staff to ensure that the school's Catholicism is rooted in the world into which their sons will go; unusually for a Catholic school, numbers have held steady over the past 10 years.

Admissions Entry at 11 (to the junior school, mostly from the state sector) by school's own exams, at 13 by Common Entrance; not unduly selective (a boy who really wants to be here is unlikely to be turned away). Applicants must be Roman Catholic or happy to accept the Catholic ethos but no proof of religious credentials required (head believes there is a potential mission to the sons of the lapsed).

The head Quiet, diffident, clearly loves the school: previously a housemaster here for 20 years and deputy head. Teaches history to first-years to get to know them; any boy free to see him without an appointment, day or night. Married; two children (one a pupil here).

The teaching Generally good: traditional in approach; long-serving, well-qualified staff (mostly male). Broad curriculum: science taught as three separate subjects; languages include German, Italian, Latin, classical Greek. Pupils grouped by ability from the start; extra help for dyslexics (of at least average ability); average class size 16 up to GCSE, smaller thereafter; wide choice of 29 subjects at A-level (all combinations accommodated). First-rate art (many take it at A-level), drama, music (particularly choral). Lots of extra-curricular activities, including popular cadet force (compulsory for first year). Annual retreat for each year group, led by the chaplain.

Results (1997) GCSE: 94% obtained at least five grades A–C. A-level: 43% of entries graded A or B (250th in the league table – its worst position ever).

Destinations Nearly all go to university (about six a year to Oxbridge).

Sport Lots on offer; good coaching; first-rate facilities, including sports centre, indoor pool, indoor rifle range, Real Tennis court, nine-hole golf course.

Remarks Attractive, caring school. Recommended.

ORMSKIRK GRAMMAR ♂ ♀
Ruff Lane, Ormskirk, Lancashire L39 4QY. Tel (01695) 572405

Synopsis
Comprehensive (voluntary-controlled) ★ Co-educational ★ Ages 11–18 ★ 1,280 pupils (roughly equal numbers of girls and boys) ★ 255 in sixth form
Head: Tony Richardson, 55, appointed 1987.
Successful, well-run school; good GCSE results; strong sport.

Profile
Background Founded 1612; moved to present site close to the town centre 1850; girls admitted 1904; went comprehensive 1976. Varied, rather crowded buildings; some classrooms in 35-year-old 'temporary' huts; recent additions include drama studio, music room, new science labs.

Atmosphere Lively, orderly; emphasis on high expectations and trust. Formal assemblies: head in gown, all stand when he enters. Library staffed daily by volunteer parents; very strong bonds between home and school.

Admissions School heavily over-subscribed but (despite its title) not academically selective; priority to siblings; rest chosen by lottery. Most from relatively prosperous backgrounds in Ormskirk, Aughton and further afield including Liverpool, Sefton, St Helens.

The head   Strong leader; warm, shrewd, widely experienced. Read English at King's College, London; MSc in education from Bradford; previously a head in Bury. Married; two children.

The teaching   Fairly traditional in style (Ofsted inspectors complained about the 'bias towards a formal teacher-centred approach' – head unimpressed). Hard-working, long-serving staff of 85, more than half appointed by present head. Standard national curriculum; sciences taught by specialists; choice of 18 subjects at GCSE, 22 at A-level. Pupils grouped by ability in maths from first year and in most other subjects thereafter; extra help for those who need it; average class size 30, smaller for GCSE, 12 at A-level. Strong drama and music; four choirs, orchestra, brass and jazz bands; high quality musicals mounted. Good record in public speaking and debating. First-rate careers service.

Results   (1997) GCSE: creditable 68% gained at least five grades A–C. A-level 35% of entries graded A or B.

Destinations   About 65% stay on for A-levels; of these, most proceed to university.

Sport   Strong; regular county honours. Main games: rugby, soccer, hockey, netball. Good facilities include first-rate playing fields (a quarter of a mile away), sports hall, gym (but no swimming pool).

Remarks   A thriving school in big demand; caters for all levels of ability and interests.

OUNDLE ♂ ♀
New Street, Oundle, Peterborough PE8 4EN. Tel (01832) 273536

Synopsis
Independent ★ Co-educational ★ Boarding (plus associated day school) ★ Ages 11–18 (plus associated junior school) ★ 829 pupils (75% boys) ★ 413 in sixth form ★ Fees: £10,635–£13,920
Head: David McMurray, 60, appointed 1984 (retiring August 1999).
Fine, well-run school; very good teaching and results; first-rate facilities; lots on offer.

Profile
Background   Founded 1556 by Sir William Laxton, Master of the Grocers' Company (who are still the governors); school divided in two in 1876 – the boarding half, Oundle, for the sons of the landed gentry, the day half, Laxton, for the sons of local traders; today, boarding and day pupils are taught together but retain separate heads, allegiances and uniforms; co-educational since 1990. Buildings dating from 17th, 18th and 19th centuries scattered round the town; extensive later additions; very good facilities; idyllic rural surroundings.

Atmosphere   Busy, well-ordered, firmly traditional. High expectations of work, play and behaviour; dedicated staff; confident pupils. Compulsory chapel (fine building, windows by John Piper); strong house system; lessons on Saturday mornings.

Admissions   At 11 by tests in English, maths; at 13 by Common Entrance (55%–60% mark required); school is over-subscribed and quite selective. Many pupils from privileged backgrounds; catchment area extends to Scotland and London; 10% from abroad. Generally pleasant boarding accommodation; girls more luxuriously housed than boys. Scholarships: academic, art, music, technology.

The head   Very able; relaxed, humorous; leads from the front; highly regarded by staff and pupils. Read English at Cambridge; previously head of Loretto (qv), where he was a pupil. Married (wife much involved in school life); three daughters.

The teaching   First-rate; dedicated, well-qualified staff (70% male). Broad curriculum; all do three languages for first three years (French, Latin plus German, Spanish or Greek); sciences taught (but not examined) separately; good maths; long technology tradition (both manufacturing and design – auto engineering a speciality). Pupils grouped by ability in most subjects; some take GCSE maths, French a year early; extra help for dyslexics; average class size 21, reducing to 11 in the sixth form. Strong art, drama, music; 65% learn an instrument; choir, three orchestras, various ensembles. Extra-curricular activities include thriving cadet force (compulsory for one year, 70% continue), Duke of Edinburgh award scheme. Regular exchanges with schools in France, Hungary, Poland, Russia.

Results   (1997) GCSE: all gained at least five grades A–C. A-level: 65% of entries graded A or B.

Destinations   Nearly all go on to university (average of 30 a year to Oxbridge).

Sport   Compulsory; wide range on offer. Rugby particularly strong but good record too in rowing, cricket, hockey, netball, tennis. Fives, squash, aerobics, dance, badminton, horse-riding also on offer. Facilities include extensive playing fields, all-weather pitch, sports hall, indoor pool.

Remarks   HMC inspectors concluded (1995): 'This is a good school. Pupils reach high standards of achievement in their work. The overall standard of teaching ranges from good to excellent. The school places a strong emphasis on social and moral development, and provides many opportunities for pupils to develop and share their spiritual beliefs.'

OXFORD HIGH ♀
Belbroughton Road, Oxford 0X2 6XA. Tel (01865) 559888

Synopsis
Independent ★ Girls ★ Day ★ Ages 9–18 (plus associated pre-prep) ★ 650 pupils (556 in senior school) ★ 144 in sixth form ★ Fees: £2,988–£4,152
Head: Miss Felicity Lusk, 41, appointed January 1997.
Strong academic school; able staff; talented pupils; good results.

Profile
Background   Founded 1875 by the Girls' Day School Trust (which accounts for the modest fees). Dreary 1950s buildings plus later additions, including junior school (soon to move to another site) and sixth-form block; some classrooms in 'temporary' huts. Merger with The Squirrel (ages three to seven) and, later, with Greycotes (ages seven to 11) will provide 'a seamless education' from three to 18 (on three sites); numbers planned to rise to 900.

Atmosphere   This is a first-rate grammar school that should not be judged by its appearance. Energy and a shared assumption that everyone believes in learning and wants to get on (tempered by humanity and openness) is the secret. Pastoral care taken seriously; girls given talks on stress management, assertiveness training. Simple uniform; sixth-formers wear what they like without showing off or looking too scruffy (if there is any snobbery here, it is intellectual). Demanding, vocal parents.

Admissions   Heavily over-subscribed, but the message seems to be that if a girl is good the school will try to fit her in somewhere, sometime. Entry at ages nine and 11 by exam: competition is hot; the race is won by those showing spark, regardless of background. Fleet of school buses brings pupils from up to an hour away. Some scholarships (academic, music); trust will replace the assisted places scheme.

The head   Recent appointment. Brought up in New Zealand; formerly head of music (plays the organ) and deputy head of Hasmonean High (qv). Smart (girls impressed that her nail varnish matches her outfit) and confident; keen to foster individual talents, raise expectations; 'pops up everywhere', say pupils, who find her approachable and appreciative. Divorced; young son at boarding school.

The teaching   Good quality: formal but warm; demanding pupils (staff say modestly it is the girls who make the school); average class size 28. Standard curriculum; choice of French, German, Spanish, Russian; classics still holds its own; design/technology gaining a foothold. Half take maths at A-level; good results in sciences. Thriving music (four orchestras, six choirs); strong, varied art.

Results   (1997) GCSE: all gained at least five grades A–C. A-level: impressive 84% of entries graded A or B (15th in the league table – its best position ever).

Destinations   Virtually all go to university (including about 25% to Oxbridge).

Sport   Energetic; hockey a particular strength. Netball, volleyball, gymnastics, badminton, tennis, athletics, swimming also on offer.

Remarks   Good school facing changes that should make it even better.

PANGBOURNE ♂ ♀
Pangbourne, Reading, Berkshire RG8 8LA. Tel (01189) 842101

Synopsis
Independent ★ Co-educational ★ Boarding and day ★ Ages 11–18 ★ 375 pupils (87% boys, 65% boarding) ★ 165 in sixth form ★ Fees: £9,060–£12,480 boarding; £6,330–£8,730 day
Head: Anthony Hudson, 58, appointed 1988.
Strongly traditional school; wide range of abilities; very good sport.

Profile
Background   Founded 1917 to train boys for a career at sea ('an education both general and vocational'); fully co-educational since September 1996. Functional, purpose-built premises on attractive, 230-acre, hill-top campus (fine views); later additions include design/technology centre.

Atmosphere   Strong ethos of tradition and service (whole school stands to attention for daily flag raising and lowering). High standards of courtesy and respect instilled (pupils stand for visitors, open doors – 'strangely polite in this modern day,' says the head). Fairly formal relations between staff and pupils; Navy-style uniform (epaulettes, chevrons, brightly polished shoes) worn throughout; lessons on Saturday mornings. Drugs, alcohol, tobacco strictly out of bounds.

Admissions   Wide range of abilities ('the college pursues a deliberate policy of recruiting a broad spectrum of academic ability' – about 100 have special educational needs). Entry at 11 (mostly from primary schools) by cognitive ability test; at 13 by Common Entrance and interview. Most come from within a 40–mile radius; 14% from abroad (mainly Hong Kong). Boarding accommodation ('cabins') clean, carpeted, cheerful but short of home comforts (cramped for juniors);

substantial but dull institutional cooking (served on plastic plates). Nine scholarships a year and many bursaries.

The head Has worked hard to revive the school's flagging fortunes. Educated at Tonbridge, Grenoble and Oxford; formerly deputy head of Radley. Teaches history to 13-year-olds, ballroom dancing to 16-year-olds; keen amateur magician. Married; three grown-up children. Retires 2000.

The teaching Sound; fairly formal in style. Standard national curriculum; sciences taught separately; German, Latin on offer; A-level options include art, theatre studies, music. Pupils grouped by ability in most subjects; extra help for dyslexics and those who speak English as a foreign language; average class size 15. Good quality art (drawing skills taught) and design/technology (inspirational artefacts). Lots of music: 25% learn an instrument; orchestra, choirs; 60-strong military band. Well-supported cadet force; lots of adventure training.

Results (1997) GCSE: 63% gained at least five grades A–C grades. A-level: extremely modest 17% of entries graded A or B (bottom of the league table).

Destinations About 85% go on to university.

Sport Outstanding for such a small school. Particular strengths in rugby, hockey, rowing (boathouse on the Thames), sailing, judo. Also on offer: swimming (heated outdoor pool), badminton, basketball, tennis, golf, shooting etc.

Remarks Sound school, particularly for robust children who enjoy making and doing things.

PARKSTONE GRAMMAR ♀
Sopers Lane, Poole, Dorset BH17 7EP. Tel (01202) 697456

Synopsis
Grammar (grant-maintained) ★ Girls ★ Ages 12–18 ★ 919 pupils ★ 285 in sixth form
Head: Mrs Janet Morrison, 44, appointed September 1997.
Traditional grammar school; good teaching and results; strong sport.

Profile
Background Founded 1905 as a co-educational independent school; joined the state sector 1934; divided into girls' and boys' (Poole Grammar, qv) sections 1937; moved to present suburban site and purpose-built, flat-roof premises 1961; opted out of council control 1992, since when numbers have steadily increased (school feels over-crowded); latest additions include new sixth-form centre; some classrooms in 'temporary' huts.

Atmosphere Busy, purposeful; work hard, play hard; standards and expectations laid down and adhered to; uniform strictly enforced below the sixth form ('smart working dress' required). Mission statement: 'We aim to make the most of our talents in order to serve others and be happy.' Parents kept in the picture (and invited to 'back-to-school' evenings to learn about what is happening in education).

Admissions School is over-subscribed (350 apply to 150 places) and highly selective; entry by tests; top 16% of the ability range. Children come from a wide range of social backgrounds in an extensive catchment area (including Dorchester, Swanage, Ringwood).

The head Recent appointment (predecessor resigned after being criticised by Ofsted – and became an Ofsted inspector). Read English at Hull; previously deputy head of Old Palace, Croydon (qv). Married; two children.

The teaching Good quality; fairly formal in style; substantial staff turn-over after recent upheavals. Standard national curriculum; science taught (but not examined) as three separate subjects; all add German to French for at least two years; lots of computing; choice of 20 subjects at A-level. Pupils grouped by ability in maths, French from second year; extra help for those with special needs, including the gifted; average class size 28, smaller in the sixth form. Lots of drama, music (some in conjunction with Poole Grammar); three choirs, three orchestras. Regular language exchanges with pupils in France, Germany.

Results (1997) GCSE: all gained at least five grades A–C. A-level: respectable 55% of entries graded A or B.

Destinations About 85% go on to university (up to eight a year to Oxbridge).

Sport A strength. Good record in swimming, cricket, volleyball, soccer, athletics, netball, tennis, trampolining. Extensive playing fields but no sports hall.

Remarks Good all round, despite recent turbulence.

PARMITER'S ♂ ♀

High Elms Lane, Garston, Watford, Hertfordshire WD2 7JU. Tel (01923) 671424

Synopsis

Partially selective comprehensive (grant-maintained) ★ Co-educational ★ Ages 11–18 ★ 1,145 pupils (more boys than girls) ★ 217 in sixth form
Head: Brian Coulshed, 47, appointed 1993.
Well-ordered, disciplined school; good teaching and results; flourishing music and sport.

Profile

Background Founded 1681 under the will of Thomas Parmiter, wealthy silk merchant, as a boys' grammar school in Bethnal Green; moved 1977 to present site (17 acres expanded to 60 by purchase of adjacent farmland) and became a co-educational comprehensive; opted out of council control 1991. Sprawling, unlovely (but well-maintained), flat-roofed buildings plus later additions, including £1.7 million sports centre.

Atmosphere Lively, purposeful, disciplined; strong Christian ethos. Tradition much in evidence: head wears a gown; school cups and portraits of former heads adorn the entrance hall; prefects help run things. Strict uniform below the sixth form (badges and special ties according to seniority and office); seniors wear formal clothes in specified colours. Parents very supportive.

Admissions Heavily over-subscribed (750 apply for 185 places); up to 50% of places allocated on the basis of tests set in conjunction with three other local schools. Fairly wide range of abilities and backgrounds but most come from relatively well-off homes; catchment area extends to St Albans and Stanmore.

The head Calm, friendly, very able; clearly on good terms with staff. Immensely proud of school's traditions and character. Read geography at Manchester; previously deputy head of Goffs (qv). Practising Roman Catholic; enthusiastic sportsman; keen to increase Oxbridge numbers. Married; two children.

The teaching Good: fairly traditional in style; experienced, committed staff. Much emphasis in junior years on 'old-fashioned' standards of presentation, accuracy; many classrooms (some a bit bleak) have desks in rows facing the board; others arranged less formally. Pupils divided into two broad ability bands; further setting in maths, science (taught as three separate subjects), French; good support for those with special needs (both in and out of the classroom); some classes rather crowded (up to 32). Options include Latin, German, Spanish; good computer provision. Drama popular (lively teaching); music thriving and enthusiastic (two wind bands, two orchestras, choirs, countless ensembles); some musical activity every break and lunchtime. Busy extra-curricular programme includes Duke of Edinburgh award scheme, numerous clubs; school owns a field centre in Wales. Well-structured careers advice. Regular exchanges with schools in France, Germany.

Results (1997) GCSE: 77% gained at least five grades A–C. A-level: 39% of entries graded A or B.

Destinations About 65% continue into the sixth form; most of these proceed to university (four or five a year to Oxbridge).

Sport Lots on offer, including: soccer (very strong), rugby, hockey, netball, basketball, cricket, athletics, cross-country, tennis. Very good facilities.

Remarks Ofsted inspectors concluded (1997): 'This is a strong school with high standards...The quality of teaching is one of the strengths.'

PARRS WOOD ♂ ♀

Wilmslow Road, East Didsbury, Manchester M20 5PG. Tel (0161) 445 8786

Synopsis
Comprehensive ★ Co-educational ★ Ages 11–18 ★ 1,500 pupils (equal numbers of girls and boys) ★ 240 in sixth form
Head: Iain Hall, 54, appointed 1991.
Very well-run school; good teaching and results; lots on offer.

Profile
Background Opened 1967 as a purpose-built comprehensive on a 40-acre suburban site; flat-roofed buildings in a shocking state of decay (they were only meant to last 25 years); school hopes a private developer will replace them in exchange for half the site; £600,000 sixth-form centre recently added.

Atmosphere Enthusiastic, orderly; big emphasis on target-setting, monitoring, rewards (pupils receive public praise in 'celebration assemblies' and letters of congratulation from head and governors). High level of pastoral care; strong homework policy; uniform below the sixth form; regular 'surgeries' for parents.

Admissions Heavily over-subscribed (more than 600 apply for 250 places); no academic selection; priority to children living in East and West Didsbury (those outside have little hope of admission, except to the sixth form). Full range of abilities but weighted towards the more able; 28% Asian.

The head Very able: motivator, innovator, entrepreneur; leads from the front. Knows his pupils well; sets staff termly performance targets. Read maths and physics at Liverpool; previously head for 10 years of a Liverpool comprehensive.

The teaching Mixture of styles: lessons delivered in a firm but friendly way; pupils respond to encouragement and praise. Broad curriculum: science on offer as three separate subjects; choice of French, Spanish, German (all do two in third year); all take 10 GCSEs. Pupils grouped by ability in main subjects; extra help for those who need it. Wide choice of subjects at A-level; GNVQ in business studies available. Lots of music to suit all tastes (orchestra, steel band, rock bands). Wide range of extra-curricular activities.

Results (1997) GCSE: 55% gained at least five grades A–C. A-level: 42% of entries graded A or B.

Destinations Most of those who stay on into the sixth form proceed to university (average of four a year to Oxbridge).

Sport Wide range; high level of participation. Main games: football, hockey, netball. Lacrosse, tennis, cricket, athletics, fencing also on offer. Lots of playing fields but indoor facilities limited.

Remarks Ofsted inspectors concluded (1996): 'This is a good school of which the community should be proud.' The buildings are a disgrace.

PATE'S GRAMMAR ♂ ♀
Princess Elizabeth Way, Cheltenham, Gloucestershire GL51 0HG. Tel (01242) 523169

Synopsis
Grammar (grant-maintained) ★ Co-educational ★ Ages 11–18 ★ 920 pupils (equal numbers of girls and boys) ★ 320 in sixth form
Head: David Barnes, 57, appointed 1986.
First-rate academic school; very good teaching and results; lots of music and sport.

Profile
Background Founded 1574 by Richard Pate for 'local poor boys'; amalgamated with a girls' grammar school 1986; opted out of council control 1990. School completely rebuilt and re-equipped in 1995 at a cost of £8 million; facilities include fine hall, library (25,000 volumes), 14 labs, performing arts suite.

Atmosphere Purposeful, academic ('traditional values combined with up-to-date methods'); high expectations all round. Formal but friendly relations between staff and pupils. Compulsory uniform throughout, strictly adhered to.

Admissions School heavily over-subscribed (700 apply for 120 places); priority to those scoring highest in verbal reasoning test; pupils need an IQ of over 120. Another 40 a year join the sixth form: minimum of six GCSEs at grades A–C. Most from professional/middle-class backgrounds.

The head Enthusiastic, donnish. Read classics at Oxford; wide experience in independent and Direct Grant schools. Strong believer in co-education; emphasises that good results (see below) can be achieved without separating the sexes.

The teaching Challenging: varied styles; emphasis on participation, rote learning not neglected. Exceptionally committed, experienced staff of 60 (most over the age of 45). Broad curriculum: most take French and German; Latin, Spanish on offer; particularly good results in science; all sixth-formers do at least three A-levels plus general studies. Lots of drama (theatre studies popular at A-level) and music; more than 200 learn an instrument; two orchestras, good choir, regular concerts. Extra-curricular activities include debating, Duke of Edinburgh award scheme, cadet force (own rifle range), lots of charity fundraising (up to £4,000 a year).

Results (1997) GCSE: all gained at least five grades A–C. A-level: 57% of entries graded A or B.

Destinations Nearly all stay on for A-levels and proceed to university (average of 15 a year to Oxbridge).

Sport High profile; good record in all major team games; particular strengths in rugby, netball (national finalists in 1996 and 1997). Facilities include extensive

on-site playing fields, sports hall, gym, eight tennis courts.
Remarks   Very good all round: more than a hot-house.

THE PERSE ♂
Hills Road, Cambridge CB2 2QF. Tel (01223) 568300

Synopsis
Independent ★ Boys (plus girls in sixth form) ★ Day ★ Ages 11–18 (plus associated prep school) ★ 535 pupils ★ 150 in sixth form (88% boys) ★ Fees: £5,250
Head: Nigel Richardson, 49, appointed 1994.
Good, well-run, academic school.

Profile
Background   Founded 1615 under the will of Dr Stephen Perse, Fellow of Gonville and Caius; moved from the city centre to present purpose-built premises 1960; formerly Direct Grant, became fully independent 1976; sixth-form girls admitted 1995. Award-winning buildings have a non-institutional feel (light, airy classrooms); later additions grouped together to form a harmonious whole on a green, 30-acre site; school steadily expanding. Prep school (ages seven to 11) near by.
Atmosphere   Welcoming, civilised (a seat of learning); good pastoral care (including careful induction procedures); warm relations between staff and pupils. School day ends at 4.15 pm; team players expected to be available for Saturday matches. Flourishing parents' association.
Admissions   By interview and tests in English, maths, verbal reasoning; school is over-subscribed (by about 2:1) and fairly selective. Those joining the sixth form need at least six grade Bs at GCSE. Catchment area extends into Hertfordshire, Bedfordshire, Essex, Suffolk.
The head   Very able and experienced. Read history at Cambridge; previously second master at Uppingham, head of The Dragon, deputy head of King's Macclesfield. Married (to a children's author); two sons
The teaching   Stimulating; well-qualified, committed staff. Broad curriculum; sciences taught separately (good results); all do Latin for at least two years; Greek, German on offer; choice of 22 subjects at A-level (sixth-formers spend a third of their time on 'non-specialist work'). Long tradition of teaching English to juniors through drama ('It is found that in this way boys become less self-conscious and acquire much accuracy and clearness in expression'). Pupils grouped by ability in maths, French; average class size 25, reducing to 12 at A-level. Very good art (displayed around the school); music expanding (25% play an instrument). Extra-curricular activities include cadet force, Scouts, debating. Regular language exchanges with pupils in France, Germany; classicists visit Greece.
Results   (1997) GCSE: all gained at least five grades A–C. A-level: 69% of entries graded A or B (not a good year).
Destinations   Nearly all go on to university (up to a third to Oxbridge).
Sport   Two full games afternoons a week; hockey very strong; rugby, cricket, the other main sports. Facilities include 28 acres of playing fields, all-weather pitch.
Remarks   Strong all round.

PERSE GIRLS' ♀
Union Road, Cambridge CB2 1HF. Tel (01223) 359589

Synopsis
Independent ★ Girls ★ Day ★ Ages 11–18 (plus associated junior school) ★ 541 pupils ★ 118 in sixth form ★ Fees: £5,172
Head: Miss Helen Smith, 55, appointed 1989.
Well-run, academic school; very good teaching and results; lots of art, drama, music.

Profile
Background Founded 1881 above a grocery shop in Trumpington Street; moved to present, surprisingly spacious site (entered through a small black door) soon afterwards; formerly Direct Grant, became fully independent 1976. Good facilities for science, languages, computing, music; attractive, well-lit classrooms; ambitious £3 million appeal launched. Well-run junior school (160 girls aged seven to 10) near by.

Atmosphere Confident, well-ordered; good pastoral care system. Navy uniform below the sixth form. Weekly newsletter keeps parents informed.

Admissions By interview and tests; majority of 81 places a year taken by girls from the junior school. Bursary fund aims to replace assisted places, which about 100 hold.

The head Quietly effective leader; very much in command. Read maths at Oxford; came here in 1971; deputy head 1988. Strong believer in single-sex education for girls.

The teaching Very good: generally traditional in style; well-qualified, predominantly female staff (a third appointed by present head); highly motivated pupils. Broad curriculum ('subjects chosen from the finest traditions and promoting newer technologies'): sciences taught separately; all do two modern languages (choice includes German, Italian, Russian, Spanish) and at least one year's Latin; Greek on offer; A-level options include psychology, theology, economics. Pupils grouped by ability in maths, science, French, Latin. Lots of art, drama, music (orchestras, choirs, 27 specialist teachers). Extra-curricular activities include well-supported Duke of Edinburgh award scheme. Regular language exchanges with schools in France, Germany, Italy, Russia, Spain.

Results (1997) GCSE: all gained at least five grades at A–C. A-level: creditable 74% of entries graded A or B.

Destinations Nearly all go on to university (15–20 a year to Oxbridge).

Sport On-site facilities for netball, tennis, dance, gymnastics; six-acre sports ground 10 minutes' walk away; inter-school fixtures in hockey, athletics.

Remarks Efficient, happy school.

PHILIP MORANT ♂ ♀
Rembrandt Way, Colchester, Essex CO3 4QS. Tel (01206) 545222

Synopsis
Comprehensive (grant-maintained) ★ Co-educational ★ Ages 11–18 ★ 1,470 pupils (equal numbers of girls and boys) ★ 200 in sixth form
Head: David Jones, 56, appointed 1984.
Popular, ambitious comprehensive; good teaching and results.

Profile

Background Opened as a secondary modern 1963 (named after Philip Morant, 18th-century Colchester cleric who wrote an acclaimed *History of Essex* – copy displayed in the library); went comprehensive 1971; opted out of council control 1992; achieved technology college status 1994; sixth form restored 1996. Unlovely 1960s buildings; many corridors and stairways not designed for the numbers now using them; latest additions include new sixth-form block. Specialist unit for pupils with hearing difficulties: staff trained in sign language; speech therapy also available.

Atmosphere Crowded, workmanlike, slightly soulless; pupils breezy, boisterous, demanding. House system attempts to break down the institution's scale – not entirely successfully – but discipline is generally good. Strict application of uniform rules (neat green blazer plus house tie) a cause of some resentment among older pupils. Honours boards opposite a portrait of the Queen echo an earlier educational age.

Admissions School heavily over-subscribed: more than 450 apply for 270 places; priority to pupils at five 'feeder' primaries and those living nearest. Generally above-average ability children from middle-class backgrounds.

The head Only the second in the school's history. Well-groomed, assured executive; spent four years in industry before teaching. Read history at Cambridge; taught here for eight years up to mid-1970s; previously head of another Essex comprehensive; recently gained an MBA in education management from Leeds Metropolitan. Married; two grown-up sons.

The teaching First-rate; varied styles. Fairly broad curriculum; science on offer as three separate subjects; choice of French or German; GCSE options include child development, photography. Pupils allocated before entry into two ability bands, Alpha and A (plus small special needs group) according to primary school reports; bandings can be changed, usually after end-of-term tests; average class size 25, reducing to 20 for GCSE. Imaginative, out-of-hours studies programme offers introductions to philosophy, Japanese, Oriental studies etc, plus off-beat technological and environmental projects. Lots of music: one in six learns an instrument. European links include annual history trip to World War One battlefields, work-experience in Hamburg, music exchange with Holland, environmental projects in Finland.

Results (1997) GCSE: creditable 73% gained at least five grades A–C. First A-level results in August 1998.

Destinations About 40% stay on for A-levels; most expected to proceed to university.

Sport Strong soccer, cricket. Good facilities, including sports hall and flood-lit all-weather courts for netball and tennis.

Remarks Highly effective, slightly functional mass education. Identified by Ofsted (1996) as 'outstandingly successful'.

PIGGOTT ♂ ♀
Twyford Road, Wargrave, Reading, Berkshire RG10 8DS. Tel (0118) 940 2357

Synopsis
Comprehensive (voluntary-controlled, Church of England) ★ Ages 11–18 ★ 813 pupils (roughly equal numbers of girls and boys) ★ 126 in sixth form
Head: Dr Keith Atton, 51, appointed 1989.
Successful, well-run school; good teaching and results; strong sport.

Profile
Background Founded 1796 by Robert Piggott, wealthy landowner; moved to sprawling, rural site between Reading and Maidenhead 1940; went comprehensive 1973. Main building looks like a cottage hospital; later additions a less attractive mixture of wood and glass; lots of pupils' work on display.

Atmosphere Warm, purposeful; discipline firm but unobtrusive (withdrawal unit for disruptive children seldom used); good pastoral care; friendly rapport between staff and pupils; all classrooms open to visitors (first-year parents encouraged to spend a morning in class).

Admissions School is not full but numbers have been rising; most pupils from six 'feeder' primaries in an affluent catchment area; 30% from outside.

The head Very able; good leader and manager; makes a daily tour of the classrooms to make his presence felt. PhD in history from London; previously deputy head of two schools in Kent.

The teaching Formal but friendly; long-serving staff (slightly more women than men). Standard national curriculum; two-thirds add German to French from second year; choice of 18 subjects at A-level; GNVQs available in business, health & social care. Pupils grouped by ability in maths, modern languages from second year, science from third year, English for GCSE; plenty of extra help for those who need it (some pupils have 'statements'); average class size 26, reducing to 22 for GCSE, 10 in the sixth form. Strong musical tradition (good choir). Regular language exchanges with pupils in France, Germany.

Results (1997) GCSE: 58% gained at least five grades A–C (has been higher). A-level: respectable 38% of entries graded A or B.

Destinations About 80% proceed to university.

Sport A strength. Good record in rugby, soccer, hockey, netball, athletics and, particularly, cross-country (county and national honours).

Remarks Ofsted inspectors concluded (1994): 'This is a good school. It provides an effective education. Teachers have high expectations of work and behaviour.'

POOLE GRAMMAR ♂
Gravel Hill, Poole, Dorset BH17 7JU. Tel (01202) 692132

Synopsis
Grammar (grant-maintained) ★ Boys ★ Ages 12–18 ★ 844 pupils ★ 275 in sixth form
Head: Alex Clarke, 51, appointed 1990.
Well-run academic school; good teaching and GCSE results; strong sport.

Profile
Background Opened 1904 as a co-educational grammar school; became

single-sex in 1937 with the creation of Parkstone Grammar (qv) for girls; moved 1966 to present purpose-built premises on a landscaped, semi-rural site; opted out of council control 1994. School has steadily expanded; new classrooms being built.

Atmosphere   Orderly, good-natured; well-organised pastoral care helps break down size; high-achieving and improving pupils personally congratulated by the head. Blazer-and-tie uniform below the sixth form.

Admissions   By 12-plus exam; school takes top 16% of the ability range from more than 40 primaries (and some prep schools) in an extensive catchment area (Dorchester, Blandford, Swanage, Ringwood); 25% of the sixth form join from other schools (with at least five GCSEs, grades A–C).

The head   Good leader; warm personality; popular with staff and pupils. Read German at Durham (teaches it to third-years); was deputy head of a comprehensive; previously a schools inspector. Married; two daughters.

The teaching   Good; generally formal in style. Experienced staff of 54 (13 women), half appointed by present head. Broad curriculum: sciences taught (and examined) as three separate subjects (chemistry particularly strong); all add German to French from second year; choice of 21 A-levels. Pupils grouped by ability for GCSE maths; some extra help for dyslexics; maximum class size 30. Good art; lots of music (Dixieland jazz a speciality). Extra-curricular activities include Duke of Edinburgh award scheme. Work experience in France, Germany for A-level linguists.

Results   (1997) GCSE: 97% gained at least five grades A–C. A-level: 38% of entries graded A or B (should be higher).

Destinations   About 80% go on to good universities (average of 12 a year to Oxbridge).

Sport   Taken seriously; up to 30 staff involved; lots of Saturday fixtures. Particular strengths in rugby, soccer, cricket, tennis. Athletics, cross-country, swimming, sailing also popular. Facilities include first-rate playing fields, good tennis courts.

Remarks   Ofsted inspectors concluded (1996): 'The school provides a very good education for all its pupils across the whole range of subjects.'

PORTSMOUTH GRAMMAR ♂ ♀
High Street, Portsmouth, Hampshire POI 2LN. Tel (01705) 819125

Synopsis
Independent ★ Co-educational ★ Day ★ Ages 11–18 (plus associated junior school) ★ 809 pupils (70% boys) ★ 192 in sixth form ★ Fees: £4,890
Head: Dr Timothy Hands, 41, appointed September 1997.
Traditional, academic school; good teaching and results; lots of extra-curricular activities.

Profile
Background   Founded 1732; formerly Direct Grant, became fully independent 1976; fully co-educational since 1991. Stark, rather barrack-like buildings dating from the 1920s on a spacious, city-centre site close to the cathedral; later additions include theatre, music school, sports hall, sixth-form centre; some facilities are stretched. Junior school (ages four to 11) on same campus.

Atmosphere   Energetic, busy, well-disciplined (Saturday morning detention for miscreants); girls, though a minority, have helped soften the feel of the place; good pastoral care.

Admissions   At 11 by tests, at 13 by Common Entrance; school is over-subscribed and fairly selective but likely to become less so with the phasing out of assisted places, which more than 200 hold; numbers expected to fall. Pupils from a mix of backgrounds; some travel long distances.

The head   Recent appointment. Read English at Oxford (DPhil); was a house-master at King's, Canterbury; previously second master at Whitgift (qv). Married; two sons. Keen musician; has written books about Thomas Hardy.

The teaching   Good quality; fairly formal in style; expectations are high. Broad curriculum: science on offer as three separate subjects (taken by 75%); all do Latin for first two years; choice of French or German; strong maths; plenty of computing; more than 20 options at A-level – most take three plus one AS-level. Average class size 24, smaller in sixth form. Good art (especially sculpture); strong music (more than a third learn an instrument); lots of drama. Extra-curricular activities include well-supported cadet and Duke of Edinburgh award scheme. Regular exchanges with schools in France, Germany, Spain, USA.

Results   (1997) GCSE: all gained at least five grades A–C. A-level: 62% of entries graded A or B.

Destinations   Nearly all go on to good universities (up to 10 a year to Oxbridge).

Sport   Strong tradition. Main sports: rugby, hockey (single and mixed), net-ball, cricket, athletics, rounders. Squash, fencing, tennis, swimming, cross--country, sea rowing also available. Facilities include 16 acres of playing fields four miles away.

Results   Good all round.

PORTSMOUTH HIGH ♀

Kent Road, Southsea, Hampshire PO5 3EG. Tel (01705) 826714

Synopsis

Independent ★ Girls ★ Day ★ Ages 11–18 (plus associated junior school) ★ 475 pupils ★ 100 in sixth form ★ Fees: £4,115
Head: Mrs Judith Dawtrey, 50, appointed 1984 (retiring December 1988).
Well-run, academic school; very good teaching and results; strong music.

Profile

Background   Founded 1882; a member of the estimable Girls' Day School Trust. Modest Victorian buildings plus many later additions (science labs across the road); classrooms carpeted, spacious. Junior school (220 girls aged four to 11) five minutes' walk away.

Atmosphere   Hard-working, well-ordered; rules couched in positive terms ('Punctuality on the part of all ensures the efficient running of the PHS commu-nity'). Burgundy and grey uniform below the sixth form. Regular lectures for parents on 'living with a teenage girl'.

Admissions   By competitive entrance exam (up to two apply for each place); policy is to maintain academic standards rather than fill desks 'at any cost'. About 150 hold assisted places, which the trust aims to replace with a scheme of its own. Catchment area extends to Chichester, Petersfield, Southampton, Isle of Wight (parents organise coaches).

The head   Able, experienced, inspires confidence; has the school running like clockwork. Read French and Spanish at London; teaches personal, social and health education to first-years. Married; two grown-up children.

The teaching   Good quality; well-qualified, long-serving, predominantly female staff. Broad curriculum: sciences taught (and examined) separately; strong maths; lots of computing; all do French or Spanish (some take GCSE a year early); up to half add German or Latin; usual range of A-levels (including Latin and Greek). Pupils grouped by ability in maths, languages; some extra help for dyslexics; average class size 20–25, reducing to 10 in the sixth form. Good music; up to 70% learn an instrument; two orchestras, various ensembles. First-rate careers advice. Regular language exchanges with pupils in France, Germany, Spain.

Results   (1997) GCSE: 99% gained at least five grades A–C. A-level: 65% of entries graded A or B (has been higher).

Destinations   About 80% stay on for A-levels; of these, nearly all proceed to university (average of six a year to Oxbridge).

Sport   All major sports offered (including lacrosse) but facilities limited; tennis and netball courts on site.

Remarks   Good school for able girls.

POYNTON HIGH   ♂ ♀
Yew Tree Lane, Poynton, Stockport, Cheshire SK12 1PU. Tel (01625) 871811

Synopsis
Comprehensive ★ Co-educational ★ Ages 11–19 ★ 1,755 pupils (roughly equal numbers of girls and boys) ★ 326 in sixth form
Head: Mark Wasserberg, 45, appointed January 1998.
First-rate comprehensive; good teaching and GCSE results; strong sport.

Profile
Background   Opened as a comprehensive 1972; pleasant, well-maintained 23-acre site in a largely affluent area of Macclesfield; functional, rather drab buildings, bursting at the seams. School enjoys strong support from parents and the community.

Atmosphere   Calm, well-ordered (despite the school's size); rules clearly stated and well understood; truancy rate virtually nil; no serious disciplinary problems; no feeling of coercion but a definite sense of authority and high expectations. Well-organised pastoral care system (staff get to know the children well). Corridors adorned with pupils' work; display cabinet groans with sporting silverware. Many teachers send their children here, always a good sign.

Admissions   School over-subscribed (more than 350 apply for 273 places); no selection; basic requirement is that child must have attended one of eight 'feeder' primaries in Poynton, Adlington and Disley. Middle-class backgrounds predominate.

The head   New appointment (predecessor had been in post 18 years). Read English at York; previously head of a comprehensive in Congleton. Married; four children (all in state schools).

The teaching   Hard-working, professional staff of 110 (equal numbers of women and men); full range of teaching methods used. Wide, varied curriculum; four languages on offer, including Italian (but no classics). GCSE options include childcare, computing, office technology, graphic communication, home economics; choice of 25 subjects at A-level; vocational alternatives available; all do general studies. Pupils grouped by ability from third year in maths, science, languages; extra help for those with special needs; largest classes 30, reducing to 12–15 in sixth form. Homework strictly monitored by teachers and parents. Good drama, dance, music; three choirs, orchestra, swing band; instrumental lessons from visiting teachers. Extra-curricular activities include outstanding community services programme involving the elderly, the young, the handicapped, and the environment (school has won a Rotary Club award for 'wholehearted service to the community'). Regular exchanges with schools in Germany, France, Spain.

Results   (1997) GCSE: creditable 73% gained at least five grades A–C. A-level: 36% of entries graded A or B.

Destinations   About 60% continue into the sixth form; of these, 65% proceed to university (about five a year to Oxbridge).

Sport   Facilities include fully equipped leisure centre (shared with the public after school hours), indoor pool, extensive on-site playing fields. All the usual games are played to a high level; tennis, rounders, squash, badminton also on offer.

Remarks   Happy, well-run school; highly recommended. Ofsted inspectors concluded (1993): 'The school provides an excellent education. The quality of the teaching is high. The pupils are strongly motivated, willing to learn and prepared to work hard.'

PRESDALES ♀
Hoe Lane, Ware, Hertfordshire SG12 9NX. Tel (01920) 462210

Synopsis
Comprehensive ★ Girls ★ Ages 11–18 ★ 980 pupils ★ 165 in sixth form
Head: Mrs Janine Robinson, 49, appointed 1988.
Successful school; good teaching and results; first-rate languages; strong music.

Profile
Background   Originally Ware Grammar School; went comprehensive 1975; acquired language college status 1995. Victorian mansion (reduced to a rather functional shell) in parkland setting at the end of a sweeping drive; 1960s classroom block behind (part refurbished, part dowdy).

Atmosphere   Safe, civilised; orderly, well-motivated girls; code of conduct firmly enforced.

Admissions   School is over-subscribed but non-selective; places allocated by Hertfordshire County Council according to seven criteria, including 'social reasons' and 'reasons put forward by parents': expressing a desire for single-sex education likely to carry most weight. Catchment area limited only by willingness to travel; includes Stevenage, Welwyn Garden City, South & East Herts, Essex. Pupils mostly of above-average ability from middle-class homes with high educational expectations.

The head   Efficient, enthusiastic, hard-working; delegates widely but runs a tight ship. Read modern languages at Birmingham; teaches French. Married (to a teacher); no children.

The teaching   Good quality, challenging. Predominantly female staff, most appointed by present head. Girls grouped by ability into three bands from the start; further setting thereafter in maths, science, English, French; less able pupils taught in smaller classes. Commendably broad curriculum: science on offer as three separate subjects; all take French and German for first two years; Russian, Italian, Spanish, Portuguese, Japanese also on offer (all rooms labeled in several foreign languages); Latin, Greek available. GCSE options include drama, expressive arts, graphic art & design; GNVQ in business studies offered as an alternative to A-levels; no shortage of audio-visual equipment or computers (IT taught to 12-year-olds in French). Lots of drama; strong music. Regular language exchanges with schools in France, Germany, Spain, Russia, Italy.

Results   (1997) GCSE: very creditable 80% gained at least five grades A–C. A-level: 43% of entries graded A or B.

Destinations   Most go on to university.

Sport   Good facilities (playing fields, tennis courts, outdoor pool); full programme of matches. Main games: netball, hockey, tennis; also athletics, swimming.

Remarks   Attractive, purposeful school; identified by Ofsted (1995) as 'outstandingly successful'.

PRIORY   ♂ ♀
Longden Road, Shrewsbury, Shropshire SY3 9EE. Tel (01743) 343769

Synopsis
Comprehensive ★ Co-educational ★ Ages 11–16 ★ 686 pupils (58% girls)
Head: Mrs Sylvia Johnes, 58, appointed 1976.
First-rate, well-run school; very good teaching and GCSE results; flourishing music and sport.

Profile
Background   Opened as a girls' grammar school 1938; became a co-educational comprehensive 1981. Uninspiring buildings on a pleasant, six-acre site in a residential area of the town.

Atmosphere   Big emphasis on high standards of achievement, behaviour and dress; grammar school ethos lingers. Fairly formal relations between staff and well-mannered pupils; rules firmly enforced. Good provision for children with special needs, including those who are blind or in wheelchairs.

Admissions   School over-subscribed (about 170 apply for 130 places) but no academic selection: places allocated by county council on a first-come-first-served basis. Catchment area covers Shrewsbury and surrounding villages; large proportion of pupils from middle-class, professional/managerial backgrounds.

The head   Shrewd, long-serving; runs a tight ship. Read history at Swansea (and teaches it to the younger pupils).

The teaching   Good quality; traditional in style (designed to produce results). Long-serving, committed staff of 43 (roughly equal numbers of women and men), all appointed by present head; qualifications well matched to subjects taught. National curriculum plus: all do French and German from the start, Latin from second year (and can continue it to GCSE); particular strengths in English, maths. Pupils grouped by ability from second year in most subjects; plenty of extra help for those who need it; average class size 25. Unsatisfactory homework leads to detention. Good music: choir, orchestra, various ensembles. Wide range of extra-curricular activities, including drama, cadet force, Duke of Edinburgh award scheme.

Results (1997) GCSE: very creditable 75% gained at least five grades A–C.
Destinations About 90% remain in full-time education.
Sport Particular strengths in gymnastics, rugby; soccer, cricket, tennis, netball, rounders, hockey also on offer; emphasis on participating for enjoyment. Facilities include well-equipped gym, all-weather cricket strip, five playing fields.
Remarks Ofsted inspectors concluded (1995): 'Standards are high at all levels; this is a school in which achievement is prized'. Recommended.

PURCELL ♂ ♀
Aldenham Road, Bushey, Hertfordshire WD2 3TS. Tel (01923) 331100

Synopsis
Independent ★ Co-educational ★ Ages 8–18 ★ Boarding and day ★ 162 pupils ★ (62% girls, 63% boarders) ★ 75 in sixth form ★ Fees: £17,343 boarding; £11,283 day
Head: John Bain, 58, appointed 1983.
Specialist music school of great distinction; good academic results; very happy atmosphere.

Profile
Background Founded 1962 to educate young musicians of outstanding talent and promise – one of a handful of specialist music schools. Moved here July 1997 from Harrow-on-the-Hill; fine Edwardian red-brick building plus later additions in 20 acres; excellent concert hall.
Atmosphere Happy, vibrant, very purposeful. Music everywhere; terrific sense of creative endeavour and common purpose – but not a temperamental hot-house. These are 'normal' children who happen to be prodigiously talented; any pressure comes from the pupils' own extremely high standards not from the school, which is constantly protecting them from too much too soon. No uniform (usual student gear – long skirts, floppy tops, scarves, jeans, sweatshirts); teachers in casual clothes. Relations between teachers and pupils mutually respectful (teachers feel privileged to be here, most visiting instrumentalists are professors at major conservatoires). Very close community ('We've so much in common'); pupils say it is like a large family. Former pupils include composers Oliver Knussen and Simon Bainbridge, cellist Robert Cohen, oboist Nicholas Daniel and pianist Julius Drake.
Admissions By musical audition only: at any age or stage between eight and 16 'when the child is ready'. Head interviews all applicants (without their parents) to ensure the school is right for them. Children must demonstrate exceptional musical talent and promise plus 'intuitive music spark' and inner steel; they (not their parents) must be dedicated. Funding found for any deserving child; most supported by bursaries or scholarships – 60% by DfEE music and ballet scheme. Two-thirds of pupils from Britain (wide range of social backgrounds), rest from abroad (mainly Asian Pacific rim); three full-time teachers of English as a foreign language. All boarders accommodated on site; juniors in small separate house (with sanatorium); seniors in small dormitories or study bedrooms (some with pianos).
The head Read classics at Oxford (choral scholar – knows the demands made on dedicated musicians); previously housemaster at Cranleigh (qv). Dedicated, compassionate, approachable (open door policy throughout the school). On

very good terms with children and staff. Married, with grown up children; likely to retire at 60.

The teaching   Musical education is outstanding: one-to-one instrumental lessons of conservatoire standard; excellent ensemble and orchestral work; academic music department particularly good (aim is to produce 'thinking musicians'); electronic music expanding rapidly. Pupils spend between 25% and 60% of their time on musical activities: two one-hour lessons a week on main instrument plus up to an hour on second; up to four hours practice a day for senior string players; choir, orchestra, chamber groups, Kodaly and regular concerts. However, not all children go on to study music, and options are kept as open as possible. Most take seven GCSEs (compulsory English, maths, science, music); French and German on offer; good art but no IT or design/technology. At A-level all take music plus one other subject from fairly limited range. Stimulating teaching; committed staff, all appointed by present head; very small classes. Lots of concerts and expeditions.

Results   (1997) GCSE: 91% gained at least five grades A–C. A-level: creditable 59% of entries graded A or B.

Destinations   Most to music colleges (particularly the Royal College, Guildhall School of Music and Drama, and the Royal Academy); others to university (many to Oxbridge) to read a variety of subjects (including music).

Sport   Enthusiastic but not a strength. Good football pitches (but no competitive games against other schools); gym, basketball court, small indoor pool.

Remarks   Excellent school for those fortunate enough to have the talent and motivation.

PUTNEY HIGH ♀
35 Putney Hill, London SW15 6BH. Tel (0181) 788 4886

Synopsis
Independent ★ Girls ★ Day ★ Ages 11–18 (plus associated junior school) ★ 570 pupils ★ 138 in sixth form ★ Fees: £4,968
Head: Mrs Eileen Merchant, 53, appointed 1991.
Sound academic school; good teaching and results.

Profile
Background   Founded 1893 by the Girls' Day School Trust; outwardly attractive Victorian buildings (but dreary inside) in pleasant grounds; later additions include £700,000 sports hall; good facilities for technology, computing. Junior school (270 girls aged four to 11) near by.

Atmosphere   Friendly, outgoing girls encouraged but not pressurised (failing to work leads to detention); good pastoral care system.

Admissions   School heavily over-subscribed (350 apply for 86 places – 50 of which go to the junior school); entry by highly competitive tests in English, maths. Trust aims to replace assisted places, which 20% hold, with a scheme of its own. Predominantly local catchment area: Fulham, Wimbledon, Barnes.

The head   Thoughtful, encouraging. Read chemistry at Sheffield; previously deputy head of Latymer (qv). Teaches maths and thinking skills to first-years. Keen bird-watcher. Married; two grown-up sons.

The teaching   Good; varied styles; predominantly female staff, nearly half appointed by present head. Fairly broad curriculum; strong languages (including German, Spanish); all do Latin; choice of 22 subjects at A-level, including business studies, art history. Pupils grouped by ability in maths, French from second year; progress closely monitored; average class size 28. Lots of music: a third learn an instrument; orchestra, choir. Extra-curricular activities include Duke of Edinburgh award scheme.

Results (1997) GCSE: all gained at least five grades A–C. A-level: creditable 71% of entries graded A or B.

Destinations Virtually all go on to university (average of seven a year to Oxbridge).

Sports Netball and tennis are strong, athletics popular. Badminton, fencing, rowing also on offer.

Remarks Solid school; good results without gloss or pressure.

QUEEN ANNE'S
Henley Road, Caversham, Reading RG4 6DX. Tel (0118) 947 1582

Synopsis
Independent ★ Girls ★ Boarding and day ★ Ages 11–18 ★ 310 pupils (64% boarding) ★ 105 in sixth form ★ Fees: £12,465 boarding; £8,160 day
Head: Mrs Deborah Forbes, 51, appointed 1993.
Sound academic school; friendly atmosphere; strong sport.

Profile
Background Founded 1698 (part of the Grey Coat Hospital foundation); established here 1894 on the 30-acre site of a former boys' school. Attractive, well-maintained grounds (behind an unprepossessing frontage); original classroom block dreary, battered, unadorned; later additions, including fine performing arts centre and some study-bedrooms, are models of design and practicality; £2 million sports centre planned.

Atmosphere Warm, 'community' feel: friendly, informal relations between staff and pupils; plenty of cheerful chatter but no hysterical shouting or running about ('We explain the rules to the girls and they keep them'). Non-Christians required to attend daily prayers in chapel. Day girls stay for evening prep; lessons on Saturday mornings. Boarding accommodation tidy, if slightly impersonal; refurbishment under way. Parents kept in touch through regular newsletter.

Admissions By Common Entrance or school's own exam. Entry is fairly selective; head weeds out unsuitable applicants in preliminary interview. Pupils predominantly British with a scattering from Hong Kong, Thailand. Scholarships, bursaries available.

The head Pleasant, approachable, well-regarded. Read English at Oxford; previously head of English at Cheltenham Ladies' (qv). Married (to a poet); two grown-up children.

The teaching Generally good; well-qualified, predominantly female staff. Broad curriculum: science on offer as three separate subjects; all do French from first year, Latin from second and may add German or Spanish from third. Pupils grouped by ability in maths, French; class sizes average 16–20; English taught as a foreign language to non-native speakers. Lots of computers; good labs for sciences and languages. Lots of music: most learn an instrument; two orchestras, large choir. Wide array of extra-curricular activities, including ballroom dancing, debating, Duke of Edinburgh award scheme; weekends filled with matches, excursions etc.

Results (1997) GCSE: 98% gained at least five grades A–C. A-level: 66% of entries graded A or B.

Destinations Most continue into the sixth form and proceed to university (three or four a year to Oxbridge).

Sport Good record, particularly in lacrosse; netball, tennis, athletics, squash, basketball, badminton, judo, volleyball, rowing (on the Thames) also on offer. Facilities include indoor pool; new sports hall planned.

Remarks Good all round.

QUEEN ELIZABETH'S, BARNET ♂

Queen's Road, Barnet, Hertfordshire EN5 4DQ. Tel (0181) 441 4646

Synopsis

Grammar (grant-maintained) ★ Boys ★ Ages 11–18 ★ 1,100 pupils ★ 200 in sixth form
Head: Eamonn Harris, 50, appointed 1984.
First-rate, well-run school; distinctive ethos; very good teaching and results; strong music and sport.

Profile

Background Founded 1573 by Elizabeth I as a grammar school for 'the training of boys in manners and learning' ('and this,' says the prospectus, 'remains our purpose to this day'). Moved to present 23-acre site 1930; went comprehensive 1971; opted out of council control 1989 (among the first to do so); won permission (unusually) to become fully selective again 1995. Solid, purpose-built premises plus some dismal later additions ('the accommodation,' observed Ofsted inspectors, 'does not always make a positive contribution to the quality of pupils' learning'); sixth-form block opened September 1997.

Atmosphere Firmly traditional: big emphasis on competitiveness in the classroom and on the sports field (blue plastic 'ducats' awarded for effort and achievement); high standards of behaviour expected and achieved (immaculate uniform); close links forged with parents (who are enjoined to work with, not against, the school for the benefit of their children – those not in sympathy with its ethos are strongly advised to look elsewhere). Bursaries (sponsored by local companies) in lieu of prizes for those whose 'work and motivation is consistently excellent'.

Admissions Heavily over-subscribed: all applicants take verbal and non-verbal reasoning tests; the top-scoring 500 are recalled for tests in English, maths. Of the 180 places, 160 are allocated on the basis of academic ability, 20 for musical ability. Pupils come from a wide range of backgrounds; many travel long distances (coaches arranged).

The head Tough, long-serving; leads from the front. Formerly a Dominican friar; has wide experience of the state sector. Demands success and has presided over a steady rise in standards. Not all parents warm to his laconic style but few question the thoroughness of their son's education.

The teaching Unquestionably good; generally formal in style. Experienced, hard-working staff (a third female). Broad curriculum: science on offer as three separate subjects; languages include German, Russian; very good art; lots of computing (impressive facilities). Pupils grouped by ability from first year and moved up or down on the basis of half-termly tests (Ofsted fretted that this could lead to 'low self esteem'); extension work for the able, help for the struggling; homework set regularly; parents kept closely informed. Sixth-form options include GNVQ in business studies. Lots of music (choirs, orchestras, bands). Wide range of lunch-time and after-school clubs. Good links with local commerce and industry. Regular trips abroad, including exchange with a Russian school.

Results (1967) GCSE: 83% gained at least five grades A–C. A-level: impressive 72% of entries graded A or B.

Destinations Virtually all go on to university (including Oxbridge).

Sport Played hard and fast; good on-site facilities. Main game rugby; water polo strong; Eton-fives, tennis, athletics also popular.

Remarks Identified by Ofsted (1995) as an 'outstandingly successful' school.

QUEEN ELIZABETH'S GRAMMAR, BLACKBURN ♂
West Park Road, Blackburn, Lancashire BB2 6DF. Tel (01254) 59911

Synopsis
Independent ★ Boys (plus girls in sixth form) ★ Day ★ Ages 11–18 (plus associated junior school) ★ 885 pupils ★ 278 in sixth form (85% boys) ★ Fees: £4,389
Head: Dr David Hempsall, 50, appointed 1995.
Successful, well-run school; good teaching; lots on offer.

Profile
Background Founded 1509; move to present urban site and purpose-built premises 1883; formerly Direct Grant, became independent 1979. Later additions include £1.75 million sixth-form centre; 13 acres of playing fields a short distance away.

Atmosphere Lively, purposeful; clear Christian ethos; well-organised pastoral care system; good relations between staff and well-disciplined pupils. Competitive house system.

Admissions By tests; school not unduly selective and likely to become even less so with the phasing out of assisted places, which 25% hold; numbers likely to drop, too. Pupils from a wide range of social and ethnic backgrounds in a North Lancashire catchment area with a 25-mile radius.

The head Able, experienced, innovative. Read history at Cambridge; PhD from Kent; was head of history at Rugby; his second headship. Married; two grown-up children.

The teaching Traditional in style; long-serving, predominantly male staff. Broad curriculum: science on offer as three separate subjects; all do French; German, Latin, Greek available; choice of 22 subjects at A-level. Pupils grouped by ability in most subjects. Lots of music (choirs, orchestra, various ensembles). Extra-curricular activities include well-supported Duke of Edinburgh award scheme. Regular language exchanges with schools in France, Germany.

Results (1997) GCSE: 98% gained at least five grades A–C. A-level: 47% of entries graded A or B.

Destinations Nearly all go on to university (average of 12 a year to Oxbridge).

Sport Strong soccer, cricket; regular county and national honours; girls play

netball, tennis, mixed hockey. Facilities include sports hall, indoor pool.
Remarks   Good all round.

QUEEN ELIZABETH'S GRAMMAR, HORNCASTLE ♂ ♀
West Street, Horncastle, Lincolnshire LN9 5AD. Tel (01507) 522465

Synopsis
Grammar (grant maintained) ★ Co-educational ★ Ages 11–18 ★ 678 pupils
(roughly equal numbers of girls and boys) ★ 160 in sixth form
Head: Tim Peacock, 48, appointed 1986.
Traditional academic school; good teaching and results; strong sport.

Profile
Background   Granted a charter by Elizabeth I 1571 (but roots go back to 14th
century); opted into the state sector 1944; opted out of council control 1991.
Solid, red-brick Edwardian buildings (wide corridors, big windows) plus later
additions – including technology centre, electronics workshop, business education suite – close to the town centre; some classrooms in huts; further building
under way.
Atmosphere   Calm, purposeful, well-disciplined; mutually respectful relations
between staff and pupils ('It is a school of quiet speech rather than shrill command and this gives dignity to all,' Ofsted inspectors reported). Blazer-and-tie
uniform for all.
Admissions   By Lincolnshire 11-plus: two verbal reasoning tests of 100 questions each; top 25% of the ability range from an extensive rural catchment area.
The head   Able, energetic, strong leader. Read geography at Cambridge;
taught at Manchester Grammar, Merchant Taylor's Northwood; teaches geography to first-years and sixth-formers. Married (to a librarian); three children (all
pupils here).
The teaching   Good quality; generally formal in style. Well-qualified, stable
staff. Standard national curriculum; science on offer as three separate subjects;
GCSE options include drama, media studies, home economics; choice of 20 subjects at A-level, including German, social biology, business studies. Pupils
grouped by ability in maths only from third year; average class size 25–27, reducing to 12–15 at A-level. Homework closely monitored by school and parents. Lots
of music (more than 100 learn an instrument or sing).
Results   (1997) GCSE: 99% gained at least five grades A–C. A-level: 41% of
entries graded A or B.
Destinations   About 80% stay on for A-levels; of these, 90% proceed to higher
education (average of three a year to Oxbridge).
Sport   A strength. Main games: football, cricket, hockey, tennis, netball.
Athletics, badminton, dance, cross-country, gymnastics, swimming, volleyball
also on offer. Facilities include large sports hall, 12 acres of playing fields.
Remarks   Ofsted inspectors concluded (1995): 'Standards of achievement are
high, commendably consistent and generally in line with pupils' ability. The
school offers a secure, stimulating and orderly environment.'

QUEEN ELIZABETH GRAMMAR, PENRITH ♂ ♀
Penrith, Cumbria CA11 7EG. Tel (01768) 864621

Synopsis
Grammar (grant-maintained) ★ Co-educational ★ Ages 11–18 ★ 692 pupils (55% girls) ★ 190 in sixth form
Head: Colin Birnie, 55, appointed 1994.
Traditional academic school; good teaching and results; very strong sport.

Profile
Background Founded 1564; moved to present site 1915; opted out of council control 1992; became academically selective 1993. Dispiriting collection of buildings (many classrooms in 'temporary' huts) on a pleasant campus; fine new technology block; sixth form in neighbouring annexe (a former primary school).

Atmosphere Hard-working, traditional, offset by Cumbrian friendliness; pupils happy to be here; good pastoral care. Competitive house system; uniform enforced 'with tact and sympathy'.

Admissions By primary school performance and interview with parents and children to determine 'aptitude for and interest in the academic nature of the education offered'; about 190 apply for 90 places. Pupils drawn from 25 primaries in a 400-square-mile catchment area (shared with Ullswater, qv); most from middle-class backgrounds.

The head Friendly, hard-working; devoted to the school (and keen that its buildings should match its achievements). Came here as deputy head 1978. Married; two grown-up children.

The teaching Relaxed, 'pupil-centred'; committed staff (equal numbers of men and women, 25% appointed by present head). Broad curriculum: all do French and German for first three years; first-rate technology; good results in history, geography; wide choice of 25 subjects at A-level. Pupils grouped by ability from third year; average class size 24, reducing to maximum of 16 in the sixth form. Plenty of extra-curricular activities.

Results (1997) GCSE: creditable 88% gained at least five grades A–C. A-level: 35% of entries graded A or B (modest for a grammar school but the selective intake has yet to work its way through).

Destinations About 60% proceed to higher education.

Sport Very strong; emphasis on participation; wide range of activities on offer. Particular strengths in PE, rugby (outstanding record in both), cricket, athletics; girls play hockey, lacrosse, netball. First-rate playing fields; archaic gym.

Remarks Ofsted inspectors concluded (1996): 'The school provides a very good education for its pupils with some outstanding features. Staff and pupils work hard to maximise achievement.'

QUEEN ELIZABETH GRAMMAR, WAKEFIELD ♂
Northgate, Wakefield, West Yorkshire WF1 3QX. Tel (01924) 373943

Synopsis
Independent ★ Boys ★ Ages 11–18 (plus associated junior school) ★ 726 pupils
★ 204 in sixth form ★ Fees: £4,674
Head: Robert Mardling, 53, appointed 1985.
Well-run school; fairly wide range of abilities; good teaching and results; lots of music, sport.

Profile
Background Granted a charter by Elizabeth I in 1591; moved to present rather cramped site and purpose-built 'Early Gothic Revival' premises 1854; later additions in a variety of styles. Junior school (235 boys aged seven to 11) on same site (acts as the choir school for Wakefield Cathedral).

Atmosphere Busy, friendly, well-ordered. Sixth-formers wear suits; prefects in gowns.

Admissions By tests in English, maths, verbal reasoning or Common Entrance; school is not unduly selective and likely to become even less so with the phasing out of assisted places, which nearly 200 hold. Most come from within a 20-mile radius.

The head Humane, kindly; gets on well with staff and pupils. Read German and French at Oxford; previously deputy head of Arnold (qv). Married; two children (one a pupil here).

The teaching Sound; hard-working, predominantly male staff; expectations are high. Fairly broad curriculum; science on offer as three separate subjects; all add German to French from second year; Latin on offer; wide range of A-levels (some run jointly with sister school, Wakefield Girls', qv); all do general studies. Pupils grouped by ability in maths; extra help for dyslexics; maximum class size 28, reducing to 22–24 for GCSE, smaller for A-levels. Lots of music: choirs, two orchestras, various ensembles. Extra-curricular activities include popular Duke of Edinburgh award scheme.

Results (1997) GCSE: 98% gained at least five grades A–C. A-level: 49% of entries graded A or B (not a good year).

Destinations About 90% go on to university (average of 10 a year to Oxbridge).

Sport Wide range on offer; particular strengths in rugby, cricket, hockey, athletics. Facilities include 37 acres of playing fields (a short walk away), athletics track, all-weather pitch.

Remarks Good all round.

QUEEN ELIZABETH'S HOSPITAL ♂
Berkeley Place, Clifton, Bristol BS8 1JX. Tel (0117) 929 1856

Synopsis
Independent ★ Boys ★ Day and boarding ★ Ages 11–18 ★ 534 pupils (87% day) ★ 143 in sixth form ★ Fees: £4,335 day; £7,899 boarding
Head: Dr Richard Gliddon, 57, appointed 1985.
Sound, traditional school; nearly half receive help with fees; strong sport.

Profile

Background Founded 1590 on the model of Christ's Hospital (qv) to educate bright boys who could not afford the fees (and still does - see below); formerly Direct Grant. Moved to present, rather restricted, urban site 1847; main building is mock-Gothic and forbidding (quadrangle reminiscent of a prison exercise yard); interior gloomy (narrow corridors, steep staircases) and fairly shabby; some classrooms dismal. Assembly hall accommodates the whole school; library houses 12,000 volumes. Later additions include well-equipped science labs, new design/technology centre, superb theatre.

Atmosphere Happy, purposeful, tightly-disciplined (mandatory expulsion for drugs, stealing, bullying); strong pastoral care system. Ofsted noted carefully (1996): 'The school has made a start in teaching pupils the importance of respect for women.' Formal uniform (suit and tie) but socially unpretentious ('An unvarnished grammar school,' says head). Saturday morning lessons discontinued in response to parents' wishes. Cheerful, spacious boarding accommodation (some beds empty – numbers declining); endearingly homely atmosphere in junior dormitories.

Admissions At 11 and 13 by interview and tests in English, maths, verbal reasoning shared with Bristol Grammar and Bristol Cathedral School (qv): parents state first choice; candidates 'sifted' rather than failed. School prides itself on being academically selective (pupils all in the top half of the ability range) but socially comprehensive. Phasing out of the assisted places scheme, from which 176 benefit, likely to lead to lower numbers and entry standards; co-education under consideration. Thanks to substantial endowment income (from property in Bristol) 25% hold scholarships, bursaries; 60% of boarders on reduced fees.

The head Compassionate, shrewd, enthusiastic. Strong leader; 'hands-on' style (visits classes unannounced); finds it hard to delegate. Warm relations with pupils (knows them all); teaches personal and social education to first- and fourth-years. Read zoology at London; PhD from Bristol; previously a housemaster at Clifton. Married (wife, a JP, much involved in school life); two daughters, both teachers.

The teaching Generally traditional in style (overly so in Ofsted's opinion); well-qualified staff of 50 (75% men, though proportion is decreasing), 60% appointed by present head. Fairly broad curriculum: science on offer as three separate subjects; all do Latin for first three years; GCSE options include German, music, theatre studies (but nearly half do not take an arts subject). Pupils grouped by ability in maths only from second year; extra help for the gifted and the less able; maximum class size 20 for GCSE. Art, drama, music beginning to improve. Good careers department.

Results (1997) GCSE: 99% gained at least five grades A–C. A-level: 61% of entries graded A or B.

Destinations About 90% stay on for A-levels; of these, nearly all proceed to university (about six a year to Oxbridge).

Sport Big emphasis on rugby (14 teams) and cricket (eight teams): county representatives in both. All play team games for two years then may choose alternatives: archery, fencing, gymnastics, hiking, squash, badminton, tennis, weight-training, basketball, swimming. Good facilities.

Remarks Rather old-fashioned; not for the faint-hearted.

QUEEN ELIZABETH, KIRKBY LONSDALE ♂ ♀
Kirkby Lonsdale, Carnforth, Lancashire LA6 2HJ. Tel (015242) 71275

Synopsis
Comprehensive (grant-maintained) ★ Co-educational ★ Ages 11–18 ★ 950 pupils ★ 150 in sixth form
Head: Chris Clarke, 43, appointed 1992.
Warm, hard-working school; good teaching and results.

Profile
Background   Royal charter granted 1591 but roots go back further; went comprehensive 1978; opted out of council control 1994. Attractive mixture of buildings – many recently refurbished at a cost of £1.5 million – on a beautiful site in a graceful rural town on the banks of the Lune serving areas of Cumbria, North Yorkshire and Lancashire. Bright, welcoming classrooms; well-designed art/technology centre; good library.

Atmosphere   Informal family feel, but purposeful; staffroom relaxed, friendly, endearingly chaotic; enthusiastic, well-behaved pupils here to learn.

Admissions   Extensive catchment area; most of above average ability.

The head   Youthful, shrewd; combines leadership with a team approach ('Every decision should be taken by at least two'); previously a deputy head in Dorset.

The teaching   Generally good: a well-judged mix of classroom teaching and directed study; well-qualified staff. Standard national curriculum; choice of 20 subjects at A-level; GNVQ alternatives available. Pupils grouped by ability from second year; well-organised support for those who need it; average class size 25, reducing to 20 for lower sets. Strict homework policy. Lots of drama, art, music (in good instrumental rooms). Regular language exchanges with schools in France, Germany.

Results   (1997) GCSE: creditable 68% gained at least five grades A–C. A-level: 32% of entries graded A or B.

Destinations   About 90% remain in full-time education after 16, most of them here; of these, 80% proceed to higher education (a few a year to Oxbridge).

Sport   All encouraged to participate; staff and pupils turn out on Saturday mornings. Main strengths: hockey, cricket, tennis, athletics, netball, rugby. Football, badminton, basketball, cross-country also on offer. Adequate facilities; good on-site playing fields.

Remarks   A rural comprehensive with a grammar school heritage, tailor-made for its catchment area. Recommended.

QUEEN ELIZABETH'S, WIMBORNE ♂ ♀
Wimborne Minster, Dorset BH21 4DT. Tel (01202) 885233

Synopsis
Comprehensive (voluntary-controlled) ★ Co-educational ★ Ages 13–18 ★ 1,310 pupils (roughly equal numbers of girls and boys) ★ 340 in sixth form
Head: Simon Tong, 54, appointed 1987.
Well-run, poorly funded comprehensive; good results; strong music.

Profile
Background   Result of a 1971 merger of a grammar school founded in 1497

('to teach freely Grammar to all them that will come thereunto perpetually while the world shall endure') and two secondary moderns; bleak post-war buildings (some in very poor condition – dismally designed, cheaply constructed, poorly maintained) on a lofty site on the northern edge of the town. Recent additions include European business centre, drama studio; school is short of textbooks.

Atmosphere   Mature, well-ordered: a school at ease with itself. Strong Anglican ethos; serious-minded, responsible pupils (no sign of graffiti or vandalism); supportive parents. 'Among the majority of the British public,' the prospectus notes, 'there is a long association of high standards in dress with high standards in education. QE's reputation is influenced by the behaviour and appearance of its students.'

Admissions   Pupils drawn from a 150-square-mile, semi-rural catchment area (socially and intellectually a cross-section of middle England); most from four middle schools (ages nine to 13) in Wimborne, Cranborne, Verwood, Colehill.

The head   Able, experienced. Read English at Cambridge; has taught extensively in the state sector ('It's heartbreaking: everything's in place here; all that's missing is the cash'). Keen on Renaissance Italy and old cars.

The teaching   Sound. Staff of 84, half appointed by present head. Standard national curriculum; wide choice of 23 subjects at A-level; all do general studies; a third take vocational courses. Pupils grouped by ability in most subjects; extra help for those who need it, including the gifted; maximum class size 25. Lots of art, drama; first-rate music (orchestra, wind band etc). Regular language exchanges with schools in France and Germany; some sixth-formers do work experience in Dusseldorf.

Results   (1997) GCSE: 55% gained at least five grades A–C. A-level: 30% of entries graded A or B.

Destinations   About 65% continue into the sixth form; of these, 60% proceed to university.

Sport   Emphasis on sport for all; particular strengths in swimming, athletics, hockey. Extensive playing fields; school has day-time use of on-site council leisure centre.

Remarks   Ofsted inspectors concluded (1996): 'Queen Elizabeth's is a very good school. Standards of achievement are generally good. Students are courteous and friendly, and behave very well in the great majority of lessons. The accommodation varies greatly in quality.'

QUEEN MARGARET'S ♀
Escrick Park, York YO4 6EU. Tel (01904) 728261

Synopsis
Independent ★ Girls ★ Boarding and some day ★ Ages 11–18 ★ 360 pupils (91% boarding) ★ 100 in sixth form ★ Fees: £11,316 boarding; £7,170 day
Head: Dr Geoffrey Chapman, 54, appointed 1993.
Fine, traditional school; very good teaching and results; first-rate facilities.

Profile
Background   Founded 1901 in Scarborough; moved to present site 1949. Magnificent 18th-century mansion (former home of Sir Thomas Knyvet, discoverer of the Gunpowder Plot) plus later additions in 50 acres of serenely beautiful

parkland; riding school has stabling for girls' own horses; art & design centre in restored mill house.

Atmosphere   Gracious setting heightens the sense of privilege: girls drift happily about, unconcerned, unpressurised, appreciative. Strong emphasis on Christian values; voluntary eucharist in tiny, basement Lady Chapel.

Admissions   By Common Entrance; school is quite selective. Comfortable boarding accommodation: juniors in four- to six-bed dormitories; sixth-formers have study bedrooms in a group of converted cottages. Good choice of food; vegetarian alternative always available. Some scholarships, occasional bursaries.

The head   Courteous, reserved, scholarly. Read classics at Oxford; became professor of classics at Natal University, South Africa; returned to Britain and became head of classics at Christ's Hospital (qv). Married (wife is head of drama here); two children.

The teaching   Good quality; varied styles. Fairly broad curriculum: science on offer as three separate subjects (seven labs); all do two years' Latin; good facilities for home economics ('for examination or for leisure'), art & design (including pottery, sculpture); lots of computing. Wide choice of subjects at A-level, including business studies, theatre studies, Spanish; extra preparation for Oxbridge entry. Pupils grouped by ability in maths, languages from second year; progress carefully monitored. Good drama (400-seat theatre); high standard of music (large choral society). Extra-curricular activities include public speaking, thriving Duke of Edinburgh award scheme.

Results   (1997) GCSE: all gained at least five grades A–C. A-level: 67% of entries graded A or B.

Destinations   About 85% stay on for A-levels; of these, virtually all proceed to university (about three a year to Oxbridge).

Sport   Plays an important role in school life. Very strong lacrosse, hockey, tennis. Netball, badminton, squash, golf, swimming and riding also on offer. Facilities include sports hall, large indoor pool, nine-hole golf course, and squash courts.

Remarks   Very good all round; balances academic goals with a country way of life. Recommended.

QUEEN MARY'S GRAMMAR ♂
Sutton Road, Walsall WS1 2PG. Tel (01922) 720696

Synopsis
Grammar (grant-maintained) ★ Boys (plus a few girls in sixth form) ★ Day ★ Ages 11–18 (plus associated prep school) ★ 653 pupils ★ 179 in sixth form
Head: Stuart Holtam, 48, appointed 1995.
Traditional grammar school; very good teaching and results.

Profile
Background   Founded 1554 (part of the Queen Mary's foundation, which includes Queen Mary's High, qv); has always produced many of the town's doctors, dentists, lawyers, accountants, teachers and business people (known locally as the 'Queen Mary's mafia'). Moved to present site on an affluent edge of town early 1960s; opted out of council control 1993. Attractive (but ageing) purpose-built premises: spacious, airy classrooms around two quadrangles; lots of wood panelling and parquet floors; hall holds entire school. Some facilities

need up-grading; £1 million appeal in progress. School owns outdoor centre in North Wales.

Atmosphere   Energetic, formal, traditional. Firm discipline; staff wear academic gowns to assembly; strict uniform; school conscious of its history.

Admissions   Heavily over-subscribed: nearly 700 apply for 96 places; verbal reasoning test identifies the top 200, who take further tests in non-verbal reasoning and maths. Extensive catchment area includes Handsworth, Sutton Coldfield, Rugeley, Lichfield; pupils drawn from 50 'feeder' primaries; 20% ethnic minorities.

The head   Promoted from within; has taught here for 25 years; lives on site. Read geography at Manchester. Married; two daughters.

The teaching   High quality; formal in style; long-serving staff; interested, responsive pupils. National curriculum plus; science on offer as three separate subjects (but computing is rather rudimentary). Pupils grouped by ability in maths, French (top sets take GCSE in both a year early) and Latin; average class size 24 up to GCSE; progress carefully monitored. All take three A-levels plus general studies. Lots of music, singing. Extra-curricular activities include well-supported cadet force, Duke of Edinburgh award scheme; very strong chess.

Results   (1997) GCSE: 99% gained at least five grades A–C. A-level: 37% of entries graded A or B (not a good year).

Destinations   Nearly all go on to university (up to 10 a year to Oxbridge).

Sport   Particular strengths in rugby, cricket, cross-country; hockey, athletics, tennis, squash also on offer. Facilities include 24 acres of playing fields.

Remarks   Ofsted inspectors concluded (1995): 'An emphasis on rigorous thinking and varied teaching methods leads to high achievement'. Money is tight.

QUEEN MARY'S HIGH ♀
Upper Forster Street, Walsall WS4 2AE. Tel (01922) 721013

Synopsis
Grammar (grant-maintained) ★ Girls ★ Ages 11–18 ★ 686 pupils ★ 210 in sixth form
Head: Mrs Ann Denny, 54, appointed 1991.
First-rate traditional grammar school; very good teaching and results.

Profile
Background   Founded 1893 next door to Queen Mary's Grammar (qv); took over the premises when the boys moved to a new site in 1966; opted out of council control 1993; achieved language college status 1996. Shabby but oddly attractive Victorian-Gothic and hugger-mugger brick buildings; spacious, high-ceilinged classrooms; cloisters enclosed to make room for canteen; basement converted for technology; home economics block looks like a small factory.

Atmosphere   Happy, hard-working; school firmly rooted in local academic tradition and belief in bettering oneself; head tells pupils to 'reach for the stars' in life; strong feeling of community, shared identity. Distinctive striped blazers (known as 'deck-chairs').

Admissions   Heavily over-subscribed (more than 700 apply annually for 96 places); entry by school's own tests in maths, verbal and non-verbal reasoning.

The head   Very able: firm leadership spiced with humanity. Educated at grammar school and Liverpool University; extensive teaching experience in different types of school. Champions single-sex education for girls (has two daughters).

The teaching   Strong right across the academic spectrum: enthusiastic staff (a third appointed by present head) run themselves into the ground. Science is particularly good (on offer as three separate subjects); also languages (all do two from French, German, Spanish, Japanese); Latin compulsory for three years; technology becoming popular (the cerebral end of it); lots of computers. Good music (choirs, orchestras); drama less high-profile. Lots of theatre trips, language exchanges, charity events.

Results   (1997) GCSE: all gained at least five grades A–C. A-level: 51% of entries graded A or B.

Destinations   Almost all stay for A-levels and proceed to university (up to 10 a year to Oxbridge).

Sport   Cramped site affords few opportunities but most girls play something without seeming to make much song and dance about it. Gym is adequate but hardly state of the art.

Remarks   Ofsted inspectors concluded (1996): 'This is a very good school with some outstanding features. The behaviour of pupils is excellent and they are eager to learn. An atmosphere of purpose pervades the school at all levels.'

QUEEN'S, CHESTER ♀
City Walls Road, Chester, Cheshire CH1 2NN. Tel (01244) 312078

> ### Synopsis
> Independent ★ Girls ★ Day ★ Ages 11–18 (plus associated junior school) ★
> 468 pupils ★ 130 in sixth form ★ Fees: £4,725
> Head: Miss Diana Skilbeck, 55, appointed 1989.
> *First-rate academic school; very good teaching and results; strong sport.*

Profile
Background   Founded 1878 for the 'education of the daughters of the middle classes'; moved to present rather restricted site (donated by the first Duke of Westminster) 1884; formerly Direct Grant, became fully independent 1976; strong links maintained with Chester Cathedral. Original Victorian buildings (cloisters, pepperpot towers, terracotta tiles) much extended and modernised; further refurbishment urgently needed; new science labs under construction. Junior school about a mile away.

Atmosphere   Traditional, busy, highly academic; portraits of founders, former heads and pupils line the walls. Smart, distinctive uniform worn with pride; sixth-formers in smart casual wear.

Admissions   Over-subscribed (about 130 apply for 72 places, 26 of which are virtually guaranteed to girls from the junior school); very selective. Entry at 11 by exams in English, maths, verbal reasoning and interview (with parents only); about 40% join from primary schools. Catchment area extends to North Wales, Shropshire, Cheshire, The Wirral. Phasing out of assisted places, which about 50 hold, will reduce the social mix. Scholarships, bursaries available.

The head   Shrewd, kind, matter-of-fact; runs a harmonious school. Read geography at London, taught in grammar schools; previously head for six years of Sheffield High (qv). Teaches history to first-years; keen on inland waterways.

The teaching   Challenging; formal in style. Experienced, well-qualified staff of 46 (six men). Broad curriculum: science (very strong – many go on to read medicine, veterinary sciences) offered as three separate subjects; Latin, Greek, German on offer; all take at least nine GCSEs followed by three A-levels (from a choice of 24) plus general studies and a foreign language. Pupils grouped by ability in maths, French from second year; maximum class size 24, reducing to 20 for GCSE, maximum of 12 at A-level. Strong music (some in conjunction with boys at King's, Chester, qv): two choirs, two orchestras, various ensembles. Extracurricular activities include well-supported Christian Union, Duke of Edinburgh award scheme, debating, drama. Annual language exchanges with schools in France, Germany.

Results (1997) GCSE: 98% gained at least five grades A–C. A-level: 65% of entries graded A or B.

Destinations Virtually all go on to university (average of seven or eight to Oxbridge).

Sport Main sports (all strong): hockey, lacrosse, tennis; regular district, county, national honours. Netball, rounders, swimming, athletics, badminton, cricket, croquet, gymnastics, volleyball also on offer. Facilities include two playing fields, indoor pool.

Remarks Very good all round.

QUEEN'S, TAUNTON ♂ ♀

Trull Road, Taunton, Somerset TA1 4QS. Tel (01823) 272559

Synopsis

Independent ★ Co-educational ★ Day and boarding ★ Ages 12–18 (plus associated junior school) ★ 481 pupils (53% boys, 61% day) ★ 152 in sixth form ★ Fees: £6,606 day; £10,080 boarding
Head: Christopher Bradnock, 55, appointed 1991.
Sound, traditional school; good teaching and results; lots of music, sport.

Profile

Background Founded by Methodists 1843; moved 1846 to purpose-built premises in 30 acres on the outskirts of the town; later additions include design/technology centre, music school. Nursery, pre-prep and junior schools on same site.

Atmosphere Happy, unpretentious, well-ordered; good pastoral care; full-time chaplain. Uniform worn throughout. Lessons on Saturday mornings.

Admissions By Common Entrance or school's own tests in English, maths, verbal reasoning; 60% join from the junior school (but strugglers weeded out). School is not unduly selective, and may become even less so with the phasing out of assisted places, which 80 hold. Day pupils from 25-mile radius; some boarders from abroad (English taught as a foreign language). Boarding accommodation comfortable but not luxurious; juniors in dormitories; most sixth-formers have single study-bedrooms. Scholarships (academic, music) and bursaries available.

The head Caring, sympathetic, has time for everyone; practising Methodist; keen to promote family values. Read theology and English at Cambridge; choral singer; accomplished sportsman (rugby, tennis, cricket); previously deputy head of a Methodist school in Harrogate. Married (to a GP); three sons.

The teaching Generally good; hard-working, long-serving staff (one third female). Fairly broad curriculum; science on offer as three separate subjects; all do French and Spanish for GCSE; religious studies compulsory; choice of 21 subjects at A-level. Pupils grouped by ability from the start; further setting in most subjects thereafter; progress closely monitored (half-termly assessment cards to parents); specialist help for dyslexics; maximum class size 26, reducing to 14 in the sixth form. Plenty of art, drama; good music (half learn an instrument; large orchestra, choir). Extra-curricular activities include debating, bridge, strongly supported Duke of Edinburgh award scheme. Regular language exchanges with pupils in France, Spain.

Results (1997) GCSE: 96% gained at least five grades A–C. A-level: 55% of entries graded A or B.

Destinations Up to 80% go on to university.

Sport Good facilities; lots on offer; full fixture lists. Main games: rugby, hockey (boys' and girls'), cricket, netball, tennis. Fencing, athletics, swimming, badminton also on offer.

Remarks A thorough education for average children.

QUEENSWOOD ♀
Shepherd's Way, Brookmans Park, Hatfield, Hertfordshire AL9 6NS. Tel (01707) 652262

Synopsis
Independent ★ Girls ★ Boarding and day ★ Ages 11–18 ★ 386 pupils (82% boarding) ★ 103 in sixth form ★ Fees: £11,469–£12,495 boarding; £7,707–£7,174 day
Head: Ms Clarissa Farr, 39, appointed 1996.
Good small school in attractive setting; strong sport; lots of music, art, drama.

Profile
Background Founded 1894 by two Methodist ministers; moved to beautiful Green Belt site 1925. Buildings in a variety of styles (country house vernacular to 1960s monstrosity) surrounded by 120 acres of gardens and woodlands; some classes in 'temporary' huts; recent additions include new teaching block (bright, airy classrooms), luxurious sports centre.

Atmosphere Calm, spacious, orderly. Friendly relations between staff and pupils; well-organised pastoral care system. School work on display everywhere. Strict (purple and grey) uniform below sixth form. Boarding accommodation being upgraded: juniors in small carpeted dormitories; seniors in attractive attic rooms (but bathrooms are spartan). Day girls can stay for supper (good choice of food). Drugs dealt with 'on an individual basis'; fines or community service for smoking, drinking. Strong parental involvement. Carol Thatcher was a pupil here.

Admissions By Common Entrance at 11, 12, 13; school is fairly selective (top 30% of the ability range); pupil numbers holding steady. Entry to sixth form is more competitive (six GCSEs A–C – A or B grades in intended A-level subjects). About 80% live within 50-mile radius; significant numbers are Muslim, Jewish, Hindu; 15% from abroad (mainly Far East). Scholarships (academic, music, tennis) and bursaries available.

The head Friendly, sensible; clear sense of direction and purpose. Recent (and youthful) appointment; was previously a deputy here (her mother was a pupil). Read English at Exeter; taught in state schools and Hong Kong; runs marathons. Married (to a sports journalist); two children.

The teaching   Generally good; relatively youthful staff, 25% male. Broad curriculum; all do French and German from the start; Spanish, Italian also on offer (but no classics); computing, seen as a 'life skill', used across the curriculum (13-year-olds have laptops). Pupils grouped by ability in English, maths, science (dual award), languages; limited help for those with special needs; English as a foreign language on offer. Most take nine GCSEs and three A-levels (emphasis on arts and humanities – options include theatre studies, Christian theology); all sixth-formers do general studies, computing, PE. Strong music: 60% learn at least one instrument (recital hall, 20 practice rooms); orchestra, various ensembles, three choirs. Art popular (artist in residence) but facilities rather cramped. Popular Duke of Edinburgh award scheme. Regular exchange visits to France, Germany, Denmark, Spain.

Results   (1997) GCSE: 99% gained at least five grades A–C. A-level: 45% of entries graded A or B.

Destinations   Nearly all go to university (four or five a year to Oxbridge).

Sport   Strong: policy is sport for all. Tennis taken seriously; facilities include largest clay court centre in UK; 200 have individual or group coaching; many girls play at national or county level. Also on offer: hockey (eight pitches, one all-weather) athletics, badminton, netball, trampolining, swimming (indoor pool).

Remarks   Friendly school; good all round.

RADLEY ♂
Abingdon, Oxford OX14 2HR. Tel (01235) 543000

Synopsis
Independent ★ Boys ★ Boarding ★ Ages 13–18 ★ 610 pupils ★ 240 in sixth form ★ Fees: £13,650
Head: Richard Morgan, 57, appointed 1991.
Fine, traditional boarding school; very good teaching and results; superb facilities.

Profile
Background   Founded 1847 to reform and civilise public schooling, placing religious observance and Christian values at the centre of the community, with an emphasis on beautiful artefacts, art, buildings and grounds. Gracious 18th-century country house plus numerous additions in 800 idyllic acres (some laid out by 'Capability' Brown) five miles south of Oxford; most recent additions include new (circular) classroom block and library.

Atmosphere   Very traditional; elaborate rules and customs; first-years ('shells') take two weeks to learn a whole new vocabulary. All boys wear short hair and academical gowns; any tempted to be different are reminded of a previous head's dictum, 'Suede shoes lead to drug abuse'; seniors complain it is like a very large prep school. Warm relations between staff ('dons') and pupils (in accordance with the founder's intentions); nearly all staff live on site. Compulsory chapel five times a week (two resident chaplains); all given a pocket Bible when they join.

Admissions   By Common Entrance; average mark 55%–60% (though some pupils are less able than that implies – yet thrive, none the less); demand for places is strong. Most from upper and upper-middle class homes 'where parents have traditional values'; many are sons of Old Radleians; catchment area stretches from Scotland to Cornwall. Early registration advised; waiting list currently for 2005. Eight boarding houses ('socials'); younger boys have their own cubicles, older boys their own bedsits; HMC inspectors noted a lack of privacy in showers and bathrooms. Good food in oak-panelled dining hall (complete with high table and portraits). Scholarships available (academic, art, music).

The head (Warden) Relentlessly enthusiastic; firm disciplinarian ('If there is no discipline there are no standards'); has introduced many changes (more than half the staff have been replaced) and overseen a steady rise up the league table. Believes a good school is one that 'expects you to show mental toughness and a quality of steel in your spiritual life, your intellect and in your games'. Read economics and law at Cambridge; taught here for 15 years and then became head of Cheltenham, where he stayed 12 years. Married; three daughters.

The teaching First-rate: able, hard-working staff; well-prepared, well-informed lessons. Broad curriculum: science taught as three separate subjects; all do French; Latin, Greek, German, Spanish, Mandarin on offer (all study one foreign language throughout their time here 'with the intention of attaining a high degree of fluency by the time they leave'); lots of computing ('a high degree of competence is essential'). All take 10 or 11 GCSEs and three A-levels plus general studies and religious education. Pupils grouped by ability in maths, languages; work marked with grades and copious comments; detailed reports to parents. Facilities for technology, art and music are outstanding. Wide range of extra-curricular activities, including beagling (twice a week in winter), campanology, racing, stocks and shares, trout fishing, compulsory cadet force, well-supported Duke of Edinburgh award scheme; all participate in 'declamations' (public speaking).

Results (1997) GCSE: all gained at least five grades A–C. A-level: very creditable 80% of entries graded A or B (school has risen steadily from 75th in the league table in 1993 to 20th).

Destinations Nearly all stay on for A-levels and proceed to university (average of 20 a year to Oxbridge).

Sports Magnificent facilities include indoor sports complex (used by local schools and the community), heated pool (with a very deep end for sub-aqua diving), floodlit all-weather hockey pitch, nine-hole golf course, 20 hard tennis courts, athletics track, boathouse (130 boats) on the college's four-mile stretch of river. Main activities: rugby (up to 20 teams fielded), rowing, cricket, tennis, athletics. Basketball, cross-country, judo, fencing, squash, fives, rackets also on offer.

Remarks HMC inspectors concluded (1995): 'Radley is running well. The academic standards achieved are high; motivation and learning are good. The dons are energetic and their dedication is impressive. The pupils' behaviour is excellent. The college has a very pleasant atmosphere and is following the founder's intentions remarkably closely.'

RADYR ♂ ♀

Heol Islaf, Radyr, Cardiff CF4 8XG. Tel (01222) 842059

Synopsis

Comprehensive ★ Co-educational ★ Ages 11–18 ★ 1,224 pupils (equal numbers of girls and boys) ★ 275 in sixth form
Head: Steven Fowler, 46, appointed 1995.
First-rate school; good teaching and results; strong sport.

Profile

Background   Purpose-built in 1972; attractive 44-acre campus surrounded by farms and woodland on the edge of an expanding, up-market residential area five miles north of Cardiff. Functional, flat-roofed buildings plus some recent additions on inconvenient split-level site (numerous inter-connecting flights of steps); school feels crowded.

Atmosphere   A school with real heart – a bustling community. Enthusiastic staff encourage lively pupils to make the most of their opportunities. Firm and consistent discipline; misdemeanours picked up immediately. Supportive parents maintain the mini-bus fleet and raise £12,000–£14,000 a year.

Admissions   Heavy pressure on places; most pupils from middle-class, professional backgrounds.

The head   Read geography; taught in comprehensives and community colleges in Humberside and Devon. Married; two children.

The teaching   Big emphasis on academic excellence, but in a friendly, non-threatening way. Impressive, hard-working staff of 72 (roughly equal numbers of women and men). Standard national curriculum; particularly good results in maths, science, modern languages; first-rate art. Pupils grouped by ability from second year. Extra-curricular activities include music, drama, photography, debating, community service. Regular language exchanges with schools in France, Germany.

Results   (1997) GCSE: creditable 68% gained at least five grades A–C. A-level: 43% of entries graded A or B.

Destinations   About 65% continue into the sixth form; of these, 90% proceed to university.

Sport   Enthusiastic staff; committed PE teaching for all. Main activities: hockey, netball, dance for girls; rugby, soccer, cricket for boys; joint athletics, tennis (12 courts), swimming (good indoor pool). County representatives in every sport. Well-equipped gym but no sports hall.

Remarks   Successful, welcoming school. Recommended.

RAINFORD HIGH ♂ ♀
Higher Lane, Rainford, St Helens WA11 8NY. Tel (01744) 885914

Synopsis
Comprehensive ★ Co-educational ★ Ages 11–18 ★ 1,709 pupils (equal numbers of girls and boys) ★ 298 in sixth form
Head: Brian Arnold, 54, appointed 1994.
Large, well-run school; good teaching and results; strong sport.

Profile

Background   Founded 1940; became a secondary modern and then a comprehensive. Variety of buildings (none distinguished but all adequate) in 25 acres bordering open country; purpose-built sixth-form centre.

Atmosphere   Crowded, bustling; everywhere scrupulously clean. Strong (and competitive) house system; good pastoral care. Relaxed but professional relations between pupils and staff (many of whom send their own children here). Neat blazer-and-tie uniform below the sixth form. Cabinets full of silverware attest to sporting prowess.

Admissions   Over-subscribed but non-selective; priority to those attending six 'feeder' primaries; fairly wide social mix but predominantly middle-class.

The head Read chemistry at Leeds and has taught widely in both the independent and state sectors; previously the successful head of a comprehensive in Lancashire. Accepts the need for innovation but also values the traditional virtues. Married (to a teacher); two grown-up children.

The teaching High quality; well-motivated, stable staff of 110 (equal numbers of women and men). Standard national curriculum; science on offer as three separate subjects; choice of 30 subjects for GCSE, including German and Spanish, 23 at A-level, including psychology, theatre studies, PE; GNVQs available in business, health & social care, art & design. Pupils grouped by ability after first half-term; extra help for those who need it (at both ends of the ability range); class sizes 20–22, reducing to a maximum of 14 at A-level. Strong music department; choirs, bands, orchestra; regular drama productions. Big choice of out-of-school activities; 300 take part in Duke of Edinburgh award scheme. Strong links with European schools.

Results (1997) GCSE: 64% gained at least five grades A–C. A-level: 42% of entries graded A or B.

Destinations About 60% stay on for A-levels; of these, 90% proceed to higher education (average of seven a year to Oxbridge).

Sport Wide range of activities, chiefly rugby, football, hockey, cricket, athletics; town, regional and national honours. First-rate facilities include large sports hall, all-weather pitch (but no swimming pool).

Remarks First-class all-round education.

RAINHAM MARK ♂ ♀
Pump Lane, Gillingham, Kent ME8 7AJ. Tel (01634) 364151

Synopsis
Grammar (grant-maintained) ★ Co-educational ★ Ages 11–18 ★ 1,100 pupils (57% boys) ★ 302 in sixth form
Head: Peter Limm, 47, appointed 1996.
Traditional grammar school; good teaching; sound results.

Profile
Background Opened 1966 as a boys' technical school; went co-educational 1972; became a grammar school in the early 1980s; opted out of council control 1992. Functional buildings, recently up-graded, on a 22-acre site overlooking the Medway estuary.

Atmosphere Friendly, business-like; emphasis on 'reward rather than punishment, self-control rather than regimentation, achievement rather than failure'. Prefect system; blazer-and-tie uniform below the sixth form.

Admissions School over-subscribed (about two apply for each place); entry by Kent selections tests in English, maths, verbal reasoning; top 25% of the ability range. Most pupils from middle-class homes.

The head Crisp, energetic, very experienced. Read history at Cambridge; has taught in both state and independent schools and worked as an inspector; previously deputy head at Tunbridge Wells Girls' Grammar and Tonbridge Girls' Grammar. Teaches A-level history, government & politics. Married; two children.

The teaching Good quality; experienced staff (60% male). Standard national curriculum; French, German, Spanish on offer (some take all three); wide choice of 25 subjects at A-level. Pupils grouped by ability in maths, modern languages; some take GCSEs a year early; extra help for dyslexics; average class size 22, reducing to a maximum of 17 at A-level. Lots of music; more than 100 learn an instrument; choirs, orchestra, various ensembles. Regular language exchanges with pupils in France, Germany.

Results (1997) GCSE: 98% gained at least five grades A–C. A-level: 40% of entries graded A or B.

Destinations About 80% go on to higher education.

Sport Main strengths: soccer, netball, hockey. Adequate playing fields; community facilities near by.

Remarks Ofsted inspectors concluded (1994): 'The school has achieved a balance between the demands of an academically rigorous and successful institution and the aim to create a caring and mutually respectful community.'

RANELAGH ♂ ♀

Ranelagh Drive, Bracknell, Berkshire RG12 9DA. Tel (01344) 421233

Synopsis

Comprehensive (voluntary-aided, Church of England) ★ Co-educational ★ Ages 11–18 ★ 635 pupils (equal number of girls and boys) ★ 185 in sixth form
Head: Mrs Kathy Winrow, 45, appointed 1993.
First-rate comprehensive; good teaching and results; strong Christian ethos.

Profile

Background Founded 1709 by Lord Ranelagh for 12 boys and 12 girls; subsequently became a co-educational grammar school; went comprehensive 1981. Traditional early 20th-century grammar school buildings with many later additions (including new music centre) on a pleasant (but rapidly filling) site. Ofsted reported (1995): 'The accommodation is barely adequate for current needs.'

Atmosphere Noticeably friendly. High standards of behaviour; respectful but relaxed relations between pupils and teachers; well-organised pastoral care system. Strong Christian ethos; much community work; supportive parents.

Admissions School is heavily over-subscribed: selection by religious criteria not academic ability; priority to those with close affiliation to the Church in four Berkshire deaneries.

The head Friendly without being effusive; has high expectations of staff and pupils. Read geography at London; previously a local education authority inspector. Teaches religious education to the sixth form.

The teaching Mainly good: a mixture of formal instruction and modern, more pupil-friendly methods geared to a fairly wide range of abilities; progress carefully monitored; on-site unit for those with special needs. French a particular strength; German, Latin on offer; GNVQs available in business and health & social care. Good music, drama; wide range of extra-curricular activities.

Results (1997) GCSE: creditable 84% gained at least five grades A–C. A-level: 47% of entries graded A or B.

Destinations Nearly all go on to university, including up to eight a year to Oxbridge.

Sport A strength. Main games: rugby, hockey, football, basketball, netball, tennis, cricket, rounders, athletics; volleyball, softball, baseball, gymnastics, dance, aerobics also on offer. Good sports centre near by.

Remarks   Ofsted inspectors concluded: 'This is a good school, held in high esteem by the local community.'

RANGE HIGH ♂ ♀
Stapleton Road, Formby, Liverpool L37 2YN. Tel (01704) 879315

Synopsis
Comprehensive ★ Co-educational ★ Ages 11–18 ★ 1,108 pupils (more boys than girls) ★ 165 in sixth form
Head: Michael Dixon, 46, appointed 1992.
First-rate school; good teaching and results; lots of extra-curricular activities.

Profile
Background   Opened 1975; neat, single-storey buildings on a 20-acre campus in an affluent, residential area of the town; some classrooms in huts.
Atmosphere   Busy, well-ordered; cordial relations between staff and pupils. Good work, effort and social skills recognised by gold, silver, bronze merit awards (pupils respond eagerly); smart uniform worn by all. Physically disabled children well provided for and fully integrated. Supportive parents help raise funds.
Admissions   Over-subscribed; no academic selection. Priority to siblings, those from traditional 'feeder' primaries and physically disabled children suitable for mainstream education. About 80% come from Formby, mostly from middle-class backgrounds; catchment area extends from Southport to Liverpool.
The head   Dignified, scholarly; totally committed to the school; gets on well with staff and pupils. Read English at Cambridge. Married; three children.
The teaching   Good quality: varied styles; pupils actively involved. Experienced staff of 72 (25% have been here more than 15 years). Standard national curriculum; all do French and German. Pupils grouped by ability in maths from second year, English, French, German from third year; extra help for the more able; average class size 27. Choice of 20 subjects at A-level; GNVQs on offer. Wide range of extra-curricular activities, including music (choir, orchestra), drama, computing, gardening, well-supported Duke of Edinburgh award scheme.
Results   (1997) GCSE: 65% gained at least five grades A–C. A-level: 49% of entries graded A or B.
Destinations   About half continue into the sixth form; of these, 75% proceed to university.
Sport   Lots on offer, ranging from team sports to leisure pursuits; everyone participates. Facilities include extensive playing fields (football, hockey, rugby), all-weather pitch, large sports hall.
Remarks   Identified by Ofsted (1996) as an 'outstanding' school with a deservedly high reputation for academic success.

RANNOCH ♂ ♀
Rannoch, By Pitlochry, Perthshire PH17 2QQ. Tel (01882) 632332

Synopsis
Independent ★ Co-educational ★ Boarding (and some day) ★ Ages 10–18 ★ 230 pupils (67% boys, 96% boarding) ★ 80 in sixth form ★ Fees: £9,330–£11,205 boarding; £5,880 day
Head: Dr John Halliday, 41, appointed April 1997.
Fine outdoor school; magnificent setting; wide range of abilities; small classes.

Profile
Background Founded 1959 by three teachers from Gordonstoun (qv) on the character-building principles expounded by Kurt Hahn; splendidly isolated 120-acre Highland estate on the south shore of Loch Rannoch, 25 miles from the nearest town (surrounding countryside used as an adventure playground). Main building is an eye-catching mid-Victorian Scottish baronial mansion recently restored and re-decorated; later additions include new technology centre. Co-educational since 1983.
Atmosphere Happy, close-knit community (compulsory chapel in converted farm building); confident, cheerful, refreshingly natural pupils. Regime still fairly robust but less rugged and spartan than it was: not, however, for the unadventurous or comfort-loving. Staff-pupil relations are excellent without being over-familiar (teachers get to know the children well out of the classroom).
Admissions At ages 10–12 by test and interview, at 13 by Common Entrance; school is barely selective and is prepared to accept those with mild learning difficulties; decline in numbers is likely to be exacerbated by phasing out of assisted places (which about 50 hold). Pupils' backgrounds include business, farming, industry, professions; 55% from Scotland, 10% foreign nationals. Boys' boarding accommodation recently refurbished (but creature comforts are few); girls better provided for in new purpose-built house. Good food.
The head New appointment (predecessor had been in post 15 years). Read German and linguistics at Exeter; PhD from Cambridge; previously a housemaster at Sedbergh (qv). Married; three young children.
The teaching Sound; emphasis on a good grounding for younger pupils in English, maths, French; science taught as three separate subjects from age 13 (labs recently refurbished); German on offer in addition to French. Pupils grouped by ability in most subjects; extra help for those with special needs; average class size 14, smaller in the sixth form. Nearly all take at least seven Standard Grades from choice of 15 (English and maths compulsory); 85% stay on for four or five Highers (over two years); a few take A-levels. Lots of music: nearly three-quarters learn an instrument; 60-strong choir; regular informal concerts. Pupil-run services (in the Hahn tradition) include ambulance, fire, loch patrol, mountain rescue; well-supported Duke of Edinburgh award scheme (500th gold award gained in 1995). Outdoor expeditions a regular feature of school life: hill walking, mountain climbing, cycling, canoeing, skiing, camping.
Results (1997) Standard Grade: 47% gained at least five grades 1–2.
Destinations About 85% continue into the sixth form; of these, 90% proceed to higher education.
Sport Strong. Main games: rugby, netball, hockey, skiing, athletics. Soccer, cricket, sailing, canoeing, basketball, badminton also on offer. Facilities include extensive playing fields, sports hall, three all-weather tennis courts, six-hole golf course, rifle range, heated pool.
Remarks A challenging (but unstressful) regime that breeds self-reliance.

Good choice for less academically able children who enjoy the outdoor life: many do better here academically than they would in a narrower educational environment. Recommended.

READING ♂
Erleigh Road, Reading RG1 5LW. Tel (0118) 926 1406

Synopsis
Grammar (grant-maintained) ★ Boys ★ Day and some boarding ★ Ages 11–18 ★ 766 pupils (90% day) ★ 225 in sixth form ★ Fees (boarding only): £4,650
Head: Dr Andrew Linnell, 40, appointed September 1997.
First-rate, traditional, academic school; very good teaching and results; lots of art, drama, music; strong sport.

Profile
Background   Founded 1125; re-founded 1560 by Elizabeth I (who made its upkeep the responsibility of Reading borough); moved to present 16-acre site and imposing, purpose-built premises 1870; opted out of council control 1991; technology college status achieved 1995. Despite recent building and refurbishment, many classrooms are in shabby 'temporary' huts – having a 'detrimental effect on the quality of provision,' Ofsted inspectors said.

Atmosphere   A firmly traditional grammar school: purposeful, busy; clear Christian ethos (daily act of worship in own chapel); mutually respectful relations between staff and articulate, confident pupils; vigorously competitive house system. Uniform of grey suit and house tie. Lessons on Saturday mornings, followed by sport.

Admissions   By highly competitive tests in English, maths, verbal reasoning; about four apply for every place. Pupils mostly from professional backgrounds in a wide and relatively prosperous catchment area; 20% join from prep schools, rest from up to 120 primaries. Two boarding houses (for 83 boys), recently refurbished (not before time); most are weekly boarders; 20% from abroad.

The head   New appointment. Read geography (PhD); previously at a boys' grammar school in Kent. Married; two young children.

The teaching   First-rate; formal in style; committed, long-serving, predominantly male staff. Fairly broad curriculum; sciences (a particular strength) taught separately; good maths (but rather rudimentary computing); all do Latin for first two years; German on offer; all take at least 10 GCSEs and three A-levels (from a choice of 17). Pupils grouped by ability in maths, French from second year, science from third year; average class size 28, reducing to a maximum of 15 in the sixth form. Lots of art, drama, music; choir, two orchestras, various ensembles. Extra-curricular activities include well-supported cadet force (up to 50% take part). Regular trips abroad for study and recreation.

Results   (1997) GCSE: all gained at least five grades A–C. A-level: very creditable 67% of entries graded A or B.

Destinations   All go on to university (average of 15 a year to Oxbridge).

Sport   Rugby and cricket (spectacular ground) are particularly strong (matches against leading independent schools); hockey, rowing, tennis, squash, cross-country, swimming also available. Facilities include indoor pool, boathouse on the Thames; some playing fields about a quarter of a mile away.

Remarks   Ofsted inspectors concluded (1996): 'This is an excellent school with an outstanding record of success in public examinations.' Recommended.

REDLAND HIGH ♀
Redland Court, Bristol BS6 7EF. Tel (0117) 924 5796

Synopsis
Independent ★ Girls ★ Day ★ Ages 11–18 (plus associated junior school) ★ 475 pupils ★ 125 in sixth form ★ Fees: £4,431
Head: Mrs Carol Lear, 56, appointed 1989.
Well-run, academic school; very good teaching and results; strong art, music, sport.

Profile
Background   Founded 1882; moved to Redland Court, a handsome 18th-century mansion, 1885; formerly Direct Grant, reverted to full independence 1976. Later additions include spacious sixth-form centre, music suite, fine library. Junior school (212 pupils aged three to 11) across the road.

Atmosphere   Calm, friendly, non-authoritarian; good relations between staff and pupils; well-developed pastoral care.

Admissions   Nearly half come from the junior school; two apply for each remaining place; entry by competitive entry tests shared with Colston's and Red Maids'; school is fairly selective.

The head   Very able; much liked and respected by staff and pupils. Read classics at University College, London; came here to teach it in 1971; previously deputy head. Still teaches Latin and Greek. Married; no children.

The teaching   Very good: mostly formal in style; professional, committed, predominantly female staff. Broad curriculum: sciences taught separately; languages (particularly good results) include Latin, Greek, German. Pupils grouped by ability in some subjects; average class size 20–25, smaller in the sixth form. First-rate art; lots of music (choirs, orchestras); annual performance of a French play in French. Extra-curricular activities include Young Enterprise (national finalists four times), well-supported Duke of Edinburgh award scheme. Regular language exchanges with pupils in France, Germany.

Results   (1997) GCSE: 94% gained at least five grades A–C. A-level: very creditable 72% of entries graded A or B.

Destinations   More than 90% go on to university (two or three a year to Oxbridge).

Sport   Flourishing tradition; particular strengths in hockey, netball, tennis. Cricket, rugby, fencing also on offer. Extensive playing fields a short distance away.

Remarks   Attractive school; recommended.

RED MAIDS' ♀
Westbury-on-Trym, Bristol BS9 3AW. Tel (0117) 962 2641

Synopsis
Independent ★ Girls ★ Day and boarding ★ Ages 11–18 (plus associated junior school) ★ 500 pupils (80% day) ★ 130 in sixth form ★ Fees: £8,160 boarding; £4,080 day
Head: Miss Susan Hampton, 56, appointed 1987.
Sound, traditional school; good teaching and results; lots of art, music, drama.

Profile
Background   Founded 1634 (the oldest surviving girls' school) for '40 poor

women children, daughters of burgesses deceased or decayed', who were to 'go apparelled in Red Cloth' and be taught to read, do fine needlework and be trained in some useful trade. Moved 1910 to attractive 12-acre site and purpose-built premises; later additions include good science labs, design/technology centre, music studio. Formerly Direct Grant, became fully independent 1976.

Atmosphere Calm, well-ordered; girls anxious to please (and conform). Good pastoral care; strong sense of community. Red uniform still worn (with bonnets and aprons on Founder's Day).

Admissions By tests (shared with five other Bristol schools) in English, maths, verbal reasoning); school is not unduly selective and likely to become less so with the phasing out of assisted places, which more than a third hold. Vast catchment area. Boarders (a third from Hong Kong) pleasantly accommodated but not given much to do. Some scholarships, bursaries (priority to children of one-parent families).

The head Experienced, determined; strong supporter of single-sex education for girls; knows her pupils well. Read maths at London; previously deputy head of comprehensive.

The teaching Lively. Well-qualified, predominantly female staff, a third appointed by present head. Broad curriculum: science taught (and examined) as three separate subjects; languages include Latin, Greek, Spanish, Italian, Russian; nearly all take 10 GCSEs (from a choice of 24); good results in maths. Pupils grouped by ability in maths only from third year; average class size 25. Strong music: two-thirds learn an instrument; two orchestras, choirs, various ensembles. Lots of art, drama. Regular language exchanges with schools in France, Spain, Russia.

Results (1997) GCSE: 99% gained at least five grades A–C. A-level: 64% of entries graded A or B.

Destinations About 70% stay on for A-levels; of these, 85% proceed to university (four or five a year to Oxbridge).

Sport Encouraged as 'part of healthy lifestyle'. Facilities include new sports hall, tennis courts, netball and hockey pitches.

Remarks Good all round.

REIGATE GRAMMAR ♂ ♀
Reigate Road, Reigate, Surrey RH2 0QS. Tel (01737) 222231

Synopsis
Independent ★ Becoming co-educational ★ Day ★ Ages 10–18 ★ 789 pupils (80% boys) ★ 210 in sixth form ★ Fees: £5,472
Head: Paul Dixon, 46, appointed 1996.
Unpretentious, traditional school; good teaching; strong sporting tradition.

Profile
Background Founded 1675 (on this site) by vicar of Reigate for 10 poor boys; modern foundation dates from 1862; became independent when Direct Grant status was abolished in 1976; co-educational since 1993. Victorian brick building (backing on to asphalt playground) plus many later additions, including concert hall, computing centre and ambitious new art/technology block; some classes in 'temporary' huts.

Atmosphere Structured, orderly, slightly old-fashioned ('a broadly based education of body, mind and character'); strong ethos of hard work, high standards; close links with parish church. Girls in every year from September 1998.

Admissions   Entry by school's own exam or Common Entrance: not unduly selective – and likely to become less so with the phasing out of assisted places, which more than 100 hold. Large catchment area (fleet of buses). Some scholarships.

The head   Read zoology at Oxford (Blue for basketball); previously deputy head for six years of Stockport Grammar (qv). Strongly committed to co-education ('the way to well-adjusted attitudes') and extra-curricular activities ('mere academic success is not enough'). Married (to a PE teacher); three children.

The teaching   Sound; styles range from traditional (tables in rows facing the blackboard, vocabulary tests, dictated notes) to a less formal, more lively approach; either way, academic standards are high. All do Latin for two years and two modern languages (German, Spanish on offer); science taught as three separate subjects; lots of computers. Choice of 20 subjects for A-level, including economics (very popular), business studies, theatre studies; all do general studies. Pupils grouped by ability in maths, French; average class size 25, smaller in sixth form. Very good drama; regular productions. Music thrives, but not outstanding. Good range of extra-curricular activities, including cadet force, Sea Scouts, Duke of Edinburgh award scheme. Numerous school trips, several abroad.

Results   (1997) GCSE: all gained at least five grades A–C. A-level: 61% of entries graded A or B.

Sport   Well-established tradition of rugby (up to 15 XVs), hockey, cricket; girls play hockey, netball, rounders, athletics, badminton. Sports centre, all-weather pitch and 23 acres of playing fields two miles away.

Remarks   Solid, in the best grammar school tradition.

REPTON ♂ ♀
The Hall, Repton, Derby DE65 6FH. Tel (01283) 559200

Synopsis
Independent ★ Co-educational ★ Boarding and day ★ Ages 13–18 (plus associated prep school) ★ 550 pupils (70% boys, 70% boarding) ★ 250 in sixth form ★ Fees: £12,720 boarding; £9,555 day
Head: Graham Jones, 52, appointed 1987.
Good, traditional school; first-rate teaching; strong art, music, sport.

Profile
Background   Founded 1557 on the site of a 12th-century priory 'dissolved' by Henry VIII (picturesque ruins survive); attractive buildings in 80 acres of grounds dominate the village (indeed, the school virtually is the village); some classes in original schoolroom. Magnificent library; beautiful chapel (seats everyone). Sixth-form girls admitted 1970; fully co-educational since 1992. Day pupils attend from 8 am to 9 pm. Co-educational prep school (Foremarke Hall, ages eight to 13) two miles away.

Atmosphere   Busy, hard-working: a strong sense that all know what they are supposed to be doing, and are trying their best to do it as well as possible.

Admissions   By Common Entrance (50%–55% mark required) or tests in maths, English, verbal reasoning; 40% join from associated prep school. Most from professional/business/farming families within 90 minutes' travelling time of the school. Ten comfortable boarding houses (overlooking pretty gardens), including three purpose-built for girls; younger pupils in large, carpeted dormitories ('bedders'); seniors in double or single study-bedrooms. All eat in their houses, which differ in character and engender strong loyalties. Scholarships (academic, music, art, design) and bursaries available.

The head Thoughtful, courteous. Read economics at Cambridge (First); taught at Charterhouse for 20 years (head of economics, housemaster); still teaches for a third of the timetable. Gets to know the pupils by lunching at each house in turn. Married; no children.

The teaching Good quality; dedicated staff of 65 (eight women), half appointed by the present head (all required to live within a mile of the school). Broad curriculum: science taught as three separate subjects; Latin, Greek, German on offer; most take nine GCSEs (some do maths, French a year early) and three A-levels (from a choice of 17) plus general studies. Pupils grouped by ability in all subjects from first year; performance monitored monthly; termly form orders; average class size 20. Very good art: three artists-in-residence; superb facilities. First-rate music; regular concerts (hall seats 250); lots of drama. Compulsory cadet force for two years (girls included); Duke of Edinburgh award scheme; lots of expeditions (Bolivia, Himalayas).

Results (1997) GCSE: 97% gained at least five grades A–C. A-level: 50% of entries graded A or B.

Destinations About 95% continue into the sixth form and proceed to university (average of 10 a year to Oxbridge).

Sport Very good match record, especially in cricket, lawn tennis; all participate in something every day; lots of inter-house competitions. Marvellous facilities, including 14 football pitches, three all-weather pitches, 14 tennis courts (two indoors), running track, sports hall, indoor pool etc.

Remarks Very good all round.

RINGMER ♂ ♀

Ringmer, Lewes, East Sussex BN8 5RB. Tel (01273) 812220

Synopsis

Comprehensive ★ Co-educational ★ Ages 11–16 ★ 840 pupils (equal numbers of girls and boys)
Head: John Wakely, 55, appointed 1983.
Well-run school; wide range of opportunities, including lively performing arts.

Profile

Background Opened as a secondary modern 1958; went comprehensive 1976. Unassuming, two-storey red-brick building on a spacious green-field site; some departments in 'temporary' huts; everything clean, well-maintained.

Atmosphere Busy but relaxed. Good-natured, co-operative pupils; committed, friendly staff; strong community spirit. Lively school council: pupils campaign for election and make suggestions which are often implemented. Prefects, who are given considerable responsibility, have to apply formally for the job and are interviewed by the head. Uniform basic but universally worn.

Admissions Non-selective; a third come from outside the official catchment area; a genuine, relatively unsophisticated, cross-section of rural East Sussex, mainly from farming, professional, small-business backgrounds.

The head Strong leader; firm sense of direction (describes his ideal pupil as 'one who has the sensitivity to care, the determination to work hard and the enthusiasm to join in the community life of the school'). Physicist; has taught in both grammar schools and comprehensives. Married; three grown-up daughters.

The teaching Varied, stimulating styles; core subjects conscientiously taught. Broad curriculum; all do German and French for first two years; good work in art & design; technology well-equipped but still finding its feet; GCSE options include music, drama (good results in both), dance, physical education, business studies; vocational alternatives available. Pupils grouped by ability in maths from first year, science, languages from second year; those with special needs carefully monitored and helped; extra challenges for the very able; average class size 28, smaller for GCSE. Regular grades for homework, effort, organisation and presentation. Good music (links with Glyndebourne): more than 200 learn an instrument; full orchestra, smaller ensembles, choirs; regular dance and drama productions. Extra-curricular activities include lively school newspaper run as a business, well-supported Duke of Edinburgh award scheme. Strong work experience programme and language exchanges with schools in France, Germany.

Results (1997) GCSE: 43% gained at least five grades A–C (not a good year).

Destinations Up to 90% remain in full-time education after 16.

Sport Chiefly rugby for the boys, netball for the girls; football, cricket, basketball, hockey, stoolball, badminton, athletics, swimming, gymnastics for both. Good facilities include heated indoor pool, large gym, extensive playing fields.

Remarks Thriving school; pupils of all abilities given a chance to shine. Identified by Ofsted (1995) as 'outstandingly successful'.

RIPON GRAMMAR ♂ ♀
Clotherholme Road, Ripon, North Yorkshire HG4 2DG. Tel (01765) 602647

Synopsis
Grammar ★ Co-educational ★ Day and some boarding ★ Ages 11–18 ★ 720 pupils (53% girls, 91% day) ★ 160 in sixth form ★ Fees (boarding only): £3,500–£4,740
Head: Alan Jones, 50, appointed 1992.
Strong, traditional grammar school; good teaching and results.

Profile

Background Founded 1556 (but roots go back further – claims to be the oldest grammar school in England); moved to its present wooded site on the edge of the city in the 19th century. Mixture of Victorian buildings and functional later additions; extensive building and refurbishment programme recently completed. Became co-educational 1962; now one of the few state schools to provide boarding for both boys and girls.

Atmosphere Civilised, friendly, well-disciplined. A proud school conscious of its traditions (staff and prefects wear gowns); big emphasis on hard work and high academic standards.

Admissions By county council's 11-plus test; top 30% of the ability range from a wide catchment area. Modern boarding accommodation for girls (eight-bed dormitories, seniors in single rooms); boys' house older, more spartan (but recently upgraded). Appetising meals served by friendly staff.

The head Pragmatic, purposeful. Has taught in both independent and state

schools; formerly deputy head of a comprehensive in Berkshire. Married.
The teaching   Good: mixture of traditional chalk-and-talk and more up-to-
date methods; able, long-serving staff (some here more than 20 years). National
curriculum plus; science taught as three separate subjects; all do two years' Latin
(many take it for GCSE); Greek and German on offer. Most do nine or 10 GCSEs
from a wide range; choice of 18 subjects at A-level, including good general studies course. Good library (professional librarian). Lots of music.
Results   (1997) GCSE: 96% gained at least five grades A–C. A-level: 57% of
entries graded A or B.
Destinations   Nearly all stay on for A-levels and proceed to university (about
10 a year to Oxbridge).
Sport   Strong – particularly in cricket, rugby, hockey, athletics, cross- country.
Facilities include extensive playing fields, first-class cricket pitch, good indoor
pool, all-weather tennis courts (but no sports hall).
Remarks   Ofsted inspectors concluded (1995): 'The school serves its community well and its reputation is justifiably high. Standards of achievement are high
in all subjects.' Boarding is a best buy.

ROBERT GORDON'S ♂ ♀
Schoolhill, Aberdeen AB10 1FE. Tel (01224) 646346

Synopsis
Independent ★ Co-educational ★ Day ★ Ages 4–18 ★ 1,350 pupils (920 in se-
nior school, 66% boys) ★ 285 in sixth form ★ Fees: £2,700–£4,470
Head: Brian Lockhart, 52, appointed 1996.
Traditional school; fairly wide range of abilities; good teaching and results.

Profile
Background   Founded 1732 by Robert Gordon, successful Aberdonian merchant, for the 'maintenance, aliment, entertainment and education of young
boys'; classical 18th-century building plus many later additions, including five-
storey teaching block, on crowded city-centre site. School is still expanding and
recently acquired a 40-acre site three miles away. Became fully independent with
the abolition of Direct Grant status 1985; girls first admitted 1989; boarding
ended 1995. Appeal has raised £750,000 for new facilities.
Atmosphere   Busy, well-ordered. Cheerful, well turned-out pupils (blazer-
and-tie uniform for all).
Admissions   By assessment or tests and interview. Fairly wide range of abilities; more than 20% receive help with fees (including assisted places). Most from
professions and oil industry-related backgrounds.
The head   Read history at Aberdeen; previously deputy head for 15 years of
Glasgow High.
The teaching   Well-qualified staff of 106 (equal numbers of women and men).
Broad curriculum; emphasis on maths, English; all do Latin, German, French.
All take seven subjects at Standard Grade from a choice of 20, including accounting, Greek, graphic communication; 95% stay on to take five Highers (choice of
20); vocational alternative available; 90% return for a sixth year to do a variety
of modular courses, repeat Highers or take the Certificate of Sixth Year Studies
(CSYS); A-levels offered in accounting, business studies, economics. Senior
school pupils grouped by ability; average class size 25. Lots of drama and music;

choir, orchestra and a variety of smaller ensembles, including thriving drum and pipe band. Well-supported cadet force and Duke of Edinburgh award scheme.
Results (1997) Standard Grade: 96% gained at least five grades 1–2. Highers: 48% gained at least five grades A–C.
Destinations More than 90% go on to university.
Sport Chiefly: rugby, hockey, cricket, athletics, tennis for the boys; hockey, netball, tennis, athletics for the girls. Facilities include two gyms, heated indoor pool; good playing fields and floodlit all-weather hockey pitch/tennis courts three miles away.
Remarks Sound school.

ROBERT MAY'S ♂ ♀
West Street, Odiham, Hampshire RG29 1NA. Tel (01256) 702700

Synopsis
Comprehensive (voluntary-controlled) ★ Co-educational ★ Ages 11–16 ★ 1,115 pupils (roughly equal numbers of girls and boys)
Head: Will Sarell, 47, appointed 1987.
Successful, well-run school; good teaching and GCSE results; wide range of extra-curricular activities.

Profile
Background Founded 1694 by Robert May, local mercer; became a secondary modern 1951; went comprehensive 1975 and moved to present 17-acre site on the edge of town (fine views over Hampshire countryside). Purpose-built premises plus attractive later additions (but space at a premium); everything well cared for, litter-free. Identified by Ofsted (1996) as an 'outstanding' school.
Atmosphere Busy, well-disciplined; big emphasis on praise and reward (stickers, well-done certificates). Smart uniform (girls can wear trousers). Parents kept well informed (weekly news bulletin). Full programme of extra-curricular activities every afternoon from 2.40 to 3.45.
Admissions Over-subscribed (and expanding) but no selection; priority to those living (or at primary school) in the (predominantly middle-class) catchment area of Odiham, Hook, Hartley Witney and surrounding villages.
The head Calm, firm, well-respected; has worked hard to raise academic and behavioural standards. Read PPE at Oxford; formerly a deputy head in Cambridgeshire. Married (to a teacher at a neighbouring school); two daughters (both pupils here).
The teaching Lively, good quality: pupils impressively 'on task'. Stable staff of 75 (65% female), 65% appointed by present head. Standard national curriculum; all do French or German in first year and may add the other in second; most take 10 GCSEs; vocational diploma on offer. Art and textiles particularly popular; computing equipment outdated. Pupils grouped by ability in most subjects from second year; effective help for those with special needs (at both ends of the ability range); average class size 29 in first year, reducing to 23 for GCSE. Lots of drama and music: 140 learn an instrument; choir, various ensembles. Extra-curricular activities include chess, woodwork, computing, Duke of Edinburgh award scheme. Regular language exchanges with pupils in France, Germany.
Results (1997) GCSE: 66% gained at least five grades A–C.
Destinations Nearly 90% remain in full-time education, mostly at one of three

local sixth-form colleges; about 50% proceed to university.
Sport Strong (full trophy cabinet); girls do particularly well in netball, hockey, athletics; boys add soccer, cricket, athletics. Facilities include sports hall, gym; playing fields inadequate.
Remarks Ofsted inspectors concluded: 'The school is a well-ordered community providing a very good all-round education.'

ROEDEAN ♀
Brighton, East Sussex BN2 5RQ. Tel (01273) 603181

Synopsis
Independent ★ Girls ★ Boarding and some day ★ Ages 10–18 ★ 403 pupils, 97% boarding ★ 163 in sixth form ★ Fees: £14,265 boarding; £8,700 day
Head: Mrs Patricia Metham, 52, appointed January 1998.
Fine, traditional school; very good teaching and results.

Profile
Background Founded 1885 by three sisters in strict imitation of a boys' public school: emphasis on games, competitive houses, fresh air, plain food, cold baths. Moved 1899 to present Jacobean-style fortress in a commanding but exposed position on the Downs above Rottingdean; premises clean, functional, well-equipped; latest additions include new theatre and dance studio, £1 million science block, innovative languages centre. Delightful 1930s chapel seats the whole school.
Atmosphere Busy, well-ordered; big emphasis on self-discipline ('rarely do girls get into much trouble here'); pupils address teachers as 'Madam' or 'Sir' (and shake hands with each member of staff at the beginning and end of term); good pastoral care; strongly competitive house system. One aim is that by the time she leaves a girl should have the presence to command the 340-seat theatre ('The single-sex environment has particular advantages for girls; it prevents stereotyping, raises expectations and develops self-confidence by offering many opportunities for leadership and responsibility').
Admissions By Common Entrance; 55% mark preferred but allowances made (numbers have fallen). Most from southern counties and London; a third from abroad. Junior boarders in cubicled dormitories; seniors in shared or single study-bedrooms.
The head New appointment. Read English and drama at Bristol; has taught in a wide range of state and independent schools; her third headship. Married (to an academic); two grown-up daughters.
The teaching First-rate; quite formal, very professional; high-calibre staff (75% female). Broad curriculum: sciences taught separately; good maths; lots of computing (140 terminals); all do Latin for first two years; modern languages include German, Spanish; choice of 22 subjects at GCSE, 20 at A-level (including business, theatre and computer studies). Pupils grouped by ability in maths, French, Latin; progress closely monitored; maximum class size 20, reducing to 10–12 in sixth form. Strong art, drama; 50% take dance lessons; 70% learn an instrument (two choirs, two orchestras, various ensembles); well-supported Duke of Edinburgh award scheme.
Results (1997) GCSE: all gained at least five grades A–C. A-level: very creditable 73% of entries graded A or B.

Destinations   Virtually all stay on for A-levels and proceed to university (up to 10 a year to Oxbridge).

Sport   Chiefly: lacrosse, netball, hockey, tennis, swimming, athletics, cricket, rounders. Basketball, badminton, volleyball, squash, fencing, karate also available. Facilities include extensive playing fields, 18 tennis courts, sports hall, indoor pool.

Remarks   Ofsted inspectors concluded (1994): 'Roedean is an excellent school with a deservedly high reputation. The pupils achieve very high standards across an impressively wide range of subjects and activities. They are taught and cared for by well-qualified and dedicated staff in a safe environment which affords them a wealth of opportunity. They grow into confident, articulate, competent and independent young women.'

ROMSEY ♂ ♀
Greatbridge Road, Romsey, Hampshire SO51 8ZB. Tel (01794) 512334

Synopsis
Comprehensive ★ Co-educational ★ Ages 11–16 ★ 1,025 pupils (roughly equal numbers of girls and boys)
Head: Dr Richard Skinner, 58, appointed 1981 (retiring August 1998).
First-rate, well-run comprehensive; good GCSE results; strong music and sport.

Profile
Background   Opened as a secondary modern 1958; went comprehensive 1973. Variety of buildings on a fine site on the edge of the town; latest additions include performing arts centre, science labs, technology centre; some class-rooms in 'temporary' huts. Grounds and buildings well maintained; no litter, vandalism, graffiti.

Atmosphere   Notably courteous, mature, orderly. School takes a strong line on bullying ('Any behaviour which is the illegitimate use of power in order to hurt others is bullying and will not be tolerated'). Blazer-and-tie uniform strictly enforced (popular with parents).

Admissions   School over-subscribed and non-selective; priority to those living nearest or attending a 'feeder' primary; 30% come from outside the official catchment area (including fugitives from Southampton).

The head   Able, determined; an old-fashioned head ('I'm not a modern man-ager'). Read politics at Leicester; PhD from Open University; wide experience in the state sector. Teaches history, runs public speaking. Keen Rotarian.

The teaching   Rigorous. First-rate staff of 66 (40 women), nearly all appointed by present head. Standard national curriculum; half do a second language (French or German) for at least one year; sciences taught by specialists; good computing across the curriculum. Pupils grouped by ability in maths, languages from first year and in most other subjects thereafter; lots of extra help for those who need it. Very good music; orchestra, choir.

Results   (1997) GCSE: 60% gained at least five grades A–C.

Destinations   About 80% remain in full-time education after 16 – 60% to do A-levels, 20% to take vocational courses.

Sport   Big variety of individual and team games available; county centre of excellence for rugby and basketball.

Remarks   Ofsted inspectors concluded (1994): 'The school provides a very good education for its pupils. The quality of teaching and learning is extremely good.'

ROSEBERY ♀
White Horse Drive, Epsom, Surrey KT18 7NQ. Tel (01372) 720439

Synopsis
Partially selective comprehensive (grant-maintained) ★ Girls ★ Ages 11–18 ★
1,205 pupils ★ 210 in sixth form
Head: Miss Heather Saunders, 49, appointed 1991.
Well-run, successful school; good teaching and results; strong design/technology.

Profile
Background   Founded as a grammar school 1927; went comprehensive 1977;
opted out of council control 1992; re-introduced selection 1996. Attractive, brick
buildings (long corridors, tall sash windows) in well-maintained, spacious
grounds; later additions mostly of high quality but some classes in huts; first-rate
technology centre. The only all-girls' state school in Surrey.

Atmosphere   Orderly, pleasant; strong work ethic; clear, sensible discipline;
well-mannered, friendly girls (in an unusually becoming uniform of white
shirts, blue jerseys and plaid kilt-style skirts). Supportive parents.

Admissions   School is over-subscribed; 15% of 210 places allocated to those
scoring highest in a 'general ability' test and living within three-and-a-half miles
('measured in a straight line from the main gate'); rest to those living nearest.

The head   Energetic, elegant, charming; ambitious for the school. Studied
science at London; previously deputy head of a comprehensive in Kent.

The teaching   Highly effective. Long-serving staff, some dating from the
grammar school era. Broad curriculum: all do French, German and Latin for
first three years; outstanding technology; very good maths results. All take 10
GCSEs; options include business studies, expressive arts, sociology. Wide
choice of 26 subjects at A-level; vocational alternatives available, including
GNVQ in business studies. Pupils grouped by ability in most subjects; extra
help for those with special needs, including the most able; progress regularly
monitored; largest classes 27, reducing to 22 for practical lessons. Lots of
music; opportunities for instrumentalists of all kinds. Active Duke of Edinburgh award scheme.

Results   (1997) GCSE: 67% gained at least five grades A–C. A-level: 46% of
entries graded A or B.

Destinations   About 60% stay on for A-levels; most of these proceed to higher
education (up to 6 a year to Oxbridge).

Sport   Teams and individuals do well at district and county levels. Main games:
hockey, netball, tennis, athletics, cross-country, swimming. Aerobics, badminton, lacrosse, trampolining also on offer. Good facilities include gym, swimming pool, tennis courts.

Remarks   Good all round: far from old-fashioned, but something of the grammar school ethos has survived. Ofsted inspectors concluded (1997): 'This is a
good school. Teachers are expert in their field and show a high level of commitment to achieving the best for the girls.'

ROUNDWOOD PARK ♂ ♀
Harpenden, Hertfordshire AL5 3AE. Tel (01582) 765344.

Synopsis
Comprehensive ★ Co-educational ★ Ages 11–18 ★ 970 pupils (65% boys) ★ 160 in sixth-form
Head: Andrew Cunningham, 47, appointed September 1997.
Successful, unpretentious school; good GCSE and A-level results.

Profile
Background Opened as a secondary modern 1956; went comprehensive early 1970s. Modern, unlovely buildings (some classrooms in 'temporary' huts) on an extensive site on the edge of town; much-needed £750,000 building programme (including six new classrooms) in progress.

Atmosphere Functional, a bit rough at the edges: school feels over-crowded; pupils (predominantly middle-class) can be noisy and careless both of adults and each other; staff appear to set no great store by displays of good manners or tidy uniforms (head of pastoral care complained that lack of parental control in some affluent homes contributed to disciplinary problems). Active governors; generally supportive parents.

Admissions Over-subscribed; application via primary schools to Hertford-shire County Council. No rigidly defined catchment area; most come from five local 'feeder' schools but others from Luton, Hemel Hempstead (buses to outly-ing districts).

The head New appointment (predecessor had been in post 17 years). BEd from London; taught physics; previously head of a comprehensive in Watford. Married; two grown-up children.

The teaching Often informal in style – children allowed to chat as they work, leading to fairly high levels of background noise. Pupils divided from the start into six groups of 26/27: three fast-track, three average; further grouping by abil-ity in maths, science (dual award) and modern languages (unusually, all do French and German for first three years). Good choice of GCSEs, including design/technology, business studies, drama; good results in maths, science, geography. A-level options include expressive arts; almost all take general stud-ies. Lots of help for those with special needs; well-resourced learning support room seen as a 'haven'. Plenty of music: 200 learn an instrument.

Results (1997) GCSE: 65% gained at least five grades A–C. A-level: 46% of entries graded A or B.

Destinations Nearly all proceed to university (including a few to Oxbridge).

Sport Extensive playing fields but inadequate gym (older pupils use local sports centre). Good range of team games, including rugby, soccer, netball, cricket, tennis, hockey; athletics a particular strength.

Remarks Popular with demanding parents in a highly competitive local mar-ket. Deserves better facilities. Ofsted inspectors concluded (1995): 'A good school with many good features.'

ROYAL HIGH, BATH ♀
Lansdown Road, Bath BA1 5SZ. Tel (01225) 313877

Synopsis
Independent ★ Girls ★ Day (and boarding from September 1998) ★ Ages 11–18 (plus associated junior school) ★ 600 pupils (75% day from September 1998) ★ 175 in sixth form (from September 1998) ★ Fees: £4,152 day; £11,000 boarding
Head: Miss Margaret Winfield, 58, appointed (to Bath High) 1985.
Strong, newly merged school under a successful head; very good teaching; improving facilities.

Profile
Background   Result of merger between Bath High, founded 1875 by Girls' Day School Trust, and Royal Bath, founded 1865 for daughters of Army officers, on the premises of the latter. Bath High needed new buildings and space; Royal Bath, situated near by, needed pupils. Junior school (300 girls aged three to 11) on the site of Bath High.

Atmosphere   Calm, purposeful, very feminine; good pastoral care; discipline not a problem (head encourages the girls to help set the rules); friendly relations between staff and pupils (who are, nonetheless, required to work hard); 'independent thought encouraged'. Highly supportive parents.

Admissions   By interview and tests in English, maths, verbal and non-verbal reasoning; Bath High has been fairly selective (top 25% of the ability range), Royal Bath much less so; trust plans to replace assisted places with a scheme of its own. Extensive catchment area served by fleet of buses. Pleasant boarding accommodation for up to 200; sixth-formers in modern, self-contained premises.

The head   Enthusiastic, experienced, beady-eyed; clear, open leadership style. Read history at Leicester; previously head of Bolton Girls' (qv). Strong role model; inspires great loyalty. No immediate plans to retire.

The teaching   Good quality; traditional in style; well-qualified, dedicated, predominantly female staff. Broad curriculum: science on offer as three separate subjects; languages include German, Spanish, Latin, Greek; wide choice of academic subjects at both GCSE and A-level. Pupils grouped by ability in maths only; extra help for dyslexics and the gifted; average class size 25. Good art; lots of music. Extra-curricular activities include Duke of Edinburgh award scheme, Air Training Corps. Regular language exchanges with pupils in France, Germany, Spain.

Results   (1997) Bath High. GCSE: all gained at least five grades A–C. A-level: creditable 65% of entries graded A or B. Royal Bath. GCSE: 84% gained at least five grades A–C. A-level: 47% of entries graded A or B.

Destinations   Nearly all go on to higher education (average of five a year to Oxbridge).

Sport   Good results in hockey, netball. Lacrosse, tennis, badminton, swimming also on offer. Merged school will benefit from the superior facilities at Royal Bath.

Remarks   One to watch.

ROYAL HOSPITAL ♂ ♀
Holbrook, Ipswich, Suffolk IP9 2RX. Tel (01473) 326210

Synopsis
Independent ★ Co-educational ★ Boarding ★ Ages 11–18 ★ 660 pupils (66% boys) ★ 170 in sixth from ★ Fees: £4,956–£9,867
Head: Nicholas Ward, 48, appointed 1995.
Unusual school; respectable results; subsidised fees.

Profile
Background   Roots go back to Greenwich Hospital, founded 1694 by William and Mary for 'sick and wounded sailors, their widows and orphans': teaching of writing, arithmetic and navigation to boys started 1712. School moved 1933 to present 200-acre site overlooking the Stour (stunning views); boys and girls from non-seafaring backgrounds first admitted 1990. Imposing Queen Anne-style buildings (chapel seats 1,000) plus later additions, including marvellous £1.3 million art and design centre; 11 boarding houses (named after famous sailors – Anson, Blake, Collingwood etc) modernised at a cost of £300,000 each. All fees subsidised by Greenwich Hospital Trust ('one of the Navy's best-kept secrets').

Atmosphere   School proud of its Naval traditions: standards still remarkably high; pupils immaculately turned out (shoes are the shiniest ever). Naval jargon (prefects are 'petty officers') and customs (daily raising of school colours, marching to meals 'up mess') retained. All uniforms – school, Naval, even games kit – supplied free. Exceptionally tidy boarding accommodation; every pupil has a 'captain's bunk' – bed above a desk with cupboards at the side; clusters of four for juniors, doubles and singles for seniors. Effective pastoral care system; lots going on at weekends ('A seven-day-a-week boarding school,' says the head). Appetising food.

Admissions   Priority to those with Naval connections (currently 30%). Entrance by exam (in maths, English, verbal reasoning) and interview: school is not unduly selective but 'the child must want to come here'; applicants expected to be capable of achieving at least five GCSEs grades A–C; requirements lowered for those with real social or financial need. All fees subsidised – significantly in the case of the children, grandchildren of seafarers.

The head   Read engineering at Leicester, later qualified as a solicitor; his second headship; teaches maths to less able pupils. Keen to promote self-discipline and team spirit; determined to raise the school's profile. Married (wife much involved in school life); two grown-up children.

The teaching   Traditional in style. Pupils grouped by ability in English, maths, science; average class size 22, reducing to 12 in the sixth form. National curriculum followed; GCSE options include Latin, German, sport studies, media studies; choice of 17 subjects at A-level; GNVQ in business studies available. Particularly good art, design/technology. Enthusiastic music (marching band performs at the Royal Tournament); first-class choir (regular tours at home and abroad). Strong cadet force (compulsory for at least two years) and Duke of Edinburgh award scheme.

Results   (1997) GCSE: 78% gained at least five grades A–C. A-level: more modest 31% of entries graded A or B.

Destinations   Most go to university; three or four a year into the Navy.

Sport   Main games: rugby, hockey, netball, basketball; lots of canoeing, sailing. Facilities include 80 acres of playing fields, large gym, nine-hole golf course.

Remarks   School shaking off its austere image and deserves to be more widely known. Not, though, for couch potatoes.

RUGBY ♂ ♀
Rugby, Warwickshire CV22 5EH. Tel (01788) 543465

Synopsis
Independent ★ Co-educational ★ Boarding and day ★ Ages 13–18 ★ 740 pupils (65% boys, 80% boarding) ★ 350 in sixth form ★ Fees: £13,830 boarding; £10,860 day
Head: Michael Mavor, CVO, 50, appointed 1990.
Distinguished, well-led school; very good teaching and results; fine facilities; strong music and sport.

Profile
Background Endowed 1567 by Lawrence Sheriff, grocer, with income from land he owned in London (now Great Ormond Street, producing £1 million a year); steeped in history ('Tom Brown' spent his schooldays here, William Webb Ellis first ran with the ball in his arms); fully co-educational since 1995. Early 19th-century buildings (including fine chapel) plus many later additions (£16 million spent in the past 10 years) on a 150-acre site on the edge of the town. First-rate facilities include attractive design centre, multi-media language lab, fully computerised library, theatre, sports hall; science block to be re-built at a cost of £4 million.

Atmosphere Clear Christian ethos ('Sermon-on-the-Mount-type things,' says the head); well-organised pastoral care (house system is very strong); respectful relations between staff and pupils; disciplinary code clearly set out (and reasons given). Uniform 'allows some scope for individual choice'. Parents required to consent to drug-testing should 'suspicious behavioural circumstances' make it necessary.

Admissions By Common Entrance (55% mark required); average IQ 110. Pupils mostly from professional backgrounds; 13% from overseas. Twelve boarding houses (through which entry is arranged) varying in standards of privacy, comfort and decor but all commanding strong loyalties (pupils eat in their houses). Scholarships (art, design/technology, music) and bursaries worth £750,000 a year (more than a tenth of the school's income).

The head Very able, highly experienced; gentle manner belies strong convictions; introduced co-education and has given the school a new sense of direction ('Traditions are like your children – you love them but you have to let them go'). Read English at Cambridge; taught at Tonbridge; formerly head of Gordonstoun (qv). Married; two children.

The teaching Good: generally formal in style but lively. Well-qualified full-time staff of 87 (75% male), 35% appointed by present head. Broad curriculum: science taught as three separate subjects; languages include Latin, German, Spanish, Russian, Italian, Japanese; choice of 21 subjects at A-level (all lower-sixth do general studies and computing). Pupils grouped by ability in English, maths, science, history; specialist help available for dyslexics; average class size 20, reducing to 10 in the sixth form. Lots of music: half learn an instrument; two choirs, two orchestras, various ensembles. Drama includes annual Latin play. Extra-curricular activities include cadet force, very popular Duke of Edinburgh award scheme. Lots of trips abroad for study and sport.

Results (1997) GCSE: 99% gained at least five grades A–C. A-level: very creditable 75% of entries graded A or B (34th in the league table – its best position ever).

Destinations   About 90% go on to university (average of 12 a year to Oxbridge).
Sport   A prominent feature: choice of 25; all play at least three times a week;
regular county and national honours. Main games: rugby, cricket, hockey for
boys; netball, hockey, tennis for girls. Fencing, lacrosse, clay-pigeon shooting,
golf also available.
Remarks   HMC inspectors concluded (1996): 'This is a very good school with
high standards of achievement and learning across the whole range of subjects.'
Highly recommended.

RUGBY HIGH ♀
Longrood Road, Rugby CV22 7RE. Tel (01788) 810518

Synopsis
Grammar (grant-maintained) ★ Girls ★ Ages 11–18 ★ 672 pupils ★ 224 in
sixth form
Head: Mrs Margaret Thornton, 58, appointed 1988.
Hard-working, well-run school; good teaching and results; strong music.

Profile
Background   Founded 1903; moved to present outer-suburban site and purpose-built premises (practical but uninspiring) 1961; opted out of council control 1993. Main buildings shabby in places; recent additions include
well-equipped music centre, new language and technology blocks; 10 classrooms
in 'temporary' huts.
Atmosphere   Serious, hard-working; friendly relations between staff and
pupils; few disciplinary problems ('you can reason with intelligent girls'); navy
blue uniform strictly enforced. Parents have high expectations.
Admissions   Heavily over-subscribed (350 apply for 90 places a year); academically selective (top 20% of the ability range). Entry at 11-plus by East
Warwickshire verbal reasoning tests; catchment area extends to outskirts of
Coventry. About 50 join the large sixth form from other schools: five GCSEs
required at grade C or above (plus at least grade B in chosen A-level subjects).
The head   Strong leader; enthusiastic, approachable; forges close links with
parents. Read maths at London (and still teaches it); previously deputy head of
a comprehensive. Married (to a retired teacher); two grown-up children (one
was a pupil here).
The teaching   Good quality; formal but friendly. Well-qualified staff of 31 (six
men), a third appointed by present head. Standard national curriculum plus
Latin (which all do for at least two years); lots of computing; choice of 16 subjects for GCSE, 24 at A-level (some in conjunction with boys at Lawrence Sheriff,
qv). Girls grouped by ability in maths, languages for GCSE. Very good music: a
third learn an instrument; two orchestras, two choirs.
Results   (1997) GCSE: 97% gained at least five grades A–C. A-level: 43% of
entries graded A or B.
Destinations   Most go on to university (average of two a year to Oxbridge).
Sport   Facilities include gym, eight tennis courts, six netball courts, four hockey pitches; sixth-formers use local sports centre.
Remarks   Ofsted inspectors concluded (1994): 'The quality of education is very
good. This is a caring school where personal development is secured and learning flourishes.'

SACRED HEART OF MARY ♀
St Mary's Lane, Upminster, Essex RM14 2QR. Tel (01708) 222660

Synopsis
Comprehensive (grant-maintained, Roman Catholic) ★ Girls ★ Ages 11–18 ★
760 pupils ★ 160 in sixth form
Head: Barry Welch, 60, appointed 1987.

Profile

Background Founded as an independent school in 1927 by the Sisters of
the Sacred Heart of Mary; joined the state sector 1950; went comprehensive
1978; opted out of council control 1993. Slightly scruffy 1930s buildings plus
later additions in pleasant grounds adjoining the convent; new classrooms
added 1996.

Atmosphere Busy, purposeful, well-ordered; strong (but not oppressive)
Catholic ethos ('a community of faith committed to the pursuit of excellence').
Girls polite, friendly; they enjoy being here and are quietly determined to succeed. Blazer-and-tie uniform for all ('make-up and nail varnish may not be
worn'); Saturday detention for truancy or other serious misdemeanours.

Admissions School over-subscribed; girls admitted 'without regard to academic ability'; 15% of 120 places a year reserved for those of 'good musical potential'; priority for the rest to 'practising Catholic girls resident in the Diocese of
Brentwood who are recommended by their parish priest'; all applicants interviewed. Wide range of abilities and social and ethnic backgrounds.

The head (Pater familias) Has raised academic standards; strong proponent of
single-sex education for girls.

The teaching Good quality: predominantly female staff; attentive pupils,
encouraged to take responsibility for their own learning. Broad curriculum: sciences taught separately; all do French and Italian for at least first two years and
Latin for at least one; lots of computing; GCSE options include Greek, business
studies, childcare, textiles (a particular strength); religious studies compulsory;
vocational alternatives to A-level available; most do general studies. Pupils set
targets from first year and grouped by ability in maths from second year;
English, languages, science from third year; extra help for those who need it;
special tuition for Oxbridge entry; maximum class size 32. First-rate drama;
good art, music (choirs, orchestras), dance. Regular language exchanges with
schools in France, Italy.

Results (1997) GCSE: creditable 79% gained at least five grades A–C. A-level:
40% of entries graded A or B.

Destinations About two-thirds go on to university (including Oxbridge).

Sport Usual range but not a big feature of school life.

Remarks Ofsted inspectors concluded (1994): 'This is a very good school.
Results are beyond what may reasonably be expected for the ability range of
the pupils.'

ST AIDAN'S ♂ ♀
Oatlands Drive, Harrogate, North Yorkshire HG2 8JR. Tel (01423) 885814

Synopsis
Comprehensive (voluntary-aided) ★ Co-educational ★ Ages 11–18 ★ 1,550 pupils (equal numbers of girls and boys) ★ 460 in sixth form
Head: Dennis Richards, 51, appointed 1989.
Successful, well-run comprehensive; good teaching and results; strong music and sport.

Profile
Background   Result of a 1968 merger between two Church of England secondary modern schools; went comprehensive 1973. Mainly 1960s buildings plus 'temporary' huts on a spacious, wooded campus (sprinkled with picnic tables); recent additions include new 500-seat chapel hall; particularly good facilities for science, technology, drama; good library; everything meticulously clean and well cared for. Huge, ecumenical sixth form shared with a neighbouring Roman Catholic school.

Atmosphere   Air of academic rigour and purposefulness; strong Christian ethos ('Commitment to the Christian way of life is at the heart of all we do and is reflected in every undertaking'); caring, family approach. Friendly but not over-familiar relations between staff and very well-behaved pupils; strict uniform below the sixth form (where 'smart, business-like appearance' is required). Much fund-raising for charity.

Admissions   School heavily over-subscribed; 146 places for those living within the catchment area, 70 for those outside; priority to those earning the most points for frequency of the attendance of the child and parent(s) at Christian services. Pupils predominantly middle-class.

The head   Strong leader: a very visible presence around the school. Has degrees in modern languages and theology; formerly deputy head of a church school in Northamptonshire. Married; youngest daughter is a pupil here (as are the children of many members of staff).

The teaching   First-rate: hard-working, enthusiastic staff; styles range from traditional 'chalk-and-talk' to group and individual learning. Standard national curriculum; particularly good work in technology, English and modern languages (all are introduced to French and German); first-rate science, taught as three separate subjects; computers used across the curriculum. Pupils grouped by ability in all subjects except religious studies (which all do for GCSE) and design; extra help for those with special needs; progress closely monitored; average class size 27. Choice of 22 subjects at A-level; half do at least one science; vocational alternatives include GNVQs in business & finance, health and social care. Strong drama and music: orchestra, famous concert band, many other ensembles.

Results   (1997) GCSE: very creditable 80% gained at least five grades A–C. A-level: 42% of entries graded A or B.

Destinations   About 70% continue into the sixth form; of those who take A-levels, 90% proceed to higher education (about six a year to Oxbridge).

Sport   Wide choice; strong soccer, cricket, basketball, athletics. Facilities include good on-site playing fields, all-weather track, sports hall, tennis courts.

Remarks   Very attractive school; all abilities catered for. Ofsted inspectors concluded (1996): 'This is an outstanding school which provides an extremely high quality of education for its pupils. It is a very well ordered and happy community.'

ST ALBANS ♂
Abbey Gateway, St Albans, Hertfordshire AL3 4HB. Tel (01727) 855521

Synopsis
Independent ★ Boys (plus girls in sixth form) ★ Day ★ Ages 11–19 ★ 680 pupils ★ 213 in sixth form (85% boys) ★ Fees: £6,210
Head: Andrew Grant, 43, appointed 1993.
Successful, traditional school; good teaching and results; lively drama and music; strong sport.

Profile
Background Founded 984, one of the oldest schools in England; moved to present site 1871; formerly Direct Grant, became fully independent 1976; sixth-form girls admitted 1991. Imposing, harmonious buildings (of which the 14th century Gateway is an integral part) in a calm, beautiful setting; facilities are modern and extensive. School is non-denominational but morning prayers are held in the Abbey.

Atmosphere Friendly, informal. High standards expected; individuality encouraged. Particularly good relations between pupils and staff. Traditional uniform (blue blazers with crest) strictly imposed; sixth-form boys wear suits; equivalent smart 'office' wear for girls.

Admissions By school's own tests or Common Entrance; top 30% of the ability range from an extensive catchment area (school coaches run from Mill Hill to Luton). Many parents were grammar-school educated – 80% are 'first-time buyers' of independent education; phasing out of assisted places, which nearly 200 pupils hold, likely to have a considerable impact. Scholarships on offer.

The head Wiry, energetic, enthusiastic; committed to excellence in every field; insists on decent standards of dress and behaviour but equally determined to retain the school's easy atmosphere. Read English at Cambridge; taught at Merchant Taylors' and Whitgift; previously second master at Royal Grammar, Guildford. Married; two young sons.

The teaching Lively, stimulating. Well-qualified, experienced staff (42 men, 13 women); low turnover. Broad curriculum: all do two languages and three sciences; most take GCSE maths (a particular strength) and French a year early; all do at least three A-levels and one AS; language options include German, Spanish, Italian, Swedish, Russian, Latin, Greek; good facilities for science, technology, computing. Academic progress closely monitored; maximum class size 22, reducing to 10 in sixth form. Strong drama: numerous productions in well-equipped theatre and outdoor amphitheatre. Well-established music tradition: joint orchestra with St Albans High (qv); numerous ensembles; choir performs regularly. Extra-curricular activities include popular cadet force, Duke of Edinburgh award scheme, social service. School owns farm house in Brecon Beacons.

Results (1997) GCSE: 99% gained at least five grades A–C. A-level: 57% of entries graded A or B.

Destinations About 90% stay on for A-levels; of these, 80% proceed to university (about 10 a year to Oxbridge).

Sport Wide range on offer, including soccer, hockey, cricket, athletics, aerobics, orienteering; particular strengths in rugby, cross-country. Extensive playing fields near by.

Remarks Good all round, with a very congenial atmosphere. Recommended.

ST ALBANS HIGH   ♀
Townsend Avenue, St Albans, Hertfordshire AL1 3SJ. Tel (01727) 853800

Synopsis
Independent ★ Girls ★ Day ★ Ages 11–18 (plus associated junior school) ★
550 pupils ★ 130 in sixth form ★ Fees: £6,210
Head: Mrs Carol Daly, 46, appointed 1994.
Lively, fairly traditional school; good teaching and results.

Profile
Background   Founded 1889; close links with St Albans Abbey ('the Christian ethos is very important in the life of the school'). Handsome, purpose-built, Edwardian premises plus later additions in a quiet road near the town centre. Junior school (180 girls aged seven to 11) opposite.

Atmosphere   Friendly, even casual, within a disciplined framework; easy relations between staff and pupils. Competitive houses; uniform (below the sixth form) accommodates short skirts and Doc Martens.

Admissions   By tests in English, maths, verbal reasoning, supplemented by interview and observation; school is not unduly selective; half the places go to girls from the junior department. Extensive Hertfordshire/North London catchment catchment area (fleet of buses). Phasing out of assisted places, which about 80 hold, will reduce the social mix.

The head   Read chemistry and geology at Nottingham; has taught in both the state and independent sectors; previously head of the girls' section at Forest (qv). Married; one daughter (was a pupil here).

The teaching   Generally traditional in style but plenty of discussion and investigative work too; well-qualified, predominantly female staff. Broad curriculum: sciences taught separately; most take two languages; Latin on offer; all do drama, music (a strength) for first three years; good art. Pupils grouped by ability in maths; average class size 26/27, reducing to 20 at GCSE, smaller at A-level. Extra-curricular activities include Duke of Edinburgh award scheme. Regular exchanges with European schools and one in St Albans, Vermont.

Results   (1997) GCSE: all gained at least five grades A–C. A-level: 63% of entries graded A or B (school has slipped steadily down the league table from 20th in 1993 to 115th).

Destinations   About 75% stay on for A-levels; of these, nearly all proceed to university (average of five a year to Oxbridge).

Sport   Main games: lacrosse, netball, tennis (all to a high standard). Gymnastics, dance, athletics, swimming also on offer. Facilities include sports hall; playing fields within walking distance.

Remarks   Sound, safe school.

ST ANDREW'S ♂ ♀
Warrington Road, Croydon CR0 4BJ. Tel (0181) 686 8306

Synopsis
Comprehensive (voluntary-aided, Church of England) ★ Co-educational ★ Ages 11–16 ★ 400 pupils (roughly equal numbers of girls and boys)
Head: John Coatman, 55, appointed 1985.
Small, well-run school; good GCSE results; outstanding music.

Profile
Background   Founded 1857; moved to present four-acre site and purpose-built premises 1964. School is over-crowded: has no library, needs more classrooms.
Atmosphere   Friendly, well-ordered. Cheerful, courteous pupils feel they are known and cared for (in a relatively intimate environment); strong Christian ethos. Smart uniform for all. Parents enthusiastically involved (they help with trips, clubs, Duke of Edinburgh award scheme).
Admissions   Heavily over-subscribed: priority to siblings and those whose parents worship regularly in the Archdeaconry of Croydon.
The head   Able, hard-working, very experienced; his second headship. Read civil engineering at Imperial College then trained as a teacher. Involved in all aspects of school life; teaches most of the pupils religious education and knows them all well.
The teaching   First-rate. Stable staff of 21 (17 women), nearly all appointed by present head; 'They never give up on you,' say pupils. Standard national curriculum; pupils grouped by ability in English, maths, science, languages; average class size 27, slightly smaller for GCSE. Exceptional music: 60% learn an instrument; choirs, 100-strong orchestra; pupils regularly perform in public. Annual exchanges with schools in France, Germany.
Results   (1997) GCSE: creditable 67% gained at least five grades A–C.
Destinations   Nearly all remain in full-time education, including 30% who take A-levels at Archbishop Tenison's (qv), with which the school shares a sixth form.
Sport   Good choice: mainly soccer, cricket, athletics, volleyball for boys; netball, rounders, athletics for girls. Limited facilities; much-needed sports hall planned.
Remarks   Deservedly popular school.

ST ANNE'S ♀
Rockstone Place, Southampton SO15 2WZ. Tel (01703) 328200

Synopsis
Comprehensive (grant-maintained, Roman Catholic) ★ Girls ★ Ages 11–18 ★ 1,200 pupils ★ 160 in sixth form
Head: Miss Catherine Hargaden, 50, appointed 1989.
Attractive, Catholic school; very good teaching and results; flourishing music.

Profile
Background   Founded 1904 by the Sisters of La Sainte Union (who remain trustees); formerly Direct Grant; went comprehensive 1967; opted out of council control 1994. Diverse, characterful buildings (red-brick, yellow-brick, white stucco, flat roofs, pitched roofs) on a very cramped island site near the city centre; good, modern facilities; recent additions include labs, dance/drama studio,

new classrooms. No playing fields (playground just about large enough to hold a fire practice for the whole school).

Atmosphere Purposeful, civilised; strong Catholic tradition ('an essentially religious foundation'); emphasis on spiritual welfare and pastoral care. Each year-group has a (voluntary) day of reflection at the local retreat house; each house supports a charity of its choice (which must be of benefit to human beings not animals).

Admissions Over-subscribed (about 260 apply for 210 places): entry by interview ('to establish the family's affirmation of the school's principles'); 75% are practising Catholics (entry supported by their parish priest – 'This child is known to me and has been a regular church-goer'). Priority for remaining places to girls showing enthusiasm and aptitude for music, and practising Christians of other communions. Catchment area extends to Winchester and Romsey.

The head Strong leader; the school's first lay head. Read history and geography at National University of Ireland; taught in Zambia, Australia, Ireland; came here as deputy head.

The teaching Rigorous: staff have high expectations; big emphasis on 'learning by doing'. Standard national curriculum; half take two languages (from French, German, Spanish). Most do three A-levels from choice of 15; GNVQs in health & social care and business available. Pupils divided into two ability bands on entry; further setting thereafter in maths, science; extra help for the least and most able. Very strong music: 200 learn an instrument; two orchestras, two choirs. Lots of extra-curricular activities.

Results (1997) GCSE: creditable 76% gained at least five grades A–C. A-level: 40% of entries graded A or B.

Destinations About 65% stay on for A-levels, 30% for vocational courses; of these, 75% proceed to university.

Sport All encouraged to participate. Hockey, netball, tennis, cross-country available (using the facilities of the local sports centre).

Remarks Ofsted inspectors concluded (1996): 'The school provides a very good education for its pupils, who achieve high standards and make good progress. Pupils show respect for each other and are courteous, articulate and responsible.'

ST AUGUSTINE'S, TROWBRIDGE ♂ ♀
Wingfield Road, Trowbridge, Wiltshire BA14 9EN. Tel (01225) 350001

Synopsis
Comprehensive (grant-maintained, Roman Catholic) ★ Co-educational ★ Ages 11–18 ★ 800 pupils ★ 150 in sixth form
Head: Robert Cook, 48, appointed 1987.
First-rate Catholic school; very good teaching and GCSE results; strong ethos.

Profile
Background Opened 1967 as a purpose-built secondary modern; went comprehensive 1988; opted out of council control 1991; sixth form opened 1996. Later additions include sixth-form block, well-equipped technology centre; some classrooms in 'temporary' huts; well-kept grounds include a small farm.

Atmosphere Purposeful, well-ordered ('The school is uncompromising on the standards of discipline it expects'); strong Catholic ethos (lessons start with a prayer); good relations between staff and courteous pupils. Blazer-and-tie uniform (sixth-formers have their own) strictly enforced. Parental involvement encouraged.

Admissions   School over-subscribed (two apply for each place). Priority to: children from 'feeder' Catholic primaries; Catholic families outside the catchment area with a letter of support from their parish priest; other practising Christians with support from their minister. Pupils drawn from a wide range of social and economic backgrounds.

The head   Enthusiastic; good leader. Music and drama specialist; teaches religious education; produces musicals; plays the organ at his parish church. Married; two children (both pupils here).

The teaching   Challenging; formal in style; predominantly female staff. Standard national curriculum; good technology; choice of 19 subjects at A-level. Pupils grouped by ability in maths, science, languages; maximum class size 25, reducing to 18 in the sixth form. Good music; three choirs, many ensembles. Regular language exchanges with schools in France, Germany; pilgrimages to Lourdes.

Results   (1997) GCSE: creditable 79% gained at least five grades A–C. First A-level results in 1998.

Destinations   Majority expected to go on to university.

Sports   Usual range; regular fixtures. No sports hall (though one is planned).

Remarks   Identified by Ofsted (1996) as 'outstandingly successful'. Inspectors said: 'This is an excellent school. It sets high standards of behaviour, attendance, attainment and relationships. These targets are achieved.'

ST BARTHOLOMEW'S   ♂ ♀
Andover Road, Newbury, Berkshire RG14 6JP. Tel (01635) 521255

Synopsis
Comprehensive (grant-maintained) ★ Co-educational ★ Ages 11–18 ★ 1,664 pupils (52% girls) ★ 660 in sixth form
Head: Stewart Robinson, 48, appointed 1994.
Successful, well-run comprehensive; high standards of work and behaviour; good teaching and results; first-rate art, music, drama.

Profile
Background   Result of 1975 amalgamation of two single-sex grammar schools (one founded 1466); opted out of council control 1991. Solid, two-storey, Edwardian buildings plus numerous later additions in quiet, residential area; juniors and sixth-formers on adjoining sites (staff move between them). Sixth form is one of the largest in the country.

Atmosphere   Well-ordered, business-like but very friendly. High standards of behaviour and appearance expected (sanctions include head's Saturday detention). Strong house system. Traditional uniform worn throughout.

Admissions   School full but not over-subscribed; pupils admitted 'without reference to ability or aptitude'; applications to Berkshire County Council. Fairly wide spread of abilities; most from relatively advantaged social backgrounds.

The head   Read economics at Newcastle; taught at an independent boarding school and comprehensives in Cheshire and Devon; previously head for six years of a comprehensive in Wiltshire. Keen sportsman; coaches cricket, hockey.

The teaching   High standards across the curriculum, outstanding in some

areas (particularly good results in maths, English). Committed staff of 110 (almost all involved in extra-curricular activities), some very long-serving. Broad curriculum: half take German as a second foreign language from second year; science taught as three separate subjects from third year; computers used across the curriculum; good facilities for art (pottery, textiles, ceramics, sculpture), design/technology, home economics. Wide choice of 25 subjects at A-level, including business studies, computing, home economics, Christian theology, politics. Pupils grouped by ability in maths, French after first year, and in most other subjects for GCSE; lots of extra help for those who need it (including from volunteer sixth-formers); maximum class size 25. Very enthusiastic music (lots of informal concerts); strong drama (large numbers take GCSE drama, A-level theatre studies). Wide range of extra-curricular activities, including cadet force, social service programme (one or the other is compulsory). Regular foreign exchanges.
Results (1997) GCSE: 66% gained at least five grades A–C. A-level: 33% of entries graded A or B.
Destinations About 75% continue into the sixth form; of these, 80% proceed to university (about 12 a year to Oxbridge).
Sport Strong tradition; enthusiastic house competitions; good facilities (including extensive playing fields, new sports hall). Main games: rugby, soccer, hockey, cricket, athletics for boys; lacrosse (a particular strength), netball, rounders, tennis for girls. Numerous minor sports.
Remarks Ofsted inspectors concluded (1996): 'This is a good school. The focus on high academic achievement and the attainment of pupils in sport, drama and music are strengths. Progress is particularly good in the sixth form.'

ST BEDE'S, THE DICKER ♂ ♀
The Dicker, Hailsham, East Sussex, BN27 3QH. Tel (01323) 843252

Synopsis
Independent ★ Co-educational ★ Boarding and day ★ Ages 13–19 ★ 470 pupils (60% boys, 65% boarding) ★ 180 in sixth form ★ Fees: £12,450 boarding; £7,500 day
Head: Roger Perrin, 56, appointed 1978.
Stimulating, unusual school; wide range of academic and extra-curricular choices; pupils of all abilities and many nationalities.

Profile
Background Founded 1978 by the present head with 22 pupils in a converted garage in Eastbourne; moved 1979 to Horatio Bottomley's Edwardian country house (complete with stables and kennels) in Upper Dicker, where it owns 85 acres and a variety of buildings (including the shop, post office and church). Most of the classrooms were built on site by resident carpenters; the biology lab was once part of East Croydon station; another classroom used to be the gym at a distant prep school – all of which the prospectus describes as a 'welcome change from the over-bearing institutional character of much school architecture'.
Atmosphere Warm, relaxed, well-ordered; clear rules and regulations (prompt expulsion for drugs and being found in an opposite-sex boarding house); strongly cosmopolitan (25% of pupils come from 61 countries). Boys wear jackets and ties; girls an equally smart equivalent.
Admissions First come, first served; no academic selection; tests to determine

correct placement only. Some pupils are destined for Oxbridge, others have statements of special educational needs. Boarding accommodation varies from attractive (new boys' house opened September 1997) to very basic ('It's better to share with a nice person than have a nice room,' says the head); good food, wide choice. Up to 20 bursaries and scholarships a year.

The head A gifted, if unorthodox, educationist; believes that schools, instead of creating a system into which pupils must fit, should cater for the needs of those who come to it; St Bede's is his enthusiastic creation. Married; wife looks after the domestic side.

The teaching Large staff of 56 (pupil-teacher ratio 8:1) offer an impressive 30 subjects at GCSE and A-level (including such options as agricultural science and ceramics) plus GNVQs in business and art & design; most pupils have what amounts to individual timetables. Science taught (and examined) as three separate subjects ('real scientists will want to study them separately, the rest should choose the ones that interest them'); all introduced to two languages (out of French, German, Spanish); the only compulsory GCSEs are maths, English and IT – because the head thinks they alone are unavoidable in later life and there is no merit in requiring children to study subjects at which they are hopeless. Pupils grouped by ability from the start; further setting in most subjects for GCSE; extra help for dyslexics; average class size 14 but many taught in smaller groups. High quality art; lively music (more than a third learn an instrument); well-equipped drama studio (pupils take Shakespeare to neighbouring prep schools). Choice of more than 90 extra-curricular activities, including fly-fishing, riding, golf, video production, electronics, jewellery making, vehicle maintenance, yoga, mountain biking, horticulture, clay-pigeon shooting.

Results (1997) GCSE: 69% gained at least five grades A–C. A-level: 38% of entries graded A or B.

Destinations Up to 90% go on to higher education (a few to Oxbridge).

Sport Nearly 30 games to choose from (the school believes success in one of them could hold the key to a child's self-confidence) but none is compulsory. Good tennis (nine all-weather courts) athletics, judo. Facilities include fine indoor pool, riding school.

Remarks Delightful school; something for everyone; highly recommended.

ST BEDE'S HIGH
St Anne's Road, Ormskirk, Lancashire L39 4TA. Tel (01695) 570335

Synopsis
Comprehensive (voluntary-aided, Roman Catholic) ★ Co-educational ★ Ages 11–16 ★ 560 pupils (roughly equal numbers of girls and boys)
Head: Philip Entwistle, 55, appointed 1983.
Well-run, caring school; good teaching and GCSE results; strong sport.

Profile
Background Opened 1956 as a secondary modern; became fully comprehensive 1970. Undistinguished, functional buildings in fine, spacious grounds and semi-rural setting. School is an adult education centre four nights a week.

Atmosphere Warm, courteous, civilised; strong sense of order. Pious statues and pictures symbolise the school's Roman Catholic character and commitment; genuine Christian assemblies. Arresting displays of pupils' art in classrooms and corridors. Blazer-and-tie uniform strictly enforced ('as a form of control and an aid to discipline').

Admissions   School is full but not over-subscribed; priority to Catholic children attending four 'feeder' primaries; maximum 10% non-Catholic. Most from professional/middle-class homes.

The head   Well-liked and respected; values tradition and is not afraid to reject the merely novel; quiet, purposeful management style. Educated at Manchester; was a professional cricketer. Taught at several Lancashire schools before coming here as deputy head in 1974. Married; two children.

The teaching   Energetic, imaginative; professional, committed staff of 32 (nearly all appointed by present head). Standard national curriculum; all learn French; more able add German from second year; choice of 16 subjects at GCSE. Pupils grouped by ability in most subjects; extra help for the less able (21 pupils have 'statements' of special need); average class size 30. Strong music: visiting tutors; 47–piece orchestra. Extra-curricular activities include community service.

Results   (1997) GCSE: 66% gained at least five grades A–C.

Destinations   About 90% remain in full-time education.

Sport   Main games: soccer (many district and county players), cricket, athletics, badminton, basketball, volleyball, netball, rounders. Adequate gym but no sports hall or swimming pool.

Remarks   Every child treated with respect and sympathy, regardless of academic ability. Ofsted inspectors concluded (1994): 'This is a very good school with many outstanding features. The life and work of the school is set within a strong and supportive Christian ethos.'

ST BEDE'S, REDHILL   ♂ ♀

Carlton Road, Redhill, Surrey RH1 2DD. Tel (01737) 212108

Synopsis

Comprehensive (voluntary-aided, ecumenical) ★ Co-educational ★ Ages 11–18
★ 1,485 pupils (slightly more girls than boys) ★ 285 in sixth form
Head: Chris Curtis, 39, appointed September 1997.
First-rate comprehensive; strong Christian ethos; good academic record.

Profile

Background   Founded 1976 as a joint Anglican/Roman Catholic school (very avant-garde at the time); small site in quiet, residential area. Main school in functional block plus new, well-equipped additions (including impressive technology centre); juniors housed separately on far side of playing field.

Atmosphere   Friendly, relaxed; large numbers move about in harmonious, noisy bustle between classes (no hurtling round corners); amiable relations between staff and pupils. Everyone encouraged to achieve personal best, but not a competitive environment. Underlying Christian ethos: commitment assumed (regular assemblies, crucifix in every room) but not forced; Mass, Eucharist and Free Church services led in rotation by three chaplains (the largest ecumenical school in the country); pastoral care taken very seriously. Uniform until sixth form, then sensible dress (nothing outrageous on view).

Admissions   School is over-subscribed; entry criteria based on church membership (predominantly Anglican and Roman Catholic, but some Free Church children). Wide range of abilities (some very bright) from large area of Surrey.

The head New appointment. Capable, thoughtful; a practising Catholic strongly committed to ecumenism; previously head of a Catholic comprehensive in Northampton. Read theology at Heythrop College, London; became a social worker then switched to teaching; MEd from King's, London in computing. Married; two sons (both pupils here).

The teaching Stimulating, imaginative, aims to 'stretch'; emphasis on good standards of work and presentation; dedicated, well-qualified staff. Standard national curriculum; well-equipped science labs; first facilities for technology, computing. Wide choice of subjects at A-level (sixth form is one of the biggest in Surrey); vocational alternatives available. Pupils grouped by ability in English, maths, languages from second year; extra help for those who need it; class sizes range from 16–27. Flourishing music: orchestras, choirs, lunchtime concerts. Very good art and drama (numerous productions, theatre studies at GCSE and A-level). Extra-curricular activities include well-supported Duke of Edinburgh award scheme. Regular exchanges with schools in New York, Tanzania, Europe.

Results (1997) GCSE: creditable 71% gained at least five grades A–C. A-level: 45% of entries graded A or B.

Destinations About 65% continue into the sixth form and proceed to university (a few each year to Oxbridge).

Sport Considered important. Wide range of individual and team activities, including athletics, badminton, cricket, dance, football, netball, rugby, tennis. Facilities include large gym, all-weather pitch.

Remarks Impressive, school; comprehensive education at its best.

ST BEES ♂ ♀
St Bees, Cumbria CA27 0DS. Tel (01946) 822263

Synopsis
Independent ★ Co-educational ★ Day and boarding ★ Ages 11–18 ★ 280 pupils (55% boys, 61% day) ★ 82 in sixth form ★ Fees: £6,486–£7,995 day; £8,502–£11,622 boarding
Head: Mrs Janet Pickering, 48, appointed January 1998.
Small, friendly school between the mountains and the sea; good teaching; wide range of abilities; strong sport.

Profile
Background Founded 1583 (original schoolroom complete with 16th-century pupils' carved initials); girls admitted 1976. Victorian, sandstone buildings plus later additions, including £1 million international business centre (languages, computing), on a beautifully situated 150-acre campus half-a-mile from the sea. Good, up-to-date facilities.

Atmosphere Small, intimate, relaxed; 'Christian principles are fundamental to the school's philosophy and practice'; an endearingly old world air (staff, some in gowns, served tea and toast for elevenses). Traditional blazer-and-tie uniform.

Admissions By interview and Common Entrance or tests in English, maths, reasoning; school is barely selective (minimum IQ 100). Phasing out of assisted places, which about 25% hold, will have a considerable impact: recruitment efforts being stepped up at home and abroad; centre for teaching English as a foreign language being established. Day pupils from up to 20 miles away; weekly boarders from surrounding counties; some full boarders from abroad.

Homely boarding accommodation; juniors in small dormitories; seniors have single or shared study-bedrooms. Scholarships (academic, music, art, sport) and bursaries available.

The head New appointment (school's first woman head). Read biochemistry at Sheffield (First); taught at Gordonstoun; previously deputy head of King's Canterbury (qv). Married; two sons.

The teaching Good: generally formal in style; hard-working staff (a third female). Fairly broad curriculum: sciences taught separately ('contrary to the policy in most schools'); all do Latin for first two years; German added to French in third year; rather narrow choice of 15 subjects for GCSE, 17 at A-level. Average class size 18–20; extra help for those who need it, including dyslexics; extra coaching for Oxbridge entry. High-quality art, drama, music. Extra-curricular activities include adventure training, cadet force (compulsory for three years), Duke of Edinburgh award scheme.

Results (1997) GCSE: 95% gained at least five grades A–C. A-level: 39% of entries graded A or B.

Destinations About 95% proceed to university.

Sport Very strong (especially rugby); first-rate coaching. Excellent facilities include extensive playing fields, modern sports hall, indoor pool, nine-hole golf course, shooting range, tennis and Eton fives courts.

Remarks Good school for all-rounders.

ST CATHERINE'S, BRAMLEY ♀
Bramley, Guildford, Surrey GU5 0DF. Tel (01483) 893363

Synopsis
Independent ★ Girls ★ Day and boarding ★ Ages 11–18 (plus associated junior school) ★ 478 pupils (76% day) ★ 110 in sixth form ★ Fees: £6,200 day; £9,100–£10,350 boarding
Head: Mrs Claire Oulton, 35, appointed 1994.
Happy, well-run, academic school; very good teaching and results; strong creative arts and sport.

Profile
Background Founded 1885 as a Church of England school under the same Royal Charter as Cranleigh (qv); purpose-built, red-brick premises (including fine chapel) in 25 acres of beautiful Surrey countryside; extensive later additions include well-equipped science labs, excellent creative arts centre. Junior school (185 girls aged four to 11) across the road.

Atmosphere Busy, cheerful, welcoming ('a happy school for bright girls'); good pastoral care; warm relations between staff and pupils; light-touch discipline based on 'old-fashioned' values; girls 'gently but firmly reminded of the importance of Christian faith, thoughts and deeds'. Neat, sensible uniform. Much fund-raising for charity.

Admissions By Common Entrance or school's own tests; school is highly selective; no automatic promotion for juniors. Most from professional/business backgrounds; many have brothers at Cranleigh. Comfortable boarding accommodation; juniors in small, cheerful dormitories; sixth-formers have individual study-bedrooms; most are weekly boarders; few foreign nationals. Scholarships: academic, music.

The head   Able, energetic; an unusually youthful appointment. Read history at Oxford; previously head of history at Charterhouse. Married (to a teacher); two young children (both pupils here).

The teaching   First-rate: academically demanding; formal in style; well-qualified, predominantly female staff. Fairly broad curriculum: science on offer as three separate subjects; all do Latin from 11, German or Spanish from 12; Greek on offer; good design/technology; all do at least nine GCSEs; choice of 21 subjects at A-level, including business studies, history of art. Pupils grouped by ability in maths, science, French; average class size 20–25. Very good art (painting, drawing, sculpture, pottery, ceramics); lots of drama (state-of-the-art studio), dance, music; 50% learn an instrument, six choirs, orchestra, various ensembles. Extra-curricular activities include Duke of Edinburgh award scheme, Young Enterprise. Regular language exchanges with pupils in France, Germany, Spain.

Results   (1997) GCSE: all gained at least five grades A–C. A-level: very creditable 71% of entries graded A or B.

Destinations   About 70% continue into the sixth form; of these, nearly all proceed to university.

Sport   Strong (regular county honours); lots on offer, including lacrosse, netball, athletics, gymnastics, even rugby. Facilities include indoor pool, squash and tennis courts.

Remarks   Very good all round; recommended.

ST CLEMENT DANES ♂ ♀
Chenies Road, Chorleywood, Hertfordshire WD3 6EW. Tel (01923) 284169

Synopsis
Partially selective comprehensive (voluntary-aided, grant-maintained) ★ Co-educational ★ Ages 11–18 ★ 1,056 pupils (equal numbers of girls and boys) ★ 200 in sixth form
Head: Dr Josephine Valentine, 38, appointed January 1998.
Successful school; good teaching and GCSE results; strong music and sport.

Profile
Background   Founded 1862 in central London as a boys' grammar school; moved 1975 to present purpose-built premises (reminiscent of a pleasant supermarket) and became a co-educational comprehensive; some classrooms in 'temporary' huts.

Atmosphere   Calm, well-ordered, fairly traditional (senior staff wear academic gowns in assembly). Strict uniform below the sixth form. Unusually good food.

Admissions   Heavily over-subscribed: 18 places a year (10%) allocated on the basis of academic ability (as recorded in previous school reports); 18 for special aptitude in music, art, drama, sport; 18 for 'other educational reasons', including need for learning support (14 have statements of special needs); most of the rest on the basis of proximity to the school.

The head   New appointment (predecessor had been in post 15 years); came here as deputy 1995. Bright, articulate, very enthusiastic. Read microbiology at Liverpool; PhD in oral pathology, then switched to teaching. Married; two children.

The teaching   Fairly formal in style. Standard national curriculum; all take French and may add German or Spanish; go-ahead IT; A-level options include sports studies, photography; history entirely post-1832. Pupils grouped by ability in maths from the first year, English from the second year, science from the third year; other classes contain a fairly wide range of abilities; first-rate specialist support for those who need it. Good music: a quarter learn an instrument (proportion rising); orchestra, various ensembles. Regular language exchanges with schools in France, Germany, Spain.

Results   (1997) GCSE: creditable 67% gained at least five grades A–C. A-level: 41% of entries graded A or B.

Destinations   About half go on to university (up to six a year to Oxbridge).

Sport   A strength: wide range on offer, including volleyball (outstanding), yachting (annual regatta). Facilities include all-weather hockey pitch paid for by the National Lottery.

Remarks   Good school for children of a wide range of abilities.

ST EDWARD'S ♂ ♀
Oxford OX2 7NN. Tel (01865) 319200

Synopsis
Independent ★ Becoming co-educational ★ Boarding and day ★ Ages 13–18 ★ 570 pupils (78% boarding) ★ 260 in sixth form (73% boys) ★ Fees: £13,425 boarding; £9,600 day
Head: David Christie, 55, appointed 1988.
Sound school; good teaching and results; fine facilities.

Profile
Background   Founded 1863; moved 1873 to present site (115 acres connected by a subway) in salubrious North Oxford. Fine, red-brick buildings around an immaculate quadrangle; many attractive later additions; school has a spacious feel but some classrooms are cramped. Good library: stained-glass windows, vaulted ceiling, 12,000 volumes. Girls in the sixth form since 1982; first 13–year-old girls admitted September 1997 ('We have taken note of changes in society').

Atmosphere   Purposeful, friendly; hard-working, unpretentious pupils; strong sense of community; good pastoral care system; bullying strongly discouraged. sixth-form girls made to feel an integral part of the school. Full-time woman chaplain.

Admissions   At 13 by interview and Common Entrance (minimum 50% mark required); at 16 (when about 40 join) with at least five GCSEs grade B or above plus school's own tests and interview; most pupils from professional/business backgrounds in Berkshire, Buckinghamshire, Oxfordshire. Boarding accommodation, dating from 1870 to 1991, is of a uniformly high standard; day pupils stay until 9 pm. Large number of scholarships – for which pupils compete by sitting an eight-paper examination during a five-day stay at the school.

The head   (Warden) A Scot whose soft accent and manner belies a steeliness of purpose. Keen to emphasise the school's academic record (which has begun to improve) rather than its traditional hearty image. Read economics at Strathclyde; trained teachers (but felt much of what they were being taught was 'unhelpful'); taught at the European School in Luxembourg (keen on Europe but thinks 'a lot of nonsense is talked about a European spirit') and Winchester.

Describes himself as 'not very sociable' but is charming and gets on well with parents. Married; three children.

The teaching Generally good; mainly front-of class; pupils clearly expected to think for themselves. Hard-working, well-qualified staff of 63 (12 women), some long-serving. National curriculum plus: science taught as three separate subjects; all do Latin; Greek, German, Spanish on offer in addition to French. Most take 10 GCSEs and three A-levels plus general studies and religious education. Pupils grouped by ability after first term; additional setting in maths, modern languages thereafter. Strong music; numerous concerts and recitals. Extra-curricular activities include compulsory cadet force, well-supported Duke of Edinburgh award scheme, community service.

Results (1997) GCSE: 99% gained at least five grades A–C. A-level: 50% of entries graded A or B (209th in the league table – its lowest position ever).

Destinations Nearly all stay on for A-levels; 90% proceed to university (up to 18 a year to Oxbridge).

Sport Wide variety; superb facilities, including sports centre, 90 acres of playing fields, all-weather pitch, 16 tennis courts, two swimming pools, six-hole golf course, boathouse on the Thames (rowing is strong).

Remarks HMC inspectors concluded (1996): 'This is a very good school catering well for pupils of a wide range of ability.'

ST EDWARD'S, ROMFORD ♂ ♀
London Road, Romford, Essex RM7 9NX. Tel (01708) 730462

Synopsis
Comprehensive (voluntary-aided) ★ Co-educational ★ Ages 11–18 ★ 1,078 pupils (equal numbers of girls and boys) ★ 180 in sixth form
Head: Giles Drew, 48, appointed 1992.
Very well-run school; strong Christian ethos; good teaching and GCSE results; lots of sport.

Profile
Background Founded as a charity school 1710; became a secondary modern 1944; went comprehensive and moved to present site and purpose-built, concrete and glass premises 1965; some classrooms in 'temporary' huts. School is generally well-equipped; computing facilities are first rate.

Atmosphere A well-ordered, close-knit community: strong commitment to Christian values; good pastoral care; friendly relations between staff and lively, articulate pupils; uniform strictly enforced. Security system includes registration by electronic swipe cards. Supportive parents donate £40,000 a year and raise another £8,000.

Admissions Heavily over-subscribed (more than 300 apply for 180 places) but no academic selection; principal criterion for admission is strength of family commitment to Christian (not necessarily Church of England) worship; clergy reference essential (no non-Christians). Pupils drawn from a wide range of social and ethnic backgrounds in an extensive catchment area. School shares the same foundation as St Edward's primary (from where 40% come).

The head Friendly, approachable; strongly committed to comprehensive education. Read English at Leicester; has taught widely in the state sector; previously head of a secondary modern in Kent (the results improved dramatically).

Married (to a former teacher); three children.

The teaching Good: orderly classes; enthusiastic, youthful staff (equal numbers of women and men), more than half appointed by present head. Big emphasis on languages (all start French and German); good art (a third take it for GCSE); lots of computers. Pupils grouped by ability in maths (some take GCSE a year early) and modern languages from second year, in English and religious studies for GCSE; lots of extra help for the gifted and those with special needs (13 have 'statements'); average class size 30, reducing to 23 for GCSE, 10–15 at A-level. A-level options include Christian theology, theatre studies; GNVQ in business studies on offer. Music strong, drama popular.

Results (1997) GCSE: 61% gained at least five grades A–C. A-level: rather modest 29% of entries graded A or B.

Destinations About half go on to university (one or two a year to Oxbridge).

Sport Good facilities for hockey, netball, volleyball (a strength), tennis, football, rugby, cricket, basketball (particularly popular), athletics, swimming (indoor pool). Highly committed staff: practices before and after school and during lunch-time.

Remarks Good school for children of all abilities; highly praised by Ofsted (1994).

ST FELIX ♀
Southwold, Suffolk IP18 6SD. Tel (01502) 722175

Synopsis
Independent ★ Girls ★ Boarding and day ★ Ages 11–18 (plus associated junior school) ★ 200 pupils (55% boarding) ★ 50 in sixth form ★ Fees: £11,550 boarding; £7,650 day.
Head: Richard Williams, 50, appointed January 1998.
Small, remote school; good GCSE results; lots of music, art, drama, sport.

Profile
Background Founded 1897 by Margaret Isabella Gardiner, an educational pioneer, as a school where 'girls can be treated as sensible beings'. Handsome, purpose-built, red-brick premises on attractive, 75-acre site overlooking the Blyth estuary, a mile-and-a-half from the sea; good facilities for art, design, sculpture, music. Numbers have steadily declined. Adjacent co-educational junior school under its own head.

Atmosphere Friendly; emphasis on self-discipline; aim is to 'turn girls into lively, confident and successful young women'. Relaxed relations between staff and pupils; good pastoral care; qualified counsellor available. Sunday evening chapel services conducted by female chaplain.

Admissions By Common Entrance; top 50% of the ability range (ie barely selective); specialist provision for those with dyslexia and English as a foreign language. Most pupils from East Anglia; handful of foreigners (despite efforts to boost recruitment in the Far East). Junior boarders in four-to-five-bed rooms; seniors in pairs or singles. Scholarships (academic, music, sport) available.

The head New appointment (well-regarded predecessor left suddenly after six years); the school's first male head. Read maths at London; previously deputy head of Queen Margaret's, York (qv). Married; three children.

The teaching Blend of formal classes and informal tutorial groups; long-serving staff (75% female). Fairly broad curriculum; all do Latin for first three years; languages include German, Spanish, Italian, Russian; lots of computing; choice of 20 subjects at A-level, including business studies, theatre studies. Pupils grouped by ability in maths, French. Good music (75% learn an instrument), art, drama. Extra-curricular activities include well-supported Duke of Edinburgh award scheme.

Results   (1997) GCSE: all gained at least five grades A–C. A-level: very modest 24% of entries graded A or B.

Destinations   Most stay on for A-levels; of these, 80% proceed to university.

Sport   Good reputation in team games: hockey, netball, tennis. Riding, sailing, canoeing, wind-surfing on offer. Facilities include new £500,000 indoor pool, squash courts, gymnasium.

Remarks   Pleasant school; arresting the decline in numbers a priority.

ST GEORGE'S GIRLS' ♀
Garscube Terrace, Edinburgh EH12 6BG. Tel (0131) 332 4575

Synopsis
Independent ★ Girls ★ Day and boarding ★ Ages 11–18 (plus associated junior school) ★ 550 pupils (86% day) ★ 160 in sixth form ★ Fees: £1,005–£4,800 day; £8,130–£9,525 boarding
Head: Dr Judith McClure, 51, appointed 1994.
Traditional, academic school; first-rate teaching and results; good music.

Profile
Background   Founded 1888 to 'prepare young women for a full and equal role in society' (and still does); moved 1912 to purpose-built 'colonial neo-classical' premises (some areas in need of refurbishment) on an 11-acre site in a quiet, residential part of the city; recent additions include sports hall, fine music centre.

Atmosphere   Courteous, hard-working, strongly traditional (wooden desks and blackboards; corridors lined with portraits of founders and former headmistresses). Big emphasis on pastoral care, personal development.

Admissions   Most join at five; entry at nine and 11 by interview and test. School is fairly selective; pupils drawn from the cream of the Edinburgh professional classes. Comfortable, spacious boarding accommodation in two large Victorian houses; sixth-formers in own purpose-built bungalow.

The head   Able, astute, progressive (known to the girls as 'Jude the Dude'). Former nun; read history at Oxford (First, followed by a PhD); previously head of Royal School, Bath (qv); teaches philosophy to the sixth form. Married (husband shares her enthusiasm for ecclesiastical history).

The teaching   Good: long-serving, predominantly female staff; highly motivated girls. Broad curriculum (choice of 19 subjects at Standard Grade); average class size 20–24; specialist help for those with learning difficulties. About 85% take one-year Highers; rest (the more able) do A-levels; Certificate of Sixth Year Studies and Scotvec modules also on offer. Strong music (choirs, four orchestras, various ensembles). Regular study trips abroad.

Results   (1997) Standard Grade: 50% gained at least five grades 1–2. Highers: 49% gained at least five grades A–C. A-level: 73% of entries graded A or B.

Destinations   About 85% continue into the sixth form; of these, more than 90% proceed to university (average of six a year to Oxbridge).

Sport   Main games: hockey, lacrosse, tennis. Skiing, squash, swimming also on offer. Facilities include floodlit, all-weather pitch.

Remarks   Good all round; less academically-able girls may struggle.

ST GEORGE'S, HARPENDEN ♂ ♀
Sun Lane, Harpenden, Hertfordshire AL5 4TD. Tel (01582) 765477

Synopsis
Comprehensive (voluntary-aided) ★ Co-educational ★ Day and boarding ★ Ages 11–18 ★ 932 pupils (55% boys, 86% day) ★ 215 in sixth form ★ Fees (boarding only): £5,175
Head: Norman Hoare, 47, appointed 1988.
Exceptionally successful, well-run school; strong Christian ethos; very good teaching and results.

Profile
Background   Founded 1907 as an independent co-educational boarding school; joined the state sector as grammar school 1967; went comprehensive 1970. Victorian buildings plus later additions; school is poorly funded ('We haven't got the bare minimum,' says the head); new classroom block represents the first major funding for 25 years.

Atmosphere   A school to gladden any traditionalist's heart: daily chapel (a prayer and a properly-sung hymn); uniformed pupils stand when an adult enters a classroom. Sixth-formers mentor younger children with learning difficulties; parents provide thousands of pounds for textbooks, furniture and equipment (and paint the school at weekends).

Admissions   School is over-subscribed; no catchment area, no academic selection; priority to siblings, those whose parents or earlier ancestors were pupils here, those who can prove Christian commitment with a letter from their parish priest (attendance at chapel compulsory on at least one Sunday in three). Prospective boarders interviewed 'to ensure they will benefit from the boarding experience' (half have parents living abroad). Boarding accommodation cheerful, if austere; younger pupils in dormitories of up to eight; seniors share with one or two others.

The head   Forceful, dedicated; passionately committed to comprehensive education (failed the 11-plus, transferred to a grammar school at 13). Read history and geography at Leicester (MA in local history); formerly deputy head of a Cambridgeshire comprehensive. Teaches religious education and general studies. Married (to a teacher); two children (both pupils here).

The teaching   First-rate; experienced, hard-working staff. Broad curriculum; all do French from first year and add German and Latin in second year (a few take all three to GCSE); all do religious studies; particularly good results in history. Pupils grouped by ability in most subjects from second year; extra help for those who need it; average class size 26. Lots of music: a third learn an instrument; choirs, orchestras, various ensembles. Regular language exchanges with pupils in France, Germany. Extra-curricular activities include Duke of Edinburgh award scheme.

Results   (1997) GCSE: very creditable 84% gained at least five grades A–C. A-level: 43% of entries graded A or B (as good as most grammar schools).

Destinations   About 70% stay on for A-levels; of these, about 70% proceed to

university (average of five a year to Oxbridge).
Sport Strong. Main games: rugby, lacrosse, cricket, netball; matches on Saturdays. Tennis (hard and grass courts), athletics, squash, swimming, basketball, soccer, sailing also on offer.
Remarks Highly praised by Ofsted, which said some of the teaching was 'inspirational'.

ST GREGORY'S, BATH ♂ ♀
Combe Hay Lane, Odd Down, Bath BA2 8PA. Tel (01225) 832873

Synopsis
Comprehensive (voluntary-aided, Roman Catholic) ★ Co-educational (slightly more girls than boys) ★ Ages 11–16 ★ 720 pupils
Head: David Byrne, 50, appointed 1986.
First-rate Catholic comprehensive; very good teaching and results; exceptionally strong creative arts.

Profile
Background Opened 1979 on the site of a secondary modern as part of a diocesan reorganisation of local Roman Catholic schools; functional, well-maintained 1960s buildings plus later additions on a grassy 12-acre site overlooking a picturesque valley; space at a premium.
Atmosphere Vibrant, happy, secure. Strong Christian identity (crucifix in every classroom, regular religious assemblies, chapel for mass, private prayer); formal, respectful relations between staff and pupils (they stand when teachers enter the class); high expectations of work and behaviour (certificates awarded in assembly); good pastoral care system. Pupils' work effectively and colourfully displayed throughout the school. Distinctive uniform (brown with gold shirts) strictly adhered to. Many staff, including the head, send their own children here.
Admissions School 50% over-subscribed; a genuine social mix from a wide catchment area (some travel 25 miles); 80% Catholic (non-Catholics are all Christians and require supporting letter from local vicar or similar).
The head Devout Roman Catholic (as are all senior staff); Christianity his 'constant reference point' (school motto, Ad Deum Per Discendum – to God through learning); listens and consults but makes the decisions; says fostering pupils' self-esteem is a priority (negative comments in reports are not permitted). Read electrical engineering at Bangor.
The teaching Good quality across the board. Lively, dedicated staff of 42, half appointed by present head. Standard national curriculum; some take three languages for GCSE (French, German, Italian – strong European awareness); Latin on offer; religious education compulsory. Pupils grouped by ability in most subjects after first term; lots of extra help for those who need it; average class size 23. First-rate creative arts; nearly a third learn a musical instrument; half take drama for GCSE; lots of trips to theatres, operas, concerts. Regular exchanges with schools in France, Germany.
Results (1997) GCSE: 70% gained at least five grades A–C.
Destinations About 90% remain in full-time education after 16 (most at St Brendan's Catholic sixth-form college); 60% proceed to higher education.
Sport Enthusiastic; all usual team games; particularly strong rugby. Good gym but no sports hall or swimming pool.

Remarks   Ofsted inspectors (in unusually lyrical mood) concluded (1995): 'St Gregory's is an excellent school. Expert teachers have clear objectives and demonstrate an eagerness for all pupils to achieve their potential. There is a happy combination of seriousness of purpose and sheer enjoyment. The headteacher provides visionary and purposeful leadership.'

ST GREGORY'S RC HIGH ♂ ♀
Cromwell Avenue, Westbrook, Warrington, Cheshire WA5 1HG. Tel (01925) 574888

Synopsis
Comprehensive (voluntary-aided, Roman Catholic) ★ Co-educational ★ Ages 11–16 ★ 960 pupils (slightly more girls than boys)
Head: Tom Brophy, 55, appointed 1979.
Fine comprehensive; strong Christian ethos; good teaching and GCSE results.

Profile
Background   Opened as a purpose-built, co-educational comprehensive on a green-field site 1979. Pleasing, well-maintained, two-storey buildings (red brick, sloping roofs); many recent additions, including new classrooms, labs, computer rooms, dance studio, superb sports hall; all blend in with the original design. Numbers have been growing steadily. Good provision for handicapped pupils, including a lift.

Atmosphere   Friendly, courteous; strong Christian ethos ('Our vocation at St Gregory's is to strive to ensure that Christ's message permeates our formal and informal curriculum'). A sense of civilised order; very good pastoral care. Blazer-and-tie uniform for all. Lots of pupils' work on display. Everywhere clean and well-maintained.

Admissions   School heavily over-subscribed; priority to Catholic children at five main 'feeder' schools and up to 15 others; maximum 5% of places allocated to others seeking a Christian education. Wide range of abilities and social backgrounds from a catchment area that includes Penketh, Great Sankey, Bewsey, Longford.

The head   In post from the start. Able leader and manager; demands high standards, hard work. Read chemistry at Liverpool. Married; five children (one a pupil here).

The teaching   Wide range of styles; committed, hard-working (and largely Catholic) staff of 52, all appointed by present head. Standard national curriculum; science taught as three separate subjects (but, unusually, 80% do only one); religious education taken seriously but technology is not; all do French, some add Spanish. GCSE options include media studies, home economics. Pupils grouped by ability in maths, French from first year, in religious education, English for GCSE; first-rate help for those with special needs (at a cost to the school of £20,000 a year); average class size 30, reducing to 26 for GCSE. Vigorous drama and music; 170 learn an instrument; choirs, ensembles. Extra-curricular activities include Duke of Edinburgh award scheme, Christian retreats, visits to France, Spain.

Results   (1997) GCSE: creditable 64% gained at least five grades A–C.

Destinations   About 80% remain in full-time education after 16, up to 60% to do A-levels.

Sport Main games: rugby league, soccer, cricket, netball, hockey, rounders (regular county honours). First-rate facilities include extensive playing fields and sports hall (but no swimming pool).

Remarks A school that lives its faith. Ofsted inspectors concluded (1996): 'This is a high achieving school with many excellent features. Pupils' behaviour is exceptionally good and parents are exceptionally supportive of the school.'

ST GREGORY'S, TUNBRIDGE WELLS ♂ ♀
Reynold's Lane, Tunbridge Wells, Kent TN4 9XL. Tel (01892) 527444

Synopsis
Comprehensive (grant-maintained) ★ Co-educational ★ Ages 11–18 ★ 965 pupils (57% boys) ★ 180 in sixth form
Head: Miss Rosemary Olivier, 49, appointed 1994.
Well-run school; good teaching and results; strong Catholic ethos.

Profile
Background Opened 1966 as a purpose-built secondary modern; went comprehensive 1982; opted out of council control 1993. Some of the accommodation – in a warren of buildings – is inadequate; new sixth-form centre planned.

Atmosphere Lively, well-ordered; clear Catholic ethos ('School life is centred on prayer and an openness to the Holy Spirit'); good pastoral care; full-time chaplain. Parents reminded that 'successful education occurs when school and home are working in harmony to provide consistent support'. Uniform for all ('sensitively implemented').

Admissions School is over-subscribed but non-selective ('proudly comprehensive'). Parents asked for proof of church membership or their commitment to the 'life and worship of the parish'; most pupils from middle-class backgrounds in an extensive catchment area; 25%–30% non-Catholic.

The head Capable, experienced. Read modern languages at London; MA in education management from Sussex; previously deputy head of a Catholic comprehensive in Surrey.

The teaching Good: fairly long-serving staff (equal numbers of women and men). Fairly broad curriculum; science on offer as three separate subjects; good results in English, history; compulsory religious education; choice of 17 subjects at A-level; GNVQ available in hospitality & catering. Pupils grouped by ability in maths, English, languages, history; extra help for those who need it (about 15 have 'statements'). Art, drama and music have a high profile; 20% learn an instrument; two choirs. Regular language exchanges with pupils in France, Germany.

Results (1997) GCSE: creditable 61% gained at least five grades A–C. A-level: 31% of entries graded A or B.

Destinations About 75% continue into the sixth form; of these, nearly all proceed to higher education.

Sport Hockey, football, athletics are particular strengths; rugby, athletics, tennis, rounders, swimming, cross-country, dance, gymnastics also on offer. Facilities include adequate playing fields, tennis courts, use of adjacent sports centre.

Remarks Ofsted inspectors concluded (1994): 'This is a very good school which provides an education of high quality. Teaching is skilful in all departments. The ethos of the school is caring but also rigorous and purposeful.'

ST HELEN & ST KATHARINE ♀
7 Faringdon Road, Abingdon, Oxfordshire OX14 1BE. Tel (01253) 520173

Synopsis
Independent ★ Girls ★ Day ★ Ages 9–18 ★ 564 pupils ★ 128 in sixth form ★
Fees: £4,962
Head: Mrs Cynthia Hall, 44, appointed 1993.
Well-run, academic school; good teaching and results; strong music and sport.

Profile
Background Founded 1903; solid, red-brick buildings plus later additions in
pleasant, well-kept grounds; some classrooms in huts. Boarding phased out 1995.
Atmosphere Cheerful, hard-working, well-ordered. Good pastoral care system (confidential counsellor available by appointment). Day starts with traditional assembly (choir, Bible reading). Neat maroon and green uniform below
the sixth form.
Admissions Entry at nine (mostly from primary schools) by assessment, at 11
by tests in English, maths, science; school has become increasingly selective but
phasing out of assisted places, which more than 100 hold, will make recruitment
harder. Most pupils from professional/business backgrounds. Wide catchment
area (elaborate system of buses overseen by seniors).
The head Able, ambitious; has worked hard to modernise the school (her predecessor had been in post 19 years). Read English at Oxford; taught at St Paul's Girls'
for 13 years (head of English). Married (to a BBC senior executive); two children.
The teaching Good quality; largely traditional in style. Well-qualified staff of 47
(seven men). Broad curriculum: science taught as three separate subjects; all do
Latin for three years; Italian, German, Greek on offer. Wide choice of 24 subjects at
A-level (some in conjunction with boys at Abingdon, qv). Pupils grouped by ability in maths from second year, French from third year; progress closely monitored
(regular tests); average class size 26. Lots of music (some in conjunction with boys
at Radley, qv); half learn an instrument; three orchestras, five choirs. Extracurricular activities include Duke of Edinburgh award scheme, much charity work
and fund-raising. Regular exchanges with schools in France, Germany, Italy, Spain.
Results (1997) GCSE: 99% gained at least five grades A–C. A-level: impressive
86% of entries graded A or B (eighth in the league table – its best performance
ever).
Destinations Nearly all stay on for A-levels and proceed to university (a few
to Oxbridge).
Sport Strong – particularly lacrosse, netball, tennis.
Remarks Good school for able girls.

ST HELEN'S, NORTHWOOD ♀
Eastbury Road, Northwood, Middlesex HA6 3AS. Tel (01923) 828511

Synopsis
Independent ★ Girls ★ Day and some boarding ★ Ages 11–18 (plus associated junior school) ★ 614 pupils (95% day) ★ 170 in sixth form ★ Fees: £5,361
day; £10,101 boarding
Head: Mrs Diana Jefkins, 54, appointed 1995.
Successful, academic school; good teaching and results; strong sport.

Profile

Background   Founded 1899; converted Victorian houses plus later additions on attractive 22-acre campus; good facilities. Junior school (350 pupils aged four to 11) on same site.

Atmosphere   Courteous, friendly; big emphasis on traditional values; good relations between staff and pupils; well-structured pastoral care; strongly competitive house system.

Admissions   By interview and tests in English, maths, verbal reasoning; school heavily over-subscribed (300 apply for 90 places) and fairly selective. Most from professional backgrounds; 25% Jewish, 25% Muslim. Two pleasant boarding houses for up to 60 girls; 75% weekly boarders. Scholarships: academic, music.

The head   Able; good leader. Read natural sciences at Cambridge; previously deputy head of Henrietta Barnett (qv). Teaches physics to juniors; keen choral singer. Married; three daughters.

The teaching   Good quality; generally traditional in style; experienced, well-qualified, predominantly female staff. Fairly broad curriculum; science available as three separate subjects; all do Latin for at least one year; German, Spanish on offer; good results in English; choice of 20 subjects at A-level. Pupils grouped by ability in maths, French (more able take GCSE a year early); average class size 23, reducing to 10 in sixth form. Strong art, music; up to 50% learn an instrument. Good careers guidance; work experience in France, Germany, Spain. Extra-curricular activities include well-supported Duke of Edinburgh award scheme, cadet force (in conjunction with Merchant Taylors', qv), community service.

Results   (1997) GCSE: all gained at least five grades A–C. A-level: creditable 66% of entries graded A or B.

Destinations   About 98% go on to university (average of six a year to Oxbridge).

Sport   Very strong lacrosse (county and national honours); netball, badminton, tennis, fencing, dance also on offer. Facilities include indoor pool, courts for squash, tennis.

Remarks   Good all round.

ST HILDA'S ♀

Croxteth Drive, Sefton Park, Liverpool L17 3AL. Tel (0151) 733 2709

Synopsis

Comprehensive (grant-maintained, Church of England) ★ Girls ★ Ages 11–18
★ 820 pupils ★ 151 in sixth form
Head: Christopher Yates, 44, appointed January 1997.
Successful school; firm Christian ethos; good teaching and results.

Profile

Background   Founded 1894 as a grammar school by the Community of the Sisters of the Church; moved to present, cramped site 1967; went comprehensive 1980; opted out of council control 1995. School is bursting at the seams; new classrooms urgently needed.

Atmosphere   Very orderly; strong Christian ethos; high expectations. Uniform taken seriously; a 'neatly cut and well-groomed head of hair sets the tone for a pleasing personal appearance,' says the prospectus.

Admissions   School heavily over-subscribed (300 apply for 128 places); entry by interview and strict points system. Priority to children of: committed Anglicans (regularity of worship attested to by local vicar, children quizzed on Bible stories etc); other Christians; other faiths whose parents agree to support the school's ethos. Wide range of abilities and backgrounds; from September 1998 (unless the Government intervenes) 15% will be selected on ability.

The head   Scholarly, single-minded; committed Christian. Read maths at London (First); MSc in management from Manchester; previously a college lecturer; came here as head of maths in 1995. Married; three children.

The teaching   Largely formal in style (head favours 'tried and tested methods'). Standard national curriculum but science on offer as three separate subjects. Girls grouped by ability from the start; further setting in English, maths; extra help for dyslexics; average class size 32, smaller for GCSE and A-levels. Extra-curricular activities include Duke of Edinburgh award scheme.

Results   (1997) GCSE: creditable 68% gained at least five grades A–C. A-level: 34% of entries graded A or B.

Destinations   About 75% stay on for A-levels; of these, 55% proceed to university.

Sport   Very strong cross-country, athletics, swimming. Badminton, dance, tennis, squash, netball, hockey also on offer.

Remarks   Popular school: parents prefer its traditional values to glossy, more spacious alternatives.

ST HILDA'S HIGH ♀
Coal Clough Lane, Burnley, Lancashire BB11 5BT. Tel (01282) 436314

Synopsis
Comprehensive (voluntary-aided, Roman Catholic) ★ Girls ★ Ages 11–16 ★ 700 pupils
Head: Miss Bernadette Bleasdale, 41, appointed 1992.
Successful, well-run school; strong commitment to the Catholic faith; good teaching and results.

Profile
Background   Founded 1954 as secondary modern; went comprehensive 1966. Main school in typical 1960s flat-roofed buildings; rolling programme of refurbishment (£1.5 million spent recently); well-maintained grounds.

Atmosphere   Warm, welcoming, civilised; strong, but unforced, sense of order; Roman Catholic character expressed in sacred statues and pictures at strategic points ('The aim of our school is to develop the whole child by fostering, in a Catholic atmosphere, qualities of mind, body and spirit, feeling and imagination'). Excellent relations between teachers and pupils: warm, caring but essentially professional. Neat uniform (prefects wear coloured house sashes).

Admissions   No academic entry tests but detailed religious requirements: RC children have preference; non-Catholic baptised Christians accepted (to a limit of 9% of the total). Socially-mixed catchment area: council estate on one side, private housing on the other.

The head   Energetic, shrewd, approachable; a good communicator with a clear educational philosophy grounded in her faith; first lay head in the school's history. Studied maths at Lancaster; previously deputy head of a Roman Catholic comprehensive in St Helens.

The teaching   First-class. Loyal, devoted staff of 40 (12 men); some have been here more than 20 years. Day begins with a prayer in the staff room. Standard national curriculum; 'linguistically-able' pupils add German to French from second year; religious education taken very seriously; GCSE options include business studies, child care and development. Pupils grouped by ability in most subjects from first year; extra help for those who need it; GCSE pupils' progress monitored half-termly. Good drama and music: 120 learn an instrument; two fine choirs, orchestra. Members of Legion of Mary make regular visits to local old people's homes; large sums raised for charity.

Results   (1997) GCSE: creditable 73% gained at least five grades A–C.

Destinations   About 80% remain in full-time education after 16.

Sport   Hockey, rounders, netball, tennis, cross-country running. Netball and tennis courts within the grounds; playing fields adjacent.

Remarks   A genuine community; good all round; recommended.

ST JAMES ♂ ♀
91 Queen's Gate, London SW7 5AB. Tel (0171) 373 5638

Synopsis
Independent ★ Co-educational (but run as two single-sex schools) ★ Day ★ Ages 10–18 (plus associated junior schools) ★ 333 pupils (55% boys) ★ 62 in sixth form ★ Fees: £4,320
Joint heads: Nicholas Debenham, 64, appointed 1975; Laura Hyde, 42, appointed 1995.
Distinctive school; wide range of abilities; good teaching and results.

Profile
Background   Founded 1975 by parents and teachers from the School of Economic Science (itself founded in 1937 'to study and teach economics and the natural laws which govern men in society'), regarded by some as a cult; links between the two are strong (all the staff and a third of the parents are students of philosophy at the SES); idealistic but without 'isms' or 'ologies' (philosophical sources range from Socrates to the Upanishads – 'We seek to discover and teach the unifying principles common to all the great faiths of the world'). Boys in 19th-century Gothic-Tudor premises (topped by a bell tower in the shape of a tea-caddy) beside the Thames in Twickenham; girls in two converted houses in Notting Hill. Juniors elegantly housed in Queen's Gate.

Atmosphere   'The growth of a boy into a young man requires nourishment of body, mind and spirit,' declares the boys' school prospectus. 'Happiness and beauty in body, mind and heart are natural to all young girls,' echoes the girls' prospectus. Both emphasise the virtues of meditation (introduced at the age of 10, with parental consent) to 'bring stillness of mind' (all lessons begin and end with a Sanskrit dedication) and discipline: boys' school retains corporal punishment ('rarely used and reserved for grave offences' – parents asked for written consent). Strong insistence on good manners, particularly at meal-times when staff and pupils eat together: grace is said; pupils wait on each other (and must offer food to their neighbours before eating themselves).

Admissions   Non-selective at age four-and-a-half; interview and test thereafter; ability range is wide. A quarter of the pupils are Indians, their parents attracted by the school's culture and discipline (they are asked to ensure that their children do not listen to pop music, watch too much television or read bad literature). Catchment area includes Chiswick, Dulwich, Croydon, Wimbledon; daily transport to boys' school from Harrow and Victoria Station. A few bursaries available.

The heads Nicholas Debenham, the school's founder, read economics at Cambridge and then spent many years in industry; became a teacher owing to lack of fulfilment. Laura Hyde was previously an assistant head.

The teaching Dedicated, appropriately-qualified staff who believe what the school offers is of real and unusual value. Big emphasis in the junior school on handwriting ('fine calligraphy'), reading and arithmetic (taught with old-fashioned thoroughness – no calculators, tables learnt by heart). Sanskrit ('its regular practice leads naturally to a refinement in English speech') and philosophy – Christian, Hindu, Greek – introduced at four-and-a-half, Greek at nine, French at 10; science taught as three separate subjects from 13; Latin on offer. Extra help for those with dyslexia or who are learning English as a second language; classes are small. Good art, drama (lots of Shakespeare), music (all sing daily). Extra-curricular activities include cadet force, Duke of Edinburgh award scheme.

Results (1997) GCSE: 92% of boys and 89% of girls gained at least five grades A–C. A-level: 58% of boys' and 53% of girls' entries graded A or B.

Destinations About 75% stay on for A-levels; of these, virtually all proceed to university.

Sport All have to take some form of exercise daily; rugby, cricket, swimming, cross-country for the boys; lacrosse, gymnastics, athletics, swimming, riding for the girls. Boys' school has a playing field.

Remarks Unusual school; pupils seem happy and achieve sound standards.

ST LAURENCE ♂ ♀
Ashley Road, Bradford-on-Avon, Wiltshire BA15 1DZ. Tel (01225) 867691

Synopsis
Comprehensive (voluntary-controlled, Church of England) ★ Co-educational
★ Ages 11–18 ★ 1,170 pupils (roughly equal numbers of girls and boys) ★ 290 in sixth form
Head: Nicholas Sorensen 42, appointed April 1997.
Busy school; good teaching and results; first-rate drama and music.

Profile
Background Result of a 1980 merger of a grammar school and a secondary modern; well-maintained 1950s brick buildings on pleasant 18-acre site. Premises used in the evenings by the community.

Atmosphere Stimulating, purposeful, family-like (attention paid to everyone's needs); bad behaviour marginalised by consistent praise (letters home to commend effort and contribution). Lots of colourful art work on display. Supportive parents.

Admissions Mostly middle-class pupils from a relatively affluent catchment area.

The head New appointment. Read English and drama at Exeter, MA in education from Sussex; previously deputy head for seven years of a community college in West Sussex. Has worked in community theatre; keen jazz musician. Married; two young children.

The teaching   Good quality. Enthusiastic, committed staff of 66; strong team spirit (they share good practice); independent learning encouraged. Standard national curriculum; good science, lots of computing; GNVQ available in business. Pupils grouped by ability in maths, modern languages; average class size 21–22. First-rate drama (big take-up at GCSE and A-level) and music (more than 200 learn an instrument – orchestras, choirs etc). Lots of extra-curricular activities. Regular exchanges with schools in France, Germany, India; educational trips to Russia.

Results   (1997) GCSE: very creditable 72% gained at least five grades A–C. A-level: 37% of entries graded A or B.

Destinations   About 70% continue into the sixth form; of these, 90% proceed to university (two or three a year to Oxbridge).

Sport   All encouraged to participate; usual team games; competitive fixtures. Facilities include sports hall but no swimming pool.

Remarks   Good all round.

ST LEONARDS ♀
St Andrews, Fife KY16 9QU. Tel (01334) 472126

Synopsis
Independent ★ Girls ★ Boarding and Day ★ Ages 12–18 (plus associated prep school) ★ 280 pupils (82% boarding) ★ 99 in sixth form ★ Fees: £13,110 boarding; £6,930 day
Head: Mrs Mary James, 54, appointed 1988.
Attractive, well-run school; fairly wide range of abilities; good teaching and results; strong music and sport.

Profile
Background   Founded 1877 by academics at St Andrews University, 'in the belief that a girl should receive an education that is as good as her brother's, if not better'; imposing, stone buildings (ranging from 16th to 20th century) on a splendid, 30-acre, sea-side site overlooking the ruins of a medieval abbey; £2 million spent recently on refurbishment.

Atmosphere   Calm, civilised, well-ordered; the gardens and tree-lined walks help diminish the gravity of the buildings. According to the head, the St Leonards girl can be distinguished 'by the easy way she is able to combine feminism, in the sense of being independent and well-qualified, with the femininity in which pride and pleasure in being female are represented'; girls tend to be robust, straightforward, uncomplicated; individuality encouraged. Daily hymn and prayer (but school is secular in spirit). Jade-green uniform ('suits all colourings'). Junior school (ages seven to 12) in separate premises on same site under its own head.

Admissions   By Common Entrance or tests; school is not severely selective ('beggars can't be choosers – most children are educable, some are more of a challenge than others'). Most from farming or professional backgrounds; 60% Scottish, 20% from abroad; 13% from England. Very pleasant boarding accommodation: juniors in small, cosy dormitories (four to six beds); seniors have study-bedrooms; new, well-appointed house for sixth formers.

The head   Dynamic, determined; believes strongly in the value of single-sex education for girls. Was a pupil here ('I was naughty and not very successful');

read history at York (First); did post-graduate research at Oxford; taught at Sedbergh and Casterton; formerly head of Queen Ethelburga's, Harrogate. Strongly opposed to the 'finishing school philosophy'; wants her girls to be ambitious, independent, assertive. Married (to a historian); two grown-up sons.

The teaching   Good. Hard-working, well-qualified staff of 38 (nine men). Broad curriculum: all do Latin for first two years; choice of French, German, Spanish; science taught as three separate subjects; good art; lots of computing (first-class facilities). Most take eight GCSEs and three A-levels ('an English school in a Scottish setting') plus general studies; vocational courses in word-processing, office skills available. Pupils grouped by ability; progress closely monitored; average class size 16. Strong music: a third learn an instrument (numerous practice rooms); three orchestras, two choirs. Wide range of extra-curricular activities (cookery and dress-making classes regularly over-subscribed); well-supported Duke of Edinburgh award scheme (up to 14 gold medals a year). Regular language exchanges with schools in France, Germany, Spain.

Results   (1997) GCSE: all gained at least five grades A–C. A-level: creditable 71% of entries graded A or B.

Destinations   About 95% continue to the sixth form; of these, virtually all proceed to university (average of six a year to Oxbridge).

Sport   Proud tradition (the first British girl's school to play lacrosse – in 1890, a former headmistress having seen it in New Hampshire); all play games four afternoons a week plus matches on Saturdays. Main sports: hockey, lacrosse (county and national honours), athletics, tennis (numerous courts). Skiing, sailing, squash, fencing, golf, cross-country also on offer. Facilities include extensive playing fields, gym, indoor heated pool.

Remarks   Fine school; recommended.

ST LEONARDS, MAYFIELD ♀
The Old Palace, Mayfield, East Sussex TN20 6PH. Tel (01435) 873383

Synopsis
Independent ★ Roman Catholic ★ Girls ★ Boarding and day ★ Ages 11–18 ★ 500 pupils (60% boarding) ★ 160 in sixth form ★ Fees: £10,935 boarding; £7,290 day
Head: Sister Jean Sinclair, 62, appointed 1980.
First-rate school; high academic standards; fairly wide range of abilities; good music and drama.

Profile
Background   Founded 1872 by Cornelia Connelly, foundress of the Society of the Holy Child Jesus, in the grounds of the former residence of the pre-Reformation Archbishops of Canterbury; merged 1976 with an earlier foundation at St Leonards on Sea. Peaceful, rural setting; new buildings, including music school and science block, blend harmoniously with the medieval; chapel – said to have the widest unsupported arches in Europe – is exceptionally fine.

Atmosphere   Informal, tolerant, gentle; no dogmatic attitudes or rigid structures; school run on a system of trust. Christian values fundamental; emphasis on kindliness and concern for others; older girls given responsibility for younger ones. A general sense of quiet purpose and underlying self-discipline. No prizes until sixth form; commendation cards ensure everyone is congratulated and encouraged for something. Mass on Sundays (after 10 am breakfast) but no compulsory daily chapel. Strong links with parents.

Admissions By Common Entrance; fairly wide range of abilities; borderline children accepted for special reasons. Most from the South East; large expatriate contingent (Services, diplomatic, business, medical); boarders all Roman Catholic. Dormitories functional rather than cosy (though some recently refurbished); sixth-formers have study-bedrooms. Outstandingly good food (dedicated and very popular chef). Means-tested scholarships, some bursaries.

The head Very able and experienced; dedicated, devout, forgiving (with a humorous light in her eyes). Called to join the Society of the Holy Child Jesus after reading maths at London; taught Greek, Latin and maths at the society's schools in London, Birmingham and Preston; came here 1971 as director of studies; deputy head 1972. Commands enormous respect from pupils, staff and parents; constantly assessing how the school is living up to the high-minded ideals of its founder.

The teaching High standards encouraged in all areas; girls expected to work seriously – but through individual commitment rather than competitive pressure. Long-serving staff, including several men. Broad curriculum; all do computing and word processing (good facilities); science taught as three separate subjects from third year (very good results – many go on to do medicine, veterinary science, engineering); strong maths and languages; all do drama for first three years. Wide choice of subjects at A-level; lower-sixth do general studies course. Pupils grouped by ability in English, French, science, maths; average class size 20, reducing to eight in the sixth form. Good pottery in modern, well-equipped art block; strong drama and music tradition; excellent singing, five choirs, orchestra.

Results (1997) GCSE: 95% gained at least five grades A–C. A-level: 53% of entries graded A or B.

Destinations About 90% stay on for A-levels; of these, 95% proceed to university (average of six a year to Oxbridge).

Sport Chiefly: hockey, netball, tennis, volleyball, athletics, swimming. Facilities include superb indoor pool, two gyms, all-weather pitch, riding school and cross-country riding course.

Remarks Nurturing Christian school with high all-round standards. Warmly recommended. HMI reported (1995) that the school achieved at least as well for its least able pupils as for its high-fliers.

ST MARGARET'S
Magdalen Road, Exeter, Devon EX2 4TS. Tel (01392) 273197

Synopsis
Independent ★ Girls ★ Day ★ Ages 11–18 (plus associated junior school) ★ 456 pupils ★ 79 in sixth form ★ Fees: £4,542
Head: Mrs Maureen D'Albertanson, 52, appointed 1993.
Traditional, academic school; good teaching and results; strong music.

Profile
Background Founded 1904 to give a sound Christian education to the 'daughters of gentlemen'; joined the Anglo-Catholic Woodard Corporation 1975. Eight

Georgian houses (a rabbit warren of rooms, corridors, staircases) a mile from the city centre; space at a premium; £5 million building and refurbishment programme under way (funded by the sale of a now-redundant boarding house).

Atmosphere Purposeful, well-ordered; strong emphasis on traditional values; religious life 'based on the eucharistic tradition of the Anglican church' (all faiths welcomed). Uniform alters with seniority (sixth-formers in formal 'office wear'); competitive house system. Strong links with neighbouring Exeter School, qv (joint A-level teaching on both sites). Parents not regarded as intruders.

Admissions Over-subscribed and fairly selective – but likely to become less so: phasing out of assisted places, which 60 hold, will make recruiting more difficult; at the same time, Exeter School is going fully co-educational. Of the 60 who join each year at 11, 25 come from the junior school. Most from business/ professional backgrounds; extensive catchment area (parents organise buses). Some scholarships, bursaries (particularly for music).

The head Able, energetic. Read history at Coventry; formerly academic head of the Royal Ballet School. Teaches 14 periods a week (history, general studies). Married; two children.

The teaching Formal in style but lively. Broad curriculum: all do Latin for first three years; science taught as three separate subjects; good art. Pupils grouped by ability in maths, French; extra help for those who need it; average class size 15–20. All take three-year vocational course in keyboard skills, use of spreadsheets etc. Wide choice of 26 subjects at A-level, some in conjunction with Exeter. Exceptionally strong music: three orchestras, jazz band, madrigal group, chamber choir; frequent concerts. Extra-curricular activities include thriving cadet force, Duke of Edinburgh award scheme. Regular language exchanges with schools in France, Germany, Spain.

Results (1997) GCSE: all gained at least five grades A–C. A-level: 48% of entries graded A or B.

Destinations Nearly all go on to university (including Oxbridge).

Sport All participate but not a school for the very sporty; facilities are limited and some distance away. Main sports: netball, hockey, athletics. Badminton, lacrosse, tennis, golf on offer.

Remarks Good all round.

ST MARY'S, ASCOT ♀
Ascot, Berkshire SL5 9JF. Tel (01344) 23721

Synopsis
Independent ★ Roman Catholic ★ Girls ★ Boarding (and some day) ★ Ages 11–18 ★ 346 pupils (95% boarding) ★ 95 in sixth form ★ Fees: £12,798 boarding; £8,316 day
Head: Sister Frances Orchard, 52, appointed 1982 (retiring December 1998).
Distinguished Catholic school; very good teaching and results; lots on offer.

Profile
Background Founded 1885 by the Institute of the Blessed Virgin Mary to 'provide an excellent education in a Christian atmosphere'. Fine, purpose-built, red-brick premises (no gloomy Gothicism here) on a beautiful 44-acre site; lovely chapel (seats the whole school); first-rate sixth-form centre; recent additions include new art complex, music school.

Atmosphere   Warm, cheerful, highly academic; strong Catholic ethos and sense of community (isolating, say some); easy relations between staff and pupils; very good pastoral care (a family feel). Sisters of the Order live in a house in the grounds.

Admissions   At 11 and 13 by assessment and exams in maths, English; school is over-subscribed and highly selective. All from Catholic families (baptismal certificate required); 9% from abroad (mainly Spain). Good quality boarding accommodation; juniors in dormitories; sixth-formers have single rooms. Scholarships available.

The head   Very able: has modernised and transformed the school. Her mind is keen, her speech direct, her manner a mixture of the caring and downright practical. Was a pupil here; joined the Order; read history at Royal Holloway; taught at St Mary's, Cambridge for 10 years; returned here as head, taking over from her elder sister (who had been in post since 1976). Greatly respected by staff and pupils (and will be greatly missed). From January 1999: Mrs Mary Breen, head of physics at Eton.

The teaching   First-rate: generally formal in style; dedicated, stable staff. Broad curriculum: sciences taught separately; very good languages (Spanish, Italian, French, German, Portuguese); all do Latin for at least two years; religious education 'an integral part of the curriculum'; lots of computing; choice of 19 subjects at A-level. Pupils grouped by ability in maths from second year, Latin, French from third year, science for GCSE; more able take GCSE maths, French a year early; average class size 22, reducing to a maximum of 15 in sixth form. Strong art (all gain As at GCSE) and music; two-thirds learn an instrument. Extra-curricular activities include well-supported Duke of Edinburgh award scheme; ballet, tap dancing, pottery, drama, dress-making also on offer.

Results   (1997) GCSE: all gained at least five grades A–C. A-level: creditable 69% of entries graded A or B.

Destinations   Virtually all go on to university (average of five a year to Oxbridge).

Sport   Chiefly hockey, netball, tennis, swimming, athletics. Facilities include all-weather tennis courts, indoor pool.

Remarks   Highly recommended.

ST MARY'S, CALNE ♀
Calne, Wiltshire SN11 0DF. Tel (01249) 815899

Synopsis
Independent ★ Girls ★ Boarding and day ★ Ages 11–18 ★ 300 pupils (85% boarding) ★ 75 in sixth form ★ Fees: £12,840 boarding; £7,635 day
Head: Mrs Carolyn Shaw, 50, appointed 1996.
Strongly academic school; excellent results; good music and drama.

Profile
Background   Founded 1873 by the Vicar of Calne; moved to present, attractive 25-acre site 1907. Buildings of varied periods and styles, some in Cotswold stone, some bleak 1960s; modern, architecturally striking chapel (daily prayers attended by all). Co-educational junior school (ages four to 11) on same site.

Atmosphere   Friendly, purposeful; hard-working rather than glamorous. Strong feeling of community; good pastoral care system. Many former pupils send their daughters here. Uniform below the sixth form (where a dress code applies).

Admissions By Common Entrance. School is highly selective: girls must be able to cope with a substantial workload as well as at least two extra-curricular activities; those from the junior school have to compete for places. Boarding by age group: juniors in dormitories (up to 11 beds); seniors have more privacy (and more modern accommodation). Few foreigners (school does not recruit abroad). A few scholarships, bursaries.

The head Recent appointment. Read English; has taught in state and independent schools here and abroad (Solomon Islands, Bermuda); spent 12 years out of teaching; previously at Cheltenham Ladies' (qv). Married; two children.

The teaching First-rate: formal in style; well-qualified, predominantly female staff. Broad curriculum: all do French and Latin from the start and can add classical Greek, German or Spanish from third year; big emphasis on maths, science (taken by most as three separate subjects); good art; lots of computing. Most do nine GCSEs and three A-levels; options include divinity, drama, history of art. Pupils grouped by ability in maths, French; maximum class size 19, smaller in the sixth form; lots of individual help (well-established tutorial system). Very strong music (75% learn an instrument, extensive facilities) and drama (purpose-built theatre). Extra-curricular activities include cookery, needlework, woodwork, photography, Duke of Edinburgh award scheme.

Results (1997) GCSE: all gained at least five grades A–C. A-level: very impressive 86% of entries graded A or B.

Destinations Nearly all continue into the sixth form; about 95% proceed to university (eight or nine a year to Oxbridge).

Sport Chiefly: lacrosse, hockey, netball, tennis, swimming (outside pool), athletics. Basketball, volleyball, football, cricket also on offer. Facilities include nine tennis courts, floodlit pitch, ageing gymnasium (sports hall needed).

Remarks Very good school for able, hard-working girls.

ST MARY'S, CAMBRIDGE ♀
Bateman Street, Cambridge CB2 1LY. Tel (01223) 353253

Synopsis
Independent ★ Roman Catholic ★ Girls ★ Day and weekly boarding ★ Ages 11–18 ★ 517 pupils (90% day) ★ 107 in sixth form ★ Fees: £4,484 day; £8,025 weekly boarding
Head: Miss Michele Conway, 47, appointed 1989 (leaving August 1998).
Sound school; good teaching and results; lots of art, drama, music.

Profile
Background Founded 1898 by the Institute of the Blessed Virgin Mary; moved 1904 to handsome Victorian house over-looking the university botanic garden; functional later additions; many areas in need of refurbishment.

Atmosphere Busy, friendly; clear Catholic ethos (but 65% of the girls are non-Catholics); very good pastoral care; warm relations between staff and pupils; 'an education of the grammar school type within the setting of a Christian community'. Uniform of navy jumpers, tartan skirts; sixth-formers wear mufti. Much fund-raising for charity.

Admissions By tests in English, maths, verbal reasoning; school is not unduly selective and likely to become even less so with the phasing out of assisted places, which more than 120 hold. Weekly boarders from North London, Norfolk, Essex; cheerful dormitories; sixth-formers have individual study-bedrooms.

The head School's first lay head (a practising Catholic); good leader; gets on well with staff and girls. Read maths at Oxford; previously head of maths at St Leonards Mayfield (qv).

The teaching Formal in style but lively; well-qualified, predominantly female staff of 60 (60% appointed by present head). Fairly broad curriculum; sciences taught separately; languages include Latin, Greek, Italian, Spanish, German; lots of computing (but girls also learn italic handwriting); religious education 'an integral part' of the curriculum; choice of 23 subjects at A-level, including sociology, theatre studies, business studies; all do general studies. Pupils grouped by ability; some extra help for dyslexics; average class size 20, reducing to a maximum of 12 in the sixth form. Lots of art, drama, music; a third learn an instrument; several choirs, chamber orchestra, various ensembles. Extra-curricular activities include well-supported Duke of Edinburgh award scheme, Young Enterprise. Regular language exchange with pupils in Germany.

Results (1997) GCSE: all gained at least five grades A–C. A-level: 53% of entries graded A or B.

Destinations Nearly all go on to university (three or four a year to Oxbridge).

Sport Hockey, netball, tennis, rounders, athletics, swimming, gymnastics on offer; regular county, regional honours. Facilities include five acres of playing fields some distance away.

Remarks Good all round.

ST MARY'S, ILKLEY ♂ ♀
Menston, Ilkley, West Yorkshire LS29 6AE. Tel (01943) 872951

Synopsis
Comprehensive (voluntary-aided, Roman Catholic) ★ Co-educational ★ Ages 11–18 ★ 1,054 pupils (roughly equal numbers of girls and boys) ★ 197 in sixth form
Head: Michael Pyle, 44, appointed September 1997.
Popular but poorly resourced school; good GCSE results; very strong sport.

Background Opened as a secondary modern 1964; went comprehensive 1973. Cramped, undistinguished 1960s buildings (full of dark corridors) but well maintained; some subjects (technology, science, music) inadequately accommodated.

Atmosphere Strong Catholic ethos (daily services, lively chaplain); emphasis on hard work, good behaviour, high expectations. Well-organised pastoral care. Uniform worn by all. Parents highly supportive.

Admissions Over-subscribed; no academic selection (but general ability level is above average); 90% of 160 places reserved for Catholic children. Priority to those at 'feeder' primaries in six mid-Wharfedale parishes (includes parts of Leeds, Bradford, North Yorkshire).

The head New appointment. Read science at Aston and Bath; previously deputy head for eight years of a Yorkshire comprehensive. Married; three children.

The teaching Generally good: predominantly formal in style; well-qualified, long-serving staff of 62 (58% male). Standard national curriculum but science on offer as three separate subjects; more able may take both French and German for GCSE; good

results in maths, English. Most take 10 GCSEs, including compulsory religious studies; choice of 20 subjects at A-level (most do three plus general studies); sports studies popular; GNVQs available in business studies, leisure and tourism. Pupils grouped by ability in maths from second year, English, languages, science from third year; extra help for those with special needs (13 have 'statements'); maximum class size 30, smaller for GCSE and A-level. Lots of music (choirs, orchestra). Extra-curricular activities include public speaking, well-supported Duke of Edinburgh award scheme.
Results (1997) GCSE: creditable 67% gained at least five grades A–C. A-level: 32% of entries graded A or B.
Destinations About 70% continue into the sixth form; of these, 75% proceed to university (average of four a year to Oxbridge).
Sport Very strong: more than 300 fixtures a year in football, netball, rugby, cross-country, basketball, tennis, cricket, athletics; representative honours at local, regional, national levels.
Remarks Ofsted inspectors concluded (1996): 'Standards in the school are good overall. Pupils work hard and with perseverance. Religious, moral and social values are vigorously promoted.'

ST MARY'S RC HIGH ♂ ♀
Newbold Road, Upper Newbold, Chesterfield, Derbyshire S41 8AG. Tel (01246) 201191

Synopsis
Comprehensive (Roman Catholic, grant-maintained) ★ Co-educational ★ Ages 11–18 ★ 1,100 pupils (roughly equal numbers of girls and boys) ★ 210 in sixth form
Head: Tom Moore, 50, appointed 1992.
First-rate, well-run comprehensive; strong ethos; very good teaching and results.

Profile
Background Roots go back to the 1890s; became a secondary modern in the 1960s; went comprehensive 1974, after which numbers rose sharply; opted out of council control 1994. Sandy-brick buildings (under a splendid pitched roof) plus later additions; light, airy classrooms; all exceptionally neat and well maintained.
Atmosphere Scholarly, disciplined, co-operative; school aims to turn out pupils 'able to cope confidently with the demands of society and to contribute to its improvement'. Strong Catholic commitment spelt out to parents; day begins with class prayers; every classroom and office has a crucifix; religious education compulsory throughout. Smart navy uniform.
Admissions School over-subscribed; priority to Catholic children from 12 parishes across much of industrial and rural north Derbyshire; about 15% of places go to non-Catholics. Genuine cross-section of ability and social class.
The head Open, clear-sighted with an easy authority. Left school at 15 without O-levels to work at the same pit as Arthur Scargill; later sponsored by employers to take a degree in mechanical engineering; became a maths teacher at 25; previously head of a Catholic comprehensive in Nottinghamshire (a superb role-model for early under-achievers). Keen on soccer, poetry, opera. Married; two children.
The teaching Energetic, didactic, well-structured; pupils expected to work hard and develop self-discipline (ballpoint pens and other signs of sloppiness firmly discouraged). Stable staff of 65 (the majority are Catholics, most of the

rest practising members of other denominations). Standard national curriculum; particular strengths in languages (French and German), maths, science, history, English; GCSE options include 'lunchtime Latin' (about five pupils a year); vocational alternatives include keyboarding, office studies, child development. Choice of 21 subjects at A-level, including computing and theology. Pupils placed in one of two ability bands after first year; further setting in English, maths, languages; average class size 30, reducing to 24 for GCSE, 13 at A-level. Ambitious music: about 200 learn an instrument.

Results   (1997) GCSE: very creditable 72% gained at least five grades A–C. A-level: 48% of entries graded A or B.

Destinations   About 65% continue into the sixth form; up to 80% proceed to university (two or three a year to Oxbridge).

Sport   Soccer most popular, but main strengths are in hockey and basketball; enthusiastic cricket (but no turf wicket). Facilities include ample pitches, large gym – but absence of sports hall keenly felt.

Remarks   Very effective school, awash with old-fashioned values. Recommended for any Christian parent resident in north Derbyshire or happy to relocate there.

ST MICHAEL'S GRAMMAR ♀
Nether Street, North Finchley, London N12 7NJ. Tel (0181) 446 2256

Synopsis
Grammar (grant-maintained, Roman Catholic) ★ Girls ★ Ages 11–18 ★ 628 pupils ★ 150 in sixth form
Head: Miss Ursula Morrissey, 48, appointed 1995.
Lively school; good teaching and results; strong Christian ethos.

Profile
Background   Founded 1908 as a convent school by the Congregation of Sisters of the Poor Child Jesus; became a voluntary-aided grammar school 1958; opted out of council control 1993. Compact site in peaceful north London suburb; lower school in original, purpose-built yellow-brick building (now slightly battered); sixth form in large Victorian house (high ceilings, elegant conservatory); rest in functional 1950s premises; latest additions include new technology block. Considerable, but disciplined, movement between them.

Atmosphere   Lively, purposeful; supportive, almost family, feel (older girls voluntarily help the younger ones with sport at lunch time). Roman Catholicism is fundamental: day starts with a prayer, crucifix in every classroom, regular voluntary mass in chapel ('The prime aim of the school is the formation of responsible and committed Catholic citizens'). Respect for others and good manners expected; compulsory blazer-and-kilt uniform (sixth-formers expected to 'exercise good taste and judgement'). High turnout at parents' evenings.

Admissions   School over-subscribed; entry by interview ('to establish the Catholicity of the child') and tests in English, maths, reasoning; top 10% of the ability range. Wide social and ethnic mix drawn from a big catchment area (Barnet, Enfield, Haringey, Camden, Islington, Westminster); all from practising Roman Catholic families (reference required from parish priest).

The head   Read history at London; came here as head of history 1973. Practising Catholic: sees working in the parish as complementary to her job.

The teaching Challenging; wide range of styles; predominantly long-serving staff (a third male). Grammar school curriculum: particular strength in languages (choice of French, German, Spanish); all start Latin; sciences taught by specialists (six well-equipped labs); lots of computing. Wide range of subjects at A-level; all do three plus one AS-level. Pupils grouped by ability in maths only; regular testing; homework ('regarded as an essential feature of the curriculum') carefully monitored. Very good art; lively, enthusiastic music (two orchestras, choir, wind band).
Results (1997) GCSE: all gained at least five grades A–C. A-level: 57% of entries graded A or B.
Destinations Most stay on for A-levels; of these, nearly 90% proceed to university (up to five a year to Oxbridge).
Sport Strong tradition, and taken seriously – despite limited space and facilities (one large field, four netball/tennis courts). Netball, badminton, tennis played to high standard. Large gym (doubles as assembly hall).
Remarks Ofsted inspectors concluded (1995): 'St Michael's is a high achieving school where relationships are excellent. The pupils are happy and well cared for morally, socially and spiritually; their attitudes to learning are exemplary. The school's national reputation in the Catholic community is justifiably high.'

ST NICHOLAS HIGH ♂ ♀
Greenbank Lane, Hartford, Northwich, Cheshire CW8 1JW. Tel (01606) 75420

Synopsis
Comprehensive (voluntary-aided, Roman Catholic) ★ Co-educational ★ Ages 11–18 ★ 1,065 pupils (52% girls) ★ 160 in sixth form
Head: Gerard Boyle, 48, appointed 1995.
First-rate comprehensive; good teaching and results.

Profile
Background Opened 1965 as a secondary modern; went comprehensive 1972; numbers have risen steadily ever since. Functional, well-maintained premises; recent additions include good science labs, music suite, sixth-form centre, new classroom block, chapel. Large campus shared with other schools and a college; council estate on one side, private housing on the other.
Atmosphere Orderly, civilised, welcoming: a general air of calm efficiency. Strong emphasis on moral and spiritual values; relaxed, friendly relations between teachers and serious, hard-working pupils. Strict uniform for all; truancy not an issue.
Admissions School over-subscribed; priority to Roman Catholics from six 'feeder' primaries; about 10% are non-Catholic but expected to be committed Christians and participate in morning worship and RE lessons. Wide range of abilities and social backgrounds from a steadily expanding catchment area: Northwich, Knutsford, Sale, Frodsham, Weaverham, Middlewich, Holmes Chapel.
The head Committed Catholic; previously head of a Catholic school in Bolton. Teaches four periods a week (believes in keeping in touch with his pupils). Married (to a deputy head); three children.
The teaching Experienced, committed staff of 60 (equal numbers of women and men); very few leave, which gives the school a strong sense of stability and continuity. Wide range of teaching styles; pupils constantly challenged to participate. Broad curriculum in which religious education plays a leading role; science on offer as three

separate subjects; choice of French, Spanish, German, Latin. Pupils grouped by ability in English, maths, science from first year: progress carefully monitored; average class size 22/23, reducing to 15–18 in sixth form. Homework taken seriously. Good drama and music: 130 learn an instrument; prize-winning choir. Wide choice of extra-curricular activities; close links with a schools in Provence, Hamburg.

Results   (1997) GCSE: 67% gained at least five grades A–C. A-level: 44% of entries graded A or B.

Destinations   About 60% stay on for A-levels; of these, 97% proceed to university.

Sport   Main games (regular county honours): rugby, soccer, hockey, netball, basketball, golf. Facilities include extensive playing fields, sports hall (but no swimming pool).

Remarks   Very good all round; recommended.

ST OLAVE'S & ST SAVIOUR'S   ♂

Goddington Lane, Orpington, Kent BR6 9SH. Tel (01689) 820101

Synopsis

Grammar (grant-maintained) ★ Boys ★ Day ★ Ages 11–18 ★ 666 pupils ★ 187 in sixth form
Head: Anthony Jarvis, 52, appointed 1994.
Successful, traditional grammar school; high academic standards; strong music, sport.

Profile

Background   Result of 1899 merger of two 16th-century grammar schools near Tower Bridge; moved to present 20-acre site and attractive, purpose-built premises in a pleasant residential area 1968; opted out of council control 1993.

Atmosphere   Lively, friendly, well-disciplined; good pastoral care; strong sense of community ('We require hard work, good conduct and a high level of commitment and loyalty to the school'). Emphasis on rewards, Saturday detention if necessary. Smart blazer-and-tie uniform; sixth-formers wear suits. Large sums raised annually for charity.

Admissions   School is heavily over-subscribed (more than 600 apply for 112 places); entry by competitive tests in English, maths, reasoning. Pupils drawn from nearly 60 primary schools.

The head   Able, charming; good leader. Read English at Sussex; previously head of Sir Thomas Rich's (qv). Teaches English literature to the juniors, general studies to the sixth form. Married (to a teacher); two children (one a pupil here).

The teaching   Good; generally traditional in style. Experienced staff of 48 (75% male). Fairly broad curriculum: science on offer as three separate subjects; all take two languages (from French, German, Spanish); Latin, Greek available; choice of 19 subjects at A-level. Pupils grouped by ability in maths only from third year; extra help for those who need it; average class size 29, reducing to 19 for GCSE, nine in the sixth form. Strong music; a third learn an instrument; several choirs, orchestra, various other ensembles. Extra-curricular activities include debating, chess, Duke of Edinburgh award scheme. Close links with business (work experience, work shadowing, sponsorship). Regular language exchanges with pupils in France, Germany, Spain.

Results   (1997) GCSE: all gained at least five grades A–C. A-level: creditable 60% of entries graded A or B.

Destinations Nearly all proceed to university (about 10 a year to Oxbridge).
Sport A strength. Main activities: rugby, cricket, athletics, basketball, swimming; matches after school and on Saturdays; local, regional and national honours. Facilities include gym, indoor pool, five rugby pitches, courts for tennis, squash, Eton-fives (national champions).
Remarks Ofsted inspectors concluded (1996): 'This is a good school with some outstanding features. The pupils have high expectations of themselves.'

ST PAUL'S ♂
Lonsdale Road, Barnes, London SW13 9JT. Tel (0181) 748 9162

Synopsis
Independent ★ Boys ★ Day and boarding ★ Ages 13–18 ★ 770 pupils (90% day) ★ 300 in sixth form ★ Fees: £8,985 day; £13,560 boarding
Head: Stephen Baldock, 52, appointed 1992.
Distinguished academic school; broad range of sports and other activities; achieves great things with tough, committed boys.

Profile
Background Founded 1509 by John Colet, Dean of St Paul's, who, combining piety and humanism in the curriculum, rooted it in the secular world of the City of London by making the Mercers' Company trustees of the foundation. Moved 1884 to West Kensington (where it grew and became academically pre-eminent) and in 1968 to a 45-acre riverside site in Barnes (drab, featureless buildings but plenty of space); later additions include Milton building (John Milton was a Pauline) for art, drama, technology. Ethos is still that of Colet's original foundation: hard work, broad thinking and scholarship.
Atmosphere Efficient yet warm: this is a highly motivated, highly organised school (though some might think it has a touch of the well-run academic factory as bells ring and people move with measured speed and purpose from place to place). Pupils are ambitious and intellectually demanding: a good lesson is an earnest dialogue between teacher and taught; no time for posturing or airs and graces. Discipline not really an issue, but the authorities are strict on smoking and drugs and there is a tight absence note system. (This is no school for the shrinking violet or the un-motivated: some boys in each year are unable to cope, despite the well-organised pastoral structure and school counsellor). Instead of assembly (for which there is no hall), notices and announcements are relayed to classrooms by intercom. Utilitarian image somewhat softened during the two-hour lunch break, when a great array of extra-curricular activities takes place.
Admissions Highly competitive: minimum 65% mark required at Common Entrance; compulsory Latin. Most from within a 10-mile radius but some boys travel long distances. Boarders can choose whether to stay for the weekend; some have parents abroad, but others live as near as Kensington and still prefer to board (facilities, though, do not compare with those in a well-run boarding school). At any one time, there are 153 foundation scholars, as many as the Biblical miraculous draught of fishes. Phasing out assisted places, which about 70 hold, will reduce the social mix.
The head (High Master) A Pauline born and bred; came here as a pupil 1958; read classics and theology at Cambridge (double First); returned 1970 to teach Greek; became surmaster (deputy head) 1984. Efficient, reliable administrator; devoted to the school. Member of the MCC; referees junior rugby; plays the

organ. Married; four children.

The teaching   At its best, absolutely outstanding; knowledge imparted at a fast pace by lively, friendly teachers (73 men, eight women). Broad curriculum: science on offer as three separate subjects (well-equipped labs); languages include French, German, Italian; classics still attract some; sixth-formers encouraged to mix arts and sciences; good facilities for computing and technology. No Saturday morning school, which explains the hectic school day; two hours' homework on weekdays, three at weekends. No acceleration for extra-bright boys, but all classes streamed, with setting as needed. A third learn a musical instrument (joint concerts with St Paul's Girls' qv); enthusiastic art department; 300-seat theatre.

Results   (1997) GCSE: all gained at least five grades A–C (it takes a strong-minded young man to fail here). A-level: impressive 81% of entries graded A or B.

Destinations   About 95% continue into the sixth form; of these, 95% proceed to university (50 a year to Oxbridge).

Sport   All expected to take some part in sport. Large range of activities on offer, including golf, sailing, fencing. The rugby is impressive, and sometimes the rowing equally so; athletics taken seriously (naturally). Big sports centre; swimming pool.

Remarks   If you have an intelligent, self-motivated, capable boy, ambitious but without pretensions, enter him for St Paul's and watch them make a success of him. HMC inspectors concluded (1995): 'St Paul's fully deserves its fine reputation, its high academic, sporting and cultural standing and its popularity with the parents of its pupils. The quality of learning is what most impressed the inspectors; even more so on occasions than the quality of the teaching.'

ST PAUL'S GIRLS'   ♀
Brook Green, London W6 7BS. Tel (0171) 603 2288

Synopsis
Independent ★ Girls ★ Day ★ Ages 11–18 ★ 630 pupils ★ 200 in sixth form
★ Fees: £6,993
Head: Miss Janet Gough, 57, appointed 1993 (retiring August 1998).
Fine academic school; excellent teaching and results; first-rate music; strong sport.

Profile
Background   Founded 1904 by the John Colet Foundation; administered (like St Paul's, qv) by the Mercers' Company. Handsome Edwardian buildings and many later additions (including fine theatre, four new science labs) on a fairly restricted site in a pleasant part of Hammersmith.

Atmosphere   A palpable air of academic seriousness and liberal learning (girls need emotional, intellectual and physical stamina to cope). Friendly, respectful relations between staff and hard-working, highly motivated pupils. No uniform: girls dress without fuss in sweatshirts, jeans, trainers.

Admissions   Highly competitive: about 300 apply for 88 places; entry by searching interview and three 75-minute tests in English, maths. Successful candidates drawn from up to 40 prep schools; 25% from state primaries. Up to 30 a year join the sixth form from other schools after a two-day 'entrance exercise'. Phasing out of assisted places, which up to 70 hold, deeply regretted. Some scholarships (including art, music).

The head   (High Mistress) Exceptionally able; intensely proud of 'idiosyncratic' Paulinas; believes all pupils flourish best in a 'gender-free context'. Disguises her humour and firmness of purpose ('We are uncompromising in our commitment to intellectual rigour') behind a quiet, self-effacing manner. Read English at Cambridge; came here to teach it in 1964 and has spent only two years away; previously deputy and acting head; successfully saw the school through a troubled period. Stands at the hub ('on the Marble') every morning to make herself available to all; study door open at lunch-time; greatly respected by senior girls. From September 1998: Miss Elizabeth Diggory, 51, head of Manchester High (qv).

The teaching   Conducted at a brisk pace by an expert, totally professional staff of 60 (10 men); methods are on the whole traditional. Standard curriculum; outstanding English; strong sciences (dual award); very good languages (all do Latin plus French or German); lots of computing; flourishing art. Pupils grouped by ability in maths only; no competitive grading (girls encouraged to compete against themselves, not each other); average class size 20. Standard of music is legendary (Gustav Holst taught here); four choirs, three orchestras, various other ensembles; every girl expected to learn an instrument. First-rate careers advice. Extra-curricular activities include well-supported Duke of Edinburgh award scheme.

Results   (1997) GCSE: 99% gained at least five grades A–C. A-level: stunning 90% of entries graded A or B (the top girls' school three years in succession).

Destinations   Nearly all stay on for A-levels; 95% proceed to university (about a third to Oxbridge).

Sport   Compulsory up to the end of the fifth year: most carry on. Good record at lacrosse; the girls also shine in athletics, play tennis, netball and squash and row. Old-style gym but no sports hall; fine indoor pool, 300-metre running track.

Remarks   Unbeatable all-round education for able, confident girls.

ST PETER'S ♂ ♀
York YO3 6AB. Tel (01904) 623213

Synopsis
Independent ★ Co-educational ★ Day and boarding ★ Ages 13–18 (plus associated prep school) ★ 492 pupils (60% boys, 67% day) ★ 209 in sixth form ★ Fees: £6,933 day; £11,019 boarding
Head: Andrew Trotman, 41, appointed 1995.
Successful, well-run school; good teaching and results; strong art, music, sport.

Profile
Background   Founded 627 by Paulinus, first bishop of York; moved to present, attractive 27-acre site (looks like an Oxbridge college) 1832; became co-educational 1987. Facilities are good. Prep school (St Olave's – 280 pupils aged eight to 13) on adjoining site under its own head.

Atmosphere   Busy, purposeful; clear-cut rules (possession of drugs leads to expulsion); chapel three times a week. Day pupils may stay until 8 pm; lessons on Saturday mornings.

Admissions   By tests in English, maths, verbal reasoning; school is fairly selective but phasing out of assisted places, which about 100 hold, is likely to have a significant impact. Boarding accommodation (two boys' houses, two girls') is of a high standard; most boarders from within 50 miles; 20% are children of expatriates.

The head   Youthful, able; strong, effective leader. Read English at Oxford; taught it at Radley and Abingdon; previously deputy head of Edinburgh Academy (qv). Plays the bagpipes; coaches under-15 rugby. Widowed; two children (both in the prep school); brother is head of Bishop's Stortford (qv).

The teaching   Enthusiastic; generally traditional in style. Standard curriculum; strong maths, science (dual award); good languages (with IT and satellite equipment); choice of 20 subjects at A-level. Pupils grouped by ability in maths, French; average class size 21, reducing to 13 in the sixth form. Very good art (Scottish sculptor in residence) and music (choirs, orchestras, various ensembles). Extracurricular activities include cadet force (popular with both sexes), Duke of Edinburgh award scheme. Regular language exchange with schools in France.

Results   (1997) GCSE: all gained at least five grades A–C. A-level: 63% of entries graded A or B.

Destinations   Virtually all proceed to higher education (up to 10 a year to Oxbridge).

Sport   Wide range, including rugby, netball, hockey, cricket, rowing (on the Ouse), swimming. Facilities include extensive playing fields, sports hall, indoor pool, tennis and squash courts.

Remarks   Good all round.

ST PETER'S RC HIGH   ♂ ♀
Howards Lane, Orrell, Wigan WN5 8NU. Tel (01942) 747693

Synopsis
Comprehensive (voluntary-aided, Roman Catholic) ★ Co-educational ★ Ages 11–16 ★ 930 pupils (roughly equal numbers of girls and boys)
Head: Alan Edwards, 48, appointed 1992.
First-rate comprehensive; good teaching and results; strong sport.

Profile
Background   Opened 1964 as a secondary modern; went comprehensive 1973. Flat-roofed 1960s buildings set in 18 acres adjacent to the M6; recent additions include well-designed science, art, technology blocks.

Atmosphere   Relaxed, cheerful, orderly; big emphasis on self-discipline. Roman Catholic values implicit rather than obtrusive ('Gospel values are at the heart of the curriculum'); very good relations between staff and lively, ambitious pupils; well-organised pastoral care system. Lots of pupil work on display (bold, imaginative paintings, textile, pottery) but the architecture makes some areas seem cold and dismal. Strict blazer-and-tie uniform ('A school is often judged by the appearance and conduct of its pupils in public'). Strong tradition of self-help: funds generated from tuck shop, parent-run club, commercial sponsorship etc.

Admissions   School over-subscribed (about 190 apply for 170 places); priority to those from six Roman Catholic 'feeder' primaries in Shevington, Orrell, Wrightington, Standish, Birchley, Up Holland. Most from middle-class backgrounds.

The head   Gentle, courteous Welshman; read English at Aberystwyth; has spent most of his career in Roman Catholic comprehensives. Says he believes in trusting children, and they rarely let him down; on excellent terms with his staff. Married; two children.

The teaching   Able, hard-working staff of 58 (43 women) fully committed to the school's humane philosophy: they care about their pupils and get the best from them, whatever their abilities (20 have 'statements' of special needs). Standard national curriculum; sciences taught by specialists; energetic modern languages; all do religious education. Choice of 25 subjects for GCSE including business studies, food technology, drama, sports studies; vocational alternatives available. Pupils grouped by ability in English, maths; average class size 30, reducing to 20 for GCSE; homework is 'an important feature of life at St Peter's'. First-rate art; active music (choirs, orchestra, brass band). Good careers department. Extra-curricular activities include Duke of Edinburgh award scheme, residential visits to the Lake District, regular language trips to France, Germany.

Results (1997) GCSE: 65% gained at least five grades A–C.

Destinations About 85% go on to sixth-form or further education colleges.

Sport Strong tradition; many town and county representatives. Main games: soccer, rugby league, hockey, netball, athletics, tennis. Facilities include good playing fields, all-weather pitch, large gym, first-rate sports hall.

Remarks Caring, challenging school; recommended.

ST SWITHUN'S ♀
Alresford Road, Winchester, Hampshire SO21 1HA. Tel (01962) 861316

Synopsis
Independent ★ Girls ★ Day and boarding ★ Ages 11–18 ★ 460 pupils (52% day) ★ 112 in sixth form ★ Fees: £7,290 day; £12,075 boarding
Head: Dr Helen Harvey, 47, appointed 1995.
First-rate academic school; very good teaching and results; fine facilities; lots of music, sport.

Profile
Background Founded 1884 to inculcate 'sound learning and true religion'; moved 1931 to present 22-acre hill-top site and purpose-built, Queen-Anne-style premises; many later additions; very good facilities. Junior school (200 girls aged three to 11) on same site.

Atmosphere Bright, cheerful, efficient ('Emphasis is placed on Christian values and consideration for others'); happy girls determined to get on and succeed; sensible discipline; supportive pastoral care. Neat uniform below the sixth form.

Admissions By Common Entrance and previous school report; school is very selective. Most live within 50 miles; 8% expatriates; few foreign nationals. Comfortable boarding houses; first-years in cheerful dormitories; upper-sixth have own study-bedrooms; weekly boarding available. Scholarships: academic, music.

The head Able, quietly spoken, precise. Read human physiology at London (PhD in tumour immunology); previously head of a girls' school on the Isle of Wight. Married (to a retired doctor); two children.

The teaching First-rate; experienced, well-qualified staff (two-thirds female). Broad curriculum; sciences taught separately; all do French and German from the start, Latin from second year; very good technology; lots of computing; choice of 19 subjects at GCSE, 24 at A-level; all do general studies. Pupils grouped by ability in maths, modern languages; extra help for dyslexics; average class size 20. Strong music; choirs, orchestras, ensembles. Wide range of extra-curricular activities, including cookery, dress-making, engineering, Duke of Edinburgh award scheme.

Results (1997) GCSE: all gained at least five grades A–C. A-level: impressive 82% of entries graded A or B (17th in the league table).

Destinations Almost all go to university (average of 10 a year to Oxbridge).

Sport Very strong lacrosse (compulsory for first three years); netball, tennis, athletics, fencing, trampolining, archery, golf, volleyball also available. Facilities

include fine sports hall, indoor pool.
Remarks   Fine school for able girls.

ST THOMAS À BECKET ♂ ♀
Barnsley Road, Wakefield WF2 6EQ. Tel (01924) 250408

Synopsis
Comprehensive (Roman Catholic) ★ Co-educational ★ Day ★ Ages 11–16 ★
750 pupils
Head: Paul Heitzman, 41, appointed 1995.
Successful, popular school; strong Catholic ethos; good teaching.

Profile
Background   Opened as a secondary modern 1963; went comprehensive 1974.
Undistinguished-looking buildings on the edge of a middle-class suburb.
Atmosphere   Firm Catholic ethos (local priest is a regular presence in the
school); high expectations in work and behaviour are the norm; good pastoral
care ('The teachers are always there for you,' say pupils). Parents actively
involved and regularly consulted: very much a community.
Admissions   Over-subscribed; no academic selection. Priority to: Catholic
pupils in named local Catholic primaries; other Catholics; non-Catholics whose
parents can demonstrate a desire for a Christian education (strong reference
from a minister required). Fairly wide range of abilities drawn mostly from
Wakefield and surrounding villages, some from further afield; 15% non-
Catholic. Breakfast served from 8.15 am.
The head   Energetic, hard-working; gets on well with staff and pupils. Read history
at Manchester; has worked only in Catholic schools and still believes his place is in
the classroom (teaches for a third of the timetable). Married; four children.
The teaching   Staff of 40 (some non-Catholic but all must have a faith and espouse
the general ethos of the school). Standard national curriculum. Pupils grouped by
ability in maths from the start, in science and languages from second year; progress
closely monitored; good provision for special needs; extra help out of hours for any
falling behind. Lots of extra-curricular activities, including popular Duke of Edinburgh award scheme. Regular language exchanges with schools in France, Germany.
Results   (1996) GCSE: 48% gained at least five grades A–C (not a good year).
Destinations   About 90% remain in full-time education.
Sport   Strong rugby, soccer, athletics; martial arts popular.
Remarks   Good all round; deservedly popular.

ST THOMAS MORE, ELTHAM ♂ ♀
Footscray Road, Eltham, London SE9 2SU. Tel (0181) 850 6700

Synopsis
Comprehensive (voluntary-aided, Roman Catholic) ★ Co-educational ★ Day
★ Ages 11–16 ★ 532 pupils (roughly equal numbers of girls and boys)
Head: Gerry Murray, 49, appointed 1995.
*First-rate comprehensive; very good teaching and GCSE results; lots of extra-
curricular activities.*

Profile

Background Opened 1964 as a secondary modern; went comprehensive 1974. No-frills concrete and glass building on a small site in a pleasant, residential area; space at a premium (school is expanding); financial constraints evident (premises look shabby though spotlessly clean); facilities are basic. Chapel funded, designed and built by parents.

Atmosphere Orderly, friendly (a close community); strong Christian ethos (crucifixes in every classroom); teachers addressed in class as 'Sir' or 'Madam'. First-rate pastoral care system (school has the lowest truancy rate in the borough); uniform strictly enforced. Pupils' work neatly displayed throughout.

Admissions Heavily over-subscribed (nearly 200 apply for 120 places); no academic selection. Catchment area restricted to radius of 3.2 miles; priority to children of parents who are committed Catholics (attested to by the parish priest) and attend weekly Mass. Pupils' backgrounds range from affluent to deprived (20% qualify for free school meals); 10% ethnic minority.

The head Came here as deputy head 1986. Strong leader; gets on well with staff, parents, pupils. Read history at Queen's, Belfast and Trinity, Dublin; has taught in independent and grammar schools. Married (no children).

The teaching Good: able, long-serving staff (equal numbers of women and men); well-planned lessons; eager, well-disciplined children. Standard national curriculum; Spanish on offer as a second language; big emphasis on the arts and humanities; lots of computing; all take nine or 10 GCSEs (including compulsory religious studies). Pupils grouped by ability from the start (on the basis of tests in verbal and non-verbal reasoning); further setting in maths from second year and in English, French, science for GCSE; specialist help for those who need it. Strong music (choir, ensembles), good art (but limited facilities), lots of drama.

Results (1997) GCSE: very creditable 71% gained at least five grades A–C (among the best state school results in London).

Destinations Virtually all remain in full-time education.

Sport Limited facilities (two playgrounds, one gym) but a surprisingly large range: football, hockey, tennis, athletics, basketball, volleyball, rounders, netball, cricket.

Remarks Ofsted inspectors concluded (1996): 'This is a very good school with many outstanding features.'

ST THOMAS MORE, GATESHEAD ♂ ♀
Croftdale Road, Blaydon-on-Tyne, Gateshead NE21 4BQ. Tel (0191) 499 0111

Synopsis
Comprehensive (voluntary-aided, Roman Catholic) ★ Co-educational ★ Ages 11–18 ★ 1,213 pupils (roughly equal numbers of girls and boys) ★ 265 in sixth form
Head: Michael Zarraga, 54, appointed 1980.
First-rate, well-run comprehensive; very good teaching and results; strong sport.

Profile

Background Opened 1967 as a secondary modern; went comprehensive 1977; achieved technology college status 1994 (one of the first to do so). Solid buildings plus numerous later additions (school has more than doubled in size) on a hill overlooking the Tyne; bright, welcoming classrooms; first-rate facilities for science, design/technology, computing.

Atmosphere Highly disciplined; strong Catholic ethos. Prospectus opens with an account of the martyrdom of St Thomas More ('Pray for me as I will for you, that we may meet merrily in heaven') and continues, 'There is, we believe, a direct link between our high standard of discipline, the caring, Christian ethos of the school and high examination performance.' Pupils may be expelled for being insolent to a member of staff, making an unprovoked physical assault on another pupil or persistently playing truant. Corridors ablaze with pupils' art work. House-based pastoral system fosters family feeling; smart uniform worn with pride. Parents and visitors warmly welcomed.

Admissions Over-subscribed (275 apply for 190 places); priority to those from 11 parishes and eight 'feeder' primaries in Gateshead; 40 a year admitted from outside the catchment area; 15% ceiling on non-Catholics. Wide range of abilities and social backgrounds

The head Very able. His enthusiasm, vision and understanding have created a school that attracts staff of the highest quality. Brought up in one of the poorer areas of Newcastle; read physics at university; has made teaching his life. Married, two sons.

The teaching Styles that were once too didactic have been liberalised and broadened to cope with a wide range of abilities and to raise staff expectations and pupil performance. Broad curriculum: science taught as three separate subjects; 60% take a second foreign language; choice of 16 subjects at A-level; GNVQs available in health & social care, business & finance, science, engineering. First-years grouped into broad ability bands; further setting thereafter; average class size 25, reducing to 15 in sixth form. Lots of drama, music, dance; full programme of community work ('Christianity in action'). Regular language exchanges with schools in Germany, France.

Results (1997) GCSE: creditable 66% gained at least five grades A–C. A-level: 40% of entries graded A or B. Good results, too, in vocational courses.

Destinations More than 70% continue into the sixth form; the vast majority proceed to university (about 40% of those who join at 11).

Sport All team games are strong; athletics, badminton, basketball also thrive. Facilities include playing fields carved out of the hillside, all-weather tennis courts and half a sports hall (badly in need of completion – fund-raising continues).

Remarks Outstanding school providing an education of breadth and quality. With an intake close to the national average, it achieves well above average results: added value plain to see. Highly recommended.

ST THOMAS MORE HIGH ♂ ♀
Dane Bank Avenue, Crewe, Cheshire CW2 8AE. Tel (01270) 68014

Synopsis
Comprehensive (voluntary-aided, Roman Catholic) ★ Co-educational ★ Ages 11–16 ★ 530 pupils (equal numbers of girls and boys)
Head: Ron Steele, 43, appointed September 1997.
Successful, small comprehensive; good GCSE results; strong emphasis on moral and spiritual values.

Profile
Background Opened as a secondary modern 1965; went comprehensive 1978. Compact campus fronting a fairly busy road in the middle of a large housing

estate; extensive playing fields behind. Bright, airy classrooms in good decorative order but space is tight; technology areas need updating.

Atmosphere Exceptionally orderly, quiet; strong Christian ethos (dignified assemblies). Good relations between staff and pupils; a friendly, cohesive community. School highly regarded locally; parents strongly supportive.

Admissions No academic selection; priority to Catholics, then non-Catholics from three 'feeder' primaries (25% are non-Catholic). About 60% come from Crewe; rest from Alsager, Nantwich, Sandbach. Numbers are increasing.

The head Recent appointment. Has spent his career in Catholic schools (apart from a spell training as a police officer); previously head of a tough comprehensive in Salford.

The teaching Good quality; generally traditional in style. Long-serving staff of 35 (60% female). Standard national curriculum; strengths in languages (French, German), religious education. Pupils grouped by ability from first year in maths, French; from second year in English, science (dual award), humanities; average class size 29, reducing to 24 for GCSE. Most take nine GCSEs; big emphasis on homework. Some music (choir, orchestras), but extra-curricular activities are limited.

Results (1997) GCSE: 61% gained at least five grades A–C.

Destinations About 80% remain in full-time education.

Sport Usual mix of soccer, hockey, rugby, netball, cricket, athletics. Indoor facilities limited.

Remarks Small, no-frills school enabling pupils to achieve academic success and develop strong Christian principles. Ofsted inspectors concluded (1994): 'This is a good school providing education of a high standard fully in accord with its stated aims. Its lively Catholic ethos pervades all aspects of school life.'

SANDBACH HIGH ♀
Middlewich Road, Sandbach, Cheshire CW11 9EB. Tel (01270) 765031

Synopsis
Comprehensive ★ Girls ★ Ages 11–18 ★ 1,100 pupils ★ 180 in sixth form
Head: John Leigh, 38, appointed 1993.
Successful, well-run comprehensive; good teaching and results; strong music.

Profile
Background Originally a co-educational secondary modern; turned into a girls' comprehensive 1979 in the belief that girls would do better in a single-sex environment. Functional buildings plus many recent additions, including new sixth-form centre; six classrooms in 'temporary' huts; funding is tight (and paint is peeling).

Atmosphere Studious, busy, well-ordered; big emphasis on courtesy, self-discipline, service to others. Competitive house system (honours boards, silver cups, shields proudly displayed); uniform regarded as a sign of commitment to the school; emphasis on partnership with parents.

Admissions Places guaranteed to all in the official catchment area; another 50 a year available to those outside it (priority to those attending 'feeder' primaries, living closest). Ability level slightly above average.

The head Youthful, energetic, good manager; gets on well with staff and pupils. Read economics at Nottingham Trent; came here as deputy head in 1990; teaches GCSE computing.

The teaching Good quality. Standard national curriculum; GCSE options include dance, child development, business studies; wide choice of 26 subjects at A-level; vocational alternatives available. Pupils grouped by ability from the start; extra help for those who need it; average class size 25, reducing to 23 for GCSE. Strong musical tradition: 160 learn an instrument; choir (European tours), large orchestra, various ensembles. Lots of extra-curricular activities, including popular Duke of Edinburgh award scheme. Regular language exchanges with schools in France, Spain.

Results   (1997) GCSE: 65% gained at least five grades A–C. A-level: 44% of entries graded A or B.

Destinations   Most continue into the sixth form; of these, about 75% proceed to university (average two a year to Oxbridge).

Sport   Participation strongly encouraged. Main sports: hockey, netball, tennis, athletics, swimming. First-rate facilities at neighbouring leisure centre.

Remarks   Praised by Ofsted (1995) as a 'high-achieving, successful and flourishing school community'.

SEDBERGH ♂
Sedbergh, Cumbria LA19 5HG. Tel (015396) 20535

Synopsis
Independent ★ Boys ★ Boarding (and some day) ★ Ages 11–18 ★ 336 pupils ★ 120 in sixth from ★ Fees: £9,060–£12,945 boarding; £9,210–£12,945 day
Head: Christopher Hirst, 50, appointed 1995.
Well-run boarding school with lots to offer; good teaching and results; strong sport.

Profile
Background   Founded 1525; reconstituted 1874, from when many of the stately buildings date; vast campus encircling the town (marvellous views over the Cumbrian hills); facilities include first-rate library, graceful assembly hall, fine chapel. Keeping up numbers is a struggle; £2 million appeal launched.

Atmosphere   Calm, civilised (stern motto, Dura Virum Nutrex – 'a hard nurse of men' – no longer applies). Good pastoral support; links with girls at Casterton (qv) encouraged; temptations of urban life kept at bay. Day begins and ends with prayers ('the school lays emphasis on introducing boys to the Christian faith'). Close links with parents.

Admissions   At 11 by interview and tests, at 13 by Common Entrance; school is not really selective, though A-level study is the ultimate goal. Scholarships, bursaries available; phasing out of assisted places will add to recruiting difficulties. Strong house system ('flagships staffed by admirals'); boarding accommodation recently modernised (juniors in dormitories of up to 12, seniors in small bed-sits).

The head   Enthusiastic; strongly committed to single-sex boarding (in defiance of the trend); emphasises the importance of academic achievement. Read history at Cambridge; previously head for 10 years of Kelly College, Devon. Keen on sport. Married (wife teaches general studies); three young daughters.

The teaching   Formal but friendly; well-qualified staff of 52 (seven women). Broad curriculum: science on offer as three separate subjects; all do Latin; most add French and German; Greek on offer; lots of computing. Pupils grouped by ability in main subjects; progress carefully monitored; maximum class size 24. Good music, drama, art (A-level options include sculpture, graphics). Extra-curricular activities include numerous expeditions, popular cadet force (marching band, corps of drums), Duke of Edinburgh award scheme.

Results   (1997) GCSE: 97% gained at leave five grades A–C. A-level: 40% of entries graded A or B.

Sport   Full programme; all expected to take part. First-rate facilities include sports hall, indoor pool, all-weather tennis courts, golf course, indoor shooting range. Main sports: rugby, cricket, cross-country (annual 10-mile run over unforgiving Cumbrian fells), fives, squash, hockey, soccer.

Remarks   Good school for active, gregarious boys.

SEVENOAKS ♂ ♀

Sevenoaks, Kent TN13 1HU. Tel (01732) 455133

Synopsis

Independent ★ Co-educational ★ Day and boarding ★ Ages 11–18 ★ 900 pupils (56% boys, 67% day) ★ 400 in sixth form ★ Fees: £8,676 day; £13,680 boarding
Head: Tommy Cookson, 55, appointed 1996.
Fine, well-rounded school; strong international flavour (IB on offer); good art, drama, music; wide range of games and extra-curricular activities.

Profile

Background   Founded 1432 (one of the three oldest lay foundations); 100-acre town-centre site (tunnel under the High Street) overlooking Knole Park; buildings range from 18th-century to uncompromisingly modern (and some 'temporary' huts); some classrooms due for refurbishment. First-rate facilities include £1.6 million international sixth-form centre, IT centre (computer:pupil ratio 1:6), 32,000-volume library, music school.

Atmosphere   Purposeful, tightly run; big emphasis on achievement (learning by doing); nearly 200 pupils from 40 countries, many attracted by the International Baccalaureate. Discipline assumed rather than imposed; easy relations between staff and pupils. Parents kept closely informed (and given all teachers' home phone numbers). Lessons on Saturday mornings; busy programme of weekend activities. Good food; lots of choice (but rather noisy, soulless dining room).

Admissions   At 11, by school's own exams in English, maths, science, reasoning; at 13, by Common Entrance (60% mark required). Fifty scholarships a year – academic, music, art, sport – but changes may follow the phasing out of the assisted places scheme. Boarding accommodation (seven houses) ranges from small dormitories for juniors to five-star luxury for sixth-formers.

The head   An enabler rather than a driver: bursting with ideas; an education romantic (keen on breadth, cross-curricular initiatives, sport for all). Read English at Oxford; taught at Manchester Grammar, Winchester (housemaster); previously head of King Edward VI, Southampton (qv). Married (wife teaches religious studies here); three daughters (the youngest a pupil here).

The teaching   Stimulating; varied styles. Highly committed staff of 95 (roughly equal numbers of women and men); attentive, well-motivated pupils. Broad curriculum: languages include Dutch, Greek, Italian, Arabic, Japanese; all do Latin from 11 to 13; science taught as three separate subjects (particularly good results); strong design/technology (in converted outbuildings). Pupils grouped by ability in maths, science, French; average class size 20–22, reducing to nine in sixth form; no special help (yet) for dyslexics. About 90 a year (out of 200) take the (broader, more challenging) International Baccalaureate in preference to A-levels (choice of 23 subjects). First-rate art (under less-than-ideal conditions), drama (40 a year take it for GCSE), music (three choirs, orchestras, various ensembles). Masses of extra-curricular activities, including well-supported cadet force, Duke of Edinburgh award scheme; 'Digweed' (estate management) cheerfully undertaken. Regular language exchanges with schools in France (all go for six weeks – included in the fees), Germany, Spain, Russia; many other trips abroad for study and sport.

Results (1997) GCSE: all gained at least five grades A–C. A-level (including IB): creditable 74% of entries graded A or B (among the best co-educational school results).

Destinations Virtually all go on to university (up to 40 a year to Oxbridge).

Sport Huge range; vast fixture list; all required to participate. Main sports: rugby, cricket, athletics (all-weather track) for boys; netball, hockey for girls; tennis (indoor and outdoor courts) for both. Fencing, golf, shooting, etc, also on offer; no indoor pool.

Remarks Very good all round: experimentation encouraged within a tight framework; great care taken to identify and nurture individual talent. Recommended – but not for the lethargic or those who need spoon-feeding.

SEXEY'S ♂ ♀
Cole Road, Bruton, Somerset BA10 0DF. Tel (01749) 813393

Synopsis
Comprehensive (grant-maintained) ★ Co-educational ★ Boarding and day ★ Ages 11–18 ★ 394 pupils (55% boys, 75% boarding) ★ 188 in sixth form ★ Fees (boarding only): £4,350
Head: Stephen Burgoyne, 49, appointed 1996.
Unusual state boarding school; good teaching and results; lots of sport.

Profile
Background Founded 1638 by Sir Huge Sexey, chancellor to Elizabeth I; re-established 1889 as a trade school; became a boys' grammar school 1944; girls admitted 1977; went comprehensive 1978; opted out of council control 1991. Variety of buildings, some modern and pleasant, on a cramped site; many classrooms in ageing 'temporary' huts; sixth form over-crowded. All pupils board between 11 and 16.

Atmosphere Busy, friendly, well-ordered; strong Christian ethos (but those of all faiths and none welcomed); good relations between staff and pupils. Uniform worn casually; seniors' dress code liberally interpreted. According to the prospectus: 'Boarding without snobbery, academic success without elitism, and manners without moulding.'

Admissions By interview to assess suitability for boarding, ability to benefit from the academic programme and a genuine desire to enter the school; entry restricted to UK nationals and EU passport-holders; school over-subscribed. Admission to sixth form requires five GCSEs grades A–C. Purpose-built boarding accommodation is attractive and spacious; good pastoral care.

The head Read history at Manchester; previously deputy head of a Kent grammar school. Keen sportsman; teaches RE and philosophy. Married (to a teacher); two children (one a pupil here).

The teaching Challenging; traditional in style; experienced, committed staff (equal numbers of women and men). Standard national curriculum; sciences taught separately; good maths; strong design/technology. Pupils grouped by ability in some subjects from second year; maximum class size 20. Little music (creative and aesthetic subjects not a strength). Extra-curricular activities include Duke of Edinburgh award scheme. Regular language exchanges with schools in France, Germany.

Results (1997) GCSE: very creditable 90% gained at least five grades A–C. A-level: 36% of entries graded A or B.

Destinations About 90% proceed to higher education.

Sport Lots on offer; regular county honours. Facilities include extensive playing fields, sports hall, covered pool.

Remarks Ofsted inspectors concluded (1996): 'This is a good school which gives a very effective education to its pupils. Standards of behaviour and courtesy are very high.'

SHARNBROOK ♂ ♀

Odell Road, Sharnbrook, Bedfordshire MK44 1JX. Tel (01234) 782211

Synopsis

Comprehensive (grant-maintained) ★ Co-educational ★ Ages 13–18 ★ 1,425 pupils (roughly equal numbers of girls and boys) ★ 500 in sixth form
Head: David Jackson, 48, appointed 1987.
Successful school; good teaching and results; strong sport.

Profile

Background Opened 1975; well-maintained, purpose-built premises on the edge of a village in lovely countryside (school has its own, partly self-financing, farm unit); later additions include new classroom block. School has expanded steadily; £1.1 million sixth-form centre planned. Community college status means 3,000 students of all ages enrol annually for day and evening classes, weekend workshops.

Atmosphere Calm, mature, well-ordered; no graffiti or litter. First rule: 'Students are expected to try to be friendly, polite and considerate at all times to all people'. Strong links with local industry and business; school benefits considerably from commercial sponsorship.

Admissions Over-subscribed but no academic selection: catchment area based on three 'feeder' middle schools which draw from 32 Bedfordshire villages and further afield ('What parents want,' says the head, 'is access to their local school and for that school to be a good one'); pupils from a wide variety of backgrounds; general level of ability above average.

The head Very experienced: came here as deputy 1983. Married; three daughters (all pupils here).

The teaching Effective, innovative. Standard national curriculum with big emphasis on technology (own TV studio, closed-circuit network, satellite broadcasting system), expressive arts, personal and social education. All take at least nine GCSEs (particularly good results in science); unusually wide choice of 30 subjects at A-level; GNVQs available. Pupils grouped by ability in some subjects from the start; extra help for those who need it. Extra-curricular activities include excellent Duke of Edinburgh award scheme (250 a year take part), farm club. Regular language exchanges to France, Italy, Germany, Spain.

Results (1996) GCSE: creditable 68% gained at least five grades A–C. A-level:

40% of entries graded A or B.

Destinations About 80% continue into the sixth form; of these, 85% proceed to university.

Sport Excellent facilities, well-qualified staff, good links with local clubs; virtually everything on offer. Main sports: rugby, hockey, soccer, netball, basketball, cross-country, cricket, tennis, badminton, volleyball.

Remarks Attractive mixture of the traditional and innovative. Recommended.

SHEFFIELD HIGH ♀
10 Rutland Park, Sheffield S10 2PE. Tel (0114) 266 1435

Synopsis
Independent ★ Girls ★ Day ★ 11–18 (plus associated junior school) ★ 583 pupils ★ 140 in sixth form ★ Fees: £4,152
Head: Mrs Margaret Houston, 52, appointed 1989.
Well-run, academic school; good teaching and results.

Profile
Background Founded 1878 by the Girls' Day School Trust; moved 1884 to present imposing, purpose-built premises (high ceilings, huge windows) in residential conservation area ('Betjeman Sheffield'). First-rate facilities, including sixth-form centre (with own car park); juniors in neighbouring old vicarage.

Atmosphere Unpressured, friendly; dedicated staff, able girls (who could ask for more?) Notice boards groan with posters, dates, fixtures. Sixth-formers regarded as students and not expected to wear uniform. Good relations between school and parents.

Admissions For younger pupils by oral and practical activities (administered 'as sympathetically as possible'), at 11 by tests in English, maths; school is fairly selective. Pupils travel by special coaches from a 20-mile radius. Scholarships, bursaries available; trust aims to replace the assisted places scheme (from which many girls benefit) with one of its own.

The head Very much in charge; loves her job (describes the school as 'my work, my hobby, my passion'). Read English at Leeds, formerly deputy head of a large comprehensive in North Yorkshire. Married; two grown-up daughters.

The teaching Good; well-qualified, predominantly female staff. Broad curriculum: all do Latin plus French and German for first three years; science taught as three separate subjects. GCSE options include Greek, Russian, geology; wide choice of 23 subjects at A-level (extra coaching for Oxbridge entry). Pupils grouped by ability in some subjects; homework regarded as essential. Extra-curricular activities include thriving Duke of Edinburgh award scheme.

Results (1997) GCSE: all gained at least five grades A–C. A-level: 65% of entries graded A or B.

Destinations Nearly all go on to university (about eight a year to Oxbridge).

Sport Taken seriously. Main games; hockey, netball, tennis, rounders athletics. Playing fields a short bus ride away.

Remarks Good school, admirably continuing to meet the purpose for which it was founded.

SHERBORNE ♂
Sherborne, Dorset DT9 3AP. Tel (01935) 812249

Synopsis
Independent ★ Boys ★ Boarding and day ★ Ages 13–18 ★ 588 pupils (93% boarding) ★ 268 in sixth form ★ Fees: £13,680 boarding; £10,350 day
Head: Peter Lapping, 56, appointed 1988.
Traditional, academic boarding school; good teaching and results; lots of art, drama, music; strong sport.

Profile
Background   Roots go back to an 8th-century Benedictine abbey; re-founded 1550 by Edward VI. Venerable, beautifully maintained buildings (medieval and Jacobean in style) grouped around a vast gravel quadrangle; fine library (33,000 volumes); first-rate, modern facilities (£5 million spent recently). International study centre prepares non-English-speaking boys aged 10–16 for entry to independent schools. John le Carré was a pupil here.

Atmosphere   Civilised, traditional, well-disciplined; respectful relations between staff and pupils; emphasis on team spirit, house loyalty. Prefects given leadership training and have limited punishment powers; urine tests may be required of suspected drug users. Day boys stay until 9 pm.

Admissions   By Common Entrance or school's own tests; school is not full (numbers have fallen recently) but will not admit those unlikely to cope academically (head determined to remain in *The Daily Telegraph*'s first division); abilities range from average to high. Most from business, farming, professional backgrounds; 18% have parents in the Services ('majors and above'); catchment area extends from Bristol to London; 10% ethnic minorities (mainly Hong Kong Chinese). Boarding accommodation in nine houses, some still to be renovated; juniors in dormitories of 12; seniors have double or single study-bedrooms; house influence is powerful and varies in character (careful choice advised); no weekly boarding. About 25 scholarships a year (academic, music, art).

The head   Dignified, scholarly, strongly principled ('change should come by evolution, not revolution'). South-African-born; read history at Natal and Oxford; his second headship. Married (wife much involved in school life); two grown-up children.

The teaching   Good quality: enthusiastic, well-qualified, predominantly male staff, half appointed by present head. Broad curriculum ('as wide as possible for as long as possible'); all do Latin, French plus German or Spanish; Greek on offer; sciences taught (and examined) separately; good results in maths; choice of 21 traditional, mainstream subjects at A-level (economics rather than business studies). Pupils grouped by ability in most subjects from second year; extra help for dyslexics; progress closely monitored; average class size 27/28, reducing to maximum of 12 in the sixth form. Strong art, music (a third learn an instrument) and drama, some in association with neighbouring girls' schools. Outstanding careers department. Masses of extra-curricular activities ('a seven-day-a-week school'), including well-supported cadet force, Duke of Edinburgh award scheme.

Results   (1997) GCSE: all gained at least five grades A–C. A-level: 62% of entries graded A or B.

Destinations   About 95% proceed to university (average of 15 a year to Oxbridge).

Sport An important aspect of school life; good coaching; regular county and national honours. Main games: rugby, hockey, cricket. Athletics, cross-country, soccer, squash, tennis, swimming, fencing, golf also on offer. Facilities include 50 acres of playing fields, sports hall, indoor pool, squash courts.

Remarks Good school for able, energetic boys; resourceful extroverts likely to thrive best.

SHERBORNE GIRLS' ♀
Sherborne, Dorset DT9 3QN. Tel (01935) 812245

Synopsis
Independent ★ Girls ★ Boarding and some day ★ Ages 11–18 ★ 418 pupils (96% boarding) ★ 155 in sixth form ★ Fees: £12,960 boarding; £9,060 day
Head: Miss June Taylor, 54 appointed 1985.
Traditional academic school; good teaching and results; lots of music, sport.

Profile
Background Founded 1899 to provide girls with an education equal to that of boys; imposing Victorian buildings plus elegant modern additions on a 40-acre site on the outskirts of the town; some classrooms in wooden huts; £10 million spent on premises and facilities since 1986.

Atmosphere Pleasant, fairly formal; big emphasis on discipline, good manners; regular worship in the Abbey a focal point of school life.

Admissions By Common Entrance; school is full and quite selective (girls must be capable of achieving three A-levels). Most join from prep schools; a third live within 50 miles; a third live abroad. Eight vertical-age boarding houses; comfortable accommodation ranges from small dormitories to single rooms according to seniority; upper-sixth housed separately. Scholarships: academic, music, art.

The head Formal, business-like; was a pupil here (and head girl). Read maths at Sussex; returned here to teach it in 1966; still teaches it to the juniors.

The teaching Good quality; long-serving, predominantly female staff. Broad curriculum; science on offer as three separate subjects; first-rate languages (French, German, Spanish); strong art, design/technology; choice of 24 subjects at A-level (including Italian, Russian, Christian theology, home economics). Pupils grouped by ability in maths, French, Latin; extra help for dyslexics; maximum class size 24. Lots of music; choirs, orchestras. Extra-curricular activities include Duke of Edinburgh award scheme, cadet force (in conjunction with boys at Sherborne, qv).

Results (1997) GCSE: all gained at least five grades A–C. A-level: creditable 67% of entries graded A or B.

Destinations Nearly all go on to university; some to art, music colleges.

Sport Taken seriously. Main sports: hockey, lacrosse, tennis, athletics. Archery, badminton, golf also available. First-rate facilities include all-weather pitch, sports hall, 27 tennis courts.

Remarks Good school for able, sociable girls.

SHREWSBURY ♂
The Schools, Shrewsbury, Shropshire SY3 7BA. Tel (01743) 344537

Synopsis
Independent ★ Boys ★ Boarding and day ★ Ages 13–18 ★ 696 pupils (80% boarding) ★ 272 in sixth form ★ Fees: £13,650 boarding; £9,600 day
Head: Ted Maidment, 54, appointed 1988.
Distinguished school; first-rate teaching and results; superb facilities; very strong sport.

Profile
Background   Founded 1552 by Edward VI ('When Edward the Sixth was a stripling/And Warwick believed him a fool,/The Severn went placidly rippling/Past Shrewsbury, lacking a school'); regarded by the Victorians as one of the nine 'great' schools. Moved 1882 from town-centre premises to beautiful 105-acre site on a hill across the river overlooking the town. Elegant Victorian buildings plus sensitively designed additions, including fine theatre. Pleasant, large, well-lit classrooms; superb facilities, especially for sciences, languages, design/technology, art, IT. Most famous old boy, Charles Darwin (who recalled his education here, dominated by the classics, as 'simply a blank').

Atmosphere   Individuality treasured, even in its extremes; the only requirements are that all give of their best and recognise the rights of others. Strong house system; good pastoral care ('If I can't recognise a boy's mood by the way he walks down the corridor, I don't know him well enough' – housemaster); every boy has a tutor with whom he spends an hour a week discussing academic and other matters.

Admissions   At 13 by school's own exam or Common Entrance; minimum 55% mark required ('They're good, solid, engine-room boys – reliable rather than brilliant,' says the head); parents predominantly from Shropshire and the Midlands (few foreign nationals). All nine boarding houses recently refurbished at a cost of £4 million (part of the head's policy of 'unbrutalising' the school); comfortable, carpeted dormitories (four to six beds); sixth-formers in bed-sits; all eat in central dining hall (five minutes' walk from main school buildings).

The head   Very able; much liked and widely respected; knows every boy. Read history at Cambridge (choral scholar); previously a housemaster at Lancing and head (at 37) of Ellesmere. Careful to strike a balance between preserving the school's traditions and 'keeping it alive' (enthusiastic about Europe, technology, computing). Says 'delivering on A-levels' is very important but he is more concerned with the development of personal qualities, such as self-reliance, the ability to handle success or failure. Still sings; travels regularly to Kenya, where he advises a school. Bachelor.

The teaching   First-rate: well-prepared teachers clearly in charge, enjoying their work; eager, responsive pupils enjoying their work. Very well-qualified staff of 82 (seven women); styles a judicious mixture of front-of-class ('well tried, traditional methods of teaching work best') and new technology. Broad curriculum; science – a particular strength – taught (and examined) as three separate subjects; very good languages, including Greek, German. All take an average of 10 GCSEs and three A-levels. Pupils grouped by ability in most subjects from the start; progress closely monitored. Vast range of extra-curricular activities, including Outward Bound, cadet force, Young Enterprise; just about everything else, from beekeeping to mountaineering, also on offer. Service to society taken seriously: strong links with a youth club in Liverpool. Good careers department.

Regular exchanges with schools in Europe and Russia.

Results (1997) GCSE: 99% gained at least five grades A–C. A-level: creditable 71% of entries graded A or B

Destinations Virtually all stay on for A-levels and proceed to university (about 20 a year to Oxbridge).

Sport Taken seriously. Huge selection: all the traditional games plus extras such as martial arts, fencing; first-rate coaching, especially in soccer and cricket. Excellent facilities include a beautiful stretch of the Severn for rowing (more Oxbridge Blues in the past 10 years than any other school), numerous playing fields, athletics track, indoor pool, gym, and courts for tennis, squash, fives.

Remarks Fine, well-run school: aims to turn out 'whole men – courtier, diplomat, soldier, poet' and very largely succeeds. Ofsted inspectors concluded (1994): 'Shrewsbury is an excellent school with a deservedly high reputation for academic, sporting and artistic achievement. It is a lively and friendly community, characterised by good, well-disciplined behaviour and supportive relationships amongst the boys. They develop into articulate, self-confident and independent young men.' Highly recommended.

SHREWSBURY HIGH ♀
32 Town Walls, Shrewsbury, Shropshire SY1 1TN. Tel (01743) 362872

Synopsis
Independent ★ Girls ★ Day ★ Ages 11–18 (plus associated junior school) ★ 360 pupils ★ 90 in sixth form ★ Fees: £4,167
Head: Miss Susan Gardner, 53, appointed 1990.
Traditional, academic school; good teaching and results; lovely setting.

Profile
Background Founded 1885 by the Girls' Day School Trust (entrance adorned with ornate stone carving of Minerva's head – the trust's logo – inscribed, 'Knowledge no more a fountain sealed'); became fully independent 1975 when Direct Grant status was abolished. Moved to present site beside the Severn (stunning outlook over games fields) 1897; lofty, purpose-built Victorian premises plus eclectic mix of later additions (described by head as Sixties brutal, Nineties pleasant) grouped around pretty squares of garden; £250,000 performing arts centre added 1996. Junior school (ages four to 11) a short distance away.

Atmosphere Secure, bright, cosy: close, higgledy arrangement of buildings encourages companionship, discussion, pooling of ideas. Girls exude interest in, and enjoyment of, all activities; little need for discipline, so obvious is the willingness to learn; relaxed relationships between staff and pupils.

Admissions Most enter from the junior school; entry at 11 by interview and tests; school is fairly selective (though numbers have declined). Girls mainly from professional/farming/business backgrounds (some travel 30 miles from Welsh border villages). Some scholarships, bursaries; trust aims to replace assisted places scheme with one of its own.

The head Efficient, practical; keen to encourage girls to be independent and have a strong sense of self-awareness. Read history at London; previously deputy head of a comprehensive in Essex. Teaches general studies and religious education. Married.

The teaching Good all round (starting with a first-rate grounding in the junior school); generally traditional in style; pupils stretched and challenged. Committed, friendly staff, most in their 40s. Pupils grouped by ability in French, maths, science (on offer as three separate subjects). Most take nine GCSEs (options include home economics, classics, art, music, design) and three A-levels (options include Latin, business, sociology). Lots of music: three choirs, orchestra. Extra-curricular activities include Duke of Edinburgh award scheme. Regular foreign exchanges.

Results   (1997) 99% gained at least five grades A–C. A-level: 58% of entries graded A or B.

Destinations   Nearly 90% proceed to university (two or three year to Oxbridge).

Sport   Chiefly: athletics, tennis, volleyball, cross-country, hockey, rounders, netball, badminton; county/regional level often achieved. Sixth-formers row with boys from Shrewsbury (just across the river).

Remarks   Safe, well-run school; recommended.

SIBFORD ♂ ♀
Sibford Ferris, Banbury, Oxfordshire OX15 5QL. Tel (01295) 780444

Synopsis
Independent ★ Co-educational ★ Boarding and day ★ Ages 5–18 ★ 300 pupils (250 in senior school, 65% boys, 55% boarding) ★ 40 in sixth form ★ Fees: £7,635–£10,485 boarding; £2,850–£5,580 day
Head: Mrs Susan Freestone 42, appointed January 1997.
Attractive school; wide range of abilities; dyslexia a speciality.

Profile
Background   Founded 1842 by Society of Friends as a self-sufficient community growing its own food (horticultural tradition continues – rows of beautifully-tended vegetables in tranquil walled garden). Cotswold stone manor house plus slightly battered 1930s addition (institutional appearance relieved by colourful artwork) in delightful 70-acre estate. School was one of the first (in the 1970s) to recognise the needs of dyslexics and provide first-class support. Co-educational from the start; junior school (Orchard Close) opened 1989.

Atmosphere   Gentle, informal, very relaxed. Quaker ethos fundamental (though only 10% are the children of Quakers); individual achievement recognised and delighted in. Pupils thrive in the supportive, encouraging atmosphere; no one here feels second best. Daily meeting based, in Quaker tradition, on silence; individuals encouraged to take responsibility for their own behaviour instead of having standards enforced by rigid rules; no prefects but sixth-formers expected to lead by example. Parents made to feel welcome.

Admissions   By interview and tests; wide range of abilities and backgrounds; a third are dyslexic. Day pupils come from as far afield as Stratford and Oxford; some boarders from the Far East (English taught as a foreign language). Some children have official statements of special needs and are paid for by their local education authority. Pleasant boarding accommodation; sixth-formers housed separately; meals served cafeteria-style in main dining room. Scholarships (academic, music) bursaries available.

The head   Recent appointment. Studied at Royal Academy of Music, Masters from Bristol. Married; two teenage children.

The teaching   Highly committed staff; variety of styles and approach; emphasis throughout on the needs of each child. Outstanding support for dyslexics (up to a third of each class) and those in need of extra help (no stigma here). Dyslexia unit (a cosy suite of rooms in the heart of the school) has five full-time teachers; several other members of staff have attended dyslexia courses. Pupils grouped by ability in maths, English; regular reporting to parents; classes are small. Curriculum embraces usual academic subjects (including French and German) in addition to a wide range of practical courses. For first three years all do textiles, drama, music, design/technology, art, home economics, word processing (25% use laptops) alongside academic subjects; most take seven or eight GCSEs; business studies on offer. Sixth form offers a choice between academic and vocational courses. Thriving drama in small memorial theatre; nearly a third learn a musical instrument. Extra-curricular activities include Duke of Edinburgh award scheme.

Results (1997) GCSE: 47% gained at least five grades A–C. A-level: no entries.
Destinations About half continue into the sixth form; some proceed to further or higher education.
Sport Wide range on offer, including rugby, hockey, athletics, cricket, tennis, netball. Extensive well-tended pitches; first rate sports hall; heated indoor pool.
Remarks Happy school that does wonders for many children who might not thrive elsewhere. Recommended.

SILVERDALE ♂ ♀
Bents Crescent, Sheffield S11 9RT. Tel (0114) 236 9991

Synopsis
Comprehensive ★ Co-educational ★ Ages 11–18 ★ 1,136 pupils (equal numbers of girls and boys) ★ 260 in sixth form
Head: Enid Butler, 46, appointed 1995.
First-rate, well-run school in disgraceful accommodation; good teaching and results; plenty of art, drama, music.

Profile
Background Opened 1956 as a secondary modern; went comprehensive and added a sixth form 1976. Atrociously maintained buildings (literally falling apart at the seams) on a 17-acre suburban site. Leaking roofs (one collapsed); corridors bereft of masonry; many classrooms in drab 'temporary' huts; exterior unpainted for years. 'There are parts of the school,' observed Ofsted, 'where the quality of the education is adversely affected by the poor quality of the buildings.' School has a unit for the hard of hearing.
Atmosphere Through the dismal portals, the school hums like a Japanese car factory: targets are set; quality control is maintained; bad behaviour is stamped on (and out); the finished product is excellent (polite, articulate pupils). Good pastoral care (first-years placed in class with at least one friend from primary school); code of conduct emphasises courtesy, awareness of others; pupil effort acknowledged by credit and reward system; close links maintained with parents. Staff send their children here, as do the city's university lecturers.
Admissions School heavily over-subscribed (two apply for each place); admissions handled by Sheffield council; priority to those living in the catchment area (parents move house) and attending one of three 'feeder' primaries. Three-quarters come from comfortably-off homes.

The head   High-octane, plain-speaking; strides the crumbling corridors with verve and purpose, 'I'm in charge' written all over her; dispenses praise and admonition in machine-gun volleys; knows every pupil; insists passionately on the highest standards. Read English at Lancaster; previously deputy head of a comprehensive in Milton Keynes; still loves teaching. She is, quite rightly, revered.

The teaching   Straight-forward, up-front, no-nonsense, good teaching; stable, committed staff. Broad curriculum: science on offer as three separate subjects; some take two languages (augmented by visits to France, Spain, Germany – target language used from the moment the pupil boards the bus in Sheffield); good history (trips to Russia). Class sizes average 25; parents receive two full reports a year. Lunch-times busy with rehearsals for drama club, orchestra, choir, wind band and brass band; flourishing art.

Results   (1997) GCSE: 81% gained at least five grades A–C. A-level: 38% of entries graded A or B.

Destinations   About 95% of those who stay on for A-levels proceed to university.

Sport   Most participate, making full use of meagre facilities. All major sports on offer.

Remarks   Fine school; pity Sheffield council is so hard of hearing.

SIR HENRY FLOYD ♂ ♀
Oxford Road, Aylesbury, Buckinghamshire HP21 8PE. Tel (01296) 24781

Synopsis
Grammar ★ Co-educational ★ Ages 12–18 (11–18 from 1998) ★ 746 pupils ★ 257 in sixth form
Head: Mrs Susan Powell, 51, appointed 1996.
Sound school; good teaching and GCSE results; lots of art, drama, music; strong business, industry links.

Profile

Background   Founded 1947 as a technical school; became a grammar school and moved to present site and purpose-built premises 1962; later additions include sixth-form centre; inadequate library; some classrooms in ageing 'temporary' huts; further building planned (but money is short).

Atmosphere   Cheerful, friendly, supportive; good pastoral care; big emphasis on recognising achievement. Sixth-formers help the juniors; lots of fund raising for charity.

Admissions   School is heavily over-subscribed (nearly 500 apply for 131 places); entry by county council 12-plus.

The head   Shrewd, down-to-earth, approachable ('my style is interactive'); good manager. Read history at Bristol came here as deputy head; previously deputy head of Beaconsfield High (qv). Married; two children

The teaching   Sound; experienced, hard-working staff (equal numbers of women and men). Standard national curriculum; all take French and German for first two years; good results in history; limited computing; choice of 20 subjects at A-level. Pupils grouped by ability in some subjects for GCSE; progress closely monitored (half-termly grades). Strong drama; lively art; lots of music. Good business and industry links. Many trips abroad for study and recreation; regular language exchanges with pupils in France, Germany.

Results (1997) GCSE: 97% gained at least five grades A–C. A-level rather modest 36% of entries graded A or B.
Destinations About 70% stay on for A-levels; of these, 90% proceed to higher education (mostly to newer universities).
Sport Wide choice; rugby, hockey are strong. Facilities include extensive playing fields, good gym.
Remarks Identified by Ofsted (1995) as 'outstandingly successful'.

SIR THOMAS RICH'S ♂
Oakleaze, Longlevens, Gloucester GL2 0LF. Tel (01452) 528467

Synopsis
Grammar ★ Boys (plus girls in sixth form) ★ Ages 11–18 ★ 727 pupils ★ 163 in sixth form (75% boys)
Head: Ian Kellie, 47, appointed 1994.
Well-run, traditional school; sound teaching and results; strong sport.

Profile
Background Founded 1666; became a grammar school 1945. Moved to present suburban 18-acre site and solid, purpose-built premises 1964; recent additions (numbers are rising) include new classroom block and library; some classrooms in 'temporary' huts. Sports hall being doubled in size.
Atmosphere Cheerful, orderly, hard-working (parents assured that 'no pupil here is prevented from working by an unruly atmosphere' – head recently declined to offer places to two sixth-formers whom he considered 'rude, arrogant and sarcastic'). Traditions respected: prefects ('observators') in gowns; honours boards around the assembly hall; blue blazers worn below the sixth form. Supportive parents run school shop, raise funds.
Admissions By local council 11-plus; minimum IQ of 105–110 required (less selective than most grammar schools). Half the pupils come from the city, the rest from across the county and beyond.
The head Strong-minded northerner; gets on well with staff and (most) pupils. Read chemistry at Durham; came here as deputy head in 1988. Married; two sons (both pupils here).
The teaching Mainly traditional in style. Hard-working staff of 40 (11 women). Standard national curriculum. Pupils grouped by ability from third year in maths, science, languages; average class size 27, reducing to 20 for GCSE, smaller at A-level.
Results (1997) GCSE: 96% gained at least five grades A–C. A level: 53% of entries graded A or B.
Destinations Majority proceed to university (about six a year to Oxbridge).
Sport Particular strengths in rugby, cricket; girls play squash, hockey, netball, lacrosse (and cricket). Cross-country, soccer, tennis, athletics also on offer. Playing fields adequate.
Remarks Successful school, well-regarded locally.

SIR WILLIAM BORLASE'S ♂ ♀
West Street, Marlow, Buckinghamshire SL7 2BR. Tel (01628) 482256

Synopsis
Grammar (voluntary-controlled) ★ Co-educational ★ Ages 12–18 ★ 854 pupils
(roughly equal numbers of girls and boys) ★ 319 in sixth form
Head: Dr Peter Holding, 43, appointed April 1997.
Close-knit, friendly school; good teaching and results; strong sport.

Profile
Background Founded on present site 1624 by Sir William Borlase in memory
of his son Henry; became co-educational 1988; voluntary-controlled (own board
of trustees) since 1992. Compact premises (incorporating the original brick and
flint 17th-century building); at the heart is a cloister, which makes the school feel
small and intimate, despite the numerous additional buildings and large numbers of children. Some classrooms in huts; many areas the worse for wear; major
building programme scheduled for completion September 1998. Chapel (built as
a memorial to Borlasians killed in World War One) used daily for assemblies.
Co-educational since 1988.

Atmosphere Orderly, friendly, buzzing with energy; activities of every sort,
every minute of the day. Very good pastoral care: a close-knit, supportive
community. Traditional blazer-and-tie uniform for all (special merit ties for
achievement). Prefects apply for the job, help run the school.

Admissions School is over-subscribed; entry by Buckinghamshire County
Council 12-plus tests; top 30% of the ability range.

The head Recent appointment. Read English at Pennsylvania; further degrees
from the Open University and Michigan; has taught in a wide variety of independent and state schools. Teaches first-years to get to know them. Hoping to
expand numbers and facilities by 15% by 2000.

The teaching Lively, stimulating; varied styles; each class designed to 'get
them thinking'. Well-qualified, enthusiastic staff, most of whom contribute to
extra-curricular activities. Broad curriculum: science on offer as three separate
subjects; all first-years do French and German; Latin survives; impressive provision for computing; flourishing art. Pupils grouped by ability in maths, modern
languages; average class size 24, reducing to 15 in sixth form. Wide range of
extra-curricular activities.

Results (1997) GCSE: 97% gained at least five grades A–C. A-level: 37% of
entries graded A or B.

Destinations About 90% stay on for A-levels; of these, 90% proceed to university (about 10 a year to Oxbridge).

Sport Strong tradition; outstanding hockey and rowing. Facilities not extensive: four pitches on site (one all-weather), small outdoor pool, three new tennis
courts. Main sports: netball, football, rugby, cricket, cross-country, tennis, athletics. Good record against other schools.

Remarks Ofsted inspectors concluded (1997): 'This is a good, popular and
highly regarded school in which the high standards that pupils attain are substantially helped by their positive attitudes to learning and their attentive
response to good teaching.'

SIR WILLIAM PERKINS'S ♀
Guildford Road, Chertsey, Surrey KT16 9BN. Tel (01932) 562161

Synopsis
Independent ★ Girls ★ Day ★ Ages 11–18 ★ 580 pupils ★ 130 in sixth form
★ Fees: £4,530
Head: Miss Susan Ross, 46, appointed 1994.
Successful, academic school; very good teaching and results.

Profile
Background Founded 1725; moved to present 12-acre site 1819; formerly a
grammar school, opted for independence 1978 to avoid being turned into a comprehensive. Fine Edwardian building plus attractive later additions.

Atmosphere Orderly without regimentation; a sense of purpose pervades;
strong Christian ethos (but no formal church affiliation). Friendly staff; polite,
confident pupils. Blazer-and-tie uniform (plus very short skirts); sixth-formers
wear own clothes 'within reasonable limits'.

Admissions By competitive exams in English, maths; school is quite selective
but may become less so with the phasing out of assisted places, which about 100
hold; social mix will also be reduced (though fees are relatively low). Some scholarships, bursaries.

The head Able; friendly manner; much respected by the pupils. Read physics
at Manchester; teaches junior girls.

The teaching Good quality; traditional but lively in style; well-qualified staff.
Fairly broad curriculum: sciences taught separately; first-rate languages
(French, German, Spanish); Latin, Greek on offer; all do home economics for
first three years, religious education for GCSE; lots of computing; wide choice of
A-levels (economics and business studies popular). Pupils grouped by ability in
maths, science, French; maximum class size 24. Well-taught art, music (60%
learn an instrument, four choirs, two orchestras). Extra-curricular activities
include community service, well-supported Duke of Edinburgh award scheme.

Results (1997) GCSE: all gained at least five grades A–C. A-level: very creditable 74% of entries graded A or B (best league table position for five years).

Destinations About 80% stay on for A-levels; of these, nearly all proceed to
university (four or five a year to Oxbridge).

Sport Although strongly committed to physical activity, the school is not
aggressively sporty. Main sports: hockey, netball, tennis, athletics; five-a-side
football popular. Facilities include playing fields, fine sports hall.

Remarks Good all round.

SKEGNESS GRAMMAR ♂ ♀
Vernon Road, Skegness, Lincolnshire PE25 2QS. Tel (01754) 610000

Synopsis
Grammar (grant-maintained) ★ Co-educational ★ Day and boarding ★ Ages
11–18 ★ 663 pupils (90% day, roughly equal numbers of girls and boys) ★ 175
in sixth form ★ Fees (boarding only): £3,353–£3,583
Head: John Webster, 51, appointed 1981.
Well-run, traditional grammar school; good-value boarding.

Profile

Background Roots go back to 1459 when William of Wainflete founded a school to prepare boys for Magdalen College, Oxford; moved to present 20-acre site near the town centre 1933; opted out of council control 1989 (the first to do so). Facilities are good.

Atmosphere Easy-going but purposeful ('unashamedly traditional'); pupils confident, eager to learn. Strict blazer-and-tie uniform.

Admissions By verbal reasoning test; top 25% of the ability range from a spread of social backgrounds. Pleasant, well-run boarding house (Wainflete Hall) five miles away.

The head Imposing figure in flowing gown (everyone's idea of a grammar school master). Genial, mischievous (presents guests with a stick of Skegness rock); loves his job and is good at it. Former member of Her Majesty's Inspectorate. Plays the stock market and, in church, the organ (was once bass guitarist with a Liverpool pop group). Married; three sons.

The teaching Traditional, effective. Able staff of 45 (18 women), half appointed by present head. Broad curriculum: science taught as three separate subjects; main languages French, Spanish; superb facilities for computing. Choice of 24 subjects at A-level, including sports studies. Pupils grouped by ability in maths only; average class size 22, reducing to 10 in sixth form. Lots of music (choirs, orchestras). Regular language exchanges with schools in Madrid and near Lyons.

Results (1997) GCSE: 97% gained at least five grades A–C. A-level: rather modest 33% of entries graded A or B.

Destinations About 95% stay on for A-levels; of these, up to 85% proceed to university.

Sport Good: choice of 32 activities, including judo, fencing, water sports, land yachting.

Remarks Happy, thriving school. Ofsted inspectors concluded (1994): 'This is a good school. The ethos is based upon sound academic traditions within an ordered environment. The quality of education provided is high. Pupils are happy, secure and take pride in their school; their behaviour is exemplary.'

SKINNERS' ♂
St John's Road, Tunbridge Wells, Kent TN4 9PG. Tel (01892) 520732

Synopsis
Grammar (grant-maintained) ★ Boys ★ Ages 11–18 ★ 707 pupils ★ 192 in sixth form
Head: Peter Braggins, 52, appointed 1992.
Well-run, traditional grammar school; good teaching and results; strong sport.

Profile

Background Founded by the Skinners' Company 1887; became a voluntary-aided grammar school 1944; opted out of council control 1992. Red-brick, Victorian-Gothic buildings plus later additions (including concrete and glass dining hall) on a restricted, terraced site; some classrooms in 'temporary' huts; new £500,000 technology and art block. Parents raised £21,000 to refurbish the library.

Atmosphere Tolerant, orderly, hard-working; mutually respectful relations between staff and pupils; rules, known as 'points for observance', prescribe courtesy, good sense ('a general presumption that boys will co-operate in taking the best advantage of the education offered'); Saturday detention for serious offences. Prefect system; blazer-and-house-tie uniform; seniors wear grey suits.

Admissions   By Kent selection test (11-plus): 86 places allocated in order of merit without regard to location; 10 to boys who pass and live in Sevenoaks, Tonbridge, Tunbridge Wells; school is over-subscribed. Most from middle-class backgrounds.

The head   Able, compassionate, forward-looking; efficient manager. Read history at Cambridge; previously deputy head of Wilson's (qv). Married; three grown-up daughters.

The teaching   Good quality: attentive pupils; experienced, long-serving staff of 46 (11 women). Standard national curriculum; science (a strength) taught as three separate subjects from third year; some do both French and German; A-level options include business studies, Christian theology, theatre studies, computing. Pupils grouped by ability in maths from second year (some take GCSE a year early), modern languages from third year; extra help for dyslexics; average class size 32, reducing to 25–28 for GCSE, 12–15 at A-level. Lots of music (more than 100 learn an instrument). Extra-curricular activities include debating, cadet force, Duke of Edinburgh award scheme. Regular language exchanges with pupils in France, Germany.

Results   (1997) GCSE: all gained at least five grades A–C. A-level 45% of entries graded A or B.

Destinations   About 90% go on to university (four or five a year to Oxbridge).

Sport   Strong, particularly rugby, hockey; good coaching. Cricket, athletics, cross-country, swimming, basketball, tennis also popular. On-site facilities include gym, functional covered pool, four tennis courts; 20 acres of playing fields 15 minutes' walk away.

Remarks   Ofsted inspectors concluded (1997): 'This is an outstandingly good school which is dedicated to the achievement of excellence.'

SKIPTON GIRLS' HIGH ♀

Gargrave Road, Skipton, North Yorkshire BD23 1QL. Tel (01756) 792115

Synopsis

Grammar (voluntary-controlled) ★ Girls ★ Ages 11–18 ★ 616 pupils ★ 166 in sixth form
Head: Mrs Diana Chambers, 54, appointed 1987.
Attractive, well-run grammar school; rich curriculum; good teaching and results.

Profile

Background   Founded 1886; serves an area where grammar schools still flourish. Original well-maintained Victorian buildings plus first-rate 1960s extension in pleasant grounds on the edge of an attractive market town; some classrooms in huts (known as 'chalets'); sixth-form centre in lovely Edwardian house across the road.

Atmosphere   Liberal, unstuffy, unpretentious; school achieves its aims with aplomb and a minimum of fuss ('We maintain high academic standards, of which were are justly proud, and seek to impart a love of learning'); pupils are positive, well-motivated. Excellent food. Supportive parents raise large sums.

Admissions   School heavily over-subscribed (nearly 300 apply for 87 places); entry by county council selection tests in verbal and non-verbal reasoning; top

30% of the ability range from a catchment area that extends to Bradford, Ilkley, Burnley. Most from middle-class backgrounds.

The head Live wire; leads from the front. Read modern languages at Birmingham; previously deputy head of a Bradford comprehensive. Keen to impress on girls that privilege brings responsibility. Active member of local church and diocesan board. Married (to an educationist); two daughters.

The teaching Lively, confident staff (a quarter male). Broad curriculum; all do Latin, classical studies, two modern languages; science taught as three separate subjects; choice of 17 subjects at A-level plus general studies and a range of short courses (computing, French for business etc). Pupils grouped by ability in maths only; average class size 23, 10–15 in sixth form. Lots of music, dance, drama, art, debating; flourishing Duke of Edinburgh award scheme; strong tradition of outdoor activities. Sound careers advice; extensive work experience programme.

Results (1997) GCSE: 99% gained at least five grades A–C. A-level: 45% of entries graded A or B.

Destinations About 90% stay on for A-levels; nearly all proceed to higher education.

Sport All-weather tennis and netball courts (surrounded by trees, grass, picnic tables) but no playing fields; leisure centre near by.

Remarks First-rate, happy school; high reputation fully deserved.

SOLIHULL ♂

Warwick Road, Solihull, West Midlands B91 3DJ. Tel (0121) 705 0958

Synopsis
Independent ★ Boys (plus girls in sixth form) ★ Day ★ Ages 7–18 ★ 801 pupils (643 in senior school) ★ 260 in sixth form (70% boys) ★ Fees: £3,300–£4,740. Head: Patrick Derham, 38, appointed 1996.
Strong school; good teaching and results; first-rate facilities.

Profile
Background Founded 1560; moved to present impeccably-maintained, 50-acre parkland site 1882. Superbly appointed throughout: facilities include new £1.5 million science block, well-equipped design/technology centre, fine modern languages building (carpeted, sound-proofed, latest audio-visual equipment); elegant chapel.

Atmosphere Crisp, well-ordered; formal in a rather old-fashioned way (pupils expected to know their place). Uniform throughout; staff wear academic gowns for assembly. Supportive parents.

Admissions Juniors transfer automatically at 11; 250 compete for remaining 50 places; tests in English, maths, verbal reasoning; school is fairly selective. Generous provision for scholarships (11 a year to senior school).

The head Recent appointment. Youthful, energetic; previously a housemaster at Radley; has a First in history from Cambridge (and teaches it at A-level); coaches athletics, cross-country. Married (wife teaches in the junior school); two children (one a pupil here).

The teaching Varied styles: good balance of didactic and investigative approaches. Staff of 75 (average age 40), 70% male; average class size 20 up to GCSE, 10 at A-level. Broad curriculum: science taught as three separate subjects; all do German and Latin for at least two years; French, Spanish, Mandarin also on offer. Most take 10 GCSEs and three A-levels plus general studies. Wide range of extra-curricular activities; strong music (three orchestras, 12 other ensembles, four choirs) and drama. Regular exchanges with schools in France, Germany.

Results (1997) GCSE: all gained at least five grades A–C. A-level: 59% of entries graded A or B.

Destinations About 85% continue into the sixth form and go on to university (about 12 a year to Oxbridge).

Sports All participate (PE offered at GCSE and A-level). Particular strengths: rugby, hockey, cricket, sailing, athletics. Excellent facilities include sports hall, gymnasium, indoor pool, squash courts, five artificial cricket wickets, grass and all-weather tennis courts courts, rifle range.

Remarks Good all round – and likely to become even better.

SOUTHEND BOYS' HIGH ♂
Prittlewell Chase, Southend-on-Sea, Essex SS0 0RG. Tel (01702) 343074

Synopsis
Grammar (grant-maintained) ★ Boys (plus girls in sixth form) ★ Ages 11–18 ★ 869 pupils ★ 251 in sixth form (36 girls)
Head: Michael Frampton, 49, appointed 1988.
Industrious, civilised, old-fashioned grammar; good teaching; strong sport.

Profile
Background Founded as a science-oriented technical school 1895; moved to present suburban site in extensive grounds 1938; became a grammar school after the 1944 Education Act; opted out of council control 1993. Solid, reassuring, 1930s red-brick architecture plus recent additions; some classrooms rather cramped.

Atmosphere Ultra-traditional: parents educated in the 1950s would feel at home here; spotless corridors, well-polished floors, honour boards in the vestibule. Main hall dominated by spectacular oak-panelled organ donated by Old Boys as memorial to First World War fallen. Whole-school assemblies twice a week. Strong house system (Athens, Sparta, Troy, Tuscany). All boys smartly attired in green blazers, house ties.

Admissions School heavily over-subscribed (more than 250 apply for 125 places); entry by tests in English, maths, verbal reasoning; top 25% of the local ability range. About 25 join the sixth form from other schools, including a few girls.

The head Calm, persuasive, determined. History graduate; has spent entire career in boys' grammar schools; previously deputy head of King Edward VI, Chelmsford. Keen to encourage participation in music, drama, art. Married; two sons.

The teaching Precise, carefully paced; good balance between didactic and investigative approaches. Staff of 62 (12 women), average age 45. Broad curriculum: science on offer as three separate subjects; Latin a popular option in second year; choice of 27 subjects at A-level, including Greek, geology, ancient history; best results in maths, sciences, economics. Most subjects taught in mixed-ability groups for first three years. Good music: orchestra, choir.

Results (1997) GCSE: 98% gained at least five grades A–C. A-level: 47% of entries graded A or B.

Destinations More than 90% stay on for A-levels; of these, 80% proceed to university (about six a year to Oxbridge).

Sport A major feature of school life; strong record in soccer, hockey, cricket, athletics (borough champions in 22 of past 23 years). Facilities include 12 acres of playing fields; all-weather pitch (paid for by old boys) five minutes' drive away. No sports hall, so the ancient gymnasium takes a fearsome pounding.

Remarks Stable school with a clear character; has little reason to change and is unlikely to do so. Ofsted inspectors concluded (1995): 'This is a good, traditional, but outward looking grammar school. The ethos is purposeful and well disciplined, emphasising the importance of academic excellence.'

SOUTHEND GIRLS' HIGH ♀
Southchurch Boulevard, Southend-on-Sea, Essex SS2 4UZ. Tel (01702) 588852

Synopsis
Grammar (grant-maintained) ★ Girls (plus a few boys in sixth form) ★ Ages 11–18 ★ 825 pupils ★ 220 in sixth form
Head: Miss Ruth Alinek, 43, appointed 1995.
Down-to-earth grammar school; good teaching and results; very strong sport.

Profile
Background Founded 1912; moved from town centre to present suburban site 1957; opted out of council control 1993. Compact buildings in spacious, neatly-maintained grounds; latest additions include new science labs, sixth-form centre.

Atmosphere Civilised, relaxed, suffused with understated feminism; good rapport between staff and pupils, who speak of strong sense of 'belonging'. Very few discipline problems: girls say they are expected to 'keep quiet and get on'. Traditional values carefully preserved: daily assembly in school hall; classes automatically stand for visitors; prefect system; smart green uniform. Parents keen to maintain league table success.

Admissions School heavily over-subscribed (nearly 300 apply for 140 places); entry by tests in English, maths, verbal reasoning; top 25% of the ability range (IQs 105–140) from an extensive catchment area. Handful of boys admitted to study less common A-levels when space permits.

The head Strong, decisive. Read English at Warwick; wide experience of girls' grammar schools; previously deputy head of another in Essex.

The teaching Fairly traditional in style; lessons have clear objectives, and are often delivered with flair and humour, despite sometimes gloomy classroom decor and ageing furniture. Staff of 68 (15 men), average age slightly high at 44. Broad curriculum: science on offer as three separate subjects; all do two languages for at least two years (choice of German or Latin); most take 10 GCSEs; options include business studies, media studies. Wide choice of 23 subjects at A-level (sociology, economics, psychology); all do general studies; one-year qualifications in word-processing and secretarial skills also available. Pupils grouped by ability in maths, science, French. Lots of music: a third play an instrument. Careers education taken seriously: timetabled lessons every three or four weeks throughout third, fourth and fifth years; innovative three-day 'Insight into Management' course for all lower-sixth with the assistance of 20 local companies.

Results (1997) GCSE: 99% gained at least five grades A–C. A-level: 49% of entries graded A or B.

Destinations   More than 90% stay on for A-levels; of these, 75% proceed to university (about four a year to Oxbridge).

Sport   Good outdoor facilities; indoor less impressive (two rather worn gyms, no sports hall or pool). However, this does not prevent the school winning many of the competitions it enters: exceptionally strong athletics, powerful hockey; further strengths in cross-country, gymnastics, volleyball, swimming. PE compulsory, even for sixth-formers.

Remarks   Deservedly popular school: high standards; well-defined character. Ofsted inspectors concluded (1996): 'This is a good school with many strengths. Standards of achievement are high.'

SOUTH HAMPSTEAD ♀
3 Maresfield Gardens, London NW3 5SS. Tel (0171) 435 2899

Synopsis
Independent ★ Girls ★ Day ★ Ages 11–18 (plus associated junior school) ★ 630 pupils ★ 160 in sixth form ★ Fees: £4,968
Head: Mrs Jean Scott, 57, appointed 1993.
Good academic school; first-rate teaching and results; lots of extra-curricular activities.

Profile
Background   Founded 1876; a member of the estimable Girls' Day School Trust (GPDST). Mainly Victorian buildings on a very cramped site in the residential heart of Swiss Cottage; later additions (linked by catwalks) include grim 1970s science block, handsome sports hall (drama studio underneath). Space is tight, paint is peeling, no grass or open space to speak of. Junior school (260 girls aged four to 11) on separate site five minutes' walk away. Former pupils include Helena Bonham Carter, Fay Weldon.

Atmosphere   Intense, busy, vigorously academic. A cosmopolitan mix of Jews (52% of pupils), Christians, Hindus, Muslims (compulsory assemblies careful not to offend any); 75% have working mothers; most have their sights set on high-powered careers (a crèche for staff babies allows them to see for themselves that work and motherhood can co-exist). Motivating them is not a problem but protecting them from the pressures of their parents' expectations is (no prizes awarded below the sixth form, no class rankings). Proper emphasis on education for citizenship, including drugs (to counter 'ferocious' North London culture), sex, Aids, anorexia, self-defence. Down-to-earth uniform; sixth-formers (who choose own clothes and are allowed to wear make-up, jewellery) given lots of responsibility (and freedom). Breakfast from 7.45 am in carpeted cafeteria.

Admissions   Heavily over-subscribed; highly selective. Entry at age four by interview (list closes at 160 for 24 places); at seven and 11 by interview and tests in English, maths. At 11, 300 apply for 50 places (another 50 come through the junior school, where they are continuously assessed); 180 invited for interview. Head says she is looking for girls who will 'romp through the academic side and have time for the extra-curricular activities'. Three-quarters live within five miles, a third walk to school. Scholarships available; GPDST replacing assisted places with its own scheme.

The head   Smart, business-like Scot; has a twinkle in her eye but a steely determination; runs the school on a tight rein (which has led many staff to leave).

Read zoology at Glasgow; worked in industry before switching to teaching; previously head of St George's, Edinburgh (qv). Keen to ensure girls have a rounded education and has encouraged the growth of after-school clubs and activities; school's league table position, on the other hand, has fallen steadily – from 17th in 1993 to 45th in 1996. Widow; two grown-up sons.

The teaching   Academically challenging but surprisingly informal (teachers part of the class rather than in front of it). Well-qualified staff of 58 (10 men), about 40% appointed by present head. Broad curriculum; modern languages outstanding; maths, science (dual award) strong; good computing. Pupils not grouped by ability; no provision for dyslexics; average class size 24, reducing to 10 at A-level. Letter home to any parents whose daughter's homework is unsatisfactory: three letters result in detention. High standard of art; lots of drama, music (choirs a particular strength). Wide range of extra-curricular activities, including aerobics, debating, Duke of Edinburgh award scheme. Ambitious programme of European exchanges, work experience.

Results   (1997) GCSE: all gained at least five grades A–C. A-level: impressive 82% of entries graded A or B (16th in the league table).

Destinations   About 90% continue into the sixth form; virtually all proceed to university.

Sport   High profile, despite the absence of playing fields: leisure centre five minutes' walk away. Netball particularly good; dance, badminton, volleyball also on offer.

Remarks   Good school for girls with brains and stamina; relatively modest fees.

SOUTH WILTS GIRLS' GRAMMAR ♀
Stratford Road, Salisbury, Wiltshire SP1 3JJ. Tel (01722) 323326

> ### Synopsis
> Grammar (grant-maintained) ★ Girls ★ Ages 11–18 ★ 825 pupils ★ 210 in sixth form
> Head: Mrs Marian Freeman, 51, appointed 1991.
> *Sound school; good teaching and results; strong music.*

Profile
Background   Opened 1927; opted out of council control 1994. Undistinguished buildings of various dates; nine classrooms in 'temporary' huts; facilities functional; space is tight.

Atmosphere   Hard-working; high expectations. Emphasis on co-operation, mutual respect; good relations between staff and pupils. Uniform (including kilt) below the sixth form.

Admissions   Over-subscribed (about 300 apply for 120 places); academically selective; entry by verbal and non-verbal reasoning tests. Pupils predominantly from middle-class backgrounds in a catchment area extending eastwards from the city centre.

The head   Experienced (her second headship); strong leader; gets on well with staff and pupils. Read history at Birmingham. Married.

The teaching   Varied styles; lots of group work. Experienced staff of 61 (75% women), 40% appointed by present head. Standard national curriculum; all take two languages from second year (from French, German, Russian); good art. Pupils grouped by ability in maths from second year, science from third year;

extra help for those who need it (at both ends of the ability range); average class size 25, much smaller for A-level. Homework regularly set, marked, monitored. Strong music: 300 sing or learn an instrument; two orchestras, chamber choirs. Good careers advice (the head takes a particular interest); lots of links with business, industry.

Results (1997) GCSE: 98% gained at least five grades A–C. A-level: 49% of entries graded A or B.

Destinations About 80% go on to university (two or three a year to Oxbridge).

Sport Chiefly: netball, hockey, tennis. Facilities limited (but leisure centre near by).

Remarks Ofsted inspectors concluded (1993): 'The school provides an education of the highest quality in a well-ordered community, based upon a well-established code of conduct and sense of responsibility towards people and property'.

STAMFORD ♂
St Paul's Street, Stamford, Lincolnshire PE9 2BS. Tel (01780) 762171

Synopsis
Independent ★ Boys ★ Day and boarding ★ Ages 13–18 (plus associated junior school) ★ 550 pupils (80% day) ★ 190 in sixth form ★ Fees: £4,524 day; £9,048 boarding
Head: Dr Peter Mason, 47, appointed September 1997.
Sound school; good teaching and results; strong sport.

Profile
Background Founded 1532; re-endowed and largely rebuilt 1870s; formerly Direct Grant, reverted to full independence 1976; shares governing body and principal with Stamford Girls' High, qv (no immediate plans to merge). Buildings of varied styles and periods on an attractive 34-acre site (shared with junior school, ages three to 13).

Atmosphere Down-to-earth (no airs and graces); chapel compulsory and very traditional; big emphasis on 'character', self-discipline, games. Lessons on Saturday mornings.

Admissions Entry to co-educational pre-prep at three; to junior school at eight by internal assessment or tests; to senior school at 13 by own exams or Common Entrance; school is moderately selective. Numbers likely to fall with the phasing out of assisted places (which more than 100 hold), and the social mix will be reduced. Pleasant boarding accommodation (numbers declining); most day pupils from 30-mile radius (parents run comprehensive transport service); 15% from Service families. Scholarships (including 25 a year funded by Lincolnshire County Council), bursaries available.

The head (Principal) New appointment. Very able; PhD in chemistry from Newcastle; previously head of Reading (qv); married (two grown-up children). Immediate task is to bring the boys' and girls' schools closer together (they are eight minutes' walk apart but the staff barely know one another); neither site is large enough to accommodate a merger. Claims to relish the challenge.

The teaching Good quality. Hard-working, well-qualified staff (90% male). Broad curriculum; Latin, Greek on offer; modern languages include German, Russian; science taught as three separate subjects; good results in maths, geography. Pupils grouped by ability in maths, science from second year and in most other subjects thereafter; extra help for dyslexics. Lots of art, drama; strong music (in conjunction with girls' school), nearly half learn an instrument. Very well organised careers service. Extra-curricular activities include 350-strong cadet force, well-supported Duke of Edinburgh award scheme. Regular trips abroad for study and sport.

Results   (1997) 99% gained at least five grade A–C. A-level: 52% of entries graded A or B.

Destinations   About 85% stay on for A-levels; of these, about 90% go on to university (average of six a year to Oxbridge).

Sport   Strong: good record across the board. Main games: rugby, hockey, cricket, athletics, canoeing. Facilities, indoor and outdoor, only just adequate.

Remarks   Old-fashioned school facing change.

STAMFORD HIGH ♀
St Martin's, Stamford, Lincolnshire PE9 2LJ. Tel (01780) 484200

Synopsis
Independent ★ Girls ★ Day and boarding ★ Ages 11–18 (plus associated junior school) ★ 714 pupils (85% day) ★ 197 in sixth form ★ Fees: £4,524 day; £8,967– £9,048 boarding
Head: Dr Peter Mason, 47, appointed September 1997.
Sound academic school; good teaching and results; lots of sport.

Profile
Background   Founded 1877; formerly Direct Grant, became full independent 1976; shares governing body and principal with Stamford, qv (but no immediate plans to merge). Purpose-built Victorian premises in the High Street (of 'one of the most beautiful towns in Europe') plus spacious modern additions. Good, modern junior school near by.

Atmosphere   Friendly, well-ordered ('We associate good discipline with a relaxed atmosphere'); grammar school ethos carefully preserved; good relations between staff and pupils; uniform worn by all.

Admissions   At 11 by exams in English, maths, verbal reasoning (entrants from junior school guaranteed a place). Catchment area has 30-mile radius (parents provide comprehensive transport service); boarding accommodation pleasant, spacious; sixth-formers in study bedrooms. Numbers likely to fall with the phasing out of assisted places, which nearly 200 hold; 25 free places allocated at 11-plus to pupils living within a catchment area defined by the county.

The head   (Principal) New appointment (predecessor had been in post 20 years). Very able; PhD in chemistry from Newcastle; previously head of Reading (qv). Immediate task is to bring the girls' and boys' schools closer together (they are eight minutes' walk apart but the staff barely know one another); neither site is large enough to accommodate a merger. Claims to relish the challenge. Married (two grown-up children).

The teaching   Mostly traditional in style; well-qualified staff (25% male). Fairly broad curriculum; in addition to compulsory French (very good results), all are introduced in the second year to German, Latin, Spanish; science taught (but not examined) as three separate subjects; all take at least nine GCSEs; A-level options include business studies, Latin, performing arts. Pupils grouped by ability in maths, French from second year. Lots of music:

400 individual lessons a week; choirs, orchestras in conjunction with boys' school. Extra-curricular activities include well-supported Duke of Edinburgh award scheme.

Results (1997) GCSE: 91% gained at least five grades A–C. A-level: 52% of entries graded A or B.

Destinations About 85% stay on for A-levels; of these, nearly all go on to university (up to eight a year to Oxbridge).

Sport Strong hockey, netball, tennis, athletics, cross-country, gymnastics. Shooting, canoeing, badminton, fencing, trampolining also available. Facilities include fine sports hall/swimming pool complex.

Remarks Old-fashioned school facing change.

STANBRIDGE EARLS ♂ ♀
Romsey, Hampshire S051 0SZ. Tel (01794) 516777

Synopsis
Independent ★ Co-educational ★ Boarding and day ★ Ages 11–18 ★ 185 pupils (78% boys; 88% boarding) ★ 40 in sixth form ★ Fees: £11,565–£12,660 boarding; £8,310–£9,090 day
Head: Howard Moxon, 57, appointed 1984.
First-rate, small school for children unlikely to thrive in the mainstream; dyslexia a speciality.

Profile
Background Founded 1952 to educate pupils in art, music, drama particularly; specialises now in catering for those with specific learning difficulties, especially dyslexia (in which the school has 35 years' experience). Tudor manor house plus some less grand additions in 50 acres of attractive grounds.

Atmosphere Warm, supportive: a steady pattern of attainable achievements geared to each child. The aim is to rebuild confidence in those who may have been diminished by their inability to cope in the mainstream, or whose personal circumstances have affected their progress. The result is friendly, relaxed pupils, grateful to be here.

Admissions One main criterion: 'Do you want to learn?' Entry by tests, interview and full confidential report from pupil's current head covering character, interests, ability at work, games or other skills. Range of abilities is wide. Some pupils funded by local education authorities unable to offer such specialised help. Small, pleasantly furnished boarding houses. Scholarships, bursaries available.

The head Very able. Long-serving but has lost none of his enthusiasm or faith in the potential of his pupils, each of whom he knows well. Approachable, understanding, humorous. Read geography at Cambridge. Married; three grown-up children.

The teaching Highly skilled: cheerful, hard-working, specialist staff; very small classes; individualised learning programmes. Pupils may take up to eight GCSEs (from a choice of 20); additional courses to foster practical talents include textiles, motor mechanics (large workshop). Art, drama, physical education also popular and successful. Sixth form offers A-levels (in all main subjects), GNVQs (leisure & tourism) and other vocational qualifications. Outward bound activities are well supported; good facilities for photography.

Results   (1997) GCSE: 20% gained at least five grades A–C. A-level: 14% of entries graded A or B. Every pupil taken as far as he/she is capable.

Destinations   Virtually all continue into the sixth form, after which most remain in full-time education.

Sport   All major games played; good facilities, including indoor pool, sports hall, tennis courts. Sailing particularly popular.

Remarks   Well-regarded school; former pupils are proud of it.

STEWART'S MELVILLE   ♂
Queensferry Road, Edinburgh EH4 3EZ. Tel (0131) 332 7925

Synopsis
Independent ★ Boys (plus associated girls' school) ★ Day and boarding ★ Ages 12–18 (plus associated co-educational junior school) ★ 806 pupils (95% day) ★ 120 in (one-year) sixth form ★ Fees: £4,812 day; £9,342 boarding
Head: Patrick Tobin, 55, appointed 1989.
Successful, well-run school; good teaching and results; strong sport.

Profile
Background   Result of a 1973 merger between Daniel Stewart's Hospital (founded 1855) and Melville College (1832) on the rather cramped site of the former; school shares a governing body and principal with Mary Erskine (girls); co-educational junior school (ages three to 12) split between the two sites. Remarkable, vast stone building embellished with towers, pinnacles and minarets (a Victorian extravaganza) plus many more functional additions.

Atmosphere   Fairly boisterous: hordes of children in a relatively small space. Strong pastoral care system; staff encourage parental involvement. Bright red blazers for those awarded 'colours' for games, music, debating.

Admissions   Junior school pupils promoted automatically (taking 100 of the 140 places); rest do tests in English, maths, verbal reasoning; school is over-subscribed but not unduly selective. Recent £5.5 million bequest will fund bursaries to replace the assisted places scheme, from which one in six benefits. Small number of boarders (mainly the children of expatriates); comfortable accommodation (Mary Erskine boarders next door).

The head   (Principal) Responsible for a total of 1,450 pupils (divides his time between here and Mary Erskine). Very able; calm, courteous, efficient. Read PPE at Oxford, was head of history at Tonbridge (qv); his second headship. Chairman in 1998 of HMC.

The teaching   Good quality. Broad curriculum: all take eight Standard Grades and five Highers; 85% stay on for Certificate of Sixth Year Studies. Maximum class size 26. Very strong music (in conjunction with Mary Erskine); flourishing orchestras, choirs. Good careers department. Extra-curricular activities include cadet force, Duke of Edinburgh award scheme.

Results   (1997) Standard Grade: 80% gained at least five grades 1–2. Highers: 38% gained at least five grades A–C.

Destinations   About 80% go on to university (four or five a year to Oxbridge).

Sport   Strong. Main games: rugby, cricket (playing fields a two-mile bus ride away), hockey, tennis. Others on offer include athletics, curling, golf, swimming. Sports hall on site.

Remarks   Good all round.

STOCKPORT GRAMMAR ♂ ♀
Buxton Road, Stockport, Cheshire SK2 7AF. Tel (0161) 456 9000

Synopsis
Independent ★ Co-educational ★ Day ★ Ages 11–18 (plus associated junior school) ★ 993 pupils (equal numbers of girls and boys) ★ 251 in sixth form ★ Fees: £4,266 (plus £81 a term for compulsory lunch)
Head: Ian Mellor, 51, appointed 1996.
Successful, traditional, academic school; good teaching and results; strong music.

Profile
Background   Founded 1487 by Sir Edmond Shaa, goldsmith (to 'teche allman persons children the science of grammar'); links with the Goldsmiths' Company retained. Moved to present 28-acre site 1916: purpose-built, Tudor-style premises plus many later (far-flung) additions; school photographs line the oak-panelled corridors; all in good decorative order. Formerly Direct Grant, school reverted to full independence 1976; girls first admitted 1980. On-site junior school shares some facilities.

Atmosphere   Warm, friendly, well-ordered. Mutually respectful relations between staff and pupils; high expectations throughout. Smart uniform (gold-braided dark blue blazers) worn by all.

Admissions   By tests (in English, maths, verbal reasoning – specimen papers available) and interview; school is over-subscribed (600 apply for 125 places) and highly selective (top 10% of the ability range). Governors aim to compensate for phasing out of assisted places, which more than 200 hold, by introducing means-tested bursaries. Catchment area has a 20-mile radius.

The head   Recent appointment; his second headship. Able, enthusiastic, approachable. Read modern languages at Cambridge; still teaches French, German. Married; three sons.

The teaching   Lively: broadly traditional in style; lots of pupil participation. Hard-working, well-qualified staff of 80 (55% female); very low turnover. Traditional academic curriculum: science taught as three separate subjects; all do French, German, Latin. Pupils grouped by ability in maths only from age 14; extra provision for the gifted; average class size 25, smaller for GCSE, 12–15 at A-level. Strong drama and music (four choirs, two orchestras, regular concerts). Extra-curricular activities include debating, chess, Duke of Edinburgh award scheme.

Results   (1997) GCSE: 99% gained at least five grades A–C. A-level: very creditable 73% of entries graded A or B (among the best co-educational school results).

Destinations   Virtually all go on to university (up to 20 a year to Oxbridge).

Sports   Particular strengths in rugby, hockey; high standards, too, in lacrosse, tennis, cricket, netball. Facilities include 12 acres of playing fields, all-weather pitch; sports hall urgently needed.

Remarks   Very good school for able children.

STOKESLEY ♂ ♀

Station Road, Stokesley, North Yorkshire TS9 5AL. Tel (01642) 710050

Synopsis

Comprehensive ★ Co-educational ★ Ages 11–18 ★ 1,250 pupils (equal numbers of girls and boys) ★ 280 in sixth-form
Head: Brian Owen, 46, appointed 1994.
Excellent, well-run school; first-rate teaching; very good results; wide range of sporting and other activities.

Profile

Background Founded as a secondary modern 1958; went comprehensive 1972 and later added a sixth-form (lavishly equipped, serves as a community education centre). Attractive, airy, flat-roofed buildings (showing some signs of wear and tear) on a 14-acre site; leisure centre adjacent. Some classes in 'temporary' huts but school is not under-funded: excellent, newly renovated library (head says he can 'almost write a blank cheque for books'); computers everywhere; splendid music centre with practice rooms. Electric stair lifts for disabled.

Atmosphere Cheerful, friendly; an ethos of respect for people and the environment. Generally cordial relations between pupils and staff (nearly all of whom take part in out-of-class activities). Pastoral care system ensures individuals are not lost in the mass (though head says some tensions arise from overcrowding – he would prefer 50 fewer pupils). Discipline unobtrusive but firmly structured; simple uniform well adhered to (pupils look both civilised and comfortable). Parents exceptionally appreciative and kept well informed.

Admissions Over-subscribed; entry controlled by North Yorkshire County Council; preference to siblings and those living in the catchment area (which covers 1,000 square miles); most come from nine 'feeder' primaries. Intake is genuinely comprehensive. Sixth-form entry restricted to those capable of A-levels or Advanced GNVQs (in business or health & social care); five GCSEs required at grade C or above.

The head Highly regarded. Excellent manager with a clear vision; wears his responsibilities lightly and with good humour; presides over a loyal and harmonious staff. Keeps his finger on the pulse: lunches in the cafeteria (where he is treated with wary respect); tours the school constantly; teaches GCSE science. Read physics at Birmingham; previously head of a comprehensive in Nottingham. Great advocate of physical fitness: runs on the surrounding hills every morning before work. Married; one daughter (in the sixth form).

The teaching First-rate. Variety of styles around a core of traditional whole-class teaching; staff of 79 (60% women), many long-serving. Classroom atmosphere fairly informal; pupils are interested and get on with their work. Mixed-ability classes in early years, grouping by ability in some subjects thereafter; extra help for those with special needs. Exceptionally good results in science (dual award); strengths, too, in art, drama, design/technology. Choice of 18 subjects at A-level, including economics, sociology, music; languages particularly well taught. Lots of music. Vast range of extra-curricular activities. Regular exchanges with schools in France and Germany.

Results (1997) GCSE: creditable 72% gained at least five grades A–C. A-level: 52% of entries graded A or B.

Destinations About 60% continue into the sixth form, from where nearly all proceed to university (three or four a year to Oxbridge).

Sport Emphasis is on variety – from recreation to high-class competition in county teams; soccer is the leading boys' game. Opportunities in the neighbouring leisure centre include athletics, basketball, canoeing, circuit training, cricket, gymnastics, hockey, netball, swimming, tennis.

Remarks A richly enabling school: everything on offer; staff work hard to realise every pupil's potential. Ofsted inspectors concluded (December 1996): 'This is a highly successful school which deserves its high reputation and popularity.'

STONAR ♀
Cottles Park, Atworth, Melksham, Wiltshire SN12 8NT. Tel (01225) 702309

Synopsis
Independent ★ Girls ★ Boarding and day ★ Ages 5–18 (plus associated nursery) ★ 420 pupils (52% boarding) ★ 92 in sixth form ★ Fees: £10,260 boarding; £5,685 day
Head: Mrs Caroline Homan, 45, appointed September 1997.
Attractive small school; fairly wide range of abilities; very good riding.

Profile
Background Founded in Kent 1895; moved to present pretty country house in 80 acres of parkland 1939; converted 17th-century cottages and substantial later additions give the campus a village-like feel. Facilities include a covered riding school and floodlit outdoor arena; 'livery is available for the girls' own ponies'. Co-educational nursery school (ages two to five) on same site.

Atmosphere Relaxed, friendly, unpretentious; 'horsiness' not dominant; friendly relations between staff and pupils.

Admissions To the junior school by informal assessment; at 11 by tests. The school is not selective (or full – numbers have fallen recently). Pupils from farming, business, Service backgrounds; a few from abroad. Boarding accommodation comfortable but not luxurious; juniors in dormitories of up to six; seniors in double study-bedrooms.

The head New appointment; lively, attractive personality. Read theology at Durham, religion and sociology at Sussex; previously deputy head of Sibford (qv).

The teaching Fairly formal in style; well-qualified staff. Standard curriculum; good science; Latin, German, Spanish on offer; A-level options include geology, business studies, psychology; vocational alternatives available, including riding instructors' qualification. Pupils grouped by ability in English, French, maths, science; extra help for those who need it, including English as a foreign language; maximum class size 20, smaller in the sixth form. Art, music, drama active and popular. Extra-curricular activities include well-supported Duke of Edinburgh award scheme.

Results (1997) GCSE: 86% gained at least five grades A–C. A-level: 42% of entries graded A or B.

Destinations Most go on to university.

Sports Strong hockey, netball; tennis, rounders, athletics, squash, gymnastics, swimming, cross-country also on offer; riding skills taught to a high level. Facilities include playing fields, indoor pool, new sports hall.

Remarks Good school for girls who might not thrive in a more academically competitive environment.

STONYHURST ♂
Stonyhurst, Clitheroe, Lancashire BB7 9PZ. Tel (01254) 826345

Synopsis
Independent ★ Roman Catholic ★ Boys (plus girls in sixth form – fully co-educational from September 1999) ★ Boarding and day ★ Ages 13–18 (plus associated junior school) ★ 390 pupils (80% boarding) ★ 190 in sixth form (91% boys) ★ Fees: £12,540 boarding; £7,800 day
Head: Adrian Aylward, 39, appointed 1996.
Distinguished Jesuit school; good teaching; fairly wide range of abilities; strong sport.

Profile
Background Founded 1593 by Jesuits in St Omer, northern France, to provide a Catholic education for English boys then denied one in England; moved here (after many vicissitudes) 1794. Elizabethan house plus vast, pinnacled (and somewhat bleak) 19th-century building and later additions on a remote 200-acre estate (long driveway, ornamental lakes to left and right); £2.5 million spent recently on extensive modernisation and refurbishment; facilities first-rate. Old boys include 22 martyrs, three saints, seven VCs.

Atmosphere Busy, friendly; Jesuit traditions of intellectual and spiritual rigour combined with faith, love, service to fellows; head has re-introduced 8 am prayers 'to show boys and girls that the spiritual has an essential place in the world'. Day boys and (from 1999) 13-year-old girls admitted primarily in response to falling numbers (head says school will have to adapt its 'somewhat male-oriented attitudes').

Admissions By Common Entrance (alternative tests available): fairly wide range of abilities; 15% non-Catholic (but expected to embrace the school's ideals); 21 nationalities represented. About a third receive help with fees: phasing out of assisted places will have a big impact. Unusually, boarders all housed under one roof; juniors in dormitories, seniors in double and single study-bedrooms. Day pupils stay until 8.30 pm.

The head Very able: youthful, charming, determined; strong spiritual commitment. Read classics at Oxford; spent nine successful years in the City then switched to teaching; previously deputy head of Downside (qv). Sees a difficult road ahead: 'a school is not a business but it has to be financially sound'. Married; three young children.

The teaching Challenging; well-qualified, stable staff of 56 (eight women). Broad curriculum: science taught as three separate subjects; Latin, Greek on offer; religious studies compulsory throughout; lots of computing. Most take nine GCSEs and three A-levels (from a choice of 21). Pupils grouped by ability in maths, French; extra help for dyslexics and those who speak English as a foreign language. All learn a musical instrument (at the school's expense). Extra-curricular activities include popular cadet force (compulsory for second years), Duke of Edinburgh award scheme.

Results (1997) GCSE: 92% gained at least five grades A–C. A-level: 53% of entries graded A or B (a relatively good year).

Destinations About 95% go on to university (average of six a year to Oxbridge).

Sport Strong rugby (old boys include 12 internationals); successful cricket, athletics; clay pigeon shooting, fishing also on offer. Facilities include fine indoor pool, squash courts, nine-hole golf course.

Remarks Attractive, well-run school adapting to changing times (without departing from its Jesuit ideals).

STOWE ♂
Stowe, Buckingham MK18 5EH. Tel (01280) 813164

Synopsis
Independent ★ Boys (plus girls in sixth form) ★ Boarding (and some day) ★
Ages 13–18 ★ 570 pupils (95% boarding) ★ 300 in sixth form (66% boys) ★
Fees: £14,175 boarding; £9,130 day
Head: Jeremy Nichols, 54, appointed 1989.
Sound school in a beautiful setting; wide range of abilities; good art, music, sport.

Profile
Background   Founded 1923 (to be unlike other, harsher boarding schools); imposing colonnaded 18th-century mansion (former home of the Dukes of Buckingham and Chandos) set in 750 acres of landscaped gardens (maintained by the National Trust). Particularly good facilities for art, drama, music.

Atmosphere   Relaxed, courteous pupils ('Stoics') cite friendliness and tolerance as the qualities that make this different from their previous schools; chaplain says spiritual matters are deemed important, too. Dress code rather than uniform: boys in sports jackets, girls in long skirts.

Admissions   By Common Entrance, interview and previous school report: 'We don't apply strictly academic criteria,' says the head; abilities range from high-flying scholars to those who thought they were educational failures at 13; 12% from abroad. Boarding accommodation more functional than luxurious; juniors in six-bed dormitories; seniors have double or single study-bedrooms; girls housed separately. Good food (in grand dining room). Up to 50 scholarships and bursaries on offer (including 20 in the sixth form).

The head   Formerly a housemaster at Eton; read English and Italian at Cambridge (pro-European in outlook); teaches poetry appreciation to first-years to get to know them. 'School,' he says, 'isn't about preparing for exams at 18, but for life. Maybe we should have league tables for 40–year-olds to see how they turned out.' Married; four children.

The teaching   Traditional in style; full-time staff of 60 (80% male), 60% appointed by present head. National curriculum followed; modern languages include French, German, Spanish; Latin, Greek on offer; computing throughout. Pupils grouped by ability from the start; further setting thereafter in maths, modern languages; thorough provision for slow learners; average class size 22–24, reducing to 12–15 at A-level. First-rate art (very good A-level results); lots of music (a third learn an instrument). Well-appointed careers centre. Extra-curricular activities include cadet force, Duke of Edinburgh award scheme.

Results   (1997) GCSE: 85% gained at least five grades A–C. A-level: rather modest 40% of entries graded A or B. ('Believing passionately that the best and the rest should be educated together, we can live with a poor placing in the league table; it hurts, but it is the price we must pay to do what we believe.')

Destinations   About 90% proceed to university (average of six a year to Oxbridge); some go into the Army.

Sport   Major and minor games played to a high standard; particular strengths in girls' hockey, lacrosse, cross-country, athletics, swimming, cricket. Facilities include sports hall, all-weather pitch, heated indoor pool, nine-hole golf course, running track, shooting ranges, croquet lawn.

Remarks   Not an academic powerhouse but likely to suit children who might not settle elsewhere.

STRATFORD-UPON-AVON GIRLS' GRAMMAR ♀
Shottery Manor, Stratford-upon-Avon, Warwickshire CV37 9HA. Tel (01789) 293759

Synopsis
Grammar ★ Girls ★ Ages 11–18 ★ 490 pupils ★ 170 in sixth form
Head: Roger Stanbridge, 48, appointed 1991.
Traditional grammar school; good teaching and results.

Profile
Background   Opened 1958; well-maintained 1950s buildings set in 20 acres of landscaped gardens and playing fields; sixth-form centre in 14th-century Shottery Manor house. A spacious, tranquil setting.

Atmosphere   Relaxed, fairly traditional; easy, respectful relations between staff and polite, self-motivated pupils. Imaginative art work enlivens corridors and foyer. Close links (curricular and social) with nearby King Edward VI boys' grammar (qv).

Admissions   School severely over-subscribed (up to seven apply for each place); entry by two verbal reasoning tests (no interview); top 15% of the ability range from a mix of social backgrounds but predominantly middle-class.

The head   Friendly, approachable, good communicator. Read chemistry at Hull; came here as deputy head 1987. Teaches first-years and sixth-formers for quarter of the timetable; sits in on others' lessons 'to keep everyone on their toes'. Aims to produce 'assertive, confident young ladies'. Married; three daughters (two are pupils here).

The teaching   Sound; firmly academic in approach; diligent staff. Standard grammar school curriculum; all do Latin for first two years and add German to French in second year; science popular and strong (on offer as three separate subjects); technology not well developed. A-level options include theatre studies, politics; all do general studies. Little music (only one part-time teacher); hard-working art department (resident potter) short of space and facilities. Lots of community service ('talking' newspaper for the blind); well-supported Duke of Edinburgh award scheme. Regular exchanges with schools in France, Germany.

Results   (1997) GCSE: 98% gained at least five grades A–C. A-level: 56% of entries graded A or B.

Destinations   About 90% stay on for A-levels; of these, 90% proceed to university (average of six a year to Oxbridge).

Sport   Main games: hockey, netball, tennis; aim is to involve everyone. Facilities are adequate.

Remarks   Ofsted inspectors concluded (1995): 'This is a very good school which enables pupils to achieve high standards. It is a well ordered community where the quality of relationships is excellent and the progress and esteem of all its members nurtured.'

STRATHALLAN ♂ ♀
Forgandenny, Perth PH2 9EG. Tel (01738) 812546

Synopsis
Independent ★ Co-educational ★ Boarding and some day ★ Ages 10–18 ★
490 pupils (61% boys, 98% boarding) ★ 170 in sixth form ★ Fees: £6,660–£8,790
Head: Angus McPhail, 41, appointed 1993.
Well-run school; wide range of abilities; lots of sport, music, drama.

Profile
Background   Founded 1912; moved 1920 to present 150-acre site seven miles south of Perth. Main building an early 19th-century mock-Tudor reconstruction of an 18th-century house; recent additions include four new boarding houses and show-piece medical centre (£5 million spent since 1990); good facilities for design/technology; most classrooms decrepit and dismal. Fully co-educational since 1982.

Atmosphere   Busy, robust community that will not suit the slouch: unsophisticated, down-to-earth (but less rugged since the introduction of girls – who are unabashed by the numerical inequality). Staff live on site.

Admissions   At 10 by tests, at 13 by Common Entrance; school is not particularly selective. Pupils primarily Scots or children of expats from engineering or financial backgrounds (more than a third have parents living abroad); high proportion of 'first-time buyers' of independent education. First-rate boarding accommodation: all have well-appointed, single study-bedrooms from age 14 (business-minded school lets well as a conference centre, grossing £200,000 a year). Some scholarships; school aims to replace assisted places, which 45 hold, with a scheme of its own.

The head   Able, vigorous. Read philosophy, politics & economics at Oxford; worked at the Bank of England for four years ('so I'm OK with a balance sheet') before switching careers; taught economics at Glenalmond and Sedbergh (housemaster). Wants to raise academic standards (in the belief that the school's traditional second-division image is 'not sustainable'); keen on sport (cricket, golf, skiing) and music (plays violin and guitar and sings); has introduced school colours for art, drama, music (in addition to sport). Married (to a teacher); three children.

The teaching   Sound; experienced staff of 64, a third appointed by present head. Emphasis in first two years on the Three Rs; all do Latin for at least two years; Greek, German on offer; science taught as three separate subjects; particularly good results in maths, design/technology; first-rate art (in inadequate premises). All do at least eight GCSEs; more able half take A-levels, rest do five Highers over two years. Pupils grouped by ability in maths, science, French; maximum class size 20, reducing to 10–12 in the sixth form. Lots of drama and music; 40% learn an instrument (50 play the bagpipes); two orchestras, several choirs. Big emphasis on outdoor pursuits: cadet force, Duke of Edinburgh award scheme, adventure expeditions.

Results   (1997) GCSE: 85% gained at least five grades A–C. A-level: 50% of entries graded A or B (but see above)

Destinations   About 85% continue into the sixth form; of these, 65% proceed to higher education.

Sport   Mainly rugby, hockey, cricket for the boys; hockey, athletics for the girls. Also on offer: squash, fives, tennis, shooting, angling, sailing, skiing. Facilities include floodlit, all-weather pitch.

Remarks   Solid, no-frills school; dispiriting classrooms.

SURBITON HIGH ♀
Surbiton Crescent, Kingston-upon-Thames, Surrey KT1 2JT. Tel (0181) 546 5245

Synopsis
Independent ★ Girls (plus boys' prep school) ★ Day ★ Ages 4–18 ★ 839 pupils
(592 in senior school) ★ 116 in sixth form ★ Fees, £3,240–£5397
Head: Miss Gail Perry, 49, appointed 1993.
Popular, well-run school; good teaching and results; first-rate art; lots of sport.

Profile
Background   Founded 1884; a member of the Church Schools Company
(formed to create schools that would offer 'a good academic education based on
Christian principles'). Original (now battle-scarred) Victorian premises plus
many later additions (including impressive sixth-form centre a few hundred
yards away) on a leafy avenue near the town centre; further expansion will create 60–70 more senior school places in 1998. Separate junior schools for girls
(newly built) and boys near by.

Atmosphere   Christian, caring, well-ordered; formal but friendly relations
between staff and well-mannered girls; sixth-formers treated as 'professional
students' (and take an active role in pastoral care). Big emphasis on celebrating
success; lots of art work on display.

Admissions   Heavily over-subscribed: three or four apply for each place. Entry
at 11 (30% from junior school, 25% from primaries) by interview and school's
own tests in English, maths; top 15% of the ability range (not an academic hot-
house) from an extensive catchment area (own bus service); head is looking for
supportive parents and well-motivated pupils. School hopes to compensate for
the phasing out of assisted places, which more than 50 hold.

The head   Able, experienced, straight-forward. Read biology at Bristol; taught
it at Tiffin Girls' (qv) for 13 years; previously deputy head of Putney High (qv).

The teaching   Generally formal in style with lots of pupil participation.
Staff of 62 (seven men). Broad curriculum: French from age four; all seniors
do Latin for at least one year and most continue it to GCSE; Greek, German,
Spanish on offer; science taught as three separate subjects; technology not
neglected. Pupils grouped by ability in maths, French from 11, science from
14; average class size 22, reducing to a maximum of 12 at A-level. All take
between nine and 11 GCSEs and three A-levels (half do maths and science).
Good art (all staff practising artists), lively drama, lots of music (three choirs,
two orchestras).

Results   (1997) GCSE: 99% gained at least five grades A–C. A-level: 55% of
entries graded A or B.

Destinations   About 70% stay on into the sixth form (most of the rest switch
to local sixth-form colleges); of these, nearly all go on to university (average of
six a year to Oxbridge).

Sport   Good record. Main games: hockey, netball; rowing, sailing are strong;
tennis, athletics, squash, badminton also on offer; skiing particularly popular.
Facilities include 33 acres of playing fields a seven-minute bus rise away (all-
weather pitch, netball and tennis courts).

Remarks   Attractive school; good all round.

SUTTON COLDFIELD GIRLS' ♀
Jockey Road, Sutton Coldfield, Birmingham B73 5PT. Tel (0121) 354 1479

Synopsis
Grammar ★ Girls ★ Ages 11–18 ★ 940 pupils ★ 185 in sixth form
Head: Mrs Jennifer Jones, 56, appointed 1983.
Sound, well-run school; good teaching and results.

Profile
Background Founded as a grammar school 1929; went comprehensive 1974; reverted to selection (thanks to parental pressure) 1982. Pleasant red-brick buildings plus careful later additions in an affluent residential area. Bright, cheerful classrooms.

Atmosphere Friendly, helpful; very few discipline problems. Uniform creatively adhered to.

Admissions Entry by tests in maths, verbal and non-verbal reasoning; places offered to the first 150 (no interview); top 20% of the ability range. Pupils from all over Birmingham (and beyond).

The head Read biology and economics at Keele; wide experience in state schools; previously deputy head of a comprehensive. Believes girls have better opportunities in single-sex schools. Married, no children.

The teaching Confident, professional; varied styles but predominantly front-of-class. Well-qualified staff of 62 (14 men), 80% appointed by present head. Standard national curriculum; all take nine GCSEs (options include business studies, physical education) and four A-levels (from a choice of 23). Pupils grouped by ability in maths only from second year; progress closely monitored; average class size 27. Very good art, music.

Results (1997) GCSE: 99% gained at least five grades A–C. A-level: 44% of entries graded A or B.

Destinations Majority stay on for A-levels and proceed to university (average of two a year to Oxbridge).

Sport All the traditional girls' games plus football; creditable match record; facilities not wonderful.

Remarks Pleasant, friendly school. Ofsted inspectors concluded (1994): 'This is a good school with some strong features. Seldom are standards less than high.'

SUTTON HIGH ♀
55 Cheam Road, Sutton, Surrey SM1 2AX. Tel (0181) 642 0594

Synopsis
Independent ★ Girls ★ Ages 4–18 ★ 750 pupils (500 in senior school) ★ 160 in sixth form ★ Fees: £4,968
Head: Mrs Anne Coutts, 41, appointed 1995.
Strong academic school; good teaching and results; friendly relations between staff and pupils.

Profile
Background Founded 1884; a member of the Girls' Day School Trust. Collection of attractive Victorian houses (narrow stairs, oddly-shaped rooms) plus later additions (which make up for in facilities what they lack in character)

on a five-acre site surrounded by blocks of flats. School will not win any beauty contests (despite continuous programme of refurbishment) but it is warm, comfortable and well equipped.

Atmosphere Calm, smiling, civilised. Hard working, cheerful girls; easy relations with staff and other pupils. Slightly surprising uniform of violet pullovers and blazers; older girls dress as they please (conservatively).

Admissions Six apply for every place; entry at 11-plus by interview and searching exam. As in all GDST schools, girls are admitted 'on the basis of their academic potential and ability without reference to religious or ethnic backgrounds or beliefs'. Almost all juniors proceed to senior school. Some social and financial mix thanks to assisted places, scholarships, bursaries. Extensive catchment area (good rail links).

The head Quietly spoken, unassuming; her second headship. Anxious to temper academic rigour with kindness; gets on well with staff and pupils. Studied microbiology at Warwick (and has a degree in educational management); teaches chemistry to younger pupils; keen musician (plays the guitar). Married (to a vicar); two daughters at another GPDST school.

The teaching Very assured. Nearly all-female staff; alert, interested pupils; no feeling of rush or pressure; average class size 25. All do two modern languages (from French, German, Spanish) plus Latin; Greek on offer; sciences taught throughout as three separate subjects; numerous computers (full-time IT adviser); well-equipped rooms for home economics. Lots of art, music (choirs, ensembles) and drama. Well-supported Duke of Edinburgh award scheme.

Results (1997) GCSE: 99% gained at least five grades A–C. A-level: creditable 70% of entries graded A or B.

Destinations Virtually all go to university (five or six a year to Oxbridge).

Sport A strength; facilities include on-site hockey pitches, fine sports hall, heated indoor pool. Activities on offer include netball, tennis, basketball, athletics, badminton, gymnastics, squash, aerobics.

Remarks Attractive, kindly school for able girls.

SUTTON VALENCE ♂ ♀
Sutton Valence, Maidstone, Kent ME17 3HN. Tel (01622) 842281

Synopsis
Independent ★ Co-educational ★ Day and boarding ★ Ages 11–18 (plus associated junior school) ★ 380 pupils (60% boys, 70% day) ★ 120 in sixth form ★ Fees: £7,485 day; £11,700 boarding
Head: Nicholas Sampson, 39, appointed 1994.
Sound academic school; good GCSE results; lots of art, drama, music, sport.

Profile
Background Founded 1576; moved 1910 to present 100-acre hill-top site (fine views over the Weald of Kent); mid-Victorian, red-brick buildings plus many later additions, including music school, art centre; starkly functional dining hall. Junior school (Underhill – 250 pupils age three to 11) in neighbouring village.

Atmosphere Calm, well-ordered; Christian faith 'expressed by the prominence given to daily worship' (full-time chaplain); friendly relations between staff and pupils; good pastoral care ('an environment in which it is easy to learn and to grow as a human being'). Uniform worn throughout. Lessons on Saturday mornings.

Admissions By interview and tests in English, maths, verbal reasoning or Common Entrance; school is over-subscribed but not unduly selective and likely to become less so with the phasing out of assisted places, which about 70 hold; half join from the junior school. Girl boarders comfortably accommodated in new house; boys' arrangements less luxurious; 15% of boarders from abroad. Scholarships: academic, drama, art, music, sport.

The head Kindly, thoughtful. Read English at Cambridge; previously a housemaster at Wells Cathedral School (qv). Teaches English to third-years. Married; two young children.

The teaching Sound; long-serving staff. Fairly broad curriculum: science on offer as three separate subjects; all do Latin for at least two years; modern languages include German, Spanish; lots of computing (many pupils have palmtops); good design/technology; GCSE options include home economics, child development; choice of 22 subjects at A-level, including history of art, theatre studies. Pupils grouped by ability in maths, modern languages from the start, in English, science for GCSE; specialist help for dyslexics; progress closely monitored (termly grades for effort and achievement); maximum class size 20, reducing to 12 in the sixth form. Lots of art, drama, music; 35% learn an instrument; four choirs, orchestra. Good careers department. Wide range of extra-curricular activities, including cadet force, Duke of Edinburgh award scheme. Regular language exchanges with pupils in France, Germany.

Results (1997) GCSE: 90% gained at least five grades A–C. A-level: 38% of entries graded A or B.

Destinations About 80% proceed to university.

Sport Has a high profile; 17 activities on offer, including hockey, rugby, netball, riding, judo, fencing, badminton, fives; regular county honours. Facilities include 40 acres of playing fields, all-weather pitch, fine cricket square, indoor pool, tennis and squash courts, six-hole golf course, shooting range.

Remarks Good school for all-rounders.

SWAVESEY ♂ ♀
Gibraltar Lane, Swavesey, Cambridge CB4 5RS. Tel (01954) 230366

Synopsis
Comprehensive ★ Co-educational (equal numbers of girls and boys) ★ Ages 11–16 ★ 820 pupils
Head: Patrick Talbott, 53, appointed 1985.
Well-run comprehensive; good teaching and GCSE results; unusually good cricket.

Profile
Background Opened 1958 as a secondary modern; went comprehensive 1974; serves a ring of 11 villages between Cambridge and Huntingdon. Pleasant greenfield site (shared with adult education centre); premises showing signs of wear.

Atmosphere Cheerful, positive, open; presence of adult learners contributes to purposeful mood. Aims include helping pupils 'to appreciate how a nation earns and maintains its standard of living and properly to esteem the essential role of industry and commerce in this process'. Maroon sweatshirt uniform compulsory ('and regularly checked').

Admissions School full but not over-subscribed; 15% from outside the official catchment area; ability profile above the national average.

The head   (Warden) Sharp, unstuffy, precise. Left school at 16; became a junior civil servant before taking A-levels at night school, gaining a teaching certificate and heading the English departments in two London comprehensives by the age of 28; has an MA in educational management; previously head of a community college in Lincolnshire. Still teaches GCSE English; runs marathons. Married; two children (both were pupils here).

The teaching   Meticulously planned with plenty of pace (rated by Ofsted inspectors as 'good and often very good'); careful balance achieved between teaching of knowledge and relevant skills; standards particularly high in English, history and art (exceptionally popular). Standard national curriculum; all do French and German for first two years; GCSE options include child development, drama, physical education. Pupils grouped by ability in maths, science from second year, English from third year (but care taken to balance gender numbers); average class size 27 (top sets tend to be largest). Good communication with parents via 'day books' in which they can monitor children's work and teachers' comments. Plenty of music: 25% learn an instrument.

Results   (1997) GCSE: 65% gained at least five grades A–C.

Destinations   About 90% remain in full-time education after 16, more than 50% to take A-levels.

Sport   One of the few state schools to regard cricket as its strongest team game: several boys in current county schools side; great enthusiasm from staff, who have own XI and include a National Cricket Association coach; two artificial pitches, indoor nets. Creditable record in soccer, basketball, girls' hockey, cross-country. Good facilities include indoor pool, squash courts, floodlit all-weather games pitch and tennis courts.

Remarks   Inspectors' verdict – 'A good school with many excellent features' – fully justified.

TALBOT HEATH ♀
Rothesay Road, Bournemouth, Dorset BH4 9NJ. Tel (01202) 761881

Synopsis
Independent ★ Girls ★ Day and boarding ★ Age 11–18 (plus pre-prep and junior schools) ★ 420 pupils (95% day) ★ 98 in sixth form ★ Fees: £5,520 day; £9,630 boarding.
Head: Mrs Christine Dipple, 42, appointed 1991.
Traditional, academic school; good teaching and results; strong music.

Profile
Background   Founded 1886; moved to present 25-acre woodland site 1935; formerly Direct Grant, reverted to full independence 1976. Fine, purpose-built premises arranged around two quadrangles; some later additions less attractive.

Atmosphere   Diligent, competitive, well-disciplined; exudes efficiency. Good pastoral care (staff trained in 'listening skills'). Strict uniform below the sixth form (when rules are relaxed).

Admissions   By interview and exams; school has been fairly selective but phasing out of assisted places, which about a third hold, could lead to a lowering of entry standards. Catchment extends from Southampton to Dorchester (parents organise buses). Boarding numbers are small and declining (most from abroad, including 12 Chinese); accommodation (consequently) is spacious but the atmosphere lacks buzz.

The head Experienced; good leader. Read modern languages at Leeds; MA from Lille; taught at Millfield, Sherborne Girls', St Swithun's. Married; one stepdaughter.

The teaching Generally formal in style. Long-serving staff of 43 (10 men). National curriculum plus: all do Latin, two modern languages; strong maths; science taught as three separate subjects (facilities need up-grading). Choice of 21 subjects at A-level; extras include electronics, car maintenance, global awareness. Pupils grouped by ability in maths, science, French; lots of extra help for those who need it; average class size 20. Strong music: nearly all learn an instrument. Popular Duke of Edinburgh award scheme.

Results (1997) GCSE: all gained at least five grades A–C. A-level: creditable 70% of entries graded A or B.

Destinations About 60% stay on for A-levels; of these, nearly all go on to university (up to six a year to Oxbridge).

Sport Strong: high level of participation; good facilities, including extensive playing fields and large, well-equipped hall. Main sports: hockey, netball, cricket, tennis, swimming, athletics.

Remarks Good all round.

TANBRIDGE HOUSE ♂ ♀
Farthings Hill, Guildford Road, Horsham, West Sussex RH12 1SR. Tel (01403) 263628

Synopsis
Comprehensive ★ Co-educational ★ Ages 11–16 ★ 1,200 pupils (60% boys)
Head: Dr Peter Thomas, 43, appointed 1995.
Successful comprehensive in brand-new premises; good teaching and GCSE results.

Profile
Background Opened 1924 as a girls' high school; went co-educational and comprehensive 1976; moved to new, purpose-built £13.5 million premises September 1994. Stylish complex of buildings with steeply pitched tiled roofs on a rising, green-field site; first-rate facilities include inter-linked suites of classrooms around a 'village square', drama studio, music centre, computerised library, large sports hall, heated outdoor pool – all surrounded by playing fields.

Atmosphere Busy, well-ordered; strong sense of a caring community. Commendations for effort in all aspects of school life: no one allowed to slip through the net out of boredom, laziness or a sense of failure. Assemblies are moral rather than doctrinal. Uniform for all.

Admissions School usually over-subscribed; places allocated by county council to those living 'to the west of a line running north to south through the central part of Horsham'. Pupils from generally supportive families in a modestly prosperous area; boys outnumber girls because of the popularity of Millais, the local girls' comprehensive, qv.

The head Read English; PhD from Exeter. Wide experience of the state sector; previously deputy head of a comprehensive in Berkshire.

The teaching Mostly group work rather than whole-class instruction: emphasis on discussion, leading to a constant exchange of ideas but little irrelevant activity or distracting noise. Well-qualified, enthusiastic staff of 64 (38 women), good mix of youth and experience. Standard national curriculum; all do French, half add a second language (German or Spanish) from second year; good technology (including imaginative work in textiles); lots of computers; GCSE options include media studies, business studies, travel & tourism, drama, dance. Pupils grouped by ability in first year and in most other subjects thereafter; specialist help for those who need it (including extra tuition after hours for any falling behind, and extension work for the gifted); average class size 24–26, smaller for GCSE. Strong music: two choirs, 40-strong orchestra. Extracurricular activities include well-supported Duke of Edinburgh award scheme. Careers education taken seriously; good links with local business and industry. Regular foreign exchanges.

Results   (1997) GCSE: 61% gained at least five grades A–C.

Destinations   Up to 90% remain in full-time education after 16.

Sport   Main games: football, rugby, hockey (particularly strong) netball, basketball. Athletics, cricket, rounders, badminton, tennis, swimming also on offer.

Remarks   Good school poised to take full advantage of much improved facilities. Recommended.

TAUNTON ♂ ♀
Staplegrove Road, Taunton, Somerset TA2 6AD. Tel (01823) 349223

Synopsis
Independent ★ Co-educational ★ Day and boarding ★ Ages 13–18 (plus associated prep school) ★ 491 pupils (59% boys, 56% day) ★ 192 in sixth form ★ Fees: £7,785 day; £12,150 boarding
Head: Julian Whiteley, 40, appointed September 1997.
Sound school; respectable results; fairly wide range of abilities.

Profile
Background   Founded 1847 for the sons of dissenters; moved to present 50-acre site and imposing, purpose-built, Victorian-Gothic premises 1870; later additions include large, austere chapel (donated by a member of the Wills tobacco family); girls admitted 1971. Lively prep school (460 pupils aged three to 13) in modern premises on same site.

Atmosphere   Friendly, orderly, traditional; fairly formal relations between staff and well-mannered pupils; daily chapel service (but those of other faiths, and none, welcomed).

Admissions   By school's own tests or Common Entrance (50% mark required); school is not unduly selective and likely to become even less so with the phasing out of assisted places, which about 150 hold. Tidy, comfortable boarding accommodation; juniors in dormitories for up to six; sixth-formers have own study-bedrooms. Good food. Scholarships: academic, art, music, sport; bursaries for Service and clergy children.

The head   New appointment. Decisive, energetic. Read engineering, has an MBA; joined the Royal Navy before switching to teaching; previously deputy head of an international school in Brazil. Married; three children.

The teaching   Sound; generally formal in style. Fairly broad curriculum; sciences taught (and examined) separately (school boasts five radio telescopes); languages include Latin, Greek, German, Spanish; choice of 23 subjects at A-level (including home economics, theatre studies, PE); GNVQ in business studies available. Pupils grouped by ability in maths, French; average class size 20, reducing to a maximum of 10 in the sixth form. Quite a lot of music; up to a third learn an instrument; choirs, orchestra. Extra-curricular activities include debating, well-supported cadet force, Duke of Edinburgh award scheme.

Results   (1997) GCSE: 85% gained at least five grades A–C. A-level: 51% of entries graded A or B.

Destinations   About 85% continue into the sixth form; of these, 95% proceed to higher education (five or six a year to Oxbridge).

Sport   Main games: rugby, hockey, netball, cricket, tennis. Good facilities for squash, badminton, basketball, fencing.

Remarks   Traditional school now under new management.

THOMAS MILLS HIGH   ♂ ♀
Saxtead Road, Framlingham, Woodbridge, Suffolk IP13 9HE. Tel (01728) 723493

Synopsis
Comprehensive ★ Co-educational ★ Ages 11–18 ★ 1,005 pupils (54% girls) ★ 324 in the sixth form
Head: David Floyd, 50, appointed 1995.
Successful, well-run school; very good teaching; lots on offer.

Profile
Background   Result of a 1979 merger between a grammar school and a secondary modern on the 20-acre site of the latter; functional 1930s buildings plus later additions, including sixth-form centre; further building in progress; six classrooms in 'temporary' huts. Granted technology college status 1996 (which should lead to better facilities).

Atmosphere   Purposeful, well-disciplined; big emphasis on achievement. Uniform, prefects, competitive house system; well-organised pastoral care.

Admissions   Over-subscribed and expanding; no academic selection. Pupils drawn from extensive mid-Suffolk catchment area; above-average numbers from business/professional backgrounds. School is very popular with parents – to the dismay of Suffolk County Council, which wants to cut the intake by 10% and reduce the sixth form (which many join from other schools) to 210.

The head   Very able: energetic, good-humoured; forceful, no-nonsense management style; well respected by staff and pupils. Has degrees in education from Birmingham and Leeds; previously head of a comprehensive in Ipswich. Married; three children.

The teaching   First-rate: generally formal in style; experienced, well-qualified staff of 50 (equal numbers of women and men). Standard national curriculum. Extra help for those with dyslexia and other learning difficulties; average class size 28, reducing to 17 in the sixth form. Wide choice of 24 subjects at A-level; GNVQs in business, science, manufacturing & engineering, health & social care also on offer. Strong music: choir, orchestras, various ensembles. Lots of extra-curricular activities. Regular language exchanges with schools in France, Germany.

Results   (1997) GCSE: 68% gained at least five grades A–C. A-level: 34% of entries graded A or B.

Destinations   About 75% stay on for A-levels; of these, 70% proceed to university (four or five a year to Oxbridge).

Sport Busy programme of fixtures in football, rugby, hockey, netball, badminton, basketball, tennis, cricket, athletics. Sports centre open to the public outside school hours.

Remarks Ofsted inspectors concluded (1997): 'The school has been very successful in establishing an ethos dedicated to high standards and civilised values in which learning can flourish.' Recommended.

THOMAS TELFORD ♂ ♀
Old Park, Telford, Shropshire TF3 4NW. Tel (01952) 200000

Synopsis
Comprehensive (City Technology College) ★ Co-educational ★ Ages 11–19 ★ 1,100 pupils (roughly equal numbers of girls and boys) ★ 300 in sixth form
Head: Kevin Satchwell, 46, appointed 1991.
Progressive, well-equipped school with an emphasis on maths, science, technology; very good GCSE results; strong sport.

Profile
Background Opened 1991, one of 15 experimental, technology-oriented secondary schools; £11 million cost partly borne by Tarmac and the Mercers' Company. Attractive, purpose-built premises (like a modern office) on 11¼-acre greenfield site; technology centre in focal position. First-rate facilities; everything immaculate and gleaming.

Atmosphere Cheerful, friendly; purrs purposefully along like a successful modern business (motto – Quality in Everything We Do). Ethos based on good manners, mutual respect and a carefully-nurtured sense of communal ownership; pupils enthusiastic, unusually mature. Long school day divided into three sessions (punctuated by breakfast, lunch and tea), the last of which ends at 7 pm four days a week (staff work shifts); holidays slightly shorter than normal. Parents receive 12 detailed progress reports a year, in return for which they are asked to encourage hard work and ensure regular attendance. Teachers in smart 'business' clothes; pupils in uniform with gold logo; sixth-formers wear 'office' dress. School has strong links with local employers.

Admissions School over-subscribed by four to one; 100 places allocated to those whose parents pay Wrekin council tax, 68 to Wolverhampton. All applicants tested, interviewed with their parents and required to declare an interest in science and technology. Full range of abilities; 20% from families on income support.

The head A dynamic visionary ('but I keep my feet on the ground'); knows all pupils by name and talks rapidly, warmly, excitedly about their achievements. Has an Open University degree and an advanced diploma in education management; previously head (appointed at 36) of a comprehensive in Wolverhampton. Married; two young children (one at the on-site crèche).

The teaching Emphasis on maths, science, technology – but not at the expense of English, languages, humanities, music, drama, PE; everything taught in a task-oriented way, pupils proceeding at their own pace. Dedicated, professionally-minded staff of 75 (55 women) plus 30 support staff. Open-plan teaching areas; maximum class size 24, reducing to 16 in the sixth form. Masses of computers (220 terminals); every pupil lent a laptop. Vocational courses offered as an alternative to A-levels. Lively drama and music; extra-curricular activities include well-supported Duke of Edinburgh award scheme.

Results (1997) GCSE: creditable 79% gained at least five grades A–C. A-level: 36% of entries graded A or B.
Destinations More than 80% expected to proceed to higher education.
Sport Very strong, particularly football, hockey, athletics, cricket, gymnastics; competitive sport regarded as important. Facilities include all-weather, floodlit pitches, sports hall, fitness centre.
Remarks Ofsted inspectors concluded (1995): 'The school provides an education of high quality. Standards of achievement match, or are superior to, national norms. Technology is not so much an instrument of learning as a way of life. The school is very effectively led and efficiently managed.'

***

THORNDEN ♂ ♀
Winchester Road, Chandler's Ford, Eastleigh, Hampshire SO53 2DW. Tel (01703) 269722

Synopsis
Comprehensive ★ Co-educational ★ Ages 11–16 ★ 1,254 pupils (slightly more boys than girls)
Head: Dr Robert Sykes, 46, appointed 1993.
Successful, well-run comprehensive; good teaching and GCSE results; lots of music, sport.

Profile
Background Opened 1973 as purpose-built comprehensive; utilitarian buildings (breeze block and black plastic, meant to look like slate and stone) plus £1 million recent additions on a large, attractive site (trees artfully conceal M3 which runs along the back).
Atmosphere Busy, purposeful, well-ordered; good pastoral care system. Uniform firmly enforced.
Admissions School over-subscribed (about 300 apply for 252 places); priority to siblings, those living in the catchment area or attending designated 'feeder' primaries. Most pupils from middle-class backgrounds; ability level above average.
The head Low-key, very able; totally committed to comprehensive education 'though it doesn't seem to be very fashionable nowadays'. Read history at Manchester (PhD in early 19th-century social and economic history); entire teaching career in comprehensives; previously deputy head of Tomlinscote (qv). Teaches history to third-years. Married (to a social worker); three sons.
The teaching Varied styles; hard-working staff of 73 (40 women), more than a third appointed by present head. Standard national curriculum; first-years choose between French and German, add a second language from second year (Spanish on offer); plenty of computing; GCSE options include drama, business studies. Pupils grouped by ability in maths, science, languages; maximum class size 30, reducing to 20 for GCSE; extra help for those with special needs, including the gifted. Lots of music: 200 learn an instrument; large orchestra. Regular language exchanges with pupils in France, Germany, Spain.
Results (1997) GCSE: very creditable 79% gained at least five grades A–C.
Destinations Nearly all remain in full-time education.
Sport Wide choice; particular strengths in tennis, badminton. Facilities include extensive playing fields, sports hall, nine tennis courts.
Remarks Popular local school.

TIFFIN ♂
Queen Elizabeth Road, Kingston-upon-Thames, Surrey KT2 6RL. Tel (0181) 546 4638

Synopsis
Grammar (grant-maintained) ★ Boys ★ Ages 11–18 ★ 978 pupils ★ 320 in sixth form
Head: Dr Tony Dempsey, 53, appointed 1988.
First-rate, well-run, academic school; very good teaching and results; strong creative arts and sport.

Profile
Background Endowed 1638 by the Tiffin brothers, local merchants; moved 1929 to present cramped, town-centre site and purpose-built premises; opted out of council control 1993. Later additions include creative arts block; older buildings showing signs of wear; some areas bleak.

Atmosphere Lively, hard-working, tightly disciplined. Strongly competitive house system; blazer-and-tie uniform; prefects wear gowns. Supportive parents raise about £80,000 a year.

Admissions By 11-plus verbal and non-verbal reasoning tests (no interview); school is heavily over-subscribed (about 1,000 apply for 140 places) and highly selective; top 10% of the ability range. Most pupils come from middle-class homes within a radius of about six miles; 30% ethnic minorities.

The head Very able; strong leader; has done much to modernise the school (only the fifth head since 1880). Was a pupil here; read chemistry at Bristol (First, followed by a PhD); previously deputy head of a comprehensive. Married (to a teacher); one son.

The teaching First-rate: mostly traditional in style; dedicated, predominantly male staff, half appointed by present head. Broad curriculum: sciences (a particular strength) taught separately; classics flourish (all do at least two years' Latin); technology department bursting at the seams; choice of 20 subjects at A-level (including sports studies, theatre studies, politics & government). Pupils grouped by ability in maths only from third year; extra help for those deemed not to be reaching their potential; average class size 29, reducing to 24 at GCSE, 16 at A-level. Very good art, drama, music (excellent facilities); 40% learn an instrument; first-rate choir, orchestras. Wide range of extra-curricular activities: 40 clubs meet at lunch-time or after school. Regular language trips to France, Germany.

Results (1997) GCSE: 94% gained at least five grades A–C. A-level: 55% of entries graded A or B.

Destinations Nearly all proceed to university (average of 10 a year to Oxbridge).

Sport Strong, particularly rugby, athletics, rowing, cricket; nearly 500 fixtures a year. Facilities include new sports hall; playing fields three miles away at Hampton Court.

Remarks Ofsted inspectors concluded (1996): 'This is a very good school. The pupils make good progress in their studies and attain high standards. Their behaviour is very good and they are highly motivated to learn and willing to take on responsibilities.' Recommended.

TIFFIN GIRLS' ♀
Richmond Road, Kingston-upon-Thames, Surrey KT2 5PL. Tel (0181) 546 0773

Synopsis
Grammar ★ Girls ★ Ages 11–18 ★ 863 pupils ★ 263 in sixth form
Head: Mrs Pauline Cox, 49, appointed 1994.
*Successful, heavily over-subscribed school; very good teaching and results;
strong sport.*

Profile
Background   Founded 1880; moved to present nine-acre site 1987, taking over
the barracks-like former premises of a 1950s secondary modern, parts of which
are deteriorating (leaking roofs, inadequate heating); money (about £2,300 a
pupil) is tight, some facilities barely adequate.

Atmosphere   High achievement taken for granted; first-rate pastoral care ('the
backbone of academic achievement'); excellent relations between confident,
articulate girls and keen, hard-working staff. Elected prefects; strict uniform
(teal-blue blazers) below the sixth form. Parents raise £40,000–£50,000 a year
(mostly spent on refurbishment).

Admissions   School is massively over-subscribed (about 1,000 apply for 120
places); entry by two highly competitive tests in verbal and non-verbal reasoning; top 10% of the ability range from a cosmopolitan range of backgrounds
(65% are non-English).

The head   Relaxed, friendly: runs the school in an almost casual way but
with no loss of drive or sense of purpose. Read geography at Birmingham; MA
from London; previously deputy head of a comprehensive. Married; two
grown-up children.

The teaching   First-rate: purposeful in an informal atmosphere; experienced,
well-qualified staff. Broad curriculum: all do Latin plus two modern languages;
sciences taught separately; lots of computing, design/technology; all do art,
drama, music up to 16. Pupils grouped by ability in English, maths, French; average class size 30, reducing to 12 at A-level. Good library (27,000 volumes). Extra-
curricular activities include choirs, orchestras, Young Enterprise, public
speaking, well-supported Duke of Edinburgh award scheme.

Results   (1997) GCSE: 99% gained at least five grades A–C. A-level: creditable
60% of entries graded A or B.

Destinations   Virtually all proceed to university (up to 10 a year to Oxbridge).

Sport   Has a high profile despite the inadequate facilities. All play hockey, netball (a particular strength), tennis; frequent local and county honours. Aerobics,
basketball, badminton, dance, volleyball also on offer.

Remarks   Ofsted inspectors concluded (1995): 'This is a pleasant and orderly
community with a stimulating intellectual and cultural environment. Standards
of achievement overall are high even considering the selective nature of the
school and pupils' abilities on entry.' Recommended.

TOMLINSCOTE ♂ ♀
Tomlinscote Way, Frimley, Surrey GU16 5PY. Tel (01276) 709050

Synopsis
Comprehensive ★ Co-educational ★ Ages 11–18 ★ 1,535 pupils (roughly equal numbers of girls and boys) ★ 341 in sixth form
Head: Tony Ryles, 50, appointed 1988.
Successful, well-run school; good teaching and results; big emphasis on languages.

Profile
Background Opened 1970 as Surrey's first purpose-built comprehensive; language college status achieved 1996. Modern, multi-storey buildings plus recent £2 million additions on a pleasant, if rather cramped, site. School has a dyslexia unit.
Atmosphere Orderly, friendly; polite pupils happy to chat about their work; space tight but well utilised; lots of art work on display. Distinctive black and yellow uniform below the sixth form, tidy dress (including jeans) thereafter.
Admissions Over-subscribed; no academic selection; places allocated by Surrey County Council (even the head had to move into the catchment to ensure a place for his son). Fairly wide range of abilities but level is above average.
The head Strong leader, good manager. Has a BEd from London; previously a deputy head in Ipswich. Married; two children.
The teaching High quality; generally formal in style. Staff of 103 (60% women); relatively low turn-over. Broad curriculum; big emphasis on languages (all do two for at least two years and are introduced to Latin); strong technology; wide choice of 27 subjects at A-level, including economics, geology, communication studies; GNVQs offered in business studies, health & social care. Pupils tested on entry and grouped by ability in English, maths, science; good provision for those with special needs; average class sizes 20–24, reducing to 16 in sixth form. Lots of drama, music (orchestra, three choirs). Regular language exchanges with schools in France, Germany, Spain.
Results (1997) GCSE: 66% gained at least five grades A–C. A-level: 38% of entries graded A or B.
Destinations About 75% continue into the sixth form; of these, 90% go on to university.
Sport All major games played. Sports centre shared with the community.
Remarks Ofsted inspectors concluded (1995): 'This is a good school which provides a high quality education for its pupils. They work hard, and behaviour and relationships are of a high order. The school functions well as a community and the standards achieved are impressive.'

TONBRIDGE ♂
Tonbridge, Kent TN9 1JP. Tel (01732) 365555

Synopsis
Independent ★ Boys ★ Boarding and day ★ Ages 13–18 ★ 697 pupils (61% boarding) ★ 276 in sixth form ★ Fees: £14,400 boarding; £10,170 day
Head: Martin Hammond, 52, appointed 1990.
Fine, traditional school; very good teaching and results; strong music and sport.

Profile

Background Founded 1553; generously endowed and still governed by Worshipful Company of Skinners. Imposing range of buildings, some 18th-century most Victorian sandstone, in 150 beautifully-tended acres (a sense of solid composure). Facilities are first class. Restored Edwardian chapel (destroyed in 1988 fire) boasts one of the country's finest organs; £20 million refurbishment and development programme under way (new boarding house, social centre, lavish arts and technology centre).

Atmosphere Busy, orderly, friendly; strong Christian ethos. Very good relations between committed staff and hard-working boys (a real feeling of joint enterprise and endeavour); firm underlying discipline (drugs lead to instant expulsion). Excellent pastoral care: lots of safety nets; strong house system (boys dine in their houses). Boarding accommodation functional but acceptable: juniors in small dorms, shared studies; seniors in pleasant study-bedrooms. Traditional uniform of tweed jackets, grey flannels (and a range of ties for all manner of things); meals start and end with grace.

Admissions By Common Entrance; minimum 60% mark required; school is highly selective. Day places over-subscribed; boarding numbers 'about right' (no plans to go co-educational). Most pupils live within one-and-a-half hour's drive (plus 6% foreign, 6% expatriate); many parents are 'first-time buyers' of independent education ('This is not a posh school,' says head). Lots of scholarships (academic, music, choral, art).

The head Exceptionally able: sure touch, clear vision; well respected by staff and boys. Scholar at Winchester, read classics at Oxford; taught at St Paul's, Harrow, Eton; previously head of City of London (qv). Teaches Latin to juniors; has raised the profile of the arts (keen musician). Married (to a prep school teacher); two grown-up children.

The teaching Very good across the board; some quite exceptional. First-rate staff of 75 (90% male). Particular strengths in science (taught as three separate subjects – most do two), maths, English, modern languages (French, Spanish, German); good computing across the curriculum. Pupils grouped by ability from the start into six classes of 22; further setting in maths, French; top sets take GCSE English, maths, French, Latin a year early. Wide choice of 25 subjects at A-level, including economics, electronics, further maths. High standards of musicianship (orchestra, choirs, various ensembles) and lavish facilities (sound-proof rooms, recording studio). New theatre planned. Extra-curricular activities include thriving Duke of Edinburgh award scheme, cadet force, community service.

Results (1997) GCSE: all gained at least five grades A to C. A-level: creditable 70% of entries graded A or B.

Destinations All continue into the sixth form; 90% proceed to university (about 20 a year to Oxbridge).

Sport Wide range on offer; traditional strengths in cricket and rugby; lots of teams for all abilities; good record against other schools. Superb facilities include 100 acres of playing fields, courts for squash, fives, racquets, all-weather athletics track, indoor pool, shooting range.

Remarks Highly recommended for able, ambitious boys.

TONBRIDGE GRAMMAR ♀
Deakin Leas, Tonbridge, Kent TN9 2JR. Tel (01732) 365125

Synopsis
Grammar (grant-maintained) ★ Girls ★ Ages 11–18 ★ 976 pupils ★ 258 in sixth form
Head: Mrs Wendy Carey, 51, appointed 1990.
First-rate, well-run grammar school; very good teaching and results; strong art, music.

Profile
Background Founded 1905; opted out of council control 1993. Conglomeration of buildings on a 19-acre hill-top site over-looking the Weald; latest additions include fine £1.2 million science and technology block; many classrooms in 'temporary' huts (spread over the lawns). Numbers have risen steadily.

Atmosphere Busy, purposeful: a community not prepared to waste time; strong emphasis on achievement; friendly relations between staff and pupils. Uniform worn by all. Parents required to confirm (in writing) that their daughters will work hard and behave well (sanctions seldom needed); supportive PTA raises thousands of pounds a year.

Admissions By Kent 11-plus (tests in English, maths); school over-subscribed (about 250 qualified applicants apply for 140 places); 90% of places awarded in merit order; 10% to qualified girls living in West Kent. 'Able girls from all backgrounds,' according to the prospectus; in practice, few are from disadvantaged homes; all, however, are bright, articulate and hard-working; 20% from prep schools, rest from 85 primaries. Vast catchment area extends into Surrey and Sussex.

The head Charismatic; strong leader; has high expectations of staff and pupils. Educated in Zimbabwe (then Southern Rhodesia); took an external London degree in English; previously deputy head of King Edward VI Camp Hill Girls' (qv). Married (to the bursar); four grown-up children.

The teaching First-rate: lively, challenging; lessons enlivened by humour, quick-fire questions; committed staff of 66 (16 men), nearly half appointed by present head. Broad curriculum; particularly good results in maths, science (on offer as three separate subjects), technology; all do French plus Latin, German or Spanish; A-level options include history of art, economics, psychology, textiles & fashion. Pupils grouped by ability in maths, French (more able take GCSEs a year early); extra help for dyslexics and the exceptionally gifted; average class size 28–30, reducing to 25 for GCSE, 12 at A-level. Imaginative art, strong music (two orchestras, two choirs, more than 200 learn an instrument). Extra-curricular activities include debating, bridge, voluntary service, fund-raising for charity, well-supported Duke of Edinburgh award scheme. Frequent trips abroad; regular language exchanges with pupils in France, Germany, Spain.

Results (1997) GCSE: 99% gained at least five grades A–C. A-level: creditable 63% of entries graded A or B.

Destinations About 95% proceed to university (up to 10 a year to Oxbridge).

Sport All major activities on offer, including netball, hockey, athletics, tennis, swimming, basketball, dance. Facilities include three hockey pitches, heated outdoor pool, gym (but no sports hall).

Remarks Ofsted inspectors concluded (1996): 'This is a very good school which achieves high academic standards.' Recommended.

TORMEAD ♀
Cranley Road, Guildford, Surrey GU1 2JD. Tel (01483) 575101

Synopsis
Independent ★ Girls ★ Day ★ Ages 10–18 (plus associated junior school) ★
422 pupils ★ 79 in sixth form ★ Fees: £5,670
Head: Mrs Honor Alleyne, 56, appointed 1992.
Lively, academic school; very good teaching and results; outstanding art.

Profile
Background Founded 1905; moved to present four-acre site in quiet residential area 1915; boarding phased out 1987. Red-brick Victorian villa plus modern, well-equipped additions, including sports hall, sixth-form centre, extra science labs (no 'temporary' huts here). Well-tended grounds and a feeling of spaciousness recall a more leisured age. Junior school (ages five to 10) on the same site.

Atmosphere Lively, well-ordered: decent behaviour and consideration for others expected; pupils exceptionally friendly, well-mannered.

Admissions By school's own entrance exam; standards are high. Scholarships, exhibitions available.

The head Enthusiastic, brisk, irrepressibly energetic; highly thought of by pupils, who find her approachable and ready to listen. Read German and French at Queen's, Belfast; formerly deputy head of St Swithun's. Married (to an Anglican priest); two grown-up children.

The teaching High standard: styles range from formal to group work; all thorough, challenging. Enthusiastic, well-qualified staff (mainly women), some very long-serving. Well-equipped classrooms; good provision for computing. Broad curriculum: all take Latin for at least two years; good modern languages (all do French plus Spanish or German); lively English and history; science on offer as three separate subjects. Pupils grouped by ability in maths, French; average class size 22, much smaller at A-level. Outstanding art (painting, textiles, pottery, sculpture, graphics); technique instilled from the start; good work displayed about the school. Lively music: more than two-thirds learn an instrument; orchestra, choirs, wind band, jazz group, various ensembles; regular concerts; composer in residence. Extra-curricular activities include thriving Duke of Edinburgh award scheme. Regular exchanges with schools in USA, France, Germany.

Results (1997) GCSE: all gained at least five grades A–C. A-level: 54% of entries graded A or B (not a good year).

Destinations About 80% stay on for A-levels and proceed to university (up to five a year to Oxbridge).

Sport Lots on offer, some to a very high standard; enthusiastic inter-house competitions, regular fixtures against other schools. Main games: hockey, netball, tennis (six courts), rounders, squash (two courts), athletics, basketball, badminton, gymnastics.

Remarks Successful, well-run school; highly recommended.

TORQUAY BOY'S GRAMMAR ♂
Shiphay Manor Drive, Torquay, Devon TQ2 7EL. Tel (01803) 615501

Synopsis
Grammar (grant-maintained) ★ Boys ★ Ages 11–18 ★ 972 pupils ★ 240 in sixth form
Head: Roy Pike, 49, appointed 1986.
Traditional grammar school; good teaching and results; strong sport; lots of extra-curricular activities.

Profile
Background   Founded 1904; moved to present, purpose-built premises in 35 acres of attractive, partly-wooded grounds 1983; opted out of council control 1993; language college status achieved 1996. Some areas a little cramped; building continues.
Atmosphere   Lively, purposeful, well-disciplined (emphasis on counselling rather than punishment); relaxed but respectful relations between staff and pupils. Competitive house system; blazer-and-tie uniform.
Admissions   School heavily over-subscribed (350 apply for 140 places); entry by competitive tests in English, maths, reasoning; top 25% of the ability range.
The head   Friendly, thoughtful, determined, very much in control; has spent all his teaching career here. Read history at London and Exeter; teaches Latin seven periods a week. Married; six children.
The teaching   Sound; well-qualified, relatively youthful staff of 65 (15 women). Standard national curriculum; all do two languages; lots of computing; choice of 24 subjects at A-level (some in conjunction with Torquay Girls' Grammar, qv). Pupils grouped by ability in maths only; half termly grades for effort; average class size 25, smaller in the sixth form. Strong art, music; 115 learn an instrument. Extra-curricular activities include chess (strong), astronomy, video making, public speaking, Duke of Edinburgh award scheme. Good careers advice. Regular language exchanges with European schools.
Results   (1997) GCSE: 98% gained at least five grades A–C. A-level: 41% of entries graded A or B (not a good year).
Destinations   About 90% proceed to university (average of five a year to Oxbridge).
Sport   Strong. Main activities: soccer, rugby, swimming, water polo, hockey, cricket; many county representatives.
Remarks   Ofsted inspectors concluded (1996): 'The school attains high standards in all its activities. It has considerable knowledge of the potential of its students and, through high expectations, is able to ensure that this expectation is fulfilled.'

TORQUAY GIRLS' GRAMMAR ♀
30 Shiphay Lane, Torquay, Devon TQ2 7DY. Tel (01803) 613215

Synopsis
Grammar ★ Girls ★ Ages 11–18 ★ 817 pupils ★ 247 in sixth form
Head: Mrs Susan Roberts, 45, appointed 1996.
Sound academic school; good teaching and results; lots of sport.

Profile
Background   Founded 1915; moved to present spacious site and purpose-built

premises 1939; latest additions include new classroom block; sixth form housed separately; music school in converted stable block; some classrooms in need of refurbishment. School owns a study centre in Brittany.

Atmosphere Calm, friendly, well-ordered; good rapport between staff and highly-motivated girls.

Admissions By Devon 11-plus; places awarded to highest-scoring 120 (nearly 250 compete).

The head Brisk. Read geography at Aberystwyth. Married; two sons.

The teaching Challenging, mostly formal in style; dedicated, well-qualified staff (two-thirds female). Standard national curriculum; all do a second language from second year; choice of 23 subjects at A-level (some shared with Torquay Boys', qv). Pupils grouped by ability in maths from second year, French and German from third year, English for GCSE; extra help for those who need it; average class size 30. Lots of music. Extra-curricular activities include well-supported Duke of Edinburgh award scheme.

Results (1997) GCSE: 98% gained at least five grades A–C. A-level: 48% of entries graded A or B.

Destinations About 90% stay on into the sixth form; of these, 90% proceed to higher education.

Sport Wide range, including hockey, football, tennis, rounders, netball, sailing, swimming, athletics; lots of inter-house matches; regular county honours.

Remarks Good all round.

TOWNLEY GIRLS' GRAMMAR ♀
Townley Road, Bexleyheath, Kent DA6 7AB. Tel (0181) 304 8311

Synopsis
Grammar ★ Girls ★ Ages 11–18 ★ 1,003 pupils ★ 215 in sixth form
Head: Mrs Linda Hutchinson, 47, appointed 1992.
Successful, well-run school; good teaching and results; lots on offer.

Profile
Background Founded 1939; purpose-built premises (in need of refurbishment) plus later additions on pleasant 17-acre site in a middle-class residential area; inadequate facilities for science, drama.

Atmosphere Friendly, purposeful, orderly (or, as the prospectus puts it, 'an atmosphere conducive to enquiry and the enjoyment of learning'). Cordial relations between staff and confident, articulate pupils; good work displayed on every available wall space. Uniform for all strictly enforced; fund raising for charity taken seriously. Parents are strongly supportive.

Admissions Over-subscribed (about 220 apply for 155 places); entry by Bexley 11-plus. Girls come from a wide range of backgrounds.

The head Forthright; strong leader; highly regarded by staff, parents, pupils. Read theology at Birmingham; formerly deputy head of a girls' comprehensive in Bromley. Married; two sons.

The teaching Mostly good; well-qualified staff; varied styles. Standard national curriculum; German added to French from second year; choice of 22 subjects at A-level; GNVQ in business studies available; all take general studies. Pupils grouped by ability in maths, French; average class size 30 for first three years, smaller later. Extra-curricular activities include drama, music (choirs, orchestras),

debating. Regular language exchanges with schools in France, Germany.
Results (1997) GCSE: 96% gained at least five grades A–C. A-level: 50% of entries graded A or B.
Destinations About 80% go on to university (many the first in their family to do so).
Sport Good facilities, including two large playing fields, 10 tennis courts. Main sports: netball, volleyball, hockey, tennis, swimming, rounders, football. Dance, gymnastics also popular.
Remarks Ofsted inspectors concluded (1997): 'This is a very good school with some outstanding features including an extremely good ethos which enables girls to grow in confidence and independence in a secure and hard-working environment.'

TRINITY ♂
Shirley Park, Croydon CR9 7AT. Tel (0181) 656 9541

Synopsis
Independent ★ Boys ★ Day ★ Ages 10–18 ★ 865 pupils ★ 213 in sixth form ★ Fees: up to £5,961 (related to parents' income)
Head: Barnaby Lenon, 43, appointed 1995.
First-rate, well-run school; very good teaching and results; excellent facilities; strong music and sport.

Profile
Background Founded 1596 by John Whitgift, Archbishop of Canterbury; moved to present 27-acre site on outskirts of Croydon 1965; former site is now the town's shopping centre – the source of the school's substantial income. Well-planned, purpose-built premises; excellent facilities include ambitious new sports and technology complex, luxurious sixth-form centre. Whitgift Foundation funds buildings and equipment; means-tested fees cover running costs.
Atmosphere Relaxed, open, friendly. School runs without fuss; everyone busily occupied; well-mannered boys on easy but respectful terms with staff; good pastoral care. School is theoretically Church of England but effectively multi-faith. Parents very involved; active old boys' association.
Admissions School heavily over-subscribed (more than 500 apply for 115 places) and fairly selective. Entry by competitive exams (sample papers available); top 25% of the ability range from wide range of social and financial backgrounds (60% join from state primaries); none turned away through inability to pay; assisted places to be replaced by Whitgift bursaries. Lots of scholarships.
The head Able, energetic. Read geography at Oxford (First); taught at Eton; previously deputy head of Highgate. Writes geography textbooks. Married; two daughters.
The teaching Lively, thorough – backed by no-expense-spared equipment in bright, pleasant classrooms. Well-qualified, predominantly male staff of 74; high standards set, hard work expected. Broad curriculum: most take science as three separate subjects; all do two languages from French, German, Spanish (up-to-date language lab with satellite link); compulsory Latin re-introduced for first three years; computers used across the curriculum. Most take 10 GCSEs and three A-levels (from choice of 21) plus extensive (20% of teaching time) non-examined general studies. Pupils grouped by ability in maths, science,

languages; average class size 20–24, smaller for A-level. Outstanding music: Trinity Boys Choir sings regularly at public concerts; orchestras, string and wind ensembles, groups of every kind. Flourishing drama in modern theatre. Very strong extra-curricular programme (from electronics and chess to war-gaming and wind-surfing); well-supported cadet force and Duke of Edinburgh award scheme. Good careers programme; work experience for all fifth-years.

Results (1997) GCSE: all gained at least five grades A–C. A-level: 65% of entries graded A or B.

Destinations Nearly all stay on for A-levels; 95% proceed to university (about 10 a year to Oxbridge).

Sport Very strong and taken seriously; full fixture list in 10 sports; particularly strong rugby, water polo, swimming. Facilities include 24 acres of playing fields (half on site, rest half-a-mile away); all-weather pitch for hockey and tennis; two new sports halls with additional squash courts, fitness training centre (weightlifting a speciality); excellent indoor pool.

Remarks HMC inspectors concluded (1996): 'This is an impressive school with a strong sense of purpose.' Very good value for money; recommended.

TRINITY CATHOLIC HIGH ♂ ♀
Mornington Road, Woodford Green, Essex IG8 0TP. Tel (0181) 504 3419

Synopsis
Comprehensive (voluntary-aided, Roman Catholic) ★ Co-educational ★ Ages 11–18 ★ 1,534 pupils (52% girls) ★ 400 in sixth form
Head: Dr Paul Docherty, 51, appointed 1981.
Very well run, successful school; good teaching and results; strong art, drama, sport.

Profile
Background Result of 1976 amalgamation of two Catholic schools a quarter of a mile apart in a pleasant setting on the fringe of Epping Forest; GCSE and A-level pupils in imposing red-brick buildings of former convent school (later additions include fine sixth-form centre); juniors in functional, slightly shabby 1960s premises.

Atmosphere A thoroughly modern school bursting with energy; strong sense of order; clear Catholic ethos; good pastoral care; very good relations between staff and pupils. Blazer-and-tie uniform strictly enforced; dress code for sixth-formers.

Admissions School is heavily over-subscribed (nearly 500 apply for 240 places) but not academically selective; ability range is fairly wide. Pupils drawn exclusively from Catholic primaries in 12 parishes in Redbridge, Essex, Waltham Forest. About 60–70 join the sixth form after an interview (non-Catholics admitted).

The head Larger-than-life; very able; strong leader. Read history at Liverpool; DPhil from Oxford. Believes the school and its staff are the 'servants of the children'; greets each pupil on his/her birthday. Writes medieval mysteries (about a detective called Athelstan, who spends a good deal of time in London's sewers and brothels). Married; seven children (four are pupils here).

The teaching Good; varied styles; hard-working, committed, relatively youthful staff of 85 (40% Catholic). Standard national curriculum; lots of computing. Pupils grouped by ability in maths only. First-rate art, drama.

Results (1997) GCSE: very creditable 71% gained at least five grades A–C. A-level: 34% of entries graded A or B.

Destinations   About two-thirds go on to university (average of three a year to Oxbridge).

Sports   Particular strengths in swimming, cross-country, soccer, netball. Hockey, rugby, cricket, sailing also on offer.

Remarks   Identified by Ofsted (1996) as 'outstandingly successful'.

TRURO ♂ ♀
Trennick Lane, Truro, Cornwall TR1 1TH. Tel (01872) 72763

Synopsis
Independent ★ Co-educational ★ Day and boarding ★ Ages 11–18 ★ 770 pupils (67% boys, 83% day) ★ 243 in sixth form ★ Fees: £5,052 day; £9,495 boarding
Head: Guy Dodd, 56, appointed 1993.
Sound, well-run school; fairly wide range of abilities; good teaching and results; lots of art, drama, music; strong sport.

Profile
Background   Founded 1880 by a group of Cornish Methodists; formerly Direct Grant, reverted to full independence 1977; girls admitted 1990. Imposing, three-storey, grey sandstone, Victorian-Gothic building (clock tower, chapel) on a steep, terraced, 50-acre site above the city; non-descript classrooms scattered behind (some in 'temporary' huts); a feeling of serviceability rather than smartness. Facilities adequate; well-stocked library.

Atmosphere   Pleasant, caring, well-disciplined; cordial relations between staff and cheerful, unpretentious pupils. Ethos is Christian but head believes it 'unproductive to thrust religion down young people's throats'.

Admissions   By tests or Common Entrance; school is not particularly selective ('High-fliers to honest strugglers – three Es at A-level is fine by me,' says the head) and likely to become less so with the phasing out of assisted places, which 25% hold; numbers will probably fall. Boarders from outlying parts of Cornwall, Scilly Isles; 10% Hong Kong Chinese; accommodation pleasant, spacious, recently refurbished; weekly boarding increasingly popular. Some scholarships.

The head   Direct, energetic; leads from the front; has re-invigorated the school. Read history at Cambridge; taught at Cheltenham; previously head for 11 years of Lord Wandsworth (qv). Married; three grown-up children.

The teaching   Fairly traditional in style (pupils tend to want teachers to give them the facts 'without messing around'). National curriculum plus: science on offer as three separate subjects; all do French and German for first three years; Spanish, Latin on offer; 21 subjects ('but no wacky ones') available at A-level. Pupils grouped by ability in maths, languages from second year; extra help for dyslexics; average class size mid-20s, reducing to a maximum of 18 at A-level. Strong art (ceramics a speciality), drama and music (choir, orchestra, various ensembles). Lots of extra-curricular activities, including well-supported Duke of Edinburgh award scheme; no reasonable interest unmet. Regular language exchanges with pupils in France, Germany.

Results   (1997) GCSE: 94% gained at least five grades A–C. A-level: 58% of entries graded A or B.

Destinations   Nearly all go on to higher education (average of five a year to Oxbridge).

Sport   Important and compulsory; regular regional and county honours. Main sports: rugby, soccer, cricket for boys; netball, hockey, tennis, athletics for girls. Squash, badminton, golf, karate, fencing, archery, sailing also on offer. Facilities include ample playing fields, athletics track, large sports hall, tennis and squash courts, roofed-in pool.

Remarks   Good school being brought up to date.

TUDOR GRANGE ♂ ♀
Dingle Lane, Solihull, West Midlands B91 3PD. Tel (0121) 705 5100

Synopsis
Comprehensive ★ Co-educational ★ Ages 11–16 ★ 1,248 pupils (roughly equal numbers of girls and boys)
Head: John Evans, 50, appointed 1990.
Well-run school; firm discipline; good teaching and GCSE results.

Profile
Background   A 1974 amalgamation of two single-sex grammar schools built 100 yards apart on a 20-acre site; achieved technology college status 1995. Drab, flat-roofed, brick buildings plus later additions, including learning resource centre, music department; some classrooms in 'temporary' huts. School has been seeking permission to open a sixth form since 1994.

Atmosphere   Grammar-school ethos retained: dedicated staff, well motivated pupils. Strict rules (uniform worn by all); work ethic very apparent.

Admissions   Heavily over-subscribed (more than 400 apply for 240 places), non-selective: priority to those living nearest; admissions handled by Solihull council. Most pupils are from middle-class homes and of above-average ability.

The head   Strong leader, very ambitious for the school. Read English at Birmingham; previously deputy head of a comprehensive in Pembrokeshire. Married; two children (one was a pupil here, the other still is).

The teaching   Mostly formal in style. Full-time staff of 69 (55% female). Standard national curriculum; lots of computing; wide choice of 27 subjects at GCSE, including Latin, Italian, Russian, drama, art & design. Pupils grouped by ability in most subjects (some take GCSE maths a year early); maximum class size 28; extra help for those with special needs. Parents asked to ensure the right conditions exist for homework and that the stipulated time is spent on it.

Results   (1997) GCSE: creditable 76% gained at least five grades A–C.

Destinations   About 90% remain in full-time education, mostly at one of the two local sixth-form colleges.

Sport   Lots on offer: hockey, netball, football, rugby, basketball in winter; tennis, cricket, athletics, rounders in summer.

Remarks   Identified by Ofsted (1996) as an 'outstanding' school.

TUDOR HALL ♀
Wykham Park, Banbury, Oxfordshire OX16 9UR. Tel (01295) 263434

Synopsis
Independent ★ Girls ★ Boarding (and some day) ★ Ages 11–18 ★ 250 pupils (96% boarding) ★ 70 in sixth form ★ Fees: £11,280 boarding; £7,035 day
Head: Miss Nanette Godfrey, 53, appointed 1984.
Small, friendly school in an attractive setting; good teaching and results.

Profile
Background Founded 1850; moved 1946 to lovely 17th-century manor house in 35-acre country estate (Japanese water garden for girls to wander about or read in); careful renovations and sympathetic later additions, including excellent music block.
Atmosphere Strong family feel; cheerful, relaxed, self-assured girls (marks awarded for manners, showing consideration to others). Boarding accommodation homely, well-furnished; 3–6 beds per room; double study-bedrooms for lower sixth, single for upper sixth. Delicious food (including hot vegetarian meal, salad bar). Strict policies on alcohol, smoking and drugs ('We don't have drugs because we don't have boys').
Admissions By Common Entrance and interview: requirements flexible; head looking for potential and whether a girl will 'fit in' socially. Twenty admitted annually at 11, another 20 at 12/13; mostly Home Counties; some from Scotland. Some scholarships (academic, music) and bursaries.
The head Authoritative, approachable; popular with parents and pupils. Read English at London; teaches the younger girls.
The teaching Good quality. Well-qualified staff of 32 (four men), three-quarters appointed by present head. All take Latin, French and either Spanish or German; Italian, Japanese also on offer; science taught as three separate subjects. Pupils grouped by ability in maths, languages. Strong music: 75% learn an instrument; orchestra, various ensembles, choirs. Regular language exchanges with schools in France, Germany.
Results (1997) GCSE: all gained at least five grades A–C. A-level: 55% of entries graded A or B.
Destinations All go to university (one or two a year to Oxbridge).
Sport Choice not wide but standard good. Professional coaching offered in tennis, fencing, riding.
Remarks Warm, safe school; high all-round standards.

TUNBRIDGE WELLS BOYS' GRAMMAR ♂
St John's Road, Tunbridge Wells, Kent TN4 9XB. Tel (01892) 529551

Synopsis
Grammar ★ Boys ★ Ages 11–18 ★ 905 pupils ★ 209 in sixth form
Head: Derek Barnard, 52, appointed 1988.
Sound academic school; good GCSE results; strong sport.

Profile
Background Founded 1859 as a technical school; moved to present rather cramped site and undistinguished, purpose-built premises 1962; became a grammar school 1982. School is poorly funded and maintained (shabby corridors);

sixth-formers do their own re-decorating; many classrooms in 'temporary' huts.
Atmosphere   Well-ordered, purposeful, no frills (boys seem oblivious to their surroundings). Blazer-and-tie uniform worn throughout ('no earrings, pony-tails'). Supportive parents help raise funds.
Admissions   By tests in English, maths, verbal reasoning (Kent selection pro-cedure); school admits a wider range of abilities (top 32%) than Judd or Skinners' (qv), its principal competitors; numbers have steadily increased. Most from middle-class backgrounds in an extensive catchment area (school draws on up to 65 primaries).
The head   Direct, shrewd, plain-speaking. Read geography at St Luke's, Exeter; MSc from Birkbeck; came here as deputy head 1980. Teaches A-level geography. Married; three children.
The teaching   Formal in style (desks in rows); many long-serving staff (some here more than 20 years). Fairly broad curriculum: science on offer as three sepa-rate subjects; second-language option 'not popular'; good design/technology; choice of 20 subjects at A-level, including theatre studies, PE, computing. Pupils grouped by ability in maths only from third year; progress closely monitored (twice-termly grades for attainment and effort); extra help for dyslexics; maximum class size 30, reducing to an average of 15 at A-level. Lots of art, drama (in con-junction with Tunbridge Wells Girls' Grammar, qv) and music; 25% learn an instrument; choirs, orchestra, various ensembles (but accommodation is limited). Extra-curricular activities include chess (strong), Duke of Edinburgh award scheme.
Results   (1997) GCSE: 98% gained at least five grades A–C. A-level: 37% of entries graded A or B (modest for a grammar school).
Destinations   About 80% go on to university (one or two a year to Oxbridge).
Sport   Strong, particularly basketball, soccer, athletics, cross-country. Rugby, tennis, squash, swimming, cricket, hockey, badminton also on offer. School has use of adjacent leisure centre.
Remarks   Solid, well-run school but poorly resourced.

TUNBRIDGE WELLS GIRLS' ♀
Southfield Road, Tunbridge Wells, Kent TN4 9UJ. Tel (01892) 520902

Synopsis
Grammar ★ Girls ★ Ages 11–18 ★ 864 pupils ★ 240 in sixth form
Head: Mrs Angela Daly, 48, appointed 1993.
Traditional grammar school; good teaching and results; strong music.

Profile
Background   Founded 1905; moved to present extensive site and purpose-built Palladian-style premises 1913; most additions date from 1950s and 1960s; school is poorly funded and many classrooms are in 'temporary' huts; good facilities for music (but not much else).
Atmosphere   Traditional, purposeful, generally well-disciplined (motto, 'Give your Best'); mutually respectful relations between staff and pupils; sixth-formers ('buddies') help take responsibility for juniors. Uniform below the sixth form strictly enforced.
Admissions   By Kent 11-plus; about 170 apply for 120 places (priority to those living in the county); top 25% of the ability range. School serves a predominantly middle-class area.

The head Strong leader; takes great pride in her pupils. Read English at Bangor; previously deputy head of St Bede's, Redhill (qv). Abolished cookery; encourages girls to do woodwork and play rugby and cricket. Married (to a teacher); two children.

The teaching Good quality; generally formal in style; experienced, stable staff (25% male). Fairly broad curriculum; science on offer as three separate subjects; all do two languages (good results); Latin available; choice of 20 subjects at A-level (including theatre studies, psychology, sociology). Pupils grouped by ability in maths, French; average class size 27, reducing to 23 for GCSE. Strong art, drama, music; two-thirds learn an instrument; two orchestras, several choirs. Extra-curricular activities include well-supported Duke of Edinburgh award scheme. Regular language exchanges with pupils in France, Germany.

Results (1997) GCSE: all gained at least five grades A–C. A-level: respectable 56% of entries graded A or B.

Destinations About 90% go on to university (seven or eight a year to Oxbridge).

Sport Particular strengths in netball, hockey, cricket (county honours), gymnastics, trampolining; recent rugby tour to Denmark.

Remarks Ofsted inspectors concluded (1995): 'The school is endeavouring to uphold the best of the old grammar school tradition. The girls make very good progress in their studies.'

TURTON HIGH ♂ ♀
Bromley Cross Road, Bromley Cross, Bolton BL7 9LT. Tel (01204) 595888

Synopsis
Comprehensive ★ Co-educational ★ Ages 11–18 ★ 1,520 pupils (roughly equal numbers of girls and boys) ★ 310 in sixth form
Head: Frank Vigon, 51, appointed 1988.
Successful, popular comprehensive; good teaching and results; strong sport.

Profile
Background Opened 1954 as a secondary modern; went comprehensive 1969 and grew rapidly. Mixture of buildings, including original 1950s block (wide corridors, impressive entrance hall) in attractive, spacious grounds overlooking Pennine moorland.

Atmosphere Welcoming, caring; big emphasis on rewarding good work and behaviour; relaxed relations between staff and pupils (but no one takes advantage). Very supportive parents (they move house to secure a place here).

Admissions School heavily over-subscribed; priority to those living nearest (in a limited catchment area); most from middle-class backgrounds.

The head Voluble, witty, warm hearted; bursting with ideas; an enemy of complacency. Gets on well with children and parents (who have his home phone number); does dinner duty daily. Read history at York (teaches A-level government & politics); his second headship. Spare-time activities include writing, painting, playing the piano. Married; three children.

The teaching Styles vary: chalk-and-talk, group discussions, role play; lively, committed staff of 95 (equal numbers of men and women). Broad curriculum: choice of 27 subjects for GCSE, 22 at A-level, including sociology, psychology. Pupils grouped by ability in maths, English from second year; extra help for the least and most able; class size 20–25, reducing to 15 in sixth form. Lots of music,

drama. Wide range of extra-curricular activities; strong chess.
Results (1997) GCSE: 55% gained at least five grades A–C. A-level: 44% of entries graded A or B.
Destinations About 50% stay on for A-levels; of these, 90% proceed to university (about six a year to Oxbridge).
Sport Strong tradition, impressive record; many district and county representatives. Big choice of games: soccer, athletics, cricket, cross-country, golf, hockey, life-saving, netball, rounders, tennis, volleyball. Facilities include extensive playing fields, new sports hall, large swimming pool.
Remarks Well-run school; good pastoral care system helps overcome drawbacks of size.

TWYCROSS HOUSE ♂ ♀
Twycross, near Atherstone, Warwickshire CV9 3PL. Tel (01827) 880651

Synopsis
Independent ★ Co-educational ★ Day ★ Ages 8–18 (plus associated pre-prep) ★ 290 pupils (roughly equal numbers of girls and boys) ★ 40 in sixth form ★ Fees: £3,450–£3,720
Joint heads: Bob and Honor Kirkpatrick, mid-60s, founded the school 1978.
Outstanding school; marvellous atmosphere; first-rate teaching and results; lots of sport.

Profile
Background Listed Queen Anne farmhouse plus ancillary buildings, later additions and neighbouring properties (biology lab in a converted cottage) grouped around a village green and surrounded by playing fields, parkland and flower gardens; everything attractively adapted, decorated (carpets, curtains), well cared-for.
Atmosphere Warm, gentle, friendly (most pupils have been here since they were eight, many since five); very traditional. One of the heads takes assembly every morning; religious education unashamedly Christian, emphasis on scripture. School runs without bells but all classes begin on time. Food is excellent ('a well-fed child is a happy child'). Present and prospective parents made to feel welcome.
Admissions Selective; over-subscribed (names put down at birth – long waiting list, though school never advertises). Entry by interview and tests at age eight in verbal and non-verbal reasoning; children ('they're all a bit above average') need to be able to 'cope comfortably' with the work; 32 places a year available, most taken by pupils from the pre-prep. Extensive catchment area, elaborate school runs (many arrive by Range Rover, Shogun, BMW or Saab). Antique, two-page prospectus.
The heads Exceptionally able, experienced (and self-deprecating): Mr Kirkpatrick first became a head (of a secondary modern) in 1960; his wife taught in state schools for 25 years. School, grown from six pupils, is their creation: 'I wouldn't say we had an underlying philosophy – just an on-going pragmatism. We're a couple of old fuddy-duddies, really.' Neither has any intention of retiring.
The teaching First-rate; generally formal in style; experienced, well-qualified staff all appointed by the present heads and in tune with the school (some have been here since the start). Big emphasis on mental arithmetic, grammar, spelling, handwriting (but not on technology or computing); science taught as three separate subjects; French from age eight (five in the pre-prep), Latin from 10, German from 11, Greek on offer from 14. Mostly mixed-ability classes (maximum size 12) but some pupils take GCSE maths a year early. Exercise books

neat, carefully marked; termly reports to parents. Lots of music, drama.
Results (1997) GCSE: all gained at least five grades A–C. A-level: creditable 72% of entries graded A or B.
Destinations Nearly all to good universities and a wide variety of careers.
Sport Lots on offer; busy fixtures calendar. Main games: soccer, basketball (deputy head captained England), netball, cross-country. Facilities include new sports hall, indoor pool.
Remarks A classical English education in an idyllic English setting. Highly recommended.

ULLSWATER ♂ ♀
Wetheriggs Lane, Penrith, Cumbria CA11 8NG. Tel (01768) 864377

Synopsis
Comprehensive ★ Co-educational ★ Ages 11–18 ★ 1,300 pupils (52% boys) ★ 230 in sixth form
Head: David Robinson, 51, appointed 1990.
Big, well-run school; good teaching; lots on offer.

Profile
Background Result of a 1980 amalgamation of two single-sex secondary moderns; sixth form added 1993. Non-descript but well-maintained 1950s buildings plus sporadic later additions set in parkland close to the town centre; school hosts one of the largest adult and community centres in England (campus buzzes with activity day and night); first-rate unit for handicapped pupils.
Atmosphere Exceptionally civilised: pupils of all abilities and backgrounds immersed in positive attitudes to work, play and community; discipline firm but unobtrusive, the accent on praise and commendation; uniform worn with pride.
Admissions No academic selection but all pupils interviewed. School keen to reduce intake to avoid over-crowding; huge catchment area includes 27 primaries.
The head First-rate: inspirational, indefatigable, leads a hard-working staff from the front; previously a school inspector.
The teaching Lively; varied styles. Standard national curriculum; sixth-form options include 24 A-levels, International Baccalaureate, GNVQs in business studies, health & social care, leisure & tourism ('A rich educational diet,' said Ofsted inspectors). Pupils grouped by ability in most subjects from second year; targets set and monitored; extra help for the least and most able; average class size 27, reducing to 12 in the sixth form. Lots of extra-curricular activities, including well-supported Duke of Edinburgh award scheme.
Results (1997) GCSE: modest 39% gained at least five grades A–C. A-level: 28% of entries graded A or B (not a good year).
Destinations About 50% of those who continue into the sixth form proceed to higher education.
Sport Full range offered; netball a particular strength. Facilities include good playing fields, two floodlit hockey pitches, sports hall, dry-ski slope.
Remarks Good all round – and a true comprehensive.

UNIVERSITY COLLEGE SCHOOL ♂
Frognal, Hampstead, London NW3 6XH. Tel (0171) 435 2215

Synopsis
Independent ★ Boys ★ Day ★ Ages 11–18 (plus associated junior school) ★ 697 pupils ★ 211 in sixth form ★ Fees: £7,626
Head: Kenneth Durham, 43, appointed 1996.
Lively, academic school; first-rate teaching and results; strong liberal ethos; very good creative arts.

Profile
Background Founded 1830 as part of University College, London; Victorian free-thinking, non-denominational tradition enshrined in a charter that forbade religious affiliation or instruction; moved 1907 to present site and handsome, purpose-built, red-brick premises (William and Mary style); sympathetic later additions; facilities are good. Junior school (220 boys aged seven to 11) five minutes' walk away.

Atmosphere Very relaxed, informal, friendly, but with a palpable buzz; boys extremely articulate, open, assured. True to its original ethos, the school values independence of mind and encourages originality. Well-managed pastoral care system; no long pages of rules, but decent behaviour expected, and achieved; no prefects. Traditional blazer-and-tie uniform until sixth form, then own clothes (but jacket and tie compulsory).

Admissions School is heavily over-subscribed (about four apply for each place) and highly selective (looking for evidence of intellectual potential plus willingness to be involved and contribute). Entry at seven, eight, 11 by interview and tests; at 13 by preliminary tests and Common Entrance (minimum 60% mark required); phasing out of assisted places, which about 80 hold, unlikely to have much impact; juniors promoted automatically to the senior school. North London catchment area; most boys very local; business, banking, professional, media backgrounds.

The head Good appointment; cheerful, friendly; well-liked by staff and boys; clearly at ease with the school's liberal ethos. Read politics, philosophy, economics at Oxford; previously director of studies at King's College School, Wimbledon (qv). Married (to the deputy head of South Hampstead, qv); no children.

The teaching First-rate: stimulating, dynamic, informal (many classrooms arranged in horseshoes); lots of lively discussion; very well-qualified, predominantly male staff. Broad curriculum: sciences taught (and examined) separately; all do Latin for at least two years then choose two from Latin, Greek, German, Spanish, French; good computing; lots of choice at GCSE (drama, economics, sport – but no religious studies); 20 subjects on offer at A-level plus many non-examined courses that 'aim to enlarge a boy's curiosity, enterprise and the capacity to learn for himself'. Pupils grouped by ability in maths, French; classes rarely larger than 22. Very good drama (fine theatre), art and music; choral society, orchestras, numerous ensembles. Extra-curricular activities include active voluntary service unit.

Results (1997) GCSE: all gained at least five grades A–C. A-level: very creditable 77% of entries graded A or B.

Destinations Virtually all go on to university (average of 20 a year to Oxbridge).

Sport Main games: rugby, soccer, cricket; regular fixtures. Hockey, tennis, sailing, athletics, fives, canoeing, golf, basketball, squash, cross-country, fencing also on offer; aim is to find something at which each can excel. Facilities include 27 acres of playing fields a mile away, all-weather pitch, large sports hall.

Remarks Attractive school for able, well-motivated boys. Highly recommended.

UPPINGHAM ♂

Uppingham, Rutland LE15 9QE. Tel (01572) 822216

Synopsis

Independent ★ Boys (plus girls in sixth form) ★ Boarding and some day ★
Ages 13–18 (plus associated 11–13 day school) ★ 633 pupils (95% boarding)
★ 330 in sixth form (67% boys) ★ Fees: £13,920 boarding; £9,000 day
Head: Dr Stephen Winkley, 53, appointed 1991.
Fine school for children of a fairly wide range of abilities; good teaching and results; strong music and sport; first-rate facilities.

Profile

Background   Founded 1584 (original schoolroom still in use); made famous by Edward Thring, head from 1853–1887, who modernised the curriculum and pioneered the development of music and sport in public schools. Gracious, well-maintained Victorian buildings (fine chapel) and many later additions (including splendid art/design/technology centre) interwoven with the town. Sixth-form girls admitted since 1975; no plans to go fully co-educational. Junior school has places for up to 50 day boys.

Atmosphere   Friendly, civilised, hard-working; strong sense of order and tradition. Friendly relations between staff and pupils ('We expect them to behave as adults but we forgive them as children'); well-organised pastoral care system (anyone found guilty of bullying required to leave). Lessons on Saturday mornings.

Admissions   Entry at 13 by Common Entrance; minimum 50% mark required (school is not severely selective); 70 girls a year admitted to sixth form by interview (to gauge 'adaptability') and tests, including IQ; minimum of six GCSEs at grades A–C required. Pleasant, homely boarding houses ('We challenge our visitors to find any echoes of *Tom Brown's Schooldays* or Dotheboys Hall'); each has a degree of autonomy and engenders strong loyalties (pupils eat in their houses); heads of houses are powerful figures (many parents apply to houses chosen for their family or prep school links). Scholarships (academic, music, art, technology) available.

The head   Charming, very able; came late to headship and loves it. Educated at Oxford; previously second master at Winchester (in charge of the scholars). Teaches ancient history. Highly musical; paints water-colours. Married, five children.

The teaching   Good quality. Long-serving staff of 75, all of whom play a full part in extra-curricular activities. Broad curriculum: science taught as three separate subjects (well-equipped labs); Latin, Greek, German, Spanish on offer; lots of computing. Choice of 25 subjects at A-level; most take three plus non-examined general studies. Pupils grouped by ability in most subjects from first year; specialist help for dyslexics; largest classes 22 (and may be as small as four to five). First-rate drama (good theatre) and music (regular Oxbridge choral awards and scholarships); two-thirds learn at least one instrument; three orchestras, fine chapel choir. Choice of cadet force or community service; well-supported Duke of Edinburgh award scheme. Regular expeditions abroad.

Results   (1997) GCSE: 92% gained at least five grades A–C. A-level: creditable 62% of entries graded A or B.

Destinations   More than 90% proceed to higher education (many to Oxbridge).

Sport   Important in the life of the school and played to a high level (but not compulsory). Vast choice: rugby, soccer, hockey, cricket, athletics, cross-country, fives, badminton, fencing, golf, shooting etc. Superb facilities include 65 acres of playing fields, fine sports hall, tennis and squash courts, swimming and diving pools.

Remarks   HMC inspectors concluded (1994): 'Uppingham is a happy, friendly and successful school with dedicated teachers and a headmaster with very clear ideas for its future well-being.' Highly recommended, especially for all-rounders.

WAKEFIELD GIRLS' HIGH ♀
Wentworth Street, Wakefield WF1 2QS. Tel (01924) 372490

Synopsis
Independent ★ Girls ★ Day ★ Ages 11–18 (plus associated junior school) ★ 750 pupils ★ 201 in sixth form ★ Fees: £4,774
Head: Mrs Pat Langham, 47, appointed 1987.
Well-run, academic school; good teaching and results; strong strong music and sport.

Profile
Background   Founded 1878; Direct Grant until 1982. Victorian buildings plus many later additions (including striking sports hall) in attractive, if limited, grounds; playing fields within walking distance.

Atmosphere   Orderly, formal (but not stiff); rules implicit rather than prescribed, stemming from adherence to (non-denominational) Christian values (motto, 'Each for all, and all for God'); reverential morning worship attended by all. High academic standards underpinned by 'failure alert' system; special help to remedy weaknesses. Strict uniform; staff formally dressed. Confident, vigorous art work on display everywhere. Strong charity tradition: girls raise nearly £10,000 a year for worthy causes.

Admissions   Top 25% of the ability range; minimum criterion is ability to obtain at least five GCSEs at grades A–C. Entry tests in English, maths, general intellectual ability; school heavily over-subscribed. Children drawn from wide range of social backgrounds but mostly professional. Catchment area includes Huddersfield, Sheffield, Barnsley, Todmorden (railway station near by). Head deeply regrets Labour's phasing out of 160 assisted places; says school will adapt 'as it has always done'.

The head   Dynamic, warm, very able; school has flourished under her leadership. Read English and Russian at Leeds; previously deputy head of a neighbouring comprehensive.

The teaching   Wide range of styles, but tending to the didactic. Well-qualified staff of 62 (78% female), more than half appointed by present head; alert, interested pupils. Science on offer as three separate subjects; lots of languages, including Latin, Greek, Russian. Average class size 24, reducing to 10 in the sixth form. Very good music. Wide range of extra-curricular activities; regular exchanges with schools in France, Germany, Spain.

Results   (1997) GCSE: all gained at least five grades A–C. A-level: 61% of entries graded A or B.

Destinations   Nearly all go to university (up to 10 a year to Oxbridge).

Sport   Wide range on offer; hockey a particular strength.

Remarks   Good all round.

WALDEGRAVE GIRLS' ♀
Fifth Cross Road, Twickenham, London TW2 5LH. Tel (0181) 894 3244

Synopsis
Comprehensive ★ Girls ★ Ages 11–16 ★ 1,000 pupils
Head: Ms Heather Flint, 46, appointed 1991.
Lively, successful school; good teaching and results; first-rate art.

Profile
Background Result of 1981 amalgamation of two girls' schools on 14-acre site in residential Twickenham; 1930s brick building plus various later additions, including well-equipped technology block; some classrooms rather cramped; school full to bursting.

Atmosphere Lively, informal, unstressed; easy, respectful relations between staff and pupils. Good pastoral care; respect for others a clearly stated aim.

Admissions School heavily over-subscribed (more than 400 apply for 200 places) and non-selective; priority to those living nearest ('measured by the shortest road route') and attending a 'feeder' primary. Wide range of abilities and backgrounds (20% ethnic minorities).

The head Cheerful, energetic, professional; much liked by the girls, who find her approachable (and always about); has breathed new life into what was a fairly traditional school. Read social sciences at Birmingham; all teaching experience (RE and sociology) in single-sex state schools in London; spent four years as an adviser on technical and vocational education. Married; no children.

The teaching Good; varied styles. Experienced staff of 60 (five men); low turnover. Standard national curriculum; all do two foreign languages (German and French) for at least one year; Latin on offer; good results in science; computers used across the curriculum. Most take nine GCSEs; options include information technology, child development, sport, drama. Pupils set by ability in maths from first year, languages from second year; extra help for those who need it average class size 24. Art a particular strength (very good work displayed throughout the school); lively drama and music. Lots of extra-curricular activities. Regular foreign exchanges.

Results (1997) GCSE: 63% gained at least five grades A–C.

Destinations About 90% remain in full-time education after 16.

Sport Enthusiastic though not a particular strength. Good range of options, including hockey (pitches on site), netball, football, gymnastics (good gym), dance, health-related fitness (weight room), cricket, tennis, rounders, volleyball, basketball.

Remarks Popular, happy school; good all round.

WALLINGTON GIRLS' HIGH ♀
Woodcote Road, Wallington, Surrey SM6 0PH. Tel (0181) 647 2380

Synopsis
Grammar (grant-maintained) ★ Girls ★ Ages 11–19 ★ 926 pupils ★ 278 in sixth form
Head: Miss Margaret Edwards, 51, appointed 1992.
Vibrant, successful school; good academic record; friendly, supportive, atmosphere.

Profile
Background Founded 1888 by local clergy and residents; became a grammar school and established a strong academic record; moved to present attractive site 1965; opted out of council control 1993. Purpose-built, three-storey premises designed for 500; recent additions include new classrooms and science labs; some classes in ageing 'temporary' huts.

Atmosphere Lively, purposeful, friendly; hums with activity, corridors crowded with animated chatter; enthusiasm abounds. Decent standards of behaviour expected; respect for others encouraged. Good relations between staff and pupils (whom the staff say are a delight to teach).

Admissions Heavily over-subscribed: nearly 600 apply for 140 places. Entry by competitive exam; top 25% of the ability range. Broad social mix from Croydon area.

The head Dedicated, serious-minded; committed Christian; came here as deputy head 1988. Read chemistry at King's College, London; previously head of chemistry at Tiffin Girls'. Strong believer in single-sex education; respects traditional values but keen to equip girls to be leaders in tomorrow's world (school motto, 'Heirs of the Past and Makers of the Future', remains apposite); values joint projects with industrial sponsors. Sixth-formers find her approachable, understanding, always on hand.

The teaching Stimulating, lively, modern in approach (group work, hands-on experience) but strong emphasis on traditional standards of accuracy, presentation, grammar. Well-qualified, stable staff, nearly all women. Mixed-ability classes (of 26): no streaming except for maths. Broad curriculum: GCSE options include Latin, business studies, home economics; languages a particular strength (many do two from French, German, Spanish); A-level choices include social biology (very popular), media studies, technology, sports science, psychology. Good art; enthusiastic music (choirs, orchestra, instrumental groups). Well-planned careers advice, work experience. Numerous school trips, some abroad.

Results (1997) GCSE: 99% gained at least five grades A–C. A-level: 44% of entries graded A or B.

Destinations About 90% stay on for A-levels; of these, 85% proceed to higher education (a few to Oxbridge); regular numbers to art school.

Sport Hockey (several pitches on site), netball, football, tennis (hard and grass courts), cricket, rounders, athletics, gymnastics; good record against other schools.

Remarks Forward-looking, academic school; state education at its best. Ofsted inspectors concluded (1994): 'This is a very successful school which provides a high quality all-round education, equipping its pupils to flourish as lively and confident individuals in the adult world.'

WALLINGTON GRAMMAR ♂
Croydon Road, Wallington, Surrey SM6 7PH. Tel (0181) 647 2235

Synopsis
Grammar (grant-maintained) ★ Boys ★ Ages 11–18 ★ 776 pupils ★ 184 in sixth form
Head: Dr Martin Haworth, 48, appointed 1990.
Well-run, traditional school; good academic record.

Profile
Background Opened 1927; opted out of council control 1993. Red-brick

buildings plus various later additions, some in need of refurbishment; accommodation is cramped. Chris Woodhead, Her Majesty's Chief Inspector of Schools, was a pupil here.

Atmosphere   Friendly, industrious, well-ordered; polite, well-motivated pupils; good pastoral care. Blazer-and-tie uniform for all. Supportive parents.

Admissions   By tests in English, maths, verbal reasoning; about 600 take them, about 210 pass; all who pass and make the school their first choice get a place; top 25% of the ability range. Pupils drawn from a fairly wide range of backgrounds in an expanding catchment area.

The head   Able, hard-working; committed Christian (following a Billy Graham rally in the 1960s); member of Mensa; respected by staff and parents. Has a divinity degree from London Bible College, followed by MA and PhD from Birmingham; previously deputy head of a Sheffield comprehensive. Married (to a teacher); two grown-up daughters.

The teaching   Sound; fairly traditional in style; well-qualified staff of 45 (30% female); good balance of age and experience. National curriculum plus; science on offer as three separate subjects; languages include German, Spanish, Latin; religious education compulsory; all do 10/11 GCSEs; choice of 18 subjects at A-level. Pupils grouped by ability in maths from second year, French for GCSE; extra help for dyslexics; average class size 30, reducing to a maximum of 15 in sixth form. Lots of drama, music; choir, orchestra. Extra-curricular activities include Scouts, Duke of Edinburgh award scheme.

Results   (1997) GCSE: 94% gained at least five grades A–C. A-level: 45% of entries graded A or B.

Destinations   Up to 90% stay on for A-levels; of these, nearly all proceed to university (average of six a year to Oxbridge).

Sport   Chiefly: rugby, hockey, cricket, athletics; regular district and county honours. Facilities include small sports hall; 30 acres of playing fields shared with old boys' association.

Remarks   Ofsted inspectors concluded (1995): 'This is a school with a consistent record of high achievement that provides a safe, secure and rich learning environment'.

WALTHAMSTOW HALL ♀
Hollybush Road, Sevenoaks, Kent TN13 3UL. Tel (01732) 451334

Synopsis
Independent ★ Girls ★ Day and boarding ★ Ages 11–18 (plus associated junior school) ★ 400 pupils (90% day) ★ 100 in sixth form ★ Fees: £6,810 day; £13,290 boarding
Head: Mrs Jackie Lang, 53, appointed 1984.
Successful, well-run school; good teaching and results; lots of music, sport.

Profile
Background   Founded 1838 in East London as a home and school for daughters of missionaries; moved to present site 1882; formerly Direct Grant, reverted to full independence 1976. Gracious Victorian house plus later additions in spacious grounds; fine library, theatre. Junior school (200 pupils aged three to 10) near by.

Atmosphere   Open, engaging; girls treated as individuals; discipline not an issue; big emphasis on good manners, service, responsibility.

Admissions By interview and tests in English, maths; school is not unduly selective; phasing out of assisted places, which 50 hold, will make recruitment more difficult. Catchment area covers West Kent, East Sussex, Surrey. Boarding accommodation pleasant, well-furnished but not very spacious. Scholarships, bursaries available.

The head Able, determined; strong leader. Was a pupil here; won a scholarship to Oxford at 16; read French (First). Believes girls must be taught to gain control of their lives. Married (to the deputy head of King's College School, Wimbledon); two grown-up daughters.

The teaching Challenging, effective; well-planned lessons; wide range of styles. Well-qualified, predominantly female staff (some long serving). Broad curriculum: sciences taught separately (good labs); languages include German, Spanish, Latin; good computing; wide choice of 25 subjects at A-level. Lots of art, drama, music; two-thirds learn an instrument; three choirs, two orchestras. Extra-curricular activities include Duke of Edinburgh award scheme.

Results (1997) GCSE: all gained at least five grades A–C. A-level: 57% of entries graded A or B.

Destinations Nearly all proceed to university (including Oxbridge).

Sport Strong, particularly lacrosse. Fencing, squash, netball, tennis, athletics, swimming also on offer; facilities include indoor pool.

Remarks Attractive school.

WARDEN PARK ♂ ♀
Broad Street, Cuckfield, Haywards Heath, West Sussex RH17 5DP. Tel (01444) 457881

Synopsis
Comprehensive ★ Co-educational ★ Ages 11–16 ★ 1,465 pupils (56% boys)
Head: Brian Webb, 56, appointed 1988.
Effective, well-run school; very good teaching and GCSE results; wide range of extra-curricular activities; strong sport.

Profile
Background Opened as a purpose-built secondary modern 1956; went comprehensive 1973, since when it has grown steadily in size and reputation. Unremarkable two-storey brick buildings plus later additions, including new science labs, language block, library. Some classrooms in ageing 'temporary' huts; school is over-crowded.

Atmosphere Well disciplined and surprisingly calm, despite the numbers. High expectations create a climate in which it would be difficult not to achieve; merit certificates awarded for contributions of all kinds. Uniform worn throughout. Parents supportive and involved.

Admissions School over-subscribed; nearly two-thirds come from outside the official catchment area (some from as far as 20 miles). Fairly wide range of abilities, mostly from ambitious middle-class homes.

The head Good manager; unassuming, informal; gets on well with staff and pupils. Married; grown-up children.

The teaching Good, often stimulating; lessons carefully planned, clearly explained; little scope for day-dreaming or time-wasting. Well-qualified, relatively youthful staff of 80, equal numbers of men and women. Standard national curriculum; choice of French, German, Spanish (some do two); GCSE options include sociology, home economics, music, drama. Pupils grouped by ability in English, maths, modern languages from second year, in science from third year; average class size 27–28; extra help for those with special needs; additional classes after school in maths, technology. Regular grades for attainment and effort (parents telephoned if there is cause for concern). Strong drama (regular productions) and music (choir, 120-strong orchestra). Rich extra-curricular programme includes Duke of Edinburgh award scheme, Young Enterprise. Regular language exchanges with schools in France, Germany, Spain.

Results (1997) GCSE: creditable 66% gained at least five grades A–C.

Destinations Nearly all remain in full-time education after 16.

Sport Taken seriously; many team and individual successes, particularly in athletics. Main games (for both sexes): rugby, football, basketball, hockey, netball, cricket, tennis, badminton. Large on-site playing field, plenty of hard courts, modern gym but no sports hall.

Remarks Ofsted inspectors concluded (1996): 'This is a good school with outstanding features. It sets high standards for pupils' academic and social development. Teaching staff are well qualified and suitably experienced. The great majority of pupils have very positive attitudes to their work and show good levels of motivation.'

WARWICK ♂
Myton Road, Warwick CV34 6PP. Tel (01926) 492484

Synopsis
Independent ★ Boys ★ Day and boarding ★ Ages 11–18 (plus associated junior school) ★ 800 pupils (7% boarding) ★ 251 in sixth form ★ Fees: £4,545 day; £10,980 boarding.
Head: Dr Philip Cheshire, 57, appointed 1988.
Firmly traditional school; good teaching and results; lots of music and sport.

Profile
Background Probably dates from 914; re-endowed by Henry VIII 1545; moved to present 50-acre site on the banks of the Avon (fine views of Warwick Castle) 1879. Rococo Tudor-style buildings plus many later additions; good facilities. Junior school (seven to 11) on the same site.

Atmosphere Firmly Christian (full-time chaplain, daily chapel services); tightly disciplined; friendly relations between staff and pupils.

Admissions At 11 (100 places) by tests in English, maths, verbal reasoning; at 13 (30 places) by Common Entrance; minimum IQ 110. Phasing out of assisted places, which more than 150 hold, will have a significant impact on recruitment. About half come from the immediate vicinity (Warwick, Leamington, Kenilworth); half the 60 boarders are from abroad. Boarding accommodation in urgent need of refurbishment. Scholarships, bursaries available.

The head Runs a tight ship. Read physics at London; previously head of science at Rugby (qv). Completely immersed in his job, and expects everyone else to be the same. Married (wife much involved in the school).

The teaching Good; very well-qualified staff (including 22 Oxbridge graduates), predominantly male, 60% appointed by present head. Broad curriculum: science taught as three separate subjects (well-equipped labs); wide choice of languages, including Russian, Chinese; lots of computers. Pupils grouped by ability in most subjects; progress closely monitored (three-weekly review of every pupil's performance); maximum class size 24, reducing to 16 at A-level. Promotion to the sixth form is not automatic: at least five grade Bs at GCSE required. Lots of music: all first-years begin learning to read it and play an instrument; two choirs, two orchestras. Extra-curricular activities include chess, bridge, debating, strong cadet force. Regular study trips abroad.

Results (1997) GCSE: all gained at least five grades A–C. A-level: creditable 71% of entries graded A or B.

Destinations About 85% continue into the sixth form; of these, nearly all proceed to university (average of 10 a year to Oxbridge).

Sport Choice of 24. Main sports: rugby, hockey, cross-country, cricket, tennis, athletics, swimming (indoor pool). Archery, fencing, golf, canoeing (on the Avon), squash also available.

Remarks HMC inspectors concluded (1996): 'This is a very purposeful and effective school, with good morale and sense of community spirit.'

WATFORD BOYS' GRAMMAR ♂
Rickmansworth Road, Watford WD1 7JF. Tel (01923) 224950

Synopsis
Partially selective comprehensive (grant-maintained) ★ Boys ★ Ages 11–18 ★ 1,115 pupils ★ 300 in sixth form
Head: John Holman, 51, appointed 1994.
First-rate, academic school; very good teaching and results; strong music and sport.

Profile
Background Founded 1704 with Watford Girls' (qv) as a charity school with separate boys' and girls' divisions; moved to present town-centre site 1912; became a grammar school 1944; went comprehensive early 1970s; opted out of council control 1990. Neo-Georgian building plus later additions of varying styles and periods arranged around a quadrangle on an attractive campus (in contrast to the girls' school). Well-equipped sixth-form centre; library has space for 100 readers.

Atmosphere Very much the traditional grammar school: commanding head; slightly aloof staff; polite, neatly-uniformed pupils (jumpers not to obscure knot of school tie); strong prefect system (90 apply for the job, staff appoint 20); trappings retained too (honours boards, cups, headmasters' portraits, team photos). Good pastoral care. Supportive parents and local businesses help raise funds.

Admissions Heavily over-subscribed: nearly five apply for every place; 50% selected on the basis of tests in maths, verbal reasoning (no interview); 10% on proven musical ability. Remaining places to siblings (up to 40 a year), boys whose parents work here or at Watford Girls', those living nearest. Sixth-form entry requires seven GCSEs at grade C or above, including at least a B in chosen A-level subjects. Pupils from a wide range of social backgrounds; 25% ethnic minorities.

The head Very able: dynamic, business-like, clear sense of purpose; unusually broad background. Read natural sciences at Cambridge; first came here as head of chemistry 1976; left in 1984 to spend 10 years working on curriculum development (helped devise national curriculum science), teaching at York University and being a scientific consultant to industry. Has published 10 text books; lectures widely on science education; teaches GCSE and A-level chemistry. Married (to a primary school teacher); three children.

The teaching   Formal in style; long-serving, highly-qualified staff (75% male); attentive, lively pupils. Broad curriculum: science on offer as three separate subjects; half first-years take French, half German and can add the other from second year; other options include Latin, drama, business studies; IT used across the curriculum. Pupils grouped by ability at different times in most subjects; extra help for those with special needs (some are 'statemented'); older boys help the younger ones. Classes are 27/28, smaller for GCSE and A-level. Most take nine GCSEs and three A-levels (from a choice of 20); sciences particularly strong. Good music: 500 take part; orchestra and choir shared with girls' school. Lots of drama (first-rate facilities), art. Extra-curricular activities include debating, Duke of Edinburgh award scheme. Frequent study trips at home and abroad; language exchanges with schools in France, Germany.

Results   Good. (1997) GCSE: 90% gained at least five grades A–C. A-level: 58% of entries graded A or B.

Destinations   Nearly all go on to good universities (including up to 12 a year to Oxbridge).

Sport   High profile; good facilities, including sports hall, ample playing fields, all-weather pitch (but no swimming pool). Main games: rugby, hockey, cricket, cross-country, athletics; many teams, regular fixtures. Tennis, golf, badminton, sailing also on offer.

Remarks   Ofsted inspectors concluded (1996): 'There is a positive learning culture within which high achievement is valued.'

WATFORD GIRLS' GRAMMAR ♀
Lady's Close, Watford, Hertfordshire WD1 8AE. Tel (01923) 223403

> **Synopsis**
> Partially selective comprehensive (grant-maintained) ★ Girls ★ Ages 11–18
> ★ 1,147 pupils ★ 253 in sixth-form
> Head: Mrs Helen Hyde, 50, appointed 1987.
> *First-rate, traditional school; dynamic head; strong teaching; lively girls.*

Profile
Background   Founded 1704 with Watford Boys' (qv); moved to present eight-acre site 1907; became a grammar school 1944; went comprehensive early 1970s; opted out of council control 1991. Early Edwardian buildings plus many later additions – including, most recently, three new science labs and sports hall – on a cramped, noisy site next to the ring road; school is over-crowded. Separate premises for first-years: a delightful haven complete with walled garden.

Atmosphere   No-frills: funding is tight, nothing goes to waste (sixth-form common room full of donated sofas); parents raise funds for books and basic equipment as well as extras. Pupils from diverse backgrounds (Jewish, Asian); many languages spoken; daily religious assembly appropriate to all. Art and other school work on display everywhere. Strongly traditional ethos: strict uniform policy (staff wear the school crest as a badge); nail polish removed on sight; prefects wear boaters on formal occasions (staff in academic gowns); girls stand when a teacher enters the room.

Admissions   Severely over-subscribed: more than 700 apply for 180 places, half of which go to those who perform best in maths and verbal reasoning tests (no interview); another 10% are allocated on the basis of 'proven ability in music' (grades five to seven). Priorities for the rest: siblings (up to 60 a year); daughters of staff; girls with brothers at Watford Boys'; daughters of former pupils; next-best test performers ('in merit order'). Allocation of all places is subject to geographical banding with a maximum of 55% going to girls living in the Watford area; remaining catchment area is extensive. Sixth-form entry requires six GCSEs A–C, including A or B in in chosen A-level subjects; 110 interviewed for up to 30 places (no geographical restrictions). 'This is an academic school,' says the head. 'It's what we're good at, it's what parents want.'

The head   Passionate, enthusiastic, ambitious for her pupils (knows nearly all by name); takes enormous pride in their and the school's achievements (girls bring good work to show her at break-time). Read French and Biblical studies at Witwatersrand University, Johannesburg; MA in theology from King's, London. Teaches French to first-years; leads a bi-annual trip to Israel. Married (to a consultant paediatrician); two daughters (both were pupils here).

The teaching   Good. Traditional in style; desks in rows. Experienced, stable staff (20% male). Classes of 30 up to GCSE (up to 22 at A-level); pupils grouped by ability in maths from second year, in languages (French, German, Italian) and science (dual award) from fourth year. No provision for special needs but specialist teaching for bi-lingual pupils, and individual help for those who are struggling. Good classics (Latin available up to A-level); half take religious studies at GCSE; first-rate design/technology, computing; lots of art; strong music (half learn an instrument but facilities are limited – pupils have to share keyboards). Wide range of extra-curricular activities (all must do three); regular music and language trips to Europe; well-supported Duke of Edinburgh award scheme.

Results   (1997) GCSE: creditable 94% gained at least five grades A–C. A level: 57% of entries graded A or B.

Destinations   Up to 50 leave after GCSE for (co-educational) sixth-form colleges or vocational courses; 90% of sixth-formers proceed to higher education (a handful to Oxbridge, some to art and music colleges).

Sport   Not a strong feature but full range on offer, despite limited facilities: athletics, swimming (functional indoor pool), basketball, dance, trampolining, cross-country, rounders, volleyball, netball, hockey (on a sloping pitch), badminton, gymnastics. New sports hall (partly funded by parents) will help.

Remarks   Old-fashioned values in a multi-cultural setting. A strong alternative to local independent schools (do not be put off by the the external fabric).

WELLINGBOROUGH   ♂ ♀
Wellingborough, Northamptonshire NN8 2BX. Tel (01933) 222427

Synopsis
Independent ★ Co-educational ★ Day and boarding ★ Ages 13–18 (plus associated junior school) ★ 390 pupils (65% boys, 92% day) ★ 140 in sixth form ★ Fees: £5,880 day; £10,350 boarding
Head: Ralph Ullmann, 53, appointed 1993.
Solid, traditional school; good teaching; wide range of abilities; lots on offer.

Profile
Background   Founded 1595; moved 1881 to present 47-acre site and purpose-built, red-brick premises; less distinguished later additions, some in need of refurbishment; some classrooms in 'temporary' huts; library has more

atmosphere than utility; pleasant chapel. Pre-prep and junior schools (370 pupils aged three to 13) on same site under own heads.

Atmosphere Quietly purposeful, well-ordered; school 'firmly wedded to Christian principles'; good pastoral care; strong sense of community; amiable relations between staff and pupils. Traditional houses, prefects, blazer-and-tie uniform.

Admissions By interview and tests or Common Entrance; school is barely selective; wide range of abilities; phasing out of assisted places, which 75 hold, will make recruitment more difficult. Adequate boarding accommodation (boys in dormitories of up to eight); 40% of boarders from abroad (13 nations represented); boarding numbers have steadily declined. Day pupils can stay for supper and prep. Scholarships (academic, music, art, sport) and bursaries available.

The head Experienced, forthright; good manager. Read history at Cambridge; previously head for eight years of Ruthin, Clwyd. Married (wife much involved in school life); three children (two are pupils here).

The teaching Sound; mainly formal in style ('Pupils tend to be receptive rather than responsive', HMC inspectors observed); experienced staff (70% male). Fairly broad curriculum; sciences taught separately (20% take all three for GCSE); German, Latin on offer (good results); rather restricted choice of 19 subjects at A-level (including design/technology, psychology, PE). Pupils grouped by ability in most subjects; extra help for dyslexics; progress closely monitored; average class size 20, reducing to a maximum of 10 at A-level. Strong art; lots of drama; flourishing music (choirs, orchestra, more than a third learn an instrument). Good careers advice. Lots of extra-curricular activities, including cadet force, Duke of Edinburgh award scheme. Regular language exchanges with pupils in France, Germany.

Results (1997) GCSE: 90% of candidates gained at least five grades A–C. A-level: 50% of entries graded A or B.

Destinations About 90% go on to university (average of four a year to Oxbridge).

Sport Good; wide range on offer. Main sports: football, rugby, cross-country for boys; hockey, netball, squash for girls; cricket, tennis, athletics also on offer. Facilities include 40 acres of first-rate playing fields, all-weather tennis courts, well-equipped sports hall, squash courts, outdoor pool, nine-hole golf course.

Remarks Sound school, particularly for children who need 'drawing out'.

WELLINGTON COLLEGE ♂
Crowthorne, Berkshire RG45 7PU. Tel (01344) 771588

Synopsis
Independent ★ Boys (plus girls in sixth form) ★ Boarding and day ★ Ages 13–18 ★ 790 pupils (80% boarding) ★ 330 in sixth form (85% boys) ★ Fees: £13,350 boarding; £9,735 day
Head: Jonty Driver, 58, appointed 1989.
Fine, well-run school; good teaching and results; very strong sport.

Profile
Background Founded 1853 as a monument to the Iron Duke to provide an education for the for the 'orphan children of indigent and meritorious' Army officers (Heroum filii – the sons of the brave); paid for by public subscription and a compulsory levy of a day's pay imposed on the entire Army. Some 1,200 old boys gave their lives in two World Wars; 15 have won the VC. Splendid buildings ('Victorian version of French Grand Rococo') plus fine chapel by Sir Gilbert Scott in a

magnificent 400-acre estate (80 acres of playing fields); later additions include good design/technology centre and vast sports hall. Girls first admitted 1978.

Atmosphere   Relaxed, happy. Courteous staff-pupil relations; big emphasis on independence and leadership; sixth-form girls need to be thoroughly competent to cope. Compulsory chapel; lessons on Saturday mornings. Elegant, informative prospectus.

Admissions   By Common Entrance (minimum 55% mark required) and previous school reports; at 16 with at least GCSE grade B in proposed A-level subjects. School owns adjoining prep school but draws from up to 170. Some scholarships (including art, music); means-tested foundation bursaries for the children of deceased Service officers.   Good boarding accommodation (eight in-college houses, six others within easy walking distance, girls have their own house); nearly all have own study-bedrooms after first year.

The head   Imposing, very able; Victorian-liberal in style. South-African born; educated at Cape Town (president of National Union of South African Students, imprisoned without trial) and Oxford. Taught at Sevenoaks and a comprehensive in Humberside before becoming head of Island School, Hong Kong; formerly head of Berkhamsted. Has written four novels (including *Send War in Our Time, O Lord*), five books of poetry and a biography (of a South African liberal). Takes a tough line on discipline in general and drugs in particular; has raised academic standards and de-militarised the school's image. Married; three grown-up children.

The teaching   Well-organised curriculum; clear-cut choices. Science taught as three separate subjects; more able do Latin and Greek; rest add German or Spanish to French; all do some design/technology and computing. All take 10–12 GCSEs; choice of 24 subjects at A-level; equal numbers do arts and sciences and many mix the two; a third of the sixth-form timetable devoted to 'general education'. Maximum class size 24, reducing to 14 or fewer in the sixth form. Lots of art (good painting, pottery), drama (300-seat theatre) and music (all learn an instrument in first year, many continue). First-rate library (full-time librarian). Compulsory cadet force in second year. Regular exchanges with schools in France, Germany, India.

Results   (1997) GCSE: 99% gained at least five grades A–C. A-level: 60% of entries graded A or B.

Destinations   Nearly all proceed to university (about 25 a year to Oxbridge).

Sport   Very strong, particularly rugby (22 XVs), hockey (16 XIs), cricket (14 XIs), athletics; girls play tennis, netball, hockey, lacrosse, cricket. Fine facilities include all-weather pitch, athletics track, indoor and outdoor pools, four climbing walls, courts for tennis, squash, fives, rackets, basketball, badminton.

Remarks   Very good school, particularly for all-rounders; warmly recommended.

WELLINGTON, SOMERSET ♂ ♀
Wellington, Somerset TA2l 8NT. Tel (01823) 668800

Synopsis
Independent ★ Co-educational ★ Day and boarding ★ Ages 10–18 ★ 790 pupils (55% boys, 77% day) ★ 190 in sixth form ★ Fees: £8,856 boarding; £4,848 day
Headmaster: Alan Rogers, 50, appointed 1990
Attractive, well-run school; good teaching and results; strong sport.

Profile
Background   Founded 1837; formerly Direct Grant, reverted to full

independence 1978; girls first admitted 1979. Attractive cluster of red-brick buildings plus later additions, including award-winning science block, on a 24-acre site in a pleasant residential area; elegant chapel (uninhibited singing); good facilities for art, design & technology; more than £6 million spent recently on building and refurbishment. Jeffrey Archer was a pupil here.

Atmosphere   Calm, civilised. High-quality pastoral care; light-touch discipline; very good relations between staff and courteous pupils. Head emphasises the school's aim to 'allow the not-so-well-endowed to develop'. Smart blazer-and-tie uniform; prefects replaced by weekly rota of seniors. Parents are very supportive.

Admissions   At 11 by interview and tests in English, maths, aptitude; at 13 by Common Entrance; school is fairly selective (grammar school standard) but phasing out of assisted places, which 230 hold, will have a considerable impact (not least on the social mix). Comfortable boarding accommodation in large, Victorian houses; largest dormitories sleep seven; sixth-formers share with one other. Day pupils from 30-mile radius.

The head   Very much in charge (and says he 'lives for the school'); management style 'as consultative as time will allow'; well-respected by staff and pupils. Read geography at Oxford; came here as deputy head 1982. 'This is a pretty unpretentious school,' he says. 'The parents make brave self-sacrifices for their children's education.' Keen on sport, music. Married; three children (two were pupils here, one still is).

The teaching   Good: traditional in style; rows of desks facing the front; strong emphasis on practical activity. Well-qualified staff of 64 (20 women), a third appointed by present head. Standard grammar school curriculum: half take science as three separate subjects; choice of French or German; Latin, home economics on offer; not much computing. A-level options include social biology, ancient history, PE. Pupils grouped by ability in maths, French; average class size 22, reducing to 12–15 in sixth form. Lots of art, drama, music (170 learn an instrument). Extra-curricular activities include cadet force (corps of drums), Duke of Edinburgh award scheme. Regular language exchanges with schools in France, Germany.

Results   (1997) GCSE: 97% gained at least five grades A–C. A-level: 57% of entries graded A or B.

Destinations   Nearly all sixth-form leavers go on to higher education.

Sport   An important feature of the school; everybody expected to participate. Main activities: rugby, hockey (girls' and boys'), netball, cricket, tennis, athletics, cross-country, swimming; regular county honours. Badminton, squash, show jumping also on offer. Facilities include ample playing fields, all-weather pitch but no sports hall.

Remarks   HMC inspectors concluded (1996) that school was a 'community of exceptional quality'. Recommended.

WELLS CATHEDRAL SCHOOL ♂ ♀
Wells, Somerset BA5 2ST. Tel (01749) 672117

Synopsis
Independent ★ Co-educational ★ Day and boarding ★ Ages 11–18 (plus associated junior school) ★ 605 pupils (52% girls, 54% day) ★ 194 in sixth form ★ Fees: £6,369 day; £10,725 boarding
Head: John Baxter, 58, appointed 1986.
Mainstream school with a specialist music department; good teaching and results; lots on offer.

Profile

Background   Roots go back to 10th century; grammar and chorister schools merged 1546; specialist department for musically-gifted children opened 1970 (one of four in England); girls admitted 1972. Fine collection of medieval and 18th-century buildings (plus some that are less distinguished) in a beautiful conservation area close to the cathedral (which is the school's chapel). Junior school (180 pupils aged three to 11, including 32 boy and girl choristers) near by.

Atmosphere   Purposeful, civilised, creative; 'an education consistent with the broad principles of Christianity'. Very good relations between staff and pupils; discipline firm but not obtrusive; drugs lead to expulsion.

Admissions   By tests; minimum IQ 105 (ability range is fairly wide); voice trials for choristers (who pay reduced fees); auditions for specialist musicians (up to 70 of the 100 qualify for substantial Government assistance). Pupils drawn from a fairly wide range of social backgrounds; many from Service families. Pleasant boarding accommodation; no dormitory larger than eight.

The head   Friendly, urbane; highly regarded. Read history at Durham; previously head of history and a housemaster at Westminster; played hockey for Britain, cricket for English universities. Married (to a teacher); two grown-up sons.

The teaching   Mostly formal in style; hard-working staff (majority appointed by present head). Standard national curriculum; choice of 20 subjects at A-level. Pupils grouped by ability in some subjects; reduced academic programme for specialist musicians; extra help for those with learning difficulties; maximum class size 25. Outstanding music (about half learn at least one instrument); lots of drama. Extra-curricular activities include cadet force, Duke of Edinburgh award scheme (one of which is compulsory).

Results   (1997) GCSE: 95% gained at least five grades A–C. A-level: 55% of entries graded A or B.

Destinations   About 90% go on to university or specialist music colleges (average of six a year to Oxbridge).

Sport   Voluntary; all main games on offer; others include pot-holing, canoeing, orienteering, climbing, sailing, golf, croquet. Facilities include 18 acres of playing fields, all-weather pitch, sports hall, tennis and netball courts.

Remarks   Good all round.

WEST KIRBY GIRLS' ♀
Graham Road, West Kirby, Wirral L48 5DP. Tel (0151) 632 3449

> ### Synopsis
> Grammar ★ Girls ★ Ages 11–18 ★ 1,240 pupils ★ 320 in sixth form
> Head: Mrs Joan Erskine, 57, appointed 1984.
> *Attractive, not unduly selective grammar school; broad curriculum; good teaching and results.*

Profile

Background   Founded (on present site) 1913; dignified, spacious premises plus 1960s flat-roof extension; some classrooms in 'temporary' huts ('Very hot in summer,' said Ofsted inspectors). Much recent refurbishment; everywhere shines.

Atmosphere   Quiet, orderly, civilised ('Very good behaviour is the norm,' said Ofsted). Honours boards going back to 1916; school photographs from the gymslip era; contemporary art work along the corridors. Good relations between staff and pupils (clearly engaged in a common cause).

Admissions   School is heavily over-subscribed (more than 500 apply for 180 places). Entry by local authority 11-plus (two verbal reasoning tests); fairly wide range of abilities (top 35%–40%); most from professional/middle-class homes.

The head   Thoughtful, compassionate. Read biology at Liverpool; formerly deputy head of a comprehensive in Crosby. Married.

The teaching   Wide range of styles, all marked by high expectations. Happy, hard-working staff of 84 (14 men), 50 appointed by present head. Varied, balanced curriculum; all do French from first year and may add German, Spanish, Latin; Japanese, Russian, Italian also available; science taught by specialists; lots of computing; good art. Choice of 30 subjects at GCSE (most take 10), 27 at A-level, including business studies, theatre studies, psychology. Pupils grouped by ability in French, maths; extra tuition for Oxbridge entrants; average class size 25, reducing to 10–12 in sixth form. Active music department; 100 learn an instrument; choirs, orchestra, brass group, ensembles. Extra-curricular activities include science club, photography, Duke of Edinburgh award scheme, cadet force (shared with neighbouring boys' grammar). Much community involvement; regular European and USA exchanges.

Results   (1997) GCSE: 98% gained at least five grades A–C levels. A-level: 42% of entries graded A or B.

Destinations   More than 90% stay on for A-levels; of these, 90% proceed to university (about five a year to Oxbridge).

Sport   Main games: hockey, netball, athletics, cross-country, tennis; many local and county representatives. Facilities include netball courts, hockey pitch, large gym. No sports hall or swimming pool but sports centre adjacent.

Remarks   Well-run, well-rounded school. Identified by Ofsted (1996) as 'outstandingly successful'.

WESTMINSTER ♂
Little Dean's Yard, London SW1P 3PF. Tel (0171) 963 1003

Synopsis
Independent ★ Boys (plus girls in sixth form) ★ Day and boarding ★ Ages 13–18 (plus associated junior school) ★ 675 pupils (65% day) ★ 350 in sixth form (75% boys) ★ Fees: £9,930 day; £14,400 boarding
Head: David Summerscale, 60, appointed 1986 (retires August 1998).
Distinguished school, unique both in its historic setting and in the unfettered individualism of its highly intelligent pupils.

Profile
Background   Founded 1542 by Henry VIII from a small Benedictine monastery school; re-founded 1560 by Elizabeth I for boys to be 'liberally instructed in good books to the greater honour of the state'; pre-eminent by the early 18th-century. Historic buildings adjoining Westminster Abbey (many of them owned by the Church – Dean is chairman of the governors); science taught in large office block near by. Numbers now at saturation point.

Atmosphere   All is hurly-burly, ebb and flow; a stimulating, surging, constricting, uplifting setting quite unlike any other. A tourist could wander into the green, domestic calm of Dean's Yard without guessing the school was there; its heart lies through a low vaulted arch into Little Dean's Yard, a spacious paved courtyard, off which boarding houses, classrooms and libraries open in haphazard profusion. Hidden behind is an enclosed 10th-century garden, with three modern fives courts defying all preservation orders and planners by forming one wall of the cloister. Boys eat in what was once the abbot's state dining room, passing the doughnuts and chips down ancient tables (never stopping to think of the past in their haste towards tomorrow). The sixth-form girls are tough, confident and clever; after a few days of mutual incomprehension, both sides enjoy the challenge of classroom competition and get on well together (the girls insist this is still a boys' school and that taking a feminist stand is futile). Compulsory morning service in the Abbey three times a week.

Admissions School is severely selective. Entry by scholarship exam (known as The Challenge) or by Common Entrance (minimum 65% mark required). No guaranteed entry from the Under School (qv), though most boys transfer. Pupils drawn from a 50-mile radius (nearly all boarders are weekly); parents mostly cosmopolitan, managerial, media or executive.

The head Considerate, unassuming, shuns publicity; has none of the breezy jollity of many heads, but his authority, humanity and integrity are beyond doubt. Educated at Sherborne and Cambridge; taught English at Charterhouse for 12 years; head of Haileybury for 10 years. Married; two teenage children. From September 1998: Tristram Jones-Parry, an old boy who read maths at Oxford, returned to teach in 1973, became Under Master (deputy head), and left in September 1994 to be head of Emanuel, a lowly-ranked school in south-west London; a tough disciplinarian, not particularly at ease with girls.

The teaching Outstanding. Staff are rigorous in their demands on the pupils and equally hard on themselves. Those who teach here have to be able to deliver the goods six days a week (Saturday morning school survives) preferably with humour; the pupils are no respecters of persons when it comes to bad or boring teaching, and the faint-hearted or pretentious 'usher' is lost. Academic subjects are strong right across the board: classics still popular; history of art is easy when the galleries are a short walk away; languages have no terrors for the 50% who have parents from abroad; history and politics come alive at Westminster (Queen's scholars have the privilege of queue-jumping for Commons debates); design/technology is not a major subject but Chinese is available on demand. Most take 10 GCSEs and four A-levels. This has always been a liberal school, and there is still a genuine tolerance and enjoyment of intellectual differences; music, art and drama all rated as important. Outside the classroom, the boys' time is not nearly as structured and overseen as it is in most boarding schools.

Results (1997) GCSE: all gained at least five grades A–C. A-level: remarkable 86% of entries graded A or B.

Destinations All proceed to university (up to 50% to Oxbridge).

Sport All try something, and those who want to play seriously can. Rowing and fencing are particularly strong; soccer, cricket, tennis in Vincent Square; squash, swimming also popular.

Remarks Fine school, adapting and living on its not inconsiderable wits. HMI concluded (1995) 'The standards achieved fully reflect the often prodigious abilities of the pupils. The teaching is consistently scholarly, painstaking and challenging.'

WHEATLEY PARK ♂ ♀
Holton, Oxford OX33 1QH. Tel (01865) 872441

Synopsis
Comprehensive ★ Co-educational ★ Ages 11–18 ★ 1,382 pupils (roughly equal numbers of girls and boys) ★ 239 in sixth form
Head: Nicholas Young, 49, appointed 1993.
Successful, well-run school; good teaching.

Profile
Background Opened 1972; moved to present site 1983; castellated Georgian mansion plus bland modern additions in superb, spacious grounds (shared with a school for severely handicapped children); many classrooms in 'temporary' huts (despite recent £400,000 building programme).

Atmosphere Concern and consideration for others apparent throughout; excellent pastoral care system; good links with parents. Pupils unanimous in their praise (and volunteer that the only sort of child who will not do well here is one who does not want to work hard or behave well); annual prize-giving celebrates achievement across the ability range. School's interpretation of the legal requirement for a daily act of worship is a 'thought for the day that does not presume any belief or faith'.

Admissions School slightly over-subscribed. Largely rural catchment area to the east of Oxford; parents range from agricultural workers to Oxford dons.

The head Read social science at London; wide experience in the state sector; previously deputy head of another Oxfordshire comprehensive. Married; three children.

The teaching Enthusiastic, well-prepared; mostly formal in style; expectations uniformly high. Standard national curriculum; choice of French, German, Spanish (more able do two); Latin on offer from third year; first-rate computing, science, technology. All take up to 11 GCSEs (from a choice of 23); vocational alternatives to A-level available (good results in GNVQ art & design). Pupils grouped by ability in English, maths, modern languages from second year, in science from third year; lots of extra help for those who need it (including the gifted); average class size 25, reducing to 23 for GCSE. Good music (madrigal choir performs abroad). Wide range of extra-curricular activities. Lots of careers advice; all have work experience. Regular language exchanges with schools in France, Germany, Spain.

Results (1997) GCSE: 48% gained at least five grades A–C (has been much higher). A-level: rather modest 29% of entries graded A or B.

Destinations About 60% continue into the sixth form; of these, 80% proceed to higher education (about four a year to Oxbridge).

Sport Good facilities, including large sports hall, gym, playing fields, netball and tennis courts (but no swimming pool). Both girls and boys play football and netball.

Remarks Attractive school.

WHITGIFT ♂
Haling Park, South Croydon, CR2 6YT. Tel (0181) 688 9222

Synopsis
Independent ★ Boys ★ Day ★ Ages 10–18 ★ 1,112 pupils ★ 350 in sixth form
★ Fees: £6,147
Head: Dr Christopher Barnett, 44, appointed 1991.
First-rate academic school; good teaching; excellent facilities; strong music, sport.

Profile
Background Founded 1596 by John Whitgift, Archbishop of Canterbury; moved to attractive 45-acre site and gracious, purpose-built premises 1931 (peacocks roam the quad); later additions include splendid £11 million science, technology and art complex, fine music hall, sports centre. Whitgift Foundation derives substantial income from Croydon shopping centre – built on land it owns. Old people's home in the grounds.

Atmosphere Civilised, friendly, well-disciplined; school is divided into four sections, helping to break down the size. Smart blazer-and-tie uniform (gold-edged for sports colours); sixth-formers wear dark suits.

Admissions At 10, 11 by competitive tests in English, maths, verbal reasoning and mental ability (syllabus available on request); at 13 by Common Entrance ('The standard required is well above that accepted at most independent schools'). Pupils drawn from a wide range of social backgrounds in an extensive catchment area (good transport links). About 45% receive some help with fees, including 180 who hold assisted places, which the Whitgift Foundation aims to replace with a scheme of its own; school gives away about £1 million a year ('No parents who would like their son to come to Whitgift need be deterred by financial reasons from applying'); six East European pupils accommodated and educated free. Scholarships for music, art, technology, all-rounders; talented musicians and sportsmen particularly welcomed.

The head Good manager, strong leader, full of ideas. Read history at Oxford (DPhil); previously head of history at Bradfield, second master at Dauntsey's (qv). Speaks French, Russian; introduced Japanese. Has raised academic standards considerably. Married; four children (three are pupils here).

The teaching Challenging, lively; hard-working, relatively youthful staff of 105 (75% male). Broad curriculum: sciences taught separately; all do two languages (one a year early for GCSE), some three; choice includes Japanese, Spanish, Italian, German, Latin, Greek (classical and modern); many take 11 GCSEs; 23 subjects offered at A-level; all do general studies courses (vehicle maintenance popular). Average class size 24, reducing to 20 for GCSE, 10 in the sixth form; half-termly grades for effort and achievement. Music a real strength: 60% play an instrument (all learn a stringed instrument for the first term); wide variety of instrumental and choral groups. Extra-curricular activities include chess, debating, cadet force, Duke of Edinburgh award scheme. Regular visits to, and exchanges with, nine countries including Japan, Russia, Scandinavia, USA.

Results (1997) GCSE: all gained at least five grades at A–C. A-level: creditable 69% of entries graded A or B.

Destinations Nearly all proceed to university (up to 20 a year to Oxbridge).

Sport Fine facilities include extensive playing fields, all-weather pitch, indoor pool, climbing wall, fencing salle, shooting range, courts for squash, tennis, fives. Main sports: rugby, hockey, cricket, athletics, swimming. Water polo, basketball, canoeing, badminton, cross-country, golf, table tennis also on offer; all expected to represent the school at something; regular county, regional, national honours. **Remarks** HMC inspectors concluded (1995): 'Whitgift's academic standards are high and rising. The teaching staff are numerous, well qualified and hard working. Boys are happy and proud to be members of the school.' Recommended.

WILSON'S ♂
Mollison Drive, Wallington, Surrey SM6 9JW. Tel (0181) 773 2931

Synopsis
Grammar (grant-maintained) ★ Boys ★ Ages 11–18 ★ 816 pupils ★ 210 in sixth form
Head: Christopher Tarrant, 44, appointed 1994.
Traditional but unstuffy grammar school; consistently good results; strong sport.

Profile
Background Founded in Camberwell 1615; became a voluntary-aided Church of England grammar school 1944; moved to present purpose-built premises on the edge of Croydon airfield 1975; opted out of council control 1989 (one of the first to do so). Cheap utilitarian buildings (bare brick walls), on a flat site lack charisma but facilities are adequate; latest additions include large sixth-form centre.

Atmosphere Lively, friendly, informal; easy relations between staff and boys. Uniform adhered to.

Admissions School severely over-subscribed (800 apply for 120 places); entry by tests in English, maths, reasoning. Pupils drawn from more than 100 primaries in a catchment area that extends into Surrey, Bromley and other London boroughs; wide social mix; 22% from ethnic minorities.

The head Energetic, enthusiastic. Read geography at Cambridge; worked in Nigeria for VSO; took a degree in theology; taught at Whitgift and Aylesbury Grammar. Active Christian; has published several books on theology. Married (to a GP); three children.

The teaching Mostly traditional in style; long-serving, dedicated staff. Grammar school curriculum: all do French, German and some Latin; Greek available for enthusiasts; science on offer as three separate subjects; some take GCSE maths a year early; good facilities for design/technology. GCSE and A-level options include economics, geology, physical education, business studies, computer studies. Lots of music (choir, orchestra, wind band, string ensemble) and drama. Extra-curricular activities include active cadet force. School owns a field studies centre in the Brecon Beacons. Numerous foreign trips.

Results (1997) GCSE: 97% gained at least five grades A–C. A-level: 52% of entries graded A or B.

Destinations About 85% stay on for A-levels; of these, 95% proceed to higher education.

Sport Very strong. All major games on offer; teams do particularly well in football, cross-country, athletics, badminton, water polo. Good facilities include playing fields, gym, squash courts, first-rate swimming pool.

Remarks Ofsted inspectors concluded (1993): 'This is a very successful school. Its pupils achieve the high academic standards set in most areas of work. Responsible and mature behaviour is fostered by sound relationships which exist throughout the school.'

WILLIAM HULME'S ♂ ♀
Spring Bridge Road, Manchester M16 8PR. Tel (0161) 226 2054

Synopsis
Independent ★ Co-educational ★ Day ★ Ages 11–18 ★ 746 pupils (66% boys)
★ 193 in sixth form ★ Fees: £4,455
Head: Bryan Purvis, 50, appointed September 1997.
Sound school; good teaching and results; strong sport.

Profile
Background Founded 1887; formerly Direct Grant, became fully independent 1976; co-educational since 1988. Imposing (but ageing) red-brick Victorian building (wood-panelled assembly hall decorated with honours boards) plus a conglomeration of later additions in spacious grounds on the southern outskirts of the city.

Atmosphere Busy, well-ordered; a harmonious community.

Admissions Heavily over-subscribed (nearly 700 apply for 120 places); entry by exams in English, maths, verbal reasoning. Phasing out of assisted places will have a significant impact, including a reduction in the total roll of 140 (20 fewer places a year). Main catchment areas: Timperley, Chorlton, Bowden, Hale.

The head New appointment. Energetic; good leader, strong disciplinarian. Read botany at London, MSc from Durham; previously head of Altrincham Boys' Grammar (qv). Married; three children.

The teaching Not highly academic but offering a good all-round education. Hard-working staff of 70 (two-thirds men). Broad curriculum: science taught as three separate subjects; all do Latin in first year, Greek, German, Spanish in second; most take nine GCSEs; choice of 23 subjects at A-level. Pupils grouped by ability from second year; progress closely monitored (mid-termly grades for aptitude, attitude); average class size 30, reducing to 20 for GCSE, eight at A-level. Lots of drama, music (choir, various ensembles). Extra-curricular activities include Duke of Edinburgh award scheme, community service, popular cadet force; school owns a field study centre in Wensleydale. Regular language exchanges with schools in France, Germany, Spain.

Results (1997) GCSE: 89% gained at least five grades A–C. A-level: 43% of entries graded A or B.

Destinations About 90% go on to university (average five a year to Oxbridge).

Sport Strong; regular county and national honours. Main sports: rugby, lacrosse (boys), hockey, netball (girls). Tennis, athletics, cricket, swimming also available. Facilities include sports hall, indoor pool.

Remarks A traditional grammar school education.

WIMBLEDON HIGH ♀
Mansel Road, London SW19 4AB. Tel (0181) 946 1756

Synopsis
Independent ★ Girls ★ Day ★ Ages 4–18 ★ 852 pupils (574 in senior school)
★ 139 in sixth form ★ Fees: £4,968
Head: Dr Jill Clough, 54, appointed 1995.
Busy, well-run academic school; lots of art, music, drama.

Profile
Background Founded 1880; a member of Girls' Day School Trust, which aims

to provide 'an all-round education of high quality for girls of intellectual promise at an affordable cost' – and does. Victorian buildings have a certain grace allied to considerable inconvenience (steep stairs, narrow passages); later additions more functional; some classrooms in 'temporary' huts. Urban site (elaborate security measures); space at a premium.

Atmosphere   Intensely busy (even the four-year-olds are absorbed in the task in hand) but uniformly courteous and friendly. Aim is to encourage every girl to have a 'well-informed enthusiasm for a wide range of interests' (not a school for the faint-hearted). Junior and senior departments closely integrated; senior pupils give a strong lead. Parents always welcome, either by appointment or at the weekly 'at home'.

Admissions   School heavily over-subscribed and highly selective; entry by tests, interview and practical exercises (teamwork, problem solving etc). Girls need to be academically able and have an extra 'something': creative flair, musical ability, lateral approach to problems, articulacy, originality etc. Four-year-old applicants (120 for 22 places) assessed on approach to games, communication with peers. Scholarships, bursaries, assisted places (which the trust will replace) ensure fairly wide social and ethnic mix; religious assemblies are multi-faith.

The head   Able, enthusiastic, experienced (her second headship); good manager; gets on well with staff and pupils. First-class degree in English from London; PhD (in 'the vocabulary of good and evil in 20th-century fiction') from Hull; teaches A-level English. Grown-up daughters.

The teaching   Highly qualified, predominantly female staff; lessons orderly, businesslike; average class size 22/23. All do two modern languages (from French, German, Spanish) and at least one year's Latin; Greek on offer; sciences taught as three separate subjects; good (if cramped) facilities for computing. All take 10 or 11 GCSEs (from a choice of 17) and three or four A-levels (choice of 21, including theatre studies, economics, geology). Superb art work everywhere; lots of music (choirs, instrumental groups) and drama (some in conjunction with boys of King's College School (qv). Extra-curricular activities include Duke of Edinburgh award scheme. Good careers advice.

Results   (1997) GCSE: all gained at least five grades A–C. A-level: 70% of entries gained A or B.

Destinations   Up to 15 a year leave for sixth forms elsewhere; almost all who stay on proceed to university (up to 15 a year to Oxbridge).

Sport   All participate. Usual team games: hockey, netball, basketball plus athletics, gymnastics, swimming (indoor pool). Tennis, badminton etc also on offer in sports centre.

Remarks   Very good school for academically able girls (shy, low-achievers would not flourish here).

WINCHESTER ♂
Winchester, Hampshire SO23 9NA. Tel (01962) 621100

Synopsis
Independent ★ Boys ★ Boarding and day ★ 683 pupils (95% boarding) ★ 280 in sixth form ★ Fees: £14,544 boarding; £10,908 day
Head: James Sabben-Clare, 56, appointed 1985.
Distinguished academic school; fine teaching and results; strong music.

Profile
Background   Founded 1382 by William of Wykeham, Bishop of Winchester, so

that 'scholars to the number of 60 and 10' might be instructed in Latin – 'without doubt the foundation, gateway and mainspring of all the liberal arts'. Beautifully situated (water meadows were the inspiration for Keats's 'Ode to Autumn'), richly endowed (owns 8,000 acres of southern England). Fine collection of buildings, including 14th-century chapel and hall, 17th-century schoolroom (possibly designed by Wren); memorial cloisters by Sir Herbert Baker. First-rate facilities for art, drama, music, design/technology, sport.

Atmosphere Friendly, stimulating, decidedly intellectual; informal relations between staff and boys (but they call their teachers 'Sir'). School steeped in tradition (including an archaic language called 'notions', much of it Anglo-Saxon in origin); compulsory Sunday chapel; scholars in gowns, commoners wear own clothes.

Admissions Highly selective: 90% are in the top 10% of the ability range; 25% are in the top 1%. Applications (usually to a house) after eighth birthday; housemasters interview and test boys (in verbal reasoning, numeracy – past papers available) at 10¼–11; offer of a place is conditional on a candidate passing the three-day entry exam (similar syllabus to Common Entrance but more searching questions). Those admitted need to have the potential to excel at something – if only to keep their end up in a high-pressure, competitive environment. Ten houses (plus one for scholars) are potent communities, varying in character: careful choice advised. Up to 15 scholarships a year; means-tested bursaries available.

The head Low key, very able (and conscious of running a decentralised school in which much of the power lies with housemasters and heads of departments). Steeped in the school (and has written a history of it): came here as a scholar (as did his father); read classics at Oxford (First); became head of classics at 28; second master 10 years later. Married (to a barrister); two grown-up children.

The teaching Outstanding: enthusiastic, highly qualified staff; curriculum extends far beyond the requirements of public exams; boys encouraged to go at their own (daunting) pace (many move on to A-level courses before taking GCSE; others are doing university work well before A-levels). Compulsory Latin; many do three languages (Russian, Japanese, Mandarin on offer); exceptionally strong maths, science (taught and examined as three separate subjects), computing; vibrant design/technology; choice of 20 subjects at A-level. Pupils grouped by ability in some subjects from the start; average class size 18–22, reducing to 12–16 in the sixth form. Excellent music (about half learn at least one instrument); flourishing drama. Extracurricular activities include book-binding, campanology, chess, bridge, pot-holing.

Results (1997) GCSE: all gained at least five grades A–C. A-level: impressive 88% of entries graded A or B (fourth in the league table).

Destinations Virtually all go on to university (average of 35% to Oxbridge).

Sport Choice of 28; standards are high. Facilities include extensive playing fields, well-equipped gym, indoor pool.

Remarks Marvellous school for robust, able boys.

WINDSOR BOYS' ♂
1 Maidenhead Road, Windsor, Berkshire SL4 5EH. Tel (01753) 716060

Synopsis
Comprehensive ★ Boys ★ Ages 13–18 ★ 875 pupils ★ 210 in sixth form
Head: Jeffrey Dawkins, 46, appointed September 1997.
Strongly traditional school; good teaching and results; first-rate sport.

Profile

Background   Founded 1906; previously a grammar school, went comprehensive 1977. Original utilitarian brick buildings date from late 1930s; large, stylish, much-needed addition (new classrooms, science labs, sixth-form centre etc) opened by the Queen in 1994.

Atmosphere   Friendly: nothing formal here; liberal use of old-fashioned sticks, carrots and kindness. Staff are continually raising boys' sights, and there is a sense of shared aims (and jokes). Speech day with lots of cups; World War One memorials still on the walls. Uniform worn throughout.

Admissions   School over-subscribed; priority to those who live nearest or attend a 'feeder' primary. Full cross-section of ability.

The head   New appointment (predecessor had been in post 19 years). Has a degree in Semitic languages from Cardiff, MEd from Reading; previously head of a comprehensive in Reading. Keen on rugby, music. Married; three children.

The teaching   Good. Long-serving staff (more than a quarter have been here more than 20 years, more than a third all their teaching careers). Standard national curriculum; science on offer as three separate subjects; technology popular; GCSE options include motor vehicle studies. A-level choices carefully guided (no sociology, law or psychology); one-year vocational alternative available. Pupils grouped by ability; extra help for those who need it. Plenty of music: brass, wind, jazz; drama in new studio theatre. Lots of community and charity activities. School opens soon after 7 am, and lock-up is late.

Results   (1997) GCSE: creditable 66% gained at least five grades A–C. A-level: 41% of entries graded A or B.

Destinations   About 70% stay on after GCSE; of those, 70% proceed to university (average of three a year to Oxbridge).

Sport   Taken seriously: fiercely competitive boys have gained representative honours in 11 sports in recent years; rowing club is the most successful in the state sector, more than holding its own with much better-funded independent school clubs; rugby also strong. Facilities include new sports hall, cricket pavilion, floodlit all-weather pitch; playing fields not extensive.

Remarks   Some fathers will recognise here the type of school they once knew. Boys leave with high standards of behaviour and interests for life.

WIRRAL BOYS' GRAMMAR ♂

Cross Lane, Bebington, Wirral L63 3AQ. Tel (0151) 644 0908

Synopsis

Grammar (grant-maintained) ★ Boys ★ Ages 11–18 ★ 970 pupils ★ 250 in sixth form
Head: Tony Cooper, 52, appointed April 1997.
Successful grammar school; good teaching and results; very strong sport.

Profile

Background   Founded 1931 next door to sister school (qv); opted out of council control 1993. Solid, dignified buildings plus many later additions in pleasant residential area (good road and rail links); facilities include attractive library, lecture theatre, spacious sixth-form centre, drama studio, new £400,000 sports hall. Harold Wilson was the first head boy (1933–34).

Atmosphere   Serious, earnest; emphasis on good discipline, high expectations;

warm relations between staff and hard-working, well-mannered pupils; good pastoral care system. Corridors lined with striking art work and photographs of the assembled multitude over the years. School enjoys strong parental support.

Admissions   By local authority 11-plus; top 25% of the ability range, mostly from middle-class homes in a catchment area that extends from Liverpool and north Cheshire to North Wales.

The head   Has been here since he started teaching in 1967; became deputy head 1986. Read classics at Newcastle (having been inspired at 13 by his Latin master to become a teacher). Married; four children.

The teaching   Good quality. Professional, dedicated staff of 60 (seven PhDs); low turnover. Broad curriculum; science on offer as three separate subjects; computers everywhere; all do French; German available from second year. Wide choice of 25 subjects for GCSE, 20 at A-level, including general studies, government & politics, law (very popular and imaginatively taught). Pupils grouped by ability in maths, French from second year, science from third year; average class size 30, reducing to 14 in sixth form. Homework compulsory and rigorously monitored. Very strong drama (many productions in conjunction with girls' school). Lots of music: 140 learn an instrument; two orchestras, two choirs. Long list of extra-curricular activities, including young engineers' club, debating society, computer club, Christian Union.

Results   (1997) GCSE: 96% gained at least five grades A–C. A-level: 50% of entries graded A or B.

Destinations   More than 90% stay on for A-levels; of these, about 90% proceed to university (four or five a year to Oxbridge).

Sport   Very strong: up to 200 play on Saturdays. Main games: rugby, hockey, cricket, athletics; many gain county honours. Facilities include 26 acres of playing fields, new sports hall.

Remarks   Ofsted inspectors concluded (1996): 'This is a highly successful grammar school which enjoys a well deserved reputation for high standards of academic, cultural and athletic achievement. It is well managed and provides a very good quality of education and excellent pastoral care.'

WIRRAL GIRLS' GRAMMAR ♀
Heath Road, Bebington, Wirral, Merseyside L63 3AF. Tel (0151) 644 8282

Synopsis
Grammar ★ Girls ★ Ages 11–18 ★ 1,005 pupils ★ 235 in sixth form
Head: Miss Alice Wakefield, 54, appointed 1994.
Traditional grammar school; good teaching and results; strong sport and music.

Profile
Background   Founded 1931; main building has a red-brick, municipal dignity; many later additions, including tower block shared with neighbouring Wirral Boys' (qv). Attractive suburban setting; good transport links to Birkenhead and Liverpool.

Atmosphere   Civilised: formality ('Pupils should stand up when staff walk in') without stuffiness; emphasis on high expectations, self-discipline, minimum rules. Morning assembly includes period of silent reflection. Strong sense of a community that cares about all its members; sixth-formers notably mature. Much concern for the disadvantaged and suffering: each class adopts a charity.

Admissions   School heavily over-subscribed; entry by verbal reasoning tests;

top third of the ability range, predominantly from middle-class homes in surrounding small towns and rural areas.

The head   Widely experienced: former local authority adviser, Ofsted inspector, teacher trainer; her second headship. Read English at Oxford (and taught it first in Canada). Staff say she leads them with vision and humour; gets on well with parents.

The teaching   Formal rather than avant garde. Hard-working, dedicated staff of 66 (16 men) who enjoy excellent relationships with each other and pupils. Standard grammar school curriculum; all do French and add Spanish or German in second year; science on offer as three separate subjects; good facilities for computing; wide choice of 25 subjects for GCSE (most take 10/11), 23 at A-level, including business studies, sociology, theatre studies. Pupils grouped by ability in English, maths, languages; average class size 30, smaller for GCSE; sixth-form groups up to 20. Very strong music: 250 learn an instrument (20 visiting tutors); four choirs, two orchestras, various ensembles. Large and varied extra-curricular programme, including Duke of Edinburgh award scheme, Christian Union, debating, drama. Regular language trips to France, Germany, Spain.

Results   (1997) GCSE: 96% gained at least five grades A–C. A-level: 44% of entries graded A or B.

Destinations   About 85% stay on for A-levels; of these, 80% proceed to university.

Sport   Strong sporting tradition but poor facilities (no sports hall or swimming pool). Main games: netball (regular national finalists), lacrosse (county players), tennis, rounders, athletics, trampolining.

Remarks   Successful, happy school.

WITHINGTON GIRLS' ♀
Wellington Road, Fallowfield, Manchester M14 6BL. Tel (0161) 224 1077

Synopsis
Independent ★ Girls ★ Day ★ Ages 11–18 (plus associated junior school) ★
495 pupils ★ 144 in sixth-form ★ Fees: £4,125
Head: Mrs Margaret Kenyon, 57, appointed 1986.
Outstanding academic school; very good teaching and results; strong music, drama.

Profile
Background   Founded 1890 by a group of eminent Mancunians (including C P Scott, for 50 years editor of *The Manchester Guardian*) to give 'a thoroughly efficient education to girls'; emphasis on science and work as its own reward (no other prizes permitted); formerly Direct Grant, reverted to full independence 1976. Moved 1903 to Victorian premises of a former boys' school on a nine-acre site three miles south of the city centre; buildings substantially modernised and refurbished; later additions include centenary sports hall, new chemistry labs, modern languages suite.

Atmosphere   Strongly academic; assured, assertive, achieving ('The world makes the girls competitive, not the school'). The small size – stipulated by the founders to allow for individual development – encourages excellent, mutually respectful relations between staff and pupils, who are immensely proud of the school and its traditions. No uniform in the sixth form (a decision made by the girls). School remains open until 5.30 pm to enable working mothers to collect their daughters.

Admissions   School is heavily over-subscribed (three apply for each place). Entry by searching tests in English, maths followed by interview. Phasing out of assisted places, which 20% hold, will reduce the social mix (though fees are comparatively modest); up to 10 bursaries a year.

The head   Charming, very able. Read modern languages at Oxford; came here as head of French in 1983. Pleased to find that 'girls are thinking much more like boys now in terms of their careers'; notes that girls' schools are the 'very last institutions which exist only for girls'. Married (to a leading businessman and educationist); two grown-up sons.

The teaching   Exceptionally high-quality, largely formal in style; highly-qualified, committed staff of 40 (two men), 10% with PhDs. Broad curriculum; all do Latin for first three years; very strong maths and science (on offer as three separate subjects); lots of computing; choice of 20 subjects at A-level (maths the largest entry). Average class size 24, reducing to five–15 in the sixth form. First-rate drama (annual production in conjunction with Manchester Grammar, qv) and music; half learn an instrument; five choirs, two orchestras, various ensembles. Extra-curricular activities include Duke of Edinburgh award scheme and much charitable work.

Results   (1997) GCSE: all gained at least five grades A–C. A-level: impressive 90% of entries graded A or B (third in the league table – its best position ever).

Destinations   Nearly all stay on for A-levels and proceed to university (average of nine a year to Oxbridge), more than a third to study maths, science, medicine or engineering.

Sport   Particularly strong lacrosse, tennis, netball. Facilities include sports hall, extensive playing fields.

Remarks   First-rate school for girls who are keen to get ahead; highly recommended.

WOLDINGHAM   ♀
Marden Park, Woldingham, Surrey CR3 7YA. Tel (01883) 349431

Synopsis
Independent ★ Roman Catholic ★ Girls ★ Boarding and day ★ Ages 11–18 ★ 545 pupils (85% boarding) ★ 130 in sixth form ★ Fees: £12,612 boarding; £7,629 day
Head: Mrs Maureen Ribbins, 50, appointed September 1997.
Well-run, delightful school; good teaching and results; fine facilities.

Profile
Background   Founded as a convent school in 1842 by the Society of the Sacred Heart; moved to present premises 1946; beautifully restored late 17th-century mansion in gracious grounds surrounded by 600 acres of secluded farmland. Under lay management since 1985; the society are still the trustees (nuns no longer teach but three live here). Roman Catholic in the ecumenical tradition: other denominations welcomed.

Atmosphere   Happy yet purposeful: a real sense of community; friendly, respectful relations between staff and pupils. High standards of work and behaviour expected and achieved; individuals encouraged to aim for their personal best, take responsibility for their own lives, contribute to the community. Excellent pastoral care system: any difficulties soon picked up. Strong parental support; close liaison encouraged.

Admissions   By Common Entrance; school is not unduly selective; most have IQs of 110–120. Strong international element (20% from abroad, half from expatriate families) but most parents live within an hour's travel; many are 'first-time buyers' of independent education and tend to want their children home as often as possible at weekends. Juniors (ages 11–12) housed in functional, slightly featureless premises set a little apart; seniors in main building have own study-bedrooms; upper-sixth house is palatial. Some scholarships, bursaries.

The head New appointment; previously head for 14 years of Wolverhampton Girls' High (qv). Read physics at Oxford; further degrees in biology, solid state physics. Married (to a professor of education).

The teaching Lively, high quality; well-qualified, dedicated staff. Traditional emphasis on solid grounding, accuracy and presentation, combined with the latest equipment and up-to-the minute thinking. Broad curriculum: most take nine or 10 GCSEs, including two languages (a particular strength – Japanese recently introduced); science on offer as three separate subjects; good facilities for computing and technology. Pupils grouped by ability in some subjects; remedial help available; average class size 18. All taught study skills and use of library (superb facilities, sophisticated computer network). Good art: specialist rooms for sculpture, pottery, photography. Strong music tradition (department currently housed in wooden huts); lively singing. First-rate careers advice: starts in third year and constantly available. Lots of extra-curricular activities; many girls involved in voluntary work of various kinds. Strong links and regular exchanges with Sacred Heart schools abroad (185 in 35 countries).

Results (1997) GCSE: 99% gained at least five grades A–C. A-level: creditable 65% of entries graded A or B.

Destinations About 85% continue into the sixth form; of these, all proceed to university (about eight a year to Oxbridge).

Sport An important part of the curriculum: daily participation, high standards, reasonable record against other schools. Main activities: hockey, netball, cross-country, orienteering, swimming, athletics, tennis. Facilities include sports hall, indoor heated pool, 14 tennis courts, well-equipped (and very popular) fitness studio.

Remarks Happy, successful school; recommended.

WOLVERHAMPTON GIRLS' HIGH ♀

Tettenhall Road, Wolverhampton WV6 0BY. Tel (01902) 312186

Synopsis

Grammar (grant-maintained) ★ Girls ★ Ages 11–18 ★ 670 pupils ★ 160 in sixth form
Head: Mrs Dru James, 43, appointed September 1997.
Successful, academic school; first-rate teaching and results; strong sport.

Profile

Background Opened 1911; opted out of council control 1990; achieved language college status 1997. Traditional stone and red-brick buildings on a pleasant site; light, airy classrooms; good, new facilities for technology, science.

Atmosphere Friendly, well-disciplined, reassuring ('We cherish our traditional ethos but we know we must equip our girls for a future full of change'). 'Do follow your dreams,' girls are told. 'Be ambitious, but remember that success in any field means hard work, and a dream without application and perseverance will stay a dream'. Smart uniform (including striped tie) worn by all (leading some locals to believe it is an independent school).

Admissions School heavily over-subscribed: 460 take the (rigorous) entrance exam for 108 places. Pupils of a wide range of social and ethnic backgrounds drawn from a 20-mile radius.

The head Recent appointment but not new to the school: came here as head of English 1989, became deputy head 1994. Read English at Leeds; MEd from Birmingham; accomplished pianist. Married (to a deputy head); one daughter.

The teaching Competent, confident; varied styles; enthusiastic, youthful staff of 50 (seven men). First-rate languages: all first-years do German, Russian, Latin ('an integral part of the cultural heritage of the western world') and add French in second year; Japanese, Spanish, Italian, Mandarin Chinese also on offer; science taught (but not examined) as three separate subjects; chemistry, biology, English and maths are the most popular subjects at A-level. Pupils grouped by ability in GCSE English, maths, science. Lots of music; regular concerts. Wide range of extra-curricular activities, including Young Enterprise, debating, drama, Duke of Edinburgh award scheme.

Results (1997) GCSE: all gained at least five grades A–C. A-level: 56% of entries graded A or B.

Destinations About 85% stay on for A-levels; of these, 90% proceed to university (four or five a year to Oxbridge).

Sport 'We make a clean sweep of the leagues': girls are as competitive on the games field as in the classroom; tennis and hockey particularly strong.

Remarks Ofsted inspectors concluded (1995): 'The school sets high standards and achieves them. The quality of education is predominantly good and sometimes outstanding.'

WOLVERHAMPTON GRAMMAR ♂ ♀
Compton Road, Wolverhampton WV3 9RB. Tel (01902) 421326

Synopsis
Independent ★ Co-educational ★ Day ★ Ages 11–18 ★ 760 pupils (70% boys) ★ 224 in sixth form ★ Fees: £5,400
Head: Dr Bernard Trafford, 41, appointed 1990.
Successful, well-run school; good teaching and results; strong music and sport.

Profile
Background Founded 1512 for 'the instruction of youth in good manners and learning'; moved 1875 to present 25-acre suburban site; became a grammar school 1944; went independent 1979 (to avoid closure by the council); fully co-educational since 1992. Impressive Victorian-Gothic main building plus many later additions, including library, sixth-form centre, £1 million sports hall; dining room, though, is dreary.

Atmosphere Orderly, friendly, buzzing with activity; good relations between head, staff and (smartly-uniformed) pupils. Well-organised pastoral care system (firm action against bullying).

Admissions Main entry at 11 (from primary schools) by tests in English, maths, verbal reasoning (minimum score of 117 required); at 13 by tests in the above plus French. School has been heavily over-subscribed but Labour's phasing out of assisted places, which 40% hold, is likely to make entry less competitive and change the social mix. Catchment area covers parts of the West Midlands, Staffordshire, Shropshire, Worcestershire; 20% Asian. Scholarships, bursaries available.

The head   Able, dynamic, well-respected; keen on consultation (PhD from Birmingham in school democracy) but has given the school a clear sense of direction. Talented musician (organ scholar at Oxford); came here in 1981 as director of music. Married; two daughters (both pupils here).

The teaching   Good quality; challenging in a mixture of styles. Hard-working, fairly youthful staff of 66 (two-thirds male), half appointed by present head. Broad curriculum: all do French, German, Latin for first two years; science on offer as three separate subjects; plenty of computing. Average class size 21, reducing to 10 or fewer in the sixth form. Particularly good provision for personal, social & health education and careers advice. Stimulating music; flourishing drama; wide range of extra-curricular activities.

Results   (1997) GCSE: all gained at least five grades A–C. A-level: creditable 62% of entries graded A or B.

Destinations   Nearly all stay on for A-levels; 90% of these proceed to university (up to 10 a year to Oxbridge).

Sport   Strong, particularly in football, rugby, volleyball, cricket, athletics, hockey, netball, tennis, shooting, gymnastics. First-rate facilities, including sports hall, squash courts, well-maintained playing fields.

Remarks   '/=A fine school,' concluded HMC inspectors (1994).

WOODBRIDGE ♂ ♀
Burkitt Road, Woodbridge, Suffolk IP12 4JH. Tel (01394) 385547

Synopsis
Independent ★ Co-educational ★ Day and sixth-form boarding ★ Ages 11–18 (plus associated junior school) ★ 540 pupils (equal numbers of girls and boys, 95% day) ★ 180 in sixth form ★ Fees: £5,958 day; £9,789 boarding
Head: Stephen Cole, 45 appointed 1994.
Good teaching and results; strong music; attractive location.

Profile
Background   Founded 1662; moved 1864 to attractive, 45-acre, wooded site overlooking the town; fully co-educational since 1974; formerly Direct Grant, reverted to full independence 1976. Good facilities for science, computing, music.

Atmosphere   Supportive, caring, well-ordered; becoming more academically demanding.

Admissions   School is over-subscribed (120 apply for 80 places) and fairly selective; entry at 11 by interview and exam, at 13 by Common Entrance. Assisted places, which more than 100 hold, will be replaced by school's own bursaries (funded by generous 19th-century endowment). Catchment extends to Ipswich, Felixstowe. Sixth-form boarders (some from abroad) in small, co-educational hall of residence (a preparation for university).

The head   Open, energetic; good leader (has presided over a big improvement in results). Read physics at Oxford; formerly head of science and housemaster at Merchant Taylors', Northwood (qv). Keen sportsman, runs marathons. Married (wife much involved in school); two grown-up children.

The teaching   Traditional in style but more informal higher up the school. Staff of 60 (60% male), 40% appointed by present head (a brisk turnover). Broad curriculum: science on offer as three separate subjects; lots of computing. Extra help for dyslexics; average class size 18–20, reducing to 12 in sixth form. Strong music; two orchestras, choir. Extra-curricular activities include cadet force, well-supported Duke of Edinburgh award scheme. Regular language exchanges with schools in France, Germany.

Results   (1997) GCSE: 98% gained at least five grades A–C. A-level: 52% of entries graded A or B.

Destinations   Of those who stay on for A-levels, about 90% proceed to university.

Sport   Facilities include floodlit, all-weather pitch, sports hall, outdoor pool. Main sports: rugby, hockey, netball, cricket, tennis, athletics, sailing, swimming.

Remarks   Good school for all-rounders; one to watch.

WOODFORD COUNTY HIGH   ♀
High Road, Woodford Green, Essex IG8 9LA. Tel (0181) 504 0611

Synopsis
Grammar ★ Girls ★ Ages 11–18 ★ 785 pupils ★ 200 in sixth form
Head: Miss Helen Cleland, 46, appointed 1991.
Successful school; very good teaching and results; strong art and music; lots of extra-curricular activities.

Profile
Background   Opened 1919 in classical 18th-century manor house set in attractive and extensive grounds on a ridge between the Roding and Lee valleys; sympathetic later additions. Numbers increasing; further building planned.

Atmosphere   Work hard, play hard: able girls expected to take their studies in their stride and have time for activities and fun. Sport, music, drama, clubs and charity work all have a high profile. Strong parental support.

Admissions   By local authority tests in verbal and non-verbal reasoning; top 10% of the ability range from all social and ethnic backgrounds (all successfully integrated).

The head   Read English at Exeter; previously deputy head of a co-educational comprehensive. Married; two children at independent schools.

The teaching   Fairly traditional in style but with a big emphasis on discussion; able, committed staff, 75% women. Standard curriculum; all do French plus, from second year, Latin, German or Italian; all take nine or 10 GCSEs; art popular. Pupils grouped by ability in maths, science (dual-award) but most other teaching is in randomly selected form groups; progress carefully monitored. A-level entries equally balanced between sciences and humanities; all sixth-formers take philosophy of religion course; self-defence, yoga, secretarial skills also on offer. Very strong music: half learn an instrument; two choirs, two orchestras, various instrumental groups. Wide programme of extra-curricular activities; much charity and work and fund-raising. Regular trips to France, Italy, Greece.

Results   (1997) GCSE: 98% gained at least five grades A–C. A-level: very creditable 69% of entries graded A or B.

Destinations   About 90% continue into the sixth form; of these, 90% proceed to university (average of eight a year to Oxbridge).

Sport   Chiefly netball and hockey (county players). Rounders, athletics, tennis, volleyball, badminton, football, dance, gymnastics, trampolining also on offer.

Remarks   Ofsted inspectors concluded (1994): 'This is a very good school. Work of real excellence is done in many subjects. Standards of behaviour are exemplary, yet pupils are not suppressed.'

WORCESTER ROYAL GRAMMAR ♂
Upper Tything, Worcester WR1 1HP. Tel (01905) 613391

> ### Synopsis
> Independent ★ Boys ★ Day ★ Ages 11–18 (plus associated junior school) ★ 768 pupils ★ 205 in sixth form ★ Fees: £4,590.
> Head: Walter Jones, 48, appointed 1993.
> *Traditional academic school; good teaching and results; strong sport.*

Profile
Background   Roots go back to 1291; Elizabethan charter 1561; moved 1868 to purpose-built, red-brick premises on a city-centre site (formerly a nunnery); became a voluntary-aided grammar school 1945; reverted to independence 1983. Later additions include sixth-form centre, eye-catching design centre (in a street near by). Junior school (220 pupils aged three to 11) on same site.

Atmosphere   Purposeful, well-disciplined (detention on Saturday mornings); strong sporting ethos; down-to-earth boys. Traditional blazer-and-tie uniform.

Admissions   By school's own tests; top 25% of the ability range from a 25-mile radius catchment area; demand is strong, and the phasing out of assisted places, which about 40 hold, is not expected to have much impact. Sixth-form entry requires at least six GCSEs averaging grade B. Scholarships, bursaries available.

The head   Relaxed in style, determined in temperament; respected by staff and pupils. Read economics at Cambridge; previously deputy head of King's, Bruton. Keen on rugby; teaches economics and business studies. Married; three children.

The teaching   Good quality; mostly traditional in style; committed, predominantly male staff. Fairly broad curriculum; science on offer as three separate subjects; languages include German, Latin, Russian; A-level options include PE, ancient history. Pupils grouped by ability in maths, French from second year, in English, science for GCSE; average class size 22–24, reducing to a maximum of 16 at A-level. Plenty of music (fine organ). Duke of Edinburgh award scheme. Regular language exchanges with pupils in France, Germany, Russia.

Results   (1997) GCSE: 99% gained at least five grades A–C. A-level: 51% of entries graded A or B.

Destinations   About 80% stay on for A-levels; of these, virtually all proceed to university (average of eight a year to Oxbridge).

Sport   Strong, particularly rugby, hockey, soccer, cricket, rowing. Athletics, cross-country, swimming, badminton, basketball, tennis, golf, fencing, squash also on offer. Facilities include new sports hall; two playing fields close by.

Remarks   Solid, all-round school.

WORTH ♂
Turners Hill, Crawley, West Sussex RH10 4SD. Tel (01342) 710200

> ### Synopsis
> Independent ★ Roman Catholic ★ Boys ★ Boarding and day ★ Ages 11–18 ★ 370 pupils (70% boarding) ★ 120 in sixth form ★ Fees: £12,552 boarding; £8,595 day
> Head: Father Christopher Jamison, 46, appointed 1994.
> *Sound school; strong religious ethos; good teaching and results; lots of computing.*

Profile
Background   Founded by Benedictines in 1933 as a prep school for Downside (qv); monastery became independent 1957; senior school opened 1959. Late 19th-century country house (in constant need of repair) plus many later additions (including modern abbey church) in a beautiful 500-acre park; recent £500,000 donation has led to an inundation of computers ('a Benedictine school for a changing world'); £1.2 million performing arts centre on the way.

Atmosphere   Friendly, dignified, spacious. Five 'key features' of equal importance: work ('computers built into every aspect of learning'); play ('all major team sports'); love ('care of the boys is a central concern'); morality ('to provide stability in the moral confusion of the world today'); religion ('each person is on a spiritual journey through life').

Admissions   Barely selective: numbers (particularly boarding) have been falling; phasing out of assisted places, which about a third hold, will severely aggravate the situation. Entry at 11 by 'simple assessment of aptitude'; at 13 by Common Entrance (55% mark preferred); requirements waived for 10% who have special needs, especially dyslexia. About 85% are Catholics but there are a growing number of Christians from other denominations; 70% live within an hour of the school (buses run to nearby towns including East Grinstead, Haywards Heath); 20% expatriate; 5% foreign. Dormitories functional, some recently refurbished; some housemasters are monks. Scholarships available.

The head   Devout, fiercely intellectual monk; swims, runs, laughs a lot; very keen on computers ('Our global village is on the verge of a cultural shift'). Educated at Downside; read French and Spanish at Oxford (where he decided to become a monk), philosophy and theology at London. Has been here since 1978; became head of religious studies and a housemaster. Staff praise his vision and leadership but grumble – perhaps seriously – that he takes effort for granted. Daily 'open door' for pupils to come and talk: there is usually a queue.

The teaching   In throes of change: becoming less formal, more 'pupil-centred'; computers (one to every three boys) in the process of becoming as 'available as the book'; 40 staff (including eight monks) mastering their laptops. Standard curriculum; Latin and Greek on offer; science can be taken as three separate subjects. Pupils grouped by ability; specialist help for those who need it; average class size 20. Lots of drama, music (orchestra, flourishing choir). Extra-curricular activities include well-supported Duke of Edinburgh award scheme, extensive community service programme (soup runs to down-and-outs in Brighton).

Results   (1997) GCSE: 95% gained at least five grades 5 A–C. A-level: 64% of entries graded A or B (105th in the league table – its best position ever).

Destinations   Most stay on into the sixth form and proceed to university (including Oxbridge).

Sport   Main games: rugby, soccer, cricket. Tennis, squash (two new courts), fencing, cross-country also available.

Remarks   Good all round.

WREKIN ♂ ♀
Wellington, Telford, Shropshire TF1 3BG. Tel (01952) 242305

Synopsis
Independent ★ Co-educational ★ Day and boarding ★ Ages 11–18 ★ 300 pupils (66% day, 60% boys) ★ 135 in sixth form ★ Fees: £6,350–£7,350 day; £12,450 boarding
Head: Peter Johnson, 49, appointed 1991 (leaves August 1998).
Small, friendly school; fairly wide range of abilities; good art, drama, music, sport.

Profile
Background Founded 1880; Victorian-Gothic buildings plus various later additions on a spacious, airy campus (attractive gardens, immaculate lawns). Co-educational since 1983; proportion of day pupils has steadily increased.
Atmosphere Friendly, busy; no social airs. Traditional morning chapel. Most staff live on site.
Admissions By Common Entrance or school's own tests. Fairly wide range of abilities; mostly from farming/business backgrounds. Boarding accommodation varies from adequate to near-luxury. Scholarships, bursaries available.
The head Forceful, vigorous, enthusiastic ('work hard, play hard is my philosophy'). Read geography at Oxford (Blues for rugby, judo); spent five years in the Army before switching to teaching; 15 years at Radley (senior housemaster). Has tightened up on discipline ('but I'm not a military dictator'); determined to raise academic standards ('being good at rugby doesn't get you a job'); very keen on music, drama (introduced daily one-hour 'protected cultural time' – dubbed 'happy hour' by pupils). Met his wife when both were still at school – 'so I can't pooh-pooh school romances'. Becomes head of Millfield (qv) September 1998.
The teaching Generally formal in style. Pupils grouped by ability into four bands; further setting in maths, French; extra help for those who need it, including dyslexics; maximum class size 20. Standard curriculum; up to a third take German in addition to French; Latin on offer to GCSE; strong science (available as three separate subjects). Choice of 17 subjects at A-level, including economics, theatre studies, social biology; most take three. Particularly good art (in attractive department); first-rate drama (some inspired teaching); flourishing music (a third learn an instrument – choir, orchestra, smaller ensembles). Extra curricular activities include cadet force (compulsory for first-years), well-supported Duke of Edinburgh award scheme, popular debating.
Results (1997) GCSE: 80% gained at least five grades A–C. A-level: 41% of entries graded A or B.
Destinations About 90% stay on for A-levels; of these, 90% proceed to university.
Sport An important part of school life; regular tours abroad. Main games: rugby, cricket, hockey, netball, basketball, fencing, cross-country, gymnastics. Facilities include 50 acres of playing fields, two sports halls, six squash courts, six tennis/netball courts, outdoor pool.
Remarks Sound school.

WYCLIFFE ♂ ♀
Stonehouse, Gloucestershire GL10 2JQ. Tel (01453) 822432

Synopsis
Independent ★ Co-educational ★ Boarding and day ★ Ages 13–18 (plus associated junior school) ★ 400 pupils (65% boys; 63% boarding) ★ 200 in sixth form ★ Fees: £12,750 boarding; £9,000 day
Head: David Prichard, 63, appointed 1994 (retiring April 1998).
Successful, friendly school; sound teaching and results; good music, drama, sport.

Profile
Background Founded 1882; mellow Georgian building plus less attractive, functional additions on 60-acre site; interiors clean, presentable; further building under way. Likes to be known as the 'Pre-University College of the Cotswolds'. Junior school on adjacent campus.

Atmosphere Friendly, easy-going; nothing to intimidate (no knees would knock coming here); unsophisticated, bordering on provincial. Spiritual dimension taken seriously (fine chapel built by staff and boys in the 1950s, using material from an old church). Impressive degree of contact with parents. Sensible uniform: plaid skirts for girls, blazers for boys.

Admissions By interview and Common Entrance or tests; school is not particularly selective (and likely to become even less so with the phasing out of assisted places, which about 100 hold). Most pupils from surrounding country towns; a few from London; some from overseas join the sixth form for vocational course. Boarding accommodation has comforting feel; most sixth-formers in study-bedrooms with en suite facilities; some houses equipped with jacuzzis and saunas. Scholarships (for music, drama, sport – and vegetarians) available.

The head Very able; boundlessly enthusiastic. Read history at Oxford; previously the exceptionally successful head for 25 years of Port Regis prep school (qv). Successor from April 1998: Dr Tony Collins, 49, currently second master at Stowe (qv). Read geography at Cambridge (First); PhD from Oxford (where he taught politics); keen sportsman. Married (wife taught English at Oxford); three children (all will be pupils here).

The teaching Emphasis on individual programmes to build confidence and suit special talents. Friendly, approachable staff of 43 (10 women). Broad curriculum: science taught as three separate subjects; all introduced to Latin; some take three languages. Most do 10 GCSEs; choice of 20 subjects at A-level; alternatives include a one-year broadly vocational course with an emphasis on business skills. Pupils divided into two broad ability bands; further setting in some subjects; maximum class size 17. Strong music (most learn an instrument) and drama (scenes regularly performed in assembly). Extra-curricular activities include active cadet force, Duke of Edinburgh award scheme, Venture Scouts. Regular exchanges with school in Germany.

Results (1997) GCSE: 79% gained at least five grades A–C. A-level: 47% of entries graded A or B.

Destinations About 90% continue into the sixth form; of these, 90% proceed to university.

Sport Wide range, including: rowing, hockey, basketball, tennis, squash (national champions 1996–97), golf, swimming, cross-country, modern pentathlon, fencing. Good facilities; more on the way.

Remarks Good, unpressured school; individuals nurtured and encouraged (but vegetarians thin on the ground).

WYCOMBE ABBEY ♀
High Wycombe, Buckinghamshire HP11 1PE. Tel (01494) 520381

Synopsis
Independent ★ Girls ★ Boarding (and some day) ★ Ages 11–18 ★ 520 pupils (96% boarding) ★ 150 in sixth form ★ Fees: £13,500 boarding; £10,125 day
Head: Mrs Judith Goodland, 59, appointed 1989 (retires August 1998).
Distinguished academic school; first-rate teaching and results; strong music and sport.

Profile
Background   Founded 1896 by Dame Frances Dove, one of the pioneers of women's education. Imposing Jacobean mansion (re-built 1798) in 160 acres of lawns and woodland (Capability Brown was here); later additions include 1920s chapel, functional 1960s classroom block, fine lakeside music and drama centre.

Atmosphere   Polite, friendly, well-disciplined; girls programmed to achieve. Firm C of E ethos (compulsory daily chapel); very good pastoral care; respectful relations between staff (many of whom are old girls) and pupils. School takes a hard line on smoking and alcohol; drugs are inconceivable. Lessons on Saturday mornings.

Admissions   School is full ('We never bother to advertise – those likely to send their daughters here will know of us') and highly selective: applicants (mostly pre-selected by good prep schools) informally assessed ('joiners' preferred); those deemed to be a potential 'Wycombe' offered a place on condition they achieve 55% at Common Entrance and perform satisfactorily in verbal and non-verbal reasoning tests; 45 admitted at 11, 15 at 12, 20–30 at 13. Most from business/professional backgrounds within two hours' drive; 13% ceiling on foreign pupils ('We want to remain the sort of school we've always been'). Very pleasant boarding accommodation (£7 million spent recently on modernisation and refurbishment); juniors progress from own house to mixed-age dormitories (maximum six beds); sixth-formers have single study-bedrooms in an adult environment. Good food (attendance monitored to ensure any potential eating disorder nipped in the bud).

The head   Forthright, business-like, very much in charge; emphasises this is an academic not a social school (while making it a much friendlier place). Read modern languages at Bristol; taught briefly before marrying and spending 14 years bringing up three children; previously head of St George's, Ascot. From September 1998: Mrs Pauline Davies, head of Croydon High (qv), which HMI said was led with 'flair, energy and determination'.

The teaching   First-rate; mainly formal in style. Highly professional, enthusiastic staff of 50 (eight men), some very long serving. Broad curriculum: science on offer as three separate subjects; all do Latin for first two years (70% continue it to GCSE); Greek, German, Spanish on offer; most take nine GCSEs ('They haven't time to do more'). Pupils grouped by ability from the start in maths, French and later in English, Latin, science; average class size 20, reducing to 12 at A-level. Good drama, music (75% learn an instrument); excellent facilities for creative arts. Wide range of extra-curricular activities, including well-supported Duke of Edinburgh award scheme.

Results   (1997) GCSE: all gained at least five grades A–C. A-level: impressive 86% of entries graded A or B.

Destinations   All but a handful stay on for A-levels and proceed to university (about 15 a year to Oxbridge).

Sport   All the traditional girls' games; very strong lacrosse, tennis. Fencing, trampolining, riding, sailing also on offer. Facilities include large indoor pool, eight lacrosse pitches, 24 tennis courts, two squash courts.

Remarks   Very good all round; highly recommended.

WYCOMBE HIGH ♀
Marlow Hill, High Wycombe, Buckinghamshire HP11 1TB. Tel (01494) 523961

Synopsis
Grammar (voluntary-controlled) ★ Girls ★ Day ★ Ages 11–18 ★ 1,280 pupils
★ 400 in sixth form
Head: Mrs Muriel Pilkington, 56, appointed 1985 (retiring August 1998).
Successful, academic school; good music and sport.

Profile
Background   Founded 1901; moved to present 27-acre site in 1956; pleasant
grounds (including an open-air theatre); much new building, including technol-
ogy block, labs, sixth-form centre, drama studio, sports hall etc.
Atmosphere   Orderly, industrious. Lively, well-motivated pupils; hard-working,
committed staff; good pastoral care. Sixth-formers treated as college students.
Admissions   By tests administered by Buckinghamshire County Council.
Nearly all in top 25% of the ability range, predominantly from professional/
middle-class homes (some parents move house to be in the catchment area).
The head   Business-like; able manager. Oxford graduate. Married; three children.
The teaching   Long-serving staff of 82 (12 men); styles vary from strongly traditional to innovative; big emphasis on academic pace and achievement. Standard
national curriculum; all do French; German, Spanish, Latin on offer; maths and
science particularly strong; good computing. All take at least nine GCSEs; choice of
27 subjects at A-level, including economics, geology, sports science, psychology,
theatre studies. Pupils grouped by ability in maths, French from third year, in science
for GCSE. First-rate music: nearly a third learn an instrument; three choirs, two
orchestras, various ensembles. Dance a strong feature (links with the Royal Ballet).
Lots of work experience and links with local business community. Extra-curricular
activities include well-supported Duke of Edinburgh award scheme; £8,000 raised
annually for charity. Regular exchanges with schools in France, Germany, Spain.
Results   (1997) GCSE: 99% gained at least five grades A–C. A-level: 51% of
entries graded A or B.
Destinations   About 85% stay for A-levels; of these, more than 80% proceed to
university (about 12 a year to Oxbridge).
Sport   Very strong: good facilities, long fixture list, regular success at local and
county level. Main activities: hockey, netball, gymnastics, tennis, athletics,
swimming, basketball. Badminton, volleyball, aerobics, squash, also on offer.
Facilities include athletics track, outdoor pool, 13 tennis and netball courts.
Remarks   High-powered, well-run school.

WYMONDHAM COLLEGE ♂ ♀
Golf Links Road, Wymondham, Norfolk NR18 9SZ. Tel (01953) 605566

Synopsis
Partially selective comprehensive (grant-maintained) ★ Co-educational ★
Boarding and day ★ Ages 11–18 ★ 888 pupils (55% boys, 61% boarding) ★
285 in sixth form ★ Fees (boarding only): £4,683
Head: John Haden, 55, appointed 1992.
*Unusual state boarding school; bizarre accommodation; strongly traditional ethos;
good GCSE results.*

Profile

Background   Opened 1951 as a dual school – grammar and technical – under a single head; went comprehensive 1981; opted out of council control 1991 (after repeated threats of closure); now Europe's largest state boarding school. An astonishing collection of shabby Nissen huts (formerly a World War Two military hospital) linked by roofed walkways on an 80-acre campus 12 miles south of Norwich. (School has been reluctant to abandon the huts, which are pleasant inside and spacious, but is now slowly removing them.) Later additions include modern science block, handsome library, £1 million technology block.

Atmosphere   Traditional grammar school ethos retained; emphasis on academic standards, self-discipline, strict uniform, no litter. Staff and pupils take great pride in the school's unusual qualities. Strong commitment to boarding; copious after-school activities; 'day boarders' may stay until 9 pm.

Admissions   Prospective boarders interviewed to determine suitability and need for boarding – 'need' strictly defined as being for domestic not behavioural or emotional reasons; 20% from Service families. Ten per cent of day places reserved for those with ability and aptitude in music or sport. More than 100 a year enter the sixth form from other schools. Wide range of abilities and social backgrounds, about half from Norfolk. Most boarding accommodation (including new international house, which attracts sixth-formers from Europe) is cosy, clean and well-decorated; some, though, is drab; first-years have a house of their own. Some scholarships for the exceptionally talented.

The head   Very able. Previously head (for 10 years) of a grant-maintained comprehensive in Lincolnshire. Read chemistry at Oxford; comes from a family of teachers (father was a head); first headship at 27 – of a school in Uganda during Idi Amin's coup (so not bothered by the challenges he faces here). Married; two sons.

The teaching   Conventional academic approach (many long-serving, dedicated staff). Strong maths, science, languages (French, German, Spanish); Latin recently re-introduced; all do three A-levels from choice of 25; vocational alternatives include GNVQs in business & finance, manufacturing, leisure & tourism. Pupils grouped by ability in major subjects; some extra help for slow learners; class sizes 25 for more able children, 15 for others. Good drama and music; bands, orchestras, choirs. First-rate art; excellent computer/video/animation facilities. Extra-curricular programme includes car maintenance, aircraft restoration, cadet force, Duke of Edinburgh award scheme.

Results   (1997) GCSE: creditable 82% gained at least five grades A–C. A-level: 30% of entries graded A or B.

Destinations   More than 75% continue into the sixth form; of these, 70% proceed to university.

Sport   Main games: hockey, rugby, football, tennis, netball. Lavish sports centre, indoor pool, plenty of playing fields.

Remarks   Most of the values and facilities (if not the buildings) associated with grander, more ancient (and more costly) establishments. Ofsted inspectors concluded (1994): 'The standard of achievement is satisfactory or better at all levels throughout the school. Pupils work industriously in most lessons and exercise a high level of self-discipline.'

YARM ♂
The Friarage, Yarm, Stockton-on-Tees TS15 9EJ. Tel (01642) 786023

Synopsis
Independent ★ Boys (plus girls in sixth form) ★ Ages 11–18 (plus associated junior school) ★ 530 pupils ★ 171 in sixth form (80% boys) ★ Fees: £5,508
Head: Neville Tait, 59 appointed 1978.
Traditional (though relatively new) academic school; good teaching and results; big emphasis on technology, computing.

Profile
Background   Opened (by the present head with 17 pupils) 1978, rising like a phoenix from the ashes of Yarm Grammar School, the Victorian premises of which it occupied after the council closed it. Eighteenth-century mansion plus many later additions – including new classrooms, science block, fine theatre and music school – in 14 acres of well-tended grounds. Self-contained pre-prep and prep school (260 boys aged four to 10) on adjacent site.

Atmosphere   Bustling, workman-like; firm, old-fashioned discipline ('time off, without due notification, is regarded with great disfavour'); pupils open doors for staff. Strong house system; simple uniform; compulsory weekly service in the parish church. Parents kept closely informed ('My aim,' says the head, 'is to ensure your son's confidence and happiness').

Admissions   By school's own tests; minimum IQ 115 (grammar school standard); school has become more selective as numbers have grown. Catchment area extends to North Yorkshire, South Durham; parents organise coaches. Scholarships (academic, music) available.

The head   Avuncular, commanding, omnipresent; the school is his creation. Started as an aeronautical engineer (pilots his own plane), later read history at Durham; still has the air of a man with a mission unaccomplished (and does not relish retirement). Widower.

The teaching   Good; generally formal in style. Broad curriculum: sciences taught separately; lots of technology, computing (IT is a way of life here); choice of French or German; all first-years do Latin; Greek on offer; all take three A-levels plus general studies. Pupils grouped by ability in maths, modern languages (more able take GCSEs a year early), English, science; maximum class size 20. Lots of music, drama. Extra-curricular activities include flourishing cadet force, well-supported Duke of Edinburgh award scheme. Frequent expeditions; regular language exchanges with schools in France, Germany.

Results   (1997) GCSE: 98% gained at least five grades A–C. A-level: 43% of entries graded A or B.

Destinations   Virtually all go on to university.

Sport   Main activities: rugby, hockey, cricket, athletics. Rowing, squash, tennis, netball also on offer. Facilities include 26 acres of playing fields.

Remarks   Good all round.

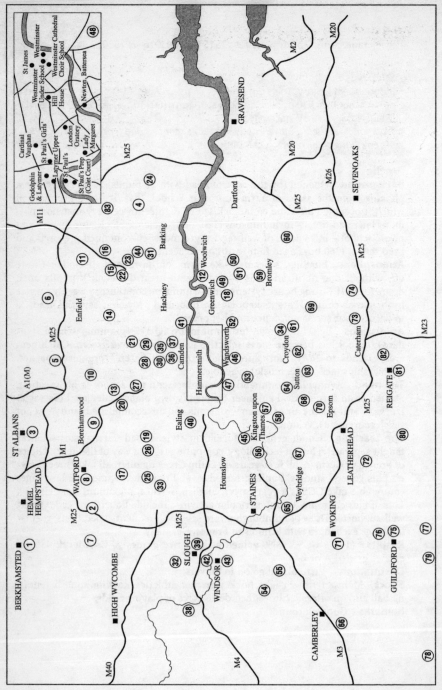

MAP 1   611

Map 1 – London Area

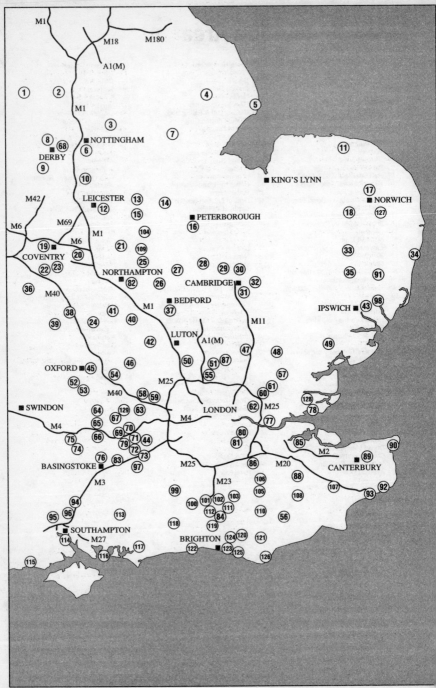

MAP 2   613

Map 2 – Eastern England

1   Lady Manners
2   St Mary's, Chesterfield
3   Minster, Southwell
4   Queen Elizabeth's Grammar, Horncastle
5   Skegness Grammar
6   Nottingham Girls' High
    Nottingham High
7   Kesteven & Sleaford High
    Carre's
8   Ecclesbourne
9   Repton
10 Loughborough Grammar
    Loughborough High
11 Gresham's, Holt
12 Leicester Grammar
    Beauchamp
13 Oakham
14 Stamford
    Stamford High
15 Uppingham
16 King's, Peterborough
    Oundle
17 Norwich
    Norwich High
    Eaton
    Notre Dame High
18 Wymondham
19 Bablake
    King Henry VIII, Coventry
    Blue Coat, Coventry
    Finham Park
20 Rugby
    Rugby High
    Bilton Grange
    Lawrence Sheriff, Rugby
21 Maidwell Hall
22 Warwick
    Warwick Prep
    King's High, Warwick
23 Arnold Lodge
24 Winchester House, Brackley
25 Wellingborough
26 Sharnbrook
27 Kimbolton
28 Hinchingbrooke
29 Swavesey
30 Cottenham
31 St Mary's, Cambridge
    King's College School
    Perse Girls'
    The Perse
    The Leys
    St John's College School
    Comberton, Cambridge
32 Bottisham
33 Riddlesworth Hall
34 St Felix
35 Debenham High
36 King Edward VI, Stratford
    Stratford-upon-Avon Girls' Grammar
37 Bedford
    Bedford Modern
    Bedford High
    Dame Alice Harpur
38 Tudor Hall
39 Sibford, Banbury
40 Swanbourne House
41 Stowe
42 Cedars
43 Ipswich
    Ipswich High
    Orwell Park
    Northgate High, Ipswich
    Royal Hospital, Ipswich

44 Lambrook & Haileybury
    Ranelagh, Bracknell
45 Oxford High
    Cherwell
    The Dragon
    Headington
    Magdalen College School
    St Edwards
    Summer Fields
    Wheatley Park
46 Aylesbury Grammar
    Aylesbury High
    Sir Henry Floyd, Aylesbury
47 Bishop's Stortford
    Bishop's Stortford High
    Hockerill
48 Felsted
49 Colchester County High
    Philip Morant
    Colchester Royal Grammar
    Holmwood House, Colchester
50 St George's, Harpenden
    Roundwood Park
51 Haileybury
52 Cothill House
53 Abingdon
    The Manor
    Radley
    St Helen & St Katharine
54 Lord Williams's
55 Queenswood
56 Vinehall, Robertsbridge
57 Chelmsford County High
    King Edward VI, Chelmsford
    New Hall, Chelmsford
58 Wycombe Abbey
    Wycombe High
    John Hampden Grammar
    Royal Grammar, High Wycombe
    Godstone, High Wycombe
59 Beaconsfield High
60 Brentwood
    Brentwood Ursuline
61 Anglo-European, Ingatestone
62 Campion, Hornchurch
63 Sir William Borlase's
64 The Oratory
65 Pangbourne
66 Bradfield
67 Piggott
68 Derby High
69 Reading
    The Abbey
    Kendrick
    Queen Anne's
70 Maiden Erlegh
71 Ludgrove
72 Wellington College
73 Collingwood
74 Downe House, Newbury
    Cheam Hawtreys
75 Horris Hill
    St Bartholomew's
    Downs, Newbury
76 Lord Wandsworth
    Bishop Challoner, Basingstoke
77 Grays Convent
78 Southend Girls' High
    Southend Boys' High
79 Holt, Wokingham
80 Townley Girls' Grammar
81 Chislehurst & Sidcup
    Bullers Wood
82 Northampton High
83 North Foreland, Hook

    Robert May's, Hook
84 Oathall, Haywards Heath
85 Rainham Mark
86 Sevenoaks
    Walthamstow Hall
87 Presdales, Ware
88 Sutton Valence
89 King's, Canterbury
90 Wellesley House
91 Thomas Mills, Framlingham
92 Duke of York's Royal Military
93 Folkestone Girls'
94 Winchester
    St Swithun's
    Pilgrims'
    Twyford, Winchester
    Henry Beaufort
95 Romsey
    Stanbridge Earls, Romsey
96 Thornden
97 Farnborough Hill
98 Woodbridge
99 Cranleigh
100 Christ's Hospital
    Millais
    Tanbridge House
101 Cottesmore
102 Worth
103 Ashdown House
    Brambletye
104 Brooke Weston, Corby
105 Tunbridge Wells Girls'
    Tunbridge Wells Boys' Grammar
    Bennett
    Holmewood House
    Skinners'
    St Gregory's, Tunbridge Wells
106 Tonbridge
    Tonbridge Grammar
    Judd
107 Ashford
108 Cranbrook
    Bedgebury
    Benenden
    Dulwich College Prep
109 Bishop Stopford, Kettering
110 St Leonards, Mayfield
111 Ardingly
112 Warden Park
113 Bedales
114 King Edward VI, Southampton
    St Anne's
115 Arnewood
116 Portsmouth Grammar
    Portsmouth High
117 Bishop Luffa
118 Windlesham House
119 Burgess Hill
120 Ringmer
121 St Bede's, The Dicker
122 Lancing
123 Brighton
    Brighton & Hove High
124 St Aubyns
125 Roedean
126 Eastbourne
    St Andrew's, Eastbourne
    St Bede's
    Moira House
127 Framlingham Earl High
128 Greensward
129 Gillott's, Henley

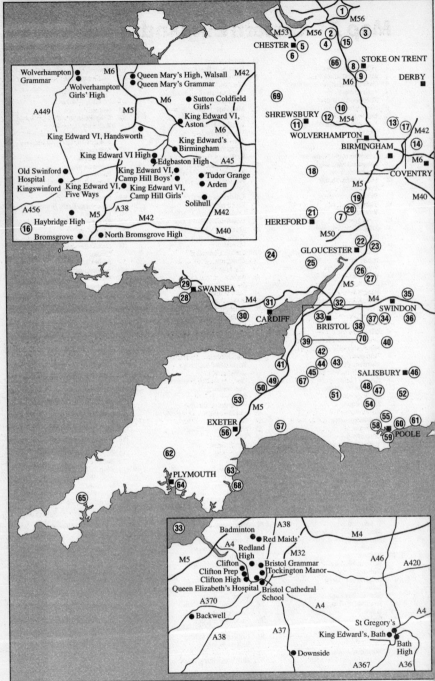

MAP 3   615

Map 3 – Western England and Wales

1 Altrincham Girls'
   Altrincham Boys'
2 Hartford County High
3 Fallibroome High
4 Grange
   St Nicholas High
5 King's, Chester
   Queen's, Chester
6 Christleton High
7 The Downs, Colwall
8 Alsager
9 Newcastle-under-Lyme
10 Newport Girls' High
   Adams' Grammar
11 Shrewsbury
   Shrewsbury High
   Packwood Haugh
   Priory, Shrewsbury
12 Thomas Telford
   Wrekin
13 King Edward VI, Lichfield
14 Higham Lane
15 Sandbach Girls'
16 Birmingham (inset):
   Arden
   Bromsgrove
   Edgbaston High
   Haybridge High
   King Edward VI High
   King Edward VI, Aston
   King Edward VI, Camp Hill,
     Boys'
   King Edward VI, Camp Hill,
     Girls'
   King Edward VI, Five Ways
   King Edward VI, Handsworth
   King Edward's, Birmingham
   Kingswinford
   Old Swinford Hospital
   Queen Mary's Grammar
   Queen Mary's High, Walsall
   Solihull
   Sutton Coldfield Girls'
   Tudor Grange
   Wolverhampton Girls' High
   Wolverhampton Grammar
17 Twycross House, Tamworth
18 Moor Park
19 King's, Worcester
   Abberley Hall

   Alice Ottley
   Worcester Royal Grammar
20 Malvern
   Malvern Girls'
21 Hereford Cathedral School
   Bishop of Hereford's Blue Coat
22 Gloucester Girls' High
   Sir Thomas Rich's, Gloucester
23 Cheltenham
   Cheltenham Ladies'
   Dean Close
   Pate's Grammar
   Cleeve
24 Crickhowell High
25 Monmouth
   Haberdashers' Monmouth
26 Wycliffe
27 Beaudesert Park
28 Bishopston
29 Olchfa
30 Cowbridge
31 Cardiff High
   Glantaf
   Radyr
   Howell's Llandaff
   Llandaff Cathedral School
32 Marlwood
33 Bristol and Bath (inset):
   Backwell
   Badminton
   Bristol Cathedral School
   Bristol Grammar
   Clifton
   Clifton High
   Clifton Prep
   Downside
   King Edward's, Bath
   Queen Elizabeth's Hospital
   Red Maids'
   Redland High
   Royal High, Bath
   St Gregory's
   Tockington Manor
34 St Mary's, Calne
35 Highworth Warneford
36 Marlborough
37 Stonar
38 St Laurence
39 The Kings of Wessex
40 Lavington

   Dauntsey's
41 Brymore
42 Wells Cathedral School
43 King's, Bruton
   Sexey's
44 Millfield Prep
45 Millfield
46 Salisbury Cathedral School
   Bishop Wordsworth's
   Godolphin
   South Wilts Girls' Grammar
47 Sandroyd
48 Port Regis
49 Taunton
   Queen's, Taunton
   King's, Taunton
50 Wellington
51 Sherborne
   Sherborne Girls'
52 Burgate
53 Blundell's
54 Bryanston
   Milton Abbey
55 Queen Elizabeth's, Wimborne
   Canford
56 Exeter
   St Margaret's, Exeter
   Maynard
57 Colyton Grammar
58 Corfe Hills
59 Poole Grammar
   Parkstone Grammar
60 Bournemouth Girls' Grammar
   Bournemouth Grammar
   Talbot Heath
61 Highcliffe
62 Mount House
63 Torquay Girls' High
   Torquay Boys' High
64 Devonport Girls' High
   Devonport Boys' High
65 Truro
66 Holmes Chapel, Crewe
   St Thomas More, Crewe
67 Huish Episcopi
68 Churston Grammar, Brixham
69 Moreton Hall, Oswestry
70 St Augustine's, Trowbridge

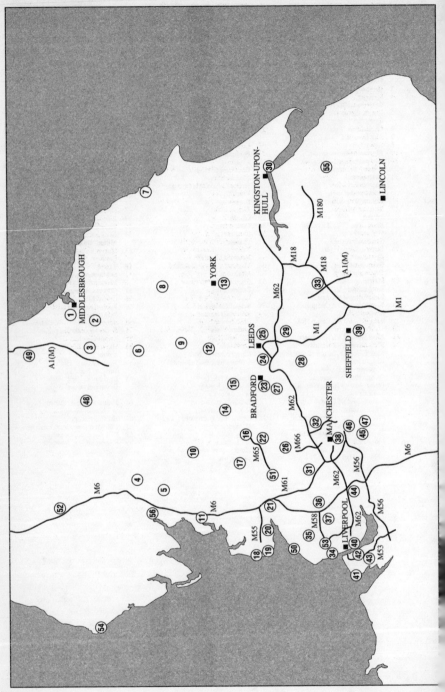

MAP 4   617

Map 4 – Northern England

1 Stokesley, Middlesborough
2 Yarm
  Conyers
3 Hummersknott
4 Sedbergh
5 Casterton, Kirkby Lonsdale
  Queen Elizabeth
6 Aysgarth
7 Bramcote
8 Ampleforth
9 Ripon Grammar
10 Giggleswick
11 Lancaster Royal Grammar
   Lancaster Girls' Grammar
12 Harrogate Grammar
   Harrogate Ladies'
   St Aidan's
13 Huntington, York
   Joseph Rowntree
   Mount
   Bootham
   St Peter's
   Queen Margaret's
14 Skipton Girls' High
   Ermysted's
15 Ilkley Grammar
   St Mary's, Ilkley
16 Malsis
17 Stonyhurst
   Clitheroe Royal Grammar
18 Baines
   Hodgson High
19 Arnold
20 Kirkham Grammar
21 All Hallows
22 St Hilda's High, Burnley

23 Bradford Girls'
   Bradford Grammar
   Dixon's City Tech
24 Fulneck
   North Halifax Grammar
25 Leeds Girls' High
   Leeds Grammar
   Benton Park
26 Bacup & Rawtenstall
   Grammar
27 Crossley Heath, Halifax
28 Heckmondwike Grammar
29 Wakefield Girls' High
   Queen Elizabeth Grammar,
   Wakefield
   St Thomas à Becket
30 Hymers, Hull
31 Bolton
   Bolton Girls'
   Canon Slade
   Turton High
32 Blue Coat, Oldham
   Hulme Grammar Girls'
   Hulme Grammar Boys'
33 Hayfield, Doncaster
34 Merchant Taylors', Crosby
   Merchant Taylors' Girls'
35 Ormskirk Grammar
   St Bede's High
36 St Peter's High, Wigan
37 Rainford High
38 Manchester Grammar
   Manchester High
   Audenshaw High, Tameside
   Fairfield High
   Chetham's

   Parrs Wood
   William Hulme's
   Withington Girls'
39 Sheffield High
   Ashdell
   Birkdale
   Silverdale
   High Storrs
40 Liverpool
   Blue Coat, Liverpool
   King David High, Liverpool
   St Hilda's
41 West Kirby Girls'
   Calday Grange
42 Birkenhead
   Birkenhead High
43 Wirral Girls' Grammar
   Wirral Boys' Grammar
44 St Gregory's High
   Helsby County High
45 Cheadle Hulme
46 Stockport Grammar
   Harrytown High
   Marple Hall High
47 Poynton High
48 Barnard Castle
49 Durham High
50 Greenbank, Southport
51 Queen Elizabeth, Blackburn
52 Queen Elizabeth, Penrith
   Ullswater Community
   College
53 Range High
54 St Bees, Cumbria
55 Caistor Grammar
56 Dallam, Cumbria

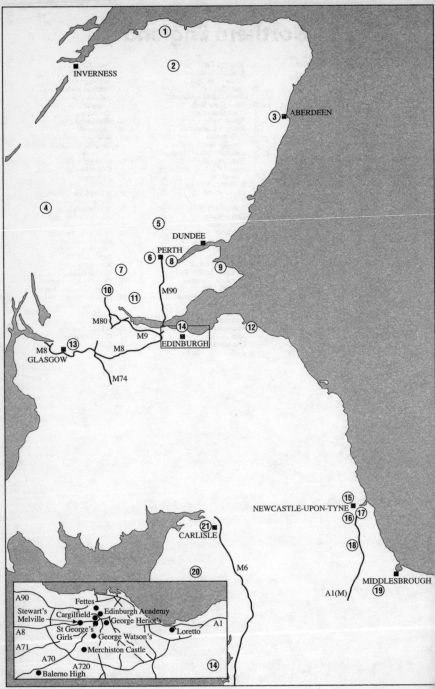

INVERNESS

①

②

③ ABERDEEN

④

⑤

DUNDEE

⑥ PERTH ⑧

⑦

⑨

⑩

⑪

M90

M80

⑭

M9

EDINBURGH

M8 ⑬

⑫

M8

GLASGOW

M74

⑮

NEWCASTLE-UPON-TYNE

⑯ ⑰

⑱

⑳

⑳

㉑ CARLISLE

M6

MIDDLESBROUGH

A1(M) ⑲

A90

Fettes

Stewart's Melville

Cargilfield

Edinburgh Academy

George Heriot's

A8

St George's Girls

Loretto

A1

A71

George Watson's

A70

Merchiston Castle

A720

⑭

Balerno High

MAP 5   619

Map 5 – Scotland and Tyneside

1   Gordonstoun
2   Aberlour House
3   Robert Gordon's
4   Rannoch
5   Butterstone, Perthshire
6   Glenalmond
7   Ardvreck
8   Craigclowan, Perth
    Strathallan
9   St Leonards
10 Dunblane High
11 Dollar Academy
12 Belhaven Hill

13 Hutchesons'
    Glasgow Academy
    Glasgow High
14 Edinburgh (inset):
    Fettes
    Stewart's Melville
    Cargilfield
    Edinburgh Academy
    George Heriot's
    George Watson's
    Loretto
    Balerno High
    St George's Girls'

    Merchiston Castle
15 Central Newcastle High
    Dame Allan's
    Newcastle Royal Grammar
16 Mowden Hall
17 Emmanuel, Gateshead
    St Thomas More, Gateshead
18 Durham Johnston
19 Egglescliffe
20 Keswick
21 Austin Friars, Carlisle

Index of Schools

Each reference gives the page on which the school's entry appears, followed by the map reference (map number in bold type).